Lecture Notes in Computer Science 10426

Commenced Publication in 1973
Founding and Former Series Editors:
Gerhard Goos, Juris Hartmanis, and Jan van Leeuwen

Editorial Board

More information about this series at http://www.springer.com/series/7407

Rupak Majumdar · Viktor Kunčak (Eds.)

Computer Aided Verification

29th International Conference, CAV 2017
Heidelberg, Germany, July 24–28, 2017
Proceedings, Part I

 Springer

Editors
Rupak Majumdar
Max Planck Institute for Software Systems
Kaiserslautern, Rheinland-Pfalz
Germany

Viktor Kunčak
School of Computer and Communication
  Sciences
EPFL - IC - LARA
Lausanne
Switzerland

ISSN 0302-9743   ISSN 1611-3349 (electronic)
Lecture Notes in Computer Science
ISBN 978-3-319-63386-2   ISBN 978-3-319-63387-9 (eBook)
DOI 10.1007/978-3-319-63387-9

Library of Congress Control Number: 2017946069

LNCS Sublibrary: SL1 – Theoretical Computer Science and General Issues

Printed on acid-free paper

This Springer imprint is published by Springer Nature
The registered company is Springer International Publishing AG
The registered company address is: Gewerbestrasse 11, 6330 Cham, Switzerland

Preface

It has been our privilege to serve as the program chairs for CAV 2017, the 29th International Conference on Computer-Aided Verification. CAV 2017 was held in beautiful Heidelberg, Germany, during July 22–28, 2017. The pre-conference workshops took place at the Crowne Plaza Hotel in Heidelberg City Centre. The main conference took place at the Stadthalle by the river Neckar.

The CAV conference series is dedicated to the advancement of the theory and practice of computer-aided formal analysis of hardware and software systems. The conference covers the spectrum from theoretical results to concrete applications, with an emphasis on practical verification tools and the algorithms and techniques that are needed for their implementation. CAV considers it vital to continue spurring advances in hardware and software verification while expanding to new domains such as biological systems and computer security.

Out of 191 submissions to the conference, we chose 50 regular papers and seven tool papers. These papers cover a wide range of topics and techniques, from algorithmic and logical foundations of verification to practical applications in distributed, networked, and cyber-physical systems. One direction of topical interest is the increasingly sophisticated combination of "traditional" techniques for reasoning and search with data-driven techniques. The program featured invited talks by Chris Hawblitzel (Microsoft), Marta Kwiatkowska (Oxford), and Viktor Vafeiadis (MPI-SWS), as well as invited tutorials, by Loris D'Antoni and Mayur Naik. As traditional, one of the winners of the CAV award also gave a presentation. We also had a special workshop to celebrate David Dill's many contributions to CAV on the occasion of his 60th birthday.

In addition to the main conference, CAV hosted the Verification Mentoring Workshop for junior scientists entering the field and six pre-conference technical workshops: the Workshop on Synthesis (SYNT), Satisfiability Modulo Theories (SMT), Verified Software: Theories, Tools, and Experiments (VSTTE), Design and Analysis of Robust Systems (DARS), Formal Approaches to Explainable Verification (FEVER), and Numerical Software Verification (NSV).

Organizing a conference is a community effort. The Program Committee for CAV consisted of 56 members; we kept the number large to ensure each PC member would have a reasonable number of papers to review and be able to provide thorough reviews. In addition, we used 104 external reviewers. All together, the reviewers drafted over 730 reviews and put in enormous effort in ensuring a good-quality program.

This year, we made artifact evaluation mandatory for tool submissions and optional but encouraged for regular submissions. We used an artifact evaluation committee of 26 members. Our goal for artifact evaluation was to provide friendly "beta-testing" to tool developers; we recognize that developing a stable tool on a cutting-edge research topic is certainly not easy and we hope the constructive comments provided by the AEC were of help to the developers. Needless to say we were impressed by the quality of the artifacts and in fact all accepted tools passed artifact evaluation. We are grateful to the reviewers for their outstanding efforts in making sure each paper got a fair chance.

We would like to thank Eva Darulova for chairing the workshop organization process, Barbara Jobstmann and Thomas Wahl for managing sponsorship and student fellowships, respectively, Mikaël Mayer for maintaining the CAV website, and the always helpful Steering Committee members Orna Grumberg, Aarti Gupta, Daniel Kroening, and Kenneth McMillan. We worked closely with Pavithra Prabhakar, Andrey Rybalchenko, and Damien Zufferey, who organized the Verification Mentoring Workshop. Finally, we would like to thank Roslyn Stricker, who helped us tremendously in the administration and organization of CAV.

We hope that you find the proceedings of CAV 2017 thought provoking!

July 2017

Rupak Majumdar
Viktor Kunčak

Organization

Program Chairs

Rupak Majumdar   Max Planck Institute for Software Systems, Germany
Viktor Kunčak   EPFL, Switzerland

Workshop Chair

Eva Darulova   Max Planck Institute for Software Systems, Germany

Sponsorship Chair

Barbara Jobstmann   EPFL, Switzerland and Cadence Design Systems

Fellowship Chair

Thomas Wahl   Northeastern University, USA

Program Committee

Aws Albarghouthi	University of Wisconsin, USA
Christel Baier	TU Dresden, Germany
Per Bjesse	Synopsys, USA
Jasmin Blanchette	Inria Nancy – Grand Est, France
Sergiy Bogomolov	Australian National University, Australia
Ahmed Bouajjani	IRIF, Paris Diderot University, France
Rohit Chadha	University of Missouri, USA
Bor-Yuh Evan Chang	University of Colorado at Boulder, USA
Swarat Chaudhuri	Rice University, USA
Wei-Ngan Chin	National University of Singapore, Singapore
Hana Chockler	King's College London, UK
Alessandro Cimatti	Fondazione Bruno Kessler, Italy
Isil Dilig	University of Texas at Austin, USA
Dino Distefano	Facebook and Queen Mary University of London, UK
Michael Emmi	Nokia Bell Labs, USA
Javier Esparza	TU Munich, Germany
Georgios Fainekos	Arizona State University, USA
Azadeh Farzan	University of Toronto, Canada
Aarti Gupta	Princeton University, USA
Gerard Holzmann	Nimble Research, USA
Marieke Huisman	University of Twente, The Netherlands
Radu Iosif	Verimag, France

Artifact Evaluation Committee

Swen Jacobs	Saarland University, Germany
Moa Johansson	Chalmers, Sweden
Dejan Jovanovic	SRI International, USA
Ralf Jung	Max Planck Institute for Software Systems, Germany
Ivan Kuraj	MIT, USA
Andreas Lochbihler	ETH Zurich, Switzerland
Jose Morales	IMDEA Software, Spain
Van Chan Ngo	Carnegie Mellon University, USA
Zvonimir Pavlinovic	New York University, USA
Markus Rabe	University of California, Berkeley, USA
Mukund Raghothaman	University of Pennsylvania, USA
Andrew Reynolds	University of Iowa, USA
Nima Roohi	University of Illinois, Urbana-Champaign, USA
Christian Schilling	University of Freiburg, Germany
Muralidaran Vijayaraghavan	MIT, USA
Nicolas Voirol	EPFL, Switzerland

Additional Reviewers

Alireza Abyaneh	Constantin Enea	K. Narayan Kumar
Mahmudul Faisal	Chuchu Fan	Sebastian Küpper
Al Ameen	Samira Farahani	Axel Legay
Sebastian Arming	Grigory Fedyukovich	Sorin Lerner
Konstantinos Athanasiou	Pierre Flener	Peizin Liu
Mohamed Faouzi Atig	Matthias Fleury	Le Quang Loc
Domagoj Babic	Wan Fokkink	Andreas Lochbihler
Michael Backenköhler	Zhoulai Fu	Alexander Lück
Gogul Balakrishnan	Nils Gesbert	Ravichandran Madhavan
Clark Barrett	Shilpi Goel	Victor Magron
Matthew Bauer	Yijia Gu	Assaf Marron
Ryan Beckett	Arie Gurfinkel	Umang Mathur
Harsh Beohar	Vahid Hashemi	Todd Millstein
Olaf Beyersdorff	Bardh Hoxha	Sergio Mover
Pavol Bielik	Johannes Hölzl	Suvam Mukherjee
Armin Biere	Catalin Hritcu	Daniel Neider
Jesse Bingham	Mens Irini-Eleftheria	Dennis Nolte
Stefan Blom	Himanshu Jain	Peter O'Hearn
Stefan Bucur	Chuan Jiang	Wytse Oortwijn
Dario Cattaruzza	George Karpenkov	Gustavo Petri
Ed Cerny	Dileep Kini	Lauren Pick
Le Ton Chanh	Hui Kong	Markus Rabe
Dmitry Chistikov	Aamod Kore	Jaideep Ramachandran
Andreea Costea	Jan Křetínský	Rajarshi Ray
Eva Darulova	Thilo Krüger	Andrew Reynolds

Nima Roohi
Philipp Ruemmer
Sarah Sallinger
Anne-Kathrin Schmuck
Peter Schrammel
Daniel
    Schwartz-Narbonne
Cristina Serban
Alexey Solovyev
Sadegh Soudjani
Benno Stein

Ofer Strichman
Kausik Subramanian
Rob Sumners
Sol Swords
Michael Tautschnig
Nguyen Toan Thanh
Dmitriy Traytel
Nikos Tzevelekos
Viktor Vafeiadis
Freark van der Berg
Jules Villard

Mike Whalen
Christoph Wintersteiger
Xiao Xu
Shakiba Yaghoubi
Eugen Zalinescu
Qirun Zhang
Yiji Zhang
Cai Zhouhong
Florian Zuleger

Steering Committee

Orna Grumberg   Technion, Israel
Aarti Gupta   Princeton University, USA
Daniel Kroening   Oxford University, UK
Kenneth McMillan   Microsoft Research, USA

CAV Award Committee

Tom Ball (Chair)   Microsoft Research, USA
Kim G. Larsen   Aalborg University, Denmark
Natarajan Shankar   SRI International, USA
Pierre Wolper   Liege University, Belgium

Verification Mentoring Workshop

Pavithra Prabhakar   Kansas State University, USA
Andrey Rybalchenko   Microsoft Research, UK
Damien Zufferey   Max Planck Institute for Software Systems, Germany

Publicity Chair

Mikaël Mayer   EPFL, Switzerland

Fast Verification of Fast Cryptography for Secure Sockets (Invited Paper)

Chris Hawblitzel

Microsoft Research, Redmond, USA

Abstract. The Everest project is a joint effort between Microsoft Research, INRIA, and CMU to build a formally verified replacement for core HTTPS components, including the TLS protocol, cryptographic primitives, and certificate processing. The goal is to build an efficient implementation of these components, and the cryptographic primitives are especially critical to performance. Therefore, the project has developed verified hand-written assembly language implementations of common cryptographic primitives such as AES, SHA, and Poly1305.

This talk will present an overview of Everest, its verified assembly language cryptography, and the tools used to verify the code, including Vale, Dafny, F*, and Z3. It will discuss challenges in using such tools to verify low-level cryptographic code, including the need to reason about bit-level operations, large integers, and polynomials. A key challenge is the speed of the verification, and the talk will discuss ongoing efforts to combine tactics with SMT solving to make verification fast without sacrificing automation.

Contents – Part I

Data Driven Techniques

Runtime Verification

Cyber-Physical Systems

Concurrency

Contents – Part II

Software Analysis

Invited Contributions

Safety Verification of Deep Neural Networks

Xiaowei Huang, Marta Kwiatkowska$^{(\boxtimes)}$, Sen Wang, and Min Wu

Department of Computer Science, University of Oxford, Oxford, UK
marta.kwiatkowska@cs.ox.ac.uk

Abstract. Deep neural networks have achieved impressive experimental results in image classification, but can surprisingly be unstable with respect to adversarial perturbations, that is, minimal changes to the input image that cause the network to misclassify it. With potential applications including perception modules and end-to-end controllers for self-driving cars, this raises concerns about their safety. We develop a novel automated verification framework for feed-forward multi-layer neural networks based on Satisfiability Modulo Theory (SMT). We focus on safety of image classification decisions with respect to image manipulations, such as scratches or changes to camera angle or lighting conditions that would result in the same class being assigned by a human, and define safety for an individual decision in terms of invariance of the classification within a small neighbourhood of the original image. We enable exhaustive search of the region by employing discretisation, and propagate the analysis layer by layer. Our method works directly with the network code and, in contrast to existing methods, can guarantee that adversarial examples, if they exist, are found for the given region and family of manipulations. If found, adversarial examples can be shown to human testers and/or used to fine-tune the network. We implement the techniques using Z3 and evaluate them on state-of-the-art networks, including regularised and deep learning networks. We also compare against existing techniques to search for adversarial examples and estimate network robustness.

1 Introduction

Deep neural networks have achieved impressive experimental results in image classification, matching the cognitive ability of humans [23] in complex tasks with thousands of classes. Many applications are envisaged, including their use as perception modules and end-to-end controllers for self-driving cars [15]. Let $\mathbb{R}^n$ be a vector space of images (points) that we wish to classify and assume that $f : \mathbb{R}^n \to C$, where C is a (finite) set of class labels, models the human perception capability, then a neural network classifier is a function $\hat{f}(x)$ which approximates $f(x)$ from M training examples $\{(x^i, c^i)\}_{i=1,..,M}$. For example,

---

This work is supported by the EPSRC Programme Grant on Mobile Autonomy (EP/M019918/1). Part of this work was done while MK was visiting the Simons Institute for the Theory of Computing.

© Springer International Publishing AG 2017
R. Majumdar and V. Kunčak (Eds.): CAV 2017, Part I, LNCS 10426, pp. 3–29, 2017.
DOI: 10.1007/978-3-319-63387-9_1

a perception module of a self-driving car may input an image from a camera and must correctly classify the type of object in its view, irrespective of aspects such as the angle of its vision and image imperfections. Therefore, though they clearly include imperfections, all four pairs of images in Fig. 1 should arguably be classified as automobiles, since they appear so to a human eye.

Classifiers employed in vision tasks are typically multi-layer networks, which propagate the input image through a series of linear and non-linear operators. They are high-dimensional, often with millions of dimensions, non-linear and potentially discontinuous: even a small network, such as that trained to classify hand-written images of digits 0–9, has over 60,000 real-valued parameters and 21,632 neurons (dimensions) in its first layer. At the same time, the networks are trained on a finite data set and expected to generalise to previously unseen images. To increase the probability of correctly classifying such an image, regularisation techniques such as dropout are typically used, which improves the smoothness of the classifiers, in the sense that images that are close (within ϵ distance) to a training point are assigned the same class label.

automobile to bird   automobile to frog   automobile to airplane   automobile to horse

Fig. 1. Automobile images (classified correctly) and their perturbed images (classified wrongly)

Unfortunately, it has been observed in [13,36] that deep neural networks, including highly trained and smooth networks optimised for vision tasks, are unstable with respect to so called *adversarial perturbations*. Such adversarial perturbations are (minimal) changes to the input image, often imperceptible to the human eye, that cause the network to misclassify the image. Examples include not only artificially generated random perturbations, but also (more worryingly) modifications of camera images [22] that correspond to resizing, cropping or change in lighting conditions. They can be devised without access to the training set [29] and are transferable [19], in the sense that an example misclassified by one network is also misclassified by a network with a different architecture, even if it is trained on different data. Figure 1 gives adversarial perturbations of automobile images that are misclassified as a bird, frog, airplane or horse by a highly trained state-of-the-art network. This obviously raises potential safety concerns for applications such as autonomous driving and calls for automated verification techniques that can verify the correctness of their decisions.

Safety of AI systems is receiving increasing attention, to mention [10,33], in view of their potential to cause harm in safety-critical situations such as autonomous driving. Typically, decision making in such systems is either solely based on machine learning, through end-to-end controllers, or involves some combination of logic-based reasoning and machine learning components, where an image classifier produces a classification, say speed limit or a stop sign, that serves as input to a controller. A recent trend towards "explainable AI" has led to approaches that learn not only how to assign the classification labels, but also additional explanations of the model, which can take the form of a justification explanation (why this decision has been reached, for example identifying the features that supported the decision) [17,31]. In all these cases, the safety of a decision can be reduced to ensuring the correct behaviour of a machine learning component. However, safety assurance and verification methodologies for machine learning are little studied.

The main difficulty with image classification tasks, which play a critical role in perception modules of autonomous driving controllers, is that they do not have a formal specification in the usual sense: ideally, the performance of a classifier should match the perception ability and class labels assigned by a human. Traditionally, the correctness of a neural network classifier is expressed in terms of *risk* [37], defined as the probability of misclassification of a given image, weighted with respect to the input distribution μ of images. Similar (statistical) robustness properties of deep neural network classifiers, which compute the average minimum distance to a misclassification and are independent of the data point, have been studied and can be estimated using tools such as DeepFool [25] and cleverhans [27]. However, we are interested in the safety of an *individual decision*, and to this end focus on the key property of the classifier being *invariant* to perturbations *at a given point*. This notion is also known as pointwise robustness [12,18] or local adversarial robustness [21].

Contributions. In this paper we propose a general framework for automated verification of safety of classification decisions made by feed-forward deep neural networks. Although we work concretely with image classifiers, the techniques can be generalised to other settings. For a given image x (a point in a vector space), we assume that there is a (possibly infinite) region η around that point that incontrovertibly supports the decision, in the sense that all points in this region must have the same class. This region is specified by the user and can be given as a small diameter, or the set of all points whose salient features are of the same type. We next assume that there is a family of operations Δ, which we call manipulations, that specify modifications to the image under which the classification decision should remain invariant in the region η. Such manipulations can represent, for example, camera imprecisions, change of camera angle, or replacement of a feature. We define a network decision to be *safe* for input x and region η with respect to the set of manipulations Δ if applying the manipulations on x will not result in a class change for η. We employ discretisation to enable a *finite exhaustive* search of the high-dimensional region η for adversarial misclassifications. The discretisation approach is justified in the case of image classifiers since they are typically represented as vectors of discrete pixels (vectors of 8 bit RGB colours). To achieve scalability, we propagate the analysis *layer by layer*, mapping the region and manipulations to the deeper layers.

We show that this propagation is sound, and is complete under the additional assumption of minimality of manipulations, which holds in discretised settings. In contrast to existing approaches [28,36], our framework can guarantee that a misclassification is found if it exists. Since we reduce verification to a search for adversarial examples, we can achieve safety *verification* (if no misclassifications are found for all layers) or *falsification* (in which case the adversarial examples can be used to fine-tune the network or shown to a human tester).

We implement the techniques using Z3 [8] in a tool called DLV (Deep Learning Verification) [2] and evaluate them on state-of-the-art networks, including regularised and deep learning networks. This includes image classification networks trained for classifying hand-written images of digits 0–9 (MNIST), 10 classes of small colour images (CIFAR10), 43 classes of the German Traffic Sign Recognition Benchmark (GTSRB) [35] and 1000 classes of colour images used for the well-known imageNet large-scale visual recognition challenge (ILSVRC) [4]. We also perform a comparison of the DLV falsification functionality on the MNIST dataset against the methods of [28,36], focusing on the search strategies and statistical robustness estimation. The perturbed images in Fig. 1 are found automatically using our tool for the network trained on the CIFAR10 dataset.

This invited paper is an extended and improved version of [20], where an extended version including appendices can also be found.

2   Background on Neural Networks

We consider feed-forward multi-layer neural networks [14], henceforth abbreviated as neural networks. Perceptrons (neurons) in a neural network are arranged in disjoint layers, with each perceptron in one layer connected to the next layer, but no connection between perceptrons in the same layer. Each layer L_k of a network is associated with an n_k-dimensional vector space $D_{L_k} \subseteq \mathbb{R}^{n_k}$, in which each dimension corresponds to a perceptron. We write P_k for the set of perceptrons in layer L_k and $n_k = |P_k|$ is the number of perceptrons (dimensions) in layer L_k.

Formally, a *(feed-forward and deep) neural* network N is a tuple (L, T, Φ), where $L = \{L_k \mid k \in \{0, \ldots, n\}\}$ is a set of layers such that layer L_0 is the *input* layer and L_n is the *output* layer, $T \subseteq L \times L$ is a set of sequential connections between layers such that, except for the input and output layers, each layer has an incoming connection and an outgoing connection, and $\Phi = \{\phi_k \mid k \in \{1, \ldots, n\}\}$ is a set of *activation functions* $\phi_k : D_{L_{k-1}} \to D_{L_k}$, one for each non-input layer. Layers other than input and output layers are called the *hidden* layers.

The network is fed an input x (point in D_{L_0}) through its input layer, which is then propagated through the layers by successive application of the activation functions. An *activation* for point x in layer k is the value of the corresponding function, denoted $\alpha_{x,k} = \phi_k(\phi_{k-1}(\ldots\phi_1(x))) \in D_{L_k}$, where $\alpha_{x,0} = x$. For perceptron $p \in P_k$ we write $\alpha_{x,k}(p)$ for the value of its activation on input x. For every activation $\alpha_{x,k}$ and layer $k' < k$, we define $Pre_{k'}(\alpha_{x,k}) = \{\alpha_{y,k'} \in D_{L_{k'}} \mid \alpha_{y,k} = \alpha_{x,k}\}$ to be the set of activations in layer k' whose corresponding activation in layer L_k is $\alpha_{x,k}$. The classification decision is made based on the activations in the output layer by, e.g., assigning to x the class $\arg\max_{p \in P_n} \alpha_{x,n}(p)$. For simplicity, we use $\alpha_{x,n}$ to denote the class assigned to input x, and thus $\alpha_{x,n} = \alpha_{y,n}$ expresses that two inputs x and y have *the same class*.

The neural network classifier N represents a function $\hat{f}(x)$ which approximates $f(x) : D_{L_0} \rightarrow C$, a function that models the human perception capability in labelling images with labels from C, from M training examples $\{(x^i, c^i)\}_{i=1,..,M}$. Image classification networks, for example convolutional networks, may contain many layers, which can be non-linear, and work in high dimensions, which for the image classification problems can be of the order of millions. Digital images are represented as 3D tensors of pixels (width, height and depth, the latter to represent colour), where each pixel is a discrete value in the range $0 \ldots 255$. The training process determines real values for weights used as filters that are convolved with the activation functions. Since it is difficult to approximate f with few samples in the sparsely populated high-dimensional space, to increase the probability of classifying correctly a previously unseen image, various regularisation techniques such as dropout are employed. They improve the smoothness of the classifier, in the sense that points that are ϵ-close to a training point (potentially infinitely many of them) classify the same.

In this paper, we work with the code of the network and its trained weights.

3   Safety Analysis of Classification Decisions

In this section we define our notion of safety of classification decisions for a neural network, based on the concept of a manipulation of an image, essentially perturbations that a human observer would classify the same as the original image. Safety is defined for an individual classification decision and is parameterised by the class of manipulations and a neighbouring region around a given image. To ensure finiteness of the search of the region for adversarial misclassifications, we introduce so called "ladders", nondeterministically branching and iterated application of successive manipulations, and state the conditions under which the search is exhaustive.

Safety and Robustness. Our method assumes the existence of a (possibly infinite) region η around a data point (image) x such that all points in the region are indistinguishable by a human, and therefore have the same true class. This region is understood as supporting the *classification decision* and can usually be inferred from the type of the classification problem. For simplicity, we identify such a region via its diameter d with respect to some user-specified norm, which intuitively measures the closeness to the point x. As defined in [18], a network $\hat{f}$ approximating human capability f is said to be *not robust at* x if there exists a point y in the region $\eta = \{z \in D_{L_0} \mid ||z - x|| \leq d\}$ of the input layer such that $\hat{f}(x) \neq \hat{f}(y)$. The point y, at a minimal distance from x, is known as an *adversarial example*. Our definition of *safety for a classification decision* (abbreviated *safety at a point*) follows he same intuition, except that we work layer by layer, and therefore will identify such a region η_k, a subspace of D_{L_k}, at each layer L_k, for $k \in \{0, \ldots, n\}$, and successively refine the regions through the deeper layers. We justify this choice based on the observation [11,23,24] that deep neural networks are thought to compute progressively more powerful invariants as the depth increases. In other words, they gradually transform images into a representation in which the classes are separable by a linear classifier.

Assumption 1. *For each activation $\alpha_{x,k}$ of point x in layer L_k, the region $\eta_k(\alpha_{x,k})$ contains activations that the human observer believes to be so close to $\alpha_{x,k}$ that they should be classified the same as x.*

Intuitively, safety for network N at a point x means that the classification decision is robust at x against perturbations within the region $\eta_k(\alpha_{x,k})$. Note that, while the perturbation is applied in layer L_k, the classification decision is based on the activation in the output layer L_n.

Definition 1. *[General Safety] Let $\eta_k(\alpha_{x,k})$ be a region in layer L_k of a neural network N such that $\alpha_{x,k} \in \eta_k(\alpha_{x,k})$. We say that N is* safe *for input x and region $\eta_k(\alpha_{x,k})$, written as $N, \eta_k \models x$, if for all activations $\alpha_{y,k}$ in $\eta_k(\alpha_{x,k})$ we have $\alpha_{y,n} = \alpha_{x,n}$.*

We remark that, unlike the notions of risk [37] and robustness of [12,18], we work with safety for a specific point and do not account for the input distribution, but such expectation measures can be considered, see Sect. 6 for comparison.

Manipulations. A key concept of our framework is the notion of a *manipulation*, an operator that intuitively models image perturbations, for example bad angles, scratches or weather conditions, the idea being that the classification decisions in a region of images close to it should be invariant under such manipulations. The choice of the type of manipulation is dependent on the application and user-defined, reflecting knowledge of the classification problem to model perturbations that should or should not be allowed. Judicious choice of families of such manipulations and appropriate distance metrics is particularly important. For simplicity, we work with operators $\delta_k : D_{L_k} \rightarrow D_{L_k}$ over the activations in the vector space of layer k, and consider the Euclidean (L^2) and Manhattan (L^1) norms to measure the distance between an image and its perturbation through δ_k, but the techniques generalise to other norms discussed in [12,18,19]. More specifically, applying a manipulation $\delta_k(\alpha_{x,k})$ to an activation $\alpha_{x,k}$ will result in another activation such that the values of *some or all* dimensions are changed. We therefore represent a manipulation as a hyper-rectangle, defined for two activations $\alpha_{x,k}$ and $\alpha_{y,k}$ of layer L_k by $rec(\alpha_{x,k}, \alpha_{y,k}) = \times_{p \in P_k}[min(\alpha_{x,k}(p), \alpha_{y,k}(p)),\ max(\alpha_{x,k}(p), \alpha_{y,k}(p))]$. The main challenge for verification is the fact that the region η_k contains potentially an uncountable number of activations. Our approach relies on discretisation in order to enable a finite exploration of the region to discover and/or rule out adversarial perturbations.

For an activation $\alpha_{x,k}$ and a set Δ of manipulations, we denote by $rec(\Delta, \alpha_{x,k})$ the polyhedron which includes all hyper-rectangles that result from applying some manipulation in Δ on $\alpha_{x,k}$, i.e., $rec(\Delta, \alpha_{x,k}) = \bigcup_{\delta \in \Delta} rec(\alpha_{x,k}, \delta(\alpha_{x,k}))$. Let Δ_k be the set of all possible manipulations for layer L_k. To ensure region coverage, we define *valid* manipulation as follows.

Definition 2. *Given an activation* $\alpha_{x,k}$, *a set of manipulations* $V(\alpha_{x,k}) \subseteq \Delta_k$ *is* valid *if* $\alpha_{x,k}$ *is an interior point of* $rec(V(\alpha_{x,k}), \alpha_{x,k})$, *i.e.,* $\alpha_{x,k}$ *is in* $rec(V(\alpha_{x,k}), \alpha_{x,k})$ *and does not belong to the boundary of* $rec(V(\alpha_{x,k}), \alpha_{x,k})$.

Figure 2 presents an example of valid manipulations in two-dimensional space: each arrow represents a manipulation, each dashed box represents a (hyper-)rectangle of the corresponding manipulation, and activation $\alpha_{x,k}$ is an interior point of the space from the dashed boxes.

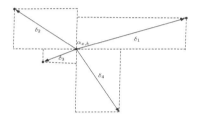

Fig. 2. Example of a set $\{\delta_1, \delta_2, \delta_3, \delta_4\}$ of valid manipulations in a 2-dimensional space

Since we work with discretised spaces, which is a reasonable assumption for images, we introduce the notion of a *minimal* manipulation. If applying a minimal manipulation, it suffices to check for misclassification just at the end points, that is, $\alpha_{x,k}$ and $\delta_k(\alpha_{x,k})$. This allows an exhaustive, albeit impractical, exploration of the region in unit steps.

A manipulation $\delta_k^1(\alpha_{y,k})$ is *finer than* $\delta_k^2(\alpha_{x,k})$, written as $\delta_k^1(\alpha_{y,k}) \leq \delta_k^2(\alpha_{x,k})$, if any activation in the hyper-rectangle of the former is also in the hyper-rectangle of the latter. It is implied in this definition that $\alpha_{y,k}$ is an activation in the hyper-rectangle of $\delta_k^2(\alpha_{x,k})$. Moreover, we write $\delta_{k,k'}(\alpha_{x,k})$ for $\phi_{k'}(...\phi_{k+1}(\delta_k(\alpha_{x,k})))$, representing the corresponding activation in layer $k' \geq k$ after applying manipulation δ_k on the activation $\alpha_{x,k}$, where $\delta_{k,k}(\alpha_{x,k}) = \delta_k(\alpha_{x,k})$.

Definition 3. *A manipulation* δ_k *on an activation* $\alpha_{x,k}$ *is* minimal *if there does not exist manipulations* δ_k^1 *and* δ_k^2 *and an activation* $\alpha_{y,k}$ *such that* $\delta_k^1(\alpha_{x,k}) \leq \delta_k(\alpha_{x,k})$, $\alpha_{y,k} = \delta_k^1(\alpha_{x,k})$, $\delta_k(\alpha_{x,k}) = \delta_k^2(\alpha_{y,k})$, *and* $\alpha_{y,n} \neq \alpha_{x,n}$ *and* $\alpha_{y,n} \neq \delta_{k,n}(\alpha_{x,k})$.

Intuitively, a minimal manipulation does not have a finer manipulation that results in a different classification. However, it is possible to have different classifications before and after applying the minimal manipulation, i.e., it is possible that $\delta_{k,n}(\alpha_{x,k}) \neq \alpha_{x,n}$. It is not hard to see that the minimality of a manipulation implies that the class change in its associated hyper-rectangle can be detected by checking the class of the end points $\alpha_{x,k}$ and $\delta_k(\alpha_{x,k})$.

Bounded Variation. Recall that we apply manipulations in layer L_k, but check the classification decisions in the output layer. To ensure *finite, exhaustive* coverage of the region, we introduce a continuity assumption on the mapping from space D_{L_k} to the output space D_{L_n}, adapted from the concept of bounded variation [9]. Given an activation $\alpha_{x,k}$ with its associated region $\eta_k(\alpha_{x,k})$, we define a "ladder" on $\eta_k(\alpha_{x,k})$ to be a set ld of activations containing $\alpha_{x,k}$ and finitely many, possibly zero, activations from $\eta_k(\alpha_{x,k})$. The activations in a ladder can be arranged into an increasing order $\alpha_{x,k} = \alpha_{x_0,k} < \alpha_{x_1,k} < ... < \alpha_{x_j,k}$ such that every activation $\alpha_{x_t,k} \in ld$ appears once and has a successor $\alpha_{x_{t+1},k}$ such that $\alpha_{x_{t+1},k} = \delta_k(\alpha_{x_t,k})$ for some manipulation $\delta_k \in V(\alpha_{x_t,k})$. For the greatest element $\alpha_{x_j,k}$, its successor should be outside the region $\eta_k(\alpha_{x,k})$, i.e., $\alpha_{x_{j+1},k} \notin \eta_k(\alpha_{x,k})$. Given a ladder ld, we write $ld(t)$ for its $t + 1$-th activation, $ld[0..t]$ for the prefix of ld up to the $t + 1$-th activation, and $last(ld)$ for the greatest element of ld. Figure 3 gives a diagrammatic explanation on the ladders.

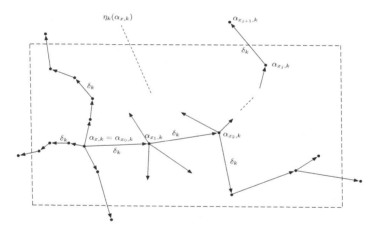

Fig. 3. Examples of ladders in region $\eta_k(\alpha_{x,k})$. Starting from $\alpha_{x,k} = \alpha_{x_0,k}$, the activations $\alpha_{x_1,k}...\alpha_{x_j,k}$ form a ladder such that each consecutive activation results from some valid manipulation δ_k applied to a previous activation, and the final activation $\alpha_{x_j,k}$ is outside the region $\eta_k(\alpha_{x,k})$.

Definition 4. *Let $\mathcal{L}(\eta_k(\alpha_{x,k}))$ be the set of ladders in $\eta_k(\alpha_{x,k})$. Then the total variation of the region $\eta_k(\alpha_{x,k})$ on the neural network with respect to $\mathcal{L}(\eta_k(\alpha_{x,k}))$ is*

$$V(N; \eta_k(\alpha_{x,k})) = \sup_{ld \in \mathcal{L}(\eta_k(\alpha_{x,k}))} \sum_{\alpha_{x_t,k} \in ld \setminus \{last(ld)\}} \mathrm{diff}_n(\alpha_{x_t,n}, \alpha_{x_{t+1},n})$$

where $\mathrm{diff}_n : D_{L_n} \times D_{L_n} \to \{0, 1\}$ is given by $\mathrm{diff}_n(\alpha_{x,n}, \alpha_{y,n}) = 0$ if $\alpha_{x,n} = \alpha_{y,n}$ and 1 otherwise. We say that the region $\eta_k(\alpha_{x,k})$ is a bounded variation if $V(N; \eta_k(\alpha_{x,k})) < \infty$, and are particularly interested in the case when $V(N; r_k(\alpha_{y,k})) = 0$, which is called a 0-variation.

The set $\mathcal{L}(\eta_k(\alpha_{x,k}))$ is *complete* if, for any ladder $ld \in \mathcal{L}(\eta_k(\alpha_{x,k}))$ of $j + 1$ activations, any element $ld(t)$ for $0 \leq t \leq j$, and any manipulation $\delta_k \in V(ld(t))$, there exists a ladder $ld' \in \mathcal{L}(\eta_k(\alpha_{x,k}))$ such that $ld'[0..t] = ld[0..t]$ and $ld'(t + 1) = \delta_k(ld(t))$. Intuitively, a complete ladder is a complete tree, on which each node represents an activation and each branch of a node corresponds to a valid manipulation. From the root $\alpha_{x,k}$, every path of the tree leading to a leaf is a ladder. Moreover, the set $\mathcal{L}(\eta_k(\alpha_{x,k}))$ is *covering* if the polyhedra of all activations in it cover the region $\eta_k(\alpha_{x,k})$, i.e.,

$$\eta_k(\alpha_{x,k}) \subseteq \bigcup_{ld \in \mathcal{L}(\eta_k(\alpha_{x,k}))} \bigcup_{\alpha_{x_t,k} \in ld \setminus \{last(ld)\}} rec(V(\alpha_{x_t,k}), \alpha_{x_t,k}). \tag{1}$$

Based on the above, we have the following definition of safety with respect to a set of manipulations. Intuitively, we *iteratively* and *nondeterministically* apply manipulations to explore the region $\eta_k(\alpha_{x,k})$, and safety means that no class change is observed by successive application of such manipulations.

Definition 5. *[Safety wrt Manipulations] Given a neural network N, an input x and a set Δ_k of manipulations, we say that N is safe for input x with respect to the region η_k and manipulations Δ_k, written as $N, \eta_k, \Delta_k \models x$, if the region $\eta_k(\alpha_{x,k})$ is a 0-variation for the set $\mathcal{L}(\eta_k(\alpha_{x,k}))$ of its ladders, which is complete and covering.*

It is straightforward to note that general safety in the sense of Definition 1 implies safety wrt manipulations, in the sense of Definition 5.

Theorem 1. *Given a neural network N, an input x, and a region η_k, we have that $N, \eta_k \models x$ implies $N, \eta_k, \Delta_k \models x$ for any set of manipulations Δ_k.*

In the opposite direction, we require the minimality assumption on manipulations.

Theorem 2. *Given a neural network N, an input x, a region $\eta_k(\alpha_{x,k})$ and a set Δ_k of manipulations, we have that $N, \eta_k, \Delta_k \models x$ implies $N, \eta_k \models x$ if the manipulations in Δ_k are minimal.*

Theorem 2 means that, under the minimality assumption over the manipulations, an *exhaustive* search through the complete and covering ladder tree from $\mathcal{L}(\eta_k(\alpha_{x,k}))$ can find adversarial examples, if any, and enable us to conclude that the network is safe at a given point if none are found. Though computing minimal manipulations is not practical, in discrete spaces by iterating over increasingly *refined* manipulations we are able to rule out the existence of adversarial examples in the region. This contrasts with *partial* exploration according to, e.g., [12,25]; for comparison see Sect. 7.

4   The Verification Framework

In this section we propose a novel framework for automated verification of safety of classification decisions, which is based on search for an adversarial misclassification within a given region. The key distinctive distinctive features of our framework compared to existing work are: a *guarantee* that a misclassification is found if it exists; the propagation of the analysis *layer by layer*; and working with *hidden* layers, in addition to input and output layers. Since we reduce verification to a search for adversarial examples, we can achieve safety *verification* (if no misclassifications are found for all layers) or *falsification* (in which case the adversarial examples can be used to fine-tune the network or shown to a human tester).

4.1   Layer-by-Layer Analysis

We first consider how to propagate the analysis layer by layer, which will involve *refining* manipulations through the hidden layers. To facilitate such analysis, in addition to the activation function $\phi_k : D_{L_{k-1}} \to D_{L_k}$ we also require a mapping $\psi_k : D_{L_k} \to D_{L_{k-1}}$ in the opposite direction, to represent how a manipulated activation of layer L_k affects the activations of layer L_{k-1}. We can simply take ψ_k as the inverse function of ϕ_k. In order to propagate safety of regions $\eta_k(\alpha_{x,k})$ at a point x into deeper layers, we assume the existence of functions η_k that map activations to regions, and impose the following restrictions on the functions ϕ_k and ψ_k, shown diagrammatically in Fig. 4.

Definition 6. *The functions $\{\eta_0, \eta_1, \ldots, \eta_n\}$ and $\{\psi_1, \ldots, \psi_n\}$ mapping activations to regions are such that*

1. $\eta_k(\alpha_{x,k}) \subseteq D_{L_k}$, *for $k = 0, \ldots, n$,*
2. $\alpha_{x,k} \in \eta_k(\alpha_{x,k})$, *for $k = 0, \ldots, n$, and*
3. $\eta_{k-1}(\alpha_{i,k-1}) \subseteq \psi_k(\eta_k(\alpha_{x,k}))$ *for all $k = 1, \ldots, n$.*

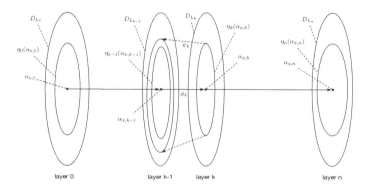

Fig. 4. Layer by layer analysis according to Definition 6

Intuitively, the first two conditions state that each function η_k assigns a region around the activation $\alpha_{x,k}$, and the last condition that mapping the region η_k from layer L_k to L_{k-1} via ψ_k should cover the region η_{k-1}. The aim is to compute functions $\eta_{k+1}, \ldots, \eta_n$ based on η_k and the neural network.

The size and complexity of a deep neural network generally means that determining whether a given set Δ_k of manipulations is minimal is intractable. To partially counter this, we define a *refinement* relation between safety wrt manipulations for consecutive layers in the sense that $N, \eta_k, \Delta_k \models x$ is a refinement of $N, \eta_{k-1}, \Delta_{k-1} \models x$ if all manipulations δ_{k-1} in Δ_{k-1} are refined by a sequence of manipulations δ_k from the set Δ_k. Therefore, although we cannot theoretically confirm the minimality of Δ_k, they are refined layer by layer and, in discrete settings, this process can be bounded from below by the unit step. Moreover, we can work gradually from a specific layer inwards until an adversarial example is found, finishing processing when reaching the output layer.

The refinement framework is given in Fig. 5. The arrows represent the implication relations between the safety notions and are labelled with conditions if needed. The goal of the refinements is to find a chain of implications to justify $N, \eta_0 \models x$. The fact that $N, \eta_k \models x$ implies $N, \eta_{k-1} \models x$ is due to the constraints in Definition 6 when $\psi_k = \phi_k^{-1}$. The fact that $N, \eta_k \models x$ implies $N, \eta_k, \Delta_k \models x$ follows from Theorem 1. The implication from $N, \eta_k, \Delta_k \models x$ to $N, \eta_k \models x$ under the condition that Δ_k is minimal is due to Theorem 2.

We now define the notion of *refinability* of manipulations between layers. Intuitively, a manipulation in layer L_{k-1} is refinable in layer L_k if there exists a sequence of manipulations in layer L_k that implements the manipulation in layer L_{k-1}.

Definition 7. *A manipulation $\delta_{k-1}(\alpha_{y,k-1})$ is refinable in layer L_k if there exist activations $\alpha_{x_0,k}, \ldots, \alpha_{x_j,k} \in D_{L_k}$ and valid manipulations $\delta_k^1 \in V(\alpha_{x_0,k}), \ldots, \delta_k^j \in V(\alpha_{x_{j-1},k})$ such that $\alpha_{y,k} = \alpha_{x_0,k}$, $\delta_{k-1,k}(\alpha_{y,k-1}) = \alpha_{x_j,k}$, and $\alpha_{x_t,k} = \delta_k^t(\alpha_{x_{t-1},k})$ for $1 \le t \le j$. Given a neural network N and an input x, the manipulations Δ_k are a refinement by layer of η_{k-1}, Δ_{k-1} and η_k if, for all $\alpha_{y,k-1} \in \eta_{k-1}(\alpha_{z,k-1})$, all its valid manipulations $\delta_{k-1}(\alpha_{y,k-1})$ are refinable in layer L_k.*

Fig. 5. Refinement framework

We have the following theorem stating that the refinement of safety notions is implied by the "refinement by layer" relation.

Theorem 3. *Assume a neural network N and an input x. For all layers $k \geq 1$, if manipulations Δ_k are refinement by layer of η_{k-1}, Δ_{k-1} and η_k, then we have that $N, \eta_k, \Delta_k \models x$ implies $N, \eta_{k-1}, \Delta_{k-1} \models x$.*

We note that any adversarial example of safety wrt manipulations $N, \eta_k, \Delta_k \models x$ is also an adversarial example for general safety $N, \eta_k \models x$. However, an adversarial example $\alpha_{x,k}$ for $N, \eta_k \models x$ at layer k needs to be checked to see if it is an adversarial example of $N, \eta_0 \models x$, i.e. for the input layer. Recall that $Pre_{k'}(\alpha_{x,k})$ is not necessarily unique. This is equivalent to checking the emptiness of $Pre_0(\alpha_{x,k}) \cap \eta_0(\alpha_{x,0})$. If we start the analysis with a hidden layer $k > 0$ and there is no specification for η_0, we can instead consider checking the emptiness of $\{\alpha_{y,0} \in Pre_0(\alpha_{x,k}) \mid \alpha_{y,n} \neq \alpha_{x,n}\}$.

4.2   The Verification Method

We summarise the theory developed thus far as a search-based recursive verification procedure given below. The method is parameterised by the region η_k around a given point and a family of manipulations Δ_k. The manipulations are specified by the user for the classification problem at hand, or alternatively can be selected automatically, as described in Sect. 4.4. The vector norm to identify the region can also be specified by the user and can vary by layer. The method can start in any layer, with analysis propagated into deeper layers, and terminates when a misclassification is found. If an adversarial example is found by manipulating a hidden layer, it can be mapped back to the input layer, see Sect. 4.5.

Algorithm 1. *Given a neural network N and an input x, recursively perform the following steps, starting from some layer $l \geq 0$. Let $k \geq l$ be the current layer under consideration.*

1. *determine a region η_k such that if $k > l$ then η_k and η_{k-1} satisfy Definition 6;*
2. *determine a manipulation set Δ_k such that if $k > l$ then Δ_k is a refinement by layer of η_{k-1}, Δ_{k-1} and η_k according to Definition 7;*
3. *verify whether $N, \eta_k, \Delta_k \models x$,*
   (a) if $N, \eta_k, \Delta_k \models x$ then
       i. report that N is safe at x with respect to $\eta_k(\alpha_{x,k})$ and Δ_k, and
       ii continue to layer $k + 1$;
   (b) if $N, \eta_k, \Delta_k \not\models x$, then report an adversarial example.

We implement Algorithm 1 by utilising satisfiability modulo theory (SMT) solvers. The SMT problem is a decision problem for logical formulas with respect to combinations of background theories expressed in classical first-order logic with equality. For checking refinement by layer, we use the theory of linear real arithmetic with existential and universal quantifiers, and for verification within a layer (0-variation) we use the same theory but without universal quantification. The details of the encoding and the approach taken to compute the regions and manipulations are included in Sect. 4.4. To enable practical verification of deep neural networks, we employ a number of heuristics described in the remainder of this section.

4.3   Feature Decomposition and Discovery

While Theorems 1 and 2 provide a *finite* way to verify safety of neural network classification decisions, the high-dimensionality of the region $\eta_k(\alpha_{x,k})$ can make any computational approach impractical. We therefore use the concept of a *feature* to partition the region $\eta_k(\alpha_{x,k})$ into a set of features, and exploit their independence and low-dimensionality. This allows us to work with state-of-the-art networks that have hundreds, and even thousands, of dimensions.

   Intuitively, a feature defines for each point in the high-dimensional space D_{L_k} the most explicit salient feature it has, e.g., the red-coloured frame of a street sign in Fig. 10. Formally, for each layer L_k, a feature function $f_k : D_{L_k} \rightarrow \mathcal{P}(D_{L_k})$ assigns a small region for each activation $\alpha_{x,k}$ in the space D_{L_k}, where $\mathcal{P}(D_{L_k})$ is the set of subspaces of D_{L_k}. The region $f_k(\alpha_{x,k})$ may have lower dimension than that of D_k. It has been argued, in e.g. [16] for natural images, that natural data, for example natural images and sound, forms a high-dimensional manifold, which embeds tangled manifolds to represent their features. Feature manifolds usually have lower dimension than the data manifold, and a classification algorithm is to separate a set of tangled manifolds. By assuming that the appearance of features is independent, we can manipulate them one by one regardless of the manipulation order, and thus reduce the problem of size $O(2^{d_1+\dots+d_m})$ into a set of smaller problems of size $O(2^{d_1}), \dots, O(2^{d_m})$.

   The analysis of activations in hidden layers, as performed by our method, provides an opportunity to *discover the features automatically*. Moreover, defining the feature f_k on each activation as a single region corresponding to a specific feature is without loss of generality: although an activation may include multiple features, the independence relation between features suggests the existence of a total relation between these features. The function f_k essentially defines for each activation one particular feature, subject to certain criteria such as explicit knowledge, but features can also be explored in parallel.

   Every feature $f_k(\alpha_{y,k})$ is identified by a pre-specified number $dims_{k,f}$ of dimensions. Let $dims_k(f_k(\alpha_{y,k}))$ be the set of dimensions selected according to some heuristic. Then we have that

$$f_k(\alpha_{y,k})(p) = \begin{cases} \eta_k(\alpha_{x,k})(p), & \text{if } p \in dims_k(f_k(\alpha_{y,k})) \\ [\alpha_{y,k}(p), \alpha_{y,k}(p)] & \text{otherwise.} \end{cases} \qquad (2)$$

Moreover, we need a set of features to partition the region $\eta_k(\alpha_{x,k})$ as follows.

Definition 8. *A set $\{f_1, \dots, f_m\}$ of regions is a partition of $\eta_k(\alpha_{x,k})$, written as $\pi(\eta_k(\alpha_{x,k}))$, if $dims_{k,f}(f_i) \cap dims_{k,f}(f_j) = \emptyset$ for $i,j \in \{1, \dots, m\}$ and $\eta_k(\alpha_{x,k}) = \times_{i=1}^m f_i$.*

   Given such a partition $\pi(\eta_k(\alpha_{x,k}))$, we define a function $acts(x,k)$ by

$$acts(x,k) = \{\alpha_{y,k} \in x \mid x \in \pi(\eta_k(\alpha_{x,k}))\} \qquad (3)$$

which contains one point for each feature. Then, we reduce the checking of 0-variation of a region $\eta_k(\alpha_{x,k})$ to the following problems:

– checking whether the points in $acts(x, k)$ have the same class as $\alpha_{x,k}$, and
– checking the 0-variation of all features in $\pi(\eta_k(\alpha_{x,k}))$.

In the above procedure, the checking of points in $acts(x, k)$ can be conducted either by following a pre-specified sequential order (*single-path* search) or by exhaustively searching all possible orders (*multi-path* search). In Sect. 5 we demonstrate that single-path search according to the prominence of features can enable us to find adversarial examples, while multi-path search may find other examples whose distance to the original input image is smaller.

4.4 Selection of Regions and Manipulations

The procedure summarised in Algorithm 1 is typically invoked for a given image in the input layer, but, providing insight about hidden layers is available, it can start from any layer L_l in the network. The selection of regions can be automated, as described below.

For the first layer to be considered, i.e., $k = l$, the region $\eta_k(\alpha_{x,k})$ is defined by first selecting the subset of $dims_k$ dimensions from P_k whose activation values are furthest away from the average activation value of the layer[1]. Intuitively, the knowledge represented by these activations is more explicit than the knowledge represented by the other dimensions, and manipulations over more explicit knowledge are more likely to result in a class change. Let $avg_k = (\sum_{p \in P_k} \alpha_{x,k}(p))/n_k$ be the average activation value of layer L_k. We let $dims_k(\eta_k(\alpha_{x,k}))$ be the first $dims_k$ dimensions $p \in P_k$ with the greatest values $|\alpha_{x,k}(p) - avg|$ among all dimensions, and then define

$$\eta_k(\alpha_{x,k}) = \times_{p \in dims_k(\eta_k(\alpha_{x,k}))}[\alpha_{x,k}(p) - s_p * m_p, \alpha_{x,k}(p) + s_p * m_p] \quad (4)$$

i.e., a $dims_k$-polytope containing the activation $\alpha_{x,k}$, where s_p represents a small span and m_p represents the number of such spans. Let $V_k = \{s_p, m_p \mid p \in dims_k(\eta_k(\alpha_{x,k}))\}$ be a set of variables.

Let d be a function mapping from $dims_k(\eta_k(\alpha_{x,k}))$ to $\{-1, 0, +1\}$ such that $\{d(p) \neq 0 \mid p \in dims_k(\eta_k(\alpha_{x,k}))\} \neq \emptyset$, and $D(dims_k(\eta_k(\alpha_{x,k})))$ be the set of such functions. Let a manipulation δ_k^d be

$$\delta_k^d(\alpha_{y,k})(p) = \begin{cases} \alpha_{y,k}(p) - s_p & \text{if } d(p) = -1 \\ \alpha_{y,k}(p) & \text{if } d(p) = 0 \\ \alpha_{y,k}(p) + s_p & \text{if } d(p) = +1 \end{cases} \quad (5)$$

for activation $\alpha_{y,k} \in \eta_k(\alpha_{x,k})$. That is, each manipulation changes a subset of the dimensions by the span s_p, according to the directions given in d. The set Δ_k is defined by collecting the set of all such manipulations. Based on this, we can define a set $\mathcal{L}(\eta_k(\alpha_{x,k}))$ of ladders, which is complete and covering.

Determining the Region η_k According to η_{k-1}. Given $\eta_{k-1}(\alpha_{x,k-1})$ and the functions ϕ_k and ψ_k, we can automatically determine a region $\eta_k(\alpha_{x,k})$

---

[1] We also considered other approaches, including computing derivatives up to several layers, but for the experiments we conduct they are less effective.

satisfying Definition 6 using the following approach. According to the function ϕ_k, the activation value $\alpha_{x,k}(p)$ of perceptron $p \in P_k$ is computed from activation values of a subset of perceptrons in P_{k-1}. We let $Vars(p) \subseteq P_{k-1}$ be such a set of perceptrons. The selection of dimensions in $dims_k(\eta_k(\alpha_{x,k}))$ depends on $dims_{k-1}(\eta_{k-1}(\alpha_{x,k-1}))$ and ϕ_k, by requiring that, for every $p' \in dims_{k-1}(\eta_{k-1}(\alpha_{x,k-1}))$, there is at least one dimension $p \in dims_k(\eta_k(\alpha_{x,k}))$ such that $p' \in Vars(p)$. We let

$$dims_k(\eta_k(\alpha_{x,k})) = \{ \arg\max_{p \in P_k}\{ |\alpha_{x,k}(p) - avg_k| \mid p' \in Vars(p)\} \mid p' \in$$

$$dims_{k-1}(\eta_{k-1}(\alpha_{x,k-1}))\} \tag{6}$$

Therefore, the restriction of Definition 6 can be expressed with the following formula:

$$\forall \alpha_{y,k-1} \in \eta_k(\alpha_{x,k-1}) : \alpha_{y,k-1} \in \psi_k(\eta_k(\alpha_{x,k})). \tag{7}$$

We omit the details of rewriting $\alpha_{y,k-1} \in \eta_k(\alpha_{x,k-1})$ and $\alpha_{y,k-1} \in \psi_k(\eta_k(\alpha_{x,k}))$ into Boolean expressions, which follow from standard techniques. Note that this expression includes variables in V_k, V_{k-1} and $\alpha_{y,k-1}$. The variables in V_{k-1} are fixed for a given $\eta_{k-1}(\alpha_{x,k-1})$. Because such a region $\eta_k(\alpha_{x,k})$ always exists, a simple iterative procedure can be invoked to gradually increase the size of the region represented with variables in V_k to eventually satisfy the expression.

Determining the Manipulation Set Δ_k According to $\eta_k(\alpha_{x,k})$, $\eta_{k-1}(\alpha_{x,k-1})$, and Δ_{k-1}. The values of the variables V_k obtained from the satisfiability of Eq. (7) yield a definition of manipulations using Eq. (5). However, the obtained values for span variables s_p do not necessarily satisfy the "refinement by layer" relation as defined in Definition 7. Therefore, we need to adapt the values for the variables V_k while, at the same time, retaining the region $\eta_k(\alpha_{x,k})$. To do so, we could rewrite the constraint in Definition 7 into a formula, which can then be solved by an SMT solver. But, in practice, we notice that such *precise* computations easily lead to overly small spans s_p, which in turn result in an unacceptable amount of computation needed to verify the relation $N, \eta_k, \Delta_k \models x$.

To reduce computational cost, we work with a weaker "refinable in layer L_k" notion, parameterised with respect to precision ε. Given two activations $\alpha_{y,k}$ and $\alpha_{m,k}$, we use $dist(\alpha_{y,k}, \alpha_{m,k})$ to represent their distance.

Definition 9. *A manipulation $\delta_{k-1}(\alpha_{y,k-1})$ is refinable in layer L_k with precision $\varepsilon > 0$ if there exists a sequence of activations $\alpha_{x_0,k}, \ldots, \alpha_{x_j,k} \in D_{L_k}$ and valid manipulations $\delta_k^1 \in V(\alpha_{x_0,k}), \ldots, \delta_k^d \in V(\alpha_{x_{j-1},k})$ such that $\alpha_{y,k} = \alpha_{x_0,k}$, $\delta_{k-1,k}(\alpha_{y,k-1}) \in rec(\alpha_{x_{j-1},k}, \alpha_{x_j,k})$, $dist(\alpha_{x_{j-1},k}, \alpha_{x_j,k}) \leq \epsilon$, and $\alpha_{x_t,k} = \delta_k^t(\alpha_{x_{t-1},k})$ for $1 \leq t \leq j$. Given a neural network N and an input x, the manipulations Δ_k are a refinement by layer of $\eta_k, \eta_{k-1}, \Delta_{k-1}$ with precision ε if, for all $\alpha_{y,k-1} \in \eta_{k-1}(\alpha_{x,k-1})$, all its legal manipulations $\delta_{k-1}(\alpha_{y,k-1})$ are refinable in layer L_k with precision ε.*

Comparing with Definition 7, the above definition replaces $\delta_{k-1,k}(\alpha_{y,k-1}) = \alpha_{x_j,k}$ with $\delta_{k-1,k}(\alpha_{y,k-1}) \in rec(\alpha_{x_{j-1},k}, \alpha_{x_j,k})$ and $dist(\alpha_{x_{j-1},k}, \alpha_{x_j,k}) \leq \varepsilon$. Intuitively, instead of requiring a manipulation to reach the activation $\delta_{k-1,k}(\alpha_{y,k-1})$ precisely, this definition allows for each $\delta_{k-1,k}(\alpha_{y,k-1})$ to be within the hyper-rectangle $rec(\alpha_{x_{j-1},k}, \alpha_{x_j,k})$. To find suitable values for V_k according to the approximate "refinement-by-layer" relation, we use a variable h to represent the maximal number of manipulations of layer L_k used to express a manipulation in layer $k-1$. The value of h (and variables s_p and n_p in V_k) are automatically adapted to ensure the satisfiability of the following formula, which expresses the constraints of Definition 9:

$$\forall \alpha_{y,k-1} \in \eta_k(\alpha_{x,k-1}) \forall d \in D(dims_k(\eta_k(\alpha_{x,k-1}))) \forall \delta_{k-1}^d \in V_{k-1}(\alpha_{y,k-1})$$
$$\exists \alpha_{y_0,k}, \ldots, \alpha_{y_h,k} \in \eta_k(\alpha_{x,k}) : \alpha_{y_0,k} = \alpha_{y,k} \wedge \bigwedge_{t=0}^{h-1} \alpha_{y_{t+1},k} = \delta_k^d(\alpha_{y_t,k}) \wedge \qquad (8)$$
$$\bigvee_{t=0}^{h-1} (\delta_{k-1,k}^d(\alpha_{y,k}) \in rec(\alpha_{y_t,k}, \alpha_{y_{t+1},k}) \wedge dist(\alpha_{y_t,k}, \alpha_{y_{t+1},k}) \leq \varepsilon).$$

It is noted that s_p and m_p for $p \in dims_k(\eta_k(\alpha_{x,k}))$ are employed when expressing δ_k^d. The manipulation δ_k^d is obtained from δ_{k-1}^d by considering the corresponding relation between dimensions in $dims_k(\eta_k(\alpha_{x,k}))$ and $dims_{k-1}(\eta_{k-1}(\alpha_{x,k-1}))$.

Adversarial examples shown in Figs. 8, 9, and 10 were found using single-path search and automatic selection of regions and manipulations.

4.5   Mapping Back to Input Layer

When manipulating the hidden layers, we may need to map back an activation in layer k to the input layer to obtain an input image that resulted in misclassification, which involves computation of $Pre_0(\alpha_{y,k})$ described next. To check the 0-variation of a region $\eta_k(\alpha_{x,k})$, we need to compute $\text{diff}_n(\alpha_{x,n}, \alpha_{y,n})$ for many points $\alpha_{y,x}$ in $\eta_k(\alpha_{x,k})$, where $\text{diff}_n : D_{L_n} \times D_{L_n} \to \{0,1\}$ is given by $\text{diff}_n(\alpha_{x,n}, \alpha_{y,n}) = 0$ if $\alpha_{x,n} = \alpha_{y,n}$ and 1 otherwise. Because $\alpha_{x,n}$ is known, we only need to compute $\alpha_{y,n}$. We can compute $\alpha_{y,n}$ by finding a point $\alpha_{y,0} \in Pre_0(\alpha_{y,k})$ and then using the neural network to predict the value $\alpha_{y,n}$. It should be noted that, although $Pre_0(\alpha_{y,k})$ may include more than one point, all points have the same class, so any point in $Pre_0(\alpha_{y,k})$ is sufficient for our purpose.

To compute $\alpha_{y,0}$ from $\alpha_{y,k}$, we use functions $\psi_k, \psi_{k-1}, \ldots, \psi_1$ and compute points $\alpha_{y,k-1}, \alpha_{y,k-2}, \ldots, \alpha_{y,0}$ such that

$$\alpha_{y,j-1} = \psi_j(\alpha_{y,j}) \wedge \alpha_{y,j-1} \in \eta_{j-1}(\alpha_{x,j-1})$$

for $1 \leq j \leq k$. The computation relies on an SMT solver to encode the functions $\psi_k, \psi_{k-1}, \ldots, \psi_1$ if they are piecewise linear functions, and by taking the corresponding inverse functions directly if they are sigmoid functions. It is possible that, for some $1 \leq j \leq k$, no point can be found by SMT solver, which means that the point $\alpha_{y,k}$ does not have any corresponding point in the input layer. We can safely discard these points. The maxpooling function ψ_j selects from every $m * m$ dimensions the maximal element for some $m > 0$. The computation of the maxpooling layer ψ_{j-1} is combined with the computation of the next layer ψ_j, that is, finding $\alpha_{y,j-2}$ with the following expression

$$\exists \alpha_{x,j-1} : \alpha_{y,j-2} = \psi_{j-1}(\psi_j(\alpha_{y,j})) \wedge \alpha_{y,j-1} \in \eta_{j-1}(\alpha_{x,j-1}) \wedge \alpha_{y,j-2} \in \eta_{j-2}(\alpha_{x,j-2})$$

This is to ensure that in the expression $\alpha_{y,j-2} = \psi_{j-1}(\psi_j(\alpha_{y,j}))$ we can reuse $m * m - 1$ elements in $\alpha_{x,j-2}$ and only need to replace the maximal element.

Figures 8, 9, and 10 show images obtained by mapping back from the first hidden layer to the input layer.

5 Experimental Results

The proposed framework has been implemented as a software tool called DLV (Deep Learning Verification) [2] written in Python, see Appendix of [20] for details of input parameters and how to use the tool. The SMT solver we employ is Z3 [8], which has Python APIs. The neural networks are built from a widely-used neural networks library Keras [3] with a deep learning package Theano [6] as its backend.

We validate DLV on a set of experiments performed for neural networks trained for classification based on a predefined multi-dimensional surface (small size networks), as well as image classification (medium size networks). These networks respectively use two representative types of layers: fully connected layers and convolutional layers. They may also use other types of layers, e.g., the ReLU layer, the pooling layer, the zero-padding layer, and the dropout layer. The first three demonstrate the single-path search functionality on the Euclidean (L^2) norm, whereas the fourth (GTSRB) multi-path search for the L^1 and L^2 norms.

The experiments are conducted on a MacBook Pro laptop, with 2.7 GHz Intel Core i5 CPU and 8 GB memory.

Two-Dimensional Point Classification Network. To demonstrate exhaustive verification facilitated by our framework, we consider a neural network trained for classifying points above and below a two-dimensional curve shown in red in Figs. 6 and 7. The network has three fully-connected hidden layers with the ReLU activation function. The input layer has two perceptrons, every hidden layer has 20 perceptrons, and the output layer has two perceptrons. The network is trained with 5,000 points sampled from the provided two-dimensional space, and has an accuracy of more than 99%.

For a given input $x = (3.59, 1.11)$, we start from the input layer and define a region around this point by taking unit steps in both directions

$$\eta_0(\alpha_{x,0}) = [3.59-1.0, 3.59+1.0] \times [1.11-1.0, 1.11+1.0] = [2.59, 4.59] \times [0.11, 2.11]$$

The manipulation set Δ_0 is shown in Fig. 6: there are 9 points, of which the point in the middle represents the activation $\alpha_{x,0}$ and the other 8 points represent the activations resulting from applying one of the manipulations in Δ_0 on $\alpha_{x,0}$. Note that, although there are class changes in the region $\eta_0(\alpha_{x,0})$, the manipulation set Δ_0 is not able to detect such changes. Therefore, we have that $N, \eta_0, \Delta_0 \models x$.

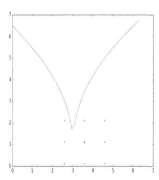

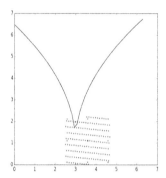

Fig. 6. Input layer

Fig. 7. First hidden layer (Colour figure online)

Now consider layer $k = 1$. To obtain the region $\eta_1(\alpha_{x,1})$, the tool selects two dimensions $p_{1,17}, p_{1,19} \in P_1$ in layer L_1 with indices 17 and 19 and computes

$$\eta_1(\alpha_{x,1}) = [\alpha_{x,1}(p_{1,17}) - 3.6, \alpha_{x,1}(p_{1,17}) + 3.6] \times [\alpha_{x,1}(p_{1,19}) - 3.52, \alpha_{x,1}(p_{1,19}) + 3.52]$$

The manipulation set Δ_1, after mapping back to the input layer with function ψ_1, is given as Fig. 7. Note that η_1 and η_0 satisfy Definition 6, and Δ_1 is a refinement by layer of η_0, Δ_0 and η_1. We can see that a class change can be detected (represented as the red coloured point). Therefore, we have that $N, \eta_1, \Delta_1 \not\models x$.

Image Classification Network for the MNIST Handwritten Image Dataset. The well-known MNIST image dataset contains images of size 28×28 and one channel and the network is trained with the source code given in [5]. The trained network is of medium size with 600,810 parameters, has an accuracy of more than 99%, and is state-of-the-art. It has 12 layers, within which there are 2 convolutional layers, as well as layers such as ReLU, dropout, fully-connected layers and a softmax layer. The images are preprocessed to make the value of each pixel within the bound $[0, 1]$.

Given an image x, we start with layer $k = 1$ and the parameter set to at most 150 dimensions (there are 21632 dimensions in layer L_1). All η_k, Δ_k for $k \geq 2$ are computed according to the simple heuristic mentioned in Sect. 4.2 and satisfy Definitions 6 and 7. For the region $\eta_1(\alpha_{x,1})$, we allow changes to the activation value of each selected dimension that are within $[-1, 1]$. The set Δ_1 includes manipulations that can change the activation value for a subset of the 150 dimensions, by incrementing or decrementing the value for each dimension by 1. The experimental results show that for most of the examples we can find a class change within 100 dimensional changes in layer L_1, by comparing the number of pixels that have changed, and some of them can have less than 30 dimensional changes. Figure 8 presents examples of such class changes for layer L_1. We also experiment on images with up to 40 dimensional changes in layer L_1; the tool is able to check the entire network, reaching the output layer and claiming that $N, \eta_k, \Delta_k \models x$ for all $k \geq 1$. While training of the network takes half an hour, finding an adversarial example takes up to several minutes.

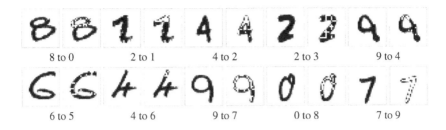

8 to 0   2 to 1   4 to 2   2 to 3   9 to 4

6 to 5   4 to 6   9 to 7   0 to 8   7 to 9

Fig. 8. Adversarial examples for a neural network trained on MNIST

Image Classification Network for the CIFAR-10 Small Image Dataset.
We work with a medium size neural network, trained with the source code from [1] for more than 12 h on the well-known CIFAR10 dataset. The inputs to the network are images of size 32×32 with three channels. The trained network has 1,250,858 real-valued parameters and includes convolutional layers, ReLU layers, max-pooling layers, dropout layers, fully-connected layers, and a softmax layer.

As an illustration of the type of perturbations that we are investigating, consider the images in Fig. 9, which correspond to the parameter setting of up to 25, 45, 65, 85, 105, 125, 145 dimensions, respectively, for layer $k = 1$. The manipulations change the activation values of these dimensions. Each image is obtained by mapping back from the first hidden layer and represents a point close to the boundary of the corresponding region. The relation $N, \eta_1, \Delta_1 \models x$ holds for the first 7 images, but fails for the last one and the image is classified as a truck. Intuitively, our choice of the region $\eta_1(\alpha_{x,1})$ identifies the subset of dimensions with most extreme activations, taking advantage of the analytical capability of the first hidden layer. A higher number of selected dimensions implies a larger region in which we apply manipulations, and, more importantly, suggests a more dramatic change to the knowledge represented by the activations when moving to the boundary of the region.

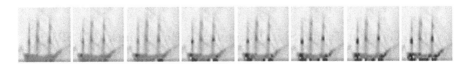

Fig. 9. An illustrative example of mapping back to input layer from the Cifar-10 mataset: the last image classifies as a truck.

We also work with 500 dimensions and otherwise the same experimental parameters as for MNIST. Figure 13 in Appendix of [20] gives 16 pairs of original images (classified correctly) and perturbed images (classified wrongly). We found that, while the manipulations lead to human-recognisable modifications to the images, the perturbed images can be classified wrongly by the network. For each image, finding an adversarial example ranges from seconds to 20 min.

Image Classification Network for the ImageNet Dataset. We also conduct experiments on a large image classification network trained on the popular ImageNet dataset. The images are of size 224×224 and have three channels. The network is the model of the 16-layer network [34], called VGG16, used by the VGG team in the ILSVRC-2014 competition, downloaded from [7]. The trained network has 138,357,544 real-valued parameters and includes convolutional layers, ReLU layers, zero-padding layers, dropout layers, max-pooling layers, fully-connected layers, and a softmax layer. The experimental parameters are the same as for the previous two experiments, except that we work with 20,000 dimensions.

Several additional pairs of original and perturbed images are included in Figure 14 in Appendix of [20]. In Fig. 10 we also give two examples of street sign images. The image on the left is reported unsafe for the second layer with 6346 dimensional changes (0.2% of the 3,211,264 dimensions of layer L_2). The one on the right is reported safe for 20,000 dimensional changes of layer L_2. It appears that more complex manipulations, involving more dimensions (perceptrons), are needed in this case to cause a class change.

Fig. 10. Street sign images. Found an adversarial example for the left image (class changed into bird house), but cannot find an adversarial example for the right image for 20,000 dimensions. (Colour figure online)

5.1   The German Traffic Sign Recognition Benchmark (GTSRB)

We evaluate DLV on the GTSRB dataset (by resizing images into size 32 * 32), which has 43 classes. Figure 11 presents the results for the multi-path search. The first case (approx. 20 min to manipulate) is a stop sign (confidence 1.0) changed into a speed limit of 30 miles, with an L_1 distance of 0.045 and L_2 distance of 0.19. The confidence of the manipulated image is 0.79. The second, easy, case (seconds to manipulate) is a speed limit of 80 miles (confidence 0.999964) changed into a speed limit of 30 miles, with an L_1 distance of 0.004 and L_2

distance of 0.06. The confidence of the manipulated image is 0.99 (a very high confidence of misclassification). Also, a "go right" sign can be easily manipulated into a sign classified as "go straight".

"stop"
to "30m speed limit"
          "80m speed limit"
to "30m speed limit"
          "go right"
to "go straight"

Fig. 11. Adversarial examples for the network trained on the GTSRB dataset by multi-path search

Figure 16 in [20] presents additional adversarial examples obtained when selecting single-path search.

6   Comparison

We compare our approach with two existing approaches for finding adversarial examples, i.e., fast gradient sign method (FGSM) [36] and Jacobian saliency map algorithm (JSMA) [28]. FGSM calculates the optimal attack for a linear approximation of the network cost, whereas DLV explores a proportion of dimensions in the feature space in the input or hidden layers. JSMA finds a set of dimensions in the input layer to manipulate, according to the linear approximation (by computing the Jacobian matrix) of the model from current output to a nominated target output. Intuitively, the difference between DLV's manipulation and JSMA is that DLV manipulates over features discovered in the activations of the hidden layer, while JSMA manipulates according to the partial derivatives, which depend on the parameters of the network.

Experiment 1. We randomly select an image from the MNIST dataset. Figure 12 shows some intermediate and final images obtained by running the three approaches: FGSM, JSMA and DLV. FGSM has a single parameter, ϵ, where a greater ϵ represents a greater perturbation along the gradient of cost function. Given an ϵ, for each input example a perturbed example is returned and we test whether it is an adversarial example by checking for misclassification against the original image. We gradually increase the parameter $\epsilon = 0.05, 0.1, 0.2, 0.3, 0.4$, with the last image (i.e., $\epsilon = 0.4$) witnessing a class change, see the images in the top row of Fig. 12. FGSM can efficiently manipulate a set of images, but it requires a relatively large manipulation to find a misclassification.

Fig. 12. FGSM vs. JSMA vs. DLV, where FGSM and JSMA search a single path and DLV multiple paths. Top row: Original image (7) perturbed deterministically by FGSM with $\epsilon = 0.05, 0.1, 0.2, 0.3, 0.4$, with the final image (i.e., $\epsilon = 0.4$) misclassified as 9. Middle row: Original image (7) perturbed deterministically by JSMA with $\epsilon = 0.1$ and $\theta = 1.0$. We show even numbered images of the 12 produced by JSMA, with the final image misclassified as 3. Bottom row: Original image (7) perturbed nondeterministically by DLV, for the same manipulation on a single pixel as that of JSMA (i.e., $s_p * m_p = 1.0$) and working in the input layer, with the final image misclassified as 3.

For the JSMA approach, we conduct the experiment on a setting with parameters $\epsilon = 0.1$ and $\theta = 1.0$. The parameter $\epsilon = 0.1$ means that we only consider adversarial examples changing no more than 10% of all the pixels, which is sufficient here. As stated in [29], the parameter $\theta = 1.0$, which allows a maximum change to every pixel, can ensure that fewer pixels need to be changed. The approach takes a series of manipulations to gradually lead to a misclassification, see the images in the middle row of Fig. 12. The misclassified image has an L^2 (Euclidean) distance of 0.17 and an L^1 (Manhattan) distance of 0.03 from the original image. While JSMA can find adversarial examples with smaller distance from the original image, it takes longer to manipulate a set of images.

Both FGSM and JSMA follow their specific heuristics to deterministically explore the space of images. However, in some cases, the heuristics may omit better adversarial examples. In the experiment for DLV, instead of giving features a specific order and manipulating them sequentially, we allow the program to nondeterministically choose features. This is currently done by MCTS (Monte Carlo Tree Search), which has a theoretical guarantee of convergence for infinite sampling. Therefore, the high-dimensional space is explored by following many different paths. By taking the same manipulation on a single pixel as that of JSMA (i.e., $s_p * m_p = 1.0$) and working on the input layer, DLV is able to find another perturbed image that is also classified as 3 but has a smaller distance (L^2 distance is 0.14 and L^1 distance is 0.02) from the original image, see the images in the last row of Fig. 12. In terms of the time taken to find an adversarial example, DLV may take longer than JSMA, since it searches over many different paths.

Experiment 2. Table 1 gives a comparison of robustness evaluation of the three appraoches on the MNIST dataset. For FGSM, we vary the input parameter ϵ according to the values $\{0.1, 0.2, 0.4\}$. For DLV, we select regions as defined in Sect. 4.4 on a single path (by defining a specific order on the features and

Table 1. FGSM vs. DLV (on a single path) vs. JSMA

	FGSM ($\epsilon = 0.1$)	(0.2)	(0.4)	DLV ($dims_l = 75$)	(150)	(450)	JSMA ($\theta = 0.1$)	(0.4)
L^2	0.08	0.15	0.32	0.19	0.22	0.27	0.11	0.11
L^1	0.06	0.12	0.25	0.04	0.06	0.09	0.02	0.02
%	17.5%	70.9%	97.2%	52.3%	79%	98%	92%	99%

manipulating them sequentially) for the first hidden layer. The experiment is parameterised by varying the maximal number of dimensions to be changed, i.e., $dims_l \in \{75, 150, 450\}$. For each input image, an adversarial example is returned, if found, by manipulating fewer than the maximal number of dimensions. When the maximal number has been reached, DLV will report failure and return the last perturbed example. For JSMA, the experiment is conducted by letting θ take the value in the set $\{0.1, 0.4\}$ and setting ϵ to 1.0.

We collect three statistics, i.e., the average L^1 distance over the adversarial examples, the average L^2 distance over the adversarial examples, and the success rate of finding adversary examples. Let $L^d(x, \delta(x))$ for $d \in \{1, 2\}$ be the distance between an input x and the returned perturbed image $\delta(x)$, and $\mathrm{diff}(x, \delta(x)) \in \{0, 1\}$ be a Boolean value representing whether x and $\delta(x)$ have different classes. We let

$$L^d = \frac{\sum_{x \text{ in test set}} \mathrm{diff}(x, \delta(x)) \times L^d(x, \delta(x))}{\sum_{x \text{ in test set}} \mathrm{diff}(x, \delta(x))}$$

and

$$\% = \frac{\sum_{x \text{ in test set}} \mathrm{diff}(x, \delta(x))}{\text{the number of examples in test set}}$$

We note that the approaches yield different perturbed examples $\delta(x)$.

The test set size is 500 images selected randomly. DLV takes 1–2 min to manipulate each input image in MNIST. JSMA takes about 10 min for each image, but it works for 10 classes, so the running time is similar to that of DLV. FGSM works with a set of images, so it is the fastest per image.

For the case when the success rates are very high, i.e., 97.2% for FGSM with $\epsilon = 0.4$, 98% for DLV with $dims_l = 450$, and 99% for JSMA with $\theta = 0.4$, JSMA has the smallest average distances, followed by DLV, which has smaller average distances than FGSM on both L^1 and L^2 distances.

We mention that a smaller distance leading to a misclassification may result in a lower rate of transferability [29], meaning that a misclassification can be harder to witness on another model trained on the same (or a small subset of) data-set.

7   Related Work

AI safety is recognised an an important problem, see e.g., [10,33]. An early verification approach for neural networks was proposed in [30], where, using the notation of this paper, safety is defined as the existence, for all inputs in a region $\eta_0 \in D_{L_0}$, of a corresponding output in another region $\eta_n \subseteq D_{L_n}$. They encode the entire network as a set of constraints, approximating the sigmoid using constraints, which can then be solved by a SAT solver, but their approach only works with 6 neurons (3 hidden neurons). A similar idea is presented in [32]. In contrast, we work layer by layer and obtain much greater scalability. Since the first version of this paper appeared [20], another constraint-based method has been proposed in [21] which improves on [30]. While they consider more general correctness properties than this paper, they can only handle the ReLU activation functions, by extending the Simplex method to work with the piecewise linear ReLU functions that cannot be expressed using linear programming. This necessitates a search tree (instead of a search path as in Simplex), for which a heuristic search is proposed and shown to be complete. The approach is demonstrated on networks with 300 ReLU nodes, but as it encodes the full network it is unclear whether it can be scaled to work with practical deep neural networks: for example, the MNIST network has 630,016 ReLU nodes. They also handle continuous spaces directly without discretisation, the benefits of which are not yet clear, since it is argued in [19] that linear behaviour in high-dimensional spaces is sufficient to cause adversarial examples.

Concerns about the instability of neural networks to adversarial examples were first raised in [13,36], where optimisation is used to identify misclassifications. A method for computing the perturbations is also proposed, which is based on box-constrained optimisation and is approximate in view of non-convexity of the search space. This work is followed by [19], which introduced the much faster FGSM method, and [22], which employed a compromise between the two (iterative, but with a smaller number of iterations than [36]). In our notation, [19] uses a *deterministic, iterative* manipulation $\delta(x) = x + \epsilon sign(\nabla_x J(x, \alpha_{x,n}))$, where x is an image in matrix representation, ϵ is a hyper-parameter that can be tuned to get different manipulated images, and $J(x, \alpha_{x,n})$ is the cross-entropy cost function of the neural network on input x and class $\alpha_{x,n}$. Therefore, their approach will test a set of discrete points in the region $\eta_0(\alpha_{x,0})$ of the input layer. Therefore these manipulations will test a lasso-type ladder tree (i.e., a ladder tree without branches) $\mathcal{L}(\eta_k(\alpha_{x,k}))$, which does not satisfy the covering property. In [26], instead of working with a single image, an evolutionary algorithm is employed for a population of images. For each individual image in the current population, the manipulation is the mutation and/or crossover. While mutations can be *nondeterministic*, the manipulations of an individual image are also following a lasso-type ladder tree which is not covering. We also mention that [38] uses several distortions such as JPEG compression, thumbnail resizing, random cropping, etc., to test the robustness of the trained network. These distortions can be understood as manipulations. All these attacks do not leverage any specific properties of the model family, and do not guarantee that they will find a misclassified image in the constraint region, even if such an image exists.

The notion of robustness studied in [18] has some similarities to our definition of safety, except that the authors work with values *averaged* over the input distribution μ, which is difficult to estimate accurately in high dimensions. As in [22,36], they use optimisation without convergence guarantees, as a result computing only an approximation to the minimal perturbation. In [12] point-wise robustness is adopted, which corresponds to our general safety; they also use a constraint solver but represent the full constraint system by reduction to a convex LP problem, and only verify an approximation of the property. In contrast, we work directly with activations rather than an encoding of activation functions, and our method *exhaustively* searches through the complete ladder tree for an adversarial example by iterative and nondeterministic application of manipulations. Further, our definition of a manipulation is more flexible, since it allows us to select a *subset* of dimensions, and each such subset can have a different region diameter computed with respect to a different norm.

8 Conclusions

This paper presents an automated verification framework for checking safety of deep neural networks that is based on a systematic exploration of a region around a data point to search for adversarial manipulations of a given type, and propagating the analysis into deeper layers. Though we focus on the classification task, the approach also generalises to other types of networks. We have implemented the approach using SMT and validated it on several state-of-the-art neural network classifiers for realistic images. The results are encouraging, with adversarial examples found in some cases in a matter of seconds when working with few dimensions, but the verification process itself is exponential in the number of features and has prohibitive complexity for larger images. The performance and scalability of our method can be significantly improved through parallelisation. It would be interesting to see if the notions of regularity suggested in [24] permit a symbolic approach, and whether an abstraction refinement framework can be formulated to improve the scalability and computational performance.

Acknowledgements. This paper has greatly benefited from discussions with several researchers. We are particularly grateful to Martin Fraenzle, Ian Goodfellow and Nicolas Papernot.

References

1. CIFAR10 model for Keras. https://github.com/fchollet/keras/blob/master/examples/cifar10_cnn.py
2. DLV. https://github.com/verideep/dlv
3. Keras. https://keras.io
4. Large scale visual recognition challenge. http://www.image-net.org/challenges/LSVRC/
5. Mnist, CNN network. https://github.com/fchollet/keras/blob/master/examples/mnist_cnn.py
6. Theano. http://deeplearning.net/software/theano/

7. VGG16 model for Keras. https://gist.github.com/baraldilorenzo/07d7802847aaa
   d0a35d3
8. Z3. http://rise4fun.com/z3
9. Ambrosio, L., Fusco, N., Pallara, D.: Functions of Bounded Variation and Free Dis-
   continuity Problems. Oxford Mathematical Monographs. Oxford University Press,
   Oxford (2000)
10. Amodei, D., Olah, C., Steinhardt, J., Christiano, P., Schulman, J., Mané, D.: Con-
    crete problems in AI safety. CoRR, abs/1606.06565 (2016)
11. Anselmi, F., Leibo, J.Z., Rosasco, L., Mutch, J., Tacchetti, A., Poggio, T.: Unsu-
    pervised learning of invariant representations. Theoret. Comput. Sci. **633**, 112–121
    (2016)
12. Bastani, O., Ioannou, Y., Lampropoulos, L., Vytiniotis, D., Nori, A., Criminisi, A.:
    Measuring neural net robustness with constraints. CoRR, abs/1605.07262 (2016).
    (To appear in NIPS)
13. Biggio, B., Corona, I., Maiorca, D., Nelson, B., Šrndić, N., Laskov, P., Giacinto,
    G., Roli, F.: Evasion attacks against machine learning at test time. In: Blockeel,
    H., Kersting, K., Nijssen, S., Železný, F. (eds.) ECML PKDD 2013. LNCS, vol.
    8190, pp. 387–402. Springer, Heidelberg (2013). doi:10.1007/978-3-642-40994-3_25
14. Bishop, C.M.: Neural Networks for Pattern Recognition. Oxford University Press,
    Oxford (1995)
15. Bojarski, M., Del Testa, D., Dworakowski, D., Firner, B., Flepp, B., Goyal, P.,
    Jackel, L.D., Monfort, M., Muller, U., Zhang, J., Zhang, X., Zhao, J., Zieba, K.:
    End to end learning for self-driving cars. arXiv:1604.07316 (2016)
16. Carlsson, G.E., Ishkhanov, T., de Silva, V., Zomorodian, A.: On the local behavior
    of spaces of natural images. Int. J. Comput. Vis. **76**(1), 1–12 (2008)
17. Hendricks, L.A., Park, D.H., Akata, Z., Schiele, B., Darrell, T., Rohrbach,
    M.: Attentive explanations: justifying decisions and pointing to the evidence.
    arXiv.org/abs/1612.04757 (2016)
18. Fawzi, A., Fawzi, O., Frossard, P.: Analysis of classifiers' robustness to adversarial
    perturbations. CoRR, abs/1502.02590 (2015)
19. Goodfellow, I.J., Shlens, J., Szegedy, C.: Explaining and harnessing adversarial
    examples. CoRR, abs/1412.6572 (2014)
20. Huang, X., Kwiatkowska, M., Wang, S., Wu, M.: Safety verification of deep neural
    networks (2016). https://arxiv.org/abs/1610.06940
21. Katz, G., Barrett, C., Dill, D., Julian, K., Kochenderfer, M.: Reluplex: an efficient
    SMT solver for verifying deep neural networks. In: CAV 2017 (2017, to appear)
22. Kurakin, A., Goodfellow, I., Bengio, S.: Adversarial examples in the physical world.
    arXiv:1607.02533 (2016)
23. LeCun, Y., Bengio, Y., Hinton, G.: Deep learning. Nature **521**, 436–444 (2015)
24. Mallat, S.: Understanding deep convolutional networks. Philos. Trans. R. Soc.
    Lond. A: Math. Phys. Eng. Sci. **374**(2065) (2016). ISSN 1364-503X. doi:10.1098/
    rsta.2015.0203
25. Moosavi-Dezfooli, S.-M., Fawzi, A., Frossard, P.: Deepfool: a simple and accurate
    method to fool deep neural networks. CoRR, abs/1511.04599 (2015)
26. Nguyen, A., Yosinski, J., Clune, J.: Deep neural networks are easily fooled: high
    confidence predictions for unrecognizable images. In: Computer Vision and Pattern
    Recognition (CVPR 2015) (2015)
27. Papernot, N., Goodfellow, I., Sheatsley, R., Feinman, R., McDaniel, P.: Cleverhans
    v1.0.0: an adversarial machine learning library. arXiv preprint arXiv:1610.00768
    (2016)

28. Papernot, N., McDaniel, P., Jha, S., Fredrikson, M., Celik, Z.B., Swami, A.: The limitations of deep learning in adversarial settings. In: Proceedings of the 1st IEEE European Symposium on Security and Privacy (2015)
29. Papernot, N., McDaniel, P.D., Goodfellow, I.J., Jha, S., Celik, Z.B., Swami, A.: Practical black-box attacks against deep learning systems using adversarial examples. CoRR, abs/1602.02697 (2016)
30. Pulina, L., Tacchella, A.: An abstraction-refinement approach to verification of artificial neural networks. In: Touili, T., Cook, B., Jackson, P. (eds.) CAV 2010. LNCS, vol. 6174, pp. 243–257. Springer, Heidelberg (2010). doi:10.1007/978-3-642-14295-6_24
31. Ribeiro, M.T., Singh, S., Guestrin, C.: "Why should i trust you?": explaining the predictions of any classifier. In: ACM SIGKDD International Conference on Knowledge Discovery and Data Mining (KDD2016) (2016)
32. Scheibler, K., Winterer, L., Wimmer, R., Becker, B.: Towards verification of artificial neural networks. In: 18th Workshop on Methoden und Beschreibungssprachen zur Modellierung und Verifikation von Schaltungen und Systemen (MBMV), pp. 30–40 (2015)
33. Seshia, S.A., Sadigh, D.: Towards verified artificial intelligence. CoRR, abs/1606.08514 (2016)
34. Simonyan, K., Zisserman, A.: Very deep convolutional networks for large-scale image recognition. arXiv:1409.1556 (2014)
35. Stallkamp, J., Schlipsing, M., Salmen, J., Igel, C.: Man vs. computer: benchmarkingmachine learning algorithms for traffic sign recognition. Neural Netw. **32**, 323–332 (2012)
36. Szegedy, C., Zaremba, W., Sutskever, I., Bruna, J., Erhan, D., Goodfellow, I., Fergus, R.: Intriguing properties of neural networks. In: International Conference on Learning Representations (ICLR-2014) (2014)
37. Vapnik, V.: Principles of risk minimization for learning theory. In: Advances in Neural Information Processing Systems 4, NIPS Conference, Denver, Colorado, USA, 2–5 December 1991, pp. 831–838 (1991)
38. Zheng, S., Song, Y., Leung, T., Goodfellow, I.: Improving the robustness of deep neural networks via stability training. In: CVPR 2016 (2016)

Program Verification Under Weak Memory Consistency Using Separation Logic

Viktor Vafeiadis[(✉)]

MPI-SWS, Kaiserslautern, Saarbrücken, Germany
viktor@mpi-sws.org

Abstract. The semantics of concurrent programs is now defined by a weak memory model, determined either by the programming language (e.g., in the case of C/C++11 or Java) or by the hardware architecture (e.g., for assembly and legacy C code). Since most work in concurrent software verification has been developed prior to weak memory consistency, it is natural to ask how these models affect formal reasoning about concurrent programs.

In this overview paper, we show that verification is indeed affected: for example, the standard Owicki-Gries method is unsound under weak memory. Further, based on concurrent separation logic, we develop a number of sound program logics for fragments of the C/C++11 memory model. We show that these logics are useful not only for verifying concurrent programs, but also for explaining the weak memory constructs of C/C++.

1 Introduction

In a uniprocessor machine with a non-optimizing compiler, the semantics of a concurrent program is given by the set of interleavings the memory accesses of its constituent threads, a model which is known as *sequential consistency* (SC) [15]. In multiprocessor machines and/or with optimizing compilers, however, more behaviors are possible; they are formally described by what is known as a weak memory model. Simple examples of such "weak" behaviors are in the SB (store buffering) and LB (load buffering) programs below:

$$
\begin{array}{ll|l}
x := 1; & & y := 1; \\
a := y; & /\!/\,0 & b := x; \quad /\!/\,0
\end{array} \text{(SB)}
\qquad
\begin{array}{ll|l}
a := x; & /\!/\,1 & b := y; \quad /\!/\,1 \\
y := 1; & & x := 1;
\end{array} \text{(LB)}
$$

Assuming all variables are 0 initially, the weak behaviours in question are the ones in which a and b have the values mentioned in the program comments. In the SB program on the left this behaviour is allowed by all existing weak memory models, and can be easily explained in terms of reordering: the hardware may execute the independent store to x and load from y in reverse order. Similarly, the behaviour in the LB program on the right, which is allowed by some memory models, can be explained by reordering the load from x and the subsequent store to y. This explanation remains the same whether the hardware itself performs

© Springer International Publishing AG 2017
R. Majumdar and V. Kunčak (Eds.): CAV 2017, Part I, LNCS 10426, pp. 30–46, 2017.
DOI: 10.1007/978-3-319-63387-9_2

out-of-order execution, or the compiler, as a part of its optimisation passes, performs these transformations, and the hardware runs a reordered program.

In this paper, we will address two questions:

1. How do such non-SC behaviours affect existing techniques for verifying concurrent programs?
2. How can we verify concurrent programs in spite of weak memory behaviours?

For the first question, we will note that even rather basic proof methods for SC concurrency are unsound under weak memory. Specifically, in Sect. 2, we will show that this is the case for the Owicki-Gries (OG) proof method [21].

To answer the second question, there are two main approaches. One approach is to determine a class of programs for which weak memory consistency does not affect their correctness. One such a class of programs are data-race-free (DRF) programs, namely programs that under SC semantics have no concurrent conflicting accesses (two accesses to the same location, at least one of which a write). Ensuring that a memory model ascribes only SC behaviours to DRF programs has become a standard sanity requirement for weak memory models [1]. For specific memory models, one can develop larger classes of programs, whose behaviour is unaffected by the weak memory consistency (e.g., [3,12,20]).

An alternative approach is to develop proof techniques for reasoning directly about programs under a certain weak memory model. To do so, we usually take an existing proof technique that has been developed for SC concurrency and adapt it to make it sound under a specific weak memory model. We may then further extend the method to make the proof technique more useful for reasoning about specific weak memory features. As an example of this approach, in [13], we applied it to the OG proof method by weakening OG's non-interference check to restore its soundness under *release-acquire* (RA) consistency.

In this paper, we will focus on this latter approach, but apply it to *concurrent separation logic* (CSL) [19]. Compared with OG, CSL is much better suited for reasoning under weak memory consistency, because by default it can reason only about DRF programs. As such, it is trivially sound under weak memory. We will then gradually extend CSL with features suitable for reasoning about the various synchronisation primitives provided by C11, and conclude with a discussion of some remaining challenges. In order to keep the exposition as simple as possible, I will elide inessential technical details and not discuss the soundness proofs of the presented proof rules. The missing details can be found in [5,6,25,27,28].

2   Owicki-Gries is Unsound Under Weak Memory!

To motivate why developing program logics for weak memory consistency is non-trivial, we start by showing that the Owicki-Gries (OG) system is unsound.

In 1976, Owicki and Gries [21] introduced a proof system for reasoning about concurrent programs, which formed the basis of rely/guarantee reasoning. Their system includes the usual Hoare logic rules for sequential programs, a rule for introducing auxiliary variables, and the following parallel composition rule:

$$\frac{\{P_1\}\,c_1\,\{Q_1\} \quad \{P_2\}\,c_2\,\{Q_2\} \quad \text{the two proofs are non-interfering}}{\{P_1 \wedge P_2\}\,c_1 \parallel c_2\,\{Q_1 \wedge Q_2\}}$$

This rule allows one to compose two verified programs into a verified concurrent program that assumes both preconditions and ensures both postconditions. The soundness of this rule requires that the two proofs are *non-interfering*, namely that every assertion R in the one proof is stable under any $\{P\}x := e$ (guarded) assignment in the other and vice versa; i.e., for every such pair, $R \wedge P \vdash R[e/x]$.

The OG system relies quite heavily on sequential consistency. In fact, OG is complete for verifying concurrent programs under SC [22], and is therefore unsound under any weakly consistent memory semantics. Auxiliary variables are instrumental in achieving completeness—without them, OG is blatantly incomplete; e.g., it cannot verify that $\{x = 0\}\,x := x + 1 \parallel x := x + 1\,\{x = 2\}$ where ":=" denotes atomic assignment.

Nevertheless, many useful OG proofs do not use auxiliary variables, and one might wonder whether such proofs are sound under weak memory models. This is sadly not the case. Figure 1 presents an OG proof that the SB program cannot return $a = b = 0$ whereas under all known weak memory models it can in fact do so. Intuitively speaking, the proof is invalid under weak memory because the two threads may have different views of memory before executing each command. Thus, when thread II terminates, thread I may perform $a := y$ reading $y = 0$ and storing 0 in a, thereby invalidating thread II's last assertion.

$$
\begin{array}{c|c}
\begin{array}{c}
\{a \neq 0\} \\
\begin{array}{l}
\{a \neq 0\} \\
x := 1; \\
\{x \neq 0\} \\
a := y \\
\{x \neq 0\}
\end{array} \;\Bigg\|\;
\begin{array}{l}
\{\top\} \\
y := 1; \\
\{y \neq 0\} \\
b := x \\
\left\{\begin{array}{l} y \neq 0 \wedge \\ (a \neq 0 \vee b = x) \end{array}\right\}
\end{array} \\
\{a \neq 0 \vee b \neq 0\}
\end{array}
&
\begin{array}{l}
\text{The non-interference checks are straightforward.} \\
\text{For example,} \\
\qquad y \neq 0 \wedge (a \neq 0 \vee b = x) \wedge a \neq 0 \\
\qquad \vdash y \neq 0 \wedge (a \neq 0 \vee b = 1) \\
\text{and} \quad y \neq 0 \wedge (a \neq 0 \vee b = x) \wedge x \neq 0 \\
\qquad \vdash y \neq 0 \wedge (y \neq 0 \vee b = x) \\
\text{show stability of the last assertion of thread II} \\
\text{under } \{a \neq 0\}x := 1 \text{ and } \{x \neq 0\}a := y.
\end{array}
\end{array}
$$

Fig. 1. OG proof that SB cannot return $a = b = 0$.

3   RC11 Preliminaries

For concreteness, we will now introduce a simple programming language containing all the features of RC11, the rectified version of the C/C++11 memory model due to Lahav et al. [14]. Programs are given by the following grammar:

$$e ::= x \mid n \mid e + e \mid e - e \mid e \leq e \mid \dots$$

$$c ::= \textbf{skip} \mid c; c \mid c \parallel c \mid \textbf{if } e \textbf{ then } c \textbf{ else } c \mid \textbf{while } e \textbf{ do } c \mid x := e \mid$$
$$\quad [e]_o := e \mid x := [e]_o \mid x := \textbf{CAS}_o(e, e, e) \mid x := \textbf{alloc} \mid \textbf{fence}_o$$

$$o ::= \textbf{na} \mid \textbf{rlx} \mid \textbf{acq} \mid \textbf{rel} \mid \textbf{acq-rel} \mid \textbf{sc}$$

Expressions, e, are built out of program variables, constants and arithmetic and logical operators. Commands, c, contain the empty command, sequential and parallel composition, conditionals and loops, assignments to local variables, memory accesses (loads, stores, und compare and swap), allocation, and fences.

Memory accesses are annotated with an access mode, o, which indicates the level of consistency guarantees provided by the access, which in turn determines its implementation cost.

The weakest access mode is *non-atomic* (na), which is intended for normal data loads and stores. Races on non-atomic accesses are treated as program errors: it is the responsibility of the programmer to ensure that such races never occur. The remaining access modes are intended for synchronisation between threads and, as such, allow races. The strongest and most expensive mode are *sequentially consistent* (sc) accesses, whose primary purpose is to restore the simple interleaving semantics of sequential consistency [15] if a program (when executed under SC semantics) has races only on SC accesses. Weaker than SC atomics are *acquire* (acq) loads and *release* (rel) stores,[1] which can be used to perform "message passing" between threads without incurring the implementation cost of a full SC access; and weaker and cheaper still are *relaxed* (rlx) accesses, which provide only minimal synchronisation guarantees.

RC11 also supports language-level fence instructions, which provide finer-grained control over where hardware fences are to be placed and can be used in conjunction with relaxed accesses to synchronise between threads. Fences are also annotated with an access mode, $o \in \{\text{acq}, \text{rel}, \text{acq-rel}, \text{sc}\}$.

We will discuss the semantics of these access modes and fences in more detail as we introduce program logic rules to reason about them.

4 Reasoning About Non-atomic Accesses Using CSL

We start with non-atomics, which have to be accessed in a data-race-free (DRF) fashion. To reason about them, it is natural to consider O'Hearn's *concurrent separation logic* (CSL) [19], because it rules out data races by construction. In CSL, accessing a memory location, ℓ, requires the command to have the permission to access that location in its precondition in the form of a points-to assertion, $\ell \mapsto v$. This formula asserts that the memory at location ℓ stores the value v, moreover it gives permission to the bearer of this assertion to access and possibly modify the contents of memory at location ℓ. Formally, the permission is generated by the allocation rule and required in the preconditions of the load and store rules.

$$\{\text{emp}\} \; x := \textbf{alloc} \; \{x \mapsto \_\} \tag{ALLOC}$$

$$\{\ell \mapsto v\} \; x := [\ell]_{\text{na}} \; \{\ell \mapsto v \wedge x = v\} \tag{R-NA}$$

$$\{\ell \mapsto v\} \; [\ell]_{\text{na}} := v' \; \{\ell \mapsto v'\} \tag{W-NA}$$

---

[1] The acquire mode is meant to be used for loads, whereas the release mode for stores: there is also a combined *acquire-release* (acq-rel) mode that can be used for CAS.

The load rule further, asserts that the value read is the one recorded in the points-to assertion, while the store rule allows one to update this value.

$$\frac{}{\{P\}\ \mathsf{skip}\ \{P\}}\ (\text{SKIP})$$

$$\frac{}{\{[e/x]P\}\ x := e\ \{P\}}\ (\text{ASSIGN})$$

$$\frac{\{P\}\ c_1\ \{Q\}\quad \{Q\}\ c_2\ \{R\}}{\{P\}\ c_1; c_2\ \{R\}}\ (\text{SEQ})$$

$$\frac{\{P\}\ c\ \{Q\}\quad P' \Rightarrow P\quad Q \Rightarrow Q'}{\{P'\}\ c\ \{Q'\}}\ (\text{CONSEQ})$$

$$\frac{\{P \wedge B\}\ c_1\ \{Q\}\quad \{P \wedge \neg B\}\ c_2\ \{Q\}}{\{P\}\ \mathsf{if}\ B\ \mathsf{then}\ c_1\ \mathsf{else}\ c_2\ \{Q\}}\ (\text{IF})$$

$$\frac{\{P_1\}\ c\ \{Q\}\quad \{P_2\}\ c\ \{Q\}}{\{P_1 \vee P_2\}\ c\ \{Q\}}\ (\text{DISJ})$$

$$\frac{\{P \wedge B\}\ c\ \{P\}}{\{P\}\ \mathsf{while}\ B\ \mathsf{do}\ c\ \{P \wedge \neg B\}}\ (\text{WHILE})$$

$$\frac{\{P\}\ c\ \{Q\}\quad x \notin \mathsf{fv}(c,Q)}{\{\exists x.\ P\}\ c\ \{Q\}}\ (\text{EX})$$

$$\frac{\begin{array}{c}\{P_1\}\ c_1\ \{Q_1\}\quad \{P_2\}\ c_2\ \{Q_2\}\\ \mathsf{fv}(P_1,c_1,Q_1) \cap \mathsf{wr}(c_2) = \emptyset\\ \mathsf{fv}(P_2,c_2,Q_2) \cap \mathsf{wr}(c_1) = \emptyset\end{array}}{\{P_1 * P_2\}\ c_1 \parallel c_2\ \{Q_1 * Q_2\}}\ (\text{PAR})$$

$$\frac{\begin{array}{c}\{P\}\ c\ \{Q\}\\ \mathsf{fv}(R) \cap \mathsf{wr}(c) = \emptyset\end{array}}{\{P * R\}\ c\ \{Q * R\}}\ (\text{FRAME})$$

Fig. 2. Proof rules of CSL (without resource invariants).

The other CSL rules are listed in Fig. 2: these include the standard rules from Hoare logic (SKIP, ASSIGN, SEQ, IF, WHILE), the parallel composition rule (PAR), the consequence rule (CONSEQ), the disjunction and existential elimination rules (DISJ, EX), and the frame rule (FRAME). In our presentation of the rules, we exclude any mention of "resource invariants" and the rules for dealing with them, as we will not ever directly use this feature of the logic. In preparation for the extensions in the next section, our formulation of the consequence rule uses ghost implication ($\Rightarrow$) instead of normal logical implication. Ghost implication is a generalisation of normal implication that in addition allows frame-preserving updates to any ghost resources mentioned in the assertions.

CSL's parallel composition rule requires the preconditions of the two threads to be disjoint (i.e., $P_1 * P_2$), which (together with the load and store rules) precludes the two threads of accessing the same location simultaneously. The disjointness conditions of the rule check that each thread does not modify any of the variables appearing in the other thread's program or specification.

5   RSL: Reasoning About Release-Acquire Synchronisation

Next, let us consider C11's *acquire loads* and *release stores*, whose main mode of use is to establish synchronisation between two threads. The basic synchronisation pattern is illustrated by the following "message passing" idiom:

$$[x]_{\mathsf{na}} := 1; \;\Big\|\; a := [y]_{\mathsf{acq}}; \quad /\!/\, 1$$
$$[y]_{\mathsf{rel}} := 1; \;\Big\|\; \mathbf{if}\ a \neq 0\ \mathbf{then}\ b := [x]_{\mathsf{na}}; \quad /\!/\, 0 \tag{MP}$$

Here, assuming that initially $[x] = [y] = 0$, the program cannot read $a = 1$ and $b = 0$. According to C11, when an acquire load reads from a release store, this results in a synchronisation. As a result, any memory access happening before the release store (by being performed previously either by the same thread or by some previously-synchronising thread) also happens before the acquire load and any access happening after it. In the MP program, this means that the $[x]_{\mathsf{na}} := 1$ write happens before the $b := [x]_{\mathsf{na}}$ load, and thus the reading thread *must* return $b = 1$ in the case it read $a = 1$.

To reason about release and acquire accesses, Vafeiadis and Narayan [28] introduced *relaxed separation logic* (RSL), which extends CSL assertions with two new assertion forms:

$$P, Q ::= \ldots \mid \mathbf{W}(\ell, \mathcal{Q}) \mid \mathbf{R}(\ell, \mathcal{Q})$$

These represent the permission to perform a release store or an acquire load respectively, and attach to location ℓ a mapping $\mathcal{Q}$ from values to assertions. This mapping describes the manner in which the location ℓ is used by the program. We can roughly consider it as an invariant stating: "if location ℓ holds value v, then the assertion $\mathcal{Q}(v)$ is true."

At any point in time, a non-atomic location may be converted into an atomic location with the following ghost implication:

$$\ell \mapsto v * \mathcal{Q}(v) \Rightarrow \mathbf{W}(\ell, \mathcal{Q}) * \mathbf{R}(\ell, \mathcal{Q}) \tag{MK-ATOM}$$

In the antecedent of the ghost move, the invariant should hold for the value of the location; as a result, we get the permissions to write and read that location.

RSL's release write rule

$$\big\{ \mathbf{W}(\ell, \mathcal{Q}) * \mathcal{Q}(v) \big\}\ [\ell]_{\mathsf{rel}} := v\ \big\{ \mathbf{W}(\ell, \mathcal{Q}) \big\} \tag{W-REL}$$

says that in order to do a release write of value v to location ℓ, we need to have a permission to do so, $\mathbf{W}(\ell, \mathcal{Q})$, and we have to satisfy the invariant specified by that permission, namely $\mathcal{Q}(v)$. After the write is done, we no longer own the resources specified by the invariant (so that readers can obtain them).

The acquire read rule

$$\big\{ \mathbf{R}(\ell, \mathcal{Q}) \big\}\ x := [\ell]_{\mathsf{acq}}\ \big\{ \mathbf{R}(\ell, \mathcal{Q}[x:=\mathsf{emp}]) * \mathcal{Q}(x) \big\} \tag{R-ACQ}$$

complements the release write rule. To perform an acquire read of location ℓ, one must have an acquire permission for ℓ. Just as with a release permission, an acquire permission carries a mapping $\mathcal{Q}$ from values to assertions. In case of an acquire permission, this mapping describes what resource will be acquired by reading a certain value; so if the value v is read, resource $\mathcal{Q}(v)$ is acquired.

This rule is slightly complicated by a technical detail. In the postcondition, we cannot simply retain the full acquire permission for location ℓ, because that would enable us to read the location again and acquire the ownership of $\mathcal{Q}(v)$ a second time. To prevent this, the acquire permission's mapping in the postcondition becomes $\mathcal{Q}[x{:=}\mathsf{emp}] \triangleq \lambda y.$ **if** $y{=}x$ **then** emp **else** $\mathcal{Q}(y)$.

As a simple application of these rules, Fig. 3 shows a slightly abbreviated proof of the MP program. Initially, the rule MK-ATOM is applied to set up the invariant for location y. By the parallel composition rule, the first thread receives the permission to access x (specifically, $x \mapsto 0$) and the release write permission to y, which it uses to transfer away the $x \mapsto 1$ resource. The second thread starts with the acquire read permission and uses it to get hold of the invariant of y, which, in the case that $a \neq 0$, gives enough permission to the thread to access x non-atomically and establish $b = 1$. In the proof outline, we often use the consequence rule to forget permissions that are no longer relevant.

$$
\begin{array}{c}
\left\{x \mapsto 0 * y \mapsto 0\right\} \\
\left\{x \mapsto 0 * \mathbf{W}(y, \mathcal{Q}) * \mathbf{R}(y, \mathcal{Q})\right\}
\end{array}
$$

$$
\begin{array}{l|l}
\left\{x \mapsto 0 * \mathbf{W}(y, \mathcal{Q})\right\} & \left\{\mathbf{R}(y, \mathcal{Q})\right\} \\
{[x]_{\mathsf{na}} := 1;} & a := [y]_{\mathsf{acq}} \\
\left\{x \mapsto 1 * \mathbf{W}(y, \mathcal{Q})\right\} & \left\{(a = 0 \vee x \mapsto 1) * \mathbf{R}(y, \mathcal{Q}[a := \mathsf{emp}])\right\} \\
{[y]_{\mathsf{rel}} := 1;} & \left\{a = 0 \vee x \mapsto 1\right\} \\
\left\{\mathbf{W}(y, \mathcal{Q})\right\} & \text{if } a \neq 0 \text{ then } b := [x]_{\mathsf{na}} \\
\left\{\top\right\} & \left\{a = 0 \vee (x \mapsto 1 \wedge b = 1)\right\}
\end{array}
$$

$$
\left\{a = 0 \vee b = 1\right\}
$$

Fig. 3. Proof outline of MP using the invariant $\mathcal{Q}(v) \triangleq (v = 0 \vee x \mapsto 1)$.

To allow multiple concurrent readers and writers, RSL's write permissions are duplicable, whereas its read permissions are splittable as follows:

$$
\mathbf{W}(\ell, \mathcal{Q}) \Longleftrightarrow \mathbf{W}(\ell, \mathcal{Q}) * \mathbf{W}(\ell, \mathcal{Q}) \tag{W-SPLIT}
$$

$$
\mathbf{R}(\ell, \lambda v.\, \mathcal{Q}_1(v) * \mathcal{Q}_2(v)) \Longleftrightarrow \mathbf{R}(\ell, \mathcal{Q}_1) * \mathbf{R}(\ell, \mathcal{Q}_2) \tag{R-SPLIT}
$$

The reason why read permissions cannot simply be duplicated is the same as why the read permission is modified in the postcondition of the R-ACQ rule. If read permissions were made duplicable, then multiple readers would incorrectly be able to acquire ownership of the same resource.

6   FSL: Reasoning About Relaxed Accesses and Fences

Next, let us consider *relaxed* accesses. Unlike release stores and acquire loads, relaxed accesses do not synchronise on their own, but only when used together with release/acquire fences. Consider the following variant of the MP example using relaxed accesses and fences.

$$
\begin{array}{c|l}
\begin{array}{l}
[x]_{\mathsf{na}} := 1; \\
\textbf{fence}_{\mathsf{rel}}; \\
[y]_{\mathsf{rlx}} := 1
\end{array}
&
\begin{array}{l}
a := [y]_{\mathsf{rlx}}; \quad /\!/ \; 1 \\
\textbf{if } a \neq 0 \textbf{ then} \\
\quad \textbf{fence}_{\mathsf{acq}}; \\
\quad b := [x]_{\mathsf{na}} \\
\textbf{end-if}
\end{array}
\end{array}
\qquad \text{(MP-fences)}
$$

Like MP, MP-fences also satisfies the postcondition, $a = 0 \lor b = 1$ (and so do the variants where either thread is replaced by the corresponding thread of MP), but if we remove any of the fences, the program will have undefined behaviour. (The reason for the latter is that in the absence of synchronisation, the non-atomic x-accesses are racy.)

In essence, we can think of resource transfer in the following way. When releasing a resource by a combination of a release fence and a relaxed write, at the fence we should decide what is going to be released, and not use that resource until we send it away by doing the write. Conversely, when acquiring a resource using a relaxed read together with an acquire fence, once we do the read, we know which resources we are going to get, but we will not be able to use those resources until we reach the synchronisation point marked by the acquire fence.

To formally represent this intuition, *fenced separation logic* (FSL) [5] introduces two modalities into RSL's assertion language:

$$
P, Q ::= \ldots \mid \triangle P \mid \triangledown P
$$

We use $\triangle$ to mark the resources that have been prepared to be released, and $\triangledown$ to mark those waiting for an acquire fence. We require the invariants appearing in $\mathbf{W}(\ell, \mathcal{Q})$ and $\mathbf{R}(\ell, \mathcal{Q})$ permissions to contain no modalities, a condition called *normalisability* in [5]. In essence, these modalities are meant to appear only in the proof outlines of individual threads and to never be nested.

FSL supports all the rules we have seen so far. In addition, it has rules for relaxed accesses and fences. The rule for relaxed writes is almost exactly the same as W-REL.

$$
\left\{ \mathbf{W}(\ell, \mathcal{Q}) * \triangle \mathcal{Q}(v) \right\} [\ell]_{\mathsf{rlx}} := v \left\{ \mathbf{W}(\ell, \mathcal{Q}) \right\}
\qquad \text{(W-RLX)}
$$

As in W-REL, we have to have a write permission as well as the resource specified by its attached invariant. The only additional requirement is that the latter resource has to be under the $\triangle$ modality stating that it can be released by a relaxed write. As we will later see, this ensures that any writes transferring away non-empty resources are placed after a release fence.

Similarly, the rule for relaxed reads differs from R-ACQ only in a single modality appearance:

$$
\left\{ \mathbf{R}(\ell, \mathcal{Q}) \right\} x := [\ell]_{\mathsf{rlx}} \left\{ \mathbf{R}(\ell, \mathcal{Q}[x := \mathsf{emp}]) * \triangledown \mathcal{Q}(x) \right\}
\qquad \text{(R-RLX)}
$$

While after acquire read, we gain ownership of the resource described by the **R** permission, in the case of a relaxed read, we get the same resource under the $\triangledown$ modality. This makes the resource unusable before we reach an acquire fence.

The fence rules simply manage the two modalities as follows:

$$\{P\}\, \mathbf{fence}_{\mathsf{rel}}\, \{\triangle P\} \qquad \text{(F-REL)} \qquad \{\triangledown P\}\, \mathbf{fence}_{\mathsf{acq}}\, \{P\} \qquad \text{(F-ACQ)}$$

Release fences protect resources that are to be released by putting them under the $\triangle$ modality, while acquire fences clear the $\triangledown$ modality making resources under it usable.

Figure 4 shows a proof outline of MP-fences using the rules presented in this section. Except for the treatment modalities, the proof itself essentially identical to that of MP. In the first thread, we use a combination of F-REL and the frame rule to put only $x \mapsto 1$ under the $\triangle$ modality. In the second thread, after the relaxed load, we use the consequence rule to forget the unnecessary **R** permission and push the $\triangledown$ modality under the disjunction.

$$
\begin{array}{c}
\{x \mapsto 0 * y \mapsto 0\} \\
\{x \mapsto 0 * \mathbf{W}(y, \mathcal{Q}) * \mathbf{R}(y, \mathcal{Q})\}
\end{array}
$$

$$
\begin{array}{l|l}
\{x \mapsto 0 * \mathbf{W}(y, \mathcal{Q})\} & \{\mathbf{R}(y, \mathcal{Q})\} \\
[x]_{\mathsf{na}} := 1; & a := [y]_{\mathsf{rlx}} \\
\{x \mapsto 1 * \mathbf{W}(y, \mathcal{Q})\} & \{\triangledown(a = 0 \vee x \mapsto 1) * \mathbf{R}(y, \mathcal{Q}[a := \mathsf{emp}])\} \\
\mathbf{fence}_{\mathsf{rel}}; & \{a = 0 \vee \triangledown x \mapsto 1\} \\
\{\triangle x \mapsto 1 * \mathbf{W}(y, \mathcal{Q})\} & \mathbf{if}\ a \neq 0\ \mathbf{then} \\
[y]_{\mathsf{rlx}} := 1; & \quad \{\triangledown x \mapsto 1\} \\
\{\mathbf{W}(y, \mathcal{Q})\} & \quad \mathbf{fence}_{\mathsf{acq}} \\
\{\top\} & \quad \{x \mapsto 1\} \\
 & \quad b := [x]_{\mathsf{na}} \\
 & \quad \{x \mapsto 1 \wedge b = 1\} \\
 & \{a = 0 \vee (x \mapsto 1 \wedge b = 1)\}
\end{array}
$$

$$\{a = 0 \vee b = 1\}$$

Fig. 4. Proof outline of MP-fences using the invariant $\mathcal{Q}(v) \triangleq (v = 0 \vee x \mapsto 1)$.

7   Reasoning About Read-Modify-Write Instructions

Next, consider compare-and-swap, which is a typical example of a read-modify-write (RMW) instruction. $\mathbf{CAS}_o(\ell, v, v')$ reads the location ℓ and if its value is v, it updates it atomically to v'. If **CAS** reads some value other than v, then the update is not performed. In either case, **CAS** returns the value read. The $o \in \{\mathsf{rlx}, \mathbf{rel}, \mathsf{acq}, \mathsf{acq\text{-}rel}, \mathbf{sc}\}$ tells us the type of event generated by a successful **CAS** operation.

To reason about **CAS**, we introduce a new type of assertion:

$$P, Q ::= \ldots \mid \mathbf{U}(\ell, \mathcal{Q})$$

which denotes the permission to perform a **CAS** on location ℓ. As with the **W** and **R** assertions, it records a mapping from values to assertions, which governs the transfer of resources via a **CAS** operation.

The **U** permission is obtained in a similar fashion as the **W** and **R** permissions. At any point in time, a non-atomic location may be converted into an atomic location with the following ghost implication:

$$\ell \mapsto v * \mathcal{Q}(v) \Rrightarrow \mathbf{U}(\ell, \mathcal{Q}) \qquad\qquad (\text{MK-ATOM-U})$$

The update permission **U** is duplicable, and interacts with the **W** and **R** permissions, allowing us to perform not only updates, but also reads and writes, when holding an update permission.

$$\mathbf{U}(\ell, \mathcal{Q}) \Lleftarrow\!\!\!\Rrightarrow \mathbf{U}(\ell, \mathcal{Q}) * \mathbf{U}(\ell, \mathcal{Q}) \qquad\qquad (\text{U-SPLIT})$$
$$\mathbf{U}(\ell, \mathcal{Q}) \Lleftarrow\!\!\!\Rrightarrow \mathbf{U}(\ell, \mathcal{Q}) * \mathbf{W}(\ell, \mathcal{Q}) \qquad\qquad (\text{UW-SPLIT})$$
$$\mathbf{U}(\ell, \mathcal{Q}) \Lleftarrow\!\!\!\Rrightarrow \mathbf{U}(\ell, \mathcal{Q}) * \mathbf{R}(\ell, \lambda v.\, \mathsf{emp}) \qquad\qquad (\text{UR-SPLIT})$$

According to UW-SPLIT, when holding the $\mathbf{U}(\ell, \mathcal{Q})$, we also have $\mathbf{W}(\ell, \mathcal{Q})$, allowing us to write to ℓ using the appropriate atomic write rule. On the other hand, UR-SPLIT tells us that we are allowed to read when holding the $\mathbf{U}(\ell, \mathcal{Q})$ permission, but we cannot gain any ownership (more precisely, no matter the value read, the acquired resource will always be the empty resource emp).

We next consider the following rule for the acquire-release **CAS**.[2]

$$\frac{\begin{array}{cc} \mathcal{Q}(v) \implies A * T & \\ P * T \implies \mathcal{Q}(v') & \mathsf{pure}(\varphi) \\ & P * \mathcal{Q}(v) \implies \varphi \end{array}}{\{\mathbf{U}(\ell, \mathcal{Q}) * P\}\; x := \mathbf{CAS}_{\mathsf{acq\text{-}rel}}(\ell, v, v') \left\{\begin{array}{l} x = v \wedge \mathbf{U}(\ell, \mathcal{Q}) * A \wedge \varphi\, \vee \\ x \neq v \wedge \mathbf{U}(\ell, \mathcal{Q}) * P \end{array}\right\}} \; (\text{CAS-AR})$$

In the precondition, we have permission to perform the **CAS** and some further resource, P, to be transferred away if the **CAS** succeeds.

If the **CAS** succeeds, we have at our disposal the resource $\mathcal{Q}(v)$, which is split into two parts, A, and T. Resource A is the part that we are going to acquire and keep it for ourselves in the postcondition. Resource T will remain in the invariant $\mathcal{Q}$. The second premise requires that the resource P (which we have in our precondition) together with the resource T (which we left behind when acquiring ownership) are enough to satisfy $\mathcal{Q}(v')$, thus reestablishing the invariant for the newly written value. If, in addition to merely reestablishing the invariant, we manage to prove some additional facts, φ, we can carry those facts into the postcondition. It is required, however, for these facts to be *pure*, meaning that the assertion φ is a logical fact and does not say anything about the ownership of resources or the state of the heap.

---

[2] This rule was proposed by Alex Summers and is a slightly stronger than the one in [6]. Its soundness has been established in Coq alongside with the other FSL rules.

If the **CAS** fails, then no resource transfer occurs, and the postcondition contains the same resources as the precondition.

$$\big\{\mathsf{U}(\ell,\mathcal{Q}) * P\big\}\; x := \mathsf{CAS_{rel}}(\ell,v,v')\; \left\{ \begin{array}{l} x = v \wedge \mathsf{U}(\ell,\mathcal{Q}) * \nabla A \wedge \varphi \vee \\ x \neq v \wedge \mathsf{U}(\ell,\mathcal{Q}) * P \end{array} \right\} \quad \text{(CAS-REL)}$$

$$\big\{\mathsf{U}(\ell,\mathcal{Q}) * \triangle P\big\}\; x := \mathsf{CAS_{acq}}(\ell,v,v')\; \left\{ \begin{array}{l} x = v \wedge \mathsf{U}(\ell,\mathcal{Q}) * A \wedge \varphi \vee \\ x \neq v \wedge \mathsf{U}(\ell,\mathcal{Q}) * \triangle P \end{array} \right\} \quad \text{(CAS-ACQ)}$$

$$\big\{\mathsf{U}(\ell,\mathcal{Q}) * \triangle P\big\}\; x := \mathsf{CAS_{rlx}}(\ell,v,v')\; \left\{ \begin{array}{l} x = v \wedge \mathsf{U}(\ell,\mathcal{Q}) * \nabla A \wedge \varphi \vee \\ x \neq v \wedge \mathsf{U}(\ell,\mathcal{Q}) * \triangle P \end{array} \right\} \quad \text{(CAS-RLX)}$$

Fig. 5. Rules for the other kinds of CAS weaker than acq-rel. All of these rules implicitly have the same premises as the CAS-AR rule.

The rules for the other types of **CAS** accesses are slight modifications of the CAS-AR rule in the same vein as the ones that get us from R-ACQ and W-REL to R-RLX and W-RLX (see Fig. 5). Namely, wherever the access type is relaxed, $\triangle$ and ∇ modalities are introduce to ensure a proper fence placement. Since the premises in these rules are the same as in CAS-AR, we avoid repeating them.

- A release **CAS** is treated as a release write and a relaxed read. Therefore, in CAS-REL sends away P without any restrictions, but the acquired resource, A, is placed under the ∇ modality, requiring the program to perform a acquire fence before accessing the resource.
- Conversely, for an acquire **CAS**, the resource to be transferred away is under the $\triangle$ modality requiring a release fence before the **CAS**, while the resource acquired is immediately usable.
- A relaxed **CAS** is relaxed as both read and write. This is reflected in the CAS-RLX rule by having both modalities in play.

$$
\begin{array}{l|l}
\begin{array}{l}
\mathsf{mk\text{-}lock}() : \\
\quad \big\{ J \big\} \\
\quad res := \mathbf{alloc} \\
\quad \big\{ res \mapsto \_ * J \big\} \\
\quad [res]_{\mathsf{na}} := 0 \\
\quad \big\{ res \mapsto 0 * \mathcal{Q}(0) \big\} \\
\quad \big\{ \mathsf{Lock}(res) \big\} \\
\mathsf{release\text{-}lock}(\ell) : \\
\quad \big\{ \mathsf{Lock}(\ell) * J \big\} \\
\quad [\ell]_{\mathsf{rel}} := 0 \\
\quad \big\{ \mathsf{Lock}(\ell) \big\}
\end{array}
&
\begin{array}{l}
\mathsf{acquire\text{-}lock}(\ell) : \\
\quad \big\{ \mathsf{Lock}(\ell) \big\} \\
\quad x := \mathsf{CAS_{acq}}(\ell,0,1); \\
\quad \big\{ \mathsf{U}(\ell,\mathcal{Q}) * (J \vee x \neq 0) \big\} \\
\quad \mathbf{while}\ x \neq 0\ \mathbf{do} \\
\quad\quad \big\{ \mathsf{U}(\ell,\mathcal{Q}) \big\} \\
\quad\quad \mathbf{while}\ x \neq 0\ \mathbf{do}\ x := [\ell]_{\mathsf{rlx}} \\
\quad\quad \big\{ \mathsf{U}(\ell,\mathcal{Q}) \big\} \\
\quad\quad x := \mathsf{CAS_{acq}}(\ell,0,1); \\
\quad\quad \big\{ \mathsf{U}(\ell,\mathcal{Q}) * (J \vee x \neq 0) \big\} \\
\quad \big\{ \mathsf{Lock}(\ell) * J \big\}
\end{array}
\end{array}
$$

Fig. 6. Lock library verification using $\mathcal{Q}(v) \triangleq (J \vee v \neq 0)$ and $\mathsf{Lock}(\ell) \triangleq \mathsf{U}(\ell,\mathcal{Q})$.

Finally, Fig. 6 presents a proof outline for verifying a spinlock implementation as an example of using the **CAS** rules. In these proof outlines, the use of the consequence rule is left implicit. Specifically, in mk-lock, we apply the MK-ATOM-U rule to generate the update permission; in acquire-lock, we apply the UR-SPLIT rule to generate a read permission, while in release-lock, we apply the UW-SPLIT rule to generate a write permission.

8   GPS: Adding Protocols

The assertions so far have attached an invariant, $\mathcal{Q}$, to each location that is meant to be used atomically. While such simple invariants suffice for reasoning about simple ownership transfer patterns, on their own they are too weak for establishing even basic coherence properties. Consider, for example, the following program, where initially $[x] = 0$.

$$\begin{array}{c|c} [x]_{\mathsf{rlx}} := 1; & a := [x]_{\mathsf{rlx}}; \\ {[x]_{\mathsf{rlx}}} := 2 & b := [x]_{\mathsf{rlx}} \end{array} \tag{COH}$$

Although RC11 ensures that $a \leq b$ in every execution of this program, it is not possible to establish this postcondition with the separation logic rules we have seen thus far. To achieve this, we need a more expressive logic incorporating some limited form of rely-guarantee reasoning (e.g., as already available in OG).

A convenient way to support such reasoning has emerged in the context of program logics for SC concurrency, such as CAP [4], CaReSL [26], TaDA [23], and Iris [9], in the form of *protocols*. The idea is to attach to each atomic location an acyclic state transition system describing the ways in which the value of the location can be updated, and to have assertions talk about the current state of a location's protocol. Formally a protocol, τ, is a tuple $\langle \Sigma_\tau, \sqsubseteq_\tau, \mathcal{Q}_\tau \rangle$, where Σ_τ is the (non-empty) set of protocol states, $\sqsubseteq_\tau$ is a partial order on Σ_τ relating a state to its possible future states, and $\mathcal{Q}_\tau$ is a mapping from protocol states and values to assertions, attaching an invariant about the value of the location to each protocol state.

We extend the language of assertions with two new assertion forms:

$$P, Q ::= \ldots \mid \mathbf{WP}_\tau(\ell, s) \mid \mathbf{RP}_\tau(\ell, s)$$

which assert that ℓ is governed by the protocol τ and its current state is reachable from the state s. $\mathbf{WP}_\tau(\ell, s)$ represents an exclusive write permission to the protocol, whereas $\mathbf{RP}_\tau(\ell, s)$ is a duplicable read permission. As usual, these permissions can be generated from a points-to assertion with a ghost move.

$$\ell \mapsto v * \tau(s, v) \Rrightarrow \mathbf{WP}_\tau(\ell, s)$$
$$\mathbf{WP}_\tau(\ell, s_1) * \mathbf{WP}_\tau(\ell, s_2) \Rightarrow \mathit{false}$$
$$\mathbf{WP}_\tau(\ell, s_1) * \mathbf{RP}_\tau(\ell, s_2) \Leftrightarrow \mathbf{WP}_\tau(\ell, s_1) \wedge s_2 \sqsubseteq_\tau s_1$$
$$\mathbf{RP}_\tau(\ell, s_1) * \mathbf{RP}_\tau(\ell, s_2) \Leftrightarrow \exists s.\, \mathbf{RP}_\tau(\ell, s) \wedge s_1 \sqsubseteq_\tau s \wedge s_2 \sqsubseteq_\tau s$$

Consider the following two simplified proof rules for relaxed reads and writes.

$$\frac{\mathsf{emp} \Rightarrow \mathcal{Q}_\tau(s', v) \wedge s \sqsubseteq_\tau s'}{\{\mathsf{WP}_\tau(\ell, s)\}\, [\ell]_{\mathsf{rlx}} := v \,\{\mathsf{WP}_\tau(\ell, s')\}} \qquad \frac{\forall s' \sqsupseteq_\tau s.\ \mathcal{Q}_\tau(s', x) \Rightarrow \varphi \qquad \mathsf{pure}(\varphi)}{\{\mathsf{RP}_\tau(\ell, s)\}\, x := [\ell]_{\mathsf{rlx}} \,\{\exists s'.\, \mathsf{RP}_\tau(\ell, s') \wedge \varphi\}}$$

To perform a relaxed write, the thread must own the exclusive write permission for that location; it then has to chose a future state s' of the current state and establish the invariant of that state. Since it is a relaxed write, no ownership transfer is possible (at least without fences). So, in this somewhat simplified rule, we require $\mathcal{Q}_\tau(s', v)$ to hold of the empty heap.

Conversely, to perform a relaxed read, the thread must own a shared read permission for that location stating that it is at least in state s. It then knows that the location is in some future protocol state s' of s, and gets to know that the invariant of $\mathcal{Q}_\tau$ holds for that state and the value that it read. Since the read is relaxed, to avoid incorrect ownership transfers, the postcondition gets only the pure part of this invariant.

$$\{x \mapsto 0\}$$
$$\{\mathsf{WP}_\tau(x, 0)\}$$
$$\{\mathsf{WP}_\tau(x, 0)\} \,\|\, \{\mathsf{RP}_\tau(x, 0)\}$$
$$[x]_{\mathsf{rlx}} := 1; \quad\|\quad a := [x]_{\mathsf{rlx}}$$
$$\{\mathsf{WP}_\tau(x, 1)\} \,\|\, \{\mathsf{RP}_\tau(x, a) \wedge 0 \le a \le 2\}$$
$$[x]_{\mathsf{rlx}} := 2; \quad\|\quad b := [x]_{\mathsf{rlx}}$$
$$\{\mathsf{WP}_\tau(x, 2)\} \,\|\, \{\mathsf{RP}_\tau(x, b) \wedge 0 \le a \le b \le 2\}$$
$$\{\mathsf{WP}_\tau(x, 2) \wedge 0 \le a \le b \le 2\}$$

Fig. 7. Proof outline of COH using the protocol $\langle \{0, 1, 2\}, \le, \lambda(s, v).\, s = v \rangle$.

These rules can be extended to use the FSL modalities to allow ownership transfer in combination with fences, but even these basic rules are sufficient for verifying the COH example. Returning to the example, we take as the protocol τ of x to consist of three states ordered linearly ($0 \sqsubseteq_\tau 1 \sqsubseteq_\tau 2$), each saying that x has the respective value. Pictorially, we have:

 $\mathcal{Q}_\tau(s, v) \triangleq s = v$

The proof outline for COH is rather straightfoward and is shown in Fig. 7. In the writer thread, each write moves to the next state. In turn, the reader can assert that each read gets a value greater or equal to the last state it observed.

Besides protocols, GPS also introduced ghost state in the form of ghost resources and escrows/exchanges. These features enable GPS to support ownership transfer over release-acquire synchronization. For an explanation of these features, we refer the reader to [10,25,27].

A Note About the Different Versions of GPS. GPS was initially developed by Turon et al. [27] for a fragment of the programming language of Sect. 3 containing only non-atomic and release/acquire accesses. It was later extended by Tassarotti et al. [25] with "exchanges" and used to verify a version of the RCU algorithm. Later, Kaiser et al. [10] developed a slight variant of GPS within the Iris framework featuring a simpler "single writer" rule. All these three works had their soundness proofs verified in Coq, but cannot handle relaxed accesses. In a different line of work, He et al. [7] have extended GPS to also cover relaxed accesses albeit without a mechanised soundness proof.

9 Conclusion: Challenges Ahead

In this section, we will review three main challenges in this line of work. The first two have to do with the soundness of the presented logic, while the third has to do with their practical usage.

9.1 Soundness Under Weaker Memory Models

All the program logics discussed so far have been proved sound with respect to the RC11 weak memory model [14], which forbids load-store reordering for atomic accesses. Reordering a relaxed-atomic load past a later relaxed-atomic store, however, is allowed in some weaker memory models, such as the "promising" model of Kang et al. [11], as it is key to explaining the weak behaviour of the LB example from the introduction.

$$\{x \mapsto 0 * y \mapsto 0 * \triangle z \mapsto 0\}$$
$$\{\mathbf{W}(x, \mathcal{Q}) * \mathbf{R}(x, \mathcal{Q}) * \mathbf{W}(y, \mathcal{Q}) * \mathbf{R}(y, \mathcal{Q}) * \triangle z \mapsto 0\}$$

$$\begin{array}{l}\{\mathbf{R}(x, \mathcal{Q}) * \mathbf{W}(y, \mathcal{Q}) * \triangle z \mapsto 0\} \\ a := [x]_{\mathsf{rlx}}; \\ \{\mathcal{Q}(a) * \mathbf{W}(y, \mathcal{Q}) * \triangle z \mapsto 0\} \\ \{a = 0 \wedge \mathbf{W}(y, \mathcal{Q}) * \triangle \mathcal{Q}(1)\} \\ [y]_{\mathsf{rlx}} := 1; \\ \{a = 0 \wedge \mathbf{W}(y, \mathcal{Q})\} \end{array} \Bigg\| \begin{array}{l}\{\mathbf{W}(x, \mathcal{Q}) * \mathbf{R}(y, \mathcal{Q})\} \\ b := [y]_{\mathsf{acq}} \\ \{\mathbf{W}(x, \mathcal{Q}) * \mathcal{Q}(b)\} \\ [x]_{\mathsf{rel}} := b \\ \{\mathbf{W}(x, \mathcal{Q})\} \end{array}$$

$$\{a = 0\}$$

Fig. 8. FSL proof outline of LB+dep where $\mathcal{Q}(v) \triangleq v = 0 \vee z \mapsto 0$.

Extending the soundness of these logics to weaker models permitting the weak behaviour of LB is rather challenging. In fact, FSL with its current model of assertions (not discussed in this paper but presented in [5]) is unsound under such models as shown by the proof outline in Fig. 8.

Under the assumption that $z \mapsto 0 * \triangle z \mapsto 0$ is unsatisfiable (used in the middle of thread I to deduce that $\mathcal{Q}(a) * \triangle z \mapsto 0 \implies a = 0 \wedge z \mapsto 0$), the proof establishes that $a = 0$, whereas the program in question may clearly yield $a = 1$ if the load and the store of thread I are reordered. Although $z \mapsto 0 * \triangle z \mapsto 0$ is unsatisfiable in the current model of assertions, it is quite possible to devise a different model of assertions, according to which the aforementioned assertion is satisfiable, and thus potentially restore the soundness of FSL under some weaker memory models.

9.2   Reasoning About SC Accesses and Fences

As the reader will have noticed, in this paper we have not presented any rules for reasoning about **sc** atomics. Naturally, since **sc** atomics are stronger than the release/acquire ones, the presented release/acquire rules are also sound for **sc** accesses and fences. The question is whether we can get any stronger proof rules for **sc** accesses and fences.

For **sc** fences, it seems quite likely that we can get better rules. An **sc** fence can be thought of as a combination of a **acq-rel** fence and an **acq-rel** RMW over a ghost location. Therefore, we should be able to extend the Hoare triples with a global invariant, J, which can be accessed at **sc** fences:

$$\frac{J * P * P' \Rrightarrow J * Q * Q'}{J \vdash \{P * \triangledown P'\} \, \text{fence}_{\text{sc}} \, \{Q * \triangle Q'\}} \tag{F-SC}$$

Such an invariant may also be used for providing rules for **sc** accesses. The fragment of RC11 restricted to accesses only of **na** or **sc** kind corresponds exactly to the language targeted by CSL [19] (by treating **sc** accesses as being surrounded by atomic blocks). Thus, for this fragment at least, one can easily derive sound rules for **sc** accesses from the CSL rules involving resource invariants. The open question is whether one can extend the soundness of such rules to the full RC11 model, especially in cases where the same location may accessed both using **sc** and non-**sc** accesses.

9.3   Tool Support

The soundness proofs of the aforementioned adaptations of separation logic have all been mechanised in the Coq proof assistant (see RSL [28], FSL [5], GPS [27], FSL++ [6]) together with some example proofs. Nevertheless, doing proofs in those program logics in Coq without any additional infrastructure is quite cumbersome. What is very much needed is some support for more automated proofs.

Such support already exists for various flavours of (concurrent) separation logic. There exist a wide range of tools, from fully automated ones for suitable fragments of the logic to tactic libraries for assisting the manual derivation of mechanised proofs (e.g., [2,8,9,16–18]). For the work described here, the two most relevant tools are probably Viper [17] and the Iris framework [9].

Viper [17] is a generic program verifier for resource-based logics. Recently, Summers and Müller [24] have encoded versions of the RSL/FSL proof rules into

Viper and have used them to verify among other examples a slightly simplified version of the ARC library verified in [6]. While their encoding is not expressive enough to verify the actual ARC implementation, it is much more convenient to use for the programs falling in its domain than the FSL's Coq formalisation.

Iris [9] is a generic logical framework built around a higher-order variant of separation logic. It is deeply embedded in Coq and comes with a useful set of Coq tactics for doing proofs in that framework. In recent work, Kaiser et al. [10] have encoded a slight variant of GPS into Iris (thereby reproving its soundness within Iris) and have used Iris's infrastructure to get a convenient way of constructing GPS proofs in Coq.

Acknowledgments. The work reported here was done in collaboration with a number of people—Hoang-Hai Dang, Marko Doko, Derek Dreyer, João Fereira, Mengda He, Jan-Oliver Kaiser, Ori Lahav, Chinmay Narayan, Shengchao Qin, Aaron Turon—who are coauthors of the relevant publications. I would also like to thank the CAV'17 chairs for inviting me to write this paper.

References

1. Adve, S.V., Boehm, H.: Memory models: a case for rethinking parallel languages and hardware. Commun. ACM **53**(8), 90–101 (2010)
2. Berdine, J., Calcagno, C., O'Hearn, P.W.: Smallfoot: modular automatic assertion checking with separation logic. In: de Boer, F.S., Bonsangue, M.M., Graf, S., de Roever, W.-P. (eds.) FMCO 2005. LNCS, vol. 4111, pp. 115–137. Springer, Heidelberg (2006). doi:10.1007/11804192_6
3. Bouajjani, A., Derevenetc, E., Meyer, R.: Checking and enforcing robustness against TSO. In: Felleisen, M., Gardner, P. (eds.) ESOP 2013. LNCS, vol. 7792, pp. 533–553. Springer, Heidelberg (2013). doi:10.1007/978-3-642-37036-6_29
4. Dinsdale-Young, T., Dodds, M., Gardner, P., Parkinson, M.J., Vafeiadis, V.: Concurrent abstract predicates. In: D'Hondt, T. (ed.) ECOOP 2010. LNCS, vol. 6183, pp. 504–528. Springer, Heidelberg (2010). doi:10.1007/978-3-642-14107-2_24
5. Doko, M., Vafeiadis, V.: A program logic for C11 memory fences. In: Jobstmann, B., Leino, K.R.M. (eds.) VMCAI 2016. LNCS, vol. 9583, pp. 413–430. Springer, Heidelberg (2016). doi:10.1007/978-3-662-49122-5_20
6. Doko, M., Vafeiadis, V.: Tackling real-life relaxed concurrency with FSL++. In: Yang, H. (ed.) ESOP 2017. LNCS, vol. 10201, pp. 448–475. Springer, Heidelberg (2017). doi:10.1007/978-3-662-54434-1_17
7. He, M., Vafeiadis, V., Qin, S., Ferreira, J.F.: Reasoning about fences and relaxed atomics. In: PDP 2016, pp. 520–527. IEEE Computer Society (2016)
8. Jacobs, B., Smans, J., Philippaerts, P., Vogels, F., Penninckx, W., Piessens, F.: VeriFast: a powerful, sound, predictable, fast verifier for C and Java. In: Bobaru, M., Havelund, K., Holzmann, G.J., Joshi, R. (eds.) NFM 2011. LNCS, vol. 6617, pp. 41–55. Springer, Heidelberg (2011). doi:10.1007/978-3-642-20398-5_4
9. Jung, R., Swasey, D., Sieczkowski, F., Svendsen, K., Turon, A., Birkedal, L., Dreyer, D.: Iris: monoids and invariants as an orthogonal basis for concurrent reasoning. In: Rajamani, S.K., Walker, D. (eds.) POPL 2015, pp. 637–650. ACM, New York (2015)

10. Kaiser, J.O., Dang, H.H., Dreyer, D., Lahav, O., Vafeiadis, V.: Strong logic for weak memory: reasoning about release-acquire consistency in Iris. In: ECOOP 2017 (2017)
11. Kang, J., Hur, C., Lahav, O., Vafeiadis, V., Dreyer, D.: A promising semantics for relaxed-memory concurrency. In: Castagna, G., Gordon, A.D. (eds.) POPL 2017, pp. 175–189. ACM, New York (2017)
12. Lahav, O., Giannarakis, N., Vafeiadis, V.: Taming release-acquire consistency. In: POPL 2016, pp. 649–662. ACM (2016)
13. Lahav, O., Vafeiadis, V.: Owicki-Gries reasoning for weak memory models. In: Halldórsson, M.M., Iwama, K., Kobayashi, N., Speckmann, B. (eds.) ICALP 2015. LNCS, vol. 9135, pp. 311–323. Springer, Heidelberg (2015). doi:10.1007/978-3-662-47666-6_25
14. Lahav, O., Vafeiadis, V., Kang, J., Hur, C., Dreyer, D.: Repairing sequential consistency in C/C++11. In: PLDI 2017. ACM (2017)
15. Lamport, L.: How to make a multiprocessor computer that correctly executes multiprocess programs. IEEE Trans. Comput. **28**(9), 690–691 (1979)
16. Leino, K.R.M.: Dafny: an automatic program verifier for functional correctness. In: Clarke, E.M., Voronkov, A. (eds.) LPAR 2010. LNCS, vol. 6355, pp. 348–370. Springer, Heidelberg (2010). doi:10.1007/978-3-642-17511-4_20
17. Müller, P., Schwerhoff, M., Summers, A.J.: Viper: a verification infrastructure for permission-based reasoning. In: Jobstmann, B., Leino, K.R.M. (eds.) VMCAI 2016. LNCS, vol. 9583, pp. 41–62. Springer, Heidelberg (2016). doi:10.1007/978-3-662-49122-5_2
18. Nanevski, A., Morrisett, J.G., Birkedal, L.: Hoare type theory, polymorphism and separation. J. Funct. Program. **18**(5–6), 865–911 (2008)
19. O'Hearn, P.W.: Resources, concurrency, and local reasoning. Theor. Comput. Sci. **375**(1–3), 271–307 (2007)
20. Owens, S.: Reasoning about the implementation of concurrency abstractions on x86-TSO. In: D'Hondt, T. (ed.) ECOOP 2010. LNCS, vol. 6183, pp. 478–503. Springer, Heidelberg (2010). doi:10.1007/978-3-642-14107-2_23
21. Owicki, S., Gries, D.: An axiomatic proof technique for parallel programs I. Acta Inform. **6**(4), 319–340 (1976)
22. Owicki, S.S.: Axiomatic proof techniques for parallel programs. Ph.D. thesis, Cornell University (1975)
23. da Rocha Pinto, P., Dinsdale-Young, T., Gardner, P.: TaDA: a logic for time and data abstraction. In: Jones, R. (ed.) ECOOP 2014. LNCS, vol. 8586, pp. 207–231. Springer, Heidelberg (2014). doi:10.1007/978-3-662-44202-9_9
24. Summers, A.J., Müller, P.: Automating deductive verification for weak-memory programs (2017)
25. Tassarotti, J., Dreyer, D., Vafeiadis, V.: Verifying read-copy-update in a logic for weak memory. In: PLDI 2015, pp. 110–120. ACM (2015)
26. Turon, A., Dreyer, D., Birkedal, L.: Unifying refinement and hoare-style reasoning in a logic for higher-order concurrency. In: Morrisett, G., Uustalu, T. (eds.) ICFP 2013, pp. 377–390. ACM (2013)
27. Turon, A., Vafeiadis, V., Dreyer, D.: GPS: navigating weak memory with ghosts, protocols, and separation. In: OOPSLA 2014, pp. 691–707. ACM (2014)
28. Vafeiadis, V., Narayan, C.: Relaxed separation logic: a program logic for C11 concurrency. In: OOPSLA 2013, pp. 867–884. ACM (2013)

The Power of Symbolic Automata
and Transducers

Loris D'Antoni[1(✉)] and Margus Veanes[2]

[1] University of Wisconsin, Madison, USA
loris@cs.wisc.edu
[2] Microsoft Research, Redmond, USA
margus@microsoft.com

Abstract. Symbolic automata and transducers extend finite automata and transducers by allowing transitions to carry predicates and functions over rich alphabet theories, such as linear arithmetic. Therefore, these models extend their classic counterparts to operate over infinite alphabets, such as the set of rational numbers. Due to their expressiveness, symbolic automata and transducers have been used to verify functional programs operating over lists and trees, to prove the correctness of complex implementations of BASE64 and UTF encoders, and to expose data parallelism in computations that may otherwise seem inherently sequential. In this paper, we give an overview of what is currently known about symbolic automata and transducers as well as their variants. We discuss what makes these models different from their finite-alphabet counterparts, what kind of applications symbolic models can enable, and what challenges arise when reasoning about these formalisms. Finally, we present a list of open problems and research directions that relate to both the theory and practice of symbolic automata and transducers.

1 Introduction

This paper summarizes the recent results in the theory and applications of symbolic automata and transducers, which are models for reasoning about lists and trees over complex domains. Finite automata and transducers are used in many applications in software engineering, including software verification [13], text processing [7], and computational linguistics [38]. Despite their many applications, these models suffer from a major drawback: in the most common forms they can only handle finite and small alphabets.

To overcome this limitation, symbolic automata and transducers allow transitions to carry predicates and functions over a specified alphabet theory, such as linear arithmetic, and therefore extend finite automata to operate over infinite alphabets, such as the set of rational numbers. Despite this generality, symbolic models retain many of the good properties of their finite-alphabet counterparts and have enabled new applications such as verification of string sanitizers [30], analysis of tree-manipulating programs [23], and program synthesis [33].

© Springer International Publishing AG 2017
R. Majumdar and V. Kunčak (Eds.): CAV 2017, Part I, LNCS 10426, pp. 47–67, 2017.
DOI: 10.1007/978-3-319-63387-9_3

Despite this success, traditional algorithms that work over finite alphabets have been proven hard to generalize to the symbolic setting, making the design of algorithms for symbolic models challenging and theoretically interesting. In certain cases, properties that hold for finite alphabets stop holding in the symbolic setting—e.g., while it is decidable to check whether a finite state transducer is injective, the same problem is undecidable for symbolic finite transducers.

Intention and Organization. The intention of this paper is to give an overview of what is currently known about symbolic automata and transducers. At the same time, we take this opportunity to present new properties that were not formally investigated in earlier papers and explain to the reader what differentiates symbolic models from their finite-alphabet counterparts. We also show what applications have been made possible thanks to the models we present.

In summary, the paper describes:

– The existing results on symbolic finite automata, their extensions (Sect. 2), and their applications (Sect. 3);
– The existing results on symbolic finite transducers, their extensions (Sect. 4), and their applications (Sect. 5); and
– A brief list of the current challenges and open problems related to symbolic automata and transducers (Sect. 6).

Related Work. It should be noted that the concept of automata with predicates instead of concrete symbols was first mentioned in [59] and was discussed in [49] in the context of natural language processing. This paper focuses on work done following the definition of symbolic finite automata presented in [55], where predicates have to be drawn from a decidable Boolean algebra. The term symbolic automata is sometimes used to refer to automata over finite alphabets where the state space is represented using BDDs [43]. This meaning is different from the one described in this paper.

Finally, it is hard to describe all the work related to symbolic automata in one paper and the authors curate an updated list of papers on symbolic automata and transducers [3]. Many of the algorithms we discuss in this paper are implemented in the open source libraries AutomataDotNet (in C#) [1] and symbolicautomata (in Java) [4], and many of the benchmarks used in the applications cited in this paper are available in the open source collection of benchmarks AutomatArk [2].

2   Symbolic Automata

In symbolic automata, transitions carry predicates over a Boolean algebra. Formally, an *effective Boolean algebra* $\mathcal{A}$ is a tuple $(\mathfrak{D}, \Psi, [\![\_]\!], \bot, \top, \vee, \wedge, \neg)$ where $\mathfrak{D}$ is a set of *domain elements*; Ψ is a set of *predicates* closed under the Boolean connectives, with $\bot, \top \in \Psi$; the component $[\![\_]\!] : \Psi \to 2^{\mathfrak{D}}$ is a *denotation function* such that (*i*) $[\![\bot]\!] = \emptyset$, (*ii*) $[\![\top]\!] = \mathfrak{D}$, and (*iii*) for all $\varphi, \psi \in \Psi$, $[\![\varphi \vee \psi]\!] = [\![\varphi]\!] \cup [\![\psi]\!]$, $[\![\varphi \wedge \psi]\!] = [\![\varphi]\!] \cap [\![\psi]\!]$, and $[\![\neg \varphi]\!] = \mathfrak{D} \setminus [\![\varphi]\!]$. We also require that checking *satisfiability* of φ—i.e., whether $[\![\varphi]\!] \neq \emptyset$—is *decidable*.

In practice, an (effective) Boolean algebra is implemented as an API with corresponding methods implementing the Boolean operations.

Example 1 (Equality Algebra). The *equality algebra* over an arbitrary set $\mathfrak{D}$ has an atomic predicate φ_a for every $a \in \mathfrak{D}$ such that $[\![\varphi_a]\!] = \{a\}$ as well as predicates $\bot$ and $\top$. The set of predicates Ψ is the Boolean closure generated from the atomic predicates—e.g., $\varphi_a \vee \varphi_b$ and $\neg\varphi_a$ where $a, b \in \mathfrak{D}$ are predicates in Ψ.

Example 2 (SMT Algebra). Consider a fixed type τ and let Ψ be the set of all quantifier free formulas with one fixed free variable x of type τ. Intuitively, SMT_τ with is a Boolean algebra representing a restricted use of an SMT solver such as Z3 [24]. Formally, $SMT_\tau = (\mathfrak{D}, \Psi, [\![\_]\!], \bot, \top, \vee, \wedge, \neg)$, where $\mathfrak{D}$ is the set of all elements of type τ, Ψ is the set of all quantifier free formulas containing a single uninterpreted constant $x : \tau$, the true predicate $\top$ is $x = x$, the false predicate $\bot$ is $x \neq x$, and the Boolean operations are the corresponding connectives in SMT formulas. The interpretation function $[\![\varphi]\!]$ is defined using the operations of satisfiability checking and model generation provided by an SMT solver. For example, we can imagine that $SMT_{\mathbb{Z}}$ is the algebra in which elements have type $\tau = \mathbb{Z}$ and predicates are in integer linear arithmetic. Examples of such predicates are $\varphi_{>0}(x) \overset{\text{def}}{=} x > 0$ and $\varphi_{odd}(x) \overset{\text{def}}{=} x \% 2 = 1$.

We can now define symbolic finite automata, which are finite automata over a symbolic alphabet, where edge labels are replaced by predicates.

Definition 1. A *symbolic finite automaton* (s-FA) is a tuple $M = (\mathcal{A}, Q, q^0, F, \Delta)$ where $\mathcal{A}$ is an effective Boolean algebra, Q is a finite set of *states*, $q^0 \in Q$ is the *initial state*, $F \subseteq Q$ is the set of *final states*, and $\Delta \subseteq Q \times \Psi_{\mathcal{A}} \times Q$ is a finite set of *transitions*.

Elements of $\mathfrak{D}$ are called *characters* and finite sequences of characters are called *strings*—i.e., elements of $\mathfrak{D}^*$. A transition $\rho = (q_1, \varphi, q_2) \in \Delta$, also denoted $q_1 \xrightarrow{\varphi} q_2$, is a transition from the *source* state q_1 to the *target* state q_2, where φ is the *guard* or *predicate* of the transition. For a character $a \in \mathfrak{D}$, an *a-transition* of M, denoted $q_1 \xrightarrow{a} q_2$ is a transition $q_1 \xrightarrow{\varphi} q_2$ such that $a \in [\![\varphi]\!]$.

An s-FA M is *deterministic* if, for all transitions $(q, \varphi_1, q_1), (q, \varphi_2, q_2) \in \Delta$, if $q_1 \neq q_2$ then $[\![\varphi_1 \wedge \varphi_2]\!] = \emptyset$—i.e., for each state q and character a there is at most one a-transition from q.

A string $w = a_1 a_2 \ldots a_k$ is *accepted at state q* iff, for $1 \leq i \leq k$, there exist transitions $q_{i-1} \xrightarrow{a_i} q_i$ such that $q_0 = q$ and $q_k \in F$. We refer to the set of strings accepted at q as the *language of M accepted at q*, denoted as $\mathcal{L}_q(M)$; the *language accepted by M* is $\mathcal{L}(M) = \mathcal{L}_{q^0}(M)$.

It is convenient to work with s-FAs that are *normalized* and have at most one transition from any state to another. For any two states p and q in Q we define $\Delta(p, q) \overset{\text{def}}{=} \bigvee \{\varphi \mid (p, \varphi, q) \in \Delta\}$ where $\bigvee \emptyset \overset{\text{def}}{=} \bot$. We can then define the normalized representation of an s-FA where for every two states p and q, we assume a single transition $p \xrightarrow{\Delta(p,q)} q$. Equivalently, in this normalized representation Δ is a function from $Q \times Q$ to Ψ with $\Delta(p, q) = \bot$ when there is no transition from p to q. We also define $dom(p) \stackrel{\text{def}}{=} \bigvee\{\varphi \mid \exists q : (p, \varphi, q) \in \Delta\}$, to denote the set of all characters for which there exists a transition from a state p. A state p of M is *complete* if $[\![dom(p)]\!] = \mathfrak{D}_{\mathcal{A}}$; p is *partial* otherwise. Observe that p is partial iff $\neg dom(p)$ is satisfiable. The s-FA M is *complete* if all states of M are complete; M is *partial* otherwise.

Example 3. Examples of s-FAs are $\mathbf{M_{pos}}$ and $\mathbf{M_{ev/odd}}$ in Fig. 1. These two s-FAs have 1 and 2 states respectively, and they both operate over the Boolean algebra $SMT_{\mathbb{Z}}$ from Example 2. The s-FA $\mathbf{M_{pos}}$ accepts all strings consisting only of positive numbers, while the s-FA $\mathbf{M_{ev/odd}}$ accepts all strings of even length consisting only of odd numbers. For example, $\mathbf{M_{ev/odd}}$ accepts the string $[2, 4, 6, 2]$ and rejects strings $[2, 4, 6]$ and $[51, 26]$. The product automaton of $\mathbf{M_{pos}}$ and $\mathbf{M_{ev/odd}}$, $\mathbf{M_{ev/odd}} \times \mathbf{M_{pos}}$, accepts the language $\mathcal{L}(\mathbf{M_{pos}}) \cap \mathcal{L}(\mathbf{M_{ev/odd}})$. Both s-FAs are partial—e.g., neither of them has transitions for character -1.

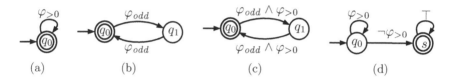

Fig. 1. Symbolic automata, (a) $\mathbf{M_{pos}}$; (b) $\mathbf{M_{ev/odd}}$; (c) $\mathbf{M_{ev/odd}} \times \mathbf{M_{pos}}$; (d) $\mathbf{M_{pos}^c}$.

2.1   Interesting Properties

In this section, we illustrate some basic properties of s-FAs and show how these models differ from finite automata. A key characteristic of all s-FAs algorithms is that there is no explicit use of characters because $\mathfrak{D}$ may be infinite and the interface to the Boolean algebra does not directly support use of individual characters.

Similarly to what happens for finite automata, nondeterminism does not add expressiveness for s-FAs.

Theorem 1 (Determinizability [55]**).** *Given an s-FA M one can effectively construct a deterministic s-FA M_{det} such that $\mathcal{L}(M) = \mathcal{L}(M_{\text{det}})$.*

The determinization algorithm is similar to the subset construction for automata over finite alphabets, but also requires combining predicates appearing in different transitions. If M contains k inequivalent predicates and n states, then the number of distinct predicates in M_{det} is at most 2^k and the number of states is at most 2^n. In other words, in addition to the classic state space explosion risk there is also a predicate space explosion risk.

Since s-FAs can be determinized, we can show that s-FAs are closed under Boolean operations using variations of classic automata constructions.

Theorem 2 (Boolean Operations [55]**).** *Given s-FAs M_1 and M_2 one can effectively construct s-FAs M_1^c and $M_1 \times M_2$ such that $\mathcal{L}(M_1^c) = \mathfrak{D}_{\mathcal{A}}^* \setminus \mathcal{L}(M_1)$ and $\mathcal{L}(M_1 \times M_2) = \mathcal{L}(M_1) \cap \mathcal{L}(M_2)$.*

The intersection of two s-FAs is computed using a variation of the classic product construction in which transitions are "synchronized" using conjunction. For example, the intersection of $\mathbf{M_{pos}}$ and $\mathbf{M_{ev/odd}}$ from Example 3 is shown in Fig. 1(c).

To complement a deterministic partial s-FA M, M is first *completed* by adding a new non-final state s with loop $s \xrightarrow{\top} s$ and for each partial state p a transition $p \xrightarrow{\neg dom(p)} s$. Then the final states and the non-final states are swapped in M^c. Following this procedure, the complement of $\mathbf{M_{pos}}$ from Example 3 is shown in Fig. 1(d).

Next, s-FAs enjoy the same decidability properties of finite automata.

Theorem 3 (Decidability [55]**).** *Given s-FAs M_1 and M_2 it is decidable to check if M_1 is empty—i.e., whether $\mathcal{L}(M_1) = \emptyset$—and if M_1 and M_2 are language-equivalent—i.e. whether $\mathcal{L}(M_1) = \mathcal{L}(M_2)$.*

Checking emptiness requires checking what transitions are satisfiable and, once unsatisfiable transitions are removed, any path reaching a final state from an initial state represents at least one accepting string. Equivalence can be reduce to emptiness using closure under Boolean operations.

Algorithms have also been proposed for minimizing *deterministic* s-FAs [18], for checking language inclusion [34], for computing forward bisimulations of s-FAs [21], and for learning s-FAs from membership and equivalence queries [25].

Alphabet Equivalence Classes. Classic automata can only describe sequences over finite alphabets. Despite this limitation, there is a way to convert every s-FA M into a finite automaton that, in some sense, preserves the set of all strings accepted by the s-FA. Although the set S of all predicates appearing in a given s-FA (or finite collection of s-FAs over the same alphabet algebra) operate over an infinite domain, the set of maximal satisfiable Boolean combinations $Minterms(S)$—also called minterms—of such predicates induces a finite set of equivalence classes. In order to perform operations over one or more s-FAs $\bar{M}$ by using classical automata algorithms, one can consider $\Sigma = Minterms(Predicates(\bar{M}))$ as the induced finite alphabet and replace each original transition $p \xrightarrow{\varphi} q$ by the transitions $\{p \xrightarrow{c} q \mid c \in \Sigma, \mathbf{SAT}(c \wedge \varphi)\}$ and consequently treat the automata as classic finite automata over the alphabet Σ.

Example 4. Consider the two s-FAs $\mathbf{M_{pos}}$ and $\mathbf{M_{ev/odd}}$ in Fig. 1. Then

$$S = Predicates(\mathbf{M_{pos}}, \mathbf{M_{ev/odd}}) = \{\varphi_{>0}, \varphi_{odd}\}$$

and

$$\Sigma = Minterms(S) = \{\underbrace{\varphi_{odd} \wedge \varphi_{>0}}_{a}, \underbrace{\neg\varphi_{odd} \wedge \varphi_{>0}}_{b}, \underbrace{\varphi_{odd} \wedge \neg\varphi_{>0}}_{c}, \underbrace{\neg\varphi_{odd} \wedge \neg\varphi_{>0}}_{d}\}$$

Then, as a DFA over the finite alphabet Σ, $\mathbf{M_{pos}}$ has the transitions $\{(q_0, a, q_0), (q_0, b, q_0)\}$ and $\mathbf{M_{ev/odd}}$ has the transitions $\{(q_0, a, q_1), (q_0, c, q_1),$ $(q_1, a, q_0), (q_1, c, q_0)\}$. In the product $\mathbf{M_{pos}} \times \mathbf{M_{ev/odd}}$ only the a-transitions remain.

Intuitively, using only the predicates in Σ there is no way to, for example, distinguish the number 1 from the number 3—i.e., given any string s, if one replaces any element 1 in s with the element 3, the new sequence s' is accepted by the s-FA iff s is also accepted by the s-FA.   ⊠

Using this argument, every s-FA M can be compiled into a symbolically equivalent finite automaton over any alphabet $Minterms(S)$ where $Predicates(M)$ forms a subset of S and S is a finite subset of Ψ. This idea, also referred to as predicate abstraction, is often used in program verification [26].

In general, computing the set $Minterms(M) \stackrel{\text{def}}{=} Minterms(Predicates(M))$ is an expensive procedure that generate exponentially many predicates. The following theorem exactly characterizes the size of the set $Minterms(M)$.

Theorem 4 (Number of minterms). *Let M be a complete and normalized s-FA with n states. Then $|Minterms(M)| \leq 2^{(n^2)}$. If M is deterministic then $|Minterms(M)| \leq 2^{n \log_2 n}$.*

Proof. Let $S = Predicates(M)$. Since M is normalized we have $|\Delta| \leq n^2$ and so $|S| \leq n^2$, and since $|Minterms(S)| \leq 2^{|S|}$ the first claim follows. Assume now that M is deterministic. Then every source state p_i of M, for $i < n$, defines a partition P_i of $\mathfrak{D}$ such that $|P_i| \leq n$ because M is normalized, where each part of P_i is defined by the guard of a transition from p_i. Given two partitions P_i and P_j of $\mathfrak{D}$ let $P_i \sqcap P_j$ denote the coarsest partition of $\mathfrak{D}$ that refines both P_i and P_j. Then $\{[\![\mu]\!] \mid \mu \in Minterms(S)\} = \prod_{i<n} P_i$. Since, for every i, $|P_i| \leq m$ implies $|\prod_{i<n} P_i| \leq m^n$, the following holds: $|Minterms(S)| \leq n^n = 2^{n \log_2 n}$.   ⊠

2.2 Parametric Complexities

In the previous paragraphs we did not discuss the complexities of the presented algorithms. Since s-FAs are parametric in an underlying alphabet theory, the complexities of the algorithms must in some way depend on the complexities of performing certain operations in the alphabet theory.

For example, checking emptiness of an s-FA requires checking satisfiability of all predicates in the s-FA and the complexity depends on "how costly" it is to check satisfiability of such predicates. Another issue arises from algorithms that generate new predicates that did not belong to the original s-FAs. In particular, repeated predicate conjunctions, unions, and complementations will cause predicates to grow in size and might therefore result in satisfiability queries with higher costs. This peculiar aspect of s-FAs opens a new set of complexity questions that have not been studied in classic automata theory.

Let's consider again the problem of checking emptiness of an s-FA. In classic automata, this problem has complexity $\mathcal{O}(kn)$ where k is the size of the alphabet and n is the number of states in the automaton. For an s-FA M, if we assume that the largest predicate in M has size ℓ and $f(x)$ is the cost of checking satisfiability of predicates of size x in the underlying alphabet theory, then checking emptiness has complexity $\mathcal{O}(m \cdot f(\ell))$, where m is the number of transitions in the s-FA M. Observe also that for s-FAs it is reasonable to work with normalized representations which implies that m is at most n^2 and m is independent of the alphabet size and the total size of M is $\mathcal{O}(m\ell)$.

For certain problems, the complexities can get more complicated and different algorithms will have different incomparable complexities. For example, consider the problem of minimizing a deterministic s-FA. For classic automata, there are two algorithms for solving this problem: (i) Moore's algorithm, which has complexity $\mathcal{O}(kn^2)$; (ii) Hopcroft's algorithm, which has complexity $\mathcal{O}(kn \log n)$. It is therefore clear that Hopcroft's algorithm has better asymptotic complexity than Moore's algorithm. In the case of s-FAs, the situation is more complicated. For an s-FAs M with n states and m transitions, if we assume that the largest predicate in M has size ℓ and $f(x)$ is the cost of checking satisfiability of predicates of size x in the underlying alphabet theory, the symbolic adaptation of Moore's algorithm has complexity $\mathcal{O}(mn \cdot f(\ell))$, while the symbolic adaptation of Hopcroft's algorithm has complexity $\mathcal{O}(m \log n \cdot f(n\ell))$. For s-FAs, the two algorithms have somewhat orthogonal theoretical complexities: Hopcroft's algorithm saves a logarithmic factor in terms of state complexity, but this saving comes at the cost of running more expensive satisfiability queries on predicates of size $n\ell$. Given the recent advances in satisfiability procedures, the second algorithm behaves better in practice.

2.3   Variants

Symbolic automata have been extended in various ways. Symbolic alternating automata (s-AFA) together with a practical equivalence algorithm are presented in [17]. s-AFAs are equivalent in expressiveness to s-FAs, but achieve succinctness by extending s-FAs with alternation [14] and, despite the high theoretical complexity, this model can at times be more practical than s-FAs. A very common extension of s-FAs is to allow multiple initial states, in particular when dealing with nondeterministic s-FAs [21].

Symbolic tree automata (s-TA) operate over trees instead of strings. s-FAs are a special case of s-TAs in which all nodes in the tree have one child or are leaves. s-TAs have the same closure and decidability properties as s-FAs [52]. Moreover, the minimization algorithms for s-FAs has been extended to s-TAs [20].

Symbolic visibly pushdown automata (s-VPA) operate over nested words, which are used to model data with both linear and hierarchical structure such—e.g., XML documents and recursive program traces. s-VPAs can be determinized and have the same closure and decidability properties of s-FAs [16].

All the previous extensions show cases in which adapting classic models to the symbolic setting does not affect closure and decidability properties. This is not the case for Symbolic Extended Finite Automata (s-EFA) [19]. s-EFAs are symbolic automata in which each transition can read more than a single character. In this model, predicates apply to finite tuples of elements up to a fixed length, but the semantics flattens the tuples.

Formally, the domain $\mathfrak{D}$ of $\mathcal{A}$ is assumed to contain tuples to enable the use of multiple variables in this setting. There are predicates $IsTup\_k$ for checking if an element is a k-tuple for $k \geq 1$ and there are projection terms x_i or *variables* such that for a k-tuple $a = (a_1, \ldots, a_k)$, and $1 \leq i \leq k$, $[\![x_i]\!](a) = a_i$. For example, using equality or disequality, one can relate elements of tuples. A predicate over k-tuples is called k-*ary*.

Example 5. A predicate $IsTup\_2 \wedge x_1 \neq x_2 \wedge \varphi$ is satisfiable iff there exists $a \in \mathfrak{D}$ such that a is a pair (a_1, a_2) and $a_1 \neq a_2$, and $[\![\varphi]\!](a_1, a_2)$ holds.   ⊠

Thus, if $[(a, b, c), (d), (e, f)] \in \mathcal{L}(M)$ where M is a considered as an s-FA then $[a, b, c, d, e, f] \in \mathcal{L}^e(M)$ when M is considered as an s-EFA. Each individual transition guard must uniquely define the length k of the tuple that determines its arity. For example, the following transition reads two adjacent symbols x_1 and x_2 and checks whether the two symbols are equal:

$$p \xrightarrow[2]{x_1=x_2} q.$$

While for automata over finite alphabet adding the the ability to consume multiple characters in a single transition does not increase expressiveness, s-EFAs are strictly more expressive than s-FAs. Moreover, s-EFAs lack many of the desirable properties s-FAs enjoy: s-EFAs are not closed under Boolean operations, nondeterministic s-EFAs are strictly more expressive than their deterministic counterpart, it is undecidable to check whether two s-EFAs are equivalent, or even to check whether their intersection is empty. An important subclass of s-EFAs, called *Cartesian* s-EFAs [19], has the same expressive power as s-FAs and allows transitions with lookahead but the guards must be predicates whose atoms only mention one variable at a time. Thus the atom $x_1 = x_2$ would not be allowed. A related problem, called *monadic decomposition* [54] arises if we want to decide if a predicate can be effectively transformed into an equivalent Cartesian form.

3   Symbolic Automata in Practice

The development of the theory of symbolic automata is motivated by concrete practical problems. Here we discuss some of them.

3.1   Analysis of Regular Expressions

The connection between automata and regular expressions has been studied for more than 50 years. However, real-world regular expressions are much more complex than the simple model described in a typical theory of computation course. In particular, in practical regular expressions the size of the alphabet is 2^{16} due to the widely adopted UTF16 standard of Unicode characters. The inability of classic automata to efficiently handle large alphabets is what started the study of symbolic automata.

Using s-FAs, the alphabet of Unicode characters can be modeled as a theory of bit-vectors where predicates are represented as Binary Decision Diagrams (BDDs) over such bit-vectors [31] or using bit-vector arithmetic in Z3 [55]. These representations turned out to be a viable way to model practical regular expressions and led to advanced analysis in the context of parametrized unit testing in the tool PEX [48], automatic SQL query exploration in QEX [56], and random password generation [18].

In applications that perform many Boolean operations on the regular expressions—e.g., in text processing and analysis of string-manipulating programs [7,57]—s-FAs may generate very large number of states despite their succinct alphabet representations. The extension of s-FAs with alternation, s-AFAs, can succinctly represent Boolean combinations of s-FAs and it was shown to be an effective model for checking equivalence of complex combinations of regular expressions.

3.2   Other Applications

Thanks to the symbolic treatment of the alphabet, symbolic automata are an executable model and can be used to generate efficient code. This idea has been used to achieve speed-ups in regular expression processing [45] and XML processing [16].

Recently, s-VPAs have been used in the context of static analysis of program failures to succinctly model properties of control-flow graphs [40]. This model is particularly helpful in modelling properties of inter-procedural programs with many different functions. In this setting, a classic automaton will need to have number of states and transitions proportional to the number of functions—i.e., when a function f is invoked, push a state remembering the name f on a stack and pop it at the function return. On the other hand, symbolic visibly pushdown automata can model this call/return interaction symbolically with a single transition that simply requires the function that is currently returning to have the same name as the last called function.

4   Symbolic Transducers

In this section, we present symbolic finite transducers, which are symbolic automata that can produce outputs. The presentation here follows the original definition from [57] but omits type annotations. In addition to predicates we use expressions for representing anonymous functions that we call *function terms*. Let $\mathcal{A}$ be a Boolean algebra as defined in Sect. 2. The set of function terms is denoted by Λ and a term $f \in \Lambda$ denotes a function $[\![f]\!]$ over $\mathfrak{D}$, such that if $f, g \in \Lambda$ then $g(f) \in \Lambda$ and it is such that for every $a \in \mathfrak{D}$:

$$[\![g(f)]\!](a) = [\![g]\!]([\![f]\!](a)).$$

Similarly, if $\varphi \in \Psi$ and $f \in \Lambda$ then $\varphi(f) \in \Psi$ such that, for $a \in \mathfrak{D}$:

$$a \in [\![\varphi(f)]\!] \Leftrightarrow [\![f]\!](a) \in [\![\varphi]\!].$$

Moreover, $f = g$ is an *equality* predicate in $\Psi_{\mathcal{A}}$ such that, for $a \in \mathfrak{D}$:

$$a \in [\![f = g]\!] \Leftrightarrow [\![f]\!](a) = [\![g]\!](a).$$

Observe that $f = g$ *does not* mean $[\![f]\!] = [\![g]\!]$. We write $f \neq g$ for $\neg f = g$. Thus, $f \neq g$ is satisfiable iff $[\![f]\!] \neq [\![g]\!]$.

Furthermore, there is an *identity* (function) term $x \in \Lambda$ such that, for all $a \in \mathfrak{D}$, $[\![x]\!](a) = a$, and for all $c \in \mathfrak{D}$ there is a *constant* term $c \in \Lambda$ such that for all $a \in \mathfrak{D}$, $[\![c]\!](a) = c$.

Example 6. Predicate $\varphi \wedge f \neq g$ is satisfiable iff there exists $a \in [\![\varphi]\!]$ such that $[\![f]\!](a) \neq [\![g]\!](a)$—i.e., when f and g are not equivalent wrt φ. Predicate $f \neq c$ for a given $c \in \mathfrak{D}$ is satisfiable iff f does not denote the constant function c. $\boxtimes$

Terms are typically typed but we omit type annotations here. We call such an extended (effective) Boolean algebra with the additional components an (*effective*) *label algebra*.

Definition 2. A *Symbolic Finite Transducer (s-FT)* T is a tuple $(\mathcal{A}, Q, q^0, \Delta, F)$ where: $\mathcal{A}$ is an effective label algebra; Q is a finite set of *states*; $q^0 \in Q$ is the *initial state*; Δ is a finite subset of $Q \times \Psi \times \Lambda^* \times Q$ called *transitions*; $F \subseteq Q$ is the set of final states.

In a transition $(p, \varphi, \bar{f}, q)$, also denoted $p \xrightarrow{\varphi/\bar{f}} q$, $\bar{f}$ is called the *output*. Observe that an s-FT in which all the transitions output the empty list corresponds to an s-FA. We also call the s-FA that is obtained from an s-FT T by removing the output component its *domain automaton*, $DOM(T)$.

Example 7. Let $\mathcal{A}$ correspond to integer linear arithmetic. So Λ contains terms such as $x\%2$ (x modulo 2), and Ψ contains atomic predicates such as $x > 0$. Here x has type $\mathbb{Z}$. The following are two examples of s-FTs:

$$T_1 = (\mathcal{A}, \{p\}, p, \{p \xrightarrow{x>0/[x,x]} p\}, \{p\}),$$

$$T_2 = (\mathcal{A}, \{q\}, q, \{q \xrightarrow{x\%2\neq0/[x]} q, q \xrightarrow{x\%2=0/[]} q\}, \{q\}).$$

Here, T_1 accepts only positive numbers and duplicates them and T_2 deletes all the even numbers. For example, on input $[1, 2, 3]$, the s-FT T_1 outputs $[1, 1, 2, 2, 3, 3]$, while the s-FT T_2 outputs $[1, 3]$. $\boxtimes$

We now define the semantics of s-FTs. In the remainder of the section, let $T = (\mathcal{A}, Q, q^0, \Delta, F)$ be a fixed s-FT. For each transition r in Δ we define the set $[\![r]\!]$ of corresponding concrete transitions as follows.

$$[\![p \xrightarrow{\varphi/[f_1,\dots,f_k]} q]\!] \stackrel{\text{def}}{=} \{(p, a) \mapsto ([[\![f_1]\!](a), \dots, [\![f_k]\!](a)], q) \mid a \in [\![\varphi]\!]\}$$

Intuitively, a transition $p \xrightarrow{\varphi/\bar{f}} q$ reads one input symbol a in state p that satisfies the guard φ and produces a sequence of output symbols by applying the output functions in $\bar{f}$ to a and enters state q. In the following, let $\llbracket \Delta \rrbracket \overset{\text{def}}{=} \bigcup_{r \in \Delta} \llbracket r \rrbracket$ and let $s_1 \cdot s_2$ denote the concatenation of two sequences s_1 and s_2. We let $\mathfrak{D}^*$ denote a *disjoint* universe from $\mathfrak{D}$ of sequences of elements over $\mathfrak{D}$, to avoid the possible ambiguity as far as concatenation is concerned.

Definition 3. For $u = [a_1, a_2, \ldots, a_n], v \in \mathfrak{D}^*, q \in Q, q' \in Q$, define $q \xrightarrow{u/v}_T q'$ iff either $u = v = []$ and $q = q'$, or there is $n \geq 1$ and $\{(p_{i-1}, a_i) \mapsto (v_i, p_i)\}_{i=1}^n \subseteq \llbracket \Delta \rrbracket$ such that $v = v_1 \cdot v_2 \cdots v_n, q = p_0$, and $q' = p_n$. The *transduction of T* is the relation $\mathscr{T}_T \subseteq \mathfrak{D}^* \times \mathfrak{D}^*$ such that $\mathscr{T}_T(u, v) \Leftrightarrow \exists q \in F : q^0 \xrightarrow{u/v} q$. Let $\mathscr{T}_T(u) \overset{\text{def}}{=} \{v \mid \mathscr{T}_T(u, v)\}$. Finally, he domain of T is defined as $\mathbf{dom}(T) \overset{\text{def}}{=} \{u \in \mathfrak{D}^* \mid \exists v : \mathscr{T}_T(u, v)\}$, and the range of T is defined as $\mathbf{ran}(T) \overset{\text{def}}{=} \{v \in \mathfrak{D}^* \mid \exists u : \mathscr{T}_T(u, v)\}$.

The s-FT T is *deterministic* when $\llbracket \Delta \rrbracket$ is a partial function from $Q \times \mathfrak{D}$ to $\mathfrak{D}^* \times Q$. The s-FT T is *single-valued* or *functional* if, for all u, $|\mathscr{T}_T(u)| \leq 1$—i.e., $\mathscr{T}_T$ represents a partial function over $\mathfrak{D}^*$. Observe that if T is deterministic then T is also functional. Both the s-FTs in Example 7 are deterministic.

4.1   Interesting Properties

In this section, we illustrate some of the basic properties of s-FTs and show what aspects differentiate these models from finite transducers [38], their finite-alphabet counterpart. First, while both the domain and the range of a finite state transduction are definable using a finite automaton, this is not the case for s-FTs. By a *regular language* here we mean a language accepted by an s-FA.

An s-FT T *admits quantifier elimination* if for every transition $(p, \varphi, [f_i]_{i=1}^k, q)$ in T where $k \geq 1$ one can effectively compute a predicate $\psi \in \Psi$ such that the following is true: for all $b \in \mathfrak{D}$, we have $b \in \llbracket \psi \rrbracket$ iff b is a k-tuple $(b_i)_{i=1}^k$ such that there exists $a \in \llbracket \varphi \rrbracket$ such that $b_i = \llbracket f_i \rrbracket(a)$ for $1 \leq i \leq k$. In other words, computation of ψ corresponds to eliminating the quantifier $\exists y$ from $\exists y : \varphi(y) \wedge \bigwedge_{i=1}^k x_i = f_i(y)$. Note that the predicate ψ is a k-ary predicate.

Theorem 5 (Domain and Range Languages). *Given an s-FT T, one can compute an s-FA $DOM(T)$ such that $\mathcal{L}(DOM(T)) = \mathbf{dom}(T)$ and, provided that T admits quantifier elimination, there is an s-EFA $RAN(T)$ such that $\mathcal{L}^e(RAN(T)) = \mathbf{ran}(T)$.*

In general, the range of an s-FT is not regular.

Example 8. Take an s-FT T with a single transition $q \xrightarrow{\varphi_{odd}(x)/[x,x]} q$ that duplicates its input if the input is odd. Then $\mathbf{ran}(T)$ is not regular, but it can be accepted by the s-EFA with one transition $q \xrightarrow[2]{x_1 = x_2} q$.   ⊠

s-FTs are closed under sequential composition. This is a property that enables several interesting program analyses [30] and optimizations.

Theorem 6 (Closure under Composition [57]**).** *Given two s-FTs T_1 and T_2, one can compute an s-FT $T_2(T_1)$ such that for $u, v \in \mathfrak{D}^*$,*

$$\mathscr{T}_{T_2(T_1)}(u, v) \Leftrightarrow \exists w : \mathscr{T}_{T_1}(u, w) \wedge \mathscr{T}_{T_2}(w, v).$$

We illustrate the role of the *substitution* operator $\cdot(\cdot)$ in a label algebra in the context of computing $T_2(T_1)$. Consider the transition $p \xrightarrow{\varphi/[f_1, f_2]} p'$ in T_1 and the transitions $q \xrightarrow{\psi/[g]} q' \xrightarrow{\gamma/[h]} q''$ in T_2. The set of states $Q_{T_2(T_1)}$ of the composed transducer is a reachable subset of $Q_1 \times Q_2$. The initial state of $T_2(T_1)$ is $(q_{T_1}^0, q_{T_2}^0)$. When a state (p, q) is explored then the transition

$$(p, q) \xrightarrow{\varphi \wedge \psi(f_1) \wedge \gamma(f_2)/[g(f_1), h(f_2)]} (p', q'')$$

is constructed from the above transitions where the substitution operator is applied to construct the combined guard and output functions. The composed transition is omitted if $\varphi \wedge \psi(f_1) \wedge \gamma(f_2)$ is unsatisfiable.

Example 9. Recall T_1 and T_2 from Example 7. Consider $T = T_2(T_1)$. Then $Q_T = \{(p, q)\}$. There are four composed candidates for the transitions in Δ_T but only the following two have satisfiable guards:

$$(p, q) \xrightarrow{x>0 \wedge x\%2 \neq 0 \wedge x\%2 \neq 0/[x,x]} (p, q), \quad (p, q) \xrightarrow{x>0 \wedge x\%2=0 \wedge x\%2=0/[]} (p, q)$$

Therefore T, given a list of positive numbers, duplicates all odd numbers and deletes the even ones. For example, on input $[1, 2, 3]$, T outputs $[1, 1, 3, 3]$.   ⊠

The following result follows from the closure properties of s-FAs and the closure under composition of s-FTs.

Corollary 1 (Type-checking). *Given an s-FTs T and s-FAs M_I and M_O, the following problem is decidable: check if for all $v \in \mathcal{L}(M_I)$: $\mathscr{T}_T(v) \subseteq \mathcal{L}(M_O)$.*

For example, using the type-checking algorithm one can prove that, for every input list, the transducer T from Example 9 always outputs a list of odd numbers of even length.

Checking whether two s-FTs are equivalent is in general undecidable (already over finite alphabets [29]). However, the problem becomes decidable when the two s-FTs are functional (single-valued), which is itself a decidable property to check.

Theorem 7 (Decidable functionality [57]**).** *Given an s-FTs T it is decidable to check whether T is functional.*

Theorem 8 (Decidable functional equivalence [57]**).** *Given two functional s-FTs T_1 and T_2 it is decidable to check whether $\mathscr{T}_{T_1} = \mathscr{T}_{T_2}$.*

Both theorems use a more general decision problem that decides for two s-FTs T_1 and T_2, if for all $u, v, w \in \mathfrak{D}^*$ it is true that if $\mathscr{T}_{T_1}(u, v)$ and $\mathscr{T}_{T_2}(u, w)$ then $v = w$. The algorithm of this decision problem [57, Fig. 3] uses the disequality operator $\neq$ and, in particular, the predicates shown in Example 6.

We conclude this section with an interesting property that is decidable for classic finite state transducers [27] but undecidable for s-FTs. We say that an s-FT T is *injective* if for all $u, v \in \mathfrak{D}^*$ we have $\mathscr{T}_T(u) \cap \mathscr{T}_T(v) = \emptyset$.

Theorem 9 (Undecidable injectivity [33]**).** *Given a deterministic s-FT T, it is undecidable to check whether T is injective.*

The proof of undecidability presented in [33, Theorem 4.8] is given for s-EFTs and is based on showing that it is undecidable to check whether there exist two different accepting paths for the same string in the s-EFA $RAN(T)$. It is easy to show that the theorem also holds for s-FTs since every s-EFA in this theory can be produced as the range language of some s-FT.

4.2 Variants

Symbolic finite transducers have been extended in various ways. The basic extension of s-FTs is to consider *finalizers*—i.e., specific transitions that are used to output final sequences upon end of input. Finite state transducers with finalizers are called *subsequential* [6,46]. Finalizers enable certain scenarios not possible without sacrificing determinism. Consider for example a decoder that decodes a string by replacing all patterns `"&amp;"` by the character `"&"`. If the input string ends with for example `"&amp"` the decoder will need to output `"&amp"` instead of `"&"` upon reaching the end of the input and finding out that `";"` is missing. Similarly, for capturing *minimality*, s-FTs may also be extended with *initial* outputs [44]. For many purposes it is enough to imagine that $\mathfrak{D}$ is extended with two new symbols that are used exclusively to detect start and end of an input sequence. In a typed universe this approach is cumbersome and complicates the notion of composition by requiring bookkeeping and special treatment of the extra symbols which have to be taken outside the type domain.

Similarly to how s-EFAs extend s-FAs, Symbolic Extended Finite Transducers (s-EFT) are symbolic transducers in which each transition can read more than a single character. Essentially, the definition of $\mathscr{T}_T$ changes to $\mathscr{T}_T^e$, similar to the change from $\mathcal{L}(M)$ to $\mathcal{L}^e(M)$, where the input is flattened. s-EFA already lack many desirable properties and s-EFTs further add to this list. s-EFTs are not closed under composition and equivalence is undecidable even for deterministic s-EFTs. However, equivalence becomes decidable when for every transition that reads n characters using a predicate $\varphi(x_1, \ldots, x_n)$, one can replace the predicate with an equivalent disjunction of predicates of the form $\varphi_1(x_1) \wedge \ldots \wedge \varphi_n(x_n)$ [19].

A further extension of s-FTs, called s-RTs, incorporates the notion of bounded *look-back* and *roll-back* in form of roll-back-transitions, not present in any other transducer formalisms, to accommodate default or exceptional behavior [50]. The key application is to simplify handling of default transitions such as the followings: if none of those patterns matches then read and output the next input character "as is". Having to hand-code state machines for such cases gets complicated and error prone very quickly—e.g., see [57, Fig. 7].

s-FTs have also been extended with *registers* [57] and are called *symbolic transducers*. The key motivation is to support loop-carried data state, such as the maximal number seen so far. This model is closed under composition, but most decision problems for it are undecidable, even emptiness.

A further extension of symbolic transducers uses *branching transitions*, which are transitions with multiple target states in form of if-then-else structures [45]. The purpose is to better facilitate code generation by maintaining code structure, sharing, and predicate evaluation order for deterministic transducers. For example, instead of two separate transitions $p \xrightarrow{\varphi/\bar{f}} q$ and $p \xrightarrow{\neg\varphi/\bar{g}} r$, there is a single branching transition $p \mapsto if\ \varphi\ then\ (\bar{f}, q)\ else\ (\bar{g}, r)$. If there is one branching transition per state then determinism is built-in. One can of course apply the same idea to s-FAs.

Symbolic *tree* transducers (s-TT) operate over trees instead of strings. s-FTs are a special case of s-TTs in which all nodes in the tree have one child or are leaves. s-TTs are only closed under composition when certain assumptions hold and their properties are studied in [28]. Equivalence of a restricted class of s-TTs is shown decidable in [51]. s-TTs with regular look-ahead are studied in [23].

5   Symbolic Transducers in Practice

Here we provide a high-level overview of the main applications involving symbolic finite transducers and their variants.

5.1   Analysis of String Encoders and Sanitizers

The original motivation for s-FTs came from analysis of string *sanitizers* [30]. String sanitizers are particular string to string functions over Unicode designed to encode special characters in text that may otherwise trigger malicious code execution in certain sensitive contexts, primarily in HTML pages. Thus, sanitizers provide a first line of defence against cross site scripting (XSS) attacks. When sanitizers can be represented as s-FTs, one can, for example, decide if two sanitizers A and B commute—i.e., if $\mathscr{T}_{A(B)} = \mathscr{T}_{B(A)}$—if a sanitizer A is idempotent—i.e., if $\mathscr{T}_{A(A)} = \mathscr{T}_A$—or if A cannot be compromised with an input attack vector—i.e., if $\mathbf{ran}(A) \subseteq SafeSet$. Checking such properties can help to ensure the correct usage of sanitizers.

One drawback of s-FTs is that they consider one input element at a time. While this is often sufficient for individual character-based transformations appearing in common sanitizers, in more complex transformations, such as BASE64 encoders and decoders, it is often necessary to be able to look at a group of characters at once in order to decode them. For example, a BASE64 encoder reads three characters at a time and outputs complex combinations and bit-level transformations of the bits appearing in the characters. This is the original motivation behind s-EFTs, which are studied in [19]. Using s-EFTs one can prove that efficient implementations of BASE64 or UTF encoders and decoders correctly invert each other. Recently, s-EFTs have been used to automatically compute inverses of encoders that are correct by construction [33].

Variants of algorithms for learning symbolic automata and transducers have been used to automatically extract models of PHP input filters [12] and string sanitizers [8]. In these applications, symbolic automata and transducers have enabled modelling of programs that were beyond the reach of existing automata-learning algorithms.

Symbolic transducers have also been used to perform static analysis of functional programs that operate over lists and trees [23]. In particular, symbolic tree transducers were used to verify HTML sanitizers, to check interference of augmented reality applications submitted to an app store, and to perform deforestation, a technique to speed-up function composition, in functional language compilation.

5.2 Code Generation and Parallelization

Symbolic transducers can be used to expose data parallelism in computations that may otherwise seem inherently sequential. This idea builds on the property that the state transition function of a DFA can be viewed as a particular kind of matrix multiplication operation which is associative and therefore lends itself to parallelization [39]. This property can be lifted to the symbolic setting and applied to many common string transformations expressed as symbolic transducers [58].

Using closure under composition, complex combinations of symbolic transducers can be composed in a manner that supports efficient code generation. The main context where this has been evaluated is in log/data processing pipelines that require loop-carried state for data processing [45]. In this context the symbolic transducers have registers and use *branching rules* that are rules with multiple target states in form of if-then-else structures. The main purpose of the branching rules is to support serial code generation.

Symbolic automata and transducers also provide the backbone of DReX, a declarative language for efficiently executing regular string transformations in a single left-to-right pass over the input [7]. DReX has also been extended to stream numerical data computations using a "numerical" extension of symbolic transducers [36].

6 Open Problems and Future Directions

We conclude this paper with a list of open theoretical questions that are unique to symbolic automata and transducers, as well as a summary of what unexplored applications could benefit from these models.

6.1   Adapting Efficient Algorithms for Finite Alphabets

Several algorithms for classic finite automata are based on efficient data structures that directly leverage the fact that the alphabet is finite. For example, Hopcroft's algorithm for automata minimization, at each step, iterates over the alphabet to find potential ways to split state partitions [32]. It turns out that this iteration can be avoided in symbolic automata using satisfiability checks on certain carefully crafted predicates [18].

Paige-Tarjan's algorithm for computing forward bisimulations of nondeterministic finite automata is similar to Hopcroft's algorithm for DFA minimization [5,41]. The efficient implementation of Paige-Tarjan's algorithm presented in [5] keeps, for every symbol a in the alphabet, for every state q in the automaton, and for every state partition P, a count of how many transitions from q on symbol a reach the partition P. Using this data-structure, the algorithm can compute the partition of forward-bisimilar states in time $\mathcal{O}(km \log n)$. Unlike Hopcroft's algorithm, this algorithm is hard to adapt to the symbolic setting. In fact, the current adaptation has complexity $\mathcal{O}(2^m \log n + 2^m f(n\ell))$ [21]. In contrast, the simpler $\mathcal{O}(km^2)$ algorithm for forward bisimulations can be easily turned into a symbolic $\mathcal{O}(m^2 f(\ell))$ algorithm [21]. This example shows how it can be hard to convert the most efficient algorithms for automata over finite alphabets to the symbolic setting. In fact, it remains open whether an efficient symbolic adaptation of Paige-Tarjan's algorithm exists.

Another example of this complexity of adaptation is the algorithm for checking equivalence of two nondeterministic unambiguous finite automata [47]. This algorithm checks equivalence of two automata in polynomial time by "counting" how many strings of all lengths smaller or equal than some small length the two automata accepts. These numbers can only be computed if the alphabet is finite and it is unclear whether one can efficiently adapt this algorithm to the symbolic setting.

Some symbolic models are still not well understood because they do not have a finite automata counterpart. In particular, s-EFAs do not enjoy many good properties, but it is possible that they have practical subclasses—e.g., deterministic, unambiguous, etc.—with good properties.

Finally, the problem of learning symbolic automata has only received limited attention [25], and there is an opportunity to develop interesting new theories in this domain. Classic learning algorithm require querying an oracle for all characters in the alphabet and this is impossible for symbolic automata. On the other hand, the learner simply needs to learn the predicates on each transition of the s-FA, which might require a finite number of queries to the oracle [25]. This is a common problem in computational learning theory and there is an opportunity to apply concepts from this domain to the problem of learning symbolic automata.

6.2   Theoretical Treatments

Complexity and expressiveness. In classic automata theory, the complexities of the algorithms are given with respect to the number of states and transitions in the automaton. We discussed in Sect. 2 how the complexities of symbolic automata and transducers operations depend on the complexities of performing certain operations in the alphabet theory. Existing structural complexity results for automata algorithms only dwell on state size, but we showed how certain algorithms pose trade-off between state complexity and alphabet complexity in the case of symbolic automata. Exactly understanding these trade-offs is an interesting research question.

There has been a lot of interest in providing algebraic and co-algebraic treatments of classic automata theory [11]. These abstract treatments are helping us understand the essence of classic algorithms and are simplifying complex proofs that were otherwise tedious. It is unclear how to extend these notions to symbolic models, making the problem intriguing from a theoretical standpoint.

Combination with Nominal Automata. In data words, each character is a pair (a, d) where a is an element of the finite alphabet and d is a data element over an infinite potentially ordered domain. Various models of automata have been introduced for data words [9]. In these models, data elements at different positions can be compared using a predefined operator—e.g., equality—but individual data elements cannot be checked against predicates in a Boolean algebra. Nominal automata [37] provide an elegant algebraic model for describing computations on data words and combining nominal automata with symbolic automata is an interesting research direction: on one hand we know that s-EFA do not enjoy good theoretical properties because they allow comparisons between different characters, and on the other hand nominal automata enjoy decidable properties by restricting what operations one can use to compare data elements.

6.3   New Potential Applications

SMT Solving with Sequences. SMT solvers such as Z3 [24] have drastically changed the world of programming languages and turned previously unsolvable problems into feasible ones. The recent interest in verifying programs operating over sequences has created a need for extending existing SMT solving techniques to handle sequences over complex theories [22,53]. Solvers that are able to handle strings, typically do so by building automata and then performing complex operations over such automata [35]. Existing solvers only handle strings over finite small alphabets [35] and s-FAs have the potential to impact the way in which such solvers for SMT are built. Recently, Z3 [24] has started incorporating s-FAs to reason about sequences. The SMT community has also been discussing how to integrate sequences and regular expressions into the SMT-lib standard [10].

Security. Dalla Preda et al. recently investigated how to use s-FAs to model program binaries [15]. s-FAs can use their state space to capture the control flow of a program and their predicates to abstract the I/O semantics of basic blocks appearing in the programs. This approach unifies existing syntactic and semantic techniques for similarity of binaries and has the promise to lead us to better understand techniques for malware detection in low-level code. The same authors recently started investigating whether, using s-FTs, the same techniques could be extended to perform analysis of reflective code—i.e., code that can self-modify itself at runtime [42].

7   Conclusion

Symbolic automata and transducers have proven to be a versatile and powerful model to reason about practical applications that were beyond the reach of models that operate over finite alphabets. In this paper, we summarized what theoretical results are known for symbolic models, described the numerous extensions of symbolic automata and transducers, and clarified why these models are different from their finite-alphabet counterparts. We also presented the following list of open problems we hope that the research community will help us solve: Can we provide theoretical treatments of the complexities of the algorithms for symbolic models? Can we extend algorithms for automata over finite alphabets to the symbolic setting? Can we combine symbolic automata with other automata models such as nominal automata? Can we use symbolic automata algorithms to design decision procedures for the SMT theory of sequences?

References

1. AutomataDotNet. https://github.com/AutomataDotNet/
2. AutomatArk. https://github.com/lorisdanto/automatark
3. Symbolic Automata. http://pages.cs.wisc.edu/~loris/symbolicautomata.html
4. symbolicautomata. https://github.com/lorisdanto/symbolicautomata/
5. Abdulla, P.A., Deneux, J., Kaati, L., Nilsson, M.: Minimization of non-deterministic automata with large alphabets. In: Farré, J., Litovsky, I., Schmitz, S. (eds.) CIAA 2005. LNCS, vol. 3845, pp. 31–42. Springer, Heidelberg (2006). doi:10.1007/11605157_3
6. Allauzen, C., Mohri, M.: Finitely subsequential transducers. Int. J. Found. Compu. Sci. **14**(6), 983–994 (2003)
7. Alur, R., D'Antoni, L., Raghothaman, M.: Drex: a declarative language for efficiently evaluating regular string transformations. In: ACM SIGPLAN Notices - POPL 2015, vol. 50, no. 1, pp. 125–137 (2015)
8. Argyros, G., Stais, I., Kiayias, A., Keromytis, A.D.: Back in black: towards formal, black box analysis of sanitizers and filters. In: 2016 IEEE Symposium on Security and Privacy (SP), pp. 91–109 (2016)
9. Benedikt, M., Ley, C., Puppis, G.: Automata vs. logics on data words. In: Dawar, A., Veith, H. (eds.) CSL 2010. LNCS, vol. 6247, pp. 110–124. Springer, Heidelberg (2010). doi:10.1007/978-3-642-15205-4_12
10. Bjørner, N., Ganesh, V., Michel, R., Veanes, M.: An SMT-LIB format for sequences and regular expressions. In: SMT Workshop (2012)
11. Bonchi, F., Bonsangue, M.M., Hansen, H.H., Panangaden, P., Rutten, J.J.M.M., Silva, A.: Algebra-coalgebra duality in Brzozowski's minimization algorithm. ACM Trans. Comput. Logic **15**(1), 3:1–3:29 (2014)
12. Botinčan, M., Babić, D.: Sigma*: symbolic learning of input-output specifications. In: ACM SIGPLAN Notices - POPL 2013, vol. 48, no. 1, pp. 443–456 (2013)

13. Bouajjani, A., Habermehl, P., Vojnar, T.: Abstract regular model checking. In: Alur, R., Peled, D.A. (eds.) CAV 2004. LNCS, vol. 3114, pp. 372–386. Springer, Heidelberg (2004). doi:10.1007/978-3-540-27813-9_29
14. Chandra, A.K., Kozen, D.C., Stockmeyer, L.J.: Alternation. J. ACM **28**(1), 114–133 (1981)
15. Dalla Preda, M., Giacobazzi, R., Lakhotia, A., Mastroeni, I.: Abstract symbolic automata: mixed syntactic/semantic similarity analysis of executables. In: ACM SIGPLAN Notices - POPL 2015, vol. 50, no. 1, pp. 329–341 (2015)
16. D'Antoni, L., Alur, R.: Symbolic visibly pushdown automata. In: Biere, A., Bloem, R. (eds.) CAV 2014. LNCS, vol. 8559, pp. 209–225. Springer, Cham (2014). doi:10.1007/978-3-319-08867-9_14
17. D'Antoni, L., Kincaid, Z., Wang, F.: A symbolic decision procedure for symbolic alternating finite automata. In: MFPS 2017 (2017)
18. D'Antoni, L., Veanes, M.: Minimization of symbolic automata. In: ACM SIGPLAN Notices - POPL 2014, vol. 49, no. 1, pp. 541–553 (2014)
19. D'antoni, L., Veanes, M.: Extended symbolic finite automata and transducers. Form. Methods Syst. Des. **47**(1), 93–119 (2015)
20. D'Antoni, L., Veanes, M.: Minimization of symbolic tree automata. In: LICS 2016, pp. 873–882. ACM, New York (2016)
21. D'Antoni, L., Veanes, M.: Forward bisimulations for nondeterministic symbolic finite automata. In: Legay, A., Margaria, T. (eds.) TACAS 2017. LNCS, vol. 10205, pp. 518–534. Springer, Heidelberg (2017). doi:10.1007/978-3-662-54577-5_30
22. D'Antoni, L., Veanes, M.: Monadic second-order logic on finite sequences. In: ACM SIGPLAN Notices - POPL'17, vol. 52, no. 1, pp. 232–245 (2017)
23. D'Antoni, L., Veanes, M., Livshits, B., Molnar, D.: Fast: a transducer-based language for tree manipulation. ACM TOPLAS **38**(1), 1–32 (2015)
24. Moura, L., Bjørner, N.: Z3: an efficient SMT solver. In: Ramakrishnan, C.R., Rehof, J. (eds.) TACAS 2008. LNCS, vol. 4963, pp. 337–340. Springer, Heidelberg (2008). doi:10.1007/978-3-540-78800-3_24
25. Drews, S., D'Antoni, L.: Learning symbolic automata. In: Legay, A., Margaria, T. (eds.) TACAS 2017. LNCS, vol. 10205, pp. 173–189. Springer, Heidelberg (2017). doi:10.1007/978-3-662-54577-5_10
26. Flanagan, C., Qadeer, S.: Predicate abstraction for software verification. ACM SIGPLAN Notices - POPL 2002, **37**(1), 191–202 (2002)
27. Fülöp, Z., Gyenizse, P.: On injectivity of deterministic top-down tree transducers. Inf. Process. Lett. **48**(4), 183–188 (1993)
28. Fülöp, Z., Vogler, H.: Forward and backward application of symbolic tree transducers. Acta Informatica **51**(5), 297–325 (2014)
29. Griffiths, T.: The unsolvability of the equivalence problem for Λ-free nondeterministic generalized machines. J. ACM **15**, 409–413 (1968)
30. Hooimeijer, P., Livshits, B., Molnar, D., Saxena, P., Veanes, M.: Fast and precise sanitizer analysis with BEK. In: Proceedings of the 20th USENIX Conference on Security, SEC 2011, Berkeley, CA, USA, p. 1. USENIX Association (2011)
31. Hooimeijer, P., Veanes, M.: An evaluation of automata algorithms for string analysis. In: Jhala, R., Schmidt, D. (eds.) VMCAI 2011. LNCS, vol. 6538, pp. 248–262. Springer, Heidelberg (2011). doi:10.1007/978-3-642-18275-4_18
32. Hopcroft, J.: An $n\log n$ algorithm for minimizing states in a finite automaton. In: Kohavi, Z. (ed.) Theory of Machines and Computations (Proceedings of International Symposium Technion, Haifa), pp. 189–196 (1971)
33. Hu, Q., D'Antoni, L.: Automatic program inversion using symbolic transducers. In: ACM SIGPLAN Notices - PLDI 2017 (2017, to appear)

34. Keil, M., Thiemann, P.: Symbolic solving of extended regular expression inequalities. In: FSTTCS 2014, LIPIcs, pp. 175–186 (2014)
35. Liang, T., Reynolds, A., Tinelli, C., Barrett, C., Deters, M.: A DPLL(T) theory solver for a theory of strings and regular expressions. In: Biere, A., Bloem, R. (eds.) CAV 2014. LNCS, vol. 8559, pp. 646–662. Springer, Cham (2014). doi:10.1007/978-3-319-08867-9_43
36. Mamouras, K., Raghotaman, M., Alur, R., Ives, Z.G., Khanna, S.: StreamQRE: modular specification and efficient evaluation of quantitative queries over streaming data. In: ACM SIGPLAN Notices - PLDI 2017 (2017, to appear)
37. Moerman, J., Sammartino, M., Silva, A., Klin, B., Szynwelski, M.: Learning nominal automata. In: ACM SIGPLAN Notices - POPL 2017, vol. 52, no. 1, pp. 613–625 (2017)
38. Mohri, M.: Finite-state transducers in language and speech processing. Comput. Linguist. **23**(2), 269–311 (1997)
39. Mytkowicz, T., Musuvathi, M., Schulte, W.: Data-parallel finite-state machines. In: ACM SIGPLAN Notices - ASPLOS 2014, vol. 49, no. 4, pp. 529–542 (2014)
40. Ohmann, P., Brooks, A., D'Antoni, L., Liblit, B.: Control-flow recovery from partial failure reports. In: ACM SIGPLAN Notices - PLDI 2017 (2017, to appear)
41. Paige, R., Tarjan, R.E.: Three partition refinement algorithms. SIAM J. Comput. **16**(6), 973–989 (1987)
42. Dalla Preda, M., Giacobazzi, R., Mastroeni, I.: Completeness in approximate transduction. In: Rival, X. (ed.) SAS 2016. LNCS, vol. 9837, pp. 126–146. Springer, Heidelberg (2016). doi:10.1007/978-3-662-53413-7_7
43. Rozier, K.Y., Vardi, M.Y.: A multi-encoding approach for LTL symbolic satisfiability checking. In: Butler, M., Schulte, W. (eds.) FM 2011. LNCS, vol. 6664, pp. 417–431. Springer, Heidelberg (2011). doi:10.1007/978-3-642-21437-0_31
44. Saarikivi, O., Veanes, M.: Minimization of symbolic transducers. In: Majumdar, R., Kunčak, V. (eds.) CAV 2017. LNCS, vol. 10426, pp. 176–196. Springer, Cham (2017)
45. Saarikivi, O., Veanes, M., Mytkowicz, T., Musuvathi, M.: Fusing effectful comprehensions. In: ACM SIGPLAN Notices - PLDI 2017. ACM (2017, to appear)
46. Schützenberger, M.P.: Sur une variante des fonctions séquentielles. Theoret. Comput. Sci. **4**, 47–57 (1977)
47. Stearns, R.E., Hunt, H.B.: On the equivalence and containment problems for unambiguous regular expressions, grammars, and automata. In: SFCS 1981, pp. 74–81, October 1981
48. Tillmann, N., Halleux, J.: Pex–white box test generation for .NET. In: Beckert, B., Hähnle, R. (eds.) TAP 2008. LNCS, vol. 4966, pp. 134–153. Springer, Heidelberg (2008). doi:10.1007/978-3-540-79124-9_10
49. van Noord, G., Gerdemann, D.: Finite state transducers with predicates and identities. Grammars **4**(3), 263–286 (2001)
50. Veanes, M.: Symbolic string transformations with regular lookahead and rollback. In: Voronkov, A., Virbitskaite, I. (eds.) PSI 2014. LNCS, vol. 8974, pp. 335–350. Springer, Heidelberg (2015). doi:10.1007/978-3-662-46823-4_27
51. Veanes, M., Bjørner, N.: Symbolic tree transducers. In: Clarke, E., Virbitskaite, I., Voronkov, A. (eds.) PSI 2011. LNCS, vol. 7162, pp. 377–393. Springer, Heidelberg (2012). doi:10.1007/978-3-642-29709-0_32
52. Veanes, M., Bjørner, N.: Symbolic tree automata. Informat. Process. Lett. **115**(3), 418–424 (2015)

53. Veanes, M., Bjørner, N., Moura, L.: Symbolic automata constraint solving. In: Fermüller, C.G., Voronkov, A. (eds.) LPAR 2010. LNCS, vol. 6397, pp. 640–654. Springer, Heidelberg (2010). doi:10.1007/978-3-642-16242-8_45

54. Veanes, M., Bjørner, N., Nachmanson, L., Bereg, S.: Monadic decomposition. J. ACM **64**(2), 14:1–14:28 (2017)

55. Veanes, M., de Halleux, P., Tillmann, N.: Rex: symbolic regular expression explorer. In: ICST 2010, pp. 498–507. IEEE (2010)

56. Veanes, M., Grigorenko, P., de Halleux, P., Tillmann, N.: Symbolic query exploration. In: Breitman, K., Cavalcanti, A. (eds.) ICFEM 2009. LNCS, vol. 5885, pp. 49–68. Springer, Heidelberg (2009). doi:10.1007/978-3-642-10373-5_3

57. Veanes, M., Hooimeijer, P., Livshits, B., Molnar, D., Bjørner, N.: Symbolic finite state transducers: algorithms and applications. In: ACM SIGPLAN Notices - POPL 2012, vol. 47, no. 1, pp. 137–150 (2012)

58. Veanes, M., Mytkowicz, T., Molnar, D., Livshits, B.: Data-parallel string-manipulating programs. In: ACM SIGPLAN Notices - POPL 2015, vol. 50, no. 1, pp. 139–152 (2015)

59. Watson, B.W.: Implementing and using finite automata toolkits. In: Extended Finite State Models of Language, pp. 19–36. Cambridge University Press (1999)

Maximum Satisfiability in Software Analysis: Applications and Techniques

Xujie Si[1], Xin Zhang[1], Radu Grigore[2], and Mayur Naik[1(✉)]

[1] University of Pennsylvania, Philadelphia, USA
mhnaik@cis.upenn.edu
[2] University of Kent, Canterbury, UK

Abstract. A central challenge in software analysis concerns balancing different competing tradeoffs. To address this challenge, we propose an approach based on the Maximum Satisfiability (MaxSAT) problem, an optimization extension of the Boolean Satisfiability (SAT) problem. We demonstrate the approach on three diverse applications that advance the state-of-the-art in balancing tradeoffs in software analysis. Enabling these applications on real-world programs necessitates solving large MaxSAT instances comprising over 10^{30} clauses in a sound and optimal manner. We propose a general framework that scales to such instances by iteratively expanding a subset of clauses while providing soundness and optimality guarantees. We also present new techniques to instantiate and optimize the framework.

1 Introduction

Designing a suitable software analysis is a challenging endeavor. Besides the fact that any non-trivial analysis problem is undecidable in general, various practical aspects drive the need for assumptions and approximations: program behaviors that the analysis intends to check may be impossible to define precisely (e.g., what constitutes a security vulnerability), computing exact answers may be prohibitively costly (e.g., worst-case exponential in the size of the analyzed program), and parts of the analyzed program may be missing or opaque to the analysis. These theoretical and practical issues in turn necessitate balancing various competing tradeoffs in designing an analysis, such as soundness, precision, efficiency, and user effort.

Constraint-based analysis [3] is a popular approach to software analysis. The core idea underlying this approach is to divide a software analysis task into two separate steps: *constraint generation* and *constraint resolution*. The former produces constraints from a given program that constitute a declarative specification of the desired information about the program, while the latter then computes the desired information by solving the constraints. This approach provides many benefits such as separating the analysis specification from the analysis implementation, and allowing to leverage sophisticated off-the-shelf constraint solvers. Due to these benefits, the constraint-based approach has achieved remarkable success, as exemplified by the many applications of SAT and SMT solvers.

ⓒ Springer International Publishing AG 2017
R. Majumdar and V. Kunčak (Eds.): CAV 2017, Part I, LNCS 10426, pp. 68–94, 2017.
DOI: 10.1007/978-3-319-63387-9_4

Existing constraint-based analyses predominantly involve formulating and solving a decision problem, which is ill-equipped to handle the tradeoffs involved in software analysis. A natural approach to address this limitation is to extend the decision problem to allow incorporating optimization objectives. These objective functions serve to effectively formulate various tradeoffs while preserving the benefits of the constraint-based approach.

Maximum Satisfiability [1], or MaxSAT for short, is one such optimization extension of the Boolean Satisfiability (SAT) problem. A MaxSAT instance comprises a system of mixed hard and soft clauses, wherein a soft clause is simply a hard clause with a weight. The goal of a (exact) MaxSAT solver is to find a solution that is *sound*, i.e., satisfies all the hard clauses, and *optimal*, i.e., maximizes the sum of the weights of satisfied soft clauses. Thus, hard clauses enable to enforce soundness conditions of a software analysis while soft clauses enable to encode different tradeoffs.

We demonstrate a MaxSAT based approach to balancing tradeoffs in software analysis. We show the versatility of this approach using three diverse applications that advance the state-of-the-art. The first concerns automated verification with the goal of finding a cheap yet precise program abstraction for a given analysis. The second concerns interactive verification with the goal of overcoming the incompleteness of a given analysis in a manner that minimizes the user's effort. The third concerns static bug detection with the goal of accurately classifying alarms reported by a given analysis by learning from a subset of labeled alarms.

Enabling these applications on real-world programs necessitates solving large MaxSAT instances comprising over 10^{30} clauses in a sound and optimal manner, which is beyond the reach of existing MaxSAT solvers. We propose a lazy grounding framework that scales to such instances by iteratively expanding a subset of clauses while providing soundness and optimality guarantees. The framework subsumes many grounding techniques in the literature. We also present two new grounding techniques, one bottom-up and one top-down, as instantiations of the framework. Finally, we propose two techniques, eager grounding and incremental solving, to optimize the framework.

The rest of the paper is organized as follows. Section 2 reviews the syntax and semantics of MaxSAT and its variants. Section 3 presents our three applications and demonstrates how to formulate them using MaxSAT. Section 4 presents our techniques and framework for MaxSAT solving. Section 5 surveys related work, Sect. 6 discusses future directions, and Sect. 7 concludes.

2   Background

In this section, we cover basic definitions and notations. We begin by defining the MaxSAT problem and its variants (Sect. 2.1). The input for MaxSAT is a CNF formula obtained by grounding a logic formula. Next, we introduce the logic used in subsequent sections (Sect. 2.2).

2.1   MaxSAT

The MaxSAT problem is a variant of the SAT problem. Given a propositional boolean formula in CNF whose clauses can be weighted, it seeks a model that maximizes the sum of the weights of the satisfied clauses. These concepts are defined formally in the next section in a more general setting. We illustrate them in this section using an example.

	edges:	source:	bias:
	$\neg x_1 \vee x_2$	x_4	$\neg x_1^{(1)}$
	$\neg x_2 \vee x_3$		$\neg x_2^{(1)}$
	$\neg x_3 \vee x_1$		$\neg x_3^{(1)}$
	$\neg x_2 \vee x_4$		$\neg x_4^{(1)}$

Fig. 1. A simple digraph and its representation as a propositional CNF formula. A clause with no weight is a hard clause; for example, x_4 is the same as $x_4^{(\infty)}$.

Consider the graph in Fig. 1. We can represent its edges by clauses which are implications. We can then ask which vertices are reachable from certain source vertices. Suppose we choose vertex 4 to be the source. Then, a possible model is $x_1 = x_2 = x_3 = x_4 = 1$, but it is not the expected one. We include a bias to indicate that variables be 0, if at all possible. The bias clauses have weight 1. None of the other clauses (encoding edges or sources) should be violated at the expense of a bias clause. Thus, we should pick their weight to be high enough. In this example, 5 would suffice. But, to avoid having to specify this high-enough weight, we allow ∞ as a weight. We call clauses with infinite weight *hard*; and we call clauses with finite weight *soft*. This leads to the most general form of the MaxSAT problem, called *weighted partial MaxSAT*, or WPMS for short. We use this form throughout the paper. We state its decision version below.

Problem 1 (WPMS). Given a weight w and a weighted propositional CNF formula $\phi := \bigwedge_i \varphi_i^{(w_i)}$, decide if ϕ has a model for which the weight of the satisfied soft clauses is $\geq w$.

2.2   Relational First-Order Logic with Weights

Propositional logic is too low level and too inefficient for our needs. Let us see why on the example in Fig. 1. There, we have two distinct concepts: the digraph structure, and the notion of reachability. However, we could not keep these concepts apart: our choice of how to represent edges is very much driven by the goal of performing reachability queries. In this section, we will see that it is possible to keep these concepts distinct if we move to quantifier-free relational first-order logic with weights. Moreover, this representation is not only more convenient, but also enables faster solving through lazy grounding.

First-order logic has been extended with quantitative notions in many ways: possibility theory [19], Bayesian probabilities [29], Markov logic networks [18], and others. Here, we present a simple extension with weights, for which ground formulas correspond to MaxSAT instances.

variable	$v ::= x \mid y \mid z \mid \ldots$	positive literal	$\ell^+ ::= r(\bar{t})$
constant symbol	$c ::= a \mid b \mid c \mid \ldots$	negative literal	$\ell^- ::= \neg \ell^+$
relation symbol	$r ::= P \mid Q \mid R \mid \ldots$	literal	$\ell ::= \ell^+ \mid \ell^-$
term	$t ::= v \mid c$	clause	$\varphi ::= \ell \vee \ldots \vee \ell$
weight	w	weighted formula	$\phi ::= \varphi^{(w)} \wedge \ldots \wedge \varphi^{(w)}$

Fig. 2. Syntax for quantifier-free relational first-order logic with weights.

Figure 2 shows the standard syntax for quantifier-free relational first-order logic formulas in CNF, but it also introduces weights on clauses. We assume a countable set of *variables* $(x, y, z, \ldots)$, and countable sets of *symbols* for *constants* $(a, b, c, \ldots)$ and *relations* $(P, Q, R, \ldots)$. A *term* is a constant symbol or a variable. Each relation has a fixed *arity* k, and takes k terms as arguments. A *literal* ℓ is either a relation or its negation; the former is a *positive literal*, the latter is a *negative literal*. A *clause* φ is a disjunction of literals. A *weight* w is a nonnegative real number. A *weighted clause* $\varphi^{(w)}$ is a clause φ together with a weight w. A *weighted formula* ϕ is a conjunction of weighted clauses. As usual, we interpret variables as universal. Occasionally, we emphasize that formula ϕ uses variables $x_1, \ldots, x_n$ by writing $\phi(x_1, \ldots, x_n)$; similarly for clauses.

Without weights, one usually defines the semantics of formulas by specifying how they evaluate to a boolean. With weights, we define the semantics of formulas by specifying how they evaluate to a weight, which is a nonnegative real. In both cases, the evaluation is done on a model.

A (finite) *model* $\sigma = \langle U, \{c_i^\sigma\}, \{P_i^\sigma\} \rangle$ consists of a finite *universe* U together with an interpretation of (i) each constant symbol c_i as an element c_i^σ of U, and (ii) each k-ary relation symbol P_i as a k-ary relation $P_i^\sigma \subseteq U^k$. This is a standard setup [36, Chap. 2].

$$\llbracket \varphi_1^{(w_1)} \wedge \ldots \wedge \varphi_n^{(w_n)} \rrbracket_\sigma := w_1 \cdot \#_\sigma(\varphi_1) + \cdots + w_n \cdot \#_\sigma(\varphi_n)$$
$$\#_\sigma(\varphi(x_1, \ldots, x_n)) := |\{ (c_1, \ldots, c_n) \in U^n \mid \sigma \models \varphi(c_1, \ldots, c_n) \}|$$
$$\sigma \models \ell_1 \vee \ldots \vee \ell_n \text{ iff } \sigma \models \ell_i \text{ for some } i$$
$$\sigma \models P(c_1, \ldots, c_n) \text{ iff } (c_1^\sigma, \ldots, c_n^\sigma) \in P^\sigma$$
$$\sigma \models \neg P(c_1, \ldots, c_n) \text{ iff } (c_1^\sigma, \ldots, c_n^\sigma) \notin P^\sigma$$

Fig. 3. Semantics for quantifier-free relational first-order logic with weights.

Figure 3 shows the semantics for quantifier-free relational first-order logic with weights. A clause/formula is said to be *ground* if it contains no variable occurrence. A ground clause φ is said to *hold* in a model σ when it contains a literal that holds in σ. A ground positive literal $P(c_1, \ldots, c_n)$ holds in σ when $(c_1, \ldots, c_n) \in P^\sigma$; a ground negative literal $\neg P(c_1, \ldots, c_n)$ holds in σ when $(c_1, \ldots, c_n) \notin P^\sigma$. For a clause $\varphi(x_1, \ldots, x_n)$ we define $\#_\sigma(\varphi)$ to be the number of groundings of φ that hold in σ. Given a model σ, the value of a weighted clause $\varphi^{(w)}$ is $w \cdot \#_\sigma(\varphi)$, and the value $[\![\phi]\!]_\sigma$ of a formula ϕ is the sum of the values of its clauses.

In the rest of the paper, we shall see how several practical problems concerning software analysis (abstraction refinement, user interaction, identifying likely bugs) can be phrased as instances of the following problem.

Problem 2. Given a formula ϕ, find a model σ that maximizes the weight $[\![\phi]\!]_\sigma$.

As in the case of WPMS, we allow infinite weights as a shorthand for very large weights. It is possible to show that the above problem is equivalent to the problem of *exact* MAP inference for Markov logic networks [18].

Example 1. Now let us revisit the example from Fig. 1. This time we represent the problem by a formula ϕ with the following clauses:

edges:	bias:	reachability:
$\texttt{edge}(1, 2)$	$\neg\texttt{path}(x, y)^{(1)}$	$\texttt{path}(x, x)$
$\texttt{edge}(2, 3)$	$\neg\texttt{edge}(x, y)^{(1)}$	$\texttt{path}(x, z) \vee \neg\texttt{path}(x, y) \vee \neg\texttt{edge}(y, z)$
$\texttt{edge}(3, 1)$		
$\texttt{edge}(2, 4)$		

There are several things to note here. First, we disentangled the representation of the digraph from the queries we want to perform. The digraph structure is represented by the relation $\texttt{edge}^\sigma$, which is specified by 5 clauses: 4 hard and 1 soft. The notion of reachability is represented by the relation $\texttt{path}^\sigma$, which is specified by 3 clauses: 2 hard and 1 soft. The maximum weight we can achieve is $[\![\phi]\!]_\sigma = 15$, for example by using model $\sigma = \langle U, 1^\sigma, 2^\sigma, 3^\sigma, 4^\sigma, \texttt{edge}^\sigma, \texttt{path}^\sigma \rangle$ with universe $U = \{1^\sigma, 2^\sigma, 3^\sigma, 4^\sigma\}$, and relations $\texttt{edge} = \{(1^\sigma, 2^\sigma), (2^\sigma, 3^\sigma), (3^\sigma, 1^\sigma), (2^\sigma, 4^\sigma)\}$ and $\texttt{path} = (\{1^\sigma, 2^\sigma, 3^\sigma\} \times \{1^\sigma, 2^\sigma, 3^\sigma, 4^\sigma\}) \cup \{(4^\sigma, 4^\sigma)\}$.

We will often omit the superscript σ when there is no danger of confusing a symbol with what it denotes. Further, in all our applications we will have constant symbols to denote all elements of the universe, so we will omit listing the constant symbols explicitly. Thus, for the model in Example 1, we simply write $\sigma = \langle \texttt{edge}, \texttt{path} \rangle$. On the topic of simplifying notation, we note that clauses are often *definite Horn*; that is, they contain exactly one positive literal. These should be thought of as implications. So, for definite Horn clauses, we may write $\ell_1^+ \wedge \ldots \wedge \ell_n^+ \xrightarrow{(w)} \ell^+$ instead of $\left(\ell_1^- \vee \ldots \ell_n^- \vee \ell^+\right)^{(w)}$.

We remark that the development so far would also work if instead of quantifier-free clauses φ we would have arbitrary first-order logic formulas. In particular, we could still define the notion of a weight $[\![\phi]\!]_\sigma$ in the same way, and Problem 2 would not change. However, we found this fragment to be expressive enough for many applications (see Sect. 3), and it has the advantage that its groundings are WPMS instances. For this, we need to see ground literals as boolean variables in a WPMS instance.

Example 2. Recall Example 1. For each ground literal $\texttt{path}(a, b)$ we introduce a boolean variable p_{ab}. Then, for example, the clause $\neg\texttt{path}(x, y)^{(1)}$ leads to 16 WPMS clauses, each containing one boolean variable: $p_{11}^{(1)}, p_{12}^{(1)}, p_{13}^{(1)}, \ldots$

3   Applications

We demonstrate our MaxSAT based approach to tackle the central challenge of balancing different tradeoffs in software analysis. We do so by illustrating the approach on three mainstream applications: automated verification (Sect. 3.1), interactive verification (Sect. 3.2), and static bug detection (Sect. 3.3). Specifically, we use the graph reachability analysis from Example 1 as an instance to explain how we can augment a conventional analysis in a systematic and general manner to balance these tradoffs. Throughout, we observe a recurring theme of using weights for encoding two conceptually different quantities: costs and probabilities.

3.1   Automated Verification

A key challenge in automated verification concerns finding a program abstraction that balances efficiency and precision. A common approach to achieve such a balance is to use a strategy called CEGAR (counter-example guided abstraction refinement) [17]. To apply this strategy, however, analysis designers often resort to heuristics that are specialized to the analysis task at hand. In this section, we show how to systematically apply CEGAR to constraint-based analyses.

```
f() { v1 = new ...;              g() { v4 = new ...;
      v2 = id1(v1);                    v5 = id1(v4);
      v3 = id2(v2);                    v6 = id2(v5);
   q2: assert(v3 != v1);           q1: assert(v6 != v1);
}                                }
id1(v) { return v; }             id2(v) { return v; }
```

Fig. 4. Example program.

Example. Consider the program in Fig. 4. We are interested in analyzing its aliasing properties; in particular, we want to check if the two assertions at labels q1 and q2 hold. Functions id1 and id2 simply return their argument. It is easy to see that the assertion at q1 holds but the assertion at q2 does not. To conclude this, however, an analysis must reason precisely about the calls to functions id1 and id2. When id1 is called from f, its variable v is of course different from its variable v when called from g. Thus, the analysis should track two variants of v, one for each *context*. In general, however, the analysis cannot track all possible contexts, because there may be an unbounded number of them due to recursive functions. It may be prohibitively expensive to track all contexts even if there are a bounded number of them. So, for both theoretical and practical reasons, some contexts cannot be distinguished. In our example, not distinguishing the two contexts leads to considering variable v in id1 to be the same, no matter from where id1 is called. Alternatively, the calls and returns to and from id1 are modelled by jumps: the return becomes a nondeterministic jump because it can go back to either f or g. This causes the analysis to conclude that the assertion at q1 might fail. Indeed, one can start the execution at the beginning of f, jump into id1 when it is called, but then 'return' after the call to id1 in g, and then continue until q1 is reached. In summary, on the one hand, we cannot distinguish all contexts for efficiency reasons; and on the other hand, merging contexts can lead to imprecision.

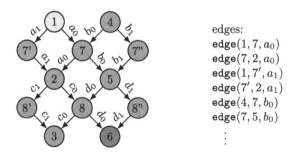

Fig. 5. Digraph model of the example program in Fig. 4. Nodes 1, 2, and 3 stand for the basic blocks of function f; nodes 4, 5, and 6 stand for the basic blocks of function g; nodes 7 and 8 stand for the bodies of id1 and id2, respectively. Nodes 7' and 7'' are clones of 7; nodes 8' and 8'' are clones of 8. Edges representing matching calls and returns have the same label.

In Fig. 5, we formulate an analysis that can answer whether assertions at q1 and q2 hold. Our formulation is similar to the reachability problem we saw earlier in Example 1. The main difference is that edges have labels, which allows us to use them selectively.

$$\texttt{path}(x, x)$$
$$\texttt{path}(x, y) \land \texttt{edge}(y, z, u) \land \texttt{abs}(u) \rightarrow \texttt{path}(x, z) \qquad \text{(Path-Def)}$$

We have two ways to model the call from f to id1: by inlining or by a jump. Intuitively, $\texttt{abs}(a_1)$ means we use inlining, and $\texttt{abs}(a_0)$ means we use a jump.

To show that the assertion at q1 holds, we need to show that there is no path from 1 to 6, for *some* choice of how to model each function call. To this end, we proceed as follows. First, we introduce the hard constraint $\neg\texttt{path}(1, 6)$. Second, we implement a CEGAR loop. In each iteration, we have some choice of how to model each function call. We can represent this choice either by selectively generating edges, or by selectively deactivating some edges. For example, we could include all edges but deactivate some of them by including clauses

$$\neg\mathsf{abs}(a_1) \qquad \neg\mathsf{abs}(b_1) \qquad \neg\mathsf{abs}(c_1) \qquad \neg\mathsf{abs}(d_1)$$

This would prevent inlining from being used. In Fig. 5, we see a path from 1 to 6 that uses only edges with labels from $\{a_0, b_0, c_0, d_0\}$. This means that $\neg\mathsf{path}(1,6)$ is inconsistent with modelling all function calls by jumps. Thus, we should change how we model some function calls. We prefer to keep as many jumps as possible so that we do as little inlining as possible:

$$\mathsf{abs}(a_0)^{(1)} \qquad \mathsf{abs}(b_0)^{(1)} \qquad \mathsf{abs}(c_0)^{(1)} \qquad \mathsf{abs}(d_0)^{(1)}$$

The solver could answer with a model in which $\mathsf{abs} = \{a_0, b_0, c_0\}$. In that case, in the next iteration we inline the call from g to $\mathsf{id2}$, by including clauses

$$\begin{array}{llll} \mathsf{abs}(a_0)^{(1)} & \mathsf{abs}(b_0)^{(1)} & \mathsf{abs}(c_0)^{(1)} & \neg\mathsf{abs}(d_0) \\ \neg\mathsf{abs}(a_1) & \neg\mathsf{abs}(b_1) & \neg\mathsf{abs}(c_1) & \mathsf{abs}(d_1) \end{array}$$

Now the solution will have to disrupt the path $1 \overset{a_0}{\to} 7 \overset{b_0}{\to} 5 \overset{d_1}{\to} 8'' \overset{d_1}{\to} 6$, by not including one of a_0 and b_0 in abs. Suppose the solver answers with $\mathsf{abs} = \{a_0, c_0, d_1\}$. Then, in the next CEGAR iteration we try to model both calls from g by inlining.

$$\begin{array}{llll} \mathsf{abs}(a_0)^{(1)} & \neg\mathsf{abs}(b_0) & \mathsf{abs}(c_0)^{(1)} & \neg\mathsf{abs}(d_0) \\ \neg\mathsf{abs}(a_1) & \mathsf{abs}(b_1) & \neg\mathsf{abs}(c_1) & \mathsf{abs}(d_1) \end{array}$$

The solver returns $\mathsf{abs} = \{a_0, b_1, c_0, d_1\}$. Since the maximum possible weight was achieved, we know that no further refinement is needed: there exists a way to model function calls that allows us to conclude the assertion at $\mathsf{q1}$ holds.

General Case. The core idea is to formulate the problem of finding a good abstraction as an optimization problem on a logic with weights (see Problem 2). In general, the encoding of the program need not be a digraph, and the analysis need not be reachability. However, the abstraction will often select between different ways of modeling program semantics, and will be represented by a relation similar to the relation abs in our example. Accordingly, we model the program, the analysis, and the query by a formula ϕ, without relying on its structure. We define the space of abstractions to be a boolean assignment to sites. (In our example, the sites are the four function calls.) Suppose the current abstraction is $A : \mathsf{Site} \to \{0, 1\}$. Then, we ask for a model of maximum weight for the formula

$$\phi \wedge \left(\bigwedge_{A(s)=0} \mathsf{abs}(s_0)^{(1)} \wedge \neg\mathsf{abs}(s_1) \right) \wedge \left(\bigwedge_{A(s)=1} \neg\mathsf{abs}(s_0) \wedge \mathsf{abs}(s_1) \right)$$

For each $s \in$ Site, we have two constant symbols, s_0 and s_1. If the formula has a model of maximum weight, which is the number of imprecise sites, then the query is proven. If the formula has no model that satisfies all its hard clauses, then no abstraction can prove the query. Otherwise, by inspecting the model, we can find a more precise abstraction to try next.

We refer the reader to [70] for instantiations of this approach to pointer analysis and typestate analysis of Java programs.

Discussion. One can design an automated analysis that balances efficiency and precision as follows: (1) design a basic constraint-based analysis; (2) parameterize the analysis; and (3) find a good abstraction by solving an optimization problem. We saw a simple example of an analysis which tracked information flow in a program. There are, however, many other analyses that use constraint-based formulations [11, 32, 64–66].

What does it mean to parameterize an analysis? Compare Example 1 with Fig. 5. In one we have edges; in the other we have edges that can be activated or deactivated. By constraining the relation **abs**, we were able to model function calls either by jumps (cheap) or by inlining (expensive). The intuition is that inlining is expensive due to nesting. This intuition also holds for other context sensitivity mechanisms, such as k-CFA and k-object sensitivity. Thus, there is often a way to introduce a relation **abs** that tells us, for each of several sites in the program, whether to use cheap or expensive semantics.

Finally, once the relation **abs** is introduced, we can implement the CEGAR loop sketched above, which achieves efficiency by increasing precision selectively. In [70], multiple queries are handled simultaneously: the result of the CEGAR loop is to classify assertions into those verified and those impossible to verify. By the latter, we mean that they would not be verified by the most expensive abstraction, if we were to try it. But the CEGAR loop will typically reach the conclusion that an assertion is impossible to verify without actually trying the most expensive abstraction. Another extension [24] describes an alternate CEGAR strategy that considers not only the relative cost of different abstractions but also their probability of success.

3.2   Interactive Verification

Sound analyses produce a large number of alarms which include a small number of real bugs. Users then sift through these alarms, classifying them into false alarms and real bugs. In other words, a computer and a user collaborate on finding bugs: in a first phase, the computer does its work; in a second phase, the user does their work. In certain situations, however, it is possible to reduce the total amount of work done by the user by interleaving: the computer and the user take turns at doing small amounts of work. The idea is that we should let users perform certain tasks they are better suited for and we should use the results of their work to guide the computer's work.

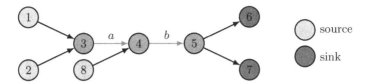

Fig. 6. First source-sink information-flow example: if some edges are spurious, then some source-sink flows are interrupted.

Example. Consider the information-flow example from Fig. 6. We wish to know if there are paths from sources to sinks. If the analysis runs with no help from the user, it presents the following alarms:

$$\mathsf{path}(1,6) \quad \mathsf{path}(1,7) \quad \mathsf{path}(2,6) \quad \mathsf{path}(2,7) \quad \mathsf{path}(8,6) \quad \mathsf{path}(8,7)$$

After inspecting all 6 alarms, the user decides that all of them are false alarms.

Now consider an alternative scenario. Suppose the analysis suspects that the edges marked as a and b may be spurious. Then, before presenting a large set of alarms to the user, it may be beneficial to ask the user if a or b are spurious. If a is spurious, then 4 alarms disappear; if b is spurious, then 6 alarms disappear. It is therefore better to ask the user about edge b. We can formulate this choice of question, between a and b, as an optimization problem.

As before (Sect. 3.1), we use labels on edges. The definition of reachability remains as in (**Path-Def**). But here labels represent something different: we use labels a and b to identify each of the possibly spurious edges, and we use one extra label c for all the other edges.

$$\begin{array}{llll}
\mathsf{edge}(3,4,a) & \mathsf{edge}(1,2,c) & \mathsf{edge}(2,3,c) & \mathsf{edge}(8,4,c) \\
\mathsf{edge}(4,5,b) & \mathsf{edge}(5,6,c) & \mathsf{edge}(5,7,c) & \mathsf{abs}(c)
\end{array}$$

We require that the non-spurious edges are selected, and that at most one of the other edges are deselected:

$$\mathsf{abs}(c) \qquad \mathsf{abs}(a) \vee \mathsf{abs}(b)$$

Finally, we want a maximum number of alarms to disappear:

$$\begin{array}{lll}
\neg\mathsf{path}(1,6)^{(1)} & \neg\mathsf{path}(2,6)^{(1)} & \neg\mathsf{path}(8,6)^{(1)} \\
\neg\mathsf{path}(1,7)^{(1)} & \neg\mathsf{path}(2,7)^{(1)} & \neg\mathsf{path}(8,7)^{(1)}
\end{array}$$

For the formula built with the clauses described so far, the model of maximum weight has $\mathsf{abs} = \{a,c\}$ and weight 6. We interpret this to mean that edge b may rule out 6 alarms.

General Case. We wish to save user time by bringing to their attention root cause of imprecision in the analysis that may be responsible for many false alarms. The core idea is to formulate the problem of finding a good question to ask the user as an optimization problem on a logic with weights (Problem 2). As before (Sect. 3.1), we assume that the analysis is described by some formula ϕ, and we assume the existence of a special relation abs. In addition, we also assume that we are given a list $\ell_1^+, \ldots, \ell_n^+$ of grounded positive literals that represent alarms. Then, we ask for a model of maximum weight for the formula

$$\phi \wedge \left(\bigwedge_{i=1}^{n} \left(\neg \ell_i^+ \right)^{(1)} \right) \wedge \left(\bigwedge_{1 \leq i < j \leq m} \mathsf{abs}(a_i) \vee \mathsf{abs}(a_j) \right) \wedge \mathsf{abs}(c)$$

The constants $a_1, \ldots, a_m$ identify the possibly spurious edges, while the constant c marks all the other edges. In a model of maximum weight, at most one of $a_1, \ldots, a_m$ will be missing from the relation abs. The missing constant identifies the question we should ask the user. The maximum weight is the number of alarms that will be classified as false, should the user answer 'no'. If none of $a_1, \ldots, a_m$ is missing from abs, then none of the alarms can be caused by imprecision of the analysis.

We refer the reader to [69] for instantiations of this approach to datarace analysis and pointer analysis of Java programs.

Discussion. What if the user labels an edge as spurious when in fact it is not? In this case, real bugs may be missed, even though the original analysis is sound. One can define a notion of *relative soundness* to accommodate this situation: bugs are not missed as long as the user makes no mistakes in handling the analysis' output. Another approach would be to check the users' answers, which would feasible if the user not only answers 'yes'/'no' but also offers extra information in the form of a certificate that supports their answer. This approach is adopted by the Ivy tool [51], which asks the user for help in finding an inductive invariant, but checks inductiveness.

Another possible concern is that the term $\bigwedge_{1 \leq i < j \leq m} \mathsf{abs}(a_i) \vee \mathsf{abs}(a_j)$, which is used to ensure that we search for a single spurious edge, grows quadratically. There exist efficient but non-obvious ways to encode such cardinality constraints [21,63] and there also exist ways to handle them directly in satisfiability solvers [55]. These techniques also work for other cardinalities: we can ask what is the best set of $\leq k$ possibly spurious edges, which may be necessary if the disappearance of any single spurious edge does not rule out any alarm. By a more involved process, it is also possible to maximize the expected number of alarms ruled out *per* spurious edge [69].

3.3   Static Bug Detection

In the previous section, we saw how user feedback can be used to reduce the number of false alarms produced by a sound analysis. While in theory we deal mostly with sound analyses, in practice, analysis designers must make pragmatic assumptions [37]. In this section, we assume that we start from such an analysis, which could be described as a bug finder. In this situation, we want to avoid not only false positives but also false negatives. The approach we take is to *probabilistically* learn from user 'likes' and 'dislikes' on bug reports. Based on this feedback, the analysis adjusts the approximations it makes.

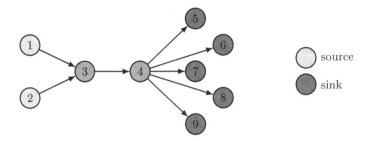

Fig. 7. Second source-sink information-flow example: if many flows with the same source lead to false bug reports, then other flows from the same source are *likely* to also lead to false bug reports.

Example. Figrue 7 gives an information-flow example, similar to the one in the previous section (Sect. 3.2). This time, however, edges are not labeled, so we use the simple definition of reachability from Example 1. While each edge in the graph is always valid, a path computed by the analysis can be spurious due to the approximations applied.

On this example, the analysis produces 10 reports, corresponding to the cross product of the 2 sources with the 5 sinks. There reports are mixed true alarms and false alarms. Suppose that all reports with node 2 as the source are false alarms because path(2, 4) is spurious. Typically, this is where the interaction between the analysis and the user stops, and the user has to inspect each report manually. In this case, the user can quickly get frustrated due to high false positive rate (50%).

To address this challenge, we allow the analysis to incorporate user feedback and therefore produce results that are more desirable to the user. For instance, if the user inspects path(2, 5) and path(2, 6) and determines them to be false alarms, we incorporate this feedback and suppress path(2, 7), path(2, 8), and path(2, 9), which are derived for the same root cause. To achieve this effect, we need to address two challenges:

1. How can we enable a conventional analysis to incorporate user feedback in a systematic and automatic manner?
2. How can we generalize the impact of feedback on limited reports to others?

For the first challenge, we notice that it is impossible to directly incorporate user feedback in a conventional analysis, which formulates the analysis problem as a decision problem. In such a decision problem, all clauses are hard, which makes the analysis rigid and define a single set of reports that cannot be changed.

As a result, if we directly add the aforementioned user feedback as hard clauses $\neg\mathtt{path}(2,5)$ and $\neg\mathtt{path}(2,6)$, it will make the constraint system inconsistent. Ideally, we want the ability to occasionally ignore certain clause groundings that can introduce imprecision and therefore guide the analysis to produce results that are more desirable to the user.

Our approach addresses this challenge by attaching weights to certain clauses whose groundings can introduce false alarms and therefore convert them from hard into soft. Intuitively, the weight of a clause represents the analysis writer's confidence in it: the higher weight it has, the less likely the writer thinks it will introduce imprecision. These weights can be specified by the analysis writer manually or automatically learnt from training programs whose bug reports are fully labeled using standard algorithms [61]. The clauses that are considered precise remain as hard clauses.

The above transformation results in a probabilistic analysis specified in logic with weights, which defines a distribution of outputs rather than a single output. We call this analysis probabilistic as the clause groundings now hold with some probability. And the final set of bug reports is the most likely one that maximizes the sum of the weights of the satisfied clause groundings. Moreover, it allows us to incorporate user feedback as new clauses in the system, which will change the output distribution and the set of bug reports. Since the user can make mistakes, we also add user feedback as soft clauses to the system, whose weights represent the user's confidence in them and can be also trained from labeled data. Intuitively, the bug reports produced after feedback are the ones that the analysis writer and the analysis user will most likely agree upon.

For the example analysis, we observe that reflexivity of $\mathtt{path}$ always holds, while transitivity of $\mathtt{path}$ can introduce imprecision. As a result we attach a weight to the clause which encodes transitivity, say 100. We also add user feedback as clauses $\neg\mathtt{path}(2,5)^{(200)}$ and $\neg\mathtt{path}(2,6)^{(200)}$. We attach high weights to user feedback clauses as we assume the user is confident in the feedback. As a result, we obtain the analysis specification with user feedback in logic with weights below:

Rules:	**Bias:**	**Feedback:**
$\mathtt{path}(x,x)$	$\neg\mathtt{edge}(x,y)^{(1)}$	$\neg\mathtt{path}(2,5)^{(200)}$
$\mathtt{path}(x,y) \wedge \mathtt{edge}(y,z) \xrightarrow{(100)} \mathtt{path}(x,z)$	$\neg\mathtt{path}(x,y)^{(1)}$	$\neg\mathtt{path}(2,6)^{(200)}$

We now discuss how our approach addresses the second challenge, of generalizing user feedback from some reports to others. We observe that all five false alarms are derived due to the spurious fact $\mathtt{path}(2,4)$, which reveals a more general insight about false alarms: most false alarms are symptoms of a few root causes. Rectifying these few root causes ($\mathtt{path}(2,4)$ in the example) can significantly improve the analysis precision. We illustrate how our approach achieves this effect by studying the MaxSAT instance generated by the above analysis specification with feedback:

$$c_1 : \texttt{path}(2,2) \qquad\qquad\qquad\qquad\qquad\qquad\qquad\qquad\quad \wedge$$
$$c_2 : \texttt{path}(2,3) \vee \neg\texttt{path}(2,2) \vee \neg\texttt{edge}(2,3)^{(100)} \qquad\qquad\quad \wedge$$
$$c_3 : \texttt{path}(2,4) \vee \neg\texttt{path}(2,3) \vee \neg\texttt{edge}(2,4)^{(100)} \qquad\qquad\quad \wedge$$
$$c_4 : \texttt{path}(2,5) \vee \neg\texttt{path}(2,4) \vee \neg\texttt{edge}(4,5)^{(100)} \qquad\qquad\quad \wedge$$
$$c_5 : \texttt{path}(2,6) \vee \neg\texttt{path}(2,4) \vee \neg\texttt{edge}(4,6)^{(100)} \qquad\qquad\quad \wedge$$
$$c_6 : \texttt{path}(2,7) \vee \neg\texttt{path}(2,4) \vee \neg\texttt{edge}(4,7)^{(100)} \qquad\qquad\quad \wedge$$
$$c_7 : \texttt{path}(2,8) \vee \neg\texttt{path}(2,4) \vee \neg\texttt{edge}(4,8)^{(100)} \qquad\qquad\quad \wedge$$
$$c_8 : \texttt{path}(2,9) \vee \neg\texttt{path}(2,4) \vee \neg\texttt{edge}(4,9)^{(100)} \qquad\qquad\quad \wedge$$
$$f_1 : \neg\texttt{path}(2,5)^{(200)} \qquad\qquad\qquad\qquad\qquad\qquad\qquad\quad \wedge$$
$$f_2 : \neg\texttt{path}(2,6)^{(200)} \qquad\qquad\qquad\qquad\qquad\qquad\qquad\quad \wedge$$

...

For the purpose of illustration, we only show the clauses that are related to the false alarms. In addition, we elide the bias clauses and assume that the computed model is always minimal. We notice that clauses c_1-c_5 form a conflict with the feedback clauses f_1 and f_2. As a result, a model of the MaxSAT instance cannot satisfy all of them. To maximize the sum of the weights of satisfied soft clauses, the model will violate c_3 while satisfying the other aforementioned clauses. Hence, variables $\texttt{path}(2,4)$, $\texttt{path}(2,5)$, $\texttt{path}(2,6)$ will be set to *false* in the solution. Since the computed model is minimal, variables $\texttt{path}(2,7)$, $\texttt{path}(2,8)$, $\texttt{path}(2,9)$ will also be set to *false*, which correspond to the other false alarms that are derived from $\texttt{path}(2,4)$. Hence, we successfully generalize the impact of the feedback on reports $\texttt{path}(2,5)$ and $\texttt{path}(2,6)$ by eliminating their common root cause $\texttt{path}(2,4)$, which in turn suppresses the other three false alarms that are derived from it.

General Case. We now discuss the general recipe for our approach. It is divided into an offline learning phase and an online inference phase. The offline phase takes a conventional analysis specified by an analysis writer and produces a probabilistic analysis specified in logic with weights. It produces the weight for each clause by learning it from training programs whose bug reports are fully labeled. The online phase applies the probabilistic analysis on a program supplied by the analysis user and produces bug reports in an interactive way. In each iteration, the user selects and inspects a subset of reports produced by the analysis, and provides positive or negative feedback. The analysis incorporates the feedback and update the reports for the next iteration. This interaction continues until all the bug reports are resolved.

We refer the reader to [39] for instantiations of this approach to datarace analysis and monomorphic call site analysis of Java programs.

Discussion. This approach is similar to the one introduced in Sect. 3.2 as they both improve the analysis accuracy by incorporating user effort. However, while the previous approach requires the user to inspect intermediate analysis facts, the current approach directly learns from user feedback on end reports. As a result, the previous approach requires the user to understand intermediate analysis results but the current approach does not. On the other hand, the previous approach can guarantee the soundness of the result if the user always gives correct answers, while the current approach may introduce false negatives due to its probabilistic nature. Hence, the current approach is more suitable for bug finding whereas the previous approach can be applied in interactive verification.

4   Techniques

We present techniques we have developed for MaxSAT solving. While primarily motivated by the domain of software analysis, they are general enough to be applicable to other domains too such as Big Data analytics and statistical AI.

We present a framework embodying our general approach (Sect. 4.1). We then present two techniques as instantiations of the framework (Sect. 4.2). Finally, we present two techniques that enable to optimize the framework (Sect. 4.3).

4.1   Framework

Our framework targets the problem of finding a model of a relational first-order logic formula with weights. The standard approach consists of two phases: *grounding* and *solving*. In the grounding phase, the formula is reduced to a WPMS instance by instantiating all variables with all possible constants. In the solving phase, the WPMS instance is solved using an off-the-shelf WPMS solver. Both phases are challenging to scale: in the grounding phase, naively instantiating all variables with all possible constants can lead to an intractable WPMS instance (comprising upto 10^{30} clauses); in the solving phase, the WPMS problem itself is also a combinatorial optimization problem, known for its intractability [4,41]. We address both these challenges by interleaving the two phases in an iterative *lazy grounding* process that progressively expands a subset of clauses while providing soundness and optimality guarantees.

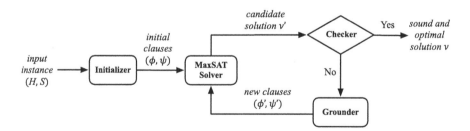

Fig. 8. Architecture of our lazy grounding framework for solving large MaxSAT instances. It scales by iteratively expanding a workset comprising a subset of clauses in the input MaxSAT instance. Our bottom-up and top-down grounding techniques, and many others in the literature, are instances of this framework.

Algorithm 1. Lazy Grounding Framework.

Input: (H, S): hard and soft clauses of input instance.
Output: ν: sound and optimal solution (assumes H is satisfiable).

1   $(\phi, \psi) \leftarrow \texttt{Init}(H, S)$
2   $(\nu, w) \leftarrow (\emptyset, 0)$
3   **while** *true* **do**
4      $(\phi', \psi') \leftarrow \texttt{Ground}(H, S, \nu, \phi, \psi)$
5      $(\nu', w') \leftarrow \texttt{MaxSAT}(\phi \cup \phi', \psi \cup \psi')$
6   **if** $\texttt{Done}(\phi, \phi', \psi, \psi', w, w')$ **then return** ν
7      $(\phi, \psi) \leftarrow (\phi \cup \phi', \psi \cup \psi')$
8      $(\nu, w) \leftarrow (\nu', w')$

The architecture of our framework is depicted in Fig. 8 and its overall algorithm is presented as Algorithm 1. For elaboration, we divide a weighted logic formula into separate hard clauses (denoted by H) and soft clauses (denoted by S). The framework is parametric in three procedures: $\texttt{Init}$, $\texttt{Ground}$, and $\texttt{Done}$. It begins by invoking the $\texttt{Init}$ procedure on line 1 to compute an initial set of hard clauses ϕ and soft clauses ψ. Next, it executes the loop defined on lines 3–8. In each iteration of the loop, the algorithm keeps track of a pair comprising the new solution ν' and its weight w', which is the sum of the weights of the soft clauses satisfied by ν'. On line 4, it invokes the $\texttt{Ground}$ procedure to compute the set of hard clauses ϕ' and soft clauses ψ' to ground next. Typically, ϕ' and ψ' correspond to the set of hard and soft clauses violated by the previous solution ν. On line 5, the current hard and soft clauses and the newly grounded hard and soft clauses are fed to an off-the-shelf WPMS solver to produce a new solution ν' and its corresponding weight w'. Initially, the solution is empty with weight zero (line 2). Next, on line 6, the algorithm checks if ν satisfies the terminating condition by invoking the $\texttt{Done}$ procedure. If not, then on line 7, both sets of grounded clauses ϕ' and ψ' are added to the corresponding sets of grounded hard clauses ϕ and grounded soft clauses ψ respectively. Accordingly, the solution ν and its corresponding weight w are updated as well.

Different instantiations of the three procedures that parameterize our framework yield different grounding algorithms proposed in the literature [14,34,38, 40,49,50,53]. We broadly classify instantiations of the framework into two categories akin to top-down and bottom-up approaches to Datalog evaluation [2]. We next present one instantiation that we have developed in each category.

4.2 Instantiations

Applications built upon constraint-based approaches are typically only concerned with the assignment to certain variables of interest, which we refer to as *queries*. The bottom-up approach computes an assignment to all variables from which one can subsequently extract the assignment to queries. The top-down approach, on the other hand, only grounds clauses that are needed to

---

Algorithm 2. Bottom-Up Approach

---

1 **Procedure** Init*(H,S)*
2 | $(\phi, \psi) \leftarrow (\emptyset, \emptyset)$
3 | **return** *(ϕ,ψ)*

4 **Procedure** Ground*(H, S, ν, ϕ, ψ)*
5 | $(\phi, \psi) \leftarrow (\emptyset, \emptyset)$
6 | **foreach** $h \in H$ **do**
7 | | **if** $\nu \nvDash [\![h]\!]_\sigma$ **then** $\phi \leftarrow \phi \cup [\![h]\!]_\sigma$
8 | **foreach** $(w, h) \in S$ **do**
9 | | **if** $\nu \nvDash [\![h]\!]_\sigma$ **then** $\psi \leftarrow \psi \cup \{(w, \rho) \mid \rho \in [\![h]\!]_\sigma\}$
10 | **return** *(ϕ,ψ)*

11 **Procedure** Done*(ϕ, ϕ', ψ, ψ', w, w')*
12 | **return** $\phi' = \emptyset \wedge w = w'$

---

compute the assignment to queries. This approach offers significant performance gains when queries comprise a small fraction of all variables, which is the case in many applications. We introduced the top-down approach for MaxSAT in [71].

Bottom-Up Approach. Algorithm 2 presents our bottom-up instantiation from [38]. Procedure Init returns an empty set of hard ground clauses and an empty set of soft ground clauses (line 2). For each hard clause in the input instance, procedure Ground checks if the current solution violates any of its groundings and includes those violated ground clauses as new hard clauses (lines 6–7). Similarly, Ground also includes violated soft ground clauses (lines 8–9), and they share the same weight as the corresponding soft clause in the input instance. Given hard and soft ground clauses and the corresponding solutions from two successive iterations, procedure Done checks whether the current solution is a sound and optimal solution. Specifically, Done returns true if no hard clauses in the input instance are violated (i.e., $\phi' = \emptyset$) and the weight of the current solution equals the weight of the last solution (i.e., $w = w'$). Intuitively, it means that we cannot improve the solution further even we consider more ground clauses.

SoftCegar [14] and Cutting Plane Inference (CPI) [50,53] are instances of the bottom-up approach. SoftCegar uses a slight variant that grounds all the soft clauses upfront but lazily grounds the hard clauses, while CPI employs a more conservative instantiation of Done.

Top-Down Approach. A top-down approach aims to find a partial assignment to queries such that there exists a completion of it that is a sound and optimum solution to the full problem. Algorithm 3 shows a naive top-down instantiation. More advanced instantiations are presented in [71]. The Init procedure returns all soft and hard ground clauses that involve at least one of the queried variables (denoted by $\mathcal{Q}$) (lines 3–6). For ease of exposition, the pseudo code of the Init procedure explicitly enumerates all ground clauses. In practice, it is implemented using symbolic approaches such as SQL queries [49] for efficiency. The Ground

Algorithm 3. Top-Down Approach

```
 1 Procedure Init(H,S)
 2 │   (φ, ψ) ← (∅, ∅)
 3 │   foreach (w, h) ∈ S do
 4 │   │   foreach ρ ∈ [[h]]_σ do
 5 │   │   └   if any variable of ρ ∈ Q then   ψ ← ψ ∪ {(w, ρ)}
 6 │   initialize φ in a similar way without considering weights
 7 └   return (φ,ψ)

 8 Procedure Ground(H, S, ν, φ, ψ)
 9 │   (φ', ψ') ← (∅, ∅)
10 │   V ← variables used in φ ∪ ψ
11 │   foreach (w, h) ∈ S do
12 │   │   foreach ρ ∈ [[h]]_σ do
13 │   │   │   if (w, ρ) ∉ ψ ∧ ν ⊭ ρ ∧ any variable of ρ ∈ V then
14 │   │   └   └   ψ' ← ψ' ∪ {(w, ρ)}
15 │   update φ' in a similar way without considering weights
16 │   w ← evaluate(ψ, ν)
17 │   (ν', w') ← MaxSAT(φ ∪ φ', ψ ∪ ψ')
18 │   if φ' = ∅ ∧ w = w' then
19 │   │   return (∅, ∅)
20 │   else
21 │   │   ψ'_s ← {(w, ρ) ∈ ψ' | ν' ⊨ ρ}
22 └   └   return (φ', ψ'_s)

23 Procedure Done(φ, φ', ψ, ψ', w, w')
24 └   return φ' = ∅ ∧ ψ' = ∅
```

---

procedure returns ground clauses that may help improve the current solution. To achieve this goal, it first searches for ground clauses (ϕ', ψ') that (1) are not in the work set, but (2) share variables with clauses int it, and (3) are not satisfied by the current solution ν (line 9–15). Then it checks whether the current solution ν violates any ground hard clauses in ϕ' and whether the weight of the solution can be improved by considering (ϕ', ψ') (line 16–22). It checks the latter condition by computing the solution (denoted by ν') to $(\phi \cup \phi', \psi \cup \psi')$ and the corresponding weight (denoted by w') (line 16–17). If neither condition holds, it returns empty sets of ground clauses and concludes that the current solution cannot be improved further. Otherwise, it returns the hard ground clauses in ϕ' that are violated by ν and the soft ground clauses in ψ' that are satisfied by ν' as these ground clauses will highly likely improve the current solution. It follows that the top-down approach terminates when **Ground** returns empty sets. The correctness of Algorithm 3 is proved in [71].

Algorithm 4. Optimization with eager proofs

---

1 **Procedure** Init(H, S)
2 $\quad$ $(\phi, \psi) \leftarrow (\emptyset, \emptyset)$
3 $\quad$ $\phi' \leftarrow$ initial facts
4 $\quad$ **while** $\phi' \not\subseteq \phi$ **do**
5 $\quad\quad$ $\phi \leftarrow \phi \cup \phi'$
6 $\quad\quad$ **foreach** $h \in H$ **do**
7 $\quad\quad\quad$ **foreach** $\rho \in [\![h]\!]_\sigma$ **do**
8 $\quad\quad\quad\quad$ **if** $\rho = \bigwedge_{i=1}^n t_i \implies t_0$ **then**
9 $\quad\quad\quad\quad\quad$ **if** $\bigwedge_{i=1}^n t_i \in \phi$ **then**
10 $\quad\quad\quad\quad\quad\quad$ $\phi' \leftarrow \phi' \cup \{t_0\}$

11 $\quad$ **return** (ϕ, ψ)
12 **Procedure** Done$(\phi, \phi', \psi, \psi', w, w')$
13 $\quad$ **return** $\phi' = \emptyset \wedge w = w'$

4.3 Optimizations

We introduce two optimizations to further improve the efficiency of our framework: eager grounding and incremental solving.

Eager Grounding. Our first observation is that most constraints in domains like software analysis are *Horn clauses*. Horn clauses form a set of proof-tree like structures. When one of them is violated by the solution of the current iteration in lazy grounding, many others will be violated in the next iteration, which in turn will cause a chain effect in the subsequent iterations. We can avoid such chain effects by *eager proof exploitation* [38], which computes an optimal initial grounding for Horn clauses. The Init procedure of Algorithm 4 shows the optimization with eager proofs, which starts with initial facts as hard clauses and iteratively applies Horn clauses to derive new facts as hard clauses. Theorem 1 shows the optimality of the Init procedure. Though Theorem 1 gives no guarantee of the necessity to ground soft Horn clauses upfront, we find that it is also helpful in practice. The eager proof exploitation procedure can be efficiently implemented using an off-the-shelf Datalog engine.

Theorem 1 (Optimal initial grounding for Horn clauses). Init *in Algorithm 4 grounds all necessary hard Horn clauses and no more hard Horn clauses need to be grounded in later phases.*

Proof. See the proof in Appendix A of [38]. $\qquad\square$

Incremental Solving. Our framework generates a sequence of MaxSAT instances such that the instance in the next iteration is obtained by adding new hard or soft clauses to the instance in the current iteration. Formally, we have a *sequential* MaxSAT problem: $(\phi^1, \psi^1), (\phi^2, \psi^2), ..., (\phi^n, \psi^n)$, with

---

Algorithm 5. *Fu & Malik* Algorithm with partial weights [4, 14]

Input: $\phi = \phi_H \cup \phi_S$
Output: optimal solution to ϕ

1 **while** true **do**
2 $\quad$ $(\mathsf{st}, \nu, \phi_C) \leftarrow \mathtt{SAT}(\phi, \mathcal{A})$
3 $\quad$ **if** $\mathsf{st} = \mathrm{SAT}$ **then return** ν $\qquad\qquad$ *// optimal solution to* ϕ
4 $\quad$ $V_R \leftarrow \emptyset$ $\qquad\qquad\qquad\qquad\quad$ *// relax variables of the core*
5 $\quad$ $w_{min} \leftarrow min\{w | c \in \phi_C \wedge (w, c) \in \phi_S\}$
6 $\quad$ **foreach** $c \in \phi_C$ **do**
7 $\quad\quad$ **if** $(w, c) \in \phi_S$ **then**
8 $\quad\quad\quad$ $V_R \leftarrow V_R \cup \{r\}$ $\qquad\qquad$ *// r is a fresh relaxation variable*
9 $\quad\quad\quad$ $\phi \leftarrow \phi \setminus \{(w, c)\} \cup \{(w - w_{min}, c), (w_{min}, c \vee r)\}$ $\quad$ *// split soft clauses*
10 $\quad$ **if** $V_R = \emptyset$ **then return** UNSAT $\qquad\quad$ *// no soft clauses in the core*
11 $\quad$ $\phi \leftarrow \phi \cup CNF(\sum_{r \in V_R} r \leq 1)$ $\qquad$ *// add hard cardinality constraint*

$\phi^k \subseteq \phi^{k+1}, \psi^k \subseteq \psi^{k+1}$. A straightforward solution is to *independently* solve each instance (ϕ^k, ψ^k) using an off-the-shelf MaxSAT solver. We propose an incremental MaxSAT solving technique [60] to solve the sequential MaxSAT problem more efficiently.

The unsat core-guided MaxSAT algorithm, also known as *Fu & Malik* algorithm [23], forms the basis of many popular MaxSAT algorithms [4,41,43, 46]. Algorithm 5 shows the *Fu & Malik* algorithm extended with partial weights. The algorithm iteratively calls a SAT solver and relaxes an unsatisfiable subformula. Initially, ϕ consists of all hard and soft clauses from the input instance. In each iteration, it calls a SAT solver on ϕ, which returns a triple (st, ν, ϕ_C). If st is satisfiable, ν is the optimal solution; otherwise, ϕ_C is an unsatisfiable subformula (or UNSAT core) of ϕ. Then, it computes the minimum weight w_{min} of the soft clauses in the UNSAT core (line-5). It then splits each soft clause in the UNSAT core into two: one with the same clause but with weight reduced by w_{min}, and the other with the original clause relaxed by a newly created variable and with weight w_{min} (lines 6–9). If there are no soft clauses in the UNSAT core, it returns UNSAT as there exists a conflict in hard clauses (line-10). Otherwise, a new hard clause is added to ϕ stating that at most one of the soft clauses in the UNSAT core can be relaxed (line-11).

There are two levels of incrementality we can explore to improve Algorithm 5. Similar to the sequential MaxSAT problem, solving an individual MaxSAT instance involves a sequence of SAT problems. So, the first level of incrementality is to use the SAT solver incrementally. Martins et al. [43] propose an *incremental blocking* technique to leverage incremental SAT solving [20]. We propose the second level of incrementality which is across MaxSAT instances. The key idea is to reuse UNSAT cores by slightly revising Algorithm 5. When the k-th MaxSAT instance is solved[1] at line-5, instead of returning the solution and exiting, we output the current solution for the k-th instance, then read the newly added clauses $(\phi^{k+1} \setminus \phi^k, \psi^{k+1} \setminus \psi^k)$ for the $(k+1)$-th instance, and jump to line-3. This approach is correct because the addition of new soft or hard clauses does not invalidate any of the previously found UNSAT cores.

An interesting empirical observation is that incremental solving does not always improve performance; on the contrary, it may even deteriorate performance. This is because UNSAT cores with low weight discovered in earlier instances can cause too many splits of soft clauses, especially when soft clauses with high weights are added later. To resolve this issue, we propose a restart mechanism, which restarts the current MaxSAT instance solving after detecting any low quality cores. We empirically find that the number of splits of each individual soft clause is an effective quality measurement, and that restarting after the number of splits is more than 5 achieves best performance on our applications.

5   Related Work

We survey work on MaxSAT applications and techniques for MaxSAT solving.

Applications. MaxSAT has been widely used in many domains [6,13,15,22, 25,30,31,33,56,67,68,72]. The Linux package manage tool OPIUM [67] uses MaxSAT to find the optimal package install/uninstall configuration. Walter et al. [68] apply MaxSAT in industry automotive configurations. Zhu et al. [72] apply MaxSAT to localize faults in integrated circuits. By combining bounded model checking and MaxSAT, BugAssist [31] performs error localization for C programs, and ConcBugAssist [33] finds concurrency bugs and recommends repairs. Jin and Orso[30] show how to improve the performance and accuracy of error localization using MaxSAT. To detect malware in Android apps, ASTROID [22] automatically learns semantic malware signatures by using MaxSAT to find the maximally suspicious common subgraph from a few samples of a malware family. Besides, MaxSAT is also helpful in visualization [13], industrial designs [15,56], reasoning about biological networks [25], and various data analysis tasks [6].

Techniques. There are a number of different approaches for exact MaxSAT solving, including branch-and-bound based, satisfiability-based, unsatisfiability-based, and their combinations [5,8,26,28,42,43,45–47]. The most successful of these on real-world instances, as witnessed in annual MaxSAT evaluations [1], perform iterative solving using a SAT solver as an oracle in each iteration [5,46]. Such solvers differ primarily in how they estimate the optimal cost (e.g., linear or binary search), and the kind of information that they use to estimate the cost (e.g. cores, the structure of cores, or satisfying assignments). Many algorithms have been proposed that perform search on either upper bound or lower bound

---

[1] We assume hard clauses can be satisfied; otherwise hard clauses of all future instances will be unsatisfied and we can exit immediately.

of the optimal cost [5, 45–47], Some algorithms efficiently perform a combined search over both bounds [26, 28]. A drawback of the most sophisticated combined search algorithms is that they modify the formula using expensive Pseudo Boolean (PB) constraints that increase the size of the formula and potentially hurt the solver's performance. A recent approach [8] avoids this problem by using succinct formula transformations that do not use PB constraints and can be applied incrementally. Lastly, similar to our optimizations in Sect. 4.3, many other techniques (e.g. [7, 27]) also focus on optimizing Horn clauses.

6   Future Directions

We plan to extend our approach in three directions to further advance constraint-based analysis using MaxSAT: constraint languages, solver techniques, and explainability of solutions.

Language Features. As discussed in Sect. 2, since propositional formulae are too low-level for effectively specifying software analyses, we use relational first-order logic with weights as our constraint language. While it suffices for applications and analyses described in our previous work [24, 39, 69, 70], it can be further improved with richer features, two of which we discuss below.

While the current logic excels at specifying analysis problems that can be succinctly expressed in relational domains, it has difficulties in expressing analysis problems in integer, real, string, and other domains. Akin to how Satisfiability Modulo Theories (SMT) extends SAT, we can handle these domains by incorporating their corresponding theories in our language via techniques similar to the Nelson-Oppen approach. One emerging language for such problem is Maximum Satisfiability Modulo Theories (MaxSMT) [9, 10, 16, 35, 48, 58, 59].

The other feature is the support for the least fixpoint operator, as almost all software analyses involve computing the least fixpoint of certain equations. Our current constraint language supports this operator indirectly by requiring additional soft clauses to bias the solution to a minimal model. However, a built-in least fixpoint operator would be much more preferred. First, it eliminates the need for the aforementioned soft constraints which can complicate the process of analysis design as they may interact with other soft constraints. Secondly, by including the operator explicitly in the language, the underlying solver can exploit more efficient algorithms that are specialized for handling least fixpoints.

Solver Techniques. We describe four techniques that can further improve the effectiveness of our solving framework.

Magic Sets Transformation. Akin to their counterparts in Datalog evaluation, the top-down approaches and the bottom-up approaches have different advantages and disadvantages. One promising idea to combine their benefits without their drawbacks is Magic Set transformation [54]. The idea is to apply the bottom-up approaches but rewrite the constraint formulation so that the constraint solving is driven by the demand of queries. In this way, we are able to only consider the clauses that are related to the queries while leveraging efficient solvers of the bottom-up approaches.

Lifted Inference. While our current grounding-based framework effectively leverages advances in MaxSAT solvers, it loses the high-level information while translating problems in our constraint language into low-level propositional formulae. Lifted inference [12,44,52,57,62] is a technique that aims to solve the constraint problem symbolically without grounding. While lifted inference can effectively avoid grounding large propositional formulae for certain problems, it fails to leverage existing efficient propositional solvers. One promising direction is to combine lifted inference with our grounding approach in a systematic way.

Compositional Solving. By exploiting modularity of programs, we envision compositional solving as an effective approach to improve the solver efficiency. The idea is to break a constraint problem into more tractable subproblems and solve them independently. It is motivated by the success of compositional and summary-based analysis techniques in scaling to large programs.

Approximate Solving. Despite all the domain insights we exploit, MaxSAT is a combinatorial optimization problem, which is known for its intractability. As a result, there will be pathological cases where none of the aforementioend techniques are effective. One idea to address this challenge is to investigate approximate solving, which trades precision for efficiency. Moreover, to trade precision for efficiency is a controlled manner, it is desirable to design an algorithm with tunable precision.

Explainability. Software analyses often return explanations along with the results, which are invaluable to their usability. For example, a typical bug finding tool not only returns the software defects it finds but also inputs that can trigger these defects. However, in the case of constraint-based analysis, the underlying constraint solver must provide explanations of the solutions to enable such functionality. While SAT and SMT solvers provide such information in the form of resolution graphs (in the case of satisfiable results) and UNSAT cores (in the case of unsatisfiable results), how to provide explanations for optimization solvers remains an open problem.

7   Conclusion

We proposed a MaxSAT based approach to tackle the central challenge of balancing different tradeoffs in software analysis. We demonstrated the approach on mainstream applications concerning automated verification, interactive verification, and static bug detection. The MaxSAT instances posed in these applications transcend the reach of existing MaxSAT solvers in terms of scalability, soundness, and optimality. We presented a lazy grounding framework to solve such instances. We proposed new grounding techniques as instantiations of this framework as well as optimizations to the framework.

Acknowledgments. This work was supported by DARPA under agreement #FA8750-15-2-0009, NSF awards #1253867 and #1526270, and a Facebook Fellowship. The U.S. Government is authorized to reproduce and distribute reprints for Governmental purposes notwithstanding any copyright thereon.

References

1. MaxSAT evaluations. http://www.maxsat.udl.cat/
2. Abiteboul, S., Hull, R., Vianu, V.: Foundations of Databases: The Logical Level. Addison-Wesley Longman Publishing Co., Inc., Boston (1995)
3. Aiken, A.: Introduction to set constraint-based program analysis. Sci. Comput. Program. (1999)
4. Ansótegui, C., Bonet, M.L., Levy, J.: Solving (weighted) partial MaxSAT through satisfiability testing. In: Kullmann, O. (ed.) SAT 2009. LNCS, vol. 5584, pp. 427–440. Springer, Heidelberg (2009). doi:10.1007/978-3-642-02777-2_39
5. AnsóTegui, C., Bonet, M.L., Levy, J.: SAT-based MaxSAT algorithms. Artif. Intell. **196**, 77–105 (2013)
6. Berg, J., Hyttinen, A., Järvisalo, M.: Applications of MaxSAT in data analysis. In: Pragmatics of SAT (2015)
7. Bjørner, N., Gurfinkel, A., McMillan, K., Rybalchenko, A.: Horn clause solvers for program verification. In: Beklemishev, L.D., Blass, A., Dershowitz, N., Finkbeiner, B., Schulte, W. (eds.) Fields of Logic and Computation II. LNCS, vol. 9300, pp. 24–51. Springer, Cham (2015). doi:10.1007/978-3-319-23534-9_2
8. Bjorner, N., Narodytska, N.: Maximum satisfiability using cores and correction sets. In: IJCAI (2015)
9. Bjørner, N., Phan, A.D.: νZ: maximal satisfaction with Z3. In: Proceedings of International Symposium on Symbolic Computation in Software Science (SCSS) (2014)
10. Bjørner, N., Phan, A.-D., Fleckenstein, L.: νZ - an optimizing SMT solver. In: Baier, C., Tinelli, C. (eds.) TACAS 2015. LNCS, vol. 9035, pp. 194–199. Springer, Heidelberg (2015). doi:10.1007/978-3-662-46681-0_14
11. Bravenboer, M., Smaragdakis, Y.: Strictly declarative specification of sophisticated points-to analyses. In: OOPSLA (2009)
12. den Broeck, G.V., Taghipour, N., Meert, W., Davis, J., Raedt, L.D.: Lifted probabilistic inference by first-order knowledge compilation. In: IJCAI (2011)
13. Bunte, K., Järvisalo, M., Berg, J., Myllymäki, P., Peltonen, J., Kaski, S.: Optimal neighborhood preserving visualization by maximum satisfiability. In: AAAI (2014)
14. Chaganty, A., Lal, A., Nori, A.V., Rajamani, S.K.: Combining relational learning with SMT solvers using CEGAR. In: Sharygina, N., Veith, H. (eds.) CAV 2013. LNCS, vol. 8044, pp. 447–462. Springer, Heidelberg (2013). doi:10.1007/978-3-642-39799-8_30
15. Chen, Y., Safarpour, S., Marques-Silva, J., Veneris, A.: Automated design debugging with maximum satisfiability. IEEE Trans. Comput. Aided Des. Integr. Circuits Syst. **29**(11), 1804–1817 (2010)
16. Cimatti, A., Franzén, A., Griggio, A., Sebastiani, R., Stenico, C.: Satisfiability modulo the theory of costs: foundations and applications. In: Esparza, J., Majumdar, R. (eds.) TACAS 2010. LNCS, vol. 6015, pp. 99–113. Springer, Heidelberg (2010). doi:10.1007/978-3-642-12002-2_8
17. Clarke, E., Grumberg, O., Jha, S., Lu, Y., Veith, H.: Counterexample-guided abstraction refinement. In: Emerson, E.A., Sistla, A.P. (eds.) CAV 2000. LNCS, vol. 1855, pp. 154–169. Springer, Heidelberg (2000). doi:10.1007/10722167_15
18. Domingos, P., Lowd, D.: Markov Logic: An Interface Layer for Artificial Intelligence. Synthesis Lectures on Artificial Intelligence and Machine Learning. Morgan & Claypool Publishers, San Rafael (2009)

19. Dubois, D., Prade, H.: Possibilistic logic - an overview. In: Computational Logic. Handbook of the History of Logic, vol. 7. Newnes (2014)

20. Eén, N., Sörensson, N.: Temporal induction by incremental SAT solving. Electron. Notes Theor. Comput. Sci. **89**(4), 543–560 (2003). http://www.sciencedirect.com/science/article/pii/S1571066105825423

21. Eén, N., Sörensson, N.: Translating pseudo-boolean constraints into SAT. JSAT (2006)

22. Feng, Y., Bastani, O., Martins, R., Dillig, I., Anand, S.: Automated synthesis of semantic malware signatures using maximum satisfiability. In: NDSS (2017)

23. Fu, Z., Malik, S.: On solving the partial MAX-SAT problem. In: Biere, A., Gomes, C.P. (eds.) SAT 2006. LNCS, vol. 4121, pp. 252–265. Springer, Heidelberg (2006). doi:10.1007/11814948_25

24. Grigore, R., Yang, H.: Abstraction refinement guided by a learnt probabilistic model. In: POPL (2016)

25. Guerra, J., Lynce, I.: Reasoning over biological networks using maximum satisfiability. In: Milano, M. (ed.) CP 2012. LNCS, pp. 941–956. Springer, Heidelberg (2012). doi:10.1007/978-3-642-33558-7_67

26. Heras, F., Morgado, A., Marques-Silva, J.: Core-guided binary search algorithms for maximum satisfiability. In: AAAI (2011)

27. Hojjat, H., Rmmer, P., McClurg, J., Černý, P., Foster, N.: Optimizing horn solvers for network repair. In: FMCAD (2016)

28. Ignatiev, A., Morgado, A., Manquinho, V., Lynce, I., Marques-Silva, J.: Progression in maximum satisfiability. In: ECAI (2014)

29. Jensen, F.V., Nielsen, T.D.: Bayesian Networks and Decision Graphs. Springer, Heidelberg (2007). doi:10.1007/978-0-387-68282-2

30. Jin, W., Orso, A.: Improving efficiency and accuracy of formula-based debugging. In: Bloem, R., Arbel, E. (eds.) HVC 2016. LNCS, vol. 10028, pp. 99–116. Springer, Cham (2016). doi:10.1007/978-3-319-49052-6_7

31. Jose, M., Majumdar, R.: Cause clue clauses: error localization using maximum satisfiability. In: PLDI (2011)

32. Kastrinis, G., Smaragdakis, Y.: Hybrid context sensitivity for points-to analysis. In: PLDI (2013)

33. Khoshnood, S., Kusano, M., Wang, C.: ConcBugAssist: constraint solving for diagnosis and repair of concurrency bugs. In: ISSTA (2015)

34. Kok, S., Sumner, M., Richardson, M., Singla, P., Poon, H., Lowd, D., Domingos, P.: The Alchemy system for statistical relational AI. Technical report, Department of Computer Science and Engineering, University of Washington, Seattle, WA (2007). http://alchemy.cs.washington.edu

35. Li, Y., Albarghouthi, A., Kincaid, Z., Gurfinkel, A., Chechik, M.: Symbolic optimization with SMT solvers. In: POPL (2014)

36. Libkin, L.: Elements of Finite Model Theory. Springer, Heidelberg (2004). doi:10.1007/978-3-662-07003-1

37. Livshits, B., Sridharan, M., Smaragdakis, Y., Lhoták, O., Amaral, J.N., Chang, B.E., Guyer, S.Z., Khedker, U.P., Møller, A., Vardoulakis, D.: In defense of soundness: a manifesto. CACM (2015)

38. Mangal, R., Zhang, X., Kamath, A., Nori, A.V., Naik, M.: Scaling relational inference using proofs and refutations. In: AAAI (2016)

39. Mangal, R., Zhang, X., Nori, A.V., Naik, M.: A user-guided approach to program analysis. In: FSE (2015)

40. Mangal, R., Zhang, X., Nori, A.V., Naik, M.: Volt: a lazy grounding framework for solving very large MaxSAT instances. In: Heule, M., Weaver, S. (eds.) SAT 2015. LNCS, vol. 9340, pp. 299–306. Springer, Cham (2015). doi:10.1007/978-3-319-24318-4_22

41. Manquinho, V., Marques-Silva, J., Planes, J.: Algorithms for weighted boolean optimization. In: Kullmann, O. (ed.) SAT 2009. LNCS, vol. 5584, pp. 495–508. Springer, Heidelberg (2009). doi:10.1007/978-3-642-02777-2_45

42. Marques-Silva, J., Planes, J.: Algorithms for maximum satisfiability using unsatisfiable cores. In: DATE (2008)

43. Martins, R., Joshi, S., Manquinho, V., Lynce, I.: Incremental cardinality constraints for MaxSAT. In: O'Sullivan, B. (ed.) CP 2014. LNCS, vol. 8656, pp. 531–548. Springer, Cham (2014). doi:10.1007/978-3-319-10428-7_39

44. Milch, B., Zettlemoyer, L.S., Kersting, K., Haimes, M., Kaelbling, L.P.: Lifted probabilistic inference with counting formulas. In: AAAI (2008)

45. Morgado, A., Dodaro, C., Marques-Silva, J.: Core-guided MaxSAT with soft cardinality constraints. In: O'Sullivan, B. (ed.) CP 2014. LNCS, vol. 8656, pp. 564–573. Springer, Cham (2014). doi:10.1007/978-3-319-10428-7_41

46. Morgado, A., Heras, F., Liffiton, M., Planes, J., Marques-Silva, J.: Iterative and core-guided MaxSAT solving: a survey and assessment. Constraints 18(4), 478–534 (2013). http://dx.doi.org/10.1007/s10601-013-9146-2

47. Narodytska, N., Bacchus, F.: Maximum satisfiability using core-guided MaxSAT resolution. In: AAAI (2014)

48. Nieuwenhuis, R., Oliveras, A.: On SAT modulo theories and optimization problems. In: Biere, A., Gomes, C.P. (eds.) SAT 2006. LNCS, vol. 4121, pp. 156–169. Springer, Heidelberg (2006). doi:10.1007/11814948_18

49. Niu, F., Ré, C., Doan, A., Shavlik, J.W.: Tuffy: scaling up statistical inference in Markov logic networks using an RDBMS. In: VLDB (2011)

50. Noessner, J., Niepert, M., Stuckenschmidt, H.: RockIt: exploiting parallelism and symmetry for MAP inference in statistical relational models. In: AAAI (2013)

51. Padon, O., McMillan, K.L., Panda, A., Sagiv, M., Shoham, S.: Ivy: safety verification by interactive generalization. In: PLDI (2016)

52. Poole, D.: First-order probabilistic inference. In: IJCAI (2003)

53. Riedel, S.: Improving the accuracy and efficiency of MAP inference for Markov logic. In: UAI (2008)

54. Ross, K.A.: Modular stratification and magic sets for DATALOG programs with negation. In: PODS (1990)

55. Roussel, O., Manquinho, V.M.: Pseudo-Boolean and Cardinality Constraints. In: Handbook of satisfiability. IOS Press (2009)

56. Safarpour, S., Mangassarian, H., Veneris, A., Liffiton, M.H., Sakallah, K.A.: Improved design debugging using maximum satisfiability. In: FMCAD (2007)

57. de Salvo Braz, R., Amir, E., Roth, D.: Lifted first-order probabilistic inference. In: IJCAI (2005)

58. Sebastiani, R., Tomasi, S.: Optimization in SMT with $\mathcal{L}A(\mathbb{Q})$ cost functions. In: Gramlich, B., Miller, D., Sattler, U. (eds.) IJCAR 2012. LNCS, vol. 7364, pp. 484–498. Springer, Heidelberg (2012). doi:10.1007/978-3-642-31365-3_38

59. Sebastiani, R., Trentin, P.: On optimization modulo theories, MaxSMT and sorting networks. In: Legay, A., Margaria, T. (eds.) TACAS 2017. LNCS, vol. 10206, pp. 231–248. Springer, Heidelberg (2017). doi:10.1007/978-3-662-54580-5_14

60. Si, X., Zhang, X., Manquinho, V., Janota, M., Ignatiev, A., Naik, M.: On incremental core-guided MaxSAT solving. In: Rueher, M. (ed.) CP 2016. LNCS, vol. 9892, pp. 473–482. Springer, Cham (2016). doi:10.1007/978-3-319-44953-1_30

61. Singla, P., Domingos, P.: Discriminative training of Markov logic networks. In: AAAI (2005)
62. Singla, P., Domingos, P.: Lifted first-order belief propagation. In: AAAI (2008)
63. Sinz, C.: Towards an optimal CNF encoding of boolean cardinality constraints. In: Beek, P. (ed.) CP 2005. LNCS, vol. 3709, pp. 827–831. Springer, Heidelberg (2005). doi:10.1007/11564751_73
64. Smaragdakis, Y., Bravenboer, M.: Using datalog for fast and easy program analysis. In: Datalog 2.0 Workshop (2010)
65. Smaragdakis, Y., Bravenboer, M., Lhoták, O.: Pick your contexts well: understanding object-sensitivity. In: POPL (2013)
66. Smaragdakis, Y., Kastrinis, G., Balatsouras, G.: Introspective analysis: context-sensitivity, across the board. In: PLDI (2014)
67. Tucker, C., Shuffelton, D., Jhala, R., Lerner, S.: OPIUM: optimal package install/uninstall manager. In: ICSE (2007)
68. Walter, R., Zengler, C., Kuchlin, W.: Applications of MaxSAT in automotive configuration. In: Proceedings of the 15th International Configuration Workshop (2013)
69. Zhang, X., Grigore, R., Si, X., Naik, M.: Effective interactive resolution of static analysis alarms (2016)
70. Zhang, X., Mangal, R., Grigore, R., Naik, M., Yang, H.: On abstraction refinement for program analyses in datalog. In: PLDI (2014)
71. Zhang, X., Mangal, R., Nori, A.V., Naik, M.: Query-guided maximum satisfiability. In: POPL (2016)
72. Zhu, C.S., Weissenbacher, G., Malik, S.: Post-silicon fault localisation using maximum satisfiability and backbones. In: FMCAD (2011)

Probabilistic Systems

Reluplex: An Efficient SMT Solver for Verifying Deep Neural Networks

Guy Katz[✉], Clark Barrett, David L. Dill,
Kyle Julian, and Mykel J. Kochenderfer

Stanford University, Stanford, USA
{guyk,clarkbarrett,dill,kjulian3,mykel}@stanford.edu

Abstract. Deep neural networks have emerged as a widely used and effective means for tackling complex, real-world problems. However, a major obstacle in applying them to safety-critical systems is the great difficulty in providing formal guarantees about their behavior. We present a novel, scalable, and efficient technique for verifying properties of deep neural networks (or providing counter-examples). The technique is based on the simplex method, extended to handle the non-convex *Rectified Linear Unit* (*ReLU*) activation function, which is a crucial ingredient in many modern neural networks. The verification procedure tackles neural networks as a whole, without making any simplifying assumptions. We evaluated our technique on a prototype deep neural network implementation of the next-generation airborne collision avoidance system for unmanned aircraft (ACAS Xu). Results show that our technique can successfully prove properties of networks that are an order of magnitude larger than the largest networks verified using existing methods.

1 Introduction

Artificial neural networks [7,32] have emerged as a promising approach for creating scalable and robust systems. Applications include speech recognition [9], image classification [23], game playing [33], and many others. It is now clear that software that may be extremely difficult for humans to implement can instead be created by training *deep neural networks* (*DNN*s), and that the performance of these DNNs is often comparable to, or even surpasses, the performance of manually crafted software. DNNs are becoming widespread, and this trend is likely to continue and intensify.

Great effort is now being put into using DNNs as controllers for safety-critical systems such as autonomous vehicles [4] and airborne collision avoidance systems for unmanned aircraft (ACAS Xu) [13]. DNNs are trained over a finite set of inputs and outputs and are expected to *generalize*, i.e. to behave correctly for previously-unseen inputs. However, it has been observed that DNNs can react in unexpected and incorrect ways to even slight perturbations of their inputs [34]. This unexpected behavior of DNNs is likely to result in unsafe systems, or restrict the usage of DNNs in safety-critical applications. Hence, there

© Springer International Publishing AG 2017
R. Majumdar and V. Kunčak (Eds.): CAV 2017, Part I, LNCS 10426, pp. 97–117, 2017.
DOI: 10.1007/978-3-319-63387-9_5

is an urgent need for methods that can provide formal guarantees about DNN behavior. Unfortunately, manual reasoning about large DNNs is impossible, as their structure renders them incomprehensible to humans. Automatic verification techniques are thus sorely needed, but here, the state of the art is a severely limiting factor.

Verifying DNNs is a difficult problem. DNNs are large, non-linear, and non-convex, and verifying even simple properties about them is an NP-complete problem (see Sect. I of the supplementary material [15]). DNN verification is experimentally beyond the reach of general-purpose tools such as *linear programming* (*LP*) solvers or existing *satisfiability modulo theories* (*SMT*) solvers [3,10,31], and thus far, dedicated tools have only been able to handle very small networks (e.g. a single hidden layer with only 10 to 20 hidden nodes [30,31]).

The difficulty in proving properties about DNNs is caused by the presence of *activation functions*. A DNN is comprised of a set of layers of nodes, and the value of each node is determined by computing a linear combination of values from nodes in the preceding layer and then applying an activation function to the result. These activation functions are non-linear and render the problem non-convex. We focus here on DNNs with a specific kind of activation function, called a *Rectified Linear Unit* (*ReLU*) [27]. When the ReLU function is applied to a node with a positive value, it returns the value unchanged (the *active* case), but when the value is negative, the ReLU function returns 0 (the *inactive* case). ReLUs are very widely used [23,25], and it has been suggested that their piecewise linearity allows DNNs to generalize well to previously unseen inputs [6,7,11,27]. Past efforts at verifying properties of DNNs with ReLUs have had to make significant simplifying assumptions [3,10]—for instance, by considering only small input regions in which all ReLUs are fixed at either the active or inactive state [3], hence making the problem convex but at the cost of being able to verify only an approximation of the desired property.

We propose a novel, scalable, and efficient algorithm for verifying properties of DNNs with ReLUs. We address the issue of the activation functions head-on, by extending the simplex algorithm—a standard algorithm for solving LP instances—to support ReLU constraints. This is achieved by leveraging the piecewise linear nature of ReLUs and attempting to gradually satisfy the constraints that they impose as the algorithm searches for a feasible solution. We call the algorithm *Reluplex*, for "ReLU with Simplex".

The problem's NP-completeness means that we must expect the worst-case performance of the algorithm to be poor. However, as is often the case with SAT and SMT solvers, the performance in practice can be quite reasonable; in particular, our experiments show that during the search for a solution, many of the ReLUs can be ignored or even discarded altogether, reducing the search space by an order of magnitude or more. Occasionally, Reluplex will still need to *split* on a specific ReLU constraint—i.e., guess that it is either active or inactive, and possibly backtrack later if the choice leads to a contradiction.

We evaluated Reluplex on a family of 45 real-world DNNs, developed as an early prototype for the next-generation airborne collision avoidance system for unmanned aircraft ACAS Xu [13]. These fully connected DNNs have 8 layers and 300 ReLU nodes each, and are intended to be run onboard aircraft. They take in sensor data indicating the speed and present course of the aircraft (the *ownship*) and that of any nearby intruder aircraft, and issue appropriate navigation advisories. These advisories indicate whether the aircraft is clear-of-conflict, in which case the present course can be maintained, or whether it should turn to avoid collision. We successfully proved several properties of these networks, e.g. that a clear-of-conflict advisory will always be issued if the intruder is sufficiently far away or that it will never be issued if the intruder is sufficiently close and on a collision course with the ownship. Additionally, we were able to prove certain *robustness* properties [3] of the networks, meaning that small adversarial perturbations do not change the advisories produced for certain inputs.

Our contributions can be summarized as follows. We (i) present Reluplex, an SMT solver for a theory of linear real arithmetic with ReLU constraints; (ii) show how DNNs and properties of interest can be encoded as inputs to Reluplex; (iii) discuss several implementation details that are crucial to performance and scalability, such as the use of floating-point arithmetic, bound derivation for ReLU variables, and conflict analysis; and (iv) conduct a thorough evaluation on the DNN implementation of the prototype ACAS Xu system, demonstrating the ability of Reluplex to scale to DNNs that are an order of magnitude larger than those that can be analyzed using existing techniques.

The rest of the paper is organized as follows. We begin with some background on DNNs, SMT, and simplex in Sect. 2. The abstract Reluplex algorithm is described in Sect. 3, with key implementation details highlighted in Sect. 4. We then describe the ACAS Xu system and its prototype DNN implementation that we used as a case-study in Sect. 5, followed by experimental results in Sect. 6. Related work is discussed in Sect. 7, and we conclude in Sect. 8.

2   Background

Neural Networks. Deep neural networks (DNNs) are comprised of an input layer, an output layer, and multiple hidden layers in between. A layer is comprised of multiple nodes, each connected to nodes from the preceding layer using a predetermined set of weights (see Fig. 1). Weight selection is crucial, and is performed during a *training* phase (see, e.g., [7] for an overview). By assigning values to inputs and then feeding them forward through the network, values for each layer can be computed from the values of the previous layer, finally resulting in values for the outputs.

The value of each hidden node in the network is determined by calculating a linear combination of node values from the previous layer, and then applying a non-linear *activation function* [7]. Here, we focus on the Rectified Linear Unit (ReLU) activation function [27]. When a ReLU activation function is applied to a node, that node's value is calculated as the maximum of the linear combination of nodes from the previous layer and 0. We can thus regard ReLUs as the function $\text{ReLU}(x) = \max(0, x)$.

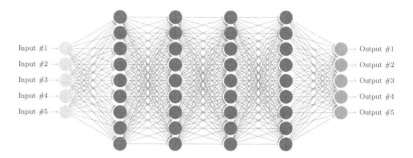

Fig. 1. A fully connected DNN with 5 input nodes (in green), 5 output nodes (in red), and 4 hidden layers containing a total of 36 hidden nodes (in blue). (Colour figure online).

Formally, for a DNN N, we use n to denote the number of layers and s_i to denote the size of layer i (i.e., the number of its nodes). Layer 1 is the input layer, layer n is the output layer, and layers $2, \ldots, n-1$ are the hidden layers. The value of the j-th node of layer i is denoted $v_{i,j}$ and the column vector $[v_{i,1}, \ldots, v_{i,s_i}]^T$ is denoted V_i. Evaluating N entails calculating V_n for a given assignment V_1 of the input layer. This is performed by propagating the input values through the network using predefined weights and biases, and applying the activation functions—ReLUs, in our case. Each layer $2 \leq i \leq n$ has a weight matrix W_i of size $s_i \times s_{i-1}$ and a bias vector B_i of size s_i, and its values are given by $V_i = \text{ReLU}(W_i V_{i-1} + B_i)$, with the ReLU function being applied element-wise. This rule is applied repeatedly for each layer until V_n is calculated. When the weight matrices $W_1, \ldots W_n$ do not have any zero entries, the network is said to be *fully connected* (see Fig. 1 for an illustration).

Figure 2 depicts a small network that we will use as a running example. The network has one input node, one output node and a single hidden layer with two nodes. The bias vectors are set to 0 and are ignored, and the weights are shown for each edge. The ReLU function is applied to each of the hidden nodes. It is possible to show that, due to the effect of the ReLUs, the network's output is always identical to its input: $v_{31} \equiv v_{11}$.

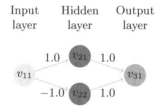

Fig. 2. A small neural network.

Satisfiability Modulo Theories. We present our algorithm as a theory solver in the context of satisfiability modulo theories (SMT).[1] A *theory* is a pair $T = (\Sigma, \mathbf{I})$ where Σ is a signature and $\mathbf{I}$ is a class of Σ-interpretations, the *models* of T, that is closed under variable reassignment. A Σ-formula φ is *T-satisfiable* (resp., *T-unsatisfiable*) if it is satisfied by some (resp., no) interpretation in $\mathbf{I}$. In this paper, we consider only *quantifier-free* formulas. The SMT problem is the problem of determining the T-satisfiability of a formula for a given theory T.

Given a theory T with signature Σ, the DPLL(T) architecture [28] provides a generic approach for determining the T-satisfiability of Σ-formulas. In DPLL(T), a Boolean satisfiability (SAT) engine operates on a Boolean abstraction of the formula, performing Boolean propagation, case-splitting, and Boolean conflict resolution. The SAT engine is coupled with a dedicated *theory solver*, which checks the T-satisfiability of the decisions made by the SAT engine. *Splitting-on-demand* [1] extends DPLL(T) by allowing theory solvers to delegate case-splitting to the SAT engine in a generic and modular way. In Sect. 3, we present our algorithm as a deductive calculus (with splitting rules) operating on conjunctions of literals. The DPLL(T) and splitting-on-demand mechanisms can then be used to obtain a full decision procedure for arbitrary formulas.

Linear Real Arithmetic and Simplex. In the context of DNNs, a particularly relevant theory is that of real arithmetic, which we denote as $\mathcal{T}_{\mathbb{R}}$. $\mathcal{T}_{\mathbb{R}}$ consists of the signature containing all rational number constants and the symbols $\{+, -, \cdot, \leq, \geq\}$, paired with the standard model of the real numbers. We focus on *linear* formulas: formulas over $\mathcal{T}_{\mathbb{R}}$ with the additional restriction that the multiplication symbol $\cdot$ can only appear if at least one of its operands is a rational constant. Linear atoms can always be rewritten into the form $\sum_{x_i \in \mathcal{X}} c_i x_i \bowtie d$, for $\bowtie \in \{=, \leq, \geq\}$, where $\mathcal{X}$ is a set of variables and c_i, d are rational constants.

The simplex method [5] is a standard and highly efficient decision procedure for determining the $\mathcal{T}_{\mathbb{R}}$-satisfiability of conjunctions of linear atoms.[2] Our algorithm extends simplex, and so we begin with an abstract calculus for the original algorithm (for a more thorough description see, e.g., [35]). The rules of the calculus operate over data structures we call *configurations*. For a given set of variables $\mathcal{X} = \{x_1, \ldots, x_n\}$, a simplex configuration is either one of the distinguished symbols $\{\texttt{SAT}, \texttt{UNSAT}\}$ or a tuple $\langle \mathcal{B}, T, l, u, \alpha \rangle$, where: $\mathcal{B} \subseteq \mathcal{X}$ is a set of basic variables; T, the *tableau*, contains for each $x_i \in \mathcal{B}$ an equation $x_i = \sum_{x_j \notin \mathcal{B}} c_j x_j$; l, u are mappings that assign each variable $x \in \mathcal{X}$ a lower and an upper bound, respectively; and α, the *assignment*, maps each variable $x \in \mathcal{X}$ to a real value. The initial configuration (and in particular the initial tableau T_0) is derived from a conjunction of input atoms as follows: for each atom $\sum_{x_i \in \mathcal{X}} c_i x_i \bowtie d$, a new basic variable b is introduced, the equation $b = \sum_{x_i \in \mathcal{X}} c_i x_i$ is added to the

---

[1] Consistent with most treatments of SMT, we assume many-sorted first-order logic with equality as our underlying formalism (see, e.g., [2] for details).

[2] There exist SMT-friendly extensions of simplex (see e.g. [17]) which can handle $\mathcal{T}_{\mathbb{R}}$-satisfiability of arbitrary literals, including strict inequalities and disequalities, but we omit these extensions here for simplicity (and without loss of generality).

tableau, and d is added as a bound for b (either upper, lower, or both, depending on $\bowtie$). The initial assignment is set to 0 for all variables, ensuring that all tableau equations hold (though variable bounds may be violated).

The tableau T can be regarded as a matrix expressing each of the basic variables (variables in $\mathcal{B}$) as a linear combination of non-basic variables (variables in $\mathcal{X} \setminus \mathcal{B}$). The rows of T correspond to the variables in $\mathcal{B}$ and its columns to those of $\mathcal{X} \setminus \mathcal{B}$. For $x_i \in \mathcal{B}$ and $x_j \notin \mathcal{B}$ we denote by $T_{i,j}$ the coefficient c_j of x_j in the equation $x_i = \sum_{x_j \notin \mathcal{B}} c_j x_j$. The tableau is changed via pivoting: the switching of a basic variable x_i (the *leaving* variable) with a non-basic variable x_j (the *entering* variable) for which $T_{i,j} \neq 0$. A $pivot(T, i, j)$ operation returns a new tableau in which the equation $x_i = \sum_{x_k \notin \mathcal{B}} c_k x_k$ has been replaced by the equation $x_j = \frac{x_i}{c_j} - \sum_{x_k \notin \mathcal{B}, k \neq j} \frac{c_k}{c_j} x_k$, and in which every occurrence of x_j in each of the other equations has been replaced by the right-hand side of the new equation (the resulting expressions are also normalized to retain the tableau form). The variable assignment α is changed via *update* operations that are applied to non-basic variables: for $x_j \notin \mathcal{B}$, an $update(\alpha, x_j, \delta)$ operation returns an updated assignment α' identical to α, except that $\alpha'(x_j) = \alpha(x_j) + \delta$ and for every $x_i \in \mathcal{B}$, we have $\alpha'(x_i) = \alpha(x_i) + \delta \cdot T_{i,j}$. To simplify later presentation we also denote:

$$\text{slack}^+(x_i) = \{x_j \notin \mathcal{B} \mid (T_{i,j} > 0 \wedge \alpha(x_j) < u(x_j)) \vee (T_{i,j} < 0 \wedge \alpha(x_j) > l(x_j))$$
$$\text{slack}^-(x_i) = \{x_j \notin \mathcal{B} \mid (T_{i,j} < 0 \wedge \alpha(x_j) < u(x_j)) \vee (T_{i,j} > 0 \wedge \alpha(x_j) > l(x_j))$$

The rules of the simplex calculus are provided in Fig. 3 in *guarded assignment form*. A rule applies to a configuration S if all of the rule's premises hold for S. A rule's conclusion describes how each component of S is changed, if at all. When S' is the result of applying a rule to S, we say that S derives S'. A sequence of configurations S_i where each S_i derives S_{i+1} is called a *derivation*.

$$\text{Pivot}_1 \quad \frac{x_i \in \mathcal{B}, \quad \alpha(x_i) < l(x_i), \quad x_j \in \text{slack}^+(x_i)}{T := pivot(T, i, j), \quad \mathcal{B} := \mathcal{B} \cup \{x_j\} \setminus \{x_i\}}$$

$$\text{Pivot}_2 \quad \frac{x_i \in \mathcal{B}, \quad \alpha(x_i) > u(x_i), \quad x_j \in \text{slack}^-(x_i)}{T := pivot(T, i, j), \quad \mathcal{B} := \mathcal{B} \cup \{x_j\} \setminus \{x_i\}}$$

$$\text{Update} \quad \frac{x_j \notin \mathcal{B}, \quad \alpha(x_j) < l(x_j) \vee \alpha(x_j) > u(x_j), \quad l(x_j) \leq \alpha(x_j) + \delta \leq u(x_j)}{\alpha := update(\alpha, x_j, \delta)}$$

$$\text{Failure} \quad \frac{x_i \in \mathcal{B}, \quad (\alpha(x_i) < l(x_i) \wedge \text{slack}^+(x_i) = \emptyset) \vee (\alpha(x_i) > u(x_i) \wedge \text{slack}^-(x_i) = \emptyset)}{\text{UNSAT}}$$

$$\text{Success} \quad \frac{\forall x_i \in \mathcal{X}. \ l(x_i) \leq \alpha(x_i) \leq u(x_i)}{\text{SAT}}$$

Fig. 3. Derivation rules for the abstract simplex algorithm.

The Update rule (with appropriate values of δ) is used to enforce that non-basic variables satisfy their bounds. Basic variables cannot be directly updated.

Instead, if a basic variable x_i is too small or too great, either the Pivot_1 or the Pivot_2 rule is applied, respectively, to pivot it with a non-basic variable x_j. This makes x_i non-basic so that its assignment can be adjusted using the Update rule. Pivoting is only allowed when x_j affords *slack*, that is, the assignment for x_j can be adjusted to bring x_i closer to its bound without violating its own bound. Of course, once pivoting occurs and the Update rule is used to bring x_i within its bounds, other variables (such as the now basic x_j) may be sent outside their bounds, in which case they must be corrected in a later iteration. If a basic variable is out of bounds, but none of the non-basic variables affords it any slack, then the Failure rule applies and the problem is unsatisfiable. Because the tableau is only changed by scaling and adding rows, the set of variable assignments that satisfy its equations is always kept identical to that of T_0. Also, the *update* operation guarantees that α continues to satisfy the equations of T. Thus, if all variables are within bounds then the Success rule can be applied, indicating that α constitutes a satisfying assignment for the original problem.

It is well-known that the simplex calculus is *sound* [35] (i.e. if a derivation ends in SAT or UNSAT, then the original problem is satisfiable or unsatisfiable, respectively) and *complete* (there always exists a derivation ending in either SAT or UNSAT from any starting configuration). Termination can be guaranteed if certain strategies are used in applying the transition rules—in particular in picking the leaving and entering variables when multiple options exist [35]. Variable selection strategies are also known to have a dramatic effect on performance [35]. We note that the version of simplex described above is usually referred to as *phase one* simplex, and is usually followed by a *phase two* in which the solution is optimized according to a cost function. However, as we are only considering satisfiability, phase two is not required.

3   From Simplex to Reluplex

The simplex algorithm described in Sect. 2 is an efficient means for solving problems that can be encoded as a conjunction of atoms. Unfortunately, while the weights, biases, and certain properties of DNNs can be encoded this way, the non-linear ReLU functions cannot.

When a theory solver operates within an SMT solver, input atoms can be embedded in arbitrary Boolean structure. A naïve approach is then to encode ReLUs using disjunctions, which is possible because ReLUs are piecewise linear. However, this encoding requires the SAT engine within the SMT solver to enumerate the different cases. In the worst case, for a DNN with n ReLU nodes, the solver ends up splitting the problem into 2^n sub-problems, each of which is a conjunction of atoms. As observed by us and others [3,10], this theoretical worst-case behavior is also seen in practice, and hence this approach is practical only for very small networks. A similar phenomenon occurs when encoding DNNs as mixed integer problems (see Sect. 6).

We take a different route and extend the theory $\mathcal{T}_{\mathbb{R}}$ to a theory $\mathcal{T}_{\mathbb{R}R}$ of reals and ReLUs. $\mathcal{T}_{\mathbb{R}R}$ is almost identical to $\mathcal{T}_{\mathbb{R}}$, except that its signature additionally includes the binary predicate ReLU with the interpretation: $\text{ReLU}(x, y)$ iff $y = \max(0, x)$. Formulas are then assumed to contain atoms that are either linear inequalities or applications of the ReLU predicate to linear terms.

DNNs and their (linear) properties can be directly encoded as conjunctions of $\mathcal{T}_{\mathbb{RR}}$-atoms. The main idea is to encode a single ReLU node v as a *pair* of variables, v^b and v^f, and then assert $\text{ReLU}(v^b, v^f)$. v^b, the *backward-facing* variable, is used to express the connection of v to nodes from the preceding layer; whereas v^f, the *forward-facing* variable, is used for the connections of x to the following layer (see Fig. 4). The rest of this section is devoted to presenting an efficient algorithm, Reluplex, for deciding the satisfiability of a conjunction of such atoms.

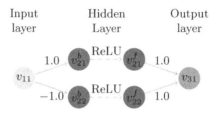

Fig. 4. The network from Fig. 2, with ReLU nodes split into backward- and forward-facing variables.

The Reluplex Procedure. As with simplex, Reluplex allows variables to temporarily violate their bounds as it iteratively looks for a feasible variable assignment. However, Reluplex also allows variables that are members of ReLU pairs to temporarily violate the ReLU semantics. Then, as it iterates, Reluplex repeatedly picks variables that are either out of bounds or that violate a ReLU, and corrects them using Pivot and Update operations.

For a given set of variables $\mathcal{X} = \{x_1, \ldots, x_n\}$, a Reluplex configuration is either one of the distinguished symbols $\{\text{SAT}, \text{UNSAT}\}$ or a tuple $\langle \mathcal{B}, T, l, u, \alpha, R \rangle$, where $\mathcal{B}, T, l, u$ and α are as before, and $R \subset \mathcal{X} \times \mathcal{X}$ is the set of ReLU connections. The initial configuration for a conjunction of atoms is also obtained as before except that $\langle x, y \rangle \in R$ iff $\text{ReLU}(x, y)$ is an atom. The simplex transition rules Pivot$_1$, Pivot$_2$ and Update are included also in Reluplex, as they are designed to handle out-of-bounds violations. We replace the Success rule with the ReluSuccess rule and add rules for handling ReLU violations, as depicted in Fig. 5. The Update$_b$ and Update$_f$ rules allow a broken ReLU connection to be corrected by updating the backward- or forward-facing variables, respectively, provided that these variables are non-basic. The PivotForRelu rule allows a basic variable appearing in a ReLU to be pivoted so that either Update$_b$ or Update$_f$ can be applied (this is needed to make progress when both variables in a ReLU are basic and their assignments do not satisfy the ReLU semantics). The ReluSplit rule is used for splitting on certain ReLU connections, guessing whether they are active (by setting $l(x_i) := 0$) or inactive (by setting $u(x_i) := 0$).

$$\text{Update}_b \quad \frac{x_i \notin \mathcal{B}, \quad \langle x_i, x_j \rangle \in R, \quad \alpha(x_j) \neq \max(0, \alpha(x_i)), \quad \alpha(x_j) \geq 0}{\alpha := update(\alpha, x_i, \alpha(x_j) - \alpha(x_i))}$$

$$\text{Update}_f \quad \frac{x_j \notin \mathcal{B}, \quad \langle x_i, x_j \rangle \in R, \quad \alpha(x_j) \neq \max(0, \alpha(x_i))}{\alpha := update(\alpha, x_j, \max(0, \alpha(x_i)) - \alpha(x_j))}$$

$$\text{PivotForRelu} \quad \frac{x_i \in \mathcal{B}, \quad \exists x_l. \langle x_i, x_l \rangle \in R \vee \langle x_l, x_i \rangle \in R, \quad x_j \notin \mathcal{B}, \quad T_{i,j} \neq 0}{T := pivot(T, i, j), \quad \mathcal{B} := \mathcal{B} \cup \{x_j\} \setminus \{x_i\}}$$

$$\text{ReluSplit} \quad \frac{\langle x_i, x_j \rangle \in R, \quad l(x_i) < 0, \quad u(x_i) > 0}{u(x_i) := 0 \qquad l(x_i) := 0}$$

$$\text{ReluSuccess} \quad \frac{\forall x \in \mathcal{X}. \, l(x) \leq \alpha(x) \leq u(x), \quad \forall \langle x^b, x^f \rangle \in R. \, \alpha(x^f) = \max(0, \alpha(x^b))}{\text{SAT}}$$

Fig. 5. Additional derivation rules for the abstract Reluplex algorithm.

Introducing splitting means that derivations are no longer linear. Using the notion of derivation trees, we can show that Reluplex is sound and complete (see Sect. II of the supplementary material [15]). In practice, splitting can be managed by a SAT engine with splitting-on-demand [1]. The naïve approach mentioned at the beginning of this section can be simulated by applying the ReluSplit rule eagerly until it no longer applies and then solving each derived sub-problem separately (this reduction trivially guarantees termination just as do branch-and-cut techniques in mixed integer solvers [29]). However, a more scalable strategy is to try to fix broken ReLU pairs using the Update_b and Update_f rules first, and split only when the number of updates to a specific ReLU pair exceeds some threshold. Intuitively, this is likely to limit splits to "problematic" ReLU pairs, while still guaranteeing termination (see Sect. III of the supplementary material [15]). Additional details appear in Sect. 6.

Example. To illustrate the use of the derivation rules, we use Reluplex to solve a simple example. Consider the network in Fig. 4, and suppose we wish to check whether it is possible to satisfy $v_{11} \in [0, 1]$ and $v_{31} \in [0.5, 1]$. As we know that the network outputs its input unchanged ($v_{31} \equiv v_{11}$), we expect Reluplex to be able to derive SAT. The initial Reluplex configuration is obtained by introducing new basic variables a_1, a_2, a_3, and encoding the network with the equations:

$$a_1 = -v_{11} + v_{21}^b \qquad a_2 = v_{11} + v_{22}^b \qquad a_3 = -v_{21}^f - v_{22}^f + v_{31}$$

The equations above form the initial tableau T_0, and the initial set of basic variables is $\mathcal{B} = \{a_1, a_2, a_3\}$. The set of ReLU connections is $R = \{\langle v_{21}^b, v_{21}^f \rangle, \langle v_{22}^b, v_{22}^f \rangle\}$. The initial assignment of all variables is set to 0. The lower and upper bounds of the basic variables are set to 0, in order to enforce the equalities that they represent. The bounds for the input and output variables are set according to the problem at hand; and the hidden variables are unbounded, except that forward-facing variables are, by definition, non-negative:

variable	v_{11}	v_{21}^b	v_{21}^f	v_{22}^b	v_{22}^f	v_{31}	a_1	a_2	a_3
lower bound	0	$-\infty$	0	$-\infty$	0	0.5	0	0	0
assignment	0	0	0	0	0	0	0	0	0
upper bound	1	∞	∞	∞	∞	1	0	0	0

Starting from this initial configuration, our search strategy is to first fix any out-of-bounds variables. Variable v_{31} is non-basic and is out of bounds, so we perform an Update step and set it to 0.5. As a result, a_3, which depends on v_{31}, is also set to 0.5. a_3 is now basic and out of bounds, so we pivot it with v_{21}^f, and then update a_3 back to 0. The tableau now consists of the equations:

$$a_1 = -v_{11} + v_{21}^b \qquad a_2 = v_{11} + v_{22}^b \qquad v_{21}^f = -v_{22}^f + v_{31} - a_3$$

And the assignment is $\alpha(v_{21}^f) = 0.5$, $\alpha(v_{31}) = 0.5$, and $\alpha(v) = 0$ for all other variables v. At this point, all variables are within their bounds, but the ReluSuccess rule does not apply because $\alpha(v_{21}^f) = 0.5 \neq 0 = \max(0, \alpha(v_{21}^b))$.

The next step is to fix the broken ReLU pair $\langle v_{21}^b, v_{21}^f \rangle$. Since v_{21}^b is non-basic, we use Update$_b$ to increase its value by 0.5. The assignment becomes $\alpha(v_{21}^b) = 0.5$, $\alpha(v_{21}^f) = 0.5$, $\alpha(v_{31}) = 0.5$, $\alpha(a_1) = 0.5$, and $\alpha(v) = 0$ for all other variables v. All ReLU constraints hold, but a_1 is now out of bounds. This is fixed by pivoting a_1 with v_{11} and then updating it. The resulting tableau is:

$$v_{11} = v_{21}^b - a_1 \qquad a_2 = v_{21}^b + v_{22}^b - a_1 \qquad v_{21}^f = -v_{22}^f + v_{31} - a_3$$

Observe that because v_{11} is now basic, it was eliminated from the equation for a_2 and replaced with $v_{21}^b - a_1$. The non-zero assignments are now $\alpha(v_{11}) = 0.5$, $\alpha(v_{21}^b) = 0.5$, $\alpha(v_{21}^f) = 0.5$, $\alpha(v_{31}) = 0.5$, $\alpha(a_2) = 0.5$. Variable a_2 is now too large, and so we have a final round of pivot-and-update: a_2 is pivoted with v_{22}^b and then updated back to 0. The final tableau and assignments are:

$$v_{11} = v_{21}^b - a_1$$
$$v_{22}^b = -v_{21}^b + a_1 + a_2$$
$$v_{21}^f = -v_{22}^f + v_{31} - a_3$$

variable	v_{11}	v_{21}^b	v_{21}^f	v_{22}^b	v_{22}^f	v_{31}	a_1	a_2	a_3
lower bound	0	$-\infty$	0	$-\infty$	0	0.5	0	0	0
assignment	0.5	0.5	0.5	-0.5	0	0.5	0	0	0
upper bound	1	∞	∞	∞	∞	1	0	0	0

and the algorithm halts with the feasible solution it has found. A key observation is that we did not ever split on any of the ReLU connections. Instead, it was sufficient to simply use updates to adjust the ReLU variables as needed.

4   Efficiently Implementing Reluplex

We next discuss three techniques that significantly boost the performance of Reluplex: use of tighter bound derivation, conflict analysis and floating point arithmetic. A fourth technique, under-approximation, is discussed in Sect. IV of the supplementary material [15].

Tighter Bound Derivation. The simplex and Reluplex procedures naturally lend themselves to deriving tighter variable bounds as the search progresses [17]. Consider a basic variable $x_i \in \mathcal{B}$ and let $\text{pos}(x_i) = \{x_j \notin \mathcal{B} \mid T_{i,j} > 0\}$ and $\text{neg}(x_i) = \{x_j \notin \mathcal{B} \mid T_{i,j} < 0\}$. Throughout the execution, the following rules can be used to derive tighter bounds for x_i, regardless of the current assignment:

$$\text{deriveLowerBound} \quad \frac{x_i \in \mathcal{B}, \;\; l(x_i) < \sum_{x_j \in \text{pos}(x_i)} T_{i,j} \cdot l(x_j) + \sum_{x_j \in \text{neg}(x_i)} T_{i,j} \cdot u(x_j)}{l(x_i) := \sum_{x_j \in \text{pos}(x_i)} T_{i,j} \cdot l(x_j) + \sum_{x_j \in \text{neg}(x_i)} T_{i,j} \cdot u(x_j)}$$

$$\text{deriveUpperBound} \quad \frac{x_i \in \mathcal{B}, \;\; u(x_i) > \sum_{x_j \in \text{pos}(x_i)} T_{i,j} \cdot u(x_j) + \sum_{x_j \in \text{neg}(x_i)} T_{i,j} \cdot l(x_j)}{u(x_i) := \sum_{x_j \in \text{pos}(x_i)} T_{i,j} \cdot u(x_j) + \sum_{x_j \in \text{neg}(x_i)} T_{i,j} \cdot l(x_j)}$$

The derived bounds can later be used to derive additional, tighter bounds.

When tighter bounds are derived for ReLU variables, these variables can sometimes be eliminated, i.e., fixed to the active or inactive state, without splitting. For a ReLU pair $x^f = \text{ReLU}(x^b)$, discovering that either $l(x^b)$ or $l(x^f)$ is strictly positive means that in any feasible solution this ReLU connection will be active. Similarly, discovering that $u(x^b) < 0$ implies inactivity.

Bound tightening operations incur overhead, and simplex implementations often use them sparsely [17]. In Reluplex, however, the benefits of eliminating ReLUs justify the cost. The actual amount of bound tightening to perform can be determined heuristically; we describe the heuristic that we used in Sect. 6.

Derived Bounds and Conflict Analysis. Bound derivation can lead to situations where we learn that $l(x) > u(x)$ for some variable x. Such contradictions allow Reluplex to immediately undo a previous split (or answer UNSAT if no previous splits exist). However, in many cases more than just the previous split can be undone. For example, if we have performed 8 nested splits so far, it may be that the conflicting bounds for x are the direct result of split number 5 but have only just been discovered. In this case we can immediately undo splits number 8, 7, and 6. This is a particular case of *conflict analysis*, which is a standard technique in SAT and SMT solvers [26].

Floating Point Arithmetic. SMT solvers typically use precise (as opposed to floating point) arithmetic to avoid roundoff errors and guarantee soundness. Unfortunately, precise computation is usually at least an order of magnitude slower than its floating point equivalent. Invoking Reluplex on a large DNN can require millions of pivot operations, each of which involves the multiplication and division of rational numbers, potentially with large numerators or denominators—making the use of floating point arithmetic important for scalability.

There are standard techniques for keeping the roundoff error small when implementing simplex using floating point, which we incorporated into our implementation. For example, one important practice is trying to avoid Pivot operations involving the inversion of extremely small numbers [35].

To provide increased confidence that any roundoff error remained within an acceptable range, we also added the following safeguards: (i) After a certain number of Pivot steps we would measure the accumulated roundoff error; and (ii) If the error exceeded a threshold M, we would *restore* the coefficients of the current tableau T using the initial tableau T_0.

Cumulative roundoff error can be measured by plugging the current assignment values for the non-basic variables into the equations of the initial tableau T_0, using them to calculate the values for every basic variable x_i, and then measuring by how much these values differ from the current assignment $\alpha(x_i)$. We define the cumulative roundoff error as:

$$\sum_{x_i \in \mathcal{B}_0} |\alpha(x_i) - \sum_{x_j \notin \mathcal{B}_0} T_{0_{i,j}} \cdot \alpha(x_j)|$$

T is restored by starting from T_0 and performing a short series of Pivot steps that result in the same set of basic variables as in T. In general, the shortest sequence of pivot steps to transform T_0 to T is much shorter than the series of steps that was followed by Reluplex—and hence, although it is also performed using floating point arithmetic, it incurs a smaller roundoff error.

The tableau restoration technique serves to increase our confidence in the algorithm's results when using floating point arithmetic, but it does not guarantee soundness. Providing true soundness when using floating point arithmetic remains a future goal (see Sect. 8).

5   Case Study: The ACAS Xu System

Airborne collision avoidance systems are critical for ensuring the safe operation of aircraft. The *Traffic Alert and Collision Avoidance System (TCAS)* was developed in response to midair collisions between commercial aircraft, and is currently mandated on all large commercial aircraft worldwide [24]. Recent work has focused on creating a new system, known as *Airborne Collision Avoidance System X (ACAS X)* [19,20]. This system adopts an approach that involves solving a partially observable Markov decision process to optimize the alerting logic and further reduce the probability of midair collisions, while minimizing unnecessary alerts [19,20,22].

The unmanned variant of ACAS X, known as ACAS Xu, produces horizontal maneuver advisories. So far, development of ACAS Xu has focused on using a large lookup table that maps sensor measurements to advisories [13]. However, this table requires over 2 GB of memory. There is concern about the memory requirements for certified avionics hardware. To overcome this challenge, a DNN representation was explored as a potential replacement for the table [13]. Initial results show a dramatic reduction in memory requirements without compromising safety. In fact, due to its continuous nature, the DNN approach can sometimes outperform the discrete lookup table [13]. Recently, in order to reduce lookup time, the DNN approach was improved further, and the single DNN was replaced by an array of 45 DNNs. As a result, the original 2 GB table can now be substituted with efficient DNNs that require less than 3 MB of memory.

A DNN implementation of ACAS Xu presents new certification challenges. Proving that a set of inputs cannot produce an erroneous alert is paramount for certifying the system for use in safety-critical settings. Previous certification methodologies included exhaustively testing the system in 1.5 million simulated encounters [21], but this is insufficient for proving that faulty behaviors do not exist within the continuous DNNs. This highlights the need for verifying DNNs and makes the ACAS Xu DNNs prime candidates on which to apply Reluplex.

Network Functionality. The ACAS Xu system maps input variables to action advisories. Each advisory is assigned a score, with the lowest score corresponding to the best action. The input state is composed of seven dimensions (shown in Fig. 6) which represent information determined from sensor measurements [20]: (i) ρ: Distance from ownship to intruder; (ii) θ: Angle to intruder relative to ownship heading direction; (iii) ψ: Heading angle of intruder relative to ownship heading direction; (iv) v_{own}: Speed of ownship; (v) v_{int}: Speed of intruder; (vi) τ: Time until loss of vertical separation; and (vii) a_{prev}: Previous advisory. There are five outputs which represent the different horizontal advisories that can be given to the ownship: Clear-of-Conflict (COC), weak right, strong right, weak left, or strong left. Weak and strong mean heading rates of 1.5 °/s and 3.0 °/s, respectively.

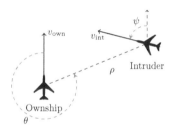

Fig. 6. Geometry for ACAS Xu horizontal logic table

The array of 45 DNNs was produced by discretizing τ and a_{prev}, and producing a network for each discretized combination. Each of these networks thus has five inputs (one for each of the other dimensions) and five outputs. The DNNs are fully connected, use ReLU activation functions, and have 6 hidden layers with a total of 300 ReLU nodes each.

Network Properties. It is desirable to verify that the ACAS Xu networks assign correct scores to the output advisories in various input domains. Figure 7 illustrates this kind of property by showing a top-down view of a head-on encounter scenario, in which each pixel is colored to represent the best action if the intruder were at that location. We expect the DNN's advisories to be consistent in each of these regions; however, Fig. 7 was generated from a finite set of input samples, and there may exist other inputs for which a wrong advisory is produced, possibly leading to collision. Therefore, we used Reluplex to prove properties from the following categories on the DNNs: (i) The system does not give unnecessary turning advisories; (ii) Alerting regions are uniform and do not contain inconsistent alerts; and (iii) Strong alerts do not appear for high τ values.

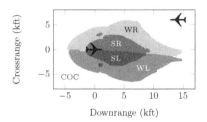

Fig. 7. Advisories for a head-on encounter with $a_{\text{prev}} = \text{COC}, \tau = 0s$.

6   Evaluation

We used a proof-of-concept implementation of Reluplex to check realistic properties on the 45 ACAS Xu DNNs. Our implementation consists of three main logical components: (i) A simplex engine for providing core functionality such as tableau representation and pivot and update operations; (ii) A Reluplex engine for driving the search and performing bound derivation, ReLU pivots and ReLU updates; and (iii) A simple SMT core for providing splitting-on-demand services. For the simplex engine we used the GLPK open-source LP solver[3] with some modifications, for instance in order to allow the Reluplex core to perform bound tightening on tableau equations calculated by GLPK. Our implementation, together with the experiments described in this section, is available online [14].

Our search strategy was to repeatedly fix any out-of-bounds violations first, and only then correct any violated ReLU constraints (possibly introducing new out-of-bounds violations). We performed bound tightening on the entering variable after every pivot operation, and performed a more thorough bound tightening on all the equations in the tableau once every few thousand pivot steps. Tighter bound derivation proved extremely useful, and we often observed that after splitting on about 10% of the ReLU variables it led to the elimination of all remaining ReLUs. We counted the number of times a ReLU pair was fixed via Update$_b$ or Update$_f$ or pivoted via PivotForRelu, and split only when this number reached 5 (a number empirically determined to work well). We also implemented conflict analysis and back-jumping. Finally, we checked the accumulated roundoff error (due to the use of double-precision floating point arithmetic) after every

---

[3] www.gnu.org/software/glpk/.

5000 Pivot steps, and restored the tableau if the error exceeded 10^{-6}. Most experiments described below required two tableau restorations or fewer.

We began by comparing our implementation of Reluplex to state-of-the-art solvers: the CVC4, Z3, Yices and MathSat SMT solvers and the Gurobi LP solver (see Table 1). We ran all solvers with a 4 h timeout on 2 of the ACAS Xu networks (selected arbitrarily), trying to solve for 8 simple satisfiable properties $\varphi_1, \ldots, \varphi_8$, each of the form $x \geq c$ for a fixed output variable x and a constant c. The SMT solvers generally performed poorly, with only Yices and MathSat successfully solving two instances each. We attribute the results to these solvers' lack of direct support for encoding ReLUs, and to their use of precise arithmetic. Gurobi solved 3 instances quickly, but timed out on all the rest. Its logs indicated that whenever Gurobi could solve the problem without case-splitting, it did so quickly; but whenever the problem required case-splitting, Gurobi would time out. Reluplex was able to solve all 8 instances. See Sect. V of the supplementary material [15] for the SMT and LP encodings that we used.

Table 1. Comparison to SMT and LP solvers. Entries indicate solution time (in seconds).

	φ_1	φ_2	φ_3	φ_4	φ_5	φ_6	φ_7	φ_8
CVC4	-	-	-	-	-	-	-	-
Z3	-	-	-	-	-	-	-	-
Yices	1	37	-	-	-	-	-	-
MathSat	2040	9780	-	-	-	-	-	-
Gurobi	1	1	1	-	-	-	-	-
Reluplex	8	2	7	7	93	4	7	9

Next, we used Reluplex to test a set of 10 quantitative properties $\phi_1, \ldots, \phi_{10}$. The properties, described below, are formally defined in Sect. VI of the supplementary material [15]. Table 2 depicts for each property the number of tested networks (specified as part of the property), the test results and the total duration (in seconds). The *Stack* and *Splits* columns list the maximal depth of nested case-splits reached (averaged over the tested networks) and the total number of case-splits performed, respectively. For each property, we looked for an input that would violate it; thus, an UNSAT result indicates that a property holds, and a SAT result indicates that it does not hold. In the SAT case, the satisfying assignment is an example of an input that violates the property.

Property ϕ_1 states that if the intruder is distant and is significantly slower than the ownship, the score of a COC advisory will always be below a certain fixed threshold (recall that the best action has the lowest score). Property ϕ_2 states that under similar conditions, the score for COC can never be maximal, meaning that it can never be the worst action to take. This property was discovered not to hold for 35 networks, but this was later determined to be acceptable

Table 2. Verifying properties of the ACAS Xu networks.

	Networks	Result	Time	Stack	Splits
ϕ_1	41	UNSAT	394517	47	1522384
	4	TIMEOUT			
ϕ_2	1	UNSAT	463	55	88388
	35	SAT	82419	44	284515
ϕ_3	42	UNSAT	28156	22	52080
ϕ_4	42	UNSAT	12475	21	23940
ϕ_5	1	UNSAT	19355	46	58914
ϕ_6	1	UNSAT	180288	50	548496
ϕ_7	1	TIMEOUT			
ϕ_8	1	SAT	40102	69	116697
ϕ_9	1	UNSAT	99634	48	227002
ϕ_{10}	1	UNSAT	19944	49	88520

behavior: the DNNs have a strong bias for producing the same advisory they had previously produced, and this can result in advisories other than COC even for far-away intruders if the previous advisory was also something other than COC. Properties ϕ_3 and ϕ_4 deal with situations where the intruder is directly ahead of the ownship, and state that the DNNs will never issue a COC advisory.

Properties ϕ_5 through ϕ_{10} each involve a single network, and check for consistent behavior in a specific input region. For example, ϕ_5 states that if the intruder is near and approaching from the left, the network advises "strong right". Property ϕ_7, on which we timed out, states that when the vertical separation is large the network will never advise a strong turn. The large input domain and the particular network proved difficult to verify. Property ϕ_8 states that for a large vertical separation and a previous "weak left" advisory, the network will either output COC or continue advising "weak left". Here, we were able to find a counter-example, exposing an input on which the DNN was inconsistent with the lookup table. This confirmed the existence of a discrepancy that had also been seen in simulations, and which will be addressed by retraining the DNN. We observe that for all properties, the maximal depth of nested splits was always well below the total number of ReLU nodes, 300, illustrating the fact that Reluplex did not split on many of them. Also, the total number of case-splits indicates that large portions of the search space were pruned.

Another class of properties that we tested is *adversarial robustness* properties. DNNs have been shown to be susceptible to adversarial inputs [34]: correctly classified inputs that an adversary slightly perturbs, leading to their misclassification by the network. Adversarial robustness is thus a safety consideration, and adversarial inputs can be used to train the network further, making it more robust [8]. There exist approaches for finding adversarial inputs [3,8], but the ability to verify their absence is limited.

We say that a network is δ-*locally-robust* at input point x if for every x' such that $\|x - x'\|_\infty \leq \delta$, the network assigns the same label to x and x'. In the case of the ACAS Xu DNNs, this means that the same output has the lowest score for both x and x'. Reluplex can be used to prove local robustness for a given x and δ, as depicted in Table 3. We used one of the ACAS Xu networks, and tested combinations of 5 arbitrary points and 5 values of δ. SAT results show that Reluplex found an adversarial input within the prescribed neighborhood, and UNSAT results indicate that no such inputs exist. Using binary search on values of δ, Reluplex can thus be used for approximating the optimal δ value up to a desired precision: for example, for point 4 the optimal δ is between 0.025 and 0.05. It is expected that different input points will have different local robustness, and the acceptable thresholds will thus need to be set individually.

Table 3. Local adversarial robustness tests. All times are in seconds.

	$\delta = 0.1$		$\delta = 0.075$		$\delta = 0.05$		$\delta = 0.025$		$\delta = 0.01$		Total
	Result	Time	Result	Time	Result	Time	Result	Time	Result	Time	Time
Point 1	SAT	135	SAT	239	SAT	24	UNSAT	609	UNSAT	57	1064
Point 2	UNSAT	5880	UNSAT	1167	UNSAT	285	UNSAT	57	UNSAT	5	7394
Point 3	UNSAT	863	UNSAT	436	UNSAT	99	UNSAT	53	UNSAT	1	1452
Point 4	SAT	2	SAT	977	SAT	1168	UNSAT	656	UNSAT	7	2810
Point 5	UNSAT	14560	UNSAT	4344	UNSAT	1331	UNSAT	221	UNSAT	6	20462

Finally, we mention an additional variant of adversarial robustness which we term *global adversarial robustness*, and which can also be solved by Reluplex. Whereas local adversarial robustness is measured for a specific x, global adversarial robustness applies to all inputs simultaneously. This is expressed by encoding two side-by-side copies of the DNN in question, N_1 and N_2, operating on separate input variables x_1 and x_2, respectively, such that x_2 represents an adversarial perturbation of x_1. We can then check whether $\|x_1 - x_2\|_\infty \leq \delta$ implies that the two copies of the DNN produce similar outputs. Formally, we require that if N_1 and N_2 assign output a values p_1 and p_2 respectively, then $|p_1 - p_2| \leq \epsilon$. If this holds for every output, we say that the network is ϵ-globally-robust. Global adversarial robustness is harder to prove than the local variant, because encoding two copies of the network results in twice as many ReLU nodes and because the problem is not restricted to a small input domain. We were able to prove global adversarial robustness only on small networks; improving the scalability of this technique is left for future work.

7   Related Work

In [30], the authors propose an approach for verifying properties of neural networks with sigmoid activation functions. They replace the activation functions with piecewise linear approximations thereof, and then invoke black-box SMT solvers. When spurious counter-examples are found, the approximation is refined. The authors highlight the difficulty in scaling-up this technique, and are able to tackle only small networks with at most 20 hidden nodes [31].

The authors of [3] propose a technique for finding local adversarial examples in DNNs with ReLUs. Given an input point x, they encode the problem as a linear program and invoke a black-box LP solver. The activation function issue is circumvented by considering a sufficiently small neighborhood of x, in which all ReLUs are fixed at the active or inactive state, making the problem convex. Thus, it is unclear how to address an x for which one or more ReLUs are on the boundary between active and inactive states. In contrast, Reluplex can be used on input domains for which ReLUs can have more than one possible state.

In a recent paper [10], the authors propose a method for proving the local adversarial robustness of DNNs. For a specific input point x, the authors attempt to prove consistent labeling in a neighborhood of x by means of discretization: they reduce the infinite neighborhood into a finite set of points, and check that the labeling of these points is consistent. This process is then propagated through the network, layer by layer. While the technique is general in the sense that it is not tailored for a specific activation function, the discretization process means that any UNSAT result only holds modulo the assumption that the finite sets correctly represent their infinite domains. In contrast, our technique can guarantee that there are no irregularities hiding between the discrete points.

Finally, in [12], the authors employ hybrid techniques to analyze an ACAS X controller given in lookup-table form, seeking to identify *safe input regions* in which collisions cannot occur. It will be interesting to combine our technique with that of [12], in order to verify that following the advisories provided by the DNNs indeed leads to collision avoidance.

8   Conclusion and Next Steps

We presented a novel decision algorithm for solving queries on deep neural networks with ReLU activation functions. The technique is based on extending the simplex algorithm to support the non-convex ReLUs in a way that allows their inputs and outputs to be temporarily inconsistent and then fixed as the algorithm progresses. To guarantee termination, some ReLU connections may need to be split upon—but in many cases this is not required, resulting in an efficient solution. Our success in verifying properties of the ACAS Xu networks indicates that the technique holds much potential for verifying real-world DNNs.

In the future, we plan to increase the technique's scalability. Apart from making engineering improvements to our implementation, we plan to explore better strategies for the application of the Reluplex rules, and to employ advanced conflict analysis techniques for reducing the amount of case-splitting required. Another direction is to provide better soundness guarantees without harming performance, for example by replaying floating-point solutions using precise arithmetic [18], or by producing externally-checkable correctness proofs [16].

Finally, we plan to extend our approach to handle DNNs with additional kinds of layers. We speculate that the mechanism we applied to ReLUs can be applied to other piecewise linear layers, such as max-pooling layers.

Acknowledgements. We thank Neal Suchy from the Federal Aviation Administration, Lindsey Kuper from Intel and Tim King from Google for their valuable comments and support. This work was partially supported by a grant from Intel.

References

1. Barrett, C., Nieuwenhuis, R., Oliveras, A., Tinelli, C.: Splitting on demand in SAT modulo theories. In: Hermann, M., Voronkov, A. (eds.) LPAR 2006. LNCS (LNAI), vol. 4246, pp. 512–526. Springer, Heidelberg (2006). doi:10.1007/11916277_35
2. Barrett, C., Sebastiani, R., Seshia, S., Tinelli, C.: Satisfiability modulo theories (Chap. 26). In: Biere, A., Heule, M.J.H., van Maaren, H., Walsh, T. (eds.) Handbook of Satisfiability. Frontiers in Artificial Intelligence and Applications, vol. 185, pp. 825–885. IOS Press, Amsterdam (2009)
3. Bastani, O., Ioannou, Y., Lampropoulos, L., Vytiniotis, D., Nori, A., Criminisi, A.: Measuring neural net robustness with constraints. In: Proceedings of the 30th Conference on Neural Information Processing Systems (NIPS) (2016)
4. Bojarski, M., Del Testa, D., Dworakowski, D., Firner, B., Flepp, B., Goyal, P., Jackel, L., Monfort, M., Muller, U., Zhang, J., Zhang, X., Zhao, J., Zieba, K.: End to end learning for self-driving cars, Technical report (2016). http://arxiv.org/abs/1604.07316
5. Dantzig, G.: Linear Programming and Extensions. Princeton University Press, Princeton (1963)
6. Glorot, X., Bordes, A., Bengio, Y.: Deep sparse rectifier neural networks. In: Proceedings of the 14th International Conference on Artificial Intelligence and Statistics (AISTATS), pp. 315–323 (2011)
7. Goodfellow, I., Bengio, Y., Courville, A.: Deep Learning. MIT Press, Cambridge (2016)
8. Goodfellow, I., Shlens, J., Szegedy, C.: Explaining and harnessing adversarial examples, Technical report (2014). http://arxiv.org/abs/1412.6572
9. Hinton, G., Deng, L., Yu, D., Dahl, G., Mohamed, A., Jaitly, N., Senior, A., Vanhoucke, V., Nguyen, P., Sainath, T., Kingsbury, B.: Deep neural networks for acoustic modeling in speech recognition: the shared views of four research groups. IEEE Sig. Process. Mag. **29**(6), 82–97 (2012)
10. Huang, X., Kwiatkowska, M., Wang, S., Wu, M.: Safety verification of deep neural networks, Technical report (2016). http://arxiv.org/abs/1610.06940
11. Jarrett, K., Kavukcuoglu, K., LeCun, Y.: What is the best multi-stage architecture for object recognition? In: Proceedings of the 12th IEEE International Conferernce on Computer Vision (ICCV), pp. 2146–2153 (2009)
12. Jeannin, J.-B., Ghorbal, K., Kouskoulas, Y., Gardner, R., Schmidt, A., Zawadzki, E., Platzer, A.: A formally verified hybrid system for the next-generation airborne collision avoidance system. In: Baier, C., Tinelli, C. (eds.) TACAS 2015. LNCS, vol. 9035, pp. 21–36. Springer, Heidelberg (2015). doi:10.1007/978-3-662-46681-0_2
13. Julian, K., Lopez, J., Brush, J., Owen, M., Kochenderfer, M.: Policy compression for aircraft collision avoidance systems. In: Proceedings of the 35th Digital Avionics Systems Conference (DASC), pp. 1–10 (2016)

14. Katz, G., Barrett, C., Dill, D., Julian, K., Kochenderfer, M.: Reluplex (2017). https://github.com/guykatzz/ReluplexCav2017

15. Katz, G., Barrett, C., Dill, D., Julian, K., Kochenderfer, M.: Reluplex: an efficient smt solver for verifying deep neural networks. Supplementary Material (2017). https://arxiv.org/abs/1702.01135

16. Katz, G., Barrett, C., Tinelli, C., Reynolds, A., Hadarean, L.: Lazy proofs for DPLL(T)-based SMT solvers. In: Proceedings of the 16th International Conference on Formal Methods in Computer-Aided Design (FMCAD), pp. 93–100 (2016)

17. King, T.: Effective algorithms for the satisfiability of quantifier-free formulas over linear real and integer arithmetic. Ph.D. thesis, New York University (2014)

18. King, T., Barret, C., Tinelli, C.: Leveraging linear and mixed integer programming for SMT. In: Proceedings of the 14th International Conference on Formal Methods in Computer-Aided Design (FMCAD), pp. 139–146 (2014)

19. Kochenderfer, M.: Optimized airborne collision avoidance. In: Decision Making Under Uncertainty: Theory and Application. MIT Press, Cambridge (2015)

20. Kochenderfer, M., Chryssanthacopoulos, J.: Robust airborne collision avoidance through dynamic programming. Project report ATC-371, Massachusetts Institute of Technology, Lincoln Laboratory (2011)

21. Kochenderfer, M., Edwards, M., Espindle, L., Kuchar, J., Griffith, J.: Airspace encounter models for estimating collision risk. AIAA J. Guidance Control Dyn. **33**(2), 487–499 (2010)

22. Kochenderfer, M., Holland, J., Chryssanthacopoulos, J.: Next generation airborne collision avoidance system. Linc. Lab. J. **19**(1), 17–33 (2012)

23. Krizhevsky, A., Sutskever, I., Hinton, G.: Imagenet classification with deep convolutional neural networks. In: Advances in Neural Information Processing Systems, pp. 1097–1105 (2012)

24. Kuchar, J., Drumm, A.: The traffic alert and collision avoidance system. Linc. Lab. J. **16**(2), 277–296 (2007)

25. Maas, A., Hannun, A., Ng, A.: Rectifier nonlinearities improve neural network acoustic models. In: Proceedings of the 30th International Conference on Machine Learning (ICML) (2013)

26. Marques-Silva, J., Sakallah, K.: GRASP: a search algorithm for propositional satisfiability. IEEE Trans. Comput. **48**(5), 506–521 (1999)

27. Nair, V., Hinton, G.: Rectified linear units improve restricted Boltzmann machines. In: Proceedings of the 27th International Conference on Machine Learning (ICML), pp. 807–814 (2010)

28. Nieuwenhuis, R., Oliveras, A., Tinelli, C.: Solving SAT and SAT modulo theories: from an abstract Davis-Putnam-Logemann-Loveland procedure to DPLL(T). J. ACM (JACM) **53**(6), 937–977 (2006)

29. Padberg, M., Rinaldi, G.: A branch-and-cut algorithm for the resolution of large-scale symmetric traveling salesman problems. SIAM Rev. **33**(1), 60–100 (1991)

30. Pulina, L., Tacchella, A.: An abstraction-refinement approach to verification of artificial neural networks. In: Touili, T., Cook, B., Jackson, P. (eds.) CAV 2010. LNCS, vol. 6174, pp. 243–257. Springer, Heidelberg (2010). doi:10.1007/978-3-642-14295-6_24

31. Pulina, L., Tacchella, A.: Challenging SMT solvers to verify neural networks. AI Commun. **25**(2), 117–135 (2012)

32. Riesenhuber, M., Tomaso, P.: Hierarchical models of object recognition in cortex. Nat. Neurosci. **2**(11), 1019–1025 (1999). doi:10.1038/14819

33. Silver, D., Huang, A., Maddison, C., Guez, A., Sifre, L., Van Den Driessche, G., Schrittwieser, J., Antonoglou, I., Panneershelvam, V., Lanctot, M., Dieleman, S.: Mastering the game of Go with deep neural networks and tree search. Nature **529**(7587), 484–489 (2016)
34. Szegedy, C., Zaremba, W., Sutskever, I., Bruna, J., Erhan, D., Goodfellow, I., Fergus, R.: Intriguing properties of neural networks, Technical report (2013). http://arxiv.org/abs/1312.6199
35. Vanderbei, R.: Linear Programming: Foundations and Extensions. Springer, Heidelberg (1996)

Automated Recurrence Analysis for Almost-Linear Expected-Runtime Bounds

Krishnendu Chatterjee[1],
Hongfei Fu[2]($\boxtimes$), and Aniket Murhekar[3]

[1] IST Austria, Klosterneuburg, Austria
[2] State Key Laboratory of Computer Science,
Institute of Software Chinese Academy of Sciences,
Beijing, People's Republic of China
fuhf@ios.ac.cn
[3] IIT Bombay, Mumbai, India

Abstract. We consider the problem of developing automated techniques for solving recurrence relations to aid the expected-runtime analysis of programs. The motivation is that several classical textbook algorithms have quite efficient expected-runtime complexity, whereas the corresponding worst-case bounds are either inefficient (e.g., QUICK-SORT), or completely ineffective (e.g., COUPON-COLLECTOR). Since the main focus of expected-runtime analysis is to obtain efficient bounds, we consider bounds that are either logarithmic, linear or almost-linear ($\mathcal{O}(\log n)$, $\mathcal{O}(n)$, $\mathcal{O}(n \cdot \log n)$, respectively, where n represents the input size). Our main contribution is an efficient (simple linear-time algorithm) sound approach for deriving such expected-runtime bounds for the analysis of recurrence relations induced by randomized algorithms. The experimental results show that our approach can efficiently derive asymptotically optimal expected-runtime bounds for recurrences of classical randomized algorithms, including RANDOMIZED-SEARCH, QUICK-SORT, QUICK-SELECT, COUPON-COLLECTOR, where the worst-case bounds are either inefficient (such as linear as compared to logarithmic expected-runtime complexity, or quadratic as compared to linear or almost-linear expected-runtime complexity), or ineffective.

1 Introduction

Static Analysis for Quantitative Bounds. Static analysis of programs aims to reason about programs without running them. The most basic properties for static analysis are qualitative properties, such as safety, termination, liveness, that for every trace of a program gives a Yes or No answer (such as assertion violation or not, termination or not). However, recent interest in analysis of resource-constrained systems, such as embedded systems, as well as for performance analysis, quantitative performance characteristics are necessary. For example, the qualitative problem of termination asks whether a given program always terminates, whereas the quantitative problem asks to obtain precise bounds on

© Springer International Publishing AG 2017
R. Majumdar and V. Kunčak (Eds.): CAV 2017, Part I, LNCS 10426, pp. 118–139, 2017.
DOI: 10.1007/978-3-319-63387-9_6

the number of steps, and is thus a more challenging problem. Hence the problem of automatically reasoning about resource bounds (such as time complexity bounds) of programs is both of significant theoretical as well as practical interest. *Worst-Case Bounds.* The worst-case analysis of programs is the fundamental problem in computer science, which is the basis of algorithms and complexity theory. However, manual proofs of worst-case analysis can be tedious and also require non-trivial mathematical ingenuity, e.g., the book *The Art of Computer Programming* by Knuth presents a wide range of involved techniques to derive such precise bounds [37]. There has been a considerable research effort for automated analysis of worst-case bounds for programs, see [23,24,26,27] for excellent expositions. For the worst-case analysis there are several techniques, such as worst-case execution time analysis [46], resource analysis using abstract interpretation and type systems [2,24,26,27,34], ranking functions [7,8,15,17,41,42,44,47] as well as recurrence relations [2–4,21].

Expected-Runtime Bounds. While several works have focused on deriving worst-case bounds for programs, quite surprisingly little work has been done to derive precise bounds for expected-runtime analysis, with the exception of [20], which focuses on randomization in combinatorial structures (such as trees). This is despite the fact that expected-runtime analysis is an equally important pillar of theoretical computer science, both in terms of theoretical and practical significance. For example, while for real-time systems with hard constraints worst-case analysis is necessary, for real-time systems with soft constraints the more relevant information is the expected-runtime analysis. Below we highlight three key significance of expected-runtime analysis.

1. *Simplicity and desired properties:* The first key aspect is *simplicity*: often much simpler algorithms (thus simple and efficient implementations) exist for expected-runtime complexity as compared to worst-case complexity. A classic example is the SELECTION problem that given a set of n numbers and $0 \leq k \leq n$, asks to find the k-th largest number (e.g., for median $k = n/2$). The classical linear-time algorithm for the problem (see [16, Chap. 9]) is quite involved, and its worst-case analysis to obtain linear time bound is rather complex. In contrast, a much simpler algorithm exists (namely, QUICK-SELECT) that has linear expected-runtime complexity. Moreover, randomized algorithms with expected-runtime complexity enjoy many desired properties, which deterministic algorithms do not have. A basic example is CHANNEL-CONFLICT RESOLUTION (see Example 7, Sect. 2.4) where the simple randomized algorithm can be implemented in a distributed or concurrent setting, whereas deterministic algorithms are quite cumbersome.
2. *Efficiency in practice:* Since worst-case analysis concerns with corner cases that rarely arise, many algorithms and implementations have much better expected-runtime complexity, and they perform extremely well in practice. A classic example is the QUICK-SORT algorithm, that has quadratic worst-case complexity, but almost linear expected-runtime complexity, and is one of the most efficient sorting algorithms in practice.

3. *Worst-case analysis ineffective:* In several important cases the worst-case analysis is completely ineffective. For example, consider one of the text-book stochastic process, namely the COUPON-COLLECTOR problem, where there are n types of coupons to be collected, and in each round, a coupon type among the n types is obtained uniformly at random. The process stops when all types are collected. The COUPON-COLLECTOR process is one of the basic and classical stochastic processes, with numerous applications in network routing, load balancing, etc. (see [39, Chap. 3] for applications of COUPON-COLLECTOR problems). For the worst-case analysis, the process might not terminate (worst-case bound infinite), but the expected-runtime analysis shows that the expected termination time is $\mathcal{O}(n \cdot \log n)$.

Challenges. The expected-runtime analysis brings several new challenges as compared to the worst-case analysis. First, for the worst-case complexity bounds, the most classical characterization for analysis of recurrences is the *Master Theorem* (cf. [16, Chap. 1]) and Akra-Bazzi's Theorem [1]. However, the expected-runtime analysis problems give rise to recurrences that are not characterized by these theorems since our recurrences normally involve an unbounded summation resulting from a randomized selection of integers from 1 to n where n is unbounded. Second, techniques like ranking functions (linear or polynomial ranking functions) cannot derive efficient bounds such as $\mathcal{O}(\log n)$ or $\mathcal{O}(n \cdot \log n)$. While expected-runtime analysis has been considered for combinatorial structures using generating function [20], we are not aware of any automated technique to handle recurrences arising from randomized algorithms.

Analysis Problem. We consider the algorithmic analysis problem of recurrences arising naturally for randomized recursive programs. Specifically we consider the following:

- We consider two classes of recurrences: (a) *univariate* class with one variable (which represents the array length, or the number of input elements, as required in problems such as QUICK-SELECT, QUICK-SORT etc.); and (b) *separable bivariate* class with two variables (where the two independent variables represent the total number of elements and total number of successful cases, respectively, as required in problems such as COUPON-COLLECTOR, CHANNEL-CONFLICT RESOLUTION). The above two classes capture a large class of expected-runtime analysis problems, including all the classical ones mentioned above. Moreover, the main purpose of expected-runtime analysis is to obtain efficient bounds. Hence we focus on the case of logarithmic, linear, and almost-linear bounds (i.e., bounds of form $\mathcal{O}(\log n)$, $\mathcal{O}(n)$ and $\mathcal{O}(n \cdot \log n)$, respectively, where n is the size of the input). Moreover, for randomized algorithms, quadratic bounds or higher are rare.

Thus the main problem we consider is to automatically derive such efficient bounds for randomized univariate and separable bivariate recurrence relations.

Our Contributions. Our main contribution is a sound approach for analysis of recurrences for expected-runtime analysis. The input to our problem is a recurrence relation and the output is either logarithmic, linear, or almost-linear as the asymptotic bound, or fail. The details of our contributions are as follows:

1. *Efficient algorithm.* We first present a linear-time algorithm for the univariate case, which is based on simple comparison of leading terms of pseudo-polynomials. Second, we present a simple reduction for separable bivariate recurrence analysis to the univariate case. Our efficient (linear-time) algorithm can soundly infer logarithmic, linear, and almost-linear bounds for recurrences of one or two variables.
2. *Analysis of classical algorithms.* We show that for several classical algorithms, such as RANDOMIZED-SEARCH, QUICK-SELECT, QUICK-SORT, COUPON-COLLECTOR, CHANNEL-CONFLICT RESOLUTION (see Sects. 2.2 and 2.4 for examples), our sound approach can obtain the asymptotically optimal expected-runtime bounds for the recurrences. In all the cases above, either the worst-case bounds (i) do not exist (e.g., COUPON-COLLECTOR), or (ii) are quadratic when the expected-runtime bounds are linear or almost-linear (e.g., QUICK-SELECT, QUICK-SORT); or (iii) are linear when the expected-runtime bounds are logarithmic (e.g., RANDOMIZED-SEARCH). Thus in cases where the worst-case bounds are either not applicable, or grossly overestimate the expected-runtime bounds, our technique is both efficient (linear-time) and can infer the optimal bounds.
3. *Implementation.* Finally, we have implemented our approach, and we present experimental results on the classical examples to show that we can efficiently achieve the automated expected-runtime analysis of randomized recurrence relations.

Novelty and Technical Contribution. The key novelty of our approach is an automated method to analyze recurrences arising from randomized recursive programs, which are not covered by Master theorem. Our approach is based on a guess-and-check technique. We show that by over-approximating terms in a recurrence relation through integral and Taylor's expansion, we can soundly infer logarithmic, linear and almost-linear bounds using simple comparison between leading terms of pseudo-polynomials.

Due to page limit, we omitted some technical details. They can be found in [12].

2   Recurrence Relations

We present our mini specification language for recurrence relations for expected-runtime analysis. The language is designed to capture running time of recursive randomized algorithms which involve (i) only one function call whose expected-runtime complexity is to be determined, (ii) at most two integer parameters, and (iii) involve randomized-selection or divide-and-conquer techniques. We present our language separately for the univariate and bivariate cases. In the sequel, we denote by $\mathbb{N}$, $\mathbb{N}_0$, $\mathbb{Z}$, and $\mathbb{R}$ the sets of all positive integers, non-negative integers, integers, and real numbers, respectively.

2.1   Univariate Randomized Recurrences

Below we define the notion of univariate randomized recurrence relations. First, we introduce the notion of univariate recurrence expressions. Since we only consider single recursive function call, we use 'T' to represent the (only) function call. We also use 'n' to represent the only parameter in the function declaration.
Univariate Recurrence Expressions. The syntax of *univariate recurrence expressions* e is generated by the following grammar:

$$e ::= c \mid n \mid \ln n \mid n \cdot \ln n \mid \frac{1}{n} \mid T(n-1) \mid T\left(\left\lfloor \frac{n}{2} \right\rfloor\right) \mid T\left(\left\lceil \frac{n}{2} \right\rceil\right)$$

$$\mid \frac{\sum_{j=1}^{n-1} T(j)}{n} \mid \frac{1}{n} \cdot \left(\sum_{j=\lceil n/2 \rceil}^{n-1} T(j) + \sum_{j=\lfloor n/2 \rfloor}^{n-1} T(j)\right) \mid c \cdot e \mid e + e$$

where $c \in [1, \infty)$ and $\ln(.)$ represents the natural logarithm function with base e. Informally, $T(n)$ is the (expected) running time of a recursive randomized program which involves only one recursive routine indicated by T and only one parameter indicated by n. Then each $T(.)$-term in the grammar has a direct algorithmic meaning:

- $T(n-1)$ may mean a recursion to a sub-array with length decremented by one;
- $T\left(\left\lfloor \frac{n}{2} \right\rfloor\right)$ and $T\left(\left\lceil \frac{n}{2} \right\rceil\right)$ may mean a recursion related to a divide-and-conquer technique;
- finally, $\frac{\sum_{j=1}^{n-1} T(j)}{n}$ and $\frac{1}{n} \cdot \left(\sum_{j=\lceil \frac{n}{2} \rceil}^{n-1} T(j) + \sum_{j=\lfloor \frac{n}{2} \rfloor}^{n-1} T(j)\right)$ may mean a recursion related to a randomized selection of an array index.

Substitution. Consider a function $h : \mathbb{N} \to \mathbb{R}$ and univariate recurrence expression e. The *substitution function*, denoted by $\mathsf{Subst}(e, h)$, is the function from $\mathbb{N}$ into $\mathbb{R}$ such that the value for n is obtained by evaluation through substituting h for T and n for n in e, respectively. Moreover, if e does not involve the appearance of 'T', then we use the abbreviation $\mathsf{Subst}(e)$ i.e., omit h. For example, (i) if $e = n + T(n-1)$, and $h : n \mapsto n \cdot \log n$, then $\mathsf{Subst}(e, h)$ is the function $n \mapsto n + (n-1) \cdot \log(n-1)$, and (ii) if $e = 2 \cdot n$, then $\mathsf{Subst}(e)$ is $n \mapsto 2n$.

Univariate Recurrence Relation. A *univariate recurrence relation* $G = (\mathsf{eq}_1, \mathsf{eq}_2)$ is a pair of equalities as follows:

$$\mathsf{eq}_1 : T(n) = e; \qquad \mathsf{eq}_2 : T(1) = c \qquad\qquad (1)$$

where $c \in (0, \infty)$ and e is a univariate recurrence expression. For a univariate recurrence relation G the *evaluation sequence* $\mathsf{Eval}(G)$ is as follows: $\mathsf{Eval}(G)(1) = c$, and for $n \geq 2$, given $\mathsf{Eval}(G)(i)$ for $1 \leq i < n$, for the value $\mathsf{Eval}(G)(n)$ we evaluate the expression $\mathsf{Subst}(e, \mathsf{Eval}(G))$, since in e the parameter n always decreases and is thus well-defined.

Finite vs Infinite Solution. Note that the above description gives a computational procedure to compute $\mathsf{Eval}(G)$ for any finite n, in linear time in n

through dynamic programming. The interesting question is to algorithmically analyze the infinite behavior. A function $T_G : \mathbb{N} \to \mathbb{R}$ is called a solution to G if $T_G(n) = \mathsf{Eval}(G)(n)$ for all $n \geq 1$. The function T_G is unique and explicitly defined as follows: (1) *Base Step.* $T_G(1) := c$; and (2) *Recursive Step.* $T_G(n) := \mathsf{Subst}(\mathfrak{e}, T_G)(n)$ for all $n \geq 2$. The algorithmic question is to reason about the asymptotic infinite behaviour of T_G.

2.2 Motivating Classical Examples

In this part we present several classical examples of randomized programs whose recurrence relations belong to the class of univariate recurrence relations described in Sect. 2.1. In all cases the base step is $T(1) = 1$, hence we discuss only the recursive case.

Example 1 (RANDOMIZED-SEARCH). Consider the Sherwood's RANDOMIZED-SEARCH algorithm (cf. [38, Chap. 9]). The algorithm checks whether an integer value d is present within the index range $[i, j]$ $(0 \leq i \leq j)$ in an integer array ar which is sorted in increasing order and is without duplicate entries. The algorithm outputs either the index for d in ar or -1 meaning that d is not present in the index range $[i, j]$ of ar. The recurrence relation for this example is as follows:

$$T(n) = 6 + \tfrac{1}{n} \cdot \left(\textstyle\sum_{j=\lceil n/2 \rceil}^{n-1} T(j) + \sum_{j=\lfloor n/2 \rfloor}^{n-1} T(j) \right) \tag{2}$$

We note that the worst-case complexity for this algorithm is $\Theta(n)$.   □

Example 2 (QUICK-SORT). Consider the QUICK-SORT algorithm [16, Chap. 7]. The recurrence relation for this example is:

$$T(n) = 2 \cdot n + 2 \cdot \left(\textstyle\sum_{j=1}^{n-1} T(j) \right) / n \tag{3}$$

where $T(n)$ represents the maximal expected execution time where n is the array length and the execution time of *pivoting* is represented by $2 \cdot n$. We note that the worst-case complexity for this algorithm is $\Theta(n^2)$.   □

Example 3 (QUICK-SELECT). Consider the QUICK-SELECT algorithm (cf. [16, Chap. 9]). The recurrence relation for this example is

$$T(n) = 4 + 2 \cdot n + \tfrac{1}{n} \cdot \left(\textstyle\sum_{j=\lfloor n/2 \rfloor}^{n-1} T(j) + \sum_{j=\lceil n/2 \rceil}^{n-1} T(j) \right) \tag{4}$$

We note that the worst-case complexity for this algorithm is $\Theta(n^2)$.   □

Example 4 (DIAMETER-COMPUTATION). Consider the DIAMETER-COMPUTATION algorithm (cf. [39, Chap. 9]) to compute the diameter of an input finite set S of three-dimensional points. Depending on Eucledian or L_1 metric we obtain two different recurrence relations. For Eucledian we have the following relation:

$$T(n) = 2 + n + 2 \cdot n \cdot \ln n + \left(\textstyle\sum_{j=1}^{n-1} T(j) \right) / n; \tag{5}$$

and for L_1 metric we have the following relation:

$$T(n) = 2 + n + 2 \cdot n + \left(\sum_{j=1}^{n-1} T(j)\right)/n \tag{6}$$

We note that the worst-case complexity for this algorithm is as follows: for Euclidean metric it is $\Theta(n^2 \cdot \log n)$ and for the L_1 metric it is $\Theta(n^2)$.   □

Example 5 (Sorting with QUICK-SELECT*).* Consider a sorting algorithm which selects the median through the QUICK-SELECT algorithm. The recurrence relation is directly obtained as follows:

$$T(n) = 4 + T^*(n) + T\left(\lfloor n/2 \rfloor\right) + T\left(\lceil n/2 \rceil\right) \tag{7}$$

where $T^*(\cdot)$ is an upper bound on the expected running time of QUICK-SELECT (cf. Example 3). We note that the worst-case complexity for this algorithm is $\Theta(n^2)$.   □

2.3 Separable Bivariate Randomized Recurrences

We consider a generalization of the univariate recurrence relations to a class of bivariate recurrence relations called *separable bivariate recurrence relations*. Similar to the univariate situation, we use 'T' to represent the (only) function call and 'n', 'm' to represent namely the two integer parameters.

Separable Bivariate Recurrence Expressions. The syntax of *separable bivariate recurrence expressions* is illustrated by $\mathfrak{e}, \mathfrak{h}$ and $\mathfrak{b}$ as follows:

$$\mathfrak{e} ::= T\left(n, m-1\right) \mid T\left(n, \lfloor m/2 \rfloor\right) \mid T\left(n, \lceil m/2 \rceil\right)$$

$$\mid \frac{\sum_{j=1}^{m-1} T(n, j)}{m} \mid \frac{1}{m} \cdot \left(\sum_{j=\lceil m/2 \rceil}^{m-1} T(n, j) + \sum_{j=\lfloor m/2 \rfloor}^{m-1} T(n, j)\right) \mid c \cdot \mathfrak{e} \mid \mathfrak{e} + \mathfrak{e}$$

$$\mathfrak{h} ::= c \mid \ln n \mid n \mid n \cdot \ln n \mid c \cdot \mathfrak{h} \mid \mathfrak{h} + \mathfrak{h} \quad \mathfrak{b} ::= c \mid \frac{1}{m} \mid \ln m \mid m \mid m \cdot \ln m \mid c \cdot \mathfrak{b} \mid \mathfrak{b} + \mathfrak{b}$$

The differences are that (i) we have two independent parameters n, m, (ii) $\mathfrak{e}$ now represents an expression composed of only T-terms, and (iii) $\mathfrak{h}$ (resp. $\mathfrak{b}$) represents arithmetic expressions for n (resp. for m). This class of separable bivariate recurrence expressions (often for brevity bivariate recurrence expressions) stresses a dominant role on m and a minor role on n, and is intended to model randomized algorithms where some parameter (to be represented by n) does not change value.

Substitution. The notion of substitution is similar to the univariate case. Consider a function $h : \mathbb{N} \times \mathbb{N} \rightarrow \mathbb{R}$, and a bivariate recurrence expression $\mathfrak{e}$. The *substitution function*, denoted by $\mathsf{Subst}(\mathfrak{e}, h)$, is the function from $\mathbb{N} \times \mathbb{N}$ into $\mathbb{R}$ such that $\mathsf{Subst}(\mathfrak{e}, h)(n, m)$ is the real number evaluated through substituting h, n, m for T, n, m, respectively. The substitution for $\mathfrak{h}, \mathfrak{b}$ is defined in a similar way, with the difference that they both induce a univariate function.

Bivariate Recurrence Relations. We consider *bivariate recurrence relations* $G = (\mathsf{eq}_1, \mathsf{eq}_2)$, which consists of two equalities of the following form:

$$\mathsf{eq}_1 : \ \mathrm{T}(\mathfrak{n}, \mathfrak{m}) = \mathfrak{e} + \mathfrak{h} \cdot \mathfrak{b}; \qquad \mathsf{eq}_2 : \ \mathrm{T}(\mathfrak{n}, 1) = \mathfrak{h} \cdot c \qquad (8)$$

where $c \in (0, \infty)$ and $\mathfrak{e}, \mathfrak{h}, \mathfrak{b}$ are from the grammar above.

Solution to Bivariate Recurrence Relations. The evaluation of bivariate recurrence relation is similar to the univariate case. Similar to the univariate case, the unique solution $T_G : \mathbb{N} \times \mathbb{N} \to \mathbb{R}$ to a recurrence relation G taking the form (8) is a function defined recursively as follows: (1) *Base Step.* $T_G(n, 1) := \mathsf{Subst}(\mathfrak{h})(n) \cdot c$ for all $n \in \mathbb{N}$; and (2) *Recursive Step.* $T_G(n, m) := \mathsf{Subst}(\mathfrak{e}, T_G)(n, m) + \mathsf{Subst}(\mathfrak{h})(n) \cdot \mathsf{Subst}(\mathfrak{b})(m)$ for all $n \in \mathbb{N}$ and $m \geq 2$. Again the interesting algorithmic question is to reason about the infinite behaviour of T_G.

2.4   Motivating Classical Examples

In this section we present two classical examples of randomized algorithms where the randomized recurrence relations are bivariate.

Example 6 (COUPON-COLLECTOR). Consider the COUPON-COLLECTOR problem [39, Chap. 3] with n different types of coupons ($n \in \mathbb{N}$). The randomized process proceeds in rounds: at each round, a coupon is collected uniformly at random from the coupon types the rounds continue until all the n types of coupons are collected. We model the rounds as a recurrence relation with two variables $\mathfrak{n}, \mathfrak{m}$, where $\mathfrak{n}$ represents the total number of coupon types and $\mathfrak{m}$ represents the remaining number of uncollected coupon types. The recurrence relation is as follows:

$$\mathrm{T}(\mathfrak{n}, 1) = \mathfrak{n} \cdot 1; \qquad \mathrm{T}(\mathfrak{n}, \mathfrak{m}) = \mathfrak{n}/\mathfrak{m} + \mathrm{T}(\mathfrak{n}, \mathfrak{m} - 1) \qquad (9)$$

where $\mathrm{T}(\mathfrak{n}, \mathfrak{m})$ is the expected number of rounds. We note that the worst-case complexity for this process is ∞.   □

Example 7 (CHANNEL-CONFLICT RESOLUTION). We consider two network scenarios in which n clients are trying to get access to a network channel. This problem is also called the RESOURCE-CONTENTION RESOLUTION [36, Chap. 13]. In this problem, if more than one client tries to access the channel, then no client can access it, and if exactly one client requests access to the channel, then the request is granted. In the distributed setting, the clients do not share any information. In this scenario, in each round, every client requests an access to the channel with probability $\frac{1}{n}$. Then for this scenario, we obtain an over-approximating recurrence relation

$$\mathrm{T}(\mathfrak{n}, 1) = \mathfrak{n} \cdot 1; \qquad \mathrm{T}(\mathfrak{n}, \mathfrak{m}) = (\mathfrak{n} \cdot e)/\mathfrak{m} + \mathrm{T}(\mathfrak{n}, \mathfrak{m} - 1) \qquad (10)$$

for the expected rounds until which every client gets at least one access to the channel. In the concurrent setting, the clients share one variable, which is the number of clients which has not yet been granted access. Also in this scenario, once a client gets an access the client does not request for access again. For this scenario, we obtain an over-approximating recurrence relation

$$T(\mathfrak{n}, 1) = 1 \cdot 1; \qquad T(\mathfrak{n}, \mathfrak{m}) = 1 \cdot e + T(\mathfrak{n}, \mathfrak{m} - 1) \tag{11}$$

We also note that the worst-case complexity for both the scenarios is ∞.   □

3   Expected-Runtime Analysis

We focus on synthesizing logarithmic, linear, and almost-linear asymptotic bounds for recurrence relations. Our goal is to decide and synthesize asymptotic bounds in the simple form: $d \cdot \mathfrak{f} + \mathfrak{g}, \mathfrak{f} \in \{\ln \mathfrak{n}, \mathfrak{n}, \mathfrak{n} \cdot \ln \mathfrak{n}\}$. Informally, $\mathfrak{f}$ is the major term for time complexity, d is the coefficient of $\mathfrak{f}$ to be synthesized, and $\mathfrak{g}$ is the time complexity for the base case specified in (1) or (8).

Univariate Case: The algorithmic problem in univariate case is as follows:

- *Input:* a univariate recurrence relation G taking the form (1) and an expression $\mathfrak{f} \in \{\ln \mathfrak{n}, \mathfrak{n}, \mathfrak{n} \cdot \ln \mathfrak{n}\}$.
- *Output: Decision problem.* Output "*yes*" if $T_G \in \mathcal{O}(\mathsf{Subst}(\mathfrak{f}))$, and "*fail*" otherwise.
- *Output: Quantitative problem.* A positive real number d such that

$$T_G(n) \leq d \cdot \mathsf{Subst}(\mathfrak{f})(n) + c \tag{12}$$

for all $n \geq 1$, or "*fail*" otherwise, where c is from (1).

Remark 1. First note that while in the problem description we consider the form $\mathfrak{f}$ part of input for simplicity, since there are only three possibilites we can simply enumerate them, and thus have only the recurrence relation as input. Second, in the algorithmic problem above, w.l.o.g, we consider that every $\mathfrak{e}$ in (1) or (8) involves at least one T($\cdot$)-term and one non-T($\cdot$)-term; this is natural since (i) for algorithms with recursion at least one T($\cdot$)-term should be present for the recursive call and at least one non-T($\cdot$)-term for non-recursive base step.   □

Bivariate Case: The bivariate-case problem is an extension of the univariate one, and hence the problem definitions are similar, and we present them succinctly below.

- *Input:* a bivariate recurrence relation G taking the form (8) and an expression $\mathfrak{f}$ (similar to the univariate case).
- *Output: Decision problem.* Output "*yes*" if $T_G \in \mathcal{O}(\mathsf{Subst}(\mathfrak{f}))$, and "*fail*" otherwise;
- *Output: Quantitative problem.* A positive real number d such that $T_G(n, m) \leq d \cdot \mathsf{Subst}(\mathfrak{f})(n, m) + c \cdot \mathsf{Subst}(\mathfrak{h})(n)$ for all $n, m \geq 1$, or "*fail*" otherwise, where $c, \mathfrak{h}$ are from (8). Note that in the expression above the term $\mathfrak{b}$ does not appear as it can be captured with $\mathfrak{f}$ itself.

Recall that in the above algorithmic problems obtaining the finite behaviour of the recurrence relations is easy (through evaluation of the recurrences using dynamic programming), and the interesting aspect is to decide the asymptotic infinite behaviour.

4   The Synthesis Algorithm

In this section, we present our algorithms to synthesize asymptotic bounds for randomized recurrence relations.

Main Idea. The main idea is as follows. Consider as input a recurrence relation taking the form (1) and an univariate recurrence expression $f \in \{\ln \mathfrak{n}, \mathfrak{n}, \mathfrak{n} \cdot \ln \mathfrak{n}\}$ which specifies the desired asymptotic bound. We first define the standard notion of a guess-and-check function which provides a sound approach for asymptotic bound. Based on the guess-and-check function, our algorithm executes the following steps for the univariate case.

1. First, the algorithm sets up a scalar variable d and then constructs the template h to be $n \mapsto d \cdot \mathsf{Subst}(f)(n) + c$ for a univariate guess-and-check function.
2. Second, the algorithm computes an over-approximation $\mathsf{OvAp}(\mathfrak{e}, h)$ of $\mathsf{Subst}(\mathfrak{e}, h)$ such that the over-approximation $\mathsf{OvAp}(\mathfrak{e}, h)$ will involve terms from $\mathfrak{n}^k, \ln^\ell \mathfrak{n}$ (for $k, \ell \in \mathbb{N}_0$) only. Note that k, ℓ may be greater than 1, so the above expressions are not necessarily linear (they can be quadratic or cubic for example).
3. Finally, the algorithm synthesizes a value for d such that $\mathsf{OvAp}(\mathfrak{e}, h)(n) \le h(n)$ for all $n \ge 2$ through truncation of $[2, \infty) \cap \mathbb{N}$ into a finite range and a limit behaviour analysis (towards ∞).

Our algorithm for bivariate cases is a reduction to the univariate case.

Guess-and-Check Functions. We follow the standard guess-and-check technique to solve simple recurrence relations. Below we first fix a univariate recurrence relation G taking the form (1). By an easy induction on n (starting from the N specified in Definition 1) we obtain Theorem 1.

Definition 1 (Univariate Guess-and-Check Functions). Let G be a univariate recurrence relation taking the form (1). A function $h : \mathbb{N} \to \mathbb{R}$ is a *guess-and-check* function for G if there exists a natural number $N \in \mathbb{N}$ such that: (1) *(Base Condition)* $T_G(n) \le h(n)$ for all $1 \le n \le N$, and (2) *(Inductive Argument)* $\mathsf{Subst}(\mathfrak{e}, h)(n) \le h(n)$ for all $n > N$.

Theorem 1 (Guess-and-Check, Univariate Case). *If a function $h : \mathbb{N} \to \mathbb{R}$ is a* guess-and-check *function for a univariate recurrence relation G taking the form (1), then $T_G(n) \le h(n)$ for all $n \in \mathbb{N}$.*

We do not explicitly present the definition for guess-and-check functions in the bivariate case, since we will present a reduction of the analysis of separable bivariate recurrence relations to that of the univariate ones (cf. Sect. 4.2).

Overapproximations for Recurrence Expressions. We now develop tight overapproximations for logarithmic terms. In principle, we use Taylor's Theorem to approximate logarithmic terms such as $\ln(n - 1), \ln \lfloor \frac{n}{2} \rfloor$, and integral to approximate summations of logarithmic terms. All the results below are technical and depends on basic calculus.

Proposition 1. *For all natural number $n \geq 2$:*

(1) $\ln n - \ln 2 - \dfrac{1}{n-1} \leq \ln \left\lfloor \dfrac{n}{2} \right\rfloor \leq \ln n - \ln 2$; (2) $\ln n - \ln 2 \leq \ln \left\lceil \dfrac{n}{2} \right\rceil \leq \ln n - \ln 2 + \dfrac{1}{n}$.

Proposition 2. *For all natural number $n \geq 2$:* $\ln n - \frac{1}{n-1} \leq \ln(n-1) \leq \ln n - \frac{1}{n}$.

Proposition 3. *For all natural number $n \geq 2$:*

- $\int_1^n \frac{1}{x}\,dx - \sum_{j=1}^{n-1} \frac{1}{j} \in \left[-0.7552, -\frac{1}{6} \right]$;
- $\int_1^n \ln x \, dx - \left(\sum_{j=1}^{n-1} \ln j \right) - \frac{1}{2} \cdot \int_1^n \frac{1}{x}\,dx \in \left[-\frac{1}{12}, 0.2701 \right]$;
- $\int_1^n x \cdot \ln x \, dx - \left(\sum_{j=1}^{n-1} j \cdot \ln j \right) - \frac{1}{2} \cdot \int_1^n \ln x \, dx + \frac{1}{12} \cdot \int_1^n \frac{1}{x}\,dx - \frac{n-1}{2} \in \left[-\frac{19}{72}, 0.1575 \right]$.

Note that Proposition 3 is non-trivial since it approximates summation of reciprocal and logarithmic terms up to a constant deviation. For example, one may approximate $\sum_{j=1}^{n-1} \ln j$ directly by $\int_1^n \ln x \, dx$, but this approximation deviates up to a logarithmic term from Proposition 3. From Proposition 3, we establish a tight approximation for summation of logarithmic or reciprocal terms.

Example 8. Consider the summation $\sum_{j=\lceil \frac{n}{2} \rceil}^{n-1} \ln j + \sum_{j=\lfloor \frac{n}{2} \rfloor}^{n-1} \ln j$ $(n \geq 4)$. By Proposition 3, we can over-approximate it as

$$2 \cdot \left(\Gamma_{\ln n}(n) + \frac{1}{12} \right) - \left(\Gamma_{\ln n}\left(\left\lceil \frac{n}{2} \right\rceil \right) + \Gamma_{\ln n}\left(\left\lfloor \frac{n}{2} \right\rfloor \right) - 0.5402 \right)$$

where $\Gamma_{\ln n}(n) := \int_1^n \ln x \, dx - \frac{1}{2} \cdot \int_1^n \frac{1}{x}\,dx = n \cdot \ln n - n - \frac{\ln n}{2} + 1$. By using Proposition 1, the above expression is roughly $n \cdot \ln n - (1 - \ln 2) \cdot n + \frac{1}{2} \cdot \ln n + 0.6672 + \frac{1}{2 \cdot n}$. □

Remark 2. Although we do approximation for terms related to only almost-linear bounds, Proposition 3 can be extended to logarithmic bounds with higher degree (e.g., $n^3 \ln n$) since integration of such bounds can be obtained in closed forms. □

4.1 Algorithm for Univariate Recurrence Relations

We present our algorithm to synthesize a guess-and-check function in form (12) for univariate recurrence relations. We present our algorithm in two steps. First, we present the decision version, and then we present the quantitative version that synthesizes the associated constant. The two key aspects are over-approximation and use of pseudo-polynomials, and we start with over-approximation.

Definition 2 (Overapproximation). Let $\mathfrak{f} \in \{\ln \mathfrak{n}, \mathfrak{n}, \mathfrak{n} \cdot \ln \mathfrak{n}\}$. Consider a univariate recurrence expression $\mathfrak{g}$, constants d and c, and the function $h = d \cdot \mathsf{Subst}(\mathfrak{f}) + c$. We define the *over-approximation function*, denoted $\mathsf{OvAp}(\mathfrak{g}, h)$, recursively as follows.

– *Base Step A.* If g is one of the following: $c', n, \ln n, n \cdot \ln n, \frac{1}{n}$, then $\mathsf{OvAp}(g, h) := \mathsf{Subst}(g)$.

– *Base Step B.* If g is a single term which involves T, then we define $\mathsf{OvAp}(g, h)$ from over-approximations Propositions 1–3. In details, $\mathsf{OvAp}(g, h)$ is obtained from $\mathsf{Subst}(g, h)$ by first over-approximating any summation through Proposition 3, then over-approximating any $\ln(n-1), \lfloor \frac{n}{2} \rfloor, \lceil \frac{n}{2} \rceil, \ln \lfloor \frac{n}{2} \rfloor, \ln \lceil \frac{n}{2} \rceil$ by Propositions 1 and 2. The details of the important over-approximations are illustrated explicitly in Table 1.

– *Recursive Step.* We have two cases: (a) If g is $g_1 + g_2$, then $\mathsf{OvAp}(g, h)$ is $\mathsf{OvAp}(g_1, h) + \mathsf{OvAp}(g_2, h)$. (b) If g is $c' \cdot g'$, then $\mathsf{OvAp}(g, h)$ is $c' \cdot \mathsf{OvAp}(g', h)$.

Table 1. Illustration for Definition 2 where the notations are given in the top-left corner.

Notation	Expression	f, T-term	Over-approximation
e_1	$T(n-1)$	$\ln n, e_1$	$\ln n - \frac{1}{n}$
e_2	$T\left(\left\lfloor \frac{n}{2} \right\rfloor\right)$	$\ln n, e_2$	$\ln n - \ln 2$
e_3	$T\left(\left\lceil \frac{n}{2} \right\rceil\right)$	$\ln n, e_3$	$\ln n - \ln 2 + \frac{1}{n}$
e_4	$\frac{1}{n} \cdot \sum_{j=1}^{n-1} T(j)$	$\ln n, e_4$	$\ln n - 1 - \frac{\ln n}{2 \cdot n} + \frac{13}{12} \cdot \frac{1}{n}$
e_5	$\frac{1}{n} \cdot \left(\sum_{j=\lceil \frac{n}{2} \rceil}^{n-1} T(j) + \sum_{j=\lfloor \frac{n}{2} \rfloor}^{n-1} T(j) \right)$	$\ln n, e_5$	$\ln n - (1 - \ln 2) + \frac{\ln n}{2 \cdot n} + \frac{0.6672}{n} + \frac{1}{2 \cdot n^2}$

f, T-term	Over-approximation	f, T-term	Over-approximation
n, e_1	$n - 1$	$n \cdot \ln n, e_1$	$n \cdot \ln n - \ln n - 1 + \frac{1}{n}$
n, e_2	$\frac{n}{2}$	$n \cdot \ln n, e_2$	$\frac{1}{2} \cdot n \cdot \ln n - \frac{\ln 2}{2} \cdot n$
n, e_3	$\frac{n+1}{2}$	$n \cdot \ln n, e_3$	$\frac{n \cdot \ln n}{2} - \frac{\ln 2}{2} \cdot n + \frac{1 - \ln 2}{2} + \frac{\ln n}{2} + \frac{1}{2 \cdot n}$
n, e_4	$\frac{n-1}{2}$	$n \cdot \ln n, e_4$	$\frac{n \cdot \ln n}{2} - \frac{n}{4} - \frac{\ln n}{2} + \frac{\ln n}{12 \cdot n} + \frac{0.5139}{n}$
n, e_5	$\frac{3}{4} \cdot n - \frac{1}{4 \cdot n}$	$n \cdot \ln n, e_5$	$\frac{3}{4} \cdot n \cdot \ln n - 0.2017 \cdot n - \frac{1}{2} \cdot \ln n$ $-0.2698 + \frac{\ln n}{8 \cdot n} + \frac{1.6369}{n} + \frac{1}{2 \cdot n \cdot (n-1)} + \frac{1}{4 \cdot n^2}$

Example 9. Consider the recurrence relation for Sherwood's RANDOMIZED-SEARCH (cf. (2)). Choose $f = \ln n$ and then the template h becomes $n \mapsto d \cdot \ln n + 1$. From Example 8, we have that the over-approximation for $6 + \frac{1}{n} \cdot \left(\sum_{j=\lceil \frac{n}{2} \rceil}^{n-1} T(j) + \sum_{j=\lfloor \frac{n}{2} \rfloor}^{n-1} T(j) \right)$ when $n \geq 4$ is $7 + d \cdot \left[\ln n - (1 - \ln 2) + \frac{\ln n}{2 \cdot n} + \frac{0.6672}{n} + \frac{1}{2 \cdot n^2} \right]$ (the second summand comes from an over-approximation of $\frac{1}{n} \cdot \left(\sum_{j=\lceil \frac{n}{2} \rceil}^{n-1} d \cdot \ln j + \sum_{j=\lfloor \frac{n}{2} \rfloor}^{n-1} d \cdot \ln j \right)$). □

Remark 3. Since integrations of the form $\int x^k \ln^l x \, dx$ can be calculated in closed forms (cf. Remark 2), Table 1 can be extended to logarithmic expressions with higher order, e.g., $n^2 \ln n$. □

Pseudo-polynomials. Our next step is to define the notion of (univariate) pseudo-polynomials which extends normal polynomials with logarithm. This notion is crucial to handle inductive arguments in the definition of guess-and-check functions.

Definition 3 (Univariate Pseudo-polynomials). A univariate pseudo-polynomial (w.r.t logarithm) is a function $p : \mathbb{N} \to \mathbb{R}$ such that there exist non-negative integers $k, \ell \in \mathbb{N}_0$ and real numbers a_i, b_i's such that for all $n \in \mathbb{N}$,

$$p(n) = \sum_{i=0}^{k} a_i \cdot n^i \cdot \ln n + \sum_{i=0}^{\ell} b_i \cdot n^i. \tag{13}$$

W.l.o.g, we consider that in the form (13), it holds that (i) $a_k^2 + b_\ell^2 \neq 0$, (ii) either $a_k \neq 0$ or $k = 0$, and (iii) similarly either $b_\ell \neq 0$ or $\ell = 0$.

Degree of Pseudo-polynomials. Given a univariate pseudo-polynomial p in the form (13), we define the *degree* $\deg(p)$ of p by: $\deg(p) = k + \frac{1}{2}$ if $k \geq \ell$ and $a_k \neq 0$ and ℓ otherwise. Intuitively, if the term with highest degree involves logarithm, then we increase the degree by $1/2$, else it is the power of the highest degree term.

Leading term $\bar{p}$. The *leading term* $\bar{p}$ of a pseudo-polynomial p in the form (13) is a function $\bar{p} : \mathbb{N} \to \mathbb{R}$ defined as follows: $\bar{p}(n) = a_k \cdot n^k \cdot \ln n$ if $k \geq \ell$ and $a_k \neq 0$; and $b_\ell \cdot n^\ell$ otherwise; for all $n \in \mathbb{N}$. Moreover, we let C_p to be the (only) coefficient of $\bar{p}$.

With the notion of pseudo-polynomials, the inductive argument of guess-and-check functions can be soundly transformed into an inequality between pseudo-polynomials.

Lemma 1. *Let $f \in \{\ln \mathfrak{n}, \mathfrak{n}, \mathfrak{n} \cdot \ln \mathfrak{n}\}$ and c be a constant. For all univariate recurrence expressions $\mathfrak{g}$, there exists pseudo-polynomials p and q such that coefficients (i.e., a_i, b_i's in (13)) of q are all non-negative, $C_q > 0$ and the following assertion holds: for all $d > 0$ and for all $n \geq 2$, with $h = d \cdot \mathsf{Subst}(f) + c$, the inequality $\mathsf{OvAp}(\mathfrak{g}, h)(n) \leq h(n)$ is equivalent to $d \cdot p(n) \geq q(n)$.*

Remark 4. In the above lemma, though we only refer to existence of pseudo-polynomials p and q, they can actually be computed in linear time, because p and q are obtained by simple rearrangements of terms from $\mathsf{OvAp}(\mathfrak{g}, h)$ and h, respectively.

Example 10. Let us continue with Sherwood's RANDOMIZED-SEARCH. Again choose $h = d \cdot \ln \mathfrak{n} + 1$. From Example 9, we obtain that for every $n \geq 4$, the inequality

$$d \cdot \ln n + 1 \geq 7 + d \cdot \left[\ln n - (1 - \ln 2) + \frac{\ln n}{2 \cdot n} + \frac{0.6672}{n} + \frac{1}{2 \cdot n^2} \right]$$

resulting from over-approximation and the inductive argument of guess-and-check functions is equivalent to $d \cdot \left[(1 - \ln 2) \cdot n^2 - \frac{n \cdot \ln n}{2} - 0.6672 \cdot n - \frac{1}{2} \right] \geq 6 \cdot n^2$.   □

As is indicated in Definition 1, our aim is to check whether $\mathsf{OvAp}(\mathfrak{g}, h)(n) \leq h(n)$ holds for sufficiently large n. The following proposition provides a sufficient and necessary condition for checking whether $d \cdot p(n) \geq q(n)$ holds for sufficiently large n.

Proposition 4. *Let p, q be pseudo-polynomials such that $C_q > 0$ and all coefficients of q are non-negative. Then there exists a real number $d > 0$ such that $d \cdot p(n) \geq q(n)$ for sufficiently large n iff $\deg(p) \geq \deg(q)$ and $C_p > 0$.*

Note that by Definition 1 and the special form (12) for univariate guess-and-check functions, a function in form (12) needs only to satisfy the inductive argument in order to be a univariate guess-and-check function: once a value for d is synthesized for a sufficiently large N, one can scale the value so that the base condition is also satisfied. Thus from the sufficiency of Proposition 4, our decision algorithm that checks the existence of some guess-and-check function in form (12) is presented below. Below we fix an input univariate recurrence relation G taking the form (1) and an input expression $\mathfrak{f} \in \{\ln \mathfrak{n}, \mathfrak{n}, \mathfrak{n} \cdot \ln \mathfrak{n}\}$.

Algorithm *UniDec*: Our algorithm, namely *UniDec*, for the decision problem of the univariate case, has the following steps.

1. *Template.* The algorithm establishes a scalar variable d and sets up the template $d \cdot \mathfrak{f} + c$ for a univariate guess-and-check function.
2. *Over-approximation.* Let h denote $d \cdot \mathsf{Subst}(\mathfrak{f}) + c$. The algorithm calculates the over-approximation function $\mathsf{OvAp}(\mathfrak{e}, h)$, where $\mathfrak{e}$ is from (1).
3. *Transformation.* The algorithm transforms the inequality $\mathsf{OvAp}(\mathfrak{e}, h)(n) \leq h(n)\,(n \in \mathbb{N})$ for inductive argument of guess-and-check functions through Lemma 1 equivalently into $d \cdot p(n) \geq q(n)\,(n \in \mathbb{N})$, where p, q are pseudo-polynomials obtained in linear-time through rearrangement of terms from $\mathsf{OvAp}(\mathfrak{e}, h)$ and h (see Remark 4).
4. *Coefficient Checking.* The algorithm examines cases on C_p. If $C_p > 0$ and $\deg(p) \geq \deg(q)$, then algorithm outputs "*yes*" meaning that "there exists a univariate guess-and-check function"; otherwise, the algorithm outputs "*fail*".

Theorem 2 (Soundness for *UniDec*). *If UniDec outputs "yes", then there exists a univariate guess-and-check function in form (12) for the inputs G and $\mathfrak{f}$. The algorithm is a linear-time algorithm in the size of the input recurrence relation.*

Example 11. Consider Sherwood's RANDOMIZED-SEARCH recurrence relation (cf. (2)) and $\mathfrak{f} = \ln \mathfrak{n}$ as the input. As illustrated in Examples 9 and 10, the algorithm asserts that the asymptotic behaviour is $\mathcal{O}(\ln n)$. $\qquad\square$

Remark 5. From the tightness of our over-approximation (up to only constant deviation) and the sufficiency and necessity of Proposition 4, the *UniDec* algorithm can handle a large class of univariate recurrence relations. Moreover, the algorithm is quite simple and efficient (linear-time). However, we do not know whether our approach is complete. We suspect that there is certain intricate recurrence relations that will make our approach fail.

Analysis of Examples of Sect. 2.2. Our algorithm can decide the following optimal bounds for the examples of Sect. 2.2.

1. For Example 1 we obtain an $\mathcal{O}(\log n)$ bound (recall worst-case bound is $\Theta(n)$).

2. For Example 2 we obtain an $\mathcal{O}(n \cdot \log n)$ bound (recall worst-case bound is $\Theta(n^2)$).
3. For Example 3 we obtain an $\mathcal{O}(n)$ bound (recall worst-case bound is $\Theta(n^2)$).
4. For Example 4 we obtain an $\mathcal{O}(n \cdot \log n)$ (resp. $\mathcal{O}(n)$) bound for Euclidean metric (resp. for L_1 metric), whereas the worst-case bound is $\Theta(n^2 \cdot \log n)$ (resp. $\Theta(n^2)$).
5. For Example 5 we obtain an $\mathcal{O}(n \cdot \log n)$ bound (recall worst-case bound is $\Theta(n^2)$).

In all cases above, our algorithm decides the asymptotically optimal bounds for the expected-runtime analysis, whereas the worst-case analysis grossly over-estimate the expected-runtime bounds.

Quantitative Bounds. We have already established that our linear-time decision algorithm can establish the asymptotically optimal bounds for the recurrence relations of several classical algorithms. We now take the next step to obtain even explicit quantitative bounds, i.e., to synthesize the associated constants with the asymptotic complexity. To this end, we derive a following proposition which gives explicitly a threshold for "sufficiently large numbers". We first explicitly constructs a threshold for "sufficiently large numbers". Then we show in Proposition 5 that $N_{\epsilon,p,q}$ is indeed what we need.

Definition 4. (Threshold $N_{\epsilon,p,q}$ for Sufficiently Large Numbers). Let p, q be two univariate pseudo-polynomials $p(n) = \sum_{i=0}^{k} a_i \cdot n^i \cdot \ln n + \sum_{i=0}^{\ell} b_i \cdot n^i$, $q(n) = \sum_{i=0}^{k'} a_i' \cdot n^i \cdot \ln n + \sum_{i=0}^{\ell'} b_i' \cdot n^i$ such that $\deg(p) \geq \deg(q)$ and $C_p, C_q > 0$. Then given any $\epsilon \in (0, 1)$, the number $N_{\epsilon,p,q}$ is defined as the smallest natural number such that both x, y (defined below) is smaller than ϵ:

- $x = -1 + \sum_{i=0}^{k} |a_i| \cdot \frac{N^i \cdot \ln N}{\overline{p}(N)} + \sum_{i=0}^{\ell} |b_i| \cdot \frac{N^i}{\overline{p}(N)}$;
- $y = -\mathbf{1}_{\deg(p)=\deg(q)} \cdot \frac{C_q}{C_p} + \sum_{i=0}^{k'} |a_i'| \cdot \frac{N^i \cdot \ln N}{\overline{p}(N)} + \sum_{i=0}^{\ell'} |b_i'| \cdot \frac{N^i}{\overline{p}(N)}$.

where $\mathbf{1}_{\deg(p)=\deg(q)}$ equals 1 when $\deg(p) = \deg(q)$ and 0 otherwise.

Proposition 5. *Consider two univariate pseudo-polynomials p, q such that $\deg(p) \geq \deg(q)$, all coefficients of q are non-negative and $C_p, C_q > 0$. Then given any $\epsilon \in (0, 1)$, $\frac{q(n)}{p(n)} \leq \frac{\mathbf{1}_{\deg(p)=\deg(q)} \cdot \frac{C_q}{C_p} + \epsilon}{1 - \epsilon}$ for all $n \geq N_{\epsilon,p,q}$ (for $N_{\epsilon,p,q}$ of Definition 4).*

With Proposition 5, we describe our algorithm *UniSynth* which outputs explicitly a value for d (in (12)) if *UniDec* outputs yes. Below we fix an input univariate recurrence relation G taking the form (1) and an input expression $\mathfrak{f} \in \{\ln \mathfrak{n}, \mathfrak{n}, \mathfrak{n} \cdot \ln \mathfrak{n}\}$. Moreover, the algorithm takes $\epsilon > 0$ as another input, which is basically a parameter to choose the threshold for finite behaviour. For example, smaller ϵ leads to large threshold, and vice-versa. Thus we provide a flexible algorithm as the threshold can be varied with the choice of ϵ.

Algorithm *UniSynth*: Our algorithm for the quantitative problem has the following steps:

1. *Calling UniDec.* The algorithm calls *UniDec*, and if it returns "*fail*", then return "*fail*", otherwise execute the following steps. Obtain the following inequality $d \cdot p(n) \geq q(n)$ $(n \in \mathbb{N})$ from the transformation step of *UniDec*.
2. *Variable Solving.* The algorithm calculates $N_{\epsilon,p,q}$ for a given $\epsilon \in (0,1)$ by e.g. repeatedly increasing n (see Definition 4) and outputs the value of d as the least number such that the following two conditions hold: (i) for all $2 \leq n < N_{\epsilon,p,q}$, we have $\mathsf{Eval}(G)(n) \leq d \cdot \mathsf{Subst}(\mathfrak{f})(n) + c$ (recall $\mathsf{Eval}(G)(n)$ can be computed in linear time), and (ii) we have $d \geq \frac{1_{\deg(p)=\deg(q)} \cdot \frac{C_q}{C_p} + \epsilon}{1-\epsilon}$.

Theorem 3 (Soundness for *UniSynth*). *If the algorithm UniSynth outputs a real number d, then $d \cdot \mathsf{Subst}(\mathfrak{f}) + c$ is a univariate guess-and-check function for G.*

Example 12. Consider the recurrence relation for Sherwood's RANDOMIZED-SEARCH (cf. (2)) and $\mathfrak{f} = \ln n$. Consider that $\epsilon := 0.9$. From Examples 9 and 10, the algorithm establishes the inequality $d \geq \frac{6}{(1-\ln 2) - \frac{\ln n}{2 \cdot n} - \frac{0.6672}{n} - \frac{1}{2 \cdot n^2}}$ and finds that $N_{0.9,p,q} = 6$. Then the algorithm finds $d = 204.5335$ through the followings: (a) $\mathsf{Eval}(G)(2) = 7 \leq d \cdot \ln 2 + 1$; (b) $\mathsf{Eval}(G)(3) = 11 \leq d \cdot \ln 3 + 1$; (c) $\mathsf{Eval}(G)(4) = 15 \leq d \cdot \ln 4 + 1$; (d) $\mathsf{Eval}(G)(5) = 17.8 \leq d \cdot \ln 5 + 1$; (e) $d \geq \frac{\frac{6}{1-\ln 2} + 0.9}{1-0.9}$. Thus, by Theorem 1, the expected running time of the algorithm has an upper bound $204.5335 \cdot \ln n + 1$. Later in Sect. 5, we show that one can obtain a much better $d = 19.762$ through our algorithms by choosing $\epsilon := 0.01$, which is quite good since the optimal value lies in $[15.129, 19.762]$ (cf. the first item R.-SEAR. in Table 2). □

4.2 Algorithm for Bivariate Recurrence Relations

In this part, we present our results for the separable bivariate recurrence relations. The key idea is to use separability to reduce the problem to univariate recurrence relations. There are two key steps which we describe below.

Step 1. The first step is to reduce a separable bivariate recurrence relation to a univariate one.

Definition 5 (From G to $\mathsf{Uni}(G)$). Let G be a separable bivariate recurrence relation taking the form (8). The univariate recurrence relation $\mathsf{Uni}(G)$ from G is defined by eliminating any occurrence of $\mathfrak{n}$ and replacing any occurrence of $\mathfrak{h}$ with 1.

Informally, $\mathsf{Uni}(G)$ is obtained from G by simply eliminating the roles of $\mathfrak{h}, \mathfrak{n}$. The following example illustrates the situation for COUPON-COLLECTOR example.

Example 13. Consider G to be the recurrence relation (9) for COUPON-COLLECTOR example. Then $\mathsf{Uni}(G)$ is as follows: $T(\mathfrak{n}) = \frac{1}{\mathfrak{n}} + T(\mathfrak{n} - 1)$ and $T(1) = 1$. □

Step 2. The second step is to establish the relationship between T_G and $T_{\mathsf{Uni}(G)}$, which is handled by the following proposition, whose proof is an easy induction on m.

Proposition 6. *For any separable bivariate recurrence relation G taking the form (8), the solution T_G is equal to $(n, m) \mapsto \mathsf{Subst}(\mathfrak{h})(n) \cdot T_{\mathsf{Uni}(G)}(m)$.*

Description of the Algorithm. With Proposition 6, the algorithm for separable bivariate recurrence relations is straightforward: simply compute $\mathsf{Uni}(G)$ for G and then call the algorithms for univariate case presented in Sect. 4.1.

Analysis of Examples in Sect. 2.4. Our algorithm can decide the following optimal bounds for the examples of Sect. 2.4.

1. For Example 6 we obtain an $\mathcal{O}(n \cdot \log m)$ bound, whereas the worst-case bound is ∞.
2. For Example 7 we obtain an $\mathcal{O}(n \cdot \log m)$ bound for distributed setting and $\mathcal{O}(m)$ bound for concurrent setting, whereas the worst-case bounds are both ∞.

Note that for all our examples, $m \leq n$, and thus we obtain $\mathcal{O}(n \cdot \log n)$ and $\mathcal{O}(n)$ upper bounds for expected-runtime analysis, which are the asymptotically optimal bounds. In all cases above, the worst-case analysis is completely ineffective as the worst-case bounds are infinite. Moreover, consider Example 7, where the optimal number of rounds is n (i.e., one process every round, which centralized Round-Robin schemes can achieve). The randomized algorithm, with one shared variable, is a decentralized algorithm that achieves $O(n)$ expected number of rounds (i.e., the optimal asymptotic expected-runtime complexity).

5   Experimental Results

We consider the classical examples illustrated in Sects. 2.2 and 2.4. In Table 2 for experimental results we consider the following recurrence relations G: R.-SEAR. corresponds to the recurrence relation (2) for Example 1; Q.-SORT corresponds to the recurrence relation (3) for Example 2; Q.-SELECT corresponds to the recurrence relation (4) for Example 3; DIAM. A (resp. DIAM. B) corresponds to the recurrence relation (5) (resp. the recurrence relation (6)) for Example 4; SORT-SEL. corresponds to recurrence relation (7) for Example 5, where we use the result from setting $\epsilon = 0.01$ in Q.-SELECT; COUPON corresponds to the recurrence relation (9) for Example 6; RES. A (resp. RES. B) corresponds to the recurrence relation (10) (resp. the recurrence relation (11)) for Example 7.

In the table, $\mathfrak{f}$ specifies the input asymptotic bound, ϵ and Dec is the input which specifies either we use algorithm *UniDec* or the synthesis algorithm *UniSynth* with the given ϵ value, and d gives the value synthesized w.r.t the given ϵ (✓ for yes). We describe d_{100} below. We need approximation for constants such as e and $\ln 2$, and use the interval $[2.7182, 2.7183]$ (resp., $[0.6931, 0.6932]$) for tight approximation of e (resp., $\ln 2$).

The Value d_{100}. For our synthesis algorithm we obtain the value d. The optimal value of the associated constant with the asymptotic bound, denoted d^*, is defined as follows. For $z \geq 2$, let $d_z := \max \left\{ \frac{T_G(n) - c}{\mathsf{Subst}(\mathfrak{f})(n)} \mid 2 \leq n \leq z \right\}$ (c is from

(1)). Then the sequence d_z is increasing in z, and its limit is the optimal constant, i.e., $d^* = \lim_{z \to \infty} d_z$. We consider d_{100} as a lower bound on d^* to compare against the value of d we synthesize. In other words, d_{100} is the minimal value such that (12) holds for $1 \leq n \leq 100$, whereas for d^* it must hold for all n, and hence $d^* \geq d_{100}$. Our experimental results show that the d values we synthesize for $\epsilon = 0.01$ is quite close to the optimal value.

We performed our experiments on Intel(R) Core(TM) i7-4510U CPU, 2.00GHz, 8GB RAM. All numbers in Table 2 are over-approximated up to 10^{-3}, and the running time of all experiments are less than 0.02 seconds. From Table 2, we can see that optimal d are effectively over-approximated. For example, for QUICK-SORT (Eq. (3)) (i.e., Q.-SORT in the table), our algorithm detects $d = 4.051$ and the optimal one lies somewhere in [3.172, 4.051]. The experimental results show that we obtain the results extremely efficiently (less than 1/50-th of a second).

Table 2. Experimental results where all running times (averaged over 5 runs) are less than 0.02 s, between 0.01 and 0.02 in all cases.

Recur. Rel	f	ϵ, Dec	d	d_{100}	Recur. Rel	f	ϵ, Dec	d	d_{100}
R.-SEAR.	ln n	UniDec	✓	15.129	SORT-SEL.	n · ln n	UniDec	✓	16.000
		0.5	40.107				0.5	50.052	
		0.3	28.363				0.3	24.852	
		0.1	21.838				0.1	17.313	
		0.01	19.762				0.01	16.000	
Q.-SORT	n · ln n	UniDec	✓	3.172	COUPON	n · ln m	UniDec	✓	0.910
		0.5	9.001				0.5	3.001	
		0.3	6.143				0.3	1.858	
		0.1	4.556				0.1	1.223	
		0.01	4.051				0.01	1.021	
Q.-SELECT	n	UniDec	✓	7.909	RES. A	n · ln m	UniDec	✓	2.472
		0.5	17.001				0.5	6.437	
		0.3	11.851				0.3	4.312	
		0.1	9.001				0.1	3.132	
		0.01	8.091				0.01	2.756	
DIAM. A	n · ln n	UniDec	✓	4.525	RES. B	m	UniDec	✓	2.691
		0.5	9.001				0.5	6.437	
		0.3	6.143				0.3	4.312	
		0.1	4.556				0.1	3.132	
		0.01	4.525				0.01	2.756	
DIAM. B	n	UniDec	✓	5.918	-	-	-	-	-
		0.5	13.001				-	-	
		0.3	9.001				-	-	
		0.1	6.778				-	-	
		0.01	6.071				-	-	

6   Related Work

Automated program analysis is a very important problem with a long tradition [45]. The following works consider various approaches for automated worst-case bounds [5, 26, 28–32, 34, 35, 43] for amortized analysis, and the SPEED project [22–24] for non-linear bounds using abstract interpretation. All these works focus on the worst-case analysis, and do not consider expected-runtime analysis.

Our main contribution is automated analysis of recurrence relations. Approaches for recurrence relations have also been considered in the literature. Wegbreit [45] considered solving recurrence relations through either simple difference equations or generating functions. Zimmermann and Zimmermann [48] considered solving recurrence relations by transforming them into difference equations. Grobauer [21] considered generating recurrence relations from DML for the worst-case analysis. Flajolet *et al.* [19] considered allocation problems. Flajolet *et al.* [20] considered solving recurrence relations for randomization of combinatorial structures (such as trees) through generating functions. The COSTA project [2–4] transforms Java bytecode into recurrence relations and solves them through ranking functions. Moreover, The PURRS tool [6] addresses finite linear recurrences (with bounded summation), and some restricted linear infinite recurrence relations (with unbounded summation). Our approach is quite different because we consider analyzing recurrence relations arising from randomized algorithms and expected-runtime analysis by over-approximation of unbounded summations through integrals, whereas previous approaches either consider recurrence relations for worst-case bounds or combinatorial structures, or use generating functions or difference equations to solve the recurrence relations.

For intraprocedural analysis ranking functions have been widely studied [7, 8, 15, 17, 41, 42, 44, 47], which have then been extended to non-recursive probabilistic programs as ranking supermartingales [9–11, 13, 14, 18]. However, existing related approaches can not derive optimal asymptotic expected-runtime bounds (such as $\mathcal{O}(\log n)$, $\mathcal{O}(n \log n)$). Proof rules have also been considered for recursive (probabilistic) programs in [25, 33, 40], but these methods cannot be automated and require manual proofs.

7   Conclusion

In this work we considered efficient algorithms for automated analysis of randomized recurrences for logarithmic, linear, and almost-linear bounds. Our work gives rise to a number of interesting questions. First, an interesting theoretical direction of future work would be to consider more general randomized recurrence relations (such as with more than two variables, or interaction between the variables). While the above problem is of theoretical interest, most interesting examples are already captured in our class of randomized recurrence relations as mentioned above. Another interesting practical direction would be automated techniques to derive recurrence relations from randomized recursive programs.

Acknowledgements. We thank all reviewers for valuable comments. The research is partially supported by Vienna Science and Technology Fund (WWTF) ICT15-003, Austrian Science Fund (FWF) NFN Grant No. S11407-N23 (RiSE/SHiNE), ERC Start grant (279307: Graph Games), the Natural Science Foundation of China (NSFC) under Grant No. 61532019 and the CDZ project CAP (GZ 1023).

References

1. Akra, M.A., Bazzi, L.: On the solution of linear recurrence equations. Comp. Opt. Appl. **10**(2), 195–210 (1998)
2. Albert, E., Arenas, P., Genaim, S., Gómez-Zamalloa, M., Puebla, G., Ramírez-Deantes, D.V., Román-Díez, G., Zanardini, D.: Termination and cost analysis with COSTA and its user interfaces. Electr. Notes Theor. Comput. Sci. **258**(1), 109–121 (2009)
3. Albert, E., Arenas, P., Genaim, S., Puebla, G.: Automatic inference of upper bounds for recurrence relations in cost analysis. In: Alpuente, M., Vidal, G. (eds.) SAS 2008. LNCS, vol. 5079, pp. 221–237. Springer, Heidelberg (2008). doi:10.1007/978-3-540-69166-2_15
4. Albert, E., Arenas, P., Genaim, S., Puebla, G., Zanardini, D.: Cost analysis of Java bytecode. In: Nicola, R. (ed.) ESOP 2007. LNCS, vol. 4421, pp. 157–172. Springer, Heidelberg (2007). doi:10.1007/978-3-540-71316-6_12
5. Avanzini, M., Lago, U.D., Moser, G.: Analysing the complexity of functional programs: higher-order meets first-order. In: Fisher, K., Reppy, J.H. (eds.) ICFP, pp. 152–164. ACM (2015)
6. Bagnara, R., Pescetti, A., Zaccagnini, A., Zaffanella, E.: PURRS: towards computer algebra support for fully automatic worst-case complexity analysis. Technical report, University of Parma (2005). https://arxiv.org/abs/cs/0512056
7. Bournez, O., Garnier, F.: Proving positive almost-sure termination. In: Giesl, J. (ed.) RTA 2005. LNCS, vol. 3467, pp. 323–337. Springer, Heidelberg (2005). doi:10.1007/978-3-540-32033-3_24
8. Bradley, A.R., Manna, Z., Sipma, H.B.: Linear ranking with reachability. In: Etessami, K., Rajamani, S.K. (eds.) CAV 2005. LNCS, vol. 3576, pp. 491–504. Springer, Heidelberg (2005). doi:10.1007/11513988_48
9. Chakarov, A., Sankaranarayanan, S.: Probabilistic program analysis with martingales. In: Sharygina, N., Veith, H. (eds.) CAV 2013. LNCS, vol. 8044, pp. 511–526. Springer, Heidelberg (2013). doi:10.1007/978-3-642-39799-8_34
10. Chatterjee, K., Fu, H.: Termination of nondeterministic recursive probabilistic programs. CoRR abs/1701.02944 (2017). http://arxiv.org/abs/1701.02944
11. Chatterjee, K., Fu, H., Goharshady, A.K.: Termination analysis of probabilistic programs through Positivstellensatz's. In: Chaudhuri, S., Farzan, A. (eds.) CAV 2016. LNCS, vol. 9779, pp. 3–22. Springer, Cham (2016). doi:10.1007/978-3-319-41528-4_1
12. Chatterjee, K., Fu, H., Murhekar, A.: Automated recurrence analysis for almost-linear expected-runtime bounds. CoRR abs/1705.00314 (2017). https://arxiv.org/abs/1705.00314
13. Chatterjee, K., Fu, H., Novotný, P., Hasheminezhad, R.: Algorithmic analysis of qualitative and quantitative termination problems for affine probabilistic programs. In: Bodík, R., Majumdar, R. (eds.) POPL, pp. 327–342. ACM (2016)
14. Chatterjee, K., Novotný, P., Žikelić, Đ.: Stochastic invariants for probabilistic termination. In: Castagna, G., Gordon, A.D. (eds.) POPL, pp. 145–160. ACM (2017)

15. Colón, M.A., Sipma, H.B.: Synthesis of linear ranking functions. In: Margaria, T., Yi, W. (eds.) TACAS 2001. LNCS, vol. 2031, pp. 67–81. Springer, Heidelberg (2001). doi:10.1007/3-540-45319-9_6

16. Cormen, T.H., Leiserson, C.E., Rivest, R.L., Stein, C.: Introduction to Algorithms, 3rd edn. MIT Press, Cambridge (2009)

17. Cousot, P.: Proving program invariance and termination by parametric abstraction, Lagrangian relaxation and semidefinite programming. In: Cousot, R. (ed.) VMCAI 2005. LNCS, vol. 3385, pp. 1–24. Springer, Heidelberg (2005). doi:10.1007/978-3-540-30579-8_1

18. Fioriti, L.M.F., Hermanns, H.: Probabilistic termination: soundness, completeness, and compositionality. In: Rajamani, S.K., Walker, D. (eds.) POPL, pp. 489–501. ACM (2015)

19. Flajolet, P., Gardy, D., Thimonier, L.: Birthday paradox, coupon collectors, caching algorithms and self-organizing search. Discret. Appl. Math. **39**(3), 207–229 (1992)

20. Flajolet, P., Salvy, B., Zimmermann, P.: Automatic average-case analysis of algorithm. Theor. Comput. Sci. **79**(1), 37–109 (1991)

21. Grobauer, B.: Cost recurrences for DML programs. In: Pierce, B.C. (ed.) ICFP, pp. 253–264. ACM (2001)

22. Gulavani, B.S., Gulwani, S.: A numerical abstract domain based on *expression abstraction* and *max operator* with application in timing analysis. In: Gupta, A., Malik, S. (eds.) CAV 2008. LNCS, vol. 5123, pp. 370–384. Springer, Heidelberg (2008). doi:10.1007/978-3-540-70545-1_35

23. Gulwani, S.: SPEED: symbolic complexity bound analysis. In: Bouajjani, A., Maler, O. (eds.) CAV 2009. LNCS, vol. 5643, pp. 51–62. Springer, Heidelberg (2009). doi:10.1007/978-3-642-02658-4_7

24. Gulwani, S., Mehra, K.K., Chilimbi, T.M.: SPEED: precise and efficient static estimation of program computational complexity. In: Shao, Z., Pierce, B.C. (eds.) POPL, pp. 127–139. ACM (2009)

25. Hesselink, W.H.: Proof rules for recursive procedures. Formal Asp. Comput. **5**(6), 554–570 (1993)

26. Hoffmann, J., Aehlig, K., Hofmann, M.: Multivariate amortized resource analysis. ACM Trans. Program. Lang. Syst. **34**(3), 14 (2012)

27. Hoffmann, J., Aehlig, K., Hofmann, M.: Resource aware ML. In: Madhusudan, P., Seshia, S.A. (eds.) CAV 2012. LNCS, vol. 7358, pp. 781–786. Springer, Heidelberg (2012). doi:10.1007/978-3-642-31424-7_64

28. Hoffmann, J., Hofmann, M.: Amortized resource analysis with polymorphic recursion and partial big-step operational semantics. In: Ueda, K. (ed.) APLAS 2010. LNCS, vol. 6461, pp. 172–187. Springer, Heidelberg (2010). doi:10.1007/978-3-642-17164-2_13

29. Hoffmann, J., Hofmann, M.: Amortized resource analysis with polynomial potential. In: Gordon, A.D. (ed.) ESOP 2010. LNCS, vol. 6012, pp. 287–306. Springer, Heidelberg (2010). doi:10.1007/978-3-642-11957-6_16

30. Hofmann, M., Jost, S.: Static prediction of heap space usage for first-order functional programs. In: Aiken, A., Morrisett, G. (eds.) POPL, pp. 185–197. ACM (2003)

31. Hofmann, M., Jost, S.: Type-based amortised heap-space analysis. In: Sestoft, P. (ed.) ESOP 2006. LNCS, vol. 3924, pp. 22–37. Springer, Heidelberg (2006). doi:10.1007/11693024_3

32. Hofmann, M., Rodriguez, D.: Efficient type-checking for amortised heap-space analysis. In: Grädel, E., Kahle, R. (eds.) CSL 2009. LNCS, vol. 5771, pp. 317–331. Springer, Heidelberg (2009). doi:10.1007/978-3-642-04027-6_24

33. Jones, C.: Probabilistic non-determinism. Ph.D. thesis, The University of Edinburgh (1989)

34. Jost, S., Hammond, K., Loidl, H., Hofmann, M.: Static determination of quantitative resource usage for higher-order programs. In: Hermenegildo, M.V., Palsberg, J. (eds.) POPL, pp. 223–236. ACM (2010)

35. Jost, S., Loidl, H.-W., Hammond, K., Scaife, N., Hofmann, M.: "Carbon credits" for resource-bounded computations using amortised analysis. In: Cavalcanti, A., Dams, D.R. (eds.) FM 2009. LNCS, vol. 5850, pp. 354–369. Springer, Heidelberg (2009). doi:10.1007/978-3-642-05089-3_23

36. Kleinberg, J., Tardos, É.: Algorithm Design. Addison-Wesley, Boston (2004)

37. Knuth, D.E.: The Art of Computer Programming, vol. I–III. Addison-Wesley, Boston (1973)

38. McConnell, J.: Analysis of Algorithms - An Active Learning Approach. Jones and Bartlett Publishers, Inc., Burlington (2008)

39. Motwani, R., Raghavan, P.: Randomized Algorithms. Cambridge University Press, Cambridge (1995)

40. Olmedo, F., Kaminski, B.L., Katoen, J., Matheja, C.: Reasoning about recursive probabilistic programs. In: Grohe, M., Koskinen, E., Shankar, N. (eds.) LICS, pp. 672–681. ACM (2016)

41. Podelski, A., Rybalchenko, A.: A complete method for the synthesis of linear ranking functions. In: Steffen, B., Levi, G. (eds.) VMCAI 2004. LNCS, vol. 2937, pp. 239–251. Springer, Heidelberg (2004). doi:10.1007/978-3-540-24622-0_20

42. Shen, L., Wu, M., Yang, Z., Zeng, Z.: Generating exact nonlinear ranking functions by symbolic-numeric hybrid method. J. Syst. Sci. Complex. **26**(2), 291–301 (2013)

43. Sinn, M., Zuleger, F., Veith, H.: A simple and scalable static analysis for bound analysis and amortized complexity analysis. In: Knoop, J., Zdun, U. (eds.) Software Engineering. LNI, vol. 252, pp. 101–102. GI (2016)

44. Sohn, K., Gelder, A.V.: Termination detection in logic programs using argument sizes. In: Rosenkrantz, D.J. (ed.) PODS, pp. 216–226. ACM Press (1991)

45. Wegbreit, B.: Mechanical program analysis. Commun. ACM **18**(9), 528–539 (1975)

46. Wilhelm, R., Engblom, J., Ermedahl, A., Holsti, N., Thesing, S., Whalley, D.B., Bernat, G., Ferdinand, C., Heckmann, R., Mitra, T., Mueller, F., Puaut, I., Puschner, P.P., Staschulat, J., Stenström, P.: The worst-case execution-time problem - overview of methods and survey of tools. ACM Trans. Embedded Comput. Syst. **7**(3), 36 (2008)

47. Yang, L., Zhou, C., Zhan, N., Xia, B.: Recent advances in program verification through computer algebra. Front. Comput. Sci. China **4**(1), 1–16 (2010)

48. Zimmermann, P., Zimmermann, W.: The automatic complexity analysis of divide-and-conquer algorithms. Technical report, HAL Inria (1989). https://hal.inria.fr/inria-00075410/

Markov Automata with Multiple Objectives

Tim Quatmann$^{(\boxtimes)}$, Sebastian Junges,
and Joost-Pieter Katoen

RWTH Aachen University, Aachen, Germany
tim.quatmann@cs.rwth-aachen.de

Abstract. Markov automata combine non-determinism, probabilistic branching, and exponentially distributed delays. This compositional variant of continuous-time Markov decision processes is used in reliability engineering, performance evaluation and stochastic scheduling. Their verification so far focused on single objectives such as (timed) reachability, and expected costs. In practice, often the objectives are mutually dependent and the aim is to reveal trade-offs. We present algorithms to analyze several objectives simultaneously and approximate Pareto curves. This includes, e.g., several (timed) reachability objectives, or various expected cost objectives. We also consider combinations thereof, such as on-time-within-budget objectives—which policies guarantee reaching a goal state within a deadline with at least probability p while keeping the allowed average costs below a threshold? We adopt existing approaches for classical Markov decision processes. The main challenge is to treat policies exploiting state residence times, even for *un*timed objectives. Experimental results show the feasibility and scalability of our approach.

1 Introduction

Markov automata [1,2] extend labeled transition systems with probabilistic branching and exponentially distributed delays. They are a compositional variant of continuous-time Markov decision processes (CTMDPs), in a similar vein as Segala's probabilistic automata extend classical MDPs. Transitions of a Markov automaton (MA) lead from states to probability distributions over states, and are either labeled with actions (allowing for interaction) or real numbers (rates of exponential distributions). MAs are used in reliability engineering [3], hardware design [4], data-flow computation [5], dependability [6] and performance evaluation [7], as MAs are a natural semantic framework for modeling formalisms such as AADL, dynamic fault trees, stochastic Petri nets, stochastic activity networks, SADF etc. The verification of MAs so far focused on single objectives such as reachability, timed reachability, expected costs, and long-run averages [8–12]. These analyses cannot treat objectives that are mutually influencing each other, like quickly reaching a target is more costly. The aim of this paper is to analyze *multiple* objectives on MAs at once and to facilitate *trade-off analysis* by approximating Pareto curves.

© Springer International Publishing AG 2017
R. Majumdar and V. Kunčak (Eds.): CAV 2017, Part I, LNCS 10426, pp. 140–159, 2017.
DOI: 10.1007/978-3-319-63387-9_7

Consider the stochastic job scheduling problem of [13]: perform n jobs with exponential service times on k identical processors under a pre-emptive scheduling policy. Once a job finishes, all k processors can be assigned any of the m remaining jobs. When $n - m$ jobs are finished, this yields $\binom{m}{k}$ non-deterministic choices.

The largest-expected-service-time-first-policy is optimal to minimize the expected time to complete all jobs [13]. It is unclear how to schedule when imposing *extra* constraints, e.g., requiring a high probability to finish a batch of c jobs within a tight deadline (to accelerate their post-processing), or having a low average waiting time. These *multiple objectives* involve non-trivial *trade-offs*. Our algorithms analyze such trade-offs. Figure 1, e.g., shows the obtained result for 12 jobs and 3 processors. It approximates the set of points (p_1, p_2) for schedules achieving that (1) the expected time to complete

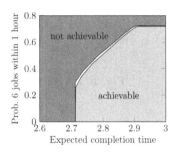

Fig. 1. Approx. Pareto curve for stochastic job scheduling.

all jobs is at most p_1 and (2) the probability to finish half of the jobs within an hour is at least p_2.

This paper presents techniques to verify MAs with multiple objectives. We consider multiple (un)timed reachability and expected reward objectives as well as their combinations. Put shortly, we reduce all these problems to instances of multi-objective verification problems on classical MDPs. For multi-objective queries involving (combinations of) untimed reachability and expected reward objectives, corresponding algorithms on the *underlying* MDP can be used. In this case, the MDP is simply obtained by ignoring the timing information, see Fig. 2(b). The crux is in relating MA schedulers—that can exploit state sojourn times to optimize their decisions—to MDP schedulers. For multiple timed reachability objectives, *digitization* [8,9] is employed to obtain an MDP, see Fig. 2(c). The key is to mimic sojourn times by self-loops with appropriate probabilities. This provides a sound arbitrary close approximation of the timed behavior and also allows to combine timed reachability objectives with other types of objectives. The main contribution is to show that digitization is sound for *all* possible MA schedulers. This requires a new proof strategy as the existing ones are tailored to optimizing a single objective. All proofs can be found in an extended version [14]. Experiments on instances of four MA benchmarks show encouraging results. Multiple untimed reachability and expected reward objectives can be efficiently treated for models with millions of states. As for single objectives [9], timed reachability is more expensive. Our implementation is competitive to PRISM for multi-objective MDPs [15,16] and to IMCA [9] for single-objective MAs.

Related Work. Multi-objective decision making for MDPs with discounting and long-run objectives has been well investigated; for a recent survey, see [17]. Etessami *et al.* [18] consider verifying finite MDPs with multiple ω-regular objectives. Other multiple objectives include expected rewards under worst-case

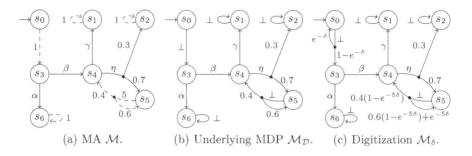

(a) MA $\mathcal{M}$.   (b) Underlying MDP $\mathcal{M}_{\mathcal{D}}$.   (c) Digitization $\mathcal{M}_\delta$.

Fig. 2. MA $\mathcal{M}$ with underlying MDP $\mathcal{M}_{\mathcal{D}}$ and digitization $\mathcal{M}_\delta$.

reachability [19,20], quantiles and conditional probabilities [21], mean pay-offs and stability [22], long-run objectives [23,24], total average discounted rewards under PCTL [25], and stochastic shortest path objectives [26]. This has been extended to MDPs with unknown cost function [27], infinite-state MDPs [28] arising from two-player timed games in a stochastic environment, and stochastic two-player games [29]. To the best of our knowledge, this is the first work on multi-objective MDPs extended with *random timing*.

2   Preliminaries

Notations. The set of real numbers is denoted by $\mathbb{R}$, and we write $\mathbb{R}_{>0} = \{x \in \mathbb{R} \mid x > 0\}$ and $\mathbb{R}_{\geq 0} = \mathbb{R}_{>0} \cup \{0\}$. For a finite set S, $Dist(S)$ denotes the set of probability distributions over S. $\mu \in Dist(S)$ is *Dirac* if $\mu(s) = 1$ for some $s \in S$.

2.1   Models

Markov automata generalize both Markov decision processes (MDPs) and continuous time Markov chains (CTMCs). They are extended with rewards (or, equivalently, costs) to allow modelling, e.g., energy consumption.

Definition 1 (Markov automaton). *A* Markov automaton (MA) *is a tuple* $\mathcal{M} = (S, Act, \rightarrow, s_0, \{\rho_1, \ldots, \rho_\ell\})$ *where S is a finite set of* states *with* initial state $s_0 \in S$, Act *is a finite set of* actions *with* $\perp \in Act$ *and* $Act \cap \mathbb{R}_{\geq 0} = \emptyset$,

- $\rightarrow \subseteq S \times (Act \cup \mathbb{R}_{>0}) \times Dist(S)$ *is a set of* transitions *such that for all $s \in S$ there is at most one transition $(s, \lambda, \mu) \in \rightarrow$ with $\lambda \in \mathbb{R}_{>0}$, and*
- $\rho_1, \ldots, \rho_\ell$ *with $\ell \geq 0$ are* reward functions $\rho_i \colon S \cup (S \times Act) \rightarrow \mathbb{R}_{\geq 0}$.

In the remainder of the paper, let $\mathcal{M} = (S, Act, \rightarrow, s_0, \{\rho_1, \ldots, \rho_\ell\})$ denote an MA. A transition $(s, \gamma, \mu) \in \rightarrow$, denoted by $s \xrightarrow{\gamma} \mu$, is called *probabilistic* if $\gamma \in Act$ and *Markovian* if $\gamma \in \mathbb{R}_{>0}$. In the latter case, γ is the rate of an exponential distribution, modeling a time-delayed transition. Probabilistic transitions fire instantaneously. The successor state is determined by μ, i.e., we move to s' with probability $\mu(s')$. Probabilistic (Markovian) states PS (MS) have an outgoing probabilistic (Markovian) transition, respectively: $\mathrm{PS} = \{s \in S \mid s \xrightarrow{\alpha} \mu, \alpha \in Act\}$ and $\mathrm{MS} = \{s \in S \mid s \xrightarrow{\lambda} \mu, \lambda \in \mathbb{R}_{>0}\}$. The *exit rate* $\mathrm{E}(s)$ of $s \in \mathrm{MS}$ is uniquely given by $s \xrightarrow{\mathrm{E}(s)} \mu$. The *transition probabilities* of $\mathcal{M}$ are given by the function $\mathbf{P} \colon S \times Act \times S \to [0,1]$ satisfying $\mathbf{P}(s, \alpha, s') = \mu(s')$ if either $s \xrightarrow{\alpha} \mu$ or $(\alpha = \perp$ and $s \xrightarrow{\mathrm{E}(s)} \mu)$ and $\mathbf{P}(s, \alpha, s') = 0$ in all other cases. The value $\mathbf{P}(s, \alpha, s')$ corresponds to the probability to move from s with action α to s'. The *enabled actions* at state s are given by $Act(s) = \{\alpha \in Act \mid \exists s' \in S \colon \mathbf{P}(s, \alpha, s') > 0\}$.

Example 1. Figure 2(a) shows an MA $\mathcal{M}$. We do not depict Dirac probability distributions. Markovian transitions are illustrated by dashed arrows.

We assume *action-deterministic* MAs: $|\{\mu \in Dist(S) \mid s \xrightarrow{\alpha} \mu\}| \leq 1$ holds for all $s \in S$ and $\alpha \in Act$. Terminal states $s \notin \mathrm{PS} \cup \mathrm{MS}$ are excluded by adding a Markovian self-loop. As standard for MAs [1,2], we impose the *maximal progress assumption*, i.e., probabilistic transitions take precedence over Markovian ones. Thus, we remove transitions $s \xrightarrow{\lambda} \mu$ for $s \in \mathrm{PS}$ and $\lambda \in \mathbb{R}_{>0}$ which yields $S = \mathrm{PS} \cup \mathrm{MS}$. MAs with *Zeno behavior*, where infinitely many actions can be taken within finite time with non-zero probability, are unrealistic and considered a modeling error.

A reward function ρ_i defines *state rewards* and *action rewards*. When sojourning in a state s for t time units, the state reward $\rho_i(s) \cdot t$ is obtained. Upon taking a transition $s \xrightarrow{\gamma} \mu$, we collect action reward $\rho_i(s, \gamma)$ (if $\gamma \in Act$) or $\rho(s, \perp)$ (if $\gamma \in \mathbb{R}_{>0}$). For presentation purposes, in the remainder of this section, rewards are omitted. Full definitions with rewards can be found in [14].

Definition 2 (Markov decision process [30]). *A* Markov decision process *(MDP) is a tuple* $\mathcal{D} = (S, Act, \mathbf{P}, s_0, \emptyset)$ *with* S, s_0, Act *as in Definition 1 and* $\mathbf{P} \colon S \times Act \times S \to [0,1]$ *are the* transition probabilities *satisfying* $\sum_{s' \in S} \mathbf{P}(s, \alpha, s') \in \{0, 1\}$ *for all* $s \in S$ *and* $\alpha \in Act$.

MDPs are MAs without Markovian states and thus without timing aspects, i.e., MDPs exhibit probabilistic branching and non-determinism. Zeno behavior is not a concern, as we do not consider timing aspects. The *underlying MDP* of an MA abstracts away from its timing:

Definition 3 (Underlying MDP). *The MDP* $\mathcal{M}_{\mathcal{D}} = (S, Act, \mathbf{P}, s_0, \emptyset)$ *is the* underlying MDP *of MA* $\mathcal{M} = (S, Act, \to, s_0, \emptyset)$ *with transition probabilities* $\mathbf{P}$.

The *digitization* $\mathcal{M}_\delta$ of $\mathcal{M}$ w.r.t. some digitization constant $\delta \in \mathbb{R}_{>0}$ is an MDP which digitizes the time [8,9]. The main difference between $\mathcal{M}_{\mathcal{D}}$ and $\mathcal{M}_\delta$ is that the latter also introduces *self-loops* which describe the probability to stay in a Markovian state for δ time units. More precisely, the outgoing transitions of states $s \in \mathrm{MS}$ in $\mathcal{M}_\delta$ represent that either (1) a Markovian transition in $\mathcal{M}$ was taken within δ time units, or (2) no transition is taken within δ time units – which is captured by taking the self-loop in $\mathcal{M}_\delta$. Counting the taken self-loops at $s \in \mathrm{MS}$ allows to approximate the sojourn time in s.

Definition 4 (Digitization of an MA). *For MA* $\mathcal{M} = (S, Act, \rightarrow, s_0, \emptyset)$ *with transition probabilities* $\mathbf{P}$ *and* digitization constant $\delta \in \mathbb{R}_{>0}$, *the* digitization of $\mathcal{M}$ *w.r.t.* δ *is the MDP* $\mathcal{M}_\delta = (S, Act, \mathbf{P}_\delta, s_0, \emptyset)$ *where*

$$\mathbf{P}_\delta(s, \alpha, s') = \begin{cases} \mathbf{P}(s, \perp, s') \cdot (1 - e^{-\mathrm{E}(s)\delta}) & \text{if } s \in \mathrm{MS}, \alpha = \perp, s \neq s' \\ \mathbf{P}(s, \perp, s') \cdot (1 - e^{-\mathrm{E}(s)\delta}) + e^{-\mathrm{E}(s)\delta} & \text{if } s \in \mathrm{MS}, \alpha = \perp, s = s' \\ \mathbf{P}(s, \alpha, s') & \text{otherwise.} \end{cases}$$

Example 2. Figure 2 shows an MA $\mathcal{M}$ with its underlying MDP $\mathcal{M}_\mathcal{D}$ and a digitization $\mathcal{M}_\delta$ for unspecified $\delta \in \mathbb{R}_{>0}$.

Paths and Schedulers. Paths represent runs of $\mathcal{M}$ starting in the initial state. Let $t(\kappa) = 0$ and $\alpha(\kappa) = \kappa$, if $\kappa \in Act$, and $t(\kappa) = \kappa$ and $\alpha(\kappa) = \perp$, if $\kappa \in \mathbb{R}_{\geq 0}$.

Definition 5 (Infinite path). *An* infinite path *of MA* $\mathcal{M}$ *with transition probabilities* $\mathbf{P}$ *is an infinite sequence* $\pi = s_0 \xrightarrow{\kappa_0} s_1 \xrightarrow{\kappa_1} \ldots$ *of states* $s_0, s_1, \cdots \in S$ *and stamps* $\kappa_0, \kappa_1, \cdots \in Act \cup \mathbb{R}_{\geq 0}$ *such that (1)* $\sum_{i=0}^\infty t(\kappa_i) = \infty$, *and for any* $i \geq 0$ *it holds that (2)* $\mathbf{P}(s_i, \alpha(\kappa_i), s_{i+1}) > 0$, *(3)* $s_i \in \mathrm{PS}$ *implies* $\kappa_i \in Act$, *and (4)* $s_i \in \mathrm{MS}$ *implies* $\kappa_i \in \mathbb{R}_{\geq 0}$.

An infix $s_i \xrightarrow{\kappa_i} s_{i+1}$ of a path π represents that we stay at s_i for $t(\kappa_i)$ time units and then perform action $\alpha(\kappa_i)$ and move to state s_{i+1}. Condition (1) excludes Zeno paths, condition (2) ensures positive transition probabilities, and conditions (3) and (4) assert that stamps κ_i match the transition type at s_i.

A *finite path* is a finite prefix $\pi' = s_0 \xrightarrow{\kappa_0} \ldots \xrightarrow{\kappa_{n-1}} s_n$ of an infinite path. The *length* of π' is $|\pi'| = n$, its *last state* is $last(\pi') = s_n$, and the *time duration* is $T(\pi') = \sum_{0 \leq i < |\pi'|} t(\kappa_i)$. We denote the sets of finite and infinite paths of $\mathcal{M}$ by $FPaths^\mathcal{M}$ and $IPaths^\mathcal{M}$, respectively. The superscript $\mathcal{M}$ is omitted if the model is clear from the context. For a finite or infinite path $\pi = s_0 \xrightarrow{\kappa_0} s_1 \xrightarrow{\kappa_1} \ldots$ the *prefix* of π of length n is denoted by $pref(\pi, n)$. The ith state visited by π is given by $\pi[i] = s_i$. The *time-abstraction* $ta(\pi)$ of π removes all sojourn times and is a path of the underlying MDP $\mathcal{M}_\mathcal{D}$: $ta(\pi) = s_0 \xrightarrow{\alpha(\kappa_0)} s_1 \xrightarrow{\alpha(\kappa_1)} \ldots$. Paths of $\mathcal{M}_\mathcal{D}$ are also referred to as the *time-abstract paths of* $\mathcal{M}$.

Definition 6 (Generic scheduler). *A* generic scheduler *for* $\mathcal{M}$ *is a measurable function* $\sigma \colon FPaths \times Act \to [0, 1]$ *such that* $\sigma(\pi, \cdot) \in Dist(Act(last(\pi)))$ *for each* $\pi \in FPaths$.

A scheduler σ for $\mathcal{M}$ resolves the non-determinism of $\mathcal{M}$: $\sigma(\pi, \alpha)$ is the probability to take transition $last(\pi) \xrightarrow{\alpha} \mu$ after observing the run π. The set of such schedulers is denoted by $\mathrm{GM}^\mathcal{M}$ (GM if $\mathcal{M}$ is clear from the context). $\sigma \in \mathrm{GM}$ is *deterministic* if the distribution $\sigma(\pi, \cdot)$ is Dirac for any π. *Time-abstract schedulers* behave independently of the time-stamps of the given path, i.e., $\sigma(\pi, \alpha) = \sigma(\pi', \alpha)$ for all actions α and paths π, π' with $ta(\pi) = ta(\pi')$. We write $\mathrm{TA}^\mathcal{M}$ to denote the set of time-abstract schedulers of $\mathcal{M}$. GM is the most general scheduler class for MAs. For MDPs, the most general scheduler class is TA.

2.2   Objectives

An objective $\mathbb{O}_i$ is a representation of a *quantitative* property like the probability to reach an error state, or the expected energy consumption. To express *Boolean* properties (e.g., the probability to reach an error state is below p_i), $\mathbb{O}_i$ is combined with a *threshold* $\rhd_i p_i$ where $\rhd_i \in \{<, \leq, >, \geq\}$ is a *threshold relation* and $p_i \in \mathbb{R}$ is a *threshold value*. Let $\mathcal{M}, \sigma \models \mathbb{O}_i \rhd_i p_i$ denote that the MA $\mathcal{M}$ under scheduler $\sigma \in \mathrm{GM}$ satisfies the property $\mathbb{O}_i \rhd_i p_i$.

Reachability Objectives. $I \subseteq \mathbb{R}$ is a *time interval* if it is of the form $I = [a, b]$ or $I = [a, \infty)$, where $0 \leq a < b$. The set of paths reaching a set of goal states $G \subseteq S$ in time I is defined as

$$\Diamond^I G = \{\pi = s_0 \xrightarrow{\kappa_0} s_1 \xrightarrow{\kappa_1} \cdots \in \mathit{IPaths} \mid \exists n \geq 0 \colon \pi[n] \in G \text{ and}$$
$$I \cap [t, t + t(\kappa_n)] \neq \emptyset \text{ for } t = T(\mathit{pref}(\pi, n))\}.$$

We write $\Diamond G$ instead of $\Diamond^{[0,\infty)} G$. A probability measure $\mathrm{Pr}_\sigma^\mathcal{M}$ on sets of infinite paths is defined, which generalizes both the standard probability measure on MDPs and on CTMCs. A formal definition is given in [14].

Definition 7 (Reachability objective). *A reachability objective has the form* $\mathbb{P}(\Diamond^I G)$ *for time interval* I *and goal states* G. *The objective is* timed *if* $I \neq [0, \infty)$ *and* untimed *otherwise. For MA* $\mathcal{M}$ *and scheduler* $\sigma \in \mathrm{GM}$, *let* $\mathcal{M}, \sigma \models \mathbb{P}(\Diamond^I G) \rhd_i p_i$ *iff* $\mathrm{Pr}_\sigma^\mathcal{M}(\Diamond^I G) \rhd_i p_i$.

Expected Reward Objectives. Expected rewards $\mathrm{ER}_\sigma^\mathcal{M}(\rho_j, G)$ define the expected amount of reward collected (w.r.t. ρ_j) until a goal state in $G \subseteq S$ is reached. This is a straightforward generalization of the notion on CTMCs and MDPs. A formal definition is found in [14].

Definition 8 (Expected reward objective). *An* expected reward objective *has the form* $\mathbb{E}(\#j, G)$ *where* j *is the index of reward function* ρ_j *and* $G \subseteq S$. *For MA* $\mathcal{M}$ *and scheduler* $\sigma \in \mathrm{GM}$, *let* $\mathcal{M}, \sigma \models \mathbb{E}(\#j, G) \rhd_i p_i$ *iff* $\mathrm{ER}_\sigma^\mathcal{M}(\rho_j, G) \rhd_i p_i$.

Expected *time* objectives $\mathbb{E}(T, G)$ are expected reward objectives that consider the reward function ρ_T with $\rho_T(s) = 1$ if $s \in \mathrm{MS}$ and all other rewards are zero.

3   Multi-objective Model Checking

Standard model checking considers objectives individually. This approach is not feasible when we are interested in multiple objectives that should be fulfilled by the same scheduler, e.g., a scheduler that maximizes the expected profit might violate certain safety constraints. *Multi-objective* model checking aims to analyze multiple objectives at once and reveals possible trade-offs.

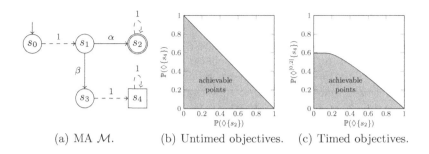

(a) MA $\mathcal{M}$.   (b) Untimed objectives.   (c) Timed objectives.

Fig. 3. Markov automaton and achievable points.

Definition 9 (Satisfaction of multiple objectives). *Let $\mathcal{M}$ be an MA and $\sigma \in$ GM. For objectives $\mathbb{O} = (\mathbb{O}_1, \ldots, \mathbb{O}_d)$ with threshold relations $\triangleright = (\triangleright_1, \ldots, \triangleright_d) \in \{<, \leq, >, \geq\}^d$ and threshold values $\mathbf{p} = (p_1, \ldots, p_d) \in \mathbb{R}^d$ let*

$$\mathcal{M}, \sigma \models \mathbb{O} \triangleright \mathbf{p} \iff \mathcal{M}, \sigma \models \mathbb{O}_i \triangleright_i p_i \text{ for all } 1 \leq i \leq d.$$

Furthermore, let $achieve^{\mathcal{M}}(\mathbb{O} \triangleright \mathbf{p}) \iff \exists \sigma \in$ GM such that $\mathcal{M}, \sigma \models \mathbb{O} \triangleright \mathbf{p}$.

If $\mathcal{M}, \sigma \models \mathbb{O} \triangleright \mathbf{p}$, the point $\mathbf{p} \in \mathbb{R}^d$ is *achievable* in $\mathcal{M}$ with scheduler σ. The *set of achievable points* of $\mathcal{M}$ w.r.t. $\mathbb{O}$ and $\mathbf{p}$ is $\{\mathbf{p} \in \mathbb{R}^d \mid achieve^{\mathcal{M}}(\mathbb{O} \triangleright \mathbf{p})\}$. This definition is compatible with the notions on MDPs as given in [16,18].

Example 3. Figure 3(b) and (c) depict the set of achievable points of the MA $\mathcal{M}$ from Fig. 3(a) w.r.t. relations $\triangleright = (\geq, \geq)$ and objectives $(\mathbb{P}(\Diamond\{s_2\}), \mathbb{P}(\Diamond\{s_4\}))$ and $(\mathbb{P}(\Diamond\{s_2\}), \mathbb{P}(\Diamond^{[0,2]}\{s_4\}))$, respectively. Using the set of achievable points, we can answer Pareto, numerical, and achievability queries as considered in [16], e.g., the Pareto front lies on the border of the set.

Schedulers. For single-objective model checking on MAs, it suffices to consider deterministic schedulers [31]. For untimed reachability and expected rewards even *time-abstract* deterministic schedulers suffice [31]. Multi-objective model checking on MDPs requires history-dependent, randomized schedulers [18]. On MAs, schedulers may also employ *timing* information to make optimal choices, even if only *untimed* objectives are considered.

Example 4. Consider the MA $\mathcal{M}$ in Fig. 3(a) with untimed objectives $\mathbb{P}(\Diamond\{s_2\}) \geq 0.5$ and $\mathbb{P}(\Diamond\{s_4\}) \geq 0.5$. A simple graph argument yields that both properties are only satisfied if action α is taken with probability exactly a half. Thus, on the underlying MDP, no deterministic scheduler satisfies both objectives. On the MA however, paths can be distinguished by their sojourn time in s_0. As the probability mass to stay in s_0 for at most $\ln(2)$ is exactly 0.5, a timed scheduler σ with $\sigma(s_0 \xrightarrow{t} s_1, \alpha) = 1$ if $t \leq \ln(2)$ and 0 otherwise does satisfy both objectives.

Theorem 1. *For some MA $\mathcal{M}$ with $achieve^{\mathcal{M}}(\mathbb{O} \triangleright \mathbf{p})$, no deterministic time-abstract scheduler σ satisfies $\mathcal{M}, \sigma \models \mathbb{O} \triangleright \mathbf{p}$.*

The Geometric Shape of the Achievable Points. Like for MDPs [18], the set of achievable points of any combination of aforementioned objectives is convex.

Proposition 1. *The set $\{\mathbf{p} \in \mathbb{R}^d \mid achieve^{\mathcal{M}}(\mathbb{O} \rhd \mathbf{p})\}$ is convex.*

For MDPs, the set of achievable points is a convex polytope where the vertices can be realized by deterministic schedulers that use memory bounded by the number of objectives. As there are finitely many such schedulers, the polytope is finite [18], i.e., it can be represented by a finite number of vertices. This result does not carry over to MAs. For example, the achievable points of the MA from Fig. 3(a) together with the objectives $(\mathbb{P}(\lozenge\{s_2\}), \mathbb{P}(\lozenge^{[0,2]}\{s_4\}))$ form the infinite polytope shown in Fig. 3(c). The insight here is that for any sojourn time $t \leq 2$ in s_0, the timing information is relevant for optimal schedulers: The shorter the sojourn time in s_0, the higher the probability to reach s_4 within the time bound.

Theorem 2. *For some MA $\mathcal{M}$ and objectives $\mathbb{O}$, the polytope $\{\mathbf{p} \in \mathbb{R}^d \mid achieve^{\mathcal{M}}(\mathbb{O} \rhd \mathbf{p})\}$ is not finite.*

As infinite convex polytopes cannot be represented by a finite number of vertices, any method extending the approach of [16] – which computes these vertices – can only approximate the set of achievable points.

Problem Statement. For an MA and objectives with threshold relations, construct arbitrarily tight over- and under-approximations of the achievable points.

4   Analysis of Markov Automata with Multiple Objectives

The state-of-the-art in single-objective model checking of MA is to reduce the MA to an MDP, cf. [8–10], for which efficient algorithms exist. We aim to lift this approach to multi-objective model checking. Assume MA $\mathcal{M}$ and objectives $\mathbb{O}$ with threshold relations $\rhd$. We discuss how the set of achievable points of $\mathcal{M}$ relates to the set of achievable points of an MDP. The key challenge is to deal with timing information—even for *untimed* objectives—and to consider schedulers beyond those optimizing single objectives. We obtain:

- For untimed reachability and expected reward objectives, the achievable points of $\mathcal{M}$ *equal* those of its *underlying* MDP, cf. Theorems 3 and 4.
- For timed reachability objectives, the set of achievable points of a *digitized* MDP $\mathcal{M}_\delta$ provides a *sound approximation* of the achievable points of $\mathcal{M}$, cf. Theorem 5. Corollary 1 gives the precision of the approximation.

4.1   Untimed Reachability Objectives

Although timing information is essential for *deterministic* schedulers, cf. Theorem 1, timing information does not strengthen randomized schedulers:

Theorem 3. *For MA $\mathcal{M}$ and untimed reachability objectives $\mathbb{O}$ it holds that $achieve^{\mathcal{M}}(\mathbb{O} \rhd \mathbf{p}) \iff achieve^{\mathcal{M}_D}(\mathbb{O} \rhd \mathbf{p})$.*

The main idea for proving Theorem 3 is to construct for scheduler $\sigma \in \mathrm{GM}^{\mathcal{M}}$ a time-abstract scheduler $\mathrm{ta}(\sigma) \in \mathrm{TA}^{\mathcal{M}_{\mathcal{D}}}$ such that they both induce the same untimed reachability probabilities. To this end, we discuss the connection between probabilities of paths of MA $\mathcal{M}$ and paths of MDP $\mathcal{M}_{\mathcal{D}}$.

Definition 10 (Induced paths of a time-abstract path). *The set of induced paths on MA $\mathcal{M}$ of a path $\hat{\pi}$ of $\mathcal{M}_{\mathcal{D}}$ is given by*

$$\langle \hat{\pi} \rangle = \mathrm{ta}^{-1}(\hat{\pi}) = \{ \pi \in FPaths^{\mathcal{M}} \cup IPaths^{\mathcal{M}} \mid \mathrm{ta}(\pi) = \hat{\pi} \}.$$

The set $\langle \hat{\pi} \rangle$ contains all paths of $\mathcal{M}$ where replacing sojourn times by $\bot$ yields $\hat{\pi}$. For $\sigma \in \mathrm{GM}$, the probability distribution $\sigma(\pi, \cdot) \in Dist(Act)$ might depend on the sojourn times of the path π. The time-abstract scheduler $\mathrm{ta}(\sigma)$ weights the distribution $\sigma(\pi, \cdot)$ with the probability masses of the paths $\pi \in \langle \hat{\pi} \rangle$.

Definition 11 (Time-abstraction of a scheduler). *The time-abstraction of $\sigma \in \mathrm{GM}^{\mathcal{M}}$ is defined as $\mathrm{ta}(\sigma) \in \mathrm{TA}^{\mathcal{M}_{\mathcal{D}}}$ such that for any $\hat{\pi} \in FPaths^{\mathcal{M}_{\mathcal{D}}}$*

$$\mathrm{ta}(\sigma)(\hat{\pi}, \alpha) = \int_{\pi \in \langle \hat{\pi} \rangle} \sigma(\pi, \alpha) \, \mathrm{dPr}_{\sigma}^{\mathcal{M}}(\pi \mid \langle \hat{\pi} \rangle).$$

The term $\mathrm{Pr}_{\sigma}^{\mathcal{M}}(\pi \mid \langle \hat{\pi} \rangle)$ represents the probability for a path in $\langle \hat{\pi} \rangle$ to have sojourn times as given by π. The value $\mathrm{ta}(\sigma)(\hat{\pi}, \alpha)$ coincides with the probability that σ picks action α, given that the time-abstract path $\hat{\pi}$ was observed.

Example 5. Consider the MA $\mathcal{M}$ in Fig. 2(a) and the scheduler σ choosing α at state s_3 iff the sojourn time at s_0 is at most one. Then $\mathrm{ta}(\sigma)(s_0 \xrightarrow{\bot} s_3, \alpha) = 1 - e^{-\mathrm{E}(s_0)}$, the probability that s_0 is left within one time unit. For $\bar{\pi} = s_0 \xrightarrow{\bot} s_3 \xrightarrow{\alpha} s_6$ we have

$$\mathrm{Pr}_{\sigma}^{\mathcal{M}}(\Diamond\{s_6\}) = \mathrm{Pr}_{\sigma}^{\mathcal{M}}(\langle \bar{\pi} \rangle) = 1 - e^{-\mathrm{E}(s_0)} = \mathrm{Pr}_{\mathrm{ta}(\sigma)}^{\mathcal{M}_{\mathcal{D}}}(\bar{\pi}) = \mathrm{Pr}_{\mathrm{ta}(\sigma)}^{\mathcal{M}_{\mathcal{D}}}(\Diamond\{s_6\}).$$

In the example, the considered scheduler and its time-abstraction induce the same untimed reachability probabilities. We generalize this observation.

Lemma 1. *For any $\hat{\pi} \in FPaths^{\mathcal{M}_{\mathcal{D}}}$ we have $\mathrm{Pr}_{\sigma}^{\mathcal{M}}(\langle \hat{\pi} \rangle) = \mathrm{Pr}_{\mathrm{ta}(\sigma)}^{\mathcal{M}_{\mathcal{D}}}(\hat{\pi})$.*

The result is lifted to untimed reachability probabilities.

Proposition 2. *For any $G \subseteq S$ it holds that $\mathrm{Pr}_{\sigma}^{\mathcal{M}}(\Diamond G) = \mathrm{Pr}_{\mathrm{ta}(\sigma)}^{\mathcal{M}_{\mathcal{D}}}(\Diamond G)$.*

As the definition of $\mathrm{ta}(\sigma)$ is independent of the considered set of goal states $G \subseteq S$, Proposition 2 can be lifted to multiple untimed reachability objectives.

Proof of Theorem 3 (sketch). By applying Proposition 2, we can show that $\mathcal{M}, \sigma \models \mathbb{O} \rhd \mathbf{p} \iff \mathcal{M}_{\mathcal{D}}, \mathrm{ta}(\sigma) \models \mathbb{O} \rhd \mathbf{p}$ for any scheduler $\sigma \in \mathrm{GM}^{\mathcal{M}}$ and untimed reachability objectives $\mathbb{O} = (\mathbb{P}(\Diamond G_1), \ldots, \mathbb{P}(\Diamond G_d))$ with thresholds $\rhd \mathbf{p}$. Theorem 3 is a direct consequence of this.

4.2   Expected Reward Objectives

The results for expected reward objectives are similar to untimed reachability objectives: An analysis of the underlying MDP suffices. We show the following extension of Theorem 3 to expected reward objectives.

Theorem 4. *For MA $\mathcal{M}$ and untimed reachability and expected reward objectives $\mathbb{O}$: $achieve^{\mathcal{M}}(\mathbb{O} \rhd \mathbf{p}) \iff achieve^{\mathcal{M}_{\mathcal{D}}}(\mathbb{O} \rhd \mathbf{p})$.*

To prove this, we show that a scheduler $\sigma \in GM^{\mathcal{M}}$ and its time-abstraction $ta(\sigma) \in TA$ induce the same expected rewards on $\mathcal{M}$ and $\mathcal{M}_{\mathcal{D}}$, respectively. Theorem 4 follows then analogously to Theorem 3.

Proposition 3. *Let ρ be some reward function of $\mathcal{M}$ and let $\rho^{\mathcal{D}}$ be its counterpart for $\mathcal{M}_{\mathcal{D}}$. For $G \subseteq S$ we have $\mathrm{ER}_{\sigma}^{\mathcal{M}}(\rho, G) = \mathrm{ER}_{ta(\sigma)}^{\mathcal{M}_{\mathcal{D}}}(\rho^{\mathcal{D}}, G)$.*

Notice that $\rho^{\mathcal{D}}$ encodes the *expected* reward of $\mathcal{M}$ obtained in a state s by assuming the sojourn time to be the expected sojourn time $1/E(s)$. Although the claim is similar to Proposition 2, its proof cannot be adapted straightforwardly. In particular, the analogon to Lemma 1 does not hold: The expected reward collected along a time-abstract path $\hat{\pi} \in FPaths^{\mathcal{M}_{\mathcal{D}}}$ does in general not coincide for $\mathcal{M}$ and $\mathcal{M}_{\mathcal{D}}$.

Example 6. We consider standard notations for rewards as detailed in [14]. Let $\mathcal{M}$ be the MA with underlying MDP $\mathcal{M}_{\mathcal{D}}$ as shown in Fig. 2. Let $\rho(s_0) = 1$ and zero otherwise. Reconsider the scheduler σ from Example 5. Let $\hat{\pi}_{\alpha} = s_0 \xrightarrow{\perp} s_3 \xrightarrow{\alpha} s_6$. The probability $\mathrm{Pr}_{\sigma}^{\mathcal{M}}(\{s_0 \xrightarrow{t} s_3 \xrightarrow{\alpha} s_6 \in \langle \hat{\pi}_{\alpha} \rangle \mid t > 1\})$ is zero since σ chooses β on such paths. For the remaining paths in $\langle \hat{\pi}_{\alpha} \rangle$, action α is chosen with probability one. The expected reward in $\mathcal{M}$ along $\hat{\pi}_{\alpha}$ is:

$$\int_{\pi \in \langle \hat{\pi}_{\alpha} \rangle} rew^{\mathcal{M}}(\rho, \pi) \, d\mathrm{Pr}_{\sigma}^{\mathcal{M}}(\pi) = \int_{0}^{1} \rho(s_0) \cdot t \cdot \mathrm{E}(s_0) \cdot e^{-\mathrm{E}(s_0)t} \, dt = 1 - 2e^{-1}.$$

The expected reward in $\mathcal{M}_{\mathcal{D}}$ along $\hat{\pi}_{\alpha}$ differs as

$$rew^{\mathcal{M}_{\mathcal{D}}}(\rho^{\mathcal{D}}, \hat{\pi}_{\alpha}) \cdot \mathrm{Pr}_{ta(\sigma)}^{\mathcal{M}_{\mathcal{D}}}(\hat{\pi}_{\alpha}) = \rho^{\mathcal{D}}(s_0, \perp) \cdot ta(\sigma)(s_0 \xrightarrow{\perp} s_3, \alpha) = 1 - e^{-1}.$$

The intuition is as follows: If path $s_0 \xrightarrow{t} s_3 \xrightarrow{\alpha} s_6$ of $\mathcal{M}$ under σ occurs, we have $t \le 1$ since σ chose α. Hence, the reward collected from paths in $\langle \hat{\pi}_{\alpha} \rangle$ is at most $1 \cdot \rho(s_0) = 1$. There is thus a dependency between the choice of the scheduler at s_3 and the collected reward at s_0. This dependency is absent in $\mathcal{M}_{\mathcal{D}}$ as the reward at a state is independent of the subsequent performed actions.

Let $\hat{\pi}_{\beta} = s_0 \xrightarrow{\perp} s_3 \xrightarrow{\beta} s_4$. The expected reward along $\hat{\pi}_{\beta}$ is $2e^{-1}$ for $\mathcal{M}$ and e^{-1} for $\mathcal{M}_{\mathcal{D}}$. As the rewards for $\hat{\pi}_{\alpha}$ and $\hat{\pi}_{\beta}$ sum up to one in both $\mathcal{M}$ and $\mathcal{M}_{\mathcal{D}}$, the expected reward along all paths of length two coincides for $\mathcal{M}$ and $\mathcal{M}_{\mathcal{D}}$.

This observation can be generalized to arbitrary MA and paths of arbitrary length.

Proof of Proposition 3 (sketch). For every $n \geq 0$, the expected reward collected along paths of length at most n coincides for $\mathcal{M}$ under σ and $\mathcal{M}_{\mathcal{D}}$ under $\mathrm{ta}(\sigma)$. The proposition follows by letting n approach infinity.

Thus, queries on MA with mixtures of untimed reachability and expected reward objectives can be analyzed on the underlying MDP $\mathcal{M}_{\mathcal{D}}$.

4.3 Timed Reachability Objectives

Timed reachability objectives cannot be analyzed on $\mathcal{M}_{\mathcal{D}}$ as it abstracts away from sojourn times. We lift the digitization approach for single-objective timed reachability [8,9] to multiple objectives. Instead of abstracting timing information, it is *digitized*. Let $\mathcal{M}_{\delta}$ denote the digitization of $\mathcal{M}$ for arbitrary digitization constant $\delta \in \mathbb{R}_{>0}$, see Definition 4. A time interval $I \subseteq \mathbb{R}_{\geq 0}$ of the form $[a, \infty)$ or $[a, b]$ with $\mathrm{di}_a := {}^a/_{\delta} \in \mathbb{N}$ and $\mathrm{di}_b := {}^b/_{\delta} \in \mathbb{N}$ is called *well-formed*. For the remainder, we only consider well-formed intervals, ensured by an appropriate digitization constant. An interval for time-bounds I is transformed to digitization step bounds $\mathrm{di}(I) \subseteq \mathbb{N}$. Let $a = \inf I$, we set $\mathrm{di}(I) = \{{}^t/_{\delta} \in \mathbb{N} \mid t \in I\} \setminus \{0 \mid a > 0\}$.

We first relate paths in $\mathcal{M}$ to paths in its digitization.

Definition 12 (Digitization of a path). *The* digitization $\mathrm{di}(\pi)$ *of path* $\pi = s_0 \xrightarrow{\kappa_0} s_1 \xrightarrow{\kappa_1} \ldots$ *in* $\mathcal{M}$ *is the path in* $\mathcal{M}_{\delta}$ *given by*

$$\mathrm{di}(\pi) = \left(s_0 \xrightarrow{\alpha(\kappa_0)}\right)^{m_0} s_0 \xrightarrow{\alpha(\kappa_0)} \left(s_1 \xrightarrow{\alpha(\kappa_1)}\right)^{m_1} s_1 \xrightarrow{\alpha(\kappa_1)} \ldots$$

where $m_i = \max\{m \in \mathbb{N} \mid m\delta \leq t(\kappa_i)\}$ *for each* $i \geq 0$.

Example 7. For the path $\pi = s_0 \xrightarrow{1.1} s_3 \xrightarrow{\beta} s_4 \xrightarrow{\eta} s_5 \xrightarrow{0.3} s_4$ of the MA $\mathcal{M}$ in Fig. 2(a) and $\delta = 0.4$, we get $\mathrm{di}(\pi) = s_0 \xrightarrow{\perp} s_0 \xrightarrow{\perp} s_0 \xrightarrow{\perp} s_3 \xrightarrow{\beta} s_4 \xrightarrow{\eta} s_5 \xrightarrow{\perp} s_4$.

The m_i in the definition above represent a digitization of the sojourn times $t(\kappa_i)$ such that $m_i\delta \leq t(\kappa_i) < (m_i+1)\delta$. These digitized times are incorporated into the digitization of a path by taking the self-loop at state $s_i \in \mathrm{MS}$ m_i times. We also refer to the paths of $\mathcal{M}_{\delta}$ as *digital paths (of $\mathcal{M}$)*. The number $|\bar{\pi}|_{\mathrm{ds}}$ of *digitization steps* of a digital path $\bar{\pi}$ is the number of transitions emerging from Markovian states, i.e., $|\bar{\pi}|_{\mathrm{ds}} = |\{i < |\bar{\pi}| \mid \bar{\pi}[i] \in \mathrm{MS}\}|$. One digitization step represents the elapse of at most δ time units—either by staying at some $s \in \mathrm{MS}$ for δ time or by leaving s within δ time. The number $|\mathrm{di}(\pi)|_{\mathrm{ds}}$ multiplied with δ yields an estimate for the duration $T(\pi)$. A digital path $\bar{\pi}$ can be interpreted as representation of the set of paths of $\mathcal{M}$ whose digitization is $\bar{\pi}$.

Definition 13 (Induced paths of a digital path). *The set of* induced paths *of a (finite or infinite) digital path* $\bar{\pi}$ *of* $\mathcal{M}_{\delta}$ *is*

$$[\bar{\pi}] = \mathrm{di}^{-1}(\bar{\pi}) = \{\pi \in \mathit{FPaths}^{\mathcal{M}} \cup \mathit{IPaths}^{\mathcal{M}} \mid \mathrm{di}(\pi) = \bar{\pi}\}.$$

For sets of digital paths Π we define the *induced paths* $[\Pi] = \bigcup_{\bar{\pi} \in \Pi}[\bar{\pi}]$. To relate timed reachability probabilities for $\mathcal{M}$ under scheduler $\sigma \in \mathrm{GM}^{\mathcal{M}}$ with ds-bounded reachability probabilities for $\mathcal{M}_{\delta}$, relating σ to a scheduler for $\mathcal{M}_{\delta}$ is necessary.

Definition 14 (Digitization of a scheduler). *The* digitization *of* $\sigma \in \mathrm{GM}^{\mathcal{M}}$ *is given by* $\mathrm{di}(\sigma) \in \mathrm{TA}^{\mathcal{M}_{\delta}}$ *such that for any* $\bar{\pi} \in \mathit{FPaths}^{\mathcal{M}_{\delta}}$ *with* $\mathrm{last}(\bar{\pi}) \in \mathrm{PS}$

$$\mathrm{di}(\sigma)(\bar{\pi}, \alpha) = \int_{\pi \in [\bar{\pi}]} \sigma(\pi, \alpha)\, \mathrm{dPr}_{\sigma}^{\mathcal{M}}(\pi \mid [\bar{\pi}]).$$

The digitization $\mathrm{di}(\sigma)$ is similar to the time-abstraction $\mathrm{ta}(\sigma)$ as both schedulers get a path with restricted timing information as input and mimic the choice of σ. However, while $\mathrm{ta}(\sigma)$ receives no information regarding sojourn times, $\mathrm{di}(\sigma)$ receives the digital estimate. Intuitively, $\mathrm{di}(\sigma)(\bar{\pi}, \alpha)$ considers $\sigma(\pi, \alpha)$ for each $\pi \in [\bar{\pi}]$, weighted with the probability that the sojourn times of a path in $[\bar{\pi}]$ are as given by π. The restriction $\mathrm{last}(\bar{\pi}) \in \mathrm{PS}$ asserts that $\bar{\pi}$ does not end with a self-loop on a Markovian state, implying $[\bar{\pi}] \neq \emptyset$.

Example 8. Let MA $\mathcal{M}$ in Fig. 2(a) and $\delta = 0.4$. Again, $\sigma \in \mathrm{GM}^{\mathcal{M}}$ chooses α at state s_3 iff the sojourn time at s_0 is at most one. Consider the digital paths $\bar{\pi}_m = (s_0 \xrightarrow{\perp})^m s_0 \xrightarrow{\perp} s_3$. For $\pi \in [\bar{\pi}_1] = \{s_0 \xrightarrow{t} s_3 \mid 0.4 \leq t < 0.8\}$ we have $\sigma(\pi, \alpha) = 1$. It follows $\mathrm{di}(\sigma)(\bar{\pi}_1, \alpha) = 1$. For $\pi \in [\bar{\pi}_2] = \{s_0 \xrightarrow{t} s_3 \mid 0.8 \leq t < 1.2\}$ it is unclear whether σ chooses α or β. Hence, $\mathrm{di}(\sigma)$ randomly guesses:

$$\mathrm{di}(\sigma)(\bar{\pi}_2, \alpha) = \int_{\pi \in [\bar{\pi}_2]} \sigma(\pi, \alpha)\, \mathrm{dPr}_{\sigma}^{\mathcal{M}}(\pi \mid [\bar{\pi}_2]) = \frac{\int_{0.8}^{1.0} \mathrm{E}(s_0)e^{-\mathrm{E}(s_0)t}\, \mathrm{d}t}{\int_{0.8}^{1.2} \mathrm{E}(s_0)e^{-\mathrm{E}(s_0)t}\, \mathrm{d}t} \approx 0.55.$$

On $\mathcal{M}_{\delta}$ we consider ds-bounded reachability instead of timed reachability.

Definition 15 (ds-bounded reachability). *The set of infinite digital paths that reach* $G \subseteq S$ *within the interval* $J \subseteq \mathbb{N}$ *of consecutive natural numbers is*

$$\Diamond_{\mathrm{ds}}^{J}G = \{\bar{\pi} \in \mathit{IPaths}^{\mathcal{M}_{\delta}} \mid \exists n \geq 0\colon \bar{\pi}[n] \in G \text{ and } |\mathit{pref}(\bar{\pi}, n)|_{\mathrm{ds}} \in J\}.$$

The timed reachability probabilities for $\mathcal{M}$ are estimated by ds-bounded reachability probabilities for $\mathcal{M}_{\delta}$. The induced ds-bounded reachability probability for $\mathcal{M}$ (under σ) coincides with ds-bounded reachability probability on $\mathcal{M}_{\delta}$ (under $\mathrm{di}(\sigma)$).

Proposition 4. *Let* $\mathcal{M}$ *be an MA with* $G \subseteq S$, $\sigma \in \mathrm{GM}$, *and digitization* $\mathcal{M}_{\delta}$. *Further, let* $J \subseteq \mathbb{N}$ *be a set of consecutive natural numbers. It holds that*

$$\mathrm{Pr}_{\sigma}^{\mathcal{M}}([\Diamond_{\mathrm{ds}}^{J}G]) = \mathrm{Pr}_{\mathrm{di}(\sigma)}^{\mathcal{M}_{\delta}}(\Diamond_{\mathrm{ds}}^{J}G).$$

Thus, induced ds-bounded reachability on MAs can be computed on their digitization. Next, we relate ds-bounded and timed reachability on MAs, i.e., we quantify the maximum difference between time-bounded and ds-bounded reachability probabilities.

Example 9. Let $\mathcal{M}$ be the MA given in Fig. 4(a). We consider the well-formed time interval $I = [0, 5\delta]$, yielding digitization step bounds $\mathrm{di}(I) = \{0, \ldots, 5\}$. The digitization constant $\delta \in \mathbb{R}_{>0}$ remains unspecified in this example. Figure 4(b) illustrates paths π_1, π_2, and π_3 of $\mathcal{M}$. We depict sojourn times by arrow length. A black dot indicates that the path stays at the current state for a multiple of δ time units. All depicted paths reach $G = \{s_3\}$ within 5δ time units. However, the digitizations of π_1, π_2, and π_3 reach G within 5, 4, and 6 digitization steps, respectively. This yields

$$\pi_1, \pi_2 \in \Diamond^I G \cap [\Diamond_{\mathrm{ds}}^{\mathrm{di}(I)} G] \quad \text{and} \quad \pi_3 \in \Diamond^I G \setminus [\Diamond_{\mathrm{ds}}^{\mathrm{di}(I)} G].$$

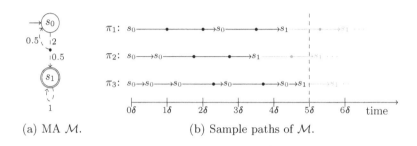

(a) MA $\mathcal{M}$.   (b) Sample paths of $\mathcal{M}$.

Fig. 4. MA $\mathcal{M}$ and illustration of paths of $\mathcal{M}$ (cf. Example 9).

Let $\lambda = \max\{\mathrm{E}(s) \mid s \in \mathrm{MS}\}$ be the maximum exit rate of $\mathcal{M}$. For $a \neq 0$ define

$$\varepsilon^{\downarrow}([a, b]) = \varepsilon^{\downarrow}([a, \infty)) = 1 - (1 + \lambda\delta)^{\mathrm{di}_a} \cdot e^{-\lambda a}, \quad \varepsilon^{\downarrow}([0, b)) = \varepsilon^{\downarrow}([0, \infty]) = 0,$$

$$\varepsilon^{\uparrow}([a, b]) = \underbrace{1 - (1 + \lambda\delta)^{\mathrm{di}_b} \cdot e^{-\lambda b}}_{=\varepsilon^{\uparrow}([0, b])} + \underbrace{1 - e^{-\lambda\delta}}_{=\varepsilon^{\uparrow}([a, \infty))}, \quad \text{and} \quad \varepsilon^{\uparrow}([0, \infty)) = 0.$$

$\varepsilon^{\downarrow}(I)$ and $\varepsilon^{\uparrow}(I)$ approach 0 for small digitization constants $\delta \in \mathbb{R}_{>0}$.

Proposition 5. *For MA $\mathcal{M}$, scheduler $\sigma \in \mathrm{GM}$, goal states $G \subseteq S$, digitization constant $\delta \in \mathbb{R}_{>0}$ and time interval I*

$$\mathrm{Pr}_{\sigma}^{\mathcal{M}}(\Diamond^I G) \in \mathrm{Pr}_{\sigma}^{\mathcal{M}}([\Diamond_{\mathrm{ds}}^I G]) + \left[-\varepsilon^{\downarrow}(I), \, \varepsilon^{\uparrow}(I)\right]$$

Proof (Sketch). The sets $\Diamond^I G$ and $[\Diamond_{\mathrm{ds}}^{\mathrm{di}(I)} G]$ are illustrated in Fig. 5. We have

$$\mathrm{Pr}_{\sigma}(\Diamond^I G) = \mathrm{Pr}_{\sigma}([\Diamond_{\mathrm{ds}}^{\mathrm{di}(I)} G]) + \mathrm{Pr}_{\sigma}(\Diamond^I G \setminus [\Diamond_{\mathrm{ds}}^{\mathrm{di}(I)} G]) - \mathrm{Pr}_{\sigma}([\Diamond_{\mathrm{ds}}^{\mathrm{di}(I)} G] \setminus \Diamond^I G).$$

One then shows

$$\mathrm{Pr}_{\sigma}^{\mathcal{M}}(\Diamond^I G \setminus [\Diamond_{\mathrm{ds}}^{\mathrm{di}(I)} G]) \leq \varepsilon^{\uparrow}(I) \quad \text{and} \quad \mathrm{Pr}_{\sigma}^{\mathcal{M}}([\Diamond_{\mathrm{ds}}^{\mathrm{di}(I)} G] \setminus \Diamond^I G) \leq \varepsilon^{\downarrow}(I).$$

Fig. 5. Illustration of the sets $\lozenge^I G$ and $[\lozenge_{\mathrm{ds}}^{\mathrm{di}(I)}G]$.

To this end, show for any $k \in \mathbb{N}$ that $1 - (1 + \lambda\delta)^k \cdot e^{-\lambda\delta k}$ is an upper bound for the probability of paths that induce more then k digitization steps within the first $k\delta$ time units. Then, this probability can be related to the probability of paths in $\lozenge^I G \setminus [\lozenge_{\mathrm{ds}}^{\mathrm{di}(I)}G]$ and $[\lozenge_{\mathrm{ds}}^{\mathrm{di}(I)}G] \setminus \lozenge^I G$, respectively.

From Propositions 4 and 5, we immediately have Corollary 1, which ensures that the value $\mathrm{Pr}_\sigma^{\mathcal{M}}(\lozenge^I G)$ can be approximated with arbitrary precision by computing $\mathrm{Pr}_{\mathrm{di}(\sigma)}^{\mathcal{M}_\delta}(\lozenge_{\mathrm{ds}}^{\mathrm{di}(I)}G)$ for a sufficiently small δ.

Corollary 1. *For MA $\mathcal{M}$, scheduler $\sigma \in \mathrm{GM}$, goal states $G \subseteq S$, digitization constant $\delta \in \mathbb{R}_{>0}$ and time interval I*

$$\mathrm{Pr}_\sigma^{\mathcal{M}}(\lozenge^I G) \in \mathrm{Pr}_{\mathrm{di}(\sigma)}^{\mathcal{M}_\delta}(\lozenge_{\mathrm{ds}}^{\mathrm{di}(I)}G) + \left[-\varepsilon^\downarrow(I),\, \varepsilon^\uparrow(I)\right]$$

This generalizes existing results [8,9] that only consider schedulers which maximize (or minimize) the corresponding probabilities. More details are given in [14].

Next, we lift Corollary 1 to multiple objectives $\mathbb{O} = (\mathbb{O}_1, \ldots, \mathbb{O}_d)$. We define the satisfaction of a *timed* reachability objective $\mathbb{P}(\lozenge^I G)$ for the digitization $\mathcal{M}_\delta$ as $\mathcal{M}_\delta, \sigma \models \mathbb{P}(\lozenge^I G) \rhd_i p_i$ iff $\mathrm{Pr}_\sigma^{\mathcal{M}_\delta}(\lozenge_{\mathrm{ds}}^{\mathrm{di}(I)}G) \rhd_i p_i$. This allows us to consider notations like $achieve^{\mathcal{M}_\delta}(\mathbb{O} \rhd \mathbf{p})$, where $\mathbb{O}$ contains one or more timed reachability objectives. For a point $\mathbf{p} = (p_1, \ldots, p_d) \in \mathbb{R}^d$ we consider the hyperrectangle

$$\varepsilon(\mathbb{O}, \mathbf{p}) = \bigtimes_{i=1}^{d} \left[p_i - \varepsilon_i^\downarrow,\, p_i + \varepsilon_i^\uparrow\right] \subseteq \mathbb{R}^d, \text{ where } \varepsilon_i^\uparrow = \begin{cases} \varepsilon^\uparrow(I) & \text{if } \mathbb{O}_i = \mathbb{P}(\lozenge^I G) \\ 0 & \text{if } \mathbb{O}_i = \mathbb{E}(\#j, G) \end{cases}$$

and $\varepsilon_i^\downarrow$ is defined similarly. The next example shows how the set of achievable points of $\mathcal{M}$ can be approximated using achievable points of $\mathcal{M}_\delta$.

Example 10. Let $\mathbb{O} = (\mathbb{P}(\lozenge^{I_1} G_1), \mathbb{P}(\lozenge^{I_2} G_2))$ be two timed reachability objectives for an MA $\mathcal{M}$ with digitization $\mathcal{M}_\delta$ such that $\varepsilon_1^\downarrow = 0.13$, $\varepsilon_1^\uparrow = 0.22$, $\varepsilon_2^\downarrow = 0.07$, and $\varepsilon_2^\uparrow = 0.15$. The blue rectangle in Fig. 6(a) illustrates the set $\varepsilon(\mathbb{O}, \mathbf{p})$ for the point $\mathbf{p} = (0.4, 0.3)$. Assume $achieve^{\mathcal{M}_\delta}(\mathbb{O} \rhd \mathbf{p})$ holds for threshold relations $\rhd = \{\geq, \geq\}$, i.e., $\mathbf{p}$ is achievable for the digitization $\mathcal{M}_\delta$. From Corollary 1, we infer that $\varepsilon(\mathbb{O}, \mathbf{p})$ contains at least one point $\mathbf{p}'$ that is achievable for $\mathcal{M}$. Hence, the bottom left corner point of the rectangle is achievable for $\mathcal{M}$. This holds for any rectangle $\varepsilon(\mathbb{O}, \mathbf{q})$ with $\mathbf{q} \in A$, where A is the set of achievable points of $\mathcal{M}_\delta$ denoted by the gray area[1] in Fig. 6(b). It follows that any point in A^- (depicted

---

[1] In the figure, A^- partly overlaps A, i.e., the green area also belongs to A.

by the green area) is achievable for $\mathcal{M}$. On the other hand, an achievable point of $\mathcal{M}$ has to be contained in a set $\varepsilon(\mathbb{O}, \mathbf{q})$ for at least one $\mathbf{q} \in A$. The red area depicts the points $\mathbb{R}^d \setminus A^+$ for which this is not the case, i.e., points that are not achievable for $\mathcal{M}$. The digitization constant δ controls the accuracy of the resulting approximation. Figure 6(c) depicts a possible result when a smaller digitization constant $\tilde{\delta} < \delta$ is considered.

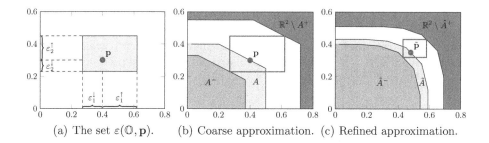

(a) The set $\varepsilon(\mathbb{O}, \mathbf{p})$.   (b) Coarse approximation.   (c) Refined approximation.

Fig. 6. Approximation of achievable points. (Color figure online)

The observations from the example above are formalized in the following theorem. The theorem also covers unbounded reachability objectives by considering the time interval $I = [0, \infty)$. For expected reward objectives of the form $\mathbb{E}(\#j, G)$ it can be shown that $\mathrm{ER}_{\sigma}^{\mathcal{M}}(\rho_j, G) = \mathrm{ER}_{\mathrm{di}(\sigma)}^{\mathcal{M}_\delta}(\rho_j^\delta, G)$. This claim is similar to Proposition 3 and can be shown analogously. This enables multi-objective model checking of MAs with timed reachability objectives.

Theorem 5. *Let $\mathcal{M}$ be an MA with digitization $\mathcal{M}_\delta$. Furthermore, let $\mathbb{O}$ be (un)timed reachability or expected reward objectives with threshold relations $\triangleright$ and $|\mathbb{O}| = d$. It holds that $A^- \subseteq \{\mathbf{p} \in \mathbb{R}^d \mid achieve^{\mathcal{M}}(\mathbb{O} \triangleright \mathbf{p})\} \subseteq A^+$ with:*

$$A^- = \{\mathbf{p}' \in \mathbb{R}^d \mid \forall \mathbf{p} \in \mathbb{R}^d \colon \mathbf{p}' \in \varepsilon(\mathbb{O}, \mathbf{p}) \text{ implies } achieve^{\mathcal{M}_\delta}(\mathbb{O} \triangleright \mathbf{p})\} \text{ and}$$
$$A^+ = \{\mathbf{p}' \in \mathbb{R}^d \mid \exists \mathbf{p} \in \mathbb{R}^d \colon \mathbf{p}' \in \varepsilon(\mathbb{O}, \mathbf{p}) \text{ and } achieve^{\mathcal{M}_\delta}(\mathbb{O} \triangleright \mathbf{p})\}.$$

5   Experimental Evaluation

Implementation. We implemented multi-objective model checking of MAs into Storm [32]. The input model is given in the PRISM language[2] and translated into a sparse representation. For MA $\mathcal{M}$, the implementation performs a multi-objective analysis on the underlying MDP $\mathcal{M}_{\mathcal{D}}$ or a digitization $\mathcal{M}_\delta$ and infers (an approximation of) the achievable points of $\mathcal{M}$ by exploiting the results from Sect. 4. For computing the achievable points of $\mathcal{M}_{\mathcal{D}}$ and $\mathcal{M}_\delta$, we apply the approach of [16]. It repeatedly checks weighted combinations of the objectives

---

[2] We slightly extend the PRISM language in order to describe MAs.

(by means of *value iteration* [30] – a standard technique in single-objective MDP model checking) to refine an approximation of the set of achievable points. This procedure is extended as follows. Full details can be found in [33].

- We support ds-bounded reachability objectives by combining the approach of [16] (which supports step-bounded reachability on MDPs) with techniques from single-objective MA analysis [8]. Roughly, we reduce ds-bounded reachability to untimed reachability by storing the digitized time-epoch (i.e., the current number of digitization steps) into the state space. A blow-up of the resulting model is avoided by considering each time-epoch separately.
- In contrast to [16], we allow a simultaneous analysis of minimizing and maximizing expected reward objectives. This is achieved by performing additional preprocessing steps that comprise an analysis of end components.

The source code including all material to reproduce the experiments is available at http://www.stormchecker.org/benchmarks.html.

Setup. Our implementation uses a single core (2 GHz) of a 48-core HP BL685C G7 limited to 20 GB RAM. The timeout (TO) is two hours. For a model, a set of objectives, and a precision $\eta \in \mathbb{R}_{>0}$, we measure the time to compute an η-approximation[3] of the set of achievable points. This set-up coincides with Pareto queries as discussed in [16]. The digitization constant δ is chosen heuristically such that recalculations with smaller constants $\tilde{\delta} < \delta$ are avoided. We set the precision for value-iteration to $\varepsilon = 10^{-6}$. We use classical value iteration; the use of improved algorithms [34] is left for future work.

Results for MAs. We consider four case studies: (i) a *job scheduler* [13], see Sect. 1; (ii) a *polling system* [35,36] containing a server processing jobs that arrive at two stations; (iii) a *video streaming client* buffering received packages and deciding when to start playback; and (iv) a randomized *mutual exclusion algorithm* [36], a variant of [37] with a process-dependent random delay in the critical section. Details on the benchmarks and the objectives are given in [14].

Table 1 lists results. For each instance we give the defining constants, the number of states of the MA and the used η-approximation. A multi-objective query is given by the triple (l, m, n) indicating l untimed, m expected reward, and n timed objectives. For each MA and query we depict the total run-time of our implementation (time) and the number of vertices of the obtained under-approximation (*pts*).

Queries analyzed on the underlying MDP are solved efficiently on large models with up to millions of states. For timed objectives the run-times increase drastically due to the costly analysis of digitized reachability objectives on the digitization, cf. [9]. Queries with up to four objectives can be dealt with within the time limit. Furthermore, for an approximation one order of magnitude better, the number of vertices of the result increases approximately by a factor three.

---

[3] An η-approximation of $A \subseteq \mathbb{R}^d$ is given by $A^-, A^+ \subseteq \mathbb{R}^d$ with $A^- \subseteq A \subseteq A^+$ and for all $\mathbf{p} \in A^+$ exists a $\mathbf{q} \in A^-$ such that the distance between $\mathbf{p}$ and $\mathbf{q}$ is at most η.

Table 1. Experimental results for multi-objective MAs.

| | benchmark | | $(\lozenge, \mathrm{ER}, \lozenge^I)$ | | $(\lozenge, \mathrm{ER}, \lozenge^I)$ | | $(\lozenge, \mathrm{ER}, \lozenge^I)$ | | $(\lozenge, \mathrm{ER}, \lozenge^I)$ | |
N(-K)	#states	$\log_{10}(\eta)$	pts	time	pts	time	pts	time	pts	time
job scheduling			$(0, 3, 0)$		$(0, 1, 1)$		$(1, 3, 0)$		$(1, 1, 2)$	
10-2	12 554	-2	9	1.8	9	41	15	435	16	2 322
		-3	44	128	21	834	TO		TO	
12-3	116 814	-2	11	42	9	798	21	2 026	TO	
		-3	53	323	TO		TO		TO	
17-2	$4.6 \cdot 10^6$	-2	14	1 040	TO		22	4 936	TO	
		-3	58	2 692	TO		TO		TO	
polling			$(0, 2, 0)$		$(0, 4, 0)$		$(0, 0, 2)$		$(0, 2, 2)$	
3-2	1 020	-2	4	0.3	5	0.6	3	130	12	669
		-3	4	0.3	5	0.8	7	3 030	TO	
3-3	9 858	-2	5	1.3	8	23	6	2 530	TO	
		-3	6	2.0	19	3 199	TO		TO	
4-4	827 735	-2	10	963	20	4 349	TO		TO	
		-3	11	1 509	TO		TO		TO	
stream			$(0, 2, 0)$		$(0, 1, 1)$		$(0, 0, 2)$		$(0, 2, 1)$	
30	1 426	-2	20	0.9	16	90	16	55	26	268
		-3	51	8.8	46	2 686	38	1 341	TO	
250	94 376	-2	31	50	15	5 830	16	4 050	TO	
		-3	90	184	TO		TO		TO	
1000	$1.5 \cdot 10^6$	-2	41	3 765	TO		TO		TO	
		-3	TO		TO		TO		TO	
mutex			$(0, 0, 3)$		$(0, 0, 3)$					
2	13 476	-2	16	351	13	1 166				
		-3	13	2 739	TO					
3	38 453	-2	15	2 333	TO					

In addition, a lower digitization constant has then to be considered which often leads to timeouts in experiments with timed objectives.

Comparison with PRISM [15] *and* IMCA [9]. We compared the performance of our implementation with both PRISM and IMCA. Verification times are summarized in Fig. 7: On points above the diagonal, our implementation is faster. For the comparison with PRISM (no MAs), we considered the multi-objective MDP benchmarks from [16,19]. Both implementations are based on [16]. For the comparison with IMCA (no multi-objective queries) we used the benchmarks from Table 1, with just a single objective. We observe that our implementation is competitive. Details are given in [14].

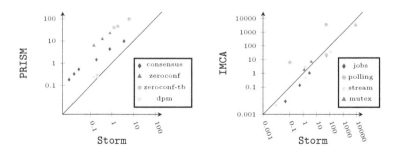

Fig. 7. Verification times (in seconds) of our implementation and other tools.

6   Conclusion

We considered multi-objective verification of Markov automata, including in particular timed reachability objectives. The next step is to apply our algorithms to the manifold applications of MA, such as generalized stochastic Petri nets to enrich the analysis possibilities of such nets.

Acknowledgement. This work was supported by the CDZ project CAP (GZ 1023).

References

1. Eisentraut, C., Hermanns, H., Zhang, L.: On probabilistic automata in continuous time. In: Proceedings of LICS, IEEE CS, pp. 342–351 (2010)
2. Deng, Y., Hennessy, M.: On the semantics of Markov automata. Inf. Comput. **222**, 139–168 (2013)
3. Boudali, H., Crouzen, P., Stoelinga, M.: A rigorous, compositional, and extensible framework for dynamic fault tree analysis. IEEE Trans. Dependable Secur. Comput. **7**(2), 128–143 (2010)
4. Coste, N., Hermanns, H., Lantreibecq, E., Serwe, W.: Towards performance prediction of compositional models in industrial GALS designs. In: Bouajjani, A., Maler, O. (eds.) CAV 2009. LNCS, vol. 5643, pp. 204–218. Springer, Heidelberg (2009). doi:10.1007/978-3-642-02658-4_18
5. Katoen, J.P., Wu, H.: Probabilistic model checking for uncertain scenario-aware data flow. ACM Trans. Embed. Comput. Sys. **22**(1), 15:1–15:27 (2016)
6. Bozzano, M., Cimatti, A., Katoen, J.P., Nguyen, V.Y., Noll, T., Roveri, M.: Safety, dependability and performance analysis of extended AADL models. Comput. J. **54**(5), 754–775 (2011)
7. Eisentraut, C., Hermanns, H., Katoen, J.-P., Zhang, L.: A semantics for every GSPN. In: Colom, J.-M., Desel, J. (eds.) PETRI NETS 2013. LNCS, vol. 7927, pp. 90–109. Springer, Heidelberg (2013). doi:10.1007/978-3-642-38697-8_6
8. Hatefi, H., Hermanns, H.: Model checking algorithms for Markov automata. ECE-ASST **53** (2012)
9. Guck, D., Hatefi, H., Hermanns, H., Katoen, J.P., Timmer, M.: Analysis of timed and long-run objectives for Markov automata. LMCS **10**(3) (2014)
10. Guck, D., Timmer, M., Hatefi, H., Ruijters, E., Stoelinga, M.: Modelling and analysis of Markov reward automata. In: Cassez, F., Raskin, J.-F. (eds.) ATVA 2014. LNCS, vol. 8837, pp. 168–184. Springer, Cham (2014). doi:10.1007/978-3-319-11936-6_13
11. Hatefi, H., Braitling, B., Wimmer, R., Fioriti, L.M.F., Hermanns, H., Becker, B.: Cost vs. time in stochastic games and Markov automata. In: Li, X., Liu, Z., Yi, W. (eds.) SETTA 2015. LNCS, vol. 9409, pp. 19–34. Springer, Cham (2015). doi:10.1007/978-3-319-25942-0_2
12. Butkova, Y., Wimmer, R., Hermanns, H.: Long-run rewards for Markov automata. In: Legay, A., Margaria, T. (eds.) TACAS 2017. LNCS, vol. 10206, pp. 188–203. Springer, Heidelberg (2017). doi:10.1007/978-3-662-54580-5_11
13. Bruno, J.L., Downey, P.J., Frederickson, G.N.: Sequencing tasks with exponential service times to minimize the expected flow time or makespan. J. ACM **28**(1), 100–113 (1981)

14. Quatmann, T., Junges, S., Katoen, J.P.: Markov automata with multiple objectives (2017). CoRR abs/1704.06648
15. Kwiatkowska, M., Norman, G., Parker, D.: PRISM 4.0: verification of probabilistic real-time systems. In: Gopalakrishnan, G., Qadeer, S. (eds.) CAV 2011. LNCS, vol. 6806, pp. 585–591. Springer, Heidelberg (2011). doi:10.1007/978-3-642-22110-1_47
16. Forejt, V., Kwiatkowska, M., Parker, D.: Pareto curves for probabilistic model checking. In: Chakraborty, S., Mukund, M. (eds.) ATVA 2012. LNCS, vol. 7561, pp. 317–332. Springer, Heidelberg (2012). doi:10.1007/978-3-642-33386-6_25
17. Roijers, D.M., Vamplew, P., Whiteson, S., Dazeley, R.: A survey of multi-objective sequential decision-making. J. Artif. Intell. Res. **48**, 67–113 (2013)
18. Etessami, K., Kwiatkowska, M., Vardi, M.Y., Yannakakis, M.: Multi-objective model checking of Markov decision processes. In: Grumberg, O., Huth, M. (eds.) TACAS 2007. LNCS, vol. 4424, pp. 50–65. Springer, Heidelberg (2007). doi:10.1007/978-3-540-71209-1_6
19. Forejt, V., Kwiatkowska, M., Norman, G., Parker, D., Qu, H.: Quantitative multi-objective verification for probabilistic systems. In: Abdulla, P.A., Leino, K.R.M. (eds.) TACAS 2011. LNCS, vol. 6605, pp. 112–127. Springer, Heidelberg (2011). doi:10.1007/978-3-642-19835-9_11
20. Bruyère, V., Filiot, E., Randour, M., Raskin, J.F.: Meet your expectations with guarantees: beyond worst-case synthesis in quantitative games. In: Proceeding of STACS. LIPIcs, vol. 25, pp. 199–213. Schloss Dagstuhl - Leibniz-Zentrum fuer Informatik (2014)
21. Baier, C., Dubslaff, C., Klüppelholz, S.: Trade-off analysis meets probabilistic model checking. In: CSL-LICS, pp. 1:1–1:10. ACM (2014)
22. Brázdil, T., Chatterjee, K., Forejt, V., Kucera, A.: Trading performance for stability in Markov decision processes. J. Comput. Syst. Sci. **84**, 144–170 (2017)
23. Brázdil, T., Brozek, V., Chatterjee, K., Forejt, V., Kucera, A.: Markov decision processes with multiple long-run average objectives. LMCS **10**(1) (2014)
24. Basset, N., Kwiatkowska, M., Topcu, U., Wiltsche, C.: Strategy synthesis for stochastic games with multiple long-run objectives. In: Baier, C., Tinelli, C. (eds.) TACAS 2015. LNCS, vol. 9035, pp. 256–271. Springer, Heidelberg (2015). doi:10.1007/978-3-662-46681-0_22
25. Teichteil-Königsbuch, F.: Path-constrained Markov decision processes: bridging the gap between probabilistic model-checking and decision-theoretic planning. In: Proceedings of ECAI. Frontiers in AI and Applications, vol. 242, pp. 744–749. IOS Press (2012)
26. Randour, M., Raskin, J.-F., Sankur, O.: Variations on the stochastic shortest path problem. In: D'Souza, D., Lal, A., Larsen, K.G. (eds.) VMCAI 2015. LNCS, vol. 8931, pp. 1–18. Springer, Heidelberg (2015). doi:10.1007/978-3-662-46081-8_1
27. Junges, S., Jansen, N., Dehnert, C., Topcu, U., Katoen, J.-P.: Safety-constrained reinforcement learning for MDPs. In: Chechik, M., Raskin, J.-F. (eds.) TACAS 2016. LNCS, vol. 9636, pp. 130–146. Springer, Heidelberg (2016). doi:10.1007/978-3-662-49674-9_8
28. David, A., Jensen, P.G., Larsen, K.G., Legay, A., Lime, D., Sørensen, M.G., Taankvist, J.H.: On time with minimal expected cost!. In: Cassez, F., Raskin, J.-F. (eds.) ATVA 2014. LNCS, vol. 8837, pp. 129–145. Springer, Cham (2014). doi:10.1007/978-3-319-11936-6_10
29. Chen, T., Forejt, V., Kwiatkowska, M., Simaitis, A., Wiltsche, C.: On stochastic games with multiple objectives. In: Chatterjee, K., Sgall, J. (eds.) MFCS 2013. LNCS, vol. 8087, pp. 266–277. Springer, Heidelberg (2013). doi:10.1007/978-3-642-40313-2_25

30. Puterman, M.L.: Markov Decision Processes: Discrete Stochastic Dynamic Programming. Wiley, New York (1994)
31. Neuhäußer, M.R., Stoelinga, M., Katoen, J.-P.: Delayed nondeterminism in continuous-time Markov decision processes. In: de Alfaro, L. (ed.) FoSSaCS 2009. LNCS, vol. 5504, pp. 364–379. Springer, Heidelberg (2009). doi:10.1007/978-3-642-00596-1_26
32. Dehnert, C., Junges, S., Katoen, J.P., Volk, M.: A storm is coming: a modern probabilistic model checker. In: Majumdar, R., Kučnak, V. (eds.) CAV 2017, Part I. LNCS, vol. 10426, pp. 592–600. Springer, Cham (2017)
33. Quatmann, T.: Multi-objective model checking of Markov automata. Master's thesis, RWTH Aachen University (2016)
34. Haddad, S., Monmege, B.: Reachability in MDPs: refining convergence of value iteration. In: Ouaknine, J., Potapov, I., Worrell, J. (eds.) RP 2014. LNCS, vol. 8762, pp. 125–137. Springer, Cham (2014). doi:10.1007/978-3-319-11439-2_10
35. Srinivasan, M.M.: Nondeterministic polling systems. Manag. Sci. **37**(6), 667–681 (1991)
36. Timmer, M., Katoen, J.-P., Pol, J., Stoelinga, M.I.A.: Efficient modelling and generation of Markov automata. In: Koutny, M., Ulidowski, I. (eds.) CONCUR 2012. LNCS, vol. 7454, pp. 364–379. Springer, Heidelberg (2012). doi:10.1007/978-3-642-32940-1_26
37. Pnueli, A., Zuck, L.: Verification of multiprocess probabilistic protocols. Distrib. Comput. **1**(1), 53–72 (1986)

Ensuring the Reliability of Your Model Checker: Interval Iteration for Markov Decision Processes

Christel Baier[1]([✉]), Joachim Klein[1]([✉]),
Linda Leuschner[1]([✉]), David Parker[2]([✉]),
and Sascha Wunderlich[1]([✉])

[1] Technische Universität Dresden, 01062 Dresden, Germany
{christel.baier,joachim.klein,linda.leuschner,sascha.wunderlich}@tu-dresden.de
[2] School of Computer Science, University of Birmingham, Birmingham, UK
d.a.parker@cs.bham.ac.uk

Abstract. Probabilistic model checking provides formal guarantees on quantitative properties such as reliability, performance or risk, so the accuracy of the numerical results that it returns is critical. However, recent results have shown that implementations of value iteration, a widely used iterative numerical method for computing reachability probabilities, can return results that are incorrect by several orders of magnitude. To remedy this, interval iteration, which instead converges simultaneously from both above and below, has been proposed. In this paper, we present interval iteration techniques for computing expected accumulated weights (or costs), a considerably broader class of properties. This relies on an efficient, mainly graph-based method to determine lower and upper bounds for extremal expected accumulated weights. To offset the additional effort of dual convergence, we also propose topological interval iteration, which increases efficiency using a model decomposition into strongly connected components. Finally, we present a detailed experimental evaluation, which highlights inaccuracies in standard benchmarks, rather than just artificial examples, and illustrates the feasibility of our techniques.

1 Introduction

Over the past twenty years, many algorithms, logics and tools have been developed for the formal analysis of probabilistic systems. They combine techniques developed by the model-checking community with methods for the analysis of stochastic models (see, e.g., [1,8,20]). A widely used model is Markov decision processes (MDPs), which represent probabilistic systems with nondeterminism, needed to model, for example, concurrency, adversarial behaviour or control.

The authors at Technische Universität Dresden are supported by the DFG through the Collaborative Research Center SFB 912 – HAEC, the Excellence Initiative by the German Federal and State Governments (cluster of excellence cfaed), the Research Training Groups QuantLA (GRK 1763) and RoSI (GRK 1907) and the DFG-project BA-1679/11-1. David Parker is part-funded by the PRINCESS project, under the DARPA BRASS programme.

© Springer International Publishing AG 2017
R. Majumdar and V. Kunčak (Eds.): CAV 2017, Part I, LNCS 10426, pp. 160–180, 2017.
DOI: 10.1007/978-3-319-63387-9_8

Various model checking problems on MDPs are reducible to the task of computing extremal (maximal or minimal) probabilities of reaching a goal state, ranging over all schedulers [2,4,12,15]. Schedulers, also often called policies, adversaries or strategies, represent the possible ways of resolving nondeterminism in an MDP. So extremal probabilities correspond to a worst-case or best-case analysis, for example, the maximal or minimal probability of a system failure.

Weighted MDPs, i.e., MDPs where rational weights are attached to the state-action pairs, provide a versatile modelling formalism that allows reasoning about, e.g., extremal values for the expected accumulation of weights until reaching a goal state. These might represent worst-case or best-case scenarios for expected costs (e.g., execution time, energy usage) or utility values. To compute schedulers that maximize or minimize the expected accumulated weight, one can rely on techniques that are known for *stochastic shortest path problems* [7,16].

The computation of extremal values for reachability probabilities or expected accumulated weights until reaching a goal can be done using linear programming techniques or iterative computation schemes. In the context of probabilistic model checking, the latter are more common since they typically scale to the analysis of larger systems. Common techniques for this are value iteration [6], policy iteration [21] or mixtures thereof [29]. We focus here on *value iteration* which relies on a fixed-point characterization $e^* = f(e^*)$ of the extremal probability or expectation vector e^* based on the Bellman equation [6] and computes an approximation thereof by successive application of the fixed-point operator f.

In practice, a stopping criterion is required to determine when this iterative approximation process can be safely terminated. For *discounted* variants of expected accumulated weights, convergence is guaranteed and the discount factor can be used to derive a safe stopping criterion ensuring that the computed vector $f^n(z)$ is indeed an ε-approximation of the desired discounted expectation vector e^* for a given tolerance $\varepsilon > 0$. (Here, z stands for the starting vector.) For the purposes of model checking, however, non-discounted variants are usually preferred, in order to compute meaningful values for properties such as execution time or energy usage, or indeed reachability probabilities, where discounting makes little sense. For the non-discounted case, with some appropriate preprocessing and model assumptions, convergence of value iteration can still be guaranteed as the fixed-point operator f can shown to be contracting [7,16], but sound stopping criteria are more difficult.

To check termination of value iteration, most practical implementations simply terminate when the last two vectors $f^{n-1}(z)$ and $f^n(z)$ differ by at most ε with respect to the supremum norm. This prevalent stopping criterion is currently realized in widely used probabilistic model checkers such as PRISM [25], MRMC [23] and IscasMC [19], as well as in other implementations such as the MDP Toolbox [10]. However, recent results from Haddad and Monmege [18] have shown that the results obtained from value iteration for reachability probabilities with this naive stopping criterion can be extremely inaccurate. On our tests using a simple example from [18], all three of the above model checkers fail. On a small MDP with 41 states (see [3] for details), MRMC returns 0 and PRISM returns ~ 0.1943 where the correct result should be 0.5.

So, [18] proposes a refinement of value iteration for computing maximal or minimal reachability probabilities, called *interval iteration*. After some graph-based preprocessing to ensure convergence, it relies on the monotonicity of the fixed-point operator f and carries out the iterative application of f to two starting vectors x and y such that $f^n(x) \leqslant e^* \leqslant f^n(y)$ for all n. Here, x is a lower bound for the required probability vector e^* and y is an upper bound. Thus, if all entries of the vector $f^n(y) - f^n(x)$ are smaller than ε, then both $f^n(x)$ and $f^n(y)$ are sound ε-approximations of z. [18] does not report on experimental studies or weights. So, it leaves open whether interval iteration is feasible in practice and yields a reasonable way to ensure the reliability of the model-checking results.

Contribution. Inspired by the work of Haddad and Monmege [18], we present an interval-iteration approach for computing maximal expected accumulated (non-discounted) weights in finite-state MDPs with a distinguished goal state *final*.[1] The weights can be negative or positive numbers. To ensure the existence of a deterministic memoryless scheduler maximizing the expected accumulated weights until reaching *final*, we assume that the MDP is contracting in the sense that the goal state will almost surely be reached, no matter which scheduler or which starting state is selected.[2] While the null vector $x = 0$ and the vector $y = 1$ where all components have value 1 obviously yield correct lower resp. upper bounds for any probability vector, the main problem for adapting the interval-iteration approach to maximal or minimal expected accumulated weights is to provide efficient algorithms for the computation of lower and upper bounds. We provide here two variants to compute lower and upper bounds that are based on bounds for the recurrence times of states under memoryless schedulers.

After presenting the foundations of the interval-iteration approach for expected accumulated weights (Sect. 3), we propose *topological* interval iteration, which embeds the basic algorithm into a stratified approach that speeds up the computation time by treating the strongly connected components separately (Sect. 4). Sections 5 and 6 will report on experimental results carried out with an implementation of the interval-iteration approaches of [18] for reachability probabilities and our approach for maximal or minimal expectations applied to MDPs with non-negative weights. Proofs omitted in this paper, as well as further details on our experiments, can be found in the appendix of the extended version [3], which is available together with our implementation at http://wwwtcs.inf.tu-dresden.de/ALGI/PUB/CAV17/.

---

[1] Analogous statements are obtained for minimal expected total weights by multiplying all weights with -1, applying the techniques for maximal expected weights and finally multiplying the result with -1.

[2] Thanks to the transformations proposed in [16], this assumption is no restriction if the weights are non-negative and the objective is to maximize the expected accumulated weight. For reasoning about minimal expected accumulated weights in MDPs with non-negative weights as well as for the general case, weaker assumptions are also sufficient (see [7,16]). Interval iteration under such relaxed assumptions will be addressed in our future work.

Related Work. Bell and Haverkort [5] reported on serious problems with the precision of the implementations for computing steady-state probabilities in continuous-time Markov chains. Wimmer et al. [31] revealed several problems with the implementations of model checking algorithms for Markov chains and properties of probabilistic computation tree logic (PCTL). They identified several sources of imprecise results, including numerical problems with floating-point arithmetic and issues that are specific to symbolic BDD-based implementations, and presented ideas for how such problems can be avoided.

Although [31] also identifies the widely used termination criterion for iterative computation schemes as a potential source of inaccuracy, they do not provide a solution for it. To the best of our knowledge, the paper by Haddad and Monmege [18] is the first one which addresses the termination problem of iterative computation schemes for MDPs. However, [18] only considers extremal probabilities and does not report on experimental studies. Prior to this, Brázdil et al. [9] presented an extension of bounded real-time dynamic programming [27], which also yields interval bounds for extremal probabilities in MDPs. The techniques were extended to handle arbitrary MDPs and full LTL model checking, but again focused on probabilities, not weights. We are not aware of any efficiently realizable safe termination conditions of value iteration proposed for expected (non-discounted) accumulated weights. The technique proposed here follows the interval-iteration approach of [18]. While – after some appropriate preprocessing – [18] can deal with 0 and 1 as lower resp. upper bound for the desired minimal or maximal probabilities, efficient computation schemes for lower and upper bounds for minimal or maximal expected accumulated weights are not obvious.

In fact, such bounds can also be interesting for different purposes. In the context of planning, [27] presents an efficient algorithm to compute an upper bound for the minimal expected accumulated weight until reaching a goal, which they call *Dijkstra Sweep for Monotone Pessimistic Initialization* (DS-MPI). This approach (which we consider in the experiments in Sect. 6) is designed for MDPs where all weights are non-negative. As it relies on the idea to generate a memoryless scheduler and an upper bound for its expected accumulated weight, there is no straightforward adaption of the approach of [27] to compute an upper bound for the maximal expected accumulated weight.

Lastly, computation of exact extremal reachability probabilities in MDPs was also considered by Giro [17], where, by exploiting the special structure of the linear programs that need to be solved for reachability probabilities, the use of simplex or other generic exact linear program solvers is avoided.

2 Preliminaries

Throughout the paper, we assume some familiarity with basic concepts of Markov decision processes (MDPs), see, e.g., [22,30]. We briefly explain our notations.

A *plain MDP* is a tuple $\mathcal{M} = (S, Act, P)$ where S is a finite state space, Act a finite set of actions, and $P : S \times Act \times S \to \mathbb{Q} \cap [0,1]$ a function such that $\sum_{t\in S} P(s,\alpha,t) \in \{0,1\}$ for all state-action pairs $(s,\alpha) \in S \times Act$. If $s \in S$, $\alpha \in Act$ and $T \subseteq S$ then $P(s,\alpha,T) = \sum_{t\in T} P(s,\alpha,t)$. We write $Act(s)$ for the set of actions $\alpha \in Act$ such that $\sum_{t\in S} P(s,\alpha,t) = 1$. State s is called a *trap state* if $Act(s)$ is empty. A *path* in $\mathcal{M}$ is a sequence $\pi = s_0\,\alpha_0\,s_1\,\alpha_1\,s_2\,\alpha_2 \ldots$ that alternates between states and actions such that $\alpha_i \in Act(s_i)$ and $P(s_i,\alpha_i,s_{i+1}) > 0$ for all i and such that π is either finite and ends in a state or infinite. π is called *maximal* if π is either infinite or finite and π's last state is a trap state. A *(deterministic) scheduler* $\mathfrak{S}$ for $\mathcal{M}$, also called policy or adversary, is a function that assigns to each finite path π ending in a non-trap state s an action in $Act(s)$. $\mathfrak{S}$ is called *memoryless* if $\mathfrak{S}(\pi) = \mathfrak{S}(\pi')$ whenever π and π' end in the same state. We write $\mathrm{Pr}^{\mathfrak{S}}_{\mathcal{M},s}$, or simply $\mathrm{Pr}^{\mathfrak{S}}_s$, to denote the standard probability measure on maximal paths induced by $\mathfrak{S}$, starting from state s. The notations $\mathrm{Pr}^{\max}_s(\varphi)$ and $\mathrm{Pr}^{\min}_s(\varphi)$ will be used for the extremal probabilities for the event φ when ranging over all schedulers. We often will use the LTL-like temporal modalities $\Diamond$ (eventually), $\Box$ (always), $\bigcirc$ (next) and U (until) to specify measurable sets of maximal paths.

A *weighted MDP*, briefly called MDP, is a tuple $\mathcal{M} = (S, Act, P, final, wgt)$ where (S, Act, P) is a plain MDP as above, $final \in S$ a distinguished trap state and $wgt : S \times Act \to \mathbb{Q}$ is a weight function that might have positive and negative values. Throughout the paper, we suppose that $\mathcal{M}$ is *contracting* in the sense that $\mathrm{Pr}^{\mathfrak{S}}_s(\Diamond final) = 1$ for all states $s \in S$. Given a finite path $\pi = s_0\,\alpha_0\,s_1\,\alpha_1 \ldots \alpha_{n-1}\,s_n$, the accumulated weight of π is $wgt(\pi) = wgt(s_0,\alpha_0) + wgt(s_1,\alpha_1) + \ldots + wgt(s_{n-1},\alpha_{n-1})$. We write $\oplus final$ to denote the function that assigns to each finite path ending in $final$ its accumulated weight. Given a scheduler $\mathfrak{S}$ for $\mathcal{M}$, let $\mathbb{E}^{\mathfrak{S}}_s(\oplus final)$ denote the expectation of $\oplus final$ under $\mathfrak{S}$ for starting state s. We consider the value iteration for computing ε-approximations for $\mathbb{E}^{\max}_{\mathcal{M},s}(\oplus final)$, or briefly $\mathbb{E}^{\max}_s(\oplus final)$, which is defined as $\max_{\mathfrak{S}} \mathbb{E}^{\mathfrak{S}}_s(\oplus final)$ where $\mathfrak{S}$ ranges over all schedulers. As $\mathcal{M}$ is supposed to be contracting, $\mathbb{E}^{\mathfrak{S}}_s(\oplus final)$ is the expected total weight from s under $\mathfrak{S}$ and there is a deterministic memoryless scheduler $\mathfrak{S}$ with $\mathbb{E}^{\max}_s(\oplus final) = \mathbb{E}^{\mathfrak{S}}_s(\oplus final)$ [7,22].

3 Interval Iteration for Weighted MDPs

Throughout the paper, $\mathcal{M} = (S, Act, P, final, wgt)$ is a weighted MDP as in Sect. 2 satisfying $\mathrm{Pr}^{\mathfrak{S}}_s(\Diamond final) = 1$ for all states $s \in S$ and schedulers $\mathfrak{S}$, i.e., that the MDP is contracting. We start in Sect. 3.1 with a brief summary of known fixed-point characterizations of the vector with maximal expected accumulated weights that yield the foundations for the standard value iteration. Sections 3.2 and 3.3 then present the details of the interval iteration and efficient computation schemes for lower and upper bounds for the maximal expected accumulated weights.

3.1 Value Iteration in Weighted MDPs

In what follows, we briefly recall known (and some simple) facts about the foundations of the value iteration to compute maximal expected total weights in MDPs. Let $f : \mathbb{R}^{|S|} \to \mathbb{R}^{|S|}$ denote the following function. Given a vector $z = (z_s)_{s \in S}$ in $\mathbb{R}^{|S|}$ then $f(z) = (f_s(z))_{s \in S}$ where $f_{final}(z) = 0$ and

$$f_s(z) = \max \left\{ wgt(s, \alpha) + \sum_{t \in S} P(s, \alpha, t) \cdot z_t : \alpha \in Act(s) \right\}$$

for all states $s \in S \setminus \{final\}$. The functions $f^n : \mathbb{R}^{|S|} \to \mathbb{R}^{|S|}$ are defined inductively by $f^0 = \text{id}$, $f^1 = f$ and $f^{n+1} = f \circ f^n$ for $n \in \mathbb{N}$, $n \geqslant 1$. Let $e^* = (e_s^*)_{s \in S}$ denote the vector with the maximal expected total weights for all states, i.e., $e_s^* = \mathbb{E}_s^{\max}(\diamond final)$. For $z = (z_s)_{s \in S} \in \mathbb{R}^{|S|}$ and $z' = (z_s')_{s \in S} \in \mathbb{R}^{|S|}$ we then write $z \leqslant z'$ if $z_s \leqslant z_s'$ for all $s \in S$. Furthermore, $\| \cdot \|$ denotes the supremum norm for vectors in $\mathbb{R}^S$. That is, $\|z\| = \max_{s \in S} |z_s|$.

The series $(f^n(z))_{n \in \mathbb{N}}$ converges to its unique fixed point e^* monotonically increasing if $z \leqslant e^* \wedge z \leqslant f(z)$ and decreasing if $z \geqslant e^* \wedge z \geqslant f(z)$ (see [3]). This provides the basis for linear programming approaches to compute the exact values e_s^* and for the value iteration that successively generates the vectors $z, f(z), f^2(z) f^3(z), \ldots$ and finally returns one of the vectors $f^n(z)$ as an approximation of e^*. However, there are two problems:

(P1) How to find a starting vector z with $z \leqslant e^* \wedge z \leqslant f(z)$ or $z \geqslant e^* \wedge z \geqslant f(z)$?
(P2) How to check whether $\|f^n(z) - e^*\| < \varepsilon$, given a tolerance $\varepsilon > 0$, a starting vector z from (P1) and the first $n+1$ vectors $z, f(z), \ldots, f^n(z)$ of the value iteration?

Problem (P1). Problem (P1) is specific to the case of maximal or minimal expectations, as (after some preprocessing to ensure the uniqueness of the fixed point) the corresponding fixed-point operator f for reachability probabilities guarantees that $0 \leqslant z \leqslant 1$ implies $0 \leqslant f(z) \leqslant 1$. For certain models with syntactic restrictions, problem (P1) can be answered directly as the null vector $z = 0$ is known to satisfy the conditions $z \leqslant e^* \wedge z \leqslant f(z)$ or $z \geqslant e^* \wedge z \geqslant f(z)$ for monotonic convergence. Prominent examples are positive bounded MDPs where each state s has an action α with $wgt(s, \alpha) \geqslant 0$, or MDPs where all weights are non-positive. In both cases, monotonic convergence of $(f^n(0))_{n \in \mathbb{N}}$ can be guaranteed even for countable state spaces (see [30]). However, for MDPs with negative and positive weights, it might be hard to find starting vectors z that ensure monotone convergence, which requires to determine lower and upper bounds for the maximal expected accumulated weight. To the best of our knowledge, even for finite-state positive bounded MDPs, techniques to determine an upper bound have not been addressed in the literature. Besides the algorithm for lower bounds for MDPs with non-positive weights proposed in [27], we are not aware of any technique proposed in the literature to find an appropriate starting vector for the lower value iteration in weighted MDPs.

Example 3.1. To illustrate that there might be vectors z that do not lead to monotonic convergence, e.g., with $z_s < e_s^* < f_s(z)$ or $e_s^* < z_s < f_s(z)$, even when all weights are non-negative, consider the MDP $\mathcal{M}$ in Fig. 1 with three states s_1, s_2 and $s_3 = final$ and $P(s_1, \alpha, s_2) = P(s_1, \beta, s_3) = 1$, $P(s_2, \beta, s_1) =$

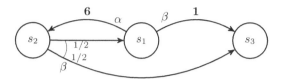

Fig. 1. Markov decision process of Example 3.1. Only non-zero probabilities and weights (in **bold**) are shown.

$P(s_2, \beta, s_3) = 1/2$, $wgt(s_1, \alpha) = 6$, $wgt(s_1, \beta) = 1$, while $P(\cdot) = 0$ and $wgt(\cdot) = 0$ in all remaining cases. Then, $e^* = (12, 6, 0)$. For the starting vector $z = (0, 9, 0)$ we have $f(z) = (15, 0, 0)$, in which case $z_s = 0 < e_s^* = 12 < f_s(z) = 15$ for $s = s_1$. Monotonic convergence can not even be guaranteed if the starting vector z satisfies $z \leqslant e^*$ or $z \geqslant e^*$ as, for instance, $z = (14, 10, 0) \geqslant (12, 6, 0) = e^*$ but $f(z) = (16, 7, 0)$, i.e., $e_s^* = 12 < z_s = 14 < f_s(z) = 16$ for $s = s_1$. ∎

Problem (P2). Many implementations of the value iteration terminate as soon as $\|f^n(z) - f^{n-1}(z)\| < \varepsilon$ for some user-defined tolerance $\varepsilon > 0$ and return the vector $f^n(z)$. The problem is that $f^n(z)$ need not be an ε-approximation of the vector e^*. This phenomenon has been first observed in [18] for value iteration to compute (maximal or minimal) reachability probabilities in Markov chains or MDPs. The following example is an adaption of an example provided in [18] for reachability probabilities to the case of expected total weights and illustrates the problem of premature termination potentially leading to serious imprecision.

Example 3.2. Let $p \in \mathbb{Q}$ with $0 < p < 1$ and let $\mathcal{C}[p]$ be the Markov chain in Fig. 2 with state space $S = \{s_0, s_1, \ldots, s_{n-1}, s_n\}$ where $s_n = \mathit{final}$, transition probabilities $P(s_i, s_{i+1}) = p$, $P(s_i, s_0) = 1 - p$ and weights $wgt(s_{n-1}) = p$ for $0 \leqslant i < n$ and $P(\cdot) = wgt(\cdot) = 0$ in all other cases.[3] Then, $\Pr_s(\Diamond \mathit{final}) = 1$ and expected total weight $e_s^* = 1$ for $s \neq \mathit{final}$. Now consider $p = 1/2$ and the tolerance $\varepsilon = 1/2^n$. The value iteration finds $0 < f_s^n(0) - f_s^{n-1}(0) = 1/2^{n+1} < \varepsilon$ and therefore returns the vector $f^n(0)$, even though the difference between $f^n(0)$ and the correct result e_s^* is significantly larger than ε, i.e., $e_s^* - f_s^n(0) = 1 - (1/2^{n+1} + 1/2^{n-i}) \geqslant 3/8 > \varepsilon$. (See [3].) ∎

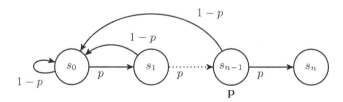

Fig. 2. Markov chain of Example 3.2. Only non-zero probabilities and weights (in **bold**) are shown.

---

[3] A Markov chain can be viewed as an MDP where Act is a singleton, say $Act = \{\tau\}$, in which case we write $P(s, t)$ rather than $P(s, \tau, t)$ and $wgt(s)$ rather than $wgt(s, \tau)$.

3.2   Lower and Upper Value Iteration

Following the ideas of [18], we present an approach with two value iterations that generate sequences of vectors in $\mathbb{Q}^{|S|}$: one that converges to the vector e^* from below (called *lower value iteration*) and one that converges to e^* from above (called *upper value iteration*). As soon as the vectors of the lower and the upper value iteration differ by components by at most ε then ε-approximations of the values e_s^* have been generated. In this way, we avoid problem (P2).

Both the lower and the upper value iteration rely on a preprocessing to determine starting vectors $x = (x_s)_{s \in S}$ and $y = (y_s)_{s \in S}$ with

$$x_{final} = y_{final} = 0 \quad \text{and} \quad x_s \leqslant e_s^* \leqslant y_s \text{ for all } s \in S \setminus \{final\} \qquad (*)$$

We then have $f^n(x) \leqslant e^* \leqslant f^n(y)$ for all $n \in \mathbb{N}$ and both sequences $(f^n(x))_{n \in \mathbb{N}}$ and $(f^n(y))_{n \in \mathbb{N}}$ converge to e^* (see [3]). Monotonicity does not hold in general as $f_s^n(x) < f_s^{n-1}(x) < e_s^*$ or $e_s^* < f_s^{n-1}(y) < f_s^n(y)$ is possible (see Example 3.1). However, with a slightly modified approach of the value iteration (see below) the assumption $x \leqslant f(x)$ or $y \leqslant f(y)$ is irrelevant. This simplifies problem (P1). The computation of starting vectors x and y satisfying $(*)$ will be addressed in Sect. 3.3.

Modified Value Iteration. We suggest a mild variant of the standard value iteration where monotonicity is ensured by construction. Suppose we are given vectors x and y satisfying $(*)$. We define inductively vectors $x^{(n)} = (x_s^n)_{s \in S}$ and $y^{(n)} = (y_s^n)_{s \in S}$ by $x^{(0)} = x$, $y^{(0)} = y$ and for all $n \in \mathbb{N}$ and $s \in S \setminus \{final\}$:

$$x_s^{(n+1)} = \max \left\{ x_s^{(n)}, f_s(x^{(n)}) \right\} \qquad y_s^{(n+1)} = \min \left\{ y_s^{(n)}, f_s(y^{(n)}) \right\}$$

and $x_{final}^{(n)} = y_{final}^{(n)} = 0$. Lemma 3.3 (see [3] for its proof) states the essential properties of the lower and upper value iteration.

Lemma 3.3. *Suppose* $(*)$ *holds. Then:*

(a) $x^{(n)} \leqslant e^* \leqslant y^{(n)}$ *for all* $n \in \mathbb{N}$

(b) $x^{(0)} \leqslant x^{(1)} \leqslant x^{(2)} \leqslant \ldots$ *and* $\lim\limits_{n \to \infty} x^{(n)} = e^*$

(c) $y^{(0)} \geqslant y^{(1)} \geqslant y^{(2)} \geqslant \ldots$ *and* $\lim\limits_{n \to \infty} y^{(n)} = e^*$

Thanks to monotonicity, we can use a Gauss-Seidel-like iteration variant with forward substitution that relies on an enumeration $s_1, s_2, \ldots, s_N$ of all states in S. The idea is to iterate values in sequence according to this enumeration. Then, in each step, the already updated values of previous states can be re-used. For this, we inductively define vectors $\tilde{x}^{(n)} = (\tilde{x}_s^n)_{s \in S}$ and $\tilde{y}^{(n)} = (\tilde{y}_s^n)_{s \in S}$ by $\tilde{x}^{(0)} = x$, $\tilde{y}^{(0)} = y$ and for all $n \in \mathbb{N}$ and $s \in S \setminus \{final\}$:

$$\tilde{x}_s^{(n+1)} = \max \left\{ \tilde{x}_s^{(n)}, f_s(\tilde{x}^{(n,i)}) \right\} \qquad \tilde{y}_s^{(n+1)} = \min \left\{ \tilde{y}_s^{(n)}, f_s(\tilde{y}^{(n,i)}) \right\}$$

and $\tilde{x}_{final}^{(n)} = \tilde{y}_{final}^{(n)} = 0$ where $\tilde{x}^{(n,i)} = \left(\tilde{x}_s^{(n,i)}\right)_{s \in S}$ with $\tilde{x}_{s_j}^{(n,i)}$ being $\tilde{x}_{s_j}^{(n+1)}$ for $j < i-1$ and $\tilde{x}_{s_j}^{(n)}$ otherwise. The definition of $\tilde{y}^{(n,i)}$ is analogous. Then, by induction and using the monotonicity of f we get the monotone convergence to e^* from below (resp. above) for the sequence $(x^{(n)})_{n \in \mathbb{N}}$ (resp. $(y^{(n)})_{n \in \mathbb{N}}$.

3.3 Computing Starting Vectors

The remaining problem is to find an efficient method for computing starting vectors x and y such that (*) holds. For this, we first use the observation that, for each memoryless deterministic scheduler $\mathfrak{S}$, the expected weight until reaching *final* can be derived by multiplying the weights by the expected number of visits to each of the states, as *final* is a trap state and is reached with probability 1:

$$\mathbb{E}_s^{\mathfrak{S}}(\Diamond final) = \sum_{t \in S} \zeta_s^{\mathfrak{S}}(t) \cdot wgt(t, \mathfrak{S}(t)) \qquad (**)$$

where $\zeta_s^{\mathfrak{S}}(t)$ denotes the expected number of times to visit t in the Markov chain induced by $\mathfrak{S}$ with starting state s and $wgt(t, \mathfrak{S}(t))$ is the weight for the action that is selected by $\mathfrak{S}$ in state t. Thus, if

$$\zeta_s^*(t) \quad \geqslant \quad \max_{\mathfrak{S}} \ \zeta_s^{\mathfrak{S}}(t) \qquad \text{for all } s, t \in S \setminus \{final\} \qquad (***)$$

where $\mathfrak{S}$ ranges over all memoryless deterministic schedulers then we may start the lower and upper value iteration with the following vectors $x = (x_s)_{s \in S}$ and $y = (y_s)_{s \in S}$. The components for the trap state are $x_{final} = y_{final} = 0$. For each state s, let R_s be the set of states reachable from s. We then define:

$$x_s = \sum_{t \in R_s} \zeta_s^*(t) \cdot wgt^{\min}(t) \qquad y_s = \sum_{t \in R_s} \zeta_s^*(t) \cdot wgt^{\max}(t)$$

Here, for $t \in S \setminus \{final\}$, $wgt^{\min}(t) = \min W(t)$, $wgt^{\max}(t) = \max W(t)$ where $W(t) = \{0\} \cup \{wgt(t, \beta) : \beta \in Act(t)\}$ and $wgt^{\min}(final) = wgt^{\max}(final) = 0$. Then, (*) follows from (**) and (***) as $wgt^{\min}(t)$ is non-positive and

$$\zeta_s^*(t) \cdot wgt^{\min}(t) \leqslant \zeta_s^{\mathfrak{S}}(t) \cdot wgt(t, \mathfrak{S}(t)) \leqslant \zeta_s^*(t) \cdot wgt^{\max}(t)$$

for all states $s, t \in S \setminus \{final\}$ and all schedulers $\mathfrak{S}$. Moreover, $\zeta_s^{\mathfrak{S}}(t) = 0$ if $t \notin R_s$.

Remark 3.4. For the special case of MDPs with non-negative weights, the starting vector x obtained by our approach for the lower value iteration agrees with the classical text-book approach (see, e.g., Sects. 7.2.4 and 7.3.3 in [30]). More precisely, as $wgt \geqslant 0$ implies $wgt^{\min} = 0$, the lower value iteration for approximating the maximal expected total weight will be started with $x^{(0)} = 0$. For computing approximations of minimal expected total weights, we switch from wgt to $-wgt$ and then apply the lower and upper value iteration. As $wgt \geqslant 0$ implies $(-wgt)^{\max} = 0$ the upper value iteration will be started with the null vector $y^{(0)} = 0$, which corresponds to the classical approach. ∎

We now present simple techniques to compute values $\zeta_s^*(t)$ satisfying (***). If $\mathcal{M}$ is acyclic then $\zeta_s^{\mathfrak{S}}(t) \leqslant 1$ for all states s, t. Thus, for acyclic MDPs we can deal with $\zeta_s^*(t) = 1$ for all states s, t. In the sequel, we suppose that $\mathcal{M}$ is cyclic.

Lemma 3.5. *Let $\mathfrak{S}$ be a memoryless deterministic scheduler. Then, for all states $s, t \in S \setminus \{final\}$:*

$$\zeta_s^{\mathfrak{S}}(t) = \frac{\Pr_s^{\mathfrak{S}}(\Diamond t)}{1 - \Pr_t^{\mathfrak{S}}(\bigcirc \Diamond t)}$$

As a consequence of Lemma 3.5 (see [3] for its proof) we get that to ensure (***) we can deal with any value

$$\zeta_s^*(t) = \frac{\Pr_s^{ub}(\Diamond t)}{1 - \Pr_t^{ub}(\bigcirc \Diamond t)}$$

where $\Pr_t^{ub}(\bigcirc \Diamond t) < 1$ is an upper bound for $\Pr_t^{max}(\bigcirc \Diamond t)$ and $\Pr_s^{ub}(\Diamond t)$ an upper bound for $\Pr_s^{max}(\Diamond t)$. One option to obtain appropriate values $\Pr_t^{ub}(\bigcirc \Diamond t)$ and $\Pr_s^{ub}(\Diamond t)$ is to apply the upper value iteration proposed in [18] for an arbitrary number of steps. However, this requires individual computations for each state t, which becomes expensive for larger models.

Then, there is a tradeoff between providing good bounds using sophisticated techniques and the time (and memory) requirements to compute such bounds. In what follows, we present two simple graph-based techniques to compute upper bounds for $\zeta_s^*(t)$. Both rely on the trivial bound 1 for $\Pr_s^{max}(\Diamond t)$, i.e., $\zeta_s^*(t)$ depends on s only implicitly by the choice of the set R_s, and compute an upper bound for the maximal recurrence probabilities $\Pr_t^{max}(\bigcirc \Diamond t)$.

Upper Bound for Maximal Recurrence Probabilities (Variant 1). For $s \in S$, we write C_s to denote the unique strongly connected component (SCC) of $\mathcal{M}$ that contains s.[4] For $t \in S \setminus \{final\}$, let X_t denotes the set of all state-action pairs (s, α) with $s \in C_t$ (hence $C_s = C_t$) and $P(s, \alpha, C_t) < 1$ and let

$$q_t = \max\{P(s, \alpha, C_t) : (s, \alpha) \in X_t\}$$

$$p_t = \min\{P(s, \alpha, u) : s, u \in C_t, \ \alpha \in Act(s), \ P(s, \alpha, u) > 0\}$$

Note that the assumption $\Pr_t^{min}(\Diamond final) = 1$ for all t ensures that X_t is nonempty. Let $q = \max_t q_t$ and p denote the minimal positive transition probability in $\mathcal{M}$, i.e., $p = \min\{P(s, \alpha, t) : s \in S, \alpha \in Act(s), P(s, \alpha, t) > 0\}$. Then, $0 < p \leqslant p_t < 1$ and $0 < q_t \leqslant q < 1$.

Lemma 3.6. *Let $\mathfrak{S}$ be a memoryless deterministic scheduler. Then, for all states $t \in S \setminus \{final\}$ (see [3] for the proof):*

$$\Pr_t^{\mathfrak{S}}(\bigcirc \Diamond t) \leqslant 1 - p_t^{|C_t|-1} \cdot (1 - q_t) \leqslant 1 - p^{|C_t|-1} \cdot (1 - q).$$

---

[4] Here, $\mathcal{M}$ is viewed as a directed graph with the node set S and the edge relation $\rightarrow$ given by $s \rightarrow t$ iff there is some action α with $P(s, \alpha, t) > 0$.

Example 3.7. In the Markov chain $\mathcal{C}[p]$ of Example 3.2, we have $\Pr_{s_i}^{\mathcal{C}[p]}(\bigcirc\Diamond s_i) = 1 - p^{n-i}$ for $i < n$. If $p \leqslant 1/2$ then $p = p_{s_i}$, $q = q_{s_i} = 1 - p$ and $|C_{s_i}| = n$. Hence, the bounds in Lemma 3.6 are tight for state s_0. ∎

We now define the values $\zeta_s^*(t)$ for variant 1 in two nuances (fine and coarse). The fine variant is based on $\Pr_t^{ub}(\bigcirc\Diamond t) = 1 - p_t^{|C_t|-1} \cdot (1 - q_t)$ and $\Pr_s^{ub}(\Diamond t) = 1$:

$$\zeta_s^*(t) = \frac{1}{p_t^{|C_t|-1} \cdot (1 - q_t)}$$

for $s, t \in S \setminus \{final\}$. For the final state we put $\zeta_s^*(final) = 1$. The coarse variant is defined analogously, except that we deal with $\Pr_t^{ub}(\bigcirc\Diamond t) = 1 - p^{|C_t|-1} \cdot (1 - q)$. Using Lemmas 3.5 and 3.6 we obtain that (***) holds.

Example 3.8. We regard again the Markov chain $\mathcal{C}[p]$ of Example 3.2. For the weight function wgt of $\mathcal{C}[p]$ given by $wgt(s_0) = 1$ and $wgt(s_i) = 0$, we obtain $e_0^* = 1/p^n$ and $e_i^* = 1/p^n - 1/p^i$ for $i = 1, \ldots, n$ (see [3]). The expected number of visits for s_i is $\zeta_{s_0}^{\mathcal{C}[p]}(s_i) = p^{i-n}$. As the states $s_0, \ldots, s_{n-1}$ constitute an SCC, the fine and coarse variant yield the same bound for the maximal recurrence probability from state s_0, namely $\zeta_{s_0}^*(s_i) = 1/p^n$ for all $i < n$. Thus, the starting vector y for the upper value iteration is $(1/p^n, 1/p^n, \ldots, 1/p^n, 0)$ as s_0 is reachable from all states $s \neq final$. In particular, $y_{s_0} = e_{s_0}^*$ is optimal. ∎

If the SCCs are large and their minimal positive transition probabilities are small then the values $\zeta_s^*(t)$ tend to be very large. Better bounds for the maximal recurrence probabilities $\Pr_t^{max}(\bigcirc\Diamond t)$ are obtained by the following variant.

Upper Bound for Maximal Recurrence Probabilities (Variant 2). Let $S_0 = \{final\}$. We then define inductively $T_{i-1} = S_0 \cup \ldots \cup S_{i-1}$ and

$$S_i = \big\{ s \in S \setminus T_{i-1} : P(s, \alpha, T_{i-1}) > 0 \text{ for all } \alpha \in Act(s) \big\}$$

The assumption $\min_{s \in S} \Pr_s^{min}(\Diamond final) = 1$ yields that if T_{i-1} is a proper subset of S then S_i is nonempty. Note that otherwise each state $s \in S \setminus T_{i-1}$ has an action α_s with $P(s, \alpha_s, T_{i-1}) = 0$. But then $P(s, \alpha_s, S \setminus T_{i-1}) = 1 - P(s, \alpha_s, T_{i-1}) = 1$ for all states $s \in S \setminus T_{i-1}$. Let $\mathfrak{S}$ be a memoryless deterministic scheduler with $\mathfrak{S}(s) = \alpha_s$ for all $s \in S \setminus T_{i-1}$. Then, $\Pr_s^{\mathfrak{S}}(\Box \neg T_{i-1}) = 1$ for each $s \in S \setminus T_{i-1}$. Hence, $\Pr_s^{\mathfrak{S}}(\Diamond final) = 0$ for $s \in S \setminus T_{i-1}$. Contradiction. Thus, $S = T_k$ for some $k \leqslant |S|$ and S is the disjoint union of the sets $S_0, S_1, \ldots, S_k$. By induction on $i \in \{0, 1, \ldots, k\}$ we define values $d_t \in \,]0, 1]$ for the states $t \in S_i$. In the basis of induction we put $d_{final} = 1$. Suppose $1 \leqslant i \leqslant k$ and the values d_u are defined for all states $u \in T_{i-1}$. Then, for each state $t \in T_i$ we define:

$$d_t = \min \big\{ \textstyle\sum_{u \in T_{i-1}} P(t, \alpha, u) \cdot d_{u,t} : \alpha \in Act(t) \big\}$$

where $d_{u,t} = 1$ if $C_t \neq C_u$ and $d_{u,t} = d_u$ if $C_u = C_t$. Recall that C_t denotes the unique SCC containing t and that the values d_t are positive as $P(t, \alpha, T_{i-1}) > 0$ for all actions $\alpha \in Act(t)$. In the appendix of [3] we show:

Lemma 3.9. $\text{Pr}_t^{\max}(\bigcirc \lozenge t) \leqslant 1 - d_t$ *for each state* $t \in S$

Using Lemma 3.5 and Lemma 3.9, condition (***) holds for $\zeta_s^*(t) = 1/d_t$.

Example 3.10. Again, consider the Markov chain $\mathcal{C}[p]$ of Example 3.2. For the weight function given by $wgt(s) = 1$ for $s \neq \text{final}$, we obtain $e_i^* = (1 - p^{n-i})/(p^n(1 - p))$. With the first variant, we get the starting vector y for the upper value iteration where $y_{s_i} = n/p^n$ for all states s_i with $i < n$. The second variant generates the decomposition $S_i = \{s_{n-i}\}$ for $i = 0, 1, \ldots, n$. Then $\zeta_{s_0}^*(s_i) = \zeta_{s_0}^{\mathcal{C}[p]}(s_i)$ as $\text{Pr}_{s_0}^{\mathcal{C}[p]}(\lozenge s_i) = 1$ and $\text{Pr}_{s_i}(\bigcirc \lozenge s_i) = 1 - p^{n-i}$ (see Example 3.7). Thus, the computed bound for the expected times to visit s_i is the exact value $\zeta_{s_0}^*(s_i) = d_{s_i} = p^{i-n}$. Here, index i ranges between 0 and $n - 1$. Thus, the second variant generates the starting vector y where $y_{s_i} = \sum_{j=0}^{n-1} p^{j-n} = (1 - p^n)(p^n(1 - p))$ for all states s_i with $i < n$, which is optimal for $i = 0$. ∎

4   Topological Interval Iteration

To increase the efficiency of the value iteration, several authors proposed a stratified approach that exploits the topological structure of the MDP [11,13,14]. In such a topological value iteration, for each strongly connected component (SCC) a value iteration is performed, which only updates the values for the states in this particular SCC. As the SCCs are computed in their topological order from the bottom up, values for the outgoing transitions of the current SCC have already been computed. For models with more than one SCC, this approach has the potential to reduce the number of state updates that are performed, as it avoids updating the values for every state in each iteration step.

To adapt such a topological approach to interval iteration, the main challenge is to ensure that the computed upper and lower bounds for the states in a given SCC S are suitably precise to allow their effective utilization during the interval iteration computation in those SCCs containing states that can reach S and thus potentially depend on its values. While we formalize our approach for the setting of maximal expected accumulated weights, the presented approach can be easily adapted to a topological interval iteration for the computation of extremal reachability probabilities in the setting of [18].

Given a subset of states $Q \subseteq S$ and, for each state $q \in Q$, an upper bound u_q and a lower bound l_q for the value $e_{\mathcal{M},q}^* = e_q^*$, i.e., $l_q \leqslant e_{\mathcal{M},q}^* \leqslant u_q$, we induce two new MDPs that arise by discarding all transitions of the states $q \in Q$ and adding a new transition from q to a trap state with weight l_q resp. u_q. Formally, we construct an MDP $\mathcal{M}_\uparrow = (S, Act', P', \text{final}, wgt_\uparrow)$ incorporating the upper-estimate and an MDP $\mathcal{M}_\downarrow = (S, Act', P', \text{final}, wgt_\downarrow)$ incorporating the lower estimate. We introduce a fresh action τ, i.e., $Act' = Act \cup \{\tau\}$, which is the only action enabled in the Q-states and goes to *final* with probability 1, replacing the original actions, i.e., $P'(s, \alpha, t) = P(s, \alpha, t)$ for all states $s \notin Q$, $\alpha \in Act$, $t \in S$ and, for all states $q \in Q$, $P'(q, \tau, \text{final}) = 1$ and $P'(q, \alpha, t) = 0$

for all $\alpha \in Act$, $t \in S$. The MDPs $\mathcal{M}_\uparrow$ and $\mathcal{M}_\downarrow$ differ in their weight functions, with $wgt_\uparrow(q, \tau) = u_q$ and $wgt_\downarrow(q, \tau) = l_q$ for $q \in Q$ while the weights for the remaining state-action pairs remain unchanged, i.e., $wgt_\uparrow(s, \alpha) = wgt_\downarrow(s, \alpha) = wgt(s, \alpha)$ for all $s \in S \setminus Q$ and $\alpha \in Act$. Intuitively, the τ transitions simulate the expected weight accumulated on the path fragments from states $q \in Q$ until *final*, replacing it with the upper or lower bound, respectively. As $\mathrm{Pr}_\mathcal{M}^{\min}(\lozenge final) = 1$, we also have $\mathrm{Pr}_{\mathcal{M}_\uparrow}^{\min}(\lozenge final) = \mathrm{Pr}_{\mathcal{M}_\downarrow}^{\min}(\lozenge final) = 1$.

Lemma 4.1. *With the notations as above (see* [3] *for the proof):*

(a) $e^*_{\mathcal{M}_\downarrow, s} \leqslant e^*_{\mathcal{M}, s} \leqslant e^*_{\mathcal{M}_\uparrow, s}$ *for all states* $s \in S$
(b) If $|u_q - l_q| < \varepsilon$ *for all* $q \in Q$, *then* $|e^*_{\mathcal{M}_\uparrow, s} - e^*_{\mathcal{M}_\downarrow, s}| < \varepsilon$ *for all* $s \in S$.

We are now interested in performing an interval iteration in the setting where we are given a desired precision threshold ε and lower and upper estimates l_q and u_q for a subset of states. Here, we assume that the bounds are within the desired precision, i.e., that $|u_q - l_q| < \varepsilon$ and that $l_q \leqslant e^*_{\mathcal{M}, q} \leqslant u_q$. As these estimates will arise from the processing of previously handled SCCs, we can ensure that the desired precision is indeed obtained. Let $\mathcal{M}_\downarrow$ and $\mathcal{M}_\uparrow$ be the two MDPs that are induced by applying the transformation detailed above for the two estimates, respectively. We now perform an interval iteration, but instead of performing both iterations in the original MDP $\mathcal{M}$, the iteration from above is performed in $\mathcal{M}_\uparrow$ and the iteration from below is performed in $\mathcal{M}_\downarrow$ in an interleaved fashion.

Let x_s and y_s be lower and upper bounds for $e^*_{\mathcal{M}, s}$, i.e., with $x_s \leqslant e^*_{\mathcal{M}, s} \leqslant y_s$ for all $s \in S$, for example computed using the methods detailed in Sect. 3.3. We obtain starting vectors $x^{(0)}$ (for the value iteration from below in $\mathcal{M}_\downarrow$) and $y^{(0)}$ (for the value iteration from above in $\mathcal{M}_\uparrow$) by setting

$$x_s^{(0)} = x_s - \varepsilon \quad \text{for } s \in S \setminus Q \quad \text{and } x_s^{(0)} = l_s \quad \text{for } s \in Q$$
$$y_s^{(0)} = y_s + \varepsilon \quad \text{for } s \in S \setminus Q \quad \text{and } y_s^{(0)} = u_s \quad \text{for } s \in Q$$

To ensure that $x_s^{(0)}$ is indeed a lower bound for $e^*_{\mathcal{M}_\downarrow, s}$ for the states $s \in S \setminus Q$, we subtract ε. Lemma 4.1(b) together with Lemma 4.1(a) yields $e^*_{\mathcal{M}_\uparrow, s} - e^*_{\mathcal{M}_\downarrow, s} < \varepsilon$, and as $e^*_{\mathcal{M}_\uparrow, s}$ is an upper bound for $e^*_{\mathcal{M}, s}$ we have $e^*_{\mathcal{M}, s} - e^*_{\mathcal{M}_\downarrow, s} < \varepsilon$. Then, due to the assumption that $x_s \leqslant e^*_{\mathcal{M}, s}$, it is guaranteed that $x_s - \varepsilon \leqslant e^*_{\mathcal{M}_\downarrow, s}$. For the upper bound $y_s^{(0)}$ similar arguments apply when adding ε to the upper bound computed for $e^*_\mathcal{M}$.

The topological interval iteration for $e^*_\mathcal{M}$ and precision ε now works as follows. We first compute lower and upper bounds x_s and y_s for $e^*_{\mathcal{M}, s}$ for all states in $\mathcal{M}$ (see Sect. 3.3). We then apply standard algorithms to compute a topological ordering $C_1, C_2, \ldots, C_n$ of the SCCs of $\mathcal{M}$. We then process each SCC according to the topological ordering, from the bottom up. We maintain the set Q of states that are contained in SCCs that have already been processed, as well as upper bounds u_q and lower bounds l_q for these states satisfying $u_q - l_q \leqslant \varepsilon$. The order of processing ensures that the successor states for all transitions that do not lead back to the current SCC are contained in Q. Let C_i be the current SCC.

If it is a singleton SCC, i.e., containing just a single state s, we can derive u_s and l_s directly. In particular, for the *final* state we can set both values to 0. For non-singleton SCCs, we consider the sub-MDP $\mathcal{M}_i$ of $\mathcal{M}$ containing the states in C_i as well as all states not in C_i but reachable from C_i. The latter states are all contained in Q. We then perform the interleaved interval iteration in $\mathcal{M}_\downarrow$ and $\mathcal{M}_\uparrow$ derived from $\mathcal{M}_i$ with the starting vectors derived from x_s and y_s and the stopping criterion $y_s^{(n)} - x_s^{(n)} < \varepsilon$ for all $s \in C_i$. Termination for C_i will eventually occur as shown in [3]. Subsequently, we add all states $s \in C_i$ to Q and set $l_s = x_s^{(n)}$ and $u_s = y_s^{(n)}$. Having processed the SCC C_i, we proceed with the next SCC in the topological order. Once all SCCs are processed, we return the vectors $(l_s)_{s \in S}$ and $(u_s)_{s \in S}$, which contain lower and upper bounds for the values $e^*_{\mathcal{M},s}$ with precision ε. The correctness of the output follows from repeated application of the termination and correctness proof for individual SCCs (see [3]).

5 Implementation

We have implemented the algorithms presented in this paper as an extension of the PRISM model checker [25]. PRISM contains four major engines: an EXPLICIT engine and three other engines (MTBDD, HYBRID, SPARSE) that either partially or fully rely on symbolic, MTBDD-based methods [28].

Interval Iteration. Since the performance of the different engines varies across benchmarks, we have implemented interval iteration for all four, extending the existing value iteration based implementations for computation of (extremal) expected accumulated rewards and reachability probabilities in MDPs. More complex probabilistic model checking problems often use these as a basic building block. Consequently, our interval iteration implementation is automatically used there as well, for example in the context of LTL model checking. We also implement interval iteration for discrete-time Markov chains (DTMCs), a special case of MDPs, to facilitate further benchmarking. We assume non-negative weights (rewards/costs), a limitation imposed by PRISM.

Our implementation supports, in addition to standard value iteration updates, two other well known variants that are implemented in PRISM for the standard value iteration approach as well: Jacobi-like updates (directly solving self-loop probabilities) and Gauss-Seidel-like updates. The latter are limited to the EXPLICIT and SPARSE engines due to the difficulty of a symbolic implementation.

To be able to apply interval iteration for the computation of maximal reachability probabilities, we support the quotienting of maximal end components as proposed in [18]. This is required to ensure that the upper value iteration converges. Interval iteration for minimal expectations is currently only supported for the EXPLICIT engine and if the MDP after preprocessing is contracting (this is always true for the special case of DTMCs).

Upper Bound Computation. For (extremal) reachability probabilities, the upper bound (=1) and lower bound (=0) for the interval iteration is set directly. For the (extremal) expected accumulated reward computation, we set the lower bound to 0, and support *variant 1 (coarse and fine)* and *variant 2* of the upper bound algorithms of Sect. 3.3, computing a single upper bound for all states (i.e., using $R_s = S$). For minimal expectations, we use the bound obtained for $\mathbb{E}^{\max}(\diamondsuit final)$ from one of the variants, and can additionally obtain an upper bound using the *Dijkstra Sweep for Monotone Pessimistic Initialization* (DS-MPI) algorithm for obtaining upper bounds on the minimal expectations proposed in [27], which we implemented for the EXPLICIT engine.

Topological Iteration. Lastly, we also implemented both topological value iteration and topological interval iteration (see Sect. 4) in the EXPLICIT engine.

6   Experiments

We have carried out extensive experiments using the PRISM benchmark suite [26], considering 294 model/property combinations in total. We give here an overview of the results; further details can be found in the appendix of [3].

Accuracy. To gauge the prevalence of imprecise results due to early termination of value iteration, we have compared the PRISM results for the benchmark instances against an exact result (if available) or the result obtained by interval iteration. We use $\varepsilon = 10^{-6}$ and evaluate both absolute and relative mode.[5] Comparing the interval iteration results against the exact results (where available) demonstrated that the interval iteration results indeed have the expected precision. We say that a value iteration result has a precision of less than 10^{-x} if the difference between the result and the reference value is larger than 10^{-x}. When the computations are done using relative termination checks, the precision is also computed relatively. For absolute mode, the results of 67 of the 294 instances were less precise than 10^{-6} (44 less precise than 10^{-5}, 17 less than 10^{-4} and 2 less than 10^{-3}, none of the benchmark instances had a precision of less than 10^{-2}). Detailed statistics, for relative mode as well, can be seen in Table 1, which shows the overall results of our accuracy check. A similar picture arises with the relative termination check, however here the absolute imprecision is magnified for values larger than 1.

The largest imprecision occurred for the "coin2.nm" model of the "consensus" case study (with model parameter $K = 16$) and the "steps-max" expectation property. The exact result for this instance is 3267. In absolute mode, the

---

[5] In addition to the termination check relying on the supremum norm (*absolute check*), probabilistic model checkers often support a *relative* check, where the criterion requires $|z'_s - z_s|/|z_s| < \varepsilon$ to hold for all states $s \in S$, where z and z' are the vectors under comparison. This takes the magnitude of the individual values into account and dynamically tightens the tolerance for values <1 and loosens it for values >1.

Table 1. Results of the accuracy benchmarks, split into the instances with probability and expectation properties and whether comparison was against exact or interval iteration results. Note that instances with precision less than 10^{-3} are also included in the count for 10^{-4}, etc.

	Number of instances	Precision less than			
		10^{-3}	10^{-4}	10^{-5}	10^{-6}
Prob., vs exact results, absolute	87	-	3	12	25
Prob., vs exact results, relative	87	-	3	9	21
Prob., vs interval iteration results, absolute	97	-	1	1	9
Prob., vs interval iteration results, relative	97	-	1	1	11
Expect., vs exact results, absolute	41	2	5	10	20
Expect., vs exact results, relative	41	2	6	12	20
Expect., vs interval iteration results, absolute	69	-	3	9	13
Expect., vs interval iteration results, relative	69	-	4	9	16

value iteration had the result 3266.9986814425756, while interval iteration had 3267.0000004994463. In relative mode, the imprecision is magnified in absolute terms, i.e., the value iteration has the result 3262.69160811823 while interval iteration yielded 3267.0016321821013. As can be seen here, interval iteration yielded the expected precision, i.e., 6 correct fractional digits for absolute mode and 6 correct first digits in relative mode. The second instance with precision of less than 10^{-3} is for the same model but the "steps-min" property.

Overall, for the benchmark instances, the imprecision was not as grave as for the example from [18]. However, in independent work on a simplified probabilistic model of an error handler, inspired by [24], we encountered a non-artificial model with probability results of 0.328597 (value iteration) vs 0.687089 (interval iteration), with $\varepsilon = 10^{-6}$. For details, see [3].

Quality of Upper Bounds and Cost of Interval Iteration. In another experiment, we were interested in (1) the quality of the upper bounds obtained by the various heuristics and (2) in the impact of using interval iteration (II) instead of value iteration (VI). Figure 3 shows statistics for a comparison of the variant 2 and the DS-MPI upper bound heuristics (for minimal expectations in MDPs and expectations in DTMCs) for the benchmark instances using expected rewards, $\varepsilon = 10^{-6}$ and a relative termination check.

The upper plot shows upper bounds, compared to the maximal (finite) value in the result vector. Clearly, no upper bound can be below that value. The benchmark instances here are sorted by this maximal result value. The plot in the middle then shows the increase in the number of iterations that are carried out for interval iteration compared to value iteration, e.g., an increase of 2 signifies that interval iteration required twice the number of iterations. Note that we count the upper and lower iteration step as a single combined iteration. To simplify the presentation, the plot in the middle omits a single data point, consisting of a 32-fold increase from 5 to 159 iterations. The plot at the bottom of Fig. 3 shows the corresponding increase in the time for model checking (including precomputations, upper bounds computations and iterations). In this plot, instances where all times are below 1 s are omitted due to their limited informative value.

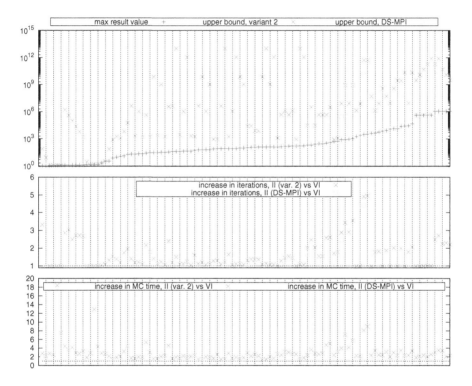

Fig. 3. Top: maximal result value versus the upper bounds. Middle: increase (2 = double, . . .) in the number of iterations. Bottom: increase in model checking time. The x-axis of the plots represents the model/property instances, sorted by maximal result value.

Generally, an increase in the number iterations required for interval iteration compared to value iteration can be due to the lower iteration requiring more iterations to reach a precise result or due to the number of iterations required by the upper iteration to converge from the initial upper bound. As can be seen, the DS-MPI heuristic (where applicable) generally provides much better upper

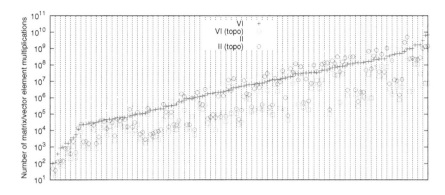

Fig. 4. Number of multiplication operations for (topological) value and interval iteration. The x-axis of both plots represents the model/property instances, sorted by the number of multiplication operations for plain value iteration.

bounds than variant 2, often by several orders of magnitude. However, for the benchmark instances, the number of required iterations does not rise by a similar factor, indicating a certain insensitivity to the quality of the upper bound. Generally, the increase in iterations for interval iteration can be considered benign. For the model checking times, a certain increase can be seen, which is to be expected due to the additional work carried out. The largest relative increases (on the left of the plot) are for instances where value iteration took less than 1 s, while in general the increases remain modest.

In [3], we also evaluate the variant 1 heuristic. The bounds obtained using this variant in general tend to be significantly larger and roughly half of the benchmark instances had no variant 1 bound that could be represented as a double-precision floating point number. However, there are instances where the variant 1 and variant 2 bounds coincide and where the variant 1 computation is faster. Additionally, we present and discuss similar experiments for the benchmark instances using probability computations. For those, the increase in the number of iterations (and model checking time) is even more limited due to the a priori availability of a rather good upper bound of 1 for probabilities.

Topological Iteration. Figure 4 shows statistics of experiments comparing topological iteration against plain iteration. We considered the MDP benchmark instances, using $\varepsilon = 10^{-6}$ and absolute checks. As the topological approach does not process all states in each iteration, we need a more fine grained measure of the operations: The plot depicts the number of *matrix element/vector element multiplications*, e.g., the operations $P(s, \alpha, t) \cdot v_t$ for MDPs and non-zero matrix entries. The potential for the topological approach is clearly demonstrated, with a reduction in the required multiplications often by an order of magnitude or more. In general, such a reduction translates into a decreased running time as well. Our experiments thus show that the known potential for topological value iteration (see, e.g., [11]) transfers to topological interval iteration as well.

7   Conclusion

In this paper, we have shown that interval iteration is a viable approach to deal with the potential termination criterion problems raised by [18], providing higher confidence in the correctness of the results of probabilistic model checkers. In particular, we have shown how the approach of [18] can be successfully extended for the context of expected accumulated weights. Clearly, even those situations where the results obtained using the standard value iteration termination criterion (or some particular parameter setting) happen to be sufficiently precise are rendered problematic in practice due to the absence of any precision guarantees. Even with interval iteration, the orthogonal question of the precision of the underlying floating-point computations remains and could be addressed by maintaining bounds on their precision. In future work, we intend to extend the implementation, e.g., using the additional knowledge provided by interval iteration in threshold problems. Additionally, the upper and lower iterations can be carried out in parallel, reducing the performance impact.

We will also focus on extending our results for the setting of non-contracting MDPs. In the case of non-negative weights, our implementation for maximal expectations handles non-contracting MDPs thanks to the preprocessing proposed in [16], while for minimal expectations the vector obtained using DS-MPI could be used as an upper starting vector, as [7] establishes the unique fixed-point characterization and convergence of value iteration under relaxed assumptions even for general weights. For general weighted MDPs, checking finiteness of the expected weight is more involved. Our results on lower and upper bounds for expectations might also be interesting for different purposes, e.g., in the context of planning as outlined in [27].

References

1. Baier, C., Haverkort, B.R., Hermanns, H., Katoen, J.: Model-checking algorithms for continuous-time Markov chains. IEEE Trans. Softw. Eng. **29**(6), 524–541 (2003)
2. Baier, C., Klein, J., Klüppelholz, S., Wunderlich, S.: Weight monitoring with linear temporal logic: complexity and decidability. In: 23rd Conference on Computer Science Logic and the 29th Symposium on Logic in Computer Science (CSL-LICS), pp. 11:1–11:10. ACM (2014)
3. Baier, C., Klein, J., Leuschner, L., Parker, D., Wunderlich, S.: Ensuring the reliability of your model checker: interval iteration for Markov decision processes (extended version) (2017). http://wwwtcs.inf.tu-dresden.de/ALGI/PUB/CAV17/
4. Baier, C., Kwiatkowska, M.Z.: Model checking for a probabilistic branching time logic with fairness. Distrib. Comput. **11**(3), 125–155 (1998)
5. Bell, A., Haverkort, B.R.: Untold horrors about steady-state probabilities: what reward-based measures won't tell about the equilibrium distribution. In: Wolter, K. (ed.) EPEW 2007. LNCS, vol. 4748, pp. 2–17. Springer, Heidelberg (2007). doi:10.1007/978-3-540-75211-0_2
6. Bellman, R.: Dynamic Programming. Princeton University Press, Princeton (1957)
7. Bertsekas, D.P., Tsitsiklis, J.N.: An analysis of stochastic shortest path problems. Math. Oper. Res. **16**(3), 580–595 (1991)

8. Bianco, A., de Alfaro, L.: Model checking of probabilistic and nondeterministic systems. In: Thiagarajan, P.S. (ed.) FSTTCS 1995. LNCS, vol. 1026, pp. 499–513. Springer, Heidelberg (1995). doi:10.1007/3-540-60692-0_70

9. Brázdil, T., Chatterjee, K., Chmelík, M., Forejt, V., Křetínský, J., Kwiatkowska, M., Parker, D., Ujma, M.: Verification of Markov decision processes using learning algorithms. In: Cassez, F., Raskin, J.-F. (eds.) ATVA 2014. LNCS, vol. 8837, pp. 98–114. Springer, Cham (2014). doi:10.1007/978-3-319-11936-6_8

10. Chades, I., Chapron, G., Cros, M., Garcia, F., Sabbadin, R.: MDPtoolbox: a multi-platform toolbox to solve stochastic dynamic programming problems. Ecography **37**, 916–920 (2014)

11. Ciesinski, F., Baier, C., Größer, M., Klein, J.: Reduction techniques for model checking Markov decision processes. In: 5th International Conference on Quantitative Evaluation of Systems (QEST), pp. 45–54. IEEE Computer Society Press (2008)

12. Courcoubetis, C., Yannakakis, M.: The complexity of probabilistic verification. J. ACM **42**(4), 857–907 (1995)

13. Dai, P., Goldsmith, J.: Topological value iteration algorithm for Markov decision processes. In: 20th International Joint Conference on Artificial Intelligence (IJCAI), pp. 1860–1865 (2007)

14. Dai, P., Mausam, M., Weld, D.S., Goldsmith, J.: Topological value iteration algorithms. J. Artif. Intell. Res. (JAIR) **42**, 181–209 (2011)

15. de Alfaro, L.: Formal verification of probabilistic systems. Ph.D. thesis, Department of Computer Science. Stanford University (1997)

16. de Alfaro, L.: Computing minimum and maximum reachability times in probabilistic systems. In: Baeten, J.C.M., Mauw, S. (eds.) CONCUR 1999. LNCS, vol. 1664, pp. 66–81. Springer, Heidelberg (1999). doi:10.1007/3-540-48320-9_7

17. Giro, S.: Optimal schedulers vs optimal bases: an approach for efficient exact solving of Markov decision processes. Theor. Comput. Sci. **538**, 70–83 (2014)

18. Haddad, S., Monmege, B.: Reachability in MDPs: refining convergence of value iteration. In: Ouaknine, J., Potapov, I., Worrell, J. (eds.) RP 2014. LNCS, vol. 8762, pp. 125–137. Springer, Cham (2014). doi:10.1007/978-3-319-11439-2_10

19. Hahn, E.M., Li, Y., Schewe, S., Turrini, A., Zhang, L.: ISCASMC: a web-based probabilistic model checker. In: Jones, C., Pihlajasaari, P., Sun, J. (eds.) FM 2014. LNCS, vol. 8442, pp. 312–317. Springer, Cham (2014). doi:10.1007/978-3-319-06410-9_22

20. Hansson, H., Jonsson, B.: A logic for reasoning about time and reliability. Form. Asp. Comput. **6**, 512–535 (1994)

21. Howard, R.: Dynamic Programming and Markov Processes. MIT Press, Cambridge (1960)

22. Kallenberg, L.: Markov decision processes. Lecture Notes, University of Leiden (2011)

23. Katoen, J.-P., Zapreev, I.S., Hahn, E.M., Hermanns, H., Jansen, D.N.: The ins and outs of the probabilistic model checker MRMC. Perform. Eval. **68**(2), 90–104 (2011)

24. Kuvaiskii, D., Faqeh, R., Bhatotia, P., Felber, P., Fetzer, C.: HAFT: hardware-assisted fault tolerance. In: 11th European Conference on Computer Systems (EuroSys), pp. 25:1–25:17. ACM (2016)

25. Kwiatkowska, M., Norman, G., Parker, D.: PRISM 4.0: verification of probabilistic real-time systems. In: Gopalakrishnan, G., Qadeer, S. (eds.) CAV 2011. LNCS, vol. 6806, pp. 585–591. Springer, Heidelberg (2011). doi:10.1007/978-3-642-22110-1_47

26. Kwiatkowska, M.Z., Norman, G., Parker, D.: The PRISM benchmark suite. In: 9th International Conference on Quantitative Evaluation of SysTems (QEST), pp. 203–204. IEEE Computer Society (2012)
27. McMahan, H.B., Likhachev, M., Gordon, G.J.: Bounded real-time dynamic programming: RTDP with monotone upper bounds and performance guarantees. In: 22nd International Conference on Machine Learning (ICML), vol. 119, pp. 569–576. ACM (2005)
28. Parker, D.: Implementation of symbolic model checking for probabilistic systems. Ph.D. thesis, University of Birmingham (2002)
29. Puterman, M., Shin, M.: Modified policy iteration algorithms for discounted Markov decision problems. Manag. Sci. **24**, 1127–1137 (1978)
30. Puterman, M.L.: Markov Decision Processes: Discrete Stochastic Dynamic Programming. Wiley, Hoboken (1994)
31. Wimmer, R., Kortus, A., Herbstritt, M., Becker, B.: Probabilistic model checking and reliability of results. In: 11th IEEE Workshop on Design and Diagnostics of Electronic Circuits and Systems (DDECS), pp. 207–212. IEEE Computer Society (2008)

Repairing Decision-Making Programs Under Uncertainty

Aws Albarghouthi, Loris D'Antoni, and Samuel Drews[(⊠)]

University of Wisconsin-Madison, Madison, USA
sedrews@wisc.edu

Abstract. The world is uncertain. Programs can be wrong. We address the problem of *repairing a program under uncertainty*, where program inputs are drawn from a probability distribution. The goal of the repair is to construct a new program that satisfies a probabilistic Boolean expression. Our work focuses on loop-free decision-making programs, e.g., classifiers, that return a Boolean- or finite-valued result. Specifically, we propose *distribution-guided inductive synthesis*, a novel program repair technique that iteratively (*i*) *samples* a finite set of inputs from a probability distribution defining the precondition, (*ii*) synthesizes a *minimal repair* to the program over the sampled inputs using an SMT-based encoding, and (*iii*) *verifies* that the resulting program is correct and is *semantically close* to the original program. We formalize our algorithm and prove its correctness by rooting it in computational learning theory. For evaluation, we focus on repairing machine learning classifiers with the goal of making them *unbiased* (fair). Our implementation and evaluation demonstrate our approach's ability to repair a range of programs.

1 Introduction

Program repair is the problem of modifying a program P to produce a new program P' that satisfies some desirable property. A majority of the investigations in automatic program repair target deterministic programs and Boolean properties, e.g., assertion violations [10,17,20,22,27]. The world, however, is uncertain, and program correctness is not always a Boolean, black-or-white property.

In this paper, we address the problem of automating program repair in the presence of uncertainty. By uncertainty, we mean that the inputs to the program are drawn from some probability distribution D. Thus, we have a *probabilistic precondition*—for instance, the input x to a program $P(x)$ may follow a Laplacian distribution. The correctness property of interest is a *probabilistic postcondition*, which we define as an expression over probabilities of program outcomes. For instance, we might be interested in ensuring that $P(r > 0) > 0.9$—the program returns a positive value at least 90% of the time—or that $P(r_1 > 0) > P(r_2 > 0)$—it is more likely that the return value r_1 is positive than that r_2 is positive. We restrict our attention to loop-free programs that return Boolean-valued (or finite-valued) results, e.g., machine learning classifiers that map inputs to a finite

© Springer International Publishing AG 2017
R. Majumdar and V. Kunčak (Eds.): CAV 2017, Part I, LNCS 10426, pp. 181–200, 2017.
DOI: 10.1007/978-3-319-63387-9_9

set of classes, and repairs that consist of altering real-valued constants in the program.

Technique: Distribution-Guided Inductive Synthesis. To address the program repair problem in the presence of uncertainty, we propose a novel program synthesis technique that we call *distribution-guided inductive synthesis* (DIGITS). The overall flow of DIGITS is illustrated in Fig. 1. Suppose we have a program P such that $\{pre\}P\{post\}$ does not hold. The goal of DIGITS is to construct a new program P' that is correct with respect to *pre* and *post* and that is *semantically close* to P. To do so, DIGITS tightly integrates three phases:

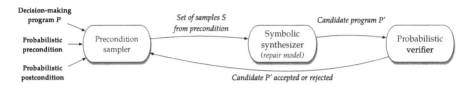

Fig. 1. Abstract, high-level view of distribution-guided inductive synthesis

Sampling: Since the precondition *pre* is a probability distribution, DIGITS begins by sampling a finite set S of program inputs from *pre*—we call S the set of *samples*. The set S is used to sidestep having to deal with arbitrary distributions directly in the synthesis process.

Synthesis: The second step is a synthesis phase, where DIGITS searches for a set of candidate programs $\{P'_1, \ldots, P'_n\}$—following a given *repair model*—where each P'_i classifies the set of samples S differently. Given that there are exponentially many ways to partition the set S, DIGITS employs a novel trie-like data structure with *conflict-driven pruning* to avoid considering redundant partitions.

Quantitative verification: Every generated candidate program P' is checked for correctness and for close *semantic distance* with P. Specifically, DIGITS employs an automated probabilistic inference technique.

Theory: Computational Learning. We formalize DIGITS by posing it as a learning algorithm, and rooting it in computational learning theory [18]. Using the concept of the *Vapnik–Chervonenkis (VC) dimension* [7] of the repair model, we show that the algorithm converges to the optimal program with a high probability when operating over postconditions that satisfy a benign property and over repair models with a finite VC dimension, which holds for many repair scenarios, e.g., *sketching*-like approaches [26].

Application: Repairing Biased Programs. Our primary motivation for this work is repairing bias in decision-making programs, e.g., programs that decide whether to hire a person, to give them a loan, or other sensitive or potentially impactful decisions like prison sentencing [5]. These programs can be generated automatically as classifiers using machine learning or can be written by hand using expert insight. The problem of algorithmic bias has received considerable attention recently, due to the increasing deployment of automated decision-making in sensitive domains [12–14,16,19,23].

Existing notions of bias in the literature neatly correspond to probabilistic postconditions. For instance, *group fairness* [11–14] stipulates that the probability that a minority job applicant is hired is almost the same as that of a majority applicant being hired. We view the underlying population of applicants as a probabilistic precondition and pose the problem of repairing biased programs within our framework: the problem is to find a new, semantically close program that is unbiased. We implemented our approach, DIGITS, and applied it to *unbias* a range of classification programs that were generated automatically. Our results demonstrate (*i*) our technique's ability to repair a range of programs and (*ii*) the importance of our algorithmic contributions.

Contributions. We summarize our contributions as follows:

- We formalize the probabilistic program repair problem as an optimization problem whose solution is a repaired program that satisfies some probabilistic pre-/post-conditions.
- We present *distribution-guided inductive synthesis*, DIGITS, a novel synthesis methodology for automatically repairing loop-free programs under uncertain inputs and probabilistic postconditions.
- We formalize correctness of our algorithm and prove its convergence using the concept of VC dimension that is standard in computational learning theory and machine learning.
- We present an implementation of our technique, DIGITS. We apply DIGITS to the increasingly important problem of ensuring that decision-making programs are not biased, for a given particular notion of bias. Our thorough evaluation demonstrates the utility of our approach and the importance of our design decisions.

2   Illustrative Example

In this section, we illustrate the operation of DIGITS on a very simple example inspired by *algorithmic bias* problems [4].

Example Program. Consider the following program, hire:

```
fun  hire(min,urank)
    dec = 1 <= urank <= 10
    return dec
```

hire is an extremely simplified automatic hiring program: it takes an applicant's information and decides whether to hire them or not, as indicated by the Boolean return variable dec. Specifically, hire takes as input the Boolean variable min, which indicates whether an applicant belongs to an underrepresented minority, and urank, which is a real-valued number indicating the rank of the university they attended. hire only hires applicants who attended top-10 universities.

Probabilistic Precondition. Let us now consider a probabilistic precondition for the program, which is a joint probability distribution over the variables min and urank. Intuitively, the precondition paints a picture of the relation between minority status and the university rank in the population of potential applicants. Consider the following precondition *pre*:

$$\text{min} \sim \text{Bernoulli}(0.1)$$
$$\text{urank} \sim \text{Gaussian}(10, 10) + 5 * \mathbb{1}(\text{min})$$

Intuitively, 10% of the possible applicants are minorities, and the university rank of an applicant is drawn from a Gaussian distribution centered at 10 (with std. 10), if the applicant is not a minority. Otherwise, if the applicant is a minority, their university rank is a Gaussian centered around 15—as shown using the indicator function, $\mathbb{1}(\text{min})$, which returns 1 when min is true and 0 otherwise.

Probabilistic Postcondition. The following postcondition formula asserts that *the probability of hiring minority applicants is at least 0.8 of the probability of hiring majority applicants*:

$$post \triangleq \frac{\mathbb{P}(\text{dec} \mid \text{min})}{\mathbb{P}(\text{dec} \mid \neg\text{min})} > 0.8$$

This is one of the many properties proposed to formalize notions of *fairness* in automated decision-making. This property is known as *group fairness* [13], and it is inspired by employment guidelines in the United States [3].

The postcondition does not hold for hire: Even though hire does not access the variable min, it only accepts applicants from top-10 universities, and, as per *pre*, minority applicants are less likely to attend top-10 universities; in fact, the value of the left hand side of *post* is ~ 0.6.

Repair Model. We would like to automatically *repair* hire in order to make it satisfy the postcondition. Additionally, we would like to avoid *obvious* repairs that result in undesirable programs. For instance, the program that hires everyone (return true) obviously satisfies the postcondition. To avoid such programs, we look for a repair that minimizes the *semantic distance* between the new program and the original program.

For our example, we will restrict the space of possible repairs as a *sketch* of the original program—we call this the *repair model*:

```
fun hireRep(min,urank)
    dec = ●₁ <= urank <= ●₂
    return dec
```

The repair model is a parametric program with two *holes* to fill, $\bullet_1$ and $\bullet_2$, which we can replace with constants to produce a program that satisfies the postcondition. Note that our approach is more general and not only restricted to filling holes with constants.

Distribution-Guided Inductive Synthesis. Now that we have set up the problem, we are ready to illustrate our approach. We are looking for a new function hireRep that satisfies *post* and that minimizes the *semantic distance* $\mathbb{P}(\text{hire} \neq \text{hireRep})$, which denotes the probability that hire and hireRep return different outputs for the same input, which is distributed according to *pre*.

To find such a repair, we present *distribution-guided inductive synthesis* (DIGITS). DIGITS begins by sampling a finite set of inputs $S = \{s_1, \ldots, s_n\}$ from the precondition *pre*. The set of samples are used to *guide* the synthesis process with concrete examples from the distribution. DIGITS considers every possible partition of the samples into positive and negative samples, (S^+, S^-). For every such partition, it attempts to find a repair that returns true for all inputs in S^+ and false for all inputs in S^-. To perform the synthesis, we encode the search problem as a quantifier-free first-order formula and ask an SMT solver to find a solution that corresponds to a filling of the holes. For each synthesized program, DIGITS uses probabilistic program verification techniques to check if the program satisfies the postcondition and to quantify the semantic distance from hire.

There are two obvious issues here: (i) The number of partitions of a given set S is exponential in $|S|$. (ii) The search finds an arbitrary repair at every step; how do we ensure that we eventually find a repair that satisfies the postcondition?

First, while the number of partitions of S is exponential, DIGITS employs an efficient binary trie data structure to guide and prune the search space. For instance, if there is no repair for a partition (S^+, S^-), DIGITS utilizes UNSAT cores to remember an unsatisfiable subset of the samples and ensure that similar partitions are not considered, thus pruning away a large family of possible partitions.

Second, we theoretically demonstrate elegant properties of DIGITS that ensure it converges to an optimal solution. The formalization is rooted in classic ideas from computational learning theory, namely, VC dimension of our repair model.

Finding Repairs. DIGITS iteratively increases the size of the sample set S by drawing more samples from *pre*. The more samples it considers, the more likely it synthesizes programs that are close to an optimal solution. Let us consider a possible trajectory of DIGITS. Figure 2 shows three programs that can be produced by DIGITS in the course of sampling and synthesis. While all programs satisfy the postcondition, the *best* repair is hireRep3, as it has the smallest distance from the original program hire. Specifically, hireRep hires all applicants from the top-15 universities, making it the semantically closest one to hire.

3   The Probabilistic Repair Problem

In this section, we formally define the probabilistic repair problem.

```
fun hireRep1(min,urank)        fun hireRep2(min,urank)        fun hireRep3(min,urank)
    dec = 10 <= urank <= 15        dec = 5 <= urank <= 17        dec = 0 <= urank <= 15
    return dec                     return dec                     return dec
```

(a) distance ≈ 0.5   (b) distance ≈ 0.4   (c) distance ≈ 0.2

Fig. 2. Repairs synthesized by DIGITS

Program Model. We consider a simple program model where a program is written in a loop-free language whose syntax is defined below:

$$P := V \leftarrow E \mid \text{if } B \text{ then } P \text{ else } P \mid P\ P \mid \text{return } V$$

P is a program, V is the set of variables used in P, E is the set of linear arithmetic expressions over V, and B is the set of Boolean expressions over V. $V \leftarrow E$ denotes assigning an expression to a variable. We assume that there is a vector of variables v_I in V that are inputs to the program and never appear on the left-hand side of an assignment. We also assume there is a single Boolean variable $v_r \in V$ that is returned by the program. All variables are real-valued or Boolean. We always assume that programs are well-typed. Given a vector of constant values c, where $|c| = |v_I|$, we use $P(c)$ to denote the result of executing P on the input c.

Probabilistic Preconditions. Given a program P with variables V, we define a probabilistic precondition *pre* as a *joint probability distribution* over the variables v_I. That is, we assume that the values of the inputs are initially drawn from the probability distribution *pre*.

Formally, we think of the distribution *pre* as a *probability space* $(\Omega, \mathcal{F}, \mathbb{P})$: Ω is the set of possible assignments to v_I, $\mathcal{F} \subseteq 2^{\Omega}$ is a set of *events*, and $\mathbb{P} : \mathcal{F} \to [0,1]$ denotes the probability of an event.

We will be interested in two kinds of events:

1. Given a Boolean expression B over v_I and v_r, overloading notation, a probability expression $\mathbb{P}(B)$ denotes

$$\mathbb{P}(\{c \in \Omega \mid \exists r.\, P(c) = r \land B[v_I/c, v_r/r] = \mathit{true}\})$$

where the notation $B[x/y]$ denotes B with all occurrences of x replaced by y. That is, $\mathbb{P}(B)$ is the probability of drawing a sample c from the precondition such that the program P returns a result satisfying B.
2. Suppose we are given two programs P and P' such that v_I and v'_I are of the same length and type. We will use $\mathbb{P}(P \neq P')$ to denote:

$$\mathbb{P}(\{c \in \Omega \mid P(c) \neq P'(c)\})$$

That is, $\mathbb{P}(P \neq P')$, which we call the *semantic distance*, is the probability that the two programs return different results on the same input.

```
1  Procedure DIGITS(P, pre, post, R, n)
      Input  : Repair problem s.t. {pre}P{post} does not hold, and a number n
      Output: Program P' ∈ R such that {pre}P{post} holds or ⊥
2     S ← ∅
3     for n times do
4        s ∼ pre
5        S ← S ∪ {s}
6     repairs ← ∅
7     foreach sets S⁺, S⁻ that partition S do
8        P' ← REPAIR(S⁺, S⁻)
9        if P' ≠ ⊥ and {pre}P'{post} then
10          | repairs ← repairs ∪ {P'}
11    if repairs ≠ ∅ then
12       | return P' ∈ repairs with minimal ℙ(P ≠ P')
13    else
14       | return ⊥
```
Algorithm 1. Distribution-Guided Inductive Synthesis

Probabilistic Postconditions. Given a program P and a precondition *pre*, we would like to refer to the probability of the program to return a specific set of values. To that end, we define a *probabilistic postcondition*, *post*, as an inequality over terms of the form $\mathbb{P}(B)$, where B is a Boolean expression over v_I and v_r. Specifically, a probabilistic postcondition is of the form $e > c$, where $c \in \mathbb{R}$ and e is an arithmetic expression over terms of the form $\mathbb{P}(B)$, e.g., $\mathbb{P}(B_1)/\mathbb{P}(B_2) > 0.75$.

Program Correctness. Given a triple $(P, pre, post)$, we say that P is *correct* with respect to *pre* and *post*, denoted $\{pre\}P\{post\}$, *iff* *post* is true.

Repair Problem. The *probabilistic repair* problem is a tuple $(P, pre, post, R)$, where $(P, pre, post)$ are as defined above, and R is a set of programs called the *repair model*, i.e., the set of possible repairs. A *solution to a repair problem* is a program $P' \in R$ such that $\{pre\}P'\{post\}$ holds, and the semantic distance $\mathbb{P}(P \neq P')$ is minimal.

The semantic distance condition is present to try to preserve as much of the original program behavior as possible.

4   Distribution-Guided Inductive Synthesis

In this section, we describe the distribution-guided inductive synthesis algorithm (DIGITS) for finding approximate solutions to the probabilistic repair problem.

DIGITS, shown in Algorithm 1, takes as input a repair problem and a number n that bounds the search depth. DIGITS first builds a set S of n samples from *pre*, and then, for every possible way to split S into positive and negative examples S^+ and S^-, it finds a candidate repair $P' \in R$ consistent with S^+ and S^-. DIGITS finally outputs the candidate repair semantically closest to P. Intuitively, DIGITS tries to inductively learn the correct repair from a finite set of samples.

Example 1. Recall the example from Sect. 2. Suppose we are given two samples $s_1 = 12$ and $s_2 = 17$, where we only consider the variable urank in the sample, as min is not used by the program. Suppose $S^+ = \{12, 17\}$ and $S^- = \emptyset$. Then, the program hireRep2 in Fig. 2 correctly classifies S^+ and S^-. Alternatively, suppose we consider the sets $S^+ = \{12\}$ and $S^- = \{17\}$. Then, a potential repair is hireRep3. If we were to add a new sample $s_3 = 15$, there would not be a repair for the sets $S^+ = \{12, 17\}$ and $S^- = \{15\}$.

To implement DIGITS, one needs to provide two components: (a) the procedure REPAIR that produces programs consistent with labeled examples and (b) a (sound) probabilistic inference algorithm to (i) check whether the synthesized program satisfies *post*, and (ii) compute the probability $\mathbb{P}(P \neq P')$. In the following we assume that such components are given. The DIGITS algorithm is relatively simple, but we show that it enjoys interesting convergence properties.

4.1 Convergence of Digits

In this section, we use classic concepts from computational learning theory to show that, under certain assumptions, the DIGITS algorithm quickly converges to good repaired programs when increasing the size n of the sample set.

Throughout this section we assume we are given a program P, a repair model R, a precondition *pre*, and a postcondition *post*, such that there exists an optimal solution $P^* \in R$ to the corresponding probabilistic program repair problem. The relationship between P, R, the programs which satisfy *post*, and P^* is visualized in Fig. 3(a). Given two programs P' and P'', we write $Er(P', P'') = \mathbb{P}(P' \neq P'')$ to denote the distance (error) between the two programs; we introduce this additional notation to make the connections to computational learning theory more explicit.

To state our main theorem, we need to recall the concept of Vapnik–Chervonenkis (VC) dimension from computational learning theory [18]. Intuitively, the VC dimension captures the expressiveness of a certain concept class; in our setting, the concept class is the repair model R. Given a set of examples S, we say that the repair model R *shatters* S iff, for every two sets S^+ and S^- that partition S, there exists a program $P_1 \in R$ such that (i) for every $s \in S^+$, $P_1(s) = true$, and (ii) for every $s \in S^-$, $P_1(s) = false$. The *VC dimension* of the repair model R is the largest integer k such that there exists a set of examples S with cardinality k that is shattered by R.

Example 2. Consider the class of linear separators in $\mathbb{R}^2$. For any collection and classification of three non-colinear points in $\mathbb{R}^2$, it is possible to construct a linear separator that is consistent with that classification; therefore, linear separators *shatter* any set of size 3. However, no linear separator can shatter *any* set of four points—for example, the points $\{(0,0), (1,1)\}$ cannot be separated from $\{(1,0), (0,1)\}$; Thus, the VC dimension of linear separators is 3.

We define the function $\text{VCCOST}(\varepsilon, \delta, k) = \frac{1}{\varepsilon}(4 \log_2(\frac{2}{\delta}) + 8k \log_2(\frac{13}{\varepsilon}))$ [7], which we will use in the following theorems.

Lemma 1 (Error Bound of digits). *If the repair model R has finite VC dimension k, then, for every program $P' \in R$, function* REPAIR, *bounds $\varepsilon > 0$ and $\delta > 0$, and set of samples S drawn from pre of size $n \geq \text{VCCOST}(\varepsilon, \delta, k)$, there exist sets S^+ and S^- that partition S such that, with probability $\geq 1 - \delta$, we have that $Er(P', \text{REPAIR}(S^+, S^-)) \leq \varepsilon$.*

Lemma 1 extends the classic notion of learnability of concept classes with finite VC dimension [7] to probabilistic program repair. Intuitively, if a repair model R has finite VC dimension, any function that correctly synthesizes from finitely many samples in *pre* will get arbitrarily close to a target solution—including P^*—with polynomially many samples. Lemma 1, however, does *not* guarantee that the synthesis algorithm will find a program consistent with the postcondition.

Intuitively, we need to ensure that there are *enough* programs close to P^* that satisfy *post*; to do so, we reason about how the error on the repair problem propagates to the error on the postcondition. Specifically, for a program $\hat{P}$ and $\alpha > 0$, we define the set $B_\alpha(\hat{P}) = \{P' \in R \mid Er(\hat{P}, P') \leq \alpha\}$; in other words, $B_\alpha(\hat{P})$ exactly characterizes a *ball* of programs in the repair model that are *close* to $\hat{P}$. Now, we define a notion of *robustness* of the postcondition with respect to a program $\hat{P}$: we say that the pair $(\hat{P}, post)$ (or just $\hat{P}$ when *post* is clear from context) is α-*robust* iff

$$\forall P' \in B_\alpha(\hat{P}). \{pre\}P'\{post\}$$

Figure 3(b) visualizes how the convergence of DIGITS follows from α-robustness: if $\hat{P}$ is α-robust, then DIGITS invoked on a sufficiently large set of samples S will, with high probability, encounter a split S^+, S^- where every program consistent with that split is contained in $B_\alpha(\hat{P})$. Thus if P' is the result of $\text{REPAIR}(S^+, S^-)$, then $Er(\hat{P}, P') \leq \alpha$ and P' satisfies *post*. We can now give our main theorem, which formalizes this property.

Theorem 1 (Convergence of digits). *Assume that there exist an $\alpha > 0$ and program $\hat{P}$ such that $(\hat{P}, \text{post})$ is α-robust. Let k be the VC dimension of repair model R. For all bounds $0 < \varepsilon \leq \alpha$ and $\delta > 0$, for every function* REPAIR *and $n \geq \text{VCCOST}(\varepsilon, \delta, k)$, with probability $\geq 1 - \delta$ we have that* DIGITS *enumerates a program P' with $Er(\hat{P}, P') \leq \varepsilon$ and $\{\text{pre}\}P'\{\text{post}\}$.*

Corollary 1 (Convergence to P^*). *In particular, if P^* is α-robust, and ε, δ, and n are constrained as above, and* DIGITS$(P, \text{pre}, \text{post}, R, n) = P'$, *then with probability $\geq 1 - \delta$ we have that $P' \neq \bot$, $Er(P^*, P') \leq \varepsilon$, and $\{\text{pre}\}P'\{\text{post}\}$.*

Theorem 1 and Corollary 1 represent the heart of the convergence result. However, there are two major technicalities.

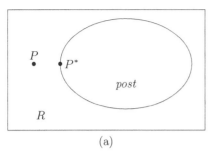 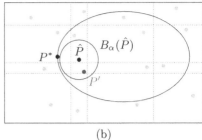

(a)   (b)

Fig. 3. Visualization of aspects of DIGITS: (a) Programs that satisfy *post* are a subset of R. (b) Samples split R into 16 regions, each with a candidate program. If $\hat{P}$ is α-robust, with high probability DIGITS finds P' close to $\hat{P}$; if $\hat{P}$ is close to P^*, so is P'.

First, P^* usually is not α-robust; in particular, if there exists $P' \in B_\alpha(P^*)$ with $Er(P, P') = Er(P, P^*) - \alpha$, then P^* is not actually optimal. In other words, We can expect P^* to lie on the boundary of the set of correct programs, as in Fig. 3(a). However, Theorem 1 still guarantees that with high probability, DIGITS will find a solution arbitrarily close to *any* α-robust program $\hat{P} \in R$; if there exist α-robust programs that are close to the optimal solution, DIGITS still converges to the optimal solution. We refine this notion in the following Corollary.

Corollary 2 (Weak convergence to P^*). *For $\alpha > 0$, let $A \subseteq R$ be the set of programs $\hat{P}$ where $(\hat{P}, post)$ is α-robust. Let $\Delta = \min_{\hat{P} \in A}\{Er(P^*, \hat{P})\}$. If ε, δ, and n are constrained as above, and DIGITS$(P, pre, post, R, n) = P'$, then with probability $\geq 1 - \delta$ we have that $P' \neq \bot$, $Er(P^*, P') \leq \Delta + \varepsilon$, and $\{pre\}P'\{post\}$.*

Extensions of Corollary 2 still provide strong results on the convergence of DIGITS: for example, if P^* is not α-robust, but there exists an α-robust $\hat{P}$ with $P^* \in B_\alpha(\hat{P})$, then one can show $\lim_{\alpha \to \infty} \Delta = 0$; in this case, running DIGITS for sufficiently large n preserves the desired convergence result from Corollary 1.

Second, an optimal P^* that satisfies *post* may not actually exist. Suppose, for example, that for some event E, *post* is the expression $\mathbb{P}(E) > 0.5$, and when evaluated on the input program P, $\mathbb{P}_P(E) = 0.4$. Then for every repaired program P' with $\mathbb{P}_{P'}(E) = 0.5 + \epsilon$, there may exist P'' that satisfies *post* with $\mathbb{P}_{P''}(E) = 0.5 + \frac{\epsilon}{2}$ and $Er(P, P'') = Er(P, P') - \frac{\epsilon}{2}$; the limit of this process could give us P^* with $\mathbb{P}_{P^*}(E) = 0.5$, but now P^* no longer satisfies *post*. To resolve this, we take P^* to be the infimum with respect to $Er(P, \cdot)$ of the set $\{P' \in R \mid \{pre\}P'\{post\}\}$. Since this P^* does not satisfy *post*, it is trivially not α-robust, and we rely on the result of Corollary 2.

The convergence of DIGITS relies on the existence of α-robust programs. Theorem 1—which follows directly from α-robustness—gives us a way to check, with high probability, whether any α-robust programs exist: we can run the algorithm for the number of iterations given by Theorem 1 for arbitrarily small δ and just see whether any solution for the program repair problem is found. If not, we can infer that with probability $1 - \delta$ no α-robust programs exist. The success of DIGITS in our evaluation (Sect. 6) suggests, as we might expect, that this would be a pathological case.

4.2 Efficient Search Strategy and Data Structure

The DIGITS algorithm is fairly abstract and opens many doors to optimizations. In this section, we present a concrete data structure for implementing DIGITS and show how it can be used to run the REPAIR algorithm on smaller inputs than with a naïve implementation.

We propose to use a binary trie of height n to describe all the possible ways to partition the set of samples $S = \{s_1, \ldots, s_n\}$ into two sets S^+ and S^-. In the trie, each node at depth i corresponds to splitting on the sample s_i; a 0-labeled edge (resp. 1-labeled edge) from depth i to depth $i+1$ denotes that, in this path, $s_i \in S^-$ (resp. $s_i \in S^+$).

We use $\{0,1\}^{\leq n}$ to denote the set of strings of length at most n over the alphabet $\{0,1\}$. A binary trie for a set of samples $S = \{s_1, \ldots, s_n\}$ is a function $f : \{0,1\}^{\leq n} \mapsto R \cup \{\bot\}$ that maps strings to repaired programs. Given a string $b = b_1 \ldots b_k \in \{0,1\}^{\leq n}$, let S_b^+ (resp. S_b^-) be the set of all $s_i \in S$ such that $b_i = true$ (resp. $b_i = false$). We define $f(b_1 \ldots b_k)$ as $\mathrm{REPAIR}(S_b^+, S_b^-)$.

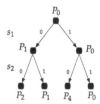

One of the many advantages of using this trie representation is that it allows us to dynamically increase the sample set size n without restarting the algorithm: whenever all strings of length at most n have been exhausted, simply sample an additional point and compute f for all strings of length $n+1$. Thus, instead of fixing the sample size a priori, the algorithm can run continuously, adding more samples as needed, until meeting some stopping criteria.

Fig. 4. Trie ex.

Example 3. Figure 4 shows a trie of height 2 for Example 1. Here only consider the samples s_1 and s_2. Each layer in the trie corresponds to a sample, and each node is assigned a candidate program consistent with the samples. For example, $f(0,1) = P_1$ is a program consistent with $S^+ = \{17\}$ and $S^- = \{12\}$. Note that P_1 is also consistent with $S^+ = \{\}$ and $S^- = \{12\}$, thus $f(0)$ can also be P_1.

Solution Propagation. Our first optimization builds on the idea illustrated at the end of Example 3 and propagates solutions down the trie, therefore reducing the number of times we call the function REPAIR and the average number of samples on which the function is called.

In the following we assume that the function REPAIR has the following property (this assumption simplifies our presentation, but does not affect convergence of our algorithm): given two sets of samples S^+, S^- and a new sample s, (i) if $\mathrm{REPAIR}(S^+, S^-) = P'$ and $P'(s) = true$, then $\mathrm{REPAIR}(S^+ \cup \{s\}, S^-) = P'$, and (ii) if $\mathrm{REPAIR}(S^+, S^-) = P'$ and $P'(s) = false$, then $\mathrm{REPAIR}(S^+, S^- \cup \{s\}) = P'$.

To compute the binary trie of height n, we also need to compute repairs for nodes $b_1 \ldots b_k$ such that $k < n$, and therefore it would seem we have to call the function REPAIR $2^{n+1} - 1$ times instead of the 2^n required by the DIGITS algorithm. The following theorem allows us to avoid this problem.

Theorem 2 (Solution propagation). *Given a string $b_1 \ldots b_k \in \{0,1\}^{\leq n}$ of length $k < n$, if $f(b_1 \ldots b_k) = P'$ and $P'(s_{k+1}) = b$, then $f(b_1 \ldots b_k b) = P'$.*

Informally, the above theorem states that the program corresponding to a certain node has to be already consistent with one of the two labeling of the following examples. Therefore, even though there are $2^{n+1} - 1$ nodes in the binary trie, we only need to call the function REPAIR for half of the 2^i nodes at depth i, or 2^n nodes total.

Additionally, the calls to REPAIR have fewer constraints: while the DIGITS algorithm as presented in Algorithm 1 always calls the function REPAIR on exactly n samples, when using the trie structure with solution propagation, REPAIR is called only on i samples at depth i. One can show that the average number of samples used by REPAIR asymptotically approaches $n - 1$.

Conflict-Driven Pruning. While solution propagation is a good strategy for reusing successful solutions, we can also learn from the instances in which REPAIR returns $\perp$. In particular, let's say that for some string $\boldsymbol{b} = b_1 \ldots b_k \in \{0,1\}^{\leq n}$, we have that $f(b_1 \ldots b_k) = \perp$. Trivially, we know that for every $b_1 \ldots b_k b_{k+1} \ldots b_{k+j} \in \{0,1\}^{\leq n}$ $f(b_1 \ldots b_k b_{k+1} \ldots b_{k+j}) = \perp$. Using this idea, we can prune the search and avoid calling the function REPAIR on partitions that are trivially going to fail. More generally, when a failure occurs, we can identify a subset of the labelings that caused the failure and use it to reduce the set of explored nodes.

Theorem 3 (Conflict-driven pruning). *Let $\boldsymbol{b} = b_1, \ldots, b_k$. Let $\boldsymbol{b}'$ be a subsequence of $\boldsymbol{b}$, e.g., $b_2 b_{10} b_{11} b_{20}$. If REPAIR$(S^+_{\boldsymbol{b}'}, S^-_{\boldsymbol{b}'}) = \perp$, then $f(b_1 \ldots b_k) = \perp$.*

While detecting what subsets of the samples caused the failure can be hard, this theorem can be used to vastly reduce the number of times the function REPAIR is called. In our implementation, we will use the *unsatisfiable cores* produced by the SMT solver to compute the subsets of the samples that induce failures.

5 Implementation

We implemented an instantiation of the DIGITS algorithm in Python. The DIGITS algorithm is abstract and modular. Therefore, to implement it we need to provide a number of components: a repair model R, the procedure REPAIR that produces programs consistent with labeled examples, and a probabilistic inference algorithm to (i) check whether the synthesized program respects the postcondition, (ii) compute the semantic difference between the synthesized program P' and the original program P. In this section, we describe the concrete choices of these components for our implementation.

Repair Model. Since we are mostly interested in repairing machine learning classifiers, a natural repair model R is only allowing modifications to real-valued constants appearing in the program. These constants are essentially the *weights* of the classifier.

Formally, let P be the program we are trying to repair, and let $c_1, \ldots, c_n$ be all of the constants appearing in P. For simplicity, assume all constants are different. Given constants $d_1, \ldots, d_k$, we write $P[c_1/d_1, \ldots, c_n/d_n]$ to denote the program in which each constant c_i has been replaced with the constant d_i. Finally, the set of allowed repairs is defined as

$$R = \{P[c_1/d_1, \ldots, c_n/d_n] \mid d_1, \ldots, d_n \in \mathbb{R}\}.$$

We only consider programs containing linear real arithmetic expressions. As such, our repair model can be viewed as a set of unions of polytopes with a bounded number of faces (bounded by the size of the program). It can be shown such polytopes have finite VC dimension [25], and therefore, so does our repair model.

Repair Implementation. The implementation of $\textsc{repair}(S^+, S^-)$ follows a sketch-like approach [26], where we encode the program and the samples as a formula whose solution is a *filling* of the *holes* defined by the repair model R.

Let P be the program we are trying to repair, and let $c_1, \ldots, c_n$ be all of the constants appearing in P, as discussed above. We will first create a new program $P_R = P[c_1/h_1, \ldots, c_n/h_n]$, where $h_1, \ldots, h_n$ are fresh variables that do not appear in P. We call h_i *holes*. We now encode the program P_R as a formula as follows, using the function $\textsc{enc}$. To simplify the encoding, and without loss of generality, we assume that P_R is in *static single assignment* (SSA) form.

$$\textsc{enc}(v \leftarrow E) \triangleq v = [\![E]\!] \qquad \textsc{enc}(P_1\ P_2) \triangleq \textsc{enc}(P_1) \wedge \textsc{enc}(P_2)$$
$$\textsc{enc}(\text{if } B \text{ then } P_1 \text{ else } P_2) \triangleq ([\![B]\!] \Rightarrow \textsc{enc}(P_1)) \wedge (\neg[\![B]\!] \Rightarrow \textsc{enc}(P_2))$$

where $[\![B]\!]$ is the denotation of an expression, which, in our setting, is a direct translation to a logical statement. For example, $[\![x + y > 0]\!] \triangleq x + y > 0$.

Once we have encoded the program P_R as a formula φ, for each sample $s_i \in S^+$, we will construct the formula

$$\varphi_i \triangleq \exists V. \varphi[\boldsymbol{v}_I/s_i] \wedge v_r = true$$

where V is the set of variables of P, which do not include the introduced holes $h_1, \ldots, h_n$. Similarly, for each sample $s_i \in S^-$, we will construct the formula

$$\varphi_i \triangleq \exists V. \varphi[\boldsymbol{v}_I/s_i] \wedge v_r = false$$

Finally, a model to the formula $\bigwedge_i \varphi_i$ is an assignment to the holes $h_1, \ldots, h_n$ that corresponds to a program in the repair model R that correctly labels the positive and negative examples. Specifically, $\textsc{repair}(S^+, S^-)$ finds a model $m \models \bigwedge_i \varphi_i$ and returns the program $P_R[h_1/m(h_1), \ldots, h_n/m(h_n)]$, where $m(h_i)$ is the value of h_i in the model m. If $\bigwedge_i \varphi_i$ is unsatisfiable, then $\textsc{repair}$ returns $\bot$.

Theorem 4 (Soundness and completeness of repair). *Suppose we are given a program P and the repair model R defined above, along with two sets of samples S^+ and S^-. Then, if REPAIR(S^+, S^-) returns a program P', P' must appear in R and correctly classifies S^+ and S^-. Otherwise, there is no program $P' \in R$ that correctly classifies S^+ and S^-.*

Probabilistic Inference. In our implementation, this component can be instantiated with any probabilistic inference tool—e.g., PSI [15]. We use the tool FairSquare [4], which is also written in Python and has already been used to verify fairness properties of decision-making programs. Moreover, unlike several other tools, the inference algorithm used in FairSquare is sound and complete and therefore meets the criteria of the DIGITS algorithm.

To speed up the search, we use sampling to approximate the probabilistic inference and quickly process obvious queries. At the end of the algorithm we use FairSquare to verify the output of DIGITS.

6   Evaluation

In this section, we evaluate the effectiveness of our algorithm on benchmarks obtained by training machine learning models on an online dataset [1]. First, we show that our algorithm can produce good repairs on many of the benchmarks. Second, we illustrate the efficacy of the optimizations discussed in Sect. 4.2.

Benchmarks. We used an online dataset [1] comprised of 14 demographic features for over 30,000 individuals to generate a number of classifiers and a probabilistic precondition. The precondition uses a graph structure represented as a probabilistic program: at each node, there is an inferred Gaussian distribution for a variable, and the edges of the graph induce correlations between variables.

We generated *support vector machines* with *linear kernels* (SVMs) and *decision trees* (DTs) to classify high- versus low-income individuals using the WEKA data mining software [2] until we obtained 3 SVMs and 3 DTs that did *not* satisfy a probabilistic postcondition describing group fairness. In particular, we used the following postcondition:

$$\frac{\mathbb{P}(\text{high income} \mid \text{female})}{\mathbb{P}(\text{high income} \mid \text{male})} \geq 0.85$$

The learned models are small and employ at most three features. Most of the generated models violated the postcondition because they were strongly influenced by a particular feature, *capital gain*, which was highly correlated with gender in the dataset.

The combined size of the precondition and decision-making program ranges from 20 to 100 lines of code. Though this is a much smaller scale than industrial applications of machine learning, the repair problems are highly non-trivial.

Effectiveness of Algorithm. Table 1 details the performance of DIGITS on our suite of benchmarks that were given 600 s to perform repair. For example, on the DT labeled DT_{16}, the table shows that in 584 s, DIGITS was able to enumerate all possible labelings for a set of 50 samples (the depth of the trie), and found a solution satisfying the postcondition that differs from the original program with probability 0.098. Despite the fact that there are $2^{50} \approx 10^{15}$ such labelings, DIGITS needed only to check 53,255 of these possibilities (nodes in the trie): among these possibilities, DIGITS calls REPAIR for just 1,903 of the labelings that have a consistent solution, avoiding 26,627 (93%) potential calls to REPAIR using solution propagation—each of these also avoids a call to the verification oracle. Additionally, DIGITS calls REPAIR for just 1,064 of the labelings that are inconsistent and return $\bot$, avoiding 23,661 (95%) potential calls to REPAIR that would also return $\bot$ using conflict-driven pruning.

It is visibly apparent that solution propagation and conflict-driven pruning save many synthesis and verification queries. However, savings from conflict-driven pruning are only possible once the depth of the search (the number of constraints) is large enough that many labelings are inconsistent—when the number of constraints exceeds the VC dimension of the repair model. Therefore, we expect the instances with a more expressive repair model to perform worse.

Accordingly, Table 1 includes multiple results for each of the SVMs, where the number of holes is varied: the SVMs compare an expression $c_0 + c_1 x_1 + c_2 x_2 + \dots$ to 0, where each c_i is replaced with a hole. The variants with fewer holes are

Table 1. Results of running DIGITS on benchmarks with a 600 s best-effort period. Solution propagation, conflict-driven pruning, and cost minimization are used for all.

Name	Holes	Result of DIGITS			Trie details				
		Samples	Time (s)	Sem. diff.	Nodes	Consistent	Soln. prop.	Incon.	Unsat pruned
DT_{16}	5	50	584	0.098	53,255	1,903	26,627	1,064	23,661
DT_{44}	3	91	553	0.03	68,051	1,741	34,025	418	31,867
DT_4	2	79	594	0.14	94,733	1,746	47,366	707	44,914
SVM_3	4	16	561	0.067	7,015	1,000	3,507	338	2,170
	3	23	587	0.0615	17,977	1,600	8,988	388	7,001
	2	91	582	0.0455	123,935	1,980	61,967	247	59,741
	1	661	599	0.0595	437,583	662	218,791	1,305	216,825
SVM_4	5	10	470	0.197	1,523	508	761	100	154
	4	13	507	0.204	4,599	1,018	2,299	205	1,077
	3	22	559	0.195	14,885	1,424	7,442	406	5,613
	2	83	598	0.04	92,495	1,674	46,247	217	44,357
	1	628	600	0.044	395,013	629	197,506	1,228	195,650
SVM_5	6	8	410	0.1305	507	240	253	11	3
	5	10	568	0.122	1,693	632	846	64	151
	4	13	559	0.1025	4,587	1,018	2,293	194	1,082
	3	23	575	0.096	15,361	1,348	7,680	332	6,001
	2	88	583	0.056	103,649	1,736	51,824	224	49,865
	1	598	599	0.067	358,203	599	179,101	1,176	177,327

generated by removing the holes for coefficients of x_i in increasing order of the mutual information between x_i and gender, as per the precondition. The last remaining hole allows only for the constant offset c_0 to be changed. The table illustrates the trade-off between expressivity and performance: though the instances with more holes have a strictly larger repair model and thus have the potential to contain solutions with better semantic difference, the search is slow, and the trie cannot enumerate as large a set of samples: the synthesis queries are over more variables and are more complex; more solutions are satisfiable, so conflict-driven pruning does not provide the same advantages. In general, as the number of holes decreases, the best solution has improving semantic difference because the trie is explored deeper. This trend continues until the only hole that remains is the constant offset, when the repair model is no longer expressive enough to capture solutions with such a minimal difference.

Optimizations. Running DIGITS as a trie allows solution propagation to avoid a synthesis query for half of all explored nodes; additionally, when the queries are performed, they are over smaller sets of constraints. Figure 5 (Left) illustrates for the benchmark DT_{44} the time saved by using the trie structure instead of explicitly enumerating the 2^n possible labelings for a sample set of size n: each point on the red line (labeled *without solution propagation*) indicates the amount of time necessary to explicitly compute the 2^n possibilities, while the blue line (labeled *with solution propagation*) denotes the total time of exploring the trie up to depth n. The plot illustrates that a run of DIGITS using the trie structure's solution propagation provides exponential savings in the size of the sample sets.

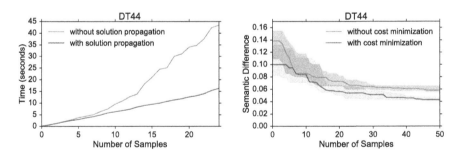

Fig. 5. (Left) efficiency of solution propagation; (Right) efficacy of cost heuristic and convergence of variance.

Syntactic Cost Minimization. Recall that our repair model consists of modifying the value of any real-valued constants in the program. As a heuristic to quickly guide the search to better solutions, we introduce a notion of the *syntactic cost* of a candidate repaired program. Specifically, if the original values of holes $h_1, \ldots, h_n$ are the values $c_1, \ldots, c_n$, then we compute the cost as $\sum_i \left| \frac{h_i - c_i}{c_i} \right|$; whenever we submit an SMT query for a set of constraints, we require that it approximately minimizes this cost function. The intuition is that since the behaviors of these programs are entirely determined by their constants' values, the amount that these values are changed is correlated with the semantic difference. Syntactic cost minimization is utilized in all our prior results.

Figure 5 (Right) contains the results of running DIGITS on DT_{44} for 20 different random seeds using cost minimization, and the same 20 different random seeds without using cost minimization. The solid lines denote the median value for the best semantic difference across the 20 runs as a function of the depth reached by the trie structure; the transparent region denotes the 90% confidence interval of the best semantic difference across all runs. It illustrates two concepts: first, that the use of the cost minimization heuristic allows for DIGITS to converge to better solutions faster. Second, it shows that while the variance between the best solutions across the different runs is high for a small number of samples, this variance decreases as the number of samples increases, suggesting DIGITS is robust with respect to the exact values of the sampled points.

7 Related Work

Program Repair and Synthesis. Automated repair has been studied in the non-probabilistic setting [10, 17, 20, 22, 27]. Closest to our work is the tool Qlose, which attempts to repair a program to match a set of test cases while attempting to minimize a mixture of syntactic and semantic distances between the original and repaired versions [10]. The approach in Qlose itself cannot be directly lifted to probabilistic programs and postconditions because it relies on a finite set of input-output examples—it finds candidates for repairs by making calls to an SMT solver with the hard constraint that the examples should be classified correctly. In our setting, the output of the optimal repair on the samples is not known a priori and our goal is to ultimately find a program that satisfies a probabilistic postcondition over an infinite set of inputs. Several of Qlose's general principles do carry over: namely, using a sketch-based approach [26] to fix portions of the code and minimizing semantic changes.

In probabilistic model checking, a number of works have addressed the model repair problem, e.g., [6, 9]. In this work, the idea is to modify transition probabilities in finite-state Markov Decision Processes to satisfy a probabilistic temporal property. Our setting is quite different, in that we are modifying a program manipulating real-valued variables to satisfy a probabilistic postcondition.

Our problem of repairing probabilistic programs is closely related to the synthesis of probabilistic programs. The technique of *smoothed proof search* [8] approximates a combination of functional correctness and maximization of an expected value as a smooth, continuous function. It then uses numerical methods to find a local optimum of this function, which translates to a synthesized program that is likely to be correct and locally maximal. Unlike our approach, smoothed proof search lacks formal convergence guarantees.

Stochastic Satisfiability. Our problem is closely related to, and subsumes, the problem of E-MAJSAT [21], a special case of *stochastic satisfiability*

(SSAT) [24] and a means for formalizing probabilistic planning problems. E-MAJSAT is of NP^{PP} complexity. In E-MAJSAT, a formula has two sets of propositional variables, a deterministic and a probabilistic set. The goal is to find an assignment of deterministic variables such that the probability that the formula is satisfied is above a given threshold. Our setting is similar, but we operate over formulas in linear real arithmetic and have an additional optimization objective stipulating semantic closeness. The deterministic variables in our setting are the holes defining the repair; the probabilistic variables are program inputs.

Algorithmic Fairness. Concerns of algorithmic fairness are recent, and there are many competing fairness definitions [11–14,16]. Approaches to enforcing fairness in machine-learned classifiers include altering the data to remove correlations with protected attributes [13] and imposing a fairness definition as a requirement of the learning algorithm [16]. However, the general problem presented in this paper of modifying an existing program (be it learned or manually constructed) to meet a quantitative probabilistic property is novel.

Acknowledgements. This material is based upon work supported by the National Science Foundation under Grant numbers 1566015 and 1652140.

A   Proofs

Proof of Lemma 1. We cite the seminal result from [7] that if a *well-behaved*[1] concept class C has VC dimension k, then for any $0 < \varepsilon, \delta < 1$ and sample size at least $\max\{\frac{4}{\varepsilon}\log_2 \frac{2}{\delta}, \frac{8k}{\varepsilon}\log_2 \frac{13}{\varepsilon}\}$ drawn from probability distribution $\mathcal{D}$ and labeled by their classification by the target concept $c^* \in C$, any concept $c \in C$ consistent with those samples has $error_{\mathcal{D}}(c) \leq \varepsilon$ with probability at least $1 - \delta$. Here, $error_{\mathcal{D}}(c)$ is the probability that a sample drawn from $\mathcal{D}$ is classified differently by c^* versus c.

Our program model satisfies the benign measure-theoretic restriction of *well-behavior* since it is equivalent to arbitrary collections of polytopes; therefore, for any $P' \in R$, some labeling of the $\geq \frac{4}{\varepsilon}\log_2 \frac{2}{\delta} + \frac{8k}{\varepsilon}\log_2 \frac{13}{\varepsilon}$ samples is consistent with P', and therefore the theorem from [7] applies.

Proof of Theorem 1. By Lemma 1, we know that with probability $\geq 1 - \delta$, one of the results $P' = \textsc{repair}(S^+, S^-)$ will have $Er(\hat{P}, P') \leq \varepsilon$. Since $(\hat{P}, post)$ is α-robust and $\varepsilon \leq \alpha$, then $P' \in B_\alpha(\hat{P})$, and so $\{pre\}P'\{post\}$ holds.

Proof of Corollary 1. This follows immediately from Theorem 1 by letting $\hat{P} = P^*$.

---

[1] See [7] Appendix 1 for a discussion of well-behaved concept classes.

Proof of Corollary 2. Observe that the Er function respects the triangle inequality, i.e. $Er(P_1, P_2) \leq Er(P_1, P_3) + Er(P_3, P_2)$.

$$
\begin{aligned}
Er(P_1, P_2) &= \mathbb{P}(P_1 \neq P_2) \\
&= \mathbb{P}(P_1 \neq P_2 \wedge P_1 \neq P_3) + \mathbb{P}(P_1 \neq P_2 \wedge P_3 = P_1) \\
&= \mathbb{P}(P_1 \neq P_2 \wedge P_1 \neq P_3) + \mathbb{P}(P_1 \neq P_2 \wedge P_3 \neq P_2) \\
&\leq \mathbb{P}(P_1 \neq P_3) + \mathbb{P}(P_3 \neq P_2) \\
&= Er(P_1, P_3) + Er(P_3, P_2)
\end{aligned}
$$

Thus if $\hat{P}$ is α-robust and $Er(P^*, \hat{P}) = \Delta$, we know P' has $Er(\hat{P}, P') \leq \varepsilon$ by Theorem 1, and the triangle inequality gives us that $Er(P^*, P') \leq \Delta + \varepsilon$.

Proof of Theorem 2. P' is consistent with the first $k + 1$ labeled samples if and only if it is consistent with the $k + 1$-th sample as well as the first k samples.

Proof of Theorem 3. Assume towards a contradiction that $f(b_1 \ldots b_k) \neq \perp$, but a subsequence b' has REPAIR$(S_{b'}^+, S_{b'}^-) = \perp$. Then *adding* constraints, which reduces the set of solutions, *introduced* a new solution.

References

1. UCI machine learning repository: Census income. https://archive.ics.uci.edu/ml/datasets/Adult/
2. Weka. http://www.cs.waikato.ac.nz/ml/weka/
3. Code of federal regulations, July 2014. https://www.gpo.gov/fdsys/pkg/CFR-2014-title29-vol4/xml/CFR-2014-title29-vol4-part1607.xml. Accessed 18 June 2016
4. Albarghouthi, A., D'Antoni, L., Drews, S., Nori, A.: Fairness as a program property. In: FATML, November 2016. http://pages.cs.wisc.edu/sdrews/papers/fatml16.pdf
5. Angwin, J., Larson, J., Mattu, S., Kirchner, L.: Machine bias: there's software used across the country to predict future criminals. And it's biased against blacks, May 2016. https://www.propublica.org/article/machine-bias-risk-assessments-in-criminal-sentencing. Accessed 18 June 2016
6. Bartocci, E., Grosu, R., Katsaros, P., Ramakrishnan, C.R., Smolka, S.A.: Model repair for probabilistic systems. In: Abdulla, P.A., Leino, K.R.M. (eds.) TACAS 2011. LNCS, vol. 6605, pp. 326–340. Springer, Heidelberg (2011). doi:10.1007/978-3-642-19835-9_30
7. Blumer, A., Ehrenfeucht, A., Haussler, D., Warmuth, M.K.: Learnability and the vapnik-chervonenkis dimension. J. ACM (JACM) **36**(4), 929–965 (1989)
8. Chaudhuri, S., Clochard, M., Solar-Lezama, A.: Bridging boolean and quantitative synthesis using smoothed proof search. In: POPL, vol. 49, pp. 207–220. ACM (2014)
9. Chen, T., Hahn, E.M., Han, T., Kwiatkowska, M., Qu, H., Zhang, L.: Model repair for markov decision processes. In: 2013 International Symposium on Theoretical Aspects of Software Engineering (TASE), pp. 85–92. IEEE (2013)
10. D'Antoni, L., Samanta, R., Singh, R.: QLOSE: program repair with quantitative objectives. In: Chaudhuri, S., Farzan, A. (eds.) CAV 2016. LNCS, vol. 9780, pp. 383–401. Springer, Cham (2016). doi:10.1007/978-3-319-41540-6_21

11. Datta, A., Sen, S., Zick, Y.: Algorithmic transparency via quantitative input influence. In: Proceedings of 37th IEEE Symposium on Security and Privacy (2016)
12. Dwork, C., Hardt, M., Pitassi, T., Reingold, O., Zemel, R.S.: Fairness through awareness. In: Innovations in Theoretical Computer Science 2012, Cambridge, MA, USA, 8–10 January 2012, pp. 214–226 (2012)
13. Feldman, M., Friedler, S.A., Moeller, J., Scheidegger, C., Venkatasubramanian, S.: Certifying and removing disparate impact. In: Proceedings of the 21th ACM SIGKDD International Conference on Knowledge Discovery and Data Mining, Sydney, NSW, Australia, 10–13 August 2015, pp. 259–268 (2015). http://doi.acm.org/10.1145/2783258.2783311
14. Friedler, S.A., Scheidegger, C., Venkatasubramanian, S.: On the (im)possibility of fairness. CoRR abs/1609.07236 (2016). http://arxiv.org/abs/1609.07236
15. Gehr, T., Misailovic, S., Vechev, M.: PSI: exact symbolic inference for probabilistic programs. In: Chaudhuri, S., Farzan, A. (eds.) CAV 2016. LNCS, vol. 9779, pp. 62–83. Springer, Cham (2016). doi:10.1007/978-3-319-41528-4_4
16. Hardt, M., Price, E., Srebro, N.: Equality of opportunity in supervised learning. CoRR abs/1610.02413 (2016). http://arxiv.org/abs/1610.02413
17. Jobstmann, B., Griesmayer, A., Bloem, R.: Program repair as a game. In: Etessami, K., Rajamani, S.K. (eds.) CAV 2005. LNCS, vol. 3576, pp. 226–238. Springer, Heidelberg (2005). doi:10.1007/11513988_23
18. Kearns, M.J., Vazirani, U.V.: An Introduction to Computational Learning Theory. MIT press, Cambridge (1994)
19. Kobie, N.: Who do you blame when an algorithm gets you fired?, January 2016. http://www.wired.co.uk/article/make-algorithms-accountable. Accessed 18 June 2016
20. Könighofer, R., Bloem, R.: Automated error localization and correction for imperative programs. In: Formal Methods in Computer-Aided Design (FMCAD 2011), pp. 91–100. IEEE (2011)
21. Littman, M.L., Goldsmith, J., Mundhenk, M.: The computational complexity of probabilistic planning. J. Artif. Intell. Res. 9(1), 1–36 (1998)
22. Mechtaev, S., Yi, J., Roychoudhury, A.: Directfix: looking for simple program repairs. In: Proceedings of the 37th International Conference on Software Engineering, vol. 1, pp. 448–458. IEEE Press (2015)
23. Miller, C.C.: When algorithms discriminate, July 2015. http://www.nytimes.com/2015/07/10/upshot/when-algorithms-discriminate.html?_r=0. Accessed 18 June 2016
24. Papadimitriou, C.H.: Games against nature. J. Comput. Syst. Sci. 31(2), 288–301 (1985)
25. Sharma, R., Nori, A.V., Aiken, A.: Bias-variance tradeoffs in program analysis. In: Proceedings of the 41st ACM SIGPLAN-SIGACT Symposium on Principles of Programming Languages, POPL 2014, NY, USA, pp. 127–137 (2014). http://doi.acm.org/10.1145/2535838.2535853
26. Solar-Lezama, A.: Program synthesis by sketching. Ph.D. thesis, University of California, Berkeley (2008)
27. Von Essen, C., Jobstmann, B.: Program repair without regret. Formal Methods Syst. Des. 47(1), 26–50 (2015)

Value Iteration for Long-Run Average Reward in Markov Decision Processes

Pranav Ashok[1], Krishnendu Chatterjee[2], Przemysław Daca[2],
Jan Křetínský[1(✉)], and Tobias Meggendorfer[1]

[1] Technical University of Munich, Munich, Germany
jan.kretinsky@gmail.com
[2] IST Austria, Klosterneuburg, Austria

Abstract. Markov decision processes (MDPs) are standard models for probabilistic systems with non-deterministic behaviours. Long-run average rewards provide a mathematically elegant formalism for expressing long term performance. Value iteration (VI) is one of the simplest and most efficient algorithmic approaches to MDPs with other properties, such as reachability objectives. Unfortunately, a naive extension of VI does not work for MDPs with long-run average rewards, as there is no known stopping criterion. In this work our contributions are threefold. (1) We refute a conjecture related to stopping criteria for MDPs with long-run average rewards. (2) We present two practical algorithms for MDPs with long-run average rewards based on VI. First, we show that a combination of applying VI locally for each maximal end-component (MEC) and VI for reachability objectives can provide approximation guarantees. Second, extending the above approach with a simulation-guided on-demand variant of VI, we present an anytime algorithm that is able to deal with very large models. (3) Finally, we present experimental results showing that our methods significantly outperform the standard approaches on several benchmarks.

1 Introduction

The analysis of probabilistic systems arises in diverse application contexts of computer science, e.g. analysis of randomized communication and security protocols, stochastic distributed systems, biological systems, and robot planning, to name a few. The standard model for the analysis of probabilistic systems that exhibit both probabilistic and non-deterministic behaviour are *Markov decision processes (MDPs)* [How60,FV97,Put94]. An MDP consists of a finite set of states, a finite set of actions, representing the non-deterministic choices, and

---

This work is partially supported by the Vienna Science and Technology Fund (WWTF) ICT15-003, the Austrian Science Fund (FWF) NFN grant No. S11407-N23 (RiSE/SHiNE), the ERC Starting grant (279307: Graph Games), the German Research Foundation (DFG) project "Verified Model Checkers", the TUM International Graduate School of Science and Engineering (IGSSE) project PARSEC, and the Czech Science Foundation grant No. 15-17564S.

© Springer International Publishing AG 2017
R. Majumdar and V. Kunčak (Eds.): CAV 2017, Part I, LNCS 10426, pp. 201–221, 2017.
DOI: 10.1007/978-3-319-63387-9_10

a transition function that given a state and an action gives the probability distribution over the successor states. In verification, MDPs are used as models for e.g. concurrent probabilistic systems [CY95] or probabilistic systems operating in open environments [Seg95], and are applied in a wide range of applications [BK08, KNP11].

Long-Run Average Reward. A *payoff* function in an MDP maps every infinite path (infinite sequence of state-action pairs) to a real value. One of the most well-studied and mathematically elegant payoff functions is the *long-run average reward* (also known as *mean-payoff* or *limit-average reward, steady-state reward* or simply *average reward*), where every state-action pair is assigned a real-valued reward, and the payoff of an infinite path is the long-run average of the rewards on the path [FV97, Put94]. Beyond the elegance, the long-run average reward is standard to model performance properties, such as the average delay between requests and corresponding grants, average rate of a particular event, etc. Therefore, determining the maximal or minimal expected long-run average reward of an MDP is a basic and fundamental problem in the quantitative analysis of probabilistic systems.

Classical Algorithms. A *strategy* (also known as *policy* or *scheduler*) in an MDP specifies how the non-deterministic choices of actions are resolved in every state. The *value* at a state is the maximal expected payoff that can be guaranteed among all strategies. The values of states in MDPs with payoff defined as the long-run average reward can be computed in polynomial-time using linear programming [FV97, Put94]. The corresponding linear program is quite involved though. The number of variables is proportional to the number of state-action pairs and the overall size of the program is linear in the number of transitions (hence potentially quadratic in the number of actions). While the linear programming approach gives a polynomial-time solution, it is quite slow in practice and does not scale to larger MDPs. Besides linear programming, other techniques are considered for MDPs, such as dynamic-programming through strategy iteration or value iteration [Put94, Chap. 9].

Value Iteration. A generic approach that works very well in practice for MDPs with other payoff functions is *value iteration (VI)*. Intuitively, a particular one-step operator is applied iteratively and the crux is to show that this iterative computation converges to the correct solution (i.e. the value). The key advantages of VI are the following:

1. *Simplicity.* VI provides a very simple and intuitive dynamic-programming algorithm which is easy to adapt and extend.
2. *Efficiency.* For several other payoff functions, such as finite-horizon rewards (instantaneous or cumulative reward) or reachability objectives, applying the concept of VI yields a very efficient solution method. In fact, in most well-known tools such as PRISM [KNP11], value iteration performs much better than linear programming methods for reachability objectives.

3. *Scalability.* The simplicity and flexibility of VI allows for several improvements and adaptations of the idea, further increasing its performance and
enabling quick processing of very large MDPs. For example, when considering
reachability objectives, [PGT03] present point-based value-iteration (PBVI),
applying the iteration operator only to a part of the state space, and [MLG05]
introduce bounded real-time dynamic programming (BRTDP), where again
only a fraction of the state space is explored based on partial strategies.
Both of these approaches are simulation-guided, where simulations are used
to decide how to explore the state space. The difference is that the former
follows an offline computation, while the latter is online. Both scale well to
large MDPs and use VI as the basic idea to build upon.

Value Iteration for Long-Run Average Reward. While VI is standard for reachability objectives or finite-horizon rewards, it does not work for general MDPs
with long-run average reward. The two key problems pointed out in [Put94,
Sects. 8.5, 9.4] are as follows: (a) if the MDP has some periodicity property,
then VI does not converge; and (b) for general MDPs there are neither bounds
on the speed of convergence nor stopping criteria to determine when the iteration can be stopped to guarantee approximation of the value. The first problem
can be handled by adding self-loop transitions [Put94, Sect. 8.5.4]. However, the
second problem is conceptually more challenging, and a solution is conjectured
in [Put94, Sect. 9.4.2].

Our Contribution. In this work, our contributions are related to value iteration
for MDPs with long-run average reward, they range from conceptual clarification
to practical algorithms and experimental results. The details of our contributions
are as follows.

- *Conceptual clarification.* We first present an example to refute the conjecture
  of [Put94, Sect. 9.4.2], showing that the approach proposed there does not
  suffice for VI on MDPs with long-run average reward.
- *Practical approaches.* We develop, in two steps, practical algorithms instantiating VI for approximating values in MDPs with long-run average reward.
  Our algorithms take advantage of the notion of maximal end-components
  (MECs) in MDPs. Intuitively, MECs for MDPs are conceptually similar to
  strongly connected components (SCCs) for graphs and recurrent classes for
  Markov chains. We exploit these MECs to arrive at our two methods:
  1. The first variant applies VI locally to each MEC in order to obtain an
     approximation of the values within the MEC. After the approximation in
     every MEC, we apply VI to solve a reachability problem in a modified
     MDP with collapsed MECs. We show that this simple combination of VI
     approaches ensures guarantees on the approximation of the value.
  2. We then build on the approach above to present a simulation-guided
     variant of VI. In this case, the approximation of values for each MEC
     and the reachability objectives are done at the same time using VI. For
     the reachability objective a BRDTP-style VI (similar to [BCC+14]) is

applied, and within MECs VI is applied on-demand (i.e. only when there is a requirement for more precise value bounds). The resulting algorithm furthermore is an *anytime* algorithm, i.e. it can be stopped at any time and give an upper and lower bounds on the result.

- *Experimental results.* We compare our new algorithms to the state-of-the-art tool MultiGain [BCFK15] on various models. The experiments show that MultiGain is vastly outperformed by our methods on nearly every model. Furthermore, we compare several variants of our methods and investigate the different domains of applicability.

In summary, we present the first instantiation of VI for general MDPs with long-run average reward. Moreover, we extend it with a simulation-based approach to obtain an efficient algorithm for large MDPs. Finally, we present experimental results demonstrating that these methods provide significant improvements over existing ones.

Further Related Work. There is a number of techniques to compute or approximate the long-run average reward in MDPs [Put94, How60, Vei66], ranging from linear programming to value iteration to strategy iteration. Symbolic and explicit techniques based on strategy iteration are combined in [WBB+10]. Further, the more general problem of MDPs with multiple long-run average rewards was first considered in [Cha07], a complete picture was presented in [BBC+14, CKK15] and partially implemented in [BCFK15]. The extension of our approach to multiple long-run average rewards, or combination of expectation and variance [BCFK13], are interesting directions for future work. Finally, VI for MDPs with guarantees for reachability objectives was considered in [BCC+14, HM14].

Proofs and supplementary material can be found in [ACD+17].

2   Preliminaries

2.1   Markov Decision Processes

A *probability distribution* on a finite set X is a mapping $\rho : X \mapsto [0,1]$, such that $\sum_{x \in X} \rho(x) = 1$. We denote by $\mathcal{D}(X)$ the set of all probability distributions on X. Further, the *support* of a probability distribution ρ is denoted by $\mathrm{supp}(\rho) = \{x \in X \mid \rho(x) > 0\}$.

Definition 1 (MDP). *A* Markov decision processes (MDP) *is a tuple of the form* $\mathcal{M} = (S, s_{init}, Act, \mathsf{Av}, \Delta, r)$, *where* S *is a finite set of* states, $s_{init} \in S$ *is the* initial *state,* Act *is a finite set of* actions, $\mathsf{Av} : S \to 2^{Act}$ *assigns to every state a set of* available *actions,* $\Delta : S \times Act \to \mathcal{D}(S)$ *is a transition function that given a state* s *and an action* $a \in \mathsf{Av}(s)$ *yields a probability distribution over successor states, and* $r : S \times Act \to \mathbb{R}^{\geq 0}$ *is a reward function, assigning rewards to state-action pairs.*

For ease of notation, we write $\Delta(s, a, s')$ instead of $\Delta(s, a)(s')$.

An *infinite path* ρ in an MDP is an infinite word $\rho = s_0 a_0 s_1 a_1 \cdots \in (S \times Act)^\omega$, such that for every $i \in \mathbb{N}$, $a_i \in \mathsf{Av}(s_i)$ and $\Delta(s_i, a_i, s_{i+1}) > 0$. A *finite path* $w = s_0 a_0 s_1 a_1 \ldots s_n \in (S \times Act)^* \times S$ is a finite prefix of an infinite path.

A *strategy* on an MDP is a function $\pi : (S \times Act)^* \times S \to \mathcal{D}(Act)$, which given a finite path $w = s_0 a_0 s_1 a_1 \ldots s_n$ yields a probability distribution $\pi(w) \in \mathcal{D}(\mathsf{Av}(s_n))$ on the actions to be taken next. We call a strategy *memoryless randomized* (or *stationary*) if it is of the form $\pi : S \to \mathcal{D}(Act)$, and *memoryless deterministic* (or *positional*) if it is of the form $\pi : S \to Act$. We denote the set of all strategies of an MDP by Π, and the set of all memoryless deterministic strategies by Π^{MD}. Fixing a strategy π and an initial state s on an MDP $\mathcal{M}$ gives a unique probability measure $\mathbb{P}^\pi_{\mathcal{M},s}$ over infinite paths [Put94, Sect. 2.1.6]. The expected value of a random variable F is defined as $\mathbb{E}^\pi_{\mathcal{M},s}[F] = \int F \, d\mathbb{P}^\pi_{\mathcal{M},s}$. When the MDP is clear from the context, we drop the corresponding subscript and write $\mathbb{P}^\pi_s$ and $\mathbb{E}^\pi_s$ instead of $\mathbb{P}^\pi_{\mathcal{M},s}$ and $\mathbb{E}^\pi_{\mathcal{M},s}$, respectively.

End Components. A pair (T, A), where $\emptyset \neq T \subseteq S$ and $\emptyset \neq A \subseteq \bigcup_{s \in T} \mathsf{Av}(s)$, is an *end component* of an MDP $\mathcal{M}$ if (i) for all $s \in T, a \in A \cap \mathsf{Av}(s)$ we have $\mathrm{supp}(\Delta(s, a)) \subseteq T$, and (ii) for all $s, s' \in T$ there is a finite path $w = s a_0 \ldots a_n s' \in (T \times A)^* \times T$, i.e. w starts in s, ends in s', stays inside T and only uses actions in A.[1] Intuitively, an end component describes a set of states for which a particular strategy exists such that all possible paths remain inside these states and all of those states are visited infinitely often almost surely. An end component (T, A) is a *maximal end component (MEC)* if there is no other end component (T', A') such that $T \subseteq T'$ and $A \subseteq A'$. Given an MDP $\mathcal{M}$, the set of its MECs is denoted by $\mathsf{MEC}(\mathcal{M})$. With these definitions, every state of an MDP belongs to at most one MEC and each MDP has at least one MEC.

Using the concept of MECs, we recall the standard notion of a *MEC quotient* [dA97]. To obtain this quotient, all MECs are merged into a single representative state, while transitions between MECs are preserved. Intuitively, this abstracts the MDP to its essential infinite time behaviour.

Definition 2 (MEC quotient [dA97]). *Let $\mathcal{M} = (S, s_{init}, Act, \mathsf{Av}, \Delta, r)$ be an MDP with MECs $\mathsf{MEC}(\mathcal{M}) = \{(T_1, A_1), \ldots, (T_n, A_n)\}$. Further, define $\mathsf{MEC}_S = \bigcup_{i=1}^n T_i$ as the set of all states contained in some MEC. The MEC quotient of $\mathcal{M}$ is defined as the MDP $\widehat{\mathcal{M}} = (\widehat{S}, \widehat{s}_{init}, \widehat{Act}, \widehat{\mathsf{Av}}, \widehat{\Delta}, \widehat{r})$, where:*

- $\widehat{S} = S \setminus \mathsf{MEC}_S \cup \{\widehat{s}_1, \ldots, \widehat{s}_n\}$,
- *if for some T_i we have $s_{init} \in T_i$, then $\widehat{s}_{init} = \widehat{s}_i$, otherwise $\widehat{s}_{init} = s_{init}$,*
- $\widehat{Act} = \{(s, a) \mid s \in S, a \in \mathsf{Av}(s)\}$,

---

[1] This standard definition assumes that actions are unique for each state, i.e. $\mathsf{Av}(s) \cap \mathsf{Av}(s') = \emptyset$ for $s \neq s'$. The usual procedure of achieving this in general is to replace Act by $S \times Act$ and adapting Av, Δ, and r appropriately.

– *the available actions* $\widehat{\mathsf{Av}}$ *are defined as*

$$\forall s \in S \setminus \mathsf{MEC}_S.\ \widehat{\mathsf{Av}}(s) = \{(s,a) \mid a \in \mathsf{Av}(s)\}$$
$$\forall 1 \le i \le n.\ \widehat{\mathsf{Av}}(\widehat{s}_i) = \{(s,a) \mid s \in T_i \wedge a \in \mathsf{Av}(s) \setminus A_i\},$$

– *the transition function* $\widehat{\Delta}$ *is defined as follows. Let* $\widehat{s} \in \widehat{S}$ *be some state in the quotient and* $(s,a) \in \mathsf{Av}(\widehat{s})$ *an action available in* $\widehat{s}$. *Then*

$$\widehat{\Delta}(\widehat{s},(s,a),\widehat{s}') = \begin{cases} \sum_{s' \in T_j} \Delta(s,a,s') & if\,\widehat{s}' = \widehat{s}_j, \\ \Delta(s,a,\widehat{s}') & otherwise,\,i.e.\ \widehat{s}' \in S \setminus \mathsf{MEC}_S. \end{cases}$$

For the sake of readability, we omit the added self-loop transitions of the form $\Delta(\widehat{s}_i,(s,a),\widehat{s}_i)$ *with* $s \in T_i$ *and* $a \in A_i$ *from all figures.*
– *Finally, for* $\widehat{s} \in \widehat{S}$, $(s,a) \in \widehat{\mathsf{Av}}(\widehat{s})$, *we define* $\widehat{r}(s,(s,a)) = r(s,a)$.

Furthermore, we refer to $\widehat{s}_1, \ldots, \widehat{s}_n$ *as* collapsed states *and identify them with the corresponding MECs.*

Example 1. Figure 1a shows an MDP with three MECs, $\widehat{A} = (\{s_2\}, \{a\}), \widehat{B} = (\{s_3, s_4\}, \{a\}), \widehat{C} = (\{s_5, s_6\}, \{a\}))$. Its MEC quotient is shown in Fig. 1b.   △

Remark 1. In general, the MEC quotient does not induce a DAG-structure, since there might be probabilistic transitions between MECs. Consider for example the MDP obtained by setting $\Delta(s_2, b, s_4) = \{s_1 \mapsto \frac{1}{2}, s_2 \mapsto \frac{1}{2}\}$ in the MDP of Fig. 1a. Its MEC quotient then has $\widehat{\Delta}(\widehat{A}, (s_2, b)) = \{s_1 \mapsto \frac{1}{2}, \widehat{B} \mapsto \frac{1}{2}\}$.

Remark 2. The MEC decomposition of an MDP $\mathcal{M}$, i.e. the computation of $\mathsf{MEC}(\mathcal{M})$, can be achieved in polynomial time [CY95]. For improved algorithms on general MDPs and various special cases see [CH11, CH12, CH14, CL13].

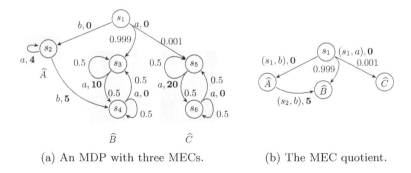

(a) An MDP with three MECs.   (b) The MEC quotient.

Fig. 1. An example of how the MEC quotient is constructed. By $a, \mathbf{r}$ we denote that the action a yields a reward of $\mathbf{r}$.

Definition 3 (MEC restricted MDP). *Let $\mathcal{M}$ be an MDP and $(T, A) \in$ MEC$(\mathcal{M})$ a MEC of $\mathcal{M}$. By picking some initial state $s'_{init} \in T$, we obtain the restricted MDP $\mathcal{M}' = (T, s'_{init}, A, \mathsf{Av}', \Delta', r')$ where*

- $\mathsf{Av}'(s) = \mathsf{Av}(s) \cap A$ *for $s \in T$,*
- $\Delta'(s, a, s') = \Delta(s, a, s')$ *for $s, s' \in T$, $a \in A$, and*
- $r'(s, a) = r(s, a)$ *for $s \in T$, $a \in A$.*

Classification of MDPs. If for some MDP $\mathcal{M}$, (S, Act) is a MEC, we call the MDP *strongly connected*. If it contains a single MEC plus potentially some transient states, it is called *(weakly) communicating*. Otherwise, it is called *multichain* [Put94, Sect. 8.3].

For a Markov chain, let $\Delta^n(s, s')$ denote the probability of going from the state s to state s' in n steps. The *period p of a pair s, s'* is the greatest common divisor of all n's with $\Delta^n(s, s') > 0$. The pair s, s' is called *periodic* if $p > 1$ and *aperiodic* otherwise. A Markov chain is called aperiodic if all pairs s, s' are aperiodic, otherwise the chain is called periodic. Similarly, an MDP is called aperiodic if every memoryless randomized strategy induces an aperiodic Markov chain, otherwise the MDP is called periodic.

Long-Run Average Reward. In this work, we consider the (maximum) *long-run average reward* (or *mean-payoff*) of an MDP, which intuitively describes the (maximum) average reward per step we expect to see when simulating the MDP for time going to infinity. Formally, let R_i be a random variable, which for an infinite path $\rho = s_0 a_0 s_1 a_1 \ldots$ returns $R_i(\rho) = r(s_i, a_i)$, i.e. the reward observed at step $i \geq 0$. Given a strategy π, the n-step average reward then is

$$v_n^\pi(s) := \mathbb{E}_s^\pi \left(\frac{1}{n} \sum_{i=0}^{n-1} R_i \right),$$

and the *long-run average reward* of the strategy π is

$$v^\pi(s) := \liminf_{n \to \infty} v_n^\pi.$$

The $\liminf$ is used in the definition, since the limit may not exist in general for an arbitrary strategy. Nevertheless, for finite MDPs the optimal limit-inferior (also called the *value*) is attained by some memoryless deterministic strategy $\pi^* \in \Pi^{\mathsf{MD}}$ and is in fact the limit [Put94, Theorem 8.1.2].

$$v(s) := \sup_{\pi \in \Pi} \liminf_{n \to \infty} \mathbb{E}_s^\pi \left(\frac{1}{n} \sum_{i=0}^{n-1} R_i \right) = \sup_{\pi \in \Pi} v^\pi(s) = \max_{\pi \in \Pi^{\mathsf{MD}}} v^\pi(s) = \lim_{n \to \infty} v_n^{\pi^*}.$$

An alternative well-known characterization we use in this paper is

$$v(s) = \max_{\pi \in \Pi^{\mathsf{MD}}} \sum_{M \in \mathsf{MEC}} \mathbb{P}_s^\pi [\Diamond \Box M] \cdot v(M), \tag{1}$$

where $\Diamond \Box M$ denotes the set of paths that eventually remain forever within M and $v(M)$ is the unique value achievable in the MDP restricted to the MEC M. Note that $v(M)$ does not depend on the initial state chosen for the restriction.

Algorithm 1. VALUEITERATION

Input: MDP $\mathcal{M} = (S, s_{\text{init}}, Act, \text{Av}, \Delta, r)$, precision $\varepsilon > 0$
Output: w, s.t. $|w - v(s_{\text{init}})| < \varepsilon$
1: $t_0(\cdot) \leftarrow 0$, $n \leftarrow 0$.
2: **while** stopping criterion not met **do**
3:     $n \leftarrow n + 1$
4:     **for** $s \in S$ **do**
5:         $t_n(s) = \max_{a \in \text{Av}(s)} \left(r(s, a) + \sum_{s' \in S} \Delta(s, a, s') t_{n-1}(s') \right)$
6: **return** $\frac{1}{n} t_n(s_{\text{init}})$

---

3   Value Iteration Solutions

3.1   Naive Value Iteration

Value iteration is a dynamic-programming technique applicable in many contexts. It is based on the idea of repetitively updating an approximation of the value for each state using the previous approximates until the outcome is precise enough. The standard value iteration for average reward [Put94, Sect. 8.5.1] is shown in Algorithm 1.

First, the algorithm sets $t_0(s) = 0$ for every $s \in S$. Then, in the inner loop, the value t_n is computed from the value of t_{n-1} by choosing the action which maximizes the expected reward plus successor values. This way, t_n in fact describes the optimal *expected n-step total reward*

$$t_n(s) = \max_{\pi \in \Pi^{\text{MD}}} \mathbb{E}_s^\pi \left(\sum_{i=0}^{n-1} R_i \right) = n \cdot \max_{\pi \in \Pi^{\text{MD}}} v_n^\pi(s).$$

Moreover, t_n approximates the n-multiple of the long-run average reward.

Theorem 1 [Put94, Theorem 9.4.1]. *For any MDP $\mathcal{M}$ and any $s \in S$ we have* $\lim_{n \to \infty} \frac{1}{n} t_n(s) = v(s)$ *for t_n obtained by Algorithm 1.*

Stopping Criteria. The convergence property of Theorem 1 is not enough to make the algorithm practical, since it is not known when to stop the approximation process in general. For this reason, we discuss stopping criteria which describe when it is safe to do so. More precisely, for a chosen $\varepsilon > 0$ the stopping criterion guarantees that when it is met, we can provide a value w that is ε-close to the average reward $v(s_{\text{init}})$.

We recall a stopping criterion for communicating MDPs defined and proven correct in [Put94, Sect. 9.5.3]. Note that in a communicating MDP, all states have the same average reward, which we simply denote by v. For ease of notation, we enumerate the states of the MDP $S = \{s_1, \ldots, s_n\}$ and treat the function t_n as a vector of values $\boldsymbol{t}_n = (t_n(s_1), \ldots, t_n(s_n))$. Further, we define the relative difference of the value iteration iterates as $\boldsymbol{\Delta}_n := \boldsymbol{t}_n - \boldsymbol{t}_{n-1}$ and introduce the *span semi-norm*, which is defined as the difference between the maximum and minimum element of a vector $\boldsymbol{w}$

$$\mathrm{sp}(\boldsymbol{w}) = \max_{s \in S} \boldsymbol{w}(s) - \min_{s \in S} \boldsymbol{w}(s).$$

The stopping criterion then is given by the condition

$$\mathrm{sp}(\boldsymbol{\Delta}_n) < \varepsilon. \tag{SC1}$$

When the criterion (SC1) is satisfied we have that

$$|\boldsymbol{\Delta}_n(s) - v| < \varepsilon \qquad \forall s \in S. \tag{2}$$

Moreover, we know that for communicating aperiodic MDPs the criterion (SC1) is satisfied after finitely many steps of Algorithm 1 [Put94, Theorem 8.5.2]. Furthermore, periodic MDPs can be transformed into aperiodic without affecting the average reward. The transformation works by introducing a self-loop on each state and adapting the rewards accordingly [Put94, Sect. 8.5.4]. Although this transformation may slow down VI, convergence can now be guaranteed and we can obtain ε-optimal values for any communicating MDP.

The intuition behind this stopping criterion can be explained as follows. When the computed span norm is small, $\boldsymbol{\Delta}_n$ contains nearly the same value in each component. This means that the difference between the expected $(n-1)$-step and n-step total reward is roughly the same in each state. Since in each state the n-step total reward is greedily optimized, there is no possibility of getting more than this difference per step.

Unfortunately, this stopping criterion cannot be applied on general MDPs, as it relies on the fact that all states have the same value, which is not true in general. Consider for example the MDP of Fig. 1a. There, we have that $v(s_5) = v(s_6) = 10$ but $v(s_3) = v(s_4) = 5$.

In [Put94, Sect. 9.4.2], it is conjectured that the following criterion may be applicable to general MDPs:

$$\mathrm{sp}(\boldsymbol{\Delta}_{n-1}) - \mathrm{sp}(\boldsymbol{\Delta}_n) < \varepsilon. \tag{SC2}$$

This stopping criterion requires that the difference of spans becomes small enough. While investigating the problem, we also conjectured a slight variation:

$$||\boldsymbol{\Delta}_n - \boldsymbol{\Delta}_{n-1}||_\infty < \varepsilon, \tag{SC3}$$

where $||\boldsymbol{w}||_\infty = \max_{s \in S} \boldsymbol{w}(s)$. Intuitively, both of these criteria try to extend the intuition of the communicating criterion to general MDPs, i.e. to require that in each state the reward gained per step stabilizes. Example 2 however demonstrates that neither (SC2) nor (SC3) is a valid stopping criterion.

Example 2. Consider the (aperiodic communicating) MDP in Fig. 2 with a parametrized reward value $\alpha \geq 0$. The optimal average reward is $v = \alpha$. But the first three vectors computed by value iteration are $\boldsymbol{t}_0 = (0,0), \boldsymbol{t}_1 = (0.9 \cdot \alpha, \alpha)$,

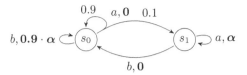

Fig. 2. A communicating MDP parametrized by the value α.

$t_2 = (1.8 \cdot \alpha, 2 \cdot \alpha)$. Thus, the values of $\mathbf{\Delta}_1 = \mathbf{\Delta}_2 = (0.9 \cdot \alpha, \alpha)$ coincide, which means that for every choice of ε both stopping criteria (SC2) and (SC3) are satisfied by the third iteration. However, by increasing the value of α we can make the difference between the average reward v and $\mathbf{\Delta}_2$ arbitrary large, so no guarantee like in Eq. (2) is possible.   △

3.2   Local Value Iteration

In order to remedy the lack of stopping criteria, we provide a modification of VI using MEC decomposition which is able to provide us with an ε-optimal result, utilizing the principle of Eq. (1). The idea is that for each MEC we compute an ε-optimal value, then consider these values fixed and propagate them through the MDP quotient.

Apart from providing a stopping criterion, this has another practical advantage. Observe that the naive algorithm updates all states of the model even if the approximation in a single MEC has not ε-converged. The same happens even when all MECs are already ε-converged and the values only need to propagate along the transient states. These additional updates of already ε-converged states may come at a high computational cost. Instead, our method adapts to the potentially very different speeds of convergence in each MEC.

The propagation of the MEC values can be done efficiently by transforming the whole problem to a reachability instance on a modified version of the MEC quotient, which can be solved by, for instance, VI. We call this variant the *weighted MEC quotient*. To obtain this weighted quotient, we assume that we have already computed approximate values $w(M)$ of each MEC M. We then collapse the MECs as in the MEC quotient but furthermore introduce new states s_+ and s_-, which can be reached from each collapsed state by a special action stay with probabilities corresponding to the approximate value of the MEC. Intuitively, by taking this action the strategy decides to "stay" in this MEC and obtain the average reward of the MEC.

Formally, we define the function f as the normalized approximated value, i.e. for some MEC M_i we set $f(\hat{s}_i) = \frac{1}{r_{\max}} w(M_i)$, so that it takes values in $[0, 1]$. Then, the probability of reaching s_+ upon taking the stay action in $\hat{s}_i$ is defined as $f(\hat{s}_i)$ and dually the transition to s_- is assigned $1 - f(\hat{s}_i)$ probability. If for example some MEC M had a value $v(M) = \frac{2}{3} r_{\max}$, we would have that $\Delta(\hat{s}, \text{stay}, s_+) = \frac{2}{3}$. This way, we can interpret reaching s_+ as obtaining the maximal possible reward, and reaching s_- to obtaining no reward. With this intuition, we show in Theorem 2 that the problem of computing the average reward is reduced to computing the value of each MEC and determining the maximum probability of reaching the state s_+ in the weighted MEC quotient.

Definition 4 (Weighted MEC quotient). *Let* $\widehat{\mathcal{M}} = (\widehat{S}, \hat{s}_{init}, \widehat{Act}, \widehat{Av}, \widehat{\Delta}, \hat{r})$ *be the MEC quotient of an MDP* $\mathcal{M}$ *and let* $\mathsf{MEC}_{\widehat{S}} = \{\hat{s}_1, \ldots, \hat{s}_n\}$ *be the set of collapsed states. Further, let* $f : \mathsf{MEC}_{\widehat{S}} \to [0,1]$ *be a function assigning a value to every collapsed state. We define the* weighted MEC quotient *of* $\mathcal{M}$ *and* f *as the MDP* $\mathcal{M}^f = (S^f, s^f_{init}, \widehat{Act} \cup \{\mathsf{stay}\}, \mathsf{Av}^f, \Delta^f, r^f)$, *where*

- $S^f = \widehat{S} \cup \{s_+, s_-\}$,
- $s^f_{init} = \hat{s}_{init}$,
- Av^f *is defined as*

$$\forall \hat{s} \in \widehat{S}. \ \mathsf{Av}^f(\hat{s}) = \begin{cases} \widehat{\mathsf{Av}}(\hat{s}) \cup \{\mathsf{stay}\} & if \, \hat{s} \in \mathsf{MEC}_{\widehat{S}}, \\ \widehat{\mathsf{Av}}(\hat{s}) & otherwise, \end{cases}$$

$$\mathsf{Av}^f(s_+) = \mathsf{Av}^f(s_-) = \emptyset,$$

- Δ^f *is defined as*

$$\forall \hat{s} \in \widehat{S}, \hat{a} \in \widehat{Act} \setminus \{\mathsf{stay}\}. \ \Delta^f(\hat{s}, \hat{a}) = \widehat{\Delta}(\hat{s}, \hat{a})$$

$$\forall \hat{s}_i \in \mathsf{MEC}_{\widehat{S}}. \ \Delta^f(\hat{s}_i, \mathsf{stay}) = \{s_+ \mapsto f(\hat{s}_i), s_- \mapsto 1 - f(\hat{s}_i)\},$$

- *and the reward function* $r^f(\hat{s}, \hat{a})$ *is chosen arbitrarily (e.g. 0 everywhere), since we only consider a reachability problem on* $\mathcal{M}^f$.

Example 3. Consider the MDP in Fig. 1a. The average rewards of the MECs are $v = \{\widehat{A} \mapsto 4, \widehat{B} \mapsto 5, \widehat{C} \mapsto 10\}$. With f defined as in Theorem 2, Fig. 3 shows the weighted MEC quotient $\mathcal{M}^f$.   △

Theorem 2. *Given an MDP* $\mathcal{M}$ *with MECs* $\mathsf{MEC}(\mathcal{M}) = \{M_1, \ldots, M_n\}$, *define* $f(\hat{s}_i) = \frac{1}{r_{\max}} v(M_i)$ *the function mapping each MEC* M_i *to its value. Moreover, let* $\mathcal{M}^f$ *be the weighted MEC quotient of* $\mathcal{M}$ *and* f. *Then*

$$v(s_{init}) = r_{\max} \cdot \sup_{\pi \in \Pi} \mathbb{P}^\pi_{\mathcal{M}^f, s^f_{init}} (\Diamond s_+).$$

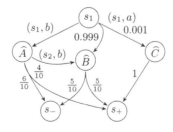

Fig. 3. The weighted quotient of the MDP in Fig. 1a and function $f = \{\widehat{A} \mapsto \frac{4}{10}, \widehat{B} \mapsto \frac{5}{10}, \widehat{C} \mapsto \frac{10}{10}\}$. Rewards and stay action labels omitted for readability.

Algorithm 2. LocalVI

Input: MDP $\mathcal{M} = (S, s_{\mathrm{init}}, Act, \mathsf{Av}, \Delta, r)$, precision $\varepsilon > 0$
Output: w, s.t. $|w - v(s_{\mathrm{init}})| < \varepsilon$
1: $f = \emptyset$
2: **for** $M_i = (T_i, A_i) \in \mathsf{MEC}(\mathcal{M})$ **do**   ▷ Determine values for MECs
3:     Compute the average reward $w(M_i)$ on M, such that $|w(M_i) - v(M_i)| < \frac{1}{2}\varepsilon$,
4:     $f(\hat{s}_i) \leftarrow \frac{1}{r_{\max}} w(M_i)$
5: $\mathcal{M}^f \leftarrow$ the weighted MEC quotient of $\mathcal{M}$ and f
6: Compute p s.t. $|p - \sup_{\pi \in \Pi} \mathbb{P}^{\pi}_{\mathcal{M}^f, s^f_{\mathrm{init}}}(\lozenge s_+)| < \frac{1}{2 r_{\max}}\varepsilon$ ▷ Determine reachability
7: **return** $r_{\max} \cdot p$

The corresponding algorithm is shown in Algorithm 2. It takes an MDP and the required precision ε as input and returns a value w, which is ε-close to the average reward $v(s_{\mathrm{init}})$. In the first part, for each MEC M the algorithm computes an approximate average reward $w(M)$ and assigns it to the function f (normalized by $r_{\max}$). Every MEC is a communicating MDP, therefore the value $w(M)$ can be computed using the naive VI with (SC1) as the stopping criterion. In the second part, the weighted MEC quotient of $\mathcal{M}$ and f is constructed and the maximum probability p of reaching s_+ in $\mathcal{M}^f$ is approximated.

Theorem 3. *For every MDP $\mathcal{M}$ and $\varepsilon > 0$, Algorithm 2 terminates and is correct, i.e. returns a value w, s.t. $|w - v(s_{init})| < \varepsilon$.*

For the correctness, we require that p is $\frac{\varepsilon}{2 r_{\max}}$-close to the real maximum probability of reaching s_+. This can be achieved by using the VI algorithms for reachability from [BCC+14] or [HM14], which guarantee error bounds on the computed probability. Note that p can also be computed by other methods, such as linear programming. In Sect. 4 we empirically compare these approaches.

3.3   On-Demand Value Iteration

Observe that in Algorithm 2, the approximations for all MECs are equally precise, irrespective of the effect a MEC's value has on the overall value of the MDP. Moreover, the whole model is stored in memory and all the MECs are computed beforehand, which can be expensive for large MDPs. Often this is unnecessary, as we illustrate in the following example.

Example 4. There are three MECs $\widehat{A}, \widehat{B}, \widehat{C}$ in the MDP of Fig. 1a. Furthermore, we have that $\mathbb{P}^{\pi}_{s_{\mathrm{init}}}(\lozenge \widehat{C}) \leq 0.001$. By using the intuition of Eq. (1), we see that no matter where in the interval $[0, r_{\max} = 20]$ its value lies, it contributes to the overall value $v(s_{\mathrm{init}})$ at most by $0.001 \cdot r_{\max} = 0.02$. If the required precision were $\varepsilon = 0.1$, the effort invested in computing the value of $\widehat{C}$ would not pay off at all and one can completely omit constructing $\widehat{C}$.

Further, suppose that $\widehat{A}$ was a more complicated MEC, but after a few iterations the criterion (SC1) already shows that the value of $\widehat{A}$ is at most 4.4. Similarly, after several iterations in $\widehat{B}$, we might see that the value of $\widehat{B}$ is greater than 4.5. In this situation, there is no point in further approximating the value of $\widehat{A}$ since the action b leading to it will not be optimal anyway, and its precise value will not be reflected in the result. $\triangle$

To eliminate these inefficient updates, we employ the methodology of *bounded real-time dynamic programming* (BRTDP) [MLG05] adapted to the undiscounted setting in [BCC+14]. The word *bounded* refers to keeping and updating both a lower and an upper bound on the final result. It has been shown in [Put94,CI14] that bounds for the value of a MEC can be derived from the current maximum and minimum of the approximations of VI. The idea of the BRTDP approach is to perform updates not repetitively for all states in a fixed order, but more often on the *more important* states. Technically, finite runs of the system are sampled, and updates to the bounds are propagated only along the states of the current run. Since successors are sampled according to the transition probabilities, the frequently visited (and thus updated) states are those with high probability of being reached, and therefore also having more impact on the result. In order to guarantee convergence, the non-determinism is resolved by taking the *most promising action*, i.e. the one with the current highest upper bound. Intuitively, when after subsequent updates such an action turns out to be worse than hoped for, its upper bound decreases and a more promising action is chosen next time.

Since BRTDP of [BCC+14] is developed only for MDP with the reachability (and LTL) objective, we decompose our problem into a reachability and MEC analysis part. In order to avoid pre-computation of all MECs with the same precision, we instead compute the values for each MEC only when they could influence the long-run average reward starting from the initial state. Intuitively, the more a particular MEC is encountered while sampling, the more it is "reached" and the more precise information we require about its value.

To achieve this, we store upper and lower bounds on its value in the functions u and l and refine them on demand by applying VI. We modify the definition of the weighted MEC quotient to incorporate these lower and upper bounds by introducing the state $s_?$ (in addition to s_+, s_-). We call this construction the *bounded MEC quotient*. Intuitively, the probability of reaching s_+ from a collapsed state now represents the lower bound on its value, while the probability of reaching $s_?$ describes the gap between the upper and lower bound.

Definition 5 (Bounded MEC quotient). *Let* $\widehat{\mathcal{M}} = (\widehat{S}, \hat{s}_{init}, \widehat{Act}, \widehat{\mathsf{Av}}, \widehat{\Delta}, \hat{r})$ *be the MEC quotient of an MDP* $\mathcal{M}$ *with collapsed states* $\mathsf{MEC}_{\widehat{S}} = \{\hat{s}_1, \ldots, \hat{s}_n\}$ *and let* $l, u : \{\hat{s}_1, \ldots, \hat{s}_n\} \to [0, 1]$ *be functions that assign a lower and upper bound, respectively, to every collapsed state in* $\widehat{\mathcal{M}}$*. The* bounded MEC quotient $\mathcal{M}^{l,u}$ *of* $\mathcal{M}$ *and* l, u *is defined as in Definition 4 with the following changes.*

- $S^{l,u} = \widehat{S} \cup \{s_?\}$,
- $\mathsf{Av}^{l,u}(s_?) = \emptyset$,
- $\forall \hat{s} \in \mathsf{MEC}_{\widehat{S}}.\ \Delta^{l,u}(\hat{s}, \mathsf{stay}) = \{s_+ \mapsto l(\hat{s}), s_- \mapsto 1 - u(\hat{s}), s_? \mapsto u(\hat{s}) - l(\hat{s})\}$.

The unshortened definition can be found in [ACD+17, Appendix D].

Algorithm 3. ONDEMANDVI

Input: MDP $\mathcal{M} = (S, s_{\text{init}}, Act, Av, \Delta, r)$, precision $\varepsilon > 0$, threshold $k \geq 2$
Output: w, s.t. $|w - v(s_{\text{init}})| < \varepsilon$
 1: Set $u(\cdot, \cdot) \leftarrow 1$, $u(s_-, \cdot) \leftarrow 0$; $l(\cdot, \cdot) \leftarrow 0$, $l(s_+, \cdot) \leftarrow 1$ ▷ Initialize
 2: Let $A(s) := \arg\max_{a \in Av^{l,u}(s)} u(s, a)$
 3: Let $u(s) := \max_{a \in A(s)} u(s, a)$ and $l(s) := \max_{a \in A(s)} l(s, a)$
 4: **repeat**
 5:     $s \leftarrow s_{\text{init}}^{l,u}, w \leftarrow s$ ▷ Generate path
 6:     **repeat**
 7:         $a \leftarrow$ sampled uniformly from $A(s)$
 8:         $s \leftarrow$ sampled according to $\Delta^{l,u}(s, a)$
 9:         $w \leftarrow w, a, s$
10:     **until** $s \in \{s_+, s_-, s_?\}$ or $\mathsf{Appear}(s, w) = k$ ▷ Terminate path
11:     **if** $\mathsf{pop}(w) = s_?$ **then**   ▷ Refine MEC in which stay was taken
12:         $\mathsf{pop}(w)$
13:         $\hat{q} \leftarrow \mathsf{top}(w)$
14:         Run VI on $\hat{q}$, updating u and l, until $u - l$ is halved
15:         Update $\Delta^{l,u}(\hat{q}, \mathsf{stay})$ according to Definition 5
16:     **else if** $\mathsf{Appear}(s, w) = k$ **then**   ▷ Update EC-collapsing
17:         ONTHEFLYEC
18:     **repeat**   ▷ Back-propagate values
19:         $a \leftarrow \mathsf{pop}(w)$, $s \leftarrow \mathsf{pop}(w)$
20:         $u(s, a) \leftarrow \sum_{s' \in S} \Delta(s, a, s') \cdot u(s')$
21:         $l(s, a) \leftarrow \sum_{s' \in S} \Delta(s, a, s') \cdot l(s')$
22:     **until** $w = \emptyset$
23: **until** $u(s_{\text{init}}) - l(s_{\text{init}}) < \frac{2\varepsilon}{r_{\max}}$ ▷ Terminate
24: **return** $r_{\max} \cdot \frac{1}{2}(u(s_{\text{init}}) + l(s_{\text{init}}))$

The probability of reaching s_+ and the probability of reaching $\{s_+, s_?\}$ give the lower and upper bound on the value $v(s_{\text{init}})$, respectively.

Corollary 1. *Let $\mathcal{M}$ be an MDP and l, u functions mapping each MEC M_i of $\mathcal{M}$ to (normalized) lower and upper bounds on the value, respectively, i.e. $l(\hat{s}_i) \leq \frac{1}{r_{\max}} v(M_i) \leq u(\hat{s}_i)$. Then*

$$r_{\max} \cdot \sup_{\pi \in \Pi} \mathbb{P}^{\pi}_{\mathcal{M}^{l,u}, s_{init}^{l,u}}(\lozenge s_+) \leq v(s_{init}) \leq r_{\max} \cdot \sup_{\pi \in \Pi} \mathbb{P}^{\pi}_{\mathcal{M}^{l,u}, s_{init}^{l,u}}(\lozenge \{s_+, s_?\}),$$

where $\mathcal{M}^{l,u}$ is the bounded MEC quotient of $\mathcal{M}$ and l, u.

Algorithm 3 shows the on-demand VI. The implementation maintains a partial model of the MDP and $\mathcal{M}^{l,u}$, which contains only the states explored by the runs. It interleaves two concepts: (i) naive VI is used to provide upper and lower bounds on the value of discovered end components, (ii) the method of [BCC+14] is used to compute the reachability on the collapsed MDP.

In lines 6–10 a random run is sampled following the "most promising" actions, i.e. the ones with maximal upper bound. The run terminates once it reaches s_+, s_- or $s_?$, which only happens if stay was one of the most promising actions.

Procedure 4. ONTHEFLYEC

1: **for** $(T_i, A_i) \in \mathsf{MEC}(\mathcal{M}^{l,u})$ **do**
2:    Collapse (T_i, A_i) to $\hat{s}_i$ in $\mathcal{M}^{l,u}$
3:    **for** $s \in T_i, a \in \mathsf{Av}(s) \setminus A_i$ **do**
4:       $u(\hat{s}_i, (s, a)) \leftarrow u(s, a)$
5:       $l(\hat{s}_i, (s, a)) \leftarrow l(s, a)$
6:    Add the **stay** action according to Definition 5.

A likely arrival to $s_?$ reflects a high difference between the upper and lower bound and, if the run ends up in $s_?$, this indicates that the upper and lower bounds of the MEC probably have to be refined. Therefore, in lines 11–15 the algorithm resumes VI on the corresponding MEC to get a more precise result. This decreases the gap between the upper and lower bound for the corresponding collapsed state, thus decreasing the probability of reaching $s_?$ again.

The algorithm uses the function $\mathsf{Appear}(s, w) = |\{i \in \mathbb{N} \mid s = w[i]\}|$ to count the number of occurrences of the state s on the path w. Whenever we encounter the same state k times (where k is given as a parameter), this indicates that the run may have got stuck in an end component. In such a case, the algorithm calls ONTHEFLYEC [BCC+14], presented in Procedure 4, to detect and collapse end components of the partial model. By calling ONTHEFLYEC we compute the bounded quotient of the MDP on the fly. Without collapsing the end components, our reachability method could remain forever in an end component, and thus never reach s_+, s_- or $s_?$. Finally, in lines 18–22 we back-propagate the upper and lower bounds along the states of the simulation run.

Theorem 4. *For every MDP $\mathcal{M}$, $\varepsilon > 0$ and $k \geq 2$, Algorithm 3 terminates almost surely and is correct, i.e. returns a value w, s.t. $|w - v(s_{init})| < \varepsilon$.*

4   Implementation and Experimental Results

In this section, we compare the runtime of our presented approaches to established tools. All benchmarks have been run on a 4.4.3-gentoo x64 virtual machine with 3.0 GHz per core, a time limit of one hour and memory limit of 8GB. The precision requirement for all approximative methods is $\varepsilon = 10^{-6}$. We implemented our constructions as a package in the PRISM Model Checker [KNP11]. We used the 64-bit Oracle JDK version `1.8.0_102-b14` as Java runtime for all executions. All measurements are given in seconds, measuring the total user CPU time of the PRISM process using the UNIX tool `time`.

4.1   Models

First, we briefly explain the examples used for evaluation. **virus** [KNPV09] models a virus spreading through a network. We reward each attack carried out by an infected machine. Note that in this model, no machine can "purge" the virus, hence eventually all machines will be infected. **cs_nfail** [KPC12] models a client-server mutual exclusion protocol with probabilistic failures of the clients. A reward is given for each successfully handled connection. **investor** [MM07, MM02] models an investor operating in a stock market. The investor can decide to sell his stocks and keep their value as a reward or hold them and wait to see how the market evolves. The rewards correspond to the value of the stocks when the investor decides to sell them, so maximizing the average reward corresponds to maximizing the expected selling value of the stocks. **phil_nofair** [DFP04] represents the (randomised) dining philosophers without fairness assumptions. We use two reward structures, one where a reward is granted each time a philosopher "thinks" or "eats", respectively. **rabin** [Rab82] is a well-known mutual exclusion protocol, where multiple processes repeatedly try to access a shared critical section. Each time a process successfully enters the critical section, a reward is given. **zeroconf** [KNPS06] is a network protocol designed to assign IP addresses to clients without the need of a central server while still avoiding address conflicts. We explain the reward assignment in the corresponding result section. **sensor** [KPC12] models a network of sensors sending values to a central processor over a lossy connection. A reward is granted for every *work* transition.

4.2 Tools

We will compare several different variants of our implementations, which are described in the following.

- Naive value iteration (NVI) runs the value iteration on the whole MDP as in Algorithm 1 of Sect. 3.1 together with the stopping criterion (SC2) conjectured by [Put94, Sect. 9.4.2]. As the stopping criterion is incorrect, we will not only include the runtime until the stopping criterion is fulfilled, but also until the computed value is ε-close to the known solution.
- Our MEC decomposition approach presented in Algorithm 2 of Sect. 3.2 is denoted by MEC-*reach*, where *reach* identifies one of the following reachability solver used on the quotient MDP.
  - PRISM's value iteration (VI), which iterates until none of the values change by more than 10^{-8}. While this method is theoretically imprecise, we did not observe this behaviour in our examples.[2]
  - An exact reachability solver based on linear programming (LP) [Gir14].
  - The BRTDP solver with guaranteed precision of [BCC+14] (BRTDP). This solver is highly configurable. Among others, one can specify the heuristic which is used to resolve probabilistic transitions in the simulation. This can happen according to transition probability (PR), round-robin (RR) or maximal difference (MD). Due to space constraints, we only compare to the MD exploration heuristic here. Results on the other heuristics can be found in [ACD+17, Appendix E]

---

[2] PRISM contains several other methods to solve reachability, which all are imprecise and behaved comparably in our tests.

– ODV is the implementation of the on-demand value iteration as in Algorithm 3 of Sect. 3.3. Analogously to the above, we only provide results on the MD heuristic here. The results on ODV together with the other heuristics can also be found in [ACD+17, Appendix E].

Furthermore, we will compare our methods to the state-of-the-art tool Multi-Gain, version 1.0.2 [BCFK15] abbreviated by MG. MultiGain uses linear programming to exactly solve mean payoff objectives among others. We use the commercial LP solver Gurobi 7.0.1 as backend[3]. We also instantiated *reach* by an implementation of the interval iteration algorithm presented in [HM14]. This variant performed comparable to MEC-VI and therefore we omitted it.

Table 1. Runtime comparison of our approaches to MultiGain on various, reasonably sized models. Timeouts (1h) are denoted by TO. Strongly connected models are denoted by "scon" in the MEC column. The best result in each row is marked in bold, excluding NVI due to its imprecisions. For NVI, we list both the time until the stopping criterion is satisfied and until the values actually converged.

Model	States	MECs	MG	NVI	MEC-VI	MEC-LP	MEC-BRTDP	ODV
virus	809	1	**3.76**	3.50/3.71	4.09	4.41	4.40	TO
cs_nfail4	960	176	4.86	10.2/TO	**4.38**	TO	9.39	16.0
investor	6688	837	16.75	4.23/TO	**8.83**	TO	64.5	18.7
phil-nofair5	93068	scon	TO	23.5/30.3	**70**	**70**	**70**	TO
rabin4	668836	scon	TO	87.8/164	**820**	**820**	**820**	TO

4.3 Results

The experiments outlined in Table 1 show that our methods outperform Multi-Gain significantly on most of the tested models. Furthermore, we want to highlight the **investor** model to demonstrate the advantage of MEC-VI over MEC-LP. With higher number of MECs in the initial MDP, which is linked to the size of the reachability LP, the runtime of MEC-LP tends to increase drastically, while MEC-VI performs quite well. Additionally, we see that NVI fails to obtain correct results on any of these examples.

ODV does not perform too well in these tests, which is primarily due to the significant overhead incurred by building the partial model dynamically. This is especially noticeable for strongly connected models like **phil-nofair** and **rabin**. For these models, every state has to be explored and ODV does a lot of superfluous computations until the model has been explored fully. On **virus**, the bad performance is due to the special topology of the model, which obstructs the back-propagation of values.

---

[3] MultiGain also supports usage of the LP solver lp_solve 5.5 bundled with PRISM, which consistently performed worse than the Gurobi backend.

Moreover, on the two strongly connected models all MEC decomposition based methods perform worse than naive value iteration as they have to obtain the MEC decomposition first. Furthermore, all three of those methods need the same amount of for these models, as the weighted MEC quotient only has a single state (and the two special states), thus the reachability query is trivial.

In Table 2 we present results of some of our methods on **zeroconf** and **sensors**, which both have a structure better suited towards ODV. The **zeroconf** model consists of a big transient part and a lot of "final" states, i.e. states which only have a single self-loop. **sensors** contains a lot of small, often unlikely-to-be-reached MECs.

Table 2. Runtime comparison of our on-demand VI method with the previous approaches. All of those behaved comparable to MEC-VI or worse, and due to space constraints we omit them. MO denotes a memory-out. Aside from runtime, we furthermore list the number of explored states and MECs of ODV

Model	States	MEC-VI	ODV	ODV States	ODV MECs
zeroconf(40,10)	3001911	MO	5.05	481	3
avoid				582	3
zeroconf(300,15)	4730203	MO	16.6	873	3
avoid				5434	3
sensors(2)	7860	18.9	20.1	3281	917
sensors(3)	77766	2293	37.2	10941	2301

On the **zeroconf** model, we evaluate the average reward problem with two reward structures. In the default case, we assign a reward of 1 to every final state and zero elsewhere. This effectively is solving the reachability question and thus it is not surprising that our method gives similarly good results as the BRTDP solver of [BCC+14]. The *avoid* evaluation has the reward values flipped, i.e. all states except the final ones yield a payoff of 1. With this reward assignment, the algorithm performed slightly slower, but still extremely fast given the size of the model. We also tried assigning pseudo-random rewards to every non-final state, which did not influence the speed of convergence noticeably. We want to highlight that the mem-out of MEC-VI already occurred during the MEC-decomposition phase. Hence, no variant of our decomposition approach can solve this problem.

Interestingly, the naive value iteration actually converges on **zeroconf**(40,10) in roughly 20 min. Unfortunately, as in the previous experiments, the used incorrect stopping criterion was met a long time before that.

Further, when comparing **sensors**(2) to **sensors**(3), the runtime of ODV only doubled, while the number of states in the model increased by an order of magnitude and the runtime of MEC-VI even increased by two orders of magnitude.

These results show that for some models, ODV is able to obtain an ε-optimal estimate of the mean payoff while only exploring a tiny fraction of the state space. This allows us to solve many problems which previously were intractable simply due to an enormous state space.

5 Conclusion

We have discussed the use of value iteration for computing long-run average rewards in general MDPs. We have shown that the conjectured stopping criterion from literature is not valid, designed two modified versions of the algorithm and have shown guarantees on their results. The first one relies on decomposition into VI for long-run average on separate MECs and VI for reachability on the resulting quotient, achieving global error bounds from the two local stopping criteria. The second one additionally is simulation-guided in the BRTDP style, and is an anytime algorithm with a stopping criterion. The benchmarks show that depending on the topology, one or the other may be more efficient, and both outperform the existing linear programming on all larger models. For future work, we pose the question of how to automatically fine-tune the parameters of the algorithms to get the best performance. For instance, the precision increase in each further call of VI on a MEC could be driven by the current values of VI on the quotient, instead of just halving them. This may reduce the number of unnecessary updates while still achieving an increase in precision useful for the global result.

References

[ACD+17] Ashok, P., Chatterjee, K., Daca, P., Křetínský, J., Meggendorfer, T.: Value iteration for long-run average reward in Markov decision processes. Technical report arXiv:1705.02326, arXiv.org (2017)

[BBC+14] Brázdil, T., Brožek, V., Chatterjee, K., Forejt, V., Kučera, A.: Markov decision processes with multiple long-run average objectives. LMCS **10**(1), 1–29 (2014). doi:10.2168/LMCS-10(1:13)2014

[BCC+14] Brázdil, T., Chatterjee, K., Chmelík, M., Forejt, V., Křetínský, J., Kwiatkowska, M., Parker, D., Ujma, M.: Verification of Markov decision processes using learning algorithms. In: Cassez, F., Raskin, J.-F. (eds.) ATVA 2014. LNCS, vol. 8837, pp. 98–114. Springer, Cham (2014). doi:10.1007/978-3-319-11936-6_8

[BCFK13] Brázdil, T., Chatterjee, K., Forejt, V., Kucera, A.: Trading performance for stability in Markov decision processes. In: LICS, pp. 331–340 (2013)

[BCFK15] Brázdil, T., Chatterjee, K., Forejt, V., Kučera, A.: MULTIGAIN: a controller synthesis tool for MDPs with multiple mean-payoff objectives. In: Baier, C., Tinelli, C. (eds.) TACAS 2015. LNCS, vol. 9035, pp. 181–187. Springer, Heidelberg (2015). doi:10.1007/978-3-662-46681-0_12

[BK08] Baier, C., Katoen, J.-P.: Principles of Model Checking. MIT Press, Cambridge (2008)

[CH11] Chatterjee, K., Henzinger, M.: Faster and dynamic algorithms for maximal end-component decomposition and related graph problems in probabilistic verification. In: SODA, pp. 1318–1336. SIAM (2011)

[CH12] Chatterjee, K., Henzinger, M.: An $O(n^2)$ time algorithm for alternating büchi games. In: SODA, pp. 1386–1399. SIAM (2012)

[CH14] Chatterjee, K., Henzinger, M.: Efficient and dynamic algorithms for alternating büchi games and maximal end-component decomposition. J. ACM **61**(3), 15:1–15:40 (2014)

[Cha07] Chatterjee, K.: Markov decision processes with multiple long-run average objectives. In: Arvind, V., Prasad, S. (eds.) FSTTCS 2007. LNCS, vol. 4855, pp. 473–484. Springer, Heidelberg (2007). doi:10.1007/978-3-540-77050-3_39

[CI14] Chatterjee, K., Ibsen-Jensen, R.: The complexity of ergodic mean-payoff games. In: Esparza, J., Fraigniaud, P., Husfeldt, T., Koutsoupias, E. (eds.) ICALP 2014. LNCS, vol. 8573, pp. 122–133. Springer, Heidelberg (2014). doi:10.1007/978-3-662-43951-7_11

[CKK15] Chatterjee, K., Komárková, Z., Křetínský, J.: Unifying two views on multiple mean-payoff objectives in Markov decision processes. In: LICS, pp. 244–256 (2015)

[CL13] Chatterjee, K., Łącki, J.: Faster algorithms for Markov decision processes with low treewidth. In: Sharygina, N., Veith, H. (eds.) CAV 2013. LNCS, vol. 8044, pp. 543–558. Springer, Heidelberg (2013). doi:10.1007/978-3-642-39799-8_36

[CY95] Courcoubetis, C., Yannakakis, M.: The complexity of probabilistic verification. J. ACM **42**(4), 857–907 (1995)

[dA97] de Alfaro, L.: Formal verification of probabilistic systems. Ph.D. thesis, Stanford University (1997)

[DFP04] Duflot, M., Fribourg, L., Picaronny, C.: Randomized dining philosophers without fairness assumption. Distrib. Comput. **17**(1), 65–76 (2004)

[FV97] Filar, J., Vrieze, K.: Competitive Markov Decision Processes. Springer, New York (1997). doi:10.1007/978-1-4612-4054-9

[Gir14] Giro, S.: Optimal schedulers vs optimal bases: an approach for efficient exact solving of Markov decision processes. Theor. Comput. Sci. **538**, 70–83 (2014)

[HM14] Haddad, S., Monmege, B.: Reachability in MDPs: refining convergence of value iteration. In: Ouaknine, J., Potapov, I., Worrell, J. (eds.) RP 2014. LNCS, vol. 8762, pp. 125–137. Springer, Cham (2014). doi:10.1007/978-3-319-11439-2_10

[How60] Howard, R.A.: Dynamic Programming and Markov Processes. MIT Press, New York, London, Cambridge (1960)

[KNP11] Kwiatkowska, M., Norman, G., Parker, D.: PRISM 4.0: verification of probabilistic real-time systems. In: Gopalakrishnan, G., Qadeer, S. (eds.) CAV 2011. LNCS, vol. 6806, pp. 585–591. Springer, Heidelberg (2011). doi:10.1007/978-3-642-22110-1_47

[KNPS06] Kwiatkowska, M., Norman, G., Parker, D., Sproston, J.: Performance analysis of probabilistic timed automata using digital clocks. Formal Methods Syst. Des. **29**, 33–78 (2006)

[KNPV09] Kwiatkowska, M., Norman, G., Parker, D., Vigliotti, M.G.: Probabilistic mobile ambients. Theoret. Comput. Sci. **410**(12–13), 1272–1303 (2009)

[KPC12] Komuravelli, A., Păsăreanu, C.S., Clarke, E.M.: Assume-guarantee abstraction refinement for probabilistic systems. In: Madhusudan, P., Seshia, S.A. (eds.) CAV 2012. LNCS, vol. 7358, pp. 310–326. Springer, Heidelberg (2012). doi:10.1007/978-3-642-31424-7_25

[MLG05] McMahan, H.B., Likhachev, M., Gordon, G.J.: Bounded real-time dynamic programming: RTDP with monotone upper bounds and performance guarantees. In: ICML, pp. 569–576 (2005)

[MM02] McIver, A.K., Morgan, C.C.: Games, probability, and the quantitative μ-calculus $qM\mu$. In: Baaz, M., Voronkov, A. (eds.) LPAR 2002. LNCS, vol. 2514, pp. 292–310. Springer, Heidelberg (2002). doi:10.1007/3-540-36078-6_20

[MM07] McIver, A., Morgan, C.: Results on the quantitative μ-calculus qMu. ACM Trans. Comput. Logic 8(1), 3 (2007)

[PGT03] Pineau, J., Gordon, G.J., Thrun, S.: Point-based value iteration: an anytime algorithm for POMDPs. In: IJCAI, pp. 1025–1032 (2003)

[Put94] Puterman, M.L.: Markov Decision Processes: Discrete Stochastic Dynamic Programming. Wiley, Hoboken (1994)

[Rab82] Michael, O.: N-Process mutual exclusion with bounded waiting by 4 Log2N-valued shared variable. J. Comput. Syst. Sci. 25(1), 66–75 (1982)

[Seg95] Segala, R.: Modelling and verification of randomized distributed real time systems. Ph.D. thesis, Massachusetts Institute of Technology (1995)

[Vei66] Veinott, A.F.: On finding optimal policies in discrete dynamic programming with no discounting. Ann. Math. Statist. 37(5), 1284–1294 (1966)

[WBB+10] Wimmer, R., Braitling, B., Becker, B., Hahn, E.M., Crouzen, P., Hermanns, H., Dhama, A., Theel, O.E.: Symblicit calculation of long-run averages for concurrent probabilistic systems. In: QEST, pp. 27–36 (2010)

Data Driven Techniques

STLInspector: STL Validation with Guarantees

Hendrik Roehm[1(✉)], Thomas Heinz[1],
and Eva Charlotte Mayer[2]

[1] Robert Bosch GmbH, Corporate Research, Renningen, Germany
{hendrik.roehm,thomas.heinz2}@de.bosch.com
[2] Universität Tübingen, Fachbereich Informatik, Tübingen, Germany
eva-charlotte.mayer@student.uni-tuebingen.de

Abstract. STLInspector is a tool for systematic validation of Signal Temporal Logic (STL) specifications against informal textual requirements. Its goal is to identify typical faults that occur in the process of formalizing requirements by mutating a candidate specification. STLInspector computes a series of representative signals that enables a requirements engineer to validate a candidate specification against all its mutated variants, thus achieving full mutation coverage. By visual inspection of the signals via a web-based GUI, an engineer can obtain high confidence in the correctness of the formalization – even if she is not familiar with STL. STLInspector makes the assessment of formal specifications accessible to a wide range of developers in industry, hence contributes to leveraging the use of formal specifications and computer-aided verification in industrial practice. We apply the tool to several collections of STL formulas and show its effectiveness.

Keywords: Specification validation · Temporal logic · STL · MTL · SMT · Mutation testing

1 Introduction

Recently, Signal Temporal Logic (STL) [14] became increasingly popular as a specification formalism for requirements of cyber-physical systems (CPS) [13,17] [1,5–7,9,20]. An STL specification can be thought of as a set of discrete and continuous signals that represent correct behavior of a CPS over time. Since many safety-critical industrial systems are CPS, checking correctness of their behavior is crucial. A variety of methods for checking STL specifications have been developed including signal monitoring [5,17], model-based falsification [1], and formal verification of STL specifications [20]. However, to be able to trust the testing/verification machinery, it is crucial to trust the formalization of requirements. It has been observed that industrial requirements can be fairly nontrivial, thus resulting in complex formulas that are not easily understandable [19]. If a formal specification does not conform to the corresponding natural language requirement, which is the common representation of requirements in industry today,

© Springer International Publishing AG 2017
R. Majumdar and V. Kunčak (Eds.): CAV 2017, Part I, LNCS 10426, pp. 225–232, 2017.
DOI: 10.1007/978-3-319-63387-9_11

verification results based on the specification are useless. Therefore, our tool STLInspector addresses the problem of checking an STL specification against an informal natural language requirement involving the requirements engineer as an oracle. STLInspector provides the requirements engineer with a systematic way of validating candidate STL specifications and gives her high confidence in the correctness of the formalization.

We use the example given by Dokhanchi et al. [4] to illustrate the problem and our solution. Suppose an engineer formalizes the textual requirement.

"At some time in the first 30 s, the vehicle speed (vel) will go over 100 $\frac{km}{h}$ and stay above 100 $\frac{km}{h}$ for 20 s."

by the STL formula

$$\varphi_c = \mathcal{F}_{[0,30]}((vel > 100) \Rightarrow \mathcal{G}_{[0,20]}(vel > 100)). \tag{1}$$

However, a test signal which is generated by STLInspector and depicted in Fig. 1 shows that φ_c does not conform to the textual requirement because the test signal satisfies φ_c but not the textual requirement. The engineer can detect the faulty specification by visual inspection of the signal which requires no knowledge of STL or temporal logics in general. Hence, specification validation becomes accessible to a wide range of developers in industry.

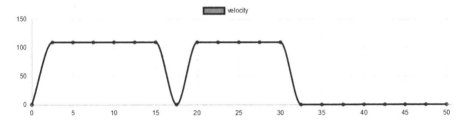

Fig. 1. A test signal – as visualized in STLInspector – that does not satisfy the textual requirement. Yet the signal satisfies its formalization φ_c, thus revealing that φ_c is incorrect.

STLInspector generates a series of such test signals that allows to show absence of typical errors made during formalization and increases confidence in its correctness. Inspired by ideas from mutation testing [3,10], typical classes of errors are formalized by mutation operators. For instance, the stuck-at-one operator produces the mutant $\varphi_c' = \mathcal{F}_{[0,30]}(true \Rightarrow \mathcal{G}_{[0,20]}(vel > 100))$ for φ_c from above. A signal is generated which does only satisfy the mutant φ_c' but not the candidate φ_c and thus represents a corner case of the formula φ_c. If the engineer identifies the behaviour as non-conforming to the textual requirement, the particular error associated with the mutation is shown to be absent. In this sense, STLInspector provides coverage guarantees for the considered set of error classes. By adding additional mutation operators, the tool can easily be extended to also handle domain specific error classes. Signal generation is performed using an SMT encoding of STL formulas (Sect. 4). We apply the tool to several collections of STL formulas and show its effectiveness (Sect. 5). STLInspector is an academic prototype and available under Apache 2.0 license at https://github.com/STLInspector.

Related Work: Vispec [9] is a tool that provides a graphical formalism based on template patterns to formalize specifications without requiring knowledge of temporal logics. STLInspector complements Vispec by enabling validation of such formalizations. It is however not restricted to templates. Vispec was extended by Dokhanchi et al. [4] to detect validity, redundancy and vacuity in MTL formalizations. These properties can be considered simple mutations and may be incorporated in STLInspector as a special case. Mutation testing has been applied to specification validation [10, Section V.B] without considering continuous-time signals. RATSY [2] is another tool that focuses on debugging specifications via a game-based approach. In contrast to STLInspector, RATSY specifications are based on a subset of PSL (expressively equivalent to ω-regular languages). Thus, it cannot be applied to continuous-time and real-valued signals. EGRET is a similar tool for string-based specifications which generates test strings for regular expressions [12].

Signal Temporal Logic: STL was introduced by Maler and Nickovic [13,14]. A signal s is a mapping from time to the valuation of Boolean and real-valued variables. We consider bounded time signals only, i.e., $s : [0, T] \rightarrow \mathbb{B}^n \times \mathbb{R}^m$ with n Boolean variables $P = \{p_1, \ldots, p_n\}$ and m real-valued variables given by the vector $R = (r_1, \ldots, r_m)$. STL is a logic to specify temporal properties of s. It consists of Boolean variables, constraints on real-valued variables, logical and temporal operators. We focus on the linear fragment of STL and signals whose real-valued components are continuous. Its syntax is as follows.

$$\alpha := p \mid D^T R \leq e, \quad \varphi := \alpha \mid \neg\varphi \mid \varphi_1 \vee \varphi_2 \mid \varphi_1 \mathcal{U}_I \varphi_2$$

with $p \in P$, $D \in \mathbb{R}^m$, $e \in \mathbb{R}$, and I being an interval $[a, b]$ with $a, b \in \mathbb{R}$. Note that STL semantics slightly differ across publications. We use the semantics as published in [20] and omit its definition due to space restrictions. While there exist different options to interpret unbounded time formulas over bounded time signals, for practical purposes bounded time formulas seem to be sufficient.

2 Mutation Testing and Coverage

In this section, we give a short introduction on mutation testing based on Fraser and Wotawa [8] and describe how we are able to guarantee that certain errors are not present in an STL formula φ by a set of test signals. Mutation testing involves the notion of a mutant of φ, i.e., another formula φ' which is obtained by applying a syntactic modification to φ. For example, $\varphi'_c = \mathcal{F}_{[0,30]}((vel < 100) \Rightarrow \mathcal{G}_{[0,20]}(vel > 100))$ is a mutation of φ_c in Eq. (1) where ">" is replaced by "<" in the first constraint. This type of syntactic modification is made precise by the *relation replacement operator* (rro):

$$rro(D^T R \sim_1 e) = \{D^T R \sim_2 e| \sim_2 \in RO, \sim_2 \neq \sim_1\} \qquad \sim_1 \in RO$$
$$rro(X \star Y) = \{x \star Y | x \in rro(X)\} \cup \{X \star y | y \in rro(Y)\} \qquad \star \in BO$$
$$rro(\star X) = \{\star \ x | x \in rro(X)\} \qquad \star \in MO$$

with $RO = \{\equiv, \neq, >, \leq, <\}$, $BO = \{\vee, \wedge, \rightarrow, \mathcal{U}_{[a,b]}, \mathcal{R}_{[a,b]}\}$, and $MO = \{\neg, \mathcal{F}_{[a,b]}, \mathcal{G}_{[a,b]}, \mathcal{N}_{[a]}\}$[1]. For φ_c, the relation replacement operator produces the list $rro(\varphi_c)$ of 8 mutants including φ'_c.

A signal s distinguishes φ and a mutant φ' if $s \models \varphi$ and $s \not\models \varphi'$ holds or $s \not\models \varphi$ and $s \models \varphi'$ holds. In such a case, s is said to kill the mutant φ'. For each such test signal s, the user must determine whether it conforms to the textual requirement ($\uparrow$) or not ($\downarrow$). Four cases can be distinguished.

– $s \models \varphi, s \not\models \varphi', \uparrow$: error represented by φ' is not present in φ
– $s \models \varphi, s \not\models \varphi', \downarrow$: φ contains illegitimate behavior
– $s \not\models \varphi, s \models \varphi', \uparrow$: φ' contains legitimate behavior that is missing in φ
– $s \not\models \varphi, s \models \varphi', \downarrow$: error represented by φ' is not present in φ

We consider the following mutation operators, which are adaptions of mutation operators defined by Fraser and Wotawa [8] to real-valued and continuous-time signals. In Sect. 5, we illustrate that they are in fact suitable to detect errors.

– Relation replacement
– Temporal operator insertion
– Temporal interval replacement
– Missing temporal operator
– Atomic proposition negation
– Expression negation
– Operand replacement
– Logical operator replacement
– Temporal operator replacement
– Stuck at zero
– Stuck at one
– Missing condition
– Associate shift

Due to space restrictions, we do not give additional operator definitions but refer to the documentation of STLInspector and the work by Fraser and Wotawa [8] and Mayer [15]. For a given list of mutants M, the mutation coverage of a set of signals can be defined as the percentage of mutants in M which are killed by these signals, not considering mutants that are semantically equivalent to the candidate formula. STLInspector generates sets of test signals which have 100% mutation coverage for all mutants generated by the mutation operators given above. Hence, we can guarantee that a formalization candidate does not contain any errors from a finite set of error classes where each class is

---

[1] Note that $\varphi \ \mathcal{R}_{[a,b]} \ \psi = \neg(\neg\varphi \ \mathcal{U}_{[a,b]} \ \neg\psi)$, $\mathcal{F}_{[a,b]} \ \varphi = \top \ \mathcal{U}_{[a,b]} \ \varphi$, $\mathcal{G}_{[a,b]} \ \varphi = \neg\mathcal{F}_{[a,b]} \ \neg\varphi$, $\mathcal{N}_{[a]} \ \varphi = \mathcal{G}_{[a,a]} \ \varphi$.

represented by a finite set of mutants. If a formula contains multiple errors, we cannot guarantee that the errors are detected unless there is a mutation operator for those specific multiple errors. However, the empirical evaluation in Sect. 5 indicates that we typically find errors also in the multiple error case. Note that the tool can be easily adapted to similar notions of coverage, for instance UFC and PICC [8].

3   Architecture of STLInspector

The tool is written in Python. STLInspector can be used as a command line tool, via the browser-based graphical user interface, or integrated into existing programs. In the following, we describe the GUI and the core components which are structured as visualized in Fig. 2.

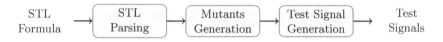

Fig. 2. Structure of the core functionality.

STL Parsing: The STL formula – written in textual form – is parsed into a syntax tree with Antlr [18]. The input format is described in the documentation. Examples are `G[1,3] vel >= 10` and `vel == 0 U[0,30] seatBeltFastened`.

Mutants Generation: In this component, all mutation operators listed in Sect. 2 are applied to the input formula. Every mutation operator outputs a list of mutants which are merged into one list containing all possible mutants.

Test Signal Generation: For a mutant φ' of the STL formula φ, STLInspector randomly chooses between the generation of a test signal s such that $s \models \varphi \wedge \neg \varphi'$ and $s \models \neg \varphi \wedge \varphi'$ to avoid bias on the satisfaction of φ. A test signal s is generated using the SMT encoding described in Sect. 4. Furthermore, it is checked whether the test signal s can be used to kill additional mutants. Test signal generation is repeatedly performed until a set S of test signals is obtained such that every mutant – except equivalent mutants – is killed by at least one element of S. Note that one test signal typically kills multiple mutants, thus less test signals are required than mutants (Sect. 5).

Web-Based GUI: STLInspector includes a front-end similar to Jupyter [11]. The user can enter an STL formula and the corresponding informal textual requirement. The front-end shows the generated test signals and the user decides whether or not the signal satisfies the informal requirement. STLInspector outputs which one of the four cases of Sect. 2 applies. If an error was found, the user can change the STL candidate and continue the visual inspection. For one STL candidate, the evaluation results of different users can be saved and easily compared on the project overview page.

4 Test Signal Encoding and Generation

For a given STL formula $\overline{\varphi}$, a test signal s which satisfies $s \models \overline{\varphi}$ is generated using the SMT-solver Z3 [16]. In the following, the SMT encoding of $s \models \overline{\varphi}$ is sketched. Time is partitioned into an alternating sequence of points and open intervals, similar to Maler and Ničković [13], however with a fixed time step c:

$$I_T = \{\{0\}, (0, c), \{c\}, (c, 2c), \ldots\}, \quad [0, T] = \bigcup_{I \in I_T} I$$

The parameters c and T are selected automatically where c must divide T and all bounds of temporal operator intervals in the formula $\overline{\varphi}$. Signals are generated such that the value of Boolean variables is constant for intervals in I_T. The set of such signals satisfying a formula can be encoded as an SMT formula using the rewriting technique by Roehm et al. [20]. For instance, the formula $\overline{\varphi}_c = \overline{\varphi}_1 \mathcal{U}_{[0,1]} \overline{\varphi}_2$ can be rewritten as follows:

$$s \models \overline{\varphi}_c \Leftrightarrow s \models (\overline{\varphi}_1 \mathcal{U}_{[0,0]} \overline{\varphi}_2) \vee (\overline{\varphi}_1 \mathcal{U}_{(0,1)} \overline{\varphi}_2) \vee (\overline{\varphi}_1 \mathcal{U}_{[1,1]} \overline{\varphi}_2)$$
$$\Leftarrow s \models \overline{\varphi}_2 \vee (\overline{\varphi}_1 \wedge \mathcal{G}_{(0,1)} \overline{\varphi}_1 \wedge \mathcal{F}_{(0,1)} \overline{\varphi}_2) \vee (\overline{\varphi}_1 \wedge \mathcal{G}_{(0,1)} \overline{\varphi}_1 \wedge \mathcal{F}_{[1,1]} \overline{\varphi}_2)$$

The rewritten formula can be expressed by the SMT formula $\overline{\varphi}_2^0 \vee (\overline{\varphi}_1^0 \wedge \overline{\varphi}_1^{0.5} \wedge \overline{\varphi}_2^{0.5}) \vee (\overline{\varphi}_1^0 \wedge \overline{\varphi}_1^{0.5} \wedge \overline{\varphi}_2^1)$ using $\overline{\varphi}_1^0 = \overline{\varphi}_1$, $\overline{\varphi}_1^{0.5} = \mathcal{G}_{(0,1)} \overline{\varphi}_1$, etc., and solved by Z3 [16]. The encoding ensures that for a real variable, the continuous signal obtained from piecewise linear interpolation of the sample points satisfies $\overline{\varphi}$ for the linear fragment of STL. The full theory [15] is omitted due to space restrictions.

5 Evaluation

We evaluate the effectiveness of mutation-based test signals in finding errors by two case studies. First, we use STLInspector to check STL formulas published as part of the UnCoVerCPS EU project [21]. They identified 8 common requirement patterns and formalized them by STL formulas and timed monitor automata. Since the patterns contain unbounded operators, we replace them by bounded ones. For the 4th requirement, one signal shows that the bounded STL formula does not conform to the requirement. Furthermore, the same signal shows that the original unbounded STL formula (as well as the monitor automaton) does not conform to the requirement either[2]. Our second evaluation is based on data of an online survey[3] by Dokhanchi et al. [4]. They requested participants to

---

[2] In fact, the proposed formula is equivalent to $\mathcal{G}_{[0,\infty)}(q \Rightarrow \mathcal{G}_{[0,\infty)}(p \Rightarrow \mathcal{G}_{[0,\infty)}p))$, which formalizes "after q, once p becomes true, p holds forever".

[3] We gratefully acknowledge the support of Bardh Hoxha and his colleagues to get access to some results of their survey.

write STL formalizations for several informal textual requirements. For each of the 66 formalizations φ_i, that we have access to from the survey, we generate a set S_i of test signals with 100% mutation coverage. For each formalization, STLInspector generates 6 test signals on average (minimum 3, maximum 11). We check whether φ_i can be distinguished from the correct formalization φ_c based on the test signals of S_i. Out of the 66 formalizations with 31 being unique, we are able to distinguish all of the 44 faulty ones (26 unique ones) from the correct formalizations. Since we are able to detect all faulty formalizations with our test generation, our list of mutation operators is sufficient to detect errors for the given formalizations. Since 12 of the 26 unique faulty formalizations need more than one mutation to transform them into the correct formula, we are able to discover the faulty formalizations even in the case where we do not have a guarantee to do so. We conclude from both case studies that mutation-based specification validation with STLInspector helps in finding errors and increasing confidence in correctness of STL formalizations.

References

1. Annpureddy, Y., Liu, C., Fainekos, G., Sankaranarayanan, S.: S-TaLiRo: A tool for temporal logic falsification for hybrid systems. In: Abdulla, P.A., Leino, K.R.M. (eds.) TACAS 2011. LNCS, vol. 6605, pp. 254–257. Springer, Heidelberg (2011). doi:10.1007/978-3-642-19835-9_21
2. Bloem, R., Cimatti, A., Greimel, K., Hofferek, G., Könighofer, R., Roveri, M., Schuppan, V., Seeber, R.: RATSY – A new requirements analysis tool with synthesis. In: Touili, T., Cook, B., Jackson, P. (eds.) CAV 2010. LNCS, vol. 6174, pp. 425–429. Springer, Heidelberg (2010). doi:10.1007/978-3-642-14295-6_37
3. Chow, T.S.: Testing software design modeled by finite-state machines. IEEE Trans. Softw. Eng. 4(3), 178–187 (1978)
4. Dokhanchi, A., Hoxha, B., Fainekos, G.E.: Metric interval temporal logic specification elicitation and debugging. In: MEMOCODE 2015, pp. 70–79 (2015)
5. Donzé, A., Ferrère, T., Maler, O.: Efficient robust monitoring for STL. In: Sharygina, N., Veith, H. (eds.) CAV 2013. LNCS, vol. 8044, pp. 264–279. Springer, Heidelberg (2013). doi:10.1007/978-3-642-39799-8_19
6. Dreossi, T., Dang, T., Donzé, A., Kapinski, J., Jin, X., Deshmukh, J.V.: Efficient guiding strategies for testing of temporal properties of hybrid systems. In: Havelund, K., Holzmann, G., Joshi, R. (eds.) NFM 2015. LNCS, vol. 9058, pp. 127–142. Springer, Cham (2015). doi:10.1007/978-3-319-17524-9_10
7. Fainekos, G.E., Pappas, G.J.: Robustness of temporal logic specifications for continuous-time signals. Theoret. Comput. Sci. 410(42), 4262–4291 (2009)
8. Fraser, G., Wotawa, F.: Complementary criteria for testing temporal logic properties. In: Dubois, C. (ed.) TAP 2009. LNCS, vol. 5668, pp. 58–73. Springer, Heidelberg (2009). doi:10.1007/978-3-642-02949-3_6
9. Hoxha, B., Mavridis, N., Fainekos, G.E.: VISPEC: A graphical tool for elicitation of MTL requirements. In: IROS 2015, Hamburg, Germany, 28 September–2 October 2015, pp. 3486–3492 (2015)
10. Jia, Y., Harman, M.: An analysis and survey of the development of mutation testing. IEEE Trans. Softw. Eng. 37(5), 649–678 (2011)

11. Kluyver, T., et al.: Jupyter notebooks - a publishing format for reproducible computational workflows. In: Positioning and Power in Academic Publishing: Players, Agents and Agendas, 20th International Conference on Electronic Publishing, Göttingen, Germany, 7–9 June 2016, pp. 87–90 (2016)

12. Larson, E., Kirk, A.: Generating evil test strings for regular expressions. In: ICST 2016, Chicago, IL, USA, 11–15 April 2016, pp. 309–319 (2016)

13. Maler, O., Ničković, D.: Monitoring properties of analog and mixed-signal circuits. Int. J. Softw. Tools Technol. Transfer **15**, 247–268 (2013)

14. Maler, O., Nickovic, D.: Monitoring temporal properties of continuous signals. In: Lakhnech, Y., Yovine, S. (eds.) FORMATS/FTRTFT 2004. LNCS, vol. 3253, pp. 152–166. Springer, Heidelberg (2004). doi:10.1007/978-3-540-30206-3_12

15. Mayer, E.C.: Mutation-based validation of temporal logic specifications with guarantees. Bachelor's thesis, Universität Tübingen (2017)

16. de Moura, L.M., Bjørner, N.: Z3: An efficient SMT solver. In: Ramakrishnan, C.R., Rehof, J. (eds.) TACAS 2008. LNCS, vol. 4963, pp. 337–340. Springer, Heidelberg (2008). doi:10.1007/978-3-540-78800-3_24

17. Nickovic, D., Maler, O.: AMT: A property-based monitoring tool for analog systems. In: Raskin, J.-F., Thiagarajan, P.S. (eds.) FORMATS 2007. LNCS, vol. 4763, pp. 304–319. Springer, Heidelberg (2007). doi:10.1007/978-3-540-75454-1_22

18. Parr, T.: The Definitive ANTLR 4 Reference, 2nd edn. Pragmatic Bookshelf, Raleigh (2013)

19. Roehm, H., Gmehlich, R., Heinz, T., Oehlerking, J., Woehrle, M.: Industrial examples of formal specifications for test case generation. In: ARCH@CPSWeek 2015, Seattle, WA, USA, pp. 80–88 (2015)

20. Roehm, H., Oehlerking, J., Heinz, T., Althoff, M.: STL model checking of continuous and hybrid systems. In: Artho, C., Legay, A., Peled, D. (eds.) ATVA 2016. LNCS, vol. 9938, pp. 412–427. Springer, Cham (2016). doi:10.1007/978-3-319-46520-3_26

21. Schuler, S., Walsch, A., Woehrle, M.: Deliverable D1.1 - Assessment of languages and tools for the automatic formalisation of system requirements. Technical report, as part of the EU-Project UnCoverCPS (2015). http://cps-vo.org/node/24197

Learning a Static Analyzer from Data

Pavol Bielik[(⊠)], Veselin Raychev, and Martin Vechev

Department of Computer Science, ETH Zürich, Zürich, Switzerland
{pavol.bielik,veselin.raychev,martin.vechev}@inf.ethz.ch

Abstract. To be practically useful, modern static analyzers must precisely model the effect of both, statements in the programming language as well as frameworks used by the program under analysis. While important, manually addressing these challenges is difficult for at least two reasons: (i) the effects on the overall analysis can be non-trivial, and (ii) as the size and complexity of modern libraries increase, so is the number of cases the analysis must handle.

In this paper we present a new, automated approach for creating static analyzers: instead of manually providing the various inference rules of the analyzer, the key idea is to learn these rules from a dataset of programs. Our method consists of two ingredients: (i) a synthesis algorithm capable of learning a candidate analyzer from a given dataset, and (ii) a counter-example guided learning procedure which generates new programs beyond those in the initial dataset, critical for discovering corner cases and ensuring the learned analysis generalizes to unseen programs.

We implemented and instantiated our approach to the task of learning JavaScript static analysis rules for a subset of points-to analysis and for allocation sites analysis. These are challenging yet important problems that have received significant research attention. We show that our approach is effective: our system automatically discovered practical and useful inference rules for many cases that are tricky to manually identify and are missed by state-of-the-art, hand tuned analyzers.

1   Introduction

Static analysis is a fundamental method for automating program reasoning with a myriad of applications in verification, optimization and bug finding. While the theory of static analysis is well understood, building an analyzer for a practical language is a highly non-trivial task, even for experts. This is because one has to address several conflicting goals, including: (i) the analysis must be scalable enough to handle realistic programs, (ii) be precise enough to not report too many false positives, (iii) handle tricky corner cases and specifics of the particular language (e.g., JavaScript), (iv) decide how to precisely model the effect of the environment (e.g., built-in and third party functions), and other concerns. Addressing all of these manually, by-hand, is difficult and can easily result in suboptimal static analyzers, hindering their adoption in practice.

© Springer International Publishing AG 2017
R. Majumdar and V. Kunčak (Eds.): CAV 2017, Part I, LNCS 10426, pp. 233–253, 2017.
DOI: 10.1007/978-3-319-63387-9_12

Problem Statement. The goal of this work is to help experts design robust static analyzers, faster, by automatically learning key parts of the analyzer from data.

We state our learning problem as follows: given a domain-specific language $\mathcal{L}$ for describing analysis rules (i.e., transfer functions, abstract transformers), a dataset $\mathcal{D}$ of programs in some programming language (e.g., JavaScript), and an abstraction function α that defines how concrete behaviors are abstracted, the goal is to learn an analyzer $pa \in \mathcal{L}$ (i.e., the analysis rules) such that programs in $\mathcal{D}$ are analyzed as precisely as possible, subject to α.

Key Challenges. There are two main challenges we address in learning static analyzers. First, static analyzers are typically described via rules (i.e., type inference rules, abstract transformers), designed by experts, while existing general machine learning techniques such as support vector machines and neural networks only produce weights over feature functions as output. If these existing techniques were applied to program analysis [25,29], the result would simply be a (linear) combination of existing rules and no new interesting rules would be discovered. Instead, we introduce domain-specific languages for describing the analysis rules, and then learn such analysis rules (which determine the analyzer) over these languages.

The second and more challenging problem we address is how to avoid learning a static analyzer that works well on some training data $\mathcal{D}$, but fails to generalize well to programs outside of $\mathcal{D}$ – a problem known in machine learning as *overfitting*. We show that standard techniques from statistical learning theory [23] such as *regularization* are insufficient for our purposes. The idea of regularization is that picking a simpler model minimizes the expected error rate on unseen data, but a simpler model also contradicts an important desired property of static analyzers to *correctly handle tricky corner cases*. We address this challenge via a counter-example guided learning procedure that leverages program semantics to generate new data (i.e., programs) for which the learned analysis produces wrong results and which are then used to further refine it. To the best of our knowledge, we are the first to replace model regularization with a counter-example guided procedure in a machine learning setting with large and noisy training datasets.

We implemented our method and instantiated it for the task of learning production rules of realistic analyses for JavaScript. We show that the learned rules for points-to and for allocation site analysis are indeed interesting and are missed by existing state-of-the-art, hand crafted analyzers (e.g., Facebook's Flow [5]) and TAJS (e.g., [17]).

Our main contributions are:

- A method for learning static analysis rules from a dataset of programs. To ensure that the analysis *generalizes* beyond the training data we carefully generate counter-examples to the currently learned analyzer using an oracle.
- A decision-tree-based algorithm for learning analysis rules from data that *learns to overapproximate* when the dataset cannot be handled precisely.

– An end-to-end implementation of our approach and an evaluation on the
challenging problem of learning tricky JavaScript analysis rules. We show
that our method produces interesting analyzers which generalize well to new
data (i.e. are sound and precise) and handle many tricky corner cases.

2   Our Approach

We begin by describing components of our learning approach as shown in Fig. 1.

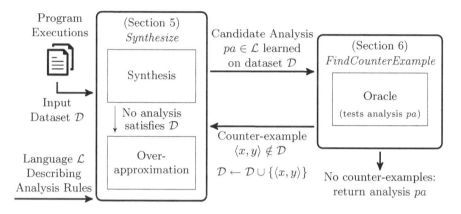

Fig. 1. Overview of our approach to learning static analysis rules from data consisting
of three components – a language $\mathcal{L}$ for describing the rules, a learning algorithm and
an oracle – that interact in a counter-example based refinement loop.

Obtaining Training Data $\mathcal{D}$. Our learning approach uses dataset of examples
$\mathcal{D} = \{\langle x^j, y^j \rangle\}_{j=1}^{N}$ consisting of pairs $\langle x^j, y^j \rangle$ where x^j is a program and y^j is
the desired output of the analysis when applied to x^j. In general, obtaining such
labeled training data for machine learning purposes is a tedious task. In our setting, however, this process can be automated because: (i) in static analysis, there
is a well understood notion of soundness, namely, the analyzer must *approximate*
(in the sense of lattice ordering) the concrete program behaviors, and (ii) thus,
we can simply run a large amount of programs in a given programming language with some inputs, and obtain a subset of the concrete semantics for each
program. We note that our learning method is independent of how the labels
are obtained. For example, the labels y^j can be obtained by running static or
dynamic analyzers on the programs x^j in $\mathcal{D}$ or they can be provided manually.

Synthesizer and Language $\mathcal{L}$. To express interesting rules of a static analyzer,
we use a loop-free domain-specific language $\mathcal{L}$ with branches. The synthesizer
then takes as input the dataset $\mathcal{D}$ with a language $\mathcal{L}$ and produces a candidate
program analysis $pa \in \mathcal{L}$ which correctly handles the pairs in $\mathcal{D}$. The synthesizer
we propose phrases the problem of learning a static analysis over $\mathcal{L}$ as a problem
in learning decision trees over $\mathcal{L}$. These components are described in Sect. 5.

Oracle. Our goal is to discover a program analysis that not only behaves as described by the pairs in the dataset $\mathcal{D}$, but one that generalizes to programs beyond those in $\mathcal{D}$. To address this challenge, we introduce the oracle component (*FindCounterExample*) and connect it with the synthesizer. This component takes as input the learned analysis *pa* and tries to find another program x for which *pa* fails to produce the desired result y. This counter-example $\langle x, y \rangle$ is then fed back to the synthesizer which uses it to generate a new candidate analyzer as illustrated in Fig. 1. To produce a counter-example, the oracle must have a way to quickly and effectively test a (candidate) static analyzer. In Sect. 6, we present two techniques that make the testing process more effective by leveraging the current set $\mathcal{D}$ as well as current candidate analysis *pa* (these techniques for testing a static analyzer are of interest beyond learning considered in our work).

Counter-Example Guided Learning. To learn a static analyzer *pa*, the synthesizer and the oracle are linked together in a counter-example guided loop. This type of iterative search is frequently used in program synthesis [31], though its instantiation heavily depends on the particular application task at hand. In our setting, the examples in $\mathcal{D}$ are programs (and not say program states) and we also deal with notions of (analysis) approximation. This also means that we cannot directly leverage off-the-shelf components (e.g., SMT solvers) or existing synthesis approaches. Importantly, the counter-example guided approach employed here is of interest to machine learning as it addresses the problem of overfitting with techniques beyond those typically used (e.g., regularization [23], which is insufficient here as it does not consider samples not in the training dataset).

Practical Applicability. We implemented our approach and instantiated it to the task of learning rules for points-to and allocation site analysis for JavaScript code. This is a practical and relevant problem because of the tricky language semantics and wide use of libraries. Interestingly, our system learned inference rules missed by manually crafted state-of-the-art tools, e.g., Facebook's Flow [5].

3   Overview

This section provides an intuitive explanation of our approach on a simple points-to analysis for JavaScript. Assume we are learning the analysis from one training data sample given in Fig. 2 (a). It consists of variables a, b and b is assigned an object s_0. Our goal is to learn that a may also point to that same object s_0.

Points-to analysis is typically done by applying inference rules until fixpoint. An example of an inference rule modeling the effect of assignment is:

$$\frac{\texttt{VarPointsTo}(v_2, h) \qquad \texttt{Assignment}(v_1, v_2)}{\texttt{VarPointsTo}(v_1, h)} \text{ [ASSIGN]}$$

This rule essentially says that if variable v_2 is assigned to v_1 and v_2 may point to an object h, then the variable v_1 may also point to this object h.

```
var b = {}; // empty object s₀
a = b;
```

(a) Training data

Expected points-to set
$\mathcal{D} = \{(\mathtt{a} \rightarrow \{s_0\})\}$

```
┣ VarDeclaration:b
│   ┗ ObjectExpression:{}
┣ Assignment
    ┣ Identifier:a
    ┗ Identifier:b
```

(b) Abstract syntax tree (AST) representation of (a)

$f_{desired}(x) ::=$

y	**if there is** Assignment(x,y)
y	**if there is** VarDeclaration:x(y)
$\perp$	**otherwise**

$f_{overfit}(x) ::=$

y	**if** y **is** VarDeclaration:y **preceding** x
y	**if there is** VarDeclaration:x(y)
$\perp$	**otherwise**

(c) Learned functions to resolve points-to queries from (a)

Fig. 2. Example data for learning points-to analysis.

Domain specific language (DSL) for analysis rules. Consider the following general shape of inference rules:

$$\frac{\mathtt{VarPointsTo}(v_2, h) \qquad v_2 = f(v_1)}{\mathtt{VarPointsTo}(v_1, h)} \text{ [GENERAL]}$$

Here, the function f takes a program element (a variable) and returns another program element or $\perp$. The rule says: use the function f to find a variable v_2 whose points-to set will be used to determine what v_1 points to. The ASSIGN rule is an instance of the GENERAL rule that can be implemented by traversing the AST and checking if the parent node of x is of type Assignment and if x is its first child. In this case, the right sibling of x is returned. Otherwise f returns $\perp$.

Problem Statement. The problem of learning a points-to analysis can now be stated as follows: find an analysis $pa \in \mathcal{L}$ such that when analyzing the programs in the training data $\mathcal{D}$, the resulting points-to set is as outlined in $\mathcal{D}$.

The Overfitting Problem. Consider Fig. 2(b) which shows the AST of our example. In addition to ASSIGN, we need to handle the case of variable initialization (first line in the program). Note that the dataset $\mathcal{D}$ does not uniquely determine the best function f. In fact, instead of the desired one $f_{desired}$, other functions can be returned such as $f_{overfit}$ shown in Fig. 2(c). This function inspects the statement prior to an assignment instead of at the assignment itself and yet it succeeds to produce the correct analysis result on our dataset $\mathcal{D}$. However, this is due to the specific syntactic arrangement of statements in the training data $\mathcal{D}$ and may not generalize to other programs, beyond those in $\mathcal{D}$.

Our Solution. To address the problem of overfitting to $\mathcal{D}$, we propose a counter-example guided procedure that biases the learning towards semantically meaningful analyses. That is, the oracle tests the current analyzer and tries to find a counter-example on which the analysis fails. Our strategy to generating candidate programs is to modify the programs in $\mathcal{D}$ in ways that can change both the syntax and the semantics of those programs. As a result, any analysis that depends on such properties would be penalized in the next iteration of *Synthesize*. As we show in the evaluation, our approach results in a much faster oracle than if we had generated programs blindly. This is critical as faster ways of finding counter-examples increase the size of the search space we can explore, enabling us to discover interesting analyzers in reasonable time.

For example, a possible way to exclude $f_{overfit}$ is to insert an unnecessary statement (e.g., var c = 1) before the assignment a = b in Fig. 2(a). Here, the analysis defined by $f_{overfit}$ produces an incorrect points-to set for variable a (as it points-to the value 1 of variable c). Once this sample is added to $\mathcal{D}$, $f_{overfit}$ is penalized as it produces incorrect results and the next iteration will produce a different analysis until eventually the desired analysis $f_{desired}$ is returned.

Soundness of the Approach. Our method produces an analyzer that is guaranteed to be sound w.r.t to all of the examples in $\mathcal{D}$. Even if the analyzer cannot exactly satisfy all examples in $\mathcal{D}$, the synthesis procedure always returns an *over-approximation* of the desired outputs. That is, when it cannot match the target output exactly, *Synthesize* learns to approximate (e.g., can return $\top$ in some cases). A formal argument together with a discussion on these points is provided in Sect. 5. However, our method is not guaranteed to be sound for all programs in the programming language. We see the problem of certifying the analyzer as orthogonal and complementary to our work: our method can be used to predict an analyzer which is likely correct, generalize well, and to sift through millions of possibilities quickly, while a follow-up effort can examine this analyzer and decide whether to accept it or even fully verify it. Here, an advantage of our method is that the learned analyzer is expressed as a program, which can be easily examined by an expert, as opposed to standard machine learning models where interpreting the result is nearly impossible and therefore difficult to verify with standard methods.

4   Checking Analyzer Soundness

In this section, following [4], we briefly discuss what it means for a (learned) analyzer to be sound. The concrete semantics of a program p include all of p's concrete behaviors and are captured by a function $[\![p]\!] : \mathbb{N} \to \wp(\mathcal{C})$. This function associates a set of possible concrete states in $\mathcal{C}$ with each position in the program p, where a position can be a program counter or a node in the program's AST.

A static analysis pa of a program p computes an abstract representation of the program's concrete behaviors, captured by a function $pa(p) : \mathbb{N} \to \mathcal{A}$ where $(\mathcal{A}, \sqsubseteq)$ is typically an abstract domain, usually a lattice of abstract facts equipped with an ordering $\sqsubseteq$ between facts. An abstraction function $\alpha : \wp(\mathcal{C}) \to \mathcal{A}$ then establishes a connection between the concrete behaviors and the abstract facts. It defines how a set of concrete states in $\mathcal{C}$ is abstracted into an abstract element in $\mathcal{A}$. The function is naturally lifted to work point-wise on a set of positions in $\mathbb{N}$ (used in the definition below).

Definition 1 (Analysis Soundness). *A static analysis pa is sound if:*

$$\forall p \in \mathcal{T}_{\mathcal{L}}.\ \alpha(\llbracket p \rrbracket) \sqsubseteq pa(p) \tag{1}$$

Here $\mathcal{T}_{\mathcal{L}}$ denotes the set of all possible programs in the target programming language ($\mathcal{T}_{\mathcal{L}}$). That is, a static analysis is sound if it over-approximates the concrete behaviors of the program according to the particular lattice ordering.

4.1 Checking Soundness

One approach for checking the soundness of an analyzer is to try and automatically verify the analyzer itself, that is, to prove the analyzer satisfies Definition 1 via sophisticated reasoning (e.g., as the one found in [10]). Unfortunately, such automated verifiers do not currently exist (though, coming up with one is an interesting research challenge) and even if they did exist, it is prohibitively expensive to place such a verifier in the middle of a counter-example learning loop where one has to discard thousands of candidate analyzers quickly. Thus, the soundness definition that we use in our approach is as follows:

Definition 2 (Analysis Soundness on a Dataset and Test Inputs). *A static analysis pa is sound w.r.t a dataset of programs P and test inputs ti if:*

$$\forall p \in P.\ \alpha(\llbracket p \rrbracket_{ti}) \sqsubseteq pa(p) \tag{2}$$

The restrictions over Definition 1 are: the use of a set $P \subseteq \mathcal{T}_{\mathcal{L}}$ instead of $\mathcal{T}_{\mathcal{L}}$ and $\llbracket p \rrbracket_{ti}$ instead of $\llbracket p \rrbracket$. Here, $\llbracket p \rrbracket_{ti} \subseteq \llbracket p \rrbracket$ denotes a subset of a program p's behaviors obtained after running the program on some set of test inputs ti.

The advantage of this definition is that we can automate its checking. We run the program p on its test inputs ti to obtain $\llbracket p \rrbracket_{ti}$ (a finite set of executions) and then apply the function α on the resulting set. To obtain $pa(p)$, we run the analyzer pa on p; finally, we compare the two results via the inclusion operator $\sqsubseteq$.

5 Learning Analysis Rules

We now present our approach for learning static analysis rules from examples.

5.1 Preliminaries

Let $\mathcal{D} = \{\langle x^j, y^j \rangle\}_{j=1}^{N}$ be a dataset of programs from a target language $\mathcal{T}_{\mathcal{L}}$ together with outputs that a program analysis should satisfy. That is, $x^j \in \mathcal{T}_{\mathcal{L}}$ and y^j are the outputs to be satisfied by the learned program analysis.

Definition 3 (Analysis Soundness on Examples). *We say that a static analysis* $pa \in \mathcal{L}$ *is sound on* $\mathcal{D} = \{\langle x^j, y^j \rangle\}_{j=1}^N$ *if:*

$$\forall j \in 1 \ldots N \quad . \quad y^j \sqsubseteq pa(x^j) \tag{3}$$

This definition is based on Definition 2, except that the result of the analysis is provided in $\mathcal{D}$ and need not be computed by running programs on test inputs.

Note that the definition above does not mention the precision of the analysis pa but is only concerned with soundness. To search for an analysis that is both sound, precise and avoids obvious, but useless solutions (e.g., always returns $\top$ element of the lattice $(\mathcal{A}, \sqsubseteq)$), we define a precision metric.

Precision Metric. First, we define a function $r : \mathcal{T}_{\mathcal{L}} \times \mathcal{A} \times \mathcal{L} \rightarrow \mathbb{R}$ that takes a program in the target language, its desired program analysis output and a program analysis and indicates if the result of the analysis is exactly as desired:

$$r(x, y, pa) \quad = \quad \textbf{if } (y \neq pa(x)) \textbf{ then } 1 \textbf{ else } 0 \tag{4}$$

We define a function *cost* to compute precision on the full dataset $\mathcal{D}$ as follows:

$$cost(\mathcal{D}, pa) = \sum_{\langle x,y \rangle \in \mathcal{D}} r(x, y, pa) \tag{5}$$

Using the precision metric in Eq. 5, we can state the following lemma:

Lemma 1. *For a program analysis* $pa \in \mathcal{L}$ *and a dataset* $\mathcal{D}$, *if* $cost(\mathcal{D}, pa) = 0$, *then the analysis is sound according to Definition 3.*

Proof: The proof is direct. Because $cost(\mathcal{D}, pa) = 0$ and r is positive, then for every $\langle x, y \rangle \in \mathcal{D}$, $r(x, y, pa) = 0$. This means that $y = pa(x)$ and so $y \sqsubseteq pa(x)$, which is as defined in Definition 3. □

5.2 Problem Formulation

Given a language $\mathcal{L}$ that describes analysis inference rules (i.e., abstract transformers) and a dataset $\mathcal{D}$ of programs with the desired analysis results, the *Synthesize* procedure should return a program analysis $pa \in \mathcal{L}$ such that:

1. pa is sound on the examples in $\mathcal{D}$ (Definition 3), and
2. $cost(\mathcal{D}, pa)$ is minimized.

The above statement essentially says that we would like to obtain a sound analysis which also minimizes the over-approximation that it makes. As the space of possible analyzers can be prohibitively large, we discuss a restriction on the language $\mathcal{L}$ and give a procedure that efficiently searches for an analyzer such that soundness is enforced and *cost* is (approximately) minimized.

5.3   Language Template for Describing Analysis Rules

A template of the language $\mathcal{L}$ for describing analysis rules is shown in Fig. 3(a). The template is simple and contains actions and guards that are to be instantiated later. The statements in the language are either an action or a conditional if-then-else statements that can be applied recursively.

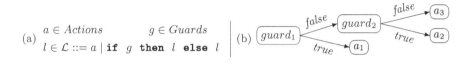

(a)
$$a \in Actions \qquad g \in Guards$$
$$l \in \mathcal{L} ::= a \mid \textbf{if}\ g\ \textbf{then}\ l\ \textbf{else}\ l$$

(b)

Fig. 3. (a) Syntax of a template language $\mathcal{L}$ with branches for expressing analysis rules. (b) Example of a function from the $\mathcal{L}$ language shown as a decision tree.

An analysis rule of a static analyzer is expressed as a function built from statements in $\mathcal{L}$. As usual, the function is executed until a fixed point [4]. The semantics of the if statements in pa is standard: guards are predicates (side-effect free) that inspect the program being analyzed and depending on their truth value, the corresponding branch of the if statement is taken. The reason such if statements are interesting is because they can express analysis rules such as the ones of our running example in Fig. 2.

We provide a formal semantics and detailed description of how the language $\mathcal{L}$ is instantiated for learning points-to and allocation site analysis in an extended version of this paper [1].

5.4   ID3 Learning for a Program Analyzer

A key challenge in learning program analyzers is that the search space of possible programs over $\mathcal{L}$ is massive as the number of possible combinations of branches and subprograms is too large. However, we note that elements of $\mathcal{L}$ can be represented as trees where internal nodes are guards of if statements and the leafs are actions as shown in Fig. 3(b). Using this observation we can phrase the problem of learning an analyzer in $\mathcal{L}$ as the problem of learning a decision tree, allowing us to adapt existing decision tree algorithms to our setting.

Towards that, we extend the ID3 [27] algorithm to handle action programs in the leafs and to enforce soundness of the resulting analysis $pa \in \mathcal{L}$. Similarly to ID3, our algorithm is a greedy procedure that builds the decision tree in a top-down fashion and locally maximizes a metric called information gain.

Our learning shown in Algorithm 1 uses three helper functions that we define next. First, the *genAction* function returns best analysis a_{best} for a dataset $\mathcal{D}$:

$$a_{best} = genAction(\mathcal{D}) = \underset{a \in Actions}{\arg\min}\ cost(\mathcal{D}, a) \qquad (6)$$

That is, *genAction* returns the most precise program analysis consisting only of *Actions* (as we will see later, an action is just a sequence of statements, without branches). If a_{best} is such that $cost(\mathcal{D}, a_{best}) = 0$, the analysis is both precise and sound (from Lemma 1), which satisfies our requirements stated in Sect. 5.2 and we simply return it. Otherwise, we continue by generating an `if` statement.

Generating Branches. The ID3 decision tree learning algorithm generates branches based on an information gain metric. To define this metric, we first use a standard definition of entropy. Let the vector $\boldsymbol{w} = \langle w_1, ..., w_k \rangle$ consist of elements from a set C. Then the entropy H on $\boldsymbol{w}$ is:

$$H(\boldsymbol{w}) = - \sum_{c \in C} \frac{count(c, \boldsymbol{w})}{k} \log_2 \left(\frac{count(c, \boldsymbol{w})}{k} \right) \tag{7}$$

where $count(c, \boldsymbol{w}) = | \{ i \in 1 \ldots k \mid w_i = c \} |$.

For a dataset $d \subseteq \mathcal{D}$, let $d = \{x_i, y_i\}_{i=1}^{|d|}$. Then, we define the following vector:

$$\boldsymbol{w}_d^{a_{best}} = \langle r(x_i, y_i, a_{best}) \mid i \in 1 \ldots |d| \rangle \tag{8}$$

That is, for every program in d, we record if a_{best} is a precise analysis (via the function r defined previously). Let $g \in Guards$ be a predicate that is to be evaluated on a program x. Let $\mathcal{D}^g = \{ \langle x, y \rangle \in \mathcal{D} \mid g(x) \}$ and $\mathcal{D}^{\neg g} = \mathcal{D} \setminus \mathcal{D}^g$.

The information gain on a set of examples $\mathcal{D}$ for analysis a_{best} and predicate guard g is then defined as:

$$IG^{a_{best}}(\mathcal{D}, g) = H(\boldsymbol{w}_{\mathcal{D}}^{a_{best}}) - \frac{|\mathcal{D}^g|}{|\mathcal{D}|} H(\boldsymbol{w}_{\mathcal{D}^g}^{a_{best}}) - \frac{|\mathcal{D}^{\neg g}|}{|\mathcal{D}|} H(\boldsymbol{w}_{\mathcal{D}^{\neg g}}^{a_{best}}) \tag{9}$$

For a given predicate g, what the information gain quantifies is how many bits of information about the analysis precision will be saved if instead of using the imprecise analysis a_{best} directly, we split the dataset with a predicate g. Using the information gain metric we define *genBranch* as follows:

$$g_{best} = genBranch(a_{best}, \mathcal{D}) = \arg\max_{g \in Guards} {}^{\perp} IG^{a_{best}}(\mathcal{D}, g) \tag{10}$$

Here, $\arg\max^{\perp}$ is defined to return $\perp$ if the maximized information gain is 0, or otherwise to return the guard g which maximizes the information gain.

Back to Algorithm 1, if *genBranch* returns a predicate with positive information gain, we split the dataset with this predicate and call *Synthesize* recursively on the two parts. In the end, we return an `if` statement on the predicate g and the two recursively synthesized analysis pieces.

Approximation. If the information gain is 0 (i.e. $g_{best} = \perp$), we could not find any suitable predicate to split the dataset and the analysis a_{best} has non-zero cost. In this case, we define a function *approximate* that returns an approximate, but sound program analysis – in our implementation we return analysis that loses precision by simply returning $\top$, which is always a sound analysis.

```
def Synthesize(D)
    Input: Dataset D = {⟨x^j, y^j⟩}_{j=1}^N
    Output: Program pa ∈ L
    a_best ← genAction(D)
    if cost(D, a_best) = 0 then return a_best;
    g_best ← genBranch(a_best, D)
    if g_best = ⊥ then  return approximate(D) ;
    p_1 ← Synthesize({⟨x, y⟩ ∈ D | g_best(x)})
    p_2 ← Synthesize({⟨x, y⟩ ∈ D | ¬g_best(x)})
    return if g_best then p_1 else p_2
```

Algorithm 1: Learning algorithm for programs from language $\mathcal{L}$.

Note that this approximation does not return $\top$ for the entire analysis but only for few of the branches in the decision tree for which the synthesis procedure fails to produce a good program using both *genAction* and *getBranch*.

In terms of guarantees, for Algorithm 1, we can state the following lemma.

Lemma 2. *The analysis pa ∈ $\mathcal{L}$ returned by Synthesize is sound according to Definition 3.*

The proof of this lemma simply follows the definition of the algorithm and uses induction for the recursion. For our induction base, we have already shown that in case $cost(D, a_{best}) = 0$, the analysis is sound. By construction, the analysis is also sound if *approximate* is called. In our induction step we use the fact that analyses p_1 and p_2 from the recursion are sound and must only show that the composed analysis if g_{best} then p_1 else p_2 is also sound.

6   The Oracle: Testing an Analyzer

A key component of our approach is an oracle that can quickly test whether the current candidate analyzer is sound, and if not, to find a counter-example. The oracle takes as an input a candidate analyzer pa and the current dataset $\mathcal{D}$ used to learn pa and outputs a counter-example program on which pa is unsound. More formally, if $P_{\mathcal{D}} = \{x \mid \langle x, y \rangle \in \mathcal{D}\}$, our goal is to find a counter-example program $p \in \mathcal{T}_{\mathcal{L}}$ such that $p \notin P_{\mathcal{D}}$ and the soundness condition in Definition 2 is violated for the given analysis pa and program p. That is, our oracle must generate new programs beyond those already present in $P_{\mathcal{D}}$.

Key Challenge. A key problem the oracle must address is to *quickly* find a counter-example in the search space of all possible programs. As we show in Sect. 7, finding such a counter-example by blindly generating new programs does not work as the search space of programs in $\mathcal{T}_{\mathcal{L}}$ is massive (or even infinite).

Speeding up the Search. We address this challenge by designing a general purpose oracle that *prioritizes* the search in $\mathcal{T}_{\mathcal{L}}$ based on ideas inspired by state-of-the-art testing techniques [11,22]. In particular, we generate new programs by performing modifications of the programs in $P_{\mathcal{D}}$. These modifications are carefully selected by exploiting the structure of the current analysis pa in two ways: (i) to select a program in $\mathcal{T}_{\mathcal{L}}$ and the position in that program to modify, and (ii) to determine what modification to perform at this position.

6.1   Choosing Modification Positions

Given a program $x \in P_{\mathcal{D}}$ and analysis pa, we prioritize positions that are *read* while executing the program analysis pa and changing them would trigger different *execution path* in the analyzer pa itself (not the analyzed program). Determining these positions is done by instrumenting the program analyzer and recording the relevant instructions affecting the branches the analyzer takes.

For example, for Fig. 2(a), we defined the analysis by the function $f_{overfit}$. For this function, only a subset of all AST nodes determine which of the three cases in the definition of $f_{overfit}$ will be used to compute the result of the analysis. Thus, we choose the modification position to be one of these AST nodes.

6.2   Defining Relevant Program Modifications

We now define two approaches for generating interesting program modifications that are potential counter-examples for the learned program analysis pa.

Modification via Equivalence Modulo (EMA) Abstraction. The goal of EMA technique is to ensure that the candidate analysis pa is robust to certain types of program transformations. To achieve this, we transform the statement at the selected program position in a semantically-preserving way, producing a set of new programs. That is, while the transformation is semantic-preserving, it is also one that should not affect the result of the analysis pa.

More formally, an EMA transformation is a function $F_{ema} : \mathcal{T}_{\mathcal{L}} \times \mathbb{N} \rightarrow \wp(\mathcal{T}_{\mathcal{L}})$ which takes as input a program p and a position in the program, and produces a set of programs that are a transformation of p at position n. If the analysis pa is sound, then these functions (transformations) have the following property:

$$\forall p' \in F_{ema}(p, n).pa(p) = pa(p') \tag{11}$$

The intuition behind such transformations is to ensure stability by exploring *local program modifications*. If the oracle detects the above property is violated, the current analysis pa is unsound and the counter-example program p' is reported. Examples of applicable transformations are dead code insertion, variable names renaming or constant modification, although transformations to use can vary depending on the kind of analysis being learned. For instance, inserting dead code that reuses existing program identifiers can affect flow-insensitive analysis, but should not affect a flow-sensitive analysis. The EMA property is similar to notion of algorithmic stability used in machine learning where the output of a classifier should be stable under small perturbations of the input as well as the concept of equivalence modulo inputs used to validate compilers [22].

Modification via Global Jumps. The previous modifications always generated semantic-preserving transformations. However, to ensure better generalization we are also interested in exploring changes to programs in P_D that may not be semantic preserving, defined via a function $F_{gj} : \mathcal{T}_\mathcal{L} \times \mathbb{N} \to \wp(\mathcal{T}_\mathcal{L})$. The goal is to discover a new program which exhibits behaviors not seen by any of the programs in P_D and is not considered by the currently learned analyzer pa.

Overall, as shown in Sect. 7, our approach for generating programs to test the analysis pa via the functions F_{gj} and F_{ema} is an order of magnitude more efficient at finding counter-examples than naively modifying the programs in P_D.

7   Implementation and Evaluation

In this section we provide an implementation of our approach shown in Fig. 1 as well as a detailed experimental evaluation instantiated to two challenging analysis problems for JavaScript: learning points-to analysis rules and learning allocation site rules. In our experiments, we show that:

- The approach can learn practical program analysis rules for tricky cases involving JavaScript's built-in objects. These rules can be incorporated into existing analyzers that currently handle such cases only partially.
- The counter-example based learning is critical for ensuring that the learned analysis generalizes well and does not overfit to the training dataset.
- Our oracle can effectively find counter-examples (orders of magnitude faster than random search).

These experiments were performed on a 28 core machine with 2.60 Ghz Intel(R) Xeon(R) CPU E5-2690 v4 CPU, running Ubuntu 16.04. In our implementation we parallelized both the learning and the search for the counter-examples.

Training Dataset. We use the official ECMAScript (ECMA-262) conformance suite (https://github.com/tc39/test262) – the largest and most comprehensive test suite available for JavaScript containing over 20 000 test cases. As the suite also includes the latest version of the standard, all existing implementations typically support only a subset of the testcases. In particular, the `NodeJS` interpreter v4.2.6 used in our evaluation can execute (i.e., does not throw a syntax error) 15 675 tests which we use as the training dataset for learning.

Program Modifications. We list the program modifications used to instantiate the oracle in Table 1. The semantic preserving program modifications that should not change the result of analyses considered in our work F_{ema} are: inserted dead code, renamed variables and user functions, renamed parameters as well as generated side-effect free expressions (e.g., declaring new variables). Note that these mutations are very general and should apply to almost arbitrary property. To explore new program behaviours by potentially changing program semantics we use program modifications F_{gj} that change values of constants (strings and numbers), add method arguments and parameters.

Table 1. Program modifications used to instantiate the oracle (Sect. 6) that generates counter-examples for points-to analysis and allocation site analysis.

Program modifications	
F_{ema}	F_{gj}
Adding dead code	Adding method arguments
Renaming variables	Adding method parameters
Renaming user functions	Changing constants
Side-effect free expressions	

7.1   Learning Points-to Analysis Rules for JavaScript

We now evaluate the effectiveness of our approach on the task of learning a points-to analysis for the JavaScript built-in APIs that affect the binding of this object. This is useful because existing analyzers currently either model this only partially [5,12] (i.e., cover only a subset of Function.prototype API behaviors) or not at all [16,24], resulting in potentially unsound results.

We illustrate some of the complexity for determining the objects to which this points-to within the same method in Fig. 4. Here, this points-to different objects depending on how the method is invoked and what values are passed in as arguments. In addition to the values shown in the example, other values may be seen during runtime if other APIs are invoked, or the method isBig is used as an object method or as a global method.

```
global.length = 4;              // this points to global
var dat = [5, 3, 9, 1];         dat.filter(isBig); // [5, 9]
function isBig(value) {         // this points to boxed 42
   return value >=              dat.filter(isBig, 42); // []
      this.length;              // this points to dat object
}                               dat.filter(isBig, dat); // [5, 9]
```

Fig. 4. JavaScript code snippet illustrating subset of different objects to which this can point to depending on the context method isBig is invoked in.

Language $\mathcal{L}$. To learn points-to analysis, we use a domain-specific language $\mathcal{L}_{pt}$ with if statements (to synthesize branches for corner cases) and instructions to traverse the JavaScript AST in order to provide the specific analysis of each case. A detailed list of the instructions with their semantics is provided in [1].

Learned Analyzer. A summary of our learned analyzer is shown in Table 2. For each API we collected all its usages in the ECMA-262 conformance suite, ranging from only 6 to more than 600, and used them as initial training dataset for the learning. In all cases, a significant amount of counter-examples were needed to refine the analysis and prevent overfitting to the initial dataset. On average,

Table 2. Dataset size, number of counter-examples found and the size of the learned points-to analysis for JavaScript APIs that affect the points-to set of `this`.

Function name	Dataset size	Counter-examples found	Analysis size*
Function.prototype			
call()	26	372	97 (18)
apply()	6	182	54 (10)
Array.prototype			
map()	315	64	36 (6)
some()	229	82	36 (6)
forEach()	604	177	35 (5)
every()	338	31	36 (6)
filter()	408	76	38 (6)
find()	53	73	36 (6)
findIndex()	51	96	28 (6)
Array			
from()	32	160	57 (7)
JSON			
stringify()	18	55	9 (2)

* Number of instructions in $\mathcal{L}_{pt}$ (Number of `if` branches)

for each API, the learning finished in 14 min, out of which 4 min were used to synthesize the program analysis and 10 min used in the search for counter-examples (cumulatively across all refinement iterations). The longest learning time was 57 min for the `Function.prototype.call` API for which we also learn the most complex analysis – containing 97 instructions in $\mathcal{L}_{pt}$. We note that even though the APIs in `Array.prototype` have very similar semantics, the learned programs vary slightly. This is caused by the fact that different number and types of examples were available as the initial training dataset which also means that the oracle had to find different types of counter-examples. We provide an example of the learned analysis in [1].

7.2 Learning Allocation Site Analysis for JavaScript

We also evaluate the effectiveness of our approach on a second analysis task – learning allocation sites in JavaScript. This is an analysis that is used internally by many existing analyzers. The analysis computes which statements or expressions in a given language result in an allocation of a new heap object.

We illustrate the expected output and some of the complexities of allocation site analysis on a example shown in Fig. 5. In JavaScript, there are various ways for how an object can be allocated including creating new object without calling a constructor explicitly (for example by creating new array or object expression inline), creating new object by calling a constructor explicitly using `new`,

```
var obj = {a: 7};
var arr = [1, 2, 3, 4];
if (obj.a == arr.slice(0,2)) { ... }          Allocation Sites
var n = new Number(7);                     (new object allocated)
var obj2 = new Object(obj);
try { ... } catch (err) { ... }
```

Fig. 5. Illustration of program locations (underlined) for which the allocation site analysis should report that a new object is allocated.

creating a new object by calling a method or new objects created by throwing an exception. In addition, some of the cases might further depend on actual values passed as arguments. For example, calling a `new Object(obj)` constructor with `obj` as an argument does not create a new object but returns the `obj` passed as argument instead. The goal of the analysis is to determine all such program locations (as shown in Fig. 5) at which a new object is allocated.

Consider the following simple, but unsound and imprecise allocation site analysis:

$$f_{alloc}(x) = \begin{cases} true & \text{if there is } \texttt{Argument:x} \text{ or } \texttt{NewExpression:x} \\ false & \textbf{otherwise} \end{cases}$$

which states that a location x is an allocation site if it is either an argument or a new expression. This analysis is imprecise because there are other ways to allocate an object (e.g., when creating arrays, strings, boxed values or by calling a function). It is also unsound, because the JavaScript compiler might not create a new object even when `NewExpression` is called (e.g., `new Object(obj)` returns the same object as the given *obj*).

Instead of defining tricky corner cases by hand, we use our approach to learn this analyzer automatically from data. We instantiate the approach in a very similar way compared to learning points-to analysis by adjusting the language and how the labels in the training dataset are obtained (details provided in [1]). For this task, we obtain 134 721 input/output examples from the training data, which are further expanded with additional 905 counter-examples found during 99 refinement iterations of the learning algorithm. For this (much higher than in the other analyzer) number of examples the synthesis time was 184 min while the total time required to find counter-examples was 7 h.

The learned program is relatively complex and contains 135 learned branches, including the tricky case where `NewExpression` does not allocate a new object. Compared to the trivial, but wrong analysis f_{alloc}, the synthesized analysis marks over twice as many locations in the code as allocation sites ($\approx$21K vs $\approx$45K).

7.3 Analysis Generalization

We study how well the learned analyzer for points-to analysis works for unseen data. First, we manually inspected the learned analyzer at the first iteration of the *Synthesize* procedure (without any counter-examples generated). We did that to check if we overfit to the initial dataset and found that indeed, the initial analysis would *not* generalize to some programs outside the provided dataset. This happened because the learned rules conditioned on unrelated regularities found in the data (such as variable names or fixed positions of certain function parameters). Our oracle, and the counter-example learning procedure, however, eliminate such kinds of non-semantic analyses by introducing additional function arguments and statements in the test cases.

Overfitting to the initial dataset was also caused by the large search space of possible programs in the DSL for the analysis. However, we decided not to restrict the language, because a more expressive language means more automation. Also, we did not need to provide upfront partial analysis in the form of a sketch [31].

Oracle Effectiveness for Finding Counter-Examples. We evaluate the effectiveness of our oracle to find counter-examples by comparing it to a random ("black box") oracle that applies all possible modifications to a randomly selected program from the training dataset. For both oracles we measure the average number of programs explored before a counter-example is found and summarize the results in Table 3. In the table, we observe two cases: (i) early in the analysis loop when the analysis is imprecise and finding a counter-example is *easy*, and (ii) later in the loop when *hard* corner cases are not yet covered by the analysis. In both cases, our *oracle guided by analysis* is orders of magnitude more efficient.

Table 3. The effect of using the learned analysis to guide the counter-example search.

Difficulty	Programs explored until first counter-example is found	
	"Black box"	Guided by analysis
Easy ($\approx 60\%$)	146	13
Hard ($\approx 40\%$)	> 3000	130

Is Counter-Example Refinement Loop Needed? Finally, we compare the effect of learning with a refinement loop to "one-shot" learning without the loop, but with more data provided up-front. For this experiment, we automatically generate a huge dataset $\mathcal{D}_{huge}$ by applying all possible program modifications (as defined by the oracle) on all programs in $\mathcal{D}$. For comparison, let the dataset obtained at the end of the counter-example based algorithm on $\mathcal{D}$ be $\mathcal{D}_{ce}$. The size of $\mathcal{D}_{ce}$ is two orders of magnitude smaller than $\mathcal{D}_{huge}$.

An analysis that generalizes well should be sound and precise on both datasets $\mathcal{D}_{ce}$ and $\mathcal{D}_{huge}$, but since we use one of the datasets for training, we use the other one to validate the resulting analyzer. For the analysis that is learned using counter-examples (from $\mathcal{D}_{ce}$), the precision is around 99.9% with the remaining 0.01% of results approximated to the top element in the lattice (that is, it does not produce a trivially sound, but useless result). However, evaluating the analysis learned from $\mathcal{D}_{huge}$ on $\mathcal{D}_{ce}$ has precision of only 70.1% with the remaining 29.1% of the cases being *unsound*. This means that $\mathcal{D}_{ce}$ indeed contains interesting cases critical to analysis soundness and precision.

Summary. Overall, our evaluation shows that the learning approach presented in our work can learn static analysis rules that handle various cases such as the ones that arise in JavaScript built-in APIs. The learned rules generalize to cases beyond the training data and can be inspected and integrated into existing static analyzers that miss some of these corner cases. We provide an example of both learned analyses in the extended version of this paper [1].

8   Related Work

Synthesis from Examples. Similar to our work, synthesis from examples typically starts with a domain-specific language (DSL) which captures a hypothesis space of possible programs together with a set of examples the program must satisfy and optionally an oracle to provide additional data points in the form of counter-examples using CEGIS-like techniques [31]. Examples of this direction include discovery of bit manipulation programs [19], string processing in spreadsheets [13], functional programs [7], or data structure specifications [9]. A recent work has shown how to generalize the setting to large and noisy datasets [28].

Other recent works [15,18] synthesize models for library code by collecting program traces which are then used as a specification. The key differences with our approach are that we (i) use large dataset covering hundreds of cases and (ii) we synthesize analysis that generalizes beyond the provided dataset.

Program Analysis and Machine Learning. Recently, several works have used machine learning in the domain of program analysis for task such as probabilistic type prediction [20,29], reducing the false positives of an analysis [25], or as a way to speed up the analysis [2,14,26] by learning various strategies used by the analysis. A key difference compared to our work is that we present a method to learn the static analysis rules which can then be applied in an iterative manner. This is a more complex task than [20,29] which do not learn rules that can infer program specific properties and [2,14,25,26] which assume the rules are already provided and typically learn a classifier on top of them.

Learning Invariants. In an orthogonal effort there has also been work on learning program invariants using dynamic executions. For recent representative examples of this direction, see [8,21,30]. The focus of all of these works is rather different: they work on a per-program basis, exercising the program, obtaining observations and finally attempting to learn the invariants. Counter-example guided abstraction refinement (CEGAR) [3] is a classic approach for learning an abstraction (typically via refinement). Unlike our work, these approaches do not learn the actual program analysis and work on a per-program basis.

Scalable Program Analysis. Another line of work considers scaling program analysis in hard to analyse domains such as JavaScript at the expense of analysis soundness [6,24]. These works are orthogonal to us and follow the traditional way of designing the static analysis components by hand, but in the future they can also benefit from automatically learned rules by techniques such as ours.

9   Conclusion and Future Work

We presented a new approach for learning static analyzers from examples. Our approach takes as input a language for describing analysis rules, an abstraction function and an initial dataset of programs. Then, we introduce a counterexample guided search to iteratively add new programs that the learned analyzer should consider. These programs aim to capture corner cases of the programming language being analyzed. The counter-example search is made feasible thanks to an oracle able to quickly generate candidate example programs for the analyzer.

We implemented our approach and applied it to the setting of learning a points-to and allocation site analysis for JavaScript. This is a very challenging problem for learning yet one that is of practical importance. We show that our learning approach was able to discover new analysis rules which cover corner cases missed by prior, manually crafted analyzers for JavaScript.

We believe this is an interesting research direction with several possible future work items including learning to model the interfaces of large libraries w.r.t to a given analysis, learning the rules for other analyzers (e.g., type analysis), or learning an analysis that is semantically similar to analyses written by hand.

References

1. Bielik, P., Raychev, V., Vechev, M.T.: Learning a static analyzer from data. CoRR, abs/1611.01752 (2016)
2. Cha, S., Jeong, S., Oh, H.: Learning a strategy for choosing widening thresholds from a large codebase. In: Igarashi, A. (ed.) APLAS 2016. LNCS, vol. 10017, pp. 25–41. Springer, Cham (2016). doi:10.1007/978-3-319-47958-3_2
3. Clarke, E., Grumberg, O., Jha, S., Lu, Y., Veith, H.: Counterexample-guided abstraction refinement. In: Emerson, E.A., Sistla, A.P. (eds.) CAV 2000. LNCS, vol. 1855, pp. 154–169. Springer, Heidelberg (2000). doi:10.1007/10722167_15
4. Cousot, P., Cousot, R.: Abstract interpretation: a unified lattice model for static analysis of programs by construction or approximation of fixpoints. In: Proceedings of the 4th ACM SIGACT-SIGPLAN Symposium on Principles of Programming Languages, pp. 238–252. ACM, New York (1977)
5. Facebook: Facebook Flow: Static typechecker for JavaScript (2016). https://github.com/facebook/flow
6. Feldthaus, A., Schäfer, M., Sridharan, M., Dolby, J., Tip, F.: Efficient construction of approximate call graphs for JavaScript IDE services. In: Proceedings of the 2013 International Conference on Software Engineering, pp. 752–761 (2013)
7. Feser, J.K., Chaudhuri, S., Dillig, I.: Synthesizing data structure transformations from input-output examples. In: Proceedings of the 36th ACM SIGPLAN Conference on Programming Language Design and Implementation, Portland, OR, USA, 15–17 June 2015, pp. 229–239 (2015)

8. Garg, P., Neider, D., Madhusudan, P., Roth, D.: Learning invariants using decision trees and implication counterexamples. In: Proceedings of the 43rd Annual ACM SIGPLAN-SIGACT Symposium on Principles of Programming Languages, POPL 2016, pp. 499–512 (2016)

9. Gehr, T., Dimitrov, D., Vechev, M.: Learning commutativity specifications. In: Kroening, D., Păsăreanu, C.S. (eds.) CAV 2015. LNCS, vol. 9206, pp. 307–323. Springer, Cham (2015). doi:10.1007/978-3-319-21690-4_18

10. Giacobazzi, R., Logozzo, F., Ranzato, F.: Analyzing program analyses. In: Proceedings of the 42nd Annual ACM SIGPLAN-SIGACT Symposium on Principles of Programming Languages, POPL 2015, pp. 261–273. ACM (2015)

11. Godefroid, P., Levin, M.Y., Molnar, D.: SAGE: whitebox fuzzing for security testing. Queue **10**(1), 20:20–20:27 (2012)

12. Guarnieri, S., Livshits, B.: GATEKEEPER: mostly static enforcement of security and reliability policies for JavaScript code. In: Proceedings of the 18th Conference on USENIX Security Symposium, SSYM 2009, pp. 151–168 (2009)

13. Gulwani, S.: Automating string processing in spreadsheets using input-output examples. In: Proceedings of the 38th ACM SIGPLAN-SIGACT Symposium on Principles of Programming Languages, pp. 317–330 (2011)

14. Heo, K., Oh, H., Yang, H.: Learning a variable-clustering strategy for octagon from labeled data generated by a static analysis. In: Rival, X. (ed.) SAS 2016. LNCS, vol. 9837, pp. 237–256. Springer, Heidelberg (2016). doi:10.1007/978-3-662-53413-7_12

15. Heule, S., Sridharan, M., Chandra, S.: Mimic: computing models for opaque code. In: Proceedings of the 2015 10th Joint Meeting on Foundations of Software Engineering, ESEC/FSE 2015, pp. 710–720 (2015)

16. Jang, D., Choe, K.-M.: Points-to analysis for JavaScript. In: Proceedings of the 2009 ACM Symposium on Applied Computing, SAC 2009, pp. 1930–1937 (2009)

17. Jensen, S.H., Møller, A., Thiemann, P.: Type analysis for JavaScript. In: Palsberg, J., Su, Z. (eds.) SAS 2009. LNCS, vol. 5673, pp. 238–255. Springer, Heidelberg (2009). doi:10.1007/978-3-642-03237-0_17

18. Jeon, J., Qiu, X., Fetter-Degges, J., Foster, J.S., Solar-Lezama, A.: Synthesizing framework models for symbolic execution. In: Proceedings of the 38th International Conference on Software Engineering, ICSE 2016, pp. 156–167 (2016)

19. Jha, S., Gulwani, S., Seshia, S.A., Tiwari, A.: Oracle-guided component-based program synthesis. In: Proceedings of the 32nd ACM/IEEE International Conference on Software Engineering, ICSE 2010, vol. 1, pp. 215–224 (2010)

20. Katz, O., El-Yaniv, R., Yahav, E.: Estimating types in binaries using predictive modeling. In: Proceedings of the 43rd Annual ACM SIGPLAN-SIGACT Symposium on Principles of Programming Languages, POPL 2016, pp. 313–326 (2016)

21. Kowalewski, S., Philippou, A. (eds.): TACAS 2009. LNCS, vol. 5505. Springer, Heidelberg (2009)

22. Le, V., Afshari, M., Su, Z.: Compiler validation via equivalence modulo inputs. In: Proceedings of the 35th ACM SIGPLAN Conference on Programming Language Design and Implementation, PLDI 2014, pp. 216–226 (2014)

23. Von Luxburg, U., Schoelkopf, B.: Statistical learning theory: models, concepts, and results. In: Inductive Logic, pp. 651–706 (2011)

24. Madsen, M., Livshits, B., Fanning, M.: Practical static analysis of JavaScript applications in the presence of frameworks and libraries. In: Proceedings of the 2013 9th Joint Meeting on Foundations of Software Engineering, ESEC/FSE 2013, pp. 499–509. ACM, New York (2013)

25. Mangal, R., Zhang, X., Nori, A.V., Naik, M.: A user-guided approach to program analysis. In: Proceedings of the 2015 10th Joint Meeting on Foundations of Software Engineering, ESEC/FSE 2015, pp. 462–473 (2015)
26. Oh, H., Yang, H., Yi, K.: Learning a strategy for adapting a program analysis via Bayesian optimisation. In: Proceedings of the 2015 ACM SIGPLAN International Conference on Object-Oriented Programming, Systems, Languages, and Applications, OOPSLA 2015, pp. 572–588 (2015)
27. Quinlan, J.R.: Induction of decision trees. Mach. Learn. **1**(1), 81–106 (1986)
28. Raychev, V., Bielik, P., Vechev, M., Krause, A.: Learning programs from noisy data. In: Proceedings of the 43rd Annual ACM SIGPLAN-SIGACT Symposium on Principles of Programming Languages, POPL 2016, pp. 761–774 (2016)
29. Raychev, V., Vechev, M., Krause, A.: Predicting program properties from big code. In: Proceedings of the 42nd Annual ACM SIGPLAN-SIGACT Symposium on Principles of Programming Languages, POPL 2015, pp. 111–124 (2015)
30. Sharma, R., Gupta, S., Hariharan, B., Aiken, A., Nori, A.V.: Verification as learning geometric concepts. In: Logozzo, F., Fähndrich, M. (eds.) SAS 2013. LNCS, vol. 7935, pp. 388–411. Springer, Heidelberg (2013). doi:10.1007/978-3-642-38856-9_21
31. Solar-Lezama, A., Tancau, L., Bodík, R., Seshia, S.A., Saraswat, V.A.: Combinatorial sketching for finite programs. In: Proceedings of the 12th International Conference on Architectural Support for Programming Languages and Operating Systems, ASPLOS 2006, pp. 404–415 (2006)

Synthesis with Abstract Examples

Dana Drachsler-Cohen[1(✉)], Sharon Shoham[2], and Eran Yahav[1]

[1] Technion, Haifa, Israel
ddana@cs.technion.ac.il
[2] Tel Aviv University, Tel Aviv, Israel

Abstract. Interactive program synthesizers enable a user to communicate his/her intent via input-output examples. Unfortunately, such synthesizers only guarantee that the synthesized program is correct on the provided examples. A user that wishes to guarantee correctness for all possible inputs has to manually inspect the synthesized program, an error-prone and challenging task.

We present a novel synthesis framework that communicates only through (abstract) examples and guarantees that the synthesized program is correct on all inputs. The main idea is to use *abstract examples*—a new form of examples that represent a potentially unbounded set of concrete examples. An abstract example captures how part of the input space is mapped to corresponding outputs by the synthesized program. Our framework uses a generalization algorithm to compute abstract examples which are then presented to the user. The user can accept an abstract example, or provide a counterexample in which case the synthesizer will explore a different program. When the user accepts a set of abstract examples that covers the entire input space, the synthesis process is completed.

We have implemented our approach and we experimentally show that our synthesizer communicates with the user effectively by presenting on average 3 abstract examples until the user rejects false candidate programs. Further, we show that a synthesizer that prunes the program space based on the abstract examples reduces the overall number of required concrete examples in up to 96% of the cases.

1 Introduction

We address the problem of interactive synthesis, where a user and synthesizer interact to generate a program that captures the user's intent. Interactive synthesis enables users to express their intent by providing the synthesizer with input-output examples. Unfortunately, such synthesizers only guarantee that the synthesized program is correct on the provided examples. A user that wishes to guarantee correctness for all possible inputs has to manually inspect the synthesized program, an error-prone and challenging task.

Motivating Example. Eli Gold is a crisis manager at a respected law firm that due to a crisis has to meet all office members personally. After setting up times and storing the meeting times in an Excel spreadsheet (Fig. 1), Eli wants

R. Majumdar and V. Kunčak (Eds.): CAV 2017, Part I, LNCS 10426, pp. 254–278, 2017.
DOI: 10.1007/978-3-319-63387-9_13

to send emails with a personal message notifying each member the time of the meeting. He starts typing the messages in Excel. While typing the third message, Flash Fill [21] (a PBE synthesizer integrated in Excel) synthesizes a program and creates messages for all members on the list.

	A	B	C	D	E
1	First	Last	Meeting	Email	Message
2	Diane	Lockhart	11:00	d.lockhart@lockhart-gardner.com	Hi Diane, please come to my office at 11:00. -EG
3	Will	Gardner	12:00	w.gardner@lockhart-gardner.com	Hi Will, please come to my office at 12:00. -EG
4	David	Lee	13:00	d.lee@lockhart-gardner.com	Ha David, please come to my office at 13:00. -EG
5	Alicia	Florrick	14:00	a.florrick@lockhart-gardner.com	HI Alicia, please come to my office at 14:00. -EG
6	Cary	Agos	15:00	c.agos@lockhart-gardner.com	Ha Cary, please come to my office at 15:00. -EG

Fig. 1. Using flash fill to send meeting appointments.

At first glance, Flash Fill seems to have learned the correct program. However, careful inspection reveals that instead of the desired "Hi" greeting, the message's first word is an "H" followed by the second letter of the person's first name. This demonstrates the importance of inspecting the synthesis result before relying on it to handle additional examples (e.g., lines 4–6 in the Excel spreadsheet).

Goal. In this work, we wish to ensure correctness of the synthesized program on all inputs, while still interacting with the user through examples.

Existing Techniques. Interactive synthesis with correctness guarantees can be viewed as a special case of *exact learning* [10], where a learner (the synthesizer) and a teacher (the user) interact to find the target concept known to the teacher. In exact learning, the learner interacts with the teacher by asking two kinds of questions: (i) *membership questions*, where the learner asks for the output of a given input, and (ii) *validation questions*, where the learner asks whether a hypothesis (a synthesized program) is correct and if not, asks for a counterexample.

The popular counterexample-guided inductive synthesis (CEGIS) [41] approach can be viewed as an instance of exact learning where the teacher is realized as a verifier with a formal specification (rather than a user). The formal specification provides an efficient way to answer validation questions automatically. Using validation questions ensures correctness on all inputs, but requires a formal specification of the user intent, a specification which often does not exist.

In contrast, in *programming by example* (PBE), the user provides a set of input-output examples which correspond to membership questions (and answers). Classical PBE approaches (e.g., [5, 29, 33]) do not use any validation questions, and never present the synthesized program to the user. These techniques tradeoff exactness for ease of interaction with an end-user. In terms of correctness, they only guarantee that the synthesized program is *consistent with the user-provided examples*. Other techniques (e.g., [26]) obtain correctness but make additional assumptions (see Sect. 6).

Relying solely on membership questions is limited in its ability to ensure correctness. Without validation queries or additional assumptions on the program space, correctness is only guaranteed if *the entire input space is covered by membership questions (examples)*. When the input space is finite, this is usually impractical. When the input space is infinite, asking membership questions about all inputs is clearly impossible.

Our Approach. We present a novel interactive synthesis framework that communicates with a user only through *abstract membership queries*—asking the user whether an *abstract* example of the current candidate program should be accepted or rejected—and guarantees that the synthesized program is correct on all inputs. Abstract examples are a new form of examples that represent a potentially unbounded set of concrete examples of a candidate program. Abstract examples are natural for a user to understand and inspect (similarly to examples), and at the same time enable validation of the synthesis result without enumerating all concrete examples (which is only possible for a finite domain, and even then is often prohibitively expensive). In fact, an abstract membership question can also be viewed as a *partial validation question*. Instead of presenting the user with a program and asking him/her to determine whether it is correct or not (a validation question), we present an abstract example, which describes (declaratively) how the candidate program transforms part of the input space. In this way, abstract examples allow us to perform *exact synthesis without a predefined specification*.

Throughout the synthesis process, as the synthesizer explores the space of candidate programs to find the one that matches the user intent, the synthesizer presents to the user abstract examples of candidate programs. The user can accept an abstract example, or provide a counterexample in which case the synthesizer will explore a different candidate program. If the user accepts an abstract example, he/she confirms the behavior of the candidate program on part of the input space. That is, the synthesizer learns the desired behavior for an *unbounded number of concrete inputs*. Thus, it can prune every program that does not meet the confirmed abstract example. This pruning is correct even if later the candidate program is rejected by another abstract example. Generally, pruning based on an abstract example removes more programs than pruning based on a concrete example. Thus, our synthesizer is likely to converge faster to the target program compared to the current alternative (see Sect. 5). When the user accepts a set of abstract examples that covers the entire input space, our synthesizer returns the corresponding candidate program and the synthesis process is completed.

A key ingredient of our synthesizer is a generalization algorithm, called L-SEP. L-SEP takes a concrete example and a candidate program, and generalizes the example to a *maximally general* abstract example consistent with the candidate program. To illustrate, consider our motivating example, and assume the candidate program is the one synthesized by Flash Fill (that returns "H" followed by the second letter of the person's first name, etc.) and the initial concrete example is the first member on the list (i.e., Diane). Our generalization algorithm produces the following abstract example:

$$\mathbf{a_0 a_1 A_2 \ B \ C} \rightarrow \underline{\mathbf{H} a_1 \ \mathbf{a_0 a_1 A_2}, \text{ please come to my office at } \mathbf{C} . \text{-EG}}$$

This example describes the program behavior on the cells at columns A, B, and C, for the case where the string at cell A has at least two characters, denoted by a_0 and a_1, followed by a string sequence of an arbitrary size (including 0), denoted by A_2. For such inputs, the example describes the output as a sequence consisting of: (i) the string "H" followed by a_1, (ii) the entire string at A followed by a comma, (iii) the string: "please come to my office at", (iv) the string at C, and (v) the string: ". -EG".

This abstract example is presented to the user. The user rejects it and provides a concrete counterexample (e.g., line 4 in the Excel spreadsheet). Thus, the synthesizer prunes the space of candidate programs and generates a new candidate program. Eventually, the synthesizer generates the target program (as a candidate program), and our synthesizer presents the following abstract example:

$$\mathbf{A \ B \ C} \rightarrow \underline{\mathbf{Hi} \ \mathbf{A}, \text{ please come to my office at } \mathbf{C} . \text{-EG}}$$

This time, the user accepts it. Since this abstract example covers the entire input space, the synthesizer infers that this program captures the user intent on all inputs and returns it. In general, covering the input space may require multiple abstract examples.

We have implemented our synthesizer and experimentally evaluated it on two domains: strings and bit vectors. Results indicate that our synthesizer can communicate with the user effectively by presenting on average 3 abstract examples until the user rejects false candidate programs (on our most challenging benchmark, consisting of programs that require a large number of examples to differentiate them from the other programs). Further, results show that pruning the program space based on the abstract examples reduces the overall number of required concrete examples in up to 96% of the cases.

Main Contributions. The main contributions of this paper are:

- A new notion of abstract examples, which capture a (potentially unbounded) set of concrete examples, and a realization via a language inspired by regular expressions (Sect. 2).
- A generalization algorithm for learning a maximally generalizing abstract example from a concrete example and a candidate program (Sect. 3).
- A novel synthesis framework that communicates only through abstract examples and guarantees that the synthesized program is correct on all inputs (Sect. 4).
- An implementation and experimental evaluation that shows that our synthesizer requires few abstract examples to reject false programs, and that it reduces the number of concrete examples required to find the target program (Sect. 5).

2   Abstract Specifications and Sequence Expressions

In this section, we define the key terms pertaining to abstract examples. We then present a special class of abstract examples for programs that manipulate strings. For simplicity's sake, from here on we assume that programs take one input. This is not a limitation as multiple inputs (or outputs) can be joined with a predefined delimiter (e.g., the inputs in the motivating example can be considered as one string separated by spaces).

2.1   Abstract Examples

Program Semantics. The semantics of a program P is a function over a domain D: $[\![P]\!] : D \to D$. We equate $[\![P]\!]$ with its input-output pair set: $\{(in, [\![P]\!](in)) \mid in \in D\}$.

Abstract Examples. An abstract example ae defines a set $[\![ae]\!] \subseteq D \times D$, which represents a partial function: if $(in, out_1), (in, out_2) \in [\![ae]\!]$, then $out_1 = out_2$. An abstract example ae is *an abstract example for program* P if $[\![ae]\!] \subseteq [\![P]\!]$. We define the domain of ae to be $dom(ae) = \{in \in D \mid \exists out. \, (in, out) \in [\![ae]\!]\}$.

Abstract Example Specifications. An abstract example specification of P is a set of abstract examples A for P such that $\bigcup_{ae \in A} dom(ae) = D$. Note that A need not be finite and the example domains need not be disjoint.

2.2   Sequence Expressions

In this work, we focus on programs that manipulate strings, i.e., $D = \Sigma^*$ for a finite alphabet Σ. Thus, it is desirable to represent abstract examples as expressions that represent collections of concrete strings and can be readily interpreted by humans. A prominent candidate for this goal is regular expressions, which are widely used to succinctly represent a set of strings. However, regular expressions are restricted to constant symbols (from Σ). Thus, they cannot relate outputs to inputs, which is desirable when describing partial functions (abstract examples). To obtain this property, we introduce a new language, *Sequence Expressions* (SE), that extends regular expressions with the ability to relate the outputs to their inputs via shared variables. We begin this section with a reminder of regular expressions, and then introduce the two types of sequence expressions: input SEs, for describing inputs, and output SEs, for describing outputs.

Regular Expressions (RE). The set of regular languages over a finite alphabet Σ is the minimal set containing $\epsilon, \sigma_1, ..., \sigma_{|\Sigma|}$ that is closed under concatenation, union, and Kleene star. A regular expression r is a text representation of a regular language over the symbols in Σ and the operators $\cdot, |, ^*$ (concatenation, or, and Kleene star).

Input SE Syntax. Figure 2(a) shows the grammar of input SEs. Compared to RE, SEs are extended with three kinds of variables that later help to relate the output to the input:

$S_I ::= S_I \cdot S_I \mid \epsilon \mid \sigma \mid x_R \mid X_R \mid \sigma^k$

(a) Input SE

$S_O ::= S_O \cdot S_O \mid \epsilon \mid \sigma \mid x \mid f(x) \mid X \mid f(X) \mid \sigma^k$

(b) Output SE

Fig. 2. SE grammar: $\sigma \in \Sigma, x \in \mathbf{x}, X \in \mathbf{X}, k \in \mathbf{K}, R \in \mathcal{R}, f \in \mathcal{F}$.

- Character variables, denoted $x \in \mathbf{x}$, used to denote an arbitrary letter from Σ.
- Sequence variables, denoted $X \in \mathbf{X}$, used to denote a sequence of arbitrary size.
- Star variables, denoted $k \in \mathbf{K}$, used instead of the Kleene star to indicate the number of consecutive repeating occurrences of a symbol. For example, 0^k has the same meaning as the RE 0^*.

To eliminate ambiguity, in our examples we underline letters from Σ. For example, $xX\underline{a}$ represents the set of words that have at least two letters and end with an a (a $\in \Sigma$).

We limit each variable (i.e., x, X, k) to appear at most once at an input SE. We also limit the use of a Kleene star to single letters from the alphabet. Also, since the goal of each SE is to describe a single behavior of the program, we exclude the 'or' operator. Instead, we extend the grammar to enable to express 'or' to some extent via predefined *predicates* that put constraints on the variables. We denote these predicates by $R \in \mathcal{R}$, and their meaning (i.e., the set of words that satisfy them) by $[\![R]\!] \subseteq \Sigma^*$. We note that we do not impose restrictions on the set $\mathcal{R}$, however our algorithm relies on an SMT-solver, and thus predicates in $\mathcal{R}$ have to be encodable as formulas.

Some examples for predicates and their meaning are: $[\![num]\!] = \{w \in \Sigma^* \mid w \text{ consists of digits only}\}$, $[\![anum]\!] = \{w \in \Sigma^* \mid w \text{ consists of letters and digits only}\}$, $[\![del]\!] = \{., \backslash t, ; \}$, $[\![no\_del]\!] = \Sigma^* \setminus [\![del]\!]$. We assume that the predicate satisfied by any string, T, (where $[\![T]\!] = \Sigma^*$) is always in $\mathcal{R}$. We abbreviate x_T, X_T to x, X. In the following, we refer to these as atomic constructs: $\sigma, x_R, X_R, \sigma^k$. Given an input SE se we denote by $\mathbf{x}_{se}, \mathbf{X}_{se}$, and $\mathbf{K}_{se}$ the set of variables in se.

Input SE Semantics. To define the semantics, we first define *interpretations* of an SE, which depend on *assignments*. An assignment env for an input SE se maps every $x \in \mathbf{x}_{se}$ to a letter in Σ, every $X \in \mathbf{X}_{se}$ to a sequence in Σ^*, and every $k \in \mathbf{K}_{se}$ to a natural number (including 0). We denote by $env[se]$ the sequence over Σ obtained by substituting the variables with their interpretations. Formally: (i) $env[\epsilon] = \epsilon$ (ii) $env[\sigma] = \sigma$ (iii) $env[x_R] = env(x)$ (iv) $env[X_R] = env(X)$ (v) $env[\sigma^k] = \sigma^{env(k)}$ (vi) $env[S_1 \cdot S_2] = env[S_1] \cdot env[S_2]$ (where $\cdot$ denotes string concatenation). An assignment is *valid* if for every x_R and X_R in se, $env(x), env(X) \in [\![R]\!]$. In the following we always refer to valid assignments.

The semantics of an input SE se, denoted by $[\![se]\!]$, is the set of strings obtained by the set of all valid assignments, i.e. $[\![se]\!] = \{s \in \Sigma^* \mid \exists env.\ env[se] = s\}$. For example, $[\![\sigma]\!] = \{\sigma\}$, $[\![x]\!] = \Sigma$, $[\![X]\!] = \Sigma^*$, and $[\![\sigma^k]\!] = \{\epsilon, \sigma, \sigma\sigma, ...\}$.

Output SE. Figure 2(b) shows the grammar of output SEs. Output SEs are defined *with respect to an input SE* and they can only refer to its variables. Formally, given an input SE *se*, an output SE over *se* is restricted to variables in $\mathbf{x}_{se}$, $\mathbf{X}_{se}$, and $\mathbf{K}_{se}$. Unlike input SEs, an output SE is allowed to have multiple occurrences of the same variable, and variables are not constrained by predicates. In addition, output SEs can express invocations of unary functions over the variables. Namely, the grammar is extended by $f(x)$ and $f(X)$, where $x \in \mathbf{x}_{se}$ and $X \in \mathbf{X}_{se}$, and $f : \Sigma \to \Sigma^*$ is a function.

An interpretation of an output SE is defined with respect to an assignment, similarly to the interpretation of an input SE. We extend the interpretation definition for the functions as follows: $env[f(x)] = f(env(x))$ and if $env(X) = \sigma_1 \cdots \sigma_n$ then $env[f(X)] = f(\sigma_1) \cdots f(\sigma_n)$, i.e., $env[f(X)]$ is the concatenation of the results of invoking f on the characters of the interpretation of X. (If $env(X) = \epsilon$, $env[f(X)] = \epsilon$.)

Input-Output SE Pairs. An input-output SE (interchangeably, an SE pair) is a pair $io = se_{in} \to se_{out}$ consisting of an input SE, se_{in}, and an output SE, se_{out}, defined over se_{in}. Given $io = se_{in} \to se_{out}$, we denote $in(io) = se_{in}$ and $out(io) = se_{out}$. The semantics of io is the set of pairs: $[\![io]\!] = \{(s_{in}, s_{out}) \in \Sigma^* \times \Sigma^* \mid \exists env.\ s_{in} = env[in(io)] \land s_{out} = env[out(io)]\}$. The domain of io is $dom(io) = [\![in(ae)]\!]$.

Example. An input-output SE for the pattern of column D based on columns A, B in Fig. 1 is:

$$x_{0\text{no\_del}}X_{1\text{no\_del}}\_X_2 \to f_{\text{lowercase}}(x_0)\underset{\cdot}{.}f_{\text{lowercase}}(X_2)\underline{@\text{lockhart-gardner.com}}$$

where x_0 is a character variable, X_1 and X_2 are sequence variables and $\_$ denotes a column delimiter (taken from Σ). The predicate *no_del* is satisfied by words that do not contain a delimiter. The semantics of this SE pair is the set of all word pairs whose first element is a string consisting of a first name, a delimiter, and a last name, and the second element is the email address which is the sequence of the first letter of the first name in lower case, a dot, the lower-cased last name, and the suffix "@lockhart-gardner.com".

2.3   Sequence Expressions as Abstract Examples

SE pairs provide an intuitive mean to describe relation between outputs to inputs. In this work, we focus on learning abstract examples that can be described with SE pairs. For simplicity's sake, in the following we ignore predicates and functions (i.e., $\mathcal{R}, \mathcal{F}$). Our definitions and algorithms can be easily extended to arbitrary (but finite) sets $\mathcal{R}$ and $\mathcal{F}$.

We say that an input-output SE is an abstract example if $[\![io]\!]$ describes a partial function. Note that in general, an SE pair is not necessarily an abstract example. For example, the pair $io_{XY} = XY \to XaY$, can be interpreted to $(bbb, babb)$ (by $env_1 = \{X \mapsto b, Y \mapsto bb\}$) and $(bbb, bbab)$ (by $env_2 = \{X \mapsto bb, Y \mapsto b\}$). Thus, $[\![io_{XY}]\!]$ is not a partial function and hence not an abstract example.

Given a program P, we say that *an input-output SE is an abstract example for P* if $[\![io]\!] \subseteq [\![P]\!]$. Since $[\![P]\!]$ is a function, this requirement subsumes the requirement of abstract example. Given an input SE se_{in}, we say that an output SE se_{out} over se_{in} is a *completion* of se_{in} for P if $se_{in} \to se_{out}$ is an abstract example for P.

Example. We next exemplify how SEs can provide an abstract example specification to describe a program behavior. Assume a user has a list of first names and middle names (space delimited), some are only initials, and he/she wants to create a greeting message of the form "Dear <name>". The name in the greeting is the first string if it is identified as a name, i.e., has at least two letters; otherwise, the name is the entire string. For example: (i) Adam $\to$ Dear Adam, (ii) Adam R. $\to$ Dear Adam, (iii) A. Robert $\to$ Dear A. Robert (iv) A.R. $\to$ Dear A.R.. In this example, we assume the predicate set contains the predicates $\mathcal{R} = \{T, \text{name}, \text{other}\}$, where $[\![\text{name}]\!] = \{A, a, ..., Z, z\}^{+} \setminus \{A, a, ..., Z, z\}$, $[\![\text{other}]\!] = (\Sigma \setminus \{\_\})^{*} \setminus [\![\text{name}]\!]$. An abstract example specification is: (i) $X_{0_{\text{name}}} \to \underline{\text{Dear } X_0}$ (ii) $X_{0_{\text{name}}}\_X_1 \to \underline{\text{Dear } X_0}$ (iii) $X_{0_{\text{other}}} \to \underline{\text{Dear } X_0}$ (iv) $X_{0_{\text{other}}}\_X_1 \to \underline{\text{Dear } X_0}\_X_1$.

Discussion. While SEs can capture many program behaviors, they have limitations. One limitation is that an SE can only describe relations between output characters to input characters, but not among input characters. For example, it cannot capture inputs that are palindromes or inputs of the form XX (e.g., *abab*). This limitation arises because we chose input SEs to be (a subset of) regular expressions, which cannot capture such languages. Also, tasks that are not string manipulations are likely to have a specification that contains (many) trivial abstract examples (i.e., concrete input-output examples). For example, consider a program that takes two digits and returns their multiplication. Some abstract examples describing it are $X\ 1 \to X$ and $1\ X \to X$. However, the specification also contains $9\ 2 \to 18$, $9\ 3 \to 27, ..., 9\ 9 \to 81$. Also, an abstract example specification consists of a *set* of independent abstract examples, with no particular order. As a result, describing if-else rules requires encoding the negation of the "if" condition explicitly in order to obtain the same case splitting as an if-else structure.

Generalization Order. We next define a partial order between SEs that are abstract examples. This order is leveraged by our algorithm in the next section. We call this order the *generalization order* and if an abstract example is greater than another one, we say it is more general or abstract. We begin with defining a partial order $\preceq$ on the atomic constructs of SEs, as follows:

$$\begin{array}{ccc} & X & \\ \nearrow & & \nwarrow \\ x & & \sigma^k \\ \nwarrow & & \nearrow \\ & \sigma & \end{array}$$

where $\sigma \in \Sigma$, $x \in \mathbf{x}$, $X \in \mathbf{X}$ and $k \in \mathbf{K}$.

We say that an input SE se' is more general than se, $se \preceq se'$, if its atomic constructs are *pointwise* more general than the atomic constructs of se. Namely, for $se = a_1 \cdots a_n$ and $se' = a_1' \cdots a_n'$ (where a_i and a_i' are atomic constructs), $se \preceq se'$ if for every $1 \leq i \leq n$, $a_i \preceq a_i'$. If $se \preceq se' \wedge se \neq se'$, we write $se \prec se'$. For example, $\underline{abc} \prec \underline{ab^k\underline{c}} \prec xYZ$. In addition, we define that for any atomic construct a, $a \npreceq \epsilon$ and $\epsilon \npreceq a$. The generalization order implies the following:

Lemma 1. *Let* se, se' *be two input SEs. If* $se \preceq se'$, *then* $[\![se]\!] \subseteq [\![se']\!]$.

The proof follows directly from the definition of $\preceq$ and the semantics of an input SE. Note that the converse does not necessarily hold. For example, $[\![XY]\!] = [\![Z]\!]$, but $XY \npreceq Z$ and $Z \npreceq XY$. In fact, $\preceq$ may only relate SEs of the same length. In practice, we partly support generalizations beyond $\preceq$ (see Sect. 3).

The generalization order of input SEs induces a generalization order on input-output SEs: $io \preceq io'$ if $in(io) \preceq in(io')$. If io and io' are abstract examples for the same program P, this implies that $[\![io]\!] \subseteq [\![io']\!]$. Moreover, in that case $[\![io]\!] \subseteq [\![io']\!]$ if and only if $[\![in(io)]\!] \subseteq [\![in(io')]\!]$. This observation enables our algorithm to focus on generalizing the input SE instead of generalizing the pair as a whole.

3   An Algorithm for Learning Abstract Examples

In this section, we describe L-SEP, our algorithm for automatically **L**earning an **SE P**air. This pair is an abstract example for a given program and it generalizes a given concrete example. In Sect. 4, we will use L-SEP repeatedly in order to generate an abstract example specification.

L-SEP (Algorithm 1) takes as input a program P (e.g., the program Flash Fill learned) and a (concrete) input in (e.g., *Diane*). These two define the initial SE to start with: $(in, [\![P]\!](in))$ (namely, the concrete example). The algorithm outputs an input-output SE, $io = s_{in} \rightarrow s_{out}$, such that $(in, [\![P]\!](in)) \in [\![io]\!] \subseteq [\![P]\!]$. Namely, io generalizes (or abstracts) the concrete example and is consistent with P. L-SEP's goal is to find an io that is *maximal* with respect to $\preceq$.

The high-level operation of L-SEP is as follows. First, it sets $io = in \rightarrow [\![P]\!](in)$. Then, it gradually generalizes io while this results in pairs that are abstract examples for P. The main insight of L-SEP is that instead of generalizing io as a whole, it generalizes the input SE, $in(io)$, and then checks whether there is a completion of $in(io)$ for P, namely an output SE over $in(io)$ such that the resulting pair is an abstract example for P. This is justified by the property that $io \preceq io'$ if and only if $in(io) \preceq in(io')$.

3.1   Input Generalization

We now explain the pseudo code of L-SEP. After initializing io by setting $s_{in} = in$ and $s_{out} = [\![P]\!](in)$, L-SEP stores in $InCands$ the set of candidates generalizing s_{in} (which are the input components of io's generalizations). Then, a loop attempts to generalize s_{in} as long as $InCand \neq \emptyset$. Each iteration picks a minimal element from $InCands$, s_{in}', which is a candidate to generalize s_{in}. To determine if s_{in}' can generalize s_{in}, findCompletion is called. If it succeeds, it returns s_{out}'

Algorithm 1. L-SEP(P, in)

---

1 $s_{in} = in$; $s_{out} = [\![P]\!](in)$
2 $InCands = \{s \in SE_{in} \mid s \succ s_{in}\}$
3 **while** $InCands \neq \emptyset$ **do**
4 | s'_{in} = pick a minimal element from $InCands$
5 | s'_{out} = findCompletion(P, s'_{in})   // if succeeds, $[\![s'_{in} \to s'_{out}]\!] \subseteq [\![P]\!]$
6 | **if** $s'_{out} \neq \perp$ **then**
7 | | $s_{in} = s'_{in}$; $s_{out} = s'_{out}$
8 | |_ $InCands = InCands \cap \{s \in SE_{in} \mid s \succ s_{in}\}$
9 | **else**
10 | |_ $InCands = InCands \setminus \{s \in SE_{in} \mid s \succeq s'_{in}\}$

11 **return** (s_{in}, s_{out})

---

such that $s'_{in} \to s'_{out}$ is an abstract example for P. If it fails, $\perp$ is returned. Either way, the search space, $InCands$, is pruned: if the generalization succeeds, then the candidates are pruned to those generalizing s'_{in}; otherwise, to those *except* the ones generalizing s'_{in}. If the generalization succeeds, s_{in} and s_{out} are updated to s'_{in} and s'_{out}.

Our next lemma states that if findCompletion returns $\perp$, pruning $InCands$ does not remove input SE that have a completion for P. The lemma guarantees that L-SEP cannot miss abstract examples for P because of this pruning.

Lemma 2. *If $s''_{in} \succeq s'_{in}$ and s'_{in} has no completion for P, s''_{in} has no completion for P.*

Proof (sketch). We prove by induction on the number of generalization steps required to get from s'_{in} to s''_{in}. Base is trivial. Assume the last generalization step is to replace a'_i in $s_{in'}$ with a''_i in s''_{in}. If s''_{in} has a completion s''_{out} for P, then substitute a''_i in s''_{out} by a'_i to obtain a completion for s'_{in}. However, this contradicts our assumption.   □

InCands. For ease of presentation, L-SEP defines $InCand$ as the set of all generalizations of in that remain to be checked, where initially it contains all generalizations. However, the size of this set is exponential in the length of in, and thus practically, L-SEP does not maintain it explicitly. Instead, it maintains two sets: $MinCands$, which records the *minimal* generalizations of the current candidate s_{in} that remain to be checked, and $Pruned$, which records the minimal generalizations that were overruled (and hence none of their generalizations need to be inspected). Technically, in Line 2 and Line 8 L-SEP initializes $MinCands$ based on the current candidate s_{in} by computing all of its minimal generalizations. In Line 10 it removes from $MinCand$ the generalization that was last checked and failed, and also records this generalization in $Pruned$ to indicate that none of its generalizations needs to be inspected. $Pruned$ is used immediately after initializing $MinCand$ in Line 8 to remove from $MinCands$

any generalization that generalizes a member of *Pruned* – this efficiently implements the update of *InCands* in Line 10. Using this representation of *InCands* we can now establish:

Lemma 3. *The number of iterations of L-SEP is* $O(|in|^2 \cdot |\mathcal{R}|^2)$.

Proof. The number of iterations is at most the maximal size of *MinCands* multiplied by the number of initializations of *MinCands* based on a new candidate s_{in} in Line 8. The size of *MinCands* computed based on some s_{in} is at most $|in| \cdot (|\mathcal{R}| + 1)$. This follows since a minimal generalization of s_{in} differs from s_{in} in a single construct that is more general than the corresponding construct in s_{in} (with respect to the partial order of constructs). The number of initializations of *MinCands* at Line 8 is bounded by the longest (possible) chain of generalizations. This follows because each such initialization is triggered by the update of s_{in} to a more general SE. Since the longest chain of generalizations is at most $|in| \cdot (|\mathcal{R}| + 1)$, the number of iterations is $O(|in|^2 \cdot |\mathcal{R}|^2)$. □

Lemma 3 implies that *MinCands* and *Pruned* provide a polynomial representation of *InCands* (even though the latter is exponential). Further, the use of these sets enables L-SEP to run in polynomial time because they provide a quadratic bound on the number of iterations, and because findCompletion is also polynomial, as we shortly prove.

Picking a Minimal Generalization. We now discuss how L-SEP picks a minimal generalization of s_{in} in Line 4. One option is to arbitrarily pick a minimal generalization. However, this greedy approach may result in a sub-optimal maximal generalization, namely a maximal generalization that concretizes to fewer concrete inputs than some other possible maximal generalization. On the other hand, to obtain an optimal generalization, all generalizations that have a completion have to be computed and only then the best one can be picked by comparing the number of concretizations. Unfortunately, this approach results in an exponential time complexity and is thus impractical. Instead, our implementation of L-SEP takes an intermediate approach: it considers all *minimal* generalizations that have a completion and picks one that concretizes to a maximal number of inputs. To avoid counting the number of inputs (which may be computationally expensive), our implementation employs the following heuristic. It syntactically compares the generalizations by comparing the construct in each of them that is not in s_{in} (i.e., where generalization took place). It then picks the generalization whose construct is maximal with respect to the order: $X > \sigma^k > x$. If there are generalized constructs incomparable w.r.t. this order (e.g., σ_1^k vs. σ_2^k), one is picked arbitrarily.

3.2   Completion

findCompletion (Algorithm 2) takes P and an input generalization s'_{in} and returns a completion of s'_{in} for P, if exists; or $\bot$, otherwise.

Unlike input SEs, the fact that a certain candidate s''_{out} is not a completion of s'_{in} for P, does not imply that its generalizations are also not completions of s'_{in}.

Algorithm 2. findCompletion(P, s'_{in})

---

1 **return** findOutputPrefix(P, s'_{in}, ϵ)

2 **Function** findOutputPrefix$(P, s'_{in}, s^{pref}_{out})$:

3 $\quad$ **if** $[\![s'_{in} \rightarrow s^{pref}_{out}]\!] \subseteq [\![P]\!]$ **then return** s^{pref}_{out}

4 $\quad$ $Cands = \{s \in SE_{out}(s'_{in}) \mid s$ is an atomic construct$\}$

5 $\quad$ **while** $Cands \neq \emptyset$ **do**

6 $\quad\quad$ $sym =$ pick and remove a minimal element from $Cands$

7 $\quad\quad$ **if** $[\![s'_{in} \rightarrow s^{pref}_{out} \cdot sym]\!] \subseteq \{(in, o_p) \mid \exists o_s \in \Sigma^*.(in, o_p \cdot o_s) \in [\![P]\!]\}$ **then**

8 $\quad\quad\quad$ $s^{pref}_{out} = s^{pref}_{out} \cdot sym$

9 $\quad\quad\quad$ $s'_{out} =$ findOutputPrefix$(P, s'_{in}, s^{pref}_{out})$

10 $\quad\quad\quad$ **if** $s'_{out} \neq \perp$ **then return** s'_{out}

11 $\quad$ **return** $\perp$

Thus, a pruning similar to the one of L-SEP may result in missing completions. To exemplify this, consider a program P whose abstract example specification is $\{xX \rightarrow \underline{b}X\}$. Assume that while L-SEP looks for a completion for $s'_{in} = \underline{a}x$ it considers $s'_{out} = \underline{ba}$, which is not a completion. Pruning SEs that are more general than s'_{out}, will result in pruning the completion $\underline{b}x$. Likewise, pruning elements that are more specific than a candidate that is not a completion may result in pruning completions.

Since the former pruning cannot be used to search the output SE, findCompletion searches differently. Its search involves attempts to gradually construct a completion s'_{out} construct-by-construct. If an attempt fails, it backtracks and attempts a different construction. This is implemented via the recursive function findOutputPrefix. At each step, a current prefix s^{pref}_{out} (initially ϵ) is extended with a single atomic construct sym (i.e., σ, x, X, σ^k). Then, it checks whether the current extended construction is *partially consistent* with P (Line 7). If the check fails, this extended prefix is discarded, thereby pruning its extensions from the search space. Otherwise, the extended prefix is attempted to be further extended. We next define *partial consistency*.

Definition 1. An SE pair $s'_{in} \rightarrow s^{pref}_{out}$ is *partially consistent* with P if for every assignment env, $env[s^{pref}_{out}]$ is a prefix of $[\![P]\!](env[s'_{in}])$.

When s'_{in} is clear from the context, we say that s^{pref}_{out} is partially consistent with P.

By the semantics definition, a pair $s'_{in} \rightarrow s^{pref}_{out}$ is partially consistent with P if and only if $[\![s'_{in} \rightarrow s^{pref}_{out}]\!] \subseteq \{(in, o_p) \mid \exists o_s \in \Sigma^*.(in, o_p \cdot o_s) \in [\![P]\!]\}$ (which is the check of line 7). Partial consistency is a necessary condition (albeit not sufficient) for $s^{pref}_{out} \cdot sym$ to be a prefix of a completion s'_{out}. Thus, if $s^{pref}_{out} \cdot sym$ is not partially consistent, there is no need to check its extensions. Note that even if a certain prefix $s^{pref}_{out} \cdot sym$ is partially consistent, it may be that this prefix cannot be further extended (namely, the suffixes cannot be realized by an SE). In this case, this prefix will be discarded in later iterations and s_{out}^{pref} will be attempted to be extended differently. This extension process terminates when an extension results in a completion, in which case it is returned, or when all extensions fail, in which case $\bot$ is returned.

Lemma 4. *The recursion depth of Algorithm 2 is bounded by the length of* $[\![P]\!](in)$.

Proof. Denote by n the length of $[\![P]\!](in)$. Assume to the contrary that the recursion depth exceeds n. Namely, the current prefix, s_{out}^{pref}, is strictly longer than n. We show that in this case, the partial consistency check is guaranteed to fail. To this end, we show an assignment env to s_{in}' such that $env[s_{out}^{pref}]$ is not a prefix of $[\![P]\!](env[s_{in}'])$. Consider the assignment env that maps each variable in s_{in}' to its original value in in (namely, $env[s_{in}'] = in$). This assignment maps each variable to exactly one letter. By our assumption, the length of $env[s_{out}^{pref}]$ is greater than n. Thus, $env[s_{out}^{pref}]$ (of length $> n$) cannot be a prefix of $[\![P]\!](in)$ (of length n). □

3.3   Guarantees

Lemmas 3 and 4 ensure that both the input generalization and the completion algorithms terminate in polynomial time. Thus, the overall runtime of L-SEP is polynomial. Finally, we discuss the guarantees of these algorithms.

Lemma 5. `findCompletion` *is sound and complete: if it returns* s_{out}', *then* s_{out}' *is a completion of* s_{in}' *for* P, *and if it returns* $\bot$, *then* s_{in}' *has no completion for* P.

Soundness follows since `findOutputPrefix` returns s_{out}' only after validating that $[\![s_{in}' \rightarrow s_{out}']\!] \subseteq [\![P]\!]$. Completeness follows since s_{out}' is gradually constructed and every possible extension is examined.

Lemma 6. *L-SEP is sound and complete: for every* (in, out) *pair, an SE pair is returned, and if L-SEP returns an SE pair, then it is an abstract example for* P.

Soundness is guaranteed from `findCompletion`. Completeness follows since even if all generalizations fail, L-SEP returns the concrete example as an SE pair.

Theorem 1. *L-SEP returns an abstract example* io *for* P *such that* $(in, [\![P]\!](in)) \in [\![io]\!]$ *and* io *is maximal w.r.t.* $\preceq$.

This follows from Lemmas 2 and 5, and since L-SEP terminates only when $InCands$ is empty (i.e., when there are no more input generalizations to explore).

We note that in our implementation, `findCompletion` runs heuristics instead of the expensive backtracking. In this case, maximality is no longer guaranteed.

3.4   Running Example

We next exemplify L-SEP on the (shortened) example from the introduction, where we start from a concrete example $in = $ Diane and we wish to obtain the abstract example $a_0a_1A_2 \rightarrow \underline{H}a_1\_a_0a_1A_2$. L-SEP starts with: $s_{in} = \underline{\text{Diane}}$ and $s_{out} = \underline{\text{Hi Diane}}$. It then picks a minimal candidate that generalizes s_{in}. A minimal candidate differs from s_{in} in one atomic construct in some position i. By $\preceq$, if $s_{in}[i] = \sigma$, then $s'_{in}[i]$ is x or σ^k.

Assume that L-SEP first tests this minimal candidate: $s'_{in} = D^{k_0}\underline{\text{iane}}$. To test it, L-SEP calls findCompletion to look for a completion. The completion is defined over s'_{in} and in particular can use the variable k_0. Then, findCompletion invokes findOutputPrefix(P, $D^{k_0}\underline{\text{iane}}$, ϵ). In the first call of findOutputPrefix, all extensions of the current prefix, ϵ, except for $\underline{\text{H}}$, fail in the partial consistency check. This follows since the output of P always starts with an 'H' (and not, e.g., with 'H^{k_0}'). Thus, a recursive call is invoked (only) for the output SE prefix $\underline{\text{H}}$. In this call, all extensions (i.e., $\underline{\text{H}}\sigma$ or $\underline{\text{H}}\sigma^{k_0}$) fail. For example, $\underline{\text{H}i}$ fails since the output prefix is not always "Hi" (e.g., P(DDiane) = HD DDiane). Since the prefix $\underline{\text{H}}$ cannot be extended further, $\perp$ is returned. This indicates that the input generalization $s'_{in} = D^{k_0}\underline{\text{iane}}$ fails. Thus, L-SEP removes from $InCands$ all generalizations whose first construct generalizes D^{k_0}.

L-SEP then tests another minimal generalization: $s'_{in} = x_0\underline{\text{iane}}$. It then calls findCompletion (which can use x_0). As before, (only) the prefix SE $\underline{\text{H}}$ is found partially consistent. Next, a second call attempts to extend $\underline{\text{H}}$. This time, the extension $\underline{\text{H}i}$ succeeds because for all interpretations of $x_0\underline{\text{iane}}$, the output prefix is "Hi". The recursion continues, until obtaining and returning the completion $\underline{\text{Hi }}x_0\underline{\text{iane}}$.

When L-SEP learns that s'_{in} is a feasible generalization, it updates s_{in} and s_{out}, and prunes $InCands$ to candidates generalizing $x_0\underline{\text{iane}}$ (for example, $InCands$ contains $x_0x_1\underline{\text{ane}}$). Eventually, s_{in} is generalized to $s'_{in} = x_0x_1X_2X_3X_4$ with the completion $s'_{out} = \underline{\text{H}}x_1\_x_0x_1X_2X_3X_4$. In a postprocessing step (performed when L-SEP is done), $X_2X_3X_4$ is simplified to Y, resulting in the abstract example $x_0x_1Y \rightarrow \underline{\text{H}}x_1\_x_0x_1Y$. Note that the last "generalization" is no longer according to $\preceq$.

4   Synthesis with Abstract Examples

In this section, we present our framework for synthesis with abstract examples. We assume the existence of an oracle $\mathcal{O}$ (e.g., a user) that has fixed a target program P_{tar}. Our framework is parameterized with a synthesizer $\mathcal{S}$ that takes concrete or abstract examples and returns a consistent program. Note that the guarantee to finally output a program equivalent to P_{tar} is the responsibility of our framework, and not $\mathcal{S}$. Nonetheless, candidate programs are provided by $\mathcal{S}$.

Goal. The goal of our framework is to learn a program *equivalent* to the target program. Note that this is different from the traditional goal of PBE synthesizers, which learn a program that agrees with the target program *at least* on the observed inputs. More formally, our goal is to learn a program P' such that $[\![P_{tar}]\!] = [\![P']\!]$, whereas PBE synthesizers that are given a set of input-output examples $E \subseteq D \times D$ can only guarantee to output a program P'' such that $[\![P_{tar}]\!] \cap E = [\![P'']\!] \cap E$.

Interaction Model. We assume that the oracle $\mathcal{O}$ can accept abstract examples or reject them and provide a counterexample. If the oracle accepts an abstract example io, then $[\![io]\!] \subseteq [\![P_{tar}]\!]$. If it returns a counterexample $cex = (in', out')$, then (i) $(in', out') \in [\![P_{tar}]\!]$, (ii) $(in', out') \notin [\![io]\!]$, and (iii) $in' \in [\![in(io)]\!]$.

Operation. Our framework (Algorithm 3) takes an initial (nonempty) set of input-output examples $E \subseteq D \times D$. This set may be extended during the execution. The algorithm consists of two loops: an outer one that searches for a candidate program and an inner one that computes abstract examples for a given candidate program. The inner loop terminates when one of the abstract examples is rejected (in which case a new iteration of the outer loop begins) or when the input space is covered (in which case the candidate program is returned along with the abstract example specification).

The framework begins with initializing A to the empty set. This set accumulates abstract examples that eventually form an abstract example specification of P_{tar}. Then the outer loop begins (Lines 2–10). Each iteration starts by asking the synthesizer for a program P consistent with the current set of concrete examples in E and abstract examples in A. Then, the inner loop begins (Lines 4–9). At each inner iteration, an input in is picked and L-SEP(P, in) is invoked. When an abstract example io is returned, it is presented to the oracle. If the oracle provides a counterexample $cex = (in', out')$, then $[\![P]\!] \neq [\![P_{tar}]\!]$ (see Lemma 7). In this case, E is extended with cex, and a new outer iteration begins. If the oracle accepts the abstract example, io, the abstract example is added to A (since it is an abstract example for P_{tar}). Conceptually, the synthesizer extends its set of examples with more examples (potentially an infinite number). This (potentially) enables faster convergence to P_{tar} (in case additional outer iterations are needed). If the inner loop terminates without encountering counterexamples, then A covers the input domain D. At this point it is guaranteed that $[\![P]\!] = [\![P_{tar}]\!]$ (see Theorem 2). Thus, P is returned, along with the abstract example specification A. Note that A has already been validated and need not be inspected again.

We remark that although abstract examples can help the synthesizer to converge faster to the target program, still the convergence speed (and the number of counterexamples required to converge) depends on the synthesizer (which is a parameter to our framework) and not on L-SEP or our synthesis framework.

Lemma 7. *If $\mathcal{O}(io) = (in', out')$ $(\neq \bot)$, then $[\![P]\!] \neq [\![P_{tar}]\!]$.*

Proof. From the oracle properties $(in', out') \in [\![P_{tar}]\!]$, $(in', out') \notin [\![io]\!]$, and $in' \in [\![in(io)]\!]$. Thus, there exists $out'' \neq out'$ such that $(in', out'') \in [\![io]\!]$. Since by construction, $[\![io]\!] \subseteq [\![P]\!]$, it follows that $(in', out'') \in [\![P]\!]$. Thus, $[\![P]\!] \neq [\![P_{tar}]\!]$. ☐

Algorithm 3. synthesisWithAbstractExamples(*E*)

---

1 $A = \emptyset$ // initialize the set of abstract examples
2 **while** *true* **do**
3     $P = \mathcal{S}(E, A)$ // obtain a program consistent with the examples
4   **while** $\cup_{io \in A} \llbracket in(io) \rrbracket \neq D$ **do**   // A does not cover D
5   Let $in \in D \setminus \cup_{io \in A} \llbracket in(io) \rrbracket$ // obtain uncovered input
6        $io = \text{L-SEP}(P, in)$ // learn abstract example
7        $cex = \mathcal{O}(io)$ // ask the oracle
8   **if** $cex = \bot$ **then** $A = A \cup \{io\}$ // abstract example is correct
9   **else** $E = E \cup \{cex\}$; **break**   // add a counterexample
10   **return** *(P, A)*

Theorem 2. *Upon termination, Algorithm 3 returns a program P s.t. $\llbracket P \rrbracket = \llbracket P_{tar} \rrbracket$.*

Proof. Upon termination, for every $in \in D$ there exists $io \in A$ s.t. $in \in \llbracket in(io) \rrbracket$. By construction $\llbracket io \rrbracket \subseteq \llbracket P \rrbracket$, thus $(in, \llbracket P \rrbracket(in)) \in \llbracket io \rrbracket$. By the oracle properties, $\llbracket io \rrbracket \subseteq \llbracket P_{tar} \rrbracket$, thus $(in, \llbracket P_{tar} \rrbracket(in)) \in \llbracket io \rrbracket$. Altogether, $\llbracket P \rrbracket(in) = \llbracket P_{tar} \rrbracket(in)$. $\square$

We emphasize that the interaction with the oracle (user) is only after obtaining both a candidate program and an abstract example, and the goal of the interaction is to determine whether the candidate program is correct. If the user rejects an abstract example, it means he/she rejects the candidate program, in which case the PBE synthesizer $\mathcal{S}$ looks for a new candidate program. In particular, the interaction goal is *not* to confirm the correctness of the abstract examples – L-SEP always returns (without any interaction) a correct generalization with respect to the candidate program.

Example. We next exemplify our synthesis framework in the bit vector domain. We consider a program space $\mathcal{P}$ defined inductively as follows. The identity function and all constant functions are in $\mathcal{P}$. For every $op \in \{\text{Not}, \text{Neg}\}$ and $P \in \mathcal{P}$, $op(P) \in \mathcal{P}$, and for every $op \in \{\text{AND}, \text{OR}, +, -, \text{SHL}, \text{XOR}, \text{ASHR}\}$ and $P_1, P_2 \in \mathcal{P}$, $op(P_1, P_2) \in \mathcal{P}$. We assume a naïve synthesizer that enumerates the program space by considering programs of increasing size and returning the first program consistent with the examples. In this setting, we consider the task of flipping the rightmost 0 bit, e.g., $10101 \rightarrow 10111$ (taken from the SyGuS competition [3]). While this task is quite intuitive to explain through examples, phrasing it as a logical formula is cumbersome. Assume a user provides to Algorithm 3 the set of examples $E = \{(10101, 10111)\}$. Table 1 shows the execution steps taken by our synthesis framework: E shows the current set of examples, $P(x)$ shows the candidate program synthesized by the naïve synthesizer, *Abstract Examples* shows the abstract examples computed by L-SEP and *Counterexample?* is either *No* if the user accepts the current abstract example (to its left) or a pair of input-output example contradicting the current abstract example. In this example, L-SEP uses the set of functions $\mathcal{F} = \{f_{neg}\}$

in the output SE, where $f_{neg}(0) = 1, f_{neg}(1) = 0$, and we abbreviate $f_{neg}(y)$ with $\bar{y}$. Further, since the bit vector domain consists of vectors of a fixed size (namely, Σ^n for a fixed n instead of Σ^*), the SE's semantics in this domain is defined as the *suffixes of size* n of its (normal) interpretation. Formally, $[\![se]\!]_n = \{s \in \Sigma^n \mid \exists env. \ s$ is a suffix of $env[se]\}$. The semantics of an input-output SE is defined similarly. In the example, the first couple of programs are eliminated immediately by the user, whereas the third program is eliminated only after showing the third abstract example describing it. This enables the synthesizer to prune a significant portion of the search space. Note that since abstract examples are interpreted over fixed sized vectors (as explained above), the last abstract example covers the input space: if $k = n$, the input is $\overbrace{11...1}^{n \text{ times}}$; if $k = 0$, the input takes the form of $b_0...b_{n-1}0$ (where the b_i-s are bits); and if $0 < k < n$, the input takes the form of $b_0...b_{n-k-1}01^k$.

Table 1. A running example for learning a program that flips the rightmost 0 bit with our synthesis framework. Target program is $P_{tar}(x) = \text{OR}(x + 1, x)$.

E	$P(x)$	Abstract examples	Counterexample?
(10101,10111)	$P(x) = 10111$	$X \rightarrow 10111$	$1 \rightarrow 11$
(10101,10111), (1,11)	$P(x) = \text{OR}(x, 2)$	$X_0 x_1 x_2 \rightarrow X_0 \underline{1} x_2$	$0 \rightarrow 1$
(10101,10111), (1,11),(0,1)	$P(x) = \text{OR}(x + 1, 1)$	$X_0 \underline{0} x_2 \rightarrow X_0 x_2 \underline{1}$ $X_0 \underline{0} \rightarrow X_0 \underline{1}$ $X_0 \underline{0} x_1 \underline{1} \rightarrow X_0 x_1 \bar{x}_1 \underline{1}$	No No $11 \rightarrow 111$
(10101,10111), (1,11),(0,1), (11,111)	$P(x) = \text{OR}(x + 1, x)$	$X_0 \underline{01}^k \rightarrow X_0 \underline{1}^k \underline{1}$	No

Leveraging Counterexamples for Learning Abstract Examples. A limitation of L-SEP is that it only generalizes the existing characters of the concrete input. For example, consider a candidate program generated by S that returns the first and last character of the string, which can be summarized by the abstract example $x_0 X_1 x_2 \rightarrow x_0 x_2$. If, in the process of generating an abstract example specification for the candidate program, the first example provided by Algorithm 3 to L-SEP for generalization is ab, then it is generalized to $x_0 x_1 \rightarrow x_0 x_1$. On the other hand, if the first example is acb, then it is generalized to $x_0 X_1 x_2 \rightarrow x_0 x_1$, whose domain is a strict superset of the former's domain. This exemplifies that some inputs may provide better generalizations than others. Although eventually our framework will learn the better generalizations, if Algorithm 3 starts from the less generalizing examples, then the termination of our framework is delayed, and unnecessary questions are presented to the oracle (in our example, it will present $x_0 x_1 \rightarrow x_0 x_1$, and then $x_0 X_1 x_2 \rightarrow x_0 x_2$, which are both accepted, but the former perhaps could be avoided). We believe that the way to avoid this is by picking "good" examples. We leave the question of how to identify them to future work, but note that if the oracle is assumed to provide "good" examples (e.g., representative) then Line 5 can be changed to first look for an uncovered input in E.

5 Evaluation

In this section, we discuss our implementation and evaluate L-SEP and our synthesis framework. We evaluate our algorithms in two domains: strings and bit vectors (of size 8). The former domain is suitable for end users, as targeted by approaches like Flash Fill or learning regular expressions. The latter domain is of interest to the synthesis community (evident by the SyGuS competition [3]). We begin with our implementation and then discuss the experiments. All experiments ran on a Sony Vaio PC with Intel(R) Core(TM) i7-3612QM processor and 8 GB RAM.

5.1 Implementation

We implemented our algorithms in Java. We next provide the main details.

Program Spaces. The program space we consider for bit vectors is the one defined in the example at the end of Sect. 4.

The program space $\mathcal{P}$ we consider for the string domain is defined inductively as follows. The identity function and all constant functions are in $\mathcal{P}$. For every $P_1, P_2 \in \mathcal{P}$, $concat(P_1, P_2) \in \mathcal{P}$.

For $P \in \mathcal{P}$ and integers i_1, i_2, $Extract(P, i_1, i_2) \in \mathcal{P}$. For $P_1, P_2 \in \mathcal{P}$, and a condition e over string programs and integer symbols, $ITE(e, P_1, P_2) \in \mathcal{P}$.

SE Spaces. In the bit vector domain we consider $\mathcal{F} = \{f_{neg}\}$ where $f_{neg}(b) = 1 - b$.

FindCompletion. To answer the containment queries (Lines 3 and 7), we use the Z3 SMT-solver [15]. To this end, we encode the candidate program P and the SEs as formulas.

Roughly speaking, an SE is encoded as a conjunction of *sequence predicates*, each encodes a single atomic construct. A sequence predicate extends the equality predicate with a start position and is denoted by $t_1 \overset{i}{=} t_2$. An interpretation d_1, d_2 for t_1, t_2 satisfies $t_1 \overset{i}{=} t_2$ if starting from the ith character of d_1 the next $|d_2|$ characters are equal to d_2. The term t_1 is either a unique variable t_{in}, representing the input (for input SEs), or $P(t_{in})$ (for output SEs). The term t_2 can be (i) σ (a letter from Σ), (ii) σ^k where k is a star variable, or (iii) a character or sequence variable. For example, $X_0 \underline{a} b^{k_2} x_3$ is encoded as: $t_{in} \overset{0}{=} X_0 \wedge t_{in} \overset{|X_0|}{=} a \wedge (\forall i. 1 + |X_0| \leq i < 1 + |X_0| + k_2 \rightarrow t_{in} \overset{i}{=} b) \wedge t_{in} \overset{1+|X_0|+k_2}{=} x_3$. Note that the positions can be a function of the variables. In the string domain, the formulas are encoded in the string theory (except for i and k_2 that are integers). In the bit vector domain, entities are encoded as bit vectors and $\overset{i}{=}$ is implemented with masks.

Synthesis Framework. To check whether A covers the input domain and obtain an uncovered input in if not, we encode the abstract examples in A as formulas. We then check whether one of the concrete examples from E does not satisfy any of these formulas. If so, it is taken as in. Otherwise, we check if there is another input that does not satisfy the formulas, and if so it is taken as in; otherwise the input domain is covered.

Synthesizer. Our synthesizer is a naïve one that enumerates the program space by considering programs of increasing size and returning the first program consistent with the examples. Technically, we check consistency by submitting the formula $P(in) = out$ to an SMT-solver for every $(in, out) \in E$. Likewise, P is checked to be consistent with the abstract examples by encoding them as formulas and testing whether they imply P. More sophisticated PBE synthesizers, such as Flash-Fill, can in many cases be extended to handle abstract examples in a straight-forward way.

5.2   Synthesis Framework Evaluation

In this section, we evaluate our synthesis framework on the bit vector domain. We consider three experimental questions: (1) Do abstract examples reduce the number of concrete examples required from the user? (2) Do abstract examples enable better pruning for the synthesizer? (3) How many abstract examples are presented to the user before he/she rejects a program? To answer these questions, we compare our synthesis framework (denoted AE) to a baseline that implements the current popular alternative (e.g., [41]) that guarantees that a synthesized program is correct. The baseline acts as follows. It looks for the first program that is consistent with the provided examples and then asks the oracle whether this program is correct. The oracle checks whether there is an input for which the synthesized program and the target program return different outputs. If so, the oracle provides this input and its correct output to the synthesizer, which in turn looks for a new program. If there is no such input, the oracle reports success, and the synthesis completes. We assume a knowledgable user (oracle), implemented by an SMT-solver, which is oblivious to whether the program is easy for a human to understand, making the comparison especially challenging.

Benchmarks. We consider three benchmarks, $B(4)$, $B(6)$, and $B(8)$, each consists of 50 programs. A program is in $B(n)$ if $baseline$ required at least n examples to find it. To find such programs, we randomly select programs of size 4, for each we execute $baseline$ (to find it), and if it required at least n examples, we add it to $B(n)$ and execute our synthesis framework (AE) to find the same (or an equivalent) program.

Consistency of Examples. The convergence of these algorithms highly depends on the examples the oracle provides. To guarantee a fair comparison, we make sure that the *same examples* are presented to both algorithms whenever possible. To this end, we use a cache that stores the examples observed by the baseline. When our algorithm asks the oracle for an example, it first looks for an example in the cache. Only if none meets its requirements, it can ask (an SMT-solver) for a new concrete example.

Results. Table 2 summarizes the results. It reports the following:

- #Concrete examples: the average number of concrete examples the oracle provided, which is also the number of candidate programs.
- Spec-final: the average size of the final abstract example specification (after removing implied abstract examples).
- #AE-intermediate: the average number of abstract examples shown to the user before he/she rejected the corresponding candidate program.
- %Better/equal/worse than baseline: the percentage of all programs in the benchmark that required fewer/same/more (concrete) examples than the baseline.

We note that we observed that the time to generate a single abstract example is a few seconds (≈ 6 s).

Results indicate that our synthesis framework (AE), which prunes the program space based on the abstract examples, improves the baseline in terms of the examples the user needs to provide. This becomes more significant as the number of examples required increases: AE improves the baseline on $B(4)$ by 22%, on $B(6)$ by 30%, and on $B(8)$ by 37%. Moreover, in each benchmark AE performed worse than the baseline only in a single case – and the common case was that it performed better (in $B(8)$, AE performed better on all cases except two).

Figure 3 provides a detailed evidence on the improvement: it shows for each experiment (the x-axis) the number of concrete examples each algorithm required (the y-axis). The figure illustrates that the improvement can be significant. For example, in the 47th experiment, AE reduced the number of examples from 17 to 7.

The number of concrete examples is also the number of candidate programs generated by the synthesizer. Thus, the lower number of examples indicates that the abstract examples improve the pruning of the program space. Namely,

Table 2. Experimental results on the bit vector domain.

	B(4)		B(6)		B(8)	
	AE	Baseline	AE	Baseline	AE	Baseline
#Concrete examples (candidate programs)	4.42	5.64	5.50	7.68	6.62	10.26
Spec-final	11.04		9.36		13.22	
#AE-intermediate	1.98		2.00		3.23	
%Better than baseline	68%		76%		96%	
%Equal to baseline	30%		22%		2%	
%Worse than baseline	2%		2%		2%	

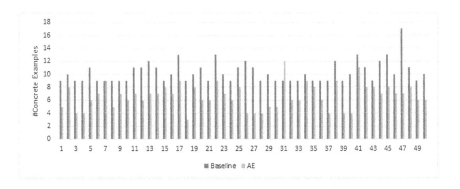

Fig. 3. Detailed results for B(8).

abstract examples help the overall synthesis to converge faster to the target program.

5.3   Abstract Example Specification Evaluation

In this section, we evaluate our generalization algorithm, L-SEP, in the string domain and check how well it succeeds in learning small specifications. To this end, we fix a program and a concrete example to start with and run L-SEP. We repeat this with uncovered inputs until the set of abstract examples covers the string domain. We then check how many abstract examples were computed.

The programs we considered are related to the motivating example. For each program, we run five experiments. Each experiment uses a different Excel row (lawyer) as the first concrete example. We note that our implementation assumes that the names and meeting times are non-empty strings and are space-delimited. Table 3 reports the programs and the average number of abstract examples. Results indicate that the average number of abstract examples required to describe the entire string domain is low.

Table 3. Experimental results on the string domain.

The string program	#Abstract examples
Concatenates the string "Dear" to the last name	1
Concatenates the first letter of the first name to the last name	1
Concatenates the first letter of the first name to the last name and to "@lockhart-gardner.com"	1
Generates the message presented in the motivating example	2
Concatenates the first two characters of the first name to the third and forth characters of the last name and to the second digit of the meeting time	6.57

6   Related Work

In this section, we survey the work closely related to ours.

Learning Specifications. Learning regular languages from examples has been extensively studied in the computational learning theory, under different models: (i) identification in the limit (Gold [20]), (ii) query learning (Angluin [4]), and (iii) PAC learning (Valiant [44]). Our setting is closest to Angluin's setting that defines a teacher-student model and two types of queries: membership (concrete examples) and equivalence (validation). The literature has many results for this setting, including learning automata, context-free grammars, and regular expressions (see [37]). In the context of learning regular expressions, current algorithms impose restrictions on the target regular expression. For example, [9] allows at most one union operator, [27] prevents unions and allows loops up to depth 2 , [17] assumes that input samples are finite and Kleene stars are not nested, and [6] assumes that expressions consist of *chains* that have at most one occurrence of every symbol. In contrast, we learn an extended form of regular expressions but we also impose some restrictions. In the context of learning specifications, [43] learns specifications for programs in the form of logical formulas, which are not intuitive for most users. Symbolic transducers [8,45] describe input-output specifications, but these are more natural to describe functions over streams than input manipulations.

Least General Generalization. L-SEP takes the approach of least general generalization to compute an abstract example. The approach of least general generalization was first introduced by Plotkin [32] that pioneered inductive logic programming and showed how to generalize formulas. This approach was later used to synthesize programs from examples in a PBE setting [31,35]. In contrast, we use this approach not to learn the low-level program, but the high-level specification in the form of abstract examples.

Pre/Post-condition Inference. Learning specifications is related to finding the weakest pre-conditions, strongest post-conditions, and inductive invariants [12,13,16,19,24,36]. Current inference approaches are mostly for program analysis and aim to learn the conditions under which a bad behavior cannot occur. Our goal is different: we learn the (good and bad) behaviors of the program and present it through a high-level language.

Applications of Regular Expressions. There are many applications of regular expressions, for example in data filtering (e.g., [46]), learning XML files' schemes (DTD) (e.g., [6,17]), and program boosting (e.g., [11]). All of these learn expressions that are *consistent* with the provided examples and have no guarantee on the target expression. In contrast, we learn expressions that precisely capture program specifications.

Synthesis. Program synthesis has drawn a lot of attention over the last decade, and especially in the setting of synthesis from examples, known as PBE (e.g., [1,5,14,18,21–23,25,28–30,33,34,38,39,47]). Commonly, PBE algorithms synthesize programs consistent with the examples, which may not capture the user intent. However, some works guarantee to output the target program. For example, CEGIS [41] learns a program via equivalence queries, and oracle-based synthesis [26] assumes that the program space is finite, which allows them to guarantee correctness by exploring all distinguishing inputs (i.e., without validation queries). Synthesis has also been studied in a setting where a specification and the program's syntax are given and the goal is to find a program over this syntax meeting the specification (e.g., [2,7,40,42]).

7 Conclusion

We presented a novel synthesizer that interacts with the user via abstract examples and is guaranteed to return a program that is correct on all inputs. The main idea is to use abstract examples to describe a program behavior on multiple concrete inputs. To that end, we showed L-SEP, an algorithm that generates maximal abstract examples. L-SEP enables our synthesizer to describe candidate programs' behavior through abstract examples. We implemented our synthesizer and experimentally showed that it required few abstract examples to reject false candidates and reduced the overall number of concrete examples required.

Acknowledgements. The research leading to these results has received funding from the European Union, Seventh Framework Programme (FP7) under grant agreement n° 908126, as well as from Len Blavatnik and the Blavatnik Family foundation.

References

1. Albarghouthi, A., Gulwani, S., Kincaid, Z.: Recursive program synthesis. In: Sharygina, N., Veith, H. (eds.) CAV 2013. LNCS, vol. 8044, pp. 934–950. Springer, Heidelberg (2013). doi:10.1007/978-3-642-39799-8_67
2. Alur, R., Bodik, R., Juniwal, G., Martin, M.M.K., Raghothaman, M., Seshia, S.A., Singh, R., Solar-Lezama, A., Torlak, E., Udupa, A.: Syntax-guided synthesis. In: FMCAD 2013 (2013)
3. Alur, R., Fisman, D., Singh, R., Solar-Lezama, A.: SyGuS-Comp 2016: results and analysis. In: SYNT@CAV 2016 (2016)
4. Angluin, D.: Queries and concept learning. Mach. Learn. **2**(4), 319–342 (1988)
5. Barowy, D.W., Gulwani, S., Hart, T., Zorn, B.: FlashRelate: extracting relational data from semi-structured spreadsheets using examples. In: PLDI 2015 (2015)
6. Bex, G.J., Neven, F., Schwentick, T., Tuyls, K.: Inference of concise DTDs from XML data. In: VLDB 2006 (2006)
7. Bornholt, J., Torlak, E., Grossman, D., Ceze, L.: Optimizing synthesis with metasketches. In: POPL 2016 (2016)
8. Botinčan, M., Babić, D.: Sigma*: symbolic learning of input-output specifications. In: POPL 2013, pp. 443–456 (2013)
9. Brāzma, A., Čerāns, K.: Efficient learning of regular expressions from good examples. In: Arikawa, S., Jantke, K.P. (eds.) AII/ALT -1994. LNCS, vol. 872, pp. 76–90. Springer, Heidelberg (1994). doi:10.1007/3-540-58520-6_55

10. Bshouty, N.H.: Exact learning from membership queries: some techniques, results and new directions. In: Jain, S., Munos, R., Stephan, F., Zeugmann, T. (eds.) ALT 2013. LNCS, vol. 8139, pp. 33–52. Springer, Heidelberg (2013). doi:10.1007/978-3-642-40935-6_4

11. Cochran, R.A., D'Antoni, L., Livshits, B., Molnar, D., Veanes, M.: Program boosting: program synthesis via crowd-sourcing. In: POPL 2015 (2015)

12. Cousot, P., Cousot, R., Fähndrich, M., Logozzo, F.: Automatic inference of necessary preconditions. In: Giacobazzi, R., Berdine, J., Mastroeni, I. (eds.) VMCAI 2013. LNCS, vol. 7737, pp. 128–148. Springer, Heidelberg (2013). doi:10.1007/978-3-642-35873-9_10

13. Cousot, P., Cousot, R., Logozzo, F.: Precondition inference from intermittent assertions and application to contracts on collections. In: Jhala, R., Schmidt, D. (eds.) VMCAI 2011. LNCS, vol. 6538, pp. 150–168. Springer, Heidelberg (2011). doi:10.1007/978-3-642-18275-4_12

14. Das Sarma, A., Parameswaran, A., Garcia-Molina, H., Widom, J.: Synthesizing view definitions from data. In: ICDT 2010 (2010)

15. De Moura, L., Bjørner, N.: Z3: an efficient SMT solver. In: Ramakrishnan, C.R., Rehof, J. (eds.) TACAS 2008. LNCS, vol. 4963, pp. 337–340. Springer, Heidelberg (2008). doi:10.1007/978-3-540-78800-3_24

16. Dijkstra, E.W.: Guarded commands, nondeterminacy and formal derivation of programs. Commun. ACM 18(8), 453–457 (1975)

17. Fernau, H.: Algorithms for learning regular expressions from positive data. Inf. Comput. 207, 521–541 (2009)

18. Feser, J.K., Chaudhuri, S., Dillig, I.: Synthesizing data structure transformations from input-output examples. In: PLDI 2015 (2015)

19. Garg, P., Löding, C., Madhusudan, P., Neider, D.: ICE: a robust framework for learning invariants. In: Biere, A., Bloem, R. (eds.) CAV 2014. LNCS, vol. 8559, pp. 69–87. Springer, Cham (2014). doi:10.1007/978-3-319-08867-9_5

20. Gold, E.M.: Language identification in the limit. Inf. Control 10(5), 447–474 (1967)

21. Gulwani, S.: Automating string processing in spreadsheets using input-output examples. In: POPL 2011 (2011)

22. Gulwani, S.: Dimensions in program synthesis. In: PPDP 2010 (2010)

23. Gulwani, S., Harris, W.R., Singh, R.: Spreadsheet data manipulation using examples. Commun. ACM 55(8), 97–105 (2012)

24. Gulwani, S., Tiwari, A.: Computing procedure summaries for interprocedural analysis. In: Nicola, R. (ed.) ESOP 2007. LNCS, vol. 4421, pp. 253–267. Springer, Heidelberg (2007). doi:10.1007/978-3-540-71316-6_18

25. Harris, W.R., Gulwani, S.: Spreadsheet table transformations from examples. In: PLDI 2011 (2011)

26. Jha, S., Gulwani, S., Seshia, S.A., Tiwari, A.: Oracle-guided component-based program synthesis. In: ICSE 2010 (2010)

27. Kinber, E.: Learning regular expressions from representative examples and membership queries. In: Sempere, J.M., García, P. (eds.) ICGI 2010. LNCS, vol. 6339, pp. 94–108. Springer, Heidelberg (2010). doi:10.1007/978-3-642-15488-1_9

28. Lau, T.A., Wolfman, S.A., Domingos, P., Weld, D.S.: Programming by demonstration using version space algebra. Mach. Learn. 53, 111–156 (2003)

29. Le, V., Gulwani, S.: Flashextract: a framework for data extraction by examples. In: PLDI 2014 (2014)

30. Menon, A.K., Tamuz, O., Gulwani, S., Lampson, B.W., Kalai, A.: A machine learning framework for programming by example. In: ICML 2013 (2013)

31. Muggleton, S., Feng, C.: Efficient induction of logic programs. In: First Conference on Algorithmic Learning Theory, pp. 368–381 (1990)
32. Plotkin, G.D.: A note on inductive generalization. Mach. Intell. **5**, 153–163 (1970)
33. Polozov, O., Gulwani, S.: Flashmeta: a framework for inductive program synthesis. In: OOPSLA 2015 (2015)
34. Raychev, V., Bielik, P., Vechev, M., Krause, A.: Learning programs from noisy data. In: POPL 2016 (2016)
35. Raza, M., Gulwani, S., Milic-Frayling, N.: Programming by example using least general generalizations. In: AAAI 2014 (2014)
36. Rival, X.: Understanding the origin of alarms in Astrée. In: Hankin, C., Siveroni, I. (eds.) SAS 2005. LNCS, vol. 3672, pp. 303–319. Springer, Heidelberg (2005). doi:10.1007/11547662_21
37. Sakakibara, Y.: Recent advances of grammatical inference. Theor. Comput. Sci. **185**(1), 15–45 (1997)
38. Singh, R., Gulwani, S.: Learning semantic string transformations from examples. In: VLDB 2012 (2012)
39. Singh, R., Gulwani, S.: Transforming spreadsheet data types using examples. In: POPL 2016 (2016)
40. Singh, R., Solar-Lezama, A.: Synthesizing data structure manipulations from storyboards. In: ESEC/FSE 2011 (2011)
41. Solar-Lezama, A.: Program Synthesis by Sketching. ProQuest, Ann Arbor (2008)
42. Solar-Lezama, A., Jones, C.G., Bodik, R.: Sketching concurrent data structures. In: PLDI 2008 (2008)
43. Tripakis, S., Lickly, B., Henzinger, T.A., Lee, E.A.: A theory of synchronous relational interfaces. ACM Trans. Program. Lang. Syst. **33**(4), 14 (2011)
44. Valiant, L.G.: A theory of the learnable. Commun. ACM **27**(11), 1134–1142 (1984)
45. Veanes, M., Hooimeijer, P., Livshits, B., Molnar, D., Bjorner, N.: Symbolic finite state transducers: algorithms and applications. In: POPL 2012 (2012)
46. Wang, X., Gulwani, S., Singh, R.: Fidex: filtering spreadsheet data using examples. In: OOPSLA 2016 (2016)
47. Yessenov, K., Tulsiani, S., Menon, A.K., Miller, R.C., Gulwani, S., Lampson, B.W., Kalai, A.: A colorful approach to text processing by example. In: UIST 2013 (2013)

Data-Driven Synthesis of Full Probabilistic Programs

Sarah Chasins$^{(\boxtimes)}$ and Phitchaya Mangpo Phothilimthana

University of California, Berkeley, USA
schasins@cs.berkeley.edu

Abstract. Probabilistic programming languages (PPLs) provide users a clean syntax for concisely representing probabilistic processes and easy access to sophisticated built-in inference algorithms. Unfortunately, writing a PPL program by hand can be difficult for non-experts, requiring extensive knowledge of statistics and deep insights into the data. To make the modeling process easier, we have created a tool that synthesizes PPL programs from relational datasets. Our synthesizer leverages the input data to generate a program sketch, then applies simulated annealing to complete the sketch. We introduce a data-guided approach to the program mutation stage of simulated annealing; this innovation allows our tool to scale to synthesizing complete probabilistic programs from scratch. We find that our synthesizer produces accurate programs from 10,000-row datasets in 21 s on average.

1 Introduction

Probabilistic programming languages (PPLs) enable users who are not experts in statistics to cleanly and concisely express probabilistic models [10,11,20]. They offer users simple abstractions and easy access to sophisticated statistical inference algorithms [4,16,18,22] for analyzing their models.

However, writing a PPL model by hand is still challenging for non-statisticians and non-programmers. First, understanding data is difficult. Reviewing large amounts of data to develop a mental model is time-consuming, and humans are prone to misinterpretations and biases. Second, translating insights to a precise statistical model of the data is difficult. To write probabilistic models that reflect their insights, users must first learn some probability theory, understand the subtleties of various probability distributions, and express the details of how different variables in a model should depend on each other.

For these reasons, we believe PPL models should be synthesized from datasets automatically. PPL models offer an interesting point in the modeling design space. Expressing models in PPLs does not make them more expressive or more accurate, but it does give users access to powerful abstractions. They can easily ask how likely an event is in a model, performing complicated inference tasks with a single line of code. They can turn a generative model into a classifier or a predictor in under a minute. They can hypothesize alternative worlds or insert

© Springer International Publishing AG 2017
R. Majumdar and V. Kunčak (Eds.): CAV 2017, Part I, LNCS 10426, pp. 279–304, 2017.
DOI: 10.1007/978-3-319-63387-9_14

interventions and observe how those edits change outcomes. The PPL synthesis in this paper is not aimed at producing models that exceed the accuracy of state-of-the-art ML on important problems, but we believe a PL-centric approach does put usable, powerful models in the hands of non-experts.

To date, we know of one tool, PSketch [23], that synthesizes PPL programs. PSketch takes as input a PPL sketch and a dataset. A sketch, in this case, is a nearly complete PPL program, with some holes. Once a user expresses which variables may affect each hole, PSketch synthesizes expressions to fill the holes. While synthesizing partial PPL programs is already a tremendous step forward, the sketch writing process still requires users to carefully inspect the data, write most of the program structure, and specify causal dependencies. Ultimately, the user still writes a piece of code that is quite close to a complete model.

We introduce DaPPer (_Da_ta-Guided _P_robabilistic _P_rogram Synthesiz_er_), a tool that synthesizes full PPL models from relational datasets. Our system decomposes the PPL synthesis problem into three stages. In the first stage, we generate a graph of dependencies between variables using one of three techniques: including all possible dependencies, analyzing the correlation between variables, or applying network deconvolution [8]. We use the dependency graph to write a program sketch that restricts the program structure. Second, we fill the holes in our sketch using a data-guided stochastic synthesis approach built on top of simulated annealing. At each iteration of our search, we mutate the candidate program and use the input dataset to tune some program parameters. We follow PSketch in computing the candidate's score—its likelihood given the dataset—using Mixtures of Gaussian distributions. Finally, after we obtain an accurate program from the prior stage, we use a redundancy reduction algorithm to make the output program more readable while maintaining its accuracy.

We have evaluated our synthesizer on a suite of 14 benchmarks, a mix of existing PPL models and models designed to stress our tool. Each benchmark in the suite has 10,000 rows of training data and 10,000 rows of test data, both generated from the same probabilistic model; thus, each benchmark is also associated with a ground truth PPL program to which we can compare synthesized programs. In our experiments, our synthesizer produced accurate models in 21 s on average. To test whether our approach works on real data, we also used DaPPer to synthesize a model of airline delay data. Leveraging our target PPL's built-in inference functionality, we used this model to predict flight delays.

This paper makes the following contributions:

- We present a tool for synthesizing PPL models from data. To our knowledge, this is the first synthesizer that generates full PPL models.
- We introduce a data-guided stochastic technique for generating candidate programs. Data-guidance improves synthesis time by two orders of magnitude compared to a data-blind approach.
- We compare three techniques for generating dependency graphs from data.
- We present an algorithm for improving program readability after synthesis while maintaining accuracy. We can reduce the size of a synthesized program by up to 8x with less than a 1% penalty in accuracy.

2   Probabilistic Programs

Probabilistic programming languages are standard languages with two additional constructs: (i) random variables whose values are drawn from probability distributions, and (ii) mechanisms for conditioning variable values on the observed values of other variables [12]. Although these constructs form a common backbone, other language features vary greatly from PPL to PPL [10,11,20]. Probabilistic programs offer a natural way to represent probabilistic models. For example, the classic burglary model can be expressed with the PPL program in Fig. 1.

```
random Boolean Burglary ~ BooleanDistrib(0.001);
random Boolean Earthquake ~ BooleanDistrib(0.002);
random Boolean Alarm ~
  if Burglary then
    if Earthquake then BooleanDistrib(0.95) else  BooleanDistrib(0.94)
  else
    if Earthquake then BooleanDistrib(0.29) else BooleanDistrib(0.001);
random Boolean JohnCalls ~ if Alarm then BooleanDistrib(0.9) else BooleanDistrib(0.05);
random Boolean MaryCalls ~ if Alarm then BooleanDistrib(0.7) else BooleanDistrib(0.01);
```

Fig. 1. The classic burglary model in BLOG (a PPL).

The output of a probabilistic program is not a value but a probability distribution over all possible values. While a deterministic program produces the same value for a given variable during every execution, a probabilistic program may produce different values. The value of each variable is drawn from one or more probability distributions, as defined by the programmer. We can obtain an approximation of the distribution of a variable by running the program many times. For example, if we run the burglary program in Fig. 1 many times, we observe that `Burglary` has the value true in approximately 0.001 of the executions. `Alarm` only becomes common if `Burglary` or `Earthquake` is true, but both are rare, so running the program also reveals that `Alarm` is often false.

Programmers can add observations in PPLs to obtain posterior probability distributions conditioned on the observations. For example, if we run our sample program with an observation statement `obs JohnCalls = true`, the program rejects executions in which `JohnCalls` is false, and we observe that in many runs `Burglary` is also true. For a thorough introduction to PPLs, we recommend [12].

3   System Overview

We will explain DaPPer with a working example, a model of how a student's tiredness and skill level affect performance on a test. The inputs to our tool are a relational dataset (e.g. Table 1) and a hypothesis about the direction of causal links between variables. Each column in a dataset is treated as a variable in the output program, and each row represents an independent run of the program. A causation hypothesis is an ordering of the dataset column identifiers; for our running example, the hypothesis might be `tired` →

Table 1. Dataset with the tiredness, skill level, and test performance of several students.

tired	skill Level	testPer formance
True	10.591	27.437
False	12.862	67.976
False	8.727	70.787
True	10.333	31.113
True	11.440	31.592

```
random Boolean tired ~ BooleanDistrib(.5);
random Real skillLevel ~ Gaussian(10, 7);
random Real testPerformance ~
  if skillLevel > 13.0 then
    if tired then Gaussian(70, 15) else Gaussian(95, 5)
  else
    if tired then Gaussian(30, 15) else Gaussian(70, 5);
```

Fig. 2. Running example, a program that expresses a model of how a student's tiredness and skill level affect test performance.

skillLevel → testPerformance. The order specifies the direction of dependencies but does not restrict which variables are connected. From the given order, we can conclude that if tired and testPerformance are related, tired affects testPerformance, rather than testPerformance affecting tired. While this means that our tool still demands some insights from users, they only have to use their knowledge of the world to guess in which direction causality may flow; that is, our tool does not ask 'is there a relationship between tiredness and test performance?' but it asks 'if there is a relationship between the two, does tiredness affect test performance, or does test performance affect tiredness?' In Fig. 2, we show the ground truth program that produced the data in Table 1.

DaPPer generates PPL programs by decomposing the synthesis task into three subtasks: (i) dependency graph generation, (ii) data-guided stochastic synthesis, and (iii) redundancy reduction. In this section, we briefly discuss their roles, and how they interoperate, as illustrated in Fig. 3.

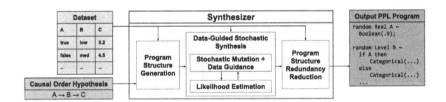

Fig. 3. A system diagram illustrating the workflow of the synthesizer.

3.1 Dependency Graph Generation

The synthesizer's first task is to determine whether any given random variable—any given dataset column—depends on any other random variables. This problem corresponds to the model selection problem in Bayesian networks. In our context, this is the *dependency graph generation problem* because a directed graph of which variables affect which other variables defines a program structure.

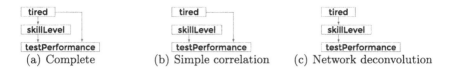

(a) Complete   (b) Simple correlation   (c) Network deconvolution

Fig. 4. The dependency graphs generated for the dataset sampled in Table 1.

```
random Boolean tired ~
  BooleanDistrib(??);
random Real skillLevel ~
  if tired then ?? else ??;
random Real testPerformance ~
  if tired then
    if (skillLevel ?? ??)
      then ?? else ??
  else
    if (skillLevel ?? ??)
      then ?? else ??;
```

```
random Boolean tired ~
  BooleanDistrib(??);
random Real skillLevel ~ ??;
random Real testPerformance ~
  if tired then
    if (skillLevel ?? ??)
      then ?? else ??
  else
    if (skillLevel ?? ??)
      then ?? else ??;
```

```
random Boolean tired ~
  BooleanDistrib(??);
random Real skillLevel ~
  if tired then ?? else ??;
random Real testPerformance ~
  if (skillLevel ?? ??)
    then ?? else ??;
```

(a) Complete   (b) Simple correlation   (c) Network deconvolution

Fig. 5. The program skeletons generated from the dependency graphs in Fig. 4. We use ?? to represent a part of the program that we have not yet synthesized.

We explore three techniques for generating dependency graphs. First, a Complete approach produces the largest possible dependency graph that the user's causation hypothesis permits. Second, a Simple Correlation approach adds edges greedily in order of correlation, from highest to lowest, excluding edges for which there already exists a path. Third, we use an existing Network Deconvolution algorithm [8]. Given a dataset like the one in Table 1 and the causation hypothesis represented by the order of the columns (tired → skillLevel → testPerformance), the three techniques produce the dependency graphs depicted in Fig. 4.

Given a dependency graph, we generate a sketch. For each variable x depending on $\{x_1, x_2, ...\}$, we define x as a nested conditional expression with holes:

```
x ~ if ( x1 ?? ?? )
      then if ( x2 ?? ?? ) ...
      else if ( x2 ?? ?? ) ...
```

For each condition (xi ?? ??), the first ?? is a comparison operator, and the second ?? is an expression. Figure 5 shows the sketches generated from the dependency graphs in Fig. 4.

3.2 Data-Guided Stochastic Synthesis

The second task is to complete the holes ?? in the program sketch generated by the previous step. We use simulated annealing (SA) to complete this task.

In each SA iteration, DaPPer creates a new program candidate from a current candidate by (i) mutating an expression, then (ii) deterministically updating all parameters in the program associated with the mutated expression, using knowledge about the data. Consider the candidate program in Fig. 6(a), a completion of the Fig. 5(c) program sketch. To generate a new candidate, our tool randomly mutates one condition, changing the RHS of a comparison from 15 to 16; this

```
random Boolean tired ~
  BooleanDistrib(.500);
random Real skillLevel ~
  if tired
    then Gaussian(9.987, 7.000)
    else Gaussian(10.000, 7.003);
random Real testPerformance ~
  if (skillLevel < 15)
    then Gaussian(44.875, 7.729)
    else UniformReal(25.300, 120.276);
```

```
random Boolean tired ~
  BooleanDistrib(.500);
random Real skillLevel ~
  if tired
    then Gaussian(9.987, 7.000)
    else Gaussian(10.000, 7.003);
random Real testPerformance ~
  if (skillLevel < 16)
    then Gaussian(??, ??)
    else UniformReal(?? , ??);
```

```
random Boolean tired ~
  BooleanDistrib(.500);
random Real skillLevel ~
  if tired
    then Gaussian(9.987, 7.000)
    else Gaussian(10.000, 7.003);
random Real testPerformance ~
  if (skillLevel < 16)
    then Gaussian(46.227, 7.663)
    else UniformReal(25.300, 125.113);
```

(a) Current candidate   (b) Stochastic mutation   (c) Data-guided completion

Fig. 6. One mutation of the program in Fig. 5(c). <u>Pink</u> highlights the changes. (Color figure online)

produces the sketch in Fig. 6(b). With the condition changed, the parameters for the distributions are out of date. DaPPer identifies all rows of the input data in which skillLevel is less than 16, then uses those rows to select parameters for the distributions in the true branch, and the remaining rows for the false branch, producing the new program in Fig. 6(c).

To evaluate programs, DaPPer uses a custom likelihood estimation approach.

3.3 Redundancy Reduction

Sometimes the most accurate model that results from the synthesis step is a model that distinguishes between many cases, even more than the ground truth. Such models can be very large, often unreadable. Because our goal is to produce readable programs from which users can extract high-level insights, this is undesirable for our purposes.

To improve the readability of our outputs, we developed a redundancy reduction algorithm that collapses similar branches. Because this is applied as a final processing stage to an already synthesized program, the reduction process is very fast, and users can easily and quickly tune the amount of reduction to their needs, based on the output at hand.

4   Language

DaPPer generates programs from the grammar shown in Fig. 7. This grammar represents a subset of the BLOG language [20], centered on the features necessary for declaring random variables.[1] While BLOG has many interesting features that set it apart from other PPLs, such as open-universe semantics, our synthesized programs do not make use of these. DaPPer needs only the features that allow it to introduce random variables drawn from distributions and describe how they depend on other random variables.

Many PPLs can express such programs, so many PPLs would be reasonable target languages. We chose to synthesize programs in the BLOG language, but with small changes to our code generator, DaPPer could easily target others.

---

[1] We leave out details of type declarations, which BLOG requires and our tool synthesizes, but which present no interesting technical challenges.

prog	::=	**statement prog** | ϵ
statement	::=	'random' **type ident** '~' **expr** ';'
type	::=	'Boolean' | 'Real' | **categoricalTypeIdent**
expr	::=	**distrib** | **condExpr**
condExpr	::=	'if' **cond** 'then' **expr** 'else' **expr**
distrib	::=	'BooleanDistrib(' real ')' | 'Categorical({' **categoricalMap** '})' | 'Gaussian(' real ',' real ')' | 'UniformReal(' real ',' real ')' | 'Gamma(' real ',' real ')' | 'Beta(' real ',' real ')'
categoricalMap	::=	**categoricalValue** '->' real | **categoricalMap** ',' **categoricalMap**
cond	::=	**ident** | **ident cmpOp cmpExpr** | **cond** '|' **cond**
cmpOp	::=	'==' | '>' | '<'
cmpExpr	::=	**ident** | **boolean** | **categoricalValue** | **real** | **cmpExpr numOp cmpExpr**
numOp	::=	'+' | '-' | '*'

Fig. 7. The subset of the BLOG language used by our synthesizer.

5   Generating Dependency Graphs

We use dependency graphs to generate a skeleton program structure, a program with variable declarations and partial conditional expressions in their definitions, but without the conditions or bodies. To generate these dependency graphs, we have tested three approaches, which we describe here.

5.1   Complete

The complete approach constructs a dependency graph based on the assumption that each variable depends on all other variables that precede it in the user's causation hypothesis. Note that this approach does not use the input dataset. If the user provides the hypothesis $A \rightarrow B \rightarrow C \rightarrow D$, the complete approach produces a graph in which A depends on no other variables, B depends on $\{A\}$, C depends on $\{A, B\}$, and D depends on $\{A, B, C\}$.

If the causation hypothesis is correct, this approach is always sufficient to express the ground truth. It breaks the outcomes into the largest number of cases and thus theoretically allows the greatest customization of the program to the input data. However, it may also introduce redundancy, distinguishing between cases even when the distinction does not affect the outcome.

5.2   Correlation Heuristic

The correlation heuristic approach uses information from the input dataset as well as the causation hypothesis. It calculates the correlation for every pair of columns in the dataset. The pairs are sorted according to the effect size of the correlation. We iterate through the sorted list of pairs, checking for each pair (A, B) whether there is already a path in the dependency graph between A and B. If yes, we do nothing. If no, we add an edge between A and B; the direction of the edge is determined by the positions of A and B in the causation hypothesis ordering. If we reach a point in the list of pairs where the correlation effect size or statistical significance is very low, we stop adding edges.

See Appendix A for a summary of how we produce correlation measures for columns with incompatible types.

5.3   Network Deconvolution

Our final approach uses the network deconvolution algorithm, developed by Feizi et al. [8], a method for inferring which nodes in a network directly affect each other, based on an observed correlation matrix that reflects both direct and indirect effects. To build a PPL model, we can observe the correlation between each pair of columns, but should only condition a variable on the variables that directly affect it. Thus, a direct link from x to y in network deconvolution corresponds to an immediate dependence of y on x in a PPL model.

Network deconvolution takes as input a *similarity* matrix. We use a symmetric square matrix of correlations, reflecting the association of each column with each other column in the dataset. Each entry in the network deconvolution output matrix represents the likelihood that a column pair is connected by a direct edge. For each entry in the output matrix, we add an edge to the dependency graph if it is above a low threshold.

6   Data-Guided Stochastic Synthesis

DaPPer applies simulated annealing (SA) to synthesize PPL programs. We use an exponential cooling schedule and the standard Kirkpatrick acceptance probability function. To apply SA, we must generate new candidate programs that are 'adjacent' to existing programs. Our synthesizer decomposes the process of creating a new candidate program into two stages: make a random mutation of the current candidate program (Sect. 6.1), then tune all parameters in the affected subtree of the AST to best match the input dataset (Sect. 6.2). Once a new candidate has been produced, SA scores the candidate to decide whether to accept or reject it (Sect. 6.3).

6.1   Mutations

The first step in creating a new adjacent program is to randomly mutate the current program. We allow three classes of mutation, described below.

Conditions. Our synthesizer is permitted to synthesize conditions of a restricted form (see **cond** in Fig. 7). They must have a single identifier (fixed based on the dependency graph) on the LHS, and an expression on the RHS. Because we deterministically generate fixed RHSs for conditions with Boolean and categorical variables in the LHS (e.g., `boolVar == true`, `boolVar == false`), the mutation process may not manipulate those conditions. Instead, its primary role is to generate new RHSs for conditions associated with real-valued variables. To alter a RHS, the mutator may: (i) replace any constant or use of a real-valued variable with a new constant or real-valued variable, (ii) slightly adjust a current constant, (iii) add, remove, or change a **numOp**, (iv) change a **cmpOp**.

Branches. Less commonly, the mutator may add or remove a condition associated with a real-valued variable. The mutator may not alter the structure of the dependency graph, but it may add a branch to an existing case split or remove a branch if it has more than two.

Distribution Selection. Finally, the mutator may alter what type of distribution appears in the body of a conditional, for definitions of real-valued variables. For instance, it may change a `Gaussian` to a `UniformReal` distribution.

6.2 Data Guidance

Once we obtain the control flow for a new candidate program from the mutator, we tune the distribution parameters to fit the dataset. For each distribution node in the abstract syntax tree, we identify the path condition associated with the node. We convert the path condition into a filter on the input dataset. For instance, consider the control flow in Fig. 8(a). To produce the parameter for the first Boolean distribution node, we would produce the path condition *Burglary* ∧ *Earthquake*. Using this as a filter over the input dataset would produce the rows highlighted in Fig. 8(b). Once we have identified the subset of the dataset consistent with a distribution's path condition, we use the subset to calculate appropriate distribution parameters. For instance, if the distribution is a Gaussian, we calculate the mean and variance.

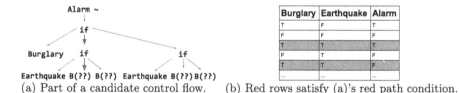

(a) Part of a candidate control flow.   (b) Red rows satisfy (a)'s red path condition.

Fig. 8. Filtering a dataset for a path condition in the classic burglary model. (Color figure online)

Once DaPPer completes this process for all distributions whose path conditions are affected by the mutation, the candidate generation stage is complete.

6.3 Likelihood Estimation

To evaluate how well a program models a dataset, we must compute the likelihood $\mathcal{L}(P|D)$ of a candidate program P given the input data D. Computing the exact likelihood [6] requires expensive integral computations, which makes scoring slow. Thus, we adopt the method used by PSketch [23] for approximating likelihood using Mixtures of Gaussian (MoG) distributions, which they show is three orders of magnitude faster than precise likelihood calculation [23].

The approach is to symbolically approximate every variable in a candidate program with MoG or Bernoulli distributions. We approximate real-valued expressions using a MoG, whose probability density function (PDF) is:

$$MoG(x; n, \boldsymbol{w}, \boldsymbol{\mu}, \boldsymbol{\sigma}) = \sum_{i=1}^{n} w_i \cdot g(x; \mu_i, \sigma_i)$$

where $\boldsymbol{w}$, $\boldsymbol{\mu}$, and $\boldsymbol{\sigma}$ are vectors of size n, representing the weight, mean, and standard deviation of each Gaussian distribution in the mixture. The function g is the PDF of a univariate Gaussian distribution. A Boolean expression is simply modeled as a Bernoulli distribution, $Brn(x; p)$. Therefore, we approximate each variable v in a program as a MoG with the PDF $MoG_v(x) = MoG(x; n_v, \boldsymbol{w_v}, \boldsymbol{\mu_v}, \boldsymbol{\sigma_v})$ or a Bernoulli with the PDF $Brn(x; p_v)$.

The approximation of $\mathcal{L}(P|D)$ is the product of the likelihood of all possible values of all variables from D given the program P:

$$\mathcal{L}(P|D) = \prod_{v \in P_{RV}} \prod_{x \in D[v]} MoG_v(x) \times \prod_{v \in P_{BV}} \prod_{x \in D[v]} Brn(x; p_v)$$

where P_{RV} is a set of real variables and P_{BV} is a set of Boolean variables in the program P that appear in data D. $D[v]$ is a set of values of the variable v in D.

In addition to the distributions supported by PSketch, we add support for categorical distributions and uniform distributions, which we describe here.

Categorical Distribution. A categorical distribution specifies probabilities for each value in a finite discrete set. The PDF of a categorical distribution is:

$$Ctg(x; \{(x_i \rightarrow p_i) | i \in \{1, ..., k\}\}) = p_i \text{ when } x = x_i$$

We introduce reduction rules to symbolically evaluate expressions with categorical distributions, shown in Fig. 9. The first rule evaluates an if expression, which may contain categorical distributions. The second rule evaluates a case expression. Although a case expression can be desugared to a nested if expression, the PDF that results is often less precise. In particular, $case([(Ctg_v(x) == x_1, Y_1), (Ctg_v(x) == x_2, Y_2), ...])$ can be desugared to $ite(Ctg_v(x) == x_1, Y_1, ite(Ctg_v(x) == x_2, Y_2, ...))$, where $Ctg_v(x) = Ctg(x; \{(x_i \rightarrow p_i) | i \in \{1, ..., k_v\}\})$. When we evaluate the former expression, we expect the resulting distribution to be the summation of $Y_1, Y_2, ..., Y_{k-1}, Y_k$ weighted by $p_1, p_2, ..., p_{k-1}, p_k$ respectively. However, if we evaluate the latter expression using the first rule, we will obtain the summation of $Y_1, Y_2, ..., Y_{k-1}, Y_k$ weighted by $p_1, (1-p_1)p_2, ..., (\prod_{i=1}^{k-2}(1-p_i))p_{k-1}, \prod_{i=1}^{k-1}(1-p_i)$ respectively. This is because the ite rule is designed for the scenario in which path conditions are independent. Therefore, we introduce the case rule to handle case expressions whose conditions are dependent and mutually exclusive in order to obtain better likelihood estimations. The remaining rules in Fig. 9 define how to evaluate $\oplus$ and $\otimes$ used in the ite and case rules.

$$[\![ite(Brn(x;p),Y_1,Y_2)]\!] := \quad [\![(p \otimes Y_1) \oplus ((1-p) \otimes Y_2)]\!]$$

$$[\![case([(Ctg_v(x) == x_1, Y_1), (Ctg_v(x) == x_2, Y_2), ...,$$
$$(Ctg_v(x) == x_k, Y_k)])]\!] := \quad [\![(p_1 \otimes Y_1) \oplus (p_2 \otimes Y_2) \oplus ... \oplus (p_k \otimes Y_k)]\!]$$
$$\text{where } Ctg_v(x) = Ctg(x; \{(x_i \to p_i) | i \in \{1, ..., k\}\}) \quad \text{where } Y_i \text{ is either Bernoulli, categorical, or MoG}$$

$$[\![Brn(x;p_1) \oplus Brn(x;p_1)]\!] := \quad Brn(x;p_1 + p_2)$$

$$[\![Ctg(x; \{(x_i \to p_i^1) | i \in \{1, ..., k\}\}) \oplus$$
$$Ctg(x; \{(x_i \to p_i^2) | i \in \{1, ..., k\}\})]\!] := \quad Ctg(x; \{(x_i \to p_i^1 + p_i^2) | i \in \{1, ..., k\}\})$$
$$[\![MoG(x; n_1, \boldsymbol{w_1}, \boldsymbol{\mu_1}, \boldsymbol{\sigma_1}) \oplus MoG(x; n_2, \boldsymbol{w_2}, \boldsymbol{\mu_2}, \boldsymbol{\sigma_2})]\!] := \quad MoG(x; n_1 + n_2, \boldsymbol{w_1} \| \boldsymbol{w_2}, \boldsymbol{\mu_1} \| \boldsymbol{\mu_2}, \boldsymbol{\sigma_1} \| \boldsymbol{\sigma_2})$$
$$\text{where } \| \text{ represents vector concatenation}$$

$$[\![c \otimes Brn(x;p)]\!] := \quad Brn(x; c \times p)$$
$$[\![c \otimes Ctg(x; \{(x_i \to p_i) | i \in \{1, ..., k\}\})]\!] := \quad Ctg(x; \{(x_i \to c \times p_i) | i \in \{1, ..., k\}\})$$
$$[\![c \otimes MoG(x; n, \boldsymbol{w}, \boldsymbol{\mu}, \boldsymbol{\sigma})]\!] := \quad MoG(x; n, c \times \boldsymbol{w}, \boldsymbol{\mu}, \boldsymbol{\sigma})$$

Fig. 9. Reduction rules to symbolically execute expressions that use categorical distributions.

Uniform Real Distribution. A uniform real distribution has constant probability for any real number between a lower bound a and an upper bound b. The PDF of a uniform real distribution is defined as:

$$Uniform(x; a, b) = \begin{cases} \frac{1}{b-a} & \text{if } a \leq x \leq b \\ 0 & \text{otherwise} \end{cases}$$

We approximate a uniform distribution as follows:

$$[\![Uniform(x; a, b)]\!] := MoG(x; n, w, \boldsymbol{\mu}, \boldsymbol{\sigma})$$
$$\text{where } w_i = \frac{1}{n}, \mu_i = a + (i + \frac{1}{2}) \cdot \frac{b-a}{n}, \sigma_i = \frac{b-a}{n}$$

We use $n = 32$. We can obtain better approximations by increasing n, but at the cost of slower evaluation.

7   Redundancy Reduction

To improve the readability of our outputs, we have developed a simple redundancy reduction algorithm that combines the similar branches of a given conditional expression. The key idea is to compare the parameters of branches' descendant distributions. For a pair of branches, we align the two sets of descendant distributions according to their associated path condition suffixes. These distribution pairs are the pairs that we combine if we collapse the branches into a single branch for executions that satisfy *either* of their path conditions. The decision to collapse them is based on both the differences in distribution pairs' parameters and on how much data DaPPer used to tune them.

For a concrete example, recall that in the classic Burglary model, `MaryCalls` does not depend on `JohnCalls`. After stochastic synthesis, we might see the following snippet within the `MaryCalls` definition: `if JohnCalls then Boolean(0.010) else Boolean(0.008)`. The parameters of the distributions in these two branches are very close. Further, we know both parameters were trained on a small number of rows. Given normal reduction parameters, this would lead our algorithm to collapse the two branches into something like `Boolean(0.009)` – essentially to conclude that `MaryCalls` does not depend on `JohnCalls`.

Our algorithm accepts two user-selected threshold parameters. By manipulating these parameters, users can explore different levels of readability without having to re-synthesize. Reduction is applied as a fast post-processing step, after the bulk of the synthesis is completed, so users can quickly and easily tune the amount of redundancy reduction to their needs. They can choose to edit and run analyzes on a readable version, knowing how much accuracy they have sacrificed, or they can temporarily adjust reduction parameters to extract high-level insights about program structure without permanently sacrificing accuracy.

See Appendix B for the full algorithm and details of the motivation.

8   Limitations

We see several limitations of the current synthesizer, all of which suggest interesting directions for future work.

Relational Input Data. Our approach handles only relational datasets, specifically relational datasets that treat each row as an independent run of the program. While there are many such datasets and our tool already allows us to model many interesting processes, our current technique does not apply for datasets that cannot be transformed into this format. Thus, we cannot take advantage of some of the BLOG language's more interesting features (e.g., open-universe semantics, which allows programs in the language to represent uncertainty about whether variables exist, or how many variables there are of a given type). For our current synthesis model, we must know the number of variables.

Hidden Variables. Our synthesis model assumes there are no hidden variables, that no additional columns of data about the world are necessary to produce a correct output. Our decision to exclude hidden variables is one of the crucial differences from the PSketch [23] approach. While PSketch is targeted at programmers looking to write functions that include randomness, we want our tool to be accessible to scientists and social scientists modeling real world phenomena. For these purposes, we expect that hypothesizing the existence of a hidden variable—which may have no correspondence to any real world variable—would only confuse the user and make output models less intelligible and less useful to the target audience. We see the addition of *optional* hidden variable introduction as an interesting technical challenge and a good direction for future work. However, we would never make hidden variable hypotheses the default. Although we believe this is a improvement over PSketch from the perspective of our target user, this is a limitation from the perspective of a PSketch user.

Restricted Grammar. For this first foray into synthesis of full PPL programs, we selected a fairly restricted grammar. We examined many existing BLOG models and designed a grammar that would express the sorts of models people already like to write. However, we find it easy to imagine models we would like to obtain that cannot be expressed in our chosen subset of BLOG. Although this may be the most serious limitation, it is also the most easily addressed, since we can cleanly extend our technique by simply expanding the grammar and the set of allowable mutations. Because each increase in the grammar size also expands the search space, this will probably be more than a trivial extension. We expect it may offer a good setting for exploring the use of a probabilistic language model and weighted search for a program synthesis application.

9   Evaluation

We evaluated DaPPer on a suite of 14 benchmarks. Each benchmark consists of 10,000 rows of training data, 10,000 rows of test data, and the ground truth BLOG program used to generate both datasets. Some benchmarks were taken directly from the sample programs packaged with the BLOG language. Since these were quite simple, we also wrote new programs to test whether our tool can synthesize more complex models. The DaPPer source and all benchmark programs and associated datasets are available at github.com/schasins/PPL-synthesis. DaPPer synthesized accurate programs for all benchmarks, taking less than 21 s on average. We also used DaPPer to generate a model of a real flight delay dataset.

9.1   Dependency Graph Generation

We start with an exploration of how dependency graphs affect synthesis time and accuracy. Recall that the Complete approach produces the largest possible dependency graph. The Correlation approach produces graphs smaller than Complete graphs but usually larger than Network Deconvolution (ND) graphs.

Figure 10(a) shows how the choice of dependency graph affects synthesis time. Each bar represents the average time DaPPer took to synthesize a program whose score on the test dataset is within 10% of the ground truth program's. Each synthesis task ran for a fixed number of SA iterations. The Fig. 10(a) timing numbers represent the first point during those iterations at which the current candidate program achieves the target likelihood score on the test (holdout) dataset. For all benchmarks except 'students,' all dependency graphs were sufficient to reach the target accuracy within the allotted SA iterations. The average times to reach the target accuracy using the Complete and Correlation approaches were 20.90 and 55.77 s, respectively. If we exclude 'students,' we can compare all three; Complete averaged 12.54 s, Correlation 44.40, and ND 15.02.

We observe a number of trends playing out in the timing numbers. First, Complete gains a small early time advantage by generating a dependency graph without examining the input data, while Correlation and ND both face the overhead of calculating correlations. This head start gave Complete the win for the first six benchmarks. Second, using the dependency graph closest to that of

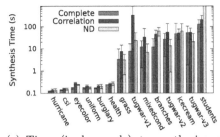
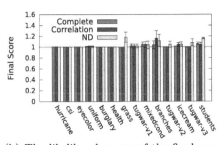

(a) Time (in log scale) to synthesize a program that achieves a target likelihood score on the test data. For each benchmark, the target is a score within 10% of the ground truth's score.

(b) The likelihood scores of the final synthesized programs on the test data, normalized by the score of the ground truth programs. Lower scores are better.

Fig. 10. Comparison of the three dependency graph generation approaches.

the ground truth confers a time advantage. If the ground truth dependency graph is dense, Complete is typically closest, so Complete finishes first (e.g., 'tugwar-v1'). If the ground truth dependency graph is sparse, ND is usually closest, so ND finishes first (e.g., 'tugwar-v3'). Finally, if any approach eliminates a necessary dependency, synthesis may fail to reach the target accuracy. Recall from Fig. 4 that ND dropped the direct dependence of testPerformance on tired. Thus, ND never reached the target accuracy for the 'students' benchmark.

Next, we evaluate whether DaPPer's performance is within the acceptable range. We cannot make a direct comparison to the most similar tool, PSketch, because the PSketch task is substantially different. Instead, we include some PSketch performance numbers to give a sense of the acceptable timescale. PSketch synthesized partial PPL programs using small datasets (100–400 rows) in 146 s on average. Note that large datasets are desirable because they result in more accurate programs, but they make synthesis slower because the likelihood estimator must use all the data to calculate a score at each iteration. To synthesize part of the 'burglary' model, PSketch took 89 s, while DaPPer synthesized a full 'burglary' model in 0.17 s. Again, since the tasks are very different, these numbers do not indicate that DaPPer outperforms PSketch. However, we are satisfied with DaPPer's synthesis times overall.

Figure 10(b) shows the likelihood scores of the final synthesized programs on the test datasets, normalized by the scores of the ground truth programs. Overall, the scores reached by the Complete, Correlation, and ND approaches, averaged across benchmarks, were 1.014, 1.024, and 1.051, respectively. As expected, larger dependency graphs typically allowed the synthesizer to reach better scores. Thus, Complete always produced likelihoods very close to those of the ground truth programs, with Correlation performing slightly worse, and ND worst of all. Still, even ND always produced likelihoods within 20% of the ground truth.

Given Complete's dominance in both synthesis time and accuracy, we conclude that Complete is the best dependency graph approach of the three we tried. If we were to select an approach on a case-by-case basis, we would only switch away from the Complete strategy when faced with a dataset for which we strongly suspect the dependency graph is sparse, and even then only if faster synthesis time is more critical than accuracy. The dominance of the Complete approach drove us to develop our redundancy reduction algorithm, which allows us to recover small, readable programs from large ones.

9.2   Data-Guided vs. Data-Blind Stochastic Synthesis

One of the primary innovations of our tool is its use of input data not only to score candidate programs but also to generate them. We evaluate DaPPer against DaPPer-blind. DaPPer-blind is a simple data-blind variation on our tool. It is identical to DaPPer in every way except: (i) in addition to DaPPer mutations, it may mutate distribution parameters and (ii) it does not run data-guided parameter adjustment after mutations.

Recall that after each mutation, DaPPer identifies affected distributions and tunes their parameters to reflect the input data that corresponds to the new path condition. Thus, the data-guided approach has the advantage of always producing programs tuned to the input data. However, filtering the data and calculating the appropriate parameters does impose a time penalty. For this reason, DaPPer-blind can complete more mutations per unit of time than DaPPer. Thus, it is not immediately clear which approach will perform better.

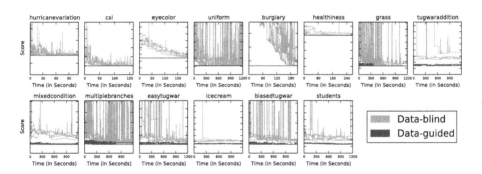

Fig. 11. Score over time for data-blind vs. data-guided synthesis. Lower is better.

Our empirical evaluation reveals that the data-guided approach outperforms the data-blind approach. Figure 11 shows how the likelihood score changed over time for five runs of DaPPer and DaPPer-blind, for each benchmark. While 100% of the data-guided runs reached a likelihood within 10% of the ground truth's likelihood, only 36% of the data-blind runs reached that same target level. For the data-guided runs, the average time to achieve the target likelihood was 20.9 s. For the 36% of data-blind runs that did reach the target likelihood, the average time was 151.6 s. Thus, using a data-guided program generation approach offers at least a 7x speedup compared to a data-blind approach.

We can acquire a better speedup estimate by including the benchmarks for which the data-blind approach never reached the target accuracy. For each benchmark, we identified the best (lowest) score that all runs managed to reach (i.e. the best score of the worst run). Reaching these scores took data-blind synthesis an average of 347.63 s and took data-guided synthesis an average of 0.54 s, indicating that data-guidance provides a 648.9x speedup.

9.3   Redundancy Reduction

To explore the tradeoff between accuracy and readability, we evaluated how much accuracy we lose by applying our redundancy reduction algorithm to our synthesized programs. While Network Deconvolution offers small, readable programs by default, the other techniques do not. In this section, we explore the effects of redundancy reduction on programs synthesized using Complete dependency graphs on a subset of the 14 benchmarks[2]. We observe up to a 7.9x reduction in program size, with negligible decreases in accuracy.

Recall that we synthesize programs in which all AST leaf nodes are distribution nodes. For this reason, the number of distribution nodes is the most informative measure of program size and complexity.

As Fig. 12(a) reveals, the reduction process does not make program alterations that substantially alter the likelihood score. However, it does significantly reduce the size of the program, producing output programs that are much more readable. Figure 12(b) shows the effects on program size, depicting the ratio of the number of distribution nodes in the output to the number of distribution nodes required to express the ground truth. We see that as the reduction parameter α increases, the synthesized programs ultimately converge to the ground truth range, but do so gradually enough that the user can explore a variety of different structures. As we see in Fig. 12(a), even when users set α quite aggressively, the reduction algorithm does not tend to make merges that substantially alter the likelihood score. Most importantly, we think the benefits for readability and for extracting high-level insights are clear. For instance, in the case of the 'healthiness' model, reduction collapses a program with 127 distinct distribution nodes to a much more readable program with 16 distribution nodes.

Overall, we find that redundancy reduction allows us to benefit from the accuracy and fast synthesis times of the Complete approach without sacrificing readability and editability. For a more concrete illustration of the resultant readability, see Appendix C's side-by-side comparison of a ground truth program and a synthesized program after redundancy reduction.

9.4   Case Study: Airline Delay Dataset

Although testing on data for which we have a ground truth model is the best way to investigate whether DaPPer produces correct programs, we also want to

---

[2] We test on the subset of benchmarks for which we can align branches using exact path condition matches. We expect to expand the path condition matching scheme to align branches with close conditions in future work.

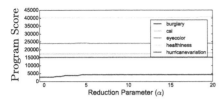
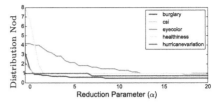

(a) Likelihood scores of the reduced programs.
Lower is better. We vary α, a parameter of the
reduction algorithm that users can adjust.

(b) Number of distribution nodes in the reduced programs, normalized by the ground
truth programs' number of distribution nodes.

Fig. 12. Effects of redundancy reduction with varying α parameter values.

be sure that DaPPer functions well on real data. To that end, we completed a
case study using our tool to produce a probabilistic model of a popular airline
delay dataset from the U.S. Department of Transportation [1]. We selected this
dataset because it has already been thoroughly studied, explored, and visualized.
Thus, although we lacked a ground truth PPL model for this dataset, we knew
from past work that we should expect delays to vary according to days of the
week [15] and to increase over the course of the day [35].

We ran DaPPer on a dataset with 447,013 rows. The output program indicates that delays vary by day, reflecting the findings of Hofmann et al. [15]. It
also indicates that delays rise as the departure time (time of day) rises, reflecting
the findings of Wicklin et al. [35]. Taking advantage of BLOG's built-in inference
algorithms, we used this model to predict flight delays on a holdout set of 10,000
dataset rows. On average, the model's predictions were off by less than 15 min.
While 15 min is substantial, it is worth noting that delays in the dataset range
from −82 to 1971. For comparison, a baseline predictor that always guessed the
average flight delay had a root-mean-square-error (RMSE) of 39.4, while the
DaPPer predictor had an RMSE of 24.1.

10 Related Work

The body of research that addresses learning programs from data is far greater
than we can cover, encompassing the entire fields of machine learning and program synthesis. Since we are interested in generating models that are both readable and probabilistic, we will limit our discussion to approaches that offer at
least one of those characteristics.

10.1 Readable and Probabilistic

Of the related work, our goals are most closely aligned with the goals of PSketch
[23]. The primary difference between our tool and PSketch is the target user.
We want DaPPer to be accessible to a user who would not manually code even a
partial PPL model. Naturally, this difference in target user comes with a number
of technical differences. First and foremost, while PSketch requires the user to

write a program sketch—including specifying which variables may affect each program hole—our tool requires no coding. This brings us to the second primary difference, which is that while PSketch can work over any dataset for which the user can write most of the model, our tool is targeted specifically at relational datasets in which each row represents an independent draw from the model. Third, our tool does not hypothesize the existence of hidden variables that do not appear in the input dataset. Fourth, PSketch is designed for small datasets (they tested on datasets up to size 400), while DaPPer is designed to handle datasets with hundreds of thousands of rows. To make this feasible, DaPPer uses data-guided mutations, while PSketch's mutations are data-blind.

10.2 Readable and Deterministic

There has been a massive body of work in deterministic program synthesis and program induction, some of which may be useful in future iterations of our tool. Many synthesizers use off-the-shelf constraint solvers to search for candidate programs and verify their correctness [13,32,33]. We cannot directly apply these techniques to our problem since we do not have precise correctness constraints. Some recent work uses constraint solving to synthesize programs that optimize a cost function, with no precise correctness constraint [7]; unfortunately, this approach is only applicable to cost functions without floating-point computations, which makes it incompatible with likelihood estimation.

On the other hand, stochastic synthesis is a good fit for our problem. Our synthesizer is among the many that apply simulated annealing. Other stochastic synthesizers perform MCMC sampling [3,29]. Some use symbolic regression or other forms of genetic programming [26,30,36,37]. In the future, we may investigate how varying the search technique affects DaPPer's performance.

Some tools use enumerative search. Previous work has shown that enumerative synthesizers outperform other synthesizers for some problems [2,3,5,25,34]. With custom pruning strategies, this may be another path to faster synthesis.

10.3 Unreadable and Probabilistic

The machine learning literature includes a rich body of work on learning Bayesian networks. Mainstream techniques fall into two categories: *constraint-based* and *search-and-score*. Constraint-based techniques focus on generating only the program structure. Search-and-score treats the problems of learning program structure and learning program parameters together.

Constraint-based techniques use statistical methods (e.g., chi-squared and mutual information) to identify relationships between variables in order to produce a network structure. In short, these techniques perform the same task as the first stage of our synthesizer. We have intentionally factored out the generation of the dependency graph from the rest of the synthesis process, which makes it easy to customize DaPPer with new structure learning approaches, including constraint-based Bayesian learning approaches. This is a direction we hope to explore in the future.

Search-and-score techniques produce not just the network structure but a complete Bayesian network. Often these techniques produce outputs that can be translated directly to PPL programs. This makes them seem like a natural fit with our goals. Unfortunately, existing Bayesian learning techniques cannot produce readable models in the presence of continuous variables.

There are many search-and-score techniques for learning Bayesian networks that can be applied to discrete variables [14,19]. To extend them to continuous variables, one approach is standard discretization [17,31,38]. Where our approach first synthesizes a program structure, then searches over the space of conditionals, search-and-score first fixes the set of conditionals (via discretization), then searches over the space of program structures. This approach leads discretization-based tools to produce dense ASTs with high branching factors. An alternative technique uses mixtures of truncated exponentials (MTEs) to do discretization more flexibly [21,28]. Despite the attempt to reduce discretization, this approach still produces models that use large sets of massive switch statements with a different exponential distribution at each of hundreds of leaf nodes. In short, discretized search-and-score methods produce models that are difficult to read, understand, and adapt. The output models are accurate, but they do not succinctly express high-level insights into data.

Aside from Bayesian networks, a new class of models called sum-product networks (SPNs) [9,27] is both probabilistic and learnable. SPNs are not suitable for our use case because they are much less readable and editable even than machine-written Bayesian networks.

Although modeling multiple interacting variables is a more common goal, some work learns probabilistic models of individual distributions. We know of one tool designed to generate a fast sampler with outputs that mimic the distribution of a set of input numbers [24]. If it is fed samples from a Gaussian distribution, rather than learning that the input can be modeled by a Gaussian, it learns a fast sampling procedure that produces Gaussian-like data. This tool does not meet our needs because it can only model a single random variable, not interacting variables, but also because its outputs are difficult to read and interpret.

11   Conclusion

This paper offers an alternative way for users without statistics expertise to create probabilistic models of their data. DaPPer synthesizes models quickly and produces human-readable PPL programs that users can explore, expand, and adapt. We introduce data-guided program mutation, which allows PPL synthesis to scale to generating full programs. We hope this extends the class of users willing to venture into using probabilistic models. We believe offering users full PPL programs without asking them to write even a single line of code is an important step towards making PPLs more accessible.

Acknowledgements. We thank Dawn Song and Rastislav Bodik for their thoughtful feedback. This work is supported in part by NSF Grants CCF–1139138, CCF–1337415,

NSF ACI–1535191, and Graduate Research Fellowship DGE–1106400, a Microsoft Research PhD Fellowship, a grant from the U.S. Department of Energy, Office of Science, Office of Basic Energy Sciences Energy Frontier Research Centers program under Award Number FOA–0000619, and grants from DARPA FA8750–14–C–0011 and DARPA FA8750–16–2–0032, as well as gifts from Google, Intel, Mozilla, Nokia, and Qualcomm.

A   Appendix: Correlation of Incompatible Types

For both the simple correlation and network deconvolution approaches to dependency graph generation, we need to be able to measure the correlation between every pair of columns in a dataset. Between columns with the same type, this is relatively straightforward, but since we must produce correlation measures for every pair, we must take a somewhat unusual approach.

As our correlation measure for the correlation technique and our similarity score for deconvolution, we use Spearman correlation, a measure of rank correlation. This measure is suitable for quantitative, ordinal, and dichotomous nominal data. Thus it can be applied to all numeric distributions we use, as well as to boolean distributions, which are nominal and dichotomous. In contrast, categorical random variables are nominal but may take on more than two values. Many categorical random variables are used to represent ordinal data (data with an implied ranking, such as a variable with values 'low', 'medium', and 'high'). On the other hands, they may also be used for nominal data (data with no implied ranking, such as a variable with values 'linen', 'silk', 'cotton'). Also, even when they are used for ordinal data, the mapping from values to ranks is not provided. In other circumstances, for comparing nominal datasets, one might use nominal-specific measures of association, such as Cramer's V. However, for our purposes (and especially for the network deconvolution technique), it is important that all measures in the similarity matrix are comparable. Since a single dataset may include both quantitative and nominal data, using different metrics for different variable types would be unacceptable.

We address this problem with the observation that any categorical variable can be replaced with a set of boolean variables (one for each value of the categorical variable) to produce an equivalent model. Then, any variable that has a direct dependence on any of the boolean variables in the altered model would have a direct dependence on the original categorical variable. Thus, for any categorical variable with m available values, we produce columns of data to represent m boolean variables, one for each value v, such that the boolean variable takes value true if and only if the categorical variable produces value v. To compare the categorical variable with another variable A, we then calculate Spearman's rank correlation for each boolean variable with A. Our tool takes the conservative approach of using the highest correlation produced by any of the boolean variables as the final correlation value.

B   Appendix: Reducing the Incidence of Redundant Branches in Synthesized Programs

In this appendix, we describe our approach to reducing redundancy in program structures.

B.1   Design

For a concrete illustration of redundancy reduction, consider our running example. The output program from the synthesis step, shown in Fig. 13(a), contains two similar branches. Our redundancy reduction approach aligns the distributions of the two branches (based on path conditions) and compares their parameters. Since both parameters are similar, our approach chooses to collapse the branches, producing the output program in Fig. 13(b).

```
random Boolean tired ~
  BooleanDistrib(.500);
random Real skillLevel ~
  if tired
    then Gaussian(9.987, 7.000)
    else Gaussian(10.000, 7.003);
random Real testPerformance ~
  if (skillLevel < 16)
    then Gaussian(46.227, 7.663)
  else if (skillLevel > 18.2)
    then Gaussian(46.358, 7.549)
  else
    UniformReal(25.300, 125.113);
```

```
random Boolean tired ~
  BooleanDistrib(.500);
random Real skillLevel ~
  if tired
    then Gaussian(9.987, 7.000)
    else Gaussian(10.000, 7.003);
random Real testPerformance ~
  if (skillLevel < 16 | skillLevel > 18.2)
    then Gaussian(46.296, 7.599)
  else
    UniformReal(25.300, 125.113);
.
```

(a) Before reduction   (b) After reduction

Fig. 13. When two different branches have very similar bodies, our redundancy reduction algorithm can merge them to make the output program smaller and more readable. Pink highlights the reduction. (Color figure online)

As detailed in Algorithm 1, for each pair of distribution parameters, our algorithm makes a decision on whether they match based on how close their parameters are, but also on how much data was used to tune the parameters. If one distribution is Boolean(.987) and the other is Boolean(.986), we are probably willing to collapse them. In contrast, if one distribution is Boolean(.987) and the other is Boolean(.345), and both were tuned with many rows, we probably should not collapse them. However, if one of the distributions was tuned with only two rows of data, we may believe the discrepancy comes only from random chance and be willing to collapse them despite the large difference in the parameters. In this regard, we believe our algorithm follows much the same approach as a human programmer attempting to simplify such a program, comparing parameters, considering how much a parameter is likely to have been affected by chance. When redundancy reduction collapses two branches, it next tunes the distribution parameters for the descendant distributions.

```
for each pair (b1, b2) of branches do
    if not structureMatch(b1, b2) then
    |    continue
    end
    match = True
    for i in 0 to b1.distribs().length do
        distrib1 = b1.distribs()[i] ;                // the ith distribution in branch 1
        distrib2 = b2.distribs()[i]
        /* each distribution is associated with a rows value, the number of
           dataset rows used to tune its parameters                          */
        minNumRows = min(distrib1.rows, distrib2.rows)
        /* if one of these distributions has params based on very little data,
           expect it may reflect randomness rather than ground truth          */
        threshold = α/(minNumRows^0.7) - β
        for j in 0 to distrib1.length do
            param1 = distrib1[j] ;                   // the jth param of distribution 1
            param2 = distrib2[j]
            match = match ∧ (| param1 - param2 | < threshold)
        end
    end
    if match then
    |    collapse(b1, b2)
    end
end
```

Algorithm 1: A redundancy reduction algorithm for making synthesized programs more human-readable. The α and β parameters can be adjusted by the user to control the size and readability of the output program.

Our algorithm uses two threshold parameters, α and β. Low α values lead the algorithm to do little reduction, while high α values produce small, highly reduced programs. The β parameter gives users direct control over the difference between parameter values that should always result in a reduction. For instance, if users anticipate that they will not benefit from seeing separate branches for `Boolean(0.94)` and `Boolean(0.96)`, they should set β to 0.02 to indicate that parameters with differences no more than 0.02 should always be collapsed, regardless of the amount of data used to estimate them. Although α is the primary determinant of how aggressively the algorithm collapses branches, users may find manipulation of β convenient if they know some magnitude of difference is unimportant for their use cases.

Applying this algorithm after the synthesis process offers both advantages and disadvantages. The primary and obvious disadvantage is that by reducing redundancy after SA, we give up the opportunity to reduce the SA time by running on a smaller program structure. However, we believe the advantages may make up for the reduction in synthesis time. With this approach, we allow SA to use all the distinctions it can use to obtain high accuracy, and only eliminate distinctions from the learned program after the fact, when it is clear they have not offered significant advantages. At this point in the process, redundancy reduction has access to all the information that has been learned during the earlier synthesis stages, and can make very informed decisions about which conditions to combine. It receives more information than the dependency graph generation stage receives. Also, as discussed in Sect. 7, because this modification is applied as a post-processing step, the user can quickly and easily explore different readability levels, tuning the amount of redundancy reduction to his or her needs.

We also feel this approach may be a more natural way to reduce program sizes, compared to aggressive dependency graph approaches like Network Deconvolution. This is because the individual branch collapse actions are intuitive to human users and could even be presented to the programmer for approval.

```
random Boolean Burglary ~
  BooleanDistrib(0.001);

random Boolean Earthquake ~
  BooleanDistrib(0.002);

random Boolean Alarm ~
  if Burglary
  then
    if Earthquake
    then BooleanDistrib(0.95)
    else BooleanDistrib(0.94)
  else
    if Earthquake
    then BooleanDistrib(0.29)
    else BooleanDistrib(0.001);

random Boolean JohnCalls ~
  if Alarm
  then BooleanDistrib(0.9)
  else BooleanDistrib(0.05);

random Boolean MaryCalls ~
  if Alarm
  then BooleanDistrib(0.7)
  else BooleanDistrib(0.01);
```

```
random Boolean Burglary ~
  BooleanDistrib(0.0008);

random Boolean Earthquake ~
  BooleanDistrib(0.0018);

random Boolean Alarm ~
  if Burglary
  then

    BooleanDistrib(1.0)

  else
    if Earthquake
    then BooleanDistrib(0.33333333)
    else BooleanDistrib(0.00110286);

random Boolean JohnCalls ~
  if Alarm
  then BooleanDistrib(0.96)
  else BooleanDistrib(0.049824561);

random Boolean MaryCalls ~
  if Alarm
  then BooleanDistrib(0.76)
  else BooleanDistrib(0.008621553);
```

(a) The ground truth program for our 'burglary' benchmark.

(b) The program DaPPer synthesizes for the 'burglary' benchmark.

Fig. 14. A side-by-side comparison of the ground truth 'burglary' program and the program DaPPer synthesizes for the 'burglary' dataset. This program was synthesized with the Complete dependency graph, then processed with redundancy reduction.

B.2   Future Work for Redundancy Reduction

Although we are satisfied with the outputs of the current redundancy reduction technique, we are also interested in pursuing a more principled approach. The current algorithm is excellent for allowing users to explore quickly, since it is fast and offers simple tuning parameters. It is also a clean way to handle many different distribution types with a unified algorithm. However, we see redundancy reduction as a natural place to apply methods for identifying whether a difference is statistically significant. Rather than use our magnitude of difference vs. magnitude of data heuristics, why not use real statistical hypothesis testing?

We see one potential drawback to this approach, which is that our redundancy reduction approach is intended to increase readability rather than reduce overfitting. We want users to be able to remove detail even when it is *not* the result of random chance or overfitting. In short, users should be able to eliminate a distinction even if it is statistically significant. We intentionally placed the redundancy reduction stage at the end so that users can quickly explore various levels of program size and readability, tuning programs to their individual needs. If we transition to a more principled approach, we would want to find a way to maintain this flexibility and the current level of user control. In future, we expect to explore this direction.

C   Appendix: Examples of Synthesized Programs

To give a sense of how readable DaPPer's output programs are, we include programs DaPPer produces for the two running examples we use throughout the paper, 'burglary' (Fig. 14) and 'students' (Fig. 15).

```
random Boolean tired ~
  BooleanDistrib(.5);

random Real skillLevel ~
  Gaussian(10, 7);

random Real testPerformance ~
  if skillLevel > 13.0
  then
    if tired
    then Gaussian(70, 15)
    else Gaussian(95, 5)
  else
    if tired
    then Gaussian(30, 15)
    else Gaussian(70, 5);
```

```
random Boolean tired ~
  BooleanDistrib(0.5009);

random Real skillLevel ~
  Gaussian(9.947325,6.981384);

random Real testPerformance ~
  if tired
  then
    if (skillLevel > 13.0266062)
    then Gaussian(70.079381,13.760027)
    else Gaussian(30.156086,20.582181)
  else
    if (skillLevel < 12.5535461)
    then Gaussian(70.005204,5.063899)
    else UniformReal(64.2285,104.1120);
```

(a) The ground truth program for our 'students' benchmark.

(b) The program DaPPer synthesizes for the 'students' benchmark.

Fig. 15. A side-by-side comparison of the ground truth 'students' program and a program DaPPer synthesizes for the 'students' dataset. We use colors to highlight the bodies of corresponding branches. This program was synthesized with the Correlation dependency graph and did not require redundancy reduction.

References

1. RITA | BTS | Transtats. http://www.transtats.bts.gov/DL_SelectFields.asp? Table_ID=236&DB_Short_Name=On-Time. Accessed 05 Feb 2016
2. Akiba, T., Imajo, K., Iwami, H., Iwata, Y., Kataoka, T., Takahashi, N., Moskal, M., Swamy, N.: Calibrating research in program synthesis using 72,000 hours of programmer time. Technical report MSR (2013)
3. Alur, R., Bodik, R., Dallal, E., Fisman, D., Garg, P., Juniwal, G., Kress-Gazit, H., Madhusudan, P., Martin, M.M.K., Raghothaman, M., Saha, S., Seshia, S.A., Singh, R., Solar-Lezama, A., Torlak, E., Udupa, A.: Syntax-guided synthesis. In: SyGus Competition (2014)
4. Arora, N.S., Russell, S.J., Sudderth, E.B.: Automatic inference in BLOG. In: Statistical Relational Artificial Intelligence, AAAI Workshops, vol. WS-10-06. AAAI (2010)
5. Barthe, G., Crespo, J.M., Gulwani, S., Kunz, C., Marron, M.: From relational verification to SIMD loop synthesis. In: PPoPP (2013)
6. Bhat, S., Borgström, J., Gordon, A.D., Russo, C.: Deriving probability density functions from probabilistic functional programs. In: Piterman, N., Smolka, S.A. (eds.) TACAS 2013. LNCS, vol. 7795, pp. 508–522. Springer, Heidelberg (2013). doi:10.1007/978-3-642-36742-7_35
7. Bornholt, J., Torlak, E., Grossman, D., Ceze, L.: Optimizing synthesis with metasketches. In: POPL (2016)
8. Feizi, S., Marbach, D., Médard, M., Kellis, M.: Network deconvolution as a general method to distinguish direct dependencies in networks. Nat. Biotechnol. **31**(8), 726–733 (2013)
9. Gens, R., Domingos, P.M.: Learning the structure of sum-product networks. In: ICML (2013)
10. Gilks, W.R., Thomas, A., Spiegelhalter, D.J.: A language and program for complex Bayesian modelling. J. R. Stat. Soc. Ser. D (Stat.) **43**(1), 169–177 (1994)
11. Goodman, N.D., Mansinghka, V.K., Roy, D.M., Bonawitz, K., Tenenbaum, J.B.: Church: a language for generative models. In: UAI, pp. 220–229 (2008)
12. Gordon, A.D., Henzinger, T.A., Nori, A.V., Rajamani, S.K.: Probabilistic programming. In: FOSE 2014 (2014)
13. Gulwani, S., Jha, S., Tiwari, A., Venkatesan, R.: Synthesis of loop-free programs. In: PLDI (2011)
14. Heckerman, D.: A tutorial on learning with Bayesian networks. In: Learning in Graphical Models, pp. 301–354. MIT Press, Cambridge (1999)
15. Hofmann, H., Cook, D., Kielion, C., Schloerke, B., Hobbs, J., Loy, A., Mosley, L., Rockoff, D., Huang, Y., Wrolstad, D., Yin, T.: Delayed, canceled, on time, boarding.. flying in the USA. J. Comput. Graph. Stat. **20**(2), 287–290 (2011)
16. Koller, D., McAllester, D., Pfeffer, A.: Effective Bayesian inference for stochastic programs. In: AAAI/IAAI (1997)
17. Kozlov, A.V., Koller, D.: Nonuniform dynamic discretization in hybrid networks. In: UAI (1997)
18. Li, L., Wu, Y., Russell, S.J.: SWIFT: compiled inference for probabilistic programs. Technical report UCB/EECS-2015-12, EECS Department, University of California, Berkeley, March 2015. http://www.eecs.berkeley.edu/Pubs/TechRpts/2015/EECS-2015-12.html
19. Lowd, D., Domingos, P.M.: Learning arithmetic circuits. In: UAI (2008)

20. Milch, B., Marthi, B., Russell, S., Sontag, D., Ong, D.L., Kolobov, A.: BLOG: probabilistic models with unknown objects. In: IJCAI, pp. 1352–1359 (2005)
21. Moral, S., Rumi, R., Salmerón, A.: Mixtures of truncated exponentials in hybrid Bayesian networks. In: Benferhat, S., Besnard, P. (eds.) ECSQARU 2001. LNCS, vol. 2143, pp. 156–167. Springer, Heidelberg (2001). doi:10.1007/3-540-44652-4_15
22. Nori, A.V., Hur, C.K., Rajamani, S.K., Samuel, S.: R2: an efficient MCMC sampler for probabilistic programs. In: AAAI, July 2014
23. Nori, A.V., Ozair, S., Rajamani, S.K., Vijaykeerthy, D.: Efficient synthesis of probabilistic programs. In: PLDI (2015)
24. Perov, Y.N., Wood, F.D.: Learning probabilistic programs. CoRR abs/1407.2646 (2014). http://arxiv.org/abs/1407.2646
25. Phothilimthana, P.M., Thakur, A., Bodik, R., Dhurjati, D.: Scaling up superoptimization. In: ASPLOS (2016)
26. Poli, R., Graff, M., McPhee, N.F.: Free lunches for function and program induction. In: FOGA (2009)
27. Poon, H., Domingos, P.: Sum-product networks: a new deep architecture. In: ICCV Workshops (2011)
28. Romero, V., Rumí, R., Salmerón, A.: Learning hybrid Bayesian networks using mixtures of truncated exponentials. Int. J. Approx. Reason. **42**(1–2), 54–68 (2006)
29. Schkufza, E., Sharma, R., Aiken, A.: Stochastic superoptimization. In: ASPLOS (2013)
30. Schmidt, M., Lipson, H.: Distilling free-form natural laws from experimental data. Science **324**, 81–85 (2009)
31. Shah, A., Woolf, P.J.: Python environment for bayesian learning: inferring the structure of bayesian networks from knowledge and data. J. Mach. Learn. Res. **10**, 159–162 (2009)
32. Solar-Lezama, A., Tancau, L., Bodik, R., Seshia, S., Saraswat, V.: Combinatorial sketching for finite programs. In: ASPLOS (2006)
33. Torlak, E., Bodik, R.: A lightweight symbolic virtual machine for solver-aided host languages. In: PLDI (2014)
34. Udupa, A., Raghavan, A., Deshmukh, J.V., Mador-Haim, S., Martin, M.M., Alur, R.: TRANSIT: specifying protocols with concolic snippets. In: PLDI (2013)
35. Wicklin, R.: An analysis of airline delays with SAS/IMLr Studio (2009)
36. Wong, M.L., Leung, K.S.: Evolutionary program induction directed by logic grammars. Evol. Comput. **5**(2), 143–180 (1997)
37. Woodward, J.R., Bai, R.: Why evolution is not a good paradigm for program induction: a critique of genetic programming. In: ACM/SIGEVO GEC, GEC 2009 (2009)
38. Yoo, C., Thorsson, V., Cooper, G.F.: Discovery of causal relationships in a gene-regulation pathway from a mixture of experimental and observational DNA microarray data. In: Proceedings of PSB, pp. 498–509 (2002)

Logical Clustering and Learning for Time-Series Data

Marcell Vazquez-Chanlatte[1(✉)],
Jyotirmoy V. Deshmukh[2],
Xiaoqing Jin[2], and Sanjit A. Seshia[1]

[1] University of California Berkeley, Berkeley, USA
{marcell.vc,sseshia}@eecs.berkeley.edu
[2] Toyota Motors North America R&D, Gardena, USA
{jyotirmoy.deshmukh,xiaoqing.jin}@toyota.com

Abstract. In order to effectively analyze and build cyberphysical systems (CPS), designers today have to combat the data deluge problem, i.e., the burden of processing intractably large amounts of data produced by complex models and experiments. In this work, we utilize monotonic parametric signal temporal logic (PSTL) to design features for unsupervised classification of time series data. This enables using off-the-shelf machine learning tools to automatically cluster similar traces with respect to a given PSTL formula. We demonstrate how this technique produces interpretable formulas that are amenable to analysis and understanding using a few representative examples. We illustrate this with case studies related to automotive engine testing, highway traffic analysis, and auto-grading massively open online courses.

1 Introduction

In order to effectively construct and analyze cyber-physical systems (CPS), designers today have to combat the *data deluge* problem, i.e., the burden of processing intractably large amounts of data produced by complex models and experiments. For example, consider the typical design process for an advanced CPS such as a self-driving car. Checking whether the car meets all its requirements is typically done by either physically driving the car around for millions of miles [2], or by performing virtual simulations of the self-driving algorithms. Either approach can generate several gigabytes worth of time-series traces of data, such as sensor readings, variables within the software controllers, actuator actions, driver inputs, and environmental conditions. Typically, designers are interested not in the details of these traces, but in discovering higher-level insight from them; however, given the volume of data, a high level of automation is needed.

The key challenge then is: "How do we automatically identify logical structure or relations within such data?" One possibility offered by unsupervised learning algorithms from the machine learning community is to cluster similar behaviors to identify higher-level commonalities in the data. Typical clustering

R. Majumdar and V. Kunčak (Eds.): CAV 2017, Part I, LNCS 10426, pp. 305–325, 2017.
DOI: 10.1007/978-3-319-63387-9_15

algorithms define similarity measures on signal spaces, e.g., the dynamic time warping distance, or by projecting data to complex feature spaces. We argue later in this section that these methods can be inadequate to learn logical structure in time-series data.

In this paper, we present *logical clustering*, an *unsupervised learning* procedure that utilizes *Parametric Signal Temporal Logic* (PSTL) templates to discover logical structure within the given data. Informally, Signal Temporal Logic (STL) enables specifying temporal relations between constraints on signal values [3,10]. PSTL generalizes STL formulas by replacing, with parameters, time constants in temporal operators and signal-value constants in atomic predicates in the formula. With PSTL templates, one can use the template parameters as *features*. This is done by projecting a trace to parameter valuations that correspond to a formula that is *marginally satisfied* by the trace. As each trace is projected to the finite-dimensional space of formula-parameters, we can then use traditional clustering algorithms on this space; thereby grouping traces that satisfy the same (or similar) formulas together. Such *logical clustering* can reveal heretofore undiscovered structure in the traces, albeit through the lens of an user-provided template. We illustrate the basic steps in our technique with an example.

Consider the design of a lane-tracking controller for a car and a scenario where a car has effected a lane-change. A typical control designer tests design performance by observing the "overshoot" behavior of the controller, i.e., by inspecting the maximum deviation (say a) over a certain duration of time (say, τ) of the vehicle position trajectory $x(t)$ from a given desired trajectory $x_{ref}(t)$. We can use the following PSTL template that captures such an overshoot:

$$\varphi_{\text{overshoot}} \stackrel{\text{def}}{=} \mathbf{F}\left(\texttt{lane\_change} \wedge \mathbf{F}_{(0,\tau]}\left(x - x_{\texttt{ref}} > a\right)\right) \tag{1}$$

When we project traces appearing in Fig. 1 through $\varphi_{\text{overshoot}}$, we find three behavior-clusters as shown in the second row of the figure: (1) Cluster 0 with traces that track the desired trajectory with small overshoot, (2) Cluster 1 with traces that fail to track the desired trajectory altogether, and (3) Cluster 2 with traces that *do* track the desired trajectory, but have a large overshoot value. The three clusters indicate a well-behaved controller, an incorrect controller, and a controller that needs tuning respectively. The key observation here is that though we use a single overshoot template to analyze the data, qualitatively different behaviors form separate clusters in the induced parameter space; furthermore, each cluster has higher-level meaning that the designer can find valuable.

In contrast to our proposed method, consider the clustering induced by using the dynamic time warping (DTW) distance measure as shown in Fig. 1. Note that DTW is one of the most popular measures to cluster time-series data [17]. We can see that traces with both high and low overshoots are clustered together due to similarities in their shape. Such shape-similarity based grouping could be quite valuable in certain contexts; however, it is inadequate when the designer is interested in temporal properties that may group traces of dissimilar shapes.

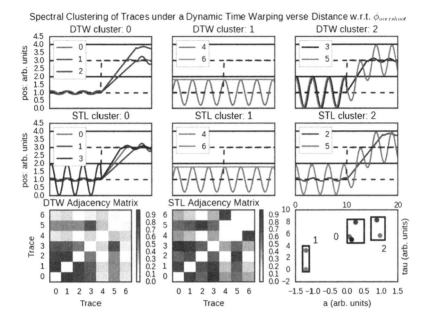

Fig. 1. An example of a pitfall when using the DTW measure compared to projection using a PSTL template. We perform spectral clustering [24] on a similarity graph representation of 7 traces. Nodes of the graph represent traces and edges are labeled with the normalized pairwise distance using (1) the DTW measure and (2) the Euclidean distance between features extracted using the PSTL template $\varphi_{\text{overshoot}}$. Note how under the DTW measure, the black and cyan traces are grouped together due to their behavior before the lane change, despite the cyan trace having a much larger overshoot. Contrast with the STL labeling in the second row, where both overshooting traces are grouped together. The bottom right figure provides the projection of the traces w.r.t. $\varphi_{\text{overshoot}}$ with the associated cluster-labels shown in the second row.

In Sect. 3, we show how we can use feature extraction with PSTL templates to group traces with similar logical properties together. An advantage of using PSTL is that the enhanced feature extraction is computationally efficient for the fragment of monotonic PSTL formulas [5,14]; such a formula has the property that its satisfaction by a given trace is monotonic in its parameter values. The efficiency in feature extraction relies on a multi-dimensional binary search procedure [20] that exploits the monotonicity property.

A different view of the technique presented here is as a method to perform temporal logic inference from data, such as the work on learning STL formulas in a supervised learning context [5–7,18], in the unsupervised anomaly detection context [15], and in the context of active learning [16]. Some of these approaches adapt classical machine learning algorithms such as decision trees [7] and one-class support vector machines [15] to learn (possibly, arbitrarily long) formulas in a restricted fragment of STL. Formulas exceeding a certain length are often considered inscrutable by designers. A key technical contribution of this paper is to show that using simple shapes such as specific Boolean combinations of axis-aligned hyperboxes in the parameter space of monotonic PSTL to represent clusters yields a formula that may be easier to interpret. We support this in Sect. 4, by showing that such hyperbox-clusters correspond to STL formulas that have length linear in the number of parameters in the given PSTL template, and thus of bounded descriptive complexity.

Mining parametric temporal logic properties in a model-based design has also been explored [12,14]. We note that our proposed methods does not require such a model, which may not be available either due to the complexity of the underlying system or lack of certainty in the dynamics. We also note that there is much work on mining discrete temporal logic specifications from data (e.g. [21]): our work instead focuses on unsupervised learning of STL properties relevant to CPS.

The reader might wonder how much insight is needed by a user to select the PSTL template to use for classification. We argue the templates do not pose a burden on the user and that our technique can have high value in several ways. First, we observe that we can combine our technique with a human-guided (or automated) enumerative learning procedure that can exploit high-level template pools. We demonstrate such a procedure in the diesel engine case study. Second, consider a scenario where a designer has insight into the data that allows them to choose the correct PSTL template. Even in this case, our method automates the task of labeleing trace-clusters with STL labels which can then be used to automatically classify new data. Finally, we argue that many unsupervised learning techniques on time-series data must "featurize" the data to start with, and such features represent relevant domain knowledge. Our features happen to be PSTL templates. As the lane controller motivating example illustrates, a common procedure that doesn't have some domain specific knowledge increases the risk of wrong classifications. This sentiment is highlighted even in the data mining literature [22]. To illustrate the value of our technique, in Sect. 5, we demonstrate the use of logic-based templates to analyze time-series data in case studies from three different application domains.

2   Preliminaries

Definition 1 (Timed Traces). *A timed trace is a finite (or infinite) sequence of pairs* $(t_0, \mathbf{x}_0)$, ..., $(t_n, \mathbf{x}_n)$, *where,* $t_0 = 0$, *and for all* $i \in [1, n]$, $t_i \in \mathbb{R}_{\geq 0}$, $t_{i-1} < t_i$, *and for* $i \in [0, n]$, $\mathbf{x}_i \in \mathcal{D}$, *where* $\mathcal{D}$ *is some compact set. We refer to the interval* $[t_0, t_n]$ *as the time domain* T.

Real-time temporal logics are a formalism for reasoning about finite or infinite timed traces. Logics such as the Timed Propositional Temporal Logic [4], and Metric Temporal Logic (MTL) [19] were introduced to reason about signals representing Boolean-predicates varying over dense (or discrete) time. More recently, Signal Temporal Logic [23] was proposed in the context of analog and mixed-signal circuits as a specification language for real-valued signals.

Signal Temporal Logic. Without loss of generality, atoms in STL formulas can be be reduced to the form $f(\mathbf{x}) \sim c$, where f is a function from $\mathcal{D}$ to $\mathbb{R}$, $\sim \in \{\geq, \leq, =\}$, and $c \in \mathbb{R}$. Temporal formulas are formed using temporal operators, "always" (denoted as $\mathbf{G}$), "eventually" (denoted as $\mathbf{F}$) and "until" (denoted as $\mathbf{U}$) that can each be indexed by an interval I. An STL formula is written using the following grammar:

$$
\begin{aligned}
I &:= (a, b) \mid (a, b] \mid [a, b) \mid [a, b] \\
\varphi &:= true \mid f(\mathbf{x}) \sim c \mid \neg \varphi \mid \varphi_1 \wedge \varphi_2 \mid \varphi_1 \, \mathbf{U}_I \, \varphi_2
\end{aligned}
\tag{2}
$$

In the above grammar, $a, b \in T$, and $c \in \mathbb{R}$. The always ($\mathbf{G}$) and eventually ($\mathbf{F}$) operators are defined for notational convenience, and are just special cases of the until operator: $\mathbf{F}_I \varphi \triangleq true \, \mathbf{U}_I \, \varphi$, and $\mathbf{G}_I \varphi \triangleq \neg \mathbf{F}_I \neg \varphi$. We use the notation $(\mathbf{x}, t) \models \varphi$ to mean that the suffix of the timed trace $\mathbf{x}$ beginning at time t satisfies the formula φ. The formal semantics of an STL formula are defined recursively:

$$
\begin{aligned}
(\mathbf{x}, t) &\models f(\mathbf{x}) \sim c &\Longleftrightarrow& \quad f(\mathbf{x}(t)) \sim c \text{ is true} \\
(\mathbf{x}, t) &\models \neg \varphi &\Longleftrightarrow& \quad (\mathbf{x}, t) \not\models \varphi \\
(\mathbf{x}, t) &\models \varphi_1 \wedge \varphi_2 &\Longleftrightarrow& \quad (\mathbf{x}, t) \models \varphi_1 \, And \, (\mathbf{x}, t) \models \varphi_2 \\
(\mathbf{x}, t) &\models \varphi_1 \, \mathbf{U}_I \, \varphi_2 &\Longleftrightarrow& \quad \exists t_1 \in t \oplus I : (\mathbf{x}, t_1) \models \varphi_2 \, \wedge \\
& & & \quad \forall t_2 \in [t, t_1) : (\mathbf{x}, t_2) \models \varphi_1
\end{aligned}
$$

We write $\mathbf{x} \models \varphi$ as a shorthand of $(\mathbf{x}, 0) \models \varphi$.

Parametric Signal Temporal Logic (PSTL). PSTL [5] is an extension of STL introduced to define *template formulas* containing unknown parameters. Formally, the set of parameters $\mathcal{P}$ is a set consisting of two disjoint sets of variables $\mathcal{P}^V$ and $\mathcal{P}^T$ of which at least one is nonempty. The parameter variables in $\mathcal{P}^V$ can take values from their domain, denoted as the set V. The parameter variables in $\mathcal{P}^T$ are time-parameters that take values from the time domain T. We define a valuation function ν that maps a parameter to a value in its domain. We denote a vector of parameter variables by $\mathbf{p}$, and extend the definition of the valuation function to map parameter vectors $\mathbf{p}$ into tuples of respective values over V or T. We define the *parameter space* $\mathcal{D}_{\mathcal{P}}$ as a subset of $V^{|\mathcal{P}^V|} \times T^{|\mathcal{P}^T|}$.

A PSTL formula is then defined by modifying the grammar specified in (2) by allowing a, b to be elements of $\mathcal{P}^T$, and c to be an element of $\mathcal{P}^V$. An STL formula is obtained by pairing a PSTL formula with a valuation function that assigns a value to each parameter variable. For example, consider the PSTL formula $\varphi(c, \tau) = \mathbf{G}_{[0,\tau]} x > c$, with parameters variables c and τ. The STL formula $\mathbf{G}_{[0,10]} x > 1.2$ is an instance of φ obtained with the valuation $\nu = \{\tau \mapsto 10, \ c \mapsto 1.2\}$.

Monotonic PSTL. Monotonic PSTL is a fragment of PSTL introduced as the polarity fragment in [5]. A PSTL formula φ is said to be monotonically increasing in parameter p_i if condition (3) holds for all $\mathbf{x}$, and is said to be monotonically decreasing in parameter p_i if condition (4) holds for all $\mathbf{x}$.

$$\nu(p_i) \leq \nu'(p_i) \implies \qquad [\mathbf{x} \models \varphi(\nu(p_i)) \implies \mathbf{x} \models \varphi(\nu'(p_i))] \qquad (3)$$

$$\nu(p_i) \geq \nu'(p_i) \implies \qquad [\mathbf{x} \models \varphi(\nu(p_i)) \implies \mathbf{x} \models \varphi(\nu'(p_i))] \qquad (4)$$

To indicate the direction of monotonicity, we now introduce the polarity of a parameter [5], $\mathrm{sgn}(p_i)$, and say that $\mathrm{sgn}(p_i) = +$ if the $\varphi(\mathbf{p})$ is monotonically increasing in p_i and $\mathrm{sgn}(p_i) = -$ if it is monotonically decreasing, and $\mathrm{sgn}(p_i) = \perp$ if it is neither. A formula $\varphi(\mathbf{p})$ is said to be monotonic in p_i if $\mathrm{sgn}(p_i) \in \{+, -\}$, and say that $\varphi(\mathbf{p})$ is monotonic if for all i, φ is monotonic in p_i.

While restrictive, the monotonic fragment of PSTL contains many formulas of interest, such as those expressing steps and spikes in trace values, timed-causal relations between traces, and so on. Moreover, in some instances, for a given non-monotonic PSTL formula, it may be possible to obtain a related monotonic PSTL formula by using distinct parameters in place of a repeated parameter, or by assigning a constant valuation for some parameters (Example in Appendix A).

Example 1. For formula (1), we can see that $\mathrm{sgn}(a) = -$, because if a trace has a certain overshoot exceeding the threshold a^*, then for a fixed τ, the trace satisfies any formula where $a < a^*$. Similarly, $\mathrm{sgn}(\tau) = +$, as an overshoot over some interval $(0, \tau^*]$ will be still considered an overshoot for $\tau > \tau^*$.

Orders on Parameter Space. A monotonic parameter induces a total order $\trianglelefteq_i$ in its domain, and as different parameters for a given formula are usually independent, valuations for different parameters induce a partial order:

Definition 2 (Parameter Space Partial Order). *We define $\trianglelefteq_i$ as a total order on the domain of the parameter p_i as follows:*

$$\nu(p_i) \trianglelefteq_i \nu'(p_i) \overset{\mathrm{def}}{=} \begin{cases} \nu(p_i) \leq \nu'(p_i) & \text{if } \mathrm{sgn}(p_i) = + \\ \nu(p_i) \geq \nu'(p_i) & \text{if } \mathrm{sgn}(p_i) = - \end{cases} \qquad (5)$$

Under the order $\trianglelefteq_i$, the parameter space can be viewed as a partially ordered set $(\mathcal{D}_P, \trianglelefteq)$, where the ordering operation $\trianglelefteq$ is defined as follows:

$$\nu(\mathbf{p}) \trianglelefteq \nu'(\mathbf{p}) \overset{\mathrm{def}}{=} \forall i : \nu(p_i) \trianglelefteq_i \nu'(p_i). \qquad (6)$$

When combined with Eqs. (3), (4) this gives us the relation that $\nu(\mathbf{p}) \trianglelefteq \nu'(\mathbf{p})$ implies that $[\varphi(\nu(\mathbf{p})) \implies \varphi(\nu'(\mathbf{p}))]$. In order to simplify notation, we define the subset of X that satisfies $\varphi(\nu(\mathbf{p}))$ as $[\![\varphi(\nu(\mathbf{p}))]\!]_X$. If X and $\mathbf{p}$ are obvious from context, we simply write: $[\![\varphi(\nu)]\!]$. It follows that $(\nu \trianglelefteq \nu') \implies ([\![\varphi(\nu)]\!] \subseteq [\![\varphi(\nu')]\!])$. In summary: $\trianglelefteq$ operates in the same direction as implication and subset. Informally, we say that the ordering is from a stronger to a weaker formula.

Example 2. For formula (1), the order operation $\trianglelefteq$ is defined as $\nu \trianglelefteq \nu'$ iff $\nu(\tau) < \nu'(\tau)$ and $\nu(a) > \nu'(a)$. Consider $\nu_1(\mathbf{p}) \overset{\mathrm{def}}{=} (\tau : 0.1, a : -1.1)$ and $\nu_2(\mathbf{p}) \overset{\mathrm{def}}{=} (\tau : 3.3, a : -1.3)$. As $\mathrm{sgn}(a) = -$, $\mathrm{sgn}(\tau) = +$, $\nu_1 \trianglelefteq \nu_2$, and

$\varphi_{\text{overshoot}}(\nu_1(\mathbf{p})) \implies \varphi_{\text{overshoot}}(\nu_2(\mathbf{p}))$. Intuitively this means that if $x(t)$ satisfies a formula specifying a overshoot > -1.1 (undershoot < 1.1) over a duration of 0.1 time units, then $x(t)$ trivially satisfies the formula specifying an undershoot of < 1.3 over a duration of 3.3 time units.

Next, we define the downward closure of $\nu(\mathbf{p})$ and relate it to $[\![\varphi(\nu(\mathbf{p}))]\!]$.

Definition 3 (Downward closure of a valuation). *For a valuation ν, its downward closure (denoted $D(\nu)$) is the set $\{\nu' \mid \nu' \trianglelefteq \nu\}$.*

In the following lemma we state that the union of the sets of traces satisfying formulas corresponding to parameter valuations in the downward closure of a valuation ν is the same as the set of traces satisfying the formula corresponding to ν. The proof follows from the definition of downward closure.

Lemma 1. $\bigcup_{\nu' \in D(\nu)} [\![\varphi(\nu')]\!] \equiv [\![\varphi(\nu)]\!]$

Lastly, we define the validity domain of a set of traces and φ.

Definition 4 (Validity domain). *Let X be a (potentially infinite) collection of timed traces, and let $\varphi(\mathbf{p})$ be a PSTL formula with parameters $\mathbf{p} \in \mathcal{P}$. The validity domain[1] $\mathcal{V}(\varphi(\mathbf{p}), X)$ of $\varphi(\mathbf{p})$ is a closed subset of $\mathcal{D}_{\mathcal{P}}$, such that:*

$$\forall \nu(\mathbf{p}) \in \mathcal{V}(\varphi(\mathbf{p}), X) : \forall \mathbf{x} \in X : \mathbf{x} \models \varphi(\nu(\mathbf{p})) \tag{7}$$

Remark 1. The validity domain for a given parameter set $\mathcal{P}$ essentially contains all the parameter valuations s.t. for the given set of traces X, each trace satisfies the STL formula obtained by instantiating the given PSTL formula with the parameter valuation.

Example 3. In Fig. 2, we show the validity domain of the PSTL formula (1) for the three traces given in the subplot labeled STL cluster 0 in Fig. 1. The hatched red region contains parameter valuations corresponding to STL formulas that are not satisfied by any trace, while the shaded-green region is the validity domain of the formula. The validity domain reflects that till the peak value a^* of the black trace is reached (which is the smallest among the peak values for the three signals), the curve in τ-a space follows the green trace (which has the lowest slope among the three traces). For any value of τ, for which $a > a^*$, the formula is trivially satisfied by all traces.

3   Trace-Projection and Clustering

In this section, we introduce the projection of a trace to the parameter space of a given PSTL formula, and discuss mechanisms to cluster the trace-projections using off-the-shelf clustering techniques.

---

[1] If X is obvious from context (or does not matter), we write $\mathcal{V}(\varphi(\mathbf{p}), X)$ as $\mathcal{V}(\varphi)$.

Trace Projection. The key idea of this paper is defining a projection operation π that maps a given timed trace $\mathbf{x}$ to a suitable parameter valuation[2] $\nu^*(\mathbf{p})$ in the validity domain of the given PSTL formula $\varphi(\mathbf{p})$. We would also like to project the given timed trace to a valuation that is as close a representative of the given trace as possible (under the lens of the chosen PSTL formula).

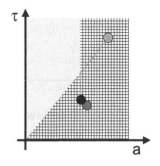

One way of mapping a given timed trace to a single valuation is by defining a total order $\preceq$ on the parameter space by an appropriate *linearization* of the partial order on parameter space. The total order then provides a minimum valuation to which the given timed trace is mapped.

Fig. 2. Validity domain and projection of traces in STL Cluster 0 from Fig. 1.

Remark 2. For technical reasons, we often adjoin two special elements $\top$ and $\bot$ to $\mathcal{V}(\varphi(\mathbf{p}), X)$ such that $\forall \nu(\mathbf{p}) \in \mathcal{V}(\varphi(\nu(\mathbf{p})), X), \bot \trianglelefteq \nu(\mathbf{p}) \trianglelefteq \top$ and $\forall x \in X, x \models \varphi(\top(\mathbf{p}))$ and $\neg(x \models \varphi(\bot(\mathbf{p})))$. These special elements mark whether $\mathcal{V}(\varphi(\nu(\mathbf{p})))$ is the whole parameter space or empty.

We present the lexicographic order on parameters as one possible linearization; other linearizations, such as those based on a weighted sum in the parameter space could also be used (presented in Appendix A for brevity).

Lexicographic Order. A lexicographic order (denoted $\preceq_{\text{lex}}$) uses the specification of a total order on parameter indices to linearize the partial order. We formalize lexicographic ordering as follows.

Definition 5 (Lexicographic Order). *Suppose we are given a total order on the parameters* $j_1 > \cdots > j_n$. *The total order* $\preceq_{\text{lex}}$ *on the parameter space* $\mathcal{D}_\mathcal{P}$ *is defined as:*

$$\nu(\mathbf{p}) \preceq_{\text{lex}} \nu'(\mathbf{p}) \iff \exists j_k \in (j_1, \ldots, j_n) \;\; s.t. \;\; \nu(p_{j_k}) \trianglelefteq_i \nu'(p_{j_k}) \text{ and,} \atop \forall \ell < k, \;\; \nu(p_{j_\ell}) = \nu'(p_{j_\ell}). \tag{8}$$

Note that for a given total or partial order, we can define inf and sup under that order in standard fashion. Formally, the projection function using lexicographic order is defined as follows:

$$\pi_{\text{lex}}(\mathbf{x}) = \inf_{\preceq_{\text{lex}}} \{\nu(\mathbf{p}) \in \mathcal{V}(\varphi(\mathbf{p}), \{x\})\} \tag{9}$$

---

[2] For canonicity, π need not be a function from timed traces to $\mathcal{D}_\mathcal{P}$. For example, it may be expedient to project a trace to a subset of $\mathcal{D}_\mathcal{P}$. For simplicity, we defer more involved projections to future exposition.

Algorithm 1. Iterated Binary Search to compute $\pi_{\text{lex}}(\mathbf{x})$

Input: $\mathbf{x}(t)$, $\varphi(\mathbf{p})$, $\mathcal{P}$, $\mathcal{D}_\mathcal{P}$, $(j_1, \ldots, j_n)$, $\epsilon > 0$, $\preceq_{\text{lex}}$
Result: $\pi_{\text{lex}}(\mathbf{x})$
1 $\nu^\ell(\mathbf{p}) \leftarrow \inf_{\preceq_{\text{lex}}} \mathcal{D}_\mathcal{P};\ \nu^u(\mathbf{p}) \leftarrow \sup_{\preceq_{\text{lex}}} \mathcal{D}_\mathcal{P}$
2 **if** $\neg(\mathbf{x} \models \varphi(\nu^u(\mathbf{p})))$ **then return** $\top$
3 **if** $\mathbf{x} \models \varphi(\nu^\ell(\mathbf{p}))$ **then return** $\bot$
4 **for** $i = 1$ *to* $|\mathcal{P}|$ **do**
5 $\quad$ **while** $|\nu^u(p_i) - \nu^\ell(p_i)| > \epsilon_i$ **do**
6 $\quad\quad$ $\nu(p_i) \leftarrow \frac{1}{2}\left(\nu^\ell(p_i) + \nu^u(p_i)\right)$
7 $\quad\quad$ **if** $\mathbf{x} \models \nu(\mathbf{p})$ **then** $\nu^u(\mathbf{p}) \leftarrow \nu(\mathbf{p})$
8 $\quad\quad$ **else** $\nu^\ell(\mathbf{p}) \leftarrow \nu(\mathbf{p})$

9 **return** $\pi_{\text{lex}}(\mathbf{x}) \leftarrow \nu^u(\mathbf{p})$

Computing π_{lex}. To approximate $\pi_{\text{lex}}(\mathbf{x})$, we recall Algorithm 1 from [14] that uses a simple lexicographic binary search[3].

We begin by setting the interval to search for a valuation in $\mathcal{V}(\varphi(\mathbf{p}))$. We set the initial valuation to $\top$ since it induces the most permissive STL formula. Next, for each parameter, (in the order imposed by $\preceq_{\text{lex}}$), we perform bisection search on the interval to find a valuation in $\mathcal{V}(\varphi(\mathbf{p}))$. Once completed, we return the lower bound of the search-interval as it is guaranteed to be satisfiable (if a satisfiable assignment exists).

Crucially, this algorithm exploits the monotonicity of the PSTL formula to guarantee that there is at most one point during the bisection search where the satisfaction of φ can change. The number of iterations for each parameter index i is bounded above by $\log\left\lceil \frac{\sup(\mathcal{D}_{\mathcal{P}i}) - \inf(\mathcal{D}_{\mathcal{P}i})}{\epsilon_i} \right\rceil$, and the number of parameters. This gives us an algorithm with complexity that grows linearly in the number of parameters and logarithmically in the desired precision.

Remark 3. Pragmatically, we remark that the projection algorithm is inherently very parallel at the trace level and as such scales well across machines.

Example 4. For the running example (PSTL formula (1)), we use the order $a \preceq_{\text{lex}} \tau$. As $\text{sgn}(a) = -$, and $\text{sgn}(\tau) = +$, lexicographic projection has the effect of first searching for the largest a, and then searching for the smallest τ such that the resulting valuation is in $\mathcal{V}(\varphi_{\text{overshoot}})$. The projections of the three traces from STL cluster 0 from Fig. 1 are shown in Fig. 2. We use the same color to denote a trace and its projection in parameter space.

---

[3] For simplicity, we have omitted a number of optimizations in Algorithm 1. For example, one can replace the iterative loop through parameters with a binary search over parameters.

Clustering and Labeling. What does one gain by defining a projection, π? We posit that applying unsupervised learning algorithms for clustering in $\mathcal{D}_{\mathcal{P}}$ lets us glean insights about the logical structure of the trace-space by grouping traces that satisfy similar formulas together. Let L be a finite, nonempty set of labels. Let $Y \subset X$ represent a user-provided set of traces. In essence, a clustering algorithm identifies a *labeling* function $\ell : Y \to 2^L$ assigning to each trace in Y zero or more labels. We elaborate with the help of an example.

Example 5. In Fig. 3, we show a possible clustering induced by using Gaussian Mixture Models[4] (GMMs) for the trace-projections for the traces in Fig. 1. The figure shows that the traces colored green,

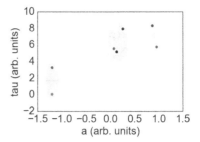

Fig. 3. Three clusters represented using the level sets of Gaussian functions learned from Gaussian Mixture Models (GMMs) (see Example 5). The user specifies the number of clusters to discover (3 in this case), and specifies that the GMM algorithm use a diagonal covariance matrix (which restricts cluster shape to axis-aligned ellipsoids).

red and black are grouped in the same cluster; this matches the observation that all three traces have behaviors indicating overshoots, but of reasonable magnitudes. On the other hand, traces colored magenta and yellow have no overshoot and are grouped into a second cluster. The final cluster contains the blue and cyan traces, both with a large overshoot.

Supposing the clustering algorithm reasonably groups traces satisfying similar parameter valuations/logical formulas, one may ask: "Can we describe this group of traces in terms of an easily interpretable STL formula?" Using an ellipsoid to represent a cluster, unfortunately, the answer is negative.

Example 6. For the cluster labeled 0 in Fig. 1, in (10), we show the formula describing the ellipsoidal cluster. Here the c_is are some constants.

$$\mathbf{F}\left(\texttt{lane\_change} \wedge \mathbf{F}_{[0,\tau]}\left(x - x_{ref} > a\right)\right) \wedge \left(\left(c_1\tau - c_2\right)^2 + \left(c_3 a - c_4\right)^2 < c_5^2\right) \tag{10}$$

It is clear that formula (10) is inscrutable, and actually represents an infinite number of STL formulas. In case of GMMs, we can at least have an abstract

---

[4] A GMM assumes that the given parameter space can be modeled as a random variable distributed according to a set of Gaussian distributions with different mean and variance values. A given parameter valuation is labeled l if the probability of the valuation belonging to the lth Gaussian distribution exceeds the probability of the valuation belonging to other distributions. Another way to visualize clusters in the parameter space is by level-sets of the probability density functions associated with the clusters. For example, for the lth cluster, we can represent it using the smallest level-set that includes all given points labeled l.

description of clusters using ellipsoid shapes in the parameter-space. If we use spectral clustering (as described in Sect. 1), the representation of a cluster in the parameter space is even less obvious. To mitigate this problem, we observe that the distance between points in $\mathcal{D}_{\mathcal{P}}$ is a "good" proxy for whether they receive the same label. Thus, another way to define the labeling function ℓ, is via parameter ranges. We argue that the use of axis-aligned hyperboxes enclosing points with the same labels is a useful approximation of the clusters, particularly because as we see in the next section, it has a compact STL encoding.

Remark 4. For a given set of points, the tightest-enclosing hyperbox may include points that would not have received the same label by an off-the-shelf clustering algorithm. This can lead to a scenario where hyperbox-clusters intersect (see Fig. 5c in for an example). This means that we can now have points in the parameter space that can have possibly two or more labels. We argue that this can be addressed in two ways: (1) introduce a new hyperbox cluster for points in the intersection, (2) indicate that points in the intersection represent traces for which there is additional guidance required from the designer.

Hyperbox Clusters. In the previous section, we showed that we can construct a labeling function ℓ to assign labels to the user-provided set of traces Y. We now see how we can extend this labeling function to all possible traces X.

Let $\nu_\top \overset{\text{def}}{=} \sup \mathcal{D}_{\mathcal{P}}$. A valid hyperbox B in the parameter space is defined in terms of its extreme points $(\nu_s(\mathbf{p}), \nu_w(\mathbf{p}))$, (where $\nu_s \trianglelefteq \nu_w$), where ν_s and ν_w are the infimum and supremum resp. over the box w.r.t. $\trianglelefteq$. Formally,

Definition 6 (Hyperbox)

$$B(\nu_s, \nu_w) \overset{\text{def}}{=} \begin{cases} \prod_i [\nu_s(p_i), \nu_w(p_i)] \text{ if } \nu_w(p_i) \neq \nu_\top(p_i) \\ \prod_i [\nu_s(p_i), \nu_w(p_i)] \text{ otherwise.} \end{cases} \quad (11)$$

In other words, we assume that a hyperbox is open on all faces not connected to the infimum of the box, unless the face is connected to the supremum of $\mathcal{D}_{\mathcal{P}}$. Let $\mathcal{B}$ denote the set of all such hyperboxes.

Definition 7 (Hyperbox Labeling Function). *Given a trace x and a hyperbox B, s.t. $\pi(x) \in B$, we define ℓ_{box} as the hyperbox labeling function from X to $\mathbf{2}^L$ as follows:*

$$l \in \ell_{\text{box}}(x) \iff \{\pi(x') \mid x' \in Y \wedge \ell(x') = l\} \subset B \quad (12)$$

In other words, we only consider hyperboxes that contain the projections of all traces with a specific label (say l), and then any trace that projects to some point in the hyperbox gets all such labels l. We extend the definition $\ell_{\text{box}}(x)$ to boxes, such that $\ell_{\mathcal{B}}(B) = \{l \mid \pi(x) \in B \wedge l \in \ell_{\text{box}}(x)\}$. We note that $B^* \overset{\text{def}}{=} \inf\{B \mid l \in \ell_{\mathcal{B}}(B)\}$ represents the smallest set containing all parameter valuations that are labeled l. However, B^* does not satisfy the definition of a hyperbox as per Definition 6 as it is a closed set. Hence, we define an ϵ relaxation of this set as the smallest bounding hyperbox satisfying Definition 6 at Hausdorff distance ϵ from B^*, and call it the *ϵ-bounding hyperbox*. In the next section, we show how we can translate a cluster represented as an ϵ-bounding hyperbox to an STL formula. We will further examine how, in some cases, we can represent a cluster by a superset B' of the ϵ-bounding hyperbox that satisfies $l \in \ell_{\mathcal{B}}(B')$, but allows a simpler STL representation.

Example 7. For the example shown in Fig. 1, for each of the red, green and black traces x, $\ell_{\text{box}}(x) = \{0\}$, while for the blue and cyan traces, $\ell_{\text{box}}(x) = \{2\}$. Any hyperbox B satisfying Definition 6 that is a superset of the hyperbox enclosing the red, green and black points shown in the bottom right figure has $\ell_{\mathcal{B}}(B) = \{0\}$, while the hyperbox shown in the figure is an ϵ-bounding hyperbox.

4   Learning STL Formulas from Clusters

A given ϵ-bounding hyperbox B simply specifies a range of valuations for the parameters in a PSTL template φ. We now demonstrate that because φ is monotonic, there exists a simple STL formula that is satisfied by the set of traces that project to some valuation in B. Recall that we use $[\![\varphi(\nu)]\!]$ to denote the set of traces that satisfies $\varphi(\nu(\mathbf{p}))$. We define X_B as the set of traces that have a satisfying valuation in B: $X_B \stackrel{\text{def}}{=} \bigcup\limits_{\nu(\mathbf{p}) \in B} [\![\varphi(\nu(\mathbf{p}))]\!]$.

Theorem 1. *There is an STL formula ψ_B such that $\{x \in X \mid x \models \psi_B\} \equiv X_B$.*

Before proving this theorem, we introduce some notation:

Definition 8 (Essential Corners, E_B). *Let $\nu_w(\mathbf{p}) = (w_1, \ldots, w_n)$, and let $\nu_s(\mathbf{p}) = (s_1, \ldots, s_n)$. A valuation corresponding to an essential corner has exactly one i such that $\nu(p_i) = s_i$, and for all $j \neq i$, $\nu(p_j) = w_j$.*

Proof (Theorem 1). We first introduce the notion of essential corners of a box B.

Note that B can be written in terms of downward closures of valuations: $B = D(\nu_w) \cap \bigcap_{\nu \in E_B} \overline{D(\nu)}$. From Lemma 1, the set of traces satisfying a formula in $\varphi(D(\nu))$ is equivalent to $[\![\varphi(\nu)]\!]$. Further, using the equivalence between intersections ($\cap$) of sets of traces and conjunctions ($\wedge$) in STL, and equivalence of set-complements with negations, we define ψ_B below and note that the set of traces satisfying the formula ψ_B below is X_B.   ∎

$$\psi_B \stackrel{\text{def}}{=} \varphi(\nu_w) \wedge \bigwedge_{\nu \in E_B} \neg\varphi(\nu) \tag{13}$$

Example 8. Consider the $B \in \mathcal{B}$ enclosing the projections for the yellow and magenta traces (Cluster 1). The corner-points of the cluster in clockwise order from bottom right corner are: $(-1.3, 0.1)$, $(-1.3, 3.3)$, $(-1.1, 3.3)$, $(-1.1, 0.1)$.

Observe that as $\text{sgn}(a) = -$ and $\text{sgn}(\tau) = +$, $\nu_s = (a \mapsto -1.1, \tau \mapsto 0.1)$, $\nu_w = (a \mapsto -1.3, \tau \mapsto 3.3)$. Thus, $E_B = \{(-1.3, 0.1), (-1.1, 3.3)\}$. Thus:

$$\varphi_{\text{overshoot}}(a, \tau) \equiv \mathbf{F}\left(\texttt{lane\_change} \wedge \mathbf{F}_{[0,\tau]}\left(x - x_{ref} > a\right)\right)$$
$$\psi_B \equiv \varphi_{\text{overshoot}}(-1.3, 3.3) \wedge \neg\varphi_{\text{overshoot}}(-1.3, .1) \wedge \neg\varphi_{\text{overshoot}}(-1.1, 3.3) \tag{14}$$

Lemma 2. $|\psi_B| \leq (|\mathcal{P}| + 1)(|\varphi| + 2)$

Proof. Recall from Definition 8 that corners in E_B have exactly 1 param set to s_i. There are $|\mathcal{P}|$ params, thus by pigeon hole principle, $|E_B| \leq |\mathcal{P}|$. In ψ_B for each corner in E_B, the corresponding formula is negated, adding 1 symbol. Between each $|\mathcal{P}| + 1$ instantiations of φ is a $\wedge$. Thus $|\psi_B| \leq (|\mathcal{P}| + 1)(|\varphi| + 2)$ ∎

Simplifying STL Representation. To motivate this section, let us re-examine Example 8. From Fig. 1, we can observe that there is no hyperbox cluster to the left of or above the chosen hyperbox cluster B, i.e., the one containing the magenta and yellow trace-projection. What if we consider supersets of B that are hyperboxes and have the same infimum point? For Example 8, we can see that any hyperbox that extends to the supremum of the parameter space in τ or $-a$ direction would be acceptable as an enclosure for the yellow and magenta traces (as there are no other traces in those directions). We formalize this intuition in terms of relaxing the set of corners that can appear in E_B.

For instance, suppose that we replace E_B in Eq. (13) with E_B', where E_B' is any subset of the corners of B (excluding ν_w). We call the collection of shapes induced by this relaxation as $\mathcal{B}_2$. For $|\mathcal{P}| = 2$, the possible shapes of elements in $\mathcal{B}_2$ are shown in Fig. 4. For convenience, we use a bit-vector encoding for hyperbox corners, where ν_s corresponds to the bit-vector with all 0s, ν_w has all 1s, and essential corners are bit-vectors with exactly one 0. Consider the L shaped region, C_L, created by $E_B' = \{00\}$.

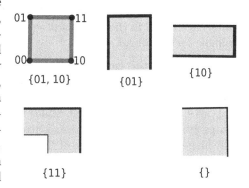

Fig. 4. 2D shapes generated by different subsets of corners.

The formula corresponding to C_L has obviously less descriptive complexity than $E_B = \{01, 10\}$. Further notice, $\mathcal{B}2 \setminus \mathcal{B}$ would have less descriptive complexity than elements of $\mathcal{B}$.

One critical feature that $\mathcal{B}_2$ (and thus $\mathcal{B}$) has is *comparable convexity*:

Definition 9 (Comparable Convexity). *If* $\forall \nu, \nu' \in B \subset \mathcal{D}_{\mathcal{P}}$ *if* $\nu \trianglelefteq \nu'$ *or* $\nu' \trianglelefteq \nu$ *then all* convex *combinations of* ν *and* ν' *are in* B.

Comparable convexity allows us to argue that one can gain some insight into the set of traces by just examining the extremal cases and just "interpolating" the cases because of the associated parameters. We call these extremal cases the "representatives" of a cluster.

Theorem 2. *Each element in $\mathcal{B}_2$ is comparably convex. See Fig. 4 for examples.*

Proof. Note that all elements of $\mathcal{B} \subset \mathcal{B}_2$ are trivially comparably convex since hyperboxes are convex. Thus we focus on elements of $\mathcal{B}_2 \setminus \mathcal{B}$. Now observe that any element $C \in \mathcal{B}_2$ is the union of a finite set, $\mathcal{H}$, of boxes in $\mathcal{B}$. C s.t. $C = \bigcup_{B_i \in \mathcal{H} \subset \mathcal{B}} B_i$ where $\nu_1 \in B_1$ and $\nu_2 \in B_2$. If $B_1 \subset B_2$ or the other way around or $\nu_1 \in B_1 \cap B_2$ or $\nu_2 \in B_1 \cap B_2$, then again there trivially the convex combination of ν_1 and ν_2 is in C because hyperboxes are convex (and the intersection of two hyperboxes is a hyperbox).

This leaves the case where $\nu_1 \in B_1 \setminus B_2$ and $\nu_2 \in B_2 \setminus B_1$ and neither $B_1 \subset B_2$ nor $B_2 \subset B_1$. This implies that $\inf(B_1)$ is not comparable to $\inf(B_2)$. W.L.O.G assume $\nu_1 \trianglelefteq \nu_2$ and that the convex combination of ν_1 and ν_2 is not a subset C. Note that the definition of downward closure and the fact that $\nu_1 \trianglelefteq \nu_2 \implies \nu_1 \in B(\sup(C), \nu_2) \overset{\text{def}}{=} B'$. But, B' is convex and $B' \subset B_2 \subset C$, thus the convex combination of ν_1 and ν_2 is in C which is a contradiction. ∎

5   Case Studies

Implementation Details. We leveraged Breach [9] for performing projections π_{lex}, `scikit-learn` toolkit [11] for clustering and custom Python code for learning STL formulas for clusters. An IPython notebook with compressed versions of the datasets studied in the case studies (and a replementation of π_{lex} in Python) is available for download at [1].

Diesel Engine. In this case study, we are provided with timed traces for a signal representing the Exhaust Gas Recirculation (EGR) rate for an early prototype of a Diesel Engine airpath controller. As the example comes from an automotive setting, we suppress actual signal values for proprietary reasons. The controller computes an EGR reference rate and attempts to track it. Typically, engineers visually inspect the step-response of the control system and look for patterns such as unusual overshoots, slow responsiveness, *etc.* The ST-Lib library [13] defines a pool of PSTL formulas designed to detect violations of such properties. Using a property from ST-Lib requires correctly setting the parameters in the PSTL templates therein. In this case study, we show how we can use our technique to determine parameters that characterize undesirable behavior. We focus on two templates: Rising Step and Overshoot. Many ST-Lib formulas are "step-triggered", *i.e.*, they are of the form: $\mathbf{F}(\text{step} \wedge \phi)$ We first identify parameters for the step template, as it is used as a primitive in further analysis. For example, in the overshoot analysis we seek to characterize by what margin traces overshoot the reference. We use the following templates for **rising**-step and overshoot:

$$\text{step}_{(m,w)} \triangleq \mathbf{F}(\ddot{x} > m \wedge \mathbf{F}_{[0,w]}(\ddot{x} < -m)) \tag{15}$$

$$\varphi_{\text{overshoot}}(c, w) \triangleq \text{step}^* \wedge \mathbf{F}_{[0,w]}(x - x_r) > c \tag{16}$$

Equation (15) first reduces step detection (via a discrete derivative) to spike detection and then applies the ST-Lib spike detection template (that introduces a second derivative). As the view of PSTL is signal-centric, such operations can be introduced as new timed traces of a new signal, and do not require any modification of the logic. The step* that appears in Eq. (16) is result step primitive we learn during our analysis. Finally, the lexicographic ordering used in the projections of Eqs. (15) and (16) are: $m \preceq_{lex} w$ and $c \preceq_{lex} w$ resp. Finally, each parameter is in $\mathbb{R}_{>0}$.

Experiments. We have 33 traces of variable time-length. As a preprocessing step, we used a sliding window with a size of 1 second and a sliding offset of 0.5 s to generate equal length traces. The sliding window size and the offset was chosen by observation and experience to capture the significant local behaviors. In general, such a selection could be automated based on statistical criteria. Further, as we did not exploit the relationship between traces generated by the sliding window, we effectively analyzed over 2×10^6 traces (1 GB). Each trace generated is then prepossessed by numerically computing the second derivative[5]. After projecting to the parameter space for each template, we normalize the parameters to lie between 0, 1 and fit a Gaussian Mixture Model to generate labels, and learn the STL formulas for each cluster.

Results. The Step template revealed 3 clusters (Fig. 5a), of which the cluster labeled Step (Fig. 5b), was identified as an admissible "step" primitive. In picking

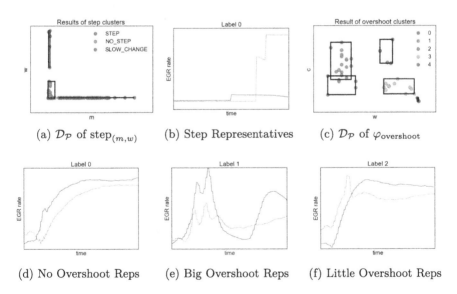

(a) $\mathcal{D}_\mathcal{P}$ of $\text{step}_{(m,w)}$ (b) Step Representatives   (c) $\mathcal{D}_\mathcal{P}$ of $\varphi_{overshoot}$

(d) No Overshoot Reps   (e) Big Overshoot Reps   (f) Little Overshoot Reps

Fig. 5. $\mathcal{D}_\mathcal{P}$ for the overshoot and step experiments and representatives of select clusters.

---

[5] As the discrete-time derivative can introduce considerable noise, we remark that the discrete-time derivative can often be approximated by a noise-robust operation (such as the difference from a rolling mean/median.).

the appropriate bounding box in $\mathcal{B}$ we noted spikes have no inherit upper limit to their peaks. Thus, we derived the characterizing STL: $\text{step}^* \overset{\text{def}}{=} \text{step}(m^*, w^*)$, where m^*, w^* are suppressed for proprietary reasons. The overshoot analysis revealed 5 clusters. We note that there are actually 2 distinct clusters which can reasonably be called overshoots, given by label 1 and 4 in Fig. 5c. The interpretation, is that while the majority of the overshoots occur soon after the step, there is a cluster that occurred later, either due to slow rise time or non-linear effects causing the oscillation about the reference to increasing before dying away. In either case, as with spike, we declare that any overshoot is still an overshoot as the amplitude c rises. Thus for cluster 1 we again chose to use a box from $\mathcal{B}$ that does not bound c. This lead to: $\varphi^*_{\text{overshoot}} \overset{\text{def}}{=} \varphi_{\text{overshoot}}(c^*, w_2^*) \wedge \neg \varphi_{\text{overshoot}}(c^*, w_1^*)$ again suppressing values.

Traffic Behavior on the US-101 Highway. In order to model and predict driver behavior on highways, the Federal Highway Administration collected detailed traffic data on southbound US-101 freeway, in Los Angeles [8]. The preselected segment of the freeway is about 640 m in length and consists of five main lanes and some auxiliary lanes. Traffic through the segment was monitored and recorded through eight synchronized cameras, mounted on top of the buildings next to the freeway. A total of 45 min of traffic data was recorded including vehicle trajectory data providing lane positions of each vehicle within the study area.

Here, we apply our method to analyze lane switching "aggressiveness" characterized by how often a driver switches lanes and the dwell time in each lane before switching. We focus on lanes 2, 3, and 4, ignoring the outer lanes 1 and 5 since they are used entering and exiting the freeway, and thus have qualitatively different behavior. Each vehicle trajectory $x(t)$, stores the lane position for the vehicle, and we use the following STL formula to capture the dwell time in L_i:

$$\mathbf{F}\left(x \neq L_i \wedge (\mathbf{F}_{[0,\epsilon]}x = L_i \mathbf{U}_{[\epsilon, \tau_i]}x \neq L_i)\right) \tag{17}$$

Results. For this experiment, from 4824 total vehicle trajectories, we discard trajectories with no lane switching behavior and group them with the conservative driving behaviors. We analyze the remaining 896 targeted trajectories that have at least one lane-switch behavior, and each trajectory is at most 100 s long. As all parameters are independent, lexicographic ordering has no impact on π_{lex}. After normalizing the parameters by centering and scaling, we apply GMMs to label and generate bounding hyperboxes/STL formulas.

The resulting clusters are shown in Fig. 6a. Upon examining the representatives, we classified the behaviors of each cluster into 4 groups:

- T1: No Weaving: only switching to adjacent lanes and never changing back.
- T2: Normal driving behavior, from switching to adjacent lanes and coming back to overtake a slow vehicle in front.
- T3: Slightly aggressive behavior, weaving between 2 lanes.
- T4: Aggressive behavior, weaving between all three lanes.

C	τ_2	τ_3	τ_4	T	|C|
0	$\top$	$\top$	$\top$	T1	626
1	$\top$	$\top$	$[\perp, 78]$	T2	115
2	$[\perp, 67]$	$\top$	$\top$	T2	44
3	$\top$	$[.26, 30]$	$[\perp, 65]$	T3	52
4	$\top$	$[\perp, 70]$	$\top$	T2	32
5	$[.56, 54]$	$[\perp, 40]$	$\top$	T3	14
6	$[.56, 32]$	$[1.8, 24]$	$[\perp, 31]$	T4	12
7	76	$\top$	$\top$	T1	1

(a) Lane Clusters

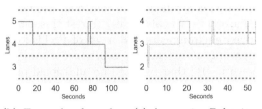

(b) Examples from lane cluster C= 1

(c) Aggressive Behavior

Fig. 6. (a) Lane Switching Behavior results. Columns: Cluster, parameters, cluster type, num(traces). (b) shows the representatives of cluster 1, which upon the inspection are qualitatively very different. The blue car moves from lane 5 to lane 4, remains for ≈60 s and then moves to lane 3. The red car appears to use lane 5 to pass another car, move's back into lane 4 and then to lane 3 shortly after. Inspecting the data, most of cluster 1 large τ_4 value. We subdivided the behavior further using a one class svm and interpreted the small τ_4 values as "aggressive". New "aggressive" representatives given in (c). (Color figure online)

The largest cluster, 0, contains behaviors without any weaving behavior. Cluster 3 and 5 represent the weaving behavior involving 2 lanes. Cluster 6 represents aggressive behavior and one of the representative is shown in Fig. 6c. We consider Cluster 7 as an anomaly for Cluster 2 as it has only 1 trajectory.

For clusters 1, 2, and 4, we cannot distinguish if drivers were rapidly weaving or weaving within a short period of time, due to the scarcity of the data. As seen in Fig. 6b, the representatives for cluster 1, demonstrated two different behaviors; one involving rapid lane-switching (red trace), one where the driver switched lanes more slowly (blue trace). Applying an additional 1-class SVM to the points in cluster 1 was used to distinguish these two cases.

CPS Grader. Massively Open Online Courses (MOOCs) present instructors the opportunity to learn from a large amount of collected data. For example, the data could be clustered to identify common correct solutions and mistakes. Juniwal et al. [16] demonstrated a semi-supervised procedure for a CPS MOOC; this involved first using DTW and K-Nearest Neighbors (KNN) to cluster traces of student solutions, and then picking representatives from clusters to ask the instructor to label. From the labeled data, they extract a characterizing STL formula given a PSTL template. The techniques demonstrated in this paper offer an alternative approach that can overcome some limitations of [16]. Firstly, as demonstrated in the opening example (see Fig. 1), DTW does not necessarily group traces in a way consistent with their logical classification. Second, the burden of labeling traces can still be quite large for instructors if the number of clusters is very large. Instead, unsupervised our approach offers a fully unsupervised approach (e.g., based on GMMs or K-Means) which still offers some degree of confidence that elements in the same cluster are similar w.r.t. a given PSTL template.

The tests in [16] involved the simulation of an IRobot Create and student generated controllers. The controller needed to navigate the robot up an incline and around static obstacles. To test this, the authors created a series of parameterized environments and a set of PSTL formula that characterized failure. In this work, we attempt to reproduce a somewhat arbitrary subset of the results shown in [16] that required no additional preprocessing on our part.

Obstacle Avoidance. We focus on 2 tests centered around obstacle avoidance. The authors used an environment where an obstacle is placed in front of a moving robot and the robot is expected to bypass the obstacle and reorient to it's pre-collision orientation before continuing. The relevant PSTL formulas were "Failing simple obstacle avoidance" and "Failing re-orienting after obstacle avoidance" given below as φ_{avoid} and $\varphi_{reorient}$ resp.:

$$\varphi_{avoid}(\tau, y_{\min}) = \mathbf{G}_{[0,\tau]}(pos.y < y_{\min}) \tag{18}$$

$$\varphi_{reorient}(y_{\min}, x_{\max}) = \mathbf{G}_{[0,\tau]}(pos.y < y_{\min} \lor pos.x > x_{\max}) \tag{19}$$

Results. A surprising observation for both templates is that the vast majority of data is captured in a relatively small parameter range. Upon investigation, it was revealed that the students were able to submit multiple solutions for grading— each corresponding to a trace. This biased the dataset towards incorrect solutions since one expects the student to produce many incorrect solutions and then a few final correct solutions. As seen in Fig. 7a, the results imply that a classifier for label 0, which corresponded to the robot not passing the obstacle, would have a low misclassification rate when compared against the STL artifact from [16]. Moreover, for obstacle avoidance, there are two other families of correct solutions uncovered. One is the set of traces that just barely pass the obstacle in time

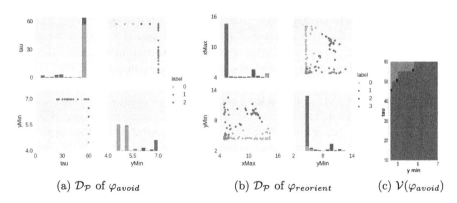

(a) $\mathcal{D}_{\mathcal{P}}$ of φ_{avoid} (b) $\mathcal{D}_{\mathcal{P}}$ of $\varphi_{reorient}$ (c) $\mathcal{V}(\varphi_{avoid})$

Fig. 7. CPS Grader Study Results, w. $\mathcal{V}(\varphi_{avoid})$, (c), from [16] included for comparison (valuations in the green region of (c) correspond to mistakes). We note that in (b) we are able to identify 3 modes of failure (obstacle not avoided, 2x obstacle avoided but did not reorient), an insight not present in [16]. (Color figure online) (label 2 in Fig. 7a), and the other is the spectrum of traces that pass the minimum threshold with a healthy margin (label 1 in Fig. 7a). For the reorient template, we discovered 3 general types of behaviors (again with GMMs), see Fig. 7b. The first (label 1) is a failure to move past the obstacle (echoing the large group under the obstacle avoidance template). The other 3 groups seem to move passed the obstacle, but two (labels 0 and 3) of them display failure to reorient to the original orientation of 45°. One could leverage this behavior to craft diagnostic feedback for these common cases.

Conclusion. In this work we explored a technique to leverage PSTL to extract features from a time series that can be used to group together qualitatively similar traces under the lens of a PSTL formula. Our approach produced a simple STL formula for each cluster, which along with the extremal cases, enable one to develop insights into a set of traces. We then illustrated with a number of case studies how this technique could be used and the kinds of insights it can develop. For future work, we will study extensions of this approach to supervised, semi-supervised, and active learning. A key missing component in this work is a principled way to select a projection function (perhaps via learning or posterior methods). Other possible extensions involve integration with systematic PSTL enumeration, and learning non-monotonic PSTL formulas.

Acknowledgments. We thank Dorsa Sadigh, Yasser Shoukry, Gil Lederman, Shromona Ghosh, Oded Maler, Eamon Keogh, and our anonymous reviewers for their invaluable feedback, and Ken Butts for the Diesel data. This work is funded in part by the DARPA BRASS program under agreement number FA8750–16–C–0043, the VeHICaL Project (NSF grant #1545126), and the Toyota Motor Corporation under the CHESS center.

A   Appendix

Related Monotonic Formula for a Non-monotonic PSTL Formula

Example 9. Consider the PSTL template: $\varphi(h, w) \stackrel{\text{def}}{=} \mathbf{F}((x \leq h) \wedge \mathbf{F}_{[0,w]}(x \geq h))$. We first show that the given formula is not monotonic.

Proof. Consider the trace $x(t) = 0$. Keep fixed $w = 1$. Observe that $h = 0$, $x(t)$ satisfies the formula. If $h = -1$, then $x(t) \not\models \varphi(h, w)$, since $x(t) \leq h$ is not eventually satisifed. If $h = 1$, then $x(0) \leq 1$ implying that for satisfaction, within the next 1 time units, the signal must becomes greater than 1. The signal is always 0, so at $h = 1$, the formula is unsatisfied. Thus, while increasing h from -1 to 0 to 1, the satifaction has changed signs twice. Thus, $\varphi(h, w)$ is not monotonic.

Now consider the following related PSTL formula in which repeated instances of the parameter h are replaced by distinct parameters h_1 and h_2. We observe that this formula is trivially monotonic: $\varphi((w, h_1, h_2)) \stackrel{\text{def}}{=} \mathbf{F}\left((x \leq h_1) \wedge \mathbf{F}_{[0,w]}(x \geq h_2)\right)$.

Linearization Based on Scalarization

Borrowing a common trick from multi-objective optimization, we define a cost function on the space of valuations as follows: $J(\nu(\mathbf{p})) = \sum_{i=1}^{|\mathcal{P}|} \lambda_i \nu(p_i)$. Here, $\lambda_i \in \mathbb{R}$, are weights on each parameter. The above cost function implicitly defines an order $\preceq_{scalar}$, where, $\nu(\mathbf{p}) \preceq_{scalar} \nu'(\mathbf{p})$ iff $J(\nu(\mathbf{p})) \leq J(\nu'(\mathbf{p}))$. Then, the projection operation π_{scalar} is defined as: $\pi_{scalar}(\mathbf{x}) = \operatorname{argmin}_{\nu(\mathbf{p}) \in \partial \mathcal{V}(\varphi(\mathbf{p}))} J(\nu(\mathbf{p}))$. We postpone any discussion of how to choose such a scalarization to future work.

References

1. Logical Clustering CAV2017 Artifact. https://archive.org/details/Logical_Clustering_CAV2017_Artifact. Accessed 29 Apr 2017
2. Ackerman, E.: Google's autonomous cars are smarter than ever at 700,000 miles. IEEE Spectr. (2014). http://spectrum.ieee.org/cars-that-think/transportation/self-driving/google-autonomous-cars-are-smarter-than-ever
3. Akazaki, T., Hasuo, I.: Time robustness in MTL and expressivity in hybrid system falsification. In: Kroening, D., Păsăreanu, C.S. (eds.) CAV 2015. LNCS, vol. 9207, pp. 356–374. Springer, Cham (2015). doi:10.1007/978-3-319-21668-3_21
4. Alur, R., Henzinger, T.A.: A really temporal logic. JACM **41**(1), 181–203 (1994)
5. Asarin, E., Donzé, A., Maler, O., Nickovic, D.: Parametric identification of temporal properties. In: Khurshid, S., Sen, K. (eds.) RV 2011. LNCS, vol. 7186, pp. 147–160. Springer, Heidelberg (2012). doi:10.1007/978-3-642-29860-8_12
6. Bartocci, E., Bortolussi, L., Sanguinetti, G.: Learning temporal logical properties discriminating ECG models of cardiac arrhytmias. arXiv preprint arXiv:1312.7523 (2013)
7. Bombara, G., Vasile, C.I., Penedo, F., Yasuoka, H., Belta, C.: A decision tree approach to data classification using signal temporal logic. In: Proceedings of HSCC, pp. 1–10 (2016)
8. Colyar, J., Halkias, J.: US highway 101 dataset. Federal Highway Administration (FHWA), Technical report FHWA-HRT-07-030 (2007)
9. Donzé, A.: Breach, a toolbox for verification and parameter synthesis of hybrid systems. In: Touili, T., Cook, B., Jackson, P. (eds.) CAV 2010. LNCS, vol. 6174, pp. 167–170. Springer, Heidelberg (2010). doi:10.1007/978-3-642-14295-6_17
10. Donzé, A., Maler, O., Bartocci, E., Nickovic, D., Grosu, R., Smolka, S.: On temporal logic and signal processing. In: Chakraborty, S., Mukund, M. (eds.) ATVA 2012. LNCS, pp. 92–106. Springer, Heidelberg (2012). doi:10.1007/978-3-642-33386-6_9
11. Pedregosa, F., et al.: Scikit-learn: machine learning in python. J. Mach. Learn. Res. **12**, 2825–2830 (2011)
12. Hoxha, B., Dokhanchi, A., Fainekos, G.: Mining parametric temporal logic properties in model-based design for cyber-physical systems. Int. J. Softw. Tools Technol. Transf. 1–15 (2017)
13. Kapinski, J., et al.: ST-lib: a library for specifying and classifying model behaviors. In: SAE Technical Paper. SAE (2016)
14. Jin, X., Donzé, A., Deshmukh, J.V., Seshia, S.A.: Mining requirements from closed-loop control models. IEEE TCAD ICS **34**(11), 1704–1717 (2015)
15. Jones, A., Kong, Z., Belta, C.: Anomaly detection in cyber-physical systems: a formal methods approach. In: Proceedings of CDC, pp. 848–853 (2014)

16. Juniwal, G., Donzé, A., Jensen, J.C., Seshia, S.A.: CPSGrader: synthesizing temporal logic testers for auto-grading an embedded systems laboratory. In: Proceedings of EMSOFT, p. 24 (2014)
17. Keogh, E.J., Pazzani, M.J.: Scaling up dynamic time warping for data mining applications. In: Proceedings of KDD, pp. 285–289 (2000)
18. Kong, Z., Jones, A., Medina Ayala, A., Aydin Gol, E., Belta, C.: Temporal logic inference for classification and prediction from data. In: Proceedings of HSCC, pp. 273–282 (2014)
19. Koymans, R.: Specifying real-time properties with metric temporal logic. Real-Time Syst. **2**(4), 255–299 (1990)
20. Legriel, J., Guernic, C., Cotton, S., Maler, O.: Approximating the pareto front of multi-criteria optimization problems. In: Esparza, J., Majumdar, R. (eds.) TACAS 2010. LNCS, vol. 6015, pp. 69–83. Springer, Heidelberg (2010). doi:10. 1007/978-3-642-12002-2_6
21. Li, W., Forin, A., Seshia, S.A.: Scalable specification mining for verification and diagnosis. In: Proceedings of the Design Automation Conference (DAC), pp. 755–760, June 2010
22. Lin, J., Keogh, E., Truppel, W.: Clustering of streaming time series is meaningless. In: Proceedings of the 8th ACM SIGMOD Workshop on Research Issues in Data Mining and Knowledge Discovery, pp. 56–65. ACM (2003)
23. Maler, O., Nickovic, D.: Monitoring temporal properties of continuous signals. In: Lakhnech, Y., Yovine, S. (eds.) FORMATS/FTRTFT 2004. LNCS, vol. 3253, pp. 152–166. Springer, Heidelberg (2004). doi:10.1007/978-3-540-30206-3_12
24. von Luxburg, U.: A tutorial on spectral clustering. Stat. Comput. **17**(4), 395–416 (2007)

Runtime Verification

Montre: A Tool for Monitoring Timed Regular Expressions

Dogan Ulus[✉]

Verimag, Université Grenoble-Alpes,
Grenoble, France
doganulus@gmail.com

Abstract. We present Montre, a monitoring tool to search patterns specified by timed regular expressions over real-time behaviors. We use timed regular expressions as a compact, natural, and highly-expressive pattern specification language for monitoring applications involving quantitative timing constraints. Our tool essentially incorporates online and offline timed pattern matching algorithms so it is capable of finding all occurrences of a given pattern over both logged and streaming behaviors. Furthermore, Montre is designed to work with other tools via standard interfaces to perform more complex and versatile tasks for analyzing and reasoning about cyber-physical systems. As the first of its kind, we believe Montre will enable a new line of inquiries and techniques in these fields.

1 Introduction

Temporal behaviors are sequences of actions and observations in time generated by various systems and the environment around us. A temporal pattern is a set of compositions of different temporal behaviors satisfying some relations among their components such as precedence and coincidence or possessing some properties such as repetition and a certain duration. Searching good [bad, desirable, undesirable] patterns over their temporal behaviors is an important task while we reason about systems and the environment.

Timed regular expressions (TREs) [2] extend regular expressions, a well-established formalism for specifying sequences of symbols, with the notion of real-time and timing constraints. Many patterns requiring both qualitative and quantitative temporal properties can be specified by TREs in a compact and natural way. Given a TRE that specifies a temporal pattern and a real-time behavior the problem of timed pattern matching is defined as locating all segments that satisfy the expression. This problem has been solved by an offline algorithm in [14]. It is further endowed with an online algorithm that incrementally matches patterns over streaming behaviors [15].

In this paper, we describe Montre a new tool for timed pattern matching whose applications are numerous and diverse. First of all, Montre can naturally check execution traces of software and hardware systems against real time properties specified in TRE (e.g. [5,7]), thus complementing temporal logic based

© Springer International Publishing AG 2017
R. Majumdar and V. Kunčak (Eds.): CAV 2017, Part I, LNCS 10426, pp. 329–335, 2017.
DOI: 10.1007/978-3-319-63387-9_16

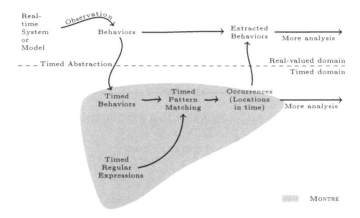

Fig. 1. The work flow and extent of the monitoring tool MONTRE

property checkers such as [1,4,11]. Further, MONTRE can be used for specification mining such as [3,8] as matching is a basic task for mining. Outside the verification context, MONTRE has a potential use in temporal data mining [10] and (vehicle or human) trajectory data mining [9,16] as it can label time segments with meaningful tags such as overtaking (another car) or sprinting. To illustrate our tool in action, we present such an example from the domain of sports analytics in Sect. 3 where we find all sprints of a soccer player.

2   Tool Description

The tool MONTRE essentially incorporates online and offline timed pattern matching algorithms extended with some practical features such as anchors and a Boolean layer. It takes a timed behavior and a timed regular expression as inputs, and produces a finite set of two dimensional zones representing the (possibly uncountable) set of segments that watch the pattern. MONTRE provides a standard text-based interface for easy integration with other tasks such as data preparations and visualization as we consider them necessary but outside the scope of MONTRE. In Fig. 1, we illustrate the work flow and extent of MONTRE, and we give details for each component in the following.

Timed Behaviors. A timed behavior is a sequence of time segments where each segment has a duration value and is associated with a set of propositional variables that hold continuously in the segment. In general, we assume all propositions are concurrent. For example, $(3, pq); (2, q); (2, p)$ is a timed behavior with 3 segments over propositions p and q. It means that p and q evaluate to true for the first 3 time units, then q is true for 2 more time units, and then p is true for 2 time units again. We assume behaviors start at time 0; therefore, the example behavior can be alternatively stated such that p holds from 0 to 3 and then 5 to 7 while q holds from 0 to 5.

Table 1. MONTRE timed regular expression syntax

Construct	Description
p	A propositional variable.
!P	Boolean NOT operation on P.
P || Q	Boolean OR operation on P and Q.
P && Q	Boolean AND operator on P and Q.
P	occurs on (t, t') if P holds from t to t' continuously.
<:P	occurs on a time period (t, t') if P occurs on (t, t') and there exists a rising edge for P at t.
P:>	occurs on a time period (t, t') if P occurs on (t, t') and there exists a falling edge for P at t'.
<:P:>	occurs on a time period (t, t') if P occurs on (t, t') and there exists a rising edge for P at t as well as a falling edge for P at t'.
E;F	occurs on a time period (t, t') if E occurs on (t, t'') and F occurs on (t'', t') for $t \leq t'' \leq t'$.
E|F	occurs on a time period (t, t') if either E or F occurs on (t, t').
E&F	occurs on a time period (t, t') if E and F occur on (t, t') concurrently.
E%(m,n)	occurs on a time period (t, t') if E occurs on (t, t') and the duration of the occurrence is in the specified range such that $m \leq t' - t \leq n$.
E*	Zero-or-more repetition of E.
E+	One-or-more repetition of E.

Timed Regular Expressions. An atomic timed regular expression corresponds to a Boolean expression over a set of propositions, denoted by letters p, q, r. These propositions can stand for predicates over real-valued variables. Usual Boolean operators (!), (||), (&&) are used to build Boolean expressions. We say that an atomic expression occurs on a time period (t, t') if the corresponding Boolean expression holds from t to t' continuously. Complex timed regular expressions are built from other expressions by using TRE operators: sequential composition (concatenation) (;), time restriction (%), choice (|), coincidence (&) and zero-or-more repetition (*). Further, we add one-or-more repetition (+) and two anchoring (<: and :>) operators to the set of operators. Typically parentheses are used to group expressions. We summarize all Boolean and TRE operations in MONTRE in Table 1.

Zones. For a proposition p that holds from t_1 to t_2, all sub-periods of (t_1, t_2) satisfy the expression p. As shown in Fig. 2-(i), such a set of matches $\{(t, t') \mid t_1 \leq t < t' \leq t_2\}$ can be represented on a two-dimensional plane as a triangular zone. Then the match set of any atomic expression would be a union of such triangular zones. A triangular zone is a special case of zones, which constitutes a restricted class of convex polygons defined by orthogonal and diagonal constraints as shown Fig. 2-(ii). Zones are basic data objects for timed pattern matching as unions of zones are closed under Boolean and regular operations. It follows that the match set of any timed regular expression over a timed behavior can be representable by a finite union of zones.

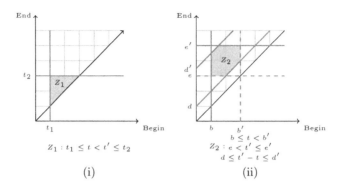

Fig. 2. (i) A triangular zone.   (ii) A zone in general.

Implementation. MONTRE is a command line program[1] that uses structured text files for input/output specification. When invoked MONTRE parses the timed regular expression passed as an argument and starts to reads the input file. According to flags set by the user MONTRE would run in either online or offline mode. For online mode it is possible that the input can be given interactively using the command line or directed from another process as usual. At its core, MONTRE contains our efficient zone manipulation library, `libmontre`, called dynamically by top-level online and offline timed pattern matching algorithms. As Boolean and regular operations over sets of zones are intensive numerical computations, we have implemented `libmontre` in C++. In the implementation, we use an integer-valued time model where all time values are represented by integers for efficiency and accuracy reasons. For the majority of applications, integers give us sufficient precision and range; and a proper scaling can be found.

We implement timed pattern matching algorithms in Pure[2], a functional programming language based on term rewriting with a support for native code compilation and native calls to dynamic libraries. For the online algorithm [15], built upon derivatives of regular expressions [12,13], we extensively use the rewriting functionality when deriving an expression with respect to a newly observed segment. The offline algorithm [14] is a recursive computation over the syntax tree of the expression; therefore, the role of Pure's rewriting engine is minimal. The worst case complexity is polynomial in the size of input behavior and expression for the offline approach. For the online approach it is polynomial in the size of the behavior and exponential in expression. In practice, however, we realistically assume patterns to be much shorter than behaviors and somewhat sparse in them. Then we expect a linear-time performance in the size of input behavior for both algorithms. Under these assumptions, MONTRE can process timed behaviors with a size of 1M segments in a few seconds (offline) and a few hundred seconds (online).

---

[1] Available at http://github.com/doganulus/montre.
[2] Available at http://purelang.bitbucket.io.

3   An Illustrative Example

We present an example use of Montre on a data set obtained by tracking positions of players in a real soccer match. In this example, we find all sprints performed by a single player where a sprint is formally specified by a timed regular expression over speed and acceleration behaviors. The data are obtained by a computer vision algorithm with a frame rate of 10 Hz so we have a xy-coordinate for each player on the field at every 100 milliseconds. Therefore we use milliseconds as our base time unit for behaviors and expressions.

In order to specify a pattern for sprints, we need to address two issues in order: (1) how to categorize continuous speed and acceleration axes, and (2) which composition of these categories defines a sprinting effort best. Clearly, there are no universal answers for these questions so we rely on the study [6] in the following. First, we partition speed and acceleration axes into four categories (near-zero, low, medium, and high), and we associate a letter for each category in Table 2. For example, a period of medium speed, denoted by r, means the speed value resides between 3.7 and 6 m/s during the period.

Often a sprint effort is characterized by any movement above a certain speed threshold for a limited time. This gives us our first sprint pattern such that a period of high speed between 1–10 s, formally written as follows:

$$(<:s:>)\%(1000,10000) \tag{P1}$$

Above we use anchor operators from both sides on the proposition s to obtain only maximal periods that satisfy s; otherwise, any sub-period satisfies the pattern as well. The operator % specifies that the duration is restricted to be in 1000 and 10000 milliseconds. Alternatively we may want to find other efforts starting with high acceleration but not reaching top speeds necessarily. This gives us our second sprint pattern such that a period of high acceleration followed by a period of medium or high speed between 1–10 s, formally written as follows:

$$(<:g);(<:(r|s):>)\%(1000,10000) \tag{P2}$$

Notice that we do not use the right-anchor on g. This allows a medium or high speed period to overlap with a high acceleration period as it is usually the case that they are concurrent. Writing an equivalent pattern using classical

Table 2. Speed and acceleration thresholds [6].

Symbol	Label	Speed thresholds $(m \cdot s^{-1})$	Symbol	Label	Acceleration thresholds $(m \cdot s^{-2})$
s	High	> 6.0	g	High	>1.60
r	Medium	3.7 - 6	f	Medium	1.17 - 1.60
q	Low	2 - 3.7	e	Low	0.57 - 1.17
p	Near Zero	0 - 2	d	Near Zero	-0.57 - 0.57

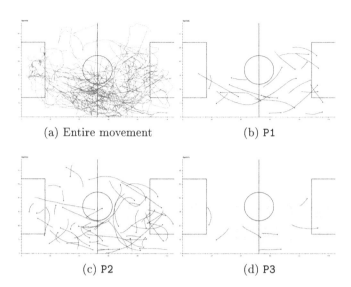

(a) Entire movement   (b) P1

(c) P2   (d) P3

Fig. 3. The trajectory of a soccer player for 45 min on the field, and his sprinting periods found by MONTRE for patterns P1-P3.

regular expressions over a product alphabet would be a very tedious task partly due to a requirement to handle such interleavings explicitly (and the lack of timing constraints). For TREs all propositions are considered to be concurrent by definition, which results in concise and intuitive expressions. Finally we give a third pattern to find rather short but intense sprints such that

$$(<:(f||g));((<:s:>)\%(1000,2000)) \tag{P3}$$

Then we visualize all sprints found by MONTRE for patterns P1-P3 in Fig. 3 over the behavior of a single player during one half of the game (45 min.) containing 27 K data points that reduces to timed behaviors of 5K segments after pre-processing. Note that we used Python to prepare data and visualize results.

4 Conclusions

Timed regular expressions can define many timed properties and MONTRE is the first tool to check such properties and detect timed patterns. Its performance is satisfactory for such monitoring tasks but we note that there is still some room for optimization especially for the online algorithm. The example we presented illustrates a complete MONTRE experience from raw data to visualization. As seen defining good patterns and categories are important to achieve intended results but it is not always obvious what a good pattern is. Such patterns should be found in the future using (unsupervised) pattern mining methods. We believe MONTRE would provide a good starting point for such research as it encapsulates timed pattern matching with an easy-to-use interface.

Acknowledgment. Thanks to Oded Maler for his helpful comments on the text, and to Hande Alemdar and Serdar Alemdar for the soccer data they provided.

References

1. Annpureddy, Y., Liu, C., Fainekos, G., Sankaranarayanan, S.: S-TALiRo: a tool for temporal logic falsification for hybrid systems. In: Abdulla, P.A., Leino, K.R.M. (eds.) TACAS 2011. LNCS, vol. 6605, pp. 254–257. Springer, Heidelberg (2011). doi:10.1007/978-3-642-19835-9_21
2. Asarin, E., Caspi, P., Maler, O.: Timed regular expressions. J. ACM **49**(2), 172–206 (2002)
3. Cutulenco, G., Joshi, Y., Narayan, A., Fischmeister, S.: Mining timed regular expressions from system traces. In: Workshop on Software Mining, pp. 3–10 (2016)
4. Donzé, A.: Breach, a toolbox for verification and parameter synthesis of hybrid systems. In: Touili, T., Cook, B., Jackson, P. (eds.) CAV 2010. LNCS, vol. 6174, pp. 167–170. Springer, Heidelberg (2010). doi:10.1007/978-3-642-14295-6_17
5. Dustdar, S., Gambi, A., Krenn, W., Nickovic, D.: A pattern-based formalization of cloud-based elastic systems. In: Principles of Engineering Service-Oriented and Cloud Systems (PESOS), pp. 31–37 (2015)
6. Dwyer, D.B., Gabbett, T.J.: Global positioning system data analysis: velocity ranges and a new definition of sprinting for field sport athletes. The. J. Strength Cond. Res. **26**(3), 818–824 (2012)
7. Ferrère, T., Maler, O., Ničković, D., Ulus, D.: Measuring with timed patterns. In: Kroening, D., Păsăreanu, C.S. (eds.) CAV 2015 Part II. LNCS, vol. 9207, pp. 322–337. Springer, Cham (2015). doi:10.1007/978-3-319-21668-3_19
8. Jin, X., Donzé, A., Deshmukh, J.V., Seshia, S.A.: Mining requirements from closed-loop control models. In: Hybrid Systems: Computation and Control, (HSCC), pp. 43–52 (2013)
9. Mazimpaka, J.D., Timpf, S.: Trajectory data mining: a review of methods and applications. J. Spat. Inf. Sci. **2016**(13), 61–99 (2016)
10. Mitsa, T.: Temporal Data Mining. CRC Press, Boca Raton (2010)
11. Nickovic, D., Maler, O.: AMT: a property-based monitoring tool for analog systems. In: Raskin, J.-F., Thiagarajan, P.S. (eds.) FORMATS 2007. LNCS, vol. 4763, pp. 304–319. Springer, Heidelberg (2007). doi:10.1007/978-3-540-75454-1_22
12. Owens, S., Reppy, J.H., Turon, A.: Regular-expression derivatives re-examined. J. Funct. Program. **19**(2), 173–190 (2009)
13. Roşu, G., Viswanathan, M.: Testing extended regular language membership incrementally by rewriting. In: Nieuwenhuis, R. (ed.) RTA 2003. LNCS, vol. 2706, pp. 499–514. Springer, Heidelberg (2003). doi:10.1007/3-540-44881-0_35
14. Ulus, D., Ferrère, T., Asarin, E., Maler, O.: Timed pattern matching. In: Legay, A., Bozga, M. (eds.) FORMATS 2014. LNCS, vol. 8711, pp. 222–236. Springer, Cham (2014). doi:10.1007/978-3-319-10512-3_16
15. Ulus, D., Ferrère, T., Asarin, E., Maler, O.: Online timed pattern matching using derivatives. In: Chechik, M., Raskin, J.-F. (eds.) TACAS 2016. LNCS, vol. 9636, pp. 736–751. Springer, Heidelberg (2016). doi:10.1007/978-3-662-49674-9_47
16. Zheng, Y.: Trajectory data mining: an overview. ACM Trans. Intell. Syst. Technol. (TIST) **6**(3), 29 (2015)

Runtime Monitoring with Recovery of the SENT Communication Protocol

Konstantin Selyunin[1]([✉]), Stefan Jaksic[1,3], Thang Nguyen[2], Christian Reidl[2], Udo Hafner[2], Ezio Bartocci[1], Dejan Nickovic[3], and Radu Grosu[1]

[1] Vienna University of Technology, Vienna, Austria
{konstantin.selyunin,ezio.bartocci,radu.grosu}@tuwien.ac.at
[2] Infineon Technologies Austria AG, Villach, Austria
{thang.nguyen,christian.reidl,udo.hafner}@infineon.com
[3] AIT Austrian Institute of Technology, Vienna, Austria
{stefan.jaksic.fl,dejan.nickovic}@ait.ac.at

Abstract. We show how the requirements of the SENT communication protocol between a magnetic sensor and an electronic control unit (ECU) can be monitored in real time, with a monitor capable of processing 70 million samples per second. We elaborate on a complete flow from formalizing electrical and timing requirements using Signal Temporal Logic (STL) and Timed Regular Expressions (TRE), to implementing runtime monitors in FPGA hardware and evaluating the results in the lab. For a class of asynchronous serial protocols, we define a procedure to obtain monitors that are capable to recover after violations. We elaborate on two different approaches to monitor the requirements of interest: (i) temporal testers with SystemC, STL and High-Level Synthesis; (ii) automata-based approach with TRE in HDL. We also present how the results of the monitoring can be used for error logging to provide users with extensive debugging information. Our approach allows to monitor requirements-specification conformance in real time for long-term tests.

Keywords: Case study · Verification in industrial practice · Runtime verification · Lightweight formal methods

1 Introduction

Strict safety standards (e.g. ISO 26262 [1]) force manufacturers in the automotive industry to develop new system-verification methods. Formal verification [2] and model-based design [3], although in principle capable of providing a formal proof of a system correctness, have limitations when applied to real-world industrial problems due to the complexity of the associated systems.

The verification and validation (V & V) phase in automotive electronic development comprises extensive product testing under different scenarios, including stress conditions. Runtime verification [4,5], a light-weight verification technique, treats the system under investigation as a black-box, and reports system's conformance to formal requirements in a current run. Since runtime verification can

© Springer International Publishing AG 2017
R. Majumdar and V. Kunčak (Eds.): CAV 2017, Part I, LNCS 10426, pp. 336–355, 2017.
DOI: 10.1007/978-3-319-63387-9_17

be applied non-intrusively to existing systems, it fits in the current V & V setting very well, allowing a rigorous treatment and a traceability of requirements, and enabling automated observation of specification compliance via monitoring.

In this case-study paper we report on the runtime verification of electrical and timing requirements of the Single Edge Nibble Transmission (SENT [6]) protocol. The SENT is mainly used in automotive applications, for instance, in an electronic power steering (EPS), or an electronic braking system (EBS). In these applications sensors transfer data about rotation of a steering wheel or position of a braking pedal, respectively; hence ensuring the correct information transfer and runtime error detection is of utter importance.

The current industry practice relies on hard-crafted checkers, that lack diagnostics information and do not runtime-check the signals on the electrical level. Existing tools for offline trace verification (e.g. the AMT [7]) are not directly applicable in this context, due to the excessive size of the resulting traces: e.g. if one records an analog signal, sampled at 70 MHz, for an hour of runtime in an array of 16-bit integers, the trace will result in 504 Gb of data. Moreover, it is also often the case that a long-term test takes several days of real-time execution. In order to be able to speed up the checking process and to produce the monitoring results during the execution of the system, we translate high-level specifications into monitors implemented in FPGA and run them in parallel with the system under investigation. We propose an approach that allows to observe the monitoring results in real time, track requirements to implementation, and report violation and debugging information for the higher level analysis.

The contributions of this paper can be summarized as follows:

1. We propose a framework for generating monitors with recovery from a class of high-level specifications;
2. We formalize the electrical and timing requirements of the SENT protocol in STL and TRE specifications;
3. We evaluate our framework on the SENT case study, demonstrating the synergy between formal methods and industrial practice in a real-world setting.

The rest of the paper is organized as follows: Sect. 2 discusses the related work, and Sect. 3 provides the preliminaries. Section 4 presents formalization of requirements in two formalisms, the necessary initial step for creating monitors. Section 5 elaborates on runtime monitoring with recovery of asynchronous serial protocols. Section 6 presents in depth the case study and experimental results. Section 7 offers our concluding remarks and directions for future work.

2   Related Work

Runtime verification of formally defined properties is an extremely diverse research area in terms of requirements-specification languages [8–14], approaches to construct the monitors [15–18], and target applications [19–24].

The FoC framework of IBM [8,25] allows to generate monitors for Property Specification Language (PSL) assertions. Although PSL allows to specify the evolution of a system, the formal semantics is based on the sequence of states and does not include a notion of time explicitly. STL [26] and TRE [27], on the other hand, were designed to deal with real time, and allow to precisely identify time intervals of interest and bound temporal modalities to these intervals.

As far as hardware implementation is concerned, Schumann et al. [16] propose an FPGA implementation of runtime monitors for the UAV applications. The authors construct FPGA monitors for security requirements and specify possible attacks that a UAV might undergo. A Bayesian network on top of Metric Temporal Logic (MTL) monitoring allows to estimate system health. The authors do not take into account neither the recovery of monitors after violations nor the electrical characteristics of signals, and define their properties on a higher level of abstraction. On the contrary, in our work we focus on formalizing the electrical and timing requirements of a sequential protocol, with a special emphasis on monitor recovery after capturing specification violations.

In a similar context we refer to the work of Reinbacher et al. [28]. The authors present a framework for monitoring past-time Metric Temporal Logic (MTL) specifications. In order to achieve the reconfigurability of the system, they introduce an over-complex hardware architecture. In our case, we specifically target asynchronous serial protocols, for which we find the TRE formalization with simpler, automaton-based architecture more appropriate.

UPPAAL [29, 30] is a well established tool for the verification of real-time systems which can be modeled with timed automata. This tool provides a description language for modelling, a simulator, and a model checker. In contrast, our goal is to create a standalone monitor in order to verify a discrete time system during runtime. Our monitors are ignorant of the model of the system. In addition, since we are using a formally proven translation from TREs to automata, our monitors are correct by construction.

We are aware of several case studies on monitoring temporal logic specifications - the automotive bus standard [31], the DDR2 memory interface [19], typical automotive functional requirements [32]. All of these works focus on offline monitoring and continuous-time semantics, which covers STL and does not consider specifications based on regular expressions, and omit monitor recovery aspects after capturing a violation. Although the authors in [33] runtime-verify a subset of requirements of the PSI5, the protocol uses different encoding scheme then the SENT; their emphasis is on how to apply runtime verification, and they by and large avoid technical details. In contrast, we compare two formalisms and implementations, to increase integration readiness level for the monitor itself and eliminate the "single source of truth" aspect from the monitoring system.

In [12] the authors also use TREs with events to evaluate the performance of a controller and sensor implementation. Orthogonally to our work, they define measurement specifications over timed patterns.

3   Preliminaries

This section presents the specification languages that we use in this work to state the requirements in a formal way.

3.1 Signal Temporal Logic

Signal Temporal Logic [10] allows specification of properties defined over analog-mixed signals. As the goal of the case study is to produce runtime monitors in digital hardware (FPGA), the monitors operate on a finite representation of originally real-valued signals (ADC is used for quantization and sampling of continuously evolving voltage). For this purpose we interpret STL over discrete time and finite-valued domain. Let w be a multi-dimensional signal of a finite length, $w : [0, d] \mapsto P^n \cup X^m$, where $d \in \mathbb{N}$ is a duration of the signal; $P^n = \{p_1, \cdots, p_n\}$ and $X^m = \{x_1, \cdots, x_m\}$ are boolean (digital) and finite-domain (analog) variables respectively. Analog variables X^m are interpreted over a domain $\mathbb{D} = [0, \gamma] \subseteq \mathbb{N}$, where $\gamma = 2^r - 1, r \in \mathbb{N}$ is defined by a resolution of an ADC. The projection of the signal w to a component $e \in P \cup X$ is denoted by $\pi_e(w)$. The syntax of an STL formula φ with past and future operators is defined by the following grammar [34]:

$$\varphi := p \mid x \sim c \mid \neg\varphi \mid \varphi_1 \vee \varphi_2 \mid \varphi_1 \mathcal{U}_I \varphi_2 \mid \varphi_1 \mathcal{S}_I \varphi_2,$$

where $p \in P, x \in X, c \in \mathbb{D}, \sim \in \{<, \leq\}$, I is a time interval $[a, b]$, where $a, b \in \mathbb{N}$ and $0 \leq a \leq b$. For intervals of the type $[a, a]$ we use a notation $\{a\}$. We derive logical and temporal operators from the definition in a standard way: $\top = \varphi \vee \neg\varphi$; $\bot = \neg\top$; eventually $\diamondsuit_I \varphi = \top \mathcal{U}_I \varphi$; once $\diamondsuit_I \varphi = \top \mathcal{S}_I \varphi$; next $\bigcirc \varphi = \diamondsuit_{\{1\}} \varphi$; previous $\ominus \varphi = \diamondsuit_{\{1\}} \varphi$; always $\square_I \varphi = \neg \diamondsuit_I \neg\varphi$; historically $\boxminus_I \varphi = \neg \diamondsuit_I \neg\varphi$. We introduce two useful macros in our notation, which capture the change in evaluation of a boolean component of w: for $p \in P$, $\texttt{enter}(p) = \ominus \neg p \wedge p$ and $\texttt{exit}(p) = \ominus p \wedge \neg p$.

The semantics of an STL formula is defined as follows:

$$
\begin{aligned}
(w, i) &\models p && \leftrightarrow \pi_p(w)[i] = \top \\
(w, i) &\models x \sim c && \leftrightarrow \pi_x(w)[i] \sim c \\
(w, i) &\models \neg\varphi && \leftrightarrow (w, i) \not\models \varphi \\
(w, i) &\models \varphi_1 \vee \varphi_2 && \leftrightarrow (w, i) \models \varphi_1 \text{ or } (w, i) \models \varphi_2 \\
(w, i) &\models \varphi_1 \mathcal{U}_I \varphi_2 && \leftrightarrow \exists j \in (i + I) \cap \mathbb{T} : (w, j) \models \varphi_2 \\
& && \quad \text{and } \forall k : i < k < j, (w, k) \models \varphi_1 \\
(w, i) &\models \varphi_1 \mathcal{S}_I \varphi_2 && \leftrightarrow \exists j \in (i - I) \cap \mathbb{T} : (w, j) \models \varphi_2 \\
& && \quad \text{and } \forall k : j < k < i, (w, k) \models \varphi_1
\end{aligned}
$$

The standard semantics of the future operators, i.e. $\varphi_1 \mathcal{U}_I \varphi_2$, $\diamondsuit_I \varphi$, $\square_I \varphi$ is defined s.t., the satisfaction of the formulae at the time step i depends on events that happen in the future, namely at $(i + I) \cap \mathbb{T}$, which makes monitoring of these specifications acausal. To overcome such limitation, our hardware monitors comprise only past-temporal operators, and we use a procedure from [35] to convert a formula with future operators to an equi-satisfiable past one.

3.2 Timed Regular Expressions

Timed regular expressions (TRE) [27] allow to pattern-match a specification over a signal. As the authors in [12] mentioned, the fundamental difference between

STL and TREs comes from a fact that the satisfaction of an STL formula is computed for a time point, while the match of a TRE results in a time interval. In this work we adapt the definition of TREs from [12] with an assumption of interpreting TREs over discrete time. We reuse definitions of a signal and its projection from the Sect. 3.1. To adhere to the definition from [12] and to allow negation in TREs, we make the following assumption: for every boolean variable $p_j \in P^n$ we admit a definition of a complementary variable p_j^- with an opposite value of p_j (to which we refer as $\neg p_j$). Every analog variable $x_j \in X^m$ is allowed to be used in TREs only in the form of $x_j \sim c$, where $\sim \in \{< . \leq\}$ and $c \in \mathbb{D}$. With every $x_j \sim c$ we associate the boolean satisfaction variable $p_{x_j \sim c}$; we then analogously define $p_{x_j \sim c}^-$ and refer to it as $\neg(x_j \sim c)$.

A timed regular expression ψ is defined according to the following syntax [12]:

$$\psi := \epsilon \mid q \mid \psi_1 \cdot \psi_2 \mid \psi_1 \cup \psi_2 \mid \psi_1 \cap \psi_2 \mid \psi^* \mid \langle \psi \rangle_I$$

where q is of the form p, $\neg p$, $x \sim c$ or $\neg(x \sim c)$; I is a time interval $[a, b] \subseteq \mathbb{N}$.

For improved readability, we will refer to discrete time instance $i \cdot T$, where T is discrete time step, simply as i. The semantics of timed regular expression φ with respect to discrete signal w and time instances $i \leq i'$ is given in terms of satisfaction relation $(w, i, i') \models \varphi$:

$$
\begin{aligned}
(w, i, i') &\models \epsilon &&\leftrightarrow i = i' \\
(w, i, i') &\models q &&\leftrightarrow i \leq i' \text{ and } \forall i'' \text{ s.t. } i \leq i'' < i', \pi_p(w)[i''] = 1 \\
(w, i, i') &\models \varphi_1 \cdot \varphi_2 &&\leftrightarrow \exists i'' \text{ s.t. } i \leq i'' < i', (w, i, i'') \models \varphi_1 \text{ and } (w, i'', i') \models \varphi_2 \\
(w, i, i') &\models \varphi_1 \cup \varphi_2 &&\leftrightarrow (w, i, i') \models \varphi_1 \text{ or } (w, i, i') \models \varphi_2 \\
(w, i, i') &\models \varphi_1 \cap \varphi_2 &&\leftrightarrow (w, i, i') \models \varphi_1 \text{ and } (w, i, i') \models \varphi_2 \\
(w, i, i') &\models \varphi^* &&\leftrightarrow (w, i, i') \models \epsilon \text{ or } (w, i, i') \models \varphi \cdot \varphi^* \\
(w, i, i') &\models \langle \varphi \rangle_I &&\leftrightarrow i' - i \in I \text{ and } (w, i, i') \models \varphi
\end{aligned}
$$

We reuse the notation $\{a\}$ for intervals of the form $[a, a]$. We introduce the following macros for describing transitions of a boolean signal: $\texttt{enter}(p) = \langle \neg p \rangle_{\{1\}} \cdot \langle p \rangle_{\{1\}}$ and $\texttt{exit}(p) = \langle p \rangle_{\{1\}} \cdot \langle \neg p \rangle_{\{1\}}$. We also use a superscript with a TRE to denote a number of concatenations of this TRE (e.g. if ψ is a TRE, then ψ^3 stands for $\psi \cdot \psi \cdot \psi$). Finally, we use ψ^+ as syntactic sugar for $\psi \cdot \psi^*$.

4   Formalization of the SENT Protocol

In this section we introduce the communication protocol under study: the Single Edge Nibble Transmission Protocol (SENT), and then formalize a subset of its electrical and timing requirements.

4.1   Single Edge Nibble Transmission Protocol

The SENT protocol is an industry standard (SAE J2716 [6]) for transmitting data between a sensor and a controller.

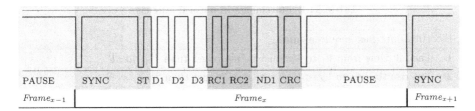

PAUSE	SYNC	ST D1 D2 D3 RC1 RC2 ND1 CRC	PAUSE	SYNC
$Frame_{x-1}$		$Frame_x$		$Frame_{x+1}$

Fig. 1. A SENT frame starts with a mandatory synchronisation pulse (SYNC), followed by a status nibble (ST), data nibbles (D1, D2, D3), rolling counters (RC1, RC2), bit inverse of D1 (ND1), cyclic redundancy check (CRC), and finishes with an optional pause.

SENT communication is unidirectional from a sensor to a controller; the information is partitioned into frames with the structure shown in Fig. 1. The transmitted data is split in four-bit data chunks, so-called nibbles, which encode the data in their length. Each nibble has the shape depicted in Fig. 2, where the length of the 'H' region determines the transmitted value (from 0 to 15). In the case study we build runtime monitors for magnetic sensors, which transfer angular information encoded in the three data nibbles D1–D3.

The SAE J2716 standard admits several frame configurations (e.g. the number of data nibbles may vary). SENT devices are configured prior to operation, and the configuration does not change on-the-fly; we take this into account and also assume that the frame structure is static and cannot change at runtime.

To be able to correctly decode sensor data, a controller needs to receive a signal that satisfies electrical and timing requirements of the SENT protocol. We now state these requirements formally, both in STL and TRE and elaborate on checking the frame correctness. Figure 2 shows a SENT nibble and graphically depicts the requirements to be checked. Table 1 presents in natural language a subset of electrical and timing requirements of the SENT protocol.

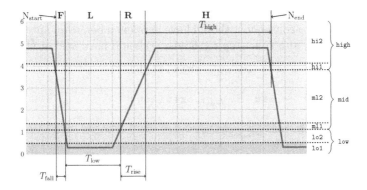

Fig. 2. SENT nibble pulse: a pulse starts (N_{start}) with a falling edge F, followed by a low region L, followed by a rising edge R, followed by a high region H.

Table 1. Requirements in natural language

Electrical interface requirements		
1	The fall time from V_1 to V_2 must be no longer than T_{fall} μs	F
2	The rise time from V_2 to V_1 must be no longer than T_{rise} μs	R
3	The signal stabilization time below low threshold V_1 or above high threshold V_2 must be at least T_{stable} μs	ST_{low},L ST_{high}
Transmission properties of synchronization & nibble pulses		
4	The synchronization pulse shall have a nominal period of 56 clock ticks	SYNC
5	Five clock ticks of the synchronization pulse shall be driven low	L
6	All remaining clock ticks of the calibration/synchronization pulse shall be driven high	SYNC, H_{sync}
7	Five clock ticks of the nibble pulse shall be driven low	L
8	All remaining clock ticks of the nibble pulse shall be driven high	NIBBLE, H_{nibble}
9	The minimum pulse period of Properties of Synchronization shall be 12 clock ticks	NIBBLE, H_{nibble}
10	The maximum pulse period of the nibble pulse shall be 27 clock ticks	NIBBLE, H_{nibble}

4.2 Formalization in STL

Electrical Interface Requirements specify the duration of the slopes, as well as the minimum stable time of the SENT signal. The STL formulae (Eqs. 1–4) capture the temporal order in which the signal should cross voltage regions from Fig. 2. F and R (Eqs. 1, 2) are the formal representations of falling and rising time requirements (Table 1, Req. 1, 2). The signal stabilization requirement (Table 1, Req. 3) is mapped to two STL formulae (Eqs. 3, 4) that deal separately with both thresholds. The STL formulae are written using past temporal operators: in this type of formulation a consequent should have happened before an antecedent (i.e. the form "whenever at a time step i φ holds, ψ should have held at $(i - I) \cap \mathbb{T}$").

$$F = \texttt{enter(low)} \rightarrow \texttt{mid}\ \mathcal{S}_{[0,T_{fall}]}\ \texttt{exit(high)} \tag{1}$$

$$R = \texttt{enter(high)} \rightarrow \texttt{mid}\ \mathcal{S}_{[0,T_{rise}]}\ \texttt{exit(low)} \tag{2}$$

$$ST_{low} = \texttt{exit(low)} \rightarrow \boxminus_{[0,T_{stable}]}\ \texttt{low} \tag{3}$$

$$ST_{high} = \texttt{exit(high)} \rightarrow \boxminus_{[0,T_{stable}]}\ \texttt{high} \tag{4}$$

Transmission Properties of Synchronization and Nibble Pulses. The synchronization and the nibble pulse requirements (Table 1, 4–6 and 7–10 respectively) describe the timing properties these pulses should adhere to. A synchronization pulse has a pre-defined length and is considered as the start of a frame. The shape of synchronization and nibble pulses is to be checked as well (see Fig. 2).

To verify the form of the synchronization, nibble, and pause pulses, we split each pulse in regions F, L, R, H (see Fig. 2) and check temporal precedence of the regions. The total length of the pulses and the length of the low region L are given in "clock ticks" (Table 1, 4–5, 7, 9–10), which are generated by a sensor's internal clock. Let us denote $\delta = (T_{\text{rise}} + T_{\text{fall}})$, then the allowed durations of the H region for the nibble pulse and synchronization pulse are $[7\text{tick} - \delta, 22\text{tick} - \delta]$ and $(51\text{tick} - \delta)$, respectively. Similarly, the length of the H region of the pause pulse is within the following bounds: $[7\text{tick} - \delta, 122\text{tick} - \delta]$.

Requirements for L and H regions can be written directly in past-STL:

$$\texttt{L} \quad = \quad \texttt{exit(low)} \ \rightarrow \ \boxminus_{[0,5\text{ticks}]} \ \texttt{low} \tag{5}$$

$$\texttt{H}_{\text{sync}} \quad = \quad \texttt{exit(high)} \ \rightarrow \ \texttt{high} \ \mathcal{S}_{\{51\text{tick}-\delta\}} \ \texttt{enter(high)} \tag{6}$$

$$\texttt{H}_{\text{nibble}} = \quad \texttt{exit(high)} \ \rightarrow \ \texttt{high} \ \mathcal{S}_{[7\text{tick}-\delta, \ 22\text{tick}-\delta]} \ \texttt{enter(high)} \tag{7}$$

$$\texttt{H}_{\text{pause}} = \quad \texttt{exit(high)} \ \rightarrow \ \texttt{high} \ \mathcal{S}_{[7\text{tick}-\delta, \ 122\text{tick}-\delta]} \ \texttt{enter(high)} \tag{8}$$

The general way of capturing precedence relation in STL is by using the bounded until operator $\mathcal{U}_I$. As the authors in [36] show, the hardware implementation of $\mathcal{U}_I$ is not scalable w.r.t. operator time bounds. In order to overcome this issue, we avoid using nested $\mathcal{U}_I$ operators in the formulation, and reformulate the properties. Each SYNC, NIBBLE, and PAUSE patterns of the SENT protocol are the requirements F, L, R, and the corresponding $\texttt{H}_{\{\text{sync}|\text{nibble}|\text{pause}\}}$ requirement put in a sequence. In order to attain efficient hardware implementation, we (i) re-state assertions from $\varphi \rightarrow \psi$ to $\psi \wedge \varphi$, to capture the events when the corresponding requirement has been satisfied; (ii) we then define precedence relation with following macro: $\varphi_1 \textbf{before}_{[t_1,t_2]} \varphi_2 = \varphi_2 \wedge \boxminus_{[0,t_1]} \neg \varphi_1 \wedge \diamondsuit_{[t_1,t_2]} \varphi_1$. This allows to use hardware-cheap bounded historically $\boxminus_{[0,t_1]}$ and bounded once $\diamondsuit_{[t_1,t_2]}$ operators and significantly reduce hardware resources.

The requirement for NIBBLE is then defined as follows (STL formulae for SYNC and PAUSE are constructed analogously):

$$\texttt{NIBBLE} = (\texttt{F} \wedge \texttt{enter(low)}) \ \textbf{before}_{[t_1,t_2]} \ (\texttt{L} \wedge \texttt{exit(low)})$$
$$\textbf{before}_{[t_3,t_4]} \ (\texttt{R} \wedge \texttt{enter(high)}) \ \textbf{before}_{[t_5,t_6]} \ (\texttt{H}_{\text{nibble}} \wedge \texttt{exit(high)})$$

The top-level FRAME requirement captures precedence relation between SYNC, NIBBLEs, and the PAUSE. The monitor construction is compositional: a frame correctness is reported only when all the lower-level requirements for all the frame components (SYNC, NIBBLEs, PAUSE) are met.

4.3   Formalization in TRE

Although it is possible to formulate TREs in an STL-like style and express the same intent: e.g. the requirements $\texttt{F}^\dagger$ and $\texttt{R}^\dagger$ match falling and rising time intervals of the signal; using the syntax features of the TRE and composing the requirements hierarchically allows to obtain a concise and clear formalization for the requirements of interest. F and R regions (Eqs. 9, 10) are defined as follows:

$$F = \langle mid \rangle_{[0,T_{fall}]} ; \quad F^{\dagger} = exit(high) \cdot \langle mid \rangle_{[0,T_{fall}]} \cdot enter(low) \tag{9}$$

$$R = \langle mid \rangle_{[0,T_{rise}]} ; \quad R^{\dagger} = exit(low) \cdot \langle mid \rangle_{[0,T_{rise}]} \cdot enter(high) \tag{10}$$

The L TRE (Eq. 11) combines the requirements 3 and 5 from Table 1. The H TRE (Eq. 12) will match when the requirement 3 is fulfilled. The two are the necessary building blocks for checking the shape of pulses:

$$L = \langle low \rangle_{[T_{stable},5tick]} \tag{11}$$

$$H = \langle high \rangle_{[T_{stable},127]} \tag{12}$$

We are now able to define the TRE for synchronization, nibble, and pause pulses as a concatenation of regions, restricting the length of the pulses with appropriate time bounds. The SYNC TRE (Eq. 13) will match only when the requirements 1–6 (Table 1) are met. The sensor signal will match the NIBBLE TRE (Eq. 14) if the requirements 1–3, 7–10 are fulfilled.

$$SYNC = \langle F \cdot L \cdot R \cdot H \rangle_{\{56tick\}} \tag{13}$$

$$NIBBLE = \langle F \cdot L \cdot R \cdot H \rangle_{[12tick,27tick]} \tag{14}$$

$$PAUSE = \langle F \cdot L \cdot R \cdot H \rangle_{[12tick,127tick]} \tag{15}$$

The frame and protocol requirements in TRE are formulated as follows:

$$SENT\_FRAME = SYNC \cdot NIBBLE^8 \cdot PAUSE \tag{16}$$

$$SENT\_PROTOCOL = (SENT\_FRAME)^{+} \tag{17}$$

5   Runtime Monitoring with Recovery

A runtime monitor typically partitions the execution traces in those that either satisfy or violate system's specification, possibly providing a quantitative metric of satisfaction (violation). However, for data-driven applications, such as serial protocols, test executions may last for hours and it is required to continue monitoring even after detecting errors. Similarly to compilers, a monitor in such a case must be able to recover after observing a violation, collect the encountered errors, and report them to the user.

For a class of serial protocols, the asynchronous serial protocols (e.g. SENT [6], RS-232 [37], DMX512 [38], etc.), we propose a procedure to construct monitors with *error recovery*. To apply monitoring with recovery, the protocol must fulfil the following requirement: the devices communicate over a single line, where synchronization symbol, control and payload data, respectively, are multiplexed in time. As control signals are absent, the devices rely on the synchronization symbol to successfully capture the beginning of a useful portion of a frame.

By creating runtime monitors with recovery, we are able to: (i) Continue monitoring after detecting violations; (ii) Collect the errors and report them together with their violation type.

5.1 TRE Monitors with Recovery

In the case of asynchronous serial protocols, the devices communicate with sequences that form certain patterns over time; the communication is cyclic, where the data is split in subsequently following frames. These protocols admit a natural formalization in TREs: A frame begins with a unique synchronization pattern (START), followed by n PAYLOAD patterns, and ends with a STOP pattern. The asynchronous serial protocol is then defined as a sequence of frames:

$$\texttt{ASYNC\_SERIAL\_PROTOCOL} = \texttt{FRAME}^+, \tag{18}$$

$$\texttt{FRAME} = \texttt{START} \cdot \texttt{PAYLOAD}^n \cdot \texttt{STOP}. \tag{19}$$

The above expression exactly generalizes the TRE formalization of the SENT protocol from Sect. 4.3. It is important to mention that the Kleene star (*) operator should not be used in the specification of START, PAYLOAD and STOP in TREs, as these patterns are finite sequences of symbols; we use the Kleene star operator only at the top TRE (i.e. Eq. 18).

The sketch of construction procedure for a monitor with recovery is shown in Fig. 3. For each of the START, PAYLOAD, and STOP patterns, we construct the corresponding automata with discrete-time clocks $\mathcal{A}_{\texttt{start}}$, $\mathcal{A}_{\texttt{payload}}$, and $\mathcal{A}_{\texttt{stop}}$, respectively. We also create an additional copy of $\mathcal{A}_{\texttt{start}}$, called $\mathcal{A}_{\texttt{rec}}$, which enables the runtime monitor to recover from an error. In this work we take an optimistic approach, and use a weak interpretation of regular expression over finite traces. In case when a trace ends and only a prefix of the regular expression is matched, we decide to accept the input sequence. Therefore all the states in $\mathcal{A}_{\texttt{start}}$, $\mathcal{A}_{\texttt{payload}}$, and $\mathcal{A}_{\texttt{stop}}$ are accepting. The automaton-construction procedure from a given TRE, is adopted from [27] to the discrete interpretation of time. The state transitions are protected by a set C of symbolic transition guards C, where $C = \{c_1^{\texttt{start}}, \ldots, c_m^{\texttt{start}}, c_1^{\texttt{payload}}, \ldots, c_p^{\texttt{payload}}, c_1^{\texttt{stop}}, \ldots, c_q^{\texttt{stop}}\}$.

For each $c_i \in C$ we associate a complementary transition $\neg c_i$ to the global error state. The error state silently transitions to the starting state of the recovery automaton $\mathcal{A}_{\texttt{rec}}$ which consumes garbage symbols until a correct synchronization symbol is observed. The correct START pattern is a necessary pre-requisite for a monitor to analyze subsequent frames, and for the decoder to analyze the transferred data: as long as the synchronization symbol of the next frame is not received, the recovery automaton $\mathcal{A}_{\texttt{rec}}$ goes back to the error state.

We introduce a diagnostic variable out, defined over a finite set of symbolic values: {ok, ok_start, ok_payload$_{1,\ldots,N}$, ok_frame, rec, err$_{1,\ldots,m}$}. The values have the following meaning: ok: the trace has been correct so far; ok_start: the starting synchronization symbol has been matched; ok_payload$_i$: the ith payload symbol has been matched; ok_frame: the frame has met all the requirements;

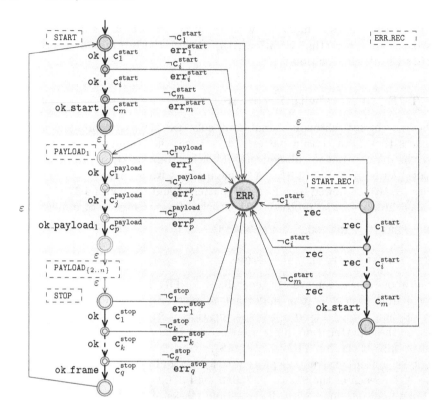

Fig. 3. Monitoring an asynchronous serial protocol with recovery (For clarity of the presentation, we keep ε-transitions in the Fig. 3; these transitions are removed in implementation though keeping the monitor deterministic.)

rec: the monitor is in the recovery state; err_i: the specification is violated by an error of type i.

We then transform $\mathcal{A}_{\texttt{start}}$, $\mathcal{A}_{\texttt{payload}}$, $\mathcal{A}_{\texttt{stop}}$ and $\mathcal{A}_{\texttt{rec}}$ to transducers $\mathcal{A}'_{\texttt{start}}$, $\mathcal{A}'_{\texttt{payload}}$, $\mathcal{A}'_{\texttt{stop}}$ and $\mathcal{A}'_{\texttt{rec}}$ as follows: (i) For each transition in $\mathcal{A}_i$, we output ok value; (ii) For each transition leading to a sink state, we output appropriate ok_{start|payload|frame} value; (iii) For each transition guarded by $\neg c_i$ we output err_i; (iv) For each recovery automaton transition, except the synchronization symbol matching transition, we associate rec value. The transition in $\mathcal{A}'_{\texttt{rec}}$ which matches synchronization symbol outputs ok_start (see Fig. 3). For the top-level expression FRAME, we create the automaton $\mathcal{A}_{\texttt{frame}}$ by concatenating the $\mathcal{A}_{\texttt{start}}$, $\mathcal{A}_{\texttt{payload}}$, and $\mathcal{A}_{\texttt{stop}}$ with ε transitions. This way the user is capable to receive the information about the number of frames that meet the specification, as well as errors and their type.

5.2   STL Monitors with Recovery

The STL monitors are transducers (temporal testers [18]) by construction and are composed hierarchically to output the satisfaction signal of the top-level requirement. The sketch of construction procedure for monitoring with recovery is as follows: (i) we first formalize the START, PAYLOAD, and STOP patterns in STL; (ii) we then change the semantic meaning of STL assertions from (1) $\varphi \rightarrow \psi$ to (2) $\varphi \wedge \psi$: in the first formulation the transducer outputs '1' even if the requirement has never been checked, and '0' when the requirement has been violated (e.g. the F requirement from Sect. 4.2 is fulfilled even the line stays always at '1'); the second case the transducer manifests with the signal the precise time stamp when the requirement has been satisfied (i.e. outputting '1' when the correct falling edge occurred); (iii) for each requirement we identify a set of possible violations and assign an error code err_i to each violation type. Each violation is guarded by an STL assertion $\varphi \wedge \neg\psi \wedge v_i$, where v_i identifies a violation type (e.g. mid $\mathcal{S}_{[T_{\text{fall}+1},\infty)}$ exit(high) is a v_i clause to capture the violation of the type "too slow falling time" for the STL assertion F from Sect. 4.2).

Finally we check the temporal precedence of the START, n PAYLOAD sequences and the STOP pattern with the before$_{[t_1,t_2]}$ macro defined in Sect. 4.2. Using temporal testers allows to monitor all the requirements in parallel, and extending with violation clauses v_i provides the necessary debugging information.

6   Runtime Monitoring of the SENT Protocol

This section describes building runtime monitors in FPGA and evaluating the results in industrial environment. A general overview of the framework is followed by implementation and evaluation details.

6.1   From Requirements to Hardware Monitors

Figure 4 summarizes the process of creating runtime monitors; the proposed framework is not limited to the SENT, and can be applied for other protocols as well.

Requirements Formalization. The initial step for creating runtime monitors is to obtain formal representation of the system requirements. Formal semantics allows to eliminate ambiguities in interpretations and precisely define what is to be monitored. In order to evaluate the power of different formalisms, and to eliminate "single source of truth" from the system we use STL and TRE as specification languages. This phase results in a set of formulae (STL & TRE) which describe natural-language requirements.

For STL requirements we admit an automated pre-processing step (see Fig. 4) to obtain formulae that allow efficient hardware realization: on the parse tree of the formula we (i) eliminate duplicate sub-trees (Simplification); (ii) apply a recursive procedure from [35] to convert bounded future STL temporal operators to an equi-satisfiable past operators, resulting in a causal formula with the

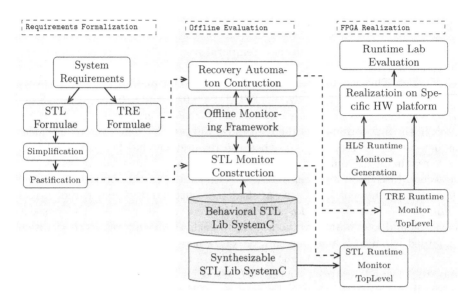

Fig. 4. Monitor generation

past temporal operators only (Pastification). The second step is achieved by (i) calculating the temporal depth $\mathcal{D}$ of the formula; (ii) re-writing a formula with past operators which results in postponing a monitoring verdict by $\mathcal{D}$.

Offline Evaluation. In this phase we evaluate monitors offline on short trace fragments, previously recorded from an oscilloscope or an ADC via the Chipscope [39] in order to speed-up debugging and identify implementation bottlenecks.

The monitors for STL formulae are built compositionally from the formula parse tree [18]. With each node of the STL parse tree, which represents either a temporal or a logical operator, we associate a transducer $\mathcal{T}$ which takes as inputs satisfaction signals of its child nodes and outputs the satisfaction signal for the corresponding operator. The satisfaction signal of the root node produces output of the monitor. *Behavioral STL Lib SystemC* (see Fig. 4) is a SystemC implementation of STL transducers, which are used to obtain a monitor. We use SystemC simulation kernel to run the monitor on the pre-recorded traces.

The runtime monitors for the TRE requirements are also implemented in hierarchical fashion: the $\mathcal{A}'_{\text{sync}}$, $\mathcal{A}'_{\text{nibble}}$, and $\mathcal{A}'_{\text{stop}}$ transducers are combined in the top-level recovery automaton described in Sect. 5.1. We use Vivado Behavioural Simulation to evaluate VHDL code of the top-level $\mathcal{A}'_{\text{frame}}$ transducer.

Runtime Monitoring in FPGA is the final phase; the monitors are synthesized in a digital reconfigurable hardware and evaluated in the lab environment. After the off-line phase we obtain the validated monitors for STL and TRE, which follow different paths of hardware implementation.

In case of STL monitoring, we use High-Level Synthesis [40] to generate HDL code for monitors written in SystemC. During the HLS step, the SystemC monitors are transformed to an equivalent synthesizable VHDL or Verilog. We use an alternative implementation of transducers (*Synthesizable STL Lib SystemC*, Fig. 4), which is suitable for HDL code generation. *Behavioral* and *Synthesizable* implementations are functionally equivalent, but HLS imposes constraints on the SystemC code to be hardware-synthesizeable. Keeping *behavioral* and *synthesizable* versions allows quick prototyping using all C++ features and then produce a hardware-optimized *synthesized* version.

Since transducers $\mathcal{A}'_{sync}$, $\mathcal{A}'_{nibble}$, $\mathcal{A}'_{stop}$, and $\mathcal{A}'_{frame}$ in the TRE approach are implemented in VHDL, we directly use Vivado Synthesis, Logic & Power Optimization, Place & Route tools to obtain a bitstream for FPGA programming.

6.2   FPGA Implementation

We implemented runtime monitors for the SENT protocol in Xilinx Virtex 7 FPGA. The monitors are embedded in the *Line Emulizer* hardware (see Fig. 5), which combines an analog front-end (AFE) capable to interface various sensors with a high-performance Virtex 7 FPGA. This hardware also models a transmission line with adjustable parameters between a sensor and an ECU.

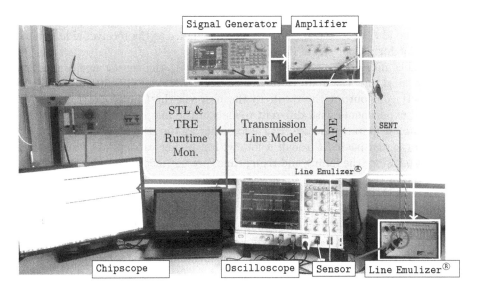

Fig. 5. Runtime monitoring of the SENT: hardware setup

The signal from the SENT sensor (see Fig. 5) comes to the *Line Emulizer*, where it is passed through the AFE and sampled with a high-speed ADC, which results in its finite value representation. During operation in a car, a sensor and

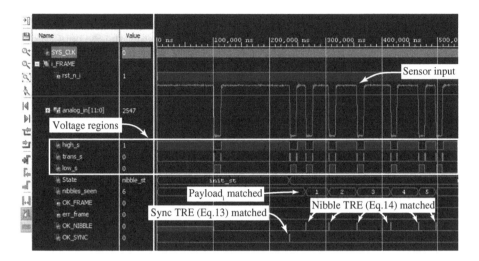

Fig. 6. Runtime TRE monitoring: Vivado functional simulation

an ECU are placed in different locations, hence the sensor signal is affected by a transmission line. To take into account the effects of physical wires, the sensor signal is passed through a digital model of a transmission line. We attach the STL and TRE runtime monitors at the end of the transmission line model (see Fig. 5), to be able to report specification conformance at the receiver side, which is important for proper signal decoding.

The STL and TRE monitors observe at 70 MHz the sensor signal affected by the physical line, calculate verdicts at every clock cycle (i.e. 70 million times per second), and output the result to the user via the Chipscope (Fig. 5). We performed experiments with different models of the line, and conclude that the appropriate line parameters are critical for ensuring the specification compliance. The sensor signal passed through a line with a higher capacitance violates the specification, since the falling and rising times are not met, which can be directly observed from the monitor.

Table 2 reports the estimated FPGA hardware resources (flip-flops, FF & look-up tables, LUT), and the estimated maximum clock period of the runtime monitors. For each HLS-generated monitor we also present its generation time and peak memory usage during HDL-code generation. The monitors in HLS are constructed in a hierarchic fashion, hence the **FRAME** monitor (see Table 2) subsumes monitors for other requirements and results the highest hardware footprint. The last row of the Table 2 reports the total hardware resources consumed by the top-level TRE monitor: the direct hardware implementation results in an order of magnitude lower footprint.

Figure 6 shows a result of offline evaluation for TRE requirements. The original SENT signal is observed by the monitor, which outputs OK_NIBBLE, OK_SYNC and the corresponding ERR signals. The figure depicts a nominal case, where all the requirements are met.

Table 2. STL monitors generation: FPGA & HLS resources

Requirement		FF	LUT	Clock	HLS: time	HLS: memory
F	HLS	61	118	5.81 ns	114.203 s	225 MB
L		53	85	4.24 ns	96.490 s	159 MB
R		61	113	5.81 ns	109.784 s	224 MB
H_{nibble}		125	249	5.81 ns	175.716 s	225 MB
H_{sync}		28	407	5.81 ns	253.507 s	224 MB
H_{pause}		73	98	4.24 ns	162.637 s	212 MB
NIBBLE		435	1123	7.7 ns	394.671 s	611 MB
SYNC		207	1062	7.7 ns	723.690 s	605 MB
PAUSE		217	710	7.7 ns	206.767 s	317 MB
FRAME		1198	4322	7.7 ns	1675.52 s	1.39 GB
FRAME	TRE	68	350	4.5 ns	-	-

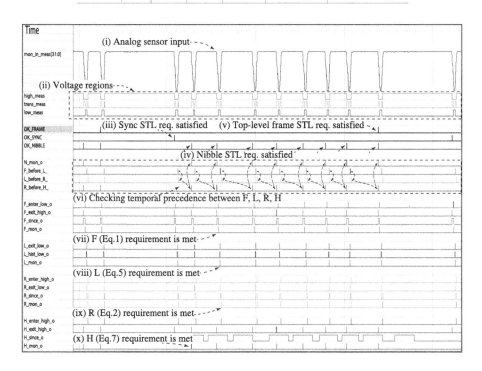

Fig. 7. Runtime monitoring of the STL requirements

Runtime monitoring of the SENT signal against STL requirements is shown in the Fig. 7. For this test case the optional pause pulse was deactivated, hence the correct frame is manifested after observing eight correct nibbles (signals OK_NIBBLE, OK_SYNC, OK_FRAME). The OK_NIBBLE signal is asserted when the corresponding precedence between the requirements F, L, R, and H is met. The output of the monitors F, L, R, and H, and the corresponding sub-formulae are presented in the lower part of the Fig. 7.

7   Conclusion and Outlooks

The case study focuses on assessing STL and TRE for formalizing requirements of the SENT protocol and obtaining hardware monitors for these requirements. We evaluate the two approaches in terms of applicability for formalizing typical protocol requirements, consumption of hardware resources, and monitor reuse.

The hardware resource consumption in Table 2 shows that (i) both approaches can be easily mapped to state-of-the-art FPGAs, (ii) STL-based monitors consume an order of magnitude more resources than the TRE monitors. Obtaining hardware monitors based on STL Synthesizable-SystemC library requires an intermediate transformation using HLS, which comes at price of increased hardware footprint. As described in the paper, TREs can be directly translated to automata with recovery which admit efficient hardware realization.

Besides low-level hardware monitoring, which both of the approaches facilitate, SystemC STL monitors can be re-used to check SystemC models. Trace verification in this setting happens during the runtime of the simulation kernel and the monitoring results are obtained at the end of the run. The re-usability of HLS-based monitors though comes at price of FPGA resource consumption.

We found both formalisms applicable for the SENT requirements formalization. TREs allow natural formulation of requirements that are concerned with repetitive sequences of groups of symbols, while formalizing precedence constraints with STL requires in general additional effort to be hardware-efficient.

As it is often the case, specifications comprise both textual and graphical information; we would like to investigate how to combine the information from both representations in a systematic way.

Acknowledgment. This research is supported by the project HARMONIA (845631), funded by a national Austrian grant from FFG (Österreichische Forschungsförderungsgesellschaft) under the program IKT der Zukunft, the EU ICT COST Action IC1402 on Runtime Verification beyond Monitoring (ARVI), the Austrian National Research Network RiSE/SHiNE (S11405-N23 and S11412-N23) project funded by the Austrian Science Fund (FWF) and the Fclose (Federated Cloud Security) project funded by UnivPM. This manuscript benefited from comments of Alena Rodionova, who we kindly acknowledge.

References

1. ISO 26262: "Road vehicles – Functional safety". International Organization for Standardization (ISO) (2011)
2. Baier, C., Katoen, J.-P.: Principles of Model Checking (Representation and Mind Series). The MIT Press, Cambridge (2008)

3. Broy, M., Krcmar, H., Kirstan, S., Schätz, B.: What is the benefit of a model-based design of embedded software systems in the car industry? In: Emerging Technologies for the Evolution and Maintenance of Software Models, pp. 310–337 (2012)
4. Leucker, M.: Teaching runtime verification. In: Khurshid, S., Sen, K. (eds.) RV 2011. LNCS, vol. 7186, pp. 34–48. Springer, Heidelberg (2012). doi:10.1007/978-3-642-29860-8_4
5. Bartocci, E., Falcone, Y., Bonakdarpour, B., Colombo, C., Decker, N., Havelund, K., Joshi, Y., Klaedtke, F., Milewicz, R., Reger, G., Rosu, G., Signoles, J., Thoma, D., Zalinescu, E., Zhang, Y.: First international competition on runtime verification: rules, benchmarks, tools, and final results of CRV 2014. Int. J. Softw. Tools Technol. Transf., 1–40 (2017)
6. SAE International. SENT - Single Edge Nibble Transmission for Automotive Applications, J2716, Standard (2016). http://standards.sae.org/j2716_201001/. Accessed 21 Jan 2017
7. Nickovic, D., Maler, O.: AMT: a property-based monitoring tool for analog systems. In: Raskin, J.-F., Thiagarajan, P.S. (eds.) FORMATS 2007. LNCS, vol. 4763, pp. 304–319. Springer, Heidelberg (2007). doi:10.1007/978-3-540-75454-1_22
8. Eisner, C.: PSL for runtime verification: theory and practice. In: Sokolsky, O., Taşiran, S. (eds.) RV 2007. LNCS, vol. 4839, pp. 1–8. Springer, Heidelberg (2007). doi:10.1007/978-3-540-77395-5_1
9. Vijayaraghavan, S., Ramanathan, M.: A Practical Guide for SystemVerilog Assertions. Springer Publishing Company Incorporated, Heidelberg (2014)
10. Donzé, A., Maler, O., Bartocci, E., Nickovic, D., Grosu, R., Smolka, S.: On temporal logic and signal processing. In: Chakraborty, S., Mukund, M. (eds.) ATVA 2012. LNCS, pp. 92–106. Springer, Heidelberg (2012). doi:10.1007/978-3-642-33386-6_9
11. Maler, O., Ničković, D.: Monitoring properties of analog and mixed-signal circuits. Int. J. Softw. Tools Technol. Transf. **15**(3), 247–268 (2013)
12. Ferrère, T., Maler, O., Ničković, D., Ulus, D.: Measuring with timed patterns. In: Kroening, D., Păsăreanu, C.S. (eds.) CAV 2015 Part II. LNCS, vol. 9207, pp. 322–337. Springer, Cham (2015). doi:10.1007/978-3-319-21668-3_19
13. Aydin-Gol, E., Bartocci, E., Belta, C.: A formal methods approach to pattern synthesis in reaction diffusion systems. In: Proceedings of CDC 2014: The 53rd IEEE Conference on Decision and Control, pp. 108–113. IEEE (2014)
14. Haghighi, I., Jones, A., Kong, Z., Bartocci, E., Grosu, R., Belta, C.: SpaTeL: a novel spatial-temporal logic and its applications to networked systems. In: Proceedings of HSCC 2015: The 18th International Conference on Hybrid Systems: Computation and Control, pp. 189–198. IEEE (2015)
15. Tabakov, D., Rozier, K.Y., Vardi, M.Y.: Optimized temporal monitors for systemc. Form. Methods Syst. Des. **41**(3), 236–268 (2012)
16. Schumann, J., Moosbrugger, P., Rozier, K.Y.: R2U2: monitoring and diagnosis of security threats for unmanned aerial systems. In: Bartocci, E., Majumdar, R. (eds.) RV 2015. LNCS, vol. 9333, pp. 233–249. Springer, Cham (2015). doi:10.1007/978-3-319-23820-3_15
17. Boule, M., Zilic, Z.: Efficient automata-based assertion-checker synthesis of PSL properties. In: 2006 IEEE International High Level Design Validation and Test Workshop, pp. 69–76 (2006)
18. Pnueli, A., Zaks, A.: On the merits of temporal testers. In: Grumberg, O., Veith, H. (eds.) 25 Years of Model Checking. LNCS, vol. 5000, pp. 172–195. Springer, Heidelberg (2008). doi:10.1007/978-3-540-69850-0_11

19. Jones, K.D., Konrad, V., Nickovic, D.: Analog property checkers: a DDR2 case study. Form. Methods Syst. Des. **36**(2), 114–130 (2010)
20. Nguyen, T., Nickovic, D.: Assertion-based monitoring in practice - checking correctness of an automotive sensor interface. Sci. Comput. Program. **118**, 40–59 (2016)
21. Bartocci, E., Liò, P.: Computational modeling, formal analysis, and tools for systems biology. PLoS Comput. Biol. **12**(1), e1004591 (2016)
22. Bartocci, E., Bortolussi, L., Nenzi, L.: A temporal logic approach to modular design of synthetic biological circuits. In: Gupta, A., Henzinger, T.A. (eds.) CMSB 2013. LNCS, vol. 8130, pp. 164–177. Springer, Heidelberg (2013). doi:10.1007/978-3-642-40708-6_13
23. Bufo, S., Bartocci, E., Sanguinetti, G., Borelli, M., Lucangelo, U., Bortolussi, L.: Temporal logic based monitoring of assisted ventilation in intensive care patients. In: Margaria, T., Steffen, B. (eds.) ISoLA 2014. LNCS, vol. 8803, pp. 391–403. Springer, Heidelberg (2014). doi:10.1007/978-3-662-45231-8_30
24. Reinbacher, T., Rozier, K.Y., Schumann. J.: Temporallogic based runtime observer pairs for system health management of real-time systems. In: Proceedings of Tools and Algorithms for the Construction and Analysis of Systems - 20th International Conference (TACAS), Grenoble, France, pp. 357–372 (2014)
25. Dahan, A., Geist, D., Gluhovsky, L., Pidan, D., Shapir, G., Wolfsthal, Y., Benalycherif, L., Kamdem, R., Lahbib, Y.: Combining system level modeling with assertion based verification. In: 6th International Symposium on Quality of Electronic Design (ISQED) 21–23 March 2005, San Jose, CA, USA, pp. 310–315 (2005)
26. Maler, O., Nickovic, D., Pnueli, A.: Checking temporal properties of discrete, timed and continuous behaviors. In: Avron, A., Dershowitz, N., Rabinovich, A. (eds.) Pillars of Computer Science. LNCS, vol. 4800, pp. 475–505. Springer, Heidelberg (2008). doi:10.1007/978-3-540-78127-1_26
27. Asarin, E., Caspi, P., Maler, O.: Timed regular expressions. J. ACM **49**(2), 172–206 (2002)
28. Reinbacher, T., Függer, M., Brauer, J.: Real-time runtime verification on chip. In: Qadeer, S., Tasiran, S. (eds.) RV 2012. LNCS, vol. 7687, pp. 110–125. Springer, Heidelberg (2013). doi:10.1007/978-3-642-35632-2_13
29. Bengtsson, J., Larsen, K., Larsson, F., Pettersson, P., Yi, W.: UPPAAL—a tool suite for automatic verification of real-time systems. In: Alur, R., Henzinger, T.A., Sontag, E.D. (eds.) HS 1995. LNCS, vol. 1066, pp. 232–243. Springer, Heidelberg (1996). doi:10.1007/BFb0020949
30. Pettersson, P., Yi, W.: UPPAAL in a nutshell. STTT **1**(1–2), 134–152 (1997)
31. Nguyen, T., Ničković, D.: Assertion-based monitoring in practice – checking correctness of an automotive sensor interface. In: Lang, F., Flammini, F. (eds.) FMICS 2014. LNCS, vol. 8718, pp. 16–32. Springer, Cham (2014). doi:10.1007/978-3-319-10702-8_2
32. Fainekos, G.E., Sankaranarayanan, S., Ueda, K., Yazarel, H.: Verification of automotive control applications using S-TaLiRo. In: American Control Conference, ACC 2012, Montreal, QC, Canada, pp. 3567–3572 (2012)
33. Selyunin, K., Nguyen, T., Bartocci, E., Grosu, R.: Applying runtime monitoring for automotive electronic development. In: Falcone, Y., Sánchez, C. (eds.) RV 2016. LNCS, vol. 10012, pp. 462–469. Springer, Cham (2016). doi:10.1007/978-3-319-46982-9_30
34. Maler, O., Nickovic, D., Pnueli, A.: From MITL to timed automata. In: Asarin, E., Bouyer, P. (eds.) FORMATS 2006. LNCS, vol. 4202, pp. 274–289. Springer, Heidelberg (2006). doi:10.1007/11867340_20

35. Maler, O., Nickovic, D., Pnueli, A.: On synthesizing controllers from bounded-response properties. In: Damm, W., Hermanns, H. (eds.) CAV 2007. LNCS, vol. 4590, pp. 95–107. Springer, Heidelberg (2007). doi:10.1007/978-3-540-73368-3_12

36. Jaksic, S., Bartocci, E., Grosu, R., Kloibhofer, R., Nguyen, T., Nickovic, D.: From signal temporal logic to FPGA monitors. In: Proceedings of 13th ACM/IEEE International Conference on Formal Methods and Models for Codesign, pp. 218–227 (2015)

37. Axelson, J.: Serial Port Complete: COM Ports, USB Virtual COM Ports, and Ports for Embedded Systems, 2nd edn. Lakeview Research, Madison (2007)

38. ANSI E1.11-2008 (R2013). Entertainment Technology – USITT DMX512-A – Asynchronous Serial Digital Data Transmission Standard for Controlling Lighting Equipment and Accessories (2008). http://webstore.ansi.org/RecordDetail.aspx?sku=ANSI+E1.11-2008+(R2013). Accessed 20 Jan 2017

39. Xilinx Inc. Vivado Design Suite Tutorial, Programming and Debugging (2016). http://www.xilinx.com/support/documentation/sw_manuals/xilinx2016_2/ug936-vivado-tutorial-programming-debugging.pdf. Accessed 12 Jan 2017

40. Xilinx Inc. Vivado High-Level Synthesis. http://www.xilinx.com/products/design-tools/vivado/integration/esl-design.html. Accessed 18 Jan 2017

Runtime Verification of Temporal Properties over Out-of-Order Data Streams

David Basin[1], Felix Klaedtke[2]([⊠]), and Eugen Zălinescu[3]

[1] Department of Computer Science, ETH Zurich, Zurich, Switzerland
[2] NEC Laboratories Europe, Heidelberg, Germany
felix.klaedtke@neclab.eu
[3] Technische Universität München, München, Germany

Abstract. We present a monitoring approach for verifying systems at runtime. Our approach targets systems whose components communicate with the monitors over unreliable channels, where messages can be delayed or lost. In contrast to prior works, whose property specification languages are limited to propositional temporal logics, our approach handles an extension of the real-time logic MTL with freeze quantifiers for reasoning about data values. We present its underlying theory based on a new three-valued semantics that is well suited to soundly and completely reason online about event streams in the presence of message delay or loss. We also evaluate our approach experimentally. Our prototype implementation processes hundreds of events per second in settings where messages are received out of order.

1 Introduction

Verifying systems at runtime can be accomplished by instrumenting system components so that they inform monitors about the actions they perform. The monitors update their states according to the information received and check whether the properties they are monitoring are fulfilled or violated. Various runtime-verification approaches exist for different kind of systems and property specification languages, see for example [2,5,8,11,18,19,22].

Many of these specifications languages are based on temporal logics or finite-state machines, which describe the correct system behavior in terms of *infinite* streams of system actions. However, at any point in time, a monitor has only partial knowledge about the system's behavior. In particular, a monitor can at best only be aware of the previously performed actions, which correspond to a finite prefix of the infinite action stream. When communication channels are unreliable, a monitor's knowledge about the previously performed actions may even be incomplete since messages can be lost or delayed and thus received out of order. Nevertheless, a monitor should output a verdict promptly when the monitored property is fulfilled or violated. Moreover, the verdict should remain correct when some of the monitor's knowledge gaps are subsequently closed.

Many runtime-verification approaches rely on an extension of the standard Boolean semantics of the linear-time temporal logic LTL with a third truth value,

© Springer International Publishing AG 2017
R. Majumdar and V. Kunčak (Eds.): CAV 2017, Part I, LNCS 10426, pp. 356–376, 2017.
DOI: 10.1007/978-3-319-63387-9_18

proposed by Bauer et al. [10]. Namely, a formula evaluates to the Boolean truth value b on a finite stream of performed actions σ if the formula evaluates to b on all infinite streams that extend σ; otherwise, the formula's truth value is unknown on σ. This semantics, however, only accounts for settings where monitors are always aware of all previously performed actions. It is insufficient to reason soundly and completely about system behavior at runtime when, for example, unreliable channels are used to inform the monitors about the performed actions.

In this paper, we present an extension of the propositional real-time logic MTL [1,17], which we name MTL$^\downarrow$. First, MTL$^\downarrow$ comprises a freeze quantifier [16] for reasoning about data values in action streams. The freeze quantifier $\downarrow$ can be seen as a restricted version of the first-order quantifiers $\exists$ and $\forall$. More concretely, at a position of the action stream, the formula $\downarrow x.\,\varphi$ uniquely binds a data value of the action at that position to the logical variable x.

Second, we equip MTL$^\downarrow$ with a new three-value semantics that is well suited for settings where system components communicate with the monitors over unreliable channels. Specifically, we define the semantics of MTL$^\downarrow$'s connectives over the three truth values t, f, and $\bot$. We interpret these truth values as in Kleene logic and conservatively extend the logic's standard Boolean semantics, where t and f stand for "true" and "false" respectively, and the third truth value $\bot$ stands for "unknown" and accounts for the monitor's knowledge gaps. The models of MTL$^\downarrow$ are finite words where knowledge gaps are explicitly represented. Intuitively, a finite word corresponds to a monitor's knowledge about the system behavior at a given time and the knowledge gaps may result from message delays, losses, crashed components, and the like. Critically in our setting, reasoning is monotonic with respect to the partial order on truth values, where $\bot$ is less than t and f, and t and f are incomparable. This monotonicity property guarantees that closing knowledge gaps does not invalidate previously obtained Boolean truth values.

Third, we present an online algorithm for verifying systems at runtime with respect to MTL$^\downarrow$ specifications. Our algorithm is based on, and extends, the algorithm for MTL by Basin et al. [6] to additionally handle the freeze quantifier. The algorithm's output is sound and complete for MTL$^\downarrow$'s three-valued semantics and with respect to the monitor's partial knowledge about the performed actions at each point in time.

Our algorithm works roughly as follows. It receives messages from the system components describing the actions they perform. As with the algorithm in [6], no assumptions are made on the order in which messages are received. The algorithm updates its state for each received message. This state comprises a graph structure for reasoning about the system behavior, i.e., computing verdicts about the monitored property's fulfillment. The graph's nodes store the truth values of the subformulas at the different times for the data values to which quantified variables are frozen. In each update, the algorithm propagates data values down to the graph's leaves and propagates Boolean truth values for subformulas up along the graph's edges. When a Boolean truth value is propagated to a root node of the graph, the algorithm outputs a verdict.

Our main contribution is a runtime-verification approach that makes no assumptions about message delivery. It handles a significantly richer specification language than previous approaches, namely, an extension of the real-time logic MTL with a quantifier for reasoning about the data processed by the monitored system. Furthermore, our approach guarantees sound and complete reasoning with partial knowledge about system behavior. Finally, we experimentally evaluate the performance of a prototype implementation of our approach, illuminating its current capabilities, tradeoffs, and performance limitations.

The remainder of this paper is structured as follows. In Sect. 2, we introduce relevant notation and terminology. In Sect. 3, we extend MTL with the freeze quantifier and give the logic's semantics. In Sect. 4, we describe our monitoring approach, including its algorithmic details. In Sect. 5, we report on our experimental evaluation. Finally, in Sects. 6 and 7, we discuss related work and draw conclusions. Details that have been omitted due to space restrictions can be found in [7].

2   Preliminaries

In this section, we introduce relevant notation and terminology.

Intervals. An *interval* I is a nonempty subset of $\mathbb{Q}_{\geq 0}$ such that if $a, b \in I$ then $c \in I$, for any $c \in \mathbb{Q}_{\geq 0}$ with $a \leq c \leq b$. We use standard notation and terminology for intervals. For example, $(a, b]$ denotes the interval that is left-open with bound a and right-closed with bound b. Note that an interval I with cardinality $|I| = 1$ is a singleton $\{\tau\} = [\tau, \tau]$, for some $\tau \in \mathbb{Q}_{\geq 0}$. An interval I is *unbounded* if its right bound is ∞, and *bounded* otherwise. Let $I - J := \{\tau - \tau' \mid \tau \in I \text{ and } \tau' \in J\} \cap \mathbb{Q}_{\geq 0}$.

Partial Functions. For a partial function $f : A \nrightarrow B$, let $\mathrm{def}(f) := \{a \in A \mid f(a) \text{ is defined}\}$. If $\mathrm{def}(f) = \{a_1, \dots, a_n\}$, for some $n \in \mathbb{N}$, we also write $[a_1 \mapsto f(a_1), \dots, a_n \mapsto f(a_n)]$ for f, when f's domain A and its codomain B are irrelevant or clear from the context. Note that $[]$ denotes the partial function that is undefined everywhere. Furthermore, for partial functions $f, g : A \nrightarrow B$, we write $f \sqsubseteq g$ if $\mathrm{def}(f) \subseteq \mathrm{def}(g)$ and $f(a) = g(a)$, for all $a \in \mathrm{def}(f)$. We write $f[a \mapsto b]$ to denote the update of a partial function $f : A \nrightarrow B$ at $a \in A$, i.e., $f[a \mapsto b]$ equals f, except that a is mapped to b if $b \in B$, and $a \notin \mathrm{def}(f[a \mapsto b])$ if $b \notin B$.

Truth Values. Let $\mathbf{3}$ be the set $\{\mathsf{t}, \mathsf{f}, \bot\}$, where t (true) and f (false) denote the standard Boolean values, and $\bot$ denotes the truth value "unknown." Table 1 shows the truth tables of some standard logical operators over $\mathbf{3}$. Observe that these operators coincide with their Boolean counterparts when restricted to the set $\mathbf{2} := \{\mathsf{t}, \mathsf{f}\}$. We partially order the elements in $\mathbf{3}$ by their knowledge: $\bot \prec \mathsf{t}$ and $\bot \prec \mathsf{f}$, and t and f are incomparable as they carry the same amount of knowledge. Note that $(\mathbf{3}, \prec)$ is a lower semilattice where $\curlywedge$ denotes the meet. We remark that

Table 1. Truth tables for three-valued logical operators (strong Kleene logic).

$\neg$		$\vee$	t	f	$\bot$		$\wedge$	t	f	$\bot$		$\rightarrow$	t	f	$\bot$
t	f	t	t	t	t		t	t	f	$\bot$		t	t	f	$\bot$
f	t	f	t	f	$\bot$		f	f	f	f		f	t	t	t
$\bot$	$\bot$	$\bot$	t	$\bot$	$\bot$		$\bot$	$\bot$	f	$\bot$		$\bot$	t	$\bot$	$\bot$

the operators in Table 1 are monotonic. This ensures that reasoning is monotonic in knowledge. Intuitively, when closing a knowledge gap, represented by $\bot$, with t or f, we never obtain a truth value that disagrees with the previous one.

Timed Words. Let Σ be an alphabet. A *timed word* over Σ is an infinite word $(\tau_0, a_0)(\tau_1, a_1) \ldots \in (\mathbb{Q}_{\geq 0} \times \Sigma)^\omega$, where the sequence of τ_is is strictly monotonic and nonzeno, that is, $\tau_i < \tau_{i+1}$, for every $i \in \mathbb{N}$, and for every $t \in \mathbb{Q}_{\geq 0}$, there is some $i \in \mathbb{N}$ such that $\tau_i > t$.

3 Metric Temporal Logic Extensions

In this section, we extend the propositional real-time logic MTL [1,17] with a freeze quantifier [16]. The logic's three-valued semantics conservatively extends the standard Boolean semantics and accounts for knowledge gaps during monitoring.

3.1 Syntax

Let P be a finite set of predicate symbols, where $\iota(p)$ denotes the arity of $p \in P$. Furthermore, let V be a set of variables and R a finite set of registers. The syntax of the real-time logic $\text{MTL}^{\downarrow}$ is given by the grammar:

$$\varphi ::= \text{t} \mid p(x_1, \ldots, x_{\iota(p)}) \mid \downarrow^r x. \, \varphi \mid \neg \varphi \mid \varphi \vee \varphi \mid \varphi \, \mathsf{U}_I \, \varphi,$$

where $p \in P$, $x, x_1, x_2 \ldots, x_{\iota(p)} \in V$, $r \in R$, and I is an interval. For the sake of brevity, we limit ourselves to the future fragment and omit the temporal connective for "next." A formula is *closed* if each variable occurrence is bound by a freeze quantifier. A formula is *temporal* if the connective at the root of the formula's syntax tree is U_I. We denote by $Sub(\varphi)$ the set of φ's subformulas.

We employ standard syntactic sugar. For example, $\varphi \rightarrow \psi$ abbreviates $(\neg \varphi) \vee \psi$, and $\Diamond_I \varphi$ ("eventually") and $\Box_I \varphi$ ("always") abbreviate $\text{t} \, \mathsf{U}_I \, \varphi$ and $\neg \Diamond_I \neg \varphi$, respectively. The nonmetric variants of the temporal connectives are also easily defined, e.g., $\Box \varphi := \Box_{[0,\infty)} \varphi$. Finally, we use standard conventions concerning the connectives' binding strength to omit parentheses. For example, $\neg$ binds stronger than $\wedge$, which binds stronger than $\vee$, and the connectives $\neg$, $\vee$, etc. bind stronger than the temporal connectives, which bind stronger than the freeze quantifier. To simplify notation, we omit the superscript r in formulas like $\downarrow^r x. \, \varphi$ whenever $r \in R$ is irrelevant or clear from the context.

Example 1. Before defining the logic's semantics, we provide some intuition. The following formula formalizes the policy that whenever a customer executes a transaction that exceeds some threshold (e.g. \$2,000) then this customer must not execute any other transaction for a certain period of time (e.g. 3 days).

$$\Box \downarrow^{cid} c. \downarrow^{tid} t. \downarrow^{sum} a. \, trans(c, t, a) \wedge a \geq 2000 \rightarrow \Box_{(0,3]} \downarrow^{tid} t'. \downarrow^{sum} a'. \, \neg trans(c, t', a')$$

We assume that the predicate symbol *trans* is interpreted as a singleton relation or the empty set at any point in time. For instance, the interpretation $\{(Alice, 42, 99)\}$ of *trans* at time τ describes the action of *Alice* executing a transaction with identifier 42 with the amount \$99 at time τ. When the interpretation is the empty set, no transaction is executed. We further assume that when the interpretation of the predicate symbol *trans* is nonempty, the registers *cid*, *tid*, and *sum* store (a) the transaction's customer, (b) the transaction identifier, and (c) the transferred amount, respectively. If the interpretation is the empty set, the registers store a dummy value, representing undefinedness.

The variables c, t, a, t', and a' are frozen to the respective register values. For example, c is frozen to the value stored in the register *cid* at each point in time and is used to identify later transactions from this customer. Furthermore, note that, e.g., the variables t and t' are frozen to values stored in the registers *tid* at different times. The freeze quantifier can be seen as a weak form of the standard first-order quantifiers [16]. Since a register stores exactly one value at any time, it is irrelevant whether we quantify existentially or universally over a register's value. □

3.2 Semantics

$\text{MTL}^{\downarrow}$'s models under the three-valued semantics are finite words (see Definition 2 below). Such a model represents a monitor's partial knowledge about the system behavior at a given point in time. This is in contrast to the models for the standard Boolean semantics for MTL, which are infinite timed words and capture the complete system behavior in the limit.

Definition 2. *Let D be the* data domain, *a nonempty set of values with $\bot \notin D$.*
Observations are finite words with letters of the form (I, σ, ϱ), where I is an interval, $\sigma : P \nrightarrow 2^{\bigcup_{\iota \in \mathbb{N}} D^{\iota}}$, and $\varrho : R \nrightarrow D$. We define observations inductively.

- *The word $([0, \infty), [], [])$ of length 1 is an observation.*
- *If w is an observation, then the word obtained by applying one of the following transformations to w is an observation.*
  (T1) Some letter (I, σ, ϱ) of w, where $|I| > 1$, is replaced by the three-letter word $(I \cap [0, \tau), \sigma, \varrho)(\{\tau\}, \sigma, \varrho)(I \cap (\tau, \infty), \sigma, \varrho)$, where $\tau \in I$ and $\tau > 0$. If $\tau = 0$, then (I, σ, ϱ) is replaced by $(\{\tau\}, \sigma, \varrho)(I \cap (\tau, \infty), \sigma, \varrho)$.
  (T2) Some letter (I, σ, ϱ) of w, where $|I| > 1$ and I is bounded, is removed.
  (T3) Some letter (I, σ, ϱ) of w, where $|I| = 1$, is replaced by (I, σ', ϱ'), where $\sigma \sqsubseteq \sigma'$ and $\varrho \sqsubseteq \varrho'$, and $\sigma \neq \sigma'$ or $\varrho \neq \varrho'$.

For an observation w of length $n \in \mathbb{N}$, let $pos(w) := \{0, \ldots, n - 1\}$. We call $i \in pos(w)$ a *time point* in w if the interval I_i of the letter at position i in w is a singleton. In this case, the element of I_i is the *timestamp* of the time point i. We note that for any letter (I, σ, ϱ) of an observation, if $|I| > 1$ then $\sigma = \varrho = [\,]$.

Example 3. A monitor's initial knowledge is represented by the observation $w_0 = ([0, \infty), [\,], [\,])$. Suppose a transaction of \$99 with identifier 42 from *Alice* is executed at time 3.0. The monitor's initial knowledge w_0 is then updated by (T1) and (T3) to $w_1 = ([0, 3.0), [\,], [\,]) (\{3.0\}, \sigma, \varrho) ((3.0, \infty), [\,], [\,])$, where $\sigma(trans) = \{(Alice, 42, 99)\}$ and $\varrho = [cid \mapsto Alice, tid \mapsto 42, sum \mapsto 99]$. If the monitor also receives the information that no action has occurred in the interval $[0, 3.0)$, then its updated knowledge is represented by $(\{3.0\}, \sigma, \varrho) ((3.0, \infty), [\,], [\,])$, obtained from w_1 by (T2). The information that no action has occurred in an interval can be communicated explicitly or implicitly by the monitored system to the monitor, for instance, by attaching a sequence number to each action. See [6] for details. Finally, note that the interval of the last letter of any observation is always unbounded. This reflects that a monitor is unaware of what it will observe in the future. □

Definition 4. *The observation w' refines the observation w, written $w \sqsubset_1 w'$, iff w' is obtained from w by one of the transformations (T1), (T2), or (T3). The reflexive-transitive closure of $\sqsubset_1$ is $\sqsubseteq$.*

MTL$^{\downarrow}$'s three-valued semantics is defined by a function $\varphi \mapsto [\![w, i, \nu \not\approx \varphi]\!] \in 3$, for a given observation w, time point $i \in \mathbb{N}$, and partial valuation $\nu : V \nrightarrow D$. We define this function inductively over the formula structure. For a predicate symbol $p \in P$, we write in the following $p(\bar{x})$ instead of $p(x_1, \ldots, x_{\iota(p)})$. Furthermore, we abuse notation by abbreviating, e.g., $\nu(x_1), \ldots, \nu(x_n)$ as $\nu(\bar{x})$, for a partial valuation $\nu : V \nrightarrow D$ and variables $x_1, \ldots, x_n$. Also, the notation $\bar{x} \in def(\nu)$ means that $x \in def(\nu)$, for each x occurring in $\bar{x}$. Finally, we identify the logic's constant symbol t with the Boolean value $\mathsf{t} \in 3$, and the connectives $\neg$ and $\vee$ with the corresponding three-valued logical operators in Table 1.

$$[\![w, i, \nu \not\approx \mathsf{t}]\!] := \mathsf{t}$$

$$[\![w, i, \nu \not\approx p(\bar{x})]\!] := \begin{cases} \mathsf{t} & \text{if } \bar{x} \in def(\nu), \ p \in def(\sigma_i), \text{ and } \nu(\bar{x}) \in \sigma_i(p) \\ \mathsf{f} & \text{if } \bar{x} \in def(\nu), \ p \in def(\sigma_i), \text{ and } \nu(\bar{x}) \notin \sigma_i(p) \\ \bot & \text{otherwise} \end{cases}$$

$$[\![w, i, \nu \not\approx \downarrow^r x.\, \varphi]\!] := [\![w, i, \nu[x \mapsto \varrho_i(r)] \not\approx \varphi]\!]$$

$$[\![w, i, \nu \not\approx \neg\varphi]\!] := \neg[\![w, i, \nu \not\approx \varphi]\!]$$

$$[\![w, i, \nu \not\approx \varphi \vee \psi]\!] := [\![w, i, \nu \not\approx \varphi]\!] \vee [\![w, i, \nu \not\approx \psi]\!]$$

$$[\![w, i, \nu \not\approx \varphi \, \mathsf{U}_I \, \psi]\!] := \bigvee_{j \in pos(w), j \geq i} \Big(tp_w(j) \wedge tc_{w,I}(j, i) \wedge [\![w, j, \nu \not\approx \psi]\!] \wedge$$

$$\bigwedge_{i \leq k < j} \big(tp_w(k) \rightarrow [\![w, k, \nu \not\approx \varphi]\!] \big) \Big)$$

The auxiliary functions $\mathrm{tp}_w : pos(w) \to 3$ and $\mathrm{tc}_{w,I} : pos(w) \times pos(w) \to 3$, are defined as follows, where I_k denotes the interval at position $k \in pos(w)$ in w.

$$\mathrm{tp}_w(j) := \begin{cases} \mathsf{t} & \text{if } j \text{ is a time point in } w \\ \bot & \text{otherwise} \end{cases}$$

$$\mathrm{tc}_{w,I}(i,j) := \begin{cases} \mathsf{t} & \text{if } \tau - \tau' \in I, \text{ for all } \tau \in I_i \text{ and } \tau' \in I_j \\ \mathsf{f} & \text{if } \tau - \tau' \notin I, \text{ for all } \tau \in I_i \text{ and } \tau' \in I_j \\ \bot & \text{otherwise} \end{cases}$$

We comment on the semantics of $\varphi \mathsf{U}_I \psi$. The auxiliary functions account for the positions in w that are not time points. For example, at position i, for a position $j \leq i$ to be a "valid anchor" for the formula, j must be a time point (in this case $\mathrm{tp}_w(j) = \mathsf{t}$). Otherwise, the truth value $\bot$ is used to express that it is not yet known whether the interval at position j in w will contain a time point. Note that using the truth value f would be incorrect since a refinement of w might contain a time point with a timestamp in I_j. Furthermore, $\mathrm{tc}_{w,I}(i,j)$ is used to account for the metric constraint of the temporal connective. In particular, $\mathrm{tc}_{w,I}(i,j)$ is $\bot$ if it is unknown in w whether the formula's metric constraint is always satisfied or never satisfied for the positions i and j. Finally, suppose that φ's truth value is f at a position k between j and i. If the interval I_k at position k is not a singleton, the function $\mathrm{tp}_w(k)$ "downgrades" this value to $\bot$, since it will be irrelevant in refinements of w that do not contain any time points with timestamps in I_k.

Note that it may be the case that $[\![w, i, \nu \not\approx \varphi]\!] \in 2$ when i is not a time point in w (i.e., I_i is not a singleton). A trivial example is when $\varphi = \mathsf{t}$. In a refinement of w, it might turn out that there are no time points with timestamps in I_i, and hence a monitor should not output a verdict for the specification φ at position i in w. We address this artifact by downgrading (with respect to the partial order $\prec$) a Boolean truth value $[\![w, i, \nu \not\approx \varphi]\!]$ to $\bot$ when i is not a time point. To this end, we introduce the following variant of the semantics.

Definition 5. *For a formula φ, an observation w, $\tau \in \mathbb{Q}_{\geq 0}$, and ν a partial valuation, we define $[\![w, \tau, \nu \not\approx \varphi]\!] := [\![w, i, \nu \not\approx \varphi]\!]$, provided that τ is the timestamp of some time point $i \in pos(w)$ in w, and $[\![w, \tau, \nu \not\approx \varphi]\!] := \bot$, otherwise.*

3.3   Properties

The following theorem states that $\mathrm{MTL}^\downarrow$'s three-valued semantics is monotonic in $\sqsubseteq$ (on observations and partial valuations) and $\preceq$ (on truth values). This property is crucial for monitoring since it guarantees that a verdict output for an observation stays valid for refined observations.

Theorem 6. *Let φ be a formula, μ and ν partial valuations, u and v observations, and $\tau \in \mathbb{Q}_{\geq 0}$. If $u \sqsubseteq v$ and $\mu \sqsubseteq \nu$ then $[\![u, \tau, \mu \not\approx \varphi]\!] \preceq [\![v, \tau, \nu \not\approx \varphi]\!]$.*

A similar theorem shows that MTL$^\downarrow$'s three-valued semantics conservatively extends the standard Boolean semantics (see [7] for details). Intuitively speaking, if a formula φ evaluates to a Boolean value for an observation at time $\tau \in \mathbb{Q}_{\geq 0}$, then φ has the same Boolean value at time τ for any timed word[1] that refines the observation. Formally, a timed word w' *refines* an observation w, $w \sqsubseteq w'$ for short, if for every $j \in \mathbb{N}$, there is some $i \in pos(w)$, such that $\tau_j \in I_i$, $\sigma_i \sqsubseteq \sigma'_j$, and $\varrho_i \sqsubseteq \varrho'_j$, where $(I_\ell, \sigma_\ell, \varrho_\ell)$ and $(\tau_k, \sigma'_k, \varrho'_k)$, for $\ell \in pos(w)$ and $k \in \mathbb{N}$, are the letters of w and w', respectively.

We investigate next the decision problem that underlies monitoring.

Theorem 7. *For an arbitrary formula φ, observation w, partial valuation ν, time $\tau \in \mathbb{Q}_{\geq 0}$, and truth value $b \in 2$, the question of whether $[w, \tau, \nu \not\approx \varphi]$ equals b is PSPACE-complete.*

In a propositional setting, the corresponding decision problem can be solved in polynomial time using dynamic programming, where the truth values at the positions of an observation are propagated up the formula structure. Note that the truth value of a proposition at a position is given by the observation's letter at that position. This is in contrast to MTL$^\downarrow$, where atomic formulas can have free variables and their truth values at the positions in an observation w may depend on the data values stored in the registers and frozen to these variables at different time points of w. Before truth values are propagated up, the bindings of variables to data values must be propagated down.

4   Monitoring Algorithm

In this section, we present an online algorithm that computes verdicts for MTL$^\downarrow$ specifications. To support scalable monitoring, the computation is incremental in that, when refining an observation according to the transformations (T1)–(T3), the results from previous computations are reused, including the propagated data values and Boolean values. We also define correctness requirements for monitoring and establish the algorithm's correctness.

4.1   Correctness Requirements

We define when a sequence of observations is valid for representing a monitor's knowledge over time. We assume that the monitor receives in the limit infinitely many messages containing information about the system behavior. This assumption is invalid if the system ever terminates. Nevertheless, we make this assumption to simplify matters and it is easy to adapt the definitions and results to the general case.

Definition 8. *The infinite sequence $\bar{w} = (w_i)_{i \in \mathbb{N}}$ of observations is valid if $w_0 = ([0, \infty), [\,], [\,])$ and $w_i \subsetneq w_{i+1}$, for all $i \in \mathbb{N}$.*

---

[1] We assume here that the timed words are over the alphabet Σ that consists of the pairs (σ, ϱ), where (i) σ is a total function over P with $\sigma(p) \subseteq D^{\iota(p)}$ for $p \in P$, and (ii) ϱ is a total function over R with $\varrho(r) \in D$ for $r \in R$.

Let M be a monitor and $\bar{w}$ a valid sequence of observations. In the following, we view w_i as the input to M at iteration i. For the input w_i, M outputs a set of *verdicts*, which is a finite set of pairs (τ, b) with $\tau \in \mathbb{Q}_{\geq 0}$ and $b \in 2$. We denote this set by $M(w_i)$. Note that in practice, M would receive at iteration $i > 0$ a message that describes just the differences between w_{i-1} and w_i. Furthermore, the w_is can be understood as abstract descriptions of M's states over time, representing M's knowledge about the system behavior, where w_0 represents M's initial knowledge. Also note that if the timed word v is the system behavior in the limit, then $w_i \sqsubseteq v$, for all $i \in \mathbb{N}$, assuming that components do not send bogus messages. However, for every $i \in \mathbb{N}$, there are infinitely many timed words u with $w_i \sqsubseteq u$. Since messages sent to the monitor can be lost, it can even be the case that there are timed words u with $u \neq v$ and $w_i \sqsubseteq u$, for all $i \in \mathbb{N}$.

Definition 9. *Let M be a monitor, φ a formula, and $\bar{w}$ a valid observation sequence.*

- *M is observationally sound for $\bar{w}$ and φ if for all partial valuations ν and $i \in \mathbb{N}$, if $(\tau, b) \in M(w_i)$ then $[w_i, \tau, \nu \approx \varphi] = b$.*
- *M is observationally complete for $\bar{w}$ and φ if for all partial valuations ν, $i \in \mathbb{N}$, and $\tau \in \mathbb{Q}_{\geq 0}$, if $[w_i, \tau, \nu \approx \varphi] \in 2$ then $(\tau, b) \in \bigcup_{j \leq i} M(w_j)$, for some $b \in 2$.*

We say that M is observationally sound if M is observational sound for all valid observation sequences and formulas φ. The definition of M being observationally complete is analogous.

It follows from Theorem 7 that there exist monitors for MTL$^\downarrow$ that are both observationally sound and complete. This is in contrast to correctness requirements that demand that a monitor outputs a verdict as soon as the specification has the same Boolean value on every extension of the monitor's current knowledge. It is easy to see that, for a given specification language, such monitoring is at least as hard as checking satisfiability for the language. The propositional fragment of MTL$^\downarrow$ is already undecidable [21]. Thus monitors satisfying such strong requirements do not exist for MTL$^\downarrow$. For LTL, such stronger requirements are standardly formalized using a three-valued "runtime-verification" semantics, as introduced by Bauer et al. [11], and adopted by other runtime-verification approaches, e.g. [9]. We refer to [7, Appendix A.2] for a formal definition of these requirements in our setting.

Example 10. Consider the formula $\varphi = \Box(p \wedge \Diamond \neg p)$. Under the classical Boolean semantics, φ is logically equivalent to f, however not under our semantics. For example, $[w, 0, \nu \approx \varphi] = \bot$, for $w = ([0, \infty), [\,], [\,])$ and any valuation ν. Given a valid observation sequence $\bar{w}$, an observationally sound and complete monitor for $\bar{w}$ and φ will first output the verdict $(0, f)$ for the minimal i such that w_i contains a letter that assigns p to false. □

4.2 Monitoring Algorithm

We sketch the algorithm's state, its main procedure, and its main data structure. We provide further algorithmic details in [7].

4.2.1 Monitor State

Before explaining the algorithm, we first rephrase the MTL$^{\downarrow}$'s semantics such that it is closer to the representation used by the monitor. Given an $i \in \mathbb{N}$, a position $j \in pos(w_i)$, and a subformula γ of φ, we denote by Φ_i^{γ, J_j}, where J_k is the interval of the kth letter of w_i, the propositional formula:

$$
\Phi_i^{\gamma, J_j} := \begin{cases}
\gamma^{J_j} & \text{if } \gamma \text{ is atomic} \\
\neg \alpha^{J_j} & \text{if } \gamma = \neg \alpha \\
\alpha^{J_j} \vee \beta^{J_j} & \text{if } \gamma = \alpha \vee \beta \\
\alpha^{J_j} & \text{if } \gamma = \downarrow^r x. \alpha \\
\bigvee_{k \geq j} \left(tp^{J_k} \wedge tc_\gamma^{J_k, J_j} \wedge \beta^{J_k} \wedge \bigwedge_{j \leq h < k} (tp^{J_h} \rightarrow \alpha^{J_h}) \right) & \text{if } \gamma = \alpha \, \mathsf{U}_I \, \beta,
\end{cases}
$$

where α^K, tp^K, and $tc_\psi^{H,K}$ denote atomic propositions, for each proper subformula α of φ, each temporal subformula ψ of φ, and all intervals H, K of letters in w_i. Next, we define, for any partial valuation ν, the substitution θ_i^ν of Boolean values for these atomic propositions as follows:

$$
\begin{aligned}
\theta_i^\nu(\alpha^{J_j}) &:= [\![w_i, j, \nu \not\approx \alpha]\!] && \text{if } [\![w_i, j, \nu \not\approx \alpha]\!] \in 2, \\
\theta_i^\nu(tp^{J_j}) &:= \mathrm{tp}_{w_i}(j) && \text{if } \mathrm{tp}_{w_i}(j) \in 2, \\
\theta_i^\nu(tc_{\alpha \mathsf{U}_I \beta}^{J_j, J_k}) &:= \mathrm{tc}_{w_i, I}(j, k) && \text{if } \mathrm{tc}_{w_i, I}(j, k) \in 2,
\end{aligned}
$$

and θ_i^ν is undefined otherwise. In what follows, the symbol $\equiv$ denotes semantic equivalence between propositional formulas. It is easy to see that

$$
\theta_i^\mu(\Phi_i^{\gamma, J_j}) \equiv [\![w_i, j, \nu \not\approx \gamma]\!] \quad \text{iff} \quad [\![w_i, j, \nu \not\approx \gamma]\!] \in 2,
$$

where $\mu = \nu[x \mapsto \varrho_j(r)]$ if $\gamma = \downarrow^r x. \alpha$ and $\mu = \nu$ otherwise, with ϱ_j being the third component of the jth letter of w_i. Note that the formula $\theta_i^\mu(\Phi_i^{\gamma, J_j})$ tells us more than the truth value $[\![w_i, j, \nu \not\approx \gamma]\!]$. Indeed, when $\theta_i^\mu(\Phi_i^{\gamma, J_j}) \not\equiv b$, for each $b \in 2$, then we know not only that $[\![w_i, j, \nu \not\approx \gamma]\!] = \bot$, but we also know what the causes of uncertainty are, namely the direct subformulas α of γ and indexes k with $[\![w_i, k, \mu \not\approx \alpha]\!] = \bot$.

The monitor maintains as state between its iterations a variant of the propositional formulas $\theta_i^\mu(\Phi_i^{\gamma, J_j})$. The reason for using variants is that it is not algorithmically convenient to transform $\theta_i^\mu(\Phi_i^{\gamma, J})$ into $\theta_{i+1}^\mu(\Phi_{i+1}^{\gamma, K})$, where K is an interval (of a letter) in w_{i+1} that originates from the interval J in w_i. Such a transformation is needed for obtaining an incremental monitoring algorithm that reuses information already computed at previous iterations.

The formulas that the monitors maintains, denoted $\Psi_i^{\gamma, J_j, \nu}$, can be obtained from the formulas $\theta_i^\mu(\Phi_i^{\gamma, J_j})$ as follows. When γ is a nontemporal formula, then

$\Psi_i^{\gamma,J_j,\nu}$ equals $\theta_i^\mu(\Phi_i^{\gamma,J_j})$. When γ is a temporal formula $\alpha \cup_I \beta$, then, to each disjunct for index k in Φ_i^{γ,J_j}, we add the subformula $(tp^{J_k} \vee \alpha^{J_k})$ as a conjunct. This is sound, based on the equivalence $tp^{J_k} \equiv tp^{J_k} \wedge (tp^{J_k} \vee \alpha^{J_k})$. Furthermore, the monitor treats the subformulas $(tp^{J_k} \wedge \beta^{J_k})$, $(tp^{J_h} \rightarrow \alpha^{J_h})$, and $(tp^{J_k} \vee \alpha^{J_k})$ in a special way: they are not simplified in $\Psi_i^{\gamma,J,\nu}$ when they are still needed to obtain $\Psi_{i+1}^{\gamma,K,\nu}$. That is, even if one of the atomic propositions q of these subformulas could be instantiated (i.e. $q \in \text{def}(\theta_i^\mu)$) this is not always done, as explained in the next section. Instead, these three types of subformulas are represented in $\Psi_i^{\gamma,J_j,\nu}$ by the atomic propositions $\bar{\beta}^{J_k}$, $\bar{\alpha}^{J_h}$, and $\bar{\bar{\alpha}}^{J_k}$, respectively.

Example 11. We illustrate here the definitions of the propositional formulas $\Phi_i^{\gamma,J,\nu}$ and $\Psi_i^{\gamma,J,\nu}$ for temporal formulas γ. We also suggest why variants of the formulas $\theta_i^\mu(\Phi_i^{\gamma,J_j})$ are needed.

Let $\gamma = p \cup q$, where p and q are 0-ary predicates. Assume that in w_1 we have the intervals $L = [0,\tau_1)$, $N = \{\tau_1\}$, and $R = (\tau_1,\infty)$, and in w_2 we have the intervals $L_1 = [0,\tau_0)$, $L_2 = \{\tau_0\}$, $L_3 = (\tau_0,\tau_1)$, N, and R, with $\tau_0 \in L$. Assume also that neither p nor q holds at τ_1. Then

$$\theta_1^{[]}(\Phi_1^{\gamma,L}) \equiv tp^L \wedge q^L \qquad \theta_2^{[]}(\Phi_2^{\gamma,L_2}) \equiv q^{L_2} \vee (tp^{L_3} \wedge q^{L_3} \wedge p^{L_2})$$
$$\Psi_1^{\gamma,L,[]} = \bar{q}^L \wedge \bar{p}^L \qquad \Psi_2^{\gamma,L_2,[]} = \bar{q}^{L_2} \vee (\bar{q}^{L_3} \wedge \bar{p}^{L_3} \wedge \bar{p}^{L_2})$$

Note that p^L is not an atomic proposition of $\Phi_1^{\gamma,L}$, while $\bar{p}^L$ is an atomic proposition of $\Psi_1^{\gamma,L,[]}$. This last fact allows the monitoring algorithm to obtain $\Psi_2^{\gamma,L_2,[]}$ from $\Psi_1^{\gamma,L,[]}$, by introducing the needed new propositions $\bar{p}^{L_2}$, $\bar{p}^{L_3}$, and $\bar{p}^{L_2}$. □

To recapitulate, the monitor's state at iteration i consists of propositional formulas $\Psi_i^{\gamma,J,\nu}$, one for each subformula γ of φ, interval J occurring in a letter of w_i, where i is the current iteration, and partial valuation ν that is *relevant* for the current subformula and position corresponding to J in w_i. Intuitively, a valuation ν is relevant for ψ and a position $j \in pos(w_i)$, if $[\![w_i,j,\nu \not\approx \psi]\!]$ is reached when unfolding the formula that defines $[\![w_i,k,[] \not\approx \varphi]\!]$, for some $k \in pos(w_i)$.[2] For instance, $[]$ is relevant for φ and any $j \in pos(w_i)$. Furthermore, if ν is relevant for $\downarrow^r x.\,\psi$ and j, then $\nu[x \mapsto \varrho_j(r)]$ is relevant for ψ and j.

Example 12. Let $\varphi := \downarrow^r x.\,\diamondsuit_{(0,1]}\, p(x)$. For brevity, we treat the temporal connective $\diamondsuit_{(0,1]}$ as a primitive. Also, for readability, we let $\alpha := \diamondsuit_{(0,1]}\, p(x)$ and $\beta := p(x)$. Consider an observation w_1 that has the same interval structure as in the previous example and the second letter is $(\tau_1, \sigma, \varrho)$ with $\varrho(r) = d$ for some data value d and $p \notin \text{def}(\sigma)$. The monitor's state for w_1 consists of the formulas:

$$\Psi_1^{\varphi,K,[]} = \alpha^K, \text{ for any } K \in \{L,N,R\}, \qquad \Psi_1^{\alpha,L,[]} = \bar{\beta}^L \vee \bar{\beta}^N \vee \bar{\beta}^R,$$
$$\Psi_1^{\beta,K,[]} = \beta^K, \text{ for any } K \in \{L,N,R\}, \qquad \Psi_1^{\alpha,N,[x \mapsto d]} = \bar{\beta}^R,$$
$$\Psi_1^{\beta,R,[x \mapsto d]} = \beta^R, \qquad\qquad\qquad\qquad \Psi_1^{\alpha,R,[]} = \bar{\beta}^R.$$

---

[2] We consider here that the formulas defining the semantics are first simplified. E.g., assuming that $[\![w_i,j,\nu \not\approx \alpha \cup_I \beta]\!]$ is reached, $k \in pos(w_i)$, and $k \geq j$, if $tc_{w_i,I}(k,j) = \text{f}$, then $[\![w_i,k,\nu \not\approx \beta]\!]$ is not reached, otherwise (i.e. $tc_{w_i,I}(k,j) \neq \text{f}$) it is reached.

Note that there are two relevant valuations for β and position 2 (which is the position of the interval R in w_1), namely $[\,]$ and $[x \mapsto d]$. This follows from the definition and it corresponds to the fact that $\bar{\beta}^R$ is an atomic proposition of a formula both of the form $\Psi_1^{\alpha,K,[\,]}$ (namely, when $K \in \{L, R\}$) and of the form $\Psi_1^{\alpha,K,[x \mapsto d]}$ (namely, when $K = N$). □

4.2.2 Main Procedure

The monitor's pseudocode is shown in Listing 1. After initializing the monitor's state, the monitor loops. In each loop iteration, the monitor receives a message, updates its state according to the information extracted from the message, and outputs the computed verdicts.

We assume that each received message describes a new time point in an observation, i.e., a letter of the form $(\{\tau\}, \sigma, \varrho)$. Furthermore, we assume that each received message m contains information that identifies the *component* that has sent the message to the monitor and a *sequence number*, i.e., the number of messages, including m, that the component has sent to the monitor so far. Using this information, the monitor can detect *complete* intervals, i.e., the non-singleton intervals that do not contain the timestamp of any message that the monitor processes in later iterations. Thus, the received messages describe the "deltas" of a valid observation sequence (cf. Sect. 4.1), where the next observation is obtained from the previous one by applying transformation (T1), followed by (T3), possibly followed by several applications of (T2).

With the procedure NewMessage, the monitor receives a new message, for instance over a channel or a log file. Next, the monitor parses the message to recover the corresponding letter $(\{\tau\}, \sigma, \varrho)$, the component, and the sequence number. Afterwards, using the procedure Split, the monitor determines the interval J that is split (namely, the one where $\tau \in J$) and the resulting new, incomplete intervals, stored in the sequence new. Concretely, the intervals in new consist of those intervals among $J \cap [0, \tau)$, $\{\tau\}$, and $J \cap (\tau, \infty)$ that are not complete. Note that new contains at least the singleton $\{\tau\}$. The detection of complete intervals by the Split procedure is done in the same manner as in [6].

Listing 1.

```
procedure Monitor(φ)
    Init(φ)
    loop
        m ← NewMessage()
        τ, σ, ϱ, comp, seq_num := Parse(m)
        J, new := Split(τ, comp, seq_num)
        NewTimePoint(φ, J, new)
        foreach ↓ʳx.ψ in Sub(φ) with r ∈ def(ϱ) do
            PropagateDown(ψ, {τ}, x, ϱ(r))
        foreach Ψᵖ⁽ˣ̄⁾,{τ},ν ≠ nil with x̄ ∈ def(φ), p ∈ def(σ) do
            b := (ν(x̄) ∈ σ(p))
            Ψᵖ⁽ˣ̄⁾,{τ},ν := b
            PropagateUp(p(x̄), {τ}, b)
        NewVerdicts()
```

The remaining pseudocode updates the monitor's state to reflect the new observation. It first transforms formulas $\Psi^{\gamma,K,\nu}$ so that they reflect the interval structure of the new observation, with NewTimePoint. Afterwards, the monitor propagates the new data values down (the formula φ's syntax tree) with PropagateDown, and propagates newly obtained Boolean values up with PropagateUp. The procedures NewTimePoint and PropagateUp are conceptually similar to analogous procedures given in [6], although the formulas $\Psi^{\gamma,K,\nu}$ were implicit in [6]. We outline next these three procedures. Finally, the monitor reports the verdicts computed during the current iteration by calling the procedure NewVerdicts.

In the rest of the section, we use the convention that whenever γ or ν are not specified in a formula $\Psi^{\gamma,J_j,\nu}$ then we assume they are an arbitrary subformula of φ and respectively an arbitrary partial valuation that is relevant for γ and j.

Adding a New Time Point. The procedure NewTimePoint builds new formulas $\Psi^{\gamma,K,\nu}$ with $K \in$ new from the corresponding formulas $\Psi^{\gamma,J,\nu}$. It also updates all formulas $\Psi^{\gamma,J,\nu}$ such that they use atomic propositions α^K with $K \in$ new instead of α^J. For nontemporal formulas γ, the update is straightforward. For instance, if $\gamma = \alpha \vee \beta$ and $\Psi^{\gamma,J,\nu} = \beta^J$, then $\Psi^{\gamma,K,\nu} = \beta^K$, for each $K \in$ new. For temporal formulas γ, the update is more involved, although it can be performed easily by applying well-suited substitutions. To illustrate the kind of updates that are needed, suppose for example that $\gamma = \alpha \, \mathsf{U}_I \, \beta$ and that $\Psi^{\gamma,J',\nu}$, for some $J' < J$, contains the atomic proposition $\bar{\alpha}^J$. Then $\Psi^{\gamma,J',\nu}$ is updated by replacing $\bar{\alpha}^J$ with the conjunct $\bigwedge_{K \in \text{new}} \bar{\alpha}^K$. Finally, we note that formulas $\Psi^{\gamma,K,\nu}$ with $K \neq J$ and without atomic propositions α^J need not be updated.

Downward Propagation. Whenever a variable x is frozen to a data value at time τ, the procedure PropagateDown updates the monitor's state to account for this fact. Concretely, this value is propagated according to the semantics through partial valuations to atomic formulas $p(\bar{y})$. The propagation is performed by starting from formulas $\Psi^{\downarrow^r x.\psi,\{\tau\},\mu}$ and recursively visiting formulas $\Psi^{\alpha,K,\nu}$ with α a subformula of ψ. For each visited formula, a new formula $\Psi^{\alpha,K,\nu[x \mapsto \varrho(r)]}$ is created, where the new formula is simply a copy of $\Psi^{\alpha,K,\nu}$. Note that the old formula $\Psi^{\alpha,K,\nu}$ may still be relevant in the future. For instance, suppose a value d is propagated from $\Psi^{\diamondsuit_I \beta,\{\tau\},\nu}$ to $\Psi^{\beta,K,\nu}$, copying it to $\Psi^{\beta,K,\nu[x \mapsto d]}$, and suppose also that $\bar{\beta}^K$ is an atomic proposition in $\Psi^{\diamondsuit_I \beta,J',\nu}$. Then $\Psi^{\beta,K,\nu}$ might be used again later when another data value d' is propagated downwards from $\Psi^{\diamondsuit_I \beta,\{\tau'\},\nu}$ with $\tau' \in J'$, to copy it to $\Psi^{\beta,K,\nu[x \mapsto d']}$.

Upward Propagation. The procedure PropagateUp performs the following update of the monitor's state. When a formula $\Psi^{\alpha,K,\mu}$ simplifies to a Boolean value b, then this Boolean value is propagated up the syntax tree of φ as follows: α^K is instantiated to b in every formula $\Psi^{\gamma,J',\nu}$ that has α^K as an atomic proposition, except when γ is itself an atom of φ. The formula is then simplified (using rules like $z \vee \mathsf{t} \equiv \mathsf{t}$) and if it simplifies to a Boolean value then propagation continues recursively. Note that γ is a parent of α. When $\Psi^{\varphi,\{\tau'\},[]}$ is simplified to a Boolean value b', then (τ', b') is marked as a new verdict. Propagation starts from the atoms of φ. The Boolean value t is propagated from the atom t only once, in the Init procedure. For an atom $\alpha = p(\bar{x})$, the monitor sets $\Psi^{p(\bar{x}),\{\tau\},\mu}$ to a Boolean value, if possible, according to the semantics, for all relevant valuations μ.

Recall that for temporal formulas $\gamma = \alpha \ \mathsf{U}_I \ \beta$, the formula $\Psi^{\gamma,J',\nu}$ contains atomic propositions of the form $\bar{\alpha}^K$, $\bar{\bar{\alpha}}^K$, and $\bar{\beta}^K$ instead of α^K and β^K. These atomic propositions are treated specially: they are not instantiated when K is not a singleton and the value b to be propagated is t for β formulas and f for α formulas (otherwise they are instantiated). This behavior corresponds to the meaning of these atomic proposition given in Sect. 4.2.1. For instance, $\bar{\beta}^K$ stands for $tp^K \vee \beta^K$ and thus it is not instantiated to t in $\Psi^{\gamma,J',\nu}$ when K is not a singleton even when $\Psi^{\gamma,K,\nu} = \mathsf{t}$, because the existence of a time point in K is not guaranteed: it might turn out that K is a complete interval. The propagation will be done later for singletons $\{\tau'\}$ with $\tau' \in K$, if and when a message with timestamp τ' arrives.

4.2.3   Data Structure

We have not yet described the data structure used in our pseudocode, which is needed for an efficient implementation. The data structure that we use is similar to that described in [6]. Namely, it is a directed acyclic graph. The graph's *nodes* are tuples of the form (ψ, J, ν), where ψ is a subformula of φ, J an interval, and ν a partial valuation. Each node (γ, J, ν) stores the associated propositional formula $\Psi^{\gamma,J,\nu}$. Nodes are linked via *triggers*: a trigger of a node (α, K, μ) points to a node (γ, J, ν) if and only if α^K, $\bar{\alpha}^K$, or $\bar{\bar{\alpha}}^K$ is an atomic proposition of $\Psi^{\gamma,J,\nu}$, γ is a nonatomic formula, and $\mu = \nu[x \mapsto \varrho_j^i(r)]$ if $\gamma = \downarrow^r x. \alpha$ and $\mu = \nu$ otherwise. Triggers are actually bidirectional: for any (outgoing) trigger there is a corresponding ingoing trigger.

This data structure allows us to directly access, given a formula $\Psi^{\alpha,K,\mu}$, all the formulas $\Psi^{\gamma,J,\nu}$ that have α^K as an atomic proposition. Also, conversely, for any formula $\Psi^{\gamma,J,\nu}$ the data structure allows us to directly access the formula $\Psi^{\alpha,K,\mu}$ for any atomic proposition α^K of $\Psi^{\gamma,J,\nu}$. These two operations are used for upward and downward propagation respectively. We note also that a node for which the associated propositional formula has simplified to a Boolean value that has been propagated can be deleted.

Figure 1 illustrates the data structure at the end of iterations 0 and 1, that is, corresponding to the observations w_0 and w_1, for the setting in Example 12. A box in the figure corresponds to a node of the graph structure, where the node's formula is given by the row, the interval by the box's column, and the valuation by the box's content. The valuation in the partially covered box in the lower right corner is $\nu = [x \mapsto d]$, the same as in the box in the middle of Fig. 1(b). Arrows correspond to triggers.

4.2.4   Correctness

The following theorem establishes the monitor's correctness. We refer to [7] for proof details.

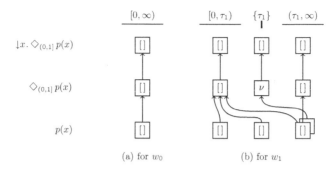

Fig. 1. Graph structures.

Theorem 13. *Let $\bar{w}$ be the valid observation sequence derived from the messages received by Monitor. Furthermore, let φ be a closed $\mathrm{MTL}^{\downarrow}$ formula. Monitor(φ) is observationally complete and sound for $\bar{w}$ and φ.*

An important property class in monitoring are safety properties. We note that our monitor is not limited to formulas in this class, and the monitor is observationally complete and sound for any formula. For instance, for the formula $\varphi = \square \diamond p$, which states that p holds infinitely often, the monitor will not output a verdict, as expected. It is nevertheless observationally complete for any valid observation sequence $\bar{w}$, since $[w_i, \tau, \nu \not\approx \varphi] = \bot$, for any $i \in \mathbb{N}$, $\tau \in \mathbb{Q}_{\geq 0}$, and partial valuation ν.

Besides correctness requirements, time and space requirements are also important. Recall Theorem 7 showing that the underlying decision problem is PSPACE-complete. Furthermore, note that the monitor's space usage cannot be bounded in general, even in the setting without message loss and with in-order delivery. To see this, consider the formula $\square \downarrow x. p(x) \rightarrow \square_{(0,\infty)} \neg p(x)$ stating that the parameter of p events are fresh at each time point. Any monitor must store the parameters seen. A thorough investigation of the time and space complexity of the monitoring procedure is however left for future work.

5   Experiments

We have implemented our monitor in a prototype tool, written in the programming language Go. Our tool either reads messages from a log file or over a UDP socket. Our experimental evaluation focuses on the prototype's performance in settings with different message orderings.

Setup. We monitor the formulas in Fig. 2, which vary in their temporal requirements and the data involved. They express compliance policies from the banking domain and are variants of policies that have been used in previous case studies [5]. Furthermore, we synthetically generate log files. Each log spans over 60 time units (i.e., a minute) and contains one event per time point. The number of

$$\Box \downarrow^{cid} c. \downarrow^{tid} t. \downarrow^{sum} a. \; trans(c, t, a) \wedge a > 2000 \rightarrow \Diamond_{[0,3]} \; report(t) \qquad \text{(P1)}$$

$$\Box \downarrow^{cid} c. \downarrow^{tid} t. \downarrow^{sum} a. \; trans(c, t, a) \wedge a > 2000 \rightarrow \Box_{(0,3]} \downarrow^{tid} t'. \downarrow^{sum} a'. \; trans(c, t', a') \rightarrow a' \leq 2000 \qquad \text{(P2)}$$

$$\Box \downarrow^{cid} c. \downarrow^{tid} t. \downarrow^{sum} a. \; trans(c, t, a) \wedge a > 2000 \rightarrow \big((\downarrow^{tid} t'. \downarrow^{sum} a'. \; trans(c, t', a') \rightarrow t = t') \; \mathsf{W} \; report(t) \big) \qquad \text{(P3)}$$

$$\Box \downarrow^{cid} c. \downarrow^{tid} t. \downarrow^{sum} a. \; trans(c, t, a) \wedge a > 2000 \rightarrow \Box_{[0,6]} \downarrow^{tid} t'. \downarrow^{sum} a'. \; trans(c, t', a') \rightarrow \Diamond_{[0,3]} \; report(t') \qquad \text{(P4)}$$

Fig. 2. $\text{MTL}^{\downarrow}$ formulas used in the experimental evaluation.

events in a log is determined by the *event rate*, which is the approximate number of events per time unit (i.e., a second). For each time point i, with $0 \leq i < 60$, the number of events with a timestamp in the time interval $[i, i + 1)$ is randomly chosen within $\pm 10\%$ of the event rate. The events and their parameters are randomly chosen such that the number of violations is in a provided range. For instance, a log with event rate 100 comprises approximately 6000 events. Finally, we use a standard desktop computer with a 2.8 GHz Intel Core i7 CPU, 8 GB of RAM, and the Linux operating system.

In-order Delivery. In our first setting, messages are received ordered by their timestamps and are never lost. Namely, all events of the log are processed in the order of their timestamps. Figure 3(a) shows the running times of our prototype tool for different event rates. Note that each log spans 60 s and a running time below 60 s essentially means that the events in the log could have been processed online. The dashed horizontal lines mark this border.

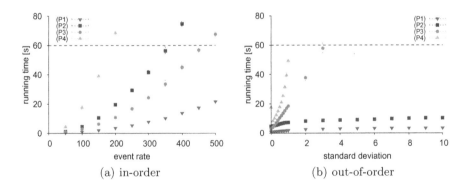

(a) in-order   (b) out-of-order

Fig. 3. Running times (where each data point shows the mean over five logs together with the minimum and maximum, which are very close to the mean).

Out-of-Order Delivery. In our second setting, messages can arrive out of order but they are not lost. We control the degree of message arrival disruption as follows. For the events in a generated log file, we choose their *arrival times*, which provide the order in which the monitor processes them. The arrival time of an event is derived from the event's timestamp by offsetting it by a random delay with respect to the normal distribution with a mean of 10 time units and a chosen standard deviation. In particular, for an event's timestamp τ and for a standard deviation $\sigma > 0$, it holds that an arrival time τ' is in the interval $[\tau + 10 - \sigma, \tau + 10 + \sigma]$ with probability 0.68 and in $[\tau + 10 - 2\sigma, \tau + 10 + 2\sigma]$ with probability 0.95. For the degenerate case $\sigma = 0$, the reordered log is identical to the original log. We remark that the mean value does not impact the event reordering because it does not influence the difference between arrival times.

Figure 3(b) shows the prototype's running times on logs with the fixed event rate 100 for different deviations. For instance, for (P1), the logs are processed in around 1 s when $\sigma = 0$ and in 3.5 s when $\sigma = 10$.

Interpretation. The running times are nonlinear in the event rate for all four formulas. This is expected from Theorem 7. The growth is caused by the data values occurring in the events. A log with a higher event rate contains more different data values and the monitor's state must account for those. As expected, (P1) is the easiest to monitor. It has only one block of freeze quantifiers. Note that (P1)–(P3) have two temporal connectives, where one is the outermost connective $\square$, which is common to all formulas, whereas (P4) has an additional nesting of temporal connectives. The time window is also larger than in (P1) and (P2).

Also expected, the running times increase when messages are received out of order. Again, (P4) is worst. For (P1) and (P2), however, the growth rate decreases for larger standard deviations. This is because, as the standard deviation increases, all the events within the relevant time window for a given time point arrive at the monitor in an order that is increasingly close to the uniformly random one. The running times thus stabilize. Due to the larger time window, this effect does not take place for (P4). The running times for (P3) increase more rapidly than for (P1) and (P2) because of the data values and the "continuation formula" of the derived unbounded temporal connective W ("weak until").

To put the experimental results in perspective, we carried out two additional experiments. First, we conducted similar experiments on formulas with their freeze quantifiers removed and further transformed into propositional formulas; see [7] for details. We make similar observations in the propositional setting. However, in the propositional setting the running times increase linearly with respect to the event rate and logs are processed several orders of magnitude faster. Overall, one pays a price at runtime for the expressivity gain given by the freeze quantifier. Second, we compared our prototype with the MONPOLY tool [3]. MONPOLY's specification language is, like MTL$^{\downarrow}$, a point-based real-time logic. It is richer than MTL$^{\downarrow}$ in that it admits existential and universal quantification over domain elements. However, MONPOLY specifications are syntactically restricted in that temporal future connectives must be bounded (except for the outermost connective $\square$). Thus, (P3) does not have a counterpart in MONPOLY's specification language. MONPOLY handles the counterparts of (P1), (P2), and (P4) significantly faster, up to three orders of magnitude. Comparing the performance of both tools should, however, be taken with a grain of salt. First, MONPOLY only handles the restrictive setting where messages must be received in-order. Second, MONPOLY outputs violations for specifications with (bounded) future only after all events in the relevant time window are available, whereas our prototype outputs verdicts promptly.[3] Finally, while MONPOLY is optimized, our prototype is not.

In summary, our experimental evaluation shows that one pays a high price to handle an expressive specification language together with message delays. Nevertheless, our prototype's performance is sufficient to monitor systems that generate hundreds of events per second, and the prototype can be used as a starting point for a more efficient implementation.

6   Related Work

Runtime verification is a well-established approach for checking at runtime whether a system's execution fulfills a given specification. Various monitoring algorithms exist, e.g., [2,5,11,19]. They differ in the specifications they can handle (some of the specification languages account for data values) and they make different assumptions on the monitored systems. A commonly made assumption is that a monitor has always complete knowledge about the system behavior up to the current time. Only a few runtime-verification approaches exist that relax this assumption. Note that this assumption is, for instance, not met in distributed systems whose components communicate over unreliable channels.

Closest to our work is the runtime-verification approach by Basin et al. [6]. We use the same system model and our monitoring algorithm extends their monitoring algorithm for the propositional real-time logic MTL. Namely, our algorithm handles the more expressive specification language MTL$^{\downarrow}$ and handles data values. Furthermore, we present a semantics for MTL$^{\downarrow}$ that is based on three truth values and uses observations instead of timed words. This enables us to cleanly state correctness requirements and establish stronger correctness guarantees for the monitoring algorithm. Basin et al.'s completeness result [6] is limited in that it assumes that all messages are eventually received. Finally, Basin et al. [6] do not evaluate their monitoring algorithm experimentally.

Colombo and Falcone [12] propose a runtime-verification approach, based on formula rewriting, that also allows the monitor to receive messages out of order. Their approach only handles the propositional temporal logic LTL with the three-valued semantics proposed by Bauer et al. [10]. In a nutshell, their approach unfolds temporal connectives as time progresses and special propositions act as placeholders for subformulas. The subsequent assignment of these placeholders to Boolean truth values triggers the reevaluation and simplification of the formula. Their approach only guarantees soundness but not completeness, since the simplification rules used for formula rewriting are incomplete. Finally, its performance with respect to out-of-order messages is not evaluated.

The monitoring approaches by Garg et al. [14] and Basin et al. [4], both targeting the auditing of policies on system logs, also account for knowledge

---

[3] For instance, for the formula $\Box_{[0,3]}\, p$, if p does not hold at time point i with timestamp τ, then our prototype outputs the corresponding verdict directly after processing the time point i, whereas MONPOLY reports this violation at the first time point with a timestamp larger than $\tau + 3$.

gaps, i.e., logs that may not contain all the actions performed by a system. Both approaches handle rich policy specification languages with first-order quantification and a three-valued semantics. Garg et al.'s approach [14], which is based on formula rewriting, is however, not suited for online use since it does not process logs incrementally. It also only accounts for knowledge gaps in a limited way, namely, the interpretation of a predicate symbol cannot be partially unknown, e.g., for certain time periods. Furthermore, their approach is not complete. Basin et al.'s approach [4], which is based on their prior work [5], can be used online. However, the problem of how to incrementally output verdicts as prior knowledge gaps are resolved is not addressed, and thus it does not deal with out-of-order events. Moreover, the semantics of the specification language handled does not reflect a monitor's partial view about the system behavior. Instead, it is given for infinite data streams that represent system behavior in the limit.

Several dedicated monitoring approaches for distributed systems have been developed [8,20,22]. These approaches only handle less expressive specification languages, namely, the propositional temporal logic LTL or variants thereof. Furthermore, none of them handles message loss or out-of-order delivery of messages, problems that are inherent to such systems because of crashing components and nonuniform delays in message delivery.

A similar extension of MTL with the freeze quantifier is defined by Feng et al. [13]. Their analysis focuses on the computational complexity of the path-checking problem. However, they use a finite trace semantics, which is less suitable for runtime verification. Out-of-order messages are also not considered.

Temporal logics with additional truth values have also been considered in model checking finite-state systems. Closest to our three-valued semantics is the three-valued semantics for LTL by Goidefroid and Piterman [15], which is based on infinite words, not observations (Definition 2). Similar to (T3) of Definition 2, a proposition with the truth value $\perp$ at a position can be refined by t or f. In contrast, their semantics does not support refinements that add and delete letters, cf. (T1) and (T2) of Definition 2.

7   Conclusion

We have presented a runtime-verification approach to checking real-time specifications given as $\text{MTL}^{\downarrow}$ formulas. Our approach handles the practically-relevant setting where messages sent to the monitors can be delayed or lost, and it provides soundness and completeness guarantees. Although our experimental evaluation is promising, our approach does not yet scale to monitor systems that generate thousands or even millions of events per second. This requires additional research, including algorithmic optimizations. We plan to do this in future work, as well as to deploy and evaluate our approach in realistic, large-scale case studies.

Acknowledgments. This work was partly performed within the 5G-ENSURE project (www.5gensure.eu) and received funding from the EU Framework Programme for

Research and Innovation Horizon 2020 under grant agreement no. 671562. David Basin acknowledges support from the Swiss National Science Foundation grant Big Data Monitoring (167162).

References

1. Alur, R., Henzinger, T.A.: Logics and models of real time: a survey. In: Bakker, J.W., Huizing, C., Roever, W.P., Rozenberg, G. (eds.) REX 1991. LNCS, vol. 600, pp. 74–106. Springer, Heidelberg (1992). doi:10.1007/BFb0031988
2. Barringer, H., Goldberg, A., Havelund, K., Sen, K.: Rule-based runtime verification. In: Steffen, B., Levi, G. (eds.) VMCAI 2004. LNCS, vol. 2937, pp. 44–57. Springer, Heidelberg (2004). doi:10.1007/978-3-540-24622-0_5
3. Basin, D., Harvan, M., Klaedtke, F., Zălinescu, E.: MONPOLY: monitoring usage-control policies. In: Khurshid, S., Sen, K. (eds.) RV 2011. LNCS, vol. 7186, pp. 360–364. Springer, Heidelberg (2012). doi:10.1007/978-3-642-29860-8_27
4. Basin, D., Klaedtke, F., Marinovic, S., Zălinescu, E.: Monitoring compliance policies over incomplete and disagreeing logs. In: Qadeer, S., Tasiran, S. (eds.) RV 2012. LNCS, vol. 7687, pp. 151–167. Springer, Heidelberg (2013). doi:10.1007/978-3-642-35632-2_17
5. Basin, D., Klaedtke, F., Müller, S., Zălinescu, E.: Monitoring metric first-order temporal properties. J. ACM 62(2), 15 (2015)
6. Basin, D., Klaedtke, F., Zălinescu, E.: Failure-aware runtime verification of distributed systems. In: Proceedings of 35th International Conference on Foundations of Software Technology and Theoretical Computer Science (FSTTCS), Leibniz International Proceedings in Informatics (LIPIcs), vol. 45, pp. 590–603. Schloss Dagstuhl - Leibniz Center for Informatics (2015)
7. Basin, D., Klaedtke, F., Zălinescu, E.: Runtime verification of temporal properties over out-of-order data streams (2017). Full version of this paper: arXiv.org
8. Bauer, A., Falcone, Y.: Decentralised LTL monitoring. In: Giannakopoulou, D., Méry, D. (eds.) FM 2012. LNCS, vol. 7436, pp. 85–100. Springer, Heidelberg (2012). doi:10.1007/978-3-642-32759-9_10
9. Bauer, A., Küster, J., Vegliach, G.: The ins and outs of first-order runtime verification. Form. Methods Syst. Des. 46(3), 286–316 (2015)
10. Bauer, A., Leucker, M., Schallhart, C.: Comparing LTL semantics for runtime verification. J. Logic Comput. 20(3), 651–674 (2010)
11. Bauer, A., Leucker, M., Schallhart, C.: Runtime verification for LTL and TLTL. ACM Trans. Softw. Eng. Meth. 20(4), 14 (2011)
12. Colombo, C., Falcone, Y.: Organising LTL monitors over distributed systems with a global clock. Form. Methods Syst. Des. 49(1), 109–158 (2016)
13. Feng, S., Lohrey, M., Quaas, K.: Path checking for MTL and TPTL over data words. In: Potapov, I. (ed.) DLT 2015. LNCS, vol. 9168, pp. 326–339. Springer, Cham (2015). doi:10.1007/978-3-319-21500-6_26
14. Garg, D., Jia, L., Datta, A.: Policy auditing over incomplete logs: theory, implementation and applications. In: Proceedings of 18th ACM Conference on Computer and Communications Security (CCS), pp. 151–162. ACM Press (2011)
15. Goidefroid, P., Piterman, N.: LTL generalized model checking revisited. Int. J. Softw. Tools Technol. Trans. 13(6), 571–584 (2011)
16. Henzinger, T.A.: Half-order modal logic: how to prove real-time properties. In: Proceedings of 9th Annual ACM Symposium on Principles of Distributed Computing (PODC), pp. 281–296. ACM Press (1990)

17. Koymans, R.: Specifying real-time properties with metric temporal logic. Real-Time Syst. **2**(4), 255–299 (1990)

18. Maler, O., Nickovic, D.: Monitoring temporal properties of continuous signals. In: Lakhnech, Y., Yovine, S. (eds.) FORMATS/FTRTFT 2004. LNCS, vol. 3253, pp. 152–166. Springer, Heidelberg (2004). doi:10.1007/978-3-540-30206-3_12

19. Meredith, P.O., Jin, D., Griffith, D., Chen, F., Rou, G.: An overview of the MOP runtime verification framework. Int. J. Softw. Tools Technol. Trans. **14**(3), 249–289 (2012)

20. Mostafa, M., Bonakdarbour, B.: Decentralized runtime verification of LTL specifications in distributed systems. In: Proceedings of 29th IEEE International Parallel and Distributed Processing Symposium (IPDPS). IEEE Computer Society (2015)

21. Ouaknine, J., Worrell, J.: On metric temporal logic and faulty turing machines. In: Aceto, L., Ingólfsdóttir, A. (eds.) FoSSaCS 2006. LNCS, vol. 3921, pp. 217–230. Springer, Heidelberg (2006). doi:10.1007/11690634_15

22. Sen, K., Vardhan, A., Agha, G., Rou, G.: Efficient decentralized monitoring of safety in distributed systems. In: Proceedings of 26th International Conference on Software Engineering (ICSE), pp. 418–427. IEEE Computer Society (2004)

Cyber-Physical Systems

Lagrangian Reachabililty

Jacek Cyranka[1], Md. Ariful Islam[2]([✉]), Greg Byrne[3], Paul Jones[4],
Scott A. Smolka[5], and Radu Grosu[6]

[1] Rutgers University, New Brunswick, USA
jcyranka@gmail.com
[2] Carnegie Mellon University, Pittsburgh, USA
mdarifui@cs.cmu.edu
[3] Metron Inc., Reston, VA, USA
gr3g.byrne@gmail.com
[4] US Food and Drug Administration, Silver Spring, USA
paul.jones@fda.hhs.gov
[5] Stony Brook University, New York, USA
sas@cs.stonybrook.edu
[6] Vienna University of Technology, Vienna, Austria
radu.grosu@tuwien.ac.at

Abstract. We introduce LRT, a new Lagrangian-based ReachTube computation algorithm that conservatively approximates the set of reachable states of a nonlinear dynamical system. LRT makes use of the Cauchy-Green stretching factor (SF), which is derived from an over-approximation of the gradient of the solution-flows. The SF measures the discrepancy between two states propagated by the system solution from two initial states lying in a well-defined region, thereby allowing LRT to compute a reachtube with a ball-overestimate in a metric where the computed enclosure is as tight as possible. To evaluate its performance, we implemented a prototype of LRT in C++/Matlab, and ran it on a set of well-established benchmarks. Our results show that LRT compares very favorably with respect to the CAPD and Flow* tools.

1 Introduction

Bounded-time reachability analysis is an essential technique for ensuring the safety of emerging systems, such as cyber-physical systems (CPS) and controlled biological systems (CBS). However, computing the reachable states of CPS and CBS is a very difficult task as these systems are most often nonlinear, and their state-space is uncountably infinite. As such, these systems typically do not admit a closed-form solution that can be exploited during their analysis.

For CPS/CBS, one can therefore only compute point solutions (trajectories) through numerical integration and for predefined inputs. To cover the infinite set of states reachable by the system from an initial region, one needs to conservatively extend (symbolically surround) these pointwise solutions by enclosing

---

J. Cyranka and M.A. Islam—These authors contributed equally to this work.

© Springer International Publishing AG 2017
R. Majumdar and V. Kunčak (Eds.): CAV 2017, Part I, LNCS 10426, pp. 379–400, 2017.
DOI: 10.1007/978-3-319-63387-9_19

them in *reachtubes*. Moreover, the starting regions of these reachtubes have to cover the initial states region.

The class of continuous dynamical systems we are interested in this paper are nonlinear, time-variant ordinary differential equations (ODEs):

$$x'(t) = F(t, x(t)), \tag{1a}$$
$$x(t_0) = x_0, \tag{1b}$$

where $x: \mathbb{R} \to \mathbb{R}^n$. We assume that F is a smooth function, which guarantees short-time existence of solutions. The class of time-variant systems includes the class of time-invariant systems. Time-variant equations may contain additional terms, e.g. an excitation variable, and/or periodic forcing terms.

For a given initial time t_0, set of initial states $\mathcal{X} \subset \mathbb{R}^n$, and time bound $T > t_0$, our goal is to compute conservative *reachtube* of (1), that is, a sequence of time-stamped sets of states $(R_1, t_1), \ldots, (R_k, t_k)$ satisfying:

$$\text{Reach}\left((t_0, \mathcal{X}), [t_{i-1}, t_i]\right) \subset R_i \text{ for } i = 1, \ldots, k,$$

where $\text{Reach}\left((t_0, \mathcal{X}), [t_{i-1}, t_i]\right)$ denotes the set of reachable states of (1) in the interval $[t_{i-1}, t_i]$. Whereas there are many sets satisfying this requirement, of particular interest to us are reasonably tight reachtubes; i.e. reachtubes whose over-approximation is the tightest possible, having in mind the goal of proving that a certain region of the phase space is (un)safe, and avoiding false positives. In practice and for the sake of comparision with other methods, we compute a discrete-time reachtube; as we discuss, a continuous reachtube can be obtained using our algorithm.

Existing tools and techniques for conservative reachtube computation can be classified by the time-space approximation they perform into three categories: (1) Taylor-expansion in time, variational-expansion in space (wrapping-effect reduction) of the solution set (CAPD [4,32,33], VNode-L [25,26], (2) Taylor-expansion in time and space of the solution set (Cosy Infinity [3,21,22], Flow* [5, 6]), and (3) Bloating-factor-based and discrepancy-function-based [10,11]. The last technique computes a conservative reachtube using a *discrepancy function* (DF) that is derived from an over-approximation of the *Jacobian of the vector field* (usually given by the RHS of the differential equations) defining the continuous dynamical system.

This paper proposes an alternative (and orthogonal to [10,11]) technique for computing a conservative reachtube, by using a *stretching factor (SF)* that is derived from an over-approximation of the *gradient of the solution-flows*, also referred to as the *sensitivity matrix* [8,9], and the *deformation tensor*. An illustration of our method is given in Fig. 1. $B_{M_0}(x_0, \delta_0)$ is a well-defined initial region given as a ball in metric space M_0 centered at x_0 of radius δ_0. The SF Λ measures the discrepancy of two states x_0, y_0 in B_{M_0} propagated by the solution flow induced by (1), i.e. $\phi_{t_0}^{t_1}$. We can thus use the SF to bound the infinite set of reachable states at time t_1 with the ball-overestimate $B_{M_1}(\phi_{t_0}^{t_1}(x_0), \delta_1)$ in an appropriate metric (which may differ from the initial M_0), where $\delta_1 = \Lambda \cdot \delta_0$.

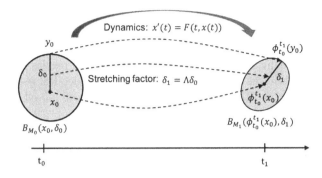

Fig. 1. An overview of LRT. The figure shows one execution step of the LRT described in detail in Sect. 3. The dashed arrows reflect the solution flow ϕ and the evolution of state discrepancy.

Similar to [10], this metric is based on a weighted norm, yielding a tightest-possible enclosure of the reach-set [7,17,19,20]. For two-dimensional system, we present an analytical method to compute M_1, but for higher dimensional system, we solve a semi-definite optimization problem. Analytical formulas derived for 2d case allow for faster computation. We point out that the output provided by LRT can be used to compute a validated bound for the so-called *finite-time Lyapunov exponent* $(FTLE = \frac{1}{T}\ln(SF))$ for a whole set of solutions. FTLE are widely computed in e.g. climate research in order to detect Lagrangian coherent structures.

We call this approach and its associated the LRT, for *Lagrangian Reachtube* computation. The LRT uses analogues of Cauchy-Green deformation tensors (CGD) from finite strain theory (FST) to determine the SF of the solution-flows, after each of its time-step iterations. The LRT algorithm is described thoroughly in Sect. 3.

To compute the gradient of the flows, we currently make use of the CAPD C^1 routine, which propagates the initial ball (box) using interval arithmetic. The CAPD library has been certified to compute a conservative enclosure of the true solution, and it has been used in many peer-reviewed computer proofs of theorems in dynamical systems, including [12,15,31].

To evaluate the LRT's performance, we implemented a prototype in C++/Matlab and ran it on a set of eight benchmarks. Our results show that the LRT compares very favorably to a direct use of CAPD and Flow* (see Sect. 4), while still leaving room for further improvement. In general, we expect the LRT to behave favorably on systems that exhibit long-run stable behavior, such as orbital stability.

We did not compare the LRT with the DF-based tools [10,11], although we would have liked to do this very much. The reason is that the publicly-available DF-prototype has not yet been certified to produce conservative results. Moreover, the prototype only considers time-invariant systems.

The rest of the paper is organized as follows. Section 2 reviews finite-strain theory and the Cauchy-Green-deformation tensor for flows. Section 3 presents the LRT, our main contribution, and proves that it conservatively computes the reachtube of a Cauchy system. Section 4 compares our results to CAPD and Flow* on six benchmarks from [6,10], the forced Van der Pol oscillator (time-variant system) [30], and the Mitchell Schaeffer cardiac cell model [23]. Section 5 offers our concluding remarks and discusses future work.

2   Background on Flow Deformation

In this section we present some background on the LRT. First, in Sect. 2.1 we briefly recall the general FST, as in the LRT we deal with matrices analogous to Cauchy-Green deformation tensors. Second, in Sect. 2.2 we show how the Cauchy-Green deformation tensor can be used to measure discrepancy of two initial states propagated by the flow inducted by Eq. (1).

2.1   Finite Strain Theory and Lagrangian Description of the Flow

In classical continuum mechanics, *finite strain theory (FST)* deals with the deformation of a continuum body in which both rotation and strain can be arbitrarily large. Changes in the configuration of the body are described by a displacement field. Displacement fields relate the initial configuration with the deformed configuration, which can be significantly different. FST has been applied, for example, in stress/deformation analysis of media like elastomers, plastically-deforming materials, and fluids, modeled by constitutive models (see e.g., [13], and the references provided there). In the *Lagrangian* representation, the coordinates describe the deformed configuration (in the material-reference-frame spatial coordinates), whereas in the *Eulerian* representation, the coordinates describe the undeformed configuration (in a fixed-reference-frame spatial coordinates).

Notation. In this section we use the standard notation used in the literature on FST. We use X to denote the position of a particle in the Eulerian coordinates, and x to denote the position of a particle in the Lagrangian coordinates. The Lagrangian coordinates depend on the initial (Eulerian) position, and the time t, so we use $x(X, t)$ to denote the position of a particle in Lagrangian coordinates.

The *displacement field* from the initial configuration to the deformed configuration in Lagrangian coordinates is given by the following equation:

$$u(X, t) = x(X, t) - X. \tag{2}$$

The dependence $\nabla_X u$ of the displacement field $u(X, t)$ on the initial condition X is called the *material displacement gradient tensor*, with

$$\nabla_X u(X, t) = \nabla_X x(X, t) - I, \tag{3}$$

where $\nabla_X x$ is called the *deformation gradient tensor*.

We now investigate how an initial perturbation $X + dX$ in the Eulerian coordinates evolves to the deformed configuration $dx(X + dX, t)$ in Lagrangian coordinates by using (2). This is called a *relative displacement vector:*

$$dx(X + dX, t) = x(X + dX, t) - x(X, t) = u(X + dX, t) + dX - u(X, t),$$

As a consequence, for small dX we obtain the following approximate equality:

$$dx(X + dX, t) \approx u(X + dX, t) - u(X, t). \tag{4}$$

Now let us compute $u(X+dX, t)$ by expressing $du(X+dX, t)$ as with $x(X+dX, t)$ above. One obtains:

$$u(X + dX, t) = u(X, t) + du(X + dX, t) = u(X, t) + \nabla_X u(X + dX, t)dX.$$

Now by replacing $u(X+dX, t)$ in Eq. (4) above, one obtains the following result:

$$dx(X + dX, t) \approx \nabla_X x(X + dX, t)dX.$$

Several rotation-independent tensors have been introduced in the literature. Classical examples include the right Cauchy-Green deformation tensor:

$$C = (\nabla_X x)^T \cdot \nabla_X x. \tag{5}$$

2.2 Cauchy-Green Deformation Tensor for Flows

Notation. By $[x]$ we denote a product of intervals (a box), i.e. a compact and connected set $[x] \subset \mathbb{R}^n$. We will use the same notation for interval matrices. By $\| \cdot \|_2$ we denote the *Euclidean norm*, by $\| \cdot \|_\infty$ we denote the max norm, we use the same notation for the inducted operator norms. Let $B(x, \delta)$ denote the closed ball centered at x with the radius δ. It will be clear from the context in which metric space we consider the ball. By $\phi_{t_0}^{t_1}$ we denote the flow inducted by (1), by $D_x \phi_{t_0}^{t_1}$ we denote the partial derivative in x of the flow with respect to the initial condition, at time t_1, which we call the *gradient of the flow*, also refereed to as the *sensitivity matrix* [8,9].

Let us now relate the finite strain theory presented in Sect. 2.1 to the study of flows inducted by the ODE (1). For expressing deformation in time of a continuum we first consider the set of initial conditions (e.g. a ball), which is being evolved (deformed) in time by the flow ϕ. For the case of flows we have that the positions in Eulerian coordinates are coordinates of the initial condition (denoted here using lower case letters with subscript 0, i.e. x_0, y_0). The equivalent of $x(X, t)$ – the Lagrangian coordinates of X at time t is $\phi_{t_0}^t(x_0)$. Obviously, the equivalent of $u(X, t)$ is $(\phi_{t_0}^t(x_0) - x_0)$, and the deformation gradient $\nabla_X x$ here is just the derivative of the flow with respect to the initial condition $D_x \phi_{t_0}^t$ (sensitivity matrix).

In this section we show that deformation tensors arise in a study of discrepancy of solutions of (1). First, we provide some basic lemmas that we use in the analysis of our reachtube-computation algorithm. We work with the metric spaces that are based on weighted norms. We aim at finding weights, such that the inducted *matrix measures* (also known as *logarithmic norms* for particular cases) [7,17,19,20] provides to be smaller than those in the Euclidean norm for the computed gradients of solutions.

Definition 1. *Given positive-definite symmetric matrix $M \in \mathbb{R}^{n \times n}$ we define the M-norm of $\mathbb{R}^n$ vectors by*

$$\|y\|_M = \sqrt{y^T M y}. \tag{6}$$

Given the decomposition

$$M = C^T C,$$

the matrix norm inducted by (6) is

$$\|A\|_M = \sqrt{\lambda_{max} \left((C^T)^{-1} \cdot A^T \cdot M \cdot A \cdot C^{-1} \right)}, \tag{7}$$

where $\lambda_{max}(\cdot)$ denotes the maximal eigenvalue of the matrix A.

Observe that the square-root is well defined, as $\lambda_{max} > 0$, M is symmetric positive definite, and hence, the matrix $(C^T)^{-1} \cdot A^T \cdot M \cdot A \cdot C^{-1}$ is also symmetric positive definite.

Lemma 1. *Consider the Cauchy problem (1). Let $x_0, y_0 \in \mathbb{R}^n$ be two initial conditions at time t_0. Let $M \in \mathbb{R}^{n \times n}$ be a positive-definite symmetric matrix and $C^T C = M$ be its decomposition. For $t_1 \geq t_0$, it holds that*

$$\|\phi_{t_0}^{t_1}(x_0) - \phi_{t_0}^{t_1}(y_0)\|_M \leq \sqrt{\lambda_{max} \left((C^T)^{-1} D_x \phi_{t_0}^{t_1}(\xi)^T M \, D_x \phi_{t_0}^{t_1}(\xi) C^{-1} \right)} \, \|x_0 - y_0\|_M \tag{8}$$

where $\xi = \omega x_0 + (1 - \omega) y_0$ for some $\omega \in [0, 1]$. For the particular case of the Euclidean norm, (8) takes the form

$$\|\phi_{t_0}^{t_1}(x_0) - \phi_{t_0}^{t_1}(y_0)\|_2 \leq \sqrt{\lambda_{max} \left(\left(D_x \phi_{t_0}^{t_1}(\xi) \right)^T \cdot D_x \phi_{t_0}^{t_1}(\xi) \right)} \, \|x_0 - y_0\|_2. \tag{9}$$

A proof can be found in Appendix A.

Remark 1. Let $\xi \in \mathbb{R}$ be a given vector. Observe that $\left(D_x \phi_{t_0}^{t_1}(\xi) \right)^T \cdot D_x \phi_{t_0}^{t_1}(\xi)$ appearing in (9) is the right *Cauchy-Green deformation tensor* (5) for two given initial vectors x_0 and y_0. We call the value $\sqrt{\lambda_{max}}$ appearing in (9) *Cauchy-Green stretching factor* for given initial vectors x_0 and y_0, which is necessarily positive as the CG deformation tensor is positive definite $\sqrt{\lambda_{max}(\cdot)} > 0$.

Lemma 1 is used when both of the discrepancy of the solutions at time t_1 as well as the initial conditions is measured in the same M-norm. In the practical Lagrangian Reachtube Algorithm the norm used is being changed during the computation. Hence we need another version of Lemma 1, where the norm in which the discrepancy of the initial condition in measured differs from the norm in which the discrepancy of the solutions at time t_1 is measured.

Lemma 2. *Consider the Cauchy problem* (1). *Let* $x_0, y_0 \in \mathbb{R}^n$ *be two initial conditions at time* t_0. *Let* $M_0, M_1 \in \mathbb{R}^{n \times n}$ *be positive-definite symmetric matrices, and* $C_0^T C_0 = M_0$, $C_1^T C_1 = M_1$ *their decompositions respectively. For* $t_1 \geq t_0$, *it holds that*

$$\|\phi_{t_0}^{t_1}(x_0) - \phi_{t_0}^{t_1}(y_0)\|_{M_1} \\ \leq \sqrt{\lambda_{max}\left((C_0^T)^{-1} \cdot \left(D_x \phi_{t_0}^{t_1}(\xi)\right)^T \cdot M_1 \cdot D_x \phi_{t_0}^{t_1}(\xi) \cdot C_0^{-1}\right)} \; \|x_0 - y_0\|_{M_0}, \quad (10)$$

where $\xi = \omega x_0 + (1 - \omega)y_0$ *for some* $\omega \in [0, 1]$.

A proof can be found in Appendix A.

Remark 2. Given a positive-definite symmetric matrix M. We call the value appearing in (10) $(C_0^T)^{-1} \cdot \left(D_x \phi_{t_0}^{t_1}(\xi)\right)^T \cdot M_1 \cdot D_x \phi_{t_0}^{t_1}(\xi) \cdot C_0^{-1}$ as the M_0/M_1-*deformation tensor*, and the value $\sqrt{\lambda_{max}}$ as the M_0/M_1-*stretching factor*.

The idea behind using weighted norms in our approach is that the stretching factor in M-norm (10) is expected to be smaller than that in the Euclidean norm (9). Ultimately, this permits a tighter reachtube computation, whose complete procedure is presented in Sect. 3.3.

3   Lagrangian Reachtube Computation

3.1   Reachtube Computation: Problem-Statement

In this section we provide first some lemmas that we then use to show that our method-and-algorithm produces a conservative output, in the sense that it encloses the set of solutions starting from a set of initial conditions. Precisely, we define what we mean by conservative enclosures.

Definition 2. *Given an initial set* $\mathcal{X}$, *initial time* t_0, *and the target time* $t_1 \geq t_0$. *We call the following compact sets:*

- $\mathcal{W} \subset \mathbb{R}^n$ *a conservative, reach-set enclosure, if* $\phi_{t_0}^{t_1}(x) \in \mathcal{W}$ *for all* $x \in \mathcal{X}$.
- $\mathcal{D} \subset \mathbb{R}^{n \times n}$ *a conservative, gradient enclosure, if* $D_x \phi_{t_0}^{t_1}(x) \in \mathcal{D}$ *for all* $x \in \mathcal{X}$.

Following the notation used in [10], and extending the corresponding definitions to our time variant setting, we introduce the notion of reachability as follows: Given an initial set $\mathcal{X} \subset \mathbb{R}^n$ and a time t_0, we call a state x in $\mathbb{R}^n$ as *reachable* within a time interval $[t_1, t_2]$, if there exists an initial state $x_0 \in \mathcal{X}$ at time t_0 and a time $t \in [t_1, t_2]$, such that $x = \phi_{t_0}^t(x_0)$. The set of all reachable states in the interval $[t_1, t_2]$ is called the *reach set* and is denoted by $\text{Reach}((t_0, \mathcal{X}), [t_1, t_2])$.

Definition 3 ([10] Definition 2.4). *Given an initial set* $\mathcal{X}$, *initial time* t_0, *and a time bound* T, *a* $((t_0, X), T)$-*reachtube of System* (1) *is a sequence of time-stamped sets* $(R_1, t_1), \ldots, (R_k, t_k)$ *satisfying the following:* (1) $t_0 \leq t_1 \leq \cdots \leq t_k = T$, (2) $\text{Reach}((t_0, \mathcal{X}), [t_{i-1}, t_i]) \subset R_i, \forall i = 1, \ldots, k$.

Definition 4. *Whenever the initial set $\mathcal{X}$ and the time horizon T are known from the context we will skip the $(\mathcal{X}, [t_0, T])$ part, and will simply use the name (conservative)* reachtube over-approximation *of the flow defined by* (1).

Observe that we do not address here the question what is the exact structure of the solution set at time t initiating at $\mathcal{X}$. In general it could have, for instance, a fractal structure. We aim at constructing an over-approximation for the solution set, and its gradient, which is amenable for rigorous numeric computations.

In the theorems below we show that the method presented in this paper can be used to construct a reachtube over-approximation $\mathcal{R}$. The theorems below is the foundation of our novel *Lagrangian Reachtube Algorithm (LRT)* presented in Sect. 3.3. In particular, the theorems below provide estimates we use for constructing $\mathcal{R}$. First, we present a theorem for the discrete case.

3.2   Conservative Reachtube Construction

Theorem 1. *Let $t_0 \leq t_1$ be two time points. Let $\phi_{t_0}^{t_1}(x)$ be the solution of* (1) *with the initial condition (t_0, x) at time t_1, let $D_x \phi_{t_0}^{t_1}$ be the gradient of the flow. Let $M_0, M_1 \in \mathbb{R}^{n \times n}$ be positive-definite symmetric matrices, and $C_0^T C_0 = M_0$, $C_1^T C_1 = M_1$ be their decompositions respectively. Let $\mathcal{X} = B_{M_0}(x_0, \delta_0) \subset \mathbb{R}^n$ be a set of initial states for the Cauchy problem* (1) *(ball in M_0-norm with the center at x_0, and radius δ_0). Assume that there exists a compact, conservative enclosure $\mathcal{D} \subset \mathbb{R}^{n \times n}$ for the gradients, such that:*

$$D_x \phi_{t_0}^{t_1}(x) \in \mathcal{D} \text{ for all } x \in \mathcal{X}. \tag{11}$$

Suppose $\Lambda > 0$ is such that:

$$\Lambda \geq \sqrt{\lambda_{max}\left((C_0^T)^{-1} D^T M_1 D C_0^{-1}\right)}, \text{ for all } D \in \mathcal{D}. \tag{12}$$

Then it holds that:

$$\phi_{t_0}^{t_1}(x) \in B_{M_1}(\phi_{t_0}^{t_1}(x_0), \Lambda \cdot \delta_0).$$

Proof. Let x_0 be the center of the ball of initial conditions $\mathcal{X} = B_{M_0}(x_0, \delta_0)$, and let us pick $x \in \mathcal{X}$. From Lemma 4 the discrepancy of the solutions initiating at x_0 and x at time t_1 is bounded in M_1-norm by:

$$\|\phi_{t_0}^{t_1}(x_0) - \phi_{t_0}^{t_1}(x)\|_{M_1} \leq \delta_0 \sqrt{\lambda_{max}\left((C_0^T)^{-1} \cdot \left(D_x \phi_{t_0}^{t_1}(\xi)\right)^T \cdot M_1 \cdot D_x \phi_{t_0}^{t_1}(\xi) \cdot C_0^{-1}\right)},$$

where $\xi = \omega x_0 + (1 - \omega)x$ for some $\omega \in [0, 1]$. Obviously, $\xi \in B_{M_0}(x_0, \delta_0)$. Hence, $D_x \phi_{t_0}^{t_1}(\xi) \in \mathcal{D}$. Moreover, if $\Lambda > 0$ satisfies (12), then

$$\Lambda \geq \sqrt{\lambda_{max}\left((C_0^T)^{-1} \cdot \left(D_x \phi_{t_0}^{t_1}(\xi)\right)^T \cdot M_1 \cdot D_x \phi_{t_0}^{t_1}(\xi) \cdot C_0^{-1}\right)},$$

and $\phi_{t_0}^{t_1}(x) \in B_{M_1}(\phi_{t_0}^{t_1}(x_0), \Lambda \delta_0)$. As x was chosen in an arbitrary way, we are done. $\qquad \square$

The next theorem is the variant of Theorem 1 for obtaining a continuous reachtube.

Theorem 2. *Let $\phi_{t_0}^{t_1}(x)$ be the solution of (1) with the initial condition (t_0, x) at time t_1, let $D_x \phi_{t_0}^{t_1}$ be the gradient of the flow. Let $M_0, M_1 \in \mathbb{R}^{n \times n}$ be positive definite symmetric matrices, and $C_0^T C_0 = M_0$, $C_1^T C_1 = M_1$ be their decompositions respectively. Let $\mathcal{X} = B_{M_0}(x_0, \delta_0) \subset \mathbb{R}^n$ be a set of initial conditions for the Cauchy problem (1) (ball in M_0-norm). Assume that there exists $\{\mathcal{D}_t\}_{t \in [t_0, t_1]}$ – a compact t-parametrized set, such that*

$$\mathcal{D}_t \subset \mathbb{R}^{n \times n} \ for \ t \in [t_0, t_1],$$
$$D_x \phi_{t_0}^t(x) \in \mathcal{D}_t \ for \ all \ x \in \mathcal{X}, \ and \ t \in [t_0, t_1].$$

If $\Lambda > 0$ is such that for all $D \colon D \in \mathcal{D}_t$ for some $t \in [t_0, t_1]$

$$\Lambda \geq \sqrt{\lambda_{max}\left((C_0^T)^{-1} D^T M_1 D C_0^{-1}\right)}$$

Then for all $t \in [t_0, t_1]$ it holds that

$$\phi_{t_0}^t(x) \in B_{M_1}(\phi_{t_0}^t(x_0), \Lambda \cdot \delta_0). \tag{13}$$

Proof. It follows from the proof of Theorem 1 applied to all times $t \in [t_0, t_1]$. □

Corollary 1. *Let $T \geq t_0$. Assume that that there exists $\{\mathcal{D}_t\}_{t \in [t_0, T]}$ – a compact t-parametrized set, such that*

$$\mathcal{D}_t \subset \mathbb{R}^{n \times n} \ for \ t \in [t_0, T],$$
$$D_x \phi_{t_0}^t(x) \in \mathcal{D}_t \ for \ all \ x \in \mathcal{X}, \ and \ t \in [t_0, T].$$

Then the existence of a $((t_0, X), T)$-reachtube of the system described in Eq. (1) in sense of Definition 3, i.e. a sequence of time-stamped sets $(R_1, t_1), \ldots, (R_k, t_k)$ is provided by an application of Lemma 2. We provide an algorithm computing the reachtube in Sect. 3.3.

Proof. Immediate application of Theorem 2 shows that if the first segment (R_1, t_1) is defined

$$(R_1, t_1) := \bigcup_{t \in [t_0, t_1]} B_{M_1}(\phi_{t_0}^t(x_0), \Lambda \cdot \delta_0),$$

then it satisfies

$$\text{Reach}((t_0, \mathcal{X}), [t_0, t_1]) \subset (R_1, t_1),$$

which is exactly provided by (13). The j-th segment (R_j, t_j) for $j = 2, \ldots, k$ is obtained by replacing in Theorem 2 the time interval $[t_0, t_1]$ with the interval $[t_{j-1}, t_j]$ (Observe that the norm may be different in each step). □

3.3 LRT: A Rigorous Lagrangian Computation Algorithm

We now present a complete description of our algorithm. In the next section we prove its correctness. First let us comment on how in practice we compute a representable enclosure for the gradients (11).

- First, given an initial ball $B_{M_0}(x_0, \delta_0)$ we compute its representable over-approximation, i.e., a product of intervals (a box in canonical coordinates $[X] \subset \mathbb{R}^n$), such that $B_{M_0}(x_0, \delta_0) \subset [X]$.
- Next, using the C^1-*CAPD algorithm* [32,33] all trajectories initiating in $[X]$ are rigorously propagated forward in time, in order to compute a conservative enclosure for $\left\{ D_x \phi_{t_0}^{t_1}(\xi) \mid \xi \in [X] \right\}$, the gradients. We use the notation $[D_x \phi_{t_0}^{t_1}([X])] \subset \mathbb{R}^{n \times n}$, to denote a representable enclosure (an interval matrix) for the set of gradients $\left\{ D_x \phi_{t_0}^{t_1}(\xi) \mid \xi \in [X] \right\}$.

The norm of an interval vector $\|[x]\|$ is defined as the supremum of the norms of all vectors within the bounds $[x]$. For an interval set $[x] \subset \mathbb{R}^n$ we denote by $\mathbb{R}^n \supset B_M([x], r) := \bigcup_{x \in [x]} B_M(x, r)$, the union of the balls in M-norm of radius r having the center in $[x]$. Each product of two interval matrices is overestimated by using the interval-arithmetic operations.

Definition 5. *We will call the* rigorous tool *the C^1-CAPD algorithm, which is currently used to generate conservative enclosures for the gradient in the LRT.*

The output of the LRT are discrete-time reachtube over-approximation cross-sections $\{t_0, t_1, \ldots, t_k\}$, $t_k = t_0 + kT$, i.e., reachtube over-approximations $B_{M_j}(x_j, \delta_j)$ of the flow induced by (1) at time t_j. We note that the algorithm can be easily modified to provide a validated bounds for the finite-time Laypunov exponent. We use the discrete-time output for the sake of comparison. However, as a byproduct, a continuous reachtube over-approximation is obtained by means of *rough enclosures* (Fig. 2) produced by the rigorous tool used and by applying Theorem 2. The implementation details of the algorithm can be found in Sect. 4.

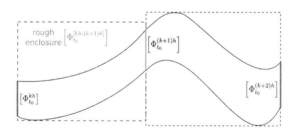

Fig. 2. Fine bounds provided at equally spaced time steps (colored), and coarse bounds provided for the intermediate times by the rough enclosure (dotted boxes). (Color figure online)

We are now ready to give the formal description of the LRT: (1) its inputs, (2) its outputs, and (3) its computation.

LRT: The Lagrangian Reachtube Algorithm
Input:

- *ODEs* (1): time-variant ordinary differential equations,
- T: time horizon, t_0: initial time, k: number of steps, $h = T/k$: time step
- M_0: initial positive-definite symmetric matrix defining the norm (6),
- $[x_0] \subset \mathbb{R}^n$: the initial bounds for the position of the center of the ball at t_0,
- $\delta_0 > 0$: the radius of the ball (in M_0 norm) about x_0 at t_0.

Output:

- $\{[x_j]\}_{j=1}^k \subset \mathbb{R}^{n \times k}$: interval enclosures for ball centers x_j at time $t_0 + jh$,
- $\{M_j\}_{j=1}^k$: norms defining metric spaces for the ball enclosures,
- $\{\delta_j\}_{j=1}^k \in \mathbb{R}_+^k$: radiuses of the ball enclosures at x_j for $j = 1, \ldots, k^1$.

Begin LRT

1. Set $t_1 = t_0 + h$. Propagate the center of the ball $[x_0]$ forward in time by the time-step h, using the rigorous tool. The result is a conservative enclosure for the solutions $[\phi_{t_0}^{t_1}([x_0])]$ and the gradients $[D_x \phi_{t_0}^{t_1}([x_0])]$.
2. Choose a matrix $D \in [D_x \phi_{t_0}^{t_1}([x_0])]$, and compute a symmetric positive-definite matrix M_1, and its decomposition $M_1 = C_1^T C_1$, such that, it minimizes the stretching factor for D. In other words, it holds that:

$$\sqrt{\lambda_{max}\left((C_1^T)^{-1}D^T M_1 D C_1^{-1}\right)} \leq \sqrt{\lambda_{max}\left((\widetilde{C}^T)^{-1}D^T \widetilde{M} D \widetilde{C}^{-1}\right)}, \quad (14)$$

for all positive-definite symmetric matrices $\widetilde{M}$. In the actual code we find the minimum with some resolution, i.e., we compute M_1, such that it is close to the optimal in the sense of (18), using the procedure presented in Subsect. 3.6.
3. Decide whether to change the norm of the ball enclosure from M_0 to M_1 (if it leads to a smaller stretching factor). If the norm is to be changed keep M_1 as it is, otherwise $M_1 = M_0$,
4. Compute an over-approximation for $B_{M_0}([x_0], \delta_0)$, which is representable in the rigorous tool employed by the LRT, and can be used as input to propagate forward in time all solutions initiating in $B_{M_0}([x_0], \delta_0)$. This is a product of intervals in canonical coordinates $[X] \subset \mathbb{R}^n$, such that:

$$B_{M_0}([x_0], \delta_0) \subset [X].$$

We compute the over-approximation using the interval arithmetic expression:

$$C_0^{-1}(C_0 \cdot [x_0] + [-\delta_0, \delta_0]^n)$$

---

[1] Observe that the radius is valid for the M_j norm, $B_{M_j}([x_j], \delta_j) \subset \mathbb{R}^n$ for $j = 1, \ldots, k$ is a conservative output, i.e. $B_{M_j}([x_j], \delta_j)$ is an over-approximation for the set of states reachable at time t_1 starting from any state (t_0, x), such that $x \in \mathcal{X}$

$$\text{Reach}((t_0, \mathcal{X}), t_j) \subset B_{M_j}([x_j], \delta_j), \text{ for } j = 1, \ldots, k.$$

5. Rigorously propagate $[X]$ forward in time, using the rigorous tool over the time interval $[t_0, t_1]$. The result is a continuous reachtube, providing bounds for $[\Phi_{t_0}^t([X])]$, and $[D_x\Phi_{t_0}^t([X])]$ for all $t \in [t_0, t_1]$. We employ an integration algorithm with a fixed time-step h. As a consequence *"fine"* bounds are obtained for $t = t_1$. We denote those bounds by:

$$[\phi_{t_0}^{t_1}([X])], \quad [D_x\phi_{t_0}^{t_1}([X])].$$

We remark that for the intermediate time-bounds, i.e., for:

$$[\phi_{t_0}^t([X])], \text{ for } t \in (t_0, t_1), \tag{15}$$

the so-called *rough enclosures* can be used. These provide *coarse* bounds, as graphically illustrated in Fig. 2 in the appendix.

6. Compute interval matrix bounds for the M_0/M_1 Cauchy-Green deformation tensors:

$$\left[\left((C_0^T)^{-1} \cdot [D_x\phi_{t_0}^{t_1}([X])]\right)^T \cdot C_1^T\right) \cdot \left(C_1 \cdot [D_x\phi_{t_0}^{t_1}([X])] \cdot C_0^{-1}\right)\right], \tag{16}$$

where C_0^T, C_0 are s.t. $C_0^T C_0 = M_0$, and C_1^T, C_1 are s.t. $C_1^T C^T = M_1$. The interval matrix operations are executed in the order given by the brackets.

7. Compute a value $\Lambda > 0$ (M_0/M_1 stretching factor) as an upper bound for the square-root of the maximal eigenvalue of each (symmetric) matrix in (16):

$$\Lambda \geq \sqrt{\lambda_{max}(C)},$$

$$\text{for all } C \in \left[\left((C_0^T)^{-1} \cdot [D_x\phi_{t_0}^{t_1}([X])]\right)^T \cdot C_1^T\right) \cdot \left(C_1 \cdot [D_x\phi_{t_0}^{t_1}([X])] \cdot C_0^{-1}\right)\right].$$

This quantity Λ can be used for the purpose of computation of validated bound for the *finite-time Lyapunov exponent*

$$FTLE(B_{M_0}([x_0], \delta_0)) = \frac{1}{t_1 - t_0} \ln(\Lambda_{prev} \cdot \Lambda),$$

where Λ_{prev} is the product of all stretching factors computed in previous steps.

8. Compute the new radius for the ball at time $t_1 = t_0 + h$:

$$\delta(t_1) = \Lambda \cdot \delta(t_0),$$

9. Set the new center of the ball at time t_1 as follows:

$$[x_1] = [\phi_{t_0}^{t_1}([x_0])].$$

10. Set the initial time to t_1, the bounds for the initial center of the ball to $[x_1]$, the current norm to M_1, the radius in M_1-norm to $\delta_1 = \Lambda \cdot \delta_0$, and the ball enclosure for the set of initial states to $B_{M_1}([x_1], \Lambda \cdot \delta(t_0))$. If $t_1 \geq T$ terminate. Otherwise go back to 1.

End LRT

3.4   LRT-Algorithm Correctness Proof

In this section we provide a proof that the LRT, our new reachtube-computation algorithm, is an overapproximation of the behavior of the system described by Eq. (1). This main result is captured by the following theorem.

Theorem 3 (LRT-Conservativity). *Assume that the rigorous tool used in the Lagrangian Reachtube Algorithm (LRT) produces conservative gradient enclosures for system (1) in the sense of Definition 2, and it guarantees the existence of the solutions within time intervals. Assume also that the LRT terminates on the provided inputs.*

Then, the output of the LRT is a conservative reachtube over-approximation of (1) at times $\{t_j\}_{j=0}^k$, that is:

$$Reach((t_0, \mathcal{X}), t_j) \subset B_{M_j}([x_j], \delta_j), \text{ for } j = 1, \ldots, k,$$

bounded solutions exists for all intermediate times $t \in (t_j, t_{j+1})$.

Proof. Let $\mathcal{X} = B_{M_0}([x_0], \delta_0)$ be a ball enclosure for the set of initial states. Without loosing generality we analyze the first step of the algorithm. The same argument applies to the consecutive steps (with the initial condition changed appropriately, as explained in the last step of the algorithm).

The representable enclosure $[X] \subset \mathbb{R}^n$ (product of intervals in canonical coordinates) computed in Step 4 satisfies $B_{M_0}([x_0], \delta_0) \subset [X]$. By the assumption the rigorous-tool used produces conservative enclosures for the gradient of the flow induced by ODEs (1). Hence, as the set $[X]$ containing $B_{M_0}([x_0], \delta_0)$ is the input to the rigorous forward-time integration procedure in Step 5, for the gradient enclosure $[D_x\phi_{t_0}^{t_1}([X])]$ computed in Step 5, it holds that

$$\left\{ D_x\phi_{t_0}^{t_1}(x) \text{ for all } x \in \mathcal{X} \right\} \subset [D_x\phi_{t_0}^{t_1}([X])].$$

Therefore, the set $[D_x\phi_{t_0}^{t_1}([X])]$ can be interpreted as the set $\mathcal{D}$, i.e., the compact set containing all gradients of the solution at time t_1 with initial condition in $B_{M_0}([x_0], \delta_0)$ appearing in Theorem 1, see (11). As a consequence, the value Λ computed in Step 7 satisfies the following inequality:

$$\Lambda \geq \sqrt{\lambda_{max}\left((C_1^T)^{-1}D^T M_0 D C_1^{-1}\right)}, \text{ for all } D \in \mathcal{D}.$$

From Theorem 2 it follows that:

$$\phi_{t_0}^{t_1}(x) \in B_{M_1}(\phi_{t_0}^{t_1}([x_0]), \Lambda \cdot \delta(t_0)) \text{ for all } x \in \mathcal{X},$$

which implies that:

$$Reach((t_0, \mathcal{X}), t_1) \subset B_{M_1}([\phi_{t_0}^{t_1}([x_0])], \Lambda \cdot \delta(t_0))$$

which proves our overapproximation (conservativity) claim. Existence of the solutions for all times $t \in (t_0, t_1)$ is guaranteed by the assumption about the rigorous tool (in the step 5 of the LRT algorithm we use rough enclosures, see Fig. 2). □

3.5   Wrapping Effect in the Algorithm

A very important precision-loss issue of conservative approximations, and therefore of validated methods for ODEs, is the *wrapping effect*. This occurs when a set of states is wrapped (conservatively enclosed) within a box defined in a particular norm. The weighted M-norms technique the LRT uses (instead of the standard Euclidean norm) is a way of reducing the effect of wrapping. More precisely, in Step 7 of every iteration, the LRT finds an appropriate norm which minimizes the stretching factor computed from the set of Cauchy-Green deformation tensors.

However, there are other sources of the wrapping effect in the algorithm. The discrete reachtube bounds are in a form of a ball in appropriate metric space, which is an ellipsoidal set in canonical coordinates, see example on Fig. 3(a). In Step 4 of the LRT algorithm, a representable enclosure in canonical coordinates for the ellipsoidal reachtube over-approximation is computed. When the ellipsoidal set is being directly wrapped into a box in canonical coordinates (how it is done in the algorithm currently), the wrapping effect is considerably larger than when the ellipsoidal set is wrapped into a rectangular set reflecting the eigencoordinates. We illustrate the wrapping effect using the following weighted norm (taken from one of our experiments):

$$M = \begin{bmatrix} 7 & -9.5 \\ -9.5 & 19 \end{bmatrix} \tag{17}$$

Figure 3 shows the computation of enclosures for a ball represented in the weighted norm given by M. It is clear from Fig. 1(c) that the box enclosure of the ball in the eigen-coordinates (blue rectangle) is much tighter than the box enclosure of it in the canonical coordinates (green square).

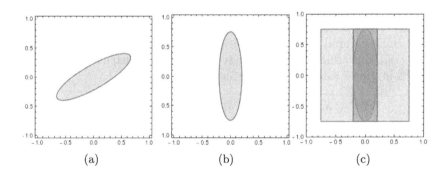

(a)   (b)   (c)

Fig. 3. (a) A ball in the weighted norm given by M of radius 1 (the ellipsoidal set). (b) The ellipsoidal set in its eigen-coordinates (unrotated). (c) Wrapping the ellipsoidal set in a box: blue rectangle in eigen-coordinates and green square in canonical-coordinates. (Color figure online)

Step 6 of the LRT is another place where reducing the wrapping effect has the potential to considerably increase the precision of the LRT. This step computes the product of interval matrices, which results in large overapproximations for wide-intervals matrices. In fact, in the experiments considered in Sect. 4, if the initial-ball radius is large, we observed that the overestimate of the stretching factor tends to worsen the LRT performance in reachtube construction, when compared to a direct application of CAPD and Flow*. We plan to find workarounds for this problem. One possible solution would be to use matrix decomposition, and compute the eigenvalues of the matrix by using this decomposition.

3.6   Direct Computation of the Optimal M-norm

The computation of the optimal M-norm enables the estimation of the streching factor. Step 7 of the LRT finds norm M_1 and decomposes it as $M_1 = C_1^T C_1$, such that, for a gradient matrix D the following inequality holds for all positive-definite symmetric matrices $\widetilde{M}$:

$$\sqrt{\lambda_{max}\left((C_1^T)^{-1}D^T M_1 DC_1^{-1}\right)} \le \sqrt{\lambda_{max}\left((\widetilde{C}^T)^{-1}D^T \widetilde{M} D\widetilde{C}^{-1}\right)}, \qquad (18)$$

Below we illustrate how to compute M_1 for 2D systems. This can be generalized to higher-dimensional systems.

(I) D has complex conjugate eigenvalues $\lambda = \alpha \pm \mathrm{i}\beta$. In this case $w \pm iv$ is the associated pair of complex conjugate eigenvectors, where $w, v \in \mathbb{R}^2$. Define:

$$C = \begin{bmatrix} w & v \end{bmatrix}^{-1}$$

As a consequence we have the following equations:

$$CDC^{-1} = \begin{bmatrix} \alpha & \beta \\ -\beta & \alpha \end{bmatrix}, \text{ and } (C^T)^{-1}D^T C^T = \begin{bmatrix} \alpha & -\beta \\ \beta & \alpha \end{bmatrix},$$

Thus, one obtains the following results:

$$(C^T)^{-1}D^T MAC^{-1} = ((C^T)^{-1}D^T C^T)(CDC^{-1}) = \begin{bmatrix} \alpha^2 + \beta^2 & 0 \\ 0 & \alpha^2 + \beta^2 \end{bmatrix},$$

Clearly, one has that:

$$\lambda_{max}((C^T)^{-1}D^T MDC^{-1}) = \alpha^2 + \beta^2.$$

As the eigenvalues of $(C^T)^{-1}D^T MDC^{-1}$ are equal, it follows from the identity of the determinants that the inequality below holds for any $\widetilde{M} = \widetilde{C}^T \widetilde{C}$:

$$\lambda_{max}((C^T)^{-1}D^T MDC^{-1}) \le \lambda_{max}((\widetilde{C}^T)^{-1}D^T \widetilde{M} D\widetilde{C}^{-1})$$

(II) D has two distinct real eigenvalues $\lambda_1 \ne \lambda_2$. In this case we do not find a positive-definite symmetric matrix. However, we can find a rotation matrix, defining coordinates in which the stretching factor is smaller than in canonical coordinates (M-norm). Let $B \in \mathbb{R}^{2 \times 2}$ be the eigenvectors matrix of D. Denote:

$$B^{-1}DB = \widetilde{D} = \begin{bmatrix} \lambda_1 & 0 \\ 0 & \lambda_2 \end{bmatrix}.$$

Let R be the rotation matrix

$$R = \begin{bmatrix} c & -s \\ s & c \end{bmatrix}, \ c, s \neq 0, \text{ hence, } R^{-1}\widetilde{D}R = \begin{bmatrix} \frac{\lambda_1 c^2 + \lambda_2 s^2}{c^2 + s^2} & \frac{(\lambda_1 - \lambda_2)cs}{c^2 + s^2} \\ -\frac{(\lambda_1 - \lambda_2)cs}{c^2 + s^2} & \frac{\lambda_1 c^2 + \lambda_2 s^2}{c^2 + s^2} \end{bmatrix}.$$

For $s, c = 1$ we have $R^T \widetilde{D}^T (R^T)^{-1} R^{-1} \widetilde{D} R = \begin{bmatrix} \left(\frac{\lambda_1 + \lambda_2}{2}\right)^2 & 0 \\ 0 & \left(\frac{\lambda_1 + \lambda_2}{2}\right)^2 \end{bmatrix}.$

Therefore, we may set $C = (BR)^{-1}$, which for $\lambda_1 < \lambda_2$ results in $\lambda_{max}(C^T D^T (C^T)^{-1} C^{-1} DC) < \lambda_{max}(D^T D)$, because $\left(\frac{\lambda_1 + \lambda_2}{2}\right)^2 < \lambda_2^2$.

(III) $D \in \mathbb{R}^{n \times n}$, where $n > 2$. In this case we call the Matlab engine part of our code. Precisely, we use the external linear-optimization packages [16,24]. We initially set $\gamma = (\lambda_1 \lambda_2 \cdots \lambda_n)^{1/n}$. Then, using the optimization package, we try to find M_1 and its decomposition, such that:

$$\sqrt{\lambda_{max}\left((C_1^T)^{-1} D^T M_1 D C_1^{-1}\right)} \leq \gamma, \tag{19}$$

If we are not successful, we increase γ until an M_1 satisfying (19) is found.

4   Implementation and Experimental Evaluation

Prototype Implementation. Our implementation is based on interval arithmetic, i.e. all variables used in the algorithm are over intervals, and all computations performed are executed using interval arithmetic. The main procedure is implemented in C++, which includes header files for the CAPD tool (implemented in C++ as well) to compute rigorous enclosures for the center of the ball at time t_1 in step 1, and for the gradient of the flow at time t_1 in step 5 of the LRT algorithm (see Sect. 3.3).

To compute the optimal norm and its decomposition for dimensions higher than 2 in step 2 of the LRT algorithm, we solve a semidefinite optimization problem. We found it convenient to use dedicated Matlab packages for that purpose [16,24], in particular for Case 3 in Sect. 3.6.

To compute an upper bound Λ for the square-root of the maximal eigenvalue of all symmetric matrices in some interval bounds, we used the VERSOFT package [27,28] implemented in Intlab [29]. To combine C++ and the Matlab/Intlab part of the implementation, we use an engine that allows one to call Matlab code within C++ using a special makefile. The source code, numerical data, and readme file describing compilation procedure for LRT can be found online [14].

We remark that the current implementation is a proof of concept; in particular, it is not optimized in terms of the runtime—a direct CAPD implementation is an order of magnitude faster. We will investigate ways of significantly improving the runtime of the implementation in future work.

Experimental Evaluation. We compare the results obtained by LRT with direct CAPD and Flow* on a set of standard benchmarks [6,10]: the Brusselator, inverse-time Van der Pol oscillator, the Lorenz equations [18], a robot arm model [2], a 7-dimensional biological model [10], and a 12-dimensional polynomial [1] system. Additionally, we consider the forced Van der Pol oscillator [30] (a time-variant system), and the Mitchell Schaeffer [23] cardiac cell model.

Our results are given in Table 1, and were obtained on a Ubuntu 14.04 LTS machine, with an Intel Core i7-4770 CPU 3.40 GHz x 8 processor and 16 GB memory. The results presented in the columns labeled *(direct) CAPD* and *Flow** were obtained using the CAPD software package and Flow*, respectively. The internal parameters used in the codes can be checked online [14]. The comparison metric that we chose is ratio of the final and initial volume, and ratio of the average and initial volume. We compute directly volumes of the reachtube over-approximations in form of rectangular sets obtained using CAPD, and Flow* software. Whereas, the volumes of the reachtube over-approximations obtained using the LRT algorithm are approximated by the volumes of the tightest rectangular enclosure of the ellipsoidal set, as illustrated on Fig. 3(c). The results in $nLRT$ column were obtained using a naive implementation of the LRT algorithm, in which the metric space is chosen to be globally Euclidean, i.e., $M_0 = M_1 = \cdots = M_k = Id$. For MS model the initial condition (i.c.) is in stable regime. For Lorenz i.c. is a period 2 unstable periodic orbit. For all the other benchmark equations the initial condition was chosen as in [10].

Some interesting observations about our experiments are as follows. Figure 4 illustrates that the volumes of the LRT reachtube of the forced Van der Pol oscillator increase significantly for some initial time-steps compared to CAPD reachtube (nevertheless reduce in the long run). This initial increase is related

Table 1. Performance comparison with Flow* and CAPD. We use the following abbreviations: B(2)-Brusselator, I(2)-Inverse Van der Pol oscillator, L(3)-Lorenz attractor, F(2)-Forced Van der Pol oscillator, M(2)-Mitchell Schaeffer cardiac cell model, R(4)-Robot arm, O(7)-Biology model, A(12)-Polynomial system (number inside parenthesis denotes dimension). T: time horizon, dt: time step, ID: initial diameter in each dimension, (F/I)V: ratio of final and initial volume, (A/I)V: ratio of average and initial volume. NA: Not applicable, Fail: Volume blow-up.

BM	dt	T	ID	LRT		Flow*		(direct) CAPD		nLRT	
				(F/I)V	(A/I)V	(F/I)V	(A/I)V	(F/I)V	(A/I)V	(F/I)V	(A/I)V
B(2)	0.01	20	0.02	**7.7e−5**	**0.09**	7.9e−5	0.15	Fail	Fail	Fail	Fail
I(2)	0.01	20	0.02	**4.3e−9**	**0.09**	5e−9	0.12	7.4e−9	0.10	1.45	1.31
L(3)	0.001	2	1.4e−6	1.6e5	9.0e3	2.1e13	7.1e12	**4.5e4**	**1.7e3**	1.2e22	4.9e19
F(2)	0.01	40	2e−3	**1.2e−42**	1.01	NA	NA	6.86e−4	**0.18**	5.64e7	3.21e5
M(2)	0.001	4	2e−3	**0.006**	**0.22**	0.29	0.54	0.29	0.52	4.01	2.24
R(4)	0.01	20	1e−2	**2.2e−19**	**0.07**	2.4e−15	0.31	2.9e−11	0.23	Fail	Fail
O(7)	0.01	4	2e−4	**71.08**	**34.35**	272	5.1e4	4.3e3	620	Fail	Fail
P(12))	5e−4	0.1	0.01	**5.25**	**4.76**	290	64.6	280	62.4	19.4	6.2

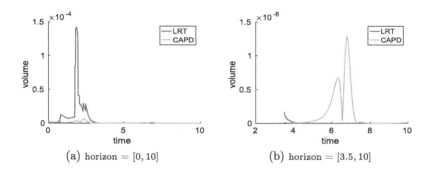

(a) horizon = [0, 10]   (b) horizon = [3.5, 10]

Fig. 4. Volume comparison for forced Van der Pol Oscillator.

to the computation of new coordinates, which are significantly different from the previous coordinates, resulting in a large stretching factor in step 7 of the LRT algorithm. Namely, we observed that it happens when the coordinates are switched from Case II to Case I, as presented in Sect. 3.6. We, however, observe that this does not happen in the system like MS cardiac model (see Fig. 5(a)). We believe those large increases of stretching factors in systems like fVDP can be avoided by smarter choices of the norms. We will further investigate those possibilities in future work.

Table 1 shows that LRT does not perform well for Lorentz attractor compared to CAPD (see also Fig. 5(b)), as the CAPD tool is current state of the art for such chaotic systems. LRT, however, performs much better than Flow* for this example. In all other examples, the LRT algorithm behaves favorably (outputs tighter reachtube, compare (F/I)V) in the long run.

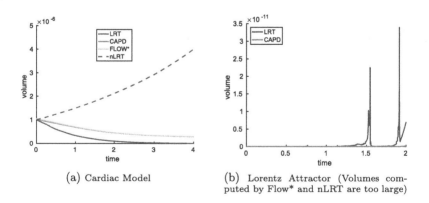

(a) Cardiac Model   (b) Lorentz Attractor (Volumes computed by Flow* and nLRT are too large)

Fig. 5. Volume comparison in two important benchmarks

5   Conclusions

We presented LRT, a rigorous procedure for computing ReachTube overapproximations based on Cauchy-Green stretching factor computation, in Lagrangian coordinates. We plan to pursue further research on our algorithm. One appealing possibility is to extend LRT to hybrid systems widely used in research on cardiac dynamics, and many other fields of study.

We also plan to implement LRT with forward-in-time integration and conservative-enclosures computation of the gradient, by just using a simple independent code (instead of CAPD). By such a code we mean a rigorous integration procedure based, for example, on the Taylor's method. This code would directly compute an interval enclosure for the Cauchy-Green deformation tensors in an appropriate metric space. It would then be interesting to compare the wrapping-reduction performance of such a code with the procedure described above.

Acknowledgments. Research supported in part by the following grants: NSF IIS-1447549, NSF CPS-1446832, NSF CPS-1446725, NSF CNS-1445770, NSF CNS-1430010, AFOSR FA9550-14-1-0261 and ONR N00014-13-1-0090.

A   Proofs of the Lemmas in Sect. 2

Lemma 3. *Consider the Cauchy problem (1). Let $x_0, y_0 \in \mathbb{R}^n$ be two initial conditions at time t_0. Let $M \in \mathbb{R}^{n \times n}$ be a positive-definite symmetric matrix and $C^T C = M$ be its decomposition. For $t_1 \geq t_0$, it holds that*

$$\|\phi_{t_0}^{t_1}(x_0) - \phi_{t_0}^{t_1}(y_0)\|_M \leq \sqrt{\hat{\lambda}\left((C^T)^{-1}\left(D_x\phi_{t_0}^{t_1}(\xi)\right)^T M \, D_x\phi_{t_0}^{t_1}(\xi)C^{-1}\right)} \, \|x_0 - y_0\|_M$$

where $\xi = \omega x_0 + (1 - \omega)y_0$ for some $\omega \in [0, 1]$. For the particular case of the Euclidean norm, (8) takes the form

$$\|\phi_{t_0}^{t_1}(x_0) - \phi_{t_0}^{t_1}(y_0)\|_2 \leq \sqrt{\lambda_{max}\left(\left(D_x\phi_{t_0}^{t_1}(\xi)\right)^T \cdot D_x\phi_{t_0}^{t_1}(\xi)\right)} \, \|x_0 - y_0\|_2.$$

Proof. Let $\xi(\omega) = \omega x_0 + (1 - \omega)y_0$. From

$$\int_0^1 D_x\phi_{t_0}^{t_1}(\xi(\omega)) \, d\omega = \frac{1}{x_0 - y_0}\left(\phi_{t_0}^{t_1}(x_0) - \phi_{t_0}^{t_1}(y_0)\right),$$

and the well known mean value theorem for integrals, it holds that

$$\phi_{t_0}^{t_1}(x_0) - \phi_{t_0}^{t_1}(y_0) = D_x\phi_{t_0}^{t_1}(\hat{\xi})(x_0 - y_0)$$

for some $\hat{\omega} \in [0, 1]$, $\xi(\hat{\omega}) = \hat{\xi}$. From taking norms in above equation we obtain

$$\|\phi_{t_0}^{t_1}(x_0) - \phi_{t_0}^{t_1}(y_0)\| = \|D_x\phi_{t_0}^{t_1}(\hat{\xi})(x_0 - y_0)\| \leq \|D_x\phi_{t_0}^{t_1}(\hat{\xi})\|\|x_0 - y_0\|.$$

Replacing $\|D_x\phi_{t_0}^{t_1}(\hat{\xi})\|_2$ with the inducted Euclidean matrix norm we obtain (9). If we use the weighted M-norm (6) we have for the matrix norm (7)

$$\|\phi_{t_0}^{t_1}(x_0)-\phi_{t_0}^{t_1}(y_0)\|_M \le \sqrt{\lambda_{max}((C^T)^{-1}\left(D_x\phi_{t_0}^{t_1}(\hat{\xi})\right)^T M\, D_x\phi_{t_0}^{t_1}(\hat{\xi})C^{-1})}\,\|x_0-y_0\|_M$$

$\square$

Lemma 4. *Consider the Cauchy problem* (1). *Let* $x_0, y_0 \in \mathbb{R}^n$ *be two initial conditions at time* t_0. *Let* $M_0, M_1 \in \mathbb{R}^{n\times n}$ *be positive-definite symmetric matrices, and* $C_0^T C_0 = M_0$, $C_1^T C_1 = M_1$ *their decompositions respectively. For* $t_1 \ge t_0$, *it holds that*

$$\|\phi_{t_0}^{t_1}(x_0) - \phi_{t_0}^{t_1}(y_0)\|_{M_1}$$
$$\le \sqrt{\lambda_{max}\left((C_0^T)^{-1}\cdot\left(D_x\phi_{t_0}^{t_1}(\xi)\right)^T\cdot M_1\cdot D_x\phi_{t_0}^{t_1}(\xi)\cdot C_0^{-1}\right)}\,\|x_0-y_0\|_{M_0},$$

where $\xi = \omega x_0 + (1-\omega)y_0$ *for some* $\omega \in [0,1]$.

Proof. Let $\xi = \omega x_0 + (1-\omega)y_0$ for some $\omega \in [0,1]$. We use the equality $\phi_{t_0}^{t_1}(x_0) - \phi_{t_0}^{t_1}(y_0) = D_x\phi_{t_0}^{t_1}(\xi)(x_0 - y_0)$ derived in the proof of Lemma 1. Let us denote $A := D_x\phi_{t_0}^{t_1}(\xi)$, and $w = (x_0 - y_0)$. It holds that

$$\|\phi_{t_0}^{t_1}(x_0) - \phi_{t_0}^{t_1}(y_0)\|_{M_1} = \|Aw\|_{M_1} = \sqrt{(Aw)^T M_1(Aw)} = \sqrt{w^T(A^T M_1 A)w} =$$
$$\sqrt{w^T C_0^T((C_0^T)^{-1}A^T M_1 A C_0^{-1})C_0 w} \le \sqrt{\lambda_{max}\left((C_0^T)^{-1}A^T M_1 A C_0^{-1}\right)}\sqrt{w^T C_0^T C_0 w}$$
$$= \sqrt{\lambda_{max}\left((C_0^T)^{-1}A^T M_1 A C_0^{-1}\right)}\,\|w\|_{M_0} \quad \square$$

References

1. Anderson, J., Papachristodoulou, A.: A decomposition technique for nonlinear dynamical system analysis. IEEE Trans. Autom. Control **57**(6), 1516–1521 (2012)
2. Angeli, D., Sontag, E.D., Wang, Y.: A characterization of integral input-to-state stability. IEEE Trans. Autom. Control **45**(6), 1082–1097 (2000)
3. Berz, M., Makino, K.: Verified integration of odes and flows using differential algebraic methods on high-order Taylor models. Reliab. Comput. **4**(4), 361–369 (1998)
4. Capinski, M., Cyranka, J., Galias, Z., Kapela, T., Mrozek, M., Pilarczyk, P., Wilczak, D., Zgliczyski, P., zelawski, M.: CAPD - computer assisted proofs in dynamics, a package for rigorous numerics. Technical report, Jagiellonian University, Kraków (2016). http://capd.ii.edu.pl
5. Chen, X., Abraham, E., Sankaranarayanan, S.: Taylor model flowpipe construction for non-linear hybrid systems. In: Proceedings of 2012 IEEE 33rd Real-Time Systems Symposium, RTSS 2012, pp. 183–192. IEEE Computer Society, Washington, DC (2012)
6. Chen, X., Ábrahám, E., Sankaranarayanan, S.: Flow*: an analyzer for non-linear hybrid systems. In: Sharygina, N., Veith, H. (eds.) CAV 2013. LNCS, vol. 8044, pp. 258–263. Springer, Heidelberg (2013). doi:10.1007/978-3-642-39799-8_18

7. Dahlquist, G.: Stability and Error Bounds in the Numerical Intgration of Ordinary Differential Equations. Transactions of the Royal Institute of Technology. Almqvist & Wiksells, Uppsala (1958)
8. Donzé, A.: Breach, A toolbox for verification and parameter synthesis of hybrid systems. In: Touili, T., Cook, B., Jackson, P. (eds.) CAV 2010. LNCS, vol. 6174, pp. 167–170. Springer, Heidelberg (2010). doi:10.1007/978-3-642-14295-6_17
9. Donzé, A., Maler, O.: Systematic simulation using sensitivity analysis. In: Bemporad, A., Bicchi, A., Buttazzo, G. (eds.) HSCC 2007. LNCS, vol. 4416, pp. 174–189. Springer, Heidelberg (2007). doi:10.1007/978-3-540-71493-4_16
10. Fan, C., Kapinski, J., Jin, X., Mitra, S.: Locally optimal reach set over-approximation for nonlinear systems. In: Proceedings of 13th International Conference on Embedded Software, EMSOFT 2016, pp. 6:1–6:10. ACM, New York (2016)
11. Fan, C., Mitra, S.: Bounded verification with on-the-fly discrepancy computation. In: Finkbeiner, B., Pu, G., Zhang, L. (eds.) ATVA 2015. LNCS, vol. 9364, pp. 446–463. Springer, Cham (2015). doi:10.1007/978-3-319-24953-7_32
12. Galias, Z., Zgliczyski, P.: Computer assisted proof of chaos in the Lorenz equations. Phys. D: Nonlinear Phenom. **115**(3), 165–188 (1998)
13. Hashiguchi, K., Yamakawa, Y.: Introduction to Finite Strain Theory for Continuum Elasto-Plasticity. Wiley Series in Computational Mechanics. Wiley, Hoboken (2012)
14. Islam, M.A., Cyranka, J.: LRT prototype implementation (2017). http://www.cs.cmu.edu/~mdarifui/cav_codes.html
15. Kapela, T., Zgliczyski, P.: The existence of simple choreographies for the N-body problem—a computer-assisted proof. Nonlinearity **16**(6), 1899 (2003)
16. Lofberg, J.: YALMIP: a toolbox for modeling and optimization in MATLAB. In: 2004 IEEE International Symposium on Computer Aided Control Systems Design, pp. 284–289. IEEE (2005)
17. Lohmiller, W., Slotine, J.-J.E.: On contraction analysis for non-linear systems. Automatica **34**(6), 683–696 (1998)
18. Lorenz, E.N.: Deterministic nonperiodic flow. J. Atmos. Sci. **20**(2), 130–141 (1963)
19. Lozinskii, S.M.: Error estimates for the numerical integration of ordinary differential equations, part i. Izv. Vyss. Uceb. Zaved. Matematica **6**, 52–90 (1958)
20. Maidens, J., Arcak, M.: Reachability analysis of nonlinear systems using matrix measures. IEEE Trans. Autom. Control **60**(1), 265–270 (2015)
21. Makino, K., Berz, M.: Cosy infinity version 9. Nucl. Instrum. Methods Phys. Res., Sect. A **558**(1), 346–350 (2006)
22. Makino, K., Berz, M.: Rigorous integration of flows and odes using Taylor models. In: Symbolic Numeric Computation, pp. 79–84 (2009)
23. Mitchell, C.C., Schaeffer, D.G.: A two-current model for the dynamics of cardiac membrane. Bull. Math. Biol. **65**(5), 767–793 (2003)
24. MOSEK ApS: The MOSEK optimization tools version 3.2 (revision 8) user's manual and reference (2002)
25. Nedialkov, N.S.: Interval tools for ODEs and DAEs. In: 12th GAMM - IMACS International Symposium on Scientific Computing, Computer Arithmetic and Validated Numerics (SCAN 2006), p. 4, September 2006
26. Nedialkov, N.S.: Vnode-Ip–a validated solver for initial value problems in ordinary differential equations. Technical report CAS-06-06-NN (2006)
27. Rohn, J.: Bounds on eigenvalues of interval matrices. ZAMM-Z. Angew. Math. Mech. **78**(3), S1049 (1998)

28. Rohn, J.: Versoft: Guide. Technical report (2011)
29. Rump, S.: Developments in Reliable Computing, pp. 77–104. INTLAB - INTerval LABoratory, Kluwer Academic Publishers, Dordrecht (1999)
30. Van Der Pol, B.: Vii. forced oscillations in a circuit with non-linear resistance. (reception with reactive triode). London, Edinb. Dublin Phil. Mag. J. Sci. **3**(13), 65–80 (1927)
31. Wilczak, D., Zgliczyński, P.: Heteroclinic connections between periodic orbits in planar restricted circular three body problem. Part ii. Commun. Math. Phys. **259**(3), 561–576 (2005)
32. Wilczak, D., Zgliczyski, P.: C^r-Lohner algorithm. In: Schedae Informaticae, 2011. vol. 20 (2012)
33. Zgliczynski, P.: C^1 Lohner algorithm. Found. Comput. Math. **2**(4), 429–465 (2002)

Simulation-Equivalent Reachability of Large Linear Systems with Inputs

Stanley Bak[1]($\boxtimes$)
and Parasara Sridhar Duggirala[2]

[1] Air Force Research Laboratory, Wright-Patterson AFB, USA
stanleybak@gmail.com
[2] University of Connecticut, Storrs, USA

Abstract. Control systems can be subject to outside inputs, environmental effects, disturbances, and sensor/actuator inaccuracy. To model such systems, linear differential equations with constrained inputs are often used, $\dot{x}(t) = Ax(t) + Bu(t)$, where the input vector $u(t)$ stays in some bound. Simulating these models is an important tool for detecting design issues. However, since there may be many possible initial states and many possible valid sequences of inputs, simulation-only analysis may also miss critical system errors. In this paper, we present a scalable verification method that computes the *simulation-equivalent reachable set* for a linear system with inputs. This set consists of all the states that can be reached by a fixed-step simulation for (i) any choice of start state in the initial set and (ii) any choice of piecewise constant inputs.

Building upon a recently-developed reachable set computation technique that uses a state-set representation called a generalized star, we extend the approach to incorporate the effects of inputs using linear programming. The approach is made scalable through two optimizations based on Minkowski sum decomposition and warm-start linear programming. We demonstrate scalability by analyzing a series of large benchmark systems, including a system with over 10,000 dimensions (about two orders of magnitude larger than what can be handled by existing tools). The method detects previously-unknown violations in benchmark models, finding complex counter-example traces which validate both its correctness and accuracy.

1 Introduction

Linear dynamical systems with inputs are a powerful formalism for modeling the behavior of systems in several disciplines such as robotics, automotive, and feedback mechanical systems. The dynamics are given as linear differential equations and the sensor noise, input uncertainty, and modeling error make up the

DISTRIBUTION A. Approved for public release; Distribution unlimited. (Approval AFRL PA #88ABW-2017-2082, 1 MAY 2017).

The rights of this work are transferred to the extent transferable according to title 17 U.S.C. 105.

R. Majumdar and V. Kunčak (Eds.): CAV 2017, Part I, LNCS 10426, pp. 401–420, 2017.
DOI: 10.1007/978-3-319-63387-9_20

bounded input signals. For ensuring the safety of such systems, an engineer would simulate the system using different initial states and input signals, and check that each simulation trace is safe. While simulations are helpful in developing intuition about the system's behavior, they might miss unsafe behaviors, as the space of valid input signals is vast.

In this paper, we present a technique to perform *simulation-equivalent reachability* and safety verification of linear systems with inputs. That is, given a linear system $\dot{x}(t) = Ax(t) + Bu(t)$, where $x(t)$ is the state of the system and $u(t)$ is the input, we infer the system to be safe if and only if all the discrete time simulations from a given initial set and an input space are safe. We restrict our attention to input signals that are piecewise constant, where the value of the input signal $u(t)$ is selected from a bounded set U every h time units. We consider piecewise constant input signals for two main reasons. First, the space of all input signals spans an infinite-dimensional space and hence is hard to analyze. To make the analysis tractable, we restrict ourselves to piecewise constant signals which can closely approximate continuous signals. Second, our approach is driven by the desire to produce concrete counterexamples if the system has an unsafe behavior. Counterexamples with input signals that are piecewise constant can be easily validated using numerical simulations.

A well-known technique for performing safety verification is to compute the *reachable set*, or its overapproximation. The reachable set includes all the states that can be reached by any trajectory of the linear system with a valid choice of inputs at each time instant. Typically, the reachable set is stored in data structures such as polyhedra [12], zonotopes [14], support functions [16], or Taylor models [8]. For linear systems, the effect of inputs can be exactly computed using the Minkowski sum operation [15]. While being theoretically elegant, a potential difficulty with this method is that Minkowski sum can greatly increase the complexity of the set representation, especially in high dimensions and after a large number of steps. This previously limited its application to reachability methods where Minkowski sum is efficient: zonotopes and support functions.

In this paper, we demonstrate that it is possible to efficiently perform the Minkowski sum operation using a recently-proposed *generalized star* representation and a linear programming (LP) formulation. The advantage of using the generalized star representation is that the reachable set of an n-dimensional linear system (without inputs) can be computed using only $n+1$ numerical simulations [10], making it scalable and fast. The method is also highly accurate (assuming the input simulations are accurate). Furthermore, it is also capable of generating concrete counterexamples, which is generally not possible with other reachability approaches.

The contributions of this paper are threefold. First, we define the notion of simulation-equivalent reachability and present a technique to compute it using the generalized star representation, Minkowski sum, and linear programming. Second, we present two optimizations which improve the speed and scalability of basic approach. The first optimization leverages a key property of Minkowski sum and decomposes the linear program that needs to be solved for verification. The second optimization uses the result of the LP at each step to warm-start the computation at the next time step. Third, we perform a thorough evaluation, examining the effect of each of the optimizations and comparing the approach versus existing reachability tools on large benchmark systems ranging from 9 to 10914 dimensions. The new approach successfully analyzes models over two orders of magnitude larger than the state-of-the-art tools, finds previously-unknown errors in the benchmark systems, and generates highly-accurate counter-example traces with complex input sequences that are externally validated to drive the system to an error state.

2   Preliminaries

2.1   Problem Definition

A system consists of several continuous variables evolving in the space of $\mathbb{R}^n$. States denoted as x and vectors denoted as v lie in $\mathbb{R}^n$. A set of states $S \subseteq \mathbb{R}^n$.

The set $S_1 \oplus S_2 \triangleq \{x_1 + x_2 \mid x_1 \in S_1, x_2 \in S_2\}$ is defined to be the Minkowski sum of sets S_1 and S_2, where $x_1 + x_2$ is addition of n-dimensional points.

The behaviors of control systems with inputs are modeled with differential equations. In this work, we consider *time-invariant affine systems with bounded inputs* given as:

$$\dot{x}(t) = Ax(t) + Bu(t); \qquad u(t) \in U, \tag{1}$$

where $A \in \mathbb{R}^{n \times n}$ and $B \in \mathbb{R}^{n \times m}$ are constant matrices, and $U \subseteq \mathbb{R}^m$ is the set of possible inputs. We assume that the system has m inputs and hence the input function $u(t)$ is given as $u : \mathbb{R} \to \mathbb{R}^m$. Given a function $u(t)$, a trajectory of the system in Eq. 1 starting from the initial state x_0 can be defined as a function $\xi(x_0, u, t)$ that is a solution to the differential equation, $\frac{d}{dt}\xi(x_0, u, t) = A\xi(x_0, u, t) + Bu(t)$. If $u(t)$ is an integrable function, the closed form expression to the unique solution to the differential equation is given as:

$$\xi(x_0, u, t) = e^{At}x_0 + \int_0^t e^{A(t-\tau)}Bu(\tau)d\tau. \tag{2}$$

If $u(t)$ is a constant function set to the value of u_0, then we abuse notation and use $\xi(x, u_0, t)$ to represent the trajectory. If the input is a constant 0, we drop the term u and denote the trajectory as $\xi(x, t)$. For performing verification of linear systems, we leverage an important property often called the *superposition principle*. Given a state $x_0 \in \mathbb{R}^n$ and vectors $v_1, v_2, \ldots, v_n \in \mathbb{R}^n$, and $\alpha_1, \alpha_2, \ldots, \alpha_n \in \mathbb{R}$, we have

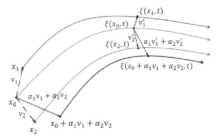

Fig. 1. The state reached at time t from $x_0 + \alpha_1 v_1 + \alpha_2 v_2$ is identical to $\xi(x_0, t) + \alpha_1(\xi(x_0 + v_1, t) - \xi(x_0, t)) + \alpha_2(\xi(x_0 + v_2, t) - \xi(x_0, t))$.

$$\xi\left(x_0 + \sum_{i=1}^{n} \alpha_i v_i, t\right) = \xi(x_0, t) + \sum_{i=1}^{n} \alpha_i(\xi(x_0 + v_i, t) - \xi(x_0, t)). \tag{3}$$

An illustration of the superposition principle in 2-d is shown in Fig. 1.

We refer to the dynamics without the input ($\dot{x} = Ax$) as the autonomous system and the system $\dot{x} = Ax + Bu(t)$ as the system with the inputs. As mentioned in the introduction, we restrict our attention to inputs that are piecewise constant. That is, the value of inputs are updated periodically with time period h. The inputs stay constant for the time duration $[k \times h, (k + 1) \times h]$. A simulation of such a system records the state of the system at time instants that are multiples of h, the same as the period when the inputs get updated. A formal definition of such a simulation is given in Definition 1.

Definition 1 (Fixed-Step Simulation of a System with Inputs). *Given an initial state x_0, a sequence of input vectors u, and a time period h, the sequence $\rho(x_0, u, h) = x_0 \xrightarrow{u_0} x_1 \xrightarrow{u_1} x_2 \xrightarrow{u_2} \ldots$, is a ($x_0, u, h$)-simulation of a system in Eq. 1 if and only if all $u_i \in U$, and for each x_{i+1} we have that x_{i+1} is the state of the trajectory starting from x_i when provided with constant input u_i for h time units, $x_{i+1} = \xi(x_i, u_i, h)$. Bounded-time variants are called (x_0, u, h, T)-simulations. We drop u to denote simulations where no input is provided.*

For simulations, h is called the *step size* and T is called *time bound*. The set of states *encountered* by a (x_0, u, h)-simulation is the set of states in $\mathbb{R}^n$ at the multiples of the time step, $\{x_0, x_1, \ldots\}$. Given a simulation $\rho(x_0, h, T)$ as defined in Definition 1, we can use the closed-form solution in Eq. 2 and substitute u to obtain the relationship between x_i and x_{i+1},

$$x_{i+1} = e^{Ah} x_i + G(A, h) B u_i \tag{4}$$

where $G(A, h) = \sum_{i=0}^{\infty} \frac{1}{(i+1)!} A^i h^{i+1}$.

Definition 2 (Simulation-Equivalent Reachable Set). *Given an initial set Θ and time step h, the **simulation-equivalent reachable set** is the set of all states that can be encountered by any (x_0, u, h)-simulation starting from any $x_0 \in \Theta$, for any valid sequence of input vectors u. This can also be extended to a time-bounded version.*

We define the system to be safe if and only if the simulation-equivalent reachable set and the unsafe set Δ are disjoint. In this paper, the initial set Θ, the space of allowed inputs U, and the unsafe set Δ are bounded polyhedra (sets of linear constraints).

2.2 Generalized Star Sets and Reachable Set Computation

Definition 3 (Generalized Star Set). *A **generalized star set** (or **generalized star**, or simply **star**) Θ is a tuple $\langle c, V, P \rangle$ where $c \in \mathbb{R}^n$ is the center, $V = \{v_1, v_2, \ldots, v_m\}$ is a set of m vectors in $\mathbb{R}^n$ called the basis vectors, and $P : \mathbb{R}^m \to \{\top, \bot\}$ is a predicate. The basis vectors are arranged to form the star's $n \times m$ basis matrix. The set of states represented by the star is given as*

$$\llbracket \Theta \rrbracket = \{x \mid x = c + \Sigma_{i=1}^m \alpha_i v_i \text{ such that } P(\alpha_1, \ldots, \alpha_m) = \top\}.$$

Sometimes we will refer to both the tuple Θ and the set of states $[\![\Theta]\!]$ as Θ. In this work, we restrict the predicates to be a conjunction of linear constraints, $P(\alpha) \triangleq C\alpha \leq d$ where, for p linear constraints, $C \in \mathbb{R}^{p \times m}$, α is the vector of m-variables i.e., $\alpha = [\alpha_1, \ldots, \alpha_m]^T$, and $d \in \mathbb{R}^{p \times 1}$.

This definition is slightly more general than the one used in existing work [10], where stars were restricted to having no more than n basis vectors. This generalization is important when computing the input effects as a star. Any set given as a conjunction of linear constraints in the standard basis can be immediately converted to the star representation by taking the center as the origin, the n basis vectors as the standard orthonormal basis vectors, and the predicate as the original conjunction linear condition with each x_i replaced by α_i. Thus, we can assume the set of initial states Θ is given as a star.

Reachable Set Computation With Stars. Due to the superposition principle, simulations can be used to accurately compute the time-bounded simulation-equivalent reachable set for an autonomous (no-input) linear system from any initial set Θ [6,10]. For an n dimensional system, only $n + 1$ simulations are necessary. The algorithm, described more fully in Appendix A, takes as input an initial set Θ, a simulation time step h, and time bound $k \times h$, and returns a tuple $\langle \Theta_1, \Theta_2, \ldots, \Theta_k \rangle$, where the sets of states that all the simulations starting from Θ can encounter at time instances $i \times h$ is given as Θ_i.

In brief, the algorithm first generates a discrete time simulation $\rho_0 = s_0[0]$, $s_0[1], \ldots, s_0[k]$ of the system from the origin at each time step. Then, n simulations are performed from the state which is unit distance along each orthonormal vector from the origin, $\rho_j = s_j[0], s_j[1], \ldots, s_j[k]$. Finally, the reachable set at each time instant $i \times h$ is returned as a star $\Theta_i = \langle c_i, V_i, P \rangle$ where $c_i = \rho_0[i]$, $V_i = \{v_1, v_2, \ldots, v_n\}$ where $v_j = \rho_j[i] - \rho_0[i]$, and P is the same predicate as in the initial set Θ. This accuracy of this approach is dependent on the errors in the $n + 1$ input simulations, which in practice can often be made arbitrarily small.

Given an unsafe set Δ as a conjunction of linear constraints, discrete-time safety verification can be performed by checking if the intersection of each $\Theta_i \cap \Delta$ is nonempty where Θ_i is the reachable set at time instant $i \times h$. This can be done by solving for the feasibility of a linear program which encodes (1) the relationship between the standard orthonormal basis and the star's basis (given by the basis matrix), (2) the linear constraints on the star's basis variables α from the star's predicate, and (3) the linear conditions on the standard basis variables from the unsafe states Δ. An example reachable set computation using this algorithm, and the associated LP formulation, is provided in Appendix B.

If the LP is feasible, then there exists a point in the star that is unsafe. Further, the trace from the initial states to the unsafe states can be produced by taking the basis point from the feasible solution ($\alpha = [\alpha_1, \ldots, \alpha_n]^T$) and multiplying it by the basis matrix the star in every preceding time step. This will give a sequence of points (one for every multiple of the time step) in the standard basis, starting from the initial set up to a point in the unsafe states.

2.3   Reachability of Linear Systems with Inputs

The reachable set of a linear system with inputs can be exactly written as the Minkowski sum of two sets, the first accounting for the autonomous system (no-input) and the second accounting for the effect of inputs [17]. From Eq. 4, this relationship is expressed as $\Theta_{i+1} = e^{Ah}\Theta_i \oplus G(A, h)BU$. Here, the $e^{Ah}\Theta_i$ represents the evolution of the autonomous system and $G(A, h)BU$ represents the effect of inputs for the time duration h. Representing $\mathcal{U} = G(A, h)BU$ and expanding the above equation, we have

$$\Theta_{i+1} = e^{A(i+1)h}\Theta \oplus e^{A(i)h}\mathcal{U} \oplus e^{A(i-1)h}\mathcal{U} \oplus \ldots \oplus e^{Ah}\mathcal{U} \oplus \mathcal{U}. \tag{5}$$

Here $e^{A(i+1)h}\Theta$ is the set reached by the autonomous system and the rest of the summation represents the accumulated effects of the inputs.

The performance of the algorithm based on Eq. 5 critically depends on the efficiency of the Minkowski sum operation of the set representation that is used. In particular, representations such as polytopes were dismissed because of the high complexity associated with computing their Minkowski sum [17], driving researchers to instead use zonotopes and support functions.

3   Reachability of Linear Systems with Inputs Using Stars

In this section, we first present the basic approach for adapting Eq. 5 for use with generalized stars. We then present two optimizations which greatly improve the efficiency of the approach when used for safety verification.

3.1   Basic Approach

Recall that the expression for the reachable set given in Eq. 5 is

$$\Theta_i = e^{Ai \times h}\Theta \oplus e^{A(i-1) \times h}\mathcal{U} \oplus e^{A(i-2) \times h}\mathcal{U} \oplus \ldots \oplus e^{Ah}\mathcal{U} \oplus \mathcal{U}.$$

where $e^{Ai \times h}\Theta$ is the reachable set of the autonomous system and the remainder of the terms characterize the effect of inputs. Consider the jth term in the remainder, namely, $e^{A(j-1) \times h}\mathcal{U}$. This term is exactly same as the reachable set of states starting from an initial set $\mathcal{U}$ after $(j-1) \times h$ time units, and evolving according to the autonomous dynamics $\dot{x} = Ax$.

Furthermore, the set $\mathcal{U} = G(A, h)BU$ can be represented as a star $\langle c, V, P \rangle$ with m basis vectors, for an n-dimensional system with m inputs. This is done by taking the origin as the center c, the set $G(A, h)B$ as the star's $n \times m$ basis matrix V, and using the linear constraints U as the predicate P, replacing each input u_i with α_i. With this, a simulation-based algorithm for computing the reachable set with inputs is given in Algorithm 1, which makes use of the AutonomousReach function that is the autonomous (no-input) reachability technique described in Sect. 2.2.

Algorithm 1, which we refer to as the Basic approach, computes the reachable set of the autonomous part for initial set Θ in line 1 and the effect of the input $\mathcal{U}$

---

input : Initial state: Θ_0, influence of inputs: $\mathcal{U}_0 = G(A, h)BU$, time bound: $k \times h$
output: Reachable states at each time step: $(\Omega_0, \Omega_1 \ldots, \Omega_k)$
1   $\langle \Theta_1, \Theta_2, \ldots, \Theta_k \rangle \leftarrow$ AutonomousReach$(\Theta_0, h, k \times h)$;
2   $\langle \mathcal{U}_1, \mathcal{U}_2, \ldots, \mathcal{U}_k \rangle \leftarrow$ AutonomousReach$(\mathcal{U}_0, h, k \times h)$;
3   $S \leftarrow \mathcal{U}_0$;
4   **for** $i = 1$ *to* k **do**
5       $\Omega_i \leftarrow \Theta_i \oplus S$;
6       $S \leftarrow S \oplus \mathcal{U}_i$;
7   **end**
8   **return** $(\Omega_1 \ldots, \Omega_k)$;

Algorithm 1. The Basic approach computes the reachable set of states at each time step up to time $k \times h$, where AutonomousReach is the reachable set computation technique presented in Sect. 2.2. For safety verification each of the returned stars should be checked for intersection with the unsafe states using LP.

in line 2. The simulation-based AutonomousReach computation avoids the need to compute and multiply by matrix exponential at every iteration. The variable S in the loop from lines 4 to 7 computes the Minkowski sum of $\mathcal{U}_i \oplus \mathcal{U}_{i-1} \oplus \ldots \oplus \mathcal{U}_1 \oplus \mathcal{U}_0$. The correctness of this algorithm follows from the expression for the reachable set given in Eq. 5. Note that although the computations of the $\mathcal{U}_i$ sets can be thought of as using an independent call to AutonomousReach, they can be computed more efficiently by reusing to simulations used to compute the Θ_i sets. Finally, Algorithm 1 needs to perform Minkowski sum with stars, for which we propose the following approach:

Minkowski Sum with Stars. Given two stars $\Theta = \langle c, V, P \rangle$ with m basis vectors and $\Theta' = \langle c', V', P' \rangle$ with m' basis vectors, their Minkowski is a new star $\overline{\Theta} = \langle \overline{c}, \overline{V}, \overline{P} \rangle$ with $m + m'$ basis vectors and (i) $\overline{c} = c + c'$, (ii) $\overline{V}$ is the list of $m + m'$ vectors produced by joining the list of basis vectors of Θ and Θ', (iii) $\overline{P}(\overline{\alpha}) = P(\alpha_m) \wedge P'(\alpha_{m'})$. Here $\alpha_m \in \mathbb{R}^m$ denotes the variables in Θ, $\alpha_{m'} \in \mathbb{R}^{m'}$ denotes the variables for Θ', and $\overline{\alpha} \in \mathbb{R}^{m+m'}$ denotes the variables for $\overline{\Theta}$ (with appropriate variable renaming).

Notice that both the number of variables in the star and the number of constraints grow with each Minkowski sum operation. In an LP formulation of these constraints, this would mean that both the number of columns and the number of rows grows at each step in the algorithm. However, even though the constraint matrix is growing in size, the number of non-zero entries added to the matrix at each step is constant, so, for LP solvers that use a sparse matrix representation, this may not be as bad as it first appears.

Example 1 (Harmonic Oscillator with Inputs). Consider a system with dynamics $\dot{x} = y + u_1$, $\dot{y} = -x + u_2$, where u_1, u_2 are inputs in the range $[-0.5, 0.5]$ that can vary at each time step, and the initial states are $x = [-6, -5]$, $y = [0, 1]$. A plot of the simulation-equivalent reachable states of this system is shown in

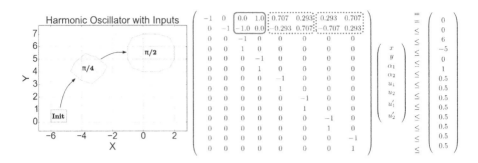

Fig. 2. A plot of the simulation-equivalent reachable states for Example 1 using a $\frac{\pi}{4}$ step size, and the associated linear constraints representing the set at time $\frac{\pi}{2}$ (after two steps).

Fig. 2 (left). The trajectories of this system generally rotate clockwise over time, although can move towards or away from the origin depending on the values of the inputs. The LP constraints which define the reachable states at time $\frac{\pi}{2}$ are given in Fig. 2 (right). Simulations are used to determine the values of the autonomous star's basis matrix (the red encircled values in the matrix). At each time step, the input-free basis matrix gets updated exactly as in the case where there were no inputs. Rows 3–6 in the constraints come from the conditions on the initial states. Additionally, at each step, two columns are added to the LP in order to account for the effects of the two inputs in the model. Rows 7–10 are the conditions on the inputs from the first step, and rows 11–14 are from the second step. The blue dotted values are the each step's input star's basis matrix, $\mathcal{U} = G(A, h)B$. The basis matrix of the combined star is the 2 by 6 matrix constructed by combining the matrices of the basis matrices from the autonomous star and each of the input-effect stars, each of which are 2 by 2. Notice that, at each step, both the number of rows and the number of columns in the LP constraints gets larger, although the number of non-zero entries added to the matrix is constant. To extract a counter-example trace to a reachable state, the LP would be solved in order to give specific assignments to each of the variables. The values of x and y would be the final position that is reachable, that could be, for example, minimized or maximized in the LP. Then, α_1 and α_2 indicate the initial starting position, u_1' and u_2' are the inputs to apply at the first step, and u_1 and u_2 are the inputs to apply at the second step.

3.2 Minkowski Sum Decomposition for Efficient Safety Verification

Algorithm 1 computes the reachable set Ω_i at each step [17] in line 5 based on Eq. 5 for safety verification with respect to an unsafe set Δ. As noted in Sect. 3.1, the number of variables in Ω_i increases linearly with i and hence for high dimensional systems, checking whether $\Omega_i \cap \Delta = \emptyset$ using linear programming becomes increasingly difficult. To improve the scalability of safety verification, we observe that it is not necessary to compute Ω_i in the star representation and then check for intersection with Δ. Consider a specific case where Δ is defined as a half-space $v \cdot x \geq a$. Checking safety of Ω_i with respect to Δ is equivalent to computing the maximum value of the cost function $v \cdot x$ over the set Ω_i and checking if $\max_{v \cdot x}(\Omega_i) \geq a$. As Ω_i is a Minkowski sum of several sets, computing $\max_{v \cdot x}(\Omega_i)$ is equivalent to computing the maximum value of $v \cdot x$ for each of the sets in the Minkowski sum and adding these maximum values. This property is described rigorously in Proposition 1. This observation was first made in [17] for zonotopes and the authors leverage this property to avoid computing Minkowski sum for safety verification. In this paper, we explicitly state the property for Minkowski sum of any two sets and any linear cost function and note that it is independent of the data structure used for representing the sets.

Proposition 1. *If $S = S_1 \oplus S_2$, then $\max_v(S) = \max_v(S_1) + \max_v(S_2)$, where $\max_v$ is defined as the maximum value of the cost function $v \cdot x$, v is any n-dimensional vector and $v \cdot x$ is the dot product.*

Proof. Let p_1 and p_2 be states in S_1 and S_2 respectively which maximize the dot product. From the definition of Minkowski sum, $p_1 + p_2 = p \in S$. Since p is in S, $\max_v(S) \geq p \cdot v$, and therefore $\max_v(S) \geq p \cdot v = p_1 \cdot v + p_2 \cdot v = \max_v(S_1) + \max_v(S_2)$.

For the other inequality, let q be the point in S which maximizes the dot product. By the definition of Minkowski sum, there exist two points $q_1 \in S_1$ and $q_2 \in S_2$ where $q = q_1 + q_2$. Therefore, $q \cdot v = q_1 \cdot v + q_2 \cdot v$. Notice now that $\max_v(S_1) \geq q_1 \cdot v$ and $\max_v(S_2) \geq q_2 \cdot v$, and so we can substitute to get $\max_v(S) = q \cdot v \leq \max_v(S_1) + \max_v(S_2)$.

Since both inequalities must hold, $\max_v(S) = \max_v(S_1) + \max_v(S_2)$.   □

As $\Omega_i = \Theta_i \oplus \mathcal{U}_{i-1} \oplus \mathcal{U}_1 \oplus \mathcal{U}$ (Eq. 5), it follows from Proposition 1 that, for safety verification in the case of unsafe set $\Delta \overset{\Delta}{=} v \cdot x \geq a$, it suffices to compute $\max_{v \cdot x} \mathcal{U}_j$ for all j and $\max_{v \cdot x} \Theta_i$; add these values; and compare the summation with a. In the general case, the unsafe states Δ may be a conjunction of half-planes, say $(v_1 \cdot x \geq a_1) \wedge (v_2 \cdot x \geq a_2) \wedge \ldots \wedge (v_l \cdot x \geq a_l)$. For such instances, if $\Omega_i \cap \Delta \neq \emptyset$, it is a necessary condition that $\forall j, \max_{v_j \cdot x}(\Omega_i) \geq a_j$. Thus, we do not compute the full Minkowski sum representation of Ω_i until the above necessary condition is satisfied. Informally, we perform *lazy computation* of Ω_i.

Additionally, all the $\mathcal{U}_j$'s appearing in Minkowski sum formulation of Ω_i also appear in Ω_{i+1}. Therefore, we keep a running sum of the maximum values for each $\mathcal{U}_j$ for all the linear functions and check the necessary conditions for all Ω_i. Only after checking the necessary conditions, we computing the Minkowski sum and formulate the linear program for checking $\Omega_i \cap \Delta = \emptyset$. We refer to this approach, shown in Algorithm 2, as the Decomp method.

The algorithm starts by extracting each constraint hyperplane's normal direction and value in lines 1 and 2. Lines 9 and 10 compute the maximum over all the normal directions in the sets Θ_i and $\mathcal{U}_i$. The tuple μ accumulates the maximum over all inputs up to the current iteration, whereas λ is recomputed at each step

---

input : Initial state: Θ, influence of inputs: $\mathcal{U}$, time bound: $k \times h$, unsafe set: Δ

output: SAFE or UNSAFE

1   $\langle v_1, v_2, \ldots, v_l \rangle \leftarrow$ NormalDirections(Δ);

2   $\langle a_1, a_2, \ldots, a_l \rangle \leftarrow$ NormalValues(Δ);

3   $\langle \Theta_1, \Theta_2, \ldots, \Theta_k \rangle \leftarrow$ AutonomousReach($\Theta, h, k \times h$);

4   $\langle \mathcal{U}_1, \mathcal{U}_2, \ldots, \mathcal{U}_k \rangle \leftarrow$ AutonomousReach($\mathcal{U}, h, k \times h$);

5   $\mathcal{U}_0 \leftarrow \mathcal{U}$;

6   $\Theta_0 \leftarrow \Theta$;

7   $\mu \leftarrow \langle 0, 0, \ldots, 0 \rangle$;

8   **for** $i = 1$ *to* k **do**

9      $\lambda \leftarrow \langle \max_{v_1}(\Theta_i), \max_{v_2}(\Theta_i), \ldots, \max_{v_l}(\Theta_i) \rangle$;

10     $\mu \leftarrow \langle \mu[1] + \max_{v_1}(\mathcal{U}_{i-1}), \mu[2] + \max_{v_2}(\mathcal{U}_{i-1}), \ldots, \mu[l] + \max_{v_l}(\mathcal{U}_{i-1}) \rangle$;

11   **if** $\forall j \in \{1, \ldots, l\}$, $\lambda[j] + \mu[j] \geq a_j$ **then**

12   **if** $\Theta_i \oplus \mathcal{U}_{i-1} \oplus \mathcal{U}_{i-2} \oplus \ldots \oplus \mathcal{U}_0 \cap \Delta \neq \emptyset$ **then**

13   **return** UNSAFE;

14   **end**

15   **end**

16 **end**

17 **return** SAFE;

Algorithm 2. The Decomp algorithm uses Minkowski sum decomposition to avoid needing to solve the full LP at each iteration.

based on the autonomous system's current generalized star. Only if all the linear constraints can exceed their constraint's value (the check on line 11), will the full LP be formulated and checked on line 12.

3.3 Optimizing with Warm-Start Linear Programming

In this section, we briefly outline the core principle behind warm-start optimization and explain why it is effective in safety verification using generalized stars. Consider a linear program given as `maximize` $c^T y$, `Subject to:` $Hy \leq g$ where $y \in \mathbb{R}^m$. To solve this LP, we use a two-phase simplex algorithm [18]. First, the algorithm finds a feasible solution and second, it traverses the vertices of the polytope defined by the set of linear conditions in the m-dimensional space to reach the optimal solution. Finding the feasible solution is performed using slack variables and the traversal among feasible solutions is done by relaxing and changing the set of active constraints. The time taken for the simplex algorithm to terminate is directly proportional to the time taken to find a feasible solution and the number of steps in the traversal from the feasible solution to the optimal solution.

The warm-start optimization allows the user (perhaps using a solution to an earlier linear program) to explicitly specify the initial set of active constraints. Internally, the slack variable associated with these constraints are assigned to be 0. This can speed-up the running time of simplex in two ways. If the set of active constraints gives a feasible solution, then the first phase of simplex terminates without any further computation. Second, if the user-provided active constraints correspond to a feasible solution is close to the optimal solution, the steps needed during the second phase are reduced.

Similar to [6], we have used warm-start optimization in this paper for improving the efficiency of safety verification. Warm-start optimization works in this context because we use the generalized star representation for sets. Consider two consecutive reachable sets of the autonomous system $\Theta_i = \langle c_i, V_i, P \rangle$ and $\Theta_{i+1} = \langle c_{i+1}, V_{i+1}, P \rangle$ represented as generalized stars. Consider solving a linear program for maximizing a cost function $v \cdot x$ over Θ_i and Θ_{i+1}. These two stars differ in the value of the *center* and the set of *basis vectors*, but the *predicate* remains unchanged. Moreover, if we choose have small time-steps, the difference between the values of center and basis vectors is also small. Therefore, the set of active constraints in the predicate P is often identical for the optimal solutions. Even in the cases where the active constraints are not identical, the corresponding vertices are often close, reducing the work needed.

In this paper, we feed the active constraints of the first linear program i.e., maximizing $v \cdot x$ over Θ_i as a warm-start to the second linear program, i.e., maximizing $v \cdot x$ over Θ_{i+1}. We apply the same principle for the input stars $\mathcal{U}_i$ and $\mathcal{U}_{i+1}$. Hence, the warm-start optimization can also be used together with the Minkowski sum decomposition optimization.

4 Evaluation

We encoded the techniques developed in this paper into a tool named Hylaa (HYbrid Linear Automata Analyzer). Using this tool, we first evaluate the effects of each of the proposed optimizations on the runtime of reachability computation. Then, we evaluate the overall approach on a benchmark set of systems ranging from 9 to 10914 coupled continuous variables. All of the measurements are run on a desktop computer running Ubuntu 16.04 x 64 with an Intel i7-3930K processor (6 cores, 12 threads) running at 3.5 GHz with 24 GB RAM.

4.1 Optimization Evaluation

We examine the effects of each of our proposed optimizations for computing reachability for linear-time invariant systems with inputs. We compare the Basic algorithm from Sect. 3.1, against the Decomp approach described in Sect. 3.2. The Warm method is the enhancement of the Basic approach with warm-start optimization as described in Sect. 3.3, and Hylaa is the approach used in our tool, which uses both Minkowski sum decomposition and LP warm-start. For reference, we also include measurements for the no-input system (NoInput), which could be considered a lower-bound for the simulation-based methods if the time to handle the inputs could be eliminated completely. Finally, we compared the approach with both optimizations (Hylaa) with other state-of-the-art tools which handle time-varying inputs. We used the support function scenario in the SpaceEx [13] tool (SpaceEx), and the linear ODE mode with Taylor model order 1 (fastest speed) in the Flow* [8] tool (Flow*).

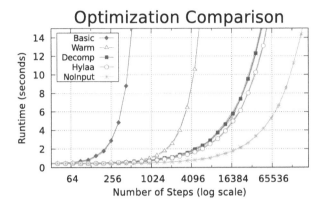

Fig. 3. The performance of the generalized star and linear programming approach for reachability computation (Basic), is improved by the warm-start linear programming optimization (Warm), but not as much as when the Minkowski sum decomposition optimization is used (Decomp). Combining both optimizations works even better (Hylaa). The reachability time for the system without inputs (NoInput) is a lower bound.

For evaluation, we use the harmonic oscillator with input system, as described in Example 1. Recall that the full LP grows at each step both in terms of the number of columns and the number of rows. The unsafe condition used is $x + y \geq 100$, which is never reached but must be checked at each step.

We varied the number of steps in the problem by changing the step size and keeping the time bound fixed at 2π. We then measured the runtime for each of the methods, recording 10 measurements in each case. Figure 3 shows the results with both the average runtime (lines), and the runtime ranges over all 10 runs (slight shaded regions around each line). Each optimization is shown to improve the performance of the method, with Minkowski sum decomposition having a larger effect on this example compared with warm-start LP. The fully optimized approach (Hylaa) is not too far from the lower bound computed by ignoring the inputs in the system (NoInput). In the tool comparison shown in Fig. 4, the approach is shown to be comparable to the other reachability tools, and outperforms both SpaceEx and Flow* when the model has a large number of steps.

4.2   High-Dimensional Benchmark Evaluation

We evaluated the proposed approach using a benchmark suite for reachability problems for large-scale linear systems [20]. This consists of nine reachability benchmarks for linear systems with inputs of various sizes, taken from "diverse fields such as civil engineering and robotics." For each benchmark, we also considered a variant with a weakened or strengthened unsafe condition, so that each system would have both a safe and an unsafe case. For all the systems, we used a step size of 0.005 and the original time bound of 20. The results are shown in Table 1.

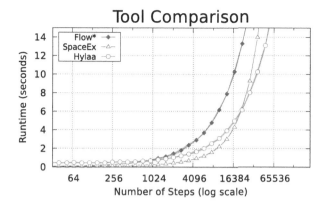

Fig. 4. The performance of our optimized generalized star representation reachability approach (Hylaa) is compared to state-of-the art tools which use support functions (SpaceEx) and Taylor Models (Flow*) as the state set representation. As the number of steps gets larger, our approach surpasses the other tools on this example.

Our Hylaa tool was able to successfully verify or disprove invariant safety conditions for all of the models, including the MNA5 model, which has 10914 dimensions. To the best of our knowledge, this is significantly (about two orders of magnitude) larger than any system that has been verified without using any type of abstraction methods to reduce the system's dimensionality.

We also attempted to run SpaceEx (0.9.8f) and Flow* (2.0.0) on the benchmark models[1]. With Flow*, in order to successfully run the Motor (9 dimensions) benchmark, we needed to use a smaller step size (0.0002), and set the Taylor Model order parameter to 20. For SpaceEx, we used the support function scenario which only requires a step size parameter. In the Motor (9 dimensions) benchmark, however, this required us to halve the step size to 0.0025 in order for SpaceEx to be able to prove the unsafe error states were not reachable with the original safety condition. Consistent with the earlier analysis [20], SpaceEx's computation only succeeded for the Motor (9 dimensions) and Building (49 dimensions) benchmarks.

We also ran the benchmarks toggling the different optimizations, and could show cases where warm-start greatly improves performance, and even outperforms Decomp. In the Beam model, for instance, Warm completes the safe case in about 4 min, whereas Decomp takes 12 min (using both optimizations takes about 1.4 min).

One important difference to keep in mind is that SpaceEx and Flow* overapproximate reachability at all times, which is slightly different than simulation-equivalent reachability computed by Hylaa. Unlike Hylaa, they may catch error

---

[1] Performance comparisons are difficult since runtime depends on the parameters used. Since the submission of this work, the Building model has been used as part of a reachability tools competition [1], in which both SpaceEx and Flow* participated. Using the parameters from the competition, which were hand-tuned by the tool authors, is likely to produce better runtimes than what we achieved in this paper.

Table 1. Benchmark results. Stars (*) indicate original specifications.

Model	Dims	Unsafe error condition	Tool	Time (s)	Safe?	CE error (Abs/Rel)	CE time
Motor*	9	$x_1 \in [0.35, 0.4] \wedge$ $x_5 \in [0.45, 0.6]$	Hylaa	2.3 s	✓	-	-
			SpaceEx	6.8 s	✓	-	-
			Flow*	13 m 19 s	✓	-	-
Motor	9	$x_1 \in [0.3, 0.4] \wedge$ $x_5 \in [0.4, 0.6]$	Hylaa	0.4 s		$2.5 \cdot 10^{-7}/2.4 \cdot 10^{-7}$	0.04
			SpaceEx	9.6 s		-	-
			Flow*	14 m 11 s		-	-
Building*	49	$x_{25} \geq 0.006$	Hylaa	2.7 s	✓	-	-
			SpaceEx	59.8 s	✓	-	-
Building	49	$x_{25} \geq 0.004$	Hylaa	0.9 s		$4.4 \cdot 10^{-8}/1.8 \cdot 10^{-6}$	0.07
			SpaceEx	59.2 s		-	-
PDE*	85	$y_1 \geq 12$	Hylaa	3.8 s	✓	-	-
PDE	85	$y_1 \geq 10.75$	Hylaa	1.2 s		$1.5 \cdot 10^{-8}/6.7 \cdot 10^{-8}$	0.025
Heat*	201	$x_{133} \geq 0.1$	Hylaa	11.8 s	✓	-	-
Heat	201	$x_{133} \geq 0.02$	Hylaa	10.1 s		$5.8 \cdot 10^{-8}/1.6 \cdot 10^{-7}$	15.67
ISS	271	$y_3 \notin$ $[-0.0007, 0.0007]$	Hylaa	1 m 28 s	✓	-	-
ISS*	271	$y_3 \notin$ $[-0.0005, 0.0005]$	Hylaa	1 m 23 s		$8.5 \cdot 10^{-6}/1.3 \cdot 10^{-5}$	13.71
Beam	349	$x_{89} \geq 2100$	Hylaa	1 m 23 s	✓	-	-
Beam*	349	$x_{89} \geq 1000$	Hylaa	1 m 19 s		$2.0 \cdot 10^{-5}/4.2 \cdot 10^{-9}$	16.045
MNA1*	579	$x_1 \geq 0.5$	Hylaa	4 m 4 s	✓	-	-
MNA1	579	$x_1 \geq 0.2$	Hylaa	3 m 49 s		$1.9 \cdot 10^{-6}/4.9 \cdot 10^{-7}$	16.555
FOM	1007	$y_1 \geq 185$	Hylaa	4 m 10 s	✓	-	-
FOM*	1007	$y_1 \geq 45$	Hylaa	1 m 7 s		$1.0 \cdot 10^{-6}/5.6 \cdot 10^{-7}$	0.29
MNA5*	10914	$x_1 \geq 0.2 \vee x_2 \geq$ 0.15	Hylaa	6 h 23 m	✓	-	-
MNA5	10914	$x_1 \geq 0.1 \vee x_2 \geq$ 0.15	Hylaa	37 m 27 s		$1.4 \cdot 10^{-6}/1.8 \cdot 10^{-6}$	1.92

cases that occur between time steps. The cost of this is that there may also be false-positives; they do not produce counterexample traces when a system is deemed unsafe. For example, choosing too small of a Taylor Model order or too large of a time step in Flow* can easily result in all states, $[-\infty, \infty]$, to be computed as potentially reachable for all variables, which is not useful.

Another important concern is the accuracy of result. Since the proposed approach uses numerical simulations that may not be exact as well as floating-point computations and a floating-point LP solver, there may be errors that accumulate in the computation. To address the issue of accuracy, we examine the counterexamples produced when the error condition is reachable.

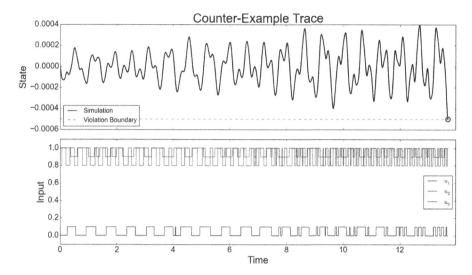

Fig. 5. Hylaa found a counterexample trace in the ISS model, generating a very specific set of inputs to use at each point in time. The post-verification analysis (external, high-accuracy simulation) confirms that the found violation is a true violation of the system.

Upon finding that an unsafe error state is reachable, Hylaa uses the approach described in Example 1 to determine the initial point and inputs to use at each step in order to reach the unsafe state. It creates a Python script using this start point and inputs to perform a simulation with high accuracy parameters in order to try to reproduce the counterexample error trace. We perform this check for each of the benchmark systems where an error state is found, and compute the l_2-norm of the difference between the expected final point given by Hylaa and the post-analysis high-accuracy simulation point. The values in the CE Error column in Table 1 indicate that the counterexamples are highly-accurate on all the models, both in terms of absolute and relative error.

Consider the structural model of component 1R (Russian Service Module) of the International Space Station (ISS model, 271 dimensions). The high-accuracy simulation of the counterexample trace found this system is shown in Fig. 5. Here, the final point in the post-analysis simulation and the Hylaa's predicted final point differ, in terms of l_2-norm, by around 10^{-5}. The figure shows the state of the output value (top) and the values of the three inputs at each point in time, computed by Hylaa. This is an extremely complicated set of inputs that would be difficult to find using random simulations.

We attempted to use a falsification tool on this system to try find the violation. A falsification tool [3,9,19] performs stochastic optimization to minimize the difference between simulation runs and the violation region. We ran S-Taliro [3] on this system for 2000 simulations, which took 4.5 hours, but it did not find a violation.

Exhaustive testing for this case would require checking simulations from each of the corner points of the initial states (270 of the dimensions can be in an initial interval range), multiplied by 8 combinations of choices of the 3 inputs at each of the 2742 steps before a counterexample was found (Hylaa found the counterexample at time 13.71). This would be $2^{270} \cdot 8^{2742} = 3.5 \cdot 10^{2557}$ individual simulations, an unfathomably large number.

In communications with the benchmark authors, the original safety specifications for all the models were chosen based on simulations of the system while holding the inputs constant. For some of the benchmarks, Hylaa was able to find cases where the original safety specification was violated. For example, in the ISS model, the shown error trace in Fig. 5 violates the original specification. This was a bit unexpected, but possible since we are considering inputs which can vary over time. When we kept the inputs constant in the ISS model, no violation was found. In other systems, for example the Beam model, the counterexample trace Hylaa finds has the same input values at every time step. This shows the incompleteness (and danger) of pure simulation-based analysis, where the safety specification was derived based on a finite set of simulations that did not include the violation. As far as we are aware, the generalized star reachability approach is the first to find violations in the benchmark's original safety conditions, as well as the first approach to verify systems of this size.

5   Related Work

Early work on handling inputs for linear systems was done for the purpose of creating abstractions that overapproximate behaviors of systems with nonlinear dynamics [4]. In this approach, a bound on the input is used to bloat a ball to account for the effect of any possible input. While sound, such an approach does not give a tight result and could not be used to generate concrete traces. Later, a formulation was given which explicitly used the Minkowski sum operation [15], along with a reachability algorithm based on zonotopes, which is a set representation that can efficiently compute both linear transformation and Minkowski sum. This allowed for more precise tracking of the reachable set of states, although the complexity of the zonotopes grew quadratically with the number of discrete time steps performed, so a reduction step was used to limit the expansion of the order of the zonotopes, leading to overapproximation. An important improvement removed this overapproximation by using two zonotopes, one to track the time-invariant system and one to track the effects of inputs [17]. The two zonotopes could be combined at any specific time step in the computation to perform operations on the reachable set at that time instant such as guard checks, but the time-elapse operation was done on the two zonotopes separately. A similar approach was applied for a support functions representation rather than zonotopes [16], which also allows for efficient Minkowski sum. The methods proposed in this paper also use this general approach, using the generalized star set data structure rather than zonotopes. The difficulty with this is that generalized star sets are similar to polytopes specified using hyperplane constraints, and the number of hyperplanes necessary to represent the

Minkowski sum can become extremely large in high dimensions [11,21]. For systems with nonlinear dynamics, a different method using Taylor models can be used for the time-elapse operation, with inputs given as bounded time-varying uncertainties [7]. This method essentially replaces time-varying parameters by their interval enclosure at every integration step.

Building on the time-elapse operation, a hybrid automaton reachability algorithm needs to perform intersections with guard sets. For zonotopes, this can be done by performing conversions to/from polytopes [2,15], although this process may introduce overapproximation error. For support functions, this can be done by converting to/from template polyhedra [13]. In non-linear reachability computation with Taylor models, guard intersections can leverage domain-contraction and range-overapproximation (converting to other representations such as polytopes) [8]. Although not explored in this work, we believe this operation can be done using generalized star sets, without conversions that may introduce error.

6   Conclusion

In this paper, we described a new approach for computing reachability for linear systems with inputs, using a generalized star set representation and linear programming. Our approach is simulation-equivalent, which means that we can detect an unsafe state is reachable if and only if a fixed-step simulation exists to the unsafe states. Furthermore, upon reaching an unsafe state, a counter-example trace is generated for the system designer to use.

The proposed method has unprecedented scalability. On the tested benchmarks, we successfully analyzed a system with 10914 dimensions, whereas the current state-of-the-art tools did not succeed on any model larger than 48 dimensions. Such large models frequently arise by discretizing partial differential equations (PDEs). For example, a 100×100 grid over a PDE model results in a 10,000 dimensional model. Thus, we believe the proposed approach opens the door to the computer-aided verification of PDE models with ranges of possible initial conditions, inputs, and uncertainties.

A   Reachability of Autonomous Systems using Stars

Here, we expand on the algorithm for computing simulation-equivalent reachability for an autonomous (no-input) system. Given an initial set Θ as a conjunction of linear predicates P, the algorithm generates one simulation from the center *origin* and one simulation from state $ortho_i$ where $ortho_i$ is unit distance along the ith vector in the orthonormal basis. The reachable set at a time instance is computed as a new star $\langle c', V', P \rangle$ where the new center and the basis vectors are calculated based on the simulations, but the predicate remains the same. This simulation-based approach is also extremely easy to parallelize. It has been shown to be quite scalable, and is capable of analyzing an certain affine 1000-dimensional systems in 10–20 min [5,6].

---

input : Initial set $\Theta \triangleq P$, time step: h, time bound: $k \cdot h$
output: Reachable states at each time step: $(\Theta_0, \Theta_1 \ldots, \Theta_k)$
1 $Sim_0 \leftarrow \rho(origin, h, k \cdot h)$;
2 **for** $j = 1$ *to* n **do**
3 $\quad$ $Sim_j \leftarrow \rho(ortho_j, h, k \cdot h)$;
4 **end**
5 **for** $i = 0$ *to* k **do**
6 $\quad$ $c_i \leftarrow Sim_0[i]$;
7 $\quad$ **for** $j = 1$ *to* n **do**
8 $\quad\quad$ $v_j \leftarrow Sim_j[i] - Sim_0[i]$;
9 $\quad$ **end**
10 $\quad$ $V_i \leftarrow \{v_1, \ldots, v_n\}$;
11 $\quad$ $\Theta_i \leftarrow \langle c_i, V_i, P \rangle$;
12 **end**
13 **return** $(\Theta_0, \Theta_1 \ldots, \Theta_k)$;

Algorithm 3. Computes the simulation-equivalent reachable set up to time $k \cdot h$ from $n + 1$ simulations, for linear system without inputs.

The procedure is given in Algorithm 3. In the algorithm, Sim_0 represents the simulation starting from the origin and Sim_j represents the simulation starting at unit distance along the jth orthonormal vector. Given a simulation Sim, $Sim[i]$ represents the ith state in the simulation, i.e., the state reached after $i \cdot h$ time units. Algorithm 3 computes the reachable set of the set Θ at time instance $i \cdot h$, returned as Θ_i as a generalized star with the center as $Sim_0[i]$, the jth basis vector as $Sim_j[i] - Sim_0[i]$ and the same predicate P as the initial set. Observe that for all Θ_i, the predicate in the star representation is the same, only the center and the basis vectors change. Applying the Eq. 2, for the closed loop system without the inputs, we have that $\Theta_i = e^{Ai \cdot h}\Theta$. The correctness of this algorithm is due to the superposition principle of linear systems [10].

B   Example of Autonomous System Reachability

We go through an example computation using the autonomous (no-input) reachability algorithm, and provide the associated LP formulation.

Example 2 (Harmonic Oscillator). Consider the 2-d harmonic oscillator with dynamics $\dot{x} = y$, $\dot{y} = -x$, and initial states $x = [-6, -5]$, $y = [0, 1]$. The trajectories of this system rotate clockwise around the origin. A plot of the simulation-equivalent reachable states of this system and the LP formulation at $\frac{\pi}{4}$ is shown in Fig. 6. Given these constraints, linear programming can quickly determine if unsafe states, provided as a conjunction of linear constraints, intersect with the reachable states. As described above, simulations are used to determine the values of the basis matrix (the red encircled values in the matrix), which gets updated at each time step, while the rest of the constraints remains unchanged. Rows 3–6 in the constraints come from the conditions on the initial states (the

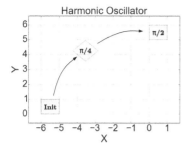

$$\begin{pmatrix} -1 & 0 & \boxed{0.707 & 0.707} \\ 0 & -1 & \boxed{-0.707 & 0.707} \\ 0 & 0 & -1 & 0 \\ 0 & 0 & 1 & 0 \\ 0 & 0 & 0 & -1 \\ 0 & 0 & 0 & 1 \end{pmatrix} \begin{pmatrix} x \\ y \\ \alpha_1 \\ \alpha_2 \end{pmatrix} \begin{matrix} = \\ = \\ \le \\ \le \\ \le \\ \le \end{matrix} \begin{pmatrix} 0 \\ 0 \\ 6 \\ -5 \\ 0 \\ 1 \end{pmatrix}$$

Fig. 6. Plot of the simulation-equivalent reachable states for the system in Example 2 with a step size of $\frac{\pi}{4}$, and the associated LP formulation at $\frac{\pi}{4}$. The red circled values are the star's basis matrix, which changes at each step. Rows 3–6 come from the initial state constraints. Additional rows could be added to check for intersection with the unsafe states.

predicate in the initial state star). The initial basis matrix is $\begin{pmatrix} 1 & 0 \\ 0 & 1 \end{pmatrix}$, where each column is the difference between a concrete simulation and the origin simulation. Since this is a 2-dimensional system ($n = 2$), 3 ($n + 1$) simulations are needed, one from the origin, one from $\begin{pmatrix} 1 \\ 0 \end{pmatrix}$, and one from $\begin{pmatrix} 0 \\ 1 \end{pmatrix}$. In this case, the simulation from the origin always stays at $\begin{pmatrix} 0 \\ 0 \end{pmatrix}$. After $\frac{\pi}{4}$ time, the simulation from state $\begin{pmatrix} 1 \\ 0 \end{pmatrix}$ goes to $\begin{pmatrix} 0.707 \\ -0.707 \end{pmatrix}$ and the simulation from state $\begin{pmatrix} 0 \\ 1 \end{pmatrix}$ goes to $\begin{pmatrix} 0.707 \\ 0.707 \end{pmatrix}$. Thus, the basis matrix at time $\frac{\pi}{4}$, which is the one shown the figure, is $\begin{pmatrix} 0.707 & 0.707 \\ -0.707 & 0.707 \end{pmatrix}$. At time $\frac{\pi}{2}$, the basis matrix in the constraints would be $\begin{pmatrix} 0 & 1 \\ -1 & 0 \end{pmatrix}$.

References

1. Althoff, M., Bak, S., Cattaruzza, D., Chen, X., Frehse, G., Ray, R., Schupp, S.: ARCH-COMP category report: continuous and hybrid systems with linear continuous dynamics. In: 4th Applied Verification for Continuous and Hybrid Systems Workshop (ARCH) (2017)
2. Althoff, M., Stursberg, O., Buss, M.: Computing reachable sets of hybrid systems using a combination of zonotopes and polytopes. Nonlinear Anal. Hybrid Syst. 4(2), 233–249 (2010)
3. Annpureddy, Y., Liu, C., Fainekos, G., Sankaranarayanan, S.: S-TaLiRo: a tool for temporal logic falsification for hybrid systems. In: Abdulla, P.A., Leino, K.R.M. (eds.) TACAS 2011. LNCS, vol. 6605, pp. 254–257. Springer, Heidelberg (2011). doi:10.1007/978-3-642-19835-9_21
4. Asarin, E., Dang, T., Girard, A.: Reachability analysis of nonlinear systems using conservative approximation. In: Maler, O., Pnueli, A. (eds.) HSCC 2003. LNCS, vol. 2623, pp. 20–35. Springer, Heidelberg (2003). doi:10.1007/3-540-36580-X_5
5. Bak, S., Duggirala, P.S.: HyLAA: a tool for computing simulation-equivalent reachability for linear systems. In: Proceedings of 20th International Conference on Hybrid Systems: Computation and Control, HSCC 2017 (2017)

6. Bak, S., Duggirala, P.S.: Rigorous simulation-based analysis of linear hybrid systems. In: Legay, A., Margaria, T. (eds.) TACAS 2017. LNCS, vol. 10205, pp. 555–572. Springer, Heidelberg (2017). doi:10.1007/978-3-662-54577-5_32

7. Chen, X.: Reachability analysis of non-linear hybrid systems using taylor models. Ph.D. thesis, RWTH Aachen University, March 2015

8. Chen, X., Abraham, E., Sankaranarayanan, S.: Taylor model flowpipe construction for non-linear hybrid systems. In: Proceedings of 2012 IEEE 33rd Real-Time Systems Symposium, RTSS 2012 (2012)

9. Donzé, A.: Breach, a toolbox for verification and parameter synthesis of hybrid systems. In: Touili, T., Cook, B., Jackson, P. (eds.) CAV 2010. LNCS, vol. 6174, pp. 167–170. Springer, Heidelberg (2010). doi:10.1007/978-3-642-14295-6_17

10. Duggirala, P.S., Viswanathan, M.: Parsimonious, simulation based verification of linear systems. In: Chaudhuri, S., Farzan, A. (eds.) CAV 2016. LNCS, vol. 9779, pp. 477–494. Springer, Cham (2016). doi:10.1007/978-3-319-41528-4_26

11. Florian, P.: Optimizing reachabiliy analysis for non-autonomous systems using ellipsoids. Master's thesis, RWTH Aachen University, Germany (2016)

12. Frehse, G.: PHAVer: algorithmic verification of hybrid systems past HyTech. In: Morari, M., Thiele, L. (eds.) HSCC 2005. LNCS, vol. 3414, pp. 258–273. Springer, Heidelberg (2005). doi:10.1007/978-3-540-31954-2_17

13. Frehse, G., et al.: SpaceEx: scalable verification of hybrid systems. In: Gopalakrishnan, G., Qadeer, S. (eds.) CAV 2011. LNCS, vol. 6806, pp. 379–395. Springer, Heidelberg (2011). doi:10.1007/978-3-642-22110-1_30

14. Girard, A.: Reachability of uncertain linear systems using zonotopes. In: Morari, M., Thiele, L. (eds.) HSCC 2005. LNCS, vol. 3414, pp. 291–305. Springer, Heidelberg (2005). doi:10.1007/978-3-540-31954-2_19

15. Girard, A., Guernic, C.: Zonotope/hyperplane intersection for hybrid systems reachability analysis. In: Egerstedt, M., Mishra, B. (eds.) HSCC 2008. LNCS, vol. 4981, pp. 215–228. Springer, Heidelberg (2008). doi:10.1007/978-3-540-78929-1_16

16. Girard, A., Le Guernic, C., et al.: Efficient reachability analysis for linear systems using support functions. In: Proceedings of 17th IFAC World Congress, pp. 8966–8971 (2008)

17. Girard, A., Le Guernic, C., Maler, O.: Efficient computation of reachable sets of linear time-invariant systems with inputs. In: Hespanha, J.P., Tiwari, A. (eds.) HSCC 2006. LNCS, vol. 3927, pp. 257–271. Springer, Heidelberg (2006). doi:10.1007/11730637_21

18. Nelder, J.A., Mead, R.: A simplex method for function minimization. Comput. J. **7**(4), 308–313 (1965)

19. Nghiem, T., Sankaranarayanan, S., Fainekos, G., Ivancić, F., Gupta, A., Pappas, G.J.: Monte-Carlo techniques for falsification of temporal properties of non-linear hybrid systems. In: Proceedings of 13th ACM International Conference on Hybrid Systems: Computation and Control, pp. 211–220. ACM (2010)

20. Tran, H.-D., Nguyen, L.V., Johnson, T.T.: Large-scale linear systems from order-reduction (benchmark proposal). In: 3rd Applied Verification for Continuous and Hybrid Systems Workshop (ARCH), Vienna, Austria (2016)

21. Zaslavsky, T.: Facing up to Arrangements: Face-Count Formulas for Partitions of Space by Hyperplanes: Face-Count Formulas for Partitions of Space by Hyperplanes. Memoirs of the American Mathematical Society (1975)

MightyL: A Compositional Translation from MITL to Timed Automata

Thomas Brihaye[1], Gilles Geeraerts[2],
Hsi-Ming Ho[1], and Benjamin Monmege[3(⊠)]

[1] Université de Mons, Mons, Belgium
{thomas.brihaye,hsi-ming.ho}@umons.ac.be
[2] Université libre de Bruxelles, Brussels, Belgium
gigeerae@ulb.ac.be
[3] Aix Marseille Univ, CNRS, LIF, Marseille, France
benjamin.monmege@univ-amu.fr

Abstract. Metric Interval Temporal Logic (MITL) was first proposed in the early 1990s as a specification formalism for real-time systems. Apart from its appealing intuitive syntax, there are also theoretical evidences that make MITL a prime real-time counterpart of Linear Temporal Logic (LTL). Unfortunately, the tool support for MITL verification is still lacking to this day. In this paper, we propose a new construction from MITL to timed automata via very-weak one-clock alternating timed automata. Our construction subsumes the well-known construction from LTL to Büchi automata by Gastin and Oddoux and yet has the additional benefits of being compositional and integrating easily with existing tools. We implement the construction in our new tool MightyL and report on experiments using Uppaal and LTSmin as back-ends.

1 Introduction

The design of critical software that respect real-time specifications is a notoriously difficult problem. In this context, verification of programs against formal specifications is crucial, in order to handle the thin timing behaviours. In the untimed setting, a logic widely used both in academia and industry is *Linear Temporal Logic* (LTL) [32]. A crucial ingredient of its success is the possibility to translate LTL formulae into (Büchi) automata. In the real-time counterpart, *Metric Interval Temporal Logic* (MITL) [3] has been introduced twenty years ago where it was established that it can be translated into (Büchi) *timed automata* (TA). Beyond verification of real-time software, there are numerous interests in MITL from other domains, e.g. automated planning and scheduling [39], control engineering [18] and systems biology [6]. The translation from MITL to TAs is complicated and has led to some simplified constructions, e.g. [17,28]. However, despite these efforts, the tool support for MITL is still lacking to this day. To the best of our knowledge, the only implementation of an automata-based

This work has been supported by the FRS/F.N.R.S. PDR grant SyVeRLo, and (partially) funded by the DeLTA project (ANR-16-CE40-0007) and the SensAS project (INS2I JCJC'17).

© Springer International Publishing AG 2017
R. Majumdar and V. Kunčak (Eds.): CAV 2017, Part I, LNCS 10426, pp. 421–440, 2017.
DOI: 10.1007/978-3-319-63387-9_21

construction is described in [10,11], but is not publicly available. Since existing verification tools based on timed automata have been around for quite some time and have been successful (e.g. UPPAAL [27] first appeared in 1995), it would be preferable if such translation can be used with these tools.

In the present paper, we attempt to amend the situation by proposing a more practical construction from MITL to (Büchi) timed automata. Compared to [10,11], our construction has the following advantages:

1. While we also use *one-clock alternating timed automata* (OCATA) [30] as an intermediate formalism, our construction exploits the 'very-weakness' of the structure of OCATAs obtained from MITL formulae to reduce state space. In particular, our construction subsumes LTL2BA [19] in the case of LTL.
2. The number of clocks in the resulting TA is reduced by a factor of up to two. This is achieved via a more fine-grained analysis of the possible clock values (see Sect. 5).
3. The construction is *compositional*: for each location of the OCATA $\mathcal{A}$ obtained from the input MITL formula, we construct a 'component' TA and establish a connection between the runs of $\mathcal{A}$ and the runs of the synchronous product of these components. Thanks to this connection, we can give the output TA in terms of components; this greatly simplifies the implementation, and speeds up its execution.
4. The construction is compatible with off-the-shelf model-checkers: our tool MIGHTYL generates output automata in the UPPAAL XML format which, besides UPPAAL [27] itself, can also be analysed by LTSMIN [24] with OPAAL front-end, TIAMO [9], ITS-TOOLS [35], DIVINE [5], etc.

Related Work. There is already a number of MITL-to-TA constructions in the literature [3,17,28]. However, most of them interpret MITL over *signals* (i.e. the *continuous* semantics of MITL) and hence generate *signal automata*. This choice unfortunately hinders the possibility to leverage existing tools based on classical timed automata over *timed words* [2] and is probably one of the reasons why the aforementioned constructions have never been implemented.[1] We, following [4, 10,11,37] (among others), interpret MITL over timed words (i.e. the *pointwise* semantics of MITL). Note that there have been some implementations that deal with peculiar specification patterns over timed words (e.g. [1]). For MITL, apart from [10,11] that we mentioned earlier, we are only aware of implementations for rather restricted cases, such as the safety fragment of $MITL_{0,\infty}$ [12] or MITL over untimed words [39]. Our construction subsumes all of these approaches.

Using alternating automata as an intermediate formalism is a standard approach in LTL model-checking [36]. However, the translation from alternating automata to Büchi automata may incur an exponential blow-up if the output automaton is constructed explicitly [19]. For this reason, an *on-the-fly* approach is proposed in [21], but it requires a specialised model-checking algorithm. Alternatively, [8] gives a *symbolic* encoding of alternating automata which can be used

---

[1] Nonetheless, it has been argued that a continuous model of time is preferable from a theoretical point of view; see e.g. [22].

directly with NuSMV [13], but minimality of transitions (which may potentially improve the performance of verification algorithms, cf. [21]) is difficult to enforce in this setting (see also [14,34]). Our construction combines the advantages of these approaches—it can be regarded as a symbolic encoding of OCATAs in TAs, enforcing some minimality criteria on transitions for efficiency (see Sect. 6)—and provides compatibility with existing tools that construct state spaces on-the-fly. By contrast, [17,28], not based on OCATAs, also give the resulting automaton in terms of smaller component automata, but they have to use specialised product constructions to synchronise the components.

Apart from automata-theoretic approaches, [7] considers 'bounded model-checking' which encodes the satisfiability problem for MITL (in the continuous semantics) into an SMT problem (*Satisfiability Modulo Theories*) [15]. This approach is complete when very large bounds (numbers of regions of equivalent TA) are used, but such bounds are clearly impractical for current SMT solvers.

Outline. Section 2 starts with preliminary definitions of timed logics and (alternating) timed automata. Sections 3, 4 and 5 then give our new translation from formulae to generalised Büchi (timed) automata for LTL, $MITL_{0,\infty}$ (a fragment of MITL where only intervals of the form $[0,a]$, $[0,a)$, $[a,+\infty)$, or $(a,+\infty)$ are allowed), and full MITL, respectively. We report on our OCaml implementation MIGHTYL and some promising experiments on several benchmarks in Sect. 6.

2   Timed Logics vs (Alternating) Timed Automata

Timed Languages. Let AP be a finite set of atomic propositions, and $\Sigma = 2^{AP}$. A timed word over Σ is an infinite sequence $\rho = (\sigma_1, \tau_1)(\sigma_2, \tau_2) \cdots$ over $\Sigma \times \mathbb{R}^+$ with $(\tau_i)_{i \geq 1}$ a non-decreasing sequence of non-negative real numbers. We denote by $T\Sigma^\omega$ the set of timed words over Σ. A *timed language* is a subset of $T\Sigma^\omega$.

Timed Logics. We consider the satisfiability and model-checking problem of Metric Interval Temporal Logic (MITL), an extension of Linear Temporal Logic (LTL) in which temporal operators can be labelled with *non-singular* timed intervals (or $[0,0]$, which is the only singular interval we allow). Formally, MITL formulae over AP are generated by the grammar

$$\varphi := p \mid \varphi \wedge \varphi \mid \neg\varphi \mid \mathbf{X}_I \varphi \mid \varphi \, \mathbf{U}_I \, \varphi$$

where $p \in$ AP and I is either a non-singular interval over $\mathbb{R}^+$ with endpoints in $\mathbb{N} \cup \{+\infty\}$ or $[0,0]$. To simplify our explanations, we will only consider closed non-singular intervals in the sequel, i.e. intervals of the form $[a,b]$ or $[a,+\infty)$, with $0 \leq a < b < +\infty$. We let $|I|$ be the length of the interval I: $|[a,b]| = b - a$ for $0 \leq a < b < +\infty$ and $|[a,+\infty)| = +\infty$.

We consider the *pointwise semantics* and interpret MITL formulae over timed words. The semantics of a formula φ in MITL is defined inductively: given $\rho = (\sigma_1, \tau_1)(\sigma_2, \tau_2) \cdots \in T\Sigma^\omega$, and a position $i \geq 1$, we let

- $(\rho, i) \models p$ if $p \in \sigma_i$;
- $(\rho, i) \models \varphi_1 \wedge \varphi_2$ if $(\rho, i) \models \varphi_1$ and $(\rho, i) \models \varphi_2$;
- $(\rho, i) \models \neg\varphi$ if $(\rho, i) \not\models \varphi$;
- $(\rho, i) \models \mathbf{X}_I\varphi$ if $(\rho, i+1) \models \varphi$ and $\tau_{i+1} - \tau_i \in I$;
- $(\rho, i) \models \varphi_1 \mathbf{U}_I \varphi_2$ if there exists $j \geq i$, $(\rho, j) \models \varphi_2$, $\tau_j - \tau_i \in I$, and, for all $i \leq k < j$, $(\rho, k) \models \varphi_1$.

We derive other Boolean operators with the following macros: $\varphi_1 \vee \varphi_2 \equiv \neg(\neg\varphi_1 \wedge \neg\varphi_2)$, $\top \equiv p \vee \neg p$, $\bot \equiv \neg\top$, and $\varphi_1 \Rightarrow \varphi_2 \equiv \neg\varphi_1 \vee \varphi_2$. We also define other temporal operators as usual: the 'eventually' operator $\mathbf{F}_I\varphi \equiv \top \mathbf{U}_I \varphi$, the 'globally' operator $\mathbf{G}_I\varphi \equiv \neg\mathbf{F}_I\neg\varphi$, the 'release' operator $\varphi_1 \mathbf{R}_I \varphi_2 \equiv \neg((\neg\varphi_1) \mathbf{U}_I (\neg\varphi_2))$, and the 'dual-next' operator $\overline{\mathbf{X}}_I\varphi \equiv \neg\mathbf{X}_I\neg\varphi$ (contrary to LTL, it is not true that $\neg\mathbf{X}_I\varphi \equiv \mathbf{X}_I\neg\varphi$). With the release and dual-next operators, we can transform every formula φ into *negative normal form*, i.e. formulae using only predicates of AP, their negations, and the operators $\vee$, $\wedge$, $\mathbf{U}_I$, $\mathbf{R}_I$, $\mathbf{X}_I$, and $\overline{\mathbf{X}}_I$. To help the understanding, let us detail the semantics of $\varphi_1 \mathbf{R}_I \varphi_2$:

- $(\rho, i) \models \varphi_1 \mathbf{R}_I \varphi_2$ if for all $j \geq i$ such that $\tau_j - \tau_i \in I$, either $(\rho, j) \models \varphi_2$, or there exists $i \leq k < j$ such that $(\rho, k) \models \varphi_1$.

We say that ρ satisfies the formula φ, written $\rho \models \varphi$ if $(\rho, 1) \models \varphi$, and we denote by $[\![\varphi]\!]$ the set of all timed words satisfying φ. When writing formulae, we omit the trivial interval $[0, +\infty)$. LTL is the fragment of MITL where all operators are labelled by $[0, \infty)$; and $\mathsf{MITL}_{0,\infty}$ is the fragment where, in all intervals, either the left endpoint is 0 or the right endpoint is $+\infty$.

Timed Automata. Let X be a finite set of real valued variables, called clocks. The set $\mathcal{G}(X)$ of *clock constraints* g over X is defined by $g := \top \mid g \wedge g \mid x \bowtie c$, where $\bowtie \in \{\leq, <, \geq, >\}$, $x \in X$ and $c \in \mathbb{N}$. A *valuation* over X is a mapping $v: X \to \mathbb{R}^+$. We denote by $\mathbf{0}$ the valuation that maps every clock to 0, and we write the valuation simply as a value in $\mathbb{R}^+$ when X is a singleton. The satisfaction of a constraint g by a valuation v is defined in the usual way and noted $v \models g$, and we denote by $[\![g]\!]$ the set of valuations v satisfying g. For $t \in \mathbb{R}^+$, we let $v + t$ be the valuation defined by $(v + t)(x) = v(x) + t$ for all $x \in X$. For $R \subseteq X$, we let $v[R \leftarrow 0]$ be the valuation defined by $(v[R \leftarrow 0])(x) = 0$ if $x \in R$, and $(v[R \leftarrow 0])(x) = v(x)$ otherwise.

We introduce the notion of *generalised Büchi timed automaton* (GBTA) as an extension of classical timed automata [2] with a generalised acceptance condition (used by [20] in the untimed setting). A GBTA is a tuple $\mathcal{A} = (L, \Sigma, \ell_0, \Delta, \mathcal{F})$ where L is a finite set of locations, Σ is a finite alphabet, $\ell_0 \in L$ is the initial location, $\Delta \subseteq L \times \Sigma \times \mathcal{G}(X) \times 2^X \times L$ is the transition relation, and $\mathcal{F} = \{F_1, \ldots, F_n\}$, with $F_i \subseteq L$ for all $1 \leq i \leq n$, is the set of sets of final locations. A timed automaton (TA), as described in [2], is a special case of GBTA where $\mathcal{F} = \{F\}$ is a singleton (F contains the accepting locations of the TA). A *state* of $\mathcal{A}$ is a pair (ℓ, v) of a location $\ell \in L$ and a valuation v of the clocks in X. A *run* of $\mathcal{A}$ over the timed word $(\sigma_1, \tau_1)(\sigma_2, \tau_2) \cdots \in T\Sigma^\omega$ is a sequence of states $C_0, C_1, \ldots$ where (i) $C_0 = (\ell_0, \mathbf{0})$ and (ii) for each $i \geq 0$ such that $C_i = (\ell, v)$, there is a transition $(\ell, \sigma_{i+1}, g, R, \ell')$ such that $C_{i+1} = (\ell', v')$, $v + (\tau_{i+1} - \tau_i) \models g$ (assuming $\tau_0 = 0$) and

$v' = (v + (\tau_{i+1} - \tau_i))[R \leftarrow 0]$. By the generalised Büchi acceptance condition, a run is *accepting* if and only if the set of locations that it visits infinitely often contains at least one location from each set F_i, for all $1 \leq i \leq n$. We let $[\![\mathcal{A}]\!]$ be the set of timed words on which there exist accepting runs of $\mathcal{A}$.

Synchronisation of Timed Automata. In the following, we will consider GBTAs described by synchronous products of several components. More precisely, given two GBTAs $\mathcal{A}^1 = (L^1, \Sigma, \ell_0^1, \Delta^1, \mathcal{F}^1)$ and $\mathcal{A}^2 = (L^2, \Sigma, \ell_0^2, \Delta^2, \mathcal{F}^2)$ over disjoint sets of clocks, we define the GBTA $\mathcal{A}^1 \times \mathcal{A}^2 = (L, \Sigma, \ell_0, \Delta, \mathcal{F})$ obtained by synchronising $\mathcal{A}^1$ and $\mathcal{A}^2$. Its set of locations is $L = L^1 \times L^2$, with $\ell_0 = (\ell_0^1, \ell_0^2)$. The acceptance condition is obtained by mimicking a disjoint union of the generalised Büchi conditions: assuming $\mathcal{F}^1 = \{F_1, \dots, F_n\}$ and $\mathcal{F}^2 = \{G_1, \dots, G_m\}$, we let $\mathcal{F} = \{F_1 \times L^2, \dots, F_n \times L^2, L^1 \times G_1, \dots, L^1 \times G_m\}$. Finally, $((\ell_1^1, \ell_1^2), \sigma, g, R, (\ell_2^1, \ell_2^2)) \in \Delta$ if there exists $(\ell_1^1, \sigma, g^1, R^1, \ell_2^1) \in \Delta^1$ and $(\ell_1^2, \sigma, g^2, R^2, \ell_2^2) \in \Delta^2$ such that $g = g^1 \wedge g^2$ and $R = R^1 \cup R^2$. This definition can be extended for the synchronisation of a set of GBTAs $\{\mathcal{A}^i \mid i \in I\}$: the product is then written as $\prod_{i \in I} \mathcal{A}^i$.

One-Clock Alternating Timed Automata. One-clock alternating timed automata (OCATA) [30] extend (non-deterministic) one-clock timed automata by adding *conjunctive transitions*. Intuitively, a conjunctive transition spawns several copies of the automaton that run in parallel from the targets of the transition. A word is accepted if and only if *all* copies accept it. An example is shown in Fig. 1, where the conjunctive transition is the hyperedge starting from ℓ_0.

Formally, we consider a single clock x and, for a set L of locations, let $\Gamma(L)$ be the set of formulae defined by

$$\gamma := \top \mid \bot \mid \gamma \vee \gamma \mid \gamma \wedge \gamma \mid \ell \mid x \bowtie c \mid x.\gamma$$

where $c \in \mathbb{N}$, $\bowtie \in \{\leq, <, \geq, >\}$, and $\ell \in L$. Compared to the clock constraints defined above for TAs, $\Gamma(L)$ allows non-determinism ($\vee$ operator), locations as atoms, and expressions of the form $x.\gamma$ (meaning that x is reset in γ). An OCATA is a tuple $\mathcal{A} = (L, \Sigma, \ell_0, \delta, F)$ where L is a finite set of locations, Σ is a finite alphabet, $\ell_0 \in L$ is the initial location, $\delta \colon L \times \Sigma \to \Gamma(L)$ is the transition function, and $F \subseteq L$ is the set of final locations. A *state* of $\mathcal{A}$ is a pair (ℓ, v) of a location in L and a valuation of the single clock x. Models of the formulae in $\Gamma(L)$, with respect to a clock valuation $v \in \mathbb{R}^+$, are sets of states M:

- $M \models_v \top$; $M \models_v \ell$ if $(\ell, v) \in M$; $M \models_v x \bowtie c$ if $v \bowtie c$; $M \models_v x.\gamma$ if $M \models_0 \gamma$;
- $M \models_v \gamma_1 \wedge \gamma_2$ if $M \models_v \gamma_1$ and $M \models_v \gamma_2$;
- $M \models_v \gamma_1 \vee \gamma_2$ if $M \models_v \gamma_1$ or $M \models_v \gamma_2$.

A set M of states is said to be a *minimal model* of the formula $\gamma \in \Gamma(S)$ with respect to a clock valuation $v \in \mathbb{R}^+$ if and only if $M \models_v \gamma$ and there is no proper subset $M' \subset M$ with $M' \models_v \gamma$. A run of $\mathcal{A}$ over a timed word $\rho = (\sigma_1, \tau_1)(\sigma_2, \tau_2) \cdots \in T\Sigma^\omega$ is a rooted directed acyclic graph (DAG) $G = (V, \to)$ with vertices of the form $(\ell, v, i) \in L \times \mathbb{R}^+ \times \mathbb{N}$, $(\ell_0, 0, 0)$ as root, and edges as

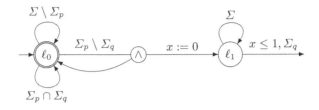

Fig. 1. An OCATA accepting the language of $\mathbf{G}(p \Rightarrow \mathbf{F}_{[0,1]}q)$.

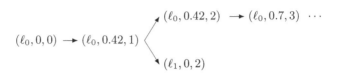

Fig. 2. A run of the OCATA of Fig. 1 over $(\emptyset, 0.42)(\{p\}, 0.42)(\{q\}, 0.7) \cdots$.

follows: for every vertex (ℓ, v, i), we choose a minimal model M of the formula $\delta(\ell, \sigma_{i+1})$ with respect to $v + (\tau_{i+1} - \tau_i)$ (again, $\tau_0 = 0$), and we have an edge $(\ell, v, i) \rightarrow (\ell', v', i+1)$ in G for every state (ℓ', v') appearing in model M. Such a run is *accepting* if and only if there is no infinite path in G that visit final locations only finitely often. We let $\llbracket \mathcal{A} \rrbracket$ be the set of timed words on which there exist accepting runs of $\mathcal{A}$.

It is also useful to see a run as a linear sequence of *configurations* (i.e. finite sets of states) which gather all states at a given DAG level. Formally, from a DAG $G = (V, \rightarrow)$ we extract the sequence of configurations $K_0, K_1, \ldots$ where $K_i = \{(\ell, v) \mid (\ell, v, i) \in V\}$ for all $i \geq 0$.[2]

Example 1. Consider the OCATA of Fig. 1 on the alphabet $\Sigma = 2^{\{p,q\}}$. For each proposition $\pi \in \{p, q\}$, we write $\Sigma_\pi = \{\sigma \in \Sigma \mid \pi \in \sigma\}$. A run over the timed word $(\emptyset, 0.42)(\{p\}, 0.42)(\{q\}, 0.7) \cdots$ is depicted in Fig. 2. It starts with the DAG rooted in $(\ell_0, 0, 0)$ (initially, there is only one copy in ℓ_0 with the clock equal to 0). This root has a single successor $(\ell_0, 0.42, 1)$, which has two successors $(\ell_0, 0.42, 2)$ and $(\ell_1, 0, 2)$ (after firing the conjunctive transition from ℓ_0). Then, $(\ell_1, 0, 2)$ has no successor since the empty model is a minimal model of the next transition (the transition from ℓ_1 points to no location). The associated sequence of configurations starts by: $\{(\ell_0, 0)\}, \{(\ell_0, 0.42)\}, \{(\ell_0, 0.42), (\ell_1, 0)\} \cdots$

Each formula φ of MITL can be translated into an OCATA $\mathcal{A}_\varphi$ that accepts the same language [11,30], and with a number of locations linear in the number of subformulae of φ. We recall the definition of $\mathcal{A}_\varphi$ for the sake of completeness. The set of locations of $\mathcal{A}_\varphi$ contains: (i) φ_{init}; (ii) all the subformulae of φ (that we suppose to be in negative normal form) whose outermost operator is $\mathbf{U}_I$ or $\mathbf{R}_I$; and (iiii) ψ^r for each subformulae ψ of φ whose outermost operator is $\mathbf{X}_I$

---

[2] In the current (infinite-word) setting, we cannot define acceptance conditions in terms of configurations as in [30].

or $\overline{\mathbf{X}}_I$. Its initial location is φ_{init}, and the accepting locations of F are all the subformulae of the form $\varphi_1 \, \mathbf{R}_I \, \varphi_2$. Finally, δ is defined inductively:

- $\delta(\varphi_{init}, \sigma) = x.\delta(\varphi, \sigma)$, $\delta(\top, \sigma) = \top$, and $\delta(\bot, \sigma) = \bot$;
- $\delta(p, \sigma) = \top$ if $p \in \sigma$, $\delta(p, \sigma) = \bot$ otherwise;
- $\delta(\neg p, \sigma) = \top$ if $p \notin \sigma$, $\delta(\neg p, \sigma) = \bot$ otherwise;
- $\delta(\varphi_1 \vee \varphi_2, \sigma) = \delta(\varphi_1, \sigma) \vee \delta(\varphi_2, \sigma)$, and $\delta(\varphi_1 \wedge \varphi_2, \sigma) = \delta(\varphi_1, \sigma) \wedge \delta(\varphi_2, \sigma)$;
- $\delta(\varphi_1 \, \mathbf{U}_I \, \varphi_2, \sigma) = (x.\delta(\varphi_2, \sigma) \wedge x \in I) \vee (x.\delta(\varphi_1, \sigma) \wedge \varphi_1 \, \mathbf{U}_I \, \varphi_2 \wedge x \leq \sup I)$;
- $\delta(\varphi_1 \, \mathbf{R}_I \, \varphi_2, \sigma) = (x.\delta(\varphi_2, \sigma) \vee x \notin I) \wedge (x.\delta(\varphi_1, \sigma) \vee \varphi_1 \, \mathbf{R}_I \, \varphi_2 \vee x > \sup I)$;
- $\delta(\mathbf{X}_I \varphi, \sigma) = x.(\mathbf{X}_I \varphi)^r$, and $\delta((\mathbf{X}_I \varphi)^r, \sigma) = x \in I \wedge x.\delta(\varphi, \sigma)$;
- $\delta(\overline{\mathbf{X}}_I \varphi, \sigma) = x.(\overline{\mathbf{X}}_I \varphi)^r$, and $\delta((\overline{\mathbf{X}}_I \varphi)^r, \sigma) = x \notin I \vee x.\delta(\varphi, \sigma)$.

As already noticed in [11], the OCATA $\mathcal{A}_\varphi$ produced from an MITL formula φ is *very-weak* [19,26,29], i.e. it comes with a partial order on its locations such that all locations appearing in $\delta(\ell, \sigma)$ are bounded above by ℓ in this order. For an OCATA $\mathcal{A}_\varphi$ obtained from an MITL formula φ, the order is given by the subformula order: φ_{init} is the greatest element in the order, and a location ψ is less than χ if ψ is a subformula of χ. We will also make use of the following properties of δ: (i) if ℓ' appears in $\delta(\ell, \sigma)$ then it is preceded by a clock reset if and only if $\ell' \neq \ell$; and (ii) each ℓ' either has no parent or has a unique parent, i.e. there is a unique $\ell \neq \ell'$ such that ℓ' appears in $\delta(\ell, \sigma)$ for some σ.

Theorem 2 ([11]). *For all formulae φ of MITL, $\llbracket \mathcal{A}_\varphi \rrbracket = \llbracket \varphi \rrbracket$.*

Remark 3. To ease the presentation, we use Boolean formulae over atomic propositions as transition labels. For instance, $\Sigma \setminus \Sigma_p$ will be written as $\neg p$.

3 Compositional Removal of Alternation

The current and next two sections are devoted to explaining the core idea of our construction: simulate the OCATA $\mathcal{A}_\varphi$ obtained from an MITL formula φ by the synchronous product of component Büchi timed automata, one for each temporal subformula (i.e. a subformula whose outermost operator is temporal). The very-weakness of $\mathcal{A}_\varphi$ is crucial for our construction to work: a run of $\mathcal{A}_\varphi$ is accepting if and only if $\mathcal{A}_\varphi$ does not get stuck at a non-accepting location in any branch. Therefore, we can keep track of each location with a separate component and simply define a suitable Büchi acceptance condition on each such component.[3] Our compositional construction preserves the structure of the formula, and thus we can hope that the model-checking tool (which is responsible for the composition) takes this into account.[4] At the very least, the model-checking tool can use an on-the-fly approach in composition (as is indeed the case for UPPAAL and LTSMIN),

---

[3] This is not possible for general (not very-weak) OCATAs since it might be the case that a branch alternates between several non-accepting location without ever hitting an accepting location.

[4] The same idea underlies the antichain-based algorithms for LTL model-checking [38], where the structure can be exploited to define a pre-order on the state space of the resulting automaton.

which is often faster in practice: the explicit construction of the whole product can be avoided when there is an accepting run.

In what follows, let φ be an MITL formula over AP in negative normal form and $\mathcal{A}_\varphi$ be the OCATA obtained from φ with the translation described earlier. For the sake of simplicity, we make the following assumptions:

- $\mathbf{X}_I$ and $\overline{\mathbf{X}}_I$ do not appear in φ;
- each temporal subformula ψ of φ appears only once in φ.

Let Φ be the set of temporal subformulae of φ. We introduce a new atomic proposition p_ψ for each subformula $\psi \in \Phi$ (i.e. for each non-initial location of the OCATA $\mathcal{A}_\varphi$) and let AP_φ be the set of these new atomic propositions. For each (not necessarily temporal) subformula ψ of φ, we denote by $\mathcal{P}_\psi$ the set of atomic propositions $p_\xi \in \mathsf{AP}_\varphi$ such that ξ is a top-level temporal subformula of ψ, i.e. the outermost operator of ξ is $\mathbf{U}_I$ or $\mathbf{R}_I$, yet ξ does not occur under the scope of another $\mathbf{U}_I$ or $\mathbf{R}_I$. For instance, $\mathcal{P}_{p\mathbf{U}_Iq\vee r\mathbf{U}_I(s\mathbf{R}t)} = \{p_{p\mathbf{U}_Iq}, p_{r\mathbf{U}_I(s\mathbf{R}t)}\}$.

Hintikka Sequences and Triggers. A *Hintikka sequence* of φ is a timed word ρ' over $2^{\mathsf{AP}\cup\mathsf{AP}_\varphi}$. Intuitively, Hintikka sequences can be regarded as an instrumented version of timed words, where the extra atomic propositions from AP_φ are *triggers* that connect timed words to their runs in the OCATA $\mathcal{A}_\varphi$; this is the central notion of our construction which, as we will prove, indeed simulates the runs of $\mathcal{A}_\varphi$. Pulling the trigger p_ψ (i.e. setting p_ψ to true) at some point means that ψ is required to hold at this point. However, the absence of a trigger p_ξ does not mean that subformula ξ must not be satisfied—its satisfaction is simply not required at this point. We denote by $\mathsf{proj}_{\mathsf{AP}}(\rho')$ the timed word obtained by hiding all the atomic propositions in AP_φ from ρ'. We also let $\mathsf{proj}_{\mathsf{AP}}(\mathcal{L}) = \{\mathsf{proj}_{\mathsf{AP}}(\rho') \mid \rho' \in \mathcal{L}\}$ for a timed language $\mathcal{L}$ over $2^{\mathsf{AP}\cup\mathsf{AP}_\varphi}$.

Formulae Over $\mathsf{AP} \cup \mathsf{AP}_\varphi$. We now introduce some syntactic operations on Boolean combinations of atomic propositions in $\mathsf{AP} \cup \mathsf{AP}_\varphi$, that will be used to construct the component Büchi automata later. Specifically, for a subformula ψ of φ, we define formulae $\overline{\psi}$, $*\psi$, $\sim\psi$, and $\widehat{\psi}$.

The formula $\overline{\psi}$ is obtained from ψ by replacing all top-level temporal subformulae by their corresponding triggers. Formally, $\overline{\psi}$ is defined inductively as follows (where $p \in \mathsf{AP} \cup \mathsf{AP}_\varphi$):

$$\overline{\psi_1 \wedge \psi_2} = \overline{\psi_1} \wedge \overline{\psi_2} \qquad \overline{\psi} = \psi \text{ when } \psi \text{ is } \top \text{ or } \bot \text{ or } p \text{ or } \neg p$$
$$\overline{\psi_1 \vee \psi_2} = \overline{\psi_1} \vee \overline{\psi_2} \qquad \overline{\psi} = p_\psi \text{ when } \psi \text{ is } \psi_1 \mathbf{U}_I \psi_2 \text{ or } \psi_1 \mathbf{R}_I \psi_2.$$

The formula $*\psi$, read as "do not pull the triggers of ψ", will be used to ensure that our component automata only follow the minimal models of the transition function of $\mathcal{A}_\varphi$ (we will see in Sect. 6 how crucial it is, for performance, to generate only minimal models). It is the conjunction of negations of all the atomic propositions in $\mathcal{P}_\psi$. As a concrete example,

$$*((\neg p \vee \psi_1 \mathbf{U} \psi_2) \wedge (q \vee \psi_3 \mathbf{R} (\psi_4 \mathbf{U} \psi_5))) = \neg p_{\psi_1\mathbf{U}\psi_2} \wedge \neg p_{\psi_3\mathbf{R}(\psi_4\mathbf{U}\psi_5)}.$$

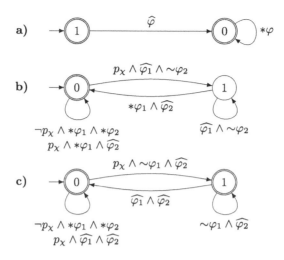

Fig. 3. The automata (a) $\mathcal{C}_{init}$ and $\mathcal{C}_\chi$ for (b) $\chi = \varphi_1 \mathbf{U} \varphi_2$, and (c) $\chi = \varphi_1 \mathbf{R} \varphi_2$.

The formula $\sim\psi$ asserts that $\overline{\psi}$ is false and none of its triggers are activated: $\sim\psi = \neg\overline{\psi} \wedge *\psi$. Finally, the formula $\widehat{\psi}$ is defined as $\mathsf{mm}(\overline{\psi})$ where $\mathsf{mm}(\alpha)$ is defined inductively as follows:

$$\mathsf{mm}(p) = p \qquad \mathsf{mm}(\neg p) = \neg p \qquad \mathsf{mm}(\top) = \top \qquad \mathsf{mm}(\bot) = \bot$$
$$\mathsf{mm}(\alpha_1 \vee \alpha_2) = \big(\mathsf{mm}(\alpha_1) \wedge \sim\alpha_2\big) \vee \big(\mathsf{mm}(\alpha_2) \wedge \sim\alpha_1\big) \vee \big((\alpha_1 \vee \alpha_2) \wedge *\alpha_1 \wedge *\alpha_2\big)$$
$$\mathsf{mm}(\alpha_1 \wedge \alpha_2) = \mathsf{mm}(\alpha_1) \wedge \mathsf{mm}(\alpha_2).$$

Intuitively, $\mathsf{mm}(\alpha)$ is satisfiable if and only if α is satisfiable, but $\mathsf{mm}(\alpha)$ only permits models of α that are minimal with respect to the triggers it contains: for $\mathsf{mm}(\alpha_1 \vee \alpha_2)$ to be true, either $\mathsf{mm}(\alpha_1)$ is true and α_2 does not hold, or vice versa, or $\alpha_1 \vee \alpha_2$ is indeed true, but not because of any of the triggers it contains.

Component Büchi Automata for LTL. We are now ready to present the construction for the case that φ is an LTL formula. Instead of building a mono-lithic Büchi automaton $\mathcal{B}_\varphi$ directly from the alternating automaton, as in [19], we build small component Büchi automata that are language-equivalent to the automaton $\mathcal{B}_\varphi$, once synchronised. There is an initial component $\mathcal{C}_{init}$, and a component Büchi automaton $\mathcal{C}_\chi$, for each $\chi \in \Phi$ (see Fig. 3). Consider, for instance, the case $\chi = \varphi_1 \mathbf{U} \varphi_2$. Component $\mathcal{C}_\chi$ has two locations 0 and 1 with the following intended meaning: $\mathcal{C}_\chi$ is in location 1 if and only if the trigger p_χ has been pulled in the past by $\mathcal{C}_{init}$, in which case $p_\chi \in \mathcal{P}_\varphi$, or by a unique component $\mathcal{C}_{\psi_1 \mathbf{U}_I \psi_2}$ (or $\mathcal{C}_{\psi_1 \mathbf{R}_I \psi_2}$) such that $p_\chi \in \mathcal{P}_{\psi_1}$ or $p_\chi \in \mathcal{P}_{\psi_2}$, and χ has not been satisfied yet. When component $\mathcal{C}_\chi$ is in location 1, we say that we have an *obligation* for χ. To satisfy this obligation, we must see a letter in the future where φ_2 holds. Thus, there is a self-loop on location 1 whose label ensures that φ_2 does not hold (because of $\sim\varphi_2$), while φ_1 still holds (this is ensured by $\widehat{\varphi_1}$, which also pulls a minimal set of triggers for φ_1 to be satisfied). $\mathcal{C}_\chi$ moves back from 1 to 0 when φ_2 holds, while no trigger of φ_1 should be pulled at this instant (which is translated by $*\varphi_1$). From location 0, if we do not read trigger p_χ, nothing has to be checked and we do not pull any trigger. However, if p_χ is pulled, then, either φ_2 holds right away and the obligation is fulfilled immediately, or we jump to location 1. The component $\mathcal{C}_\chi$ for the case $\chi = \varphi_1 \, \mathbf{R} \, \varphi_2$ is based on a similar reasoning. We state the following proposition without proof as it will be superseded by a stronger proposition in the next section.

Proposition 4. *For all* LTL *formulae* φ, $\mathsf{proj}_{\mathsf{AP}}(\llbracket \mathcal{C}_{init} \times \prod_{\chi \in \Phi} \mathcal{C}_\chi \rrbracket) = \llbracket \varphi \rrbracket$.

Example 5. Consider the LTL formula $\mathbf{G}(p \Rightarrow \mathbf{F}q)$ that can be rewritten into negative normal form as $\varphi = \bot \, \mathbf{R} \, (\neg p \vee \top \, \mathbf{U} \, q)$. Then, the three component Büchi automata $\mathcal{C}_{init}$, $\mathcal{C}_\varphi$ and $\mathcal{C}_{\mathbf{F}q}$, after the constraints on the transitions are simplified, are depicted on the top of Fig. 4, The automaton $\mathcal{C} = \mathcal{C}_{init} \times \mathcal{C}_\varphi \times \mathcal{C}_{\mathbf{F}q}$ is depicted in the middle of the figure. Once atomic propositions in AP_φ are projected away, one obtains an automaton isomorphic to the one at the bottom of the figure that accepts $\llbracket \varphi \rrbracket$.

4   The Case of MITL$_{0,\infty}$

We now describe how to lift the translation we described earlier to the timed operators of MITL$_{0,\infty}$. The new components for $\mathbf{U}_{[0,a]}$, $\mathbf{R}_{[0,a]}$, and $\mathbf{R}_{[a,\infty)}$ are depicted in Fig. 5. They have the same shape as the components for untimed $\mathbf{U}$ and $\mathbf{R}$ (see Fig. 3); only the guards are changed to reflect the more involved semantics of the timed operators. Observe that these automata have only one clock. To understand why this is sufficient, consider the formula $\mathbf{G}(p \Rightarrow \chi)$ with $\chi = p\,\mathbf{U}_{[0,2]}\,q$. After reading $(\{p\},0)(\{p\},0.4)(\{p\},1)$, the OCATA $\mathcal{A}_\varphi$ reaches the configuration $\{(\varphi,0),(\chi,0),(\chi,0.6),(\chi,1)\}$, meaning intuitively that, to satisfy the formula, one must fulfil three obligations related to χ: to see q's within 2, 1.4, and 1 time units, respectively. Hence, we can store the earliest obligation, corresponding to $(\chi,1)$, only (as already observed in [11]). Indeed, if the corresponding instance of χ is satisfied, it means that there will be a q occurring within less that 1 time unit, which will also satisfy all the other obligations. More generally, for operators $\mathbf{U}_{[0,a]}$ and $\mathbf{R}_{[a,\infty)}$, it is always the case that only the oldest obligation has to be stored, while for operators $\mathbf{R}_{[0,a]}$ and $\mathbf{U}_{[a,\infty)}$, only the earliest obligation has to be stored. This is translated in the components by the absence/presence of resets on transitions that leave state 1 (which is reached when an obligation is currently active) and read p_χ.

For $\chi = \varphi_1 \, \mathbf{U}_{[a,\infty)} \, \varphi_2$, the situation is slightly more complicated, although one clock is again sufficient. The corresponding component is in Fig. 6 and has four locations. To understand why, consider the case when there is an obligation for χ associated with the current valuation $v \geq a$ of clock x ($\mathcal{C}_\chi$ is in location 1), the current letter contains p_χ and satisfies both $\widehat{\varphi_1}$ and $\widehat{\varphi_2}$. Since the trigger has been pulled, $\mathcal{C}_\chi$ should stay in the non-accepting location 1. On the other hand, the pending obligation has also been fulfilled, and an accepting location

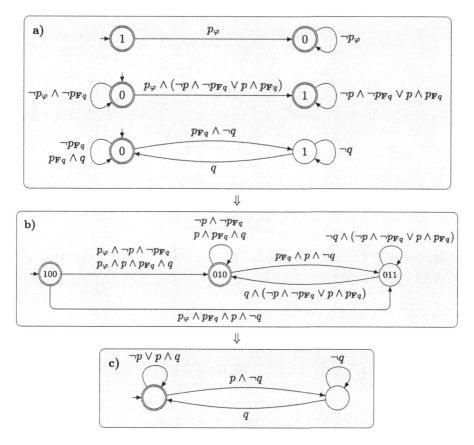

Fig. 4. (a) Component Büchi automata for the formula $\varphi = \bot\,\mathbf{R}\,(\neg p\vee\top\,\mathbf{U}\,q)$; (b) Büchi automaton obtained by the product of the components; (c) Büchi automaton obtained by projecting away AP_φ (and merging two identical locations).

should be visited. So, instead of staying in 1, $\mathcal{C}_\chi$ moves to $1'$ in this case: $1'$ is a copy of 1 as far as transitions are concerned, but it is accepting. The location $1''$ is used to deal with the situation where p_χ is launched infinitely often but no two occurrences of p_χ are separated by more than a time units; in this case, we non-deterministically move to $1''$ and add a new obligation (by resetting x) after the current obligation has been verified. Notice that this problem cannot occur for $\varphi_1\,\mathbf{U}\,\varphi_2$, or $\varphi_1\,\mathbf{U}_{[0,a]}\,\varphi_2$: in these cases, the new obligation is immediately fulfilled, and the automaton moves to the initial, accepting, location.

We now present the extension of Proposition 4 to the case of $\mathsf{MITL}_{0,\infty}$. The proof relies on a function that, given a formula $\gamma = \delta(\ell,\sigma)$ (where δ is the transition function of $\mathcal{A}_\varphi$, ℓ is a location of $\mathcal{A}_\varphi$, and $\sigma \in \Sigma = 2^{\mathsf{AP}}$) and a minimal model M of γ with respect to a clock valuation $v \in \mathbb{R}^+$, recovers the set of triggers activated. Formally, we write $\mathrm{trig}_\varphi(M,\gamma,v)$ for the subset of AP_φ inductively defined by (the rule for $x.\gamma$ where $\gamma = \delta(\ell,\sigma)$ for some $\ell \in \varPhi$ has precedence over the rule for $x.(\gamma_1 \wedge \gamma_2)$ and $x.(\gamma_1 \vee \gamma_2)$):

a) $\neg p_x \wedge {*}\varphi_1 \wedge {*}\varphi_2, x := 0$
$p_x \wedge {*}\varphi_1 \wedge \widehat{\varphi_2}, x := 0$

$p_x \wedge \widehat{\varphi_1} \wedge {\sim}\varphi_2, x = 0$

$\boxed{0}$

$\widehat{\varphi_1} \wedge {\sim}\varphi_2 \wedge x \le a$

$\boxed{1}$

${*}\varphi_1 \wedge \widehat{\varphi_2} \wedge x \le a, x := 0$

b) $\neg p_x \wedge {*}\varphi_1 \wedge {*}\varphi_2, x := 0$
$p_x \wedge \widehat{\varphi_1} \wedge \widehat{\varphi_2}, x := 0$

$p_x \wedge {\sim}\varphi_1 \wedge \widehat{\varphi_2}, x = 0$

$\boxed{0}$

$\neg p_x \wedge {\sim}\varphi_1 \wedge \widehat{\varphi_2} \wedge x \le a$
$p_x \wedge {\sim}\varphi_1 \wedge \widehat{\varphi_2}, x := 0$

$\boxed{1}$

$\neg p_x \wedge {*}\varphi_1 \wedge {*}\varphi_2 \wedge x > a, x := 0$
$\neg p_x \wedge \widehat{\varphi_1} \wedge \widehat{\varphi_2} \wedge x \le a, x := 0$
$p_x \wedge \widehat{\varphi_1} \wedge \widehat{\varphi_2}, x := 0$

c) $\neg p_x \wedge {*}\varphi_1 \wedge {*}\varphi_2, x := 0$
$p_x \wedge \widehat{\varphi_1} \wedge {*}\varphi_2, x := 0$

$p_x \wedge {\sim}\varphi_1 \wedge {*}\varphi_2, x = 0$

$\boxed{0}$

${\sim}\varphi_1 \wedge {*}\varphi_2 \wedge x < a$
${\sim}\varphi_1 \wedge \widehat{\varphi_2} \wedge x \ge a$

$\boxed{1}$

$\widehat{\varphi_1} \wedge {*}\varphi_2 \wedge x < a, x := 0$
$\widehat{\varphi_1} \wedge \widehat{\varphi_2} \wedge x \ge a, x := 0$

Fig. 5. One-clock TA for the subformulae: (a) $\chi = \varphi_1 \, \mathbf{U}_{[0,a]} \, \varphi_2$, (b) $\chi = \varphi_1 \, \mathbf{R}_{[0,a]} \, \varphi_2$, and (c) $\chi = \varphi_1 \, \mathbf{R}_{[a,\infty)} \, \varphi_2$.

- $\mathsf{trig}_\varphi(M, \gamma_1 \wedge \gamma_2, v) = \mathsf{trig}_\varphi(M, \gamma_1, v) \cup \mathsf{trig}_\varphi(M, \gamma_2, v)$;
- $\mathsf{trig}_\varphi(M, \gamma_1 \vee \gamma_2, v) = \begin{cases} \mathsf{trig}_\varphi(M, \gamma_1, v) & \text{if } M \models_v \gamma_1 \\ \mathsf{trig}_\varphi(M, \gamma_2, v) & \text{otherwise}; \end{cases}$
- $\mathsf{trig}_\varphi(M, x.\gamma, v) = \{p_\ell\} \cup \mathsf{trig}_\varphi(M, \gamma, 0)$ if $\gamma = \delta(\ell, \sigma)$ for some $\ell \in \Phi$;
- $\mathsf{trig}_\varphi(M, x.(\gamma_1 \wedge \gamma_2), v) = \mathsf{trig}_\varphi(M, x.\gamma_1, v) \cup \mathsf{trig}_\varphi(M, x.\gamma_2, v)$;
- $\mathsf{trig}_\varphi(M, x.(\gamma_1 \vee \gamma_2), v) = \begin{cases} \mathsf{trig}_\varphi(M, x.\gamma_1, v) & \text{if } M \models_v x.\gamma_1 \\ \mathsf{trig}_\varphi(M, x.\gamma_2, v) & \text{otherwise}; \end{cases}$
- $\mathsf{trig}_\varphi(M, \gamma, v) = \emptyset$ otherwise.

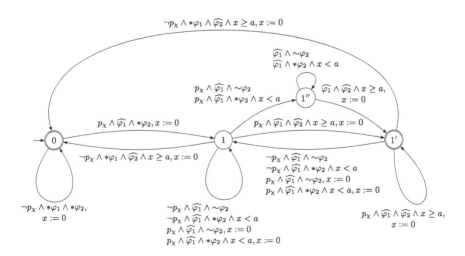

Fig. 6. One-clock TA for the subformula $\chi = \varphi_1 \, \mathbf{U}_{[a,\infty)} \, \varphi_2$.

Proposition 6. *For all* $\mathsf{MITL}_{0,\infty}$ *formulae* φ, $\mathsf{proj}_{\mathsf{AP}}(\llbracket \mathcal{C}_{init} \times \prod_{\chi \in \Phi} \mathcal{C}_\chi \rrbracket) = \llbracket \varphi \rrbracket$.

Proof (Sketch). Recall that Theorem 2 states that $\llbracket \varphi \rrbracket = \llbracket \mathcal{A}_\varphi \rrbracket$. Therefore, it suffices to relate the accepting runs of the synchronous product of all component Büchi timed automata $\mathcal{C} = \mathcal{C}_{init} \times \prod_{\chi \in \Phi} \mathcal{C}_\chi$ with the accepting runs of $\mathcal{A}_\varphi$. Let us consider a timed word $\rho \in \llbracket \mathcal{A}_\varphi \rrbracket$ and an accepting run $G = (V, \rightarrow)$ of $\mathcal{A}_\varphi$ over ρ. Let $K_0, K_1, \ldots$ be the sequence of configurations associated with G.

We first construct the instrumented timed word ρ' over $2^{\mathsf{AP} \cup \mathsf{AP}_\varphi}$ from ρ and G by adding the triggers in AP_φ according to the minimal models selected in G. More precisely, for all $i \geq 0$, we associate with every state (ℓ, v) of K_i the pair $(\gamma_{\ell,v}, M_{\ell,v})$ where $\gamma_{\ell,v} = \delta(\ell, \sigma_{i+1})$ and $M_{\ell,v}$ is the minimal model of $\gamma_{\ell,v}$ with respect to $v + \tau_{i+1} - \tau_i$ chosen in G. We then gather all the triggers in $\mathcal{Q}_i = \bigcup_{(\ell,v) \in K_i} \mathsf{trig}_\varphi(M_{\ell,v}, \gamma_{\ell,v}, v + \tau_{i+1} - \tau_i)$, and let $\rho' = (\sigma_1 \cup \mathcal{Q}_1, \tau_1)(\sigma_2 \cup \mathcal{Q}_2, \tau_2) \cdots$. Then, it can be shown that each component has an accepting run over ρ'. By definition, the generalised Büchi acceptance condition on $\mathcal{C}$ is fulfilled exactly when the Büchi acceptance condition on each of the components is fulfilled. It follows that $\mathcal{C}$ accepts ρ', and hence $\rho \in \mathsf{proj}_{\mathsf{AP}}(\llbracket \mathcal{C} \rrbracket)$. The other direction of the proof consists of building an accepting run G of $\mathcal{A}_\varphi$ over $\mathsf{proj}_{\mathsf{AP}}(\rho')$ from an accepting run of $\mathcal{C}$ over $\rho' \in \llbracket \mathcal{C} \rrbracket$. At each level of G, the truth values of the triggers in ρ' are used to guide the construction of minimal models. $\square$

5   Handling Full MITL

We can now extend our translation to full MITL, i.e. allowing operators $\mathbf{U}_{[a,b]}$ and $\mathbf{R}_{[a,b]}$ with $0 < a < b < +\infty$. For these two types of operators, we cannot rely on a single clock in the components anymore. For instance, consider the formula $\varphi = \mathbf{G}(p \Rightarrow \chi)$ with $\chi = \mathbf{F}_{[1,2]} q$. Imagine that $\mathcal{A}_\varphi$ reads the prefix

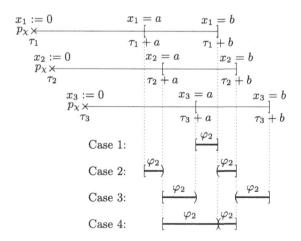

Fig. 7. How to split cases to satisfy the formula $\chi = \varphi_1 \, \mathbf{U}_{[a,b]} \, \varphi_2$.

$(\{p\},0)(\{p\},0.5)$. At this point, its configuration is $\{(\varphi,0),(\chi,0),(\chi,0.5)\}$. It is not possible, as before, to drop one of the two states in location χ as the following futures can happen: if we read $(\{q\},1)$, obligation $(\chi,0)$ is fulfilled but not $(\chi,0.5)$; if we read $(\{q\},2.5)$ then the obligation $(\chi,0.5)$ is fuilfilled but not $(\chi,0)$. Therefore, we must keep track of the two obligations separately. It is, however, not clear how to find an *a priori* bound on the number of clocks. This is the role of the *interval semantics* introduced in [11] for OCATAs resulting from MITL formulae over infinite words. In this interpretation of OCATAs, valuations of the clocks are no longer *points* but *intervals* meant to approximate sets of (singular) valuations: $(\ell,[\alpha,\beta])$ means that there *are* clock copies with valuations α and β in ℓ, yet there *could be* more copies in ℓ with valuations in (α,β). In this semantics, we can *merge* non-deterministically two copies $(\ell,[\alpha_1,\beta_1])$ and $(\ell,[\alpha_2,\beta_2])$ into a single copy $(\ell,[\alpha_1,\beta_2])$ (assuming $\alpha_1 \le \beta_2$), in order to keep the number of clock copies below a fixed threshold, and thus obtain an equivalent TA. It has been shown in [11] that, for the OCATA $\mathcal{A}_\varphi$, with $\varphi \in$ MITL, the interval semantics is sufficient to retain the language of the formula, with TAs having at most $M(\varphi) = |\varphi| \times \max_{I \in \mathcal{I}_\varphi}(\max(4 \times \lceil \inf(I)/|I| \rceil + 2, 2 \times \lceil \sup(I)/|I| \rceil + 2))$ clocks, where $\mathcal{I}_\varphi$ is the set of intervals that appear in φ: more precisely, each subformula with topmost operator $\mathbf{U}_I$ (respectively, $\mathbf{R}_I$) contributes to $4 \times \lceil \inf(I)/|I| \rceil + 2$ (respectively, $2 \times \lceil \sup(I)/|I| \rceil + 2$) more clocks.

Our solution is twofold in this context: (i) we propose a better approximation by intervals that allows us to cut, up to a factor of two, the number of clock copies we must keep in memory; (ii) instead of a single TA, as in [11], we provide a GBTA, with one component per temporal subformula of φ. The component TA are much more involved than for MITL$_{0,\infty}$, thus we do not give them explicitly, but rather explain the main ideas.

We start by developing our new merging strategy on an example, to explain how it is different from [11]. Consider $\chi = \varphi_1 \mathbf{U}_{[a,b]} \varphi_2$ with $0 < a < b < +\infty$ and the situation depicted in Fig. 7, where the trigger p_χ is pulled at three positions of time stamps τ_1, τ_2, and τ_3. We suppose that φ_1 holds at all three positions. The picture presents four different cases corresponding to the four possible situations where the occurrences of φ_2 fulfil the three pending obligations. Case 1 is when a position in $[\tau_3 + a, \tau_1 + b]$ satisfies φ_2, hence all three obligations are resolved at once. This case can be checked using only clocks x_3 and x_1. In case 2, the first obligation is resolved by an occurrence of φ_2 with time stamp in $[\tau_1 + a, \tau_2 + a)$, while the two others are resolved by an occurrence in $(\tau_1 + b, \tau_2 + b]$. Thus, case 2 can be checked using only clocks x_1 and x_2. Now consider the remaining cases: if no occurrences of φ_2 appear in $[\tau_1 + a, \tau_2 + a) \cup [\tau_3 + a, \tau_1 + b]$, one occurrence of φ_2 must necessarily happen in $[\tau_2 + a, \tau_3 + a)$, while the other should be in $(\tau_1 + b, \tau_3 + b]$, which can only be checked using three clocks x_1, x_2 and x_3. We avoid this by splitting this case into two further cases (cases 3 and 4) that can be checked with only two clocks. Specifically, case 3 can be checked using only clocks x_2 and x_3; and case 4 using only clocks x_2 and x_1.

Observe that these cases can be categorised into two groups: one where φ_2 should occur in a single interval whose endpoints use two distinct clocks (case 1), another where φ_2 should occur in two half-open intervals whose both endpoints use the same two distinct clocks (cases 2, 3 and 4). In each of the two groups, it must be understood how a new obligation (added by pulling the trigger p_χ) modifies the situation. With only one interval, if a new obligation for φ_2 appear as a new interval $[\tau + a, \tau + b]$, either the new obligation is implied by the current one, in which case we are done, or the two intervals intersect and we do a further split (non-deterministically) into cases 1, 3 and 4, or they are disjoint and we keep both intervals in memory. The latter situation cannot happen too often since intervals are non-singular; more precisely, this will happen at most $\lceil(\inf(I)/|I|)+1\rceil$ times ($I = [a, b]$). With two intervals, either the new obligation is already implied by current obligations, or $[\tau + a, \tau + b]$ is not implied by the current obligations and we add this new interval in memory as before (again, this cannot happen more than $\lceil(\inf(I)/|I|) + 1\rceil$ times).

In the end, following the same lines as [11], we can build a component $\mathcal{C}_\chi$ for each subformula $\chi = \varphi_1 \mathbf{U}_{[a,b]} \varphi_2$ with $N(\chi) = 2 \times \lceil(\inf(I)/|I|)+1\rceil+2$ clocks (the two additional clocks are used to deal easily with some special cases), which is roughly half of the previous bound on the number of clocks [11]. In the locations, we can handle the clocks in pairs and use a queue of size $N(\chi)/2$ to keep track of which case we fall into and which clocks are used to represent the endpoints of intervals. It follows that the number of locations is exponential in $N(\chi)$. A similar construction, using $2 \times \lceil(\inf(I)/|I|) + 1\rceil$ clocks, builds a component $\mathcal{C}_\chi$ for each subformula $\chi = \varphi_1 \mathbf{R}_{[a,b]} \varphi_2$. In this case, we have to consider unions of intervals, which are easier to deal with.

Theorem 7. *For all* MITL *formulae* φ, $\mathsf{proj}_{\mathsf{AP}}(\llbracket\mathcal{C}_{init} \times \prod_{\chi \in \Phi} \mathcal{C}_\chi\rrbracket) = \llbracket\varphi\rrbracket$.

Proof (Sketch). We follow the same lines of the proof of Proposition 6, i.e. relating the accepting runs of $\mathcal{A}_\varphi$ with the accepting runs of $\mathcal{C} = \mathcal{C}_{init} \times \prod_{\chi \in \Phi} \mathcal{C}_\chi$. To show that $\llbracket\mathcal{A}_\varphi\rrbracket \subseteq \mathsf{proj}_{\mathsf{AP}}(\llbracket\mathcal{C}\rrbracket)$, we use the same construction of the Hintikka sequence over $2^{\mathsf{AP}\cup\mathsf{AP}_\varphi}$. Note that we have the accepting run G, so that we know in advance *how each obligation is to be fulfilled in the future*. In particular, we use this knowledge to resolve the non-determinism in components of the form $\mathcal{C}_{\varphi_1 \mathbf{U}_{[a,b]} \varphi_2}$ or $\mathcal{C}_{\varphi_1 \mathbf{R}_{[a,b]} \varphi_2}$. The other direction is also similar.   □

6   Implementation

We have implemented our translation from MITL formulae to generalised Büchi timed automata in a tool called MIGHTYL, written in OCaml. From a formula φ, it produces the GBTA $\mathcal{C}$, described in previous sections, in the XML format used by UPPAAL, as well as the generalised Büchi condition written as a very simple LTL formula. When the input formula is in $\mathsf{MITL}_{0,\infty}$, the translation can be done in polynomial time. For the general case, it runs in exponential time (assuming a succinct encoding of constants, as is the case here). We can then use UPPAAL [27] to check the satisfiability of φ over finite timed words, or LTSMIN [24] with OPAAL front-end to check satisfiability over infinite timed words. To maximise compatibility with model-checking tools, we use several helper variables in the output

XML file, e.g. a Boolean variable for each atomic proposition and a `loc` variable in each component for the current location. The synchronisation is done in a round-robin fashion with a counter variable `N`: initially, `N` is set to 0, allowing the model (to be model-checked) to take a transition and set the truth values of the atomic propositions. Then, `N` loops from 1 to the number of components of $\mathcal{C}$, allowing each component to read the atomic propositions and take a corresponding transition. Finally, `N` is set back to 0 and we start over again. For the finite-word case, this also enables to check that all components have been synchronised properly (`N = 0`) while in the final location. Our tool is publicly available, and can even be executed directly on the website

$$\text{http://www.ulb.ac.be/di/verif/mightyl}$$

Compared to the simplified version we studied in this article, MIGHTYL also allows for (semi-)open intervals. Since it can also deal with next and dual-next operators, we can verify formulae like $\neg \mathbf{X}_{[1,2)}p$. All the following tests have been performed on a MacBook Pro 2.7 GHz with 8Go RAM.

We check the satisfiability of MITL formulae on examples, inspired by the benchmarks of [11,19]. For $k \in \mathbb{N}$ and an interval I, we consider the satisfiable formulae: $F(k,I) = \bigwedge_{i=1}^{k}\mathbf{F}_I p_i$, $G(k,I) = \bigwedge_{i=1}^{k}\mathbf{G}_I p_i$, $U(k,I) = (\cdots(p_1 \mathbf{U}_I p_2) \mathbf{U}_I \cdots) \mathbf{U}_I p_k$, $R(k,I) = (\cdots(p_1 \mathbf{R}_I p_2) \mathbf{R}_I \cdots) \mathbf{R}_I p_k$, and $\theta(k,I) = \neg((\bigwedge_{i=1}^{k}\mathbf{GF}p_i) \Rightarrow \mathbf{G}(q \Rightarrow \mathbf{F}_I r))$. We also consider an example inspired from motion planning problems via MITL specifications as in [25,31]. In this benchmark, a robot must visit some target points $t_1, t_2, t_3, \ldots, t_k$ within given time frames (in our case, t_i must be seen in time frame $[3(i-1), 3i]$), while enforcing a safety condition $\mathbf{G}\neg p$. This specification is modelled by the satisfiable MITL formula $\mu(k) = \bigwedge_{i=1}^{k}\mathbf{F}_{[3(i-1),3i]}t_i \wedge \mathbf{G}\neg p$. In Table 1, we report on the time taken by the execution of MIGHTYL; LTSMIN (split into the time taken by OPAAL front-end to translate the model into C++ code, the compilation time of the resulting C++ code, and the time taken by LTSMIN for the actual model-checking); and UPPAAL, on all these examples (for the motion planning,

Table 1. Execution time for the satisfiability check of benchmarks of [11,19]. For LTSMIN, the three columns reported correspond to the translation into C++, the compilation and the actual model-checking, respectively.

Formula	MIGHTYL	LTSMIN	UPPAAL	Formula	MIGHTYL	LTSMIN	UPPAAL
$F(5,[0,\infty))$	9ms	3.48s/2.18s/0.12s	0.75s	$U(5,[0,\infty))$	16ms	1.90s/1.44s/0.05s	0.41s
$F(5,[0,2])$	7ms	3.76s/2.23s/0.15s	0.84s	$U(5,[0,2])$	8ms	2.08s/1.54s/0.06s	0.42s
$F(5,[2,\infty))$	6ms	3.76s/2.26s/0.91s	1.64s	$U(5,[2,\infty))$	8ms	2.08s/1.53s/0.09s	0.52s
$F(3,[1,2])$	70ms	6m5.15s/38.01s/0.22s	9.00s	$U(3,[1,2])$	49ms	4m0.14s/23.54s/0.09s	4.92s
$F(5,[1,2])$	70ms	>15m	2m6s	$U(5,[1,2])$	97ms	>15m	21.80s
$G(5,[0,\infty))$	10ms	3.83s/2.43s/0.05s	0.75s	$R(5,[0,\infty))$	7ms	1.86s/1.42s/0.03s	0.40s
$G(5,[0,2])$	10ms	4.01s/2.51s/0.10s	0.82s	$R(5,[0,2])$	7ms	1.97s/1.44s/0.03s	0.40s
$G(5,[2,\infty))$	9ms	4.06s/2.47s/0.04s	0.85s	$R(5,[2,\infty))$	7ms	1.92s/1.42s/0.03s	0.42s
$G(5,[1,2])$	15ms	7.81s/2.99s/0.09s	1.12s	$R(5,[1,2])$	10ms	5.37s/2.16s/0.04s	0.62s
$\mu(1)$	13ms	-	0.39s	$\theta(1,[100,1000])$	9ms	1.88s/1.74s/0.04s	0.25s
$\mu(2)$	21ms	-	2.33s	$\theta(2,[100,1000])$	13ms	5.04s/3.17s/0.19s	0.86s
$\mu(3)$	76ms	-	15.77s	$\theta(3,[100,1000])$	14ms	36.57s/16.27s/3.20s	21.84s
$\mu(4)$	87ms	-	2m23s	$\theta(4,[100,1000])$	15ms	5m30s/4m18s/2m16s	18m39s

Table 2. Validity and redundancy checking of MITL formulae.

Formula	MIGHTYL	LTSMIN	UPPAAL	[16]
$\mathbf{F}_{[0,30]}(p \Rightarrow \mathbf{G}_{[0,20]}p)$ (tautology)	7ms	0.98s	0.32s	7s
$\mathbf{G}_{[0,30]}\neg p \vee \mathbf{F}_{[0,20]}p$ (valid, i.e. satisfiable and not tautology)	13ms	1.66s	0.30s	not considered
$\mathbf{F}_{[0,30]}p \wedge \mathbf{F}_{[0,20]}p$ (valid but redundant)	24ms	3.39s	0.79s	14s
$\mathbf{G}_{[0,20]}\mathbf{F}_{[0,20]}p \wedge \mathbf{G}_{[0,40]}p \wedge \mathbf{F}_{[20,40]}\top$ (valid but redundant)	60ms	2m58s	4.94s	not considered

only finite words are relevant, hence we report only on the UPPAAL running
time).

We also report on the benchmarks found in [16], where the debugging of formal specifications of cyber-physical systems is reduced to MITL non-satisfiability.
More precisely, we check formulae for *validity* and *redundancy*. In [16], a formula
φ is called *valid* (with respect to a specification goal) if φ is neither unsatisfiable
nor a tautology, i.e. φ and $\neg\varphi$ are both satisfiable. A conjunct φ_1 of formula
$\varphi = \bigwedge_{i=1}^{k} \varphi_i$ is redundant if and only if $\bigwedge_{i=2}^{k} \varphi_i$ implies φ_1. This is true if and
only if $\psi = \bigwedge_{i=2}^{k} \varphi_i \Rightarrow \varphi_1$ is valid, i.e. if and only if $\neg\psi$ is not satisfiable. For
instance, $\mathbf{F}_{[0,30]}p$ is redundant in $\mathbf{F}_{[0,30]}p \wedge \mathbf{F}_{[0,20]}p$, and $\mathbf{G}_{[0,20]}\mathbf{F}_{[0,20]}p$ is redundant in $\mathbf{G}_{[0,20]}\mathbf{F}_{[0,20]}p \wedge \mathbf{G}_{[0,40]}p \wedge \mathbf{F}_{[20,40]}\top$. We check the validity and redundancy
of several formulae considered in [16] and report the results in Table 2. For ref-
erence, we copy the execution time reported in [16] for these checks.[5] We also
consider some new formulae specific to our pointwise semantics.

Finally, recall that one technical part of the constructions of component Büchi
timed automata is the minimal model simplification $\mathsf{mm}(\varphi)$. Our components
remain correct if we replace everywhere $\mathsf{mm}(\varphi)$ by φ (i.e. $\widehat{\varphi}$ simply becomes $\overline{\varphi}$).
On some instances of the previous benchmarks, the influence on the execution
time of the satisfiability checks is tremendous (differences on the execution time
of MIGHTYL negligible, since the tool always answers in less than a second).
For instance, over $F(5, [0, \infty))$, LTSMIN shows a 17% overhead. For $F(5, [0, 2])$,
LTSMIN experiences a 5% overhead, while UPPAAL has a 12% overhead. For
formulae $F(5, [2, \infty))$, $F(3, [1, 2])$, $F(5, [1, 2])$, the situation is even worse since
UPPAAL stops responding before the timeout of fifteen minutes. LTSMIN also
hangs on $F(3, [1, 2])$ before the timeout. On the motion planning example, the
overhead is also significant for UPPAAL, e.g. 80% for μ_2, and, for μ_3 and μ_4,
UPPAAL does not respond anymore before the timeout. Finally, on the two unsatisfiable examples of the redundancy check, LTSMIN and UPPAAL have overheads
of 70%/3% and 630%/230%, respectively.

7   Conclusion and Perspectives

In this work, we proposed a new compositional construction from MITL to timed
automata which we implemented the tool MIGHTYL, enabling easy automata-
based model-checking of full MITL. For future work, since the structure of the

---

[5] These numbers are only for reference and should not be taken as a direct comparison
since, contrary to us, [16] considers a bounded continuous semantics of MITL.

formula is preserved in our construction, we want to investigate antichain-based heuristics to allow more performance boost. For MIGHTYL, we plan to add native support for ECL [33] operators which eases the writing of specifications, as well as past operators and counting operators [23].

Acknowledgements. We thank the reviewers of this article that help us clarify its overall presentation. The third author would like to thank Andreas Engelbredt Dalsgaard, Alfons Laarman and Jeroen Meijer for their technical help with OPAAL and LTSMIN.

References

1. Abid, N., Dal-Zilio, S., Botlan, D.L.: A formal framework to specify and verify real-time properties on critical systems. Int. J. Crit. Comput.-Based Syst. **5**(1/2), 4–30 (2014)
2. Alur, R., Dill, D.L.: A theory of timed automata. Theoret. Comput. Sci. **126**(2), 183–235 (1994)
3. Alur, R., Feder, T., Henzinger, T.A.: The benefits of relaxing punctuality. J. ACM **43**(1), 116–146 (1996)
4. Alur, R., Henzinger, T.A.: Real-time logics: complexity and expressiveness. Inf. Comput. **104**(1), 35–77 (1993)
5. Barnat, J., et al.: DiVinE 3.0 – an explicit-state model checker for multithreaded C & C++ programs. In: Sharygina, N., Veith, H. (eds.) CAV 2013. LNCS, vol. 8044, pp. 863–868. Springer, Heidelberg (2013). doi:10.1007/978-3-642-39799-8_60
6. Bartocci, E., Bortolussi, L., Nenzi, L.: A temporal logic approach to modular design of synthetic biological circuits. In: Gupta, A., Henzinger, T.A. (eds.) CMSB 2013. LNCS, vol. 8130, pp. 164–177. Springer, Heidelberg (2013). doi:10.1007/978-3-642-40708-6_13
7. Bersani, M.M., Rossi, M., San Pietro, P.: A tool for deciding the satisfiability of continuous-time metric temporal logic. Acta Inform. **53**(2), 171–206 (2016)
8. Bloem, R., Cimatti, A., Pill, I., Roveri, M.: Symbolic implementation of alternating automata. Int. J. Found. Comput. Sci. **18**(4), 727–743 (2007)
9. Bouyer, P., Colange, M., Markey, N.: Symbolic optimal reachability in weighted timed automata. In: Chaudhuri, S., Farzan, A. (eds.) CAV 2016. LNCS, vol. 9779, pp. 513–530. Springer, Cham (2016). doi:10.1007/978-3-319-41528-4_28
10. Brihaye, T., Estiévenart, M., Geeraerts, G.: On MITL and alternating timed automata. In: Braberman, V., Fribourg, L. (eds.) FORMATS 2013. LNCS, vol. 8053, pp. 47–61. Springer, Heidelberg (2013). doi:10.1007/978-3-642-40229-6_4
11. Brihaye, T., Estiévenart, M., Geeraerts, G.: On MITL and alternating timed automata over infinite words. In: Legay, A., Bozga, M. (eds.) FORMATS 2014. LNCS, vol. 8711, pp. 69–84. Springer, Cham (2014). doi:10.1007/978-3-319-10512-3_6
12. Bulychev, P.E., David, A., Larsen, K.G., Li, G.: Efficient controller synthesis for a fragment of $MTL_{0,\infty}$. Acta Inform. **51**(3–4), 165–192 (2014)
13. Cimatti, A., Clarke, E., Giunchiglia, E., Giunchiglia, F., Pistore, M., Roveri, M., Sebastiani, R., Tacchella, A.: NuSMV2: an opensource tool for symbolic model checking. In: Brinksma, E., Larsen, K.G. (eds.) CAV 2002. LNCS, vol. 2404, pp. 359–364. Springer, Heidelberg (2002). doi:10.1007/3-540-45657-0_29

14. Claessen, K., Een, N., Sterin, B.: A circuit approach to LTL model checking. In: FMCAD 2013. IEEE (2013)
15. De Moura, L., Bjørner, N.: Satisfiability modulo theories: introduction and applications. Commun. ACM **54**(9), 69–77 (2011)
16. Dokhanchi, A., Hoxha, B., Fainekos, G.: Formal requirement debugging for testing and verification of cyber-physical systems. Research report 1607.02549. arXiv (2016)
17. D'Souza, D., Matteplackel, R.: A clock-optimal hierarchical monitoring automaton construction for MITL. Research report 2013–1, IIS (2013). http://www.csa.iisc.ernet.in/TR/2013/1/lics2013-tr.pdf
18. Fu, J., Topcu, U.: Computational methods for stochastic control with metric interval temporal logic specifications. In: CDC 2015, pp. 7440–7447. IEEE (2015)
19. Gastin, P., Oddoux, D.: Fast LTL to Büchi automata translation. In: Berry, G., Comon, H., Finkel, A. (eds.) CAV 2001. LNCS, vol. 2102, pp. 53–65. Springer, Heidelberg (2001). doi:10.1007/3-540-44585-4_6
20. Gerth, R., Peled, D., Vardi, M.Y., Wolper, P.: Simple on-the-fly automatic verification of linear temporal logic. In: PSTV 1995. pp. 3–18. Chapman & Hall (1995)
21. Hammer, M., Knapp, A., Merz, S.: Truly on-the-fly LTL model checking. In: Halbwachs, N., Zuck, L.D. (eds.) TACAS 2005. LNCS, vol. 3440, pp. 191–205. Springer, Heidelberg (2005). doi:10.1007/978-3-540-31980-1_13
22. Hirshfeld, Y., Rabinovich, A.M.: Logics for real time: decidability and complexity. Fundam. Informaticae **62**(1), 1–28 (2004)
23. Hirshfeld, Y., Rabinovich, A.: An expressive temporal logic for real time. In: Královič, R., Urzyczyn, P. (eds.) MFCS 2006. LNCS, vol. 4162, pp. 492–504. Springer, Heidelberg (2006). doi:10.1007/11821069_43
24. Kant, G., Laarman, A., Meijer, J., van de Pol, J., Blom, S., van Dijk, T.: LTSmin: high-performance language-independent model checking. In: Baier, C., Tinelli, C. (eds.) TACAS 2015. LNCS, vol. 9035, pp. 692–707. Springer, Heidelberg (2015). doi:10.1007/978-3-662-46681-0_61
25. Karaman, S.: Optimal planning with temporal logic specifications. Master's thesis, Massachussetts Institute of Technology (2009)
26. Kupferman, O., Vardi, M.Y.: Weak alternating automata are not that weak. In: ISTCS 1997, pp. 147–158. IEEE (1997)
27. Larsen, K.G., Pettersson, P., Yi, W.: Uppaal in a nutshell. Int. J. Softw. Tools Technol. Transfer **1**(1–2), 134–152 (1997)
28. Maler, O., Nickovic, D., Pnueli, A.: From MITL to timed automata. In: Asarin, E., Bouyer, P. (eds.) FORMATS 2006. LNCS, vol. 4202, pp. 274–289. Springer, Heidelberg (2006). doi:10.1007/11867340_20
29. Muller, D.E., Saoudi, A., Schupp, P.E.: Alternating automata, the weak monadic theory of the tree, and its complexity. In: Kott, L. (ed.) ICALP 1986. LNCS, vol. 226, pp. 275–283. Springer, Heidelberg (1986). doi:10.1007/3-540-16761-7_77
30. Ouaknine, J., Worrell, J.: On the decidability and complexity of metric temporal logic over finite words. In: Logical Methods in Computer Science, vol. 3, no. 1 (2007)
31. Plaku, E., Karaman, S.: Motion planning with temporal-logic specifications: progress and challenges. AI Communications **29**, 151–162 (2016)
32. Pnueli, A.: The temporal logic of programs. In: FOCS 1977. pp. 46–57. IEEE (1977)
33. Raskin, J.F., Schobbens, P.Y.: The logic of event clocks: decidability, complexity and expressiveness. J. Automata Lang. Comb. **4**(3), 247–282 (1999)

34. Rozier, K.Y., Vardi, M.Y.: A multi-encoding approach for LTL symbolic satisfiability checking. In: Butler, M., Schulte, W. (eds.) FM 2011. LNCS, vol. 6664, pp. 417–431. Springer, Heidelberg (2011). doi:10.1007/978-3-642-21437-0_31

35. Thierry-Mieg, Y.: Symbolic model-checking using ITS-tools. In: Baier, C., Tinelli, C. (eds.) TACAS 2015. LNCS, vol. 9035, pp. 231–237. Springer, Heidelberg (2015). doi:10.1007/978-3-662-46681-0_20

36. Vardi, M.Y.: An automata-theoretic approach to linear temporal logic. In: Moller, F., Birtwistle, G. (eds.) Logics for Concurrency. LNCS, vol. 1043, pp. 238–266. Springer, Heidelberg (1996). doi:10.1007/3-540-60915-6_6

37. Wilke, T.: Specifying timed state sequences in powerful decidable logics and timed automata. In: Langmaack, H., de Roever, W.-P., Vytopil, J. (eds.) FTRTFT 1994. LNCS, vol. 863, pp. 694–715. Springer, Heidelberg (1994). doi:10.1007/3-540-58468-4_191

38. de Wulf, M., Doyen, L., Maquet, N., Raskin, J.-F.: Antichains: alternative algorithms for LTL satisfiability and model-checking. In: Ramakrishnan, C.R., Rehof, J. (eds.) TACAS 2008. LNCS, vol. 4963, pp. 63–77. Springer, Heidelberg (2008). doi:10.1007/978-3-540-78800-3_6

39. Zhou, Y., Maity, D., Baras, J.S.: Timed automata approach for motion planning using metric interval temporal logic. Research report 1603.08246. arXiv (2016)

DryVR: Data-Driven Verification and Compositional Reasoning for Automotive Systems

Chuchu Fan[(✉)], Bolun Qi, Sayan Mitra,
and Mahesh Viswanathan

University of Illinois at Urbana-Champaign,
Champaign, USA
{cfan10,bolunqi2,mitras,vmahesh}@illinois.edu

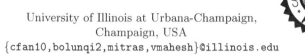

Abstract. We present the DryVR framework for verifying hybrid control systems that are described by a combination of a black-box simulator for trajectories and a white-box transition graph specifying mode switches. The framework includes (a) a probabilistic algorithm for learning sensitivity of the continuous trajectories from simulation data, (b) a bounded reachability analysis algorithm that uses the learned sensitivity, and (c) reasoning techniques based on simulation relations and sequential composition, that enable verification of complex systems under long switching sequences, from the reachability analysis of a simpler system under shorter sequences. We demonstrate the utility of the framework by verifying a suite of automotive benchmarks that include powertrain control, automatic transmission, and several autonomous and ADAS features like automatic emergency braking, lane-merge, and auto-passing controllers.

1 Introduction

The starting point of existing hybrid system verification approaches is the availability of nice mathematical models describing the transitions and trajectories. This central conceit severely restricts the applicability of the resulting approaches. Real world control system "models" are typically a heterogeneous mix of simulation code, differential equations, block diagrams, and hand-crafted look-up tables. Extracting clean mathematical models from these descriptions is usually infeasible. At the same time, rapid developments in Advanced Driving Assist Systems (ADAS), autonomous vehicles, robotics, and drones now make the need for effective and sound verification algorithms stronger than ever before. The DryVR framework presented in this paper aims to narrow the gap between sound and practical verification for control systems.

M. Viswanathan—This work is supported by the grants CAREER 1054247 and CCF 1422798 from the National Science Foundation.

R. Majumdar and V. Kunčak (Eds.): CAV 2017, Part I, LNCS 10426, pp. 441–461, 2017.
DOI: 10.1007/978-3-319-63387-9_22

Model Assumptions. Consider an ADAS feature like automatic emergency braking system (AEB). The high-level logic deciding the timing of when and for how long the brakes are engaged after an obstacle is detected by sensors is implemented in a relatively clean piece of code and this logical module can be seen as a *white-box*. In contrast, the dynamics of vehicle itself, with hundreds of parameters, is more naturally viewed as a *black-box*. That is, it can be simulated or tested with different initial conditions and inputs, but it is nearly impossible to write down a nice mathematical model.

The empirical observation motivating this work is that many control systems, and especially automotive systems, share this combination of white and black boxes (see other examples in Sects. 2.1, 2.5, [21]). In this paper, we view hybrid systems as a combination of a white-box that specifies the mode switches and a black-box that can simulate the continuous evolution in each mode. Suppose the system has a set of modes $\mathcal{L}$ and n continuous variables. The mode switches are defined by a *transition graph* G—a directed acyclic graph (DAG) annotated with allowed switching times. The black-box is a set of trajectories $\mathcal{TL}$ in $\mathbb{R}^n$ for each mode in $\mathcal{L}$.Instead of a closed form description of $\mathcal{TL}$, we have a *simulator*, that can generate sampled data points on individual trajectories. Combining a transition graph G, a set of trajectories $\mathcal{TL}$, and a set of initial states, we obtain a hybrid system for which executions, reachability, and trace containment can be defined naturally.

A number of automotive systems we have studied are naturally represented in the above style: in powertrain [30] and transmission [34] control systems the mode transitions are brought about by the driver or the control algorithm, and in either case it is standard to describe typical switching behavior using time-triggered signals; in automatic emergency braking (AEB), merge and auto-passing control, once the maneuver is activated, the mode transitions occur within certain time intervals. Similar observations hold in other examples.

Safety Verification Algorithm. With black-box modules in our hybrid systems, we address the challenge of providing guaranteed verification. Our approach is based on the idea of simulation-driven reachability analysis [15,16,22]. For a given mode $\ell \in \mathcal{L}$, finitely many simulations of the trajectories of ℓ and a *discrepancy function* bounding the sensitivity of these trajectories, is used to over-approximate the reachable states. For the key step of computing discrepancy for modes that are now represented by black-boxes, we introduce a probabilistic algorithm that learns the parameters of exponential discrepancy functions from simulation data. The algorithm transforms the problem of learning the parameters of the discrepancy function to the problem of learning a linear separator for a set of points in $\mathbb{R}^2$ that are obtained from transforming the simulation data. A classical result in PAC learning, ensures that any such discrepancy function works with high probability for all trajectories. We performed dozens of experiments with a variety of black-box simulators and observed that 15–20 simulation traces typically give a discrepancy function that works for nearly 100% of all simulations. The reachability algorithm for the hybrid system proceeds along the topologically sorted vertices of the transition graph and this gives a sound bounded verification algorithm, provided the learned discrepancy function is correct.

Reasoning. White-box transition graphs in our modelling, identify the switching sequences under which the black-box modules are exercised. Complex systems have involved transition graphs that describe subtle sequences in which the black-box modules are executed. To enable the analysis of such systems, we identify reasoning principles that establish the safety of system under a complex transition graph based on its safety under a simpler transition graph. We define a notion of forward simulation between transition graphs that provides a sufficient condition of when one transition graph "subsumes" another—if G_1 is simulated by G_2 then the reachable states of a hybrid system under G_1 are contained in the reachable states of the system under G_2. Thus the safety of the system under G_2 implies the safety under G_1. Moreover, we give a simple polynomial time algorithm that can check if one transition graph is simulated by another.

Our transition graphs are acyclic with transitions having bounded switching times. Therefore, the executions of the systems have a time bound and a bounded number of mode switches. An important question to investigate is whether establishing the safety for bounded time, enables one to conclude the safety of the system for an arbitrarily long time and for arbitrarily many mode switches. With this in mind, we define a notion of sequential composition of transition graphs G_1 and G_2, such that switching sequences allowed by the composed graph are the concatenation of the sequences allowed by G_1 with those allowed by G_2. Then we prove a sufficient condition on a transition graph G such that safety of a system under G implies the safety of the system under arbitrarily many compositions of G with itself.

Automotive Applications. We have implemented these ideas to create the **D**ata-driven System for **V**erification and **R**easoning (DRYVR). The tool is able to automatically verify or find counter-examples in a few minutes, for all the benchmark scenarios mentioned above. Reachability analysis combined with compositional reasoning, enabled us to infer safety of systems with respect to arbitrary transitions and duration.

Related Work. Most automated verification tools for hybrid systems rely on analyzing a white-box mathematical model of the systems. They include tools based on decidability results [3,24,28], semi-decision procedures that over-approximate the reachable set of states through symbolic computation [4,7,25], using abstractions [1,5,8,38], and using approximate decision procedures for fragments of first-order logic [33]. More recently, there has been interest in developing simulation-based verification tools [2,10–12,16,17,31]. Even though these are simulation based tools, they often rely on being to analyze a mathematical model of the system. The type of analysis that they rely on include instrumentation to extract a symbolic trace from a simulation [31], stochastic optimization to search for counter-examples [2,17], and sensitivity analysis [10–12,16]. Some of the simulation based techniques only work for systems with linear dynamics [26,27]. Recent work on the APEX tool [36] for verifying trajectory planning and tracking in autonomous vehicles is related our approach in that it targets the same application domain.

2 Modeling/Semantic Framework

We introduce a powertrain control system from [30] as a running example to illustrate the elements of our hybrid system modeling framework.

2.1 Powertrain Control System

This system (Powertrn) models a highly nonlinear engine control system. The relevant state variables of the model are intake manifold pressure (p), air-fuel ratio (λ), estimated manifold pressure (pe) and intergrator state (i). The overall system can be in one of four modes startup, normal, powerup, sensorfail. A Simulink® diagram describes the continuous evolution of the above variables. In this paper, we mainly work on the *Hybrid I/O Automaton Model* in the suite of powertrain control models. The Simulink® model consists of continuous variables describing the dynamics of the powertrain plant and sample-and-hold variables as the controller. One of the key requirements to verify is that the engine maintains the air-fuel ratio within a desired range in different modes for a given set of driver behaviors. This requirement has implications on fuel economy and emissions. For testing purposes, the control system designers work with sets of driver profiles that essentially define families of switching signals across the different modes. Previous verification results on this problem have been reported in [14,18] on a simplified version of the powertrain control model.

2.2 Transition Graphs

We will use $\mathcal{L}$ to denote a finite set of *modes* or locations of the system under consideration. The discrete behavior or mode transitions are specified by what we call a transition graph over $\mathcal{L}$.

Definition 1. *A* transition graph *is a labeled, directed acyclic graph $G = \langle \mathcal{L}, \mathcal{V}, \mathcal{E}, vlab, elab \rangle$, where (a) $\mathcal{L}$ is the set of vertex labels, also called the set of modes, $\mathcal{V}$ the set of vertices, $\mathcal{E} \subseteq \mathcal{V} \times \mathcal{V}$ is the set of edges, $vlab : \mathcal{V} \to \mathcal{L}$ is a vertex labeling function that labels each vertex with a mode, and $elab : \mathcal{E} \to \mathbb{R}_{\geq 0} \times \mathbb{R}_{\geq 0}$ is an edge labeling function that labels each edge with a nonempty, closed, bounded interval defined by pair of non-negative reals.*

For cyclic graph with bounded number of switches and bounded time, we can first unfold it to a required depth to obtain the DAG. Since G is a DAG, there is a nonempty subset $\mathcal{V}_{\text{init}} \subseteq \mathcal{V}$ of vertices with no incoming edges and a nonempty subset $\mathcal{V}_{\mathsf{term}} \subseteq \mathcal{V}$ of vertices with no outgoing edges. We define the set of initial locations of G as $\mathcal{L}_{\mathsf{init}} = \{\ell \mid \exists\, v \in \mathcal{V}_{\mathsf{init}}, vlab(v) = \ell\}$. A (maximal) *path* of the graph G is a sequence $\pi = v_1, t_1, v_2, t_2, \ldots, v_k$ such that, (a) $v_1 \in \mathcal{V}_{\mathsf{init}}$,(b) $v_k \in \mathcal{V}_{\mathsf{term}}$, and for each (v_i, t_i, v_{i+1}) subsequence, there exists $(v_i, v_{i+1}) \in \mathcal{E}$, and $t_i \in elab((v_i, v_{i+1}))$. Paths_G is the set of all possible paths of G. For a given path $\pi = v_1, t_1, v_2, t_2, \ldots, v_k$ its *trace*, denoted by $vlab(\pi)$, is the sequence $vlab(v_1), t_1, vlab(v_2), t_2, \ldots, vlab(v_k)$. Since G is a DAG, a trace of G can visit the same mode finitely many times. Trace_G is the set of all traces of G.

An example transition graph for the Powertrain system of Sect. 2.1 is shown in Fig. 1. The set of vertices $\mathcal{V} = \{0, \ldots, 4\}$ and the $vlab$'s and $elab$'s appear adjacent to the vertices and edges.

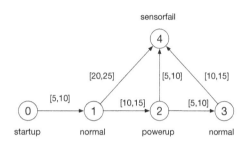

Fig. 1. A sample transition graph for Powertrain system.

Trace Containment. We will develop reasoning techniques based on reachability, abstraction, composition, and substitutivity. To this end, we will need to establish containment relations between the behaviors of systems. Here we define containment of transition graph traces. Consider transition graphs G_1, G_2, with modes $\mathcal{L}_1, \mathcal{L}_2$, and a mode map $lmap : \mathcal{L}_1 \to \mathcal{L}_2$. For a trace $\sigma = \ell_1, t_1, \ell_2, t_2, \ldots, \ell_k \in \mathsf{Trace}_{G_1}$, simplifying notation, we denote by $lmap(\sigma)$ the sequence $lmap(\ell_1), t_1, lmap(\ell_2), t_2, \ldots, lmap(\ell_k)$. We write $G_1 \preceq_{lmap} G_2$ iff for every trace $\sigma \in \mathsf{Trace}_{G_1}$, there is a trace $\sigma' \in \mathsf{Trace}_{G_2}$ such that $lmap(\sigma)$ is a prefix of σ'.

Definition 2. *Given graphs G_1, G_2 and a mode map $lmap : \mathcal{L}_1 \to \mathcal{L}_2$, a relation $R \subseteq \mathcal{V}_1 \times \mathcal{V}_2$ is a* forward simulation relation *from G_1 to G_2 iff*

(a) for each $v \in \mathcal{V}_{1\mathsf{init}}$, there is $u \in \mathcal{V}_{2\mathsf{init}}$ such that $(v, u) \in R$,
(b) for every $(v, u) \in R$, $lmap(vlab_1(v)) = vlab_2(u)$, and
(c) for every $(v, v') \in \mathcal{E}_1$ and $(v, u) \in R$, there exists a finite set $u_1, \ldots, u_k$ such that: (i) for each u_j, $(v, u_j) \in R$, and (ii) $elab_1((v, v')) \subseteq \cup_j elab_2((u, u_j))$.

Proposition 1. *If there exists a forward simulation relation from G_1 to G_2 with $lmap$ then $G_1 \preceq_{lmap} G_2$.*

Sequential Composition of Graphs. We will find it convenient to define the *sequential composition* of two transition graphs. Intuitively, the traces of the composition of G_1 and G_2 will be those that can be obtained by concatenating a trace of G_1 with a trace of G_2. To keep the definitions and notations simple, we will assume (when taking sequential compositions) $|\mathcal{V}_{\mathsf{init}}| = |\mathcal{V}_{\mathsf{term}}| = 1$; this is true of the examples we analyze. It is easy to generalize to the case when this does not hold. Under this assumption, the unique vertex in $\mathcal{V}_{\text{init}}$ will be denoted as v_{init} and the unique vertex in $\mathcal{V}_{\text{term}}$ will be denoted as v_{term}.

Definition 3. *Given graphs $G_1 = \langle \mathcal{L}, \mathcal{V}_1, \mathcal{E}_1, vlab_1, elab_1 \rangle$ and $G_2 = \langle \mathcal{L}, \mathcal{V}_2, \mathcal{E}_2, vlab_2, elab_2 \rangle$ such that $vlab_1(v_{1\text{term}}) = vlab_2(v_{2\text{init}})$, the sequential composition of G_1 and G_2 is the graph $G_1 \circ G_2 = \langle \mathcal{L}, \mathcal{V}, \mathcal{E}, vlab, elab \rangle$ where*

(a) $\mathcal{V} = (\mathcal{V}_1 \cup \mathcal{V}_2) \setminus \{v_{2\text{init}}\}$,
(a) $\mathcal{E} = \mathcal{E}_1 \cup \{(v_{1\text{term}}, u) \mid (v_{2\text{init}}, u) \in \mathcal{E}_2\} \cup \{(v, u) \in \mathcal{E}_2 \mid v \neq v_{2\text{init}}\}$,
(a) $vlab(v) = vlab_1(v)$ if $v \in \mathcal{V}_1$ and $vlab(v) = vlab_2(v)$ if $v \in \mathcal{V}_2$,
(a) For edge $(v, u) \in \mathcal{E}$, $elab((v, u))$ equals (i) $elab_1((v, u))$, if $u \in \mathcal{V}_1$, (ii) $elab_2((v_{2\text{init}}, u))$, if $v = v_{1\text{term}}$, (ii) $elab_2((v, u))$, otherwise.

Given our definition of trace containment between graphs, we can prove a very simple property about sequential composition.

Proposition 2. *Let G_1 and G_2 be two graphs with modes $\mathcal{L}$ that can be sequential composed. Then $G_1 \preceq_{\text{id}} G_1 \circ G_2$, where id is the identity map on $\mathcal{L}$.*

The proposition follows from the fact that every path of G_1 is a prefix of a path of $G_1 \circ G_2$. Later in Sect. 4.1 we see examples of sequential composition.

2.3 Trajectories

The evolution of the system's continuous state variables is formally described by continuous functions of time called *trajectories*. Let n be the number of continuous variables in the underlying hybrid model. A *trajectory* for an n-dimensional system is a continuous function of the form $\tau : [0, T] \to \mathbb{R}^n$, where $T \geq 0$. The interval $[0, T]$ is called the *domain* of τ and is denoted by $\tau.dom$. The first state $\tau(0)$ is denoted by $\tau.fstate$, last state $\tau.lstate = \tau(T)$ and $\tau.ltime = T$. For a hybrid system with $\mathcal{L}$ modes, each trajectory is labeled by a mode in $\mathcal{L}$. A *trajectory labeled by $\mathcal{L}$* is a pair $\langle \tau, \ell \rangle$ where τ is a trajectory and $\ell \in \mathcal{L}$.

A T_1-*prefix* of $\langle \tau, \ell \rangle$, for any $T_1 \in \tau.dom$, is the labeled-trajectory $\langle \tau_1, \ell \rangle$ with $\tau_1 : [0, T_1] \to \mathbb{R}^n$, such that for all $t \in [0, T_1]$, $\tau_1(t) = \tau(t)$. A set of labeled-trajectories $T\mathcal{L}$ is prefix-closed if for any $\langle \tau, \ell \rangle \in T\mathcal{L}$, any of its prefixes are also in $T\mathcal{L}$. A set $T\mathcal{L}$ is *deterministic* if for any pair $\langle \tau_1, \ell_1 \rangle, \langle \tau_2, \ell_2 \rangle \in T\mathcal{L}$, if $\tau_1.fstate = \tau_2.fstate$ and $\ell_1 = \ell_2$ then one is a prefix of the other. A deterministic, prefix-closed set of labeled trajectories $T\mathcal{L}$ describes the behavior of the continuous variables in modes $\mathcal{L}$. We denote by $T\mathcal{L}_{\text{init},\ell} = \{\tau.fstate \mid \langle \tau, \ell \rangle \in T\mathcal{L}\}$, the set of initial states of trajectories in mode ℓ. Without loss generality we assume that $T\mathcal{L}_{\text{init},\ell}$ is a connected, compact subset of $\mathbb{R}^n$. We assume that trajectories are defined for unbounded time, that is, for each $\ell \in \mathcal{L}, T > 0$, and $x \in T\mathcal{L}_{\text{init},\ell}$, there exists a $\langle \tau, \ell \rangle \in T\mathcal{L}$, with $\tau.fstate = x$ and $\tau.ltime = T$.

In control theory and hybrid systems literature, the trajectories are assumed to be generated from models like ordinary differential equations (ODEs) and differential algebraic equations (DAEs). Here, we avoid an over-reliance on the models generating trajectories and closed-form expressions. Instead, DRYVR works with sampled data of $\tau(\cdot)$ generated from simulations or tests.

Definition 4. *A simulator for a (deterministic and prefix-closed) set TL of trajectories labeled by $\mathcal{L}$ is a function (or a program) sim that takes as input a mode label $\ell \in \mathcal{L}$, an initial state $x_0 \in TL_{\text{init},\ell}$, and a finite sequence of time points $t_1, \ldots, t_k$, and returns a sequence of states $sim(x_0, \ell, t_1), \ldots, sim(x_0, \ell, t_k)$ such that there exists $\langle \tau, \ell \rangle \in TL$ with $\tau.fstate = x_0$ and for each $i \in \{1, \ldots, k\}$, $sim(x_0, \ell, t_i) = \tau(t_i)$.*

The trajectories of the Powertrn system are described by a Simulink® diagram. The diagram has several switch blocks and input signals that can be set appropriately to generate simulation data using the Simulink® ODE solver.

For simplicity, we assume that the simulations are perfect (as in the last equality of Definition 4). Formal guarantees of soundness of DRYVR are not compromised if we use *validated simulations* instead.

Trajectory Containment. Consider sets of trajectories, TL_1 labeled by $\mathcal{L}_1$ and TL_2 labeled by $\mathcal{L}_2$, and a mode map $lmap : \mathcal{L}_1 \to \mathcal{L}_2$. For a labeled trajectory $\langle \tau, \ell \rangle \in TL_1$, denote by $lmap(\langle \tau, \ell \rangle)$ the labeled-trajectory $\langle \tau, lmap(\ell) \rangle$. Write $TL_1 \preceq_{lmap} TL_2$ iff for every labeled trajectory $\langle \tau, \ell \rangle \in TL_1$, $lmap(\langle \tau, \ell \rangle) \in TL_\in$.

2.4 Hybrid Systems

Definition 5. *An n-dimensional hybrid system $\mathcal{H}$ is a 4-tuple $\langle \mathcal{L}, \Theta, G, TL \rangle$, where (a) $\mathcal{L}$ is a finite set of modes, (b) $\Theta \subseteq \mathbb{R}^n$ is a compact set of initial states, (c) $G = \langle \mathcal{L}, \mathcal{V}, \mathcal{E}, elab \rangle$ is a transition graph with set of modes $\mathcal{L}$, and (d) TL is a set of deterministic, prefix-closed trajectories labeled by $\mathcal{L}$.*

A *state* of the hybrid system $\mathcal{H}$ is a point in $\mathbb{R}^n \times \mathcal{L}$. The set of initial states is $\Theta \times \mathcal{L}_{\text{init}}$. Semantics of $\mathcal{H}$ is given in terms of executions which are sequences of trajectories consistent with the modes defined by the transition graph. An *execution* of $\mathcal{H}$ is a sequence of labeled trajectories $\alpha = \langle \tau_1, \ell_1 \rangle \ldots \langle \tau_{k-1}, \ell_{k-1} \rangle, \ell_k$ in TL, such that (a) $\tau_1.fstate \in \Theta$ and $\ell_1 \in \mathcal{L}_{\text{init}}$, (b) the sequence $\text{path}(\alpha)$ defined as $\ell_1, \tau_1.ltime, \ell_2, \ldots \ell_k$ is in Trace_G, and (c) for each pair of consecutive trajectories, $\tau_{i+1}.fstate = \tau_i.lstate$. The set of all executions of $\mathcal{H}$ is denoted by $\text{Execs}_\mathcal{H}$. The first and last states of an execution $\alpha = \langle \tau_1, \ell_1 \rangle \ldots \langle \tau_{k-1}, \ell_{k-1} \rangle, \ell_k$ are $\alpha.fstate = \tau_1.fstate$, $\alpha.lstate = \tau_{k-1}.lstate$, and $\alpha.fmode = \ell_1$ $\alpha.lmode = \ell_k$. A state $\langle x, \ell \rangle$ is *reachable* at time t and vertex v (of graph G) if there exists an execution $\alpha = \langle \tau_1, \ell_1 \rangle \ldots \langle \tau_{k-1}, \ell_{k-1} \rangle, \ell_k \in \text{Execs}_\mathcal{H}$, a path $\pi = v_1, t_1, \ldots v_k$ in Paths_G, $i \in \{1, \ldots k\}$, and $t' \in \tau_i.dom$ such that $vlab(\pi) = \text{path}(\alpha)$, $v = v_i$, $\ell = \ell_i$, $x = \tau_i(t')$, and $t = t' + \sum_{j=1}^{i-1} t_j$. The set of reachable states, reach tube, and states reachable at a vertex v are defined as follows.

$\text{ReachTube}_\mathcal{H} = \{ \langle x, \ell, t \rangle \mid \text{for some } v, \langle x, \ell \rangle \text{ is reachable at time } t \text{ and vertex } v \}$
$\text{Reach}_\mathcal{H} = \{ \langle x, \ell \rangle \mid \text{for some } v, t, \langle x, \ell \rangle \text{ is reachable at time } t \text{ and vertex } v \}$
$\text{Reach}_\mathcal{H}^v = \{ \langle x, \ell \rangle \mid \text{for some } t, \langle x, \ell \rangle \text{ is reachable at time } t \text{ and vertex } v \}$

Given a set of (unsafe) states $\mathcal{U} \subseteq \mathbb{R}^n \times \mathcal{L}$, the *bounded safety verification problem* is to decide whether $\text{Reach}_\mathcal{H} \cap \mathcal{U} = \emptyset$. In Sect. 3 we will present DRYVR's algorithm for solving this decision problem.

Remark 1. Defining paths in a graph G to be maximal (i.e., end in a vertex in $\mathcal{V}_{term}$) coupled with the above definition for executions in $\mathcal{H}$, ensures that for a vertex v with outgoing edges in G, the execution must leave the mode $vlab(v)$ within time bounded by the largest time in the labels of outgoing edges from v.

An instance of the bounded safety verification problem is defined by (a) the hybrid system for the Powertrn which itself is defined by the transition graph of Fig. 1 and the trajectories defined by the Simulink® model, and (b) the unsafe set $(\mathcal{U}_p)$: in powerup mode, $t > 4 \wedge \lambda \notin [12.4, 12.6]$, in normal mode, $t > 4 \wedge \lambda \notin [14.6, 14.8]$.

Containment between graphs and trajectories can be leveraged to conclude the containment of the set of reachable states of two hybrid systems.

Proposition 3. *Consider a pair of hybrid systems* $\mathcal{H}_i = \langle \mathcal{L}_i, \Theta_i, G_i, \mathcal{TL}_i \rangle$, $i \in \{1, 2\}$ *and mode map* $lmap : \mathcal{L}_1 \to \mathcal{L}_2$. *If* $\Theta_1 \subseteq \Theta_2$, $G_1 \preceq_{lmap} G_2$, *and* $\mathcal{TL}_1 \preceq_{lmap} \mathcal{TL}_2$, *then* $\mathsf{Reach}_{\mathcal{H}_1} \subseteq \mathsf{Reach}_{\mathcal{H}_2}$.

2.5   ADAS and Autonomous Vehicle Benchmarks

This is a suite of benchmarks we have created representing various common scenarios used for testing ADAS and Autonomous driving control systems. The hybrid system for a scenario is constructed by putting together several individual vehicles. The higher-level decisions (paths) followed by the vehicles are captured by transition graphs while the detailed dynamics of each vehicle comes from a black-box Simulink® simulator from Mathworks® [35].

Each vehicle has several continuous variables including the x, y-coordinates of the vehicle on the road, its velocity, heading, and steering angle. The vehicle can be controlled by two input signals, namely the throttle (acceleration or brake) and the steering speed. By choosing appropriate values for these input signals, we have defined the following modes for each vehicle — cruise: move forward at constant speed, speedup: constant acceleration, brake: constant (slow) deceleration, em_brake: constant (hard) deceleration. In addition, we have designed lane switching modes ch_left and ch_right in which the acceleration and steering are controlled in such a manner that the vehicle switches to its left (resp. right) lane in a certain amount of time.

For each vehicle, we mainly analyze four variables: absolute position (sx) and velocity (vx) orthogonal to the road direction (x-axis), and absolute position (sy) and velocity (vy) along the road direction (y-axis). The throttle and steering are captured using the four variables. We will use subscripts to distinguish between different vehicles. The following scenarios are constructed by defining appropriate sets of initial states and transitions graphs labeled by the modes of two or more vehicles. In all of these scenarios a primary safety requirement is that the vehicles maintain safe separation. See [21] for more details on initial states and transition graphs of each scenario.

Merge: Vehicle A in the left lane is behind vehicle B in the right lane. A switches through modes cruise, speedup, ch_right, and cruise over specified intervals to merge behind B. Variants of this scenario involve B also switching to speedup or brake.

AutoPassing: Vehicle A starts behind B in the same lane, and goes through a sequence of modes to overtake B. If B switches to speedup before A enters speedup then A aborts and changes back to right lane.

Merge3: Same as AutoPassing with a third car C always ahead of B.

AEB: Vehicle A cruises behind B and B stops. A transits from cruise to em_brake possibly over several different time intervals as governed by different sensors and reaction times.

3   Invariant Verification

A subproblem for invariant verification is to compute ReachTube$_{\mathcal{H}}$, or more specifically, the reachtubes for the set of trajectories $\mathcal{TL}$ in a given mode, up to a time bound. This is a difficult problem, even when $\mathcal{TL}$ is generated by white-box models. The algorithms in [11, 15, 20] approximate reachtubes using simulations and sensitivity analysis of ODE models generating $\mathcal{TL}$. Here, we begin with a probabilistic method for estimating sensitivity from black-box simulators.

3.1   Discrepancy Functions

Sensitivity of trajectories is formalized by the notion of discrepancy functions [15]. For a set $\mathcal{TL}$, a *discrepancy function* is a uniformly continuous function $\beta : \mathbb{R}^n \times \mathbb{R}^n \times \mathbb{R}_{\geq 0} \to \mathbb{R}_{\geq 0}$, such that for any pair of identically labeled trajectories $\langle \tau_1, \ell \rangle, \langle \tau_2, \ell \rangle \in \mathcal{TL}$, and any $t \in \tau_1.dom \cap \tau_2.dom$: (a) β upper-bounds the distance between the trajectories, i.e.,

$$|\tau_1(t) - \tau_2(t)| \leq \beta(\tau_1.fstate, \tau_2.fstate, t), \tag{1}$$

and (b) β converges to 0 as the initial states converge, i.e., for any trajectory τ and $t \in \tau.dom$, if a sequence of trajectories $\tau_1, \ldots, \tau_k, \ldots$ has $\tau_k.fstate \to \tau.fstate$, then $\beta(\tau_k.fstate, \tau.fstate, t) \to 0$. In [15] it is shown how given a β, condition (a) can used to over-approximate reachtubes from simulations, and condition (b) can be used to make these approximations arbitrarily precise. Techniques for computing β from ODE models are developed in [19, 20, 29], but these are not applicable here in absence of such models. Instead we present a simple method for discovering discrepancy functions that only uses simulations. Our method is based on classical results on PAC learning linear separators [32]. We recall these before applying them to find discrepancy functions.

Learning Linear Separators. For $\Gamma \subseteq \mathbb{R} \times \mathbb{R}$, a *linear separator* is a pair $(a, b) \in \mathbb{R}^2$ such that

$$\forall (x, y) \in \Gamma. \ x \leq ay + b. \tag{2}$$

Let us fix a subset Γ that has a (unknown) linear separator (a_*, b_*). Our goal is to discover some (a, b) that is a linear seprator for Γ by sampling points in Γ^1. The assumption is that elements of Γ can be drawn according to some (unknown) distribution $\mathcal{D}$. With respect to $\mathcal{D}$, the *error* of a pair (a, b) from satisfying Eq. 2, is defined to be $\mathsf{err}_{\mathcal{D}}(a, b) = \mathcal{D}(\{(x, y) \in \Gamma \mid x > ay + b\})$ where $\mathcal{D}(X)$ is the measure of set X under distribution $\mathcal{D}$. Thus, the error is the measure of points (w.r.t. $\mathcal{D}$) that (a, b) is not a linear separator for. There is a very simple (probabilistic) algorithm that finds a pair (a, b) that is a linear separator for a large fraction of points in Γ, as follows.

1. Draw k pairs $(x_1, y_1), \ldots (x_k, y_k)$ from Γ according to $\mathcal{D}$; the value of k will be fixed later.
2. Find $(a, b) \in \mathbb{R}^2$ such that $x_i \leq ay_i + b$ for all $i \in \{1, \ldots k\}$.

Step 2 involves checking feasibility of a linear program, and so can be done efficiently. This algorithm, with high probability, finds a linear separator for a large fraction of points.

Proposition 4. *Let $\epsilon, \delta \in \mathbb{R}_+$. If $k \geq \frac{1}{\epsilon} \ln \frac{1}{\delta}$ then, with probability $\geq 1 - \delta$, the above algorithm finds (a, b) such that $\mathsf{err}_{\mathcal{D}}(a, b) < \epsilon$.*

Proof. The result follows from the PAC-learnability of concepts with low VC-dimension [32]. However, since the proof is very simple in this case, we reproduce it here for completeness. Let k be as in the statement of the proposition, and suppose the pair (a, b) identified by the algorithm has error $> \epsilon$. We will bound the probability of this happening.

Let $B = \{(x, y) \mid x > ay + b\}$. We know that $\mathcal{D}(B) > \epsilon$. The algorithm chose (a, b) only because no element from B was sampled in Step 1. The probability that this happens is $\leq (1 - \epsilon)^k$. Observing that $(1 - s) \leq e^{-s}$ for any s, we get $(1 - \epsilon)^k \leq e^{-\epsilon k} \leq e^{-\ln \frac{1}{\delta}} = \delta$. This gives us the desired result.

Learning Discrepancy Functions. Discrepancy functions will be computed from simulation data independently for each mode. Let us fix a mode $\ell \in \mathcal{L}$, and a domain $[0, T]$ for each trajectory. The discrepancy functions that we will learn from simulation data, will be one of two different forms, and we discuss how these are obtained.

Global exponential discrepancy (GED) is a function of the form

$$\beta(x_1, x_2, t) = |x_1 - x_2| K e^{\gamma t}.$$

Here K and γ are constants. Thus, for any pair of trajectories τ_1 and τ_2 (for mode ℓ), we have

$$\forall t \in [0, T].\ |\tau_1(t) - \tau_2(t)| \leq |\tau_1.fstate - \tau_2.fstate| K e^{\gamma t}.$$

---

[1] We prefer to present the learning question in this form as opposed to one where we learn a Boolean concept because it is closer to the task at hand.

Taking logs on both sides and rearranging terms, we have

$$\forall t. \ \ln \frac{|\tau_1(t) - \tau_2(t)|}{|\tau_1.fstate - \tau_2.fstate|} \leq \gamma t + \ln K.$$

It is easy to see that a global exponential discrepancy is nothing but a linear separator for the set Γ consisting of pairs $(\ln \frac{|\tau_1(t) = \tau_2(t)|}{|\tau_1.fstate - \tau_2.fstate|}, t)$ for all pairs of trajectories τ_1, τ_2 and time t. Using the sampling based algorithm described before, we could construct a GED for a mode $\ell \in \mathcal{L}$, where sampling from Γ reduces to using the simulator to generate traces from different states in $\mathcal{TL}_{\text{init},\ell}$. Proposition 4 guarantees the correctness, with high probability, for any separator discovered by the algorithm. However, for our reachability algorithm to not be too conservative, we need K and γ to be small. Thus, when solving the linear program in Step 2 of the algorithm, we search for a solution minimizing $\gamma T + \ln K$.

Piece-Wise Exponential Discrepancy (PED). The second form of discrepancy functions we consider, depends upon dividing up the time domain $[0, T]$ into smaller intervals, and finding a global exponential discrepancy for each interval. Let $0 = t_0, t_1, \ldots t_N = T$ be an increasing sequence of time points. Let $K, \gamma_1, \gamma_2, \ldots \gamma_N$ be such that for every pair of trajectories τ_1, τ_2 (of mode ℓ), for every $i \in \{1, \ldots, N\}$, and $t \in [t_{i-1}, t_i]$, $|\tau_1(t) = \tau_2(t)| \leq |\tau_1(t_{i-1}) - \tau_2(t_{i-1})|Ke^{\gamma_i t}$. Under such circumstances, the discrepancy function itself can be seen to be given as

$$\beta(x_1, x_2, t) = |x_1 - x_2|Ke^{\sum_{j=1}^{i-1} \gamma_j(t_j - t_{j-1}) + \gamma_i(t - t_{i-1})} \quad \text{for } t \in [t_{i-1}, t_i].$$

If the time points $0 = t_0, t_1, \ldots t_N = T$ are fixed, then the constants $K, \gamma_1, \gamma_2, \ldots \gamma_N$ can be discovered using the learning approach described for GED; here, to discover γ_i, we take Γ_i to be the pairs obtained by restricting the trajectories to be between times t_{i-1} and t_i. The sequence of time points t_i are also dynamically constructed by our algorithm based on the following approach. Our experience suggests that a value for γ that is ≥ 2 results in very conservative reach tube computation. Therefore, the time points t_i are constructed inductively to be as large as possible, while ensuring that $\gamma_i < 2$.

Experiments on Learning Discrepancy. We used the above algorithm to learn discrepancy functions for dozens of modes with complex, nonlinear trajectories. Our experiments suggest that around 10–20 simulation traces are adequate for computing both global and piece-wise discrepancy functions. For each mode we use a set S_{train} of simulation traces that start from independently drawn random initial states in $\mathcal{TL}_{\text{init},\ell}$ to learn a discrepancy function. Each trace may have 100–10000 time points, depending on the relevant time horizon and sample times. Then we draw another set S_{test} of 1000 simulations traces for validating the computed discrepancy. For every pair of trace in S_{test} and for every time point, we check whether the computed discrepancy satisfies Eq. 1. We observe that for $|S_{\text{train}}| > 10$ the computed discrepancy function is correct for 96% of the points S_{test} in and for $|S_{\text{train}}| > 20$ it is correct for more than 99.9%, across all experiments.

Algorithm 1. *GraphReach*($\mathcal{H}$) computes bounded time reachtubes for each vertex of the transition G of hybrid system $\mathcal{H}$.

---
1 $RS \leftarrow \emptyset$; $VerInit \leftarrow \{\langle \Theta, v_{\text{init}} \rangle\}$; $Order \leftarrow TopSort(G)$;
2 **for** $ptr = 0 : len(Order) - 1$ **do**
3 $\quad$ $curv \leftarrow Order[ptr]$;
4 $\quad$ $\ell \leftarrow vlab(curv)$;
5 $\quad$ $dt \leftarrow \max\{t' \in \mathbb{R}_{\geq 0} \mid \exists vs \in \mathcal{V}, (curv, vs) \in \mathcal{E}, (t, t') \leftarrow elab((curv, vs))\}$;
6 $\quad$ **for** $S_{\text{init}} \in \{S \mid \langle S, curv \rangle \in VerInit\}$ **do**
7 $\quad\quad$ $\beta \leftarrow LearnDiscrepancy(S_{\text{init}}, dt, \ell)$;
8 $\quad\quad$ $RT \leftarrow ReachComp(S_{\text{init}}, dt, \beta)$;
9 $\quad\quad$ $RS \leftarrow RS \cup \langle RT, curv \rangle$;
10 $\quad\quad$ **for** $nextv \in curv.succ$ **do**
11 $\quad\quad\quad$ $(t, t') \leftarrow elab((curv, nextv))$;
12 $\quad\quad\quad$ $VerInit \leftarrow VerInit \cup \langle Restr(RT, (t, t')), nextv \rangle$;
13 **return** RS ;

3.2   Verification Algorithm

In this section, we present algorithms to solve the bounded verification problem for hybrid systems using learned exponential discrepancy functions. We first introduce an algorithm *GraphReach* (Algorithm 1) which takes as input a hybrid system $\mathcal{H} = \langle \mathcal{L}, \Theta, G, \mathcal{TL} \rangle$ and returns a set of reachtubes—one for each vertex of G—such that their union over-approximates ReachTube$_{\mathcal{H}}$.

GraphReach maintains two data-structures: (a) RS accumulates pairs of the form $\langle RT, v \rangle$, where $v \in \mathcal{V}$ and RT is its corresponding reachtube; (b) *VerInit* accumulates pairs of the form $\langle S, v \rangle$, where $v \in \mathcal{V}$ and $S \subset \mathbb{R}^n$ is the set of states from which the reachtube in v is to be computed. Each v could be in multiple such pairs in RS and *VerInit*. Initially, $RS = \emptyset$ and $VerInit = \{\langle \Theta, v_{\text{init}} \rangle\}$.

LearnDiscrepancy(S_{init}, d, ℓ) computes the discrepancy function for mode ℓ, from initial set S_{init} and upto time d using the algorithm of Sect. 3.1.

ReachComp($S_{\text{init}}, d, \beta$) first generates finite simulation traces from S_{init} and then bloats the traces to compute a reachtube using the discrepancy function β. This step is similar to the algorithm for dynamical systems given in [15].

The *GraphReach* algorithm proceeds as follows: first, a topologically sorted array of the vertices of the DAG G is computed as $Order$ (Line 1). The pointer ptr iterates over the $Order$ and for each vertex $curv$ the following is computed. The variable dt is set to the maximum transition time to other vertices from $curv$ (Line 5). For each possible initial set S_{init} corresponding to $curv$ in *VerInit*, the algorithm computes a discrepancy function (Line 7) and uses it to compute a reachtube from S_{init} up to time dt (Line 8). For each successor $nextv$ of $curv$, the restriction of the computed reachtube RT to the corresponding transition time interval $elab((curv, nextv))$ is set as an initial set for $nextv$ (Line 11–12).

The invariant verification algorithm *VerifySafety* decides safety of $\mathcal{H}$ with respect to a given unsafe set $\mathcal{U}$ and uses *GraphReach*. This algorithm proceeds in a way similar to the simulation-based verification algorithms for dynamical

---

Algorithm 2. *VerifySafety*($\mathcal{H}$,$\mathcal{U}$) verifies safety of hybrid system $\mathcal{H}$ with respect to unsafe set $\mathcal{U}$.

---

   initially: $\mathcal{I}.push(Partition(\Theta))$
1 **while** $\mathcal{I} \neq \emptyset$ **do**
2 | $S \leftarrow \mathcal{I}.pop()$;
3 | $RS \leftarrow GraphReach(\mathcal{H})$;
4 | **if** $RS \cap \mathcal{U} = \emptyset$ **then**
5 | | continue;
6 | **else if** $\exists (x,l,t) \in RT$ *s.t.* $\langle RT,v \rangle \in RS$ *and* $(x,l,t) \subseteq \mathcal{U}$ **then**
7 | | **return** UNSAFE, $\langle RT,v \rangle$
8 | **else**
9 | | $I.push(Partition(S))$;
10 | | Or, $G \leftarrow RefineGraph(G)$;
11 **return** SAFE

---

and hybrid systems [15, 22]. Given initial set Θ and transition graph G of $\mathcal{H}$, this algorithm partitions Θ into several subsets, and then for each subset S it checks whether the computed over-approximate reachtube RS from S intersects with $\mathcal{U}$: (a) If RS is disjoint, the system is safe starting from S; (b) if certain part of a reachtube RT is contained in $\mathcal{U}$, the system is declared as unsafe and RT with the the corresponding path of the graph are returned as counter-example witnesses; (c) if neither of the above conditions hold, then the algorithm performs refinement to get a more precise over-approximation of RS. Several refinement strategies are implemented in DryVR to accomplish the last step. Broadly, these strategies rely on splitting the initial set S into smaller sets (this gives tighter discrepancy in the subsequent vertices) and splitting the edge labels of G into smaller intervals (this gives smaller initial sets in the vertices).

The above description focuses on invariant properties, but the algorithm and our implementation in DryVR can verify a useful class of temporal properties. These are properties in which the time constraints only refer to the time since the last mode transition. For example, for the Powertrn benchmark the tool verifies requirements like "after 4s in normal mode, the air-fuel ratio should be contained in [14.6, 14.8] and after 4s in powerup it should be in [12.4, 12.6]".

Correctness. Given a correct discrepancy function for each mode, we can prove the soundness and relative completeness of Algorithm 2. This analysis closely follows the proof of Theorem 19 and Theorem 21 in [13].

Theorem 1. *If the β's returned by LearnDiscrepancy are always discrepancy functions for corresponding modes, then VerifySafety($\mathcal{H}$,$\mathcal{U}$) (Algorithm 2) is sound. That is, if it outputs "SAFE", then $\mathcal{H}$ is safe with respect to $\mathcal{U}$ and if it outputs "UNSAFE" then there exists an execution of $\mathcal{H}$ that enters $\mathcal{U}$.*

3.3   Experiments on Safety Verification

The algorithms have been implemented in DRYVR[2] and have been used to automatically verify the benchmarks from Sect. 2 and an Automatic Transmission System (detailed description of the models can be found in the appendix of [21]). The transition graph, the initial set, and unsafe set are given in a text file. DRYVR uses simulators for modes, and outputs either "Safe" of "Unsafe". Reachtubes or counter-examples computed during the analysis are also stored in text files.

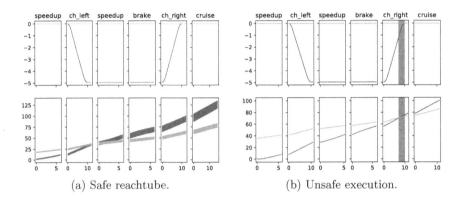

(a) Safe reachtube.   (b) Unsafe execution.

Fig. 2. AutoPassing verification. Vehicle A's (red) modes are shown above each subplot. Vehicle B (green) is in cruise. Top: sx_A, sx_B. Bottom: sy_A, sy_B. (Color figure online)

The implementation is in Python using the MatLab's Python API for accessing the Simulink® simulators. Py-GLPK [23] is used to find the parameters of discrepancy functions; either global (GED) or piece-wise (PED) discrepancy can be selected by the user. Z3 [9] is used for reachtube operations.

Figure 2 shows example plots of computed safe reachtubes and counter-examples for a simplified AutoPassing in which vehicle B stays in the cruise always. As before, vehicle A goes through a sequence of modes to overtake B. Initially, for both $i \in \{A, B\}$, $sx_i = vx_i = 0$ and $vy_i = 1$, i.e., both are cruising at constant speed at the center of the right lane; initial positions along the lane are $sy_A \in [0, 2], sy_B \in [15, 17]$. Figure 2a shows the lateral positions (sx_A in red and sx_B in green, in the top subplot), and the positions along the lane (sy_A in red and sy_B in green, in the bottom plot). Vehicle A moves to left lane (sx decreases) and then back to the right, while B remains in the right lane, as A overtakes B (bottom plot). The unsafe set ($|sx_A - sx_B| < 2$ & $|sy_A - sy_B| < 2$) is proved to be disjoint from computed reachtube. With a different initial set, $sy_B \in [30, 40]$, DRYVR finds counter-example (Fig. 2b).

---

[2] The implementation of DRYVR with the case studies can be found at https://github.com/qibolun/DryVR. We have also moved the Autonomous vehicle benchmark models and all the scenarios to Python for faster simulation..

Table 1. Safety verification results. Numbers below benchmark names: # vertices and edges of G, TH: duration of shortest path in G, Ref: # refinements performed; Runtime: overall running time.

Model	TH	Initial set	$\mathcal{U}$	Ref	Safe	Runtime
Powertrn (5 vers, 6 edges)	80	$\lambda \in [14.6, 14.8]$	$\mathcal{U}_p$	2	✓	217.4s
AutoPassing (12 vers, 13 edges)	50	$sy_A \in [-1, 1]$ $sy_B \in [14, 16]$	$\mathcal{U}_c$	4	✓	208.4s
	50	$sy_A \in [-1, 1]$ $sy_B \in [4, 6.5]$	$\mathcal{U}_c$	5	✗	152.5s
Merge (7 vers, 7 edges)	50	$sx_A \in [-5, 5]$ $sy_B \in [-2, 2]$	$\mathcal{U}_c$	0	✓	55.0s
	50	$sx_A \in [-5, 5]$ $sy_B \in [2, 10]$	$\mathcal{U}_c$	-	✗	38.7s
Merge3 (6 vers, 5 edges)	50	$sy_A \in [-3, 3]$ $sy_B \in [14, 23]$ $sy_C \in [36, 45]$	$\mathcal{U}_c$	4	✓	197.6s
	50	$sy_A \in [-3, 3]$ $sy_B \in [14, 15]$ $sy_C \in [16, 20]$	$\mathcal{U}_c$	-	✗	21.3s
ATS (4 vers, 3 edges)	50	Erpm $\in [900, 1000]$	$\mathcal{U}_t$	2	✓	109.2s

Table 1 summarizes some of the verification results obtained using DRYVR. ATS is an automatic transmission control system (see [21] for more details). These experiments were performed on a laptop with Intel Core i7-6600U CPU and 16 GB RAM. The initial range of only the salient continuous variables are shown in the table. The unsafe sets are discussed with the model description. For example $\mathcal{U}_c$ means two vehicles are too close. For all the benchmarks, the algorithm terminated in a few minutes which includes the time to simulate, learn discrepancy, generate reachtubes, check the safety of the reachtube, over all refinements.

For the results presented in Table 1, we used GED. The reachtube generated by PED for Powertrn is more precise, but for the rest, the reachtubes and the verification times using both GED and PED were comparable. In addition to the *VerifySafety* algorithm, DRYVR also looks for counter-examples by quickly generating random executions of the hybrid system. If any of these executions is found to be unsafe, DRYVR will return "Unsafe" without starting the *VerifySafety* algorithm.

4   Reasoning Principles for Trace Containment

For a fixed unsafe set $\mathcal{U}$ and two hybrid systems $\mathcal{H}_1$ and $\mathcal{H}_2$, proving $\mathsf{Reach}_{\mathcal{H}_1} \subseteq \mathsf{Reach}_{\mathcal{H}_2}$ and the safety of $\mathcal{H}_2$, allows us to conclude the safety of $\mathcal{H}_1$. Proposition 3 establishes that proving containment of traces, trajectories, and initial sets of two hybrid systems, ensures the containment of their respective reach sets. These two observations together give us a method of concluding the safety of one system, from the safety of another, provided we can check trace containment of two graphs, and trajectory containment of two trajectory sets. In our examples, the set of modes $\mathcal{L}$ and the set of trajectories $\mathcal{TL}$ is often the same between the hybrid systems we care about. So in this section we present different reasoning principles to check trace containment between two graphs.

Semantically, a transition graph G can be viewed as one-clock timed automaton, i.e., one can construct a timed automaton T with one-clock variable such that the timed traces of T are exactly the traces of G. This observation, coupled with the fact that checking the timed language containment of one-clock timed automata [37] is decidable, allows one to conclude that checking if $G_1 \preceq_{lmap} G_2$ is decidable. However the algorithm in [37] has non-elementary complexity. Our next observation establishes that forward simulation between graphs can be checked in polynomial time. Combined with Proposition 1, this gives a simple sufficient condition for trace containment that can be efficiently checked.

Proposition 5. *Given graphs G_1 and G_2, and mode map lmap, checking if there is a forward simulation from G_1 to G_2 is in polynomial time.*

Proof. The result can be seen to follow from the algorithm for checking timed simulations between timed automata [6] and the correspondence between one-clock timed automata; the fact that the automata have only one clock ensures that the region construction is poly-sized as opposed to exponential-sized. However, in the special case of transition graphs there is a more direct algorithm which does not involve region construction that we describe here.

Observe that if $\{R_i\}_{i \in I}$ is a family of forward simulations between G_1 and G_2 then $\cup_{i \in I} R_i$ is also a forward simulation. Thus, like classical simulations, there is a unique largest forward simulation between two graphs that is the greatest fixpoint of a functional on relations over states of the transition graph. Therefore, starting from the relation $\mathcal{V}_1 \times \mathcal{V}_2$, one can progressively remove pairs (v, u) such that v is not simulated by u, until a fixpoint is reached. Moreover, in this case, since G_1 is a DAG, one can guarantee that the fixpoint will be reached in $|\mathcal{V}_1|$ iterations.   □

Executions of hybrid systems are for bounded time, and bounded number of mode switches. This is because our transition graphs are acyclic and the labels on edges are bounded intervals. Sequential composition of graphs allows one to consider switching sequences that are longer and of a longer duration. We now present observations that will allow us to conclude the safety of a hybrid system with long switching sequences based on the safety of the system under short switching sequences. To do this we begin by observing simple properties about sequential composition of graphs. In what follows, all hybrid systems we consider will be over a fixed set of modes $\mathcal{L}$ and trajectory set $\mathcal{TL}$. id is the identity function on $\mathcal{L}$. Our first observation is that trace containment is consistent with sequential composition.

Proposition 6. *Let G_i, G'_i, $i \in \{1, 2\}$, be four transition graphs over $\mathcal{L}$ such that $G_1 \circ G_2$ and $G'_1 \circ G'_2$ are defined, and $G_i \preceq_{id} G'_i$ for $i \in \{1, 2\}$. Then $G_1 \circ G_2 \preceq_{id} G'_1 \circ G'_2$.*

Next we observe that sequential composition of graphs satisfies the "semi-group property".

Proposition 7. *Let G_1, G_2 be graphs over $\mathcal{L}$ for which $G_1 \circ G_2$ is defined. Let v_{1term} be the unique terminal vertex of G_1. Consider the following hybrid systems: $\mathcal{H} = \langle \mathcal{L}, \Theta, G_1 \circ G_2, \mathcal{TL} \rangle$, $\mathcal{H}_1 = \langle \mathcal{L}, \Theta, G_1, \mathcal{TL} \rangle$, and $\mathcal{H}_2 = \langle \mathcal{L}, \text{Reach}_{\mathcal{H}_1}^{v_{1term}}, G_2, \mathcal{TL} \rangle$. Then $\text{Reach}_{\mathcal{H}} = \text{Reach}_{\mathcal{H}_1} \cup \text{Reach}_{\mathcal{H}_2}$.*

Consider a graph G such that $G \circ G$ is defined. Let $\mathcal{H}$ be the hybrid system with transition graph G, and $\mathcal{H}'$ be the hybrid system with transition graph $G \circ G$; the modes, trajectories, and initial set for $\mathcal{H}$ and $\mathcal{H}'$ are the same. Now by Propositions 2 and 3, we can conclude that $\mathsf{Reach}_{\mathcal{H}} \subseteq \mathsf{Reach}_{\mathcal{H}'}$. Our main result of this section is that under some conditions, the converse also holds. This is useful because it allows us to conclude the safety of $\mathcal{H}'$ from the safety of $\mathcal{H}$. In other words, we can conclude the safety of a hybrid system for long, possibly unbounded, switching sequences (namely $\mathcal{H}'$) from the safety of the system under short switching sequences (namely $\mathcal{H}$).

Theorem 2. *Suppose G is such that $G \circ G$ is defined. Let v_{term} be the unique terminal vertex of G. For natural number $i \geq 1$, define $\mathcal{H}_i = \langle \mathcal{L}, \Theta, G^i, \mathcal{TL} \rangle$, where G^i is the i-fold sequential composition of G with itself. In particular, $\mathcal{H}_1 = \langle \mathcal{L}, \Theta, G, \mathcal{TL} \rangle$. If $\mathsf{Reach}_{\mathcal{H}_1}^{v_{\mathsf{term}}} \subseteq \Theta$ then for all i, $\mathsf{Reach}_{\mathcal{H}_i} \subseteq \mathsf{Reach}_{\mathcal{H}_1}$.*

Proof. Let $\Theta_1 = \mathsf{Reach}_{\mathcal{H}_1}^{v_{\mathsf{term}}}$. From the condition in the theorem, we know that $\Theta_1 \subseteq \Theta$. Let us define $\mathcal{H}_i' = \langle \mathcal{L}, \Theta_1, G^i, \mathcal{TL} \rangle$. Observe that from Proposition 3, we have $\mathsf{Reach}_{\mathcal{H}_i'} \subseteq \mathsf{Reach}_{\mathcal{H}_i}$.

The theorem is proved by induction on i. The base case (for $i = 1$) trivially holds. For the induction step, assume that $\mathsf{Reach}_{\mathcal{H}_i} \subseteq \mathsf{Reach}_{\mathcal{H}_1}$. Since $\circ$ is associative, using Proposition 7 and the induction hypothesis, we have $\mathsf{Reach}_{\mathcal{H}_{i+1}} = \mathsf{Reach}_{\mathcal{H}_1} \cup \mathsf{Reach}_{\mathcal{H}_i'} \subseteq \mathsf{Reach}_{\mathcal{H}_1} \cup \mathsf{Reach}_{\mathcal{H}_i} = \mathsf{Reach}_{\mathcal{H}_1}$.

Theorem 2 allows one to determine the set of reachable states of a set of modes $\mathcal{L}$ with respect to graph G^i, provided G satisfies the conditions in the statement. This observation can be generalized. If a graph G_2 satisfies conditions similar to those in Theorem 2, then using Proposition 7, we can conclude that the reachable set with respect to graph $G_1 \circ G_2^i \circ G_3$ is contained in the reachable set with respect to graph $G_1 \circ G_2 \circ G_3$. The formal statement of this observation and its proof is skipped in the interest of space, but we will use it in our experiments.

4.1 Experiments on Trace Containment Reasoning

Graph Simulation. Consider the AEB system of Sect. 2.5 with the scenario where Vehicle B is stopped ahead of vehicle A, and A transits from cruise to em_brake to avoid colliding with B. In the actual system (G_2 of Fig. 3), two different sensor systems trigger the obstacle detection and emergency braking at time intervals $[1, 2]$ and $[2.5, 3.5]$ and take the system from vertex 0 (cruise) to two different vertices labeled with em_brake.

To illustrate trace containment reasoning, consider a simpler graph G_1 that allows a single transition of A from cruise to em_brake over the interval bigger $[0.5, 4.5]$. Using Proposition 3 and checking that graph $G_2 \preceq_{\mathsf{id}} G_1$, it follows that verifying the safety of AEB with G_1 is adequate to infer the safety with G_2. Figure 3c shows that the safe reachtubes returned by the algorithm for G_1 in red, indeed contain the reachtubes for G_2 (in blue and gray).

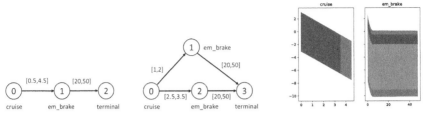

(a) Transition graph G_1.   (b) Transition graph G_2.   (c) AEB Reachtubes.

Fig. 3. Graphs and reachtubes for the automatic emergency braking AEB system. (Color figure online)

Sequential Composition. We revisit the Powertrn example of Sect. 2.1. The initial set Θ and unsafe set are the same as in Table 1. Let G_A be the graph $(v_0,\text{startup})$ $\xrightarrow{[5,10]}$ (v_1,normal) $\xrightarrow{[10,15]}$ $(v_2,\text{powerup})$, and G_B be the graph $(v_0,\text{powerup})$ $\xrightarrow{[5,10]}$ (v_1,normal) $\xrightarrow{[10,15]}$ $(v_2,\text{powerup})$. The graph $G_1 = (v_0,\text{startup})$ $\xrightarrow{[5,10]}$ (v_1,normal) $\xrightarrow{[10,15]}$ $(v_2,\text{powerup})$ $\xrightarrow{[5,10]}$ (v_3,normal) $\xrightarrow{[10,15]}$ $(v_4,\text{powerup})$, can be expressed as the composition $G_1 = G_A \circ G_B$. Consider the two hybrid systems $\mathcal{H}_i = \langle \mathcal{L}, \Theta_i, G_i, \mathcal{TL} \rangle$, $i \in \{A, B\}$ with $\Theta_A = \Theta$ and $\Theta_B = \text{Reach}^{v_2}_{\mathcal{H}_A}$. DRYVR's estimate of Θ_B had λ in the range from 14.68 to 14.71. The reachset $\text{Reach}^{v_2}_{\mathcal{H}_B}$ computed by DRYVR had λ from 14.69 to 14.70. The remaining variables also were observed to satisfy the containment condition. Therefore, $\text{Reach}^{v_2}_{\mathcal{H}_B} \subseteq \Theta_B$. Consider the two hybrid systems $\mathcal{H}_i = \langle \mathcal{L}, \Theta, G_i, \mathcal{TL} \rangle$, $i \in \{1, 2\}$, where G_1 is (defined above) $G_A \circ G_B$, and $G_2 = G_A \circ G_B \circ G_B \circ G_B$. Using Theorem 2 it suffices to analyze $\mathcal{H}_1$ to verify $\mathcal{H}_2$. $\mathcal{H}_1$ was been proved to be safe by DRYVR without any refinement. As a sanity check, we also verified the safety of $\mathcal{H}_2$. DRYVR proved $\mathcal{H}_2$ safe without any refinement as well.

5   Conclusions

The work presented in this paper takes an alternative view that complete mathematical models of hybrid systems are unavailable. Instead, the available system description combines a black-box simulator and a white-box transition graph. Starting from this point of view, we have developed the semantic framework, a probabilistic verification algorithm, and results on simulation relations and sequential composition for reasoning about complex hybrid systems over long switching sequences. Through modeling and analysis of a number of automotive control systems using implementations of the proposed approach, we hope to have demonstrated their promise. One direction for further exploration in this vein, is to consider more general timed and hybrid automata models of the white-box, and develop the necessary algorithms and the reasoning techniques.

References

1. Alur, R., Dang, T., Ivančić, F.: Counter-example guided predicate abstraction of hybrid systems. In: Garavel, H., Hatcliff, J. (eds.) TACAS 2003. LNCS, vol. 2619, pp. 208–223. Springer, Heidelberg (2003)
2. Annapureddy, Y., Liu, C., Fainekos, G., Sankaranarayanan, S.: S-taliro: a tool for temporal logic falsification for hybrid systems. In: Proceedings of the International Conference on Tools and Algorithms for the Construction and Analysis of Systems (2011)
3. Asarin, E., Dang, T., Maler, O.: The d/dt tool for verification of hybrid systems. In: Brinksma, E., Larsen, K.G. (eds.) CAV 2002. LNCS, vol. 2404, pp. 365–370. Springer, Heidelberg (2002). doi:10.1007/3-540-45657-0_30
4. Balluchi, A., Casagrande, A., Collins, P., Ferrari, A., Villa, T., Sangiovanni-Vincentelli, A.L.: Ariadne: a framework for reachability analysis of hybrid automata. In: Proceedings of the International Syposium on Mathematical Theory of Networks and Systems. Citeseer (2006)
5. Bogomolov, S., Frehse, G., Greitschus, M., Grosu, R., Pasareanu, C.S., Podelski, A., Strump, T.: Assume-guarantee abstraction refinement meets hybrid systems. In: 10th International Haifa Verification Conference, pp. 116–131 (2014)
6. Čerāns, K.: Decidability of bisimulation equivalences for parallel timer processes. In: von Bochmann, G., Probst, D.K. (eds.) CAV 1992. LNCS, vol. 663, pp. 302–315. Springer, Heidelberg (1993). doi:10.1007/3-540-56496-9_24
7. Chen, X., Ábrahám, E., Sankaranarayanan, S.: Flow*: an analyzer for non-linear hybrid systems. In: International Conference on Computer Aided Verification, pp. 258–263 (2013)
8. Clarke, E., Fehnker, A., Han, Z., Krogh, B., Stursberg, O., Theobald, M.: Verification of hybrid systems based on counterexample-guided abstraction refinement. In: Garavel, H., Hatcliff, J. (eds.) TACAS 2003. LNCS, vol. 2619, pp. 192–207. Springer, Heidelberg (2003). doi:10.1007/3-540-36577-X_14
9. de Moura, L., Bjørner, N.: Z3: an efficient SMT solver. In: Ramakrishnan, C.R., Rehof, J. (eds.) TACAS 2008. LNCS, vol. 4963, pp. 337–340. Springer, Heidelberg (2008). doi:10.1007/978-3-540-78800-3_24
10. Deng, Y., Rajhans, A., Julius, A.A.: Strong: a trajectory-based verification toolbox for hybrid systems. In: International Conference on Quantitative Evaluation of SysTems, pp. 165–168 (2013)
11. Donzé, A.: Breach, a toolbox for verification and parameter synthesis of hybrid systems. In: Touili, T., Cook, B., Jackson, P. (eds.) CAV 2010. LNCS, vol. 6174, pp. 167–170. Springer, Heidelberg (2010). doi:10.1007/978-3-642-14295-6_17
12. Donzé, A., Maler, O.: Systematic simulation using sensitivity analysis. In: Bemporad, A., Bicchi, A., Buttazzo, G. (eds.) HSCC 2007. LNCS, vol. 4416, pp. 174–189. Springer, Heidelberg (2007). doi:10.1007/978-3-540-71493-4_16
13. Duggirala, P.S.: Dynamic analysis of cyber-physical systems. Ph.D. thesis, University of Illinois at Urbana-Champaign (2015)
14. Duggirala, P.S., Fan, C., Mitra, S., Viswanathan, M.: Meeting a powertrain verification challenge. In: Kroening, D., Păsăreanu, C.S. (eds.) CAV 2015. LNCS, vol. 9206, pp. 536–543. Springer, Cham (2015). doi:10.1007/978-3-319-21690-4_37
15. Duggirala, P.S., Mitra, S., Viswanathan, M.: Verification of annotated models from executions. In: Proceedings of International Conference on Embedded Software (EMSOFT 2013), Montreal, QC, Canada, pp. 1–10. ACM SIGBED, IEEE, September 2013

16. Duggirala, P.S., Mitra, S., Viswanathan, M., Potok, M.: C2E2: a verification tool for stateflow models. In: Baier, C., Tinelli, C. (eds.) TACAS 2015. LNCS, vol. 9035, pp. 68–82. Springer, Heidelberg (2015). doi:10.1007/978-3-662-46681-0_5

17. Fainekos, G.E., Pappas, G.J.: Robustness of temporal logic specifications for continuous-time signals. Theor. Comput. Sci. **410**, 4262–4291 (2009)

18. Fan, C., Duggirala, P.S., Mitra, S., Viswanathan, M.: Progress on powertrain verification challenge with C2E2. In: Workshop on Applied Verification for Continuous and Hybrid Systems (ARCH 2015) (2015)

19. Fan, C., Kapinski, J., Jin, X., Mitra, S.: Locally optimal reach set over-approximation for nonlinear systems. In: Proceedings of the 13th ACM-SIGBED International Conference on Embedded Software (EMSOFT), EMSOFT 2016, pp. 6:1–6:10. ACM, New York (2016)

20. Fan, C., Mitra, S.: Bounded verification with on-the-fly discrepancy computation. In: Finkbeiner, B., Pu, G., Zhang, L. (eds.) ATVA 2015. LNCS, vol. 9364, pp. 446–463. Springer, Cham (2015). doi:10.1007/978-3-319-24953-7_32

21. Fan, C., Qi, B., Mitra, S., Viswanathan, M.: DRYVR: data-driven verification and compositional reasoning for automotive systems. arXiv preprint arXiv:1702.06902 (2017)

22. Fan, C., Qi, B., Mitra, S., Viswanathan, M., Duggirala, P.S.: Automatic reachability analysis for nonlinear hybrid models with C2E2. In: Chaudhuri, S., Farzan, A. (eds.) CAV 2016. LNCS, vol. 9779, pp. 531–538. Springer, Cham (2016). doi:10.1007/978-3-319-41528-4_29

23. Finley, T.: Python package PyGLPK. http://tfinley.net/software/pyglpk/

24. Frehse, G.: PHAVer: algorithmic verification of hybrid systems past HyTech. In: Morari, M., Thiele, L. (eds.) HSCC 2005. LNCS, vol. 3414, pp. 258–273. Springer, Heidelberg (2005). doi:10.1007/978-3-540-31954-2_17

25. Frehse, G., Le Guernic, C., Donzé, A., Cotton, S., Ray, R., Lebeltel, O., Ripado, R., Girard, A., Dang, T., Maler, O.: SpaceEx: scalable verification of hybrid systems. In: International Conference on Computer Aided Verification, pp. 379–395. Springer (2011)

26. Girard, A., Pappas, G.J.: Verification using simulation. In: Hespanha, J.P., Tiwari, A. (eds.) HSCC 2006. LNCS, vol. 3927, pp. 272–286. Springer, Heidelberg (2006). doi:10.1007/11730637_22

27. Girard, A., Pola, G., Tabuada, P.: Approximately bisimilar symbolic models for incrementally stable switched systems. IEEE Trans. Autom. Contr. **55**(1), 116–126 (2010)

28. Henzinger, T.A., Ho, P.-H.: HyTech: the cornell hybrid technology tool. In: Antsaklis, P., Kohn, W., Nerode, A., Sastry, S. (eds.) HS 1994. LNCS, vol. 999, pp. 265–293. Springer, Heidelberg (1995). doi:10.1007/3-540-60472-3_14

29. Huang, Z., Fan, C., Mereacre, A., Mitra, S., Kwiatkowska, M.: Invariant verification of nonlinear hybrid automata networks of cardiac cells. In: Biere, A., Bloem, R. (eds.) CAV 2014. LNCS, vol. 8559, pp. 373–390. Springer, Cham (2014). doi:10.1007/978-3-319-08867-9_25

30. Jin, X., Deshmukh, J.V., Kapinski, J., Ueda, K., Butts, K.: Powertrain control verification benchmark. In: Proceedings of the 17th International Conference on Hybrid Systems: Computation and Control, pp. 253–262. ACM (2014)

31. Kanade, A., Alur, R., Ivančić, F., Ramesh, S., Sankaranarayanan, S., Shashidhar, K.C.: Generating and analyzing symbolic traces of Simulink/Stateflow models. In: Bouajjani, A., Maler, O. (eds.) CAV 2009. LNCS, vol. 5643, pp. 430–445. Springer, Heidelberg (2009). doi:10.1007/978-3-642-02658-4_33

32. Kearns, M.J., Vazirani, U.V.: An Introduction to Computational Learning Theory. MIT Press, Cambridge (1994)
33. Kong, S., Gao, S., Chen, W., Clarke, E.: dReach: δ-reachability analysis for hybrid systems. In: Baier, C., Tinelli, C. (eds.) TACAS 2015. LNCS, vol. 9035, pp. 200–205. Springer, Heidelberg (2015). doi:10.1007/978-3-662-46681-0_15
34. Mathworks: Modeling an Automatic Transmission and Controller. http://www.mathworks.com/videos/modeling-an-automatic-transmission-and-controller-68823.html
35. Mathworks. Simple 2D Kinematic Vehicle Steering Model and Animation. https://www.mathworks.com/matlabcentral/fileexchange/54852-simple-2d-kinematic-vehicle-steering-model-and-animation?requestedDomain=www.mathworks.com
36. O'Kelly, M., Abbas, H., Gao, S., Shiraishi, S., Kato, S., Mangharam, R.: APEX: autonomous vehicle plan verification and execution (2016)
37. Ouaknine, J., Worrell, J.: On the language inclusion problem for timed automata: closing a decidability gap. In: Proceedings of the 19th Annual IEEE Symposium on Logic in Computer Science, pp. 54–63. IEEE (2004)
38. Roohi, N., Prabhakar, P., Viswanathan, M.: Hybridization based CEGAR for hybrid automata with affine dynamics. In: Chechik, M., Raskin, J.-F. (eds.) TACAS 2016. LNCS, vol. 9636, pp. 752–769. Springer, Heidelberg (2016). doi:10.1007/978-3-662-49674-9_48

Automated Formal Synthesis of Digital Controllers for State-Space Physical Plants

Alessandro Abate[1], Iury Bessa[2],
Dario Cattaruzza[1], Lucas Cordeiro[1,2(✉)],
Cristina David[1], Pascal Kesseli[1],
Daniel Kroening[1], and Elizabeth Polgreen[1]

[1] University of Oxford, Oxford, UK
lucas.cordeiro@cs.ox.ac.uk
[2] Federal University of Amazonas, Manaus, Brazil

Abstract. We present a sound and automated approach to synthesize safe digital feedback controllers for physical plants represented as linear, time-invariant models. Models are given as dynamical equations with inputs, evolving over a continuous state space and accounting for errors due to the digitization of signals by the controller. Our counterexample guided inductive synthesis (CEGIS) approach has two phases: We synthesize a static feedback controller that stabilizes the system but that may not be safe for all initial conditions. Safety is then verified either via BMC or abstract acceleration; if the verification step fails, a counterexample is provided to the synthesis engine and the process iterates until a safe controller is obtained. We demonstrate the practical value of this approach by automatically synthesizing safe controllers for intricate physical plant models from the digital control literature.

1 Introduction

Linear Time Invariant (LTI) models represent a broad class of dynamical systems with significant impact in numerous application areas such as life sciences, robotics, and engineering [4,13]. The synthesis of controllers for LTI models is well understood, however the use of digital control architectures adds new challenges due to the effects of finite-precision arithmetic, time discretization, and quantization noise, which is typically introduced by Analogue-to-Digital (ADC) and Digital-to-Analogue (DAC) conversion. While research on digital control is well developed [4], automated and sound control synthesis is challenging, particularly when the synthesis objective goes beyond classical stability. There are recent methods for verifying reachability properties of a given controller [14]. However, these methods have not been generalized to control synthesis. Note that a synthesis algorithm that guarantees stability does not ensure safety: the system might transitively visit an unsafe state resulting in unrecoverable failure.

Supported by EPSRC grant EP/J012564/1, ERC project 280053 (CPROVER) and the H2020 FET OPEN 712689 SC[2].

© Springer International Publishing AG 2017
R. Majumdar and V. Kunčak (Eds.): CAV 2017, Part I, LNCS 10426, pp. 462–482, 2017.
DOI: 10.1007/978-3-319-63387-9_23

We propose a novel algorithm for the synthesis of control algorithms for LTI models that are guaranteed to be safe, considering both the continuous dynamics of the plant and the finite-precision discrete dynamics of the controller, as well as the hybrid elements that connect them. We account for the presence of errors originating from a number of sources: quantisation errors in ADC and DAC, representation errors (from the discretization introduced by finite-precision arithmetic), and roundoff and saturation errors in the verification process (from finite-precision operations). Due to the complexity of such systems, we focus on linear models with known implementation features (e.g., number of bits, fixed-point arithmetic). We expect a safety requirement given as a reachability property. Safety requirements are frequently overlooked in conventional feedback control synthesis, but play an important role in systems engineering.

We give two alternative approaches for synthesizing digital controllers for state-space physical plants, both based on CounterExample Guided Inductive Synthesis (CEGIS) [30]. We prove their soundness by quantifying errors caused by digitization and quantization effects that arise when the digital controller interacts with the continuous plant.

The first approach uses a naïve technique that starts by devising a digital controller that stabilizes the system while remaining safe for a pre-selected time horizon and a single initial state; then, it verifies unbounded safety by unfolding the dynamics of the system, considering the full hyper-cube of initial states, and checking a *completeness threshold* [17], i.e., the number of iterations required to sufficiently unwind the closed-loop state-space system such that the boundaries are not violated for any larger number of iterations. As it requires unfolding up to the completeness threshold, this approach is computationally expensive.

Instead of unfolding the dynamics, *the second approach* employs *abstract acceleration* [7] to evaluate all possible progressions of the system simultaneously. Additionally, the second approach uses *abstraction refinement*, enabling us to always start with a very simple description regardless of the dynamics complexity, and only expand to more complex models when a solution cannot be found.

We provide experimental results showing that both approaches are able to efficiently synthesize safe controllers for a set of intricate physical plant models taken from the digital control literature: the median run-time for our benchmark set is 7.9 s, and most controllers can be synthesized in less than 17.2 s. We further show that, in a direct comparison, the abstraction-based approach (i.e., the second approach) lowers the median run-time of our benchmarks by a factor of seven over the first approach based on the unfolding of the dynamics.

Contributions

1. We compute state-feedback controllers that guarantee a given safety property. Existing methods for controller synthesis rely on transfer function representations, which are inadequate to prove safety requirements.
2. We provide two novel algorithms: the first, naïve one, relies on an unfolding of the dynamics up to a completeness threshold, while the second one

is abstraction-based and leverages abstraction refinement and acceleration to improve scalability while retaining soundness. Both approaches provide sound synthesis of state-feedback systems and consider the various sources of imprecision in the implementation of the control algorithm and in the modeling of the plant.
3. We develop a model for different sources of quantization errors and their effect on reachability properties. We give bounds that ensure the safety of our controllers in a hybrid continuous-digital domain.

2   Related Work

CEGIS - Program synthesis is the problem of computing correct-by-design programs from high-level specifications. Algorithms for this problem have made substantial progress in recent years, for instance [16] to inductively synthesize invariants for the generation of desired programs.

Program synthesizers are an ideal fit for the synthesis of digital controllers, since the semantics of programs capture the effects of finite-precision arithmetic precisely. In [27], the authors use CEGIS for the synthesis of switching controllers for stabilizing continuous-time plants with polynomial dynamics. The work extends to affine systems, but is limited by the capacity of the state-of-the-art SMT solvers for solving linear arithmetic. Since this approach uses switching models instead of linear dynamics for the digital controller, it avoids problems related to finite precision arithmetic, but potentially suffers from state-space explosion. Moreover, in [28] the same authors use a CEGIS-based approach for synthesizing continuous-time switching controllers that guarantee *reach-while-stay* properties of closed-loop systems, i.e., properties that specify a set of goal states and safe states (constrained reachability). This solution is based on synthesizing control Lyapunov functions for switched systems that yield switching controllers with a guaranteed minimum dwell time in each mode. However, both approaches are unsuitable for the kind of control we seek to synthesize.

The work in [2] synthesizes stabilizing controllers for continuous plants given as transfer functions by exploiting bit-accurate verification of software-implemented digital controllers [5]. While this work also uses CEGIS, the approach is restricted to digital controllers for stable closed-loop systems given as transfer function models: this results in a static check on their coefficients. By contrast, in the current paper we consider a state-space representation of the physical system, which requires ensuring the specification over actual traces of the model, alongside the numerical soundness required by the effects of discretisation and finite-precision errors. A state-space model has known advantages over the transfer function representation [13]: it naturally generalizes to multivariate systems (i.e., with multiple inputs and outputs); and it allows synthesis of control systems with guarantees on the internal dynamics, e.g., to synthesize controllers that make the closed-loop system *safe*. Our work focuses on the *safety* of internal states, which is usually overlooked in the literature. Moreover, our work integrates an abstraction/refinement (CEGAR) step inside the main CEGIS loop.

The tool Pessoa [21] synthesizes correct-by-design embedded control software in a Matlab toolbox. It is based on the abstraction of a physical system to an equivalent finite-state machine and on the computation of reachability properties thereon. Based on this safety specification, Pessoa can synthesize embedded controller software for a range of properties. The embedded controller software can be more complicated than the state-feedback control we synthesize, and the properties available cover more detail. However, relying on state-space discretization Pessoa is likely to incur in scalability limitations. Along this research line, [3,20] studies the synthesis of digital controllers for continuous dynamics, and [34] extends the approach to the recent setup of Network Control Systems.

Discretization Effects - The classical approach to control synthesis has often disregarded digitalization effects, whereas more recently modern techniques have focused on different aspects of discretization, including delayed response [10] and finite word length (FWL) semantics, with the goal either to verify (e.g., [9]) or to optimize (e.g., [24]) given implementations.

There are two different problems that arise from FWL semantics. The first is the error in the dynamics caused by the inability to represent the exact state of the physical system, while the second relates to rounding and saturation errors during computation. In [12], a stability measure based on the error of the digital dynamics ensures that the deviation introduced by FWL does not make the digital system unstable. A more recent approach [33] uses μ-calculus to directly model the digital controller so that the selected parameters are stable by design. The analyses in [29,32] rely on an invariant computation on the discrete system dynamics using Semi-Definite Programming (SDP). While the former uses bounded-input and bounded-output (BIBO) properties to determine stability, the latter uses Lyapunov-based quadratic invariants. In both cases, the SDP solver uses floating-point arithmetic and soundness is checked by bounding the error. An alternative is [25], where the verification of given control code is performed against a known model by extracting an LTI model of the code by symbolic execution: to account for rounding errors, an upper bound is introduced in the verification phase. The work in [26] introduces invariant sets as a mechanism to bound the quantization error effect on stabilization as an invariant set that always converges toward the controllable set. Similarly, [19] evaluates the quantization error dynamics and bounds its trajectory to a known region over a finite time period. This technique works for both linear and non-linear systems.

3   Preliminaries

3.1   State-Space Representation of Physical Systems

We consider models of physical plants expressed as ordinary differential equations (ODEs), which we assume to be controllable and under full state information (i.e., we have access to all the model variables):

$$\dot{x}(t) = Ax(t) + Bu(t), \quad x \in \mathbb{R}^n, u \in \mathbb{R}^m, A \in \mathbb{R}^{n \times n}, B \in \mathbb{R}^{n \times m}, \tag{1}$$

where $t \in \mathbb{R}_0^+$, where A and B are matrices that fully specify the continuous plant, and with initial states set as $x(0)$. While ideally we intend to work on the continuous-time plant, in this work Eq. (1) is soundly discretized in time [11] into

$$x_{k+1} = A_d x_k + B_d u_k \tag{2}$$

where $k \in \mathbb{N}$ and $x_0 = x(0)$ is the initial state. A_d and B_d denote the matrices that describe the discretized plant dynamics, whereas A and B denote the continuous plant dynamics. We synthesize for requirements over this discrete-time domain. Later, we will address the issue of variable quantization, as introduced by the ADC/DAC conversion blocks (Fig. 1).

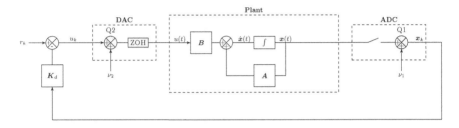

Fig. 1. Closed-loop digital control system.

3.2 Controller Synthesis via State Feedback

Models (1) and (2) depend on external non-determinism in the form of input signals $u(t)$ and u_k, respectively. Feedback architectures can be employed to manipulate the properties and behaviors of the continuous process (the plant). We are interested in the synthesis of digital feedback control algorithms, as implemented on Field-Programmable Gate Arrays or Digital Signal Processors. The most basic feedback architecture is the state feedback one, where the control action u_k (notice we work with the discretized signal) is computed by:

$$u_k = r_k - K x_k. \tag{3}$$

Here, $K \in \mathbb{R}^{m \times n}$ is a state-feedback gain matrix, and r_k is a reference signal (again digital). The closed-loop model then takes the form

$$x_{k+1} = (A_d - B_d K)x_k + B_d r_k. \tag{4}$$

The gain matrix K can be set so that the closed-loop discrete dynamics are shaped as desired, for instance according to a specific stability goal or around a specific dynamical behavior [4]. As argued later in this work, we will target more complex objectives, such as quantitative safety requirements, which are not typical in the digital control literature. Further, we will embrace the digital nature of the controller, which manipulates quantized signals as discrete quantities represented with finite precision.

3.3   Stability of Closed-Loop Systems

In this work we employ asymptotic stability in the CEGIS loop, as an objective for guessing controllers that are later proven sound over safety requirements. Asymptotic stability is a property that amounts to convergence of the model executions to an equilibrium point, starting from any states in a neighborhood of the point (see Fig. 3 for the portrait of a stable execution, converging to the origin). In the case of linear systems as in (4), considered with a zero reference signal, the equilibrium point of interest is the origin.

A discrete-time LTI system as (4) is asymptotically stable if all the roots of its characteristic polynomial (i.e., the eigenvalues of the closed-loop matrix $A_d - B_d K$) are inside the unity circle of the complex plane, i.e., their absolute values are strictly less than one [4] (this simple sufficient condition can be generalised, however this is not necessary in our work). In this paper, we express this stability specification $\phi_{stability}$ in terms of a check known as *Jury's criterion* [11]: this is an easy algebraic formula to select the entries of matrix K so that the closed-loop dynamics are shaped as desired.

3.4   Safety Specifications for Dynamical Systems

We are not limited to the synthesis of digital stabilizing controllers – a well known task in the literature on digital control systems – but target safety requirements with an overall approach that is sound and automated. More specifically, we require that the closed-loop system (4) meets given safety specifications. A safety specification gives raise to a requirement on the states of the model, such that the feedback controller (namely the choice of the gains matrix K) must ensure that the state never violates the requirement. Note that a stable, closed-loop system is not necessarily a safe system: indeed, the state values may leave the safe part of the state space while they converge to the equilibrium, which is typical in the case of oscillatory dynamics. In this work, the safety property is expressed as:

$$\phi_{safety} \iff \forall k \geq 0. \bigwedge_{i=1}^{n} \underline{x_i} \leq x_{i,k} \leq \overline{x_i}, \tag{5}$$

where $\underline{x_i}$ and $\overline{x_i}$ are lower and upper bounds for the i-th coordinate x_i of state $x \in \mathbb{R}^n$ at the k-th instant, respectively. This means that the states will always be within an n-dimensional hyper-box.

Furthermore, it is practically relevant to consider the constraints ϕ_{input} on the input signal u_k and ϕ_{init} on the initial states x_0, which we assume have given bounds: $\phi_{input} = \forall k.\underline{u} \leq u_k \leq \overline{u}$, $\phi_{init} = \bigwedge_{i=1}^{n} \underline{x_{i,0}} \leq x_{i,0} \leq \overline{x_{i,0}}$. For the former, this means that the control input might saturates in view of physical constraints.

3.5   Numerical Representation and Soundness

The models we consider have two sources of error that are due to numerical representation. The first is the numerical error introduced by the fixed-point numbers employed to model the plant, i.e., to represent the plant dynamics A_d, B_d and x_k. The second is the quantization error introduced by the digital controller, which performs operations on fixed-point numbers. In this section we outline the notation for the fixed-point representation of numbers, and briefly describe the errors introduced. A formal discussion is in Appendix B.1.

Let $\mathcal{F}_{\langle I,F \rangle}(x)$ denote a real number x represented in a fixed point domain, with I bits representing the integer part and F bits representing the decimal part. The smallest number that can be represented in this domain is $c_m = 2^{-F}$. Any mathematical operations performed at the precision $\mathcal{F}_{\langle I,F \rangle}(x)$ will introduce errors, for which an upper bound can be given [6].

We will use $\mathcal{F}_{\langle I_c,F_c \rangle}(x)$ to denote a real number x represented at the fixed-point precision of the controller, and $\mathcal{F}_{\langle I_p,F_p \rangle}(x)$ to denote a real number x represented at the fixed-point precision of the plant model (I_c and F_c are determined by the controller. We pick I_p and F_p for our synthesis such that $I_p \geq I_c$ and $F_p \geq F_c$). Thus any mathematical operations in our modelled digital controller will be in the range of $\mathcal{F}_{\langle I_c,F_c \rangle}$, and all other calculations in our model will be carried out in the range of $\mathcal{F}_{\langle I_p,F_p \rangle}$. The physical plant operates in the reals, which means our verification phase must also account for the numerical error and quantization errors caused by representing the physical plant at the finite precision $\mathcal{F}_{\langle I_p,F_p \rangle}$.

Effect on Safety Specification and Stability. Let us first consider the effect of the quantization errors on safety. Within the controller, state values are manipulated at low precision, alongside the vector multiplication Kx. The inputs are computed using the following equation:

$$u_k = -(\mathcal{F}_{\langle I_c,F_c \rangle}(K) \cdot \mathcal{F}_{\langle I_c,F_c \rangle}(x_k)).$$

This induces two types of the errors detailed above: first, the truncation error due to representing x_k as $\mathcal{F}\langle I_c, F_c \rangle(x_k)$; and second, the rounding error introduced by the multiplication operation. We represent these errors as non-deterministic additive noise.

An additional error is due to the representation of the plant dynamics, namely

$$x_{k+1} = \mathcal{F}_{\langle I_p,F_p \rangle}(A_d)\mathcal{F}_{\langle I_p,F_p \rangle}(x_k) + \mathcal{F}_{\langle I_p,F_p \rangle}(B_d)\mathcal{F}_{\langle I_p,F_p \rangle}(u_k).$$

We address this error by use of interval arithmetic [22] in the verification phase.

Previous studies [18] show that the FWL affects the poles and zeros positions, degrading the closed-loop dynamics, causing steady-state errors (see Appendix B for details) and eventually de-stabilizing the system [5]. However, since in this paper we require stability only as a precursor to safety, it is sufficient to check that the (perturbed, noisy) model converges to a neighborhood of the equilibrium within the safe set (see Appendix A.1).

In the following, we shall disregard these steady-state errors (caused by FWL effects) when stability is ensured by synthesis, and then verify its safety accounting for the finite-precision errors.

4   CEGIS of Safe Controllers for LTI Systems

In this section, we describe our technique for synthesizing safe digital feedback controllers using CEGIS. For this purpose, we first provide the synthesizer's general architecture, followed by describing our two approaches to synthesizing safe controllers: the first one is a baseline approach that relies on a naïve unfolding of the transition relation, whereas the second uses abstraction to evaluate all possible executions of the system.

4.1   General Architecture of the Program Synthesizer

The input specification provided to the program synthesizer is of the form $\exists P. \forall a. \sigma(a, P)$, where P ranges over functions (where a function is represented by the program computing it), a ranges over ground terms, and σ is a quantifier-free formula. We interpret the ground terms over some finite domain $\mathcal{D}$. The design of our synthesizer consists of two phases, an inductive synthesis phase and a validation phase, which interact via a finite set of test vectors INPUTS that is updated incrementally. Given the aforementioned specification σ, the inductive synthesis procedure tries to find an existential witness P satisfying the specification $\sigma(a, P)$ for all a in INPUTS (as opposed to all $a \in \mathcal{D}$). If the synthesis phase succeeds in finding a witness P, this witness is a candidate solution to the full synthesis formula. We pass this candidate solution to the validation phase, which checks whether it is a full solution (i.e., P satisfies the specification $\sigma(a, P)$ for all $a \in \mathcal{D}$). If this is the case, then the algorithm terminates. Otherwise, additional information is provided to the inductive synthesis phase in the form of a new counterexample that is added to the INPUTS set and the loop iterates again. More details about the general architecture of the synthesizer can be found in [8].

4.2   Synthesis Problem: Statement (Recap) and Connection to Program Synthesis

At this point, we recall the synthesis problem that we solve in this work: we seek a digital feedback controller K (see Eq. 3) that makes the closed-loop plant model safe for initial state x_0, reference signal r_k and input u_k as defined in Sect. 3.4. We consider non-deterministic initial states within a specified range, the reference signal to be set to zero, saturation on the inputs, and account for digitization and quantization errors introduced by the controller.

When mapping back to the notation used for describing the general architecture of the program synthesizer, the controller K denotes P, (x_0, u_k) represents a and $\phi_{stability} \wedge \phi_{input} \wedge \phi_{init} \wedge \phi_{safety}$ denotes the specification σ.

4.3   Naïve Approach: CEGIS with Multi-staged Verification

An overview of the algorithm for controller synthesis is given in Fig. 2. One important observation is that we verify and synthesize a controller over k time

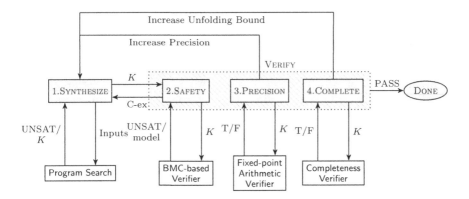

Fig. 2. CEGIS with multi-staged verification.

steps. We then compute a completeness threshold $\bar{k}$ [17] for this controller, and verify correctness for $\bar{k}$ time steps. Essentially, $\bar{k}$ is the number of iterations required to sufficiently unwind the closed-loop state-space system, which ensures that the boundaries are not violated for any other $k>\bar{k}$.

Theorem 1. *There exists a finite $\bar{k}$ such that it is sufficient to unwind the closed-loop state-space system up to $\bar{k}$ in order to ensure that ϕ_{safety} holds.*

Proof. A stable control system is known to have converging dynamics. Assume the closed-loop matrix eigenvalues are not repeated (which is sensible to do, since we select them). The distance of the trajectory from the reference point (origin) decreases over time within subspaces related to real-valued eigenvalues; however, this is not the case in general when dealing with complex eigenvalues. Consider the closed-loop matrix that updates the states in every discrete time step, and select the eigenvalue ϑ with the smallest (non-trivial) imaginary value. Between every pair of consecutive time steps kT_s and $(k+1)T_s$, the dynamics projected on the corresponding eigenspace rotate ϑT_s radians. Thus, taking $\bar{k}$ as the ceiling of $\frac{2\pi}{\vartheta T_s}$, after $k \geq \bar{k}$ steps we have completed a full rotation, which results in a point closer to the origin. The synthesized $\bar{k}$ is the completeness threshold.   □

Next, we describe the different phases in Fig. 2 (blocks 1 to 4) in detail.

1. The inductive synthesis phase (SYNTHESIZE) uses BMC to compute a candidate solution K that satisfies both the stability criteria (Sect. 3.3) and the safety specification (Sect. 3.4). To synthesize a controller that satisfies the stability criteria, we require that a computed polynomial satisfies Jury's criterion [11]. The details of this calculation can be found in the Appendix. Regarding the second requirement, we synthesize a safe controller by unfolding the transition system k steps and by picking a controller K and a single initial state, such that the states at each step do not violate the safety criteria. That is, we ask the bounded model checker if there exists a K that is

Algorithm 1. Safety check

```
 1: function safetyCheck()
 2:     assert(u ≤ u ≤ ū)
 3:     set x_0 to be a vertex state, e.g., [x_0, x_0]
 4:     for (c = 0; c < 2^{Num_States}; c++) do
 5:         for (i = 0; i < k; i++) do
 6:             u = (plant_typet)((controller_typet)K * (controller_typet)x)
 7:             x = A * x + B * u
 8:             assert(x ≤ x ≤ x̄ )
 9:         end for
10:         set x_0 to be a new vertex state
11:     end for
12: end function
```

safe for at least one x_0 in our set of all possible initial states. This is sound if the current k is greater than the completeness threshold. We also assume some precision $\langle I_p, F_p \rangle$ for the plant and a sampling rate. The checks that these assumptions hold are performed by subsequent VERIFY stages.

2. The first VERIFY stage, SAFETY, checks that the candidate solution K, which we synthesized to be safe for at least one initial state, is safe for *all* possible initial states, i.e., does not reach an unsafe state within k steps where we assume k to be under the completeness threshold. After unfolding the transition system corresponding to the previously synthesized controller k steps, we check that the safety specification holds for any initial state. This is shown in Algorithm 1.

3. The second VERIFY stage, PRECISION, restores soundness with respect to the plant's precision by using interval arithmetic [22] to validate the operations performed by the previous stage.

4. The third VERIFY stage, COMPLETE, checks that the current k is large enough to ensure safety for any $k' > k$. Here, we compute the completeness threshold $\bar{k}$ for the current candidate controller K and check that $k \geq \bar{k}$. This is done according to the argument given above and illustrated in Fig. 3.

Checking that the safety specification holds for any initial state can be computationally expensive if the bounds on the allowed initial states are large.

Theorem 2. *If a controller is safe for each of the corner cases of our hypercube of allowed initial states, it is safe for any initial state in the hypercube.*

Thus we only need to check 2^n initial states, where n is the dimension of the state space (number of continuous variables).

Proof. Consider the set of initial states, X_0, which we assume to be convex since it is a hypercube. Name v_i its vertexes, where $i = 1, \ldots, 2^n$. Thus any point $x \in X_0$ can be expressed by convexity as $x = \sum_{i=1}^{2^n} \alpha_i v_i$, where $\sum_{i=1}^{2^n} \alpha_i = 1$.

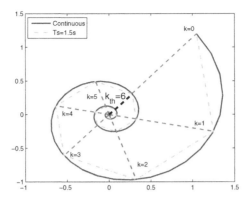

Fig. 3. Completeness threshold for multi-staged verification. T_s is the time step for the time discretization of the control matrices.

Then if $x_0 = x$, we obtain

$$x_k = (A_d - B_d K)^k x = (A_d - B_d K)^k \sum_{i=1}^{2^n} \alpha_i v_i = \sum_{i=1}^{2^n} \alpha_i (A_d - B_d K)^k v_i = \sum_{i=1}^{2^n} \alpha_i x_k^i,$$

where x_k^i denotes the trajectories obtained from the single vertex v_i. We conclude that any k-step trajectory is encompassed, within a convex set, by those generated from the vertices. □

Illustrative Example. We illustrate our approach with an example, extracted from [13]. Since we have not learned any information about the system yet, we pick an arbitrary candidate solution (we always choose $K = [0\ 0\ 0]^T$ in our experiments to simplify reproduction), and a precision of $I_p = 13$, $F_p = 3$. In the first VERIFY stage, the SAFETY check finds the counterexample $x_0 = [-0.5\ 0.5\ 0.5]$. After adding the new counterexample to its sets of INPUTS, SYNTHESIZE finds the candidate solution $K = [0\ 0\ 0.00048828125]^T$, which prompts the SAFETY verifier to return $x_0 = [-0.5\ -0.5\ -0.5]$ as the new counterexample.

In the subsequent iteration, the synthesizer is unable to find further suitable candidates and it returns UNSAT, meaning that the current precision is insufficient. Consequently, we increase the precision the plant is modelled with to $I_p = 17$, $F_p = 7$. We increase the precision by 8 bits each step in order to be compliant with the CBMC type API. Since the previous counterexamples were obtained at lower precision, we remove them from the set of counterexamples. Back in the SYNTHESIZE phase, we re-start the process with a candidate solution with all coefficients 0. Next, the SAFETY verification stage provides the first counterexample at higher precision, $x_0 = [-0.5\ 0.5\ 0.5]$ and SYNTHESIZE finds $K = [0\ 0.01171875\ 0.015625]^T$ as a candidate that eliminates this counterexample. However, this candidate triggers the counterexample $x_0 = [0.5\ -0.5\ -0.5]$ found again by the SAFETY verification stage. In the next iteration, we get the candidate $K = [0\ 0\ -0.015625]$, followed by the counterexample $x_0 = [0.5\ 0.5\ 0.5]$. Finally, SYNTHESIZE finds the candidate $K = [0.01171875\ -0.013671875\ -0.013671875]^T$, which is validated as a final solution by all verification stages.

4.4   Abstraction-Based CEGIS

The naïve approach described in Sect. 4.3 synthesizes a controller for an individual initial state and input with a bounded time horizon and, subsequently, it generalizes it to all reachable states, inputs, and time horizons during the verification phase. Essentially, this approach relies on the symbolic simulation over a bounded time horizon of individual initial states and inputs that form part of an uncountable space and tries to generalize it for an infinite space over an infinite time horizon.

Conversely, in this section, we find a controller for a continuous initial set of states and set of inputs, over an abstraction of the continuous dynamics [7] that conforms to witness proofs at specific times. Moreover, this approach uses abstraction refinement enabling us to always start with a very simple description regardless of the complexity of the overall dynamics, and only expand to more complex models when a solution cannot be found.

The CEGIS loop for this approach is illustrated in Fig. 4.

1. We start by doing some preprocessing:
   (a) Compute the characteristic polynomial of the matrix $(A_d - B_d K)$ as $P_a(z) = z^n + \sum_{i=1}^{n} (a_i - k_i) z^{n-i}$.
   (b) Calculate the noise set N from the quantizer resolutions and estimated round-off errors:

   $$N = \left\{ \nu_1 + \nu_2 + \nu_3 : \nu_1 \in \left[-\frac{q_1}{2}\ \frac{q_1}{2} \right] \wedge \nu_2 \in \left[-\frac{q_2}{2}\ \frac{q_2}{2} \right] \wedge \nu_3 \in [-q_3\ q_3] \right\}$$

   where q_1 is the error introduced by the truncation in the ADC, q_2 is the error introduced by the DAC and q_3 is the maximum truncation and rounding error in $u_k = -K \cdot \mathcal{F}_{(I_c, F_c)}(x_k)$ as discussed in Sect. 3.5. More details on how to model quantization as noise are given in Appendix B.2.
   (c) Calculate a set of initial bounds on K, ϕ_{init}^K, based on the input constraints

   $$(\phi_{init} \wedge \phi_{input} \wedge u_k = -K x_k) \Rightarrow \phi_{init}^K$$

   Note that these bounds will be used by the SYNTHESIZE phase to reduce the size of the solution space.
2. In the SYNTHESIZE phase, we synthesize a candidate controller $K \in \mathbb{R}\langle I_c, F_c \rangle^n$ that satisfies $\phi_{stability} \wedge \phi_{safety} \wedge \phi_{init}^K$ by invoking a SAT solver. If there is no candidate solution we return UNSAT and exit the loop.
3. Once we have a candidate solution, we perform a safety verification of the progression of the system from ϕ_{init} over time, $x_k \models \phi_{safety}$. In order to compute the progression of point x_0 at iteration k, we accelerate the dynamics of the closed-loop system and obtain:

$$x = (A_d - B_d K)^k x_0 + \sum_{i=0}^{k-1} (A_d - B_d K)^i B_n (\nu_1 + \nu_2 + \nu_3) : B_n = [1 \cdots 1]^T \quad (6)$$

As this still requires us to verify the system for every k up to infinity, we use abstract acceleration again to obtain the reach-tube, i.e., the set of all reachable states at all times given an initial set ϕ_{init}:

$$\hat{X}^{\#} = \mathcal{A} X_0 + \mathcal{B}_n N, \quad X_0 = \{x : x \models \phi_{init}\}, \quad (7)$$

where $\mathcal{A} = \bigcup_{k=1}^{\infty} (A_d - B_d K)^k, \mathcal{B}_n = \bigcup_{k=1}^{\infty} \sum_{i=0}^{k} (A_d - B_d K)^i B_n$ are abstract matrices for the closed-loop system [7], whereas the set N is non-deterministically chosen.

We next evaluate $\hat{X}^{\#} \models \phi_{safety}$. If the verification holds we have a solution, and exit the loop. Otherwise, we find a counterexample iteration k and corresponding initial point x_0 for which the property does not hold, which we use to locally refine the abstraction. When the abstraction cannot be further refined, we provide them to the ABSTRACT phase.

4. If we reach the ABSTRACT phase, it means that the candidate solution is not valid, in which case we must refine the abstraction used by the synthesizer.
   (a) Find the constraints that invalidate the property as a set of counterexamples for the eigenvalues, which we define as ϕ_Λ. This is a constraint in the spectrum i.e., transfer function) of the closed loop dynamics.
   (b) We use ϕ_Λ to further constrain the characteristic polynomial $z^n + \sum_{i=1}^{n} (a_i - k_i) z^{n-i} = \prod_{i=1}^{n} (z - \lambda_i) : |\lambda_i| < 1 \wedge \lambda_i \models \phi_\Lambda$. These constraints correspond to specific iterations for which the system may be unsafe.
   (c) Pass the refined abstraction $\phi(K)$ with the new constraints and the list of iterations k to the SYNTHESIZE phase.

Illustrative Example. Let us consider the following example with discretized dynamics

$$A_d = \begin{bmatrix} 2.6207 & -1.1793 & 0.65705 \\ 2 & 0 & 0 \\ 0 & 0.5 & 0 \end{bmatrix}, \quad B_d = \begin{bmatrix} 8 \\ 0 \\ 0 \end{bmatrix}$$

Using the initial state bounds $\underline{x_0} = -0.9$ and $\overline{x_0} = 0.9$, the input bounds $\underline{u} = -10$ and $\overline{u} = 10$, and safety specifications $\underline{x_i} = -0.92$ and $\overline{x_i} = 0.92$, the SYNTHESIZE phase in Fig. 4 generates an initial candidate controller $K = [0.24609375 \; -0.125 \; 0.1484375]$. This candidate is chosen for its closed-loop stable dynamics, but the VERIFY phase finds it to be unsafe and returns a list of iterations with an initial state that fails the safety specification $(k, x_0) \in \{(2, [0.9 \; -0.9 \; 0.9]), (3, [0.9 \; -0.9 \; -0.9])\}$. This allows the ABSTRACT phase to create a new safety specification that considers these iterations for these initial states to constrain the solution space. This refinement allows SYNTHESIZE to find a new controller $K = [0.23828125 \; -0.17578125 \; 0.109375]$, which this time passes the verification phase, resulting in a safe system.

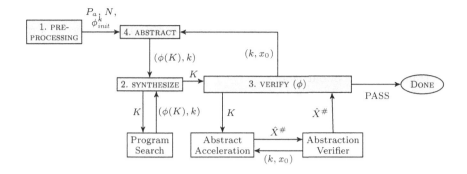

Fig. 4. Abstraction-based CEGIS

5 Experimental Evaluation

5.1 Description of the Benchmarks

A set of state-space models for different classes of systems has been taken from the literature [1, 13, 23, 31] and employed for validating our methodology.

DC Motor Rate plants describes the angular velocity of a DC Motor, respectively. The *Automotive Cruise System* plant represents the speed of a motor vehicle. The *Helicopter Longitudinal Motion* plant provides the longitudinal motion model of a helicopter. The *Inverted Pendulum* plant describes a pendulum model with its center of mass above its pivot point. The *Magnetic Suspension* plant provides a physical model for which a given object is suspended via a magnetic field. The *Magnetized Pointer* plant describes a physical model employed in analogue gauges and indicators that is rotated through interaction with magnetic fields. The *1/4 Car Suspension* plant presents a physical model that connects a car to its wheels and allows relative motion between the two parts. The *Computer Tape Driver* plant describes a system to read and write data on a storage device.

Our benchmarks are SISO models (Sect. 3). The Inverted Pendulum appears to be a two-output system, but it is treated as two SISO models during the experiments. All the state measurements are assumed to be available (current work targets the extension of our framework to observer-based synthesis).

All benchmarks are discretized with different sample times [11]. All experiments are performed considering $\underline{x_i} = -1$ and $\overline{x_i} = 1$ and the reference inputs $r_k = 0, \forall k > 0$. We conduct the experimental evaluation on a 12-core 2.40 GHz Intel Xeon E5-2440 with 96 GB of RAM and Linux OS. We use the Linux *times* command to measure CPU time used for each benchmark. The runtime is limited to one hour per benchmark.

5.2 Objectives

Using the state-space models given in Sect. 5.1, our evaluation has the following two experimental goals:

EG1 **(CEGIS)** Show that both the multi-staged and the abstraction-based CEGIS approaches are able to generate FWL digital controllers in a reasonable amount of time.

EG2 **(sanity check)** Confirm the stability and safety of the synthesized controllers outside of our model.

5.3 Results

We provide the results in Table 1. Here *Benchmark* is the name of the respective benchmark, *Order* is the number of continuous variables, $\mathcal{F}_{\langle I_p, F_p \rangle}$ is the fixed-point precision used to model the plant, while *Time* is the total time required to synthesize a controller for the given plant with one of the two methods. Timeouts are indicated by ✗. The precision for the controller, $\mathcal{F}_{\langle I_c, F_c \rangle}$, is chosen to be $I_c = 8$, $F_c = 8$.

For the majority of our benchmarks, we observe that the abstraction-based back-end is faster than the basic multi-staged verification approach, and finds one solution more (9) than the multi-staged back-end (8). In direct comparison, the abstraction-based approach is on average able to find a solution in approximately 70% of the time required using the multi-staged back-end, and has a median run-time 1.4 s, which is seven times smaller than the multi-staged approach. The two back-ends complement each other in benchmark coverage and together solve all benchmarks in the set. On average our engine spent 52% in the synthesis and 48% in the verification phase.

Table 1. Experimental results.

#	Benchmark	Order	Multi-staged		Abstraction	
			$\mathcal{F}_{\langle I_p, F_p \rangle}$	Time	$\mathcal{F}_{\langle I_p, F_p \rangle}$	Time
1	Cruise Control	1	8,16	8.40 s	16,16	2.17 s
2	DC Motor	2	8,16	9.45 s	20,20	2.06 s
3	Helicopter	3	✗	✗	16,16	1.37 s
4	Inverted Pendulum	4	8,16	9.65 s	16,16	0.56 s
5	Magnetic Pointer	2	✗	✗	28,28	44.14 s
6	Magnetic Suspension	2	12,20	10.41 s	16,16	0.61 s
7	Pendulum	2	8,16	14.02 s	16,16	0.60 s
8	Suspension	2	12,20	73.66 s	✗	✗
9	Tape Driver	3	8,16	10.10 s	16,16	68.24 s
10	Satellite	2	8,16	9.43 s	16,16	0.67 s

The median run-time for our benchmark set is 9.4 s. Overall, the average synthesis time amounts to approximately 15.6 s. We consider these times short enough to be of practical use to control engineers, and thus affirm EG1.

There are a few instances for which the system fails to find a controller. For the naïve approach, the completeness threshold may be too large, thus causing a timeout. On the other hand, the abstraction-based approach may require a very precise abstraction, resulting in too many refinements and, consequently, in a timeout. Yet another source of incompleteness is the inability of the SYNTHESIZE phase to use a large enough precision for the plant model.

The synthesized controllers are confirmed to be safe outside of our model representation using MATLAB, achieving EG2. A link to the full experimental environment, including scripts to reproduce the results, all benchmarks and the tool, is provided in the footnote as an Open Virtual Appliance (OVA).[1] The provided experimental environment runs multiple discretisations for each benchmark, and lists the fastest as the result synthesis time.

5.4   Threats to Validity

Benchmark Selection: We report an assessment of both our approaches over a diverse set of real-world benchmarks. Nevertheless, this set of benchmarks is limited within the scope of this paper and the performance may not generalize to other benchmarks.

Plant Precision and Discretization Heuristics: Our algorithm to select suitable FWL word widths to model the plant behavior increases the precision by 8 bits at each step in order to be compliant with the CBMC type API. Similarly, for discretization, we run multiple discretizations for each benchmark and retain the fastest run. This works sufficiently well for our benchmarks, but performance may suffer in some cases, for example if the completeness threshold is high.

Abstraction on Other Properties: The performance gain from abstract acceleration may not hold for more complex properties than safety, for instance "eventually reach and always remain in a given safe set".

6   Conclusion

We have presented two automated approaches to synthesize digital state-feedback controllers that ensure both stability and safety over the state-space representation. The first approach relies on unfolding of the closed-loop model dynamics up to a completeness threshold, while the second one applies abstraction refinement and acceleration to increase speed whilst retaining soundness. Both approaches are novel within the control literature: they give a fully automated synthesis method that is algorithmically and numerically sound, considering various error sources in the implementation of the digital control algorithm and in the computational modeling of plant dynamics. Our experimental results show that both approaches are able to synthesize safe controllers for most

---

[1] www.cprover.org/DSSynth/controller-synthesis-cav-2017.tar.gz.

benchmarks within a reasonable amount of time fully automatically. In particular, both approaches complement each other and together solve all benchmarks, which have been derived from the control literature.

Future work will focus the extension of these approaches to the continuous-time case, to models with output-based control architectures (with the use of observers), and to the consideration of more complex specifications.

A   Stability of Closed-Loop Models

A.1   Stability of Closed-Loop Models with Fixed-Point Controller Error

The proof of Jury's criterion [11] relies on the fact that the relationship between states and next states is defined by $x_{k+1} = (A_d - B_dK)x_k$, all computed at infinite precision. When we employ a FWL digital controller, the operation becomes:

$$x_{k+1} = A_d \cdot x_k - (\mathcal{F}_{\langle I_c, F_c \rangle}(K) \cdot \mathcal{F}_{\langle I_c, F_c \rangle}(x_k)).$$
$$x_{k+1} = (A_d - B_dK) \cdot x_k + B_dK\delta,$$

where δ is the maximum error that can be introduced by the FWL controller in one step, i.e., by reading the states values once and multiplying by K once. We derive the closed form expression for x_n as follows:

$$x_1 = (A_d - B_dK)x_0 + B_dK\delta$$
$$x_2 = (A_d - B_dK)^2x_0 + (A_d - B_dK)B_dK\delta + B_dK\delta$$
$$x_n = (A_d - B_dK)^nx_0 + (A_d - B_dK)^{n-1}B_dK\delta + ... + (A_d - B_dK)^1B_dK\delta + B_dK\delta$$
$$= (A_d - B_dK)^nx_0 + \sum_{i=0}^{i=n-1} (A_d - B_dK)^iB_dk\delta.$$

The definition of asymptotic stability is that the system converges to a reference signal, in this case we use no reference signal so an asymptotically stable system will converge to the origin. We know that the original system with an infinite-precision controller is stable, because we have synthesized it to meet Jury's criterion. Hence, $(A_d - B_dK)^nx_0$ must converge to zero.

The power series of matrices converges [15] iff the eigenvalues of the matrix are less than 1 as follows: $\sum_{i=0}^{\infty} T^i = (I - T)^{-1}$, where I is the identity matrix and T is a square matrix. Thus, our system will converge to the value

$$0 + (I - A_d + B_dK)^{-1}B_dk\delta.$$

As a result, if the value $(I - A_d + B_dK)^{-1}B_dk\delta$ is within the safe space, then the synthesized fixed-point controller results in a safe closed-loop model. The convergence to a finite value, however, will not make it asymptomatically stable.

B Errors in LTI Models

B.1 Errors Due to Numerical Representation

We have used $\mathcal{F}_{\langle I,F\rangle}(x)$ denote a real number x represented in a fixed point domain, with I bits representing the integer part and F bits representing the decimal part. The smallest number that can be represented in this domain is $c_m = 2^{-F}$. The following approximation errors will arise in mathematical operations and representation:

1. **Truncation:** Let x be a real number, and $\mathcal{F}_{\langle I,F\rangle}(x)$ be the same number represented in a fixed-point domain as above. Then $\mathcal{F}_{\langle I,F\rangle}(x) = x - \delta_T$ where the error $\delta_T = x \;\%_{c_m}\; \tilde{x}$, and $\%_{c_m}$ is the modulus operation performed on the last bit. Thus, δ_T is the truncation error and it will propagate across operations.

2. **Rounding:** The following errors appear in basic operations. Let c_1, c_2 and c_3 be real numbers, and δ_{T1} and δ_{T2} be the truncation errors caused by representing c_1 and c_2 in the fixed-point domain as above.
   (a) Addition/Subtraction: these operations only propagate errors coming from truncation of the operands, namely $\mathcal{F}_{\langle I,F\rangle}(c_1) \pm \mathcal{F}_{\langle I,F\rangle}(c_2) = c_3 + \delta_3$ with $|\delta_3| \leq |\delta_{T1}| + |\delta_{T2}|$.
   (b) Multiplication: $\mathcal{F}_{\langle I,F\rangle}(c_1) \cdot \mathcal{F}_{\langle I,F\rangle}(c_2) = c_3 + \delta_3$ with $|\delta_3| \leq |\delta_{T1} \cdot \mathcal{F}_{\langle I,F\rangle}(c_2)| + |\delta_{T2} \cdot \mathcal{F}_{\langle I,F\rangle}(c_1)| + c_m$, where $c_m = 2^{-F}$ as above.
   (c) Division: the operations performed by our controllers in the FWL domain do not include division. However, we do use division in computations at the precision of the plant. Here the error depends on whether the divisor is greater or smaller than the dividend: $\mathcal{F}_{\langle I,F\rangle}(c_1)/\mathcal{F}_{\langle I,F\rangle}(c_2) = c_3 + \delta_{T3}$ where δ_{T3} is $(\delta_{T2} \cdot c_1 - \delta_{T1} \cdot c_2)/(\delta_{T2}^2 - \delta_{T2}c_2)$,

3. **Overflow:** The maximum size of a real number x that can be represented in a fixed point domain as $\mathcal{F}_{\langle I,F\rangle}(x)$ is $\pm(2^{I-1} + 1 - 2^{-F})$. Numbers outside this range cannot be represented by the domain. We check that overflow does not occur.

B.2 Modeling Quantization as Noise

During any given ADC conversion, the continuous signal will be sampled in the real domain and transformed by $\mathcal{F}\langle I_c, F_c\rangle(x)$ (assuming the ADC discretization is the same as the digital implementation). This sampling uses a threshold which is defined by the less significant bit ($q_c = c_{m_c} = 2^{-F_c}$) of the ADC and some non-linearities of the circuitry. The overall conversion is

$$\mathcal{F}\langle I_c, F_c\rangle(y(t)) = y_k : y_k \in \left[y(t) - \frac{q_c}{2} \quad y(t) + \frac{q_c}{2} \right].$$

If we denote the error in the conversion by $\nu_k = y_k - y(t)$ where $t = nk$, and n is the sampling time and k the number of steps, then we may define some bounds for it $\nu_k \in \left[-\frac{q_c}{2} \quad \frac{q_c}{2} \right]$.

We will assume, for the purposes of this analysis, that the domain of the ADC is that of the digital controller (i.e., the quantizer includes any digital gain added in the code). The process of quantization in the DAC is similar except that it is calculating $\mathcal{F}\langle I_{dac}, F_{dac}\rangle(\mathcal{F}\langle I_c, F_c\rangle(x))$. If these domains are the same ($I_c = I_{dac}, F_c = F_{dac}$), or if the DAC resolution in higher than the ADCs, then the DAC quantization error is equal to zero. From the above equations we can now define the ADC and DAC quantization noises $\nu_{1k} \in [-\frac{q_1}{2} \quad \frac{q_1}{2}]$ and $\nu_{2k} \in [-\frac{q_2}{2} \quad \frac{q_2}{2}]$, where $q_1 = q_c$ and $q_2 = q_{dac}$. This is illustrated in Fig. 1 where Q_1 is the quantizer of the ADC and Q_2 the quantizer for the DAC. These bounds hold irrespective of whether the noise is correlated, hence we may use them to over-approximate the noise effect on the state space progression over time. The resulting dynamics are

$$x_{k+1} = A_d x_k + B_d(u_k + \nu_{2k}), \quad u_k = -Kx_k + \nu_{1k},$$

which result in the following closed-loop dynamics:

$$x_{k+1} = (A_d - B_d K_d)x_k + B_d \nu_{2k} + \nu_{1k}.$$

References

1. Control tutorials for MATLAB and SIMULINK. http://ctms.engin.umich.edu/
2. Abate, A., Bessa, I., Cattaruzza, D., Cordeiro, L.C., David, C., Kesseli, P., Kroening, D.: Sound and automated synthesis of digital stabilizing controllers for continuous plants. In: Hybrid Systems: Computation and Control (HSCC), pp. 197–206. ACM (2017)
3. Anta, A., Majumdar, R., Saha, I., Tabuada, P.: Automatic verification of control system implementations. In: EMSOFT, pp. 9–18 (2010)
4. Åström, K., Wittenmark, B.: Computer-Controlled Systems: Theory and Design. Prentice Hall Information and System Sciences Series. Prentice Hall, Upper Saddle River (1997)
5. Bessa, I., Ismail, H., Palhares, R., Cordeiro, L., Filho, J.E.C.: Formal non-fragile stability verification of digital control systems with uncertainty. IEEE Trans. Comput. **66**(3), 545–552 (2017)
6. Brain, M., Tinelli, C., Rümmer, P., Wahl, T.: An automatable formal semantics for IEEE-754 floating-point arithmetic. In: ARITH, pp. 160–167. IEEE (2015)
7. Cattaruzza, D., Abate, A., Schrammel, P., Kroening, D.: Unbounded-time analysis of guarded LTI systems with inputs by abstract acceleration. In: Blazy, S., Jensen, T. (eds.) SAS 2015. LNCS, vol. 9291, pp. 312–331. Springer, Heidelberg (2015). doi:10.1007/978-3-662-48288-9_18
8. David, C., Kroening, D., Lewis, M.: Using program synthesis for program analysis. In: Davis, M., Fehnker, A., McIver, A., Voronkov, A. (eds.) LPAR 2015. LNCS, vol. 9450, pp. 483–498. Springer, Heidelberg (2015). doi:10.1007/978-3-662-48899-7_34
9. de Bessa, I.V., Ismail, H., Cordeiro, L.C., Filho, J.E.C.: Verification of fixed-point digital controllers using direct and delta forms realizations. Des. Autom. Emb. Syst. **20**(2), 95–126 (2016)
10. Duggirala, P.S., Viswanathan, M.: Analyzing real time linear control systems using software verification. In: IEEE Real-Time Systems Symposium, pp. 216–226, December 2015

11. Fadali, S., Visioli, A.: Digital Control Engineering: Analysis and Design. Electronics & Electrical. Elsevier/Academic Press, Amsterdam/Cambridge (2009)
12. Fialho, I.J., Georgiou, T.T.: On stability and performance of sampled-data systems subject to wordlength constraint. IEEE Trans. Autom. Control **39**(12), 2476–2481 (1994)
13. Franklin, G., Powell, D., Emami-Naeini, A.: Feedback Control of Dynamic Systems, 7th edn. Pearson, Upper Saddle River (2015)
14. Frehse, G., et al.: SpaceEx: scalable verification of hybrid systems. In: Gopalakrishnan, G., Qadeer, S. (eds.) CAV 2011. LNCS, vol. 6806, pp. 379–395. Springer, Heidelberg (2011). doi:10.1007/978-3-642-22110-1_30
15. Horn, R.A., Johnson, C.: Matrix Analysis. Cambridge University Press, Cambridge (1990)
16. Itzhaky, S., Gulwani, S., Immerman, N., Sagiv, M.: A simple inductive synthesis methodology and its applications. In: OOPSLA, pp. 36–46. ACM (2010)
17. Kroening, D., Strichman, O.: Efficient computation of recurrence diameters. In: Zuck, L.D., Attie, P.C., Cortesi, A., Mukhopadhyay, S. (eds.) VMCAI 2003. LNCS, vol. 2575, pp. 298–309. Springer, Heidelberg (2003). doi:10.1007/3-540-36384-X_24
18. Li, G.: On pole and zero sensitivity of linear systems. IEEE Trans. Circuits Syst.-I: Fundam. Theory Appl. **44**(7), 583–590 (1997)
19. Liberzon, D.: Hybrid feedback stabilization of systems with quantized signals. Automatica **39**(9), 1543–1554 (2003)
20. Liu, J., Ozay, N.: Finite abstractions with robustness margins for temporal logic-based control synthesis. Nonlinear Anal.: Hybrid Syst. **22**, 1–15 (2016)
21. Mazo, M., Davitian, A., Tabuada, P.: PESSOA: a tool for embedded controller synthesis. In: Touili, T., Cook, B., Jackson, P. (eds.) CAV 2010. LNCS, vol. 6174, pp. 566–569. Springer, Heidelberg (2010). doi:10.1007/978-3-642-14295-6_49
22. Moore, R.E.: Interval Analysis, vol. 4. Prentice-Hall, Englewood Cliffs (1966)
23. Oliveira, V.A., Costa, E.F., Vargas, J.B.: Digital implementation of a magnetic suspension control system for laboratory experiments. IEEE Trans. Educ. **42**(4), 315–322 (1999)
24. Oudjida, A.K., Chaillet, N., Liacha, A., Berrandjia, M.L., Hamerlain, M.: Design of high-speed and low-power finite-word-length PID controllers. Control Theory Technol. **12**(1), 68–83 (2014)
25. Park, J., Pajic, M., Lee, I., Sokolsky, O.: Scalable verification of linear controller software. In: Chechik, M., Raskin, J.-F. (eds.) TACAS 2016. LNCS, vol. 9636, pp. 662–679. Springer, Heidelberg (2016). doi:10.1007/978-3-662-49674-9_43
26. Picasso, B., Bicchi, A.: Stabilization of LTI systems with quantized state - quantized input static feedback. In: Maler, O., Pnueli, A. (eds.) HSCC 2003. LNCS, vol. 2623, pp. 405–416. Springer, Heidelberg (2003). doi:10.1007/3-540-36580-X_30
27. Ravanbakhsh, H., Sankaranarayanan, S.: Counter-example guided synthesis of control Lyapunov functions for switched systems. In: Conference on Decision and Control (CDC), pp. 4232–4239 (2015)
28. Ravanbakhsh, H., Sankaranarayanan, S.: Robust controller synthesis of switched systems using counterexample guided framework. In: EMSOFT, pp. 8:1–8:10. ACM (2016)
29. Roux, P., Jobredeaux, R., Garoche, P.: Closed loop analysis of control command software. In: HSCC, pp. 108–117. ACM (2015)
30. Solar-Lezama, A., Tancau, L., Bodík, R., Seshia, S.A., Saraswat, V.A.: Combinatorial sketching for finite programs. In: ASPLOS, pp. 404–415. ACM (2006)

31. Tan, R.H.G., Hoo, L.Y.H.: DC-DC converter modeling and simulation using state space approach. In: IEEE Conference on Energy Conversion, CENCON, pp. 42–47, October 2015
32. Wang, T.E., Garoche, P., Roux, P., Jobredeaux, R., Feron, E.: Formal analysis of robustness at model and code level. In: HSCC, pp. 125–134. ACM (2016)
33. Wu, J., Li, G., Chen, S., Chu, J.: Robust finite word length controller design. Automatica **45**(12), 2850–2856 (2009)
34. Zamani, M., Mazo, M., Abate, A.: Finite abstractions of networked control systems. In: IEEE CDC, pp. 95–100 (2014)

Classification and Coverage-Based Falsification for Embedded Control Systems

Arvind Adimoolam[1], Thao Dang[1][✉], Alexandre Donzé[2], James Kapinski[3], and Xiaoqing Jin[3]

[1] CNRS/Verimag, Grenoble, France
{santosh.adimoolam,thao.dang}@univ-grenoble-alpes.fr
[2] Decyphir, Inc., San Francisco, CA, USA
alex@decyphir.com
[3] Toyota Motors North America R&D, Gardena, CA, USA
{james.kapinski,xiaoqing.jin}@toyota.com

Abstract. Many industrial cyber-physical system (CPS) designs are too complex to formally verify system-level properties. A practical approach for testing and debugging these system designs is falsification, wherein the user provides a temporal logic specification of correct system behaviors, and some technique for selecting test cases is used to identify behaviors that demonstrate that the specification does not hold for the system. While coverage metrics are often used to measure the exhaustiveness of this kind of testing approach for software systems, existing falsification approaches for CPS designs do not consider coverage for the signal variables. We present a new coverage measure for continuous signals and a new falsification technique that leverages the measure to efficiently identify falsifying traces. This falsification algorithm combines global and local search methods and uses a classification technique based on support vector machines to identify regions of the search space on which to focus effort. We use an industrial example from an automotive fuel cell application and other benchmark models to compare the new approach against existing falsification tools.

1 Introduction

Cyber-physical systems integrate heterogeneous components whose descriptions in high level modeling languages involve a wide array of specification paradigms, such as differential equations, difference equations, automata, and data flow graphs. Although the behavior of individual cyber-physical components may be amenable to rigorous mathematical reasoning and analysis, the complex interactions between the components are still not well-understood and pose major theoretical hurdles in formal reasoning. Also, the scalability of the existing formal verification methods and tools (see [1,3,4,12,15,16,18,26] and references therein) is still limited and therefore not suited for verifying industrial scale cyber-physical systems. Testing is an alternate approach for detecting errors, whose advantage over formal verification methods is that it can treat a system

© Springer International Publishing AG 2017
R. Majumdar and V. Kunčak (Eds.): CAV 2017, Part I, LNCS 10426, pp. 483–503, 2017.
DOI: 10.1007/978-3-319-63387-9_24

as a black box, meaning that no internal description of the system is required. In black box testing, only an interface of the system with the external environment is described. Although testing can be applied to large scale cyber-physical systems, as attested by its use in industry, it does not provide proofs of correctness. In other words, black box testing can only detect bugs, and when it does so successfully, it means that the system design has to be corrected. Nevertheless, when the testing process does not find any bugs, we cannot draw any conclusion about its correctness. If the falsification is unsuccessful, then information about the potential validity of the correct behavior of the system would be of great interest to the designer. This information can be provided in terms of a testing coverage measure.

In the existing research on cyber-physical systems testing, the focus was generally on *state-coverage measures*, that is measures to characterize the portion of the state space covered by a test suite. An example is star discrepancy [6,11], a notion borrowed from statistics that indicates how equi-distributed are a set of tested points in the state space. Some other measures are dispersion [13], which indicates the size of the largest unexplored areas, and grid-cell count [25]. Although these state-coverage measures can serve as a possible means to compare coverage of testing data generated by different algorithms, these measures exhibit the following drawbacks. Typically, a test generation algorithm guided by a state coverage measure tries to sample test cases in the areas that are not well explored; however, in industrial scale system models describing interactions among a large number of heterogeneous components, information about the state can be hard to obtain. Additionally, such systems can have low controllability, meaning that it is difficult or impossible to reach some regions of the state space. In such a case, the algorithms can expend a large amount of time attempting to explore unreachable regions. So, state coverage measures are not appropriate for analysis or guidance of the testing effort on many cyber-physical systems.

The present work addresses the shortcomings of the state-coverage-based techniques by instead focusing on *coverage of input signal spaces*. We develop a new test generation technique that is based on covering the input signal space rather than the state space. Previous test generation methods have considered coverage of a parameter space (such as in [9]); the way that we handle input signals is directly related, as we consider the class of finitely parameterized input signals.

While coverage is important during testing for providing confidence in correctness of the system behavior, bug detection is still an important goal of testing. Usually, there is a mutual tradeoff between satisfying the two criteria. Achieving good coverage entails exploring a large portion of the search space, most of which would correspond to correct behaviors. Whereas, the objective of a falsification procedure is to find incorrect behaviors, which would require focusing on behaviors close to incorrectness. Most falsification methods are based on minimizing the behavioral robustness with respect to a property under test; the robustness measure here indicates how far the behavior is from violating the property. A common drawback of such falsification methods is that the optimization procedures can spend a significant amount of computing time near local optima that may not correspond to a false behavior. Therefore, a criterion like coverage can help overcome this drawback, since seeking to improve the global coverage would drive the search process out of the areas of local optima. One way to achieve a good compromise between coverage-driven and local search-driven testing is to initiate the search procedures from points that are separated by some threshold distance. This insight was used previously in the tabu search method, which ensures that all the starting points are well separated [7]; however, apart from ensuring that the starting points are well separated, it is also desirable that they are chosen in regions in which one can reasonably expect to find an incorrect behavior. That is, heuristically speaking, a starting point should have a low robustness value.

Based on the above observations, in this work we present a falsification algorithm that combines the following three essential ideas:

– Defining a coverage measure for quantifying the exploration of input signal space during testing.
– Guiding a randomized global search procedure by performing robustness classification: the classification divides the search space into regions with different potentials of falsification characterized by the robustness of evaluated test cases. Our classification is inspired from linear *support vector machines* [8,17].
– Using local search in regions classified as less robust. The above-mentioned global search together with an iterative classification procedure does converge towards an incorrect behavior, if it exists. However, to speed up the convergence, instead of continually classifying, we can use the information obtained from classification to efficiently initialize a local search within each classified region. Note that in general, local search with arbitrary initialization can perform poorly. Therefore, by alternating classification and local search we can achieve a better convergence while assuring a good coverage of the input signal space (because in general local search does not take into account this coverage criterion).

Before proceeding further, we note that our idea of combining global and local search for black box falsification is independent of the work [22] that is concerned with falsification based on state trajectories. In the latter work [22], although the motivation is to combine local and global search, the state trajectories have to be computed, in which case the system is not a black-box. On the other hand, our work is concerned with black-box kind of systems, i.e., complex systems where the information about the state of the system is very hard, if not impossible, to know.

For implementation and evaluation purposes, for local search we use a method, called the CMA-ES (Covariance Matrix Adaptation Evolution Strategy) [21], also used by the tool Breach [9]. The CMA-ES algorithm is considered as the state-of-the-art in evolutionary computation and has been used for industrial optimization applications. The experimental results obtained using a MATLAB implementation of our falsification algorithm on some benchmark systems demonstrate its good performance and, in addition, its efficiency improvements over search algorithms like the CMA-ES. Indeed, our algorithm was tested on a difficult property of the PTC benchmark [11] and could falsify in all the tested random seeds while the methods based on pseudo-random sampling or only on the CMA-ES could not. Also, we demonstrate that the technique can be successfully applied to industrial problems by presenting results for a prototype automotive hydrogen fuel cell application.

Our approach draws inspiration from the approaches implemented in the tools S-Taliro [2] and Breach [9]. These approaches seek the worst case behaviors using the notion of robustness metrics, which are defined with respect to properties specified using the languages MTL (Metric Temporal Logic) [14] and STL (Signal Temporal Logic) [10], respectively. The tools identify property violations by employing global optimization methods to search for behaviors that minimize robustness, where negative robustness values correspond to property violations. Robustness-based approaches can be seen as complementary to coverage-based approach, since the former try to find a worst case behavior while the latter tries to cover a large number of possible behaviors. When a robustness-based approach cannot find an erroneous behavior due to the limitations of global optimization algorithms, the observed error absence cannot be used as a formal correctness proof; in this case good coverage would be desirable to enhance the confidence that the system is free from errors. By combining robustness-based and coverage-guided explorations, our approach enhances the overall testing effectiveness by providing confidence that important or representative behaviors are tested.

2   Preliminaries

We consider system models defined by a mapping from parameters and input signals to output signals,

$$y = \Phi(v, u), \tag{1}$$

where $v \in \mathcal{V}$ is a valuation of a finite collection of parameters, and $u \in \mathcal{U}$ is an input signal used to simulate the system. In this setting, v could contain a set of system initial conditions as well as some finite set of system parameters. Each input signal $u \in \mathcal{U}$ is a function $\mathcal{I}_u \mapsto U$, where $\mathcal{I}_u$ is an interval (either discrete or continuous) from 0 to some finite value, and U is some metric space of finite dimension. Similarly, we assume that each output signal $y \in \mathcal{Y}$ is a function $\mathcal{I}_y \mapsto Y$, where $\mathcal{I}_y$ is an interval (either discrete or continuous) from 0 to some finite value, and Y is some metric space of finite dimension. We assume that $\mathcal{V}$, $\mathcal{U}$, and $\mathcal{Y}$ are metric spaces. Note that the system defined by (1) does not explicitly model the behaviors of the internal system states. State behaviors could be modeled using this framework by ensuring that v includes the system state and all of the states map to system outputs, but we do not require this.

We assume that signals are finitely parameterized, i.e., an input signal u can be uniquely determined by a finite set of m parameters, whose valuation $\hat{u}$ is a in a subset $\hat{\mathcal{U}}$ of an m-dimensional metric space. For example, a right-continuous piecewise constant input signal $u : \mathcal{I}_u \to \mathbb{R}$, where $\mathcal{I}_u = [0, T]$, with discontinuities occurring at monotonically increasing instants $\tau_1, \ldots, \tau_m$, where

$0 = \tau_1 < \tau_m < T$, can be uniquely defined by the m values $u(\tau_i)$. Subsequently, our system can be defined as a mapping from a finite set of parameters to the output signals, as follows:

$$y = \widehat{\Phi}(v, \widehat{u}), \ v \in \mathcal{V} \text{ and } \widehat{u} \in \widehat{\mathcal{U}} \tag{2}$$

We call $\mathcal{V}$ the space of *nominal parameters* and $\widehat{\mathcal{U}}$ the space of *input signal parameters*.

Signal Temporal Logic. To specify correct behavior of a system defined by (1), we use signal temporal logic (STL) [23]. STL can capture behaviors of real valued signals over discrete or dense time. We present here an informal description of STL (see [23] for more details). A formula in STL consists of atomic predicates, Boolean, and temporal operators. Atomic predicates are inequalities over signal values, as in $\mu = f(y(t)) \sim 0$, where f is a scalar-valued function over the signal y evaluated at time t, and $\sim \in \{<, \le, >, \ge, =, \ne\}$. Temporal operators "always" ($\square$), "eventually" ($\lozenge$), and "until" ($\mathcal{U}$) have the usual meaning and are scoped using intervals of the form (a, b), $(a, b]$, $[a, b)$, $[a, b]$, (a, ∞), or (a, ∞), where $a, b \in \mathbb{R}_{\ge 0}$ and $a < b$. If I is such an interval, then the language of STL is given by the following grammar:

$$\varphi := \top \mid f(y(t)) \sim 0 \mid \neg \varphi \mid \varphi_1 \wedge \varphi_2 \mid \varphi_1 \mathcal{U}_I \varphi_2 : \quad \sim \in \{<, \le, >, \ge, =, \ne\} \tag{3}$$

The $\lozenge$ and $\square$ operators are defined as follows: $\lozenge_I \varphi \triangleq \top \mathcal{U}_I \varphi$, $\square_I \varphi \triangleq \neg \lozenge_I \neg \varphi$. When omitted, the interval I is assumed to be $[0, \infty)$. The semantics are described informally as follows. The signal u satisfies $f(u) > 0$ at time t if $f(u(t)) > 0$. It satisfies $\varphi = \square_{[0,1)}(f(u) = 0)$ if for all time $0 \le t < 1$, $f(y(t)) = 0$. The signal satisfies $\varphi = \lozenge_{[1,2)} f(u) < 0$ iff there exists a time t such that $1 \le t < 2$ and $u(t) < 0$. The two-dimensional signal $y = (y_1, y_2)$ satisfies the formula $\varphi = (y_1 > 0)\mathcal{U}_{[2.3, 4.5]}(y_2 < 0)$ iff there is some time t where $2.3 \le t \le 4.5$ and $y_2(t) < 0$, and $\forall t'$ in $[2.3, t)$, $y_1(t')$ is greater than 0.

Quantitative Semantics for STL. The quantitative semantics of STL tells how far a signal is from satisfying a formula. In this respect, we use the quantitative interpretation presented in [10], which we describe informally as follows. The semantics relies on a function ρ such that a positive sign of $\rho(\varphi, y, t)$ indicates that (y, t) satisfies φ, and its absolute value estimates the *robustness* of this satisfaction. If ϕ is a simple inequality of the form $f(y) > b$, then its robustness is $\rho(\varphi, y, t) = f(y(t)) - b$. For the conjunction of two formulas $\varphi := \varphi_1 \wedge \varphi_2$, we have $\rho(\varphi, y, t) = \min(\rho(\varphi_1, y, t), \rho(\varphi_2, y, t))$, while for the disjunction $\varphi := \varphi_1 \wedge \varphi_2$, we have $\rho(\varphi, y, t) = \max(\rho(\varphi_1, y, t), \rho(\varphi_2, y, t))$. For a formula with until operator as $\varphi := \varphi_1 \mathcal{U}_I \varphi_2$, the robustness is computed as $\rho(\varphi, y, t) = \max_{t' \in t + I}\left(\min\left(\rho(\varphi_2, y, t), \min_{t' \in [t, t']}(\rho(\varphi_1, y, t''))\right)\right)$.

Since the output signal is determined by the set of nominal parameters and input signal parameters according to the mapping $\widehat{\Phi}$, we can define a robustness function over the space of parameters, called *parametric robustness*, as $\widehat{\rho}(\varphi, v, \widehat{u}, t) = \rho\left(\varphi, \widehat{\Phi}(v, \widehat{u}), t\right)$.

Falsification. Finding a counterexample of φ means finding a parameter value $v \in \mathcal{V}$ and an input parameter value $\widehat{u} \in \widehat{\mathcal{U}}$ such that $y \not\models \varphi$, where $y = \widehat{\Phi}(v, \widehat{u})$. Equivalently, the counterexample is identified when its parametric robustness is less than zero, i.e., $\widehat{\rho}(\varphi, v, \widehat{u}, t) < 0$ for some time point t in the time horizon of the signal. We call any $v \in \mathcal{V}$ and $\widehat{u} \in \widehat{\mathcal{U}}$ for which $y \not\models \varphi$ a *counterexample* and we call this task of finding a counterexample as a *falsification problem.* We say that a counterexample y (that is $y \not\models \varphi$) is *robust* if there exists a neighborhood around y, $\mathcal{N}_y$, such that for all $y' \in \mathcal{N}_y$, $y' \not\models \varphi$. We call a corresponding neighborhood $\mathcal{N}_y$ a robustness neighborhood of counterexample y. If a counterexample has a robustness neighborhood that contains a closed ball of radius ϵ, then we say that the counterexample is ϵ-*robust*.

Continuity of Robustness. Recall that our input signals are assumed to be finitely parametrized and correspondingly we defined the parametric robustness function. If we assume that the predicates of an STL formula are defined by functions f in (3) which are continuous w.r.t. the value of y at any time t, and the mapping Φ defining the system dynamics is continuous w.r.t. the parameter and input signal, then we can prove that the parametric robustness is continuous w.r.t. v and $\widehat{u}$. Indeed, for any atomic predicate $\varphi = f(y(t)) \sim 0$, the parametric robustness $\widehat{\rho}(\varphi, v, \widehat{u}, t)$ is continuous because f and $\widehat{\Phi}$ are continuous. Next, for any general formula as defined in (3), the robustness is computed by a composition of min and max operators of subformulas. By using induction we thus can deduce that the parametric robustness, given the aforementioned assumptions, is continuous in the input parameter $\widehat{u}$ and the nominal parameter v.

3   Input Space Coverage - Cell Occupancy

This section presents a metric that we use to measure the coverage of signal spaces. The notion is intended to be used to define the coverage of input signals used to stimulate a dynamical system. We define a measure called cell occupancy, which has the following desirable properties:

- The measure is *monotonic*, in the sense that it is guaranteed not to decrease in value when new signals are added to an existing set;
- The measure permits computation with *efficient algorithms*;
- The measure provides numbers in *reasonable ranges*, in the sense that, for both low dimension and high dimension problems, the measure results in values that are neither too large nor too small so as to be accurately represented with standard floating point numbers.

Henceforth, we define a measure called *cell occupancy* as follows. Let M be a set of signals, which corresponds to a set of parameter vectors X_M. We call elements of X_M points. We use p to denote the size of sets M and X_M.

Choose a partition of X, $\omega = \{\omega_i | i = 1, \ldots, l\}$. For now, we assume that each partition element, which we call a *cell*, is rectangular, with each side of equal length, Δ, called *grid cell size*[1]. A vector that indicates how many points are in each cell is called a *distribution, $D = (n_1, \ldots, n_l)$*, where each n_i indicates how many points are located in cell i. Cell occupancy is based on the relative number cells occupied by points, compared to the total number of cells. Consider the total number of occupied cells, that is, the number of cells that contain at least one point, i.e., $N_c = \sum_{i=1}^{l} g_i$ where $g_i = 1$ if $n_i \geq 1$, and $g_i = 0$ otherwise. Then, the proposed cell occupancy measure is given as

$$H_c(D) = \frac{\log N_c}{\log l}.$$

Logarithm functions are used due to the fact that the total number of cells could be very large as compared to the number of occupied cells. The logarithms provide two key features for the cell occupancy measure: (1) they maintain the monotonicity of the measure, and (2) they result in reasonable measure values even for cases where the dimension m is large.

Guarantee for Finding Counterexample. We consider here falsification algorithms based on an iterative search on the nominal parameter and input signal parameter spaces. We assume that the functions in the atomic predicates of STL formulas are continuous in the value of the output signal at any fixed time point. Also, the system mapping $\widehat{\Phi}$ is assumed to be continuous w.r.t. the input signal parameters and nominal parameters. In this case, if a falsification algorithm is such that the cell occupancy is guaranteed to increase after a finite number of robustness evaluations for any partition, then because of the continuity of parametric robustness (explained in Sect. 2), there exists a sufficiently small upper bound on the grid cell size below which, the algorithm is guaranteed to find a counterexample. This is summarized by the following lemma. However, note that in general such falsification algorithms may be used for non-continuous systems as well. The following lemma gives a theoretical insight about why coverage may be taken into account for designing efficient falsification algorithms.

Lemma 1. *Given a falsification algorithm and a partition ω with l grid cells of size $\Delta > 0$, let $D(\kappa, \Delta)$ denote the cell distribution after κ robustness evaluations by the algorithm. Let us consider that there exists $\alpha \in \mathbb{Z}_{>0}$ for which the algorithm guarantees that $\forall \kappa \in \mathbb{Z}_{\geq 0} H_c(D(\kappa + \alpha, \Delta)) > H_c(D(\kappa, \Delta))$. Let us also consider that the system mapping $\widehat{\Phi}$ is continuous and an STL formula φ is formed by continuous predicates with respect to the signal value at a fixed time. In this case, if an ϵ-robust counterexample of φ exists, then there exists an upper bound $\overline{\Delta} > 0$ on the grid cell size of ω such that $\forall \Delta < \overline{\Delta}$, the algorithm finds a counterexample after a finite number of robustness evaluations.*

---

[1] We note that in the setting in which we intend to apply the following coverage metrics, we will expect to select points in X that are no closer than some ϵ distance from each other, based on some metric between signals, but this rectangularity will not be exploited in the following. Further, we assume that $\epsilon \ll \Delta$.

4   Falsification Techniques

We use the term *sampling a point* to mean selecting a parameter vector x in the parameter set X_M, to uniquely define an input signal in M. Such signals are then used as stimuli to simulate the system and determine the robustness values of the corresponding output traces. For simplicity of notation, for a given sampled parameter vector x, we write $\rho(x)$ to denote the robustness value of the corresponding output trace. And for a set S of sampled parameter vectors, $\rho(S) = \min\{\rho(x) \mid x \in S\}$. A parameter vector x is called a *falsifier* if $\rho(x) < 0$.

A rudimentary approach to search for a falsifier is repeatedly select randomly an unoccupied cell with uniform probability distribution and evaluate one point inside it. This way, we ensure that the cell occupancy always keeps increasing until we eventually find a robust bug, if it exists (see Lemma 1); however, this approach may not be efficient because the uniform search does not differentiate regions that are more likely to contain an input that falsifies from those that are less likely. Therefore, we propose to enhance it using two concepts:

1. *Using classification to bias random search.* We use robustness based classification to classify less falsifiable regions from more falsifiable regions. Then, the probability distribution of random samples is biased according to the coverage and robustness information in different regions.
2. *Combining global search and local search.* Local search approaches (such as Hill climbing, Gradient methods, Simulated annealing, Genetic algorithms) (see for example [19,24]) can be very efficient if the search procedures are appropriately initialized. Finding good initializations constitutes a major difficulty that limits the efficiency of these approaches. In our framework, the classification based global search provides useful hints at appropriate initializations for the local search. Indeed, the least robust points in regions with high potential of falsification can be used to initialize a number of local searches.

Thus, our falsification algorithm involves two phases. The first phase is a global search guided by hyperplane classifiers, coverage and the robustness information. Next is a local search phase which runs a number of local searches initiated at the least robust points of different regions formed by the classification process during the global search. We now explain the aforementioned ingredients of the algorithm.

4.1   Classification Using Hyperplane Subdivision

In the following, we say that two regions are *separate* if their intersection can only lie on their boundaries. Our classification problem can be intuitively described as follows: given a rectangle R representing a search space and a set S of sampled points in R, iteratively subdivide it, according to the robustness values of the sampled points, to obtain a rectangular partition, the elements of which have different average robustness levels. We define the average robustness of the set of samples S in R as $\mu = \dfrac{\sum_{x \in S} \rho(x)}{|S|}$. Our objective is thus to separate a region of R having higher potential of containing low robustness samples. To this end, we define a hyperplane, in view of separating samples below the average robustness μ from those above μ. Obviously, such a hyperplane does not always exist, and we therefore choose a hyperplane that does this separation as best as possible. To address this problem, we draw inspiration from *soft margin support vector machines* [5], where hyperplanes are determined so that the misclassification error is minimized. In general, a misclassification error is defined according to the locations of the misclassified samples; however, in our approach we define a misclassification error that gives weightage to the robustness values of the misclassified samples in addition to their locations. Furthermore, since it is easy to sample uniformly in rectangles, we only use axis-aligned hyperplanes, which generate only rectangular subregions. Otherwise, when allowing non-axis aligned classifiers, we generate polyhedral regions in which uniform random sampling as well as partition manipulation could be more expensive.

To explain the essence of our classification method, let us consider one rectangle R in the partition as the product of intervals $R = [a_1, b_1] \times \ldots \times [a_n, b_n]$. Let S be the set of samples in R. We denote an axis-aligned hyperplane inside R by a tuple (d, r) where $d \in \{1, \ldots, n\}$ is the axis normal to the separating hyperplane, while $r \in [a_d, b_d]$ is a coordinate at which the hyperplane is drawn. The hyperplane (d, r) subdivides R into two subrectangles $A^-(R, d, r)$ and $A^+(R, d, r)$ such that $A^-(R, d, r) = [a'_1, b_1] \times \ldots \times [a'_n, b_n]$ where $a'_j = r$ if $j = d$, and $a'_j = a_j$ otherwise; and $A^+(R, d, r) = [a_1, b'_1] \times \ldots \times [a_n, b'_n]$ where $b'_j = r$ if $j = d$, and $b'_j = b_j$ otherwise (Fig. 1).

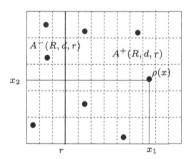

Fig. 1. Classification by subdivision. The samples in a 2-dimensional rectangle R are represented by black points labeled with their robustness values; R is divided by the hyperplane (d, r) where the axis is $d = 1$, to minimise the misclassification error. This division produces two subrectangles $A^-(R, d, r)$ (on the left) and $A^+(R, d, r)$ (on the right).

An ideal separation of samples below the average robustness from those above the average robustness by the hyperplane can be described in one of the following scenarios, identified by the following notion of *polarity*. Hyperplane (d, r)

has polarity $p = 1$ w.r.t. S, if the left subrectangle $A^-(R, d, r)$ contains all samples below the average μ, while the right subrectangle $A^+(R, d, r)$ contains all samples above the average μ. Similarly, (d, r) has polarity $p = -1$ w.r.t. S, if $A^+(R, d, r)$ contains all samples below μ, while $A^-(R, d, r)$ contains all samples above μ. When an ideal separation as above is not feasible, we identify misclassified samples as follows.

Definition 1. *A point $x \in R$ is misclassified w.r.t. a hyperplane (d, r), polarity $p \in \{-1, 1\}$ and the sampled set S, if $\mathrm{sgn}\left(p\left(\rho(x) - \mu\right)\left(x_d - r\right)\right) = 1$ where x_d is the dth coordinate of x, and sgn denotes the sign function.*

For a misclassified sample, the misclassification error is measured according to its location and robustness value. If a misclassified sample is farther from the hyperplane, it is considered to entail a higher misclassification error. Also, since the classification is based on the average robustness, samples with robustness values farther from the average get higher weightage in measuring the misclassification error. Accordingly, we define the misclassification error for a point $x \in R$ w.r.t. a hyperplane (d, r), polarity $p \in \{-1, 1\}$, and a set of samples S as $e_{d,r}(x, R, S, p) = \max\{p(\rho(x) - \mu)(x_d - r), 0\}$. Then the total misclassification error is the sum of the misclassification errors of all the samples:

$$\Gamma_{d,r}(R, S, p) = \sum_{x \in S} e_{d,r}(x, R, S, p). \tag{4}$$

An appropriate hyperplane (d_*, r_*) traversing the rectangle R, chosen for the desired separation of S, is one that minimises the total misclassification error for either a positive or negative polarity, *i.e.*,

$$\left(d_*^{R,S}, r_*^{R,S}\right) = \underset{r \in [a_d, b_d], d \in [n]}{\mathrm{argmin}} \left(\min\{\Gamma_{d,r}(R, S, -1), \Gamma_{d,r}(R, S, 1)\}\right). \tag{5}$$

We denote $A_*^-(R, S) = A^-(R, d_*^{R,S}, r_*^{R,S})$ and $A_*^+(R, S) = A^+(R, d_*^{R,S}, r_*^{R,S})$ as the subrectangles formed by dividing R by the above optimal hyperplane.

It is important to remark that in order for the classification to reflect the robustness distribution over the whole dense space, the number of samples should be sufficiently large. Henceforth, only rectangles in which the number of samples is not smaller than a (user-defined) threshold number, are subdivided as above. The classification procedure takes as input a partition encoded as a list of k rectangles and the set of points in each respective rectangle. For each rectangle if the number of points is not smaller than the threshold K_c, the rectangle is subdivided by a hyperplane that minimizes the classification error. The rectangle is replaced by the left subrectangle and the right subrectangle is added to the list of rectangles. After all rectangles are considered for subdivision, the samples inside them are updated.

4.2 Global Search

Each iteration of the global search performs 3 successive procedures:

1. Classification using hyperplanes, the goal of which is to partition the state space into regions with different robustness levels.
2. Coverage and robustness guided sampling of input signal parameters.
3. Singularity based sampling of input signal parameters inside rectangles containing very low robust samples. Here, we use *singularity* to refer to a partition element that contains a point in a low robustness range with low frequency of occurance.

Note that the term *sampling* in the description of our method refers to the consecutive execution of three steps (1) defining the input signals from the sampled parameters, (2) simulating the system under the defined input signals, and (3) evaluating the robustness of the corresponding simulated output traces.

Coverage and Robustness Based Sampling. We randomly select a number of unoccupied cells, such that the probability of picking a cell in each rectangle is based on two components: coverage based probability and robustness based probability. Then the probability of cell sampling is determined as a weighted sum of the former components. Once a cell is sampled, a point is selected by a uniform sampling inside the cell.

Coverage Based Probability Distribution. Let $\{R_1, \ldots, R_k\}$ be the set of rectangles of a partition of the parameter space. We now consider the collection of grid cells intersecting with R_i, that is $\{w_j : w_j \cap R_i \neq \emptyset\}$, and we index them as $\beta^i = \{\beta^i_1, \ldots, \beta^i_{q_i}\}$ where q_i is the number of such cells. Let $D(R_i, S_i)$ be the vector denoting the distribution of samples S_i in cells of β^i, that is $\forall j \in \{1, \ldots, l\}$ (l is the total number of grid cells), the jth component $D_j(R_i, S_i) = |S_i \cap \beta^i_j|$. Then the coverage based sampling probability in R_i is proportional to the number of unoccupied cells in this rectangle:

$$P^i_c = \frac{1 - H_c\left(D(R_i, S_i)\right)}{\sum_{j=1}^{m}(1 - H_c\left(D(R_j, S_j)\right))}, \tag{6}$$

where $H_c\left(D(R_i, S_i)\right)$ is the *local cell occupancy* of R_i, i.e., $H_c\left(D(R_i, S_i)\right) = \frac{\log(N_{ci})}{\log(l_i)}$. where l_i is the number of grid cells intersecting with R_i and N_{ci} is the number of unoccupied cells intersecting with R_i.

Robustness Based Probability Distribution. A probability distribution takes into consideraton the average robustness as well as the potential reduction in robustness below the average. The potential reduction in robustness below the average is defined as $\lambda_i = \frac{1}{|S_i|}\sum_{x \in S_i} \max(\mu_i - \rho(x), 0)$. Then a potentially reduced robustness value below the average is $\theta_i = \mu_i - \lambda_i$. Then we define a robustness based probability in a rectangle R_i as inversely proportional to θ_i, as follows.

$$P^i_r = \frac{\frac{1}{\theta_i}}{\sum_{j=1}^{m} \frac{1}{\theta_j}}. \tag{7}$$

Sampling Probability Distribution. The probability distribution for sampling is a weighted sum of the probability based on robustness and the probability based on coverage. The weightage given to either probability is a user defined constant. Let the weight assigned to the robustness based probability be denoted by w_r such that $w_r \in [0, 1]$. Then, the overall probability of sampling in rectangle R_i is

$$P_t^i = w_r P_r^i + (1 - w_r) P_c^i. \tag{8}$$

Singularity Based Sampling. Certain rectangles may contain samples whose robustness is very low compared to the lowest robustness values in other rectangles. We refer to them as *singular samples*, which we heuristically define as follows.

Let $\gamma = \{\gamma_1, \ldots, \gamma_k\}$ be the vector of lowest robustness values in each rectangle, defined as $\gamma_i = \min_{x \in S_i} \rho(x)$. The mean of γ and the average deviation below the mean are respectively defined as $\mu_\gamma = \frac{\sum_{i=1}^k \gamma_i}{k}$ and $\lambda_\gamma = \frac{\sum_{i=1}^k max\,(0, (\mu_\gamma - \gamma_i))}{k}$. If the robustness of a sample is less than λ then it is an indication that the sample may be close to a counterexample. Also, samples with very low frequency and sufficiently low robustness are also considered singular. To select such rare samples, we use the following heuristic. If γ were a large set of random samples selected from a normal distribution, then less than 15% of the samples tend to lie below the value $\mu_\gamma - 3\lambda_\gamma$. Although the actual set of samples in γ may not follow the pattern of a normal distribution, this also can be used as a heuristic to define a singular sample.

Definition 2. *A point $x \in \bigcup_{i=1}^k S_i$ for which $\rho(x) \leq max\,(\mu_\gamma - 3\lambda_\gamma, \lambda)$ is called a singular sample.*

We call the rectangles containing singular samples as *singular rectangles*. Since the frequency of singular samples can be very small, the robustness based probability in (7) may not give adequate weightage to singular rectangles. So, we have to perform additional sampling in the singular rectangles.

Overall Global Search. Suppose that we have a partition of rectangles $R_1, \ldots, R_k$ containing sets of samples $S_1, \ldots, S_k$, respectively. Let C_i be the set of unoccupied cells intersecting with a rectangle R_i, i.e., $C_i = \{\omega_j \in \omega : \omega_j \cap R_i \neq \emptyset \wedge \omega_j \cap S_i = \emptyset\}$. Let N be the number of samples to be added during probabilistically biased random sampling. We compute the probability distribution of sampling among different rectangles P^t, where the user defines a weightage w_r given to the robustness based probability distribution P^r. Then we select $(\min\{\max\{1, \lfloor P_i^t N \rfloor\}, |C_i|\})$ number of cells among C_i and sample one point in each cell. Note that if there is an unoccupied cell in a rectangle, then at least one sample is added to each rectangle irrespective of the probability P_i^t. Then update the sets of samples $S_1, \ldots, S_k$ by adding the new samples and also the sets of unoccupied cells $C_i \; \forall i \in \{1 \ldots k\}$.

Next, we perform sampling in each of the singular rectangles as follows. Let R_j be a singular rectangle, currently containing the set S_j of samples and a set C_j of unoccupied cells. Then we select $\min\{\max\{K_c - |S_j|, 0\}, |C_j|\}$ cells among the unoccupied cells C_i. Therefore, in the next iteration R_j contains at least K_c samples (if it has unoccupied cells) and is consequently subdivided. The procedure is repeated in each iteration until the time limit $\overline{T}_g$ on global search is reached. Alternatively, we can also set a limit on the total number of samples for which robustness is evaluated. If we have not falsified yet, then we perform a number of local searches initialized at the lowest robustness samples of all the separate subrectangles, as described below.

4.3 Local Search

Suppose that we have K subrectangles $R_1, \ldots, R_K$ after running global search for $\overline{T}_g$ time. Let L be the set of the lowest robustnes points of different rectangles. If the property is not yet falsified, then we use the lowest robustness points of different rectangles to initialize a local search based falsification algorithm. In our implementation, we used the state-of-the-art *Covariance matrix adaptive evolutionary search* (CMA-ES) algorithm [21] in the local search phase. The essence of the CMA-ES algorithm can be briefly described as follows. It is a randomized black box method which selects samples based on a multivariate normal distribution having a mean and a covariance matrix as parameters. Based on the robustness of a population of points evaluated in an iteration, the mean and covaraiance matrix of the search distribution are updated for the next sampling iteration. The procedure generally coverges to a locally optimum point or finds a counterexample. It may happen that the set of sampled points do not contain enough information to derive a reliable estimation of a covariance matrix for an efficient update. Therefore, good initializations of the mean and covariance matrix are crucial. In our algorithm, the global search provides initialization guidance as follows. We have a number of subrectangles formed by classification, that contain sets of samples. So, we can initialize in one the following ways: (1) Each of the lowest robustness points of different rectangles, i.e., the points in L can be selected for initialization with covariance as identity (the order of selection is according to their robustness values, with the lowest robustness tested first); (2) The mean and covariance are initialized as that of those points in L whose robustness is less than the average robustness of samples in L. (3) The mean and covariance are initialized as that of all the points in L. With such initialization guidance from our global search procedure described earlier, this local search procedure can become more effective in falsification.

4.4 Overall Falsification Algorithm

The overall falsification algorithm consists of iteratively doing global search for a threshold time and then doing local search. We give an outline of the algorithm below.

- Step 1: *Initialization.* In the first step, we evaluate the robustness of N uniformly selected points in the search space R and store them as a set of samples S.
- Step 2: *Global search phase*: We perform a number of global search iterations until a time limit is attained. Each global search iteration consists of the following three steps executed one after the other. (i) The first step is classification, where new rectangles are constructed by classifying and consequently subdividing the existing rectangles that contain more than a threshold K_c of samples. (ii) The second step involves probabilistically biased sampling based on the coverage and robustness values of samples in different rectangles. The specific procedure is explained earlier in the Section on overall global search. (iii) The third step is singularity based sampling. This procedure is also explained earlier in the Section on overall global search.
- Step 3: *Local search phase.* If no counterexample is found in the global search phase, then we perform the local search based on the set of low robustness points in different rectangles. The specific procedure is explained earlier in the Section on local search.
- Step 5: If not falsified during local search, then continue global search iterations i.e. go to Step 3.
- Step 6: If not falsified, then alternate with local search, i.e. go to Step 4.

We can now state an important completeness property of our overall falsification algorithm for the class of the systems (2) satisfying the assumption that the mapping $\widehat{\Phi}$ is continuous in the nominal parameters and the input signal parameters.

Theorem 1. *If an ϵ-robust counterexample exists, then there exists a grid cell size Δ and a global search time $\overline{T}_g$ so that our algorithm finds a counterexample.*

Sketch of proof. The theorem can be directly established from Lemma 1. Indeed, the condition in this lemma is always satisfied by our algorithm since, by construction, after each iteration the cell occupancy of the samples always strictly increases. So, for sufficient $\overline{T}_g$, the falsification is guaranteed if an ϵ-robust counterexample exists.

5 Experimental Results

In our experiments, we compare the performance of a MATLAB implementation[2] with the following standard approaches: CMA-ES, Simulated Annealing, Global Nelder-Mead algorithm implementations (integrated in Breach [9]), and the S-TaLiRo tool [2] by setting Simulated Annealing as optimization algorithm[3].

---

[2] We use the robustness evaluation function from the Breach toolbox available in October 2016, on the site https://people.eecs.berkeley.edu/~donze/breach_page.html.

[3] We used the latest version available in October 2016, on the site https://sites.google.com/a/asu.edu/s-taliro/home.

Experiments were performed on a computer with 1.4 GHz processor with 4 GB RAM, running MATLAB R2015 64-bit version. Also, we compare with a random sampling method, where in each iteration a pseudo-randomly selected point is tested only if it falls in a grid cell wherein no other point has been previously tested. The grid used in this method is the same as the grid chosen in our falsification approach. We will call this method as grid based random sampling, for the sake of reference during comparison.

5.1 Automative Powertrain Control

We consider a Simulink model of a closed loop of an Automative Powertrain Control subsystem (PTC). The model contains a representation of an internal combustion engine and an embedded software controller for the air-to-fuel ratio within the engine (see [11] for more details). Here, we focus on the input-output behavior, considering the internal model as a blackbox. The model has three input signals, Pedal Angle Engine Speed and Sensor Offset. The air-to-fuel (A/F) ratio, denoted by η, is an output signal for which the following safety requirement was stated in [11]: $\phi = \Box_{[5,10]} (\eta < 0.5)$.

Input Signal Settings. Compared to [11], we consider a smaller input range for the Pedal Angle as $[0, 40]$ and fix the Engine Speed and Sensor Offset as 1000 and 1, respectively. Reducing the ranges makes the properties more robust and consequently difficult to falsify. The time horizon is 50s. We use piecewise constant signal for testing, where the Pedal Angle is parameterized by 10 uniformly spaced control points in the time horizon. Thus, we have a 10 dimensional search space X.

Algorithm Setting. For our algorithm, the threshold number of samples for hyperplane classification K_c is 100. The global search time is $\overline{T}_g = 2000s$. The local search is initialized with the lowest robustness point found during global search and allowed to run until falsification. Cell partitioning ω consists of hypercubes of side length $\epsilon = 4$. We consider equal weightage for robustness based probability and coverage based probability for sampling during global search, i.e., $w_r = 0.5$.

Results. Our algorithm (classification guided global search + local search) successfully found a counterexample in less than 3000s for all seeds. As an estimate of the classification frequency, the final number of separate rectangles constructed for while testing the first seed were 30. In comparison, the tool S-TaLiRo could falsify but took 4481s. The grid based random sampling found a falsifier for only the seeds 15000 and 20000, but failed to do so on the other seeds before maximum time limit was reached. The other methods were not successful in finding a falsifier within the default stopping time of 5000s. Both the CMA-ES and Nelder-Mead became stuck without reduction in robustness value until the default stopping time was reached. The results are presented in Table 1. We note that for any fixed seed for random sampling, these results are reproducible.

5.2   Automatic Transmission

We consider the benchmark model of an Automatic Transmission control system, which appeared in [20][4]. The system has two input signals, called throttle and break, respectively, and two output signals, called the engine speed, denoted w (RPM), and the vehicle speed, denoted v (mph). The property states that if the engine speed stays below a value $\overline{w}$, then the vehicle speed v does not exceed a threshold $\overline{v}$ within 10s. We specify the values of $\overline{w}$ and $\overline{v}$ to be 2520 and 50, respectively, which gives the following STL property: $\phi = \neg \left(\left(\Diamond_{[0,10]} v > 50 \right) \wedge \left(\Box w \leq 2520 \right) \right)$ [20].

Input Signal and Parameter Settings. Initially, the vehicle is at rest, when $v = 0$ and $w = 0$. For the input signals, we consider smaller ranges than specified in [20], which makes the property ϕ more robust. Henceforth, the throttle signal is allowed to vary between [35, 100] and the break is allowed to vary between [0, 40]. The time horizon is set to 30s. We use piecewise constant input signals for testing, where the throttle signal is parametrized by 7 control points and the break has 3 control points. Thus, we have a $7 + 3 = 10$ dimensional search space. ϕ.

Algorithm Setting. For our algorithm, the threshold number of samples of hyperplane classification K_c is 70. The global search time is $\overline{T}_g = 500$s, while maximum time for local search is $\overline{\tau}_l = 2000$s. Cell partitioning ω consists of hypercubes of side length $\epsilon = 4$. We consider equal weightage for robustness based probability and coverage based probability for sampling during global search, i.e., $w_r = 0.5$.

Results. Our algorithm (classification guided global search + local search) successfully found a counterexample in less than 2000s for all tested seeds. As an indication of the number of classification operations that occurred, the final number of separate rectangles constructed for while testing the first seed were 31. In comparison, the CMA-ES found a falsifier for two seeds 5000 and 15000 within 2000s but failed to do so on the other seeds. The other methods were not successful in finding a falsifier within the default stopping time of 3000s. For this example, S-TaLiRo became stuck around a local optimum without any significant reduction in robustness value. The results are presented in Table 1. We note that for any fixed seed for random sampling, these results are reproducible.

5.3   Industrial Example

We present results for an air path controller for an automotive fuel cell (FC) application. The system contains an FC stack that generates electrical power to provide torque to the vehicle drivetrain. The system is composed of an air compressor and the air path through the FC stack. The system takes as input

---

[4] The model and property description of this benchmark is available at the site of the workshop Applied Verification for Continuous and Hybrid Systems, ARCH 2014–2015, http://cps-vo.org/node/12116.

Table 1. Experimental results

Solver	Seed	Computation time (secs)		Falsification	
		PTC	Aut. Trans	PTC	Aut. Trans
Hyperplane classification + CMA-ES-Breach	0	2891	996	✓	✓
	5000	2364	1382	✓	✓
	10000	2101	1720	✓	✓
	15000	2271	1355	✓	✓
CMA-ES-Breach	0	T.O. (5000)	T.O. (2000)		
	5000	T.O. (5000)	1302		✓
	10000	T.O. (5000)	T.O. (2000)		
	15000	T.O. (5000)	1325		✓
Grid based random sampling	0	T.O. (5000)	T.O. (2000)		
	5000	T.O. (5000)	T.O. (2000)		
	10000	3766	T.O. (2000)	✓	
	15000	268	T.O. (2000)	✓	
S-TaLiRo (Simulated Annealing)		4481	T.O. (3000)	✓	
S-TaLiRo (Simulated Annealing)		4481	Default stopping (3300)	✓	

T.O.: Exceeded indicated time out limit.
Seed: Index for a sequence of random numbers in MATLAB. *Solver*: Algorithm used for falsification. *Computation time*: Amount of time (in seconds) until falsification or default stopping after the time limit in parentheses. Computation time is reported for a computer with 1.4 GHz processor and 4 GB RAM, running MATLAB R2015 64-bit version. *Falsification*: Boolean variable indicating whether the algorithm could falsify the property.

requested current from the stack and ambient temperature. The outputs are desired air flow rate and the measured air flow rate through the FC stack. The goal is for the stack air flow rate to maintain accurate regulation when current request "disturbances" are presented to the system. System performance (called *responsiveness*) crucially depends on accurate and timely regulation of the air flow to the commanded reference. The corresponding specification for the system can be described informally as follows: when there is a step input of current request, there is a rise-time requirement on the output air flow that should be satisfied. Details about the system and the specifications are proprietary and so are suppressed here.

We analyze a Simulink model of the FC system, which contains representations of the FC system along with its controller. The model is complex, containing several thousands of Simulink blocks; simulations over the selected time horizon are expensive to perform, each taking approximately 1 to 2 min. The MATLAB implementation of the hyperplane classification algorithm with local search is applied to the model, and the results are compared to the same algorithms used in Sects. 5.1 and 5.2.

For our method, we performed the tests using two different cell partitions. Cell partition A is large and corresponds to a small number of grid elements; cell partition B is smaller (each dimension of the search space is 1/5 the size of the grid elements in partition A). Thus, partition B corresponds to a significantly larger number of grid elements.

Table 2 provides the results. As can be seen in the table, using cell partition A with our method performs much better than with partition B. This can be attributed to the fact that, for partition A, the classification phase of the search spends less time in regions close to regions that have already been explored, as compared to partition B. This demonstrates that the selected cell partition size has a significant impact on the performance of our technique.

Table 2. Results for fuel cell example.

Solver	Seed	Computation time (sec.)	Falsification
Hyperplane classification + CMA-ES-Breach (cell partition: A)[†]	1	406	✓
	2	1383	✓
	3	T.O.	
	4	794	✓
Hyperplane classification + CMA-ES-Breach (cell partition: B)[†]	1	409	✓
	2	T.O.	
	3	T.O.	
	4	T.O.	
CMA-ES Breach[†]	1	314	✓
	2	1418	
	3	T.O.	
	4	1316	✓
Uniform random[†] sampling	1	396	✓
	2	786	✓
	3	2241	✓
	4	T.O.	
S-TaLiRo (Simulated Annealing)[‡] sampling	1	310	✓
	2	T.O.	
	3	671	✓
	4	T.O.	
Global Nelder-Mead-Breach[†]		1501	✓

T.O.: Exceeded time out limit of 2700 s.

†: Times reported are from machines running Dell Precision, with a Xeon processor (2.13 GHz), with 24 GB of RAM, running a 64 bit version of Windows 7 Ultimate, SP1.

‡: Times reported are from machines running Dell Precision, with a Xeon processor (2.3 GHz), with 64 GB of RAM, running a 64 bit version of Windows 7 Ultimate, SP1.

Also, the table shows that the CMA-ES fails to find falsifying behaviors in 2 of the 4 cases, which demonstrates better performance than our technique using partition B but poorer performance than our technique using partition A. The uniform random sampling approach is able to find falsifying traces in all but one case, and the computation times for the successful cases are comparable to our technique using partition A, though we note that the computation times for our technique are lower than the uniform random method, for the cases where falsifying traces are found. The S-TaLiRo approach fails to find falsifying traces in 2 of the 4 cases, which is less than the number of times our technique is successful, using partition A. The Nelder-Mead algorithm is able to identify a falsifying trace in about 25 min, which is longer than the 3 successful cases of our technique, using partition A.

The above results show mixed results for our technique for this example, as compared to the other falsification approaches. This could be due to any of several factors. We observe that for this example, comparing against the falsification techniques that we selected, only a relatively small number of simulations are required to find falsifying traces, when they are found at all. This may suggest that either the model is not robust, in the sense that there may be many disconnected regions in the search space that correspond to falsifying behaviors, or that the robustness function is rather monotone or simple. It may be that for systems with these qualities, the benefits provided by the hyperplane classification approach are outweighed (or at least offset) by the overhead that it requires.

6   Conclusions

We have presented a novel falsification algorithm that maintains a balance between convergence towards low robustness points and enhancing global coverage. We accomplish this by intelligently subdividing the search space and subsequently biasing the density of random sampling in different sub-regions. For the subdivision, we use hyperplane classifiers akin to support vector machines, which tries to focus effort on low robustness regions of the search space. We demonstrated the efficiency of our algorithm by falsifying properties on benchmark examples, which other approaches failed to falsify. Also, we demonstrated that the approach could be applied to industrial systems by describing a successful application on an automotive hydrogen fuel cell example. Future work includes investigating new coverage measures, such as the combinatorial entropy notion from the domain of physics to measure the degree of randomness in the distribution of points. In addition, global search and local search can be done in a multi-resolution manner, that is if local search leads to a promising region, global search can then be done within the region using a more refined grid.

References

1. Althoff, M., Krogh, B.: Zonotope bundles for the efficient computation of reachable sets. In: 2011 50th IEEE Conference on Decision and Control and European Control Conference (CDC-ECC), pp. 6814–6821, December 2011
2. Annpureddy, Y., Liu, C., Fainekos, G., Sankaranarayanan, S.: S-TaLiRo: a tool for temporal logic falsification for hybrid systems. In: Abdulla, P.A., Leino, K.R.M. (eds.) TACAS 2011. LNCS, vol. 6605, pp. 254–257. Springer, Heidelberg (2011). doi:10.1007/978-3-642-19835-9_21
3. Bouissou, O., Goubault, E., Putot, S., Tekkal, K., Vedrine, F.: HybridFluctuat: a static analyzer of numerical programs within a continuous environment. In: Bouajjani, A., Maler, O. (eds.) CAV 2009. LNCS, vol. 5643, pp. 620–626. Springer, Heidelberg (2009). doi:10.1007/978-3-642-02658-4_46
4. Chen, X., Ábrahám, E., Sankaranarayanan, S.: Flow*: an analyzer for non-linear hybrid systems. In: Sharygina, N., Veith, H. (eds.) CAV 2013. LNCS, vol. 8044, pp. 258–263. Springer, Heidelberg (2013). doi:10.1007/978-3-642-39799-8_18
5. Cortes, C., Vapnik, V.: Support-vector networks. Mach. Learn. 20(3), 273–297 (1995)
6. Dang, T., Nahhal, T.: Coverage-guided test generation for continuous and hybrid systems. Formal Methods Syst. Des. 34(2), 183–213 (2009)
7. Deshmukh, J., Jin, X., Kapinski, J., Maler, O.: Stochastic local search for falsification of hybrid systems. In: Finkbeiner, B., Pu, G., Zhang, L. (eds.) ATVA 2015. LNCS, vol. 9364, pp. 500–517. Springer, Cham (2015). doi:10.1007/978-3-319-24953-7_35
8. Dietterich, T.G., Lathrop, R.H., Lozano-Pérez, T.: Solving the multiple instance problem with axis-parallel rectangles. Artif. Intell. 89(1), 31–71 (1997)
9. Donzé, A.: Breach, a toolbox for verification and parameter synthesis of hybrid systems. In: Touili, T., Cook, B., Jackson, P. (eds.) CAV 2010. LNCS, vol. 6174, pp. 167–170. Springer, Heidelberg (2010). doi:10.1007/978-3-642-14295-6_17
10. Donzé, A., Maler, O.: Robust satisfaction of temporal logic over real-valued signals. In: Chatterjee, K., Henzinger, T.A. (eds.) FORMATS 2010. LNCS, vol. 6246, pp. 92–106. Springer, Heidelberg (2010). doi:10.1007/978-3-642-15297-9_9
11. Dreossi, T., Dang, T., Donzé, A., Kapinski, J., Jin, X., Deshmukh, J.V.: Efficient guiding strategies for testing of temporal properties of hybrid systems. In: Havelund, K., Holzmann, G., Joshi, R. (eds.) NFM 2015. LNCS, vol. 9058, pp. 127–142. Springer, Cham (2015). doi:10.1007/978-3-319-17524-9_10
12. Dreossi, T., Dang, T., Piazza, C.: Parallelotope bundles for polynomial reachability. In: Proceedings of the 19th International Conference on Hybrid Systems: Computation and Control, HSCC 2016, Vienna, Austria, 12–14 April 2016, pp. 297–306 (2016)
13. Esposito, J.M., Kim, J., Kumar, V.: Adaptive RRTs for validating hybrid robotic control systems. In: Erdmann, M., Overmars, M., Hsu, D., van der Stappen, F. (eds.) Algorithmic Foundations of Robotics VI. STAR, vol. 17, pp. 107–121. Springer, Heidelberg (2005). doi:10.1007/10991541_9
14. Fainekos, G.E., Pappas, G.J.: Robustness of temporal logic specifications. In: Havelund, K., Núñez, M., Roşu, G., Wolff, B. (eds.) FATES/RV-2006. LNCS, vol. 4262, pp. 178–192. Springer, Heidelberg (2006). doi:10.1007/11940197_12
15. Fan, C., Qi, B., Mitra, S., Viswanathan, M., Duggirala, P.S.: Automatic reachability analysis for nonlinear hybrid models with C2E2. In: Chaudhuri, S., Farzan, A. (eds.) CAV 2016. LNCS, vol. 9779, pp. 531–538. Springer, Cham (2016). doi:10.1007/978-3-319-41528-4_29

16. Frehse, G., Guernic, C., Donzé, A., Cotton, S., Ray, R., Lebeltel, O., Ripado, R., Girard, A., Dang, T., Maler, O.: SpaceEx: scalable verification of hybrid systems. In: Gopalakrishnan, G., Qadeer, S. (eds.) CAV 2011. LNCS, vol. 6806, pp. 379–395. Springer, Heidelberg (2011). doi:10.1007/978-3-642-22110-1_30

17. Fung, G.M., Mangasarian, O.L., Shavlik, J.W.: Knowledge-based support vector machine classifiers. In: Advances in Neural Information Processing Systems, pp. 521–528 (2002)

18. Gao, S., Avigad, J., Clarke, E.M.: δ-complete decision procedures for satisfiability over the reals. In: Joint Automated Reasoning, pp. 286–300 (2012)

19. Hoos, H., Sttzle, T.: Stochastic Local Search: Foundations & Applications. Morgan Kaufmann Publishers Inc., San Francisco (2004)

20. Hoxha, B., Abbas, H., Fainekos, G.E.: Benchmarks for temporal logic requirements for automotive systems. In: 1st and 2nd International Workshop on Applied veRification for Continuous and Hybrid Systems, ARCH@CPSWeek 2014, Berlin, Germany, 14 April 2014/ARCH@CPSWeek 2015, Seattle, WA, USA, 13 April 2015, pp. 25–30 (2014)

21. Igel, C., Suttorp, T., Hansen, N.: A computational efficient covariance matrix update and a (1+1)-CMA for evolution strategies. In: Proceedings of the 8th Annual Conference on Genetic and Evolutionary Computation GECCO, pp. 453–460. ACM (2006)

22. Kuřátko, J., Ratschan, S.: Combined global and local search for the falsification of hybrid systems. In: Legay, A., Bozga, M. (eds.) FORMATS 2014. LNCS, vol. 8711, pp. 146–160. Springer, Cham (2014). doi:10.1007/978-3-319-10512-3_11

23. Maler, O., Nickovic, D.: Monitoring temporal properties of continuous signals. In: Lakhnech, Y., Yovine, S. (eds.) FORMATS/FTRTFT-2004. LNCS, vol. 3253, pp. 152–166. Springer, Heidelberg (2004). doi:10.1007/978-3-540-30206-3_12

24. Russell, S.J., Norvig, P.: Artificial Intelligence: A Modern Approach, 2nd edn. Pearson Education, Upper Saddle River (2003)

25. Skruch, P.: A coverage metric to evaluate tests for continuous-time dynamic systems. Cent. Eur. J. Eng. **1**(2), 174–180 (2011)

26. Testylier, R., Dang, T.: NLTOOLBOX: a library for reachability computation of nonlinear dynamical systems. In: Hung, D., Ogawa, M. (eds.) ATVA 2013. LNCS, vol. 8172, pp. 469–473. Springer, Cham (2013). doi:10.1007/978-3-319-02444-8_37

Concurrency

GPUDrano: Detecting Uncoalesced Accesses in GPU Programs

Rajeev Alur, Joseph Devietti, Omar S. Navarro Leija,
and Nimit Singhania$^{(\boxtimes)}$

University of Pennsylvania, Philadelphia, USA
nimits@seas.upenn.edu

Abstract. Graphics Processing Units (GPUs) have become widespread and popular over the past decade. Fully utilizing the parallel compute and memory resources that GPUs present remains a significant challenge, however. In this paper, we describe GPUDrano: a scalable static analysis that detects uncoalesced global memory accesses in CUDA programs. Uncoalesced global memory accesses arise when a GPU program accesses DRAM in an ill-structured way, increasing latency and energy consumption. We formalize the GPUDrano static analysis and compare it empirically against a dynamic analysis to demonstrate that false positives are rare for most programs. We implement GPUDrano in LLVM and show that it can run on GPU programs of over a thousand lines of code. GPUDrano finds 133 of the 143 uncoalesced static memory accesses in the popular Rodinia GPU benchmark suite, demonstrating the precision of our implementation. Fixing these bugs leads to real performance improvements of up to 25%.

1 Introduction

Graphics Processing Units (GPUs) are well-established as an energy-efficient, data parallel accelerator for an increasingly important set of workloads including image processing, machine learning, and scientific simulations. However, extracting optimal performance and energy efficiency from a GPU is a painstaking process due to the many sharp corners of current GPU programming models. One particularly sharp corner arises when interacting with the memory hierarchy. We propose the GPUDrano system, the first scalable static analysis to identify an important class of memory hierarchy performance bugs for GPU programs. To show what GPUDrano does, we first explain a bit about the GPU memory hierarchy and the specific class of performance bugs, known as *global memory coalescing bugs*, that GPUDrano targets.

Load and store instructions that reference the GPU's DRAM (known as *global memory*) must obey a certain structure to ensure that memory bandwidth is fully utilized. Accesses that do not exhibit this structure result in underutilization and can lead to significant performance problems. When a GPU program executes a load or store instruction, the memory address(es) referenced are mapped to aligned 128-byte cache blocks [18, Sect. 5.3.2], which is the physical granularity

© Springer International Publishing AG 2017
R. Majumdar and V. Kunčak (Eds.): CAV 2017, Part I, LNCS 10426, pp. 507–525, 2017.
DOI: 10.1007/978-3-319-63387-9_25

at which DRAM is accessed. GPUs bundle multiple threads together for single-instruction multiple-data (SIMD) execution, and we say that a SIMD load/store is *coalesced* if its accesses are contained within a single cache block, otherwise the access is *uncoalesced*. Uncoalesced accesses are difficult to spot, even for seasoned GPU developers, and in some cases rewriting can avoid such uncoalescing, as is the case for many of our benchmarks from an established benchmark suite.

```
int array[N]; // in global memory

int a = array[0]; // Example 1: coalesced
int b = array[tid]; // Example 2: coalesced
int c = array[8*tid]; // Example 3: uncoalesced
```

Fig. 1. Examples of coalesced and uncoalesced memory accesses.

Figure 1 shows simple examples of coalesced and uncoalesced memory accesses. Each thread in the program executes the code shown (we explain the GPU's threading model in more detail in Sect. 2), and *tid* is a numeric thread id. Memory accesses that involve each thread accessing the same address (Example 1) or consecutive threads accessing consecutive addresses (Example 2) fall within a single cache line, and so are considered coalesced. Memory accesses that have consecutive threads accessing non-consecutive addresses, as in Example 3, result in significant slowdowns: Example 3 will run about 8x slower than the other examples.

Discovering uncoalesced accesses statically introduces many challenges. Expressions used for array indexing are often complex, and their coalesced or uncoalesced nature must be propagated through arithmetic operations, to each use. The size of the data types involved in a memory access affects coalescing. The number of threads that actually execute a particular access affects coalescing as well; *e.g.*, Example 3 in Fig. 1 is coalesced if only a single active thread reaches this statement. In this paper, we define GPUDrano, a simple but effective abstraction for detecting uncoalesced accesses that uses intra-procedural dataflow analysis to identify uncoalesced memory accesses in GPU programs statically. We target GPU code written for Nvidia's CUDA programming model. GPUDrano makes the following contributions:

– To the best of our knowledge, GPUDrano is the first scalable static analysis for uncoalesced global memory accesses in GPU programs.
– We provide a formal definition of both our analysis and the memory coalescing bugs we wish to detect.
– GPUDrano leverages well-established program analysis techniques to improve scalability and is able to analyze thousand-line CUDA programs in seconds, while incorporating relevant information such as accounting for the set of active threads to reduce the number of false positives.

```
// t, N ↦ 0
if(tid+t+1 >= N) return;
x = tid+t+1; // x ↦ 1
for(y=t; y<N; y++){ // y ↦ 0
    xt = N*x + t; // xt ↦ ⊤
    xy = N*x + y; // xy ↦ ⊤
    ty = N*t + y; // ty ↦ 0
    A[xy] -= M[xt]*A[ty];
    if(y == t)
        B[x] -= M[xt]*B[t];
}
```

```
// t, N ↦ 0
if(tid+t >= N) return;
y = tid+t; // y ↦ 1
for(x=t+1; x<N; x++){ // x ↦ 0
    xt = N*x + t; // xt ↦ 0
    xy = N*x + y; // xy ↦ 1
    ty = N*t + y; // ty ↦ 1
    A[xy] -= M[xt]*A[ty];
    if(y == t)
        B[x] -= M[xt]*B[t];
}
```

(a) Original Fan2 snippet

(b) Fixed Fan2 snippet

Fig. 2. Kernel snippets from Gaussian Elimination program.

– We demonstrate that GPUDrano works in practice by implementing it in LLVM and detecting over a hundred real uncoalesced accesses in the well-established Rodinia benchmark suite. We also validate GPUDrano against a dynamic analysis to show that GPUDrano has few or no false positives on most programs.

The remainder of this paper is organized as follows. Section 2 describes the CUDA programming model and a real memory coalescing bug from our benchmarks. Section 3 presents our formalization of CUDA programs, their executions, and uncoalesced accesses. Section 4 describes the GPUDrano static analysis. Section 5 describes the dynamic analysis we use to validate our GPUDrano implementation. Section 6 discusses our experimental results, and Sect. 7 related work. Finally, Sect. 8 concludes.

2 Illustrative Example

We use an example GPU program to briefly illustrate the GPU programming model and the problem of uncoalesced accesses. GPUs follow an SIMT (Single Instruction Multiple Thread) execution model, where multiple threads execute the same sequence of instructions, often called a *kernel*. Figure 2a shows one such kernel, Fan2, from Gaussian Elimination program in Rodinia benchmark suite [5]. The comments in the kernel can be ignored for now. The kernel performs row operations on matrix A (size $N \times N$) and vector B (size $N \times 1$) using the tth column of a multiplier matrix M (size $N \times N$) and the tth row of A and B. The kernel is a sequential procedure that takes in a thread id, tid, to distinguish executions of different threads. The kernel is executed for threads with ids in range $[0, N - t - 2]$. Each thread is assigned a distinct row and updates row (tid $+ t + 1$) of matrix A and vector B. Note that A, B and M reside in global memory and are shared across threads, while the remaining variables are private to each thread.

$$
\begin{array}{lll}
S ::= & & \text{statement} \\
\quad | \quad AS & & \text{assignment} \\
\quad | \quad \textbf{if } \langle test \rangle \textbf{ then } S_1 \textbf{ else } S_2 & & \text{conditional} \\
\quad | \quad \textbf{while } \langle test \rangle \textbf{ do } S & & \text{loop} \\
\quad | \quad S_1 ; S_2 & & \text{sequence}
\end{array}
$$

Fig. 3. The grammar for kernel K.

The GPU executes threads in bundles, or *warps*, where threads in each warp consist of consecutive ids and execute instructions in lock-step. The above kernel, for example, might be executed for warps w_0 with ids $[0, 31]$, w_1 with ids $[32, 63]$, and so on ... When a warp, say w_0, accesses A using index xy in $A[xy]$ for some iteration of y, the elements $A[N(t+1)+y], A[N(t+2)+y], \ldots, A[N(t+32)+y]$ are fetched simultaneously. The elements are at least N locations apart from each other, and thus, separate transactions are required to access each element, which takes significant time and energy. This is an *uncoalesced* access. Access to $M[xt]$ is similarly uncoalesced. Now, Fig. 2b shows a fixed version of the kernel, where each thread is mapped to a column of the matrices A and M, instead of a row. The access to $A[xy]$ by warp w_0 results in elements $A[Nx+t], A[Nx+t+1], \ldots, A[Nx+t+31]$ to be accessed. These are consecutive elements, and thus, can be accessed in a single transaction. Access to $M[xt]$ is similarly coalesced, and our experiments show a 25% reduction in run-time for the fixed kernel, when run for inputs with $N = 1024$.

3   Formalization of Uncoalesced Accesses

This section describes the GPU programming model and uncoalesced accesses formally. A GPU program is a tuple $\langle T, V_L, V_G, K \rangle$, where T represents the set of all threads; V_L and V_G represent the sets of variables residing in local and global memories respectively; and K represents the kernel or the sequence of instructions executed by the threads. The kernel K is defined by the grammar in Fig. 3, and consists of assignments, conditionals and loops. The set V_L further contains a special read-only variable, tid, initialized with the thread id of the thread. The variable can appear in the right-hand-side of assignments and helps distinguish executions of different threads.

We next present a simple operational semantics for GPU programs. We use a simplified execution model, where *all* threads in the program execute instructions in lock-step. While the standard GPU execution model is more flexible, this assumption simplifies the semantics without affecting the detection of memory coalescing bugs, and has been used in a previous formalization [4].

Excluded GPU Features. The GPU programming model represents threads in a two-level hierarchy, where a bunch of threads form a *thread-block* and the thread-blocks together form the set of all threads. Further, threads have access to a block-level memory space, *shared memory*, used to share data between threads within a block. Lastly, threads within a block can synchronize on a __syncthreads() barrier. These features do not directly affect uncoalesced accesses and have been excluded here for the ease of presentation.

3.1   Semantics

To describe the semantics, we define two entities: the state σ and the active set of threads π. The state σ maps variables to a type-consistent value ν. It consists of a copy of local variables per thread and a copy of global variables, and thus, is a function $(V_L \times T) \cup V_G \rightarrow V$. We further use $\perp$ to represent an undefined or error state. The active set of threads π is a subset of T and defines a set of threads for which the execution is active. Now, the semantics for a statement S are given by the function $[\![S]\!]$, where $[\![S]\!](\sigma, \pi) = \sigma'$ represents the execution of statement S in state σ for threads in set π to generate a new state σ'.

Assignments. We first define the semantics for assignment statements when executed by a single thread t i.e. $[\![AS]\!](\sigma, t) = \sigma'$. Let $l \in V_L$ and $g \in V_G$ represent a local and global variable, respectively. Let v represent a generic variable. Further, let the variables be either scalars or arrays. An assignment is of the form $[E := e]$, where E is the expression being updated, and consists of either a scalar variable v or an array variable indexed by a local $v(l)$; and e is an expression whose value is assigned to E, and is built using scalar variables, array variables indexed by locals, constants, and arithmetic and boolean operations on them. Note that in an assignment at least one of E and e must be a local scalar variable l. We distinguish two types of assignments: *global array read* $[l' := g(l)]$, where the global array g indexed by l is read into l', i.e. $\sigma'(l', t) = \sigma(g)(\sigma(l, t))$ and $\sigma'(v, t) = \sigma(v, t)$ for all $v \neq l$; and *global array write* $[g(l) := l']$, where g indexed by l is written with value of l', i.e. $\sigma'(g)(\sigma(l, t)) = \sigma(l', t)$, $\sigma'(g)(\nu) = \sigma(g)(\nu)$ for all $\nu \neq \sigma(l, t)$, and $\sigma'(v, t) = \sigma(v, t)$ for all $v \neq g$.

We now define the semantics when an assignment is executed by a set of threads π, i.e. $[\![AS]\!](\sigma, \pi) = \sigma'$. When the set π is empty, the state remains unchanged i.e. $[\![AS]\!](\sigma, \phi) = \sigma$. When π is non-empty i.e. $\pi = \{t\} \cup \pi'$, the desired update is obtained by first executing AS for thread t, and then the other threads in π'. Thus, $[\![AS]\!](\sigma, \pi) = [\![AS]\!]([\![AS]\!](\sigma, t), \pi')$. Note that, if different threads write to the same memory location, the execution is not deterministic and the updated state is set to the undefined state, i.e. $[\![AS]\!](\sigma, t) = \perp$.

Sequences. The execution of sequence of statements $(S_1; S_2)$ is described by first executing S_1, followed by S_2 i.e. $[\![S_1; S_2]\!](\sigma, \pi) = [\![S_2]\!]([\![S_1]\!](\sigma, \pi), \pi)$.

Conditionals. Next consider $[\![\textbf{if } l \textbf{ then } S_1 \textbf{ else } S_2]\!](\sigma, \pi) = \sigma'$, where $\langle test \rangle$ consists of a local boolean variable l. The semantics *serializes* the execution of statements S_1 and S_2. Let the set of threads for which the predicate $\sigma(l, t)$ is true be π_1. The threads in π_1 first execute S_1 to get the state σ_1 i.e. $[\![S_1]\!](\sigma, \pi_1) = \sigma_1$. Next, the remaining threads execute S_2 in state σ_1 to get the final updated state i.e. $[\![S_2]\!](\sigma_1, \pi \setminus \pi_1) = \sigma'$. Note that, similar to assignments, if the same location is read or written by a thread executing the **if** branch and another thread executing the **else** branch with one of the accesses being writes, there is a potential conflict between the two accesses, and the final state σ' is set to $\bot$.

Loops. We next describe the semantics for loops $[\![\mathbf{while}\,l\,\mathbf{do}\,S]\!](\sigma, \pi) = \sigma'$. We first consider semantics for terminating loops. The loop execution terminates when there are no threads active in the loop, and it is repeated until then. Formally, if there exist $\sigma_1, \pi_1, \sigma_2, \pi_2, \ldots, \sigma_k, \pi_k$, such that σ_i and π_i represent the state and the active set of threads at the beginning of the ith iteration of the loop, i.e. $\sigma_1 = \sigma$, $\pi_1 = \{t \in \pi : \sigma(l, t) = \mathsf{true}\}$, $\sigma_{i+1} = [\![S]\!](\sigma_i, \pi_i)$, and $\pi_{i+1} = \{t \in \pi_i : \sigma_{i+1}(l, t) = \mathsf{true}\}$, and the last active set is empty, $\pi_k = \phi$, then $\sigma' = \sigma_k$. If the loop is non-terminating, σ' is assigned the undefined state $\bot$.

Reachable Configurations. We now define the set $\mathcal{R}$ of configurations reachable during a kernel's execution. A configuration is a tuple (σ, π, S), where σ is the current state, π is the current active set of threads, and S is the next statement to be executed. We give a inductive definition for $\mathcal{R}$. The initial configuration (σ_0, T, K) belongs to $\mathcal{R}$, where σ_0 is the initial state, T is the set of all threads and K is the kernel. In the recursive case, suppose (σ, π, S) belongs to $\mathcal{R}$. When $S = S_1; S_2$, the configuration (σ, π, S_1) belongs to $\mathcal{R}$, since S_1 is the next statement to be executed. Further, if the state after executing S_1, $\sigma' = [\![S_1]\!](\sigma, \pi)$, is not undefined i.e. $\sigma' \neq \bot$, then (σ', π, S_2) also belongs to $\mathcal{R}$. Similarly, when S is a conditional $[\mathbf{if}\,l\,\mathbf{then}\,S_1\,\mathbf{else}\,S_2]$, both **if** and **else** branches are reachable, and thus, (σ, π_1, S_1) and (σ, π_2, S_2) belong to $\mathcal{R}$, where $\pi_1 = \{t \in \pi : \sigma(l, t) = \mathsf{true}\}$ and $\pi_2 = \pi \setminus \pi_1$. Lastly, when S is a loop $[\mathbf{while}\,l\,\mathbf{do}\,S']$, the configuration (σ, π', S'), where $\pi' = \{t \in \pi : \sigma(l, t) = \mathsf{true}\}$, is reachable. Further, if the state after executing S' is not undefined, the configuration $([\![S']\!](\sigma, \pi'), \pi', S)$ is also reachable.

3.2   Uncoalesced Global Memory Accesses

To define uncoalesced global memory accesses, we first describe how the global memory is accessed by a GPU. Let the memory bandwidth for global memory be η bytes i.e. the GPU can access η contiguous bytes from the memory in one transaction. When a warp of threads with consecutive thread indices W issues a read or write to the global memory, the addresses accessed by the active threads are coalesced together into as few transactions as possible. If the number of transactions is above a threshold τ, there is an uncoalesced access.

We now define uncoalesced accesses formally. Consider the configuration (σ, π, AS), where AS is a global array read $[l' := g(l)]$ or a global array write $[g(l) := l']$ and g is a global array with each element of size k bytes. Let W be a warp of threads with consecutive thread indices. Let the addresses accessed by the warp, $\Gamma(\sigma, \pi, AS, W)$, be defined as,

$$\Gamma(\sigma, \pi, AS, W) = \bigcup_{t \in W \cap \pi} \big[\sigma(l, t).k, \sigma(l, t).k + k - 1\big]$$

Now, each contiguous set of η bytes is accessed in one transaction. Thus, the number of transactions $N(\sigma, \pi, AS, W)$ required for the access equals the number of unique elements in the set $\{\lfloor a/\eta \rfloor : a \in \Gamma(\sigma, \pi, AS, W)\}$. If $N(\sigma, \pi, AS, W)$ is greater than threshold τ for some warp W, the configuration (σ, π, AS) is an "uncoalesced" configuration. A global array access AS is uncoalesced, if an uncoalesced configuration involving the access is reachable.

For most current GPUs, the bandwidth $\eta = 128$ bytes, and warp size $|W| = 32$. We use the threshold $\tau = 1$, so that accesses that require more than one transaction are flagged as uncoalesced. Suppose the index variable l in a global array access is a linear function of tid, i.e. $l \equiv c.\text{tid} + c_0$. The range of addresses accessed by a completely active warp W is $(31|kc| + k - 1)$ bytes and thus, the number of transactions N required is at least $|kc|/4$. If $k \geq 4$ bytes and $|c| \geq 1$ (with one of the inequalities being strict), N is greater than 1, and hence, the access is uncoalesced. We refer to such uncoalescing, where the range of addresses accessed by a warp is large, as *range-based* uncoalescing.

Alternately, an uncoalesced access can occur due to alignment issues, where the range of accessed locations is small but mis-aligned with the cache block boundaries. Suppose $k = 4$ and $c = 1$, but $c_0 = 8$. The addresses accessed by a warp W with tids $[0, 31]$ are $[32, 159]$ and require two transactions, even though the range of locations is 127 bytes which is less than the bandwidth. We refer to such accesses as *alignment-based* uncoalesced accesses.

4   Static Analysis

This section presents a static compile-time analysis to identify uncoalesced accesses. We use abstract interpretation [8,17] for the analysis, where-in we first define an abstraction of the state and the active set of threads. The abstraction captures features of the kernel execution essential to identify uncoalesced accesses. It tracks values, particularly access indices, as a function of tid, and for the indices with potentially large linear or non-linear dependence on tid, the analysis flags the corresponding global array access as uncoalesced. Further, if a segment of code is executed only by a single thread (which is often the case when some sequential work needs to be done), a single transaction is required for an access and it cannot be uncoalesced. Hence, our abstraction also tracks whether single or multiple threads are active during the execution of a statement.

After defining the abstraction, we associate abstract semantics with the statements in kernels, computable at compile-time, that preserve the abstraction. We then present our algorithm to execute kernels abstractly and identify global array accesses which can potentially be uncoalesced. Finally, we describe our implementation for the analysis.

Example. Before diving into the details of the analysis, let's consider the example in Fig. 2a. Our abstraction tracks local variables as a function of tid. All variables that are independent of tid are assigned value 0 in the abstraction. Thus, variables t and N are assigned the value 0 initially (shown in comments). Further, variables y and ty are constructed from tid-independent variables, and hence, assigned 0. Next, all variables that are linear function of tid with coefficient 1 (i.e. of the form tid $+ c$), are assigned value 1. The variable x is therefore assigned 1. Lastly, all variables that are either non-linear function of tid or linear function with possibly greater than one coefficient are assigned $\top$. Variable xt, for example, is assigned the expression $N(\text{tid}+t+1)+t$, where the coefficient for tid is N. Since N can be greater than one, xt is assigned $\top$. Similarly, variable xy is assigned $\top$. Now, global array accesses where the index variable has value $\top$, are flagged as uncoalesced. Hence, accesses A[xy] and M[xt] are flagged as uncoalesced. Note that in the fixed kernel in Fig. 2b, none of the index variables are $\top$, and hence, none of the accesses are flagged as uncoalesced.

4.1   Abstraction

We now formally define our abstraction. Let $\alpha()$ be the abstraction function. The abstraction of state $\hat{\sigma}$ only tracks values of local scalar variables. We observe that indirect indexing through arrays is rare for coalesced accesses, and hence we consevatively flag all such accesses as uncoalesced. Further, we use a different abstraction for integer and boolean variables. We assign a single abstract value to each local variable, that tracks its dependency on tid. For integer variables, we use the set $\widehat{\mathcal{V}}_{int} = \{\bot, 0, 1, -1, \top\}$ to abstract values. The value $\bot$ represents undefined values, while $\top$ represents all values. The remaining values are defined here. Let l be a local variable.

$$\alpha(\sigma)(l) = \begin{cases} 0, & \text{exists } c_0 \text{ s.t. for all } t \in T, \ \sigma(l,t) = c_0 \\ 1, & \text{exists } c_0 \text{ s.t. for all } t \in T, \ \sigma(l,t) = \text{tid}(t) + c_0 \\ -1, & \text{exists } c_0 \text{ s.t. for all } t \in T, \ \sigma(l,t) = -\text{tid}(t) + c_0 \end{cases}$$

i.e. the abstract value 0 represents values constant across threads; 1 represents values that are a linear function of tid with coefficient 1; and, -1 represents values that are a linear function with coefficent -1. This abstraction is necessary to track dependency of access indices on tid.

We use the set $\widehat{\mathcal{V}}_{bool} = \{\bot, \mathsf{T}, \mathsf{T}^-, \mathsf{F}, \mathsf{F}^-, \mathsf{TF}, \mathsf{TT}^-, \mathsf{FF}^-, \top\}$ to abstract boolean variables. Again $\bot$ and $\top$ represent the undefined value and all values, respectively. The remaining values are defined here.

$$\alpha(\sigma)(l) \equiv \begin{cases} \mathsf{T}, & \text{for all } t \in T, \ \sigma(l,t) = \text{true} \\ \mathsf{T}^-, & \text{exists } t \in T \text{ s.t. } \sigma(l,t) = \text{false} \\ & \text{and for all } t' \in T \setminus t, \ \sigma(l,t') = \text{true} \\ \mathsf{F}, & \text{for all } t \in T, \ \sigma(l,t) = \text{false} \\ \mathsf{F}^-, & \text{exists } t \in T \text{ s.t. } \sigma(l,t) = \text{true} \\ & \text{and for all } t' \in T \setminus t, \ \sigma(l,t') = \text{false} \end{cases}$$

i.e. the abstract value T represents values true for all threads; T^- represents values true for all but one thread; F represents values false for all threads; F^- represents values false for all but one thread. Further, we construct three additional boolean values: $\mathsf{TF} = \{\mathsf{T}, \mathsf{F}\}$ representing values true or false for all threads, $\mathsf{TT}^- = \{\mathsf{T}, \mathsf{T}^-\}$ representing values false for at most one thread, and

$FF^- = \{F, F^-\}$ representing values true for at most one thread. We only use these compound values in our analysis, along with $\bot$ and $\top$. We use them to abstract branch predicates in kernels. This completes the abstraction for state. Note that $\hat{\sigma}$ is function $V_L \to \widehat{\mathcal{V}}_{int} \cup \widehat{\mathcal{V}}_{bool}$.

Now, the active set of threads π can be seen as a predicate on the set of threads T. We observe that if at most one thread is active for a global array access, a single transaction is required to complete the access and hence, it is always coalesced. Thus, in our abstraction for π, we only track if it consists of at most one thread or an arbitrary number of threads. These can be abstracted by boolean values FF^- and $\top$ respectively, and thus, $\hat{\pi} \in \{FF^-, \top\}$.

Lastly, our abstraction for boolean and integer variables induces a natural complete lattice on sets $\widehat{\mathcal{V}}_{int}$ and $\widehat{\mathcal{V}}_{bool}$. These lattices can be easily extended to complete lattices for the abstract states and active sets of threads.

Justification. We designed our abstraction by studying the benchmark programs in Rodinia. We have already motivated the abstract values 0, 1 and $\top$ for integer variables in the example above. We found coefficient -1 for tid in a few array indices, which led to the abstract value -1. There were also instances where values 1 and -1 were added together to generate 0 or tid-independent values. Next, the values FF^- and TT^- were motivated by the need to capture predicates in conditionals where one of the branches consisted of at most one active thread. Lastly, the value TF was necessary to distinguish conditionals with tid-dependent and tid-independent predicates.

4.2   Abstract Semantics

We briefly describe the abstract semantics $\widehat{[\![S]\!]}(\hat{\sigma}, \hat{\pi}) = \hat{\sigma}'$ for a statement S, which is the execution of S in an abstract state $\hat{\sigma}$ for abstract active set $\hat{\pi}$ to generate the abstract state $\hat{\sigma}'$. We first consider abstract computation of values of local expressions e (involving only local scalar variables) in state $\hat{\sigma}$, $\widehat{[\![e]\!]}(\hat{\sigma})$. Local scalar variable l evaluates to its value in $\hat{\sigma}$, $\hat{\sigma}(l)$. Constants evaluate to the abstract value 0 (TF if boolean). Index tid evaluates to 1. Arithmetic operations on abstract values are defined just as regular arithmetic, except all values that do not have linear dependency on tid with coefficient 0, 1 or -1, are assigned $\top$. For example, $[1 + 1] = \top$ since the resultant value has a dependency of 2 on tid. Boolean values are constructed from comparison between arithmetic values. Equalites $[\hat{\nu}_1 = \hat{\nu}_2]$ are assigned a boolean value FF^-, and inequalities $[\hat{\nu}_1 \neq \hat{\nu}_2]$ a boolean value TT^-, where one of ν_1 and ν_2 equals 1 or -1, and the other 0. Note that this is consistent with our abstraction. The equalities are of the form $[tid = c]$, for some constant c, and are true for at most one thread. The inequalities are of the form $[tid \neq c]$ and are true for all except one thread. For boolean operations, we observe that $\neg TT^- = FF^-$, $[FF^- \wedge b] = FF^-$, and $[TT^- \vee b] = TT^-$, for all $b \in \{TF, FF^-, TT^-, \top\}$. Other comparison and boolean operations are defined similarly.

We next define the abstract semantics for different types of assignments AS in a state $\hat{\sigma}$, $\widehat{[\![AS]\!]}(\hat{\sigma}) = \hat{\sigma}'$. For local assignments $[l := e]$ where e is a local

$$\frac{\widehat{[\![AS]\!]}(\hat{\sigma}) = \hat{\sigma}'}{\widehat{[\![AS]\!]}(\hat{\sigma}, \hat{\pi}) = \hat{\sigma}'} \ \text{ASSIGN} \qquad \frac{\begin{array}{c}\widehat{[\![S_1]\!]}(\hat{\sigma}, \hat{\pi}) = \hat{\sigma}_1 \\ \widehat{[\![S_2]\!]}(\hat{\sigma}_1, \hat{\pi}) = \hat{\sigma}_2\end{array}}{\widehat{[\![S_1; S_2]\!]}(\hat{\sigma}, \hat{\pi}) = \hat{\sigma}_2} \ \text{SEQ}$$

$$\frac{\begin{array}{c}\hat{\pi}_1 = [\hat{\pi} \wedge \hat{\sigma}(l)] \\ \hat{\pi}_2 = [\hat{\pi} \wedge \neg\hat{\sigma}(l)] \\ \widehat{[\![S_1]\!]}(\hat{\sigma}, \hat{\pi}_1) = \hat{\sigma}_1 \\ \widehat{[\![S_2]\!]}(\hat{\sigma}, \hat{\pi}_2) = \hat{\sigma}_2 \\ \hat{\sigma}_3 = \varPhi_{\{S_1, S_2\}}^{\hat{\sigma}(l)}(\hat{\sigma}_1, \hat{\sigma}_2)\end{array}}{\widehat{[\![\text{if } l \text{ then } S_1 \text{ else } S_2]\!]}(\hat{\sigma}, \hat{\pi}) = \hat{\sigma}_3} \ \text{ITE} \qquad \frac{\begin{array}{c}\hat{\pi}' = [\hat{\pi} \wedge \hat{\sigma}(l)] \\ \widehat{[\![S]\!]}(\hat{\sigma}, \hat{\pi}') = \hat{\sigma}_1 \\ \hat{\sigma}_2 = \varPhi_{\{\text{skip}, S\}}^{\hat{\sigma}(l)}(\hat{\sigma}, \hat{\sigma}_1) \\ \widehat{[\![\text{while } l \text{ do } S]\!]}(\hat{\sigma}_2, \hat{\pi}') = \hat{\sigma}_3\end{array}}{\widehat{[\![\text{while } l \text{ do } S]\!]}(\hat{\sigma}, \hat{\pi}) = \hat{\sigma}_3} \ \text{WHILE}$$

Fig. 4. Abstract semantics for compound statements.

expression, l is updated with value of expression e, $\widehat{[\![e]\!]}(\hat{\sigma})$. For reads $[l := g]$, where g is a global scalar variable, all threads receive the same value, and the new value is tid-independent. Hence, l is updated to 0 (TF if boolean). For array reads $[l := v(l')]$, where $\hat{\sigma}(l') = 0$, all threads access the same element in the array v, and recieve the same value. Thus, the updated value is again 0 (TF if boolean). Lastly for array reads where $\hat{\sigma}(l') \neq 0$, the read could return values that are arbitrary function of tid (since we do not track the values for arrays), and hence, the updated value is $\top$.

We now define abstract semantics for the compound statements. We use rules in Fig. 4 to describe them formally. Note that, our abstract semantics for assignments are oblivious to the set of threads $\hat{\pi}$, and thus, the [ASSIGN] rule extends these semantics to an arbitrary set of threads. The [SEQ] rule similarly extends the semantics to sequence of statements. The [ITE] rule describes the semantics for conditionals. The sets $\hat{\pi}_1$ and $\hat{\pi}_2$ represent the new active set of threads for the execution of S_1 and S_2. Note that $\hat{\pi}_1 = [\hat{\pi} \wedge \hat{\sigma}(l)]$, and gets a value FF$^-$, only if either $\hat{\pi}$ or $\hat{\sigma}(l)$ is FF$^-$. The new set of threads π_1 has at most one thread, only if either the incoming set π or the predicate $\sigma(l, t)$ is true for at most one thread. Hence, $\hat{\pi}_1$ correctly abstracts the new set of the threads for which S_1 is executed. A similar argument follows for $\hat{\pi}_2$. Now, the concrete value for predicate $\sigma(l, t)$ is not known at compile time, and a thread could execute either of S_1 or S_2. Hence, our abstract semantics executes both, and merges the two resulting states to get the final state, i.e. $\varPhi_{\{S_1, S_2\}}^{\hat{\sigma}(l)}(\hat{\sigma}_1, \hat{\sigma}_2)$.

The merge operation is a non-trivial operation and depends on the branch predicate $\hat{\sigma}(l)$. If $\hat{\sigma}(l)$ is TF or tid-independent, all threads execute either the **if** branch or the **else** branch, and final value of a variable l is one of the values $\hat{\sigma}_1(l)$ and $\hat{\sigma}_2(l)$. In the merged state, our semantics assigns it a merged value $\hat{\sigma}_1(l) \sqcup \hat{\sigma}_2(l)$ or the join of the two values, a value that subsumes both these values. When $\hat{\sigma}(l)$ is tid-dependent, however, this merged value does not suffice. Consider, for example, $y := (\text{tid} < N)? 10 : 20$. While on both the branches, y is assigned a constant (abstract value 0), the final value is a non-linear function of tid (abstract value $\top$), even though the join of the two values is 0. Hence, in such cases, when the predicate is tid-dependent and the variable l is assigned a value in S_1 or S_2, the merged value is set to $\top$.

The [WHILE] rule describes the abstract semantics for loops. Note that similar to conditionals, it is not known whether a thread executes S or not. Thus, the rule first transforms the original state $\hat{\sigma}$ into the merge of $\hat{\sigma}$ and the execution of S on $\hat{\sigma}$ and repeats this operation, until the fixed point is reached and the state does not change on repeating the operation. Note that our abstract semantics for different statements are monotonic. The merge operation Φ is also monotonic. The abstract state can have only finite configurations, since each variable gets a finite abstract value. Thus, the fixpoint computation always terminates.

4.3   Detecting Uncoalesced Accesses

We first define the set of abstract configurations that are reachable during the abstract execution of the kernel. An abstract configuration is the tuple $(\hat{\sigma}, \hat{\pi}, S)$. The initial abstract configuration is $(\alpha(\sigma_0), \top, K)$, and is reachable. The other abstract reachable configurations can be defined by a similar recursive definition as that for reachable configurations.

Now, an abstract configuration $(\hat{\sigma}, \hat{\pi}, AS)$ is "uncoalesced", where AS is a global array read $[l' := g(l)]$ or global array write $[g(l) := l']$ and g is a global array with elements of size k, if both these conditions hold:

- $\hat{\pi} = \top$ i.e. the access is potentially executed by more than one thread.
- $(\hat{\sigma}(l) = \top) \vee (\hat{\sigma}(l) \in \{1, -1\} \wedge k > 4)$ i.e. l is a large linear or non-linear function of tid, or it is a linear function of tid with unit coefficient and the size of elements of array g is greater than 4 bytes.

The analysis computes the set of abstract reachable configurations by executing the kernel using the abstract semantics, starting from the abstract initial configuration. It reports a global array access AS as uncoalesced, if an abstract uncoalesced configuration involving AS is reached during the abstract execution of the kernel.

Correctness. We show that for all global array accesses AS, if a range-based uncoalesced configuration involving a global array access AS is reachable, the analysis identifies it as uncoalesced. We first note that our abstract semantics preserve the abstraction. Hence, for any reachable configuration (σ, π, AS), there exists an abstract reachable configuration $(\hat{\sigma}, \hat{\pi}, AS)$ that is an overapproximation of its abstraction i.e. $\alpha(\sigma) \sqsubseteq \hat{\sigma}$ and $\alpha(\pi) \sqsubseteq \hat{\pi}$. Now, for a range-based uncoalesced configuration to occur, the access needs to be executed by more than one thread, and thus $\alpha(\pi) = \top$. Further, the access index l either has non-linear dependence on tid, in which case $\alpha(\sigma)(l) = \top$, or as noted in Sect. 3.2, the index has linear dependence with one of $k > 4$ or $|c| > 1$, which again leads to an abstract uncoalesced configuration. Hence, GPUDrano identifies all range-based uncoalesced configurations as uncoalesced. There are no guarantees for alignment-based uncoalescing, however. This gives some evidence for the correctness of the analysis.

4.4   Implementation

We have implemented the analysis in the gpucc CUDA compiler [23], an open-source compiler based on LLVM. We implement the abstract semantics defined above. We work with an unstructured control flow graph representation of the kernel, where conditionals and loops are not exposed as separate units. So, we simplify the semantics at the cost of being more imprecise. We implement the abstract computation of local expressions and the abstract semantics for assignments exactly. We however differ in our implementation for the merge operation. Consider a conditional statement $[\mathbf{if}\, l\, \mathbf{then}\, S_1\, \mathbf{else}\, S_2]$. Let the states after executing S_1 and S_2 be $\hat{\sigma}_1$ and $\hat{\sigma}_2$. The merge of states $\Phi_{\{S_1,S_2\}}^{\hat{\sigma}(l)}(\hat{\sigma}_1,\hat{\sigma}_2)$ after the conditional is contigent on tid-dependence of the value of l at the beginning of the conditional. This information requires path-sensitivity and is not available in the control flow graph at the merge point. Therefore, we conservatively assume l to be tid-dependent. We use the SSA representation of control flow graph, where variables assigned different values along paths S_1 and S_2 are merged in special phi instructions after the conditional. We conservatively set the merged value to $\top$ for such variables. The values of remaining variables remain unchanged. This completes the implementation of merge operation. We define the set of active threads $\hat{\pi}'$ after the conditional as $\hat{\pi}_1 \sqcup \hat{\pi}_2$, or the join of incoming active sets from S_1 and S_2. The new active set $\hat{\pi}'$ equals the active set $\hat{\pi}$ before the conditional. If $\hat{\pi} = \top$, it must be split into $\hat{\pi}_1$ and $\hat{\pi}_2$ such that at least one of the values is $\top$ and hence, $\hat{\pi}' = \top$. Similarly, when $\hat{\pi} = \mathsf{FF}^-$, both $\hat{\pi}_1$ and $\hat{\pi}_2$ equal FF^-, and hence, $\hat{\pi}' = \mathsf{FF}^-$.

Limitations. Our implementation does not do a precise analysis of function calls and pointers, which are both supported by CUDA. In the implementation, we assume that call-context of a kernel is always empty, and function calls inside a kernel can have arbitrary side-effects and return values. We support pointer dereferencing by tracking two abstract values for each pointer variable, one for the address stored in the pointer and the other for the value at the address. We do not implement any alias analyses, since we observe that array indices rarely have aliases. Our evaluation demonstrates that, despite these limitations, our static analysis is able to identify a large number of uncoalesced accesses in practice.

5   Dynamic Analysis

To gauge the accuracy of our GPUDrano static analysis, we have implemented a dynamic analysis for uncoalesced accesses. Being a dynamic analysis, it has full visibility into the memory addresses being accessed by each thread, as well as the set of active threads. Thus, the dynamic analysis can perfectly distinguish coalesced from uncoalesced accesses (for a given input). We use this to determine (1) whether the static analysis has missed any uncoalesced accesses and (2) how many of the statically-identified uncoalesced accesses are false positives.

The dynamic analysis is implemented as a pass in the gpucc CUDA compiler [23], which is based on LLVM. By operating on the LLVM intermediate representation (a type of high-level typed assembly), we can readily identify the instructions that access memory. So for every load and store in the program we insert instrumentation to perform the algorithm described below. A single IR instruction may be called multiple times in a program due to loops or recursion, so every store and load instruction is assigned a unique identifier (analogous to a program counter).

For every global memory access at runtime, we collect the address being accessed by each thread. Within each warp, the active thread with the lowest id is selected as the "computing thread" and it performs the bulk of the analysis. All active threads pass their addresses to the computing thread. The computing thread places all addresses into an array. This array will be at most of length n, where n is the warp size (if there are inactive threads, the size may be smaller). Next the computing thread determines all bytes that will be accessed by the warp, taking the size of the memory access into account. Note that, due to the SIMT programming model, the access size is the same for all threads in the warp since all threads execute the same instruction. Each byte accessed is divided by the size of the cache line using machine integer division. (for current generation Nvidia GPUs this number is 128 [18, Sect. 5.3.2]). Conceptually this assigns each address to a "bin" representing its corresponding cache line. For example, for a cache line of 128 bytes, $[0, 127] \mapsto 0$, $[128, 255] \mapsto 1$, etc. Finally, we count the number of unique bins, which is the total number of cache lines required. The computing thread prints the number of required cache lines, along with the assigned program counter, for post-processing.

A second, off-line step aggregates the information from each dynamic instance of an instruction by averaging. For example, if a load l executes twice, first touching 1 cache line and then touching 2 cache lines, the average for l will be 1.5 cache lines. If the average is 1.0 then l is coalesced, otherwise if the average is > 1.0 l is uncoalesced. The specific value of the average is sometimes useful, to distinguish accesses that are mildly uncoalesced (with averages just over 1.0), as we explore more in Sect. 6.

6   Evaluation

This section describes the evaluation of GPUDrano on the Rodinia benchmarks (version 3.1) [5]. Rodinia consists of GPU programs from various scientific domains. We run our static and dynamic analyses to identify existing uncoalesced accesses in these programs. We have implemented our analyses in LLVM version 3.9.0, and compile with `--cuda-gpu-arch=sm_30`. We use CUDA SDK version 7.5. We run our experiments on an Amazon EC2 instance with Amazon Linux 2016.03 (OS), an 8-core Intel Xeon E5-2670 CPU running at 2.60 GHz, and an Nvidia GRID K520 GPU (Kepler architecture).

Table 1 shows results of our experiments. It shows the benchmark name, the lines of GPU source code analyzed, the manually-validated real uncoalesced

Table 1. Results of GPUDrano's static analysis (SA) and dynamic analysis (DA) on Rodinia benchmark programs. "-" indicates the DA hit the 2-h timeout.

Benchmark	LOC	Real-bugs	SA-bugs (real)	SA-runtime (s)	DA-bugs	DA-runtime (s)
backprop	110	7	0 (0)	0.14	7	5.23
bfs	35	7	7 (7)	0.07	0–7	3.89
b+tree	115	19	19 (19)	0.35	7	16.71
CFD	550	0	22 (0)	12.41	-	-
dwt2D	1380	0	16 (0)	5.99	n/a	3.72
gaussian	30	6	6 (6)	0.07	5–6	6.82
heartwall	1310	8	25 (8)	39.87	-	-
hotspot	115	3	2 (0)	0.75	3	0.89
hotspot3D	50	2	12 (2)	0.21	2	327.00
huffmann	395	21	26 (21)	0.68	3	2.42
lavaMD	180	9	9 (9)	0.73	5	511.60
lud	160	3	0 (0)	0.34	3	0.83
myocyte	3240	19	19 (19)	1,813.72	0	134.13
nn	10	4	4 (4)	0.06	2	0.13
nw	170	7	2 (2)	0.41	6	4.17
particle filter	70	4	3 (2)	0.58	4	11.62
pathfinder	80	3	0 (0)	0.22	3	4.25
srad_v1	275	2	14 (2)	0.33	2	185.00
srad_v2	250	9	0 (0)	1.38	9	53.94
streamcluster	45	10	10 (10)	0.11	-	-
		143	180 (111)		69	

accesses, and the number of uncoalesced accesses found and running time for each analysis. The Rodinia suite consists of 22 programs. We exclude 4 (hybridsort, kmeans, leukocyte, mummergpu) as they could not be compiled due to lack of support for texture functions in LLVM. We synonymously use "bugs" for uncoalesced accesses, though sometimes they are fundamental to the program and cannot be avoided. We next address different questions related to the evaluation.

Do Uncoalesced Accesses Occur in Real Programs? We found 143 actual bugs in Rodinia benchmarks, with bugs in almost every program (Column "Real bugs" in Table 1). A few of the bugs involved random or irregular access to global arrays (bfs, particle filter). Such accesses are dynamic and data-dependent, and difficult to fix. Next, we found bugs where consecutive threads access rows of global matrices, instead of columns (gaussian). Such bugs could be fixed by assigning consecutive threads to consecutive columns or changing the layout of matrices, but this is possible only when consecutive columns can be accessed in parallel. Another common bug occurred when data was allocated as an array of structures instead of a structure of arrays (nn, streamcluster). A closely related bug was one where the array was divided into contiguous chunks and each chunk was assigned to a thread, instead of allocating elements in a round-robin fashion (myocyte, streamcluster). There were some bugs which involved reduction operations (for example, sum) on arrays (heartwall, huffmann). These bugs do not have a standard fix, and some of the above techniques could be applicable.

A few bugs were caused by alignment issues where accesses by a warp did not align with cache-block boundaries, and hence, got spilled over to multiple blocks. These were caused, first, when the input matrix dimensions were not a multiple of the warp size which led consecutive rows to be mis-aligned (backprop, hotspot3D), or when the whole array was misaligned due to incorrect padding (b+tree). These could be fixed by proper padding.

Which Real Bugs Does Static Analysis Miss? While the static analysis catches a significant number of bugs (111 out of 143), it does miss some in practice. We found two primary reasons for this. 22 of the missed bugs depend on the second dimension of the tid vector, while we only considered the smallest dimension in our analysis. Uncoalesced accesses typically do not depend on higher dimensions unless the block dimensions are small or not a multiple of the warp size. We modified our analysis to track the second dimension and observed that all these bugs were caught by the static analysis, at the cost of 20 new false positives. Eight of the remaining missed bugs were alignment bugs which were caused by an unaligned offset added to tid. The actual offsets are challenging to track via static analysis. Two missed bugs (particle filter) were due to an implementation issue with conditionals which we will address in the future.

What False Positives Does Static Analysis Report? For most programs, GPUDrano reports few or no false positives. The primary exceptions are CFD, dwt2D and heartwall, which account for the bulk of our false positives. A common case occurred when tid was divided by a constant, and multiplied back by the same constant to generate the access index (heartwall, huffman, srad_v1). Such an index should not lead to uncoalesced accesses. The static analysis, however, cannot assert that the two constants are equal, since we do not track exact values, and hence, sets the access index to $\top$, and reports any accesses involving the index as uncoalesced. Another type of false positive occurred when access indices were non-linear function of tid, but consecutive indices differed by at most one, and led to coalesced accesses. Such indices were often either generated by indirect indexing (CFD, srad_v1) or by assigning values in conditionals (heartwall, hotspot, hotspot3D). In both cases, our static analysis conservatively assumed them to be uncoalesced. Lastly, a few false positives happened because the access index was computed via a function call (__mul24) which returned a coalesced index (huffmann), though we conservatively set the index to $\top$.

How Scalable is Static Analysis? As can be noted, the static analysis is quite fast, and finishes within seconds for most benchmarks. The largest benchmark, myocyte, is 3240 lines of GPU code, with the largest kernel containing 930 lines. The kernels in myocyte consist of many nested loops, and it appears the static analysis takes significant time computing fixed points for these loops.

How Does Static Analysis Compare with Dynamic Analysis? The dynamic analysis misses nearly half the bugs in our benchmarks. We found several benchmarks where different inputs varied the number of bugs reported (bfs, gaussian, lud). Similarly, the analysis finds bugs along a single execution path, so all bugs in unexecuted branches or uncalled kernels were not found.

Due to compiler optimizations it can be difficult to map the results of dynamic analysis back to source code. In dwt2D, we were unable to do so due to multiple uses of C++ templates. Moreover, the dynamic analysis does not scale to long-running programs, as it incurs orders of magnitude of slowdown. While none of our benchmarks execute for more than 5 s natively, several did not finish with the dynamic analysis within our 2-h limit (CFD, heartwall, streamcluster).

7   Related Work

While the performance problems that uncoalesced accesses cause are well understood [18, Sect. 5.3.2], there are few static analysis tools for identifying them.

Several compilers for improving GPU performance [3,7,11,20,21,24] incorporate some static analysis for uncoalesced global memory accesses, but these analyses are described informally and not evaluated for precision. Some of these systems also exhibit additional restrictions, such as CuMAPz's [11] reliance on runtime traces, CUDA-lite's [21] use of programmer annotations, or [3,20] which are applicable only to programs with affine access patterns. Some systems for optimizing GPU memory performance, like Dymaxion [6], eschew static analysis for programmer input instead. GPUDrano's precision could likely help improve the performance of the code generated by these prior systems and reduce programmer effort. [1] describes in a short paper the preliminary implementation of CUPL, a static analysis for uncoalesced global memory accesses. While CUPL shares similar goals as GPUDrano, no formalization or detailed experimental results are described.

GKLEE [15] is a symbolic execution engine for CUDA programs. It can detect uncoalesced accesses to global memory (along with data races), but due to the limitations of its underlying SMT solver it cannot scale to larger kernels or large numbers of threads. The PUG verifier for GPU kernels [14] has also been extended to detect uncoalesced memory accesses [10], but PUG is less scalable than GKLEE. In contrast, GPUDrano's static analysis can abstract away the number of threads actually used by a kernel.

[9] uses dynamic analysis to identify uncoalesced global memory accesses, and then uses this information to drive code transformations that produce coalesced accesses. GPUDrano's static analysis is complementary, and would eliminate [9]'s need to be able to run the program on representative inputs.

There are many programming models that can generate code for GPUs, including proposals to translate legacy OpenMP code [12,13] or C code [2,3,22], and new programming models such as OpenACC [19] and C++ AMP [16]. An analysis such as GPUDrano's could help improve performance in such systems, by identifying memory coalescing bottlenecks in the generated GPU code.

8   Conclusion

This paper presents GPUDrano, a scalable static analysis for uncoalesced global memory accesses in GPU programs. We formalize our analysis, and implement

GPUDrano in LLVM. We apply GPUDrano to a range of GPU kernels from the Rodinia benchmark suite. We have evaluated GPUDrano's accuracy by comparing it to a dynamic analysis that is fully precise for a given input, and found that the GPUDrano implementation is accurate in practice and reports few false positives for most programs. Fixing these issues can lead to performance improvements of up to 25% for the gaussian benchmark.

We would like to thank anonymous reviewers for their valuable feedback. This research was supported by NSF awards CCF-1138996 and XPS-1337174.

References

1. Amilkanthwar, M., Balachandran, S.: CUPL: a compile-time uncoalesced memory access pattern locator for CUDA. In: Proceedings of the 27th International ACM Conference on International Conference on Supercomputing, ICS 2013, pp. 459–460. ACM, New York (2013). http://doi.acm.org/10.1145/2464996.2467288
2. Baskaran, M.M., Bondhugula, U., Krishnamoorthy, S., Ramanujam, J., Rountev, A., Sadayappan, P.: Automatic data movement and computation mapping for multi-level parallel architectures with explicitly managed memories. In: Proceedings of the 13th ACM SIGPLAN Symposium on Principles and Practice of Parallel Programming, PPoPP 2008, pp. 1–10. ACM, New York (2008). http://doi.acm.org/10.1145/1345206.1345210
3. Baskaran, M.M., Bondhugula, U., Krishnamoorthy, S., Ramanujam, J., Rountev, A., Sadayappan, P.: A compiler framework for optimization of affine loop nests for GPGPUs. In: Proceedings of the 22nd Annual International Conference on Supercomputing, ICS 2008, pp. 225–234. ACM, New York (2008). http://doi.acm.org/10.1145/1375527.1375562
4. Betts, A., Chong, N., Donaldson, A.F., Ketema, J., Qadeer, S., Thomson, P., Wickerson, J.: The design and implementation of a verification technique for GPU kernels. ACM Trans. Program. Lang. Syst. **37**(3), 10:1–10:49 (2015). http://doi.acm.org/10.1145/2743017
5. Che, S., Boyer, M., Meng, J., Tarjan, D., Sheaffer, J.W., Lee, S.H., Skadron, K.: Rodinia: a benchmark suite for heterogeneous computing. In: 2009 IEEE International Symposium on Workload Characterization (IISWC), pp. 44–54, October 2009
6. Che, S., Sheaffer, J.W., Skadron, K.: Dymaxion: optimizing memory access patterns for heterogeneous systems. In: Proceedings of 2011 International Conference for High Performance Computing, Networking, Storage and Analysis, SC 2011, pp. 13:1–13:11. ACM, New York (2011). http://doi.acm.org/10.1145/2063384.2063401
7. Chen, G., Wu, B., Li, D., Shen, X.: PORPLE: an extensible optimizer for portable data placement on GPU. In: Proceedings of the 47th Annual IEEE/ACM International Symposium on Microarchitecture, MICRO-47, pp. 88–100. IEEE Computer Society, Washington, DC (2014). http://dx.doi.org/10.1109/MICRO.2014.20
8. Cousot, P., Cousot, R.: Abstract interpretation: a unified lattice model for static analysis of programs by construction or approximation of fixpoints. In: Proceedings of the 4th ACM SIGACT-SIGPLAN Symposium on Principles of Programming Languages, POPL 1977, pp. 238–252. ACM, New York (1977). http://doi.acm.org/10.1145/512950.512973

9. Fauzia, N., Pouchet, L.N., Sadayappan, P.: Characterizing and enhancing global memory data coalescing on GPUs. In: Proceedings of the 13th Annual IEEE/ACM International Symposium on Code Generation and Optimization, CGO 2015, pp. 12–22. IEEE Computer Society, Washington, DC (2015). http://dl.acm.org/citation.cfm?id=2738600.2738603

10. Lv, J., Li, G., Humphrey, A., Gopalakrishnan, G.: Performance degradation analysis of GPU kernels. In: Workshop on Exploiting Concurrency Efficiently and Correctly (2011)

11. Kim, Y., Shrivastava, A.: CuMAPz: A tool to analyze memory access patterns in CUDA. In: Proceedings of the 48th Design Automation Conference, DAC 2011, pp. 128–133. ACM, New York (2011). http://doi.acm.org/10.1145/2024724.2024754

12. Lee, S., Eigenmann, R.: OpenMPC: extended OpenMP programming and tuning for GPUs. In: Proceedings of the 2010 ACM/IEEE International Conference for High Performance Computing, Networking, Storage and Analysis, SC 2010, pp. 1–11. IEEE Computer Society, Washington, DC (2010). https://doi.org/10.1109/SC.2010.36

13. Lee, S., Min, S.J., Eigenmann, R.: OpenMP to GPGPU: a compiler framework for automatic translation and optimization. In: Proceedings of the 14th ACM SIGPLAN Symposium on Principles and Practice of Parallel Programming, PPoPP 2009, pp. 101–110. ACM, New York (2009). http://doi.acm.org/10.1145/1504176.1504194

14. Li, G., Gopalakrishnan, G.: Scalable SMT-based verification of GPU kernel functions. In: Proceedings of the Eighteenth ACM SIGSOFT International Symposium on Foundations of Software Engineering, FSE 2010, pp. 187–196. ACM, New York (2010). http://doi.acm.org/10.1145/1882291.1882320

15. Li, G., Li, P., Sawaya, G., Gopalakrishnan, G., Ghosh, I., Rajan, S.P.: GKLEE: concolic verification and test generation for GPUs. In: Proceedings of the 17th ACM SIGPLAN Symposium on Principles and Practice of Parallel Programming, PPoPP 2012, pp. 215–224. ACM, New York (2012). http://doi.acm.org/10.1145/2145816.2145844

16. Microsoft: C++ Accelerated Massive Parallelism. https://msdn.microsoft.com/en-us/library/hh265137.aspx

17. Nielson, F., Nielson, H.R., Hankin, C.: Principles of Program Analysis. Springer Publishing Company Incorporated, Heidelberg (2010)

18. Nvidia: CUDA C Programming Guide v7.5. http://docs.nvidia.com/cuda/cuda-c-programming-guide/

19. OpenACC-standard.org: OpenACC: Directives for Accelerators. http://www.openacc.org/

20. Sung, I.J., Stratton, J.A., Hwu, W.M.W.: Data layout transformation exploiting memory-level parallelism in structured grid many-core applications. In: Proceedings of the 19th International Conference on Parallel Architectures and Compilation Techniques, PACT 2010, pp. 513–522. ACM, New York (2010). http://doi.acm.org/10.1145/1854273.1854336

21. Ueng, S.Z., Lathara, M., Baghsorkhi, S.S., Wen-mei, W.H.: CUDA-Lite: Reducing GPU Programming Complexity, pp. 1–15. Springer, Heidelberg (2008). http://dx.doi.org/10.1007/978-3-540-89740-8_1

22. Verdoolaege, S., Carlos Juega, J., Cohen, A., Ignacio Gómez, J., Tenllado, C., Catthoor, F.: Polyhedral parallel code generation for CUDA. ACM Trans. Archit. Code Optim. $\mathbf{9}$(4), 54:1–54:23 (2013). http://doi.acm.org/10.1145/2400682.2400713

23. Wu, J., Belevich, A., Bendersky, E., Heffernan, M., Leary, C., Pienaar, J., Roune, B., Springer, R., Weng, X., Hundt, R.: Gpucc: An open-source GPGPU compiler. In: Proceedings of the 2016 International Symposium on Code Generation and Optimization, CGO 2016, pp. 105–116. ACM, New York (2016). http://doi.acm.org/10.1145/2854038.2854041
24. Yang, Y., Xiang, P., Kong, J., Zhou, H.: A GPGPU compiler for memory optimization and parallelism management. In: Proceedings of the 31st ACM SIGPLAN Conference on Programming Language Design and Implementation, PLDI 2010, pp. 86–97. ACM, New York (2010). http://doi.acm.org/10.1145/1806596.1806606

Context-Sensitive Dynamic Partial Order Reduction

Elvira Albert[1], Puri Arenas[1($\boxtimes$)], María García de la Banda[2,4],
Miguel Gómez-Zamalloa[1], and Peter J. Stuckey[3,4]

[1] DSIC, Complutense University of Madrid, Madrid, Spain
puri@sip.ucm.es
[2] DCIS, University of Melbourne, Melbourne, Australia
[3] Faculty of IT, Monash University, Melbourne, Australia
[4] IMDEA Software Institute, Madrid, Spain

Abstract. Dynamic Partial Order Reduction (DPOR) is a powerful technique used in verification and testing to reduce the number of *equivalent* executions explored. Two executions are equivalent if they can be obtained from each other by swapping adjacent, non-conflicting (*independent*) execution steps. Existing DPOR algorithms rely on a notion of independence that is *context-insensitive*, i.e., the execution steps must be independent in all contexts. In practice, independence is often proved by just checking no execution step writes on a shared variable. We present context-sensitive DPOR, an extension of DPOR that uses *context-sensitive independence*, where two steps might be independent only in the particular context explored. We show theoretically and experimentally how context-sensitive DPOR can achieve exponential gains.

1 Introduction

A fundamental challenge in the verification and testing of concurrent programs arises from the combinatorial explosion that occurs when exploring the different ways in which processes/threads can interleave. Partial-order reduction (POR) [4,6,7] is a general theory that provides full coverage of all possible executions of concurrent programs by identifying equivalence classes of redundant executions, and only exploring one representative of each class. Two executions are said to be equivalent if one can be obtained from the other by swapping adjacent, non-conflicting (i.e., independent) execution steps. POR-based approaches avoid the exploration of such equivalent executions thanks to the use of two complementary sets: *persistent sets* and *sleep sets*. Intuitively, the former contains the execution steps that must be explored (as they might lead to non-equivalent executions), while the latter contain the steps that should no longer be explored (as they lead to executions equivalent to others already explored).

In the state-of-the-art POR algorithm [5], called DPOR (*Dynamic POR*), persistent sets are computed dynamically by only adding a step to the persistent set (called *backtracking set* in DPOR terminology) if the step is proved to be dependent on another previously explored step. Refining dependencies thus

© Springer International Publishing AG 2017
R. Majumdar and V. Kunčak (Eds.): CAV 2017, Part I, LNCS 10426, pp. 526–543, 2017.
DOI: 10.1007/978-3-319-63387-9_26

improves POR verification methods [8,15]. While very effective, DPOR is not optimal, as it sometimes explores equivalent executions. Optimality was later achieved by *optimal*-DPOR [1] thanks to the analysis of past explorations to build *source sets* and *wakeup trees*. Intuitively, the former is a relaxation of persistent sets that avoids exploring steps that will later be blocked by the sleep set. The latter stores fragments of executions that are known not to end up being blocked by the sleep set. Source sets and wakeup trees, respectively, replace persistent sets and enhance the performance of sleep sets. Together, they ensure the exploration of all equivalence classes with the minimum number of executions, regardless of scheduling decisions.

Our work stems from the observation that source sets, and their predecessors persistent sets, are computed dynamically based on a notion of *context-insensitive independence*, which requires two steps be independent in *all possible* contexts. While optimal-DPOR has indeed been proved to be optimal, it is so only under the assumption of context-insensitive independence. In existing implementations of both DPOR and optimal-DPOR [1,5], context-insensitive independence is over-approximated by requiring global variables accessed by one execution step not to be modified by the other. The contribution of this paper is to extend the DPOR framework to take advantage of *context-sensitive independence*, that is, of two steps being independent for a given state encountered during the execution, rather than for all possible states. For example, steps $\{if \ (cond) \ f = 0\}$ and $\{f+ = 3\}$ are independent for states where *cond* fails, but not for states where it holds.

Context-sensitiveness is a general, well-known concept that has been intensively studied and applied in both static analyses [13] and dynamic analyses [11]. The challenge is in incorporating this known concept into a sophisticated framework like DPOR. We do so by adding to the computation of the standard sleep sets any sequence of steps that are independent in the considered context, so that the exploration of such sequence is later avoided. Our extension is orthogonal to the previous improvements of source sets and wakeup trees, and can thus be used in conjunction with them.

Importantly, our method also provides an effective technique to improve the traditional over-approximation of context-insensitive independence. Consider, for example, the simple case where two steps add a certain amount to the value of a variable, or the more complex case of an agent-based implementation of merge sort, where each agent splits their input into two parts, gives them to child agents to sort, and then merges the result. Both cases will give the same result regardless of the execution order, and at least the merge case will be difficult to prove. Our context-sensitive approach can easily determine in both cases that the orders lead to the same result (for each particular input being tested) and, hence, only consider one execution order of the processes. Without this, the algorithm will need to consider an exponential number of executions for the merge case, even though they are all equivalent. Our experimental results confirm our method achieves exponential speedups.

2   Preliminaries

Following [1], we assume our concurrent system is composed of a finite set of *processes* (or threads) and has a unique *initial state* s_0. Each process is a sequence of atomic execution *steps* that are globally relevant, that is, might depend on and affect the global state of the system. Each such step represents the combined effect of a global statement and a finite sequence of local statements, ending just before the next global statement in the process. The set of processes enabled by state s (that is, that can perform an execution step from s) is denoted by $enabled(s)$.

An *execution sequence* E is a finite sequence of execution steps performed from the initial state s_0. For example, $q.r.r$ is an execution sequence that executes the first step of process q, followed by two steps of process r. The state reached by execution sequence E is unique and denoted by $s_{[E]}$. Executions sequences E and E' are *equivalent* if they reach the same state: $s_{[E]} = s_{[E']}$. An execution sequence is *complete* if it exhausts all processes (that is, there is no possible further step).

An *event* (p, i) denotes the i-th occurrence of process p in an execution sequence, and $proc(e)$ denotes the process of event e. The set of events in execution sequence E is denoted by $dom(E)$, and contains event (p, i) iff p appears at least i times in E. We use $e <_E e'$ to denote that event e occurs before event e' in E, and $E \leq E'$ to denote that sequence E is a prefix of sequence E'. Note that $<_E$ establishes a total order between events in E. Let $dom_{[E]}(w)$ denote the set of events in execution sequence $E.w$ that are in sequence w, that is, $dom(E.w) \backslash dom(E)$. If w is a single process p, we use $next_{[E]}(p)$ to denote $dom_{[E]}(p)$.

The core concept in POR is that of the *happens-before* partial order among the events in execution sequence E, denoted by $\to_E$. This relation defines a subset of the $<_E$ total order, such that any two sequences with the same happens-before order are equivalent. POR algorithms use this relation to reduce the number of equivalent execution sequences explored, with Optimal-DPOR ensuring that only one execution sequence in each equivalence class is explored. The happens-before partial order has traditionally been defined in terms of a *dependency* relation between the execution steps associated to those events [7]. Intuitively, two steps p and q are *dependent* if there is at least one execution sequence E for which they do not commute, either because one enables the other or because $s_{[E.p.q]} \neq s_{[E.q.p]}$. Instead, the Optimal-DPOR algorithm is based on a very general happens-before relation that is not defined in terms of a dependency relation [1]. It simply requires it to satisfy the following seven properties for all execution sequences E:

1. $\to_E$ is a partial order on $dom(E)$, which is included in $<_E$.
2. The execution steps of each process are totally ordered, i.e. $(p, i) \to_E (p, i+1)$ whenever $(p, i + 1) \in dom(E)$, as one enables the other.
3. If E' is a prefix of E, then $\to_E$ and $\to_{E'}$ are the same on $dom(E')$. That is, adding more events cannot change the order among previous events.

4. Any linearization E' of $\to_E$ on $dom(E)$ is an execution sequence with exactly the same happens-before relation $\to_{E'}$ as $\to_E$. Thus, $\to_E$ induces a set of equivalent execution sequences, all with the same happens-before relation. We use $E \simeq E'$ to denote that E and E' are linearizations of the same happens-before relation, and $[E]_\simeq$ to denote the equivalence class of E.
5. If $E \simeq E'$, then $s_{[E]} = s_{[E']}$, thus ensuring equivalent sequences commute.
6. For any sequences E, E' and w, such that $E.w$ is an execution sequence, we have $E \simeq E'$ iff $E.w \simeq E'.w$.
7. If p, q, and r are different processes, then if $next_{[E]}(p) \to_{E.p.r} next_{[E.p]}(r)$ and $next_{[E]}(p) \not\to_{E.p.q} next_{[E.p]}(q)$, then $next_{[E]}(p) \to_{E.p.q.r} next_{[E.p.q]}(r)$. This ensures that if the next step of p happens-before the next step of r, this will still be the case if we add in the middle a step independent of p.

The above relation is used for defining the concept of a *race* between two events. Event e is said to be in race with event e' in execution E, if the events have different processes, e happens-before e' in E ($e \to_E e'$), and the two events are "concurrent", i.e. there exists an equivalent execution sequence $E' \simeq E$ where the two events are adjacent. We write $e \precsim_E e'$ to denote that e is in race with e' and that the race can be reversed (i.e., the events can be executed in reversed order).

3   The Happens-Before Relation is Not Context-Sensitive

One could think the generality of the above happens-before definition allows it to capture context-sensitive independence and, thus, there is no need to modify DPOR to achieve context-sensitivity. The following example shows this is not the case and explains why Optimal-DPOR might explore sequences avoided by our method. Consider three simple processes defined by:

$$p: \texttt{write(x=5)} \qquad q: \texttt{write(x=5)} \qquad r: \texttt{read(x)}$$

All three pairs of associated execution steps will usually be considered as dependent, which means traditional DPOR methods will process the 6 sequences resulting for all permutations of $\{p, q, r\}$. However, there are only 2 different resulting states, one where r is executed after q and/or p thus reading 5, and one where it is executed before the others, thus reading 0. Let us construct a minimal (i.e., least restrictive) happens-before partial order for all execution sequences of $\{p, q, r\}$. For sequences of length 2, the only properties that need to be considered are 1, 4 and 5 (all others deal with at least three events in the execution). A minimal partial order that satisfies these three properties is:

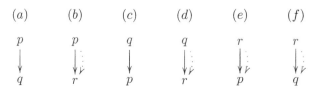

where the dotted arrows indicate a happens-before order between the two process steps, and the continuous arrows indicate the $<_E$ total order within the execution sequence. That is, the following relations hold: (a) $p \not\rightarrow_{p.q} q$, (b) $p \rightarrow_{p.r} r$, (c) $q \not\rightarrow_{q.p} p$, (d) $q \rightarrow_{q.r} r$, (e) $r \rightarrow_{r.p} p$, (f) $r \rightarrow_{r.q} q$. Note that (b), (d), (e) and (f) are needed as, otherwise, properties (4) and (5) of the happens-before definition above would require (b) and (e) to be equivalent, as well as (d) and (f). As given, only (a) and (c) are equivalent.

For sequences of length 3, all properties need to be considered, although our example makes property 2 directly satisfied, as each process has only one execution step. Property (6) requires $p \rightarrow_{p.q.r} r$ to hold, due to (a) and (b). Similarly, $q \rightarrow_{q.p.r} r$ must hold due to (c) and (d). However, these cannot be the only happens-before relations for sequences $p.q.r$ and $q.p.r$, as this would contradict property (4): $q.p.r$ is a linearization of the happens-before for $p.q.r$ and, hence, must have identical happens-before relations. Hence, $q \rightarrow_{p.q.r} r$ and $p \rightarrow_{q.p.r} r$ must also hold. Consider now sequence $p.r.q$. By property (3), $p \rightarrow_{p.r.q} r$ must hold. Again, this cannot be the only relation for the sequence as, by (4), it would also be the only relation for sequence $p.q.r$. Hence, $r \rightarrow_{p.r.q} q$ must also hold. Similarly, $q \rightarrow_{q.r.p} r$ and $r \rightarrow_{q.r.p} p$ must also hold. A similar reasoning can be done for sequences $r.p.q$ and $r.q.p$, obtaining the following minimal happens-before relation for sequences of length 3:

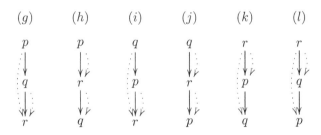

Since $g \simeq i$ and $k \simeq l$, Optimal-DPOR must explore at least 4 different sequences with this minimal happens-before relation. Furthermore, it would need to explore all 6 sequences using the traditional happens before over-approximation. In contrast, using context-sensitivity we can determine that $s_{[d]} = s_{[h]} = s_{[i]} = s_{[j]}$ and $s_{[k]} = s_{[l]}$. Hence, only two sequences must be explored. As we will see later, our algorithm explores 3 sequences when using the traditional happens-before relation.

4　Context-Sensitivity Can Give Exponential Gains

Let us motivate the relevance of our work by means of a typical producer-consumer interaction where we can see that the gain of using context-sensitive independence can be exponential. Consider two processes, a producer (p) that stores results in a bounded buffer (a FIFO queue), and a consumer (c) that takes them from the buffer, defined as follows:

```
                                   consume(Q)
          produce(Q,v)               if Q not empty
            if Q not full              let Q = [v] ++ Q'
              Q := Q ++ [v]            Q := Q'
                                       return v
                                     else return ⊥
```

Let us, for simplicity, assume that calls to produce and consume are atomic, that is, locks are used to prevent their concurrent execution. In any sequence E containing events (p, i) and (c, j), either $(p, i) \rightarrow_E (c, j)$ or $(c, j) \rightarrow_E (p, i)$ must hold, even in a minimal happens-before relation. However, as long as the buffer is neither empty, nor full, both orders lead to the same state.

Given n occurrences of the producer and n of the consumer, a context-insensitive algorithm will need to explore all their interleavings, since each occurrence happens-before the other. This means exploring $\binom{2n}{n}$ executions. However, most of these lead to the same state: if the size k of the buffer is $k \geq n$, the state is determined by the subset of consumers that read an empty buffer and, hence, there are exactly 2^n different states.

Consider an example where $n = 3$, $k = 5$, and p stores 1, 2, 3 in sequence. A DAG representing all execution sequences is given in Fig. 1. For clarity, edges for the consumer appear as dotted and labeled by the value consumed. Nodes represent states and are labeled by the number of elements in the buffer. For brevity, we denote events (p, i) and (c, j) as p_i and c_j, respectively.

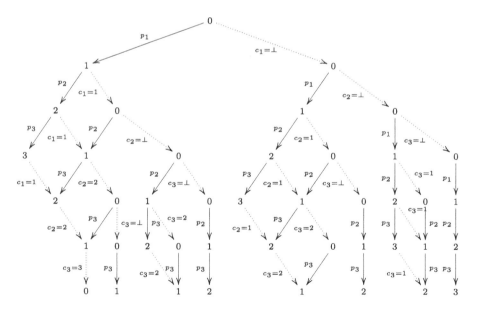

Fig. 1. All interleavings of consumers (dotted) and producers for $n = 3$ and $k = 5$.

Note that there are only $2^3 = 8$ non-equivalent execution sequences, rather than $\binom{6}{3} = 20$. The reduction given by context-sensitive independence is exponential, since each state labeled from 1 to $k-1$ has two paths leading to the same state, hence reducing the number of leaves of the resulting subtree by a factor of 2 (modulo some edge effects). Section 6.1 gives experimental results on the application of our context-sensitive method to this example.

5   Context-Sensitive DPOR

We will use the Source-DPOR algorithm [1] both to explain and to implement our method. This is because Source-DPOR is usually faster than Optimal-DPOR in practice, and its algorithm (and thus our extension) is much easier to understand. Both the original algorithm and our extension are formulated in a general setting, which only assumes the existence of a happens-before relation between the events of an execution. It can thus be used both for computational models where dependency of concurrent threads is based on modifying shared variables, and for those where dependency of asynchronous message-passing processes is based on modifying shared messages. Most examples in the paper use shared variables, as traditional in the DPOR literature, while our implementation is developed for an asynchronous message-passing language (see Sect. 6).

5.1   The Extended Algorithm

Source-DPOR can be obtained from Algorithm 1 by removing lines 11–14 and line 16, which provide our extension. Note also that we have made the sleep

---

Algorithm 1. Context-sensitive DPOR

1: **procedure** EXPLORE(E, $Sleep$)
2:     $sleep(E) := Sleep$;
3:     **if** $(\exists p \in (enabled(s_{[E]})\backslash Sleep))$ **then**
4:         $backtrack(E) := \{p\}$;
5:         **while** $(\exists p \in (backtrack(E)\backslash sleep(E)))$ **do**
6:             **for all** $(e \in dom(E)$ such that $e \precsim_{E.p} next_{[E]}(p))$ **do**
7:                 let $E' = pre(E, e)$;
8:                 let $v = notdep(e, E).p$;
9:                 **if** $(I_{[E']}(v) \cap backtrack(E') = \emptyset)$ **then**
10:                     add some q' in $I_{[E']}(v)$ to $backtrack(E')$
11:                 let $u = dep(e, E)$
12:                 **if** $(\nexists w \in sleep(E')$ where $w \leq v.u)$ **then**
13:                     **if** $(s_{[E.p]} = s_{[E'.v.u]})$ **then**
14:                         add $v.u$ to $sleep(E')$;
15:             $Sleep' := \{v \mid v \in sleep(E), E \models p \diamond v\}$
16:                     $\cup \{v \mid p.v \in sleep(E)\}$;
17:             EXPLORE($E.p$, $Sleep'$);
18:             $sleep(E) := sleep(E) \cup \{p\}$;

set for each sequence E, $sleep(E)$, global in line 2, as our modifications require the addition of new elements to previous sleep sets. Let us first describe the behaviour of the original Source-DPOR algorithm. As shown in Algorithm 1, Source-DPOR extends an execution sequence E with current sleep set $Sleep$, which contains the set of processes that previous executions have determined do not need to be explored yet from E. Initially, the algorithm starts with an empty sequence and an empty sleep set. In general, the algorithm starts by selecting any process p that is enabled by the state reached after executing E and is not already in $Sleep$. If it does not find any such process p, it stops. Otherwise, it initiates the backtrack set of E (i.e., the set of processes that must be explored from E) to be the singleton $\{p\}$, and starts exploring every element p in this set that is not in $sleep(E)$ (which is the same as $Sleep$ in the original algorithm). Note that the backtrack set of E might grow as the loop progresses (due to later executions of line 10).

For each such p, Source-DPOR performs two phases: race detection (lines 6 to 10) and state exploration (lines 15, 17 and 18). The race detection starts by finding all events e in $dom(E)$ such that $e \lesssim_{E.p} next_{[E]}(p)$. For each such e, it sets E' to $pre(E, e)$, i.e., to be the prefix of E up to, but not including e. It also sets v to $notdep(e, E).p$, where $notdep(e, E)$ is the subsequence of events of E that occur after e but do not "happen after" e (i.e., every e' such that $e <_E e'$ and $e \not\rightarrow_E e'$). It then checks whether there is any process in the backtrack set of E that appears also in $I_{[E']}(v)$, where $I_{[E']}(v)$ denotes the set of processes that perform events in $dom_{[E']}(v)$ that have no happens-before predecessors in $dom_{[E']}(v)$. If there is no such process, it adds any process in $I_{[E']}(v)$ to the backtrack set of E'. Note that this has the effect of adding new processes to the backtrack sets of earlier parts of the exploration tree (right before e was explored in E). After this, Source-DPOR continues with the state exploration phase for $E.p$, by retaining in its sleep set $Sleep'$ any element v in $sleep(E)$ that is independent of p in E (denoted as $E \models p \diamond v$), i.e., any v such that the next event $next_{[E]}(p)$ would not happen-before any event in $dom[E.p](v)$. After this, the algorithm explores $E.p$ with sleep set $Sleep'$, and finally it adds p to $Sleep$ to ensure p is not selected again.

Let us now explain the new lines added by our method. We start during the race detection phase, where event e has been detected in the original Source-DPOR to be in a reversible race with the next event $next_{[E]}(p)$. We first set u to be $dep(e, E)$, i.e., to be the sub-sequence of E that starts with e and contains all events that "happen after" e in E. We then simply need to check (line 13) whether inverting the sequences of events v and u after E' will lead to the same state and, if so, add $v.u$ to $sleep(E')$. However, none of this is needed if there is already something in $sleep(E')$ that will by itself prevent us from exploring the reversed sequence $v.u$. This is why we first check, in line 12, whether $v.u$ has a prefix w ($w \leq v.u$) in $sleep(E')$ and, if so, do nothing. The only other change occurs during the exploration phase. In the sleep set propagation step that computes $Sleep'$, any sequence $p.v$ in $sleep(E)$ that starts with the process p we are about to explore, is replaced by v in the initial sleep set of the new state. This is not needed in the original Source-DPOR, because its *Sleep* set only has processes, not sequences.

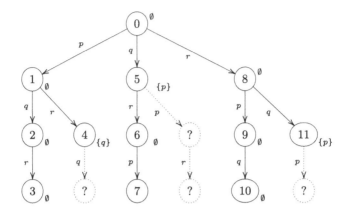

Fig. 2. Context-sensitive DPOR with initial sleep sets for each state. The dotted components would be visited by optimal-DPOR with the traditional happens-before.

Example 1. Let us follow the algorithm's execution on the example of Sect. 3 (Fig. 2) but using the traditional happens-before approximation where all p, q and r are dependent to each other. Since all processes have only one execution step, by an abuse of notation, we will refer to events by their process name. The algorithm starts with sequence ϵ and an empty sleep set, denoted as state 0 in Fig. 2. The execution first chooses p, detects no races and explores sequence p with an empty sleep set to state 1. The execution then chooses q, detects a reversible race with p, and adds q to $backtrack(\epsilon)$, i.e., state 0 in the figure. At this point our method confirms that $s_{[p.q]} = s_{[q.p]}$, and thus adds $q.p$ to $sleep(\epsilon)$, i.e., state 0, indicating there is no need to explore q from it. The execution proceeds by exploring sequence $p.q$ with an empty sleep set to state 2. Now only r can be chosen. The execution detects a reversible race with q, and adds r to $backtrack(p)$, i.e., state 1. Our method confirms that $s_{[p.q.r]} = s_{[p.r.q]}$, thus adding $r.q$ to $sleep(p)$, i.e., state 1. The execution then explores sequence $p.q.r$ to state 3 and finds the first solution, where r reads x as 5. It then backtracks to state 1, adding r to $sleep(p.q)$ and q to $sleep(p)$ on the way. Next, it chooses r, and finds a reversible race with p which adds r to $backtrack(\epsilon)$. Our method also realises $s_{[p.r]} \neq s_{[r.p]}$, which means nothing needs to be added to $sleep(\epsilon)$. The execution then explores $p.r$ to state 4 with the sleep set $sleep(p.r)$ initialized to q. Thanks to this, q cannot be selected at this point and the execution backtracks to state 0, adding r to $sleep(p)$ and p to $sleep(\epsilon)$ on the way. In the original source-DPOR algorithm q would not have been in $sleep(p.r)$, since $r.q$ would not have been in $sleep(p)$. Hence, it would have explored the full sequence $p.r.q$.

The execution then backtracks to state 0 and explores sequence q to state 5, with $sleep(q)$ initially set to $\{p\}$ (since $sleep(\epsilon)$ was $\{p, q.p\}$ at this point).

The execution can then only choose r. It finds a reversible race but does not add anything to $backtrack(\epsilon)$ since r is already there. Our method also realises $s_{[q.r]} \neq s_{[r.q]}$. It then explores $q.r$ to state 6. The execution chooses p detects a reversible race with r at state 5, and adds p to $backtrack(q)$. Since p is already in $sleep(q)$, it does not check for equivalence. The method finds an equivalent solution at state 7. In the original Source-DPOR algorithm p would not have been in $sleep(q)$, since $q.p$ would not have been in $sleep(\epsilon)$. Hence, it would have explored the full sequence $q.p.r$.

The execution now backtracks to state 0 and explores sequence r to state 8 with $sleep(r)$ initially empty. The execution then chooses p, finds a reversible race with r, but does not update anything, as the tests in lines 9 and 12 fail. The execution explores $r.p$ to state 9 with $sleep(r.p)$ initially empty. It then chooses q, finds a reversible race with p, and adds q to $backtrack(r)$. Our method then confirms $s_{[r.p.q]} = s_{[r.q.p]}$, and adds $q.p$ to $sleep(r)$. The execution then explores sequence $r.p.q$ to state 10, and finds the second solution where r reads x as 0. The execution then backtracks to state 8, adding q to $sleep(r.p)$ and p to $sleep(r)$ on the way. The execution then chooses q and finds a reversible race with r which produce no effects. It then explores $r.q$ to state 11 with $sleep(r.q)$ initially set to $\{p\}$. Since nothing can be selected, the execution terminates. In the original Source-DPOR p would not have been in $sleep(r.q)$, since $q.p$ would not have been in $sleep(r)$. Hence, it would have explored the full sequence $r.q.p$.

The execution has explored 3 complete sequences rather than the minimal 2, whereas the original Source-DPOR would have explored 6 (rather than its minimal 4). Note that while some redundant executions are not detected until their last steps, others are detected earlier, as is the case for sequence $q.p.r$.   □

The above example shows in detail how the context-sensitive DPOR algorithm works step by step, and how it can detect equivalent execution sequences. However, the example is too simple to show how the algorithm can make real reductions in the exploration. Note that the dotted derivations that the original Source-DPOR algorithm would have explored, have also been executed by our algorithm in order to do the context-sensitive checks in line 13. Hence, though the context-sensitive DPOR algorithm has obtained less solutions, it has not been able to reduce the exploration, and it has performed some recomputations. The following example illustrates how context-sensitive DPOR is able to achieve reductions while exploring execution sequences.

Example 2. Let us consider the execution of our algorithm on the producer-consumer example of Sect. 3, and let us assume it first explores the execution sequence $p_1.p_2.p_3$, shown as the leftmost sequence in Fig. 1. Up to this point no race has been detected. Now the algorithm can only select c_1 and detects a reversible race with p_3 adding c_1 to $backtrack(p_1.p_2)$. It then confirms $s_{[p_1.p_2.p_3.c_1]} = s_{[p_1.p_2.c_1.p_3]}$ and, hence, adds $c_1.p_3$ to $sleep(p_1.p_2)$. After exploring the complete leftmost branch, it backtracks to state $p_1.p_2$ and selects c_1. It then detects the race with p_2, adding c_1 to $backtrack(p_1)$. It then confirms $s_{[p_1.p_2.c_1]} = s_{[p_1.c_1.p_2]}$ and, hence, adds $c_1.p_2$ to $sleep(p_1)$. It then executes c_1, reaching state $p_1.p_2.c_1$ with p_3 in its sleep set. At this point the algorithm can only select c_2. The important point to note is that the algorithm has been able to avoid exploring the equivalent sub-sequence $p_3.c_2.c_3$ that the original DPOR algorithm would have had to explore. The reduction is made more apparent if we continue some more steps. Let us assume the algorithm has already found the second solution and backtracks to state p_1 to select c_1. After managing the race with p_1, and executing c_1, it will reach state $p_1.c_1$ with p_2 in its sleep set. Importantly, this will prevent our algorithm from exploring the whole execution tree below $p_1.c_1.p_2$. As we will see later in Sect. 6.1, our algorithm is able to obtain the minimal number of 2^n solutions for this example and, more importantly, it is able to reduce exponentially the number of states explored.   □

5.2   Soundness

Soundness relies on showing that any omitted Mazurkiewicz trace, i.e., the happens-before order of a complete execution sequence, is equivalent to an explored one in terms of the final state.

Lemma 1. *If the context-sensitive DPOR algorithm discovers that $s_{[E.p]} = s_{[E'.v.u]}$, for any complete sequence C of the form $C = E'.v.u.w$ there is a complete sequence $C' = E.p.w$ that defines a different Mazurkiewicz trace $T' =\to_{C'}$ and leads to the same final state.*

Proof. Let $C = E'.v.u.w$ be a complete execution sequence. Since $s_{[E.p]} = s_{[E'.v.u]}$, we have that $s_{[C]} = s_{[C']}$ where $C' = E.p.w$. Note that for C, $next_{[E]}(p) \to_C e$, while in C', $e \to_{C'} next_{[E]}(p)$.   □

Theorem 1. *For each Mazurkiewicz trace T defined by the happens-before relation, $\mathsf{Explore}(\epsilon, \emptyset)$ explores a complete execution sequence that either implements T, or reaches the same state as one that implements T.*

Proof. Consider an execution of $\mathsf{Explore}(\epsilon, \emptyset)$ without the additions for context-sensitivity, and assuming we always choose an enabled process that would not be sleep set blocked in the extended algorithm, wherever possible. This is exactly the source-DPOR algorithm of [1] and, hence, is guaranteed to explore a complete execution sequence that implements each T [12].

Suppose that some Mazurkiewicz trace T is omitted by our context-sensitive DPOR, C is the complete execution sequence that implements T ($T =\to_C$) and is explored by the original source-DPOR algorithm. This sequence must be cut by our algorithm. Thus, it must be of the form $C = E'.v'.u'.y$, where our algorithm added $v.u$ to $sleep(E')$ after finding $s_{[E.p]} = s_{[E'.v.u]}$, and $v'.u'$ is $v.u$ possibly with some events added that do not depend on any event in $dom_{[E']}(v.u)$, as otherwise the sleep set entry would have been removed. Hence, there exists a complete execution sequence $E'.v.u.w.y$ with the same happens-before relation as C, obtained by moving events independent of $v.u$ (those with processes in w) after $v.u$. By Lemma 1 there is a different trace T' which leads to the same state as C. Since the source-DPOR tree explores a complete execution sequence for each Mazurkiewicz trace, it must include a complete execution sequence C' that implements T'. Note that C' has the same happens before relation as $E.p.w.y$.

We now show that C' appears to the left of C in the source-DPOR tree. Sequence $E.p$ clearly appears to the left of C in the source-DPOR tree, or it could not be used to add the sleep set entry that blocked C. Suppose to the contrary that C' appears to the right of C. Let E'' be the largest common prefix of C and C'. Now $C = E''.q.w'$ for some q. Since C' appears to the right of C, then q will be in the sleep sets for (the remainder of) sequence C' unless it is removed by some dependent event. Let $e' = next_{[E'']}(q)$.

Suppose that $E''.q \leq E'$ then the first change is above E'. The happens-before relation for C' must then have some event e'' (after $E''.q$) such that $e'' \rightarrow_{C'} e'$, but this cannot be the case since $\rightarrow_{C'} = \rightarrow_{E.p.w.y}$ where this does not occur.

Suppose that $E' \leq E''$ and, thus, the first change is at or after the place where $E.p$ and $E'.v.u$ differ. Clearly C' must appear to the right of $E'.proc(e)$ (otherwise it would be left of C). Hence, $proc(e)$ is in the sleep set (for the remainder) of C' after E' until removed by dependent events. Suppose event e'' removes $proc(e)$. Then, we have that $e'' \rightarrow_{C'} e$. This is a contradiction since this does not occur in $E.p.w.y$.

Hence, C' must appear to the left of C in the source-DPOR tree. If C' exists in the tree visited by context-sensitive DPOR we are done, since we have found an equivalent complete sequence. Otherwise, we can apply the same construction to discover an equivalent complete sequence that occurs to the left in the original source-DPOR tree. The procedure must terminate since, eventually, we reach the left most branch, which cannot be removed by the context-sensitive additions to the algorithm. $\square$

5.3   Optimizations

Let us now discuss two possible optimizations that are crucial to fully exploit the algorithm's potential, as our experiments in Sect. 6.3 show.

1. Anticipating Cuts: Consider a very frequent situation, where E is an execution sequence with state s and enabled steps $p_1, p_2, q_1, \ldots, q_n$. Steps p_1 and p_2 are independent in the context of s, but considered as dependent, either because there is a context in which they are, or because of a loss of precision in the dependency over-approximation (e.g., they both increment the same variable). Steps $q_1, \ldots, q_n$ might have some dependencies among them but none is dependent with p_1 nor p_2. Let us assume our algorithm selects first p_1 and then p_2. At this point, p_2 is added to the backtrack set of E (line 10), and the sequence $p_2.p_1$ added to the sleep set of E (line 14). When the algorithm backtracks to E, the sleep set contains p_1 (due to line 18) and $p_2.p_1$. Let us assume it selects p_2. The sleep set is updated to include p_1, since line 15 removes p_1 but line 16 puts it there again. Thus, our algorithm reaches a sequence E' with enabled steps $p_1, q_1, \ldots, q_n$ and p_1 in the sleep set. If none of the steps $q_1, \ldots, q_n$ transitively generates a step that is dependent on p_1, then all execution sequences coming from this point will be sleep set blocked (since p_1 will always remain in the sleep set) and many useless computations will be performed. If we can compute a set O that over-approximates the set of steps that can arise in any future execution from the current state, and none of these depend on p, we can then block sequence E'. In general, whenever a sequence in the sleep set (added by line 14 due to a context-sensitive check) is consumed except for its last step l (by the successive executions of line 16), if no step in O is dependent on l, we block the execution at this point. Section 6 describes the analysis we implemented to compute such O for actors.

2. Guiding with Sleep Sequences: The algorithm makes three arbitrary selections: the first step to explore (line 3); the next step to backtrack with (line 5); and a step for the backtrack set (line 10). Implementations should make these selections such that the shortest sequences in the sleep set are explored first. This allows context-sensitive equivalent explorations to be discarded as soon as possible. Otherwise, potentially good sleep sequences (i.e. those that will be responsible for important exploration reductions) could be discarded.

6   Implementation and Experimental Evaluation

We have implemented and experimentally evaluated our method for actor programs within the tool SYCO [3], a systematic testing tool for ABS programs [10]. SYCO can be used online through its web interface available at http://costa.ls.fi. upm.es/syco.

6.1   Producer-Consumer with Actors

Actor programs consist of computing entities called actors, each with its own local state and thread of control, that communicate by exchanging messages asynchronously. The actor concurrency model [2,9] has been regaining popularity lately and is used in many systems such as Go, ActorFoundry, Asynchronous Agents, Charm++, E, ABS, Erlang, and Scala. It is also influencing commercial practice, with Twitter using actors for scalability and Microsoft using them in the development of its asynchronous agents library.

An actor configuration consists of the local state of the actors and a set of pending *tasks*. In response to receiving a message (or task), an actor can update its local state, send messages (tasks) to another actor or itself (using the ! function), or create new actors (using the instruction new). Actor languages often have instructions to await for an asynchronous call to terminate. The actor model is characterized by inherent concurrency of computation within and among actors (note that tasks within each actor work on a locally shared memory), dynamic creation of actors, and interaction only through direct asynchronous message passing with no restriction on message arrival order. In the computation of an actor system, there are two non-deterministic choices: selecting an actor and scheduling one of its pending tasks.

```
{ /* main Block */
  List<Data> d = D0;
  Buffer b = new Buffer();
  Producer p = new Producer(b);
  Consumer c = new Consumer(b);
  p ! produceN(d);
  c ! consumeN(size(d));
}

class Consumer(Buffer b){
  Data consumeN(Int n){
    while (n > 0){
      await b!take();
      n = n − 1;
    }
  }
}

class Producer(Buffer b){
  Unit produceN(List<Data> d){
    while (not empty(d)){
      await b!store(head(d));
      d = tail(d);
    }
  }
}
```

```
class Buffer {
  List⟨Int⟩ buffer = Nil;
  Int n = 0;
  Int max = MAX;
  Unit store(Data d){
    if (n < max){
      buffer = append(buffer, d);
      n = n + 1;
    }
  }
  Data take(){
    if (n > 0){
      Data d = head(buffer);
      buffer = tail(buffer);
      n = n − 1;
      return d;
    }
    else
      return Nil;
  }
}
```

Fig. 3. Actor-based producer-consumer program

Figure 3 shows an actor-based version of the producer-consumer program provided in Sect. 4. The execution starts from an (initially empty) actor that executes the main block, shown at the top, to create three concurrent actors representing the buffer of size MAX, the consumer and the producer. The last two receive a reference to the buffer b used for the communication. The main block then performs two asynchronous calls to add tasks on the producer and consumer to execute the corresponding methods. These tasks will in turn make asynchronous calls on the buffer to create the tasks that consume and produce data on it. The search tree that results from the execution of the main block has the same shape as the one in Fig. 1. Basically, the actor program for one producer and one consumer creates 4 tasks: consumeN, produceN, store and take. As consumeN and produceN do not modify the shared data (i.e., the buffer), they are trivially independent from all others. In contrast, store and take are detected as conflicting due to their write accesses to the buffer. As in the thread-based version, most steps lead to the same state, i.e., they are context-sensitive independent.

Table 1 experimentally compares Source-DPOR and context-sensitive DPOR (CDPOR) on the producer-consumer problem. Column *Execs* gives the number of complete executions sequences explored, *Time* the total time taken in

Table 1. Reduction gains on consumer-producer

N	Source-DPOR			CDPOR			Red. gains	
	Execs	Time	States	Execs	Time	States	Execs	Time
3	20	5	69	8	6	52	2.5x	0.9x
5	252	100	923	32	58	324	7.9x	1.8x
7	3432	1663	12869	128	357	1712	26.9x	4.7x
9	48620	30856	184755	512	2284	8428	95.0x	13.6x

milliseconds, and *States* the number of explored states obtained when executing the above example with our context-sensitive DPOR algorithm and with the original Source-DPOR algorithm, for an increasing number N of elements produced and consumed, and a buffer of size MAX $\geq N$. The last two columns show the reduction gains in *Execs* and *Time* obtained by our algorithm. Times are obtained on an Intel Core I7 at 3.4 GHz with 16 GB of RAM (Linux Kernel 4.4). Our algorithm is able to obtain the exact number (2^N) of non-equivalent executions. Furthermore, it is able to detect the equivalent sequences of executions as soon as they happen. For instance, in the example of Fig. 1, it detects that sequence $p_1.c_1.p_2$ leads to the same state as the previously explored $p_1.p_2.c_1$, and thus blocks it at this point. We therefore observe the claimed exponential reductions, not only in number of explored sequences, but also in the number of explored states and execution time.

6.2   Implementation Details

Computing the Over-Approximation for Optimization 1: Our analysis computes the over-approximation O of possibly reachable tasks from the current state s as follows: Using the flow graph of the program, we compute the set of task names reachable from the enabled tasks in s. We also compute the set of references of *alive* actors in s, which includes the references of actors with pending tasks, actors in parameters of pending tasks, and actors stored in fields. The set O of reachable tasks from s is obtained by combining each task name with each compatible alive actor.

Avoiding Recomputations: Our algorithm recomputes sub-sequences due to the context-sensitive equivalence check between the current sequence $E.p$ and the one $E'.v.u$ that reverses the race (line 13). When the algorithm later backtracks to E', it may eventually recompute the same sequence $E'.v.u$, except for the last step if the check succeeded. Our implementation avoids these recomputations as follows: In line 13, instead of checking the context sensitive equivalence of $v.u$, it adds $v.u$ together with the state $S_{[E.p]}$ to the sleep set of E'. For efficiency, in our implementation this is done right after executing event p, so that the state stored is the current one. Hence, a sequence t in the sleep set with attached state s is interpreted as "if we execute t and reach state s, then we block the sequence and add an enabled event to the backtrack set of the previous state if possible". This guarantees we do not recompute any single step due to context-sensitive checks. Note that in actor based systems the shared state between actors is typically small, therefore we never store full states, only local ones. Also, our experiments show that the peak numbers of stored local states remains quite low (see column M in Table 2). Alternatively, the check can be implemented by recording the state changes from E' to $E.p$ and comparing them against those from E' to $E'.v.u$. This would require a bounded amount of memory which can be reused for every equivalence check.

6.3 Experimental Evaluation

Table 2 shows our experimental results, which compare the performance of the original source-DPOR algorithm with three versions of our context-sensitive approach: CDPOR1 is the basic algorithm without any of the optimizations in Sect. 5.3, CDPOR2 applies the first optimization, while CDPOR3 applies both optimizations. The comparison is performed on 6 classical concurrent actor programs, borrowed from [14], each executed with 3 (size increasing) input parameters. All benchmarks can be found at the SYCO web interface. The data shown in each set of columns (*Execs*, *Time*) is computed as before. For CDPOR3 we include an additional column (M) to show the peak amount of additional memory used (measured in number of stored local states) due to the *avoiding recomputations* approach mentioned above.

The last three columns show the gains in time obtained by each version of our algorithm over the original source-DPOR algorithm. A timeout of 120 s is used and, when reached, we write $>X$ to indicate that for the corresponding measure we encountered X units up to that point. Thus, $>X$ indicates that the measure is at least X.

Table 2 shows that the less optimized implementation CDPOR1 is at least 1.3 times faster (Reg(5)) than Source-DPOR, and can be almost 3 orders of magnitude (PSort(5)) faster. The gain is much larger using the optimizations, in which case we achieve up to 4 orders of magnitude speedups. In some cases, the main reduction is achieved by the first optimization (e.g., compare G2 and G3 in PSort), while in most cases it is achieved by the second one (e.g., see Reg). The most important observation, however, is that the gain increases exponentially in all examples with the size of the input, in all three versions of our implementation. This experimentally justifies our claims about the exponential gains made in Sect. 4.

7   Conclusions

We have presented a novel technique that can be incorporated to state-of-the-art DPOR algorithms [1,7,14] to further reduce the number of redundant sequences explored. The crux of our method is the dynamic detection and use of context-sensitive independence, which allows proving independence of execution steps

Table 2. Experimental evaluation

Bench.	Source-DPOR		CDPOR1		CDPOR2		CDPOR3			Reduction gains		
	Execs	Time	Execs	Time	Execs	Time	Execs	Time	M	G1	G2	G3
Fib(5)	94	93	26	64	26	50	1	39	7	1.5x	1.9x	2.4x
Fib(6)	2148	2935	256	1407	256	683	1	39	12	2.1x	4.3x	75.3x
Fib(7)	56735	>120 s	7929	>120 s	11924	43637	1	124	20	–	>2.7x	>967.7x
QSort(9)	84	99	13	57	7	20	1	23	7	1.7x	5.0x	4.3x
QSort(12)	280	356	26	176	26	68	1	24	9	2.0x	5.2x	14.8x
QSort(15)	3166	3940	177	1132	87	249	1	40	12	3.5x	15.8x	98.5x
MSort(9)	256	259	14	84	14	32	1	18	8	3.1x	8.1x	14.4x
MSort(12)	912	1187	33	470	23	98	1	37	11	2.5x	12.1x	32.1x
MSort(15)	15872	36653	135	2051	135	374	1	51	14	17.9x	98.0x	718.7x
Pi(5)	120	83	9	26	9	17	9	15	21	3.2x	4.9x	5.5x
Pi(6)	720	556	24	51	24	60	24	43	35	10.9x	9.3x	12.9x
Pi(7)	5040	4673	74	146	74	150	74	149	53	32.0x	31.2x	31.4x
PSort(4)	288	109	8	14	2	12	2	4	13	7.8x	9.1x	27.2x
PSort(5)	34560	11921	64	128	8	15	8	15	28	93.1x	794.7x	794.7x
PSort(6)	275358	>120 s	1224	2598	72	128	72	129	53	>46.2x	>937.5x	>930.2x
Reg(4)	384	214	148	178	71	68	1	4	11	1.2x	3.1x	53.5x
Reg(5)	3840	2357	1047	1465	449	498	1	6	16	1.6x	4.7x	392.8x
Reg(6)	46080	39769	7920	13916	3145	4337	1	7	22	2.9x	9.2x	5681.3x

for the particular context encountered. As our experiments show, our method achieves exponential gains in a message-passing concurrency model. Although we have not yet evaluated it, we believe the benefits of our method for shared-memory programs with synchronized blocks of code should be similar as for message passing.

While our extension was performed on the Source-DPOR algorithm, in practice Optimal-DPOR is usually slower than Source-DPOR. Hence, we expect our context-sensitive algorithm to also be significantly faster than Optimal-DPOR.

Note that our context-sensitive extension could be applied directly to Optimal-DPOR. However, Optimal-DPOR only checks races at leaf nodes, which is unsuitable for our context sensitive check, since its too late to gain benefit. Efficiently combining them is not straightforward and it is left as future work. Further, we have shown our context-sensitive DPOR algorithm can achieve exponential gains over Source-DPOR (e.g., for the producer-consumer example).

Acknowledgments. This work was funded partially by the Spanish MINECO projects TIN2012-38137 and TIN2015-69175-C4-2-R and by the CM project S2013/ICE-3006.

References

1. Abdulla, P.A., Aronis, S., Jonsson, B., Sagonas, K.F.: Optimal dynamic partial order reduction. In: Proceedings of POPL 2014, pp. 373–384. ACM (2014)

2. Agha, G.: Actors: A Model of Concurrent Computation in Distributed Systems. MIT Press, Cambridge (1986)
3. Albert, E., Gómez-Zamalloa, M., Miguel Isabel, S.: A systematic testing tool for concurrent objects. In: Proceedings of CC 2016, pp. 269–270. ACM (2016)
4. Clarke, E.M., Grumberg, O., Minea, M., Peled, D.A.: State space reduction using partial order techniques. STTT **2**(3), 279–287 (1999)
5. Flanagan, C., Godefroid, P.: Dynamic partial-order reduction for model checking software. In: Proceedings of POPL 2005, pp. 110–121. ACM (2005)
6. Godefroid, P.: Using partial orders to improve automatic verification methods. In: Clarke, E.M., Kurshan, R.P. (eds.) CAV 1990. LNCS, vol. 531, pp. 176–185. Springer, Heidelberg (1991). doi:10.1007/BFb0023731
7. Godefroid, P.: Partial-Order Methods for the Verification of Concurrent Systems - An Approach to the State-Explosion Problem. LNCS, vol. 1032. Springer, Heidelberg (1996)
8. Godefroid, P., Pirottin, D.: Refining dependencies improves partial-order verification methods (extended abstract). In: Courcoubetis, C. (ed.) CAV 1993. LNCS, vol. 697, pp. 438–449. Springer, Heidelberg (1993). doi:10.1007/3-540-56922-7_36
9. Haller, P., Odersky, M.: Scala actors: unifying thread-based and event-based programming. Theoret. Comput. Sci. **410**(2–3), 202–220 (2009)
10. Johnsen, E.B., Hähnle, R., Schäfer, J., Schlatte, R., Steffen, M.: ABS: a core language for abstract behavioral specification. In: Aichernig, B.K., Boer, F.S., Bonsangue, M.M. (eds.) FMCO 2010. LNCS, vol. 6957, pp. 142–164. Springer, Heidelberg (2011). doi:10.1007/978-3-642-25271-6_8
11. Katz, S., Peled, D.A.: Defining conditional independence using collapses. Theoret. Comput. Sci. **101**(2), 337–359 (1992)
12. Mazurkiewicz, A.: Trace theory. In: Brauer, W., Reisig, W., Rozenberg, G. (eds.) ACPN 1986. LNCS, vol. 255, pp. 278–324. Springer, Heidelberg (1987). doi:10.1007/3-540-17906-2_30
13. Nielson, F., Nielson, F., Nielson, H.R., Hankin, C.: Principles of Program Analysis. Springer, Heidelberg (1999). doi:10.1007/978-3-662-03811-6
14. Tasharofi, S., Karmani, R.K., Lauterburg, S., Legay, A., Marinov, D., Agha, G.: TransDPOR: a novel dynamic partial-order reduction technique for testing actor programs. In: Giese, H., Rosu, G. (eds.) FMOODS/FORTE -2012. LNCS, vol. 7273, pp. 219–234. Springer, Heidelberg (2012). doi:10.1007/978-3-642-30793-5_14
15. Valmari, A.: On-the-fly verification with stubborn sets. In: Courcoubetis, C. (ed.) CAV 1993. LNCS, vol. 697, pp. 397–408. Springer, Heidelberg (1993). doi:10.1007/3-540-56922-7_33

Starling: Lightweight Concurrency Verification with Views

Matt Windsor[1]([⊠]), Mike Dodds[1]([⊠]),
Ben Simner[1], and Matthew J. Parkinson[2]

[1] University of York, York, UK
{mbw500,mike.dodds,bs829}@york.ac.uk
[2] Microsoft Research, Cambridge, UK
mattpark@microsoft.com

Abstract. Modern program logics have made it feasible to verify the most complex concurrent algorithms. However, many such logics are complex, and most lack automated tool support. We propose *Starling*, a new lightweight logic and automated tool for concurrency verification. Starling takes a proof outline written in an abstracted Hoare-logic style, and converts it into proof terms that can be discharged by a sequential solver. Starling's approach is generic in its structure, making it easy to target different solvers. In this paper we verify shared-variable algorithms using the Z3 SMT solver, and heap-based algorithms using the GRASShopper solver. We have applied our approach to a range of concurrent algorithms, including Rust's atomic reference counter, the Linux ticketed lock, the CLH queue-lock, and a fine-grained list algorithm.

1 Introduction

Shared-memory concurrent algorithms are critical components of many systems, for example as locks, reference counters, work-queues, and garbage collectors [12]. These algorithms must achieve high performance, while also enforcing properties such as mutual exclusion and safe memory reclamation. In pursuit of performance, modern algorithms have become increasingly complex. As a result, by-hand correctness arguments are unreliable, and formal verification remains very challenging.

Concurrent algorithms often depend on intangible concepts such as thread-local *ownership* of resources, and *protocols* between threads. For example, a thread that acquires a lock takes ownership of the guarded resource, and the mutual exclusion protocol forbids other threads from accessing the lock at the same time. Beginning with Concurrent Separation Logic (CSL) [18], program logics have integrated these concepts directly in reasoning, which has enabled the verification of many challenging algorithms (see Sect. 7, Related Work).

However, these logics derived from CSL are very complex, with auxiliary proof constructs such as fractional permissions, shared regions, and labelled transition systems. Complexity makes these logics difficult to learn and difficult to reason with, and non-standard proof constructs make tooling hard to develop, and therefore rare. As a result, there are substantial barriers to applying these logics in practice.

© Springer International Publishing AG 2017
R. Majumdar and V. Kunčak (Eds.): CAV 2017, Part I, LNCS 10426, pp. 544–569, 2017.
DOI: 10.1007/978-3-319-63387-9_27

We present *Starling*, a new program logic and verification tool for concurrent algorithms. Our approach is inspired by CSL and its relatives, but we dispense with heavyweight auxiliary proof concepts. Starling's proofs are lightweight, easy to read, and easy to automate – but powerful enough to verify challenging concurrent algorithms.

Starling's approach is based on *views* – units of linear, invariant information that can be held by a single thread. Proofs in Starling are written in a lightweight proof-outline style, with views annotating program points and *constraints* defining their meaning in the underlying domain. Notions such as ownership and protocol can be expressed through interactions between views. For example, we can have a view expressing that the thread holds a lock, then express mutual exclusion by forbidding two threads from holding this view at the same time.

Starling's reasoning is built on the pre-existing *Views framework* [6]: this was designed as an off-the-shelf metatheory for encoding other logics, but we instead instantiate it directly as a simple view-based logic. The Views framework works by reducing a concurrent proof to multiple applications of a single core proof rule. We use this to reduce a Starling proof to a collection of verification conditions that can be discharged using a sequential solver. Building on the Views framework means that Starling requires minimal extra metatheory and can easily be automated.

Our approach is agnostic to the underlying data domain: we require only an appropriate sequential solver. In this paper, we instantiate our approach with two domains. First, for algorithms that use shared variables and linear arithmetic, we generate SMT queries, which are discharged using Z3 [5]. For algorithms that use dynamic linked data-structures, we generate queries written in separation logic, which we discharge using GRASShopper [20]. In both cases, our approach lets us map uniformly from concurrent reasoning into sequential verification conditions.

We have tested Starling on a collection of real-world concurrent algorithms. Many of these are synchronisation algorithms, one of the most important class of concurrent algorithm. Our running example is Rust's Atomic Reference-Count algorithm, which prevents reuse of an object after it has been freed. We also verify several different lock algorithms including the CLH queue-lock algorithm, Peterson's algorithm, and a fine-grained list algorithm. As is often the case in concurrency, these algorithms are small in size but exhibit killer subtleties that make verification very challenging. Other approaches would require considerably more proof annotations, or customised auxiliary proof constructs. We show that these algorithms can be verified using a lightweight, automated approach.

Our tool is open source (MIT license) and available on GitHub:

https://github.com/septract/starling-tool

2   Motivating Example: ARC

The Atomic Reference-Count (ARC) algorithm is used to ensure that a shared object is not disposed before all threads are finished with it. In Rust, the ARC forms an important part of the concurrency model [23]. Our version of the ARC has three operations:

clone: Clone the ARC reference and increment the counter.
access: Fetch or modify the object stored in the ARC.
drop: Destroy an ARC reference by decrementing the counter. If the count is
             0, dispose the shared object.

2.1   Specification

To specify the ARC using our approach, we first declare the *view atom* arc(). A view atom is a unit of linear, invariant information that can be held by a thread. The atom arc() states the thread holds a single reference to the ARC object. We do not specify the meaning of arc() in the program state yet (in this way view atoms resemble the *abstract predicates* of Dinsdale-Young et al [8]).

View atoms can be conjoined into unboundedly large *views* using the composition operator, $*$. This operator is linear, not standard conjunction: for example the view arc() $*$ arc() $*$ arc() asserts that the thread holds three separate references to the ARC object. A thread could also hold zero references to the ARC, represented by the special unit view emp. The $*$ operator is generalised from separating conjunction in separation logic, but views need not have disjoint heap representations.

Using arc() and emp, we give the ARC operations Hoare-style specifications:

$$\{\mathsf{arc}()\}\quad \mathtt{clone}()\quad \{\mathsf{arc}() * \mathsf{arc}()\}$$
$$\{\mathsf{arc}()\}\quad \mathtt{access}()\quad \{\mathsf{arc}()\}$$
$$\{\mathsf{arc}()\}\quad \mathtt{drop}()\quad \{\mathsf{emp}\}$$

The clone method creates a new reference, represented by a duplicate arc() atom in its postcondition. The access method requires an ARC reference to ensure the object has not been disposed: the arc() atom in its precondition represents this. The drop method takes an ARC reference, represented by an arc() atom, and destroys it leaving emp.

In our tool, specifications are implicitly *framed* with arbitrary views. The frame represents other views held locally or by other threads. For example, the thread might hold three ARC references, and then call drop():

$$\{\mathsf{arc}() * \mathsf{arc}() * \mathsf{arc}()\}\quad \mathtt{drop}()\quad \{\mathsf{arc}() * \mathsf{arc}()\}$$

As can be seen, the frame arc() $*$ arc() is unaffected by calling drop(). Likewise, if some other thread held arc() $*$ arc() it would be unaffected by the call.

Framing means that every view must continue to hold irrespective of the behaviour of other threads. However, arc() atoms are not independent in their underlying representation, nor between each other. In their representation, all the arc() views refer to the same shared variables. Also, the reference count must not be smaller than the *total* number of arc() atoms across all threads – otherwise a thread could access the object after it has been disposed. Reasoning about this combination of thread-local views and inter-thread interaction is the core problem that our approach solves.

```
1  // View atom declarations
2  view iter arc();
3  view countCopy(int c);
4
5  // Create a new reference to the ARC
6  method clone() {
7    {| arc() |}
8      <| count++; |>
9    {| arc() * arc() |}
10 }
11
12 // Remove an ARC reference and dispose if possible
13 method drop() {
14   {| arc() |}
15     <| c = count--; |>
16   {| countCopy(c) |}
17     if (c == 1) {
18       {| countCopy(1) |}
19         <| free = true; |>
20       {| emp |}
21     }
22   {| emp |}
23 }
24
25 // Access the ARC contents - Model with a test of free
26 method access() {
27   {| arc() |}
28     <| f = free; |>
29   {| if (f) { false } else { arc() } |}
30     if (f) {
31       {| false |}
32         <| error; |>  // Models a bad dereference.
33       {| false |}
34     }
35   {| arc() |}
36 }
37
38 // Constraints on countCopy()
39 constraint countCopy(c)                     ->  c == 1 => (!free && count == 0);
40 constraint countCopy(m) * countCopy(n)  ->  (m != 1) || (n != 1);
41
42 // Iterated constraint on arc()
43 constraint iter[n] arc()  ->  n > 0 => (!free && n <= count);
```

Fig. 1. Shared-variable version of ARC, and proof.

2.2   Proof

Figure 1 shows an ARC implementation, and a proof that it satisfies our specification. (Here, and elsewhere, we elide some details such as variable declarations.)

In this implementation we model a single ARC instance by shared variables. The integer variable `count` holds the reference count, while disposal is modelled by the boolean variable `free`. This simplification to variables means we can discharge the proof using an SMT solver. Below, we verify a heap-allocated ARC using the GRASShopper separation-logic solver.

Our programming language is a standard while-language, with atomic commands written with angle-brackets, `<| |>`. The proof itself consists of Hoare-style assertions, written in views, that are interleaved into the program. These assertions are written using assertion brackets `{| |}` As well as plain views, views can hold conditional on local variables: for example, in Fig. 1 we write `{| if (f) { false } else { arc() } |}`. The complete syntax for Starling's input language is given in Appendix A.

In addition to the `arc()` atom discussed above, the proof uses the additional atom `countCopy(c)`, which represents the fact that c was previously observed as the value of `count`. (It does not mean that `count` is currently c, as `count` can change through the action of other threads).

The meaning of the views in the underlying program state is given by *constraints*. There are unboundedly many possible composite views, but we need only give meanings for a minimal set of *defining* views – meanings for others are derived from these. Section 3 explains how this derivation works.

In Fig. 1, the meaning of a single `countCopy(c)` atom is given by the following constraint:

```
constraint countCopy(c)  ->  c == 1 => (!free && count == 0);
```

Once a thread observes `count` as 1 in a fetch-and-decrement, the ARC cannot be disposed by any other thread, and the value of `count` will always be zero. This depends on `count` accurately recording the number of references to the ARC: once `count` is 1, the only thread with access is the current one.

Constraints can also specify interactions between views. Interactions can be between views on the same or multiple different threads – we make no distinction between the two. In Fig. 1, two `countCopy(c)` atoms have the following meaning:

```
constraint countCopy(m) * countCopy(n)  ->  (m != 1) || (n != 1);
```

If two threads take copies of `count`, only one of them can equal 1: again, this depends on the counter accurately recording the number of references.

The final important properties represented in the proof are, first, that the ARC is not disposed until all references are removed; and, second, that `count` accurately records the number of references. Each `arc()` atom represents a reference, so we need the following:

$$\overbrace{\mathsf{arc()} * \mathsf{arc()} * \cdots * \mathsf{arc()}}^{n > 0 \ atoms} \implies \neg disposed \wedge n \leq ref\text{-}count.$$

In the proof, this is expressed directly by the following constraint on views:

```
constraint iter[n] arc()  -> n > 0 => (!free && n <= count);
```

The `iter[n]` keyword indicates that we have `n` instances of the `arc()` atom on the same thread or across different threads.

2.3 Heap-Allocated ARC

The implementation in Fig. 1 modelled a single ARC by shared variables – as a result, we can discharge this proof using an SMT back-end. In Fig. 2, we give a more realistic implementation where ARCs are heap-allocated structs. To discharge this proof, we use GRASShopper, a solver for separation logic [20].

The most important implementation change is a new method `init` which allocates a new ARC. This method has the following specification:

$$\{\mathsf{emp}\}\ \ \mathsf{init()}\ \ \{\mathsf{arc}(ret)\}$$

A further difference is that heap commands are written in GRASShopper's input language. We embed these using the special brackets %{ }, and allow variables to be referenced using the inner brackets [| |]. For example, in `clone`, we write the following for an atomic increment:

```
<| %{[|x|].count := [|x|].count + 1}; |>
```

By combining heap commands we can build complex atomic operations – for example an atomic fetch-and-decrement operation, as used in `drop`:

```
<| c = %{ [|x|].count };  %{ [|x|].count := [|x|].count - 1 }; |>
```

Despite the fact that this implementation targets a much richer domain than shared variables, we can apply the same proof strategy as Fig. 1. The same views are needed, though they are now parameterised by the address of the ARC. Likewise, the same constraints are needed, modified to use GRASShopper's constraint language. As with commands, we embed GRASShopper assertions using the special brackets %{ }. For example, this is the constraint on a single countCopy(x, c) atom:

```
constraint countCopy(x, c) ->
    c == 1 => %{ [|x|] in ArcFoot && [|x|].count == 0};
```

Here, $[|x|]$ in ArcFoot requires that `x` is in the set of allocated ARCs – this corresponds to the requirement that `free` is false in Fig. 1. Likewise, $[|x|]$.count $== 0$ corresponds to the constraint on the value of `count`.

With both the variable-based and heap-based versions of the ARC, our approach gives a simple proof that captures the algorithm's linear nature. Our approach lets us convert these lightweight proofs into verification conditions that can be discharged by either SMT or GRASShopper as appropriate. We next explain how this translation works.

```
 1 struct ArcNode {
 2   var count: Int;
 3   var val: Int;
 4 }
 5
 6 view iter arc(ArcNode x);
 7 view countCopy(ArcNode x, Int c);
 8
 9 method init() {
10   {| emp |}
11     <| ret = %{new ArcNode};
12        %{ [|ret|].count := 1 }; |>
13   {| arc(ret) |}
14 }
15
16 method clone(ArcNode x) {
17   {| arc(x) |}
18     <| %{ [|x|].count := [|x|].count + 1 }; |> // Atomic increment
19   {| arc(x) * arc(x) |}
20 }
21
22 method drop(ArcNode x) {
23   {| arc(x) |}
24     <| c = %{ [|x|].count };  // Atomic fetch-and-decrement
25        %{ [|x|].count := [|x|].count - 1 }; |>
26   {| countCopy(x, c) |}
27     if (c == 1) {
28       {| countCopy(x, 1) |}
29         <| %{ free([|x|]) }; |>
30       {| emp |}
31     }
32   {| emp |}
33 }
34
35 method access(ArcNode x) {
36   {| arc(x) |}
37     <| pval = %{ [|x|].val }; |>
38   {| arc(x) |}
39 }
40
41 constraint countCopy(x, c) ->
42     c == 1 => %{ [|x|] in ArcFoot && [|x|].count == 0 };
43 constraint countCopy(x, m) * countCopy(y, n) ->
44     x == y => ((m != 1) || (n != 1));
45
46 constraint iter[n] arc(x) ->
47     n > 0 => %{ [|x|] in ArcFoot && [|n|] <= [|x|].count };
```

Fig. 2. Heap-allocated version of ARC, and proof.

3   Theory

Starling's theory works by recasting the pre-existing Views framework [6] into a form suitable for automation. As the Views framework has been proved sound in Coq, this gives us a simple way of justifying the soundness of our translation into a set of verification conditions.

3.1   Owicki-Gries

For comparison, we first consider the Owicki-Gries method [19], one of the simplest approaches to Hoare-style verification of a concurrent program. Owicki-Gries presents us with a single core rule for validating a proof outline.[1] Let Axioms be the set of atomic Hoare triples of the proof; Formula the set of all formulas used in the outline; and $\models_{\text{Hoare}}$ the entailment rule for Hoare logic. Then, the Owicki-Gries proof rule is written as:

$$\forall \{P\} c \{Q\} \in \text{Axioms. } \forall F \in \text{Formula. } \models_{\text{Hoare}} \{P \wedge F\} c \{Q \wedge F\}$$

This rule expresses two key correctness properties for a concurrent system. First, each command behaves correctly in a sequential setting – the post-state Q is established from the pre-state P. Second, no command interferes with any properties needed by other threads – the frame F is preserved by c.

To achieve completeness, Owicki-Gries needs *auxiliary variables*: additional variables that capture key aspects of the local state of each thread. To encode Starling into Owicki-Gries, we would need to use auxiliary variables to encode the more rich interactions our constraint system permits. However, these variables can hide the details of the verification and make proof discovery harder. We need a different approach.

3.2   Views

We eliminate the need for auxiliary variables, while keeping much of the shape and simplicity of Owicki-Gries, by building on the Views framework [6]. Views was originally an off-the-shelf metatheory for proving the soundness of concurrent reasoning systems; we recast it as an Owicki-Gries-style proof rule. In this paper, we introduce just enough of the Views framework to support Starling's theory – this fits with the framework's purpose as reusable metatheory.

The Views framework is designed to allow a broad range of reasoning systems to be encoded into a small set of parameters. If these parameters satisfy a few key properties, the encoded reasoning system is sound.

The parameters that must be instantiated include the sets Views, from which all assertions in the logic are derived; Cmds, containing atomic commands; and Axioms, containing the atomic Hoare triples over views and commands. The reasoning system must also define a view composition operator $*$ and unit view

---

[1] We simplify Owicki-Gries to a setting where all threads execute the same code.

emp, which together must form a monoid with Views; a reification function $\lfloor \_ \rfloor$ mapping Views to their representation in the underlying state; and a semantic function $\llbracket \_ \rrbracket$ mapping atomic commands to state transformers.

Taken together, these parameters must satisfy the key property of *axiom soundness*:

$$\forall \{P\} \, c \, \{Q\} \in \mathsf{Axioms}. \ \forall V \in \mathsf{Views}. \ \llbracket c \rrbracket \lfloor P * V \rfloor \subseteq \lfloor Q * V \rfloor \tag{1}$$

This rule requires that every atomic Hoare triple generated by the reasoning system upholds sequential correctness, and inter-thread non-interference, just as we saw in Owicki-Gries. As the Views approach makes no distinction between contexts that on the same thread or other threads, it captures both Concurrent Separation Logic's FRAME and PARALLEL rules:

$$\frac{\{P\} \, C \, \{Q\}}{\{P * F\} \, C \, \{Q * F\}} \ \text{FRAME} \qquad \frac{\{P_1\} \, C_1 \, \{Q_1\} \qquad \{P_2\} \, C_2 \, \{Q_2\}}{\{P_1 * P_2\} \, C_1 \parallel C_2 \, \{Q_1 * Q_2\}} \ \text{PARALLEL}$$

In Starling, we recast Rule (1) to generate verification conditions from proofs. In comparison to Owicki-Gries, the Views proof rule allows us to avoid auxiliary variables in most cases. In Owicki-Gries, assertions and contexts are joined by conjunction, but in the Views rule they are joined by view composition, $*$, and their reification is defined separately. This means that we can define interactions between views that go beyond their individual reifications – for example to enforce mutual exclusion between views. This gives our proof system its power.

3.3 Instantiating the Views Rule

We first instantiate the Views framework parameters in a way that is suitable for Starling's reasoning. For Starling, *view atoms* consist of a name and a sequence of value arguments, and views are multisets of view atoms. More formally, we define Views as:

$$\mathsf{ViewAtoms} \triangleq \mathsf{String} \times seq \ \mathsf{Value}$$
$$\mathsf{Views} \triangleq multiset \ \mathsf{ViewAtoms}$$

(Below we sometimes call these *plain views* to distinguish them from constructs such as view patterns.)

Starling Views form a monoid with the multiset union $\cup_m$ as the view composition $*$, and the empty multiset $\emptyset$ as the unit view emp.

We first change Rule (1) by making the state accessed by a command explicit. We model the state as a pair (l, s) of thread-local and shared components. The command semantics $\llbracket c \rrbracket$ is then a relation over these states. We write $\lfloor P \rfloor(s)$ to say that state s is in the representation of P, and (for now) ignore the local state. The resulting rule is:

$$\forall \{P\} \, c \, \{Q\} \in \mathsf{Axioms}.$$
$$\forall ((l, s), (l', s')) \in \llbracket c \rrbracket. \forall V \in \mathsf{Views}. \ \lfloor P * V \rfloor(s) \Rightarrow \lfloor Q * V \rfloor(s') \tag{2}$$

For example, in Fig. 1, of the atomic triples in Axioms is:

$$\{\mathsf{arc}()\} \quad \mathsf{<|\,count++;\,|>} \quad \{\mathsf{arc}() * \mathsf{arc}()\}$$

Rule (2) yields a proof term with the following shape for each combination of this triple and frame V:

$$\forall((l, s), (l', s')) \in [\![\mathsf{count++}]\!].\forall V \in \mathsf{Views}.\ \lfloor \mathsf{arc}() * V \rfloor(s) \Rightarrow \lfloor \mathsf{arc}() * \mathsf{arc}() * V \rfloor(s')$$

3.4 Integrating Local State

Rule (2) is not sufficient for the ARC proof in Fig. 1. First, the view atom $\mathsf{countCopy(c)}$ refers to a local variable c, not a value. Second, the view $\mathsf{arc}()$ is defined using the iterator variable n. Finally, we need the ability to choose whether atoms appear in a view based on local conditions to encode assertions such as $\{|\ \mathsf{if}\ (f)\ \{\ \mathsf{false}\ \}\ \mathsf{else}\ \{\ \mathsf{arc}()\ \}\ |\}$.

To incorporate these local-state properties into the rule, we introduce syntactic *view expressions*, with the following syntax:

$$P ::= \mathsf{emp} \mid (B \to a[n](\overline{e})) * P$$

View expressions are used to encode Starling's assertion syntax. Each view expression P is a $*$-composition of *atom expressions*. These have a name a, a list $\overline{e}$ of integer or boolean argument expressions, an integer iterator expression n, and a boolean guard expression B. The argument, iterator, and guard expressions are all interpreted in the local state.

To map a view expression to a view, we must interpret its local-state expressions. Given a local state l and expression X, we write $l(X)$ for the value of X in l. Using this, we define a function $[\![-]\!]_l$ which maps from view expressions into views:[2]

$$[\![\mathsf{emp}]\!]_l \triangleq \emptyset$$

$$[\ * P]\!]_l \triangleq [\![P]\!]_l \cup_\mathsf{m} \begin{cases} \{a(l(\overline{e})) \mapsto l(n)\} & \text{if } l(B) \\ \emptyset & \text{otherwise} \end{cases}$$

Here, the empty view expression maps to an empty multiset, i.e. the unit plain view. Other view expressions map to the appropriate view atoms, dictated by the values of the local-state expressions. The argument expressions dictate the values of the view atom's arguments. The guard expression controls whether any view atoms are created, and the iterator expression dictates the number of instances of the view atom.

---

[2] Note that we have a composition operator $*$ and unit emp in both view expressions and plain views. This definition links the two levels: to avoid confusion here, for plain views we use their semantic definitions $\cup_\mathsf{m}$ and $\emptyset$.

To integrate this into our core proof rule, we amend Axioms so that pre- and post-conditions are view expressions, not plain views. This means that they must be interpreted by the semantic function $[\![-]\!]_l$. Our modified rule is as follows:

$$\begin{array}{c} \forall\,\{P\}\,c\,\{Q\} \in \textsf{Axioms.} \\ \forall((l,s),(l',s')) \in [\![c]\!].\forall V \in \textsf{Views.}\ \lfloor[\![P]\!]_l * V\rfloor(s) \Rightarrow \lfloor[\![Q]\!]_{l'} * V\rfloor(s') \end{array} \qquad (3)$$

3.5   Context Reduction

The quantification $\forall V$ over context views means that Rule (3) cannot be used directly for automated verification. As two smaller views can be composed into a larger one, there are arbitrarily many possible values of V, and by default we must consider them all.

Other logics allow a degree of context reduction here. For example, in Owicki-Gries, if two threads separately assert F_1 and F_2, and each is preserved, we need not consider the context $F_1 \wedge F_2$. This means we can validate our proof outline for an unbounded number of threads by considering a finite set of entailments.

We cannot use this simple context reduction, because in Views any context may contribute information not represented in its sub-views. This generality is desirable – it is what gives our proof system its power. We can preserve it while gaining context reduction by defining reification in a particular way.

Defining Function. The first restriction on reification is we only consider functions where the reification of a composite view implies the conjunction of its sub-view reifications. In other words, view composition cannot lose information, which lets us avoid considering sub-views of composite views. More formally, we require that for all views, $\lfloor P * Q\rfloor \Rightarrow \lfloor P\rfloor \wedge \lfloor Q\rfloor$.

The second restriction is that we bound the set of views that can contribute information to the reification. Intuitively, this means that we only need to consider these *defining* sub-views in our proof rule. To enforce this, we require that the reification function is derived from a syntactic *defining function*.

In a Starling proof, the defining function is given precisely by the constraints. For example, in Fig. 1 we have:

```
constraint  countCopy(m) * countCopy(n)  ->  (m != 1) || (n != 1);
```

On the left we have a *view pattern* `countCopy(m) * countCopy(n)`, while on the right we have a formula giving the meaning for this pattern.

View patterns allow a definition to match many different views with similar shapes. A view pattern r has the syntax:

$$r ::= \ \textsf{emp} \ | \ a[n](\overline{x}) * r$$

A pattern is either `emp`, or a $*$-composition of *pattern atoms*. Each atom has a name a, variable arguments $\overline{x}$ which bind to the arguments of a view atom, and an iterator variable n which records the number of view atoms matched.

A *definition* is then a tuple $(\overline{y}, r, p)$ where, r is a view pattern, p is a formula of the underlying theory, and $\overline{y}$ is a set of free variables used in the definition. In the example constraint above, $\overline{y}$ is the set of variables $\{m, n\}$, the pattern r is $\mathsf{countCopy}[1](m) * \mathsf{countCopy}[1](n)$, and the formula p is $(m \neq 1) \vee (n \neq 1)$.

A defining function D is then a finite set of definitions (derived from the constraints in the proof). Using such a D, we can then induce a reification function where only definitions contribute information. The reification of a view-expression V, for a shared state s, is the conjunction of all the definitions that match some sub-view of V.

$$\lfloor V \rfloor (s) \triangleq \bigwedge_{(\overline{y}, r, p) \in D} \hat{\forall} \overline{y}.\ r \subseteq_{\mathsf{m}} V \implies p(s)$$

We write $r \subseteq_{\mathsf{m}} V$ (using multiset subset) to indicate that r is a sub-view of V, meaning there is a pattern match.

A pattern may be matched under any instantiations of its free variables $\overline{y}$. We express this using the special quantification $\hat{\forall} \overline{y}$. Given a formula X that includes r and p, $\hat{\forall} \overline{y}.X$ is shorthand for quantifying over all possible assignments to $\overline{y}$, and substituting in r and p. This has the effect of converting r into a plain view. Many theories, such as SMT, can natively handle the $\hat{\forall} \overline{y}$ construction without further expansion.

$\forall V \in \mathsf{Views}.\ \lfloor [\![P]\!]_l \cup_{\mathsf{m}} V \rfloor (s) \Rightarrow \lfloor [\![Q]\!]_{l'} \cup_{\mathsf{m}} V \rfloor (s')$
    [Definition of reification]
$\impliedby \forall V \in \mathsf{Views}.\ \lfloor [\![P]\!]_l \cup_{\mathsf{m}} V \rfloor (s) \Rightarrow \forall (\overline{y}, r, p) \in D.\ \hat{\forall} \overline{y}.\ (r \subseteq_{\mathsf{m}} ([\![Q]\!]_{l'} \cup_{\mathsf{m}} V) \Rightarrow p(s'))$
    [Lift out quantifiers]
$\impliedby \forall V \in \mathsf{Views}.\ \forall (\overline{y}, r, p) \in D.\ \hat{\forall} \overline{y}.\ \lfloor [\![P]\!]_l \cup_{\mathsf{m}} V \rfloor (s) \Rightarrow (r \subseteq_{\mathsf{m}} ([\![Q]\!]_{l'} \cup_{\mathsf{m}} V) \Rightarrow p(s'))$
    [View adjoint lemma]
$\impliedby \forall V \in \mathsf{Views}.\ \forall (\overline{y}, r, p) \in D.\ \hat{\forall} \overline{y}.\ \lfloor [\![P]\!]_l \cup_{\mathsf{m}} V \rfloor (s) \Rightarrow ((r \setminus_{\mathsf{m}} [\![Q]\!]_{l'}) \subseteq_{\mathsf{m}} V \Rightarrow p(s'))$
    [Move subset condition]
$\impliedby \forall V \in \mathsf{Views}.\ \forall (\overline{y}, r, p) \in D.\ \hat{\forall} \overline{y}.\ (r \setminus_{\mathsf{m}} [\![Q]\!]_{l'}) \subseteq_{\mathsf{m}} V \Rightarrow (\lfloor [\![P]\!]_l \cup_{\mathsf{m}} V \rfloor (s) \Rightarrow p(s'))$
    [Multiset subset is preserved under union]
$\impliedby \forall V \in \mathsf{Views}.\ \forall (\overline{y}, r, p) \in D.\ \hat{\forall} \overline{y}.$
    $(([\![P]\!]_l \cup_{\mathsf{m}} (r \setminus_{\mathsf{m}} [\![Q]\!]_{l'})) \subseteq_{\mathsf{m}} ([\![P]\!]_l \cup_{\mathsf{m}} V)) \Rightarrow (\lfloor [\![P]\!]_l \cup_{\mathsf{m}} V \rfloor (s) \Rightarrow p(s'))$
    [Reification monotone]
$\impliedby \forall V \in \mathsf{Views}.\ \forall (\overline{y}, r, p) \in D.\ \hat{\forall} \overline{y}.$
    $(([\![P]\!]_l \cup_{\mathsf{m}} (r \setminus_{\mathsf{m}} [\![Q]\!]_{l'})) \subseteq_{\mathsf{m}} ([\![P]\!]_l \cup_{\mathsf{m}} V)) \Rightarrow (\lfloor [\![P]\!]_l \cup_{\mathsf{m}} (r \setminus_{\mathsf{m}} [\![Q]\!]_{l'}) \rfloor (s) \Rightarrow p(s'))$
    [Remove V]
$\impliedby \forall (\overline{y}, r, p) \in D.\ \hat{\forall} \overline{y}.\ \lfloor [\![P]\!]_l \cup_{\mathsf{m}} (r \setminus_{\mathsf{m}} [\![Q]\!]_{l'}) \rfloor (s) \Rightarrow p(s')$

Fig. 3. Derivation of Rule (4), with outer quantifiers elided.

Rule Context Reduction. Using this definition, we can modify Rule (3) to reduce the contexts we consider to just those in the defining function.

First we introduce two lemmas. The first lemma (*reification monotone*) states that the reifications of larger views are more restrictive than those of smaller views. This justifies us considering only defining views in the premise of the proof rule, because any larger context will be more restrictive.

Lemma 1. (Reification monotone). $V_1 \subseteq_m V_2 \implies (\forall s. \lfloor V_2 \rfloor (s) \Rightarrow \lfloor V_1 \rfloor (s))$

The second lemma (*view adjoint*) defines the relationship between multiset union $\cup_m$, multiset subset $\subseteq_m$, and multiset minus $\backslash_m$. We use $\backslash_m$ in our new rule to construct a 'weakest context', analogous to a weakest precondition.

Lemma 2. (View adjoint). $(V_1 \backslash_m V_2) \subseteq_m V_3 \implies V_1 \subseteq_m (V_2 \cup_m V_3)$

Now we take Rule (3) and (eliding the two outer quantifiers) rewrite it as shown in Fig. 3. This at last gives us Starling's core proof rule:

$$\begin{aligned} \forall \{P\} \, c \, \{Q\} \in \mathsf{Axioms}. \forall ((l, s), (l', s')) \in \llbracket c \rrbracket. \\ \forall (\overline{y}, r, p) \in D. \hat{\forall} \overline{y}. \, \lfloor \llbracket P \rrbracket_l \cup_m (r \backslash_m \llbracket Q \rrbracket_{l'}) \rfloor (s) \Rightarrow p(s') \end{aligned} \tag{4}$$

This is the rule that we use to generate verification conditions from Starling input proofs such as Fig. 1. The atomic steps of the program form the set Axioms; the built-in semantics of commands specify $\llbracket c \rrbracket$; and the constraints specify the defining function D and the reification $\lfloor - \rfloor$. The significant advantage of this rule is that, rather than quantify over an infinite set of context views, it quantifies only over finite sets, and therefore generates a finite set of proof terms.

Consider the arc() proof term we examined in Sect. 3.3. If rather than using Rule (2), we apply our new rule, we get the following outcome:

$$\begin{aligned} \forall ((l, s), (l', s')) \in \llbracket \mathsf{count}{+}{+} \rrbracket. \\ \forall (\overline{y}, r, p) \in D. \hat{\forall} \overline{y}. \lfloor \llbracket \mathsf{arc}() \rrbracket_l \cup_m (r \backslash_m \llbracket \mathsf{arc}() * \mathsf{arc}() \rrbracket_{l'}) \rfloor (s) \Rightarrow p(s') \end{aligned}$$

3.6   Finite Pattern Matching

Rule (4) gives us a finite set of proof terms. However, we must also translate each term into finitely many verification conditions. The key issue is ensuring that the number of pattern matches in each reification is finite.

Most cases of pattern matching are trivially finite, but iterated views require careful treatment. An iterated view expression $B \to a[n](\overline{y})$ can produce n many subviews. As a result, if a view pattern r and view V are both iterated, there may be unboundedly many valid distinct matches (for $i = 1, 2, \ldots$).

To solve this, a definition $(\overline{y}, r, p)$ where p is dependent on an iterator n must satisfy the following *downclosure* properties:

$$\lfloor \mathsf{emp} \rfloor (s) \implies p[0/n](s) \qquad \text{(base downclosure)}$$

$$\forall x \in \mathbb{Z}^+. p[x/n](s) \implies p[x-1/n](s) \qquad \text{(inductive downclosure)}$$

These properties let us just consider the largest iterator value when constructing pattern matches. Our tool checks downclosure as an extra proof obligation.

A further subtlety is that iterated definitions can match against combinations of atoms when they can be made equal through parameter equality. For example, $A[n](x)$ matches $(B_1 \rightarrow A[i](y)) * (B_2 \rightarrow A[j](z))$ to form $((B_1 \wedge B_2 \wedge y = z) \rightarrow A[i + j](y))$. We can solve this by expanding out the equalities as if they are separate view atoms before matching – this does not change the view's meaning.

4   SMT Back-End

We now have a proof outline for the ARC (Sect. 2) and a proof rule to convert it into verification conditions (Sect. 3). We now show how to verify these conditions using an SMT solver – in our case, Z3 [5]. To do this, we must convert the defining function, multiset minus, and command semantics into forms supported by Z3.

Definition Quantification. We begin by eliminating the defining function. Consider the following term we generated from our running example at the end of Sect. 3.5:

$$\forall((l, s), (l', s')) \in [\![\mathsf{count}\texttt{++}]\!].$$
$$\forall(\overline{y}, r, p) \in D.\, \hat{\forall}\overline{y}.\, \lfloor [\![\mathsf{arc}()]\!]_l \cup_\mathsf{m} (r \setminus_\mathsf{m} [\![\mathsf{arc}() * \mathsf{arc}()]\!]_{l'}) \rfloor (s) \Rightarrow p(s')$$

As the defining function D is bounded, we can expand the quantification into a finite set of terms. For example, for the pattern $\mathsf{arc}[n]()$, we get the following term:

$$\forall((l, s), (l', s')) \in [\![\mathsf{count}\texttt{++}]\!].\forall n.$$
$$\lfloor [\![\mathsf{arc}()]\!]_l \cup_\mathsf{m} ([\]\!]_{l'} \setminus_\mathsf{m} [\![\mathsf{arc}() * \mathsf{arc}()]\!]_{l'}) \rfloor (s)$$
$$\Rightarrow (n > 0 \Rightarrow \neg free \wedge n \leq count)(s')$$

We get this by substituting the view pattern into the left of the implication in place of r, and the corresponding formula into the right in place of p. We also eliminate the $\hat{\forall}\overline{y}$ by quantifying over the single variable n that is bound in $\overline{y}$. For simplicity later, we treat r as a view expression over l'.

Multiset Minus. We next eliminate multiset minus. We can easily reduce our proof term so that all instances of $\setminus_\mathsf{m}$ have the following shape:

$$[\) * P]\!]_{l'} \setminus_\mathsf{m} [\]\!]_{l'}$$

We eliminate this shape by case-splitting on the relationship between B_1 and B_2, n_1 and n_2, and $\overline{y_1}$ and $\overline{y_2}$. The main subtlety is that some, but not all instances in the iterator $a[n_1]$ may be subtracted, i.e. we may be left with the iterator $a[n_1 - n_2]$. If we are left with anything on the right of the $\setminus_\mathsf{m}$, we then apply the simplification step to the remainder formula P.

In our example, subtracting $[\![arc() * arc()]\!]_{l'}$ from $[\]\!]_{l'}$ leaves $n-2$ copies of arc(). If $n \leq 2$, nothing is left: we express this as a guarded view. The multiset minus rewrite yields the following term:

$$\forall((l, s), (l', s')) \in [\![\text{count++}]\!].\forall n.$$
$$\lfloor [\![arc()]\!]_l \cup_m [\)]\!]_{l'} \rfloor \Rightarrow (n > 0 \Rightarrow \neg free \wedge n \leq count)(s')$$

Commands as Predicates. To eliminate the command, we recast it as a boolean predicate over pre- and post-states. To do so, we instantiate two copies of each variable: one set for (l, s), and another (primed) set for (l', s'). We conjoin this command predicate into the proof term, replacing the outer quantification with implicit ones over the variable sets. Expanding out the reification and the local-state interpretations, and ensuring we handle the subtleties in Sect. 3.6, we get:

$$\begin{pmatrix} count' = count + 1 \wedge free' = free \wedge c' = c \\ \wedge\, (1 > 0 \Rightarrow \neg free \wedge 1 \leq count) \\ \wedge\, (n > 2 \Rightarrow (n - 1 > 0 \Rightarrow \neg free \wedge n - 1 \leq count)) \\ \wedge\, (n > 2 \Rightarrow (n - 2 > 0 \Rightarrow \neg free \wedge n - 2 \leq count)) \end{pmatrix}$$
$$\implies (n > 0 \Rightarrow \neg free' \wedge n \leq count')$$

SMT Term. Finally, we negate the outer implication for each condition, so Z3 tries to find counter-example instantiations for the condition's variables. We can also simplify the term. For example, we remove the $n - 2$ case, as it is implied by the $n - 1$ case. The resulting term, in the SMT-LIB language accepted by Z3, is:

```
(and (= count' (+ count 1)) (= free' free) (= c' c) (not free) (<= 1 count)
     (=> (> n 2) (<= (- n 1) count))
     (not (=> (> n 0) (and (not free') (<= n count')))))
```

5   GRASShopper Back-End

For heap-based programs like the ARC in Fig. 2, we target the GRASShopper solver [20] rather than Z3. GRASShopper is a separation-logic solver, but its underlying model is based on sets of heap locations and reachability properties over sets. For example, the following GRASShopper predicate asserts that the set of locations Footprint contains a list with head x and tail y:

```
predicate list_segment(Footprint: Set<Node>, x: Node, y: Node) {
    acc(Footprint) &*&
    Footprint = {z: Node :: Btwn(next,x,z,y)}
}
```

Here, acc(Footprint) is a spatial assertion claiming ownership of the locations in Footprint. The Btwn(next,x,z,y) predicate asserts that z is reachable between x and y by following the next field – in other words,

z is in the list starting at x and ending at y. The set comprehension
{z: Node:: Btwn(next,x,z,y)} therefore contains the set of locations in the
list.

Most of the pipeline for producing GRASShopper proofs is similar to the
SMT case. However, the presence of a heap model causes some differences. Suppose we try to model the allocated ARC equivalent of our previous working
example,

$$\{\mathsf{arc}(x)\} \quad <|\ \ \mathtt{count++};\ \ |> \quad \{\mathsf{arc}(x) * \mathsf{arc}(x)\}$$

Given a context of $\mathsf{arc}(x) * \mathsf{arc}(x)$ (that is, the same x as in the local state of
the thread), our translation would give the following in pseudo-SMT format:

```
(and %{ [|x|].count := [|x|].count + 1; }
     %{ [|x|] in ArcFoot && 1 <= [|x|].count }
     (=> (> n 2) (and %{ [|x|] in ArcFoot } (<= (- n 1) %{ [|x|].count })))
     (not (=> (> n 0) (and %{ [|x|] in ArcFoot } (<= n %{ [|x|].count }))))))
```

As we cannot discharge this term using SMT, we convert it into a
GRASShopper procedure. Input and output variables are represented by arguments to the procedure. The command becomes the procedure body, and the
left- and right-hand sides of the proof rule body become **requires** and **ensures**
clauses.

Both the **requires** and **ensures** clause existentially quantify over a *footprint
set* representing the whole heap – in the ARC, this is the ArcFoot set. This allows
predicates to require access to the footprint, represented by acc(ArcFoot), and
to conjoin constraints on this shared footprint arising from the views.

In general, it would not be sound to introduce an arbitrary existential to
the consequent side of the term. The problem is that existential might be witnessed differently across different terms (see the derivation in Sect. 3). However,
our encoding into GRASShopper is sound, because GRASShopper will always
witness the footprint the same way, as the set of all available heap locations.

With this translation, the above pseudo-SMT query becomes:

```
procedure Example (n: Int, x: ArcNode)
requires exists ArcFoot:Set<ArcNode> :: (
        acc(ArcFoot) &*&
        ((x in ArcFoot && 1 <= x.count) &&
        (n <= 2 || (x in ArcFoot && n <= x.count)))
    )
ensures exists ArcFoot:Set<ArcNode> :: (
        acc(ArcFoot) &*&
        (n <= 0 || (x in ArcFoot && n <= x.count))
    )
{ x.count := x.count + 1; }
```

In some cases we need to model the mutation of variables. To do this, we declare fresh GRASShopper variables in the procedure body, and connect them to the input and output variables by assertion.

5.1   Example: CLH Queue Lock

GRASShopper's support for dynamic data-structures allows us to target much more complex algorithms than the ARC. In this section we verify the queue-based CLH lock [16], which also demonstrates a subtle ownership-transfer pattern between threads. For space reasons, we give the main proof in Appendix B, and here only explain the key details.

The code and inline views are given in Fig. 4. In the CLH lock, each participating thread owns a single node. To contend for the lock, a thread adds its own node to the queue, and waits on its predecessor. Releasing the lock means setting the node's lock flag to false. Once the predecessor is released, the thread can take hold of the lock.

This protocol is reflected in the views in Fig. 4. A node starts life dormant, i.e. not on the queue. It is then made active when its lock flag is set, and then is queued. Once the algorithm establishes that the node is at the end of the queue, it becomes locked. Finally, once the lock is released the node leaves the queue, and it becomes dormant again.

```
1 method lock() {                        1 method unlock() {
2   {| dormant(mynode) |}                2   {| locked(mynode, mypred) |}
3   <| %{ [|mynode|].lock := true }; |>  3   <| %{ [|mynode|].lock := false };
4   {| active(mynode) |}                 4      %{ [|mynode|].pred := null };
5   <| mypred = tail; tail = mynode;     5      head = mynode; |>
6      %{[|tail|].pred := [|mypred|]}; |> 6   {| dormant(mypred) |}
7   {| queued(mynode, mypred) |}         7   mynode = mypred;
8   do {                                 8   {| dormant(mynode) |}
9     {| queued(mynode, mypred) |}       9 }
10    <| test = %{ [|mypred|].lock }; |>
11    {| if (test) {queued(mynode, mypred)}
12       else {locked(mynode, mypred)} |}
13  } while (test);
14  {| locked(mynode, mypred) |}
15 }
```

Fig. 4. CLH queue-based lock algorithm. Note that the head pointer and pred field are ghost code necessary to verify the algorithm.

The key property of the CLH lock (and any lock) is mutual exclusion: each node is held exclusively, and the lock as a whole can only be held by one thread. In our approach, we can specify this using constraints, for example:

```
constraint queued(a, ap) * queued(b, bp) -> a != b;
constraint locked(a, ap) * locked(b, bp) -> false;
```

The queue data-structure is similarly defined by constraints. For example the locked() atom is defined using GRASShopper assertions similar to the list_segment predicate above.

```
constraint locked(node, pred) -> %{
    [|node|] in Foot && [|pred|] in Foot
    && Btwn(pred, [|tail|], [|node|], [|head|])
    && [|node|].pred == [|pred|] && [|pred|] == [|head|] };
```

The most subtle reasoning step happens in lines 2–6 of unlock in Fig. 4, when the thread releases the lock. As some other thread may be waiting on its current node, it cannot be reused immediately. Instead the thread takes ownership of its dormant *predecessor*. Thus threads always have a single exclusively-held node, but the exact node held varies over time.

This ownership transfer is reflected in the proof in Fig. 4 and the mutual exclusion constraints above. The terms passed to GRASShopper precisely encode the required properties, even though GRASShopper itself cannot reason about ownership transfer. Other reasoning approaches would capture this through regions or shared protocols: we encode it through views.

6   Examples and Performance Results

We have tested Starling on a range of examples: the ARC algorithm discussed in Sect. 2; a standard compare-and-swap spinlock; a ticket-based FIFO lock, as used in Linux [2]; a reader-writer lock which combines the classic Courtois et al. algorithm [3] with tickets; Peterson's algorithm; the CLH queue-lock discussed in Sect. 5 [16]; and a lock-coupling list algorithm previously verified by Vafeiadis [26] (note we verify memory safety, not linearizability). For several of these we have verified both a static version encoded in shared variables (using SMT) and a version allocated on the heap (using GRASShopper).

These algorithm are small in size, but all are challenging to verify, and each demonstrates an aspect of Starling's reasoning. Verifying the ARC example would typically require a primitive notion of "permissions" in separation logic – Starling can directly handle it without resorting to new metatheory. The CLH lock has an implied protocol between threads that performs ownership transfer of the node from one thread to the next, again handled directly by the theory. The other synchronisation algorithms similarly involve subtle protocols between threads that, in other reasoning systems, would need auxiliary proof constructs. The lock-coupling example shows that we can reason about complex fine-grained data-structures where the protocol is entwined with the list nodes.

Figure 5 gives performance statistics for our examples. From left to right we give statistics for: the total lines of input code and proof (including auxiliary GRASShopper code); the approximate number of which are proof annotations; the lines of generated GRASShopper output; the total number of proof terms generated; the number of those successfully discharged using SMT/Z3 (the remainder are sent to GRASShopper); the total proof time (excluding

Algorithm	No. lines Starling input	No. lines auxiliary input	No. lines proof input	No. lines gen GH	No. generated terms	No. SMT-elim terms	Time, total excl GH (s)	Time, on tool (s)	Time, SMT (s)	Time, GH (s)	Mem use, Starling (MiB)	Mem use, GH (MiB)
SMT/Z3:												
ARC (static)	52	-	19	-	40	40	1.62	1.55	0.08	-	118	-
Ticket lock (static)	47	-	16	-	18	18	1.49	1.44	0.05	-	94	-
Spinlock (static)	35	-	10	-	12	12	1.51	1.47	0.04	-	87	-
Reader/writer lock	109	-	45	-	160	160	1.85	1.67	0.19	-	192	-
Peterson's algo.	94	-	27	-	72	72	2.35	2.05	0.30	-	136	-
GRASShopper:												
ARC (alloc)	59	13	32	482	20	5	1.55	1.54	0.02	1.56	92	10.2
Ticket lock (alloc)	59	80	104	1054	66	30	1.48	1.46	0.02	3.64	87	10.8
Spin lock (alloc)	54	18	38	689	56	31	1.57	1.56	0.02	2.45	88	10.6
CLH queue-lock	124	10	58	1407	50	21	1.47	1.45	0.02	3.87	84	11.3
Lock-coupling list	79	118	154	5019	240	116	1.96	1.94	0.02	35.31	96	30.2

Fig. 5. Benchmarks for example algorithms.

GRASShopper); of that time, the total spent on the tool itself, and on SMT/Z3; the total memory in the .NET runtime working set at the end of the proof, in mebibytes; and the average maximum resident set size over 3 runs of GRASShopper on the output from Starling, in mebibytes (these loosely approximate the total memory used).

Times reported are the average of 3 runs. Benchmarks were run on a 2016 series MacBook Pro, with 8 GB RAM and a 2.9 GHz dual-core Intel Core i5.

7 Related Work

Our approach builds on Views [6], and thus is part of the family of logics descended from Concurrent Separation Logic [18]. These logics all use separating conjunction to reason about distinct threads, and many of these logics have introduced auxiliary constructs to assist with reasoning. For example, Svendsen and Birkedal's iCAP [24] combines reasoning about interference (derived from Rely-Guarantee [14]), abstraction through abstract predicates, a rich system of protocols based on capabilities, and higher-order propositions. Other significant logics include CaReSL [25], TaDA [22], FCSL [17], and others – each comes with a different collection of auxiliary constructs.

As discussed in Sect. 3, our approach also has similarities to Owicki-Gries reasoning [19]. In Owicki-Gries, many kinds of interaction between threads need to be encoded through auxiliary variables. Views allow us to capture these interactions directly in a more intuitive style.

Starling inherits much of the generality of the Views framework – see [6] for encodings of multiple previous logics. We can encode many of the auxiliary proof constructs used in other logics. For example, Boyland-style fractional permissions [1] can be encoded by a view with a permission-value argument, which can then be split and joined by entailment. iCAP-style protocols can be encoded by making each protocol state into a view, and using constraints to enforce mutual exclusion between these state-views.

A few CSL-style logics have automated tool support. FCSL [17] and Verifast [13] both support automated proof-checking, albeit with a considerable annotation burden as all steps must be given explicitly. SmallfootRG [26] supports proof-checking for the RGsep logic, but requires annotations of invariants and rely-conditions – in our system these are defined implicitly by the constraints.

Caper [7] is the tool most similar to ours. It supports reasoning about functional specifications that our tool cannot presently handle – for example that an element is correctly inserted into a bag. However, Caper's logic is built on auxiliary guard algebras, shared regions, and actions. It is therefore significantly more complex than our approach both in reasoning and in metatheory. Caper uses Z3, as do we, but its heap reasoning is custom-built, and we are uncertain whether it could verify an example of the complexity of the CLH lock or lock-coupling list. We handle these examples using the GRASShopper heap solver [20], and our approach is designed to be generic in the choice of back-end solver.

We have not undertaken a precise comparison, but we believe for our heap-based examples, all competing tools would require significantly more annotations. For example, the CLH lock is our most challenging algorithm: in Verifast, its code and proof require 343 lines, while Starling requires 134 lines.[3]

Several other tools share similarities with our approach. VCC [4] is a verifier based on Z3 which has been used to verify large-scale concurrent C programs. In VCC, concepts such as permission and ownership are encoded through auxiliary state. Our approach encodes these properties through view interactions.

QED [9] is a refinement-based approach to verification: concurrent programs are related to their atomic specifications by a series of sound refinement steps. We are hopeful that our approach could be combined with this style of reasoning as well as CSL-style program logic.

Our SMT/Z3 back-end has similarities to Threader [11], and unlike our tool, Threader can infer invariants using a Horn-clause solver. However, it only targets shared-variable algorithms – we can handle heap-based algorithms. Invariant inference in our approach is a topic of future work.

There is a lot of work on model-checking concurrent systems – e.g. [21,27]. In model-checking terms we require significant annotation, but our context reduction means that our proofs apply to an unbounded number of threads, context switches and unrolling of loops.

---

[3] https://github.com/verifast/verifast/blob/master/examples/clhlock/clhlock.c, accessed May 2017.

8   Conclusions

We have presented a new logic-based approach to verifying concurrent programs. Our approach is lightweight, automated, and based on a sound bedrock of existing theory. Because we build on the generic Views framework, we believe our approach could be reused by other concurrent logics as a way to target sequential solvers.

One next step will be invariant inference for Starling. Our proof terms are already in quasi-Horn clause form, and preliminary experiments suggest we can infer view definitions using an off-the-shelf solver such as HSF [10]. We also plan to extend Starling with modular reasoning, meaning that proofs of libraries and clients can be performed separately, as in iCAP [24]. Finally, we plan to extend Starling to prove algorithm linearizability rather than pre-post specifications, as in Vafeiadis [26] and Liang and Feng [15].

A   Starling Assertion and Command Languages

We define the syntax of the Starling assertion and command languages using the grammars below. We assume the existence of grammars for <lvalue> (assignable locations), <expr> (expressions), and <identifier> (valid identifiers).

A.1   Assertions

```
<assertion>        ::= <assertion-item>
                   |   <assertion-item> "*" <assertion>

<assertion-item> ::= "emp"
                   |   "false"
                   |   <identifier> "(" <arglist> ")"
                   |   "local" "{" <expr> "}"
                   |   "if" "(" <expr> ")" "{" <assertion> "}" <assertion-else>
                   |   "(" <assertion> ")"
<assertion-else> ::= ""   |   "else" "{" <assertion> "}"

<arglist>          ::= ""   |   <arglist-1>
<arglist-1>        ::= <expr>  |  <expr> "," <arglist-1>
```

A.2   Commands

Atomic commands, i.e. those within <| angle braces |>, are described by <atomic-cmds>, and may refer to thread-local and shared state variables in their expressions. Local commands are described by <local-cmds>, and may only refer to thread-local variables.

```
<atomic-cmds>    ::= ""   |   <atomic-cmd> <atomic-cmds>

<atomic-cmd>     ::= <primitive-cmd> ";"
                 |   "assert" "(" <expr> ")" ";"
                 |   "if" "(" <expr> ")" "{" <atomic-cmds> "}" <atomic-else>
                 |   "CAS" "(" <lvalue> "," <lvalue> ","<expr> ")" ";"
<atomic-else>    ::= ""   |   "else" "{" <atomic-cmds> "}"

<local-cmds>     ::= ""   |   <primitive-cmd> <local-cmds>

<primitive-cmd> ::= <lvalue> "=" <expr>
                 |   <lvalue> "=" <lvalue> <postfix>
                 |   "havoc" <lvalue>
                 |   <lvalue> <postfix>
                 |   "assume" "(" <expr> ")"
                 |   ""

<postfix>        ::= "++"  |  "--"
```

B   The CLH Lock Proof

```
1 typedef int Node;
2
3 // Shared pointers to nodes
4 shared Node tail;
5 shared Node head;   // (Ghost code)
6
7 // Thread-local pointers to nodes
8 thread Node mynode, mypred;
9 thread bool test;  // Used when trying to take the lock.
10
11 // Views
12 view dormant(Node node);
13 view active(Node node);
14 view queued(Node node, Node pred);
15 view locked(Node node, Node pred);
16
17 // Goal constraint
18 constraint locked(a, ap) * locked(b, bp) -> false;
19
20 // Other constraints
21 constraint emp -> %{
22     [|head|] in Foot
23     && [|tail|] in Foot
24     && Reach(pred, [|tail|], [|head|])
25     && ![|head|].lock
26     && (forall x : Node ::
```

```
27          (x in Foot && x.pred != null) ==> x.lock)
28     && (forall x : Node ::
29          (x in Foot && Reach(pred, [|tail|], x) && !x.lock)
30          ==> x == [|head|])
31 };
32
33 constraint dormant(node) -> %{
34     [|node|] in Foot && [|node|] != [|head|] && [|node|].pred == null
35     && [|node|].lock == false
36 };
37 constraint active(node) -> %{
38     [|node|] in Foot && [|node|] != [|head|] && [|node|].pred == null
39     && [|node|].lock == true
40 };
41
42 constraint queued(node, pred) -> %{
43     [|node|] in Foot
44     && [|pred|] in Foot
45     && [|node|].pred == [|pred|]
46     && [|node|].lock
47     && Btwn(pred, [|tail|], [|node|], [|head|])
48 };
49 constraint locked(node, pred) -> %{
50     [|node|] in Foot
51     && [|pred|] in Foot
52     && [|node|].pred == [|pred|]
53     && Btwn(pred, [|tail|], [|node|], [|head|])
54     && [|pred|] == [|head|]
55 };
56
57 constraint dormant(a) * dormant(b) -> a != b;
58 constraint active(a) * active(b) -> a != b;
59 constraint queued(a, ap) * queued(b, bp) -> a != b;
60 constraint queued(a, ap) * locked(b, bp) -> a != b;
61
62 // Proof outline
63 method lock() {
64   {| dormant(mynode) |}
65     <| %{ [|mynode|].lock := true }; |>
66   {| active(mynode) |}
67     <| mypred = tail; tail = mynode;
68        %{[|tail|].pred := [|mypred|]}; /* Ghost code */ |>
69   {| queued(mynode, mypred) |}
70     do {
71       {| queued(mynode, mypred) |}
72         <| test = %{ [|mypred|].lock }; |>
73       {| if (test) { queued(mynode, mypred) }
74              else { locked(mynode, mypred) } |}
75     } while (test);
76   {| locked(mynode, mypred) |}
```

```
77 }
78
79 method unlock() {
80   {| locked(mynode, mypred) |}
81     <| %{ [|mynode|].lock := false };
82       %{ [|mynode|].pred := null }; head = mynode; /* Ghost code */ |>
83   {| dormant(mypred) |}
84     mynode = mypred;
85   {| dormant(mynode) |}
86 }
```

The CLH lock proof depends on the following auxiliary definition written in GRASShopper's assertion language:

```
1 struct Node {
2     var lock: Bool;
3     var pred: Node;  // Ghost field
4 }
```

References

1. Boyland, J.: Checking interference with fractional permissions. In: Cousot, R. (ed.) SAS 2003. LNCS, vol. 2694, pp. 55–72. Springer, Heidelberg (2003). doi:10.1007/3-540-44898-5_4

2. Corbet, J.: Ticket spinlocks. LWN.net (2008). https://lwn.net/Articles/267968/

3. Courtois, P.J., Heymans, F., Parnas, D.L.: Concurrent control with "readers" and "writers". Commun. ACM **14**(10), 667–668 (1971). http://doi.acm.org/10.1145/362759.362813

4. Dahlweid, M., Moskal, M., Santen, T., Tobies, S., Schulte, W.: Vcc: contract-based modular verification of concurrent C. In: 31st International Conference on Software Engineering, pp. 429–430, May 2009

5. de Moura, L., Bjørner, N.: Z3: an efficient SMT solver. In: Ramakrishnan, C.R., Rehof, J. (eds.) TACAS 2008. LNCS, vol. 4963, pp. 337–340. Springer, Heidelberg (2008). doi:10.1007/978-3-540-78800-3_24

6. Dinsdale-Young, T., Birkedal, L., Gardner, P., Parkinson, M., Yang, H.: Views: compositional reasoning for concurrent programs. In: Proceedings of the 40th Annual ACM SIGPLAN-SIGACT Symposium on Principles of Programming Languages, POPL 2013, New York, NY, USA, pp. 287–300. ACM (2013). http://doi.acm.org/10.1145/2429069.2429104

7. Dinsdale-Young, T., da Rocha Pinto, P., Andersen, K.J., Birkedal, L.: CAPER. In: Yang, H. (ed.) ESOP 2017. LNCS, vol. 10201, pp. 420–447. Springer, Heidelberg (2017). doi:10.1007/978-3-662-54434-1_16

8. Dinsdale-Young, T., Dodds, M., Gardner, P., Parkinson, M.J., Vafeiadis, V.: Concurrent abstract predicates. In: D'Hondt, T. (ed.) ECOOP 2010. LNCS, vol. 6183, pp. 504–528. Springer, Heidelberg (2010). doi:10.1007/978-3-642-14107-2_24

9. Elmas, T.: QED: a proof system based on reduction and abstraction for the static verification of concurrent software. In: Proceedings of the 32nd ACM/IEEE International Conference on Software Engineering - Volume 2, ICSE 2010, New York, NY, USA, pp. 507–508. ACM (2010). http://doi.acm.org/10.1145/1810295.1810454

10. Grebenshchikov, S., Lopes, N.P., Popeea, C., Rybalchenko, A.: Synthesizing software verifiers from proof rules. In: Proceedings of the 33rd ACM SIGPLAN Conference on Programming Language Design and Implementation, PLDI 2012, New York, NY, USA, pp. 405–416. ACM (2012). http://doi.acm.org/10.1145/2254064.2254112

11. Gupta, A., Popeea, C., Rybalchenko, A.: Threader: a constraint-based verifier for multi-threaded programs. In: Gopalakrishnan, G., Qadeer, S. (eds.) CAV 2011. LNCS, vol. 6806, pp. 412–417. Springer, Heidelberg (2011). doi:10.1007/978-3-642-22110-1_32

12. Herlihy, M., Shavit, N.: The Art of Multiprocessor Programming. Elsevier, Amsterdam (2008)

13. Jacobs, B., Smans, J., Philippaerts, P., Vogels, F., Penninckx, W., Piessens, F.: VeriFast: a powerful, sound, predictable, fast verifier for C and Java. In: Bobaru, M., Havelund, K., Holzmann, G.J., Joshi, R. (eds.) NFM 2011. LNCS, vol. 6617, pp. 41–55. Springer, Heidelberg (2011). doi:10.1007/978-3-642-20398-5_4

14. Jones, C.B.: Tentative steps toward a development method for interfering programs. ACM Trans. Program. Lang. Syst. **5**(4), 596–619 (1983). http://doi.acm.org/10.1145/69575.69577

15. Liang, H., Feng, X.: Modular verification of linearizability with non-fixed linearization points. In: Proceedings of the 34th ACM SIGPLAN Conference on Programming Language Design and Implementation, PLDI 2013, New York, NY, USA, pp. 459–470. ACM (2013). http://doi.acm.org/10.1145/2491956.2462189

16. Magnusson, P.S., Landin, A., Hagersten, E.: Queue locks on cache coherent multiprocessors. In: Proceedings of the 8th International Symposium on Parallel Processing, Washington, DC, USA, pp. 165–171. IEEE Computer Society (1994). http://dl.acm.org/citation.cfm?id=645604.662740

17. Nanevski, A., Ley-Wild, R., Sergey, I., Delbianco, G.A.: Communicating state transition systems for fine-grained concurrent resources. In: Shao, Z. (ed.) ESOP 2014. LNCS, vol. 8410, pp. 290–310. Springer, Heidelberg (2014). doi:10.1007/978-3-642-54833-8_16

18. O'Hearn, P.W.: Resources, concurrency, and local reasoning. Theor. Comput. Sci. **375**(1–3), 271–307 (2007). http://dx.doi.org/10.1016/j.tcs.2006.12.035

19. Owicki, S., Gries, D.: Verifying properties of parallel programs: an axiomatic approach. Commun. ACM **19**(5), 279–285 (1976). http://doi.acm.org/10.1145/360051.360224

20. Piskac, R., Wies, T., Zufferey, D.: GRASShopper. In: Ábrahám, E., Havelund, K. (eds.) TACAS 2014. LNCS, vol. 8413, pp. 124–139. Springer, Heidelberg (2014). doi:10.1007/978-3-642-54862-8_9

21. Qadeer, S., Rehof, J.: Context-bounded model checking of concurrent software. In: Halbwachs, N., Zuck, L.D. (eds.) TACAS 2005. LNCS, vol. 3440, pp. 93–107. Springer, Heidelberg (2005). doi:10.1007/978-3-540-31980-1_7

22. da Rocha Pinto, P., Dinsdale-Young, T., Gardner, P.: TaDA: a logic for time and data abstraction. In: Jones, R. (ed.) ECOOP 2014. LNCS, vol. 8586, pp. 207–231. Springer, Heidelberg (2014). doi:10.1007/978-3-662-44202-9_9

23. Rust `std::sync` module. https://doc.rust-lang.org/std/sync/struct.Arc.html

24. Svendsen, K., Birkedal, L.: Impredicative concurrent abstract predicates. In: Shao, Z. (ed.) ESOP 2014. LNCS, vol. 8410, pp. 149–168. Springer, Heidelberg (2014). doi:10.1007/978-3-642-54833-8_9

25. Turon, A., Dreyer, D., Birkedal, L.: Unifying refinement and hoare-style reasoning in a logic for higher-order concurrency. In: Proceedings of the 18th ACM SIGPLAN International Conference on Functional Programming, ICFP 2013, New York, NY, USA, pp. 377–390. ACM (2013). http://doi.acm.org/10.1145/2500365.2500600
26. Vafeiadis, V.: Modular fine-grained concurrency verification. Ph.D. thesis, University of Cambridge, July 2007
27. Yahav, E., Sagiv, M.: Verifying safety properties of concurrent heap-manipulating programs. ACM Trans. Program. Lang. Syst. **32**(5), 18:1–18:50 (2008). http://doi.acm.org/10.1145/1745312.1745315

Compositional Model Checking
with Incremental Counter-Example Construction

Anton Wijs[(⊠)] and Thomas Neele

Eindhoven University of Technology, 5612 AZ
Eindhoven, The Netherlands
{A.J.Wijs,T.S.Neele}@tue.nl

Abstract. In compositional model checking, the approach is to reason about the correctness of a system by lifting results obtained in analyses of subsystems to the system-level. The main challenge, however, is that requirements, in the form of temporal logic formulae, are usually specified at the system-level, and it is not obvious how to relate these to subsystem-local behaviour. In this paper, we propose a new approach to checking regular safety properties, which we call Incremental Counter-Example Construction (ICC). Its main strong point is that it performs a series of model checking procedures, and that each one only explores a small part of the entire state space. This makes ICC an excellent approach in those cases where state space explosion is an issue. Moreover, it is frequently much faster than traditional explicit-state model checking, particularly when the model satisfies the verified property, and in most cases not significantly slower. We explain the technique, and report on experiments we have conducted using an implementation of ICC, comparing the results to those obtained with other approaches.

1 Introduction

Model checking [3] is an automatic technique to verify that a given specification of a concurrent system meets a particular functional property. The specification of a concurrent system describes a finite number of *components*, or processes, and how these can interact. Model checking involves very time and memory demanding computations. Most computations rely on state space exploration. This involves interpreting the specification, resulting in building a graph, or *state space*, describing all its potential behaviour.

However, model checking suffers from the *state space explosion problem*, meaning that a linear growth of the model tends to lead to an exponential growth of the corresponding state space. Over the years, a whole range of techniques have been proposed to mitigate this problem. One prominent technique is *compositional model checking* [10]. The aim is to break down the model checking problem into several subproblems, and solve these individually, thereby achieving a compositional approach.

© Springer International Publishing AG 2017
R. Majumdar and V. Kunčak (Eds.): CAV 2017, Part I, LNCS 10426, pp. 570–590, 2017.
DOI: 10.1007/978-3-319-63387-9_28

The main challenge in compositional model checking is that on the one hand, one wishes to reason about the correctness of subsystems or components and lift those results to the system level, but on the other hand, the functional property to be checked is usually expressed directly at the system level. Furthermore, the possible interactions between the components need to be taken into account when verifying, therefore only checking components in isolation does not suffice.

In this paper, we present a new approach to compositional model checking, which we call *Incremental Counter-Example Construction* (ICC). The main idea is that the system components are placed in a fixed order, and a sequence of verification checks is performed, each involving a single component M in the system in the specified order. Furthermore, each check involves a version of the negation of the functional property φ at the relevant level of abstraction, and a partially built counter-example c. The goal of each check is to extend c with behaviour of M in such a way that (the abstract version of) φ is still violated. If one is able to extend a counter-example with behaviour of all components in the system, then a complete counter-example has been successfully constructed. If extending c fails in some check, ICC backtracks to an earlier check to produce a new counter-example candidate. Rejected candidates are added to checks as constraints to prevent them from being proposed again.

The main benefit of ICC is that it is often very memory-efficient; frequently the individual checks explore state spaces that are orders of magnitude smaller than the full system state space. For models with sufficiently large state spaces, we observe that ICC allows us to check those models, while traditional model checking runs out of memory.

Another benefit is that, while reducing the memory-use, ICC is actually not significantly slower than traditional, explicit-state model checking. In fact, it is frequently even much faster, particularly in those cases where individual checks can quickly discard large parts of the state space.

The structure of the paper is as follows: Sect. 2 presents the preliminaries. In Sect. 3, the ICC procedure is presented. Optimisations of this algorithm are discussed in Sect. 4. Then, experimental results are presented in Sect. 5. Related work is discussed in Sect. 6, and finally, Sect. 7 contains conclusions and pointers to future work.

2   Preliminaries

Concurrent System Semantics. We capture the formal semantics of single components in concurrent systems in *Labelled Transition Systems.*

Definition 1 (Labelled Transition System). *An LTS $\mathcal{G}$ is a tuple $\langle \mathcal{S}, \mathcal{A}, \mathcal{T}, s^{in} \rangle$, with*

- *$\mathcal{S}$ a finite set of states;*
- *$\mathcal{A}$ a set of action labels, not containing the special internal, or hidden, system action τ;*

- $\mathcal{T} \subseteq \mathcal{S} \times \mathcal{A} \cup \{\tau\} \times \mathcal{S}$ a transition relation;
- $s^{in} \in \mathcal{S}$ the initial state.

An LTS $\mathcal{G}$ with accepting states *has an additional tuple element* $\mathcal{F}_\mathcal{G} \subseteq \mathcal{S}$, which is called the set of accepting states.

The set $\mathcal{A} \cup \{\tau\}$ is denoted by $\mathcal{A}_\tau$. Action labels in $\mathcal{A}$ are denoted by a, b, c, etc., while actions in $\mathcal{A}_\tau$ are denoted by ℓ. A transition $(s, \ell, s') \in \mathcal{T}$, or $s \xrightarrow{\ell} s'$ for short, denotes that LTS $\mathcal{G}$ can move from state s to state s' by performing the ℓ-action. Whenever we want to make explicit that $s \xrightarrow{\ell} s'$ is a transition of $\mathcal{G}$, we write $s \xrightarrow{\ell}_\mathcal{G} s'$. We call $\mathcal{G}$ *deterministic* iff for all $\ell \in \mathcal{A} \cup \{\tau\}$ and $s, s' \in \mathcal{S}$, if $s \xrightarrow{\ell} s'$, then there exists no $s'' \in \mathcal{S}$ with $s' \neq s''$ and also $s \xrightarrow{\ell} s''$. The reflexive, transitive closure of $\xrightarrow{}$ is indicated by $\Rightarrow$.

A *path* $\sigma = \langle s^{in} \xrightarrow{\ell_1} \xrightarrow{\ell_2} \cdots \xrightarrow{\ell_n} s_n \rangle$ through $\mathcal{G}$ of length n is a sequence of n transitions, starting from the initial state, that all exist in $\mathcal{T}$. We call a state $s \in \mathcal{S}$ *reachable* iff there exists at least one path from s^{in} to s. The *trace* described by σ is the sequence of actions $w(\sigma) = \langle \ell_1, \ldots, \ell_m \rangle \in \mathcal{A}_\tau^*$ as they appear in σ. The trace $w(\sigma_1)$ of path σ_1 is a *prefix* of $w(\sigma_2)$ of path σ_2 iff $w(\sigma_2)$ can be obtained by extending $w(\sigma_1)$. A trace v is said to be accepted by LTS $\mathcal{G}$ iff there is at least one path σ through $\mathcal{G}$ leading to a state in $\mathcal{F}_\mathcal{G}$ and $w(\sigma) = v$. When relevant, we denote this by $v\checkmark$. We refer to the empty trace with ϵ.

We write $1..n$ for the set of integers ranging from 1 to n. A vector $\bar{v}$ of size n contains n elements indexed from 1 to n. For all $i \in 1..n$, $\bar{v}_i$ represents the ith element of vector $\bar{v}$.

LTSs can be combined using *parallel composition*, for which we use the convention that LTSs must synchronise on common actions, while actions unique to one LTS represent independent actions. An exception to this is the τ-action: internal steps of an LTS are not synchronised with those of another.

Definition 2 (Parallel composition). *Given two LTSs* $\mathcal{G}_1 = \langle \mathcal{S}_1, \mathcal{A}_1, \mathcal{T}_1, s_1^{in} \rangle$ *and* $\mathcal{G}_2 = \langle \mathcal{S}_2, \mathcal{A}_2, \mathcal{T}_2, s_2^{in} \rangle$, *we say that* $\mathcal{M} = \mathcal{G}_1 \parallel \mathcal{G}_2$ *is the* parallel composition *of* $\mathcal{G}_1$ *and* $\mathcal{G}_2$. *Its LTS* $\mathcal{M} = \langle \mathcal{S}_\mathcal{M}, \mathcal{A}_\mathcal{M}, \mathcal{T}_\mathcal{M}, \bar{s}_\mathcal{M}^{in} \rangle$ *is defined as follows:*

- $\bar{s}_\mathcal{M}^{in} = \langle s_1^{in}, s_2^{in} \rangle$;
- $\mathcal{T}_\mathcal{M}$ *and* $\mathcal{S}_\mathcal{M}$ *are the smallest relation and set, respectively, satisfying* $\bar{s}_\mathcal{M}^{in} \in \mathcal{S}_\mathcal{M}$ *and for all* $\bar{s} \in \mathcal{S}_\mathcal{M}, \ell \in \mathcal{A}_1 \cup \mathcal{A}_2 \cup \{\tau\}$:
  - $\bar{s}_1 \xrightarrow{\ell}_1 t \wedge \ell \notin \mathcal{A}_2 \implies \bar{s} \xrightarrow{\ell}_\mathcal{M} \langle t, \bar{s}_2 \rangle \wedge \langle t, \bar{s}_2 \rangle \in \mathcal{S}_\mathcal{M}$;
  - $\bar{s}_2 \xrightarrow{\ell}_2 t \wedge \ell \notin \mathcal{A}_1 \implies \bar{s} \xrightarrow{\ell}_\mathcal{M} \langle \bar{s}_1, t \rangle \wedge \langle \bar{s}_1, t \rangle \in \mathcal{S}_\mathcal{M}$;
  - $\bar{s}_1 \xrightarrow{\ell}_1 t \wedge \bar{s}_2 \xrightarrow{\ell}_2 t' \wedge \ell \neq \tau \implies \bar{s} \xrightarrow{\ell}_\mathcal{M} \langle t, t' \rangle \wedge \langle t, t' \rangle \in \mathcal{S}_\mathcal{M}$.
- $\mathcal{A}_\mathcal{M} = \{a \mid \exists \bar{s}, \bar{s}' \in \mathcal{S}_\mathcal{M}.\bar{s} \xrightarrow{a}_\mathcal{M} \bar{s}'\} \setminus \{\tau\}$.

Besides the parallel composition as defined in Definition 2, we also use a special parallel composition operator $\parallel\mid$, which is identical to $\parallel$ except for the (non-)synchronisation of τ-actions: contrary to $\parallel$, $\parallel\mid$ also forces synchronisation between LTSs on τ-actions. For that reason, we refer to the latter form of parallel composition as *fully synchronised parallel composition*.

Encoding and Verifying Regular Safety Properties. A safety property φ is a linear time property that describes which infinite traces in $\mathcal{A}^*$ are considered correct. Therefore, its negation $\neg\varphi$ describes which traces violate φ by listing all finite bad prefixes of those traces. If this set of bad prefixes constitutes a regular language, then φ is said to be regular [3]. The negation $\neg\varphi$ can be encoded in an LTS with accepting states $\mathcal{P}^{\neg\varphi} = \langle \mathcal{S}_\mathcal{P}, \mathcal{A}_\mathcal{P}, \mathcal{T}_\mathcal{P}, s_\mathcal{P}^{in}, \mathcal{F}_\mathcal{P} \rangle$.

Verifying whether a system $\mathcal{M}$, consisting of n components of the form $\mathcal{M}_i = \langle \mathcal{S}_i, \mathcal{A}_i, \mathcal{T}_i, s_i^{in} \rangle$ ($i \in 1..n$) satisfies a regular safety property φ boils down to checking whether in the parallel composition $\mathcal{M}_1 \parallel \cdots \parallel \mathcal{M}_n \parallel \mathcal{P}^{\neg\varphi}$ a system state $\langle s_1, \ldots, s_n, s' \rangle$ is reachable from $\langle s_1^{in}, \ldots, s_n^{in}, s_\mathcal{P}^{in} \rangle$ in which $s' \in \mathcal{F}_\mathcal{P}$. For convenience, we also call such a system state an accepting state. In fact, in this paper, we use a generalised version of this definition of accepting state: in a parallel composition of LTSs $\mathcal{G}_1 \parallel \cdots \parallel \mathcal{G}_n$, we say that a system state $\langle s_1, \ldots, s_n \rangle$ is accepting iff for all $\mathcal{G}_i$ containing accepting states, i.e., $\mathcal{F}_{\mathcal{G}_i} \neq \emptyset$, we have that $s_i \in \mathcal{F}_{\mathcal{G}_i}$.

Trace Equivalences. As equivalence relations between LTSs, we use both trace equivalence and weak trace equivalence [7]. In contrast to trace equivalence, weak trace equivalence is sensitive to internal actions. These equivalences can be used to minimise an LTS, i.e., obtain a reduced LTS in which all the (visible) traces are preserved that are present in the original one. To define these equivalences, we first define for an LTS with accepting states $\mathcal{G} = \langle \mathcal{S}, \mathcal{A}, \mathcal{T}, s^{in}, \mathcal{F} \rangle$ the set of traces and weak traces of a state $s \in \mathcal{S}$. Sets $\mathcal{A} \cup \{\checkmark\}$ and $\mathcal{A}_\tau \cup \{\checkmark\}$ are denoted by $\mathcal{A}_\checkmark$ and $\mathcal{A}_{\tau,\checkmark}$, respectively.

Definition 3 (Traces of a state). *For a state $s \in \mathcal{S}$, Traces(s) is the minimal set satisfying:*

- $\epsilon \in$ Traces(s)*;*
- $\checkmark \in$ Traces(s) *iff $s \in \mathcal{F}$;*
- *For all $\ell \in \mathcal{A}_\tau, \sigma \in \mathcal{A}_{\tau,\checkmark}^*$, we have $\ell\sigma \in$ Traces(s) iff there exists an $s' \in \mathcal{S}$ such that $s \xrightarrow{\ell} s'$ and $\sigma \in$ Traces(s').*

Definition 4 (Weak traces of a state). *For a state $s \in \mathcal{S}$, WTraces(s) is the minimal set satisfying:*

- $\epsilon \in$ WTraces(s)*;*
- $\checkmark \in$ WTraces(s) *iff $s \in \mathcal{F}$;*
- *For all $a \in \mathcal{A}, \sigma \in \mathcal{A}_\checkmark^*$, we have $a\sigma \in$ WTraces(s) iff there exists an $s' \in \mathcal{S}$ such that $s \xrightarrow{a} s'$ and $\sigma \in$ WTraces(s');*
- *For all $\sigma \in \mathcal{A}_\checkmark^*$, we have $\sigma \in$ WTraces(s) iff there exists an $s' \in \mathcal{S}$ such that $s \xrightarrow{\tau} s'$ and $\sigma \in$ WTraces(s').*

Definition 5 (Trace equivalence). *States s, s' are* trace equivalent *iff*

$$\text{Traces}(s) = \text{Traces}(s')$$

Definition 6 (Weak trace equivalence). *States s, s' are weak trace equivalent iff*

$$\text{WTraces}(s) = \text{WTraces}(s')$$

We say that two LTSs $\mathcal{G}_1 = \langle \mathcal{S}_1, \mathcal{A}_1, \mathcal{T}_1, s_1^{in}, \mathcal{F}_1 \rangle$ and $\mathcal{G}_2 = \langle \mathcal{S}_2, \mathcal{A}_2, \mathcal{T}_2, s_2^{in}, \mathcal{F}_2 \rangle$ are trace equivalent and weak trace equivalent iff their initial states s_1^{in} and s_2^{in} are trace equivalent and weak trace equivalent, respectively. Finally, given an LTS $\mathcal{G} = \langle \mathcal{S}, \mathcal{A}, \mathcal{T}, s^{in}, \mathcal{F} \rangle$, we refer with $\text{Traces}(\mathcal{G})$ and $\text{WTraces}(\mathcal{G})$ to $\text{Traces}(s^{in})$ and $\text{WTraces}(s^{in})$, respectively.

It is known that linear-time properties are preserved by trace equivalence [3], i.e., if an LTS $\mathcal{G}_1$ satisfies a linear-time property φ and $\mathcal{G}_1$ is trace equivalent to $\mathcal{G}_2$, then also $\mathcal{G}_2$ satisfies φ. The same holds for weak trace equivalence, as long as φ does not refer to the internal action τ. The standard powerset construction algorithm to determinise finite automata [40] can be used to reduce LTSs w.r.t. trace and weak trace equivalence. Although this algorithm has worst-case complexity $O(2^{|\mathcal{S}|})$, reducing small LTSs of system components can still be done relatively fast. As an intermediate step, one could consider first reducing the LTS w.r.t. branching bisimulation, which can be done in $O(|\mathcal{T}| \cdot (\log |\mathcal{A}| + \log |\mathcal{S}|))$ [26].

Abstraction. To raise the abstraction level of an LTS, we define *action hiding* of an LTS w.r.t. a set of actions A.

Definition 7 (Action hiding). *Given an LTS $\mathcal{G} = \langle \mathcal{S}, \mathcal{A}, \mathcal{T}, s^{in} \rangle$, we define the LTS $\mathcal{G}' = \langle \mathcal{S}, \mathcal{A}', \mathcal{T}', s^{in} \rangle$ resulting from action hiding $\mathcal{G}$ w.r.t. A as follows:*

- $\mathcal{A}' = \mathcal{A} \cap A$;
- $\mathcal{T}' = \{(s, \ell, s') \mid (s, \ell, s') \in \mathcal{T} \wedge \ell \in A\} \cup \{(s, \tau, s') \mid (s, \ell, s') \in \mathcal{T} \wedge \ell \notin A\}$.

With $\mathcal{G}_{\downarrow A}$, we denote the LTS resulting from first action hiding $\mathcal{G}$ w.r.t. A, and subsequently applying weak trace equivalence reduction on the action hidden LTS. Similarly, with $\mathcal{G}_{\downarrow}$ we refer to the LTS obtained by applying trace equivalence reduction on $\mathcal{G}$. Note that $\mathcal{G}_{\downarrow}$ is in general not equivalent to $\mathcal{G}_{\downarrow A}$, in particular when τ-transitions are present in $\mathcal{G}$.

3   Incremental Counter-Example Construction

In this section, we introduce the basic approach to compositionally verify whether a system $\mathcal{M}$ satisfies a regular safety property φ via ICC.

3.1   The ICC Algorithm

We first illustrate how the algorithm works by using an example.

Example. Consider the two LTSs and the property LTS depicted in Fig. 1, where the doubly lined state denotes an accepting state, and states with a detached incoming arrow are initial. For this system, the ICC procedure works as follows:

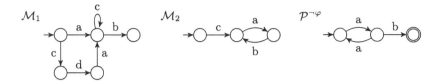

Fig. 1. Example with two LTSs and the property "after an odd amount of a's no b can be performed". The doubly-lined state is an accepting state.

first, we place LTSs $\mathcal{M}_1$ and $\mathcal{M}_2$ in some order, say the order in which they are depicted in Fig. 1. Then, we analyse the parallel composition of the first LTS and an abstract version of the property LTS w.r.t. the action set $\mathcal{A}_1$: $\mathcal{M}_1 \parallel \mathcal{P}^{\neg\varphi}{\downarrow}_{\mathcal{A}_1}$. A Breadth-First Search exploration of the state space will reach an accepting state via a path describing the traces ac^*b (it should be noted that the correctness of ICC does not depend on the exploration strategy). Next, we replace $\mathcal{M}_1$ by an LTS $\mathcal{L}_1$ with Traces($\mathcal{L}_1$) = $\{ab\checkmark, acb\checkmark, accb\checkmark, \ldots\}$, include $\mathcal{M}_2$ in the analysis, and consider another abstract version of the property LTS. This means that we search for a counter-example in $\mathcal{L}_1 \parallel \mathcal{M}_2 \parallel \mathcal{P}^{\neg\varphi}{\downarrow}_{\mathcal{A}_1\cup\mathcal{A}_2}$. In this case, note that since $\mathcal{L}_1$ has an accepting state, a system state is accepting iff both $\mathcal{L}_1$ and $\mathcal{P}^{\neg\varphi}{\downarrow}_{\mathcal{A}_1\cup\mathcal{A}_2}$ are in accepting states. Also note that the property LTS is now abstracted w.r.t. actions in both LTSs. In this system, no accepting state is reachable, therefore we have to go back to $\mathcal{M}_1 \parallel \mathcal{P}^{\neg\varphi}{\downarrow}_{\mathcal{A}_1}$ to find another accepted trace. Now, we find a path describing the traces $cdac^*b$, which we use to construct a new $\mathcal{L}_1'$. Since an accepting state can be reached in $\mathcal{L}_1' \parallel \mathcal{M}_2 \parallel \mathcal{P}^{\neg\varphi}{\downarrow}_{\mathcal{A}_1\cup\mathcal{A}_2}$, we conclude that the property does not hold.

The $\mathcal{L}_i$ and $\mathcal{L}_i'$ referred to in the example above can actually be directly extracted from the state space that was explored up to the point when the first accepting state was reached. Consider having to check the parallel composition of $\mathcal{L}_1 \parallel \cdots \parallel \mathcal{L}_{i-1} \parallel \mathcal{M}_i \parallel \mathcal{P}^{\neg\varphi}{\downarrow}_{\mathcal{A}_1\cup\ldots\cup\mathcal{A}_i}$, with $i \in 1..n$. When the state space is explored, an accepting state is searched on-the-fly, and, once detected, the state space exploration is terminated. Subsequently, *all the traces* of component $\mathcal{M}_i$ that are accepted in the state space explored so far, are taken into account to construct an LTS for the next check. Such an LTS can be constructed as follows from an LTS $\mathcal{G} = \langle \mathcal{S}, \mathcal{A}, \mathcal{T}, s^{in}, \mathcal{F}\rangle$ representing the state space explored so far, where $\mathcal{F}$ is the singleton set $\{s\}$.

1. Remove all states from $\mathcal{G}$ from which s cannot be reached. This can be efficiently done by exploring $\mathcal{G}$ in the opposite direction, starting from s, and after doing so, removing all the unreached states. Let us call the resulting LTS $\mathcal{G}'$.
2. Action hide $\mathcal{G}'$ w.r.t. $\mathcal{A}_i$, thereby only keeping the behaviour of $\mathcal{M}_i$ visible. In order for this to work correctly, it is required that during construction of $\mathcal{G}$, the explored τ-transitions that originated from $\mathcal{M}_i$ have been labelled in such a way that they can be distinguished from other τ-transitions (for instance with the label τ').
3. Finally, relabel the τ'-transitions in $\mathcal{G}'{\downarrow}_{\mathcal{A}_i}$ back to τ-transitions.

Algorithm 1. Incremental Counter-Example Construction

Require: $\langle \mathcal{M}_1, \ldots, \mathcal{M}_n \rangle$, $\mathcal{P}^{\neg \varphi}$
Ensure: true is returned if $\mathcal{M}$ satisfies φ, otherwise a counter-example is returned
1: $i \leftarrow 1$
2: **while** $i \leq n$ **do**
3:      $result \leftarrow Check_i$ ($= $ explore $\mathcal{L}_1 \mid\mid \cdots \mid\mid \mathcal{L}_{i-1} \mid\mid (\mathcal{M}_i \mid\mid\mid \mathcal{R}_{i\downarrow}) \mid\mid \mathcal{P}^{\neg \varphi} {\downarrow}_{\bigcup_{k \in 1..i} \mathcal{A}_k}$)
4:      **if** $\neg result$ **then**
5:          construct LTS $\mathcal{L}_i$ containing all the accepted traces of $\mathcal{M}_i$ in the state space
                                            // New counter-example found, update
6:          $i \leftarrow i + 1$ // Go to next $Check_i$
7:      **else if** $i = 1$ **then**
8:          **return true**   // Property is satisfied
9:      **else**
10:         identify the smallest $j < i$ for which $\mathcal{L}_j$ caused $Check_i$ to not reach an accepting state
11:         $updatePreviousRestrictions(j)$ // Update restrictions
12:         $resetRestrictions(j + 1, i)$ // Reset restriction LTSs in range $[j + 1,i]$
13:         $i \leftarrow j$ // Backtrack to $Check_j$
14: **return** counter-example from the final state space

Algorithm 1 presents the basic ICC technique. We iterate over the components of the system (lines 1-2), and in each iteration i, we construct a verification task $Check_i$ (line 3). Note that the order here in which the components are considered coincides with the order in which they appear in the system. Prior to performing ICC, one can determine a suitable ICC order. For more on this, see Sect. 4.

Initially, $Check_1$ entails placing LTS $\mathcal{M}_1$ in parallel composition with $\mathcal{P}^{\neg \varphi} {\downarrow}_{\mathcal{A}_1}$, that is, a version of the property LTS in which we have abstracted away all actions that are not present in $\mathcal{M}_1$, and on which we have applied weak trace equivalence reduction. In addition, we involve a trace equivalence reduced version of *restriction LTS* $\mathcal{R}_1$. In general, the purpose of restriction LTS $\mathcal{R}_i$ is to enable iterating over the possible traces through $\mathcal{M}_i$. We place $\mathcal{M}_i$ in a fully synchronised parallel composition with $\mathcal{R}_{i\downarrow}$ (line 3). Every time we have learned that at least one selected trace through some $\mathcal{M}_j$ cannot be part of a counter-example, we update $\mathcal{R}_j$ in such a way, that this trace is no longer accepted by $\mathcal{R}_j$, and thereby cannot be produced anymore by $\mathcal{M}_j \mid\mid\mid \mathcal{R}_{j\downarrow}$. More on the restriction LTSs and how updating is done in the next subsection. Initially, $\mathcal{R}_i$ accepts all possible traces that can be produced by $\mathcal{M}_i$.

Verifying whether we can reach an accepting state in $(\mathcal{M}_1 \mid\mid\mid \mathcal{R}_{1\downarrow}) \mid\mid \mathcal{P}^{\neg \varphi} {\downarrow}_{\mathcal{A}_1}$ will produce one of two possible results: the first possibility is that an accepting state was detected (*result* = **false**). In that case, we extract all explored and accepted behaviour of $\mathcal{M}_1$ from the state space explored so far, using the previously described procedure, which results in an LTS $\mathcal{L}_1$ (line 5). After that, we increment i (line 6).

The second option is that no accepting state was reachable. Then, we may conclude that $\mathcal{M}$ satisfies φ, since we are considering an over-approximation of the behaviour of $\mathcal{M}_1$ within the context given by $\mathcal{M}$ (parallel composition with other components can only restrict $\mathcal{M}_1$ (Definition 2)). Since after the first check, we have $i = 1$, the algorithm returns **true** and terminates (lines 7-8).

In iterations $i > 1$, we construct a verification task $Check_i$ by combining the selected traces $\mathcal{L}_1, \ldots, \mathcal{L}_{i-1}$ from previous iterations with $\mathcal{M}_i$, $\mathcal{R}_i$ and the property LTS at the right level of abstraction, i.e. $\mathcal{P}^{\neg \varphi} \downarrow_{\bigcup_{k \in 1..i} \mathcal{A}_k}$. When performing $Check_i$, we determine whether the partial counter-example obtained so far involving $\mathcal{M}_1, \ldots, \mathcal{M}_{i-1}$, represented by LTSs $\mathcal{L}_1, \ldots, \mathcal{L}_{i-1}$, is allowed by $\mathcal{M}_i$. If so, then again, we extract from the state space explored so far the accepted traces of $\mathcal{M}_i$, create an LTS $\mathcal{L}_i$ exactly containing these traces, and increment i (lines 5-6).

Alternatively, we should identify the smallest $j < i$ for which $\mathcal{L}_j$ caused $Check_i$ to not result in finding an accepting state (line 10, we skip lines 7-8 since $i > 1$). This can be achieved as follows, performing at most $i - 2$ subsequent checks $Check'_1, \ldots, Check'_{i-2}$, where each check $Check'_l$ ($l \in 1..i - 2$) is defined as follows:

$$Check'_l = \text{explore } \mathcal{L}_1 \parallel \cdots \parallel \mathcal{L}_l \parallel (\mathcal{M}_i \parallel\parallel \mathcal{R}_{i\downarrow}) \parallel \mathcal{P}^{\neg\varphi} \downarrow_{\bigcup_{k \in 1..l \cup \{i\}} \mathcal{A}_k}$$

When performing the checks in the order specified by their indices, then as soon as one of these checks results in not reaching an accepting state, we have found the smallest j and can stop this procedure. If all checks result in reaching an accepting state, then we select $j = i - 1$. It is important that we find the smallest j, as opposed to directly selecting $i - 1$, since failure to backtrack as far as possible up the ICC order of components will result in performing redundant checks.

Next, we have to reject the current combination of traces $\mathcal{L}_1, \ldots, \mathcal{L}_{i-1}$, and we do this using the value of j. Namely, we update the restriction LTS $\mathcal{R}_j$ of $\mathcal{M}_j$ in procedure *updatePreviousRestrictions* (line 11). In this case, instead of extracting the accepted traces of $\mathcal{M}_i$ from the state space explored so far, we extract a constraint concerning $\mathcal{L}_j$ from the state space that resulted either from the final $Check'_j$ (if $j < i - 1$) or from $Check_i$ (if $j = i - 1$). This can be done using almost the same procedure that is used to extract accepted traces of $\mathcal{M}_i$ (except that we skip step 1, since no accepting state was reached) provided that the state space was adequately annotated with additional information during construction. After constructing the constraint, procedure *updatePreviousRestrictions* adds this constraint to $\mathcal{R}_j$. How to extract constraints and update restriction LTSs is explained in detail in the next section.

Having updated $\mathcal{R}_j$, we reset all restriction LTSs in the range $[j+1, i]$, since those restrictions were only relevant for the combination of traces $\mathcal{L}_1, \ldots, \mathcal{L}_{i-1}$ (line 12), and jump back to verification task $Check_j$ (line 13).

Finally, if at any moment, $i > n$, then we have successfully constructed a complete counter-example. This result is returned at line 14.

3.2   Constraints and Restriction LTSs

Extracting a Constraint LTS. Whenever a check at line 3 of Algorithm 1 has failed to reach an accepting state, and subsequently, the smallest index j has been

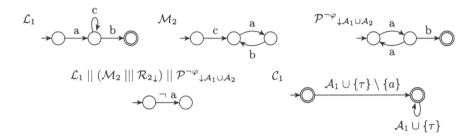

Fig. 2. Example with two LTSs and the property "after an odd amount of a's no b can be performed". The state space is constructed with annotations expressing which behaviour of $\mathcal{L}_1$ is not possible. From the result, a constraint $\mathcal{C}_1$ can be constructed.

identified corresponding with an $\mathcal{L}_j$ that causes accepting states to be unreachable (line 10), we must extract relevant information from the corresponding state space to update the restriction LTS $\mathcal{R}_j$.

In order to make this possible in the first place, we annotate, while constructing, the state space resulting from each check with information regarding the *impossibility* to perform behaviour of the component directly preceding component $\mathcal{M}_i$, i.e., component $\mathcal{L}_{i-1}$ in the checks $Check_i$ at line 3, and $\mathcal{L}_l$ in the checks $Check'_l$ performed at line 10.

Again consider the example system in Fig. 1. As illustrated in Sect. 3.1, after the first check, a path is found representing the traces ac^*b. Based on this, we construct an LTS $\mathcal{L}_1$ that accepts exactly these traces. Now, the setup is as illustrated in Fig. 2, and ICC moves on to the next check, which involves exploring $\mathcal{L}_1 \parallel (\mathcal{M}_2 \parallel\mid \mathcal{R}_{2\downarrow}) \parallel \mathcal{P}^{\neg\varphi}{\downarrow}_{\mathcal{A}_1\cup\mathcal{A}_2}$. This is a rather straightforward task in this case, since the outgoing transition from the initial state of $\mathcal{L}_1$ cannot synchronise with behaviour of $\mathcal{M}_2$, and hence the exploration is finished. But instead of only producing a single state with no transitions, we add a special *sink state* and a transition from the initial state to that sink state labelled $\neg a$, to make explicit that at that point in the exploration, an a-transition of $\mathcal{L}_1$ was not enabled. In general, we annotate each state in a state space in this manner, and furthermore, we also mark states in which the 'preceding' component state is accepting, but the overall system state is not, with a selfloop labelled $\neg accept$.

The purpose of doing this is that with the additional information, it is possible to construct a *constraint LTS* based on the result of the check. Again consider the example. Similar to the procedure of extracting accepting traces from a state space, we first action hide the state space w.r.t. $\mathcal{A}_1$ and reduce the outcome w.r.t. weak trace equivalence. Next, we add a new accepting sink state, and make the LTS complete w.r.t. $\mathcal{A}_1\cup\{\tau\}$, by adding transitions from each state s to the sink state for all labels in $\mathcal{A}_1 \cup \{\tau\}$ not occurring already on an outgoing transition of s (either normally or in negated form) and adding selfloops for all actions in $\mathcal{A}_1 \cup \{\tau\}$ to the sink state. Next, we make all states without a $\neg accept$-selfloop accepting, and finally, remove all transitions with a negated label from the LTS. Note that in the example, the resulting constraint LTS $\mathcal{C}_1$ accepts all traces except for the traces starting with an a. For convenience, we have labelled transitions with sets of actions here, to indicate that for every action in the set, a transition exists from the indicated source state to the indicated target state.

Updating a Restriction LTS. For each $\mathcal{M}_i$, we maintain a restriction LTS $\mathcal{R}_i$ to allow iterating over the traces through $\mathcal{M}_i$. Initially, for each $\mathcal{M}_i$, the structure of $\mathcal{R}_i$ is as illustrated in Fig. 3: there is a single state which is initial and accepting and it has selfloops for all labels in $\mathcal{A}$ and for τ.

Fig. 3. Initial $\mathcal{R}_i$

First of all, note that this LTS is deterministic; this is required to prevent the state space of $\mathcal{M}_i \; ||| \; \mathcal{R}_i$ from becoming very large. When updating $\mathcal{R}_i$ with new constraints, we make sure that $\mathcal{R}_i$ remains deterministic. Secondly, note that the initial $\mathcal{R}_i$ does not actually restrict the behaviour of $\mathcal{M}_i$ in $\mathcal{M}_i \; ||| \; \mathcal{R}_i$, since all traces in $(\mathcal{A}_i \cup \{\tau\})^*$ are accepted by it.

With this in mind, updating a restriction LTS $\mathcal{R}_i$ with a constraint $\mathcal{C}$ can be performed by computing the language intersection [40] of $\mathcal{R}_i$ and $\mathcal{C}$, i.e., an $\mathcal{R}'_i$ is constructed such that the language of $\mathcal{R}'_i$ (the set of accepted traces) is equal to the language of $\mathcal{R}_i$ intersected with the language of $\mathcal{C}$. In this way, we remove the bad behaviour that is encoded in $\mathcal{C}$. The intersection of LTSs is defined by Definition 8.

Definition 8 (Intersection of LTSs with accepting states). *Given two LTSs with accepting states that have a total transition relation $\mathcal{G}_1 = \langle \mathcal{S}_1, \mathcal{A}, \mathcal{T}_1, s_1^{in}, \mathcal{F}_1 \rangle$ and $\mathcal{G}_2 = \langle \mathcal{S}_2, \mathcal{A}, \mathcal{T}_2, s_2^{in}, \mathcal{F}_2 \rangle$ (note that they have the same alphabet), we call $\mathcal{K} = \mathcal{G}_1 \cap \mathcal{G}_2$ the intersection of $\mathcal{G}_1$ and $\mathcal{G}_2$. Its LTS is defined as $\mathcal{K} = \langle \mathcal{S}_1 \times \mathcal{S}_2, \mathcal{A}, \mathcal{T}_{\mathcal{K}}, \langle s_1^{in}, s_2^{in} \rangle, \mathcal{F}_{\mathcal{K}} \rangle$, where:*

- $\mathcal{T}_{\mathcal{K}} = \{\langle s_1, s_2 \rangle \xrightarrow{\ell} \langle s'_1, s'_2 \rangle \mid \ell \in \mathcal{A}, s_1 \xrightarrow{\ell}_{\mathcal{T}_1} s'_1, s_2 \xrightarrow{\ell}_{\mathcal{T}_2} s'_2\}$;
- $\mathcal{F}_{\mathcal{K}} = \{\langle s_1, s_2 \rangle \mid s_1 \in \mathcal{F}_1, s_2 \in \mathcal{F}_2\}$.

Note that the intersection of $\mathcal{G}_1$ and $\mathcal{G}_2$ can actually be computed by constructing the state space of $\mathcal{G}_1 \; || \; \mathcal{G}_2$. By applying trace equivalence reduction on the resulting LTS, and involving the reduced version in subsequent ICC checks (see line 3 of Algorithm 1), we restrict state space explosions caused by parallel composition as much as possible. Furthermore, by our interpretation of accepting system state, note that a system state is only accepting if the involved state in the corresponding restriction LTS is also accepting, i.e., if the restriction LTS accepts the trace.

Finally, resetting a restriction LTS, as referred to at line 12 of Algorithm 1, amounts to reverting it to its initial structure. One possible optimisation involves updating the initial restriction LTSs whenever applicable, such that resetting a restriction LTS does not always mean that all the learned restrictions are discarded. For more on this, see Sect. 4.

3.3 Soundness and Completeness

We provide an informal proof that ICC is both sound and complete. Completeness relies on the fact that the state space is finite-state, and hence from a finite number of states it is possible to reach an accepting state.

Lemma 1. *Algorithm 1 is sound and complete: it returns* **true** *if and only if* $\mathcal{M} \vDash \phi$.

Proof. We split the proof into two parts, one for each direction.

$\Rightarrow$ The result *true* implies that at some point, $Check_1$ returned *true*. This value indicates that no new accepted trace could be generated from $(\mathcal{M}_1 \;|||\; \mathcal{R}_{1\downarrow}) \;||\; \mathcal{P}^{\neg\varphi}{}_{\downarrow\mathcal{A}_1}$. Since we have tried all traces of $\mathcal{M}_1$ that are accepted by $\mathcal{P}^{\neg\varphi}$, and each has been rejected by other checks involving other components, there is no path in $\mathcal{M}$ with a trace accepted by $\mathcal{P}^{\neg\varphi}$. Therefore, the property holds ($\mathcal{M} \vDash \phi$).

$\Leftarrow$ $\mathcal{M} \vDash \phi$ implies that there is no trace accepted by $\mathcal{M} \;||\; \mathcal{P}^{\neg\varphi}$. Therefore, there is also no trace accepted by $\mathcal{M}_1 \;||\; \mathcal{P}^{\neg\varphi}{}_{\downarrow\mathcal{A}_1}$ that is accepted by the other components. The traces accepted by $\mathcal{M}_1 \;||\; \mathcal{P}^{\neg\varphi}{}_{\downarrow\mathcal{A}_1}$ can be captured in finitely many LTSs $\mathcal{L}_1, \mathcal{L}'_1, \ldots$, since there are only finitely many states in $\mathcal{M}_1$. The traces in each of these LTSs will be rejected by a subsequent check in ICC. Therefore, after having considered all these LTSs, execution of $Check_1$ returns *true*, causing the procedure to return *true*. $\square$

4 Optimisations

The basic ICC procedure, as explained in the previous section, is correct, but its performance in practice highly depends on applying several optimisations. In this section, we discuss the ones we identified and implemented. Identifying more opportunities to further optimise ICC remains future work.

Heuristics to Select an Initial Component Order. In Algorithm 1, the *ICC order* of the components $\mathcal{M}_1, \ldots, \mathcal{M}_n$ is fixed to the order in which they appear in the system. However, this is not required. In fact, it seems more reasonable to base such an order on the *dependency w.r.t.* φ. In general, the dependency relation D can be defined as follows:

$$D = \{(i,j) \mid i, j \in 1..n \land \mathcal{A}_i \cap \mathcal{A}_j \neq \emptyset\}$$

Relation D can be used to partition the components based on their dependency distance from $\mathcal{P}^{\neg\varphi}$. If we say that $\mathcal{P}^{\neg\varphi}$ has index $n+1$ in the combination of $\mathcal{M}$ and $\mathcal{P}^{\neg\varphi}$, then we place all components directly related via D to $n+1$ in one equivalence class E_1, all components with an index directly related to at least one of the components in E_1 in an equivalence class E_2, etc. Then, when choosing an order, we first select all components from E_1, then those from E_2, and so on. Within an equivalence class, a further ordering can be applied, for instance based on the number of states in the LTSs, or the number of transitions that require synchronisation with preceding LTSs in the ICC order. In our implementation, we currently use relation D and do not try to further order the LTSs in each class, but we are planning to investigate this further in the future.

Dynamically Changing the ICC Order During Analysis. In Algorithm 1, the ICC order, once selected, remains fixed during execution of ICC. This is not necessary for the procedure to be correct. In fact, it may be fruitful to frequently change the position of components in the order. So far, we have identified two situations in which changing the order frequently affects the performance of ICC positively.

First of all, consider the situation that after a $Check_i$ has returned $true$, with $i > 1$, at line 3 of Algorithm 1, an LTS $\mathcal{L}_j$ is identified at line 10 to be rejected. Just before line 13, in which we move to component $\mathcal{M}_j$ to perform the next check, it may be smart to move $\mathcal{M}_i$ in the ICC order to the position just after $\mathcal{M}_j$, i.e., to position $j + 1$. Apparently, the behaviour relevant for $\mathcal{P}^{\neg\varphi}$ of $\mathcal{M}_j$ depends to some extent on the behaviour of $\mathcal{M}_i$, making it likely that the next traces selected for $\mathcal{M}_j$ in $Check_j$, if they have to be rejected, will also be rejected by $\mathcal{M}_i$.

Second of all, another place where the order can be reconsidered is just before the next check is performed (line 3 of Algorithm 1). Based on the selected traces accepted by $\mathcal{L}_{i-1}$ the next component can be selected. For instance, the shortest trace accepted by $\mathcal{L}_{i-1}$ can be identified, and from the set of components still to be involved in a check, we select one of the components with the strongest dependency (in terms of number of actions and/or transitions) on that trace.

In our implementation, we have incorporated both strategies to dynamically change the order. In the second case, we use the number of actions in the shortest trace that need to synchronise with a component to select the next component for a check. Changing the order can also be done in a number of ways; we have chosen to shift each component at position $i + 1$ or higher to the right, where the component ending up at position $n + 1$ is moved to position $i + 1$, until the selected component has ended up at position $i + 1$. An alternative possibility is to swap the positions of two components, but in that way, the initially selected ICC order tends to be erased more quickly.

One final remark about changing the ICC order of components: in order not to make the procedure incorrect, the restriction LTSs of components that are moved to the left should be reset. The reason for this is that before moving such a component, say $\mathcal{M}_i$, the constraints learned about $\mathcal{M}_i$ depend on the traces that have been selected for $\mathcal{M}_1, \ldots, \mathcal{M}_{i-1}$, represented by $\mathcal{L}_1, \ldots, \mathcal{L}_{i-1}$. Once any of these are changed, the constraints learned so far for $\mathcal{M}_i$ have to be reset, similar to how the constraints also need to be reset when new constraints are added to the restriction LTS of a previous component (lines 11-12 in Algorithm 1). This observation directly leads us to the next possible optimisation.

Updating Initial Restriction LTSs. The restriction LTS of a component that is moved to the left in the ICC order needs to be reset. However, the constraints learned about $\mathcal{M}_1$ actually never require this, since that component cannot be moved to the left. This can be further explained by noting that the validity of the constraints for $\mathcal{M}_1$ does not depend on previously selected traces of other components being sufficient to construct a counter-example. In that respect, the contraints learned about $\mathcal{M}_1$ are more valuable for the progress of ICC then the constraints learned about any of the other components, since the former constraints are always relevant. For this reason, these constraints can safely be added to the *initial* restriction LTS of $\mathcal{M}_1$.

In order to also learn constraints about other components that are persistent to updates applied to restriction LTSs, an additional check *Check''* can be added right after line 10 in Algorithm 1, at the moment when the smallest j has been identified. This check can be defined as follows:

$$Check'' = \text{explore } \mathcal{L}_j \mid\mid (\mathcal{M}_i \mid\mid\mid \mathcal{R}_{i\downarrow}) \mid\mid \mathcal{P}^{\neg\varphi}{}_{\downarrow \mathcal{A}_j \cup \mathcal{A}_i}$$

The purpose of performing *Check''* is to determine whether the traces of $\mathcal{L}_j$ should also be rejected when placed in parallel composition only with $\mathcal{M}_i$. If this is the case, then those traces should never be selected anymore. If we add this insight as a new constraint to the initial restriction LTS of $\mathcal{M}_j$, then every time $\mathcal{M}_j$'s current restriction LTS is reset, we revert to an initial restriction LTS that has these constraints still in them. In our implementation, we have added this optimisation.

First Adding an Abstract Version of a Component to a Check. As a final optimisation, we propose to implement the check at line 3 of Algorithm 1 in two steps instead of one. When introducing $\mathcal{M}_i$ into check *Check_i*, note that for the possible rejection of traces in $\mathcal{L}_1, \ldots, \mathcal{L}_{i-1}$, it is only relevant to consider the behaviour in $\mathcal{M}_i$ that requires synchronisation with components $\mathcal{M}_1, \ldots, \mathcal{M}_{i-1}$; all other behaviour can be abstracted away. Also, the restriction LTS of $\mathcal{M}_i$ is not relevant for the rejection of traces, only for the case when traces through $\mathcal{M}_i$ can be selected to extend the current partial counter-example. In that case, the restriction LTS ensures that no traces will be selected that have been selected previously.

The possibility to only consider an abstract version of $\mathcal{M}_i$ provides the potential to reduce the size of state spaces in those cases where $\mathcal{M}_i$ rejects previously selected traces. In cases where no traces can be rejected, a subsequent check as defined at line 3 still has to be performed, since the abstract version of $\mathcal{M}_i$ does not suffice to extend the counter-example. Therefore, this proposed optimisation may primarily have a positive effect on the memory use of ICC, and to a lesser extent on the running time.

Formally, we redefine *Check_i* at line 3 now as the following two checks *Check$_i^1$* and *Check$_i^2$*:

$$Check_i^1 = \text{explore } \mathcal{L}_1 \mid\mid \cdots \mid\mid \mathcal{L}_{i-1} \mid\mid \mathcal{M}_{i\downarrow\bigcup_{k \in 1..i-1} \mathcal{A}_k} \mid\mid \mathcal{P}^{\neg\varphi}{}_{\downarrow\bigcup_{k \in 1..i} \mathcal{A}_k}$$

$$Check_i^2 = \text{explore } \mathcal{L}_1 \mid\mid \cdots \mid\mid \mathcal{L}_{i-1} \mid\mid (\mathcal{M}_i \mid\mid\mid \mathcal{R}_{i\downarrow}) \mid\mid \mathcal{P}^{\neg\varphi}{}_{\downarrow\bigcup_{k \in 1..i} \mathcal{A}_k}$$

This optimisation has also been incorporated in our implementation of ICC.

5   Experiments

To validate the effectiveness of ICC, we conducted a number of representative experiments, using the DAS-5 cluster [4], with nodes equipped with an INTEL HASWELL E5-2630-V3 2.4 GHz CPU, 64 GB memory, and running CENTOS LINUX 7.2. The selected models have been taken from various sources, namely the BEEM benchmark set [37], the CADP toolbox distribution [24], and the mCRL2 toolset distribution [15]. Table 1 lists the models, together with their state space characteristics, the type of safety property checked, and whether or not the property holds. The models suffixed '.1' are altered versions of the standard models. The alterations resulted in larger state spaces.

Table 1. Characteristics of the performed experiments

Model	#states	#transitions	Property	Satisfied
1394	69,518	123,614	Limited action occurrence	Y
1394.1	563,040	1,154,447	Limited action occurrence	Y
transit	3,480,248	37,394,212	Bounded response	N
wafer_stepper.1	6,099,751	29,028,530	Mandatory precedence	N
Lamport8	62,669,317	269,192,485	Mutual exclusion	N
Lann5	993,914	3,604,487	Mutual exclusion	Y
Gas station c2	165	276	Bounded response	Y
Gas station c3	1,197	2,478	Bounded response	Y
HAVi3.2	19,554,248	80,704,326	Bounded response	Y
Peterson7	142,471,098	626,952,200	Mandatory precedence	Y
Szymanski5	79,518,740	922,428,824	Mutual exclusion	Y

Regarding the property types, *limited action occurrence* states that at most two occurrences of a given action a are allowed between two consecutive occurrences of another action b. The *mandatory precedence* property says that an action a is always preceded by an action b. *Bounded response* states that after an occurrence of a, a b of a given set of actions must occur. *Limited action exclusion* is a property in which an action a cannot occur between two consecutive occurrences of actions b and c. In *exact occurrence number*, it is required that an action a occurs an exact number of times, if action b has previously occurred. *Mutual exclusion* refers to the standard property regarding access to critical sections.

We compared the following approaches:

- ICC refers to an implementation of ICC (single-threaded) in the REFINER exploration tool [45]. We have implemented the optimisations proposed in Sect. 4.

- OTF refers to on-the-fly property checking. We also used REFINER for this, running on a single thread. It explores the state space, checks on-the-fly whether the property holds and terminates if a counter-example is found. Even though there exist much faster state space exploration tools, having both ICC and OTF use the same implementation results in a fair comparison. A better implementation of state space exploration could be used to speed up both ICC and OTF, since this procedure is the main performance bottleneck for both.
- PMC refers to partial model checking [23,32]. In PMC, the state space is incrementally constructed by adding processes and minimising the intermediate results. The property can be checked once the state space is constructed. We used the (single-threaded) PMC tool of the CADP toolbox for this.

We have not compared ICC with other compositional model checking techniques, such as Assume-Guarantee [9,9,17,27,30,34], since no implementations were available to us that are directly applicable on the type of models we consider, namely networks of LTSs. In future work, we plan to perform an extensive comparison between ICC and Assume-Guarantee. In this paper, we focus on determining whether ICC is effective in breaking down the classical OTF analyses into smaller checks. We have also not compared to the SPIN model checker [31]. For the BEEM models we consider here, PROMELA models exist, however, the number of states in the resulting state spaces differ significantly from the numbers produced here.

Table 2 presents the results, providing for each approach the runtime in seconds. "T/O" indicates a timeout, which was set to 3 h. The maximum number of states involved in a check at some point during the analysis is also reported; for OTF, this is the number of explored states, for PMC this refers to the largest LTS constructed during the construction, and for ICC, this is the maximum number of states involved in a single ICC check, i.e., the total number of states in the restriction LTSs, plus the number of explored states in the check. Finally, for ICC, also the total number of performed checks is reported (#iters.).

In terms of the maximum number of involved states, which provides an indication for the maximum amount of memory used, ICC is very effective in breaking down the monolithic analysis performed by OTF into smaller analyses, particularly when the model satisfies the property. For the Peterson7 case, only 0.00002% of the state space was ever explored in one check. In this respect, ICC was much more effective than both OTF and PMC, which timed out. Notable exceptions to this are the 1394 and the gas station models. We will further investigate the exact cause of ICC not performing very well in those cases in the near future.

It is to be expected that for models that do not satisfy the property, OTF is much more effective than the compositional model checking approaches. An important concern for the latter techniques is that the size of the state space is kept small, and therefore the state space is iteratively built. A straightforward approach that directly explores the state space may therefore run into a counter-example much more quickly. However, in the cases we considered, the runtimes of ICC and OTF were still comparable. Moreover, in two of the three cases where the property is violated, ICC outperformed PMC both in runtime and the number of explored states.

As already mentioned, ICC seems to be particularly effective when the model satisfies the property. In a number of cases, ICC was even much faster than OTF. In those cases, the rejection of tested path prefixes in ICC quickly led to rejecting all potential candidates, and more importantly, it could avoid the exploration of many states. This effect is absent when checking incorrect models. In those cases, a counter-example can be constructed, but there are also many traces that are initially promising, but need to be rejected later on.

Concluding, individual ICC checks are often very small, and the runtime of ICC is often comparable to OTF. Furthermore, it should be noted that we have not yet attempted to optimise the implementation of ICC, so it is very likely that the reported runtimes can be further improved. Finally, the frequently drastic reduction in memory use of model checking when using ICC is very encouraging regarding the scalability of ICC. We expect that we can go far beyond what can currently be analysed using OTF.

Table 2. Experimental results for OTF, PMC, and ICC; Times in seconds

Model	Property satisfied	OTF		PMC		ICC		
		Time	#states	Time	#states	Time	#states	#iters
1394	Y	9.35	69,518	26.13	1,061	10.48	5,659	3
1394.1	Y	51.04	563,040	36.15	1,061	155.66	219,981	5
transit	N	7.76	50,970	1,044.03	1,437,433	5.69	10,443	5
wafer_stepper.1	N	20.27	60,809	68.09	3,821	18.67	28,227	8
Lamport8	N	2.66	30,041	56.52	301,711	11.78	22,552	6
Lann5	Y	289.65	993,914	T/O		1.39	33	35
Gas station c2	Y	0.08	165	0.54	342	0.91	595	11
Gas station c3	Y	0.21	1,197	12.53	4,532	9.15	4,930	21
HAVi3.2	Y	T/O		21.24	12	8.89	167	57
Peterson7	Y	T/O		T/O		7.11	34	73
Szymanski5	Y	T/O		T/O		2.67	48	21

6 Related Work

Regarding compositional model checking, a number of prominent approaches need to be mentioned. First of all, *partial model checking* [23,32] is an approach in which it is attempted to incrementally construct a state space bisimilar to the original one, without actually constructing the latter. It is attempted to keep the constructed state space small by carefully combining component LTSs and applying bisimulation reduction on the intermediate results. However, the order in which component LTSs are introduced in the analysis usually heavily influences the effectiveness of the technique, and the best order is a-priori not clear [16]. *Saturation* is similar to partial model checking, in that they both attempt to incrementally construct a version of the system state space [35].

Instead, ICC never involves more than one complete component LTS in a single check. Moreover, if a component order is initially chosen which is not efficiently leading to a solution, ICC with optimisations can change this order dynamically.

In [13,36], it has been investigated what the best system decompositions are for a set of benchmarks, and what the best order is in which to combine components again. Even though ICC is adaptive in this respect to some extent, we experience that its performance is greatly affected by the initially selected ICC order. In the future, we will study the results in the literature on this topic.

Another approach is to impose interaction constraints and to find relevant invariants for combinations of components [5,6]. The use of *interface automata* [1] allows reasoning about the possible interactions between components. In ICC checks, we always assume that a component being checked can interact with components not involved in the check. Subsequent checks will detect cases where this assumption was not valid. It would be interesting to investigate how the above techniques could positively influence the running time of ICC.

Assume-Guarantee (AG) [9,17,27,30,34] is another prominent technique. It construct assumptions with the goal to prove that the system satisfies the property. Given a system $M_1 \parallel M_2$ and property φ, it tries to establish that both M_1 satisfies a set of assumptions A, and that M_2 satisfies φ under assumptions A. If this holds, then $M_1 \parallel M_2$ satisfies φ. Circular AG extends this approach to N instead of 2 components, and constructs assumption LTSs using SAT solving [18].

Like restriction LTSs in ICC, assumptions are expressed in LTSs in AG. How to keep these LTSs minimal is hard, as they tend to grow rapidly. L^* [2] is frequently applied [12,38], but sometimes, this seems to be unnecessary [39], and other approaches have been investigated as well [20,21,28]. For ICC, we have not experienced that the sizes of the restriction LTSs became problematic. This is probably because ICC and AG attack the problem from opposite directions: AG tries to establish that the property holds, whereas ICC tries to construct a counter-example. In AG, the goal is that an assumption LTS overapproximates a component while still reasoning about the property, whereas in ICC, the function of a restriction LTS is merely to block certain traces in the component, and can therefore often remain a much coarser approximation of the component LTS. Finally, a fundamental difference between ICC and AG is that the latter tries to avoid involving the actual component LTSs in the verification checks and instead tries to establish that the assumptions are sufficient to prove that the property is satisfied. In this way of working, it frequently happens that spurious counter-examples are constructed, so any identified counter-examples in the complete, abstract system must first be checked against the original system to establish whether the counter-example is real. ICC, on the other hand, involves component LTSs from the very start, and selects part of their behaviour for subsequent checks instead of the complete component LTSs, with the goal to keep the parallel composition of component behaviour small. As a result, ICC never produces spurious counter-examples. Only partially constructed counter-examples can be rejected in one of the checks, but once a complete counter-example has been successfully constructed, it is by definition a real one.

Counterexample-Guided Abstraction Refinement (CEGAR) [11] is a very well established technique that computes abstractions of programs and refines them based on spurious counter-examples. In spirit, ICC and CEGAR are very similar, but the latter does not operate in a compositional manner and in contrast to ICC, reasons with behavioural over-approximations of the program being verified. Finally, the same observation regarding spurious counter-examples can be made as above for Assume-Guarantee.

Although more tailored towards programs than models, *thread-modular reasoning* [22,29] is another related technique, designed to compositionally reason about threads in multi-threaded programs. Besides the obvious similarities, the fact that the inputs of the two approaches are very different makes it hard to provide a clear comparison, or learn from these techniques to further improve ICC.

One of the motivations behind the development of ICC is to reduce the memory requirements. This makes ICC related to other memory-saving techniques [19,25,33], but different from most other techniques of this type, we observe that besides memory savings, also the runtimes can be positively affected by ICC.

Finally, ICC is pleasantly parallel, since different ICC orders can be inspected fully independently. Other parallel techniques, such as [8,41], still require frequent communication between workers. In the future, we plan to investigate the potential to perform ICC in parallel.

7 Conclusions

We presented a new compositional model checking technique, called Incremental Counter-example Construction. Experiments point out that it can very effectively reduce the number of states involved in a single check, thereby demonstrating great potential for scaling up the technique to larger models. Moreover, the runtime is frequently comparable to a traditional on-the-fly analysis, and in cases where the model is correct, ICC can actually by significantly faster.

Future Work. ICC also seems applicable to check linear-time liveness or branching time properties. For those, checks could be performed using Nested Depth-First Search [14] or by solving Boolean Equation Systems [32], respectively. We plan to investigate this.

We also plan to investigate performing ICC in parallel, by having different threads inspect different ICC orders, perhaps in line of our earlier work [42–44,46]. We will further investigate the potential to optimise ICC, in addition to the optimisations discussed in Sect. 4.

Finally, we will investigate to what extent the ICC approach is suitable for symbolic model checking techniques.

References

1. de Alfaro, L., Henzinger, T.: Interface automata. ACM SIGSOFT Softw. Eng. Notes **26**(5), 109–120 (2001)
2. Angluin, D.: Learning regular sets from queries and counterexamples. Inf. Comput. **75**, 87–106 (1987)
3. Baier, C., Katoen, J.P.: Principles of Model Checking. The MIT Press, Cambridge (2008)
4. Bal, H., Epema, D., de Laat, C., van Nieuwpoort, R., Romein, J., Seinstra, F., Snoek, C., Wijshoff, H.: A medium-scale distributed system for computer science research: infrastructure for the long term. IEEE Comput. **49**(5), 54–63 (2016)
5. Bensalem, S., Bozga, M., Legay, A., Nguyen, T.H., Sifakis, J., Yan, R.: Incremental component-based construction and verification using invariants. In: FMCAD, pp. 257–266. IEEE (2010)
6. Bensalem, S., Bozga, M., Legay, A., Nguyen, T.H., Sifakis, J., Yan, R.: Component-based verification using incremental design and invariants. Softw. Syst. Model. **15**(2), 427–451 (2016)
7. Brookes, S., Hoare, C., Roscoe, A.: A theory of communicating sequential processes. J. ACM **31**(3), 560–599 (1984)
8. Camilli, M., Bellettini, C., Capra, L., Monga, M.: CTL model checking in the cloud using MapReduce. In: SYNACS, pp. 333–340. IEEE (2014)
9. Chen, Y.-F., Clarke, E.M., Farzan, A., Tsai, M.-H., Tsay, Y.-K., Wang, B.-Y.: Automated assume-guarantee reasoning through implicit learning. In: Touili, T., Cook, B., Jackson, P. (eds.) CAV 2010. LNCS, vol. 6174, pp. 511–526. Springer, Heidelberg (2010). doi:10.1007/978-3-642-14295-6_44
10. Clarke, E., Long, D., McMillan, K.: Compositional model checking. In: LICS, pp. 353–362. IEEE (1989)
11. Clarke, E., Grumberg, O., Jha, S., Lu, Y., Veith, H.: Counterexample-guided abstraction refinement. In: Emerson, E.A., Sistla, A.P. (eds.) CAV 2000. LNCS, vol. 1855, pp. 154–169. Springer, Heidelberg (2000). doi:10.1007/10722167_15
12. Cobleigh, J.M., Giannakopoulou, D., Păsăreanu, C.S.: Learning assumptions for compositional verification. In: Garavel, H., Hatcliff, J. (eds.) TACAS 2003. LNCS, vol. 2619, pp. 331–346. Springer, Heidelberg (2003). doi:10.1007/3-540-36577-X_24
13. Cobleigh, J., Avrunin, G., Clarke, L.: Breaking up is hard to do: an evaluation of automated assume-guarantee reasoning. ACM Trans. Softw. Eng. Methodol. **17**(2), 7 (2008)
14. Courcoubetis, C., Vardi, M., Wolper, P., Yannakakis, M.: Memory efficient algorithms for the verification of temporal properties. In: Clarke, E.M., Kurshan, R.P. (eds.) CAV 1990. LNCS, vol. 531, pp. 233–242. Springer, Heidelberg (1991). doi:10.1007/BFb0023737
15. Cranen, S., Groote, J.F., Keiren, J.J.A., Stappers, F.P.M., de Vink, E.P., Wesselink, W., Willemse, T.A.C.: An overview of the mCRL2 toolset and its recent advances. In: Piterman, N., Smolka, S.A. (eds.) TACAS 2013. LNCS, vol. 7795, pp. 199–213. Springer, Heidelberg (2013). doi:10.1007/978-3-642-36742-7_15
16. Crouzen, P., Lang, F.: Smart reduction. In: Giannakopoulou, D., Orejas, F. (eds.) FASE 2011. LNCS, vol. 6603, pp. 111–126. Springer, Heidelberg (2011). doi:10.1007/978-3-642-19811-3_9
17. Elkader, K.A., Grumberg, O., Păsăreanu, C.S., Shoham, S.: Automated circular assume-guarantee reasoning. In: Bjørner, N., de Boer, F. (eds.) FM 2015. LNCS, vol. 9109, pp. 23–39. Springer, Cham (2015). doi:10.1007/978-3-319-19249-9_3

18. Abd Elkader, K., Grumberg, O., Păsăreanu, C.S., Shoham, S.: Automated circular assume-guarantee reasoning with N-way decomposition and alphabet refinement. In: Chaudhuri, S., Farzan, A. (eds.) CAV 2016. LNCS, vol. 9779, pp. 329–351. Springer, Cham (2016). doi:10.1007/978-3-319-41528-4_18

19. Evangelista, S., Pradat-Peyre, J.-F.: Memory efficient state space storage in explicit software model checking. In: Godefroid, P. (ed.) SPIN 2005. LNCS, vol. 3639, pp. 43–57. Springer, Heidelberg (2005). doi:10.1007/11537328_7

20. Finkbeiner, B., Peter, H.-J., Schewe, S.: RESY: requirement synthesis for compositional model checking. In: Ramakrishnan, C.R., Rehof, J. (eds.) TACAS 2008. LNCS, vol. 4963, pp. 463–466. Springer, Heidelberg (2008). doi:10.1007/978-3-540-78800-3_35

21. Finkbeiner, B., Schewe, S., Brill, M.: Automatic synthesis of assumptions for compositional model checking. In: Najm, E., Pradat-Peyre, J.-F., Donzeau-Gouge, V.V. (eds.) FORTE 2006. LNCS, vol. 4229, pp. 143–158. Springer, Heidelberg (2006). doi:10.1007/11888116_12

22. Flanagan, C., Freund, S., Qadeer, S., Seshia, S.: Modular verification of multi-threaded programs. TCS **338**(1–3), 153–183 (2005)

23. Garavel, H., Lang, F., Mateescu, R.: Compositional verification of asynchronous concurrent systems using CADP. Acta Inform. **52**(4–5), 337–392 (2015)

24. Garavel, H., Lang, F., Mateescu, R., Serwe, W.: CADP 2011: a toolbox for the construction and analysis of distributed processes. STTT **15**(2), 89–107 (2013)

25. Geldenhuys, J.: State caching reconsidered. In: Graf, S., Mounier, L. (eds.) SPIN 2004. LNCS, vol. 2989, pp. 23–38. Springer, Heidelberg (2004). doi:10.1007/978-3-540-24732-6_3

26. Groote, J.F., Wijs, A.: An $O(m \log n)$ algorithm for stuttering equivalence and branching bisimulation. In: Chechik, M., Raskin, J.-F. (eds.) TACAS 2016. LNCS, vol. 9636, pp. 607–624. Springer, Heidelberg (2016). doi:10.1007/978-3-662-49674-9_40

27. Grumberg, O., Meller, Y.: Learning-based compositional model checking of behavioral UML systems. In: Dependable Software Systems Engineering, NATO Science for Peace and Security Series - D: Information and Communication Security, vol. 45, pp. 117–136. IOS Press (2016)

28. Gupta, A., McMillan, K.L., Fu, Z.: Automated assumption generation for compositional verification. In: Damm, W., Hermanns, H. (eds.) CAV 2007. LNCS, vol. 4590, pp. 420–432. Springer, Heidelberg (2007). doi:10.1007/978-3-540-73368-3_45

29. Gupta, A., Popeea, C., Rybalchenko, A.: Threader: a constraint-based verifier for multi-threaded programs. In: Gopalakrishnan, G., Qadeer, S. (eds.) CAV 2011. LNCS, vol. 6806, pp. 412–417. Springer, Heidelberg (2011). doi:10.1007/978-3-642-22110-1_32

30. Henzinger, T.A., Qadeer, S., Rajamani, S.K.: You assume, we guarantee: methodology and case studies. In: Hu, A.J., Vardi, M.Y. (eds.) CAV 1998. LNCS, vol. 1427, pp. 440–451. Springer, Heidelberg (1998). doi:10.1007/BFb0028765

31. Holzmann, G.: The SPIN Model Checker: Primer and Reference Manual. Addison-Wesley, Boston (2003)

32. Lang, F., Mateescu, R.: Partial model checking using networks of labelled transition systems and Boolean equation systems. Logical Methods Comput. Sci. **9**(4:1) (2013)

33. Mateescu, R., Wijs, A.: Hierarchical adaptive state space caching based on level sampling. In: Kowalewski, S., Philippou, A. (eds.) TACAS 2009. LNCS, vol. 5505, pp. 215–229. Springer, Heidelberg (2009). doi:10.1007/978-3-642-00768-2_21

34. Mendoza, L.E., Capel, M.I., Pérez, M., Benghazi, K.: Compositional model-checking verification of critical systems. In: Filipe, J., Cordeiro, J. (eds.) ICEIS 2008. LNBIP, vol. 19, pp. 213–225. Springer, Heidelberg (2009). doi:10.1007/978-3-642-00670-8_16

35. Molnár, V., Vörös, A., Darvas, D., Bartha, T., Majzik, I.: Component-wise incremental LTL model checking. Formal Aspects Comput. **28**(3), 345–379 (2016)

36. Nam, W., Alur, R.: Learning-based symbolic assume-guarantee reasoning with automatic decomposition. In: Graf, S., Zhang, W. (eds.) ATVA 2006. LNCS, vol. 4218, pp. 170–185. Springer, Heidelberg (2006). doi:10.1007/11901914_15

37. Pelánek, R.: BEEM: benchmarks for explicit model checkers. In: Bošnački, D., Edelkamp, S. (eds.) SPIN 2007. LNCS, vol. 4595, pp. 263–267. Springer, Heidelberg (2007). doi:10.1007/978-3-540-73370-6_17

38. Păsăreanu, C., Giannakopoulou, D., Bobaru, M., Cobleigh, J., Barringer, H.: Learning to divide and conquer: applying the L* algorithm to automate assume-guarantee reasoning. Formal Methods Syst. Des. **32**(3), 175–205 (2008)

39. Siirtola, A., Tripakis, S., Heljanko, K.: When do we (not) need complex assume-guarantee rules? In: ACSD, pp. 30–39. IEEE (2015)

40. Sudkamp, T.: Languages and Machines - An Introduction to the Theory of Computer Science. Addison-Wesley, Boston (1988)

41. Verstoep, K., Bal, H., Barnat, J., Brim, L.: Efficient large-scale model checking. In: IPDPS, pp. 1–12. IEEE (2009)

42. Wijs, A.: The HIVE tool for informed swarm state space exploration. In: PDMC Electronic Proceedings in Theoretical Computer Science, vol. 72, pp. 91–98. Open Publishing Association (2011)

43. Wijs, A.: Towards informed swarm verification. In: Bobaru, M., Havelund, K., Holzmann, G.J., Joshi, R. (eds.) NFM 2011. LNCS, vol. 6617, pp. 422–437. Springer, Heidelberg (2011). doi:10.1007/978-3-642-20398-5_30

44. Wijs, A., Bošnački, D.: Many-core on-the-fly model checking of safety properties using GPUs. STTT **18**(2), 169–185 (2016)

45. Wijs, A., Engelen, L.: REFINER: towards formal verification of model transformations. In: Badger, J.M., Rozier, K.Y. (eds.) NFM 2014. LNCS, vol. 8430, pp. 258–263. Springer, Cham (2014). doi:10.1007/978-3-319-06200-6_21

46. Wijs, A.J., Lisser, B.: Distributed extended beam search for quantitative model checking. In: Edelkamp, S., Lomuscio, A. (eds.) MoChArt 2006. LNCS (LNAI), vol. 4428, pp. 166–184. Springer, Heidelberg (2007). doi:10.1007/978-3-540-74128-2_11

Pithya: A Parallel Tool for Parameter Synthesis of Piecewise Multi-affine Dynamical Systems

Nikola Beneš, Luboš Brim, Martin Demko,
Samuel Pastva, and David Šafránek(✉)

Systems Biology Laboratory, Faculty of Informatics,
Masaryk University, Brno, Czech Republic
xsafran1@fi.muni.cz

Abstract. We present a novel tool for parameter synthesis of piecewise multi-affine dynamical systems from specifications expressed in a hybrid branching-time temporal logic. The tool is based on the algorithm of parallel semi-symbolic coloured model checking that extends standard model checking methods to cope with parametrised Kripke structures. The tool implements state-of-the-art techniques developed in our previous research and is primarily intended to be used for the analysis of dynamical systems with uncertain parameters that frequently arise in computational systems biology. However, it can be employed for any dynamical system where the non-linear equations can be sufficiently well approximated by piecewise multi-affine equations.

1 Introduction

Complex dynamical systems arise in many areas such as biology, biophysics, economy, or social sciences. To study them, various kinds of models are used. Such models usually employ some parameters that either represent unknown mechanics of the real-world system or serve as a way of tuning the behaviour of the system. A popular way of modelling dynamical systems is to employ the framework of differential equations with parameters. To find an analytical solution to these equations is often intractable due to the complexity of the system, the number of parameters and their interdependencies. A different approach, the one we focus on here, is to discretise the system, thereby obtaining a parametrised transition system, a kind of a computational model in the sense of [21]. Such systems are amenable to processing by formal methods. We formalise the desired properties of the system's dynamics in a suitable (temporal) logic and then, using an algorithm similar to model checking, we find parameter valuations under which the model satisfies given properties (i.e., exhibits the desired behaviour).

This work has been supported by the Czech Science Foundation grant GA15-11089S. The authors acknowledge Matej Hajnal for functional testing and language corrections.

R. Majumdar and V. Kunčak (Eds.): CAV 2017, Part I, LNCS 10426, pp. 591–598, 2017.
DOI: 10.1007/978-3-319-63387-9_29

In this paper, we present Pithya, a new parallel semi-symbolic tool for parameter synthesis. The input to our tool is a parametrised model of a continuous-time dynamical system. Currentĺy, models represented by means of autonomous ordinary differential equations (ODEs) with sigmoidal functions are supported. This format covers most of the models commonly used in computational systems biology [22]. The model is first approximated into a piecewise multi-affine model and subsequently discretised into a parametrised direction transition system (PDTS) [7]. States of a PDTS are labelled with basic atomic propositions explicitly characterising the variable values. The transitions are indexed by parameter valuations and labelled with *directions* of change in the affected variable values. The use of directions as transition labels allows to reason about the flows in the system. To formalise the desired properties of the model we employ a hybrid extension of the UCTL logic [5] with past, called HUCTLP [7]. Action-based parts of UCTL allow to express properties about directions; the hybrid extension together with the past/future duality of operators allows to capture interesting dynamical properties of states such as sinks, sources, cycles etc.

The parameter synthesis engine of the tool thus obtains a PDTS model and an HUCTLP formula and its job is to compute the set of all parameter valuations under which the PDTS satisfies the formula. In order to do so, the engine employs the parallel algorithm for coloured model checking [11], more specifically, the semi-symbolic version presented in [6] (the extension to HUCTLP was presented in [7]). The sets of parameter valuations in the PDTS are represented symbolically as first-order arithmetic formulae (while the states are represented explicitly). To deal with these formulae, the tool makes use of an SMT solver.

The algorithm starts by partitioning the PDTS into fragments [14] and distributing them among the working nodes (workstations in a cluster setting, processors in a multi-core setting). Each node then considers each state of its own fragment and each subformula of the given formula and computes the set of parameter valuations under which the subformula holds in the given state. This computation is done in a bottom-up dynamic programming fashion akin to original CTL model checking [16]. The sets of parameter valuations are represented as first-order arithmetic formulae. At specific times during the computation, the computed (symbolic) sets are exchanged among the nodes. The algorithm stops once no new information has been computed by any node since the last exchange.

2   Architecture

The Pithya tool consists of three parts: The main part consisting of several stand-alone executables, the graphical user interface (GUI) used for model design and result visualisation, and the command-line interface (CLI). Figure 1 depicts the architecture of Pithya and all its components. The white boxes denote input, output, and the auxiliary files while the coloured boxes denote the executables.

The *model input file* defines the input model and is written using our `.bio` format. The file declares the parameters of the model and defines the variables using ODEs with predefined sigmoidal functions. For more information about the `.bio` format see the tool manual.

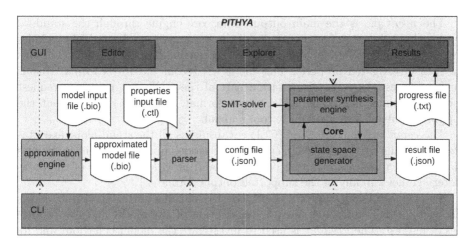

Fig. 1. The architecture of Pithya. (Colour figure online)

The *approximation engine* is a stand-alone executable that verifies the syntax of the model and performs the piecewise multi-affine approximation of the ODEs (using the approach defined in [22]). The GUI can use this executable separately to visualise the approximated model without performing the full parameter synthesis.

The *approximated model file* is an auxiliary .bio file produced by the approximation engine containing the piecewise multi-affine approximated version of the original model.

The *properties input file* defines properties of the model as HUCTLP formulae in our .ctl format. For more information about this format see the tool manual.

The *parser* is a stand-alone executable that verifies the syntax of the provided formulae with respect to the approximated model and prepares the final configuration file used by the core executable.

The *configuration file* is an auxiliary file in the JSON format that describes both the input model together with the properties of interest in a machine-readable way that is used by the core executable.

The *core* performs the parameter synthesis based on the parallel coloured model checking approach. The core consists of a model-agnostic parameter synthesis engine together with a model-specific state space generator. The space generator employs the rectangular abstraction as defined in [4,22].

The *SMT-solver* is either an internal solver (Pithya implements a very efficient solver for models with independent parameters) or an external instance of the Z3 prover [25]. Using Z3 allows Pithya to handle models with interdependent parameters.

The *progress file* is a simple text output from the core engine through the standard error channel. It contains various useful information mostly used by the GUI to inform the user about the progress of the synthesis.

The *result file* is the main output from core engine through the standard output channel containing the results of the parameter synthesis. This includes the set of satisfying states along with the corresponding parameter valuations for each investigated property. This file is written in the JSON format that is further processed by the visualisation part of the GUI. The user may request a different, more human-readable output format. For more details about the supported output formats see the tool manual.

The *command-line interface* (CLI) encapsulates all the stand-alone executables so that the user only needs to provide the model input file and the properties file. The executables are run automatically and provide the result of the parameter synthesis in any of the supported output formats.

The *graphical user interface* (GUI) consists of three parts. The *editor* allows the user to load, edit, and save the description of the model and the properties of interest. The *explorer* is used to investigate the model behaviour and its approximated transition state space. The *results* visualiser provides an interactive visual analysis of the parameter synthesis results. For more information about the possibilities of the GUI see the tool manual.

3   Implementation

Pithya is available at http://biodivine.fi.muni.cz/pithya under the GPL license. It relies on SMT solving for the core parameter synthesis procedure, however, it does so in a way that is not entirely conventional. Instead of issuing a small number of difficult queries, Pithya iteratively builds up the knowledge about the system by issuing a high amount of simple queries while maintaining a compact symbolic representation of the intermediate results.

The effectiveness of this approach relies on several key observations:

– SMT solving is the main performance bottleneck.
– Small independent queries can be easily solved concurrently, even if the solver itself does not support parallel evaluation.
– The intermediate results can immediately influence ongoing computation, therefore merging several execution paths or cutting others entirely.
– The queries can be often simplified during the solving procedure and the size of the resulting queries does not increase substantially during the whole computation.
– The complexity of SMT solving is worse than linear. Therefore, it can be faster to iteratively issue small queries and simplify their results, even if the simplification procedure costs more than just plain solving.

Assignment Caching. Except for optimisations, another relatively cheap byproduct of formula solving is often a satisfying parameter assignment. Such assignment is saved and later used to speed up solving of formulae derived from the original satisfiable formula.

Adaptive Optimiser. To achieve optimal balance between solving and simplifying, Pithya tracks the average size of the simplified formulae and adjusts the threshold for future optimisations accordingly. This ensures that the size of the formulae does not grow too much while reducing the need for costly optimisations of formulae that are already almost minimal.

4   Evaluation and Applications

The methods implemented in Pithya have been successfully employed for complex analysis in several case studies.

In [11], a well-known model of cancer-critical phase transition in mammalian cell cycle has been analysed using the prototype tool. Fully automated parameter synthesis has been used to analyse systems stability in the case of independent parameters. The achieved results are in good agreement with traditional numerical continuation analysis. In [6], the results have been extended to parameter synthesis of interdependent parameters, a very difficult task to achieve with numerical methods. When supplied with several properties the method can also be used to find the boundaries in the parametric space where the satisfiability of the properties changes. Such boundaries are called bifurcation points and the prototype has been applied [7] to complex bifurcation analysis.

In [23], the prototype has been used to explore the behaviour of various models of signalling pathways. In particular, it has been discovered under which parameter valuations the models reproduce abnormal behaviour observed in cells of organisms suffering serious illnesses such as dysplasia or cancer.

The prototype has been also applied in synthetic biology [18]. In particular, a synthetic pathway for efficient biodegradation of a toxic substance has been designed and fine-tuned with the help of parameter synthesis for the given temporal specification of desired behaviour.

Regarding the performance, the prototype has been evaluated on several different models showing that scalability of the parallel algorithm copes well with increasing number of synthesised parameters. In particular, it was possible to compute the results on multi-dimensional models (5–8 variables) for up to six parameters in tens of minutes on a common homogeneous cluster equipped with quad-core Intel Xeon 2 GHz processors [11,12].

5   Related Tools

RoVerGeNe [4] uses the same piecewise multi-affine approximation and discrete abstraction that is employed in Pithya. However, the algorithm employs different approach and heuristics to explore the parameter space. Recently, there has been developed an extension Hydentify [9] for multi-affine hybrid automata that incorporates time but is limited to reachability properties only. GNA [3] employs different approximation/abstraction techniques (piecewise affine systems) while using NuSMV as the model checker. BioPsy [24] implements parameter synthesis with respect to time-series data. It is entirely based on SMT for formulae over reals and employs δ-decidability. The limitation is that the technique is limited only to reachability analysis. Sapo [20] implements parameter synthesis for discrete-time polynomial dynamical systems specified by difference equations and supports (linear-time) Signal Temporal Logic (STL). BioCham [26], Breach [19] and Parasim [13] employ parameter synthesis for linear-time logics. Sampling is used along with numerical methods to simulate trajectories and explore the parameters w.r.t. a given formula by computing quantitative satisfaction/robustness measures.

There are several tools for discrete models based on Boolean networks (BNs). To the best of our knowledge, the only tools that offer parameter synthesis for BNs and temporal formulae are Esther [29] and TREMPPI [28]. BMA [1] is a model checker for BNs that is based on LTL. Antelope [2] is a model checker that employs branching-time hybrid logic. ANIMO [27] uses timed automata and UPPAAL [8] as the computation engine and thus is limited to reachability.

Tools for parameter synthesis have been recently developed also in the domain of stochastic models. PROPhESY [17] supports discrete-time models and reachability properties. PRISM-PSY [15] implements parametric uniformisation for Continuous Stochastic Logic and employs GPU hardware. U-check [10] employs Bayesian statistical algorithm and smoothed model checking.

References

1. Ahmed, Z., et al.: Bringing LTL model checking to biologists. In: Bouajjani, A., Monniaux, D. (eds.) VMCAI 2017. LNCS, vol. 10145, pp. 1–13. Springer, Cham (2017). doi:10.1007/978-3-319-52234-0_1
2. Arellano, G., Argil, J., Azpeitia, E., Benítez, M., Carrillo, M., Góngora, P., Rosenblueth, D.A., Alvarez-Buylla, E.R.: "Antelope": a hybrid-logic model checker for branching-time Boolean GRN analysis. BMC Bioinf. **12**(1), 1–15 (2011)
3. Batt, G., Page, M., Cantone, I., Gössler, G., Monteiro, P., de Jong, H.: Efficient parameter search for qualitative models of regulatory networks using symbolic model checking. Bioinformatics **26**(18), 603–610 (2010)
4. Batt, G., Yordanov, B., Weiss, R., Belta, C.: Robustness analysis and tuning of synthetic gene networks. Bioinformatics **23**(18), 2415–2422 (2007)
5. ter Beek, M.H., Fantechi, A., Gnesi, S., Mazzanti, F.: A state/event-based model-checking approach for the analysis of abstract system properties. Sci. Comput. Program. **76**(2), 119–135 (2011)
6. Beneš, N., Brim, L., Demko, M., Pastva, S., Šafránek, D.: Parallel SMT-based parameter synthesis with application to piecewise multi-affine systems. In: ATVA 2016. LNCS, vol. 9936, pp. 1–17. Springer, Cham (2016)
7. Beneš, N., Brim, L., Demko, M., Pastva, S., Šafránek, D.: A model checking approach to discrete bifurcation analysis. In: Fitzgerald, J., Heitmeyer, C., Gnesi, S., Philippou, A. (eds.) FM 2016. LNCS, vol. 9995, pp. 85–101. Springer, Cham (2016). doi:10.1007/978-3-319-48989-6_6
8. Bengtsson, J., Larsen, K., Larsson, F., Pettersson, P., Yi, W.: UPPAAL — a tool suite for automatic verification of real-time systems. In: Alur, R., Henzinger, T.A., Sontag, E.D. (eds.) HS 1995. LNCS, vol. 1066, pp. 232–243. Springer, Heidelberg (1996). doi:10.1007/BFb0020949

9. Bogomolov, S., Schilling, C., Bartocci, E., Batt, G., Kong, H., Grosu, R.: Abstraction-based parameter synthesis for multiaffine systems. In: Piterman, N. (ed.) HVC 2015. LNCS, vol. 9434, pp. 19–35. Springer, Cham (2015). doi:10.1007/978-3-319-26287-1_2

10. Bortolussi, L., Milios, D., Sanguinetti, G.: U-check: model checking and parameter synthesis under uncertainty. In: Campos, J., Haverkort, B.R. (eds.) QEST 2015. LNCS, vol. 9259, pp. 89–104. Springer, Cham (2015). doi:10.1007/978-3-319-22264-6_6

11. Brim, L., Češka, M., Demko, M., Pastva, S., Šafránek, D.: Parameter synthesis by parallel coloured CTL model checking. In: Roux, O., Bourdon, J. (eds.) CMSB 2015. LNCS, vol. 9308, pp. 251–263. Springer, Cham (2015). doi:10.1007/978-3-319-23401-4_21

12. Brim, L., Demko, M., Pastva, S., Šafránek, D.: High-performance discrete bifurcation analysis for piecewise-affine dynamical systems. In: Abate, A., Šafránek, D. (eds.) HSB 2015. LNCS, vol. 9271, pp. 58–74. Springer, Cham (2015). doi:10.1007/978-3-319-26916-0_4

13. Brim, L., Vejpustek, T., Šafránek, D., Fabriková, J.: Robustness analysis for value-freezing signal temporal logic. In: HSB 2013, EPTCS, vol. 125, pp. 20–36 (2013)

14. Brim, L., Yorav, K., Žídková, J.: Assumption-based distribution of CTL model checking. STTT 7(1), 61–73 (2005)

15. Češka, M., Pilař, P., Paoletti, N., Brim, L., Kwiatkowska, M.: PRISM-PSY: precise GPU-accelerated parameter synthesis for stochastic systems. In: Chechik, M., Raskin, J.-F. (eds.) TACAS 2016. LNCS, vol. 9636, pp. 367–384. Springer, Heidelberg (2016). doi:10.1007/978-3-662-49674-9_21

16. Clarke, E.M., Emerson, E.A., Sistla, A.P.: Automatic verification of finite-state concurrent systems using temporal logic specifications. ACM Trans. Program. Lang. Syst. 8(2), 244–263 (1986)

17. Dehnert, C., Junges, S., Jansen, N., Corzilius, F., Volk, M., Bruintjes, H., Katoen, J.-P., Ábrahám, E.: PROPhESY: a probabilistic parameter synthesis tool. In: Kroening, D., Păsăreanu, C.S. (eds.) CAV 2015. LNCS, vol. 9206, pp. 214–231. Springer, Cham (2015). doi:10.1007/978-3-319-21690-4_13

18. Demko, M., Beneš, N., Brim, L., Pastva, S., Šafránek, D.: High-performance symbolic parameter synthesis of biological models: a case study. In: Bartocci, E., Lio, P., Paoletti, N. (eds.) CMSB 2016. LNCS, vol. 9859, pp. 82–97. Springer, Cham (2016). doi:10.1007/978-3-319-45177-0_6

19. Donzé, A., Fanchon, E., Gattepaille, L.M., Maler, O., Tracqui, P.: Robustness analysis and behavior discrimination in enzymatic reaction networks. PLoS ONE 6(9), e24246 (2011)

20. Dreossi, T.: Sapo: Reachability computation and parameter synthesis of polynomial dynamical systems. CoRR abs/1607.02200 (2016)

21. Fisher, J., Henzinger, T.: Executable cell biology. Nat. Biotechnol. 25(11), 1239–1249 (2007)

22. Grosu, R., Batt, G., Fenton, F.H., Glimm, J., Guernic, C., Smolka, S.A., Bartocci, E.: From cardiac cells to genetic regulatory networks. In: Gopalakrishnan, G., Qadeer, S. (eds.) CAV 2011. LNCS, vol. 6806, pp. 396–411. Springer, Heidelberg (2011). doi:10.1007/978-3-642-22110-1_31

23. Hajnal, M., Šafránek, D., Demko, M., Pastva, S., Krejčí, P., Brim, L.: Toward modelling and analysis of transient and sustained behaviour of signalling pathways. In: Cinquemani, E., Donzé, A. (eds.) HSB 2016. LNCS, vol. 9957, pp. 57–66. Springer, Cham (2016). doi:10.1007/978-3-319-47151-8_4

24. Madsen, C., Shmarov, F., Zuliani, P.: BioPSy: an SMT-based tool for guaranteed parameter set synthesis of biological models. In: Roux, O., Bourdon, J. (eds.) CMSB 2015. LNCS, vol. 9308, pp. 182–194. Springer, Cham (2015). doi:10.1007/978-3-319-23401-4_16
25. de Moura, L., Bjørner, N.: Z3: an efficient SMT solver. In: Ramakrishnan, C.R., Rehof, J. (eds.) TACAS 2008. LNCS, vol. 4963, pp. 337–340. Springer, Heidelberg (2008). doi:10.1007/978-3-540-78800-3_24
26. Rizk, A., Batt, G., Fages, F., Soliman, S.: A general computational method for robustness analysis with applications to synthetic gene networks. Bioinformatics **25**(12), i169–i178 (2009)
27. Schivo, S., Scholma, J., van der Vet, P.E., Karperien, M., Post, J.N., van de Pol, J., Langerak, R.: Modelling with animo: between fuzzy logic and differential equations. BMC Syst. Biol. **10**(1), 56 (2016)
28. Streck, A.: Toolkit for reverse engineering of molecular pathways via parameter identification. Ph.D. thesis, Free University of Berlin, Germany (2016)
29. Streck, A., Kolčák, J., Siebert, H., Šafránek, D.: Esther: introducing an online platform for parameter identification of boolean networks. In: Gupta, A., Henzinger, T.A. (eds.) CMSB 2013. LNBI, vol. 8130, pp. 257–258. Springer, Heidelberg (2013)

Author Index

Printed in the United States
By Bookmasters